THE AMERICAN PEOPLE

THE AMERICAN PEOPLE

Creating a Nation and a Society

Sixth Edition
VOLUME TWO: SINCE 1865

General Editors

GARY B. NASH
University of California, Los Angeles

JULIE ROY JEFFREY
Goucher College

JOHN R. HOWE
University of Minnesota

PETER J. FREDERICK
Wabash College

ALLEN F. DAVIS
Temple University

ALLAN M. WINKLER
Miami University of Ohio

PEARSON
Longman

New York   San Francisco   Boston
London   Toronto   Sydney   Tokyo   Singapore   Madrid
Mexico City   Munich   Paris   Cape Town   Hong Kong   Montreal

Vice President and Publisher:	*Priscilla McGeehon*
Acquisitions Editor:	*Ashley Dodge*
Development Manager:	*Lisa Pinto*
Senior Development Editor:	*Dawn Groundwater*
Executive Marketing Manager:	*Sue Westmoreland*
Supplement Editor:	*Kristi Olson*
Media Editor:	*Patrick McCarthy*
Production Manager:	*Douglas Bell*
Project Coordination, Text Design, and Electronic Page Makeup:	*Elm Street Publishing Services, Inc.*
Cover Designer/Manager:	*John Callahan*
Cover Illustration:	*Patti Mollica/Superstock*
Cartographer:	*Maps.com*
Photo Research:	*Photosearch, Inc.*
Recovering the Past Spinning Wheel Image:	*George Pickow/Getty Images*
Manufacturing Buyer:	*Alfred C. Dorsey*
Printer and Binder:	*Quebecor-World-Versailles*
Cover Printer:	*The Lehigh Press, Inc.*

For permission to use copyrighted material, grateful acknowledgment is made to the following copyright holders:

p. 630 Chart from *The Changing Face of Inequality,* by Oliver Zunz © University of Chicago Press. Reprinted with permission.

p. 900 Verse from "Little Boxes" by Malvina Reynolds © 1962 Schroeder Music Co. (ASCAP)

p. 941 George C. Gallop: *The Gallop Poll: Public Opinion, 1935–1971,* vol. 2 (New York: Random House, 1972).

p. 1012–1013 From "The Times They Are A-Changin" by Bob Dylan, Copyright © 1963, 1964 by Warner Bros. Inc. Copyright renewed by Special Rider Music. All rights reserved. International copyright secured. Reprinted by permission.

p. 1023 "I Am Woman" lyrics by Helen Reddy © 1971 by Irving Music Inc. and BMI.

p. 1026 Passages from *I Am Joaquim* by Rudolfo "Corky" Gonzalez. New York: Bantam Books, 1972 © by Rudolfo Gonzalez.

p. 1078 *The New York Times,* 04/01/2001 "Portrait of a Nation" © New York Times. All rights reserved. Reprinted with permission.

p. 1090 *The New York Times,* 06/25/2002, "Mending a Trail of Broken Treaties" © New York Times. All rights reserved. Reprinted with permission.

p. 1100 *Time,* 04/08/2002, "The Scene of the Siege," p. 20 © Time Inc. Reprinted with permission.

Library of Congress Cataloging-in-Publication Data

The American people: creating a nation and a society / general editors, Gary B. Nash . . . [et al.].—6th ed.
    p. cm.
Includes biblitographical references and index.
ISBN 0-321-12526-6 (Volume Two)
1. United States—History. I. Nash, Gary B.

E178.1.A49355 2004
973—dc21   2002040662

Please visit our website at http://www.ablongman.com

Single Volume Edition ISBN 0-321-12524-X
Volume One ISBN 0-321-12525-8
Volume Two ISBN 0-321-12526-6

1 2 3 4 5 6 7 8 9 10—WCV—06 05 04 03

✦ Brief Contents

✦ DETAILED CONTENTS

✦ SPECIALIZED CONTENTS

RECOVERING THE PAST

ANALYZING HISTORY

MAPS

INTERNATIONAL MAPS, CHARTS, AND TABLES 🌎

FIGURES

TABLES

The Yoruba people of West Africa have an old saying, "However far the stream flows, it never forgets its source." Why, we wonder, do such ancient societies as the Yoruba find history so important, whereas today's American students question its relevance? This book aims to end such skepticism about the usefulness of history.

As we begin the twenty-first century in an ethnically and racially diverse society caught up in an interdependent global society, history is of central importance in preparing us to exercise our rights and responsibilities as free people. History cannot make good citizens, but without history we cannot understand the choices before us and think wisely about them. Lacking a collective memory of the past, we would be unaware of the human condition and the long struggles of men and women everywhere to deal with the problems of their day and to create a better society. Unfurnished with historical knowledge, we deprive ourselves of knowing about the huge range of approaches people have taken to political, economic, and social life; to solving problems; and to conquering the obstacles in their way. Unaware of how events beyond our national boundaries have affected our own history, we are less able to deal with the challenges of contemporary globalism.

History has a deeper, even more fundamental importance: the cultivation of the private person whose self-knowledge and self-respect provide the foundation for a life of dignity and fulfillment. Historical memory is the key to self-identity, to seeing one's place in the long stream of time, in the story of humankind.

When we study our own history, that of the American people, we see a rich and extraordinarily complex human story that stretches back to the last ice age when nomadic hunters arrived in the Americas from Siberia. This country, whose written history began thousands of years later with a convergence of Native Americans, Europeans, and Africans, has always been a nation of diverse peoples—a magnificent mosaic of cultures, religions, and skin shades. This book explores how American society assumed its present shape and developed its present forms of government; how as a nation we have conducted our foreign affairs and managed our economy; how as individuals and in groups we have lived, worked, loved, married, raised families, voted, argued, protested, and struggled to fulfill our dreams and the noble ideals of the American experiment.

Several ways of making the past understandable distinguish this book from most textbooks written in the last 20 years. While this book covers public events like presidential elections, diplomatic treaties, and economic legislation, we have attempted to integrate this broad national narrative with the private human stories that pervade them. Within a chronological framework, we have woven together our history as a nation, as a people, and as a society. When, for example, national political events are discussed, we analyze their impact on social and economic life at the state and local levels. Wars are described not only as they unfolded on the battlefield and in the salons of diplomats but also on the home front, where they are history's greatest motor of social change. The interaction of ordinary Americans with extraordinary events runs as a theme throughout this book.

Above all, we have tried to show the "humanness" of our history as it is revealed in people's everyday lives. We have often used the words of ordinary Americans to capture the authentic human voices of those who participated in and responded to epic events such as war, slavery, industrialization, and reform movements.

GOALS AND THEMES OF THE BOOK

Our primary goal is to provide students with a rich, balanced, and thought-provoking treatment of the American past. By this, we mean a history that treats the lives and experiences of Americans of all national origins and cultural backgrounds, at all levels of society, and in all regions of the country. It also means a history that seeks connections between the many factors—political, economic, technological, social, religious, intellectual, and biological—that have molded and remolded American society over four centuries. And, finally, it means a history that encourages students to think about how we have all inherited a complex past filled with both notable achievements and thorny problems. The only history befitting a democratic nation is one that inspires students to initiate a frank and searching dialogue with their past.

Historians continually revise their understanding of what happened in the past. Historians reinterpret history both because they find new evidence on old topics and also because new sensibilities inspire them to ask questions about the past that did not interest earlier historians. It is this continual questioning of the past that has led to historical research and writing on many topics previously ignored or scanted.

Through this book, we also hope to promote class discussions, which can be organized around seven questions that we see as basic to the American historical experience:

1. How has this nation been peopled, from the first inhabitants to the many groups that arrived in slavery or servitude during the colonial period down to the voluntary immigrants of today? How have these waves of newcomers contributed to the American cultural mosaic? To what extent have different immigrant groups preserved elements of their ethnic, racial, and religious heritages? How have the tensions between cultural assimilation and cultural preservation been played out, in the past and today?

2. To what extent have Americans developed a stable, democratic political system flexible enough to address the wholesale changes occurring in the last two centuries, and to what degree has this political system been consistent with the principles of our nation's founding?

3. How have economic and technological changes affected daily life, work, family organization, leisure, sexual behavior, the division of wealth, and community relations in the United States?

4. How did the European settlement of the Americas alter the landscape? How have environmental factors shaped American society, and how have Americans changed in their attitudes and policies concerning the natural environment?

5. What role has American religion played in the development of the nation? How has religion served to promote or retard social reform in our history? Whatever their varied sources, how have the recurring reform movements in our history dealt with economic, political, and social problems in attempting to square the ideals of American life with the reality?

6. In what ways have global events and trends had an impact on the shape and character of American life? How has the United States affected the rest of the world? To what extent has the United States served as a model for other peoples, as an interventionist savior of other nations around the globe, and as an interfering expansionist in the affairs of other nations?

7. How have American beliefs and values changed over more than four hundred years of history, and how have they varied between different groups—women and men; Americans of many colors and cultures; people of different regions, religions, sexual orientations, ages, and classes?

In writing a history that revolves around these themes, we have tried to convey two dynamics that operate in all societies. First, we observe people continuously adjusting to new developments, such as industrialization and urbanization, over which they seemingly have little control; yet we realize that people are not paralyzed by history but are the fundamental creators of it. They retain the ability, individually and collectively, to shape the world in which they live and thus in considerable degree to control their own lives.

Second, we emphasize the connections that always exist among social, political, economic, and cultural events. Just as our individual lives are never neatly parceled into separate spheres of activity, the life of a society is made up of a complicated and often messy mixture of forces, events, and accidental occurrences. In this text, political and economic, technological and cultural factors are intertwined like strands in a rope.

STRUCTURE OF THE BOOK

The chapters of this book are grouped into three parts that relate to major periods in American history from 1865 to 2002. The title of each part suggests a major theme that helps to characterize the period.

Every chapter begins with an outline that provides an overview of the chapter's organization. Next, a personal story, called *American Stories*, recalls the experience of an ordinary or lesser-known American. Chapter 30, for example, gives an account of a woman who, frustrated with liberalism, drifts into the Republican Party. This brief anecdote introduces the overarching themes and major concepts of the chapter, in this case the revival of conservatism in the Reagan and George H. W. Bush years. In addition, *American Stories* launches the chapter by engaging the student with a human account, suggesting that history was shaped by ordinary as well as extraordinary people. Following the personal story and easily identifiable by its visual separation from the anecdote and the body of the chapter, a *brief chapter overview* links the story to the text. Students should read these crucial transition paragraphs carefully for three reasons: first, to identify the three or four major themes of the chapter; second, to understand the organizational structure of the chapter, and third, to see how the chapter's themes are related to the organizing questions of this book.

We aim to facilitate the learning process for students in other ways as well. Every chapter ends with pedagogical features to reinforce and expand the narrative. A *Timeline* reviews the major events and developments covered in the chapter. A *Conclusion* briefly summarizes the main concepts and developments elaborated in the chapter and serves as a bridge to the following chapter. A list of *Recommended Readings* provides supplementary sources for further study or research; an annotated selection of novels and films, called *Fiction and Film,* is also included. Finally, a special annotated section of suggested Web sites, *Discovering U.S. History Online,* offers students information on electronic sources relating to chapter themes. Each map, figure, and table has been chosen to relate clearly to the narrative.

SPECIAL FEATURES

Five distinctive features help contribute to student learning of history.

- **Recovering the Past.** A distinctive feature of this book is the two-page *Recovering the Past* presented in each chapter. These RTPs, as the authors affectionately call them, introduce students to the fascinating variety of evidence—ranging from diaries to popular music—that historians have learned to employ in reconstructing the past. Each RTP gives basic information about the source and its use by historians and then raises questions, called *Reflecting on the Past,* for students to consider as they study the example reproduced for their inspection.
- **An international context for American history.** Believing that in today's global society it is particularly important for students to think across national boundaries and to understand the ways in which our history intersects with the world, we have provided an international framework. Rather than developing a separate discussion of global events, we have woven an international narrative into our analysis of the American past. Chapter 20, for example, has a discussion of American expansionism in a global context. We have shown the ways in which the United States has been influenced by events in other parts of the world and the connection between the history of other nations and our own. We have also

drawn attention to those aspects of our history that appear to set the nation apart. New tables, charts, and maps provide an additional dimension for this international context. These are identified by a global icon 🌐 and are accompanied by *Reflecting on the Past* questions.

- New to this edition, an **international context for American history.** This feature brings together, in visually engaging ways, a variety of socio-economic data that illustrates the ways in which complex changes are closely intertwined at particular moments in American history. One chart, for example, suggests how new methods of steel production during the late nineteenth century affected prices, working and living conditions, and investment in industry. Our goal is not only to show connections but also to encourage visual literacy by helping students read and interpret statistics and graphs. We have written captions for this feature to assist students in analyzing these materials and have posed *Reflecting on the Past* questions to encourage them to think about the implications of the data presented.
- **Discovering U.S. History Online.** Suggested Web sites, carefully evaluated for this edition, allow students to explore particular areas that relate to each chapter. These sites can also provide the basis for written evaluations, essays, and other learning activities.
- **Illustration Program.** Color illustrations—paintings, cartoons, photographs, maps, and figures—amplify important themes while presenting visual evidence for student reflection and analysis. Captions on all photographs, maps, and figures are designed to help students understand and interpret the information presented. Many map captions pose questions for students to think about. Summary tables, which we refer to as "talking boxes," recap points discussed in the narrative, pulling the material together in a format designed for ease of student study. An example of a "talking box" is "Conflicting Aims During the Cold War" in Chapter 27.

THE SIXTH EDITION

The sixth edition of *The American People* has benefited from both the helpful comments of scholars and the experience of teachers and students who used previous editions of the book. While some of the modifications are small, this edition incorporates substantial changes.

Major Changes

- A new chapter (Chapter 31) on the recent past called "The Post–Cold War World" concludes the book. This chapter examines the post–Cold War period of the Clinton administration, economic and social change, the election of 2000, and new foreign policy challenges, including the terrorist attacks of September 11, 2001.
- Several chapters have been reorganized and revised. Chapters 26–29 have been restructured to give students a more chronological examination of the postwar years.
- This edition also has an important new focus. Because we believe it is not enough to understand only the history of our own nation in today's world, we have reconceptualized the way in which we present the story of our past. We have woven important international materials and themes into the narrative and added many new maps and tables to illuminate the connection between the United States and the world. Chapter 17, for example, includes a new section on "American Agriculture and the World." Chapter 18 includes a new section on "American Industry and the World."
- We have strengthened our coverage on the American West, the role of Asian Americans, and religion. Chapter 17, for example, has been reorganized to reflect greater coverage of the West. Chapter 20 contains stories of California Japanese farmers. Chapter 25 features coverage of religion during World War II.
- This edition also features several smaller changes, with several new anecdotes. An expanded map program as well as carefully selected new visual materials provide students with additional ways of understanding chapter discussions. Revised bibliographies with annotated sections on film and fiction and a carefully selected list of helpful Web sites provide avenues for further explorations outside of the classroom.

Other Chapter Changes

- *Chapter 16* has been largely rewritten to reflect scholarship and language usage. There is a new section on white farmers during Reconstruction and greater emphasis on religion.
- *Chapter 17* has been retitled to reflect greater coverage of the West and has been significantly reorganized. The connection between events in rural America and the rest of the world has been highlighted.

- *Chapter 18* frames the discussion of technological and industrial development in Europe. The chapter reflects the experiences of new immigrants through new anecdotes and quotes.
- *Chapter 19* now includes material on the People's party once found in Chapter 17. While there is no special section on international themes, throughout the chapter there are references to world events and trends that help students connect them to late-nineteenth-century American politics and reform, cities, health, and the Depression. The chapter has added material on traditional religion.
- *Chapter 20* has a significant discussion of American expansionism in a global context. Quotations from foreign observers give their perspectives on American foreign policy of the period. Stories of California Japanese farmers and one Chinese activist have been included.
- *Chapter 21* places the Progressive movement, especially the social justice movement, in a global context and includes new material on Asian immigrants and the West.
- *Chapter 22* features a more extensive discussion of the global causes, military developments, and peace settlements of World War I; the chapter also contains an expanded section on the 1918 flu epidemic, "A Global Pandemic."
- *Chapter 23* places the discussion on the U.S. economy in comparative context and explores the global expansion of trade and culture (including jazz). Additional materials on Asian Americans and the West have been incorporated in the chapter.
- *Chapter 24* points out the ways in which the Great Depression was global in scope, pointing out the linkages to the war and its settlement. The importance of the New Deal in the West has been added, and there is increased coverage of Asian Americans.
- *Chapter 25* features a section entitled "Foreign Policy in a Global Age" that provides a broad picture of the national and international causes of the Second World War. The chapter increases its treatment of the Asian-American experience during the war, adds new material on the Breton Woods Conference, and a new section on religion during the war.
- *Chapter 26* now deals more fully with the period 1945–1960, pulling in the story of public policy in the Truman and Eisenhower administrations for a more chronologically based narrative than was the case in the fifth edition. A new section on the post–World War II world provides an in-

ternational perspective while the story of the civil rights movement (and other movements) has been moved here from Chapter 29. Increased material on Asian-American activism has been added.

- *Chapter 27* now focuses on the Cold War period 1945–1960. The chapter deals with Vietnam in these years, but saves the escalation of the war for the next chapter. A new section on the creation of Israel has been added. A new map on Africa since 1950 is also included.

- *Chapter 28* has been wholly reorganized to provide a chronological analysis of the years between 1960 and 1969. It deals with the administration of JFK and LBJ (including civil rights and foreign policy) and has new material on the war in the Middle East. It contains new maps on divided Berlin and Israeli conquests in 1967.

- *Chapter 29* has also been reorganized in a chronological fashion, covering the years of the Nixon administration and their aftermath (1969 to 1980). It discusses the end of the war in Vietnam and continues the story of the Middle East (the Yom Kippur War). It includes the continuing quest for social reform in these years, formerly in a separate chapter.

- *Chapter 30* now is devoted to the Reagan/Bush years, 1980–1992. It has an altogether new open-

ing vignette about a Republican Party staffer that tells how her family drifted into the Republican Party. The turn toward conservatism is put in an international framework. There is a new RTP on the Internet/World Wide Web and a new section on Asian Americans.

- *Chapter 31* takes the text up to the recent past in its account of the Clinton and George W. Bush years. It includes material about the international situation and compares Clinton's ascendancy to other leaders like Britain's Tony Blair. It makes extensive use of the 2000 census and provides an account of the terrorist attacks of September 11, 2001. It places immigration, the economy, and the AIDS epidemic in global context.

Our aim has been to write a balanced and vivid history of the development of the American nation and its society. We have also tried to provide the support materials necessary to make teaching and learning enjoyable and rewarding. The reader will be the judge of our success. We welcome your comments.

Gary B. Nash
Julie Roy Jeffrey

FOR QUALIFIED ADOPTERS: INSTRUCTOR SUPPLEMENTS

Instructor's Manual, written by Neal Brooks and Ingrid Sabio, Essex Community College. This guide was written based on ideas generated in "active learning" workshops and is tied closely to the text. In addition to suggestions on how to generate lively class discussion and involve students in active learning, this supplement also offers a file of exam questions and lists of resources, including films, slides, photo collections, records, and audiocassettes. ISBN: 0-321-18636-2.

Test Bank. This test bank, prepared by Jeanne Whitney, Salisbury State University, contains more than 3,500 objective, conceptual, and essay questions. All questions are keyed to specific pages in the text. ISBN: 0-321-18639-7.

TestGen EQ Computerized Testing System. This flexible, easy-to-master computerized test bank on a dual-platform CD includes all of the items in the printed test bank and allows instructors to select specific questions, edit existing questions, and add their own items to create exams. Tests can be printed in several different fonts and formats and can include figures, such as graphs and tables. ISBN: 0-321-18640-0.

History Digital Media Archive CD-ROM. The Digital Media Archive CD-ROM contains electronic images and interactive and static maps, along with media elements such as video. These media assets are fully customizable and ready for classroom presentation or easy downloading into your PowerPoint™ presentations or any other presentation software. ISBN: 0-321-14976-9.

Companion Website, www.ablongman.com/nash. Instructors can take advantage of the Companion Website that supports this text. The instructor section of the Website includes the instructor's manual, teaching links, downloadable maps and images from the text in PowerPoint™.

PowerPoint™ Presentations. These presentations contain an average of 15 PowerPoint™ slides for each chapter. These slides may include key points and terms for a lecture on the chapter, as well as four-color slides of some important maps, graphs, and charts within a particular chapter. The presentations are available for download at www.ablongman.com/nash.

CourseCompass®, www.ablongman.com/coursecompass. Combines the strength of the content from *The American People,* Sixth Edition, with state-of-the-art eLearning tools. CourseCompass™ is an easy-to-use online course management system that allows professors to tailor content and functionality to meet individual course needs. Every CourseCompass™ course includes a range of pre-loaded content—all designed to help students master core course objectives. Organized by era, CourseCompass™ allows you to access maps, map exercises, and primary sources as well as test questions from the print test bank and the full text of several of our best-selling supplements. *The American People* CourseCompass™ site is available at no additional charge for students whose professor has requested that a student Access Kit be bundled with the text.

BlackBoard and WebCT. Longman's extensive American history content is available in these two major course management platforms: BlackBoard and WebCT. All quickly and easily customizable for use with *The American People,* Sixth Edition, the content includes multiple primary sources, maps, and map exercises. Book specific testing is simply uploaded.

The History Place Premium Website, www.ushistoryplace.com. Available at no additional cost when requested as a bundle component by the professor, the site offers extraordinary breadth and depth, featuring unmatched interactive maps, timelines, and activities; hundreds of source documents, images, and audio clips; a powerful TestFlight student self-assessment tool; and much more.

A Guide to Teaching American History Through Film. Written by Randy Roberts, Purdue University, this guide provides instructors with a creative and practical tool for stimulating classroom discussion. The sections include "American Films: A Historian's Perspective," a list of films, practical suggestions, and bibliography. The film listing is presented in narrative form, developing connections between each film and the topics being discussed. ISBN: 0-673-99798-7.

Comprehensive American History Transparency Set. This collection includes more than 200 four-color American history map transparencies on subjects ranging from the first Native Americans to the end of the Cold War, covering wars, social trends, elections, immigration, and demographics. ISBN: 0-673-97211-9.

Discovering American History Through Maps and Views Transparency Set. Created by Gerald Danzer, the recipient of the AHA's James Harvey Robinson Prize for his work in the development of map transparencies, this set of 140 four-color acetates is a unique instructional tool. The collection includes cartographic and pictorial maps, views and photos, urban plans, building diagrams, and works of art. ISBN: 0-673-53766-8.

Text-specific Transparency Set. A set of four-color transparency acetates showing maps from the text. ISBN: 0-321-18641-9.

Video Lecture Launchers. Prepared by Mark Newman, University of Illinois at Chicago, these video lecture launchers (each two to five minutes in duration) cover key issues in American history from 1877 to the present. The launchers are accompanied by an *Instructor's Manual.* ISBN: 0-321-01869-9.

"This Is America" Immigration Video. Produced by the American Museum of Immigration, this video tells the story of American immigrants, relating their personal stories and accomplishments. By showing how the richness of our culture is due to the contributions of millions of immigrant

Americans, the videos make the point that America's strength lies in the ethnically and culturally diverse backgrounds of its citizens. ISBN: 0-321-01865-6.

FOR STUDENTS

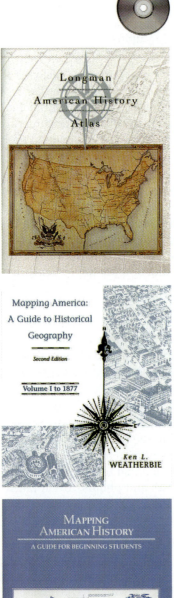

Multimedia Edition CD-ROM for The American People, **Sixth Edition.** This unique CD-ROM takes students beyond the printed page, offering them a complete multimedia learning experience. It contains the full annotatable textbook on CD-ROM, with contextually placed media—audio, video, interactive maps, photos, figures, Web links, and practice tests—that link students to additional content directly related to key concepts in the text. The CD also contains the Study Guide, Map Workbooks, a primary source reader, and more than a dozen supplementary books most often assigned in American history courses. Free when packaged with the text. ISBN: 0-321-18788-1.

Study Guide. This two-volume study guide, created by Neal Brooks and Ingrid Sabio, Essex Community College, includes chapter outlines, significant themes and highlights, a glossary, learning enrichment ideas, sample test questions, exercises for identification and interpretation, and geography exercises based on maps in the text. Volume One: ISBN: 0-321-18637-0; Volume Two: ISBN: 0-321-18638-9.

Longman American History Atlas. A four-color reference tool and visual guide to American history that includes almost 100 maps and covers the full scope of history. Atlas overhead transparencies available to adopters. *$3.00 when bundled.* ISBN: 0-321-00486-8.

Mapping America: A Guide to Historical Geography, **Second Edition.** A two-volume workbook by Ken L. Weatherbie, Del Mar College, that presents the basic geography of the United States and helps students place the history of the United States into spatial perspective. *Free when bundled.* Volume One: ISBN: 0-321-00487-6; Volume Two: ISBN: 0-321-00488-4.

Mapping American History. A workbook created by Gerald A. Danzer for use in conjunction with *Discovering American History Through Maps and Views* and designed to teach students to interpret and analyze cartographic materials as historical documents. *Free when bundled.* ISBN: 0-673-53768-4.

Companion Website for The American People, **Sixth Edition,** www.ablongman.com/nash. The online course companion provides a wealth of resources for students using *The American People,* Sixth Edition. Students can access chapter summaries, interactive practice test questions, and Web links for every chapter. The Website is a comprehensive online study guide for students.

iSearch Guide for History (with Research Navigator™). This guidebook includes exercises and tips on how to use the Internet for the study of history. It also includes an access code for Research Navigator™—the easiest way

for students to start a research assignment or research paper. Research Navigator™ is composed of three exclusive databases of credible and reliable source material including EBSCO's ContentSelect™ Academic Journal Database, New York Times Search by Subject Archive, and "Best of the Web" Link Library. This comprehensive site also includes a detailed help section. ISBN: 0-321-14282-9.

America Through the Eyes of Its People. A comprehensive anthology that makes primary sources widely available in an inexpensive format, balancing social and political history and providing up-to-date narrative material. *Free when bundled.* ISBN: 0-673-97738-2.

Sources of the African American Past. Edited by Roy Finkenbine, University of Detroit at Mercy, this collection of primary sources covers key themes in the African-American experience from the West African background to the present. Balanced between political and social history, it offers a vivid snapshot of the lives of African Americans in different historical periods and includes documents representing women and different regions of the United States. Available at a minimum cost when bundled with the text. ISBN: 0-673-99202-0.

Women and the National Experience, **Second Edition.** Edited by Ellen Skinner, Pace University, this primary source reader contains both classic and unusual documents describing the history of women in the United States. The documents provide dramatic evidence that outspoken women attained a public voice and participated in the development of national events and policies long before they could vote. Chronologically organized and balanced between social and political history, this reader offers a striking picture of the lives of women across American history. Available at a minimum cost when bundled with the text. ISBN: 0-321-00555-4.

Reading the American West. Edited by Mitchel Roth, Sam Houston State University, this primary source reader uses letters, diary excerpts, speeches, interviews, and newspaper articles to let students experience how historians research and how history is written. Every document is accompanied by a contextual headnote and study questions. The book is divided into chapters with extensive introductions. Available at a minimum cost when bundled with the text. ISBN: 0-321-04409-6.

A Short Guide to Writing About History, **Fourth Edition.** Richard Marius, Harvard University, Melvin E. Page Eastern Tennessee University. This engaging and practical text helps students get beyond merely compiling dates and facts; it teaches them how to incorporate their own ideas into their papers and to tell a story about history that interests them and their peers. Covering both brief essays and the documented resource paper, the text explores the writing and researching processes, different modes of historical writing including argument, and concludes with guidelines for improving style. ISBN: 0-321-09300-3.

Retracing the Past, **Fifth Edition.** This two-volume set of readers is edited by Ronald Schultz, University of Wyoming, and Gary B. Nash. These secondary source readings cover economic, political, and social history with special emphasis on women, racial and ethnic groups, and working-class people. Volume One: ISBN: 0-321-10137-5; Volume Two: ISBN: 0-321-10138-3.

American History in a Box. This unique primary source reader offers students the opportunity to experience written documents, visual materials, material culture artifacts, and maps in order to learn firsthand what history is and what historians actually do. It was written and put together by Julie Roy Jeffrey and Peter Frederick, two of the authors of *The American People,* Sixth Edition. Volume One (to 1877): ISBN: 0-321-30005-2; Volume Two (since 1865): ISBN: 0-321-03006-0.

The History Place Premium Website, www.ushistoryplace.com. Available at no additional cost when requested as a bundle component by the professor, the site is a continually updated American history Website of extraordinary breadth and depth, which features unmatched interactive maps, timelines, and activities; hundreds of source documents, images, and audio clips; and much more.

The Library of American Biography Series. Each of the interpretative biographies in this series focuses on a figure whose actions and ideas significantly influenced the course of American history and national life. Brief and inexpensive, they are ideal for any American history survey course. Available to students at a discount.

Penguin Books

The partnership between Penguin-Putnam USA and Longman Publishers offers students a discount on many titles when you bundle them with any Longman survey. Among these include

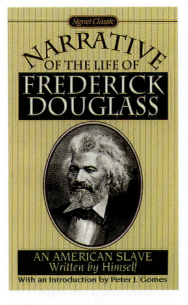

- Frederick Douglass, *Narrative of the Life of Frederick Douglass*
- L. Jesse Lemisch (Editor), *Benjamin Franklin: The Autobiography & Other Writings*
- Upton Sinclair, *The Jungle*
- Harriet Beecher Stowe, *Uncle Tom's Cabin*

♦ ACKNOWLEDGMENTS

The authors wish to thank the following reviewers who gave generously of their time and expertise and whose thoughtful and constructive work have contributed greatly to this edition:

Cara Anzilotti, *Loyola Marymount University*

Virginia H. Bellows, *Tulsa Community College*

Marjorie Berman, *Red Rocks Community College*

S. Charles Bolton, *University of Arkansas at Little Rock*

James Brett Adams, *University of Oklahoma*

Roger Bromert, *Southwest Oklahoma State University*

Neal Brooks, *Community College of Baltimore County—Essex*

Thomas P. Carroll, *John A. Logan College*

Kathleen Carter, *Highpoint University*

Mark Clark, *Oregon Institute of Technology*

Stephanie Cole, *University of Texas—Arlington*

William Furdell, *University of Great Falls*

Kathleen Gorman, *Minnesota State University—Mankato*

Amy Greenberg, *Pennsylvania State University*

Maurice Greenwald, *University of Pittsburgh*

David J. Grettler, *Northern State University*

David Gutzke, *Southwest Missouri State University*

James Hedtke, *Cabrini College*

Craig Hendricks, *Long Beach City College*

Carol Sue Humphrey, *Oklahoma Baptist University*

Edmund Irlbacher, *Orange County Community College*

Shawn Johansen, *Frostburg State University*

Jeremy Johnston, *Northwest College*

Anne Klejment, *University of St. Thomas*

Lawrence Lowther, *Central Washington University*

Robert F. Marcom, *San Antonio College*

Joanne Maypole, *Front Range Community College*

Sylvia W. McGrath, *Stephen F. Austin State University*

Thomas M. McLuen, *Spokane Falls Community College*

John McWilliams, *Pennsylvania State University*

Earl F. Mulderink III, *Southern Utah State University*

Tom Murphy, *Temple College*

Cassandra L. Newby-Alexander, *Norfolk State University*

Sean O'Neill, *Grand Valley State University*

Anne Paulet, *Humboldt State University*

Dolores Davison Peterson, *Foothill College*

Gene B. Preuss, *Texas Tech University*

David Richards, *State University College of New York at Oneonta*

Steven Riess, *Northeastern Illinois University*

Arthur T. Robinson, *Santa Rosa Junior College*

Dale J. Schmitt, *East Tennessee State University*

John A. Trickel, *Richland College*

Steve Tripp, *Grand Valley State University*

Michael P. White, *Temple College*

Over the years, as previous editions of this text were being developed, many of our colleagues read and criticized the various drafts of the manuscript. For their thoughtful evaluations and constructive suggestions, the authors wish to express their gratitude to the following reviewers:

Richard H. Abbott, *Eastern Michigan University*

John Alexander, *University of Cincinnati*

Kenneth G. Alfers, *Mountain View College*

Terry Alford, *North Virginia Community College*

Gregg Andrews, *Southwest Texas State University*

Robert Asher, *University of Connecticut, Storrs*

Harry Baker, *University of Arkansas at Little Rock*

Michael Batinski, *Southern Illinois University*

Gary Bell, *Sam Houston State University*

Virginia Bellows, *Tulsa Community College*

Spencer Bennett, *Siena Heights College*

Jackie R. Booker, *Western Connecticut State University*

James Bradford, *Texas A&M University*

Neal Brooks, *Essex Community College*

Jeffrey P. Brown, *New Mexico State University*

Dickson D. Bruce, Jr., *University of California, Irvine*

David Brundage, *University of California, Santa Cruz*

Colin Calloway, *Dartmouth University*

D'Ann Campbell, *Indiana University*

Jane Censer, *George Mason University*

Vincent A. Clark, *Johnson County Community College*

Neil Clough, *North Seattle Community College*

Matthew Ware Coulter, *Collin County Community College*

David Culbert, *Louisiana State University*

Mark T. Dalhouse, *Northeast Missouri State University*

Bruce Dierenfield, *Canisius College*

John Dittmer, *DePauw University*

Gordon Dodds, *Portland State University*

Richard Donley, *Eastern Washington University*

Dennis B. Downey, *Millersville University*

Robert Downtain, *Tarrant County Community College*

Robert Farrar, *Spokane Falls Community College*

Bernard Friedman, *Indiana University–Purdue University at Indianapolis*

Bruce Glasrud, *California State University, Hayward*

Brian Gordon, *St. Louis Community College*

Richard Griswold del Castillo, *San Diego State University*

Carol Gruber, *William Paterson College*

Colonel Williams L. Harris, *The Citadel Military College*

Robert Haws, *University of Mississippi*

Jerrold Hirsch, *Northeast Missouri State University*

Frederick Hoxie, *University of Illinois*

John S. Hughes, *University of Texas*

Link Hullar, *Kingwood College*

Donald M. Jacobs, *Northeastern University*

Delores Janiewski, *University of Idaho*

David Johnson, *Portland State University*

Richard Kern, *University of Findlay*

Robert J. Kolesar, *John Carroll University*

Monte Lewis, *Cisco Junior College*

William Link, *University of North Carolina, Greensboro*

Patricia M. Lisella, *Iona College*

Paul K. Longmore, *San Francisco State University*

Rita Loos, *Framingham State College*

Ronald Lora, *University of Toledo*

George M. Lubick, *Northern Arizona University*

Suzanne Marshall, *Jacksonville State University*

John C. Massman, *St. Cloud State University*

Vern Mattson, *University of Nevada at Las Vegas*

Art McCoole, *Cuyamaca College*

John McCormick, *Delaware County Community College*

Sylvia McGrath, *Stephen F. Austin University*

James E. McMillan, *Denison University*

Otis L. Miller, *Belleville Area College*

Walter Miszczenko, *Boise State University*

Norma Mitchell, *Troy State University*

Gerald F. Moran, *University of Michigan, Dearborn*

William G. Morris, *Midland College*

Marian Morton, *John Carroll University*

Roger Nichols, *University of Arizona*

Paul Palmer, *Texas A&I University*

Al Parker, *Riverside City College*

Judith Parsons, *Sul Ross State University*

Carla Pestana, *Ohio State University*

Neva Peters, *Tarrant County Community College*

James Prickett, *Santa Monica College*

Noel Pugash, *University of New Mexico*

Juan Gomez-Quiñones, *University of California, Los Angeles*

George Rable, *Anderson College*

Joseph P. Reidy, *Howard University*

Leonard Riforgiato, *Pennsylvania State University*

Randy Roberts, *Purdue University*

Mary Robertson, *Armstrong State University*

David Robson, *John Carroll University*

Jud Sage, *Northern Virginia Community College*

Phil Schaeffer, *Olympic College*

Sylvia Sebesta, *San Antonio College*

Herbert Shapiro, *University of Cincinnati*

David R. Shibley, *Santa Monica College*

Ellen Shockro, *Pasadena City College*

Nancy Shoemaker, *University of Connecticut*

Bradley Skelcher, *Delaware State University*

Kathryn Kish Sklar, *State University of New York at Binghampton*

James Smith, *Virginia State University*

John Snetsinger, *California Polytechnic State University, San Luis Obispo*

Jo Snider, *Southwest Texas State University*

Stephen Strausberg, *University of Arkansas*

Katherine Scott Sturdevant, *Pikes Peak Community College*

Nan M. Sumner-Mack, *Hawaii Community College*

Cynthia Taylor, *Santa Rosa Junior College*

Tom Tefft, *Citrus College*

John A. Trickel, *Richland College*

Donna Van Raaphorst, *Cuyahoga Community College*

Morris Vogel, *Temple University*

Michael Wade, *Appalachian State University*

Jackie Walker, *James Madison University*

Paul B. Weinstein, *University of Akron—Wayne College*

Joan Welker, *Prince George's Community College*

Kenneth H. Williams, *Alcorn State University*

Mitch Yamasaki, *Chaminade University*

Charles Zappia, *San Diego Mesa College*

GARY B. NASH received his Ph.D. from Princeton University. He is currently Director of the National Center for History in the Schools at the University of California, Los Angeles, where he teaches colonial and revolutionary American history. Among the books Nash has authored are *Quakers and Politics: Pennsylvania, 1681–1726* (1968); *Red, White, and Black: The Peoples of Early America* (1974, 1982, 1992, 2000); *The Urban Crucible: Social Change, Political Consciousness, and the Origins of the American Revolution* (1979); *Forging Freedom: The Formation of Philadelphia's Black Community, 1720–1840* (1988); and *First City: Philadelphia and the Forging of Historical Memory* (2002). A former president of the Organization of American Historians, his scholarship is especially concerned with the role of common people in the making of history. He wrote Part I and served as a general editor of this book.

JULIE ROY JEFFREY earned her Ph.D. in history from Rice University. Since then she has taught at Goucher College. Honored as an outstanding teacher, Jeffrey has been involved in faculty development activities and curriculum evaluation. She was Fulbright Chair in American Studies at the University of Southern Denmark, 1999–2000. Jeffrey's major publications include *Education for Children of the Poor* (1978); *Frontier Women: The Trans-Mississippi West, 1840–1880* (1979, 1997); *Converting the West: A Biography of Narcissa Whitman* (1991); and *The Great Silent Army of Abolitionism: Ordinary Women in the Antislavery Movement* (1998). She collaborated with Peter Frederick on *American History in a Box,* two volumes (2002). She is the author of many articles on the lives and perceptions of nineteenth-century women. Her research continues to focus on abolitionism as well as on history and film. She wrote Parts III and IV in collaboration with Peter Frederick and acted as a general editor of this book.

JOHN R. HOWE received his Ph.D. from Yale University. At the University of Minnesota, he has taught the U.S. history survey and courses on the American revolutionary era and the early republic. His major publications include *The Changing Political Thought of John Adams, The Role of Ideology in the American Revolution,* and *From the Revolution Through the Age of Jackson.* In 2003, The University of Massachusetts Press will publish his most recent book on conceptions of language in the political writing of the American revolutionary era. His present research deals with the social politics of verbal discourse in late eighteenth and early nineteenth century Boston. He has received a Woodrow Wilson Graduate Fellowship, a John Simon Guggenheim Fellowship, and a Research Fellowship from the Charles Warren Center for Studies in American History.

PETER J. FREDERICK received his Ph.D. in history from the University of California, Berkeley. Innovative student-centered teaching in American and African-American history has been the focus of his career at California State University, Hayward, and since 1970 at Wabash College (1992–1994 at Carleton College). Recognized nationally as a distinguished teacher and for his many articles and workshops on teaching and learning, Frederick was awarded the Eugene Asher Award for Excellence in Teaching by the AHA in 2000. He has also written several articles on life-writing and a book, *Knights of the Golden Rule: The Intellectual as Christian Social Reformer in the 1890s.* With Julie Jeffrey, he recently published *American History in a Box.* He coordinated and edited all the "Recovering the Past" sections and coauthored Parts III and IV.

ALLEN F. DAVIS earned his Ph.D. from the University of Wisconsin. A former president of the American Studies Association, he is a professor of history at Temple University and editor of *Conflict and Consensus in American History* (9th edition, 1997). He is the author of *Spearheads for Reform: The Social Settlements and the Progressive Movement* (1967); *American Heroine: The Life and Legend of Jane Addams* (1973); and *Postcards from Vermont: A Social History* (2002). He is coauthor of *Still Philadelphia* (1983); *Philadelphia Stories* (1987); and *One Hundred Years at Hull-House* (1990). Davis wrote Part V of this book.

ALLAN M. WINKLER received his Ph.D. from Yale University. He has taught at Yale and the University of Oregon, and he is now Distinguished Professor of History at Miami University of Ohio.

An award-winning teacher, he has also published extensively about the recent past. His books include *The Politics of Propaganda: The Office of War Information, 1942–1945* (1978); *Home Front U.S.A.: America During World War II* (1986, 2000); *Life Under a Cloud: American Anxiety About the Atom* (1993, 1999); and *The Cold War: A History in Documents* (2000). His research centers on the connections between public policy and popular mood in modern American history. Winkler wrote Part VI of this book.

FEATURES OF THIS BOOK

We have included a number of tools to help you in your study of American history.

- Each chapter begins with a personal story called *American Stories*, recalling the experience of an ordinary or lesser-known American. A *brief chapter overview* links this opening story to the major themes of the chapter.
- An *outline* provides an overview of the chapter topics and organization.
- *Summary* tables ("talking boxes") recap points discussed in the chapter for easy reference.
- Each international map or table is identified by a global icon 🌐 and contains *Reflecting on the Past* questions for you to consider.
- *Recovering the Past* essays in each chapter examine different kinds of historical evidence ranging from household inventories, folktales, and diaries to advertising, and popular music. *Reflecting on the Past* questions raise points for you to consider.
- *Analyzing History* graphics help you in reading and interpreting graphs and statistics. Each ends with *Reflecting on the Past* questions.
- A carefully selected program of *illustrations*—paintings, cartoons, photographs, maps, and figures—amplify important themes while presenting visual evidence for your reflection and analysis.
- A *timeline* reviews the major events and developments covered in the chapter.
- A *Conclusion* briefly summarizes the main concepts and developments discussed in the chapter.
- *Recommended Readings* are included at the end of every chapter, offering you research suggestions for scholarly resources, as well as a brief list of fiction and film (feature films and documentaries) related to chapter topics and themes.
- At the end of each chapter there is also an annotated list of suggested Web sites called *Discovering U.S. History Online* that relate to chapter topics and themes. Though these Web addresses were checked for accuracy before publication of this text, the changing nature of Web sites suggests that at least a few might be outdated links by the time you investigate them. These and additional Web suggestions will be updated regularly on the text's Web site at http://www.ablongman.com/nash.

In addition to the specific Web sites recommended for the chapters, you may also want to visit some of the following *major history Web sites* that have content that relates to all periods of American history.

Smithsonian Institution—National Museum of American History

americanhistory.si.edu/

Library of Congress Web Site

www.loc.gov/

Library of Congress American Memory Project

memory.loc.gov/ammem/amhome.html

National Archives and Records Administration Home Page

www.nara.gov

"The Digital Classroom"

www.nara.gov/education/teaching/teaching.html

"The Exhibit Hall"

www.nara.gov/exhall/

Documents for the Study of American History (AMDOCS)

www.ukans.edu/carrie/docs/amdocs_index.html

United States Census Bureau

www.census.gov/

The African-American Mosaic—A Library of Congress Resource Guide

lcweb.loc.gov/exhibits/african/intro.html

National Women's History Project

www.nwhp.org

National Gallery of Art

www.nga.gov/home.htm

Historical Maps: The Perry Castaneda Library Map Collection

www.lib.utexas.edu/Libs/PCL/Map_collection/historical/history_main.html

University of California—Berkeley Library Digital Map Collection

www.lib.berkeley.edu/EART/digital/tour.html

16 The Union Reconstructed

In this Winslow Homer painting entitled *A Visit from the Old Mistress,* imagine Adele Allston returning to her plantation to reunite with former slaves. What kind of new relationships would they form in the transformed world after a wrenching Civil War? *(National Museum of American Art, Smithsonian Institution)*

✦ *American Stories*

BLACKS AND WHITES REDEFINE THEIR DREAMS AND RELATIONSHIPS

In April 1864, a year before Lincoln's assassination, Robert Allston died, leaving his wife Adele and his daughter Elizabeth to manage their many rice plantations. Elizabeth was left with a "sense of terrible desolation and sorrow" as the Civil War raged around her. With Union troops moving through coastal South Carolina in the late winter of 1864–1865, Elizabeth's sorrow turned to "terror" as Union soldiers arrived and searched for liquor, firearms, and valuables. The Allston women endured an insulting search and then fled.

Later, Yankee troops encouraged the Allston slaves to take furniture, food, and other goods from the Big House. "My house at Chicora Wood plantation has been robbed of every article of furniture and much defaced," Adele complained to the local Union commander, adding, "all my provisions of meat, lard, coffee and tea [were] taken [and] distributed among the Negroes." Moreover, before they left, the liberating Union soldiers gave the keys to the crop barns to the semi-free slaves.

After the war, Adele Allston swore allegiance to the United States and secured a written order requiring the newly freed blacks to relinquish the keys. She and Elizabeth returned in the summer of 1865 to reclaim the plantations and reassert white authority. She was assured that although the blacks had guns and were determined to have the means to a livelihood, "no outrage has been committed against the whites except in the matter of property." But property was the issue. Possession of the keys to the barns, Elizabeth wrote, would be the "test case" of whether former masters or former slaves would control land, labor, and its fruits, as well as the subtle aspects of interpersonal relations.

Nervously, Adele and Elizabeth Allston rode up in a carriage to confront their ex-slaves at Chicora Wood. To their surprise, a pleasant reunion took place as the Allston women greeted the blacks by name, inquired after their children, and caught up on their lives. A trusted black foreman handed over the keys to the barns. This harmonious scene was repeated elsewhere.

But at one plantation, owned by a son who was absent during most of the war because he was fighting with the Confederate army, the Allston women met defiant and armed African Americans, who lined both sides of the road as the carriage arrived. Tension grew when the carriage stopped. An old black driver, Uncle Jacob, was unsure whether to yield the keys to the barns full of rice and corn, put there by black labor. Mrs. Allston insisted. As Uncle Jacob hesitated, an angry young man shouted out: "If you give up de key, blood'll flow." Uncle Jacob slowly slipped the keys back into his pocket.

The blacks sang freedom songs and brandished hoes, pitchforks, and guns to discourage anyone from going to town for help. Two blacks, however, slipped away to find some Union officers. The Allston women spent the night safely, if restlessly, in their house. Early the next morning, they were awakened by a knock at the unlocked front door. Adele slowly opened the door, and there stood Uncle Jacob. Without a word, he gave back the keys.

The story of the keys reveals most of the essential human ingredients of the Reconstruction era. Defeated southern whites were determined to resume control of both land and labor. Rebellion aside, the law and federal enforcement generally supported the original owners of the land. The Allston women were friendly to the blacks in a genuine but maternal way and insisted on restoring the deferential relationships that existed before the war. Adele and Elizabeth, in short, both feared and cared about their former slaves.

The African-American freedpeople likewise revealed mixed feelings toward their former owners: anger, loyalty, love, resentment, and pride. They paid respect to the person of the Allstons but not to their property and crops. They wanted not revenge but economic independence and freedom.

In this encounter between former slaves and their mistresses, the role of the northern federal officials is also revealing. Union soldiers, literally and symbolically, gave the keys of freedom to the freedmen and women but did not stay around long enough to guarantee that freedom. Although encouraging blacks to plunder the master's house and seize the crops, in the crucial encounter, Union officials had disappeared. Understanding the limits of northern help, Uncle Jacob handed the keys to land and liberty back to his former owner. The blacks realized that if they wanted to ensure their freedom, they would have to do it themselves.

This chapter describes what happened to the conflicting goals and dreams of three groups as they sought to redefine new social, economic, and political relationships during the postwar Reconstruction era. Amid devastation and divisions of class and race, Civil War survivors sought to put their lives back together. Victorious but variously motivated northern officials, defeated but defiant southern planters, and impoverished but hopeful African Americans could not all fulfill their conflicting goals, yet each had to try. This guaranteed that Reconstruction would be divisive, leaving a mixed legacy of human gains and losses.

THE BITTERSWEET AFTERMATH OF WAR

"There are sad changes in store for both races," the daughter of a Georgia planter wrote in her diary early in the summer of 1865, adding, "I wonder the Yankees do not shudder to behold their work." To understand the bittersweet nature of Reconstruction, we must look at the state of the nation after the assassination of President Lincoln.

The United States in 1865

The "Union" faced constitutional crisis in April 1865. What was the status of the 11 former Confederate states? The North had denied the South's constitutional right to secede but needed four years of civil war and over 600,000 deaths to win the point. Were the 11 southern states part of the Union or not? Lincoln's official position had been that they had never left the Union, which was "constitutionally indestructible," and were only "out of their proper relation" with the United States. The president, therefore, as commander in chief, had the authority to decide how to set relations right again.

Lincoln's congressional opponents argued that by declaring war on the Union, the Confederate states had broken their constitutional ties and reverted to a kind of pre-statehood status, like territories or "conquered provinces." Congress, therefore, should resolve the constitutional issues and assert its authority over the Reconstruction process.

Politically, differences between Congress and the White House mirrored a wider struggle between two branches of the national government. During war, as has usually been the case, the executive branch assumed broad powers necessary for rapid mobilization of resources and domestic security. Many

believed, however, that Lincoln had far exceeded his constitutional authority and that his successor, Andrew Johnson, was even worse. Would Congress reassert its authority?

In April 1865, the Republican party ruled virtually unchecked. Republicans had made immense achievements in the eyes of the northern public: winning the war, preserving the Union, and freeing the slaves. They had enacted sweeping economic programs on behalf of free labor and free enterprise. These included a high protective tariff, a national banking system, broad use of the power to tax and to borrow and print money, generous federal appropriations for internal improvements, the Homestead Act, and an act to establish land-grant colleges to teach agricultural and mechanical skills. Alexander Hamilton, John Quincy Adams, and Henry Clay might all have applauded. But the party remained an uneasy grouping of former Whigs, Know-Nothings, Unionist Democrats, and antislavery idealists.

The Democrats, by contrast, were in shambles. Republicans depicted southern Democrats as rebels, murderers, and traitors, and they blasted northern Democrats as weak-willed, disloyal, and opposed to economic growth and progress. Nevertheless, in the election of 1864, needing to show that the war was a bipartisan effort, the Republicans nominated a Unionist Tennessee Democrat, Andrew Johnson, as Lincoln's vice president. Now the tactless Johnson headed the government.

Economically, the United States in the spring of 1865 presented stark contrasts. Northern cities hummed with productive activity; southern cities and railroads lay in ruin. Northern banks flourished; southern financial institutions were bankrupt. Mechanized northern farms were more productive than ever, as free farmers took pride that they had

Conflicting Goals During Reconstruction

Examine these conflicting goals which, at a human level, were the challenge of Reconstruction. How could each group possibly fulfill its goals when so many of them are in conflict with other groups? You may find yourself referring back to this chart throughout the chapter. How can each group fulfill its goals?

Victorious Northern ("Radical") Republicans

- Justify the war by remaking southern society in the image of the North
- Inflict political but not physical or economic punishment on Confederate leaders
- Continue programs of economic progress begun during the war: high tariffs, railroad subsidies, national banking
- Maintain the Republican party in power
- Help the freedpeople make the transition to full freedom by providing them with the tools of citizenship (suffrage) and equal economic opportunity

Northern Moderates (Republicans and Democrats)

- Quickly establish peace and order, reconciliation between North and South
- Bestow on the southern states leniency, amnesty, and merciful readmission to the Union
- Perpetuate land ownership, free labor, market competition, and other capitalist ventures
- Promote local self-determination of economic and social issues; limit interference by the national government
- Provide limited support for black suffrage

Old Southern Planter Aristocracy (Former Confederates)

- Ensure protection from black uprising and prevent excessive freedom for former slaves
- Secure amnesty, pardon, and restoration of confiscated lands
- Restore traditional plantation-based, market-crop economy with blacks as cheap labor force
- Restore traditional political leaders in the states
- Restore traditional paternalistic race relations as basis of social order

New "Other South": Yeoman Farmers and Former Whigs (Unionists)

- Quickly establish peace and order, reconciliation between North and South
- Achieve recognition of loyalty and economic value of yeoman farmers
- Create greater diversity in southern economy: capital investments in railroads, factories, and the diversification of agriculture
- Displace the planter aristocracy with new leaders drawn from new economic interests
- Limit the rights and powers of freedpeople; extend suffrage only to the educated few

Black Freedpeople

- Secure physical protection from abuse and terror by local whites
- Achieve economic independence through land ownership (40 acres and a mule) and equal access to trades
- Receive educational opportunity and foster the development of family and cultural bonds
- Obtain equal civil rights and protection under the law
- Commence political participation through the right to vote

amply fed the Union army and cities throughout the war. By contrast, southern farms and plantations, especially those along Sherman's march, resembled a "howling waste." Said one resident, "The Yankees came through . . . and just tore up everything."

Socially, the South was largely devastated as soldiers, many missing limbs and suffering from hunger, demobilized and returned home in April 1865. One-half million southern whites faced starvation. Yet, as a later southern writer, Wilbur Cash, explained, "If this war had smashed the Southern world, it had left the essential Southern mind and will . . . entirely unshaken." Many white southerners braced to resist Reconstruction and restore their former life while the minority who had remained quietly loyal to the Union dreamed of reconciliation.

Whatever the extremes of southern white attitudes, the dominant social reality in the spring of 1865 was that nearly 4 million freedpeople faced the challenges of freedom. After initial joy and celebration in jubilee songs, the freedmen and women quickly realized their continuing dependence on former owners. A Mississippi woman said:

> I used to think if I could be free I should be the happiest of anybody in the world. But when my master come to me, and says—Lizzie, you is free! it seems like I was in a kind of daze. And when I would wake up in the morning I would think to myself, Is I free? Hasn't I got to get up before day light and go into the field of work?

For Lizzie and 4 million other blacks, everything—and nothing—had changed.

The United States in 1865:
Crises at the End of the Civil War

Given these enormous casualties, costs, and crises of the immediate aftermath of the Civil War, what attitudes, behaviors, and goals would you predict for the major combatants in the war?

Military Casualties

360,000 Union soldiers dead
260,000 Confederate soldiers dead
620,000 Total dead
375,000 Seriously wounded and maimed
995,000 Casualties nationwide in a total male population of 15 million (nearly 1 in 15)

Physical and Economic Crises

The South devastated; its railroads, industry, and some major cities in ruins; its fields and livestock wasted

Constitutional Crisis

Eleven former Confederate states not a part of the Union, their status unclear and future status uncertain

Political Crisis

Republican party (entirely of the North) dominant in Congress; a former Democratic slaveholder from Tennessee, Andrew Johnson, in the presidency

Social Crisis

Nearly 4 million black freedpeople throughout the South facing challenges of survival and freedom, along with thousands of hungry, demobilized Confederate soldiers and displaced white families

Psychological Crisis

Incalculable stores of resentment, bitterness, anger, and despair, North and South, white and black

Hopes Among the Freedpeople

Throughout the South in the summer of 1865, optimism surged through the old slave quarters. As Union soldiers marched through Richmond, prisoners in slave-trade jails chanted: "Slavery chain done broke at last! Gonna praise God till I die!" The slavery chain, however, broke slowly, link by link. After Union troops swept through an area, as one man said, "they would tell us we was free and we'd begin celebratin'." But Confederate soldiers would follow, or master and overseer would return, and "tell us to go back to work, and we would go." Another slave recalled celebrating emancipation "about twelve times" in one North Carolina county. The freedmen and women learned, therefore, not to rejoice too quickly or openly.

Gradually, though, blacks began to test the reality of freedom. Typically, their first step was to leave the plantation, if only for a few hours or days. "If I stay here I'll never know I am free," said a South Carolina woman, who went to work as a cook in a nearby town. Some freedpeople cut their ties entirely, returning to an earlier master, or, more often, going into towns and cities to find jobs, family members, churches, and schools.

The freedpeople made education a priority. A Mississippi farmer vowed, "If I nebber does do nothing more, I shall give my children a chance to go to school, for I consider education next best ting to liberty." An official in Virginia echoed the observation of many when he said that the freedmen were "down right crazy to learn." As the war ended, impatient for teachers, they set up schools "taught by colored people who have got a little learning." One traveler throughout the South counted "at least five hundred" such schools, observing that blacks were "determined to be self-taught."

Many freedpeople left the plantation in search of a spouse, parent, or child who had been sold away years before. Advertisements detailing these sorrowful searches filled African-American newspapers. For those who found a spouse and those who had been living together in slave marriages, freedom meant getting married legally, sometimes in mass ceremonies, which were common in the first months of emancipation. Legal marriage was important morally, but it also established the legitimacy of children and meant access to land titles and other economic opportunities. Marriage meant special burdens for black women who assumed the now familiar double role of housekeeper and breadwinner. Their determination to create a family life and to educate their children resulted in the withdrawal of many women from plantation field labor.

Freedpeople also demonstrated their new status by choosing surnames. Names connoting independence, such as Washington, were common. Revealing their mixed feelings toward their former masters, some would adopt their master's name, while others would pick "any big name 'ceptin' their master's." Emancipation changed black manners around whites as well. Masks fell, and expressions of humility—tipping a hat, stepping aside, feigning happiness, addressing whites with titles of deference—diminished. For the blacks, these changes were necessary expressions of selfhood, proving that social relationships were different. Whites, however, saw these new behaviors as acts of "insolence" and "insubordination."

Other than the passion for education, the primary goal for most African Americans was securing jobs and land. "All I want is to git to own fo' or five acres ob land, dat I can build me a little house on and call my home," a Mississippi black said. Only through eco-

Both white southerners and their former slaves suffered in the immediate aftermath of the Civil War, as illustrated by this engraving from *Frank Leslie's Illustrated Newspaper*, February 23, 1867. *(The Granger Collection, New York)*

nomic independence, the American means of controlling one's own labor and land, could freedpeople like Lizzie be certain that emancipation was real.

During the war, some Union generals had put liberated slaves in charge of confiscated and abandoned lands. In the Sea Islands of South Carolina and Georgia, African Americans had been working 40-acre plots of land and harvesting their own crops for several years. Farther inland, freedpeople who received land were the former slaves of Cherokees and Creeks. Some blacks held title to these lands. Northern philanthropists had organized others to grow cotton for the Treasury Department to prove the superiority of free labor over slavery. In Mississippi, thousands of blacks worked 40-acre tracts on leased lands formerly owned by Jefferson Davis. In this highly successful experiment, they made profits sufficient to repay the government for initial costs, and then lost the land to Davis's brother.

Many freedpeople expected a new economic order as fair payment for their years of involuntary work. "It's de white man's turn ter labor now," a black preacher in Florida told a group of fieldhands, adding that "de Guverment is gwine ter gie ter ev'ry Nigger forty acres of lan' an' a mule." Others were willing to settle for less: a freedman in Virginia offered to take only one acre of land—"Ef you make it de acre dat Marsa's house sets on." Another was more guarded, aware of how easy the power could shift back to white planters: "Gib us our own land and we take care ourselves; but widout land, de ole massas can hire us or starve us, as dey please."

Such cautions aside, freedpeople hoped that the promised "40 acres and a mule" was forthcoming. Once they obtained land, family unity, and education, many looked forward to civil rights and the vote—along with protection from vengeful defeated confederates.

Everything—and nothing—had changed: In the early months of freedom, the daily life of former slaves was both the same and different. Here (top) we see a photograph of freedpeople, led by a crew leader much like during slavery days, leaving the cotton fields after a full day of gang labor carrying cotton on their heads, and a sketch (above) of a Freedmen's Bureau school in 1866, which many men, women, and children attended at night. *(Top, © Collection of The New-York Historical Society; Above, The Newberry Library)*

The Promise of Land: 40 Acres

Note the progression in various documents in this chapter from promised lands (this page), to lands restored to whites (page 551), to work contracts (page 557), to semi-autonomous tenant farms (page 559). Freedom came by degrees to freedpeople.

To All Whom It May Concern
Edisto Island, August 15th, 1865

George Owens, having selected for settlement forty acres of Land, on Theodore Belab's Place, pursuant to Special Field Orders, No. 15, Headquarters Military Division of the Mississippi, Savannah, Ga., Jan. 16, 1865; he has permission to hold and occupy the said Tract, subject to such regulations as may be established by proper authority; and all persons are prohibited from interfering with him in his possession of the same.

By command of   R. SAXTON
                         Brev't Maj. Gen.,
                         Ass't Comm.
                         S.C., Ga., and Fla.

The White South's Fearful Response

White southerners had equally mixed goals and expectations. Middle-class (yeoman) farmers and poor whites stood beside rich planters in bread lines, all hoping to regain land and livelihood. Suffering from "extreme want and destitution," as a Cherokee County, Georgia, resident put it, southern whites responded to the immediate postwar crises with feelings of outrage, loss, and injustice. "I tell you it is mighty hard," said one man, "for my pa paid his own money for our niggers; and that's not all they've robbed us of. They have taken our horses and cattle and sheep and everything." Others felt the loss more personally, as former faithful slaves for whom they felt great affection suddenly left. "Something dreadful has happened," a Florida woman wrote in 1865. "My dear black mammy has left us. . . . I feel lost, I feel as if someone is dead in the house. Whatever will I do without my Mammy?"

A more dominant emotion than sorrow, however, was fear. The entire structure of southern society was shaken, and the semblance of racial peace and order that slavery had provided was shattered. Many white southerners could hardly imagine a society without blacks in bondage. Having lost control of all that was familiar and revered, whites feared everything—from losing their cheap labor supply to having blacks sit next to them on trains. Many feared the inconvenience of doing chores like housework that they had rarely done before. A Georgia woman, Eliza Andrews, complained that it seemed to her a "waste of time for people who are capable of doing something better to spend their time sweeping and dusting while scores of lazy negroes that are fit for nothing else are lying around idle." Worse yet was the "impudent and presumin'" new manners of former slaves, a North Carolinian put it, worrying, with others, that blacks wanted social equality.

Ironically, given the rape of black women during slavery, southern whites' worst fears were of rape and revenge. African-American "impudence," some thought, would lead to legal intermarriage and "Africanization," the destruction of the purity of the white race. The presence of black soldiers was especially ominous. These fears were groundless, as demobilization of black militia units came quickly, and rape and violence by blacks against whites was extremely rare.

Believing their world turned upside down, the former planter aristocracy tried to set it right again. To reestablish white dominance, southern legislatures passed "Black codes" in the first year after the war. Many of the codes granted freedpeople the right to marry, sue and be sued, testify in court, and hold property. But these rights were qualified. Complicated passages explained under exactly what circumstances blacks could testify against whites or own property (mostly they could not) or exercise other rights of free people. Rights expressly denied were bearing arms, racial intermarriage, possessing alcoholic beverages, sitting on trains (except in baggage compartments), being on city streets at night, and congregating in large groups.

Many of the qualified rights guaranteed by the Black codes—testimony in court, for example—were passed only to induce the federal government to withdraw its remaining troops from the South. This was a crucial issue, for in many places marauding groups of whites were terrorizing virtually defenseless blacks. In one small district in Kentucky, for example, a government agent reported the following in 1865:

Twenty-three cases of severe and inhuman beating and whipping of men; four of beating and shooting; two of robbing and shooting; three of robbing; five men shot and killed; two shot and wounded; four beaten to death; one beaten and roasted; three women assaulted and ravished; four women beaten; two women tied up and whipped until insensible; two men and their families beaten and driven from their homes, and their property destroyed; two instances of burning of dwellings, and one of the inmates shot.

The Black codes, widespread violence against freedpeople, and President Johnson's veto of the Civil Rights Bill gave rise to the sardonic question "Slavery Is Dead?" Note the irony of blind justice presiding over two violations of the freedpeople's rights (described in the newspaper headings at the bottom on either side of a death's head encircled by "state rights"). *(The Newberry Library, Chicago)*

Freedpeople clearly needed protection and the right to testify in court against whites.

For white planters, the violence was another sign of social disorder that could be eased only by restoring a plantation-based society. Besides, they needed African-American labor. Key provisions of the Black codes regulated freedpeople's economic status. "Vagrancy" laws provided that any blacks not "lawfully employed" (by a white employer) could be arrested, jailed, fined, or hired out to a man who would assume responsibility for their debts and behavior. The codes regulated black laborers' work contracts with white landowners, including severe penalties for leaving before the yearly contract was fulfilled and rules for proper behavior, attitude, and manners. Thus, southern leaders sought to reestablish their dominance, agreeing with the Texan who advocated adopting "a coercive system of labor." A Kentucky newspaper was more direct: "The tune . . . will not be 'forty acres and a mule,' but . . . 'work nigger or starve.'"

NATIONAL RECONSTRUCTION POLITICS

The Black codes directly challenged the national government in 1865. Would it use its power to uphold the codes or to defend freedpeople? Would the federal government support the property rights and self-interest of the few or the rights and liberties of the many? The Reconstruction drama took place both in the South and in Washington. Although the primary story pitted white landowners against black freedmen over land and labor on southern plantations, in the background of these local struggles lurked the debate over Reconstruction policy among politicians in the nation's capital. This dual drama would extend well into the twentieth century.

Presidential Reconstruction by Proclamation

After initially demanding that the defeated Confederates be punished for "treason," President

Johnson soon adopted a more lenient policy. On May 29, 1865, he issued two proclamations setting forth his Reconstruction program. Like Lincoln's, it rested on the claim that the southern states had never left the Union.

Johnson's first proclamation continued Lincoln's policies by offering "amnesty and pardon, with restoration of all rights of property" to most former Confederates who would swear allegiance to the Constitution and the Union. Johnson revealed his Jacksonian hostility to "aristocratic" planters by exempting former Confederate government leaders and rich rebels with taxable property valued over $20,000. They could, however, apply for individual pardons, which Johnson granted to nearly all applicants.

In his second proclamation, Johnson accepted the reconstructed government of North Carolina and prescribed the steps by which other southern states could reestablish state governments. First, the president would appoint a provisional governor, who would call a state convention representing those "who are loyal to the United States," including

persons who took the oath of allegiance or were otherwise pardoned. The convention must ratify the Thirteenth Amendment, which abolished slavery; void secession; repudiate Confederate debts; and elect new state officials and members of Congress.

Under this lenient plan, all southern states completed Reconstruction and sent representatives to the Congress that convened in December 1865. Defiant southern voters elected dozens of former officers and legislators of the Confederacy, including a few not yet pardoned. Some state conventions hedged on ratifying the Thirteenth Amendment, and some asserted former owners' right to compensation for lost slave property. No state convention provided for black suffrage, and most did nothing to guarantee civil rights, schooling, or economic protection for the freedpeople. Eight months after Appomattox, the southern states were back in the Union, freedpeople were working for former masters under annual contracts, and the new president seemed firmly in charge. Reconstruction seemed to be over. A young French reporter, Georges Clemenceau, wondered if the North, having made so many "painful sacrifices," would "let itself be tricked out of what it had spent so much trouble and perseverance to win."

Congressional Reconstruction by Amendment

Late in 1865, northern leaders painfully saw that almost none of their postwar goals were being fulfilled. The South seemed far from reconstructed. The freedpeople had received neither equal citizenship nor economic independence. And the Republicans were not likely to maintain their political power. Would Democrats and the South gain by postwar elections what they had been unable to achieve by civil war?

A song popular in the North in 1866 posed the question: "Who shall rule this American Nation?"—those who would betray their country and "murder the innocent freedmen" or those "loyal millions" who had shed their "blood in battle"? The answer was obvious. Congressional Republicans, led by Congressman Thaddeus Stevens of Pennsylvania and Senator Charles Sumner of Massachusetts, decided to set their own policies for Reconstruction. Although labeled "radicals," the vast majority of Republicans were moderates on the economic and political rights of African Americans.

Rejecting Johnson's position that the South had already been reconstructed, Congress exercised its constitutional authority to decide on its own membership. It refused to seat the new senators and

---

Promised Land Restored to Whites

Richard H. Jenkins, an applicant for the restoration of his plantation on Wadmalaw Island, S. C., called "Rackett Hall," the same having been unoccupied during the past year and up to the 1st of Jan. 1866, except by one freedman who planted no crop, and being held by the Bureau of Refugees, Freedmen and Abandoned Lands, having conformed to the requirements of Circular No. 15 of said Bureau, dated Washington, D. C., Sept. 12, 1865, the aforesaid property is hereby restored to his possession.

. . . The Undersigned, Richard H. Jenkins, does hereby solemnly promise and engage, that he will secure to the Refugees and Freedmen now resident on his Wadmalaw Island Estate, the crops of the past year, harvested or unharvested; also, that the said Refugees and Freedmen shall be allowed to remain at their present houses or other homes on the island, so long as the responsible Refugees and Freedmen (embracing parents, guardians, and other natural protectors) shall enter into contracts, by leases or for wages, in terms satisfactory to the Supervising Board.

Also, that the undersigned will take the proper steps to enter into contracts with the above described responsible Refugees and Freedmen, the latter being required on their part to enter into said contracts on or before the 15th day of February, 1866, or surrender their right to remain on the said estate, it being understood that if they are unwilling to contract after the expiration of said period, the Supervising Board is to aid in getting them homes and employment elsewhere.

representatives from the former Confederate states. It also established the Joint Committee on Reconstruction to investigate conditions in the South. Its report documented white resistance, disorder, and the appalling treatment and conditions of freedpeople.

Even before the report came out in 1866, Congress passed a civil rights bill to protect the fragile rights of African Americans and extended for two more years the Freedmen's Bureau, an agency providing emergency assistance at the end of the war. Johnson vetoed both bills and called his congressional opponents "traitors." His actions drove moderates into the radical camp, and Congress passed both bills over his veto—both, however, watered down by weakening the power of enforcement. Southern courts, therefore, regularly disallowed black testimony against whites, acquitted whites of violence, and sentenced blacks to compulsory labor.

In such a climate, southern racial violence erupted. In May 1866, white mobs in Memphis, encouraged by local Irish police violence against black Union soldiers stationed nearby, went on the rampage. For over 40 hours of terror, they killed, beat, robbed, and raped virtually helpless black residents and burned houses, schools, and churches. A Memphis newspaper suggested that "the negro can do the country more good in the cotton field than in the camp," and prominent local officials urged the mob to "go ahead and kill the last damned one of the nigger race." Forty-eight people died, all but two of them black. The local Union army commander took his time restoring order, arguing that his troops "hated Negroes too." A congressional inquiry found that Memphis blacks had "no protection from the law whatever."

A month later, Congress sent to the states for ratification the Fourteenth Amendment, the most significant act of the Reconstruction era. The first section of the amendment promised permanent constitutional protection of the civil rights of blacks by defining them as citizens. States were prohibited from depriving "any person of life, liberty, or property, without due process of law," and all people were guaranteed the "equal protection of the laws." Section 2 granted black male suffrage in the South, putting the word "male" into the Constitution for the first time, and stating that those states denying the black vote would have their "basis of representation" reduced proportionally. Other sections of the amendment barred leaders of the Confederacy from national or state offices (except by act of Congress), and repudiated the Confederate debt and claims of compensation to former slave owners. Johnson urged the southern states to reject the Fourteenth Amendment, and 10 immediately did so.

The Fourteenth Amendment was the central issue of the 1866 midterm election. Johnson barnstormed the country asking voters to throw out the radical Republicans and trading insults with hecklers. Democrats north and south appealed openly to racial prejudice in attacking the Fourteenth Amendment. The nation would be "Africanized," they charged, with black equality threatening both

Reconstruction Amendments

Constitutional Seeds of Dreams Deferred for 100 Years (or More)

Substance	Outcome of Ratification Process	Final Implementation and Enforcement
Thirteenth Amendment—Passed by Congress January 1865		
Prohibited slavery in the United States	Ratified by 27 states, including 8 southern states, by December 1865	Immediate, although economic freedom came by degrees
Fourteenth Amendment—Passed by Congress June 1866		
(1) Defined equal national citizenship; (2) reduced state representation in Congress proportional to number of disenfranchised voters; (3) denied former Confederates the right to hold office; (4) Confederate debts and lost property claims voided and illegal	Rejected by 12 southern and border states by February 1867; Congress made readmission depend on ratification; ratified in July 1868	Civil Rights Act of 1964
Fifteenth Amendment—Passed by Congress February 1869		
Prohibited denial of vote because of race, color, or previous servitude (but not sex)	Ratification by Virginia, Texas, Mississippi, and Georgia required for readmission; ratified in March 1870	Voting Rights Act of 1965

Note: See exact wording in U.S. Constitution in the Appendix.

A white mob burned this freedpeople's school during the Memphis riot of May 1866. *(Library Company of Philadelphia)*

the marketplace and the bedroom. Republicans responded by calling Johnson a drunkard and a traitor and by "waving the bloody shirt," reminding voters of Democrats' treason and draft dodging during the civil war. Governor Oliver P. Morton of Indiana described the Democratic party as a "common sewer and loathsome receptacle [for] inhumanity and barbarism." But self-interest and local issues moved voters more than speeches, and the result was an overwhelming Republican victory. The mandate seemed clear: presidential Reconstruction had not worked, and Congress could present its own.

Early in 1867, Congress passed three Reconstruction acts. The southern states were divided into five military districts, whose military commanders had broad powers to maintain order and protect civil and property rights. Congress also defined a new process for readmitting a state. Qualified voters—including blacks but excluding unreconstructed rebels—would elect delegates to state constitutional conventions that would write new constitutions guaranteeing black suffrage. After the new voters of the states had ratified these constitutions, elections would be held to choose governors and state legislatures. When a state ratified the Fourteenth Amendment, its representatives to

Congress would be accepted, completing readmission to the Union.

The President Impeached

Congress also restricted presidential powers and launched an era of legislative dominance over the executive branch. The Tenure of Office Act, designed to prevent Johnson from firing the outspoken Secretary of War Edwin Stanton, limited the president's appointment powers. Other measures trimmed his power as commander in chief.

Johnson responded exactly as congressional Republicans had anticipated. He vetoed the Reconstruction acts, removed cabinet officers and other officials sympathetic to Congress, hindered the work of Freedmen's Bureau agents, and limited the activities of military commanders in the South. The House Judiciary Committee investigated, charging the president with "usurpations of power" and of acting in the "interests of the great criminals" who had led the southern rebellion. But moderate House Republicans defeated the impeachment resolutions.

In August 1867, Johnson dismissed Stanton and asked for Senate consent. When the Senate refused, the president ordered Stanton to surrender his office, which he refused, barricading himself inside.

The House quickly approved impeachment resolutions, charging the president with "high crimes and misdemeanors." The three-month trial in the Senate early in 1868 featured impassioned oratory, similar to the trial of President Bill Clinton 131 years later. Evidence was skimpy, however, that Johnson, like Clinton, had committed any constitutional crime justifying his removal. With seven moderate Republicans joining Democrats against conviction, the effort to find the president guilty fell one vote short of the required two-thirds majority. Not until the late twentieth century (Nixon and Clinton) would an American president face removal from office through impeachment.

Moderate Republicans, satisfied with the changes wrought by the Civil War, may have feared the consequences of removing Johnson, for the next man in line for the presidency, Senator Benjamin Wade of Ohio, was a leading radical Republican. Wade had endorsed woman suffrage, rights for labor unions, and civil rights for blacks in both southern and northern states. As moderate Republicans gained strength in 1868 through their support of the presidential election winner, Ulysses S. Grant, radicalism lost much of its power within Republican ranks.

What Congressional Moderation Meant for Rebels, Blacks, and Women

The impeachment crisis revealed that most Republicans were more interested in protecting themselves than the freedpeople and in punishing Johnson rather than the South. Congress's political battle against the president was not matched by a commitment to African Americans. State and local elections of 1867 showed that voters preferred moderate Reconstruction policies. In the enduring national effort to embody principles of justice, freedom, and rights, it is important to look not only at what Congress did during Reconstruction but also at what it did not do.

With the exception of Jefferson Davis, Congress did not imprison rebel Confederate leaders, and only one person, the commander of the infamous Andersonville prison camp, was executed. Congress did not insist on a lengthy probation before southern states could be readmitted to the Union. It did not reorganize southern local governments. It did not mandate a national program of education for freedpeople. It did not confiscate and redistribute land to the freedpeople, nor did it prevent Johnson from taking land away from those who had gained titles during the war. It did not, except indirectly, provide economic help to black citizens.

What Congress did do was to grant citizenship and suffrage to freedpeople, although only to southern black men. Northerners were no more prepared than southerners to make all blacks fully equal citizens. Between 1865 and 1869, several states held referendums proposing black (male) suffrage. Voters in Kansas, Ohio, Michigan, Missouri, Wisconsin, Connecticut, New York, and the District of Columbia all turned down the proposals. Only in Iowa and Minnesota (on the third try, and then only by devious wording) did northern whites grant the vote to blacks.

Proposals to give black men the vote gained support in the North only after the election of 1868, when General Grant, the supposedly invincible military hero, barely won the popular vote in several states. To ensure grateful black votes, Congressional Republicans, who had twice rejected a suffrage amendment, took another look at the idea. After a bitter fight, in 1870 the Fifteenth Amendment, forbidding all states to deny the vote "on account of race, color, or previous condition of servitude," became part of the Constitution. A black preacher from Pittsburgh observed that "the Republican party had done the Negro good, but they were doing themselves good at the same time."

One casualty of the Fourteenth and Fifteenth Amendments was the goodwill of white women. They had been fighting for rights, including the right to vote, since the Seneca Falls convention in 1848, and hoped that grateful male legislators would recognize their willing suspension of their campaign in order to support the Union during the war. The Woman's Loyal League, headed by Elizabeth Cady Stanton and Susan B. Anthony, had gathered nearly 400,000 signatures petitioning Congress to pass the Thirteenth Amendment. They were therefore shocked when the Fourteenth (and later the Fifteenth) Amendments applied only to "male" voters.

Some suffragists such as Lucy Stone were willing to accept delay, recognizing the plea of Frederick Douglass, a longtime proponent of woman suffrage, that this was "the Negro's hour." But Stanton and Anthony, veteran suffragists, campaigned against an amendment that left them out, refusing to ask women to continue to rely on fathers and husbands to protect their rights. Anthony vowed to "cut off this right arm of mine before I will ever work for or demand the ballot for the Negro and not the woman."

Disappointment over the suffrage issue helped split the women's movement in 1869. Anthony and Stanton continued their fight for a national amendment for woman suffrage and a long list of property, educational, and sexual rights, while other women focused on securing the vote state by state.

Abandoned by radical and moderate men alike, women had few champions in Congress and their efforts were put off for half a century.

The moderate Congress compromised the rights of African Americans as well as women. It gave blacks the vote but not the land, the opposite of what they wanted. Almost alone, Thaddeus Stevens argued that "forty acres . . . and a hut would be more valuable . . . than the . . . right to vote." But Congress never seriously considered his plan to confiscate the land of the "chief rebels" and give a small portion of it, divided into 40-acre plots, to the freedpeople, for this would have violated deeply held American beliefs in the sacredness of private property. Moreover, northern business interests looking to develop southern industry and invest in southern land liked the prospect of a large pool of property-less black workers.

Congress did, however, pass the Southern Homestead Act of 1866 making public lands available to blacks and loyal whites in five southern states. But the land was poor and inaccessible; no transportation, tools, or seed was provided; and most blacks were bound by contracts that prevented them from making claims before the deadline. Only about 4,000 black families even applied for the Homestead Act lands, and fewer than 20 percent of them saw their claims completed. White claimants did little better. Congressional moderation, therefore, ironically strengthened southern white landowners while leaving freedmen and women economically weak and with only paper rights as they faced the challenges of freedom.

THE LIVES OF FREEDPEOPLE

Union army major George Reynolds boasted to a friend late in 1865 that in the area of Mississippi under his command, he had "kept the negroes at work, and in a good state of discipline." Clinton Fisk, a well-meaning white who helped found a black college in Tennessee, told freedmen in 1866 that they could be "as free and as happy" working again for their "old master . . . as any where else in the world." Such pronouncements reminded blacks of white preachers' exhortations during slavery to work hard and obey their masters. Ironically, Fisk and Reynolds were agents of the Freedmen's Bureau, the agency intended to aid the black transition from slavery to freedom.

The Freedmen's Bureau

Never before in American history had one small agency—underfinanced, understaffed, and under-supported—been given a harder task than the Bureau of Freedmen, Refugees and Abandoned Lands. But with amnesty restoring lands to former owners, the Bureau controlled less than 1 percent of southern lands. Its name is telling; its fate epitomizes Reconstruction.

The Freedmen's Bureau performed many essential services. It issued emergency food rations, clothed and sheltered homeless victims of the war, and established medical and hospital facilities. It provided funds to relocate thousands of freedpeople. It helped blacks search for relatives and get legally married. It represented African Americans in local civil courts to see that they got fair trials. In conjunction with northern missionary aid societies and southern black churches, the Bureau was responsible for an extensive education program, authorizing a half million dollars for freedpeople's schooling.

Many of the earliest teachers were Quaker and Yankee "schoolmarms" who volunteered through the American Missionary Association to teach in the South. In October, 1865, Esther Douglass found "120 dirty, half naked, perfectly wild black children" in her schoolroom near Savannah, Georgia. Eight months later, she reported, "their progress was wonderful"; they could read, sing hymns, and repeat Bible verses. Bureau Commissioner General O. O. Howard estimated that by 1868, one-third of southern black children had been educated by Bureau schools. By 1870, there were almost 250,000 pupils in 4,329 agency schools when Bureau funds for education were terminated.

The Bureau's largest task was to provide African-American economic survival, serving as an employment agency. This included settling blacks on abandoned lands and getting them started with tools, seed, and draft animals, as well as arranging work contracts with white landowners. But in this area, the Freedmen's Bureau, although not intending to instill a new dependency, often supported the needs of whites to find cheap labor rather than helping blacks to become independent farmers.

Although some agents were eager to help freedpeople adjust to freedom, others were Union army officers more concerned with social order than social transformation. Working in a postwar climate of resentment and violence, Freedmen's Bureau agents were overworked, underpaid, spread too thin (at its peak only 900 agents were scattered across 11 states), and constantly harassed by local whites. Even the best-intentioned agents would have agreed with General Howard's belief in the nineteenth-century American values of self-help, minimal government interference in the marketplace, the sanctity

The Freedmen's Bureau had fewer resources in relation to its purpose than any agency in the nation's history. *Harper's Weekly* published this engraving of freedpeople lining up for aid in Memphis in 1866. *(Library of Congress)*

of private property, contractual obligations, and white superiority. The Bureau's work served to uphold these values as it sought to aid the freedpeople.

On a typical day, these overburdened agents would visit local courts and schools, file reports, supervise the signing of work contracts, and handle numerous complaints, most involving contract violations between whites and blacks or property and domestic disputes among blacks. A Georgia agent wrote that he was *"tired out* and *broke down....* Every day for 6 months, day after day, I have had from 5 to 20 complaints, *generally trivial* and of no moment, yet requiring consideration & attention coming from both Black & White." Another, reflecting his growing frustrations, complained that the freedpeople were "disrespectful and greatly in need of instruction." In finding work for freedmen and imploring freedwomen to hold their husbands accountable as providers, agents often sided with white landowners by telling blacks to obey orders, trust employers, and accept disadvantageous contracts. One agent sent a man who had complained of a severe beating back to work with the advice, "Don't be sassy [and] don't be lazy when you've got work to do."

Despite numerous constraints and even threats on their lives, the agents accomplished much. In little more than two years, the Freedmen's Bureau issued 20 million rations (nearly one-third to poor whites); reunited families and resettled some 30,000 displaced war refugees; treated some 450,000 people for illness and injury; built 40 hospitals and hundreds of schools; provided books, tools, and furnishings to the freedmen; and occasionally protected their civil rights. W.E.B. Du Bois, arguably the greatest African-American scholar of the twentieth century, wrote, "In a time of perfect calm, amid willing neighbors and streaming wealth," it "would have been a herculean task" for the Bureau to fulfill its many purposes. But in the midst of hunger, hate, sorrow, suspicion, and cruelty, "the work of ... social regeneration was in large part foredoomed to failure." The Bureau's greatest success was education; providing land was its greatest failure. By 1868, all agents were gone as Congress stopped funding.

Economic Freedom by Degrees

Despite the best efforts of the Freedmen's Bureau, the failure of Congress to provide the promised 40 acres and a mule forced freedmen and women into a new economic dependency on former masters. Blacks made some progress, however, in degrees of economic autonomy and were partly responsible, along with international economic developments, in forcing the white planter class into making major changes in southern agriculture.

First, a land-intensive system replaced the labor intensity of slavery. Land ownership was concentrated into fewer and even larger holdings than before the war. From South Carolina to Louisiana, the wealthiest tenth of the population owned about 60 percent of the real estate in the 1870s. Second, these large planters increasingly concentrated on one crop, usually cotton, and were tied into the international market. This resulted in a steady drop in food production (both grains and livestock). Third, one-crop farming created a new credit system whereby most farmers—black and white—were forced into dependence on local merchants for renting seed, farm implements and animals, provisions, housing, and land. These changes affected race relations and class tensions among whites.

This new system, however, took a few years to develop after emancipation. At first, most African Americans signed contracts with white landowners and worked fields in gangs very much as during slavery. Supervised by superintendents who still used the lash, they toiled from sunrise to sunset for a meager wage and a monthly allotment of bacon and meal. All members of the family had to work to receive their rations.

Freedpeople resented this new semi-servitude, refused to sign the contracts, and sought a measure of independence working their own lands. A South

---

A Freedman's Work Contract

As you read this rather typical work contract defining the first economic relationship between whites and blacks in the early months of the postwar period, note the regulation of social behavior and deportment, as well as work and "pay" arrangements. How different is this from slavery? As a freedman or freedwoman, would you have signed such an agreement? Why or why not? What options did you have?

State of South Carolina
Darlington District
Articles of Agreement

This Agreement entered into between Mrs. Adele Allston Exect of the one part, and the Freedmen and Women of The Upper Quarters plantation of the other part Witnesseth:

That the latter agree, for the remainder of the present year, to reside upon and devote their labor to the cultivation of the Plantation of the former. And they further agree, that they will in all respects, conform to such reasonable and necessary plantation rules and regulations as Mrs. Allston's Agent may prescribe; that they will not keep any gun, pistol, or other offensive weapon, or leave the plantation without permission from their employer; that in all things connected with their duties as laborers on said plantation, they will yield prompt obedience to all orders from Mrs. Allston or his [sic] agent; that they will be orderly and quiet in their conduct, avoiding drunkenness and other gross vices; that they will not misuse any of the Plantation Tools, or Agricultural Implements, or any Animals entrusted to their care, or any Boats, Flats, Carts or Wagons; that they will give up at the expiration of this Contract, all Tools & c., belonging to the Plantation, and in case any property, of any description belonging to the Plantation shall be willfully or through negligence destroyed or injured, the value of the Articles so destroyed, shall be deducted from the portion of the Crops which the person or persons, so offending, shall be entitled to receive under this Contract.

Any deviations from the condition of the foregoing Contract may, upon sufficient proof, be punished with dismissal from the Plantation, or in such other manner as may be determined by the Provost Court; and the person or persons so dismissed, shall forfeit the whole, or a part of his, her or their portion of the crop, as the Court may decide.

In consideration of the foregoing Services duly performed, Mrs. Allston agrees, after deducting Seventy five bushels of Corn for each work Animal, exclusively used in cultivating the Crops for the present year; to turn over to the said Freedmen and Women, one half of the remaining Corn, Peas, Potatoes, made this season. He [sic] further agrees to furnish the usual rations until the Contract is performed.

All Cotton Seed Produced on the Plantation is to be reserved for the use of the Plantation. The Freedmen, Women and Children are to be treated in a manner consistent with their freedom. Necessary medical attention will be furnished as heretofore.

Any deviation from the conditions of this Contract upon the part of the said Mrs. Allston or her Agent or Agents shall be punished in such manner as may be determined by a Provost Court, or a Military Commission. This agreement to continue till the first day of January 1866.

Witness our hand at The Upper Quarters this 28th day of July 1865.

Carolina freedman said, "If I can't own de land, I'll hire or lease land, but I won't contract." Freedwomen especially wanted to send their children to school rather than to the fields and, except for small vegetable gardens, insisted on "no more outdoor work."

A Georgia planter observed that freedpeople wanted "to get away from all overseers, to hire or purchase land, and work for themselves." Many broke contracts, haggled over wages, engaged in work slowdowns or strikes, burned barns, and otherwise expressed their displeasure with the contract labor system. In the Sea Islands and rice-growing regions of coastal South Carolina and Georgia, resistance was especially strong. On the Heyward plantations, near the Allstons, blacks "refuse work at any price," a Bureau agent reported, and the women "wish to stay in the house or the garden all the time." Even when offered livestock and other incentives, the Allstons' blacks refused to sign their contracts, and in 1869 Adele Allston was forced to sell much of her vast landholdings.

Blacks' insistence on autonomy and land of their own was the major impetus for the change from the contract system to tenancy and sharecropping. Families would hitch mules to their old slave cabin and drag it to their plot as far from the Big House as possible. Sharecroppers received seed, fertilizer, implements, food, and clothing. In return, the landlord (or a local merchant) told them what and how much to grow, and he took a share—usually half—of the harvest. The croppers' half usually went to pay for goods bought on credit (at high interest rates) from the landlord. Sharecroppers remained only semi-autonomous, tied to the landlord for economic survival.

Tenant farmers had only slightly more independence. Before a harvest, they promised to sell their crop to a local merchant in return for renting land, tools, and other necessities. From the merchant's store they also had to buy goods on credit (at a higher price than whites paid) against the harvest. At "settling up" time, income from sale of the crop was compared with accumulated debts. It was possible, especially after an unusually bountiful season, to come out ahead and eventually to own one's own land. But tenants rarely did; in debt at the end of each year, they had to pledge the next year's crop. World cotton prices remained low, and whereas big landowners still generated profits through their large scale of operation, sharecroppers rarely made much money. When they were able to pay their debts, landowners frequently altered loan agreements. Thus, debt peonage replaced slavery, ensuring a continuing cheap labor supply to grow cotton and other staples in the South.

Despite this bleak picture, painstaking, industrious work by African Americans helped many gradually accumulate a measure of income, personal property, and autonomy, especially in the household economy of producing eggs, butter, meat, food

Sharecroppers and tenant farmers, though more autonomous than contract laborers, remained dependent on the landlord for their survival. *(Brown Brothers)*

The Rise of Tenancy in the South, 1880

Although no longer slaves and after resisting labor contracts and the gang system of field labor, the freedpeople (as well as many poor whites) became tenant farmers, working on shares in the New South. The former slaves on the Barrow Plantation in Georgia, for example, moved their households to individual 25 to 30 acre tenant farms, which they rented from the Barrow family in annual contracts requiring payment in cotton and other cash crops. Where was the highest percentage of tenant farms, and how do you explain it? How would you explain the low percentage areas? What do you notice about how circumstances have changed—and not changed—on the Barrow plantation?

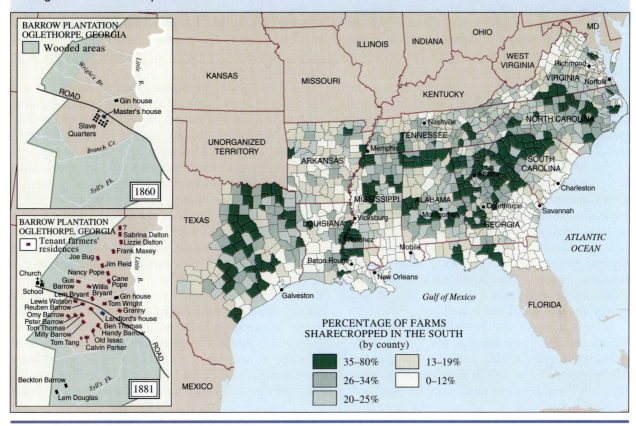

PERCENTAGE OF FARMS
SHARECROPPED IN THE SOUTH
(by county)

35–80%   13–19%
26–34%   0–12%
20–25%

crops, and other staples. Debt did not necessarily mean a lack of subsistence. In Virginia the declining tobacco crop forced white planters to sell off small parcels of land to blacks. Throughout the South, a few African Americans became independent landowners—about 3–4 percent by 1880, but closer to 25 percent by 1900.

White Farmers During Reconstruction

Changes in southern agriculture affected yeoman and poor white farmers as well, and planters worried about a coalition between poor black and pro-Unionist white farmers. As a white Georgia farmer said in 1865, "We should tuk the land, as we did the niggers, and split it, and giv part to the niggers and part to me and t'other Union fellers." But confiscation and redistribution of land was no more likely for white farmers than for the freedpeople. Whites, too, had to concentrate on growing staples, pledging their crops against high-interest credit, and facing perpetual indebtedness. In the upcountry piedmont area of Georgia, for example, the number of whites working their own land dropped from nine in ten before the Civil War to seven in ten by 1880, while cotton production doubled.

Reliance on cotton meant fewer food crops and therefore greater dependence on merchants for provisions. In 1884, Jephta Dickson of Jackson County, Georgia, purchased over $50 worth of flour, meal, meat, syrup, peas, and corn from a local store;

25 years earlier he had been almost completely self-sufficient. Fencing laws seriously curtailed the livelihood of poor whites raising pigs and hogs, and restrictions on hunting and fishing reduced the ability of poor whites and blacks alike to supplement incomes and diets.

In the worn-out flatlands and barren mountainous regions of the South, poor whites' antebellum poverty, health, and isolation worsened after the war. A Freedmen's Bureau agent in South Carolina described the poor whites in his area as "gaunt and ragged, ungainly, stooping and clumsy in build." They lived a marginal existence, hunting, fishing, and growing corn and potato crops that, as a North Carolinian put it, "come up puny, grow puny, and mature puny." Many poor white farmers, in fact, were even less productive than black sharecroppers. Some became farmhands at $6 a month and board. Others fled to low-paying jobs in cotton mills, where they would not have to compete against blacks.

The cultural life of poor southern whites reflected both their lowly position and their pride. Their religion centered on the emotional camp meeting revivals. In backwoods clearings, men and women told tall tales of superhuman feats and exchanged folk remedies for poor health. Their ballads and folklore told of debt, chain gangs, and deeds of drinking prowess. Their quilt making and house construction reflected a marginal culture in which everything was saved and reused.

In part because their lives were so hard, poor whites clung to their belief in white superiority. A federal officer reported in 1866, "The poorer classes of white people . . . have a most intense hatred of the Negro, and swear he shall never be reckoned as part of the population." Many joined the Ku Klux Klan and other southern white terror groups that emerged in 1866 to resist Reconstruction. The Klan was founded initially in Tennessee by six Confederate veterans and populated by a cross section of southern white society. With a fierce belief in white superiority, the Klan terrorized freedpeople and their white Republican allies. The Klan expressed its hatred in midnight raids on teachers in black schools, laborers who disputed their landlords' discipline, Republican voters, and any black whose "impudence" caused him not to "bow and scrape to a white man, as was done formerly."

Black Self-Help Institutions

Enforced by the Klan, African Americans were beaten, killed, sentenced to chain gangs for the slightest crimes, and bound to a life of debt, degradation, and dependency. Their hopes and dreams after emancipation had soured. Texan Felix Haywood recalled:

> We thought we was goin' to be richer than white folks, 'cause we was stronger and knowed how to work, and the whites . . . didn't have us to work for them anymore. But it didn't turn out that way. We soon found out that freedom could make folks proud but it didn't make 'em rich.

Haywood understood the limitations of programs and efforts on behalf of the freedpeople. It was clear to many black leaders, therefore, that because white people and institutions could not fulfill the promises of emancipation, blacks would have to do it themselves.

They began, significantly, with churches. The tradition of black community self-help survived in the organized churches and schools of the antebellum free Negro communities and in the "invisible" religious and cultural institutions of the slave quarters. As Union troops liberated areas of the Confederacy, blacks fled white churches for their own, causing an explosion in the growth of membership in African-American churches. The Negro Baptist Church grew from 150,000 members in 1850 to 500,000 in 1870, while the membership of the African Methodist Episcopal Church increased in the postwar decade from 50,000 to 200,000, and by 1896 to over 400,000 members. Other denominations such as the Colored (later Christian) Methodist Episcopal (CME) Church, the Reformed Zion Union Apostolic Church, and the Colored Presbyterian Church all broke with their white counterparts to establish indigenous black churches in the first decade after emancipation.

African-American ministers continued to exert community leadership. Many led efforts to oppose discrimination, some by entering politics: over one-fifth of the black officeholders in South Carolina were ministers. Most preachers, however, focused on sin, conversion, salvation, and revivalist enthusiasm. An English visitor to the South in 1867 and 1868, after observing a revivalist preacher in Savannah arouse nearly 1,000 people to "sway, and cry, and groan," noted the intensity of black "devoutness." Despite some efforts by urban blacks to restrain the emotionalism characteristic of black worship, most congregations preferred traditional forms of religious expression. One woman, when urged to pray more quietly, complained: "We make noise 'bout ebery ting else . . . I want ter go ter Heaben in de good ole way."

The freedpeople's desire for education was as strong as for religion. Even before the Freedmen's Bureau ceased operating schools, African Americans assumed more responsibility for their costs and operation. Black South Carolinians contributed

$17,000, 16 percent of the cash cost of education, and more in labor and supplies. Louisiana and Kentucky blacks contributed more to education than the Bureau itself. Georgia African Americans increased the number of "freedom schools" from 79 to 232 in 1866–1867, despite attacks by local whites who stoned them on their way home and threatened to "kill every d——d nigger white man" who worked in the schools.

Black teachers increasingly replaced whites. By 1868, 43 percent of the Bureau's teachers were African American, working for four or five dollars a month and boarding with families. Although white teachers played a remarkable role in the education of freedpeople during Reconstruction, black teachers were more persistent and positive. Charlotte Forten, for example, who taught in a school in the Sea Islands, noted that even after a half day's "hard toil" in the fields, her older pupils were "as bright and as anxious to learn as ever." Despite the taunting degradation of "the haughty Anglo-Saxon race," she said, blacks showed "a desire for knowledge, and a capability for attaining it."

Indeed, by 1870 there was a 20 percent gain in freed black adult literacy, a figure that, against difficult odds, would continue to grow for all ages to the end of the century, when there were more than 1.5 million black children in school with 28,560 black teachers. This achievement was remarkable in the face of crowded facilities, limited resources, local opposition, and absenteeism caused by the demands of fieldwork. In Georgia, for example, only 5 percent of black children went to school for part of any one year between 1865 and 1870, as opposed to 20 percent of white children. To train teachers like Forten, northern philanthropists founded Fisk, Howard, Atlanta, and other black universities in the South between 1865 and 1867.

Black schools, like churches, became community centers. They published newspapers, provided training in trades and farming, and promoted political participation and land ownership. A black farmer in Mississippi founded both a school and a society to facilitate land acquisition and better agricultural methods. These efforts made black schools objects of local white hostility. A Virginia freedman told a congressional committee that in his county, anyone starting a school would be killed and blacks were "afraid to be caught with a book." In Alabama, the Klan hanged an Irish-born teacher and four black men. In 1869, in Tennessee alone, 37 black schools were burned to the ground.

Along with equal civil rights and land of their own, what the freedpeople wanted most was education. Despite white opposition and limited facilities for black schools, one of the most positive outcomes of the Reconstruction era was education in freedpeople's schools. *(Valentine Museum, Richmond, Virginia)*

White opposition to black education and land ownership stimulated African-American nationalism and separatism. In the late 1860s, Benjamin "Pap" Singleton, a Tennessee slave who had escaped to Canada, observed that "whites had the lands and ... blacks had nothing but their freedom." Singleton urged them to abandon politics and migrate westward. He organized a land company in 1869, purchased public property in Kansas, and in the early 1870s took several groups from Tennessee and Kentucky to establish separate black towns in the prairie state. In following years, thousands of "exodusters" from the Lower South bought some 10,000 infertile acres in Kansas. But natural and human obstacles to self-sufficiency often proved insurmountable. By the 1880s, despairing of ever finding economic independence in the United States, Singleton and other nationalists urged emigration to Canada and Liberia. Frederick Douglass and other African-American leaders continued to press for full citizenship rights within the United States.

RECONSTRUCTION IN THE SOUTHERN STATES

Douglass's confidence in the power of the ballot seemed warranted in the enthusiastic early months under the Reconstruction Acts of 1867. With President Johnson neutralized, national Republican leaders finally could prevail. Local Republicans, taking advantage of the inability or refusal of many southern whites to vote, overwhelmingly elected their delegates to state constitutional conventions in the fall of 1867. Guardedly optimistic and sensing the "sacred importance" of their work, black and white Republicans began creating new state governments.

Republican Rule

Contrary to early pro-southern historians, the southern state governments under Republican rule were not dominated by illiterate black majorities intent on "Africanizing" the South by passing compulsory racial intermarriage laws, as many whites feared. Nor were these governments unusually corrupt or extravagant, nor did they use massive numbers of federal troops to enforce their will. By 1869, only 1,100 federal soldiers remained in Virginia, and most federal troops in Texas were guarding the frontier against Mexico (temporarily under French-imposed monarchial rule) and hostile Indians. Lacking strong military backing, the new state governments tried to do their work in a climate of economic distress and increasingly violent harassment.

Diverse coalitions made up the new governments elected under congressional Reconstruction. These "black and tan" governments (as opponents called them) were actually predominantly white, except for the lower house of the South Carolina legislature. Some new leaders came from the old Whig elite of bankers, industrialists, and others interested far more in economic growth and sectional reconciliation than in radical social reforms. A second group consisted of northern Republican capitalists who headed south to invest in land, railroads, and new industries. Others included Union veterans and missionaries and teachers inspired to work in Freedmen's Bureau schools. Such people were unfairly labeled "carpetbaggers."

Moderate African Americans made up a third group in the Republican state governments. A large percentage of black officeholders were mulattos, many of them well-educated preachers, teachers, and soldiers from the North. Others were self-educated tradesmen or representatives of the small landed class of southern blacks. In South Carolina, for example, of some 255 black state and federal officials elected between 1868 and 1876, two-thirds were literate and one-third owned real estate; only 15 percent owned no property at all. This class composition meant that African-American leaders often supported land policies that largely ignored the land redistribution needs of the black masses. Their goals fit squarely into the American republican tradition. Black leaders reminded whites that they, too, were southerners: "the dust of our fathers mingles with yours in the same grave yards," an 1865 petition put it, seeking only that "the same laws which govern white men shall govern black men."

The primary accomplishment of Republican rule in the South was to eliminate undemocratic features from prewar state constitutions. All states provided universal male suffrage and loosened requirements for holding office. Underrepresented counties got more legislative seats. Automatic imprisonment for debt was ended, and laws were enacted to relieve poverty and care for the handicapped. Many southern states passed their first divorce laws and provisions granting property rights to married women. Lists of crimes punishable by death were shortened, in one state from 26 to 5.

Republican governments reconstructed the South financially and physically by overhauling tax systems and approving generous railroad and other capital investment bonds. Harbors, roads, and bridges were rebuilt; hospitals and asylums were established. Most important, the Republican governments created the South's first public school systems. As in the North, these schools were largely

The Establishment of Historically Black Colleges in the South During Reconstruction

Note the scattered location of Freedmen's Bureau agencies in eight of the eleven former Confederate states. How well do you imagine agents were able to serve the 4 million freedpeople in their areas? The establishment of black colleges during Reconstruction by mostly white philanthropic monies suggests that self-help through the preparation of black preachers, teachers, and other educated leaders had more long-term potential for achieving the freedpeople's goals. What else do you see here?

Legend:
- ○ Locations of Freedmen's Bureaus
- Black colleges established during the Reconstruction Era
- Black colleges established before the Civil War
- Former Confederate states with Freedmen's Bureaus
- Former Confederate states without Freedmen's Bureaus
- Border states during Civil War

segregated, but for the first time, rich and poor, black and white alike had access to education. By the 1880s, African-American school attendance increased from 5 to over 40 percent, and white attendance increased from 20 to over 60 percent. All this cost money, and so the Republicans also increased tax rates and state debts.

These considerable achievements came in the face of opposition like that expressed at a convention of Louisiana planters, which labeled the Republican leaders the "lowest and most corrupt body of men ever assembled in the South." There was some corruption, mostly in land sales, railway bonds, and construction contracts. Such graft had become a way of life in postwar American politics, South and North.

But given their lack of experience with politics, the black role was remarkable. As Du Bois put it, "There was one thing that the White South feared more than negro dishonesty, ignorance, and incompetence, and that was negro honesty, knowledge, and efficiency."

Despite its effectiveness in modernizing southern state governments, the Republican coalition did not survive. The map on page 564 shows that Republican rule lasted for different periods in different states. A Georgia newspaper in 1868 charged that Republican rulers would "see this fair land drenched in blood from the Potomac to the Rio Grande rather than lose their power." True to their word, in Georgia and Virginia, Republicans ruled hardly at all. Situated in the shadow of Washington,

The Return of Conservative Democratic Control in Southern States During Reconstruction

Note that the length of time Republican governments were in power to implement even moderate Reconstruction programs varied from state to state. In North Carolina and Georgia, for example, Republican rule was very brief, while in Virginia it never took place at all. "Redemption," the return of conservative control, took longest in the three Deep South states where electoral votes were hotly contested in the election of 1876.

1870 Date readmitted to the Union
1870 Date of reestablishment of conservative government
○ Military districts

conservatives in Virginia professed agreement with Congress's Reconstruction guidelines while doing as they pleased. In South Carolina, white violence and African-American leaders' unwillingness to use their power to help black laborers contributed to a loss of political control to the Democrats in 1876.

Republican rule lasted longest in the Black Belt Gulf states. In Louisiana, Reconstruction began with General Ben Butler's occupation of New Orleans in 1862. Although he granted civil rights to blacks, he was quickly replaced by a succession of Republican governors in the late 1860s more interested in graft, election laws, and staying in office than in the rights and welfare of freedpeople. Class tensions and divisions among blacks in Louisiana also helped to weaken the Republican regime there. Alabama received a flood of northern capital to develop railroads and the rich coal, iron ore, and timber resources of the northern third of the state. Republican rule in Alabama typified the greater role for merchants and the emergence of a new class structure to replace the old planter aristocracy. Mississippi was another story, as we see in the next section.

Violence and "Redemption"

Democrats used violence, intimidation, and coercion to regain power. As one southern editor put it, "We must render this either a white man's government, or convert the land into a Negro man's ceme-

tery." The Ku Klux Klan was only one of several secret organizations that used violent force to drive black and white Republicans from power. Although violence was terrible throughout the South, Mississippi and North Carolina typify the pattern.

After losing a close election in North Carolina in 1868, conservatives waged a concentrated terror campaign in several piedmont counties, areas of strong Unionist support. If the Democrats could win these counties in 1870, they would most likely win statewide. In the year before the election, several prominent Republicans were killed, including a white state senator, whose throat was cut, and a leading black Union League organizer, who was hanged in the courthouse square with a sign pinned to his breast: "Bewar, ye guilty, both white and black." Scores of citizens were flogged, tortured, fired from their jobs, or driven in the middle of the night from burning homes and barns. The courts consistently refused to prosecute anyone for these crimes, which local papers blamed on "disgusting negroes and white Radicals." The conservative campaign worked. In the election of 1870, some 12,000 fewer Republicans voted in the two crucial counties than had voted two years earlier, and the Democrats swept back into power.

In Mississippi's state election 1875, Democrats used similar tactics, openly announcing that "the thieves . . . robbers, and scoundrels" in power "deserve death and ought to be killed." In what became known as the Mississippi Plan, local Democratic clubs formed armed militias, marching defiantly through black areas, breaking up Republican meetings, and provoking riots to justify killing hundreds. Armed men were posted during voter registration to intimidate Republicans. At the election itself, voters were either "helped" by gun-toting whites to cast a Democratic ballot, or they were chased away by clubs. Counties that had given Republican majorities in the thousands managed a total of less than a dozen votes in 1875.

Democrats called their victory "redemption." As conservative Democrats resumed control of each state government, Reconstruction ended. Redemption succeeded with a combination of persistent white southern resistance, including violence and coercion, and a failure of northern will. Albion Tourgée summed up the Reconstruction era in his novel *A Fool's Errand* (1879): "The spirit of the dead Confederacy was stronger than the mandate of the nation to which it had succumbed in battle."

Congress did not totally ignore southern violence. Three force acts, passed in 1870 and 1871, gave the president strong powers to use federal supervisors to ensure that citizens were not prevented from voting by force or fraud. The third act, known as the Ku Klux Klan Act, declared illegal secret organizations that used disguise and coercion to deprive others of equal protection of the laws. Congress created a joint committee to investigate Klan violence,

and in 1872 its report filled 13 huge volumes with horrifying testimony.

President Grant, who supported these measures, sent messages to Congress proclaiming the importance of the right to vote, issued proclamations condemning lawlessness, and even dispatched troops to Hamburg, South Carolina, to restore order when several blacks were killed in court by a white mob dispensing its own form of "justice" to black militiamen arrested for parading on Independence Day. Republicans, however, lost interest in defending African Americans, whose votes they took for granted or no longer thought they needed. Besides, they were much more concerned with northern issues. In 1875, Grant's advisers told him that Republicans might lose important Ohio elections if he continued protecting blacks, so he rejected appeals by Mississippi blacks for troops to guarantee free elections. He and the nation "had tired of these annual autumnal outbreaks," the president said.

The success of the Mississippi Plan in 1875, repeated a year later in South Carolina and Louisiana, indicated that congressional reports, presidential proclamations, and the Force Acts did little to stop the reign of terror against black and white Republicans throughout the South. Despite hundreds of arrests, all-white juries refused to find whites guilty of crimes against blacks. The U.S. Supreme Court backed them, in two 1874 decisions

"The negroes of the South are free—free as air," says the parliamentary Watterson. This is what the *Slate*, a well-known Democratic organ of Tennessee, says, in huge capitals, on the subject: 'Let it be known before the election that the farmers have agreed to spot every leading Radical negro in the county, and treat him as an enemy for all time to come. The rotten ring must and shall be broken at any and all costs. The Democrats have determined to withdraw all employment from their enemies. Let this fact be known."

Although the Fourteenth and Fifteenth Amendments gave African-American males the right to vote in the late 1860s, by the 1870s white southerners opposed to black suffrage found many illegal ways of influencing and eventually depriving that vote, thus returning white Democrats to office. In this cartoon, titled "Of course he wants to vote the Democratic Ticket," one of the two pistol-wielding men is saying: "You're as free as air, ain't you? Say you are, or I'll blow your black head off!" Note that another freedman is being led down the street to the polling place, no doubt to vote Democratic also. *(Corbis)*

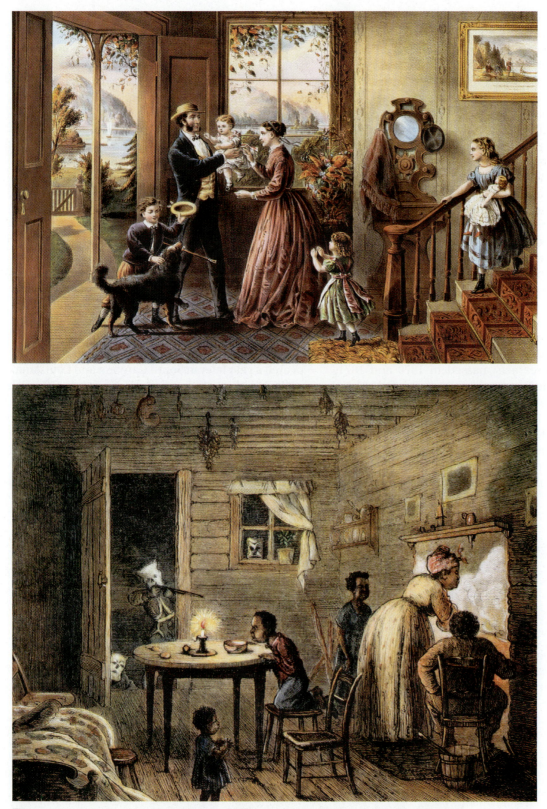

These two scenes vividly contrast family life during Reconstruction in the North and South. For most white northerners, as shown in this 1868 Currier & Ives print (top), the end of the Civil War meant renewing the good life of genteel middle-class values. *(Museum of the City of New York, The Harry T. Peters Collection)* For many freedpeople, however, family life was constantly threatened by the intrusion of Klan violence. *(The Granger Collection, New York)*

throwing out cases against whites convicted of preventing blacks from voting and declared key parts of the Force Acts unconstitutional. Although the Klan's power ended officially, the attitudes (and tactics) of Klansmen would continue long into the next century.

Shifting National Priorities

The American people in the North, like their leaders, were tired of battles over freedpeople. Frustrated with the difficulties of trying to transform an unwilling South, the easiest course was to give citizenship and the vote to African Americans, and leave them to fend for themselves. Americans of increasing ethnic diversity were primarily interested in starting families, finding work, and making money. Slovakian immigrants fired furnaces in steel plants in Pittsburgh; Chinese men pounded in railroad ties for the Central Pacific over the Sierra Nevada mountains and across the Nevada desert; Yankee women taught in one-room schoolhouses in Vermont for $23 a month; Mexican vaqueros drove Texas cattle herds to Kansas; and Scandinavian families battled heat, locusts, and high railroad rates on farmsteads in the Dakotas.

American priorities had shifted, at both the individual and national levels. Failing to effect a smooth transition from slavery to freedom for freedpeople, northern leaders focused their efforts on accelerating and solidifying their program of economic growth and industrial and territorial expansion.

As North Carolina Klansmen convened in dark forests in North Carolina in 1869, the Central Pacific and Union Pacific railroads met in Utah, linking the Atlantic and Pacific. As southern cotton production revived, northern iron and steel manufacturing and western settlement of the mining, cattle, and agricultural frontiers also surged. As black farmers haggled over work contracts with landowners in Georgia, white workers were organizing the National Labor Union in Baltimore. As Elizabeth and Adele Allston demanded the keys to their crop barns in the summer of 1865, the Boston Labor Reform Association was demanding that "our . . . education, morals, dwellings, and the whole Social System" needed to be "reconstructed." If the South would not be reconstructed, labor relations might be.

The years between 1865 and 1875 featured not only the rise (and fall) of Republican governments in the South but also a spectacular rise of working-class organizations. Stimulated by the Civil War to improve working conditions in northern factories, trade unions, labor reform associations, and labor parties flourished, culminating in the founding of the National Labor Union in 1866. Before the depression of 1873, an estimated 300,000 to 500,000 American workers enrolled in some 1,500 trade unions, the largest such increase in the nineteenth century. This growth inevitably stirred class tensions. In 1876, hundreds of freedmen in the rice region along the Combahee River in South Carolina went on strike to protest a 40-cent-per-day wage cut, clashing with local sheriffs and white Democratic rifle clubs. A year later, also fighting wage cuts, thousands of northern railroad workers went out in a nationwide wave of strikes, clashing with police and the National Guard.

As economic relations changed, so did the Republican party. Heralded by the moderate tone of state elections of 1867 and Grant's election in 1868, the Republicans changed from a party of moral reform to one of material interest. In the continuing struggle in American politics between "virtue and commerce," self-interest was again winning. Abandoning the Freedmen's Bureau as an inappropriate federal intervention, Republican politicians had no difficulty handing out huge grants of money and land to the railroads. As freedpeople were told to help themselves, the Union Pacific was getting subsidies of between $16,000 and $48,000 for each mile of track laid across western plains and mountains. As Susan B. Anthony and others tramped through the snows of upstate New York with petitions for the rights of suffrage and citizenship, Boss Tweed and other machine politicians defrauded New York taxpayers of millions of dollars. As Native Americans in the Great Plains struggled to preserve their sacred Black Hills from greedy gold prospectors protected by U.S. soldiers, corrupt government officials in the East "mined" public treasuries.

By 1869, the year financier Jay Gould almost cornered the gold market, the nation was increasingly defined by its sordid, materialistic "go-getters." Henry Adams, a descendant of two presidents, was living in Washington, D.C., during this era. As he wrote in his 1907 autobiography *The Education of Henry Adams*, he had had high expectations in 1869 that Grant, like George Washington, would restore moral order and peace. But when Grant announced his cabinet, a group of army cronies and rich friends to whom he owed favors, Adams felt betrayed, charging that Grant's administration "outraged every rule of decency."

Honest himself, Grant showed poor judgment of others. The scandals of his administration touched his relatives, his cabinet, and two vice presidents. Outright graft, loose prosecution, and generally negligent administration flourished in a half dozen

RECOVERING THE PAST

Novels

We usually read novels, short stories, and other forms of fiction for pleasure, that is, for the enjoyment of plot, style, symbolism, and character development. In addition to being well-written, "classic" novels such as *Moby Dick, Huckleberry Finn, The Great Gatsby, The Invisible Man*, and *Beloved*, explore timeless questions of good and evil, of innocence and knowledge, of noble dreams fulfilled and shattered. We enjoy novels because we often find ourselves identifying with one of the major characters. Through that person's problems, joys, relationships, and search for identity, we gain insights about our own.

Even though novels may be historically untrue, we can also read them as historical sources, for they reveal much about the attitudes, dreams, fears, and ordinary, everyday experiences of human beings in a particular period. They also show how people responded to the major events of that era. The novelist, like the historian, is a product of time and place and has an interpretive point of view. Consider the two novels about Reconstruction that are quoted here. Neither is reputed for great literary merit, yet both reveal much about the various interpretations and impassioned attitudes of the post–Civil War era. *A Fool's Errand* was written by Albion Tourgée, a northerner, while *The Clansman* was written by Thomas Dixon, Jr., a southerner.

Tourgée was a young northern teacher and lawyer who fought with the Union army and moved to North Carolina after the war, partly for health reasons and partly to begin a legal career. He became a judge and was an active Republican, supporting black suffrage and helping to shape the new state constitution and the codification of North Carolina laws. But because he boldly criticized the Ku Klux Klan for its campaign of terror against blacks, his life was threatened many times. When he left North Carolina in 1879, he published an autobiographical novel about his experiences as a judge challenging the Klan's violence against the freedpeople.

The "fool's errand" in the novel is that of the northern veteran Comfort Servosse, who, like Tourgée, seeks to fulfill humane goals on behalf of both blacks and whites in post–Civil War North Carolina. His efforts are thwarted, however, by threats, intimidation, a campaign of violent "outrages" against Republican leaders in the county, and a lack of support from Congress. Historians have verified the accuracy of many of the events in Tourgée's novel. While exposing the brutality of the Klan, Tourgée features loyal southern Unionists, respectable planters ashamed of Klan violence, and even guiltridden, poor white Klansmen who try to protect or warn intended victims.

In 1905, the year of Tourgée's death, another North Carolinian published a novel with a very different analysis of Reconstruction and its fate. Thomas Dixon was a lawyer, North Carolina state legislator, Baptist minister, pro-Klan lecturer, and novelist. *The Clansman*, subtitled *A Historical Romance of the Ku Klux Klan*, reflects turn-of-the-century attitudes most white southerners still had about Republican rule during Reconstruction. According to Dixon, once the "Great Heart" Lincoln was gone, a power-crazed, vindictive, radical Congress, led by scheming Austin Stoneman (Thaddeus Stevens), sought to impose corrupt carpetbagger and brutal black rule by bayonet on a helpless South. Only through the inspired leadership and redemptive role of the Ku Klux Klan was the South saved from the horrors of rape and revenge.

Dixon dedicated *The Clansman* to his uncle, who was a Grand Titan of the Klan in North Carolina during the time when two crucial counties were being transformed from Republican to Democratic through intimidation and terror. No such violence shows up in Dixon's novel. When the novel was made the basis of D. W. Griffith's film classic *Birth of a Nation* in 1915, the novel's attitudes were firmly imprinted on the twentieth-century American mind.

Both novels convey Reconstruction attitudes toward the freedpeople. Both create clearly defined heroes and villains. Both include exciting chase scenes, narrow escapes, daring rescues, and tragic deaths. Both include romantic subplots in which a southern man falls in love with a northern woman (both white). Yet the two novels are strikingly different.

Reflecting on the Past Even in these brief excerpts, what differences of style and attitude do you see in the descriptions of Uncle Jerry and Old Aleck? What emotional responses do you have to these passages? How do you think turn-of-the-twentieth-century Americans might have responded?

A Fool's Errand
Albion Tourgée (1879)

When the second Christmas came, Metta wrote again to her sister:

"The feeling is terribly bitter against Comfort on account of his course towards the colored people. There is quite a village of them on the lower end of the plantation. They have a church, a sabbath school, and are to have next year a school. You can not imagine how kind they have been to us, and how much they are attached to Comfort. . . . I got Comfort to go with me to one of their prayer-meetings a few nights ago. I had heard a great deal about them, but had never attended one before. It was strangely weird. There were, perhaps, fifty present, mostly middle-aged men and women. They were singing in a soft, low mono-tone, interspersed with prolonged exclamatory notes, a sort of rude hymn, which I was surprised to know was one of their old songs in slave times. How the chorus came to be endured in those days I can not imagine. It was

'Free! free! free, my Lord, free!
An' we walks de hebben-ly way!'

"A few looked around as we came in and seated our-selves; and Uncle Jerry, the saint of the settlement, came forward on his staves, and said, in his soft voice,

"'Ev'nin', Kunnel! Sarvant, Missus! Will you walk up, an' hev seats in front?'

"We told him we had just looked in, and might go in a short time; so we would stay in the back part of the audience.

"Uncle Jerry can not read nor write; but he is a man of strange intelligence and power. Unable to do work of any account, he is the faithful friend, monitor, and director of others. He has a house and piece of land, all paid for, a good horse and cow, and, with the aid of his wife and two boys, made a fine crop this season. He is one of the most promising colored men in the settle-ment: so Comfort says, at least. Everybody seems to have great respect for his character. I don't know how many people I have heard speak of his religion. Mr. Savage used to say he had rather hear him pray than any other man on earth. He was much prized by his master, even after he was disabled, on account of his faithfulness and character."

The Clansman
Thomas Dixon, Jr. (1905)

At noon Ben and Phil strolled to the polling-place to watch the progress of the first election under Negro rule. The Square was jammed with shouting, jostling, perspiring negroes, men, women, and children. The day was warm, and the African odour was supreme even in the open air. . . .

The negroes, under the drill of the League and the Freedman's Bureau, protected by the bayonet, were voting to enfranchise themselves, disfranchise their former masters, ratify a new constitution, and elect a legislature to do their will. Old Aleck was a candidate for the House, chief poll-holder, and seemed to be in charge of the movements of the voters outside the booth as well as inside. He appeared to be omnipresent, and his self-importance was a sight Phil had never dreamed. He could not keep his eyes off him. . . .

[Aleck] was a born African orator, undoubtedly descended from a long line of savage spell-binders, whose eloquence in the palaver houses of the jungle had made them native leaders. His thin spindle-shanks supported an oblong, protruding stomach, resembling an elderly monkey's, which seemed so heavy it swayed his back to carry it.

The animal vivacity of his small eyes and the flexibil-ity of his eyebrows, which he worked up and down rapidly with every change of countenance, expressed his eager desires.

He had laid aside his new shoes, which hurt him, and went barefooted to facilitate his movements on the great occasion. His heels projected and his foot was so flat that what should have been the hollow of it made a hole in the dirt where he left his track.

He was already mellow with liquor, and was dressed in an old army uniform and cap, with two horse-pistols buckled around his waist. On a strap hanging from his shoulder were strung a half-dozen tin canteens filled with whiskey.

departments. Most scandals involved large sums of public money. The Whiskey Ring affair, for example, cost the public millions of dollars in lost tax revenues siphoned off to government officials. Gould's gold scam received the unwitting aid of Grant's Treasury Department and the knowing help of the president's brother-in-law.

Nor was Congress pure. Crédit Mobilier, a dummy corporation supposedly building the transcontinental railroad, received generous bonds and contracts in exchange for giving congressmen gifts of money, stocks, and railroad lands. An Ohio congressman described the House of Representatives in 1873 as an "auction room where more valuable considerations were disposed of under the speaker's hammer than any place on earth." In Henry Adams's 1880 novel *Democracy*, written about Washington life during this period, the main character, Mrs. Madeleine Lee, sought to uncover "the heart of the great American mystery of democracy and government." What she found were corrupt legislators and lobbyists in an unprincipled pursuit of power and wealth. "Surely something can be done to check corruption?" Mrs. Lee asked her friend one evening, adding, "Is a respectable government impossible in a democracy?" His answer was that "no responsible government can long be much better or much worse than the society it represents."

The election of 1872 showed the public uninterested in moral issues. "Liberal" Republicans, disgusted with Grant, formed a third party calling for lower tariffs and fewer grants to railroads, civil service reform, and the removal of federal troops from the South. Their candidate, Horace Greeley, editor of the New York *Tribune*, was also nominated by the Democrats, whom he had spent much of his earlier career assailing. Despite his wretched record, Grant easily won a second term. Greeley was beaten so badly, he said, "I hardly knew whether I was running for the Presidency or the Penitentiary."

The End of Reconstruction

Soon after Grant's second inauguration, a financial panic, caused by commercial overexpansion into railroads, railroad mismanagement, and the collapse of some eastern banks, started a terrible depression that lasted throughout the mid-1870s. In these hard times, economic issues dominated politics, further diverting attention from the freedpeople. As Democrats took control of the House of Representatives in 1874 and looked toward winning the White House in 1876, politicians talked about new Grant scandals, unemployment and public works projects, the currency, and tariffs. No one said much about civil rights. In 1875, a guilt-ridden Congress did pass Senator Charles Sumner's civil rights bill to put teeth into the Fourteenth Amendment. But the act was not enforced, and after eight years, the Supreme Court declared it unconstitutional. Congressional Reconstruction, long dormant, was over. The election of 1876, which was the closest in American history until 2000, sealed the end.

As their presidential candidate in 1876, the Republicans chose a former governor of Ohio, Rutherford B. Hayes, partly because of his reputation for honesty, partly because he had been a Union officer (a necessity for post–Civil War candidates), and partly because, as Henry Adams put it, he was "obnoxious to no one." The Democrats nominated Governor Samuel J. Tilden of New York, a well-known civil service reformer who had broken the corrupt Tweed ring.

Like Al Gore in 2000, Tilden won a popular-vote majority and appeared to have enough electoral votes (184 to 165) for victory—except for 20 disputed votes, all but one in the Deep South states of Florida, Louisiana, and South Carolina, where some federal troops remained and where Republicans still controlled the voting apparatus despite Democratic intimidation. To settle the dispute, Congress created a special electoral commission of eight Republicans and seven Democrats, who voted along party lines to give Hayes all 20 votes and a narrow electoral-college victory, 185 to 184.

As in the election of 2000, outraged Democrats protested the outcome and threatened to stop the Senate from officially counting the electoral votes, preventing Hayes's inauguration. There was talk of a new civil war but a North–South compromise emerged. Northern investors wanted the government to subsidize a New Orleans-to-California railroad. Southerners wanted northern dollars but not northern political influence—no social agencies, no federal enforcement of the Fourteenth and Fifteenth Amendments, and no military occupation, not even the symbolic presence left in 1876.

As the March 4 inauguration date approached, and as newspapers echoed outgoing President Grant's call for "peace at any price," the forces of mutual self-interest concluded the "compromise of 1877." Democrats agreed to suspend their resistance to the counting of the electoral votes, and on March 2, Hayes was declared president. After his inauguration, he ordered the last federal troops out of the South, sending them west to fight Indians,

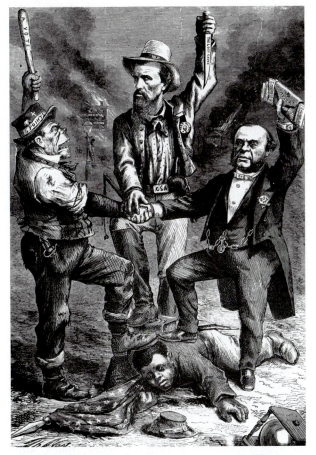

Under a caption quoting a Democratic party newspaper, "This is a white man's government," this Thomas Nast cartoon from 1868 shows three white groups (stereotyped as apelike northern Irish workers, unrepentant former Confederates, and rich northern capitalists) joining hands to bring Republican Reconstruction to an end almost before it began. The immigrant's vote, the Kluxer's knife, and the capitalist's dollars would restore a "white man's government" on the back of the freedman, still clutching the Union flag and reaching in vain for the ballot box. What else do you see here? No single image better captures the story of the end of Reconstruction. (Harper's Weekly, *September 5, 1868/The Granger Collection, New York*)

appointed a former Confederate general to his cabinet, supported federal aid for economic and railroad development in the South, and promised to let southerners handle race relations themselves. On a goodwill trip to the South, he told blacks that "your rights and interests would be safer if this great mass of intelligent white men were let alone by the general government." The message was clear: Hayes would not enforce the Fourteenth and Fifteenth Amendments, initiating a pattern of governmental inaction and white northern abandonment of African Americans that lasted to the 1960s. But the immediate crisis was averted, officially ending Reconstruction.

Timeline

1865	Civil War ends
	Lincoln assassinated; Andrew Johnson becomes president
	Johnson proposes general amnesty and Reconstruction plan
	Racial confusion, widespread hunger, and demobilization
	Thirteenth Amendment ratified
	Freedmen's Bureau established
1865–1866	Black codes
	Repossession of land by whites and freedpeople's contracts
1866	**Freedmen's Bureau renewed and Civil Rights Act passed over Johnson's veto**
	Southern Homestead Act
	Ku Klux Klan formed
	Tennessee readmitted to Union
1867	Reconstruction Acts passed over Johnson's veto
	Impeachment controversy
	Freedmen's Bureau ends
1868	Fourteenth Amendment ratified
	Senate fails to convict Johnson of impeachment charges
	Ulysses Grant elected president
1868–1870	Ten states readmitted under congressional plan
1869	Georgia and Virginia reestablish Democratic party control
1870	Fifteenth Amendment ratified
1870s–1880s	Black "exodusters" migrate to Kansas
1870–1871	Force Acts
	North Carolina and Georgia reestablish Democratic control
1872	Grant reelected president
1873	Crédit Mobilier scandal
	Panic causes depression
1874	Alabama and Arkansas reestablish Democratic control
1875	Civil Rights Act passed
	Mississippi reestablishes Democratic control
1876	Hayes–Tilden election
1876–1877	South Carolina, Louisiana, and Florida reestablish Democratic control
1877	Compromise of 1877; Rutherford B. Hayes assumes presidency and ends Reconstruction
1880s	Tenancy and sharecropping prevail in the South
	Disfranchisement and segregation of southern blacks begins

✦ *Conclusion*

A MIXED LEGACY

In the 12 years between Appomattox and Hayes's inauguration, victorious northern Republicans, defeated white southerners, and hopeful black freedpeople each wanted more than the others would give. Each saw some fulfillment of their dreams. The compromise of 1877 cemented the reunion of South and North, providing new opportunities for economic development in both regions. The Republican party achieved its economic goals and generally held the White House, though not always Congress, until 1932. The former Confederate states came back into the Union, and southerners retained their grip on southern lands and black labor, though not without struggle and some changes. Elizabeth Allston resumed authority over the family plantations for a time but eventually faced black resistance to work contracts and had to sell much of her land—to whites.

What of the freedpeople? In 1880, Frederick Douglass wrote: "Our Reconstruction measures were radically defective. . . . To the freedmen was given the machinery of liberty, but there was denied to them the steam to put it in motion. They were given the uniform of soldiers, but no arms; they were called citizens, but left subjects; they were called free, but left almost slaves. The old master class . . . retained the power to starve them to death, and wherever this power is held there is the power of slavery." The wonder, Douglass said, was "not that freedmen have made so little progress, but, rather, that they have made so much; not that they have been standing still, but that they have been able to stand at all." Freedpeople had made strong gains in education and economic and family survival. Despite sharecropping and tenancy, black laborers organized themselves to achieve a measure of autonomy and opportunity in their lives. The three great Reconstruction amendments, despite flagrant violation over the next 100 years, held out the promise that the dreams of equal citizenship and political participation would yet be realized.

But there was still an underlying tragedy to Reconstruction, as a short story by W. E. B. Du Bois, written in 1903, makes sadly clear. Two boyhood playmates, both named John, one black and one white, are sent from the fictional town of Altamaha, Georgia, north to school to prepare for leadership of their respective communities, the black John as a teacher and the white John as a judge and possibly governor. While they were away, the black and white people of Altamaha, each race thinking of its own John and not of the other, waited for "the coming of two young men, and dreamed . . . of new things that would be done and new thoughts that all would think." After several years, both Johns returned to Altamaha, but a series of tragic events shattered their hopes. Neither John understood the people of the town, and each was in turn misunderstood. Black John's school was closed because he taught ideals of liberty. Heartbroken and discouraged as he walked through the forest near town, he surprised white John in an attempted rape of his sister. Without a word, black John picked up a fallen limb, and with "all the pent-up hatred of his great black arm," killed his boyhood friend. Within hours he was lynched.

Du Bois's story captures the human cost of the Reconstruction era. The black scholar's hope for reconciliation by a "union of intelligence and sympathy across the color-line" was smashed in the tragic encounter between the two Johns. Both young men, each once filled with glorious dreams, lay dead under the pines of the Georgia forest. Dying with them were hopes that interracial harmony, intersectional trust, and equal opportunities and rights for freedpeople might be the legacies of Reconstruction. Conspicuously absent in the forest scene was the presence of northerners. They had turned their attention to other, less noble, causes.

✦ Recommended Reading

The Bittersweet Aftermath of War
W. E. B. Du Bois, *Black Reconstruction* (1935); Laura Edwards, *Gendered Strife & Confusion: The Political Culture of Reconstruction* (1997); Eric Foner, *Reconstruction: America's Unfinished Revolution, 1863–1877* (1988); John Hope Franklin, *Reconstruction After the Civil War* (1961); Leon Litwack, *Been in the Storm So Long: The Aftermath of Slavery* (1980); James M. McPherson, *Ordeal by Fire: Civil War and Reconstruction*, 3rd ed. (2000).

National Reconstruction Politics
Richard H. Abbott, *The Republican Party and the South, 1855–1877* (1986); Michael Les Benedict, *A Compromise of Principle: Congressional Republicans and Reconstruction,*

1863–1869 (1974); David Donald, *The Politics of Reconstruction* (1965); William Gillette, *Retreat from Reconstruction, 1869–1879* (1979); Ward M. McAfee, *Religion, Race, and Reconstruction: The Public Schools in the Politics of the 1870s* (1998); William McFeeley, *Grant: A Biography* (1981); Heather Cox Richardson, *The Death of Reconstruction: Race, Labor, and Politics in the post–Civil War North, 1865–1901* (2001); Brooks D. Simpson, *The Reconstruction Presidents* (1998); Hans L. Trefousse, *Thaddeus Stevens: Nineteenth-Century Egalitarian* (1997); Allen Trelease, *Andrew Johnson: A Biography* (1989).

The Lives of Freedpeople
Paul Cimbala and Randall M. Miller, eds., *The Freedmen's Bureau and Reconstruction: Reconsiderations* (1999); Paul Cimbala, *Under the Guardianship of the Nation: The Freedmen's Bureau and the Reconstruction of Georgia, 1865–1870* (1997); Eric Foner, *Nothing but Freedom: Emancipation and Its Legacy* (1983); Noralee Frankel, *Freedom's Women: Black Women and Families in Civil War Era Mississippi* (1999); Sharon Ann Holt, *Making Freedom Pay: North Carolina Freedpeople Working for Themselves, 1865–1900* (2000); Tera Hunter, *To 'Joy My Freedom: Southern Black Women's Lives and Labors after the Civil War* (1997); Jacqueline Jones, *Soldiers of Light and Love: Northern Teachers and Georgia Blacks, 1865–1873* (1980); Robert Kenzer, *Enterprising Southerners: Black Economic Success in North Carolina, 1865–1915* (1997); Leon Litwack, *Been in the Storm So Long: The Aftermath of Slavery* (1980); Roger Ransom and Richard Sutch, *One Kind of Freedom: The Economic Consequences of Emancipation* (1977); Elizabeth Regosin, *Freedom's Promise: Ex-Slaves and Citizenship in the Age of Emancipation* (2002); Edward Royce, *The Origins of Southern Sharecropping* (2002); Julie Saville, *The Work of Reconstruction: From Slave to Wage Laborer in South Carolina, 1860–1870* (1994).

Reconstruction in the Southern States
W. Fitzhugh Brundage, *Lynching in the New South: Georgia and Virginia, 1880–1930* (1993); Dan T. Carter, *When the War Was Over: The Failure of Self-Reconstruction in the South* (1985); Thomas Holt, *Black over White: Negro Political Leadership in South Carolina During Reconstruction* (1977); Edward A. Miller, *Gullah Statesman: Robert Smalls from Slavery to Congress, 1839–1915* (1995); George C. Rable, *But There Was No Peace: The Role of Violence in the Politics of Reconstruction* (1984); Scott Reynolds, *Iron Confederacies: Southern Railways, Klan Violence, and Reconstruction* (1999); Joel Williamson, *The Crucible of Race* (1984) and *A Rage for Order: Black/White Relations in the American South Since Emancipation* (1986).

Fiction and Film
W. E. B. Du Bois's *The Quest of the Silver Fleece* (1911) is a little-known novel by the sociologist-historian about the lives of sharecroppers during Reconstruction. Howard Fast's *Freedom Road* (1944) is a novel about the heroic but ultimately failed efforts of poor whites and blacks to unite for mutual benefit during the era. Ernest Gaines's *The Autobiography of Miss Jane Pittman* (1971), framed as an autobiography, is a gripping fictional account of a proud centenarian black woman who lived from the time of the Civil War to the era of civil rights. In *A Fool's Errand* (1879), as described in the "Recovering the Past" section, Albion Tourgee takes the viewpoint of a sympathetic white judge who helps the freedpeople in North Carolina during Reconstruction. Margaret Walker's *Jubilee* (1966) is a black woman novelist's epic version of the African-American experience in the Civil War era, and Alice Randall's *The Wind Done Gone* (2001) is a parody of Margaret Mitchell's *Gone With the Wind* (1936); both follow black and white families from slavery to Reconstruction. Toni Morrison's *Beloved* (1988), an extraordinary novel set near Cincinnati in 1873 that includes flashbacks, is about the lasting traumas of slavery as black women especially seek to put their lives together and pursue their dreams of freedom. The film of the same name (1998), though slow moving, follows the time disconnections of the novel well with many moving scenes. *Birth of a Nation*, the classic 1913 film by D. W. Griffith that portrays the rise of the Ku Klux Klan as the defender of white supremacy and womanhood, is based on Thomas Dixon's *The Clansman* (1905) (which is described in the "Recovering the Past" section of the chapter).

✦ Discovering U.S. History Online

A Documentary History of Emancipation, 1861–1867
www.inform.umd.edu/ARHU/Depts/History/Freedman/home.html
A rich collection of primary sources from the Freedom and Southern Society Project of the University of Maryland, containing superb links to four completed of nine projected volumes of collected documents.

Civil War, Reconstruction and Recovery in Brazoria County, Texas
www.bchm.org/wrr/
This illustrated exhibit focuses on Reconstruction and recovery in Texas as an example of these issues in the South.

Nineteenth Century African-American Legislators and Constitutional Convention Delegates of Texas
www.tsl.state.tx.us/exhibits/forever/index.html
This exhibit documents the political struggles in the post–Reconstruction South via the stories of the "52 African-American men who served Texas as either state legislative members or Constitutional Convention delegates."

The Impeachment of Andrew Johnson
www.andrewjohnson.com
Over 200 excerpts from contemporary issues of *Harper's Weekly* (1865–1869) provide in-depth information about Andrew Johnson and the impeachment process.

Images of African-Americans from the Nineteenth Century

www.digital.nypl.org/schomburg/images_aa19/

A vast collection of visual images by artists, engravers, and photographers capturing elements of African-American life in the nineteenth century.

Reports on Black America, 1857–1874

www.blackhistory.harpweek.com

Fascinating text and imagery found in the pages of *Harper's Weekly* magazine.

African-American Perspectives, 1818–1907

www.memory.loc.gov/ammem/aap/aaphome.html

This searchable collection is filled with links to Reconstruction topics and political speeches and manuscripts from the Federal Writers' Project interviews with ex-slaves in the 1930s.

Diary and Letters of Rutherford B. Hayes

www.ohiohistory.org/onlinedoc/hayes/index.cfm

The center offers a searchable database of 3,000 pages digitized from the five volume set of Hayes's presidential diaries and letters.

Central Pacific Railroad

www.cprr.org

This searchable site traces the history of the completion of the first transcontinental railroad. The Web site includes photographs, 3-D stereographs, engravings, documents, railroad and survey maps, and other related materials.

Freedmen's Bureau in Augusta County, Virginia

www.vcdh.virginia.edu/afam/reconst.html

"This student-made project traces the attempts by Augusta County African Americans and the U.S. Freedmen's Bureau to reunite families, establish fair labor practices, and build community institutions."

17 Rural America: The West and the New South

The flat landscape disappearing into the horizon, the picture of a hardworking and determined woman—these suggest some of the geographic and physical realities of rural life in the West.
(Harvey Dunn, The Homesteader's Wife, *1916/South Dakota Memorial Art Center Collection, Brookings)*

◆ *American Stories*

REALIZING DREAMS: LIFE ON THE GREAT PLAINS

In 1873, Milton Leeper, his wife, Hattie, and their baby, Anna, climbed into a wagon piled high with their possessions and set out to homestead in Boone County, Nebraska. Once on the claim, the Leepers dreamed confidently of their future. Wrote Hattie to her sister in Iowa, "I like our place the best of any around here. When we get a fine house and 100 acres under cultivation," she added, "I wouldn't trade with any one." But Milton had broken in only 13 acres when disaster struck. Hordes of grasshoppers appeared, and the Leepers fled their claim and took refuge in the nearby town of Fremont.

There they stayed for two years. Milton worked first at a store and then hired out to other farmers. Hattie sewed, kept a boarder, and cared for chickens and a milk cow. The family lived on the brink of poverty but never gave up hope. "Times are hard and we have had bad luck," Hattie acknowledged, but "I am going to hold that claim . . . there will [be] one gal that won't be out of a home." In 1876, the Leepers triumphantly returned to their claim with the modest sum of $27 to help them start over.

The grasshoppers were gone, there was enough rain, and preaching was only half a mile away. The Leepers, like others, began to prosper. Two more daughters were born and cared for in the comfortable sod house—"homely" on the outside but plastered and cozy within. As Hattie explained, the home-steaders lived "just as civilized as they would in Chicago."

Their luck did not last. Hattie, pregnant again, fell ill and died in childbirth along with her infant son. Heartbroken, Milton buried his wife and child and left the claim. The last frontier had momentarily defeated him, although he would try farming in at least four other locations before his death in 1905.

The same year that the Leepers established their Boone County home-stead, another family tried their luck in a Danish settlement about 200 miles west of Omaha. Rasmus and Ane Ebbesen and their eight-year-old son, Peter, had arrived in the United States from Denmark in 1868, lured by the promise of an "abundance" of free land "for all willing to cultivate it." By 1870, they had made it as far west as Council Bluffs, Iowa. There they stopped to earn the capital that would be necessary to begin farming. Rasmus dug ditches for the railroad, Ane worked as a cleaning woman in a local boardinghouse, and young Peter brought drinking water to thirsty laborers who were digging ditches for the town gas works.

Like the Leepers, the Ebbesens eagerly settled on their homestead and be-gan to cultivate the soil. Peter later recalled that the problems that the family had anticipated never materialized. Even the rumors that the Sioux, "flying demons" in the eyes of settlers, were on the rampage proved false. The real problems the family faced were unexpected: rattlesnakes, prairie fires, and an invasion of grasshoppers. The grasshoppers were just as devastating to the Ebbesen farm as they had been to the Leeper homestead. But unlike the Leepers, the Ebbesens stayed on the claim. Although the family "barely had enough" to eat, they survived the three years of grasshopper infestation.

In the following years, the Ebbesens thrived. Rasmus had almost all the original 80 acres under cultivation and purchased an additional 80 acres from the railroad. A succession of sod houses rose on the land and finally even a two-story frame house, paid for with money Peter earned teaching school. By the time they were in their 50s, they could look with pride at their "luxurient and promising crop." But once more natural disaster struck: a "violent hailstorm . . . which completely devastated the whole lot."

The Ebbesens were lucky, however. A banker offered to buy them out, al-though the amount was $1,000 less than what the family calculated as the farm's "real worth." But it was enough for the purchase of a "modest" house in town. Later, there was even a "dwelling of two stories and nine rooms . . . with adjacent park."

The stories of the Leepers and the Ebbesens, though different in their details and endings, hint at some of the problems confronting rural Americans in the last quarter of the nineteenth century. As a mature industrial economy transformed agriculture and shifted the balance of economic power permanently away from America's farmlands to the country's cities and factories, many farmers found it impossible to realize the traditional dream of rural independence and prosperity. Even bountiful harvests no longer guaranteed success. "We were told two years ago to go to work and raise a big crop; that was all we needed," said one farmer. "We went to work and plowed and planted; the rains fell, the sun shone, nature smiled, and we raised the big crop they told us to; and what came of it? Eight cent corn, ten cent oats, two cent beef and no price at all for butter and eggs—that's what came of it." Native Americans also discovered that changes in rural life threatened their values and dreams. As the Sioux leader Red Cloud told railroad surveyors in Wyoming, "We do not want you here. You are scaring away the buffalo."

This chapter explores several of this book's basic questions as it analyzes the agricultural transformation of the late nineteenth century. Highlighting the ways in which rural Americans—red, white, yellow, and black—joined the industrial world, it asks how diverse groups responded to new economic and social conditions. The rise of large-scale agriculture in the West, the exploitation of its natural resources, and the development of the Great Plains form a backdrop for discussing the impact of white settlement on western tribes and assessing how well native peoples were able to preserve their culture and traditions. In an analysis of the South, the efforts of whites to create a "New South" form a contrast to the underlying realities of race and cotton. Although the chapter shows that discrimination and economic peonage characterized the lives of most black southerners during this period, it also describes the rise of new black protest tactics and ideologies. Finally, the chapter highlights the ways in which agricultural problems of the late nineteenth century, which would continue to characterize much of agricultural life in the twentieth century, led American farmers to become reformers.

MODERNIZING AGRICULTURE

Between 1865 and 1900, the nation's farms more than doubled in number as Americans eagerly took up virgin land west of the Mississippi River. In both newly settled and older areas, farmers raised specialized crops with the aid of modern machinery and relied on the expanding railroad system to send them to market. The character of agriculture became increasingly capitalistic. As one New Englander pointed out, farmers had to understand "farming as a business; if they do not it will go hard with them."

While small family farms still typified American agriculture, vast mechanized operations devoted to the cultivation of one crop appeared, especially west of the Mississippi River. The bonanza farms, established in the late 1870s on the northern plains, symbolized the trend to large-scale agriculture. Thousands of acres in size, these wheat farms required large capital investments; in fact, corporations owned many of them. Like factories, they depended on machinery, hired hundreds of workers, and relied on efficient managers. Although bonanza farms were not typical, they dramatized the agricultural changes that were occurring everywhere on a smaller scale.

Despite their success in adapting farming to modern conditions, farmers were slipping from their dominant position in the workforce. In 1860, they represented almost 60 percent of the labor force; by 1900, less than 37 percent of employed Americans farmed. At the same time, farmers' contribution to the nation's wealth declined from one-third to one-quarter.

American Agriculture and the World

The expansion of American agriculture was tied to changing global patterns and demands. During the nineteenth century, the population of Europe exploded, growing from 175 million in 1800 to 435 million in 1910. While some Europeans continued to till the land, increasing numbers abandoned farming and drifted into cities to find industrial work. In Britain, farmers, who made up only 10 percent of the total workforce, could not produce nearly enough to feed the nation. Like other European countries, Great Britain had to import substantial supplies of food for its citizens. The growing demand prompted American farmers along with their counterparts in Eastern Europe, Australia, and New Zealand to expand their operations for the European market.

In their attempts to improve crop yields and livestock, American farmers both benefited from and contributed to trends in agriculture elsewhere in the world. German scientists facilitated agricultural expansion after 1850 by developing better seeds, livestock, and chemical fertilizers. The land-grant university system in the United States, established during the Civil War, ensured that American agriculturists would continue to have access to research into and development of better strains of crops and animals and more effective farming methods. For their part, American farmers led the way in using farm machinery like the horse-drawn harvester, showing farmers elsewhere in the world the way to raise bigger harvests.

This integration into the wider world depended on improved transportation at home and abroad. Reliable, cheap transportation in the United States allowed farmers to specialize: wheat on the Great Plains, corn in the Midwest. Eastern farmers turned to vegetable, fruit, and dairy farming—or sold out. Cotton, tobacco, wheat, and rice dominated in the South, and grain, fruits, and vegetables were prevalent in the Far West. The development of steamships and an ever-expanding network of railroad systems in Europe ensured that Americans goods and products could move swiftly, efficiently, and cheaply across land and sea to distant markets.

As farmers specialized for national and international markets, their success depended increasingly on outside forces and demands. Bankers and investors, many of them European, provided the capital to improve transportation and expand operations; middlemen stored and sometimes sold produce; and railroads and steamships carried it to market. A prosperous economy at home and abroad put money into laborers' pockets for food purchases. But when several European countries banned American pork imports between 1879 and 1883, fearing trichinosis, American stock raisers suffered. As Russian, Argentinean, and Canadian farmers turned to wheat cultivation, increased competition in the world market affected the United States' chief cash crop. Moreover, the world-wide deflation of prices for crops like wheat and corn affected all who raised these crops for the international market, including American farmers.

The Character of American Agriculture

Technological innovation played a major role in facilitating American agricultural expansion. Harvesters, binders, and other new machines, pulled by work animals, diminished much of the drudgery of farming life, making the production of crops easier, more efficient, and cheaper. Moreover, they allowed a farmer to cultivate far more land than possible with hand tools. But machinery was expensive, and many American farmers borrowed to buy it. In the decade of the 1880s, mortgage indebtedness grew two and a half times faster than agricultural wealth.

Only gradually did farmers only realize the perils of their new situation in the world. Productivity rose 40 percent between 1869 and 1899. But so large

Price of Wholesale Wheat Flour, 1865–1900

The plummeting price of wheat flour was just one indication of the difficulties farmers faced in the late nineteenth century.

Source: U.S. Bureau of the Census.

were the harvests for crops like wheat that the domestic market could not absorb them. Foreign competition and deflation further affected steadily declining prices. In 1867, corn sold for 78 cents a bushel. By 1873, it had tumbled to 31 cents, and by 1889, to 23 cents. Wheat similarly plummeted from about $2 a bushel in 1867 to only 70 cents a bushel in 1889. Cotton profits also spiraled downward, the value of a bale depreciating from $43 in 1866 to $30 in the 1890s.

Falling prices did not automatically hurt all farmers. Because the supply of money rose more slowly than productivity, all prices declined—by more than half between the end of the Civil War and 1900 (for a discussion of the money issue, see Chapter 19). In a deflationary period, farmers were receiving less for their crops but also paying less for their purchases.

Deflation may have encouraged overproduction, however. To make the same amount of money, many farmers believed they had to raise larger and larger crops. As they did, prices fell even lower. Furthermore, deflation increased the real value of debts. In 1888, it took 174 bushels of wheat to pay the interest on a $2,000 mortgage at 8 percent. By

George Inness's *Lackawanna Valley*—with the reclining figure in the foreground, the train, and puffing smokestacks in the background—suggests that there need be no conflict between technology and agriculture. *(Inness, George, The Lackawanna Valley, Gift of Mrs. Huttleston Rogers, © 2000 Board of Trustees, National Gallery of Art, Washington, c. 1856, oil on canvas, .860 × 1.275 [33 ⅞ × 50 ¼])*

1895, it took 320 bushels. Falling prices thus had their greatest impact on farmers in newly settled areas who had borrowed heavily to finance their new operations.

THE WEST

In 1893, the young American historian Frederick Jackson Turner addressed historians gathered at Chicago's World's Fair. Even though the hour was late, Turner's remarks must have galvanized some of his listeners. The age of the American frontier had ended, Turner declared, pointing to recent census data that suggested the disappearance of vacant land in the West. Although Turner overstated his case (for even in the twentieth century much of the West remained uninhabited), his analysis did reflect the rapid expansion into the trans-Mississippi West after the Civil War. Between 1870 and 1900, acreage devoted to farming tripled west of the Mississippi, while from 1880 to 1900, the western population grew at a faster rate than the nation as a whole.

The Frontier Thesis in National and Global Context

Turner greeted the end of the frontier as a milestone in the nation's history. The frontier had played a central role, he argued, in shaping the American character and American institutions. Over the course of American history, the struggle to tame the wilderness had changed settlers from Europeans into Americans and created a rugged individualism that "promoted democracy." Turner's thesis, emphasizing the unique nature of the American experience and linking it to the frontier, won many sup-

porters. His interpretation complemented long-held ideas about the exceptional nature of American society and character. It accorded with what many saw as a long struggle to conquer what Turner called the "wilderness."

But the American westward movement was less unusual than Turner suggested. The settlement of the trans-Mississippi West was part of a global pattern that redistributed European populations into new areas of the world. Paralleling their American counterparts, farmers, miners, and ranchers were claiming land in Argentina, Brazil, New Zealand, Australia, Canada, and South Africa. Like Americans, they argued that native occupants had failed to make the land productive, and they used their technological superiority to wrest the land from those they considered backwards and inferior. Around the world, many native peoples were facing domination by settler societies or retreating as far away from "civilization" as they could.

Turner's frontier scheme gave the place of honor to the frontier farmer who transformed and civilized the wilderness. Before the Civil War, however, real farmers avoided settling many parts of the West. Few chose to try their luck on the Great Plains, an area from 200 to 700 miles wide, extending from Canada to Texas. Much of this region, especially beyond the 98th meridian, had little rain. The absence of trees seemed to symbolize the plains' unsuitability for agriculture.

The Cattleman's West, 1860–1890

While the region of the Great Plains initially discouraged farmers, its grasses provided the founda-

Here a lone cowboy herds cattle. Although novels and movies often romanticize cowboys, their job was far from glamorous or financially rewarding. The flat, dry, and somewhat barren landscape suggests some of the realities of herding cattle. *(Brown Brothers)*

tion for the cattle kingdom. Mining discoveries in California and the Rocky Mountains established a market for meat. When cattlemen discovered before the Civil War that their animals could graze throughout the year on bunchgrass that accommodatingly turned into hay on its own, the future of the Great Plains for cattle raising became clear.

Although cattle raising dated back to Spanish mission days, the realization of the commercial possibilities for cattle ranching was partly a by-product of Union military strategy. During the war, the North had split the South, cutting Texas off from Confederate cattle markets. By the war's end, millions of longhorns roamed the Texas range. The postwar burst of railroad construction provided a way of turning these cattle into dollars. If Texas ranchers drove their steers north to Abilene, Wichita, or Dodge City, they could be loaded on rail-road cars for slaughtering and packinghouses in cities like Chicago and Kansas City. In the cattle drives of the late 1860s and 1870s, cowboys herded thousands of longhorns north with hefty profits for owners and investors.

Ranchers on the Great Plains bought some of the cattle and bred them with Hereford and Angus cows to create cattle able to withstand the region's severe winters. In the late 1870s and early 1880s, huge ranches appeared in eastern Colorado, Wyoming, and Montana and in western Kansas, Nebraska, and the Dakotas. These ventures, many owned by out-side investors, paid off handsomely. Because the cattle could roam at will over the public domain, they cost owners little as they fattened up but commanded good prices at the time of sale. The cow-boys (one-third of them Mexican and black) who herded the steers, however, shared few of the profits. Their meager wages of $25 to $40 a month were just enough to pay for a fling in the saloons, dance halls, and gambling palaces in Dodge City or Abilene when taking the cattle to market.

By the mid-1880s, the first phase of the cattle frontier was ending as farmers moved onto the Plains, bought up public lands once used for grazing, and fenced them in. But the competition between cattle ranchers and farmers was only one factor in the cattle frontier's collapse. Eager for profits, ranchers overstocked their herds in the mid-1880s. European investors added to the rush of capital into herding. Hungry cattle ate everything in sight, then weakened as grass became scarce. As was often the case on the Plains, the weather played an important role. A winter of memorable blizzards followed the very hot summer of 1886. Cattle, usually able to forage for themselves during the winter months, could not dig through the deep snow to the grass and died from starvation. By spring, 90 percent of the cattle were dead. One observer reported seeing "countless carcasses of cattle . . . going down [a stream] with the ice, rolling over and over as they went, sometimes with all four stiffened legs pointing skyward.

For days on end, tearing down with the grinding ice cakes, went Death's cattle roundup." Frantic owners dumped their surviving cattle on the market, getting $8 or even less per animal.

In the aftermath, the ranchers who remained stock raisers adopted new techniques. Experimenting with new breeds, they began to fence in their herds and to feed them grain during the winter. Since consumers were hungering for tender beef, these new methods suited the market. Ranching, like farming, was becoming a modern business.

Ranching altered the western landscape in ways that had immediate and future ecological consequences. As one Texan realized, "Grass is what counts. It's what saves us all—as far as we get saved. . . . Grass is what holds the earth together." Seeing native species as either competing with cattle for nourishment or threatening them, ranchers hunted and killed antelope, elk, wolves, and other wildlife. When cattlemen overstocked the range, their herds devoured the perennial grasses. In their place, tough, less nutritious annual grasses sprang up, and sometimes even these grasses disappeared. Lands once able to support large herds of cattle eventually were transformed into deserts of sagebrush, weeds, and dust.

Farmers on the Great Plains, 1865–1890s

Views of the agricultural possibilities of the Great Plains brightened after the Civil War, and railroads played a key role in transforming views of the region's potential. Now that rail lines crossed the continent, they needed customers, settlers, and freight to make a profit. Along with town boosters and land speculators, also hoping to capitalize on their investments, railroads joined in extravagant promotional campaigns. "This is the sole remaining section of paradise in the western world," promised one newspaper. "All the wild romances of the gorgeous orient dwindle into nothing when compared to the everyday realities of Dakota's progress." Propaganda reached beyond the United States to bring the message to Scandinavians, Germans, and others. Dismissing the fear that the plains lacked adequate rainfall to support cultivation, the promotional material assured readers that "All that is needed is to plow, plant, and attend to the crops properly; the rains are abundant." Above average rainfall in the 1880s strengthened the case.

In the first boom period of settlement, lasting from 1879 to the early 1890s, tens of thousands of eager families moved onto the Great Plains and began farming. The majority came from Illinois, Iowa, and Missouri. But like the Ebbesens, a substantial number of settlers were immigrants, making the Great Plains the second most important destination for foreign immigration. The greatest numbers came from Germany, the British Isles, and Canada, joined by smaller groups of Scandinavians, Czechs, and Poles. Unlike the single immigrant men flocking to American cities for work, these newcomers came with their families. From the beginning, they intended to put down roots in the new country.

Some settlers established their farms by making claims under the provisions of the Homestead Act, which granted 160 acres to any family head or adult who lived on the claim for five years or who paid

Agricultural Productivity, 1800–1900

The astonishing gains in the productivity of wheat farmers point to the use of reapers that cut and bound the wheat and thrashers that knocked the grain off the stalks. The combine integrated both operations and also cleared and bagged the grain.

Crop and Productivity Indicator	1800	1840	1880	1900
Wheat				
Worker-hours/acre	56	35	30	15
Yield/acre (bushels)	15	15	13	14
Worker-hours/100 bushels	373	233	152	108
Corn				
Worker-hours/acre	86	69	46	38
Yield/acre (bushels)	25	25	26	26
Worker-hours/100 bushels	344	276	180	147
Cotton				
Worker-hours/acre	185	135	119	112
Yield/acre (bushels)	147	147	179	191
Worker-hours/bale	601	439	318	280

Source: U.S. Bureau of the Census.

Routes West

On this map, you can trace the various overland routes to the West. How many railroad lines ran across the West? Notice how the railroads contributed to urban growth as trains made their way west. The transcontinental railroads also provided the basis for the economic and demographic expansion and helped to tie East and West together.

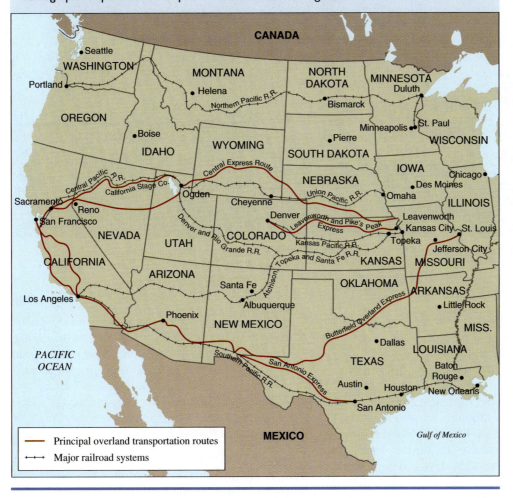

$1.25 an acre after six months of residence. Because homestead land was frequently less desirable than land held by railroads and speculators, however, most settlers bought land outright rather than taking up claims. The costs of getting started were thus more substantial than the Homestead Act would suggest. Western land was cheap compared with farmland in the East, but an individual farmer was fortunate if he could buy a good quarter section for under $500. The costs of machinery would often reach $700. Although some farmers thought it made better economic sense to lease rather than buy land, many rented only because they lacked the capital to purchase land and set up operations. In 1880, some 20 percent of the Plains farmers were tenants, and this percentage rose over time.

Achieving success on a Plains farm was much more difficult than promotional materials promised. Violent changes in the weather and temperature along with the scarcity of water and wood all demanded adjustments. Without firewood, farmers learned to burn corncobs and twisted straw for warmth. The log cabin, long the symbol of frontier life, was replaced by houses of sod "bricks." Although from a distance such houses often looked like mounds of earth—"homely old things," as Hattie Leeper described them—they frequently had glass windows, wooden shingles, and even plastered interiors. Dark and gloomy to our eyes, they were comfortable, cozy, and practical for the settlers. Walls two to three feet thick kept out the scorching summer heat and fierce cold of winter, the moaning

This sod house, surrounded by wooden planks, was the home of a Norwegian family. Note that the family are dressed in their good clothes, and have posed with some of their furniture, their houseplants, and an elaborate baby carriage. One of the children holds her doll. This scene suggests the pride the family felt in their homestead. *(The Fred Hulstrand History in Pictures Collection, NDSU, Fargo, ND)*

winds, and the prairie fires. The solidity of the sod house provided a welcome contrast to the impersonal power and scale of nature.

Late-nineteenth-century industrial innovations helped settlers overcome some of the natural obstacles. The shortage of timber for fencing and housing had encouraged early emigrants to go elsewhere. But in the 1870s, Joseph Glidden developed barbed wire as a cheap alternative to timber fencing. Having seen a simple wooden device designed to keep animals away from fences at a country fair, Glidden thought of making fencing wire with similar protruding barbs. Before long, he and a partner were producing hundreds of miles of barbed wire fencing that could be used to enclose fields on the Plains. Other innovations overcame other challenges. Twine binders, which speeded up grain harvesting, reduced the threat of losing crops to the unpredictable weather. And mail-order steel windmills for pumping water from deep underground wells relieved some of the water shortages by the 1890s.

Industrial innovations, however, could not resolve all of the problems confronting Great Plains settlers. Wrote Miriam Peckham, a Kansas homesteader:

> I tell you Auntie no one can depend on farming for a living in this country. Henry is very industrious and this year had in over thirty acres of small grain, 8 acres of corn and about an acre of potatoes. We have sold our small grain . . . and it come to $100; now deduct $27.00

for cutting, $16.00 for threshing, $19.00 for hired help, say nothing of boarding our help, none of the trouble of drawing 25 miles to market and 25 cts on each head for ferriage over the river and where is your profit. I sometimes think this a God forsaken country, the [grass]hopper hurt our corn and we have 1/2 a crop and utterly destroyed our garden. If one wants trials, let them come to Kansas.

Peckham's letter highlights the uncertainties of frontier life: the costs of machinery, the vagaries of crops and markets, the threat of pests and natural disasters, the shortage of cash. Unlike earlier emigrants to the Far West, who had to finance the six-month trip, many Plains pioneers took up their homesteads with only a few dollars in their pockets. Survival often depended on how well families managed to do during the crucial first years and how much work each member of the family, including women and children, could perform. If they succeeded in raising and selling their crops, they might accumulate the capital needed to continue. But if nature was harsh or their luck or health bad, or if they were unable to adjust to new conditions or to do the hard labor that was necessary to get the farm going, the chances of failure grew.

Life on the Plains had its compensations, however. Willa Cather, who grew up in Nebraska, showed both the harshness and the appeal of the prairie in her novels. Alexandra Bergson, the main

This 1880 photo highlights the role of machine and animal power rather than human power during the wheat harvest. With more land under cultivation, there was a strong impetus to develop larger and/or more efficient harvesting machines. *(Corbis-Bettmann)*

This photograph of immigrant women settlers, probably in North Dakota, shows some of the hard physical labor involved in homesteading. The presence of immigrants also reminds us that the West was the home of diverse peoples including Asians, European newcomers, Native Americans, black migrants, and Hispanics whose families had lived in the West for generations. *(The Fred Hulstrand History in Pictures Collection, NDSU, Fargo, ND)*

character of *O Pioneers!* (1913), loves the land: "It seemed beautiful to her, rich and strong and glorious." The thousands of letters and diaries that survive from the period also provide a positive picture of farming life. One woman reflected on the way she had softened the harsh landscape. "Our flower garden was such a vision of beauty . . . the dreary, desolate place was blossoming in all the gorgeous beauty that God has promised to those who try."

In the late 1880s and early 1890s, the first boom on the Great Plains halted abruptly. Falling agricultural prices cut profits. Then, the unusual rainfall that had lured farmers into the semiarid region near the hundredth meridian vanished. A devastating drought followed. One farmer reported in 1890 that he had earned $41.48 from his wheat crop, yet his expenses for seed and threshing amounted to $56.00. The destitute survived on boiled weeds, a few potatoes, and a little bread and butter. Many farmers had debts they now could not repay. Thousands lost their farms to creditors. Some stayed on as tenants. Homesteaders like the Leepers gave up. By 1900, two-thirds of homesteaded farms had failed. Many homesteaders fled east. In western

The New Economy of the West, 1850–1893

This map shows the importance of mining, ranching, and farming in the western part of the nation. Note the railroad links with the East.

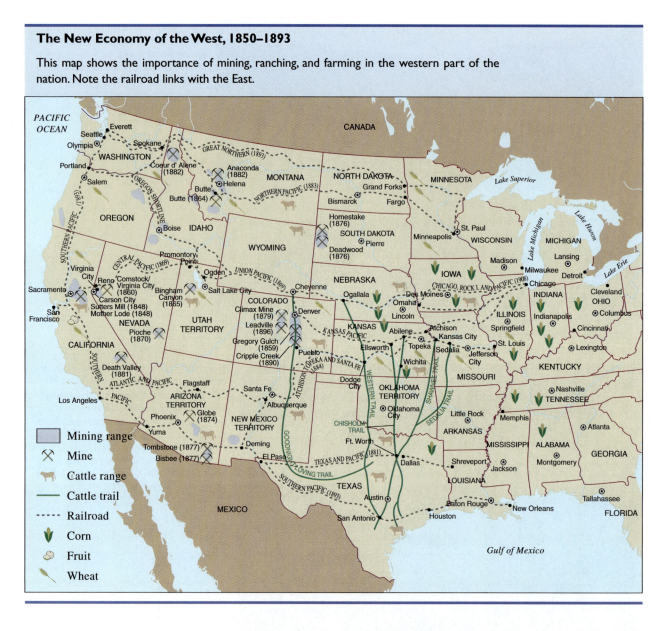

Kansas, the population declined by half between 1888 and 1892. The wagons of those who retreated bore the epitaph of their experience: "In God We Trusted: In Kansas We Busted."

Whether individual farmers remained on the Great Plains or retreated to more promising climates, collectively these new agricultural efforts had a significant long-term impact on the region's environment. When farmers removed sod to build their sod houses and broke the prairies with their plows to plant their crops, they were removing the earth's protective covering. The heavy winds so common on the prairies could lift exposed topsoil and carry it miles away. Deep plowing, which was essential for dry farming techniques introduced after the drought of the 1880s, worsened this situation. The dust bowl of the 1930s was the eventual outcome of these agricultural interventions. Other less obvious consequences of farming and settlement on the Great Plains included a lowering of the water table level as mail-order steel windmills provided the power for pumping water from deep underground. Far from the Plains, the pine forests around the Great Lakes fell to satisfy the settlers' need for wood and the railroads' voracious appetite for railroad ties.

Cornucopia on the Pacific

When gold was discovered in California, Americans rushed west to find it. But as one father told his eager son, "Plant your lands; these be your best gold fields." He was right; with the completion of a national railroad system, farming eventually became California's greatest asset. But farming in California neither resembled romanticized depictions of rural life nor the vision of the framers of the Homestead Act. The state's agricultural success would rest on railroads, machinery, and irrigation.

Although federal and state land policies supposedly promoted "homes for the homeless," little of California's land was actually homesteaded or developed as small family farms. When California entered the Union, Mexican ranchers had vast land-holdings that never became part of the public domain. Because most Mexican Americans impoverished themselves in legal efforts to establish the legitimacy of their claims, speculators eventually acquired much of their land. Consequently, farmers needed substantial sums to buy land.

By 1871, reformer Henry George described California as "not a country of farms but a country of plantations and estates." California farms were indeed substantially larger than farms in the rest of the country. In 1870, the average California farm was 482 acres, whereas the national average farm was only 153 acres. By 1900, farms of 1,000 acres or more made up two-thirds of the state's farmland. This landscape reflected the advent of large-scale farming. As one California visitor reported to the *New York Times* in 1887, "You go through miles and miles of wheat fields, you see the fertility of the land and the beauty of the scenery, but where are the hundreds of farm houses . . . that you would see in Ohio or Iowa?"

Small farmers and ranchers did exist, of course, but they found it difficult to compete with large, mechanized operators using cheap migrant laborers, usually Mexican or Chinese. One wheat farm in the San Joaquin Valley was so vast that workers started plowing in the morning at one end of the 17-mile field, ate lunch at its halfway point, and camped at its end that night.

The value of much of California's agricultural land, especially the southern half of the Central Valley, depended on water. By the 1870s, water, land, and railroad companies, using the labor and expertise of Chinese workers, were taking on the huge costs of building dams, headgates, and canals. They passed on the costs of construction to settlers now eager to acquire hitherto barren lands along with water rights. By 1890, over a quarter of California's farms benefited from irrigation. The irrigation ditches were a fitting symbol of the importance of technology and a managerial attitude toward the land that characterized late-nineteenth-century agriculture, particularly in California.

Although grain was initially California's most valuable crop, it faced stiff competition from farmers on the Plains and in other parts of the world.

Some argued that land capable of raising luscious fruits "in a climate surpassing that of Italy, is too valuable for the cultivation of simple cereals." But high railroad rates and lack of refrigeration limited the volume of fresh fruit and vegetables sent to market. As railroad managers in the 1880s realized the potential profitability of California produce, they lowered rates and introduced refrigerated railroad cars. In June 1888, fresh apricots and cherries successfully survived the trip from California to New York. Fruit and vegetable production rose, benefiting from the agricultural expertise of Chinese laborers, tenant farmers, and Chinese entrepreneurs. So important were their contributions that some have argued that Chinese know-how was mainly responsible for the shift to produce farming. By 1890, 9,000 carloads of navel oranges were heading east. Before long, California fruit appeared in London markets and on English dining tables.

The Mining West

Mining hastened rapid western growth and development. The first and best known mining rush occurred in 1848 when gold was discovered in California, but others followed as precious metals—silver, iron,

Mining was a difficult and dangerous job. This picture shows five miners inside a mine shaft in Central City, Colorado. You can just make out a lamp attached to the wall of the shaft, a reminder that much of the miner's work was done with little illumination. Two of the miners are holding their tools, while two hold a chain. Why the fifth man sits in a barrel is a mystery. The bright spot on the front of the barrel is perhaps the reflection of the flash. (*A. C. Dickerson/Denver Public Library [X-11636]*)

copper, coal, lead, zinc, and tin—lured thousands west to Colorado, Montana, Idaho, and Nevada as well as to states like Minnesota. Mining discoveries were transformative events, for they attracted people and businesses west, often to places far away from agricultural settlements. Hastily built mining communities might be eyesores, but they had bustling urban characters. If and when the strike was over, however, residents abandoned the mining camps and towns as fast as they had rushed into them. The pattern of boom and bust characterized much of mining life.

While the image of the independent miner panning for gold has passed into the nation's memory, the reality of late-nineteenth-century mining was nothing like the popular stereotype. Retrieving minerals from rock was difficult, expensive, and dangerous. A successful mine required a large labor force, industrial tools, and railroad links. Miners worked way below the earth's surface in poorly ventilated tunnels, with no means for removing human or animal waste. Temperatures could reach as high as 120 degrees. Accidents were part of the job that depended upon blasting equipment and industrial machinery. In 1884, a Montana miner drilled into an unexploded dynamite charge and lost his eyes and ear. He received no compensation, for the court decided that the accident "was the result of an unforeseen and unavoidable accident incident to the risk of mining." As the next chapter will show, in time, western miners became one of the most radical group of industrial workers.

Mining in the West

The map depicts the major areas for mining between 1848 and 1900 as well as some of the important western cities and towns. In what ways did mining stimulate urban growth in the West? What relationships between mining and regional development do you see suggested here?

Exploiting Natural Resources

Mining was a big business with high costs and a basic dynamic that encouraged rapid and thorough exploitation of the earth's resources. The decimation of the nation's forests went hand in hand with large-scale mining and the railroads that provided the links to markets. Both railroads and mining depended on wood—railroads for wooden ties, mines for shaft timber and ore reduction. The impact of these demands is captured by the California State Board of Agriculture's estimate in the late 1860s that one-third of the state's forests had already disappeared.

When lumber companies cut down timber, they affected the flow of streams and destroyed the habitat supporting birds and animals. Like the activities of farmers and cattle owners, the companies that stripped the earth of its forest cover were also contributing to soil erosion. The idea that the public lands belonging to the federal government ought to be rapidly developed supported such exploitation

of the nation's natural resources. Often, in return for royalties, the government leased parts of the public domain to companies that hoped to extract valuable minerals, not to own the land permanently. In other cases, companies bought land, but not always legally. In 1878, Congress passed the Timber and Stone Act, which initially applied to Nevada, Oregon, Washington, and California. This legislation allowed the sale of 160-acre parcels of the public domain that were "unfit for cultivation" and "valuable chiefly for timber." Timber companies were quick to see the possibilities in the new law. They hired men willing to register for claims and then to turn them over to timber interests. By the end of the century, more than 3.5 million acres of the public domain had been acquired under the legislation, and most of it was in corporate hands.

The rapacious and rapid exploitation of resources combined with the increasing pace of industrialization made some Americans uneasy. Many believed

The Natural Environment of the West

Study the patterns of rainfall and the natural features of the West, including rivers and mountain ranges. What do these patterns suggest about native vegetation and the prospects for farming? What is revealed about the role of water and irrigation in the West? What difficulties facing the settlers are revealed?

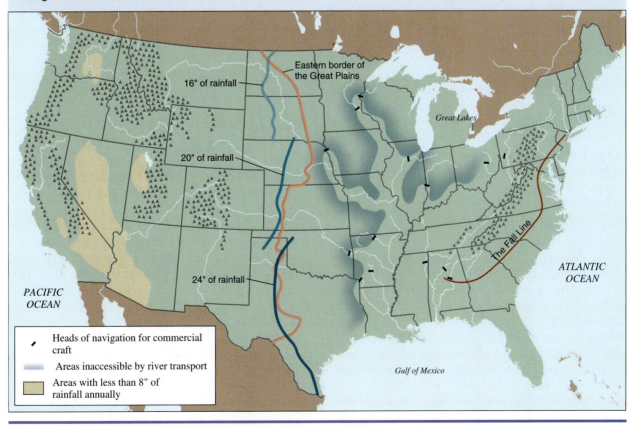

that forests played a part in causing rainfall and that their destruction would have an adverse impact on the climate. Others, like John Muir, lamented the destruction of the country's great natural beauty. In 1868, Muir came upon the Great Valley of California, "all one sheet of plant gold, hazy and vanishing in the distance . . . one smooth, continuous bed of honey-bloom." He soon realized, however, that a "wild, restless agriculture" and "flocks of hoofed locusts, sweeping over the ground like a fire" would destroy this vision of loveliness. Muir became a preservation champion. He played a part in the creation of Yosemite National Park in 1890, participated in a successful effort to allow President Benjamin Harrison to classify certain parts of the public domain as forest reserves (the Forest Reserve Act of 1891), and in 1892, established the Sierra Club. At the same time, conservation ideas were also emerging. Gifford Pinchot, who became a leading advocate of these ideas, was less interested in the preservation of the nation's wilderness areas than in careful management of its natural resources. "Conservation," he explained, "means the wise use of the earth and its resources for the lasting good of man." Both perspectives, however, were more popular in the East than in the West, where the seeming abundance of natural resources and the profit motive diminished support.

RESOLVING THE INDIAN QUESTION

Black Elk, an Oglala Sioux, listened to a story his father had heard from his father.

> A long time ago . . . there was once a Lakota [Sioux] holy man, called Drinks Water, who dreamed what was to be; and this was long before the coming of the Wasichus [white men]. He dreamed . . . that a strange race had woven a spider's web all around the Lakotas. And he said: "When this happens, you shall live in square gray houses, in a barren land, and beside those square gray houses you shall starve."

This strange dream Black Elk saw come true.

As farmers settled the western frontier and became entangled in a national economy, they clashed with the Indian tribes who lived on the land. In California, disease and violence killed 90 percent of the Native American population in the 30 years following the gold rush. Elsewhere, the struggle among Native Americans, white settlers, the U.S. Army, and government officials and reformers was prolonged and bitter. Although some tribes moved onto government reservations with little protest, most tribes, including the Nez Percé in the Northwest, the Apache in the Southwest, and the

Black Elk, pictured here on the left, perceived the deleterious changes experienced by Indians during the latter part of the nineteenth century. Although Black Elk was one of the holy men of Oglala Sioux, he became a convert to Roman Catholicism in the early twentieth century. (*Smithsonian Institution*)

Plains Indians, resisted the attempts to curb their way of life and to transform their culture.

Background to the Plains Wars

As Chapter 13 suggested, the lives of most Plains Indians revolved around the buffalo. Increased emigration to California and Oregon in the 1840s and 1850s disrupted tribal pursuits and animal migration patterns. Initially, the federal government tried, without much success, to persuade the Plains tribes to stay away from white wagon trains and white settlers. As Lone Horn, a Miniconjou chief, explained when American commissioners at the 1851 Fort Laramie Council asked him if he would be satisfied to live on the Missouri River, "When the buffalo comes close to the river, we come close to it. When the buffaloes go off, we go off after them."

During the Civil War, the eastern tribes that were forced to relocate in Oklahoma divided: some tribes, especially the slaveholders, supported the Confederacy, while other tribes supported the Union. After the war, however, all were branded as "traitors." The federal government callously nulli- fied earlier pledges and treaties, leaving Indians de- fenseless against further incursions on their lands. As settlers pushed into Kansas, the tribes living in Kansas were shunted into Oklahoma.

The White Perspective

When the Civil War ended, red and white men on the Plains were already at war. In 1864, the Colorado militia had massacred a band of friendly Cheyenne at Sand Creek, Colorado, despite the fact that Chief Black Kettle waved both a white flag of truce and an American flag. Militia leader John Chivington urged his men on. "Kill and scalp all, big and little." Before long, Cheyenne, Sioux, and Arapaho were respond- ing in kind. The Plains wars had begun.

Although not all whites condoned the militia's butchery, the deliberations of the congressional commission authorized to make peace revealed a constricted vision of the future of Native Americans. The commission, which included the commander of the army in the West, Civil War hero General William T. Sherman, accepted as fact that the future of the West lay in an "industrious, thrifty, and en- lightened population" of whites. The commission believed that all Native Americans must relocate in one of two areas: Oklahoma and the western half of present-day South Dakota. There they would learn the ways of white society and agricultural and me- chanical arts. Annuities, food, and clothes would placate the Indians and ease their transition from a "savage" to a "civilized" life.

At two major conferences in 1867 and 1868, Native American chiefs listened to these drastic pro- posals that spelled out the end of the traditional na- tive life. Some agreed. Others, like Satanta, a Kiowa chief, insisted, "I don't want to settle. I love to roam over the prairies." In any case, the agreements ex- tracted were not binding, because no chief had au- thority to speak for his tribe. For its part, the U.S. Senate dragged its feet in approving the treaties. Supplies promised to Indians who settled in the arid reserved areas failed to materialize, and wildlife proved sparse. These Indians soon drifted back to their former hunting grounds.

As General Sherman warned, however, "All who cling to their old hunting ground are hostile and will remain so till killed off." When persuasion failed, the U.S. Army adopted militant tactics. "The more we can kill this year," Sherman remarked, "the less will have to be killed the next war." In 1867, Sherman en- trusted General Philip Sheridan with the duty of dealing with the tribes. Sheridan introduced winter campaigning, which was aimed at seeking out the Indians who divided into small groups during the winter and exterminating them.

The completion of the transcontinental railroad in 1869 added yet another pressure for "solving" the Indian question. Transcontinental railroads wanted rights-of-way through tribal lands and needed white settlers to make their operations profitable. They carried not only thousands of hopeful settlers to the West, but miners and hunters as well. Few thought Native Americans had any right to the lands whites wanted.

In his 1872 annual report, the commissioner for Indian affairs, Francis Amasa Walker, addressed the two fundamental questions troubling whites: how to prevent Indians from blocking white migration to and settlement in the Great Plains and what to do with Native Americans once they had been con- trolled. Because they could mount 8,000 warriors, Walker suggested buying off the "savages." With promises of food and gifts, he hoped to lure them onto reservations and there impose a "rigid refor- matory discipline."

Coercion would be necessary, because Indians, according to Walker, were "unused to manual labor, and physically unqualified for it by the habits of the chase . . . without forethought and without self con- trol . . . with strong animal appetites and no intellec- tual tastes or aspirations to hold those appetites in check." The grim reservations he proposed resem- bled prisons more than schools. Indians could not leave without permission and could be arrested if they tried to do so. Though Walker considered him- self a "friend of humanity" and, like many reformers, wished to save the Indians from destruction, he said that there was only one choice: "yield or perish."

The Tribal View

Native Americans defied such attacks on their an- cient way of life and protested the wholesale viola- tion of treaties. Black Elk remembered that, in 1863, when he was only three, his father had his leg bro- ken in a fierce battle against the white men. "When I was older," he recalled,

I learned what the fighting was about. . . . Up on the Madison Fork the Wasichus had found much of the yel- low metal that they worship and that makes them crazy, and they wanted to have a road up through our country to the place where the yellow metal was; but my people did not want the road. It would scare the bi- son and make them go away, and also it would let the other Wasichus come in like a river. They told us that they wanted only to use a little land, as much as a wagon would take between the wheels; but our people knew better.

As the plains and prairies of the trans-Mississippi West filled up with farms and rural communities, Americans became nostalgic for the recent past. Buffalo Bill's Wild West show offered a colorful but inaccurate picture of the migration west. Native Americans were hired for the show to take part in scenes where they attacked "innocent settlers" and travelers. White audiences loved the clear picture the show provided of villains and heroes, while ironically Native Americans were often grateful for the opportunity to escape the confines of reservation life and to earn money. *(The Granger Collection, New York)*

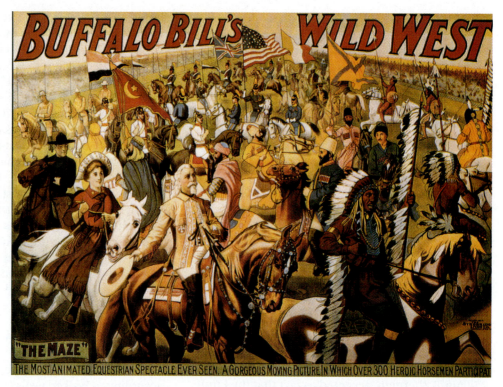

Black Elk's father and many others soon realized that fighting was the only "way to keep our country." But "wherever we went, the soldiers came to kill us."

Broken promises fired Indian resistance. In 1875, the federal government allowed gold prospectors into the Black Hills, part of the Sioux reservation and one of their sacred places. Chiefs Sitting Bull, Crazy Horse, and Rain-in-the-Face led the angry Sioux on the warpath. At the Battle of Little Big Horn in 1876, they vanquished General George Custer. But their bravery and skill could not permanently withstand the power of the well-supplied, well-armed, and determined U.S. Army. Elsewhere, the pattern of resistance and ultimate defeat was repeated. In Texas, General Sherman vanquished Native American tribes, and in the Pacific Northwest, Nez Percé Chief Joseph surrendered in 1877.

The wholesale destruction of the buffalo was an important element in white victory. The animals were central to Indian life, culture, and religion. As one Pawnee chief explained, "Am afraid when we have no meat to offer, Great Spirit . . . will be angry & punish us." Although Plains Indians could be wasteful of buffalo in areas where the animals were abundant, white miners and hunters ultimately destroyed the herds. Sportsmen shot the beasts from train windows. Railroad crews ate the meat. Ranchers' cattle competed for grass. And demand for buffalo bones for fertilizer and hides for robes and shoes encouraged the decimation.

The slaughter, which had claimed 13 million animals by 1883, was disgraceful in retrospect. The Indians considered white men demented. "They just killed and killed because they like to do that," said one, whereas when "we hunted the bison . . . [we] killed only what we needed." But the destruction of the herds pleased whites who were determined to curb the movements of Native Americans. As Secretary of the Interior Columbus Delano explained in 1872, "I cannot regard the rapid disappearance of the game from its former haunts as a matter prejudicial to our management of the Indians." Rather, he said, "as they become convinced that they can no longer rely upon the supply of game for their support, they will return to the more reliable source of subsistence furnished at their agencies."

The 1887 Dawes Act

Changing federal policy was aimed at ending Indian power and culture. In 1871, Congress abandoned the practice, in effect since the 1790s, of treating the tribes as sovereign nations. Other measures supplemented this attempt to undermine both tribal integrity and the prestige of tribal leaders, whom negotiators would no longer recognize as speaking for their tribes. The government urged tribes to replace tribal justice with a court system and extended federal jurisdiction to the reservations. Tribes were also warned not to gather for religious ceremonies.

The Dawes Severalty Act of 1887 pulled together the strands of federal Indian policy that emerged

Native Americans, 1850–1896

This map reveals the widespread appeal of the Ghost Dance movement as well as the result of efforts to force Native Americans onto reservations.

→ Flight of the Nez Perces, 1877

- - - Extent of the Ghost Dance Religion, 1888–1890

—— Extent of European Settlement, 1880

Selected Indian Reservations in 1896

✳ Battles

NAVAHO Selected Indian groups

after the Civil War and set its course for the rest of the century. Believing that tribal bonds kept Indians in savagery, reformers intended to destroy them. As Theodore Roosevelt noted approvingly, the bill was a "mighty pulverizing engine to break up the tribal mass." The reservation policy was, in effect, abandoned. Rather than allotting reservation lands to tribal groups, the act allowed the president to distribute these lands to individuals. Private property, the framers of the bill reasoned, would undermine communal norms and tribal identity and encourage Indians to settle down and farm as white men did. Although Indian agents explained that Native Americans opposed the Dawes Act, Congress, convinced that white people knew what was best for Indians, did not hesitate to legislate on their behalf.

The fact that speculators as well as reformers lobbied for the legislation betrayed another motive at work. Even if each Indian family head claimed a typical share of 160 acres, millions of "surplus" acres would remain for sale to white settlers. Within 20 years of the Dawes Act, Native Americans had lost 60 percent of their lands. The federal government held the profits from land sales "in trust" and used them for the "civilizing" mission.

The Ghost Dance: An Indian Renewal Ritual

By the 1890s, the grim reality of their plight made many Native Americans responsive to a new religious revitalization movement. Like other prophets before him, the Paiute holy man, Wovoka, held out

Magazines

Weekly and monthly magazines constitute a rich primary source for the historian, offering a vivid picture of the issues of the day and useful insights into popular tastes and values. With advances in the publishing industry and an increasingly literate population, the number of these journals soared in the years following the Civil War. In 1865, only 700 periodicals were published. Twenty years later, there were 3,300. As the *National Magazine* grumbled, "Magazines, magazines, magazines! The newsstands are already groaning under the heavy load, and there are still more coming."

Some of these magazines were aimed at the mass market. *Frank Leslie's Illustrated Newspaper,* established in 1855, was one of the most successful. At its height, circulation reached 100,000. Making skillful use of pictures (sometimes as large as two by three feet and folded into the magazine), the weekly covered important news of the day as well as music, drama, sports, and books. Although Leslie relied more heavily on graphics and sensationalism than do modern news weeklies, his publication was a forerunner of *Newsweek* and *Time.*

Another kind of weekly magazine was aimed primarily at middle- and upper-class readers. Editors like the oft-quoted Edwin Lawrence Godkin of *The Nation*, with a circulation of about 30,000, hoped to influence those in positions of authority and power by providing a forum for the discussion of reform issues. In contrast, *Scribner's* revealed a more conservative, middle-of-the-road point of view. Both magazines, however, exuded a confident, progressive tone that was characteristic of middle-class Americans.

Harper's Weekly was one of the most important magazines designed primarily for middle- and upper-class readers. Established in 1857, this publication continued in print until 1916. The success of *Harper's Weekly,* which called itself a "family newspaper," rested on a combination of its moderate point of view and an exciting use of illustrations and cartoons touching on contemporary events. The popular cartoons of Thomas Nast appeared in this magazine. In large part because of the use of graphics, the circulation of *Harper's Weekly* reached a peak of 160,000 in 1872.

Illustrated here is a page from the January 16, 1869, issue of *Harper's Weekly*. The layout immediately suggests the importance of graphics. Most of the page is taken up with the three pictures. The top and bottom pictures are wood engravings based on drawings by Theodore R. Davis, one of *Harper's* best-known illustrator-reporters. The center picture was derived from a photograph.

The story featured on this page concerns a victory of General George Custer in the war against the Cheyenne tribe that the U.S. Army was waging that winter. Davis had been a correspondent in the West covering Custer's actions in 1867. But when news of Custer's victory arrived, Davis was back in New York. He thus drew on his imagination for the two scenes reproduced on the next page. What kind of characterization of Native Americans does Davis give in the picture at the top of the page? What view of American soldiers does he suggest? At the bottom of the page, you can see soldiers slaughtering "worthless" horses while Cheyenne teepees burn in the background. Would the average viewer have any sympathy for the plight of the Cheyenne after looking at this picture? This "victory," in fact, involved the slaughter not only of horses but also of all males over age eight.

The editors' decision to insert a picture that had nothing to do with the incident being reported was obviously significant. As you can see, the subject in the center illustration is a white hunter who had been killed and scalped by Indians. By considering the choice of graphics and text, you can begin to discover how magazines provide insight, not only into the events of the day but also into the ways magazines shaped the values and perspectives of nineteenth-century men and women.

Reflecting on the Past   What kind of special relationship were the editors suggesting by placing the picture of one dead white hunter in the center of a page that primarily covered a specific conflict between the Indians and the U.S. Army? How might the reader respond to the group of pictures as a whole? How do you? How does the text contribute to the overall view of the Indian–white relationship that the pictures suggest?

CUSTER'S INDIAN SCOUTS CELEBRATING THE VICTORY OVER BLACK KETTLE.—[Sketched by Thos. R. Davis.]

THE INDIAN WAR.

THE SCALPED HUNTER.—[Photographed by Wm. S. Soule.]

Harper's Weekly delivered powerful messages about the Native Americans in its choice of illustrations.

These girls, attending an Indian school, are neatly dressed in identical dresses, with hair pulled into buns rather than braided. Their aprons and the "classroom" reveal they are learning domestic skills, part of the process of learning white ways that Indian schools taught. *(Bettmann/Corbis)*

hope that history would reverse itself. He assured his followers that a natural disaster would eliminate the white race and that their ancestors and wild game would return to earth. If Indians performed a special dance called the Ghost Dance and observed traditional customs, this transformation would come more quickly. Wovoka's prophecies spread rapidly. Believers expressed their faith and hope through the new rituals of ghost or spirit dancing, hypnosis, and meditation.

Although Wovoka's prophecies discouraged hostile actions against whites, American settlers were uneasy. Indian agents tried to prevent the ghost dances and filed hysterical reports. "Indians are dancing in the snow and are wild and crazy. . . . We need protection, and we need it now." One agent identified the Sioux medicine man Sitting Bull, who had strenuously opposed American expansion, as a leading troublemaker and decided to arrest him. In the confusion of arrest, Indian police killed Sitting Bull.

Bands of Sioux fled the reservation with the army in swift pursuit. In late December 1890, the army overtook the Sioux at Wounded Knee Creek. Although the Sioux had raised a flag of truce, a scuffle that ensued as they were turning over their weapons led to a bloody massacre. Using the most up-to-date machine guns and Hotchkiss cannons, the army killed over 200 men, women, and children. An eyewitness described the desolate scene a few

days later. "Among the fragments of burned tents . . . we saw the frozen bodies lying close together or piled one upon another."

Thus arose the lament of Black Elk, who saw his people diminished, starving, despairing:

> Once we were happy in our own country and we were seldom hungry, for then the two-leggeds and the four-leggeds lived together like relatives, and there was plenty for them and for us. But then the Wasichus came, and they have made little islands for us . . . , and always these islands are becoming smaller, for around them surges the gnawing flood of the Wasichus; . . . dirty with lies and greed.

As Black Elk recognized, white Americans had finally defeated the western tribes. Once independent, proud, and strong, Native Americans suffered dependency, poverty, and social and cultural disorganization on the reservations, in grim Indian schools, and in city slums. The country's original inhabitants seemed to have no place in the American nation.

THE NEW SOUTH

The trans-Mississippi West was transformed as native peoples were subdued, the Great Plains settled, and commercial agriculture helped knit the region into the larger world. Mining camps turned into industrial centers. Western cities grew at a fast pace; by 1900, nearly 40 percent of westerners lived in cities. The large number of itinerant workers who worked in mines, forests, and fields provided a flexible workforce that supported economic growth.

In contrast to this pattern, the southern economy sputtered. Of all the nation's agricultural regions, the South was the poorest. In 1880, southerners' yearly earnings were only half the national average. The agricultural labor force was neither efficient, mobile, nor prosperous enough to invest in needed improvements. And while some southerners dreamed of making the agricultural South rival the industrial North, their dreams were never realized. The region remained dependent on the North. Southern industrial workers were poorly paid, caught in dead-end jobs with little hope of advancement

Postwar Southerners Face the Future

After the painful war and Reconstruction, compelling arguments for regional self-sufficiency rang out. Those who wanted a "New South" argued that southern backwardness did not stem from the war itself, but from basic conditions in southern life—a rural economy based on cotton foremost among them. The defeat only made clearer the reality of the nineteenth century. Power and wealth came not from cotton but from factories, machines, and cities.

The effort to create a New South was far-ranging. In hundreds of speeches, editorials, pamphlets, articles, and books, spokesmen for the New South, like Atlanta newspaper publisher Henry Grady, encouraged fellow southerners to change. Southerners must abandon prewar ideals that glorified leisure and gentility and adopt new entrepreneurial values. To lure northern investment, critical because the South was short of capital, New South advocates also held out the possibility of "fabulous" profits. In a bid to encourage manufacturers, several southern state governments offered tax exemptions and the cheap labor of leased convicts. Texas and Florida awarded the railroads land grants, and cities like Atlanta and Louisville mounted huge industrial exhibitions. The most startling example of commitment to the vision of a New South may have come in 1886 when southern railroad companies, in a crash effort, relaid railroad tracks and adjusted rolling stock to fit the northern gauges.

During the late nineteenth century, northern money flowed south as dollars replaced the moral fervor and political involvement of the Civil War and Reconstruction years. In the 1880s, northerners increased their investment in the cotton industry sevenfold and financed the expansion of the southern railroad system. Northern capital fueled southern urban expansion. By 1900, some 15 percent of all southerners lived in cities, whereas only 7 percent had in 1860. (The national averages for these years were 40 and 20 percent, respectively.)

Birmingham, Alabama, symbolized the New South. In 1870, the site was a peaceful cornfield. The next year, two northern real estate speculators arrived on the scene, attracted by the area's rich iron deposits. Despite a siege of cholera and the depression of the 1870s, Birmingham rapidly became the center of the southern iron and steel industry. By 1890, a total of 38,414 people lived in the city. Coke ovens, blast furnaces, rolling mills, iron foundries, and machine shops belched forth polluting smoke into the air where once there had been only fields. Millions of dollars of finished goods poured forth from the city's mills and factories, and eight railroad lines carried them away.

Other southern cities flourished as well. Memphis prospered from its lumber industry and the manufacturing of cottonseed products, and Richmond became the country's tobacco capital even as its flour mills and iron and steel foundries continued to produce wealth. Augusta, Georgia, was the "Lowell of the South," a leader in the emerging textile industry that blossomed in Georgia, North and South Carolina, and Alabama. Augusta's eight cotton mills employed about 2,800 workers, many of them women and children.

The Other Side of Progress

New South leaders—a small group of merchants, industrialists, and planters—bragged about the growth of the iron and textile industries and paraded statistics to prove the success of efforts to modernize. The South, one writer boasted, was "throbbing with industrial and railroad activity." Middle-class southerners increasingly accepted new entrepreneurial values. But the South made slow progress.

Older values persisted. Indeed, New South spokesmen paradoxically kept older, chivalric values alive by romanticizing the recent past. By viewing "all Confederate veterans" rather than big businessmen as "heroes" and by clinging to genteel values that did not glorify getting ahead, many southerners resisted the demands of the new economic order. Despite the interest in modernization, southerners did not invest in a modern workforce. The southern school system lagged far behind that of the North.

Although new industries and signs of progress abounded, two of the new industries depended on tobacco and cotton—traditional crops long at the center of rural life. As they had before the war, commerce and government work drove urban growth. Moreover, the South did not better its position relative to the North. Whereas in 1860, the South had 17 percent of the country's manufacturing concerns, by 1904, it had only 15 percent. The South's achievements were not insignificant during a period in which northern industry and cities rapidly expanded, but they could not make the South the equal of the North.

Moreover, the South failed to reap many benefits from industrialization. As in the antebellum period, the South remained an economic vassal of the North. Southern businessmen grew in number, but with the exception of the American Tobacco Company, no great southern corporations arose. Instead, southerners worked for northern companies and corporations, which absorbed southern businesses or dominated them financially. Profits flowed north. "Our capitalists are going into your country," the Lowell *Manufacturers' Record* noted, "because they see a chance to make money there, but you must not think that they will give your people the benefit of the money they make. That will come North and enrich their heirs, or set up public libraries in our country towns." As dollars fled north, so, too, went the power to make critical decisions. In many cases, northern directors determined that southern mills and factories could handle only the early stages of processing, while northern factories finished the goods. Thus, southern cotton mills sent yarn and coarse cloth north for completion. Southern manufacturers who did finish their products, hoping to compete in the marketplace, found that railroad rate discrimination robbed their goods of any competitive edge.

Individual workers in the new industries may have found factory life preferable to sharecropping, but their rewards were meager. Caught in low-skill jobs with little chance for advancement, workers earned lower wages and worked longer hours in the South than elsewhere. Per capita income was the same in 1900 as it had been in 1860—and only half the national average. In North Carolina in the 1890s, workers were paid an average of 50 cents a day and toiled 70 hours a week. Black workers, who made up 6 percent of the southern manufacturing force in 1890 (but who were excluded from textile mills), usually had the worst jobs and the lowest pay.

The thousands of women and children who labored gave silent testimony to the fact that their husbands and fathers could not earn enough to support their families. As usual, women and children earned lower wages than men. Justifying these policies, one Augusta factory president claimed that the employment of children was "a matter of charity with us; some of them would starve if they were not given employment.... Ours are not overworked.

The work we give children is very light." Actually, many children at his factory were doing the same work as adults, but for children's pay.

Cotton Still King

Although New South advocates envisioned the South's transformation from a rural to an industrial society, they recognized the need for agricultural change. "It's time for an agricultural revolution," Henry Grady proclaimed. "When we once decide that southern lands are fit for something else besides cotton, and then go to work in earnest to multiply and diversify our products and industries, independence and wealth will be the certain reward of our intelligent and industrious farmers."

A new agricultural South with new class and economic arrangements did emerge, but it was not the one Grady and others envisioned. Despite the breakup of some plantations following the Civil War, large landowners proved resourceful in holding onto their property and in dealing with postwar conditions, as Chapter 16 showed. As they adopted new agricultural arrangements, former slaves sank into debt peonage.

White farmers on small- and medium-sized holdings fared only slightly better than black tenants and sharecroppers. Immediately after the war, high cotton prices tempted them to raise as much cotton as they could. Then prices began a disastrous decline, from 11 cents a pound in 1875 to less than 5 cents in 1894. Yeoman farmers became entangled in debt. Each year, farmers found themselves buying supplies on credit from merchants so that they could plant the next year's crop and support their families until harvest time. In return, merchants demanded their exclusive business and acquired a lien (or claim) on their crops. But when farmers sold their crops at declining prices, they usually discovered that they had not earned enough to settle with the merchant, who had charged dearly for store goods and whose annual interest rates might exceed 100 percent. Each year, thousands of farmers fell further behind, and many eventually lost their land. By 1900, over half the South's white farmers and three-quarters of its black farmers were tenants. Although tenancy was increasing all over rural America, nowhere did it rise more rapidly than in the Deep South.

These patterns had baneful results for individual southerners and for the South as a whole. Caught in a cycle of debt and poverty, few farmers could think of improving agricultural techniques, investing in machinery, or diversifying crops. In their desperate attempt to pay off debts, they concentrated on cotton, despite falling prices. "Cotton brings money, and money pays debt," was the small farmer's slogan. Landowners also pressured tenants to raise a market crop. Far from diversifying, as Grady had hoped, farmers increasingly limited the number of crops they raised. By 1880, the South was not growing enough food to feed its people adequately. Poor nutrition contributed to chronic bad health and sickness.

The Nadir of Black Life

Grady and other New South advocates painted a picture of a strong, prosperous, and industrialized South, a region that could deal with the troublesome race issue without interference. Grady had few regrets over the end of slavery, which he thought had contributed to southern economic backwardness. Realizing that black labor would be crucial to the transformation he sought, he advocated racial cooperation.But racial cooperation did not mean equality. Grady assumed that blacks were racially inferior and supported an informal system of segregation. "The negro is entitled to his freedom, his franchise, to full and equal legal rights," Grady wrote in 1883. But "social equality he can never have."

By the time of Grady's death in 1889, a much harsher perspective on southern race relations was replacing his view. In 1891, at a national assembly of women's clubs in Washington, D.C., Frances Watkins Harper, a black speaker, writer, and former abolitionist, anticipated efforts to strip the vote from blacks and appealed to the white women at the meeting not to abandon black suffrage. "I deem it a privilege to present the negro," she said, "not as a mere dependent asking for Northern sympathy or Southern compassion, but as a member of the body politic who has a claim upon the nation for justice, simple justice." Women, of all people, should not seek to achieve their own right to vote at the expense of the vote for black men, she explained. "Instead of taking the ballot from his hands, teach him how to use it, and add his quota to the progress, strength, and durability of the nation."

The decision by congressional leaders in 1890 to shelve a proposed act for protecting black civil rights and the defeat of the Blair bill providing federal assistance for educational institutions left black Americans vulnerable, as Harper realized. The traditional sponsor of the rights of freedpeople, the Republican party, left blacks to fend for themselves as a minority in the white South. The courts also abandoned blacks. In 1878, the Supreme Court declared unconstitutional a Louisiana statute banning discrimination in transportation. In 1882, the Court voided the Ku Klux Klan Act of 1871 that had been passed to break the power of the clan. In 1883, the provisions of the Civil Rights Act of 1875, which assured blacks of equal rights in public places, were declared unconstitutional on the grounds that the

Black dockworkers load bales of cotton in this undated photograph, which is evidence not only of the kinds of jobs that free blacks could secure but also of the continuing dominance of cotton in southern life. *(Library of Congress)*

federal government did not have the right to involve itself in the racial relations between individuals.

Northern leaders did not oppose these actions. In fact, northerners increasingly promulgated negative stereotypes in magazines, newspapers, cartoons, advertisements, "coon songs," serious art and theater, and the minstrel shows that dominated northern entertainment. The *Atlanta Monthly* in 1890 anticipated a strong current in magazine literature when it expressed doubts that this "lowly variety of man" could ever be brought up to the intellectual and moral standards of whites. Other magazines openly opposed suffrage as wasted on people too "ignorant, weak, lazy and incompetent" to make good use of it. *Forum* magazine suggested that "American Negroes" had "too much liberty." When this freedom was combined with natural "race traits" of stealing and hankering after white women, the *Forum* advised in 1893, black crime increased. Only lynching and burning would deter the "barbarous" rapist and other "sadly degenerated" Negroes corrupted since the Civil War by independence and too much education.

Encouraged by northern public opinion, and with the blessing of Congress and the Supreme Court, southern citizens and legislatures sought to make blacks permanently second-class members of southern society. In the political sphere, white southerners amended state constitutions to disenfranchise black voters. By various legal devices—the poll tax, literacy tests, "good character" and "understanding" clauses administered by white voter registrars, and all-white primary elections—blacks lost the right to vote. The most ingenious method was the "grandfather clause," which specified that only citizens whose grandfathers were registered to vote on January 1, 1867, could cast their ballots. This virtually excluded blacks. Although the Supreme Court outlawed blatantly discriminatory laws such as grandfather clauses, a series of other constitutional changes, like those just mentioned, beginning in Mississippi in 1890 and spreading to all 11 former Confederate states by 1910, effectively excluded the black vote. The results were dramatic. Louisiana, for example, contained 130,334 registered black voters in 1896. Eight years later, there were only 1,342.

In a second tactic in the 1890s, state and local laws legalized informal segregation in public facilities. Beginning with railroads and schools, "Jim Crow" laws were extended to libraries, restaurants, hospitals, prisons, parks and playgrounds, cemeteries, toilets, drinking fountains, and nearly every other place where blacks and whites might mingle. The Supreme Court upheld these laws in 1896 in *Plessy* v. *Ferguson* by declaring that "separate but equal" facilities did not violate the equal protection clause of the Fourteenth Amendment because separation did not necessarily mean the inferiority of a group. The Court's decision opened the way for as many forms of legal segregation as southern lawmakers could devise.

Political and social discrimination made it ever more possible to keep blacks permanently confined to agricultural and unskilled labor. While extended families—aunts, uncles, cousins, and other kin—all helped blacks to cope with their dire situation, the truth was that all too often blacks were dependent on whites for their material welfare. In 1900, nearly 84 percent of black workers nationwide engaged in some form of agricultural labor as farmhands, overseers, sharecroppers, or tenant or independent farmers or in service jobs, primarily domestic service and laundry work. These had been the primary slave occupations. The remaining 16 percent worked in forests, sawmills, mines, and, with northward migration, in northern cities.

Gone were the skilled black tradesmen of slavery days. At the end of the Civil War, at least half of all skilled craftsmen in the South had been black. But by the 1890s, the percentage had decreased to less than 10 percent, as whites systematically excluded blacks from the trades. The factory work that blacks had been doing was also reduced, largely to drive a wedge between poor blacks and whites in order to prevent unionization. In Greensboro, North Carolina, for example, where in 1870 some 30 percent of all blacks worked in skilled trades or factory occupations, by 1910, blacks in the skilled trades had been reduced to 8 percent, and not a single black worked in a Greensboro factory. The exclusion of blacks from industry prevented them from acquiring the skills and habits that would enable them to rise into the middle class as would many European immigrants and their children by the mid-twentieth century.

Blacks did not accept their declining position passively. In the mid-1880s, they enthusiastically joined the mass worker organization the Knights of Labor (discussed in Chapter 18), first in cities such as Richmond and Atlanta and then in rural areas. But southern whites feared that the Knights' policies of racial and economic cooperation might lead to social equality. The Charleston *News and Courier* warned of the dangers of "miscegenation" and the possibility that the South would be left "in the possession of . . . mongrels and hybrids." As blacks continued to join it, whites abandoned the order in growing numbers. The flight of whites weakened the organization in the South, and a backlash of white violence finally smashed it.

Against this backdrop, incidents of lynchings and other forms of violence against blacks increased. Lynching was a way to show both black men and white women the dire consequences of stepping out of line. On February 21, 1891, the *New York Times* reported that in Texarkana, Arkansas, a mob apprehended Ed Coy, a 32-year-old black man who was charged with the rape of a white woman. He was tied to a stake and then burned alive. As Coy proclaimed his innocence to a large crowd, his alleged victim somewhat hesitatingly put the torch to his oil-soaked body. The *Times* report concluded that only by the "terrible death such as fire . . . can inflict" could other blacks "be deterred from the commission of like crimes." Ed Coy was one of more than 1,400 black men lynched or burned alive during the 1890s. About one-third were charged with sex crimes. The rest were accused of a variety of "crimes" related to not knowing their place; this included marrying or insulting a white woman, testifying in court against whites, or having a "bad reputation."

Diverging Black Responses

White discrimination and exploitation nourished new protest tactics and ideologies among blacks. For years, Frederick Douglass had been proclaiming that blacks should remain loyal Americans and count on the promises of the Republican party. But on his deathbed in 1895, his last words were allegedly, "Agitate! Agitate! Agitate!"

Agitation had its costs. In Memphis, Tennessee, Ida B. Wells, the first female editor of an important newspaper, launched an anti-lynching campaign in 1892. So hostile was the response from the white community that Wells carried a gun to protect herself. When white citizens finally destroyed the press and threatened her partner, Wells left Memphis to pursue her activism elsewhere.

Some black leaders called called for black separatism within white America. T. Thomas Fortune wrote in the black New York *Freeman* in 1887 that "there will one day be an African Empire." Three years later, he organized the Afro-American League (a precursor of the NAACP), insisting that blacks must join together to fight the rising tide of discrimination. "Let us stand up," he urged, "in our own organization where color will not be a brand of odium." The League encouraged independent voting, opposed segregation and lynching, and urged the establishment of black institutions like banks to support black businesses. As a sympathetic journalist explained, "The solution of the problem is in our own hands. . . . The Negro must preserve his identity."

In 1896, an African American named William Biggerstaff was hung for what was labeled the murder of a white man. The picture cannot reveal the innocence or guilt of the accused. Lynching and violence aimed at blacks became common in the late nineteenth century. As the crowd suggests, lynchings were often well-attended events. *(Montana Historical Society, Helena, MT)*

Although some promoted black nationalism, most blacks worked patiently but persistently within white society for equality and social justice. In 1887, J. C. Price formed the Citizens Equal Rights Association, which supported various petitions and direct-action campaigns to protest segregation. The association also called for state laws to guarantee equal rights in the aftermath of the Supreme Court's 1883 ruling. Other blacks boycotted streetcars in southern cities and petitioned Congress, demanding reparations for unpaid labor as slaves.

Efforts to escape oppression in the South, like "Pap" Singleton's movement to found black towns in Tennessee and Kansas, continued. In the 1890s, black leaders lobbied to make the Oklahoma Territory, recently opened to white settlement, an all-black state. Blacks founded 25 towns there as well as many towns in other states and even in Mexico. But these attempts, like earlier ones, were short-lived, for they were crippled by limited funds and by the hostility of white neighbors. Singleton eventually recommended migration to Canada or

Liberia as a final solution, and later black nationalist leaders also looked increasingly to Africa. Bishop Henry McNeal Turner, a former Union soldier and prominent black leader, despaired of ever securing equal rights for American blacks. He described the Constitution as "a dirty rag, a cheat, a libel" and said that it ought to be "spit upon by every Negro in the land." In 1894, he organized the International Migration Society to return blacks to Africa, arguing that "this country owes us forty billions of dollars" to help. He succeeded in sending two boatloads of emigrants to Liberia, but this colonization effort worked no more successfully than those earlier in the century.

As Frederick Douglass had long argued, no matter how important African roots might be, blacks had been in the Americas for generations and would have to win justice and equal rights here. W. E. B. Du Bois, the first black to receive a Ph.D. from Harvard, agreed. Yet in 1900, he attended the first Pan-African Conference in London, where he argued that blacks must lead the struggle for liberation both in Africa and in the United States. It was at this conference that Du Bois first made his prophetic comment that "the problem of the Twentieth Century" would be "the problem of the color line."

Despite these vigorous voices of militant anger and nationalistic fervor, most black Americans continued to follow the slow, moderate, self-help program of Booker T. Washington, the best-known black leader in America. Born a slave, Washington had risen through hard and faithful work to become the founder (in 1881) and principal of Tuskegee Institute in Alabama, which he personally and dramatically built into the nation's largest and best-known industrial training school. At Tuskegee, young blacks received a highly disciplined education in scientific agricultural techniques and vocational skilled trades. Washington believed that economic self-help and the familiar Puritan virtues of hard work, frugality, cleanliness, and moderation would lead to success for African Americans despite the realities of racism. He spent much of his time traveling through the North to secure philanthropic gifts to support Tuskegee. In time, he became a favorite of the American entrepreneurial elite whose capitalist assumptions he shared.

In 1895, Washington was asked to deliver a speech at the Cotton States and International Exposition in Atlanta, celebrating three decades of industrial and agricultural progress since the Civil War. He took advantage of that invitation, a rare honor for a former slave, to make a significant statement about the position of blacks in the South. Without a hint of protest, Washington decided "to say something that would cement the friendship of the races." He therefore proclaimed black loyalty to the economic development of the South while accepting the lowly status of southern blacks. "It is at the bottom of life we must begin, and not at the top," he declared. "In all things that are purely social we can be as separate as the fingers, yet one as the hand in all things essential to mutual progress." Although Washington worked actively behind the scenes for black civil rights, in Atlanta, he publicly renounced black interest in either the vote or civil rights as well as social equality with whites. Whites throughout the country enthusiastically acclaimed Washington's address, but many blacks called his "Atlanta Compromise" a serious setback in the struggle for black rights.

Washington has often been charged with conceding too quickly that political rights should follow rather than precede economic well-being. In 1903, Du Bois confronted Washington directly in *The Souls of Black Folk*, arguing instead for the "manly assertion" of a program of equal civil rights, suffrage, and higher education in the ideals of liberal learning. A trip through the Black Belt of Dougherty County, Georgia, showed Du Bois the "forlorn and forsaken" condition of southern blacks. The young sociologist saw that most blacks were confined to dependent agricultural labor, "fighting a hard battle with debt" year after year. Although "here and there a man has raised his head above these murky waters . . . a pall of debt hangs over the beautiful land." Beneath all others was the cotton picker, who, with his wife and children, would have to work from sunup to sundown to pick 100 pounds of cotton to make 50 cents. The lives of most blacks were still tied to the land of the South. If they were to improve their lives, rural blacks would have to organize.

FARM PROTEST

During the post–Civil War period, many farmers, both black and white, began to realize that only by organizing could they hope to ameliorate the conditions of rural life. Farmers in the South and West, most affected by new problems and conditions, were in the vanguard of the first mass organization of farmers in American history. However, farmers in the Midwest and near city markets who had successfully adjusted to new economic conditions had less reason for discontent.

The Grange in the 1860s and 1870s

The earliest effort to organize white farmers came in 1867 when Oliver Kelley founded the Order of the Patrons of Husbandry. Originally a social and cultural organization, it was soon protesting the powerlessness of the "immense helpless mob" of farmers, victims of "human vampires." The depression of the 1870s (which will be discussed in Chapter 18) sharpened discontent. By 1875, an estimated 800,000 had joined Kelley's organization, now known as the National Grange.

The Grangers recognized some, but not all, of the forces that contributed to their problems. Middlemen seemed obvious culprits. They gouged farmers by raising the prices of finished goods farmers needed and by lowering the prices they received for their products. Some Granger "reforms" attempted to bypass middlemen by establishing buying and selling cooperatives. Although many cooperatives failed, they indicated that farmers realized the importance of collective action. Other culprits included grain elevator operators, who, midwestern farmers claimed, often misgraded their wheat and corn and paid less than its worth. The greatest oppressors were America's first big business, the railroads. As Chapter 18 will show, cut-throat competition among railroad companies generally brought lower rates. But even though rates dropped nationwide, railroads often set high rates in rural areas, and their rebates to large shippers discriminated against small operators.

Although the Grange was originally nonpolitical, farmers recognized that confronting the mighty railroads demanded political action. Other groups also wished to curb the power of the railroads. Railroad policies that favored large Chicago grain terminals and long-distance shippers victimized many western businessmen. Between 1869 and 1874, businessmen and farmers in Illinois, Iowa, Wisconsin, and Minnesota cooperated to lobby for state railroad laws. The resulting Granger laws (an inaccurate name because the Grangers do not deserve complete credit for them) established the maximum rates railroads and grain elevators could charge. Other states passed legislation setting up railroad commissions with the power to regulate railroad rates. In some states, legislators outlawed railroad pools, rebates, passes, and other practices that seemed to represent "unjust discrimination and distortion."

Railroad companies and grain elevators quickly challenged the new laws. In 1877, the Supreme Court upheld the legislation in *Munn* v. *Illinois*. The Court declared that railroads, even though they were privately owned, could be regulated for the common good, because their operation affected the public interest. Even so, it soon became apparent that although state commissions had authority over local rates and fares, they could not control long-haul rates. To make up for the money lost on local hauls, railroads often raised long-haul charges, thus frustrating the intent of the laws. Other complicated issues involved determining what was a fair rate, who was competent to decide that rate, and what was a justifiable return for the railroad. The tangle of questions that state regulation raised proved difficult to resolve at the local level.

Although the Granger laws failed to solve the questions involved in attempts to control the railroads, they established an important principle. The Supreme Court decision made clear that state legislatures could regulate businesses of a public nature like the railroads. But the failure of the Granger laws and the Supreme Court's reversal of *Munn* v. *Illinois* in its 1886 decision *Wabash* v. *Illinois* led to greater pressure on Congress to continue the struggle against big business.

The Interstate Commerce Act, 1887

In 1887, Congress responded to farmers, railroad managers who wished to control the fierce competition that threatened to bankrupt their companies, and shippers who objected to transportation rates by passing the Interstate Commerce Act. That legislation required that railroad rates be "reasonable and just," that rate schedules be made public, and that practices such as rebates be discontinued. The act also set up the first federal regulatory agency, the Interstate Commerce Commission (ICC). The ICC had the power to investigate and prosecute lawbreakers, but the legislation limited its authority to control over commerce conducted between states.

Like state railroad commissions, the ICC found it difficult to define a reasonable rate. Moreover, thousands of cases overwhelmed the tiny staff in the early months of operation. In the long run, the lack of enforcement power was most serious. The ICC's only recourse was to bring offenders into the federal courts and engage in lengthy legal proceedings. Few railroads worried about defying ICC directions on rates. When they appeared in court four or five years later, they often won their cases from judges suspicious of new federal authority. Between 1887 and 1906, a total of 16 cases made their way to the Supreme Court, which decided 15 of them in the railroads' favor. As one railroad executive candidly admitted, "There is not a road in the country that can be accused of living up to the rules of the Interstate Commerce Law."

The Southern Farmers' Alliance in the 1880s and 1890s

The Grange declined in the late 1870s as the nation recovered from depression. But neither farm organizations nor farm protest died. Depression struck farmers once again in the late 1880s and worsened as the 1890s began. Official statistics told the familiar story of falling prices for cereal crops grown on the plains and prairies. The national currency shortage, which usually reached critical proportions at harvest time, helped push agricultural prices ever lower. Agricultural debt climbed, and shipping rates were high. It sometimes cost a farmer as much as one bushel of corn to send another one to market.

A Kansas farmer's letter reveals some of the human consequences of such trends:

> At the age of 52 years, after a long life of toil, economy and self-denial, I find myself and family virtually paupers. With hundreds of cattle, hundreds of hogs, scores of good horses, and a farm that rewarded the toil of our hands with 16,000 bushels of golden corn, we are poorer by many dollars than we were years ago.

Under these pressures, farmers turned again to organization, education, and cooperation. The Southern Farmers' Alliance became one of the most important reform organizations of the 1880s as it launched an ambitious organizational drive, sending lecturers throughout the South and onto the western plains. Eventually, alliance lecturers reached 43 states and territories, bringing their message to 2 million farming families and organizing a far-reaching agrarian network.

The farmer's condition was, in the words of an alliance song, a "sin," the result of the farmer's forgetting that "he's the man that feeds them all." Lecturers pointed out that the economic and social position of farmers had slipped, even though as producers, the farming class was critical to national well-being.

The Alliance tried to reverse this dire situation. On the one hand, it experimented with buying and selling cooperatives to free farmers from the clutches of supply merchants, banks, and other credit agencies. Although these efforts often failed in the long run, they reinforced the value of cooperation to achieve common goals. On the other hand, the Alliance supported legislative efforts to regulate powerful monopolies and corporations, which they believed gouged the farmer. Many Alliance members also felt that increasing the money supply was critical to improving the position of farmers and supported a national banking system empowered to issue paper money. The Alliance also called for a variety of measures to improve the quality of rural life: better public schools for rural children, state agricultural colleges, and an improvement in the status of women.

By 1890, rural discontent was spreading. In the Midwest, where farmers were prospering by raising hogs and cattle on cheap grain, and in the East,

where farmers were growing fruit and vegetables for urban markets, discontent was muted. But that summer in Kansas, hundreds of farmers packed their families into wagons to set off for Alliance meetings or to parade in long lines through the streets of nearby towns and villages. Floats garnished with evergreens proclaimed that the farmers' new organization focused on live issues, not the dead ones Congress debated.

Similar scenes occurred through the West and the South. Never had there been such a wave of organizational activity in rural America. In 1890, more than a million farmers counted themselves as Alliance members.

The Alliance network also included black farmers. In 1888, black and white organizers established the Colored Farmers' Alliance, headed by white Baptist minister R.M. Humphrey. The Colored Farmers' Alliance recognized that since black and white farmers faced common economic problems, they must cooperate to ameliorate their shared plight. Few initially confronted the fact that many southern cotton farmers depended on black labor and had a different perspective from that of blacks. In 1891, however, cotton pickers working on plantations near Memphis, Tennessee, went on strike. White posses chased the strikers, lynched 15 of them, and demonstrated that racial tensions simmered just below the surface.

The Ocala Platform, 1890

In December 1890, the National Alliance gathered in Ocala, Florida, to develop an official platform. Most delegates felt that the federal government had failed to address the farmers' problems. "Congress must come nearer the people or the people will come nearer the Congress," warned the Alliance's president. Both parties were far too subservient to the "will of corporation and money power."

The platform called for the direct election of U.S. senators. Alliance members supported lowering the tariff, a much debated topic in Congress, but their justification, emphasizing the need to reduce prices for the "poor of our land," had a radical ring. Their money plank went far beyond what any national legislator was likely to consider. Rejecting the notion that only gold had value or, indeed, that precious metals had to be the basis for currency, Alliance leaders boldly envisioned a new banking system controlled by the federal government. They demanded that the government take an active economic role by increasing the amount of money in circulation, believing that more money would lead to inflation, higher prices, and a reduction in debt.

Timeline

1860s	Cattle drives from Texas begin
1865–1867	Sioux wars on the Great Plains
1867	National Grange founded
1869	Transcontinental railroad completed
1869–1874	Granger laws
1873	Financial panic triggers economic depression
1874	Barbed wire patented
1875	Black Hills gold rush incites Sioux war
1876	Custer's last stand at Little Big Horn
1877	*Munn v. Illinois* Bonanza farms in the Great Plains
1878	Timber and Stone Act
1880s	Attempts to create a "New South"
1881	Tuskegee Institute founded
1883–1885	Depression
1884	Southern Farmers' Alliance founded
1886	Severe winter ends cattle boom *Wabash v. Illinois*
1887	Dawes Severalty Act Interstate Commerce Act Farm prices plummet
1888	Colored Farmers' Alliance founded
1890	Afro-American League founded Sioux ghost dance movement Massacre at Wounded Knee Ocala platform Yosemite National Park established
1890s	Black disenfranchisement in the South Jim Crow laws passed in the South Declining farm prices
1891	Forest Reserve Act
1892	Populist party formed Sierra Club founded
1895	Booker T. Washington's "Atlanta Compromise" address
1896	*Plessy v. Ferguson*

The platform also called for the creation of subtreasuries (federal warehouses) to store agricultural produce at low interest rates until market prices favored selling. To tide farmers over until that time, the federal government would lend farmers up to 80 percent of the current local price for their products. Thus, the plan would free farmers from the twin evils of the credit merchant and depressed prices at harvest time. Other demands included a graduated income tax and support for the regulation of transportation and communication networks. If regulation failed, the government was called on to take over both networks and run them for the public benefit.

In the context of late-nineteenth-century political life, almost all these planks radically departed from political norms. They demanded aggressive government action to assist the country's farmers at a time when the government favored big business (see Chapter 19). Even though a minority of farmers belonged to the Alliance, many Americans feared that the organization was capable of upsetting political arrangements.

The New York *Sun* reported that the Alliance had caused a "panic" in the two major parties. The Alliance's warning that the people would replace their representatives unless they were better represented was already coming true. Although the Alliance was not formally in politics, it had supported sympathetic candidates in the fall elections of 1890. A surprising number of these local and state candidates had won. Alliance victories in the West harmed the Republican party enough to cause President Harrison to refer to "our election disaster."

Before long, many Alliance members were pressing for an independent political party, as legislators who had courted Alliance votes conveniently forgot their pledges once elected. Alliance support did not necessarily bring action on issues of interest to farmers, or even respect. One Texas farmer reported that the chairman of the state Democratic executive committee "calls us all skunks" and observed that "anything that has the scent of the plowhandle smells like a polecat" to the Democrats. On the national level, no one had much interest in the Ocala platform. As one North Carolinian observed, "I am not able to perceive any very great difference between the two parties."

Among the first to realize the necessity of forming an independent third party was Georgia's Tom Watson. "We are in the midst of a great crisis," he argued. "We have before us three or four platforms . . . [and] the Ocala platform is the best of all three. It is the only one that breathes the breath of life." Watson also realized that electoral success in the South would depend on unity between white and black farmers.

◆ *Conclusion*

FARMING IN THE INDUSTRIAL AGE

The late nineteenth century brought turbulence to rural America. The "Indian problem," which had plagued Americans for 200 years, was tragically solved for a while, but not without resistance and bloodshed. Few whites found these events troubling. Most were caught up in the challenge of responding to a fast-changing world. Believing themselves to be the backbone of the nation, white farmers brought Indian lands into cultivation, modernized their farms, and raised bumper crops. But success and a comfortable competency eluded many of them. Some, like Milton Leeper, never gave up hope or farming. Many were caught in a cycle of poverty and debt. Others fled to the cities, where they joined the industrial workforce described in the next chapter. Many turned to collective action and politics. Their actions demonstrate that they did not merely react to events but attempted to shape them.

◆ Recommended Reading

Modernizing Agriculture
David Blanke, *Sowing the American Dream: How Consumer Culture Took Root in the Rural Midwest* (2000); Fred A. Shannon, *The Farmer's Last Frontier: Agriculture, 1860–1897* (1945).

The West
Steven J. Holmes, *The Young John Muir: An Environmental Biography* (1999); Rodman W. Paul, with Martin Ridge, *The Far West and the Great Plains in Transition, 1859–1900* (1988); William G. Robbins, *Colony & Empire: The Capitalist Transformation of the American West* (1994); Donald Worster, *Rivers of Empire: Water, Aridity, and the Growth of the American West* (1985) and *An Unsettled Country: Changing Landscapes of the American West* (1994).

Resolving the Indian Question
John G. Neihardt, *Black Elk Speaks* (1932); Robert M. Utley, *The Indian Frontier of the American West* (1984) and *The Lance and the Shield: The Life and Times of Sitting Bull* (1993); Richard White, *The Roots of Dependency: Subsistence, Environment, and Social Change Among the Choctaws, Pawnees, and Navajos* (1983).

The New South
W. Fitzhugh Brundage, *Lynching in the New South; Georgia and Virginia, 1880–1930* (1993); Orville Vernon Burton and Robert C. McMath, Jr., eds., *Toward a New South? Post–Civil War Southern Communities* (1982); Glenda Elizabeth Gilmore, *Gender and Jim Crow: Women and the Politics of White Supremacy in North Carolina, 1896–1920* (1996); Lawrence H. Larsen, *The Rise of the Urban South* (1985); William E. Montgomery, *Under Their Own Vine and Fig Tree: The African-American Church in the South, 1865–1900* (1993); Michael Perman, *Struggle for Mastery: Disfranchisement in the South, 1888–1908* (2001); Edward Royce, *The Origins of Southern Sharecropping* (1993).

Farm Protest
Steven Hahn, *The Roots of Southern Populism: Yeoman Farmers and the Transformation of the Georgia Upcountry, 1850–1890* (1983); Robert W. Larson, *Populism in the Mountain West* (1986); Jeffrey Ostler, *Prairie Populism: The Fate of Agrarian Radicalism in Kansas, Nebraska, and Iowa, 1880–1892* (1993); Bruce Palmer, *"Men over Money:" The Southern Populist Critique of American Capitalism* (1980).

Fiction and Film
Willa Cather's novels *My Antonia* (1918) and *O Pioneers!* (1913) emphasize the energy and determination of those farming in the post–Civil War West as well as the presence of immigrants there. O. E. Rölvaag's *Giants in the Earth* (1927) deals with immigrant families but gives a very grim picture of their adjustment to farming life in the United States. Written in 1885 by Maria Amparo Ruiz de Burton, *The Squatter and the Don* provides insights into the views of Mexican Americans. *The Searchers* (1956), *Stagecoach* (1939), and *She Wore a Yellow Ribbon* (1949) come from the heyday of western films and reveal mid-twentieth century (and John Wayne's) views of the late frontier. *Dances with Wolves* (1990) is Kevin Costner's indictment of the white assault on Native American life and culture. His sympathetic depiction of Indian life bears marks of the consciousness of the 1990s. *Ethnic Notions* (1987), an Emmy-winning documentary by Marlon Riggs, traces the evolution of negative stereotypes of African Americans and the ways these stereotypes have been embodied in popular culture.

✦ Discovering U.S. History Online

McCormick Farm

www.vaes.vt.edu/steeles/mccormick/harvest.html

Cyrus Hall McCormick invented the McCormick Reaper, and his former farm is now owned by Virginia Polytechnic Institute and State University. This site chronicles various stages of harvesting technological development via an interactive photo essay.

Heroes and Villains

www.ukans.edu/carrie/kancoll

Part of the Kansas Collection Gallery, this site offers glimpses of heroes and villains of the West via books, letters, diaries, photos, and other materials from the past.

Fort Larned National Historic Site

www.nps.gov/fols/home.html

The companion Web site for Fort Larned, a preserved fort from the "Indian Wars Period," offers a virtual tour of the fort, information about the Buffalo Soldiers, soldier equipment, Plains Indians, and other learning tools and facts.

Yosemite History

www.yosemite.ca.us/history

This site presents articles contemporary to Yosemite's creation and biographies of key figures, maps, and photos.

Native American Documents

www.csusm.edu/projects/nadp/nadp.htm

Several documents relating to Native Americans have been transcribed and indexed for use on this site. The documents include indexed published reports of the Commissioner of Indian Affairs and the Board of Indian Commissioners for 1871, "allotment" data, as well as over 100 documents from the Rogue River War and Siletz Reservation.

Lynching in America

www.journale.com/withoutsanctuary/index.html

This site presents a stark visual history of lynching in the South. The site includes a flash movie with narration.

The Grange Society

www.indianhill.org/History/Hist018.htm

This local historical site gives an example of an agricultural society that became an increasingly "commercialized industry."

Farmers' Alliance and Colored Farmers' Alliance

www.tsha.utexas.edu/handbook/online/articles/view/FF/aaf2.html

www.tsha.utexas.edu/handbook/online/articles/view/CC/aac1.html

These two articles from this online "multidisciplinary encyclopedia of Texas history" give more detail about these allied farm-protest organizations.

The Rise of Smokestack America

This anxious scene of a strike hints at the tensions between workers and owners during the industrial era. *(Robert Koehler, The Strike [detail], 1886, Courtesy of District 1199, National Union of Hospital and Health Care Employees, RWDSW/AFL-CIO and Lee Baxandall)*

◆ *American Stories*

TELLING HIS STORY: O'DONNELL AND THE SENATORS

By 1883, Thomas O'Donnell, an Irish immigrant, had lived in the United States for more than a decade. He was 30 years old, married, with two young children. His third child had died in 1882, and O'Donnell was still in debt for the funeral. Money was scarce, for O'Donnell was a textile worker in Fall River, Massachusetts, and not well educated. "I went to work when I was young," he explained, "and have been working ever since." However, O'Donnell worked only sporadically at the mill. New machines needed "a good deal of small help," and the mill owners preferred to hire man-and-boy teams. Because O'Donnell's children were very young, he often saw others preferred for day work. Once, when he was passed over, he asked the boss "what am I to do; I have got two little boys at home . . . how am I to get something for them to eat; I can't get a turn when I come here. . . . I says, 'Have I got to starve; ain't I to have any work?' "

O'Donnell and his family were barely getting by, even though he worked with pick and shovel when he could. He estimated that he had earned only $133 the previous year. Rent came to $72. The family spent $2 for a little coal but depended for heat on driftwood that O'Donnell picked up on the beach. Clams were a major part of the family diet, but on some days there was nothing to eat at all.

The children "got along very nicely all summer," but it was now November, and they were beginning to "feel quite sickly." It was hardly surprising. "One has one shoe on, a very poor one, and a slipper, that was picked up somewhere. The other has two odd shoes on, with the heel out." His wife was healthy, but not ready for winter. She had two dresses, one saved for church, and an "undershirt that she got given to her, and . . . an old wrapper, which is about a mile too big for her; somebody gave it to her."

O'Donnell was describing his family's marginal existence to a Senate committee gathering testimony in Boston in 1883 on the relations between labor and capital. As the senators heard the tale, they asked him why he did not go west. "It would not cost you over $1,500," said one senator. The gap between the worlds of the senator and the worker could not have been more dramatic. O'Donnell replied, "Well, I never saw over a $20 bill . . . if some one would give me $1,500 I will go." Asked by the senator if he had friends who could provide him with the funds, O'Donnell sadly replied no.

The senators, of course, were far better acquainted with the world of comfort and leisure than with the poverty of families like the O'Donnells. From their vantage point, the fruits of industrial progress were clear. As the United States became a world industrial leader in the years after the Civil War, its factories poured forth an abundance of ever-cheaper goods ranging from steel rails and farm reapers to mass-produced parlor sets. These were years of tremendous growth and broad economic and social change. Manufacturing replaced agriculture as the leading source of economic growth between 1860 and 1900. By 1890, a majority of the American workforce held nonagricultural jobs; over a third lived in cities. A rural nation of farmers was becoming a nation of industrial workers and city dwellers.

As O'Donnell's appearance before the senatorial committee illustrates, industrial and technological advances profoundly changed the nature of American life. For O'Donnell and others like him, the benefits of this transformation were hard to see. Although no nationwide studies of poverty existed, estimates suggest that perhaps half the American population was too poor to take advantage of the new goods of the age. Eventually, the disparity between the reality of life for humble families like the O'Donnells and American ideals would give rise to attempts to improve conditions for working-class Americans, but it is unlikely that O'Donnell ever profited from such efforts.

This chapter examines the new order that resulted from the maturing of the American industrial economy. Focusing on the years between 1865 and 1900, it describes the rise of heavy industry, the organization and character of the new industrial workplace, and the emergence of big business. It then examines the locus of industrial life, the fast-growing city, and its varied people, classes, and social inequities. The chapter's central theme grows out of O'Donnell's story: As the United States built up its railroads, cities, and factories, its production and profit orientation resulted in the maldistribution of wealth and power. Although many Americans were too exhausted by life's daily struggles to protest new inequalities, strikes and other forms of working-class resistance punctuated the period. The social problems that accompanied the country's industrial development would capture the attention of reformers and politicians for decades to come.

THE TEXTURE OF INDUSTRIAL PROGRESS

When Americans went to war in 1861, agriculture was the country's leading source of economic growth. Forty years later, manufacturing had taken its place. During these years, the production of manufactured goods outpaced population growth. By 1900, three times as many goods per person existed as in 1860. Per capita income increased by over 2 percent a year. But these aggregate figures disguise the fact that many people did not win any gains at all.

As the nature of the American economy changed, big businesses became the characteristic form of economic organization. They could raise the capital to build huge factories, acquire expensive and efficient machinery, hire hundreds of workers, and use the most up-to-date methods. The result was more goods at lower prices.

New regions grew in industrial importance. From New England to the Midwest lay the country's industrial heartland. New England remained a center of light industry, while the Midwest still processed natural resources. Now, however, the production of iron, steel, and transportation equipment joined older manufacturing operations there. In the Far West, manufacturers concentrated on processing the region's natural resources, but heavy industry made strides as well. In the South, the textile industry put down roots by the 1890s.

Although many factors contributed to dramatically rising industrial productivity, the changing character of the industrial sector explains many of the gains. Pre–Civil War manufacturers had concentrated either on producing textiles, clothing, and leather products or on processing agricultural and natural resources like grain, logs, or lumber. Although these operations remained important, heavy industry grew rapidly after the war. The manufacturing of steel, iron, and machinery meant for other producers rather than consumers fueled economic growth.

Technological Innovations

An accelerating pace of technological change contributed to and was shaped by the industrial transformation of the late nineteenth century. Technological breakthroughs allowed more efficient production that, in turn, helped to generate new needs and further innovation. Developments in the steel and electric industries exemplify this interdependent process and highlight the contributions of entrepreneurs and new ways of organizing research and innovation.

Before the Civil War, skilled workers produced iron in a slow and expensive process. The iron was so soft that trains wore out rails in a matter of years. The need for a harder metal supported the development and introduction of new technologies. The Bessemer converter (named after its English inventor) transformed iron into steel by forcing air through the liquid iron, thus reducing the carbon (see "Analyzing History" feature on page 612). The process contributed to the rapid expansion of the steel industry and had the added advantage of reducing the need for highly paid skilled workers.

Neither an inventor nor an engineer, Andrew Carnegie recognized the promise not only of new processes but also of new ways of organizing industry. Steel companies like Carnegie's acquired access to raw materials and markets and brought all stages of steel manufacturing, from smelting to rolling, into one mill. Output soared, and prices fell. When Andrew Carnegie introduced the Bessemer process in his plant in the mid-1870s, the price of steel plummeted from $100 a ton to $12 a ton by 1900.

In turn, the production of a cheaper, stronger, more durable material than iron created new goods, new demands, and new markets, and it stimulated further technological change. Bessemer furnaces,

The Homestead Steel Works, pictured here in about 1890, were located near Pittsburgh, Pennsylvania. The vast scale of the enterprise suggests the ways in which technological innovation stimulated the expansion of the steel industry in the late nineteenth century. Although the two small figures in the foreground humanize the picture, the extent and size of the steel mills created a workplace that was anything but humane. *(Courtesy of Rivers of Steel Archives)*

geared toward making steel rails, did not produce steel for building. Experimentation with the open-hearth process that used very high temperatures resulted in steel for bridge and ship builders, engineers, architects, and even designers of subways. Countless Americans bought steel in more humble forms: wire, nails, bolts, needles, and screws.

New power sources facilitated American industry's shift to mass production and also suggest the importance of new ways of organizing research and innovation. In 1869, about half of the nation's industrial power came from water. The opening of new anthracite deposits, however, cut the cost of coal, and American industry rapidly converted to steam. By 1900, steam engines generated 80 percent of the nation's industrial energy supply. But soon electricity began to replace steam as a power source.

Experiments in generating electricity dated back to the middle of the eighteenth century and facilitated the development of the telegraph before the Civil War. In 1878, Thomas Edison, having already developed the ticker tape (to send information from the stock exchange to investors' offices) and a telegraph capable of simultaneously transmitting four messages along the wires, turned his attention to electric lighting. His ultimate success came not only from his own inventiveness but also from his understanding that professional collaboration could foster successful innovation. In 1876, he set up a research lab with a range of specialists and facilities. His work with the ticker tape ensured generous support from the business and financial community.

By 1880, Edison had not only developed a workable and safe light bulb but also created a company in New York to build the electric generating station to provide electricity to the city's customers. Since people used their electric lights mainly at night, there was a built-in incentive to find a way to use generators during the day. Electric traction trolley cars using steel tracks provided one way to maximize the potential of the generating station. Experimenting with electric generators also led to the development of the electric machine, which has transformed American life.

Railroads: Pioneers of Big Business

Completion of efficient and speedy national transportation and communications networks encouraged mass production and mass marketing. Beginning in 1862, federal and state governments

STEEL: THE ENGINE OF INDUSTRIAL GROWTH

Innovations in the steel industry affected many aspects of American life. They helped to make an efficient national transportation network a reality through the production of steel rails, stimulated urban growth and a new urban character with steel girders for bridges and high buildings, and provided working-class jobs in many different urban hubs.

Reflecting on the Past What was the relationship between production and prices? How does this relationship explain business attitudes and practices? What is its relationship to the growth of the large industrial firms? The stock market? In what ways does the information contained here relate to the creation of a mass market in the United States?

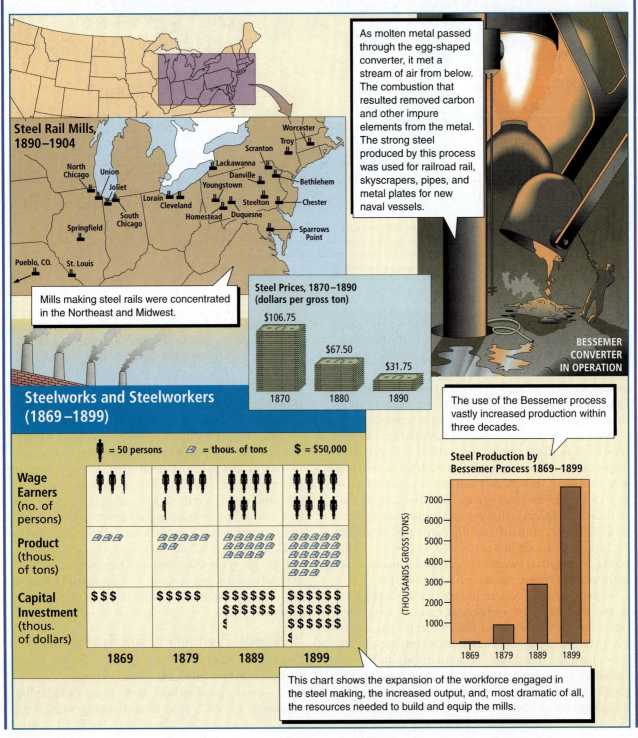

Steel Rail Mills, 1890–1904

Worcester
Troy
Scranton
Lackawanna
Danville
Youngstown
Bethlehem
North Chicago
Union
Joliet
Lorain
Cleveland
Steelton
Chester
South Chicago
Homestead
Duquesne
Springfield
Sparrows Point
Pueblo, CO.
St. Louis

Mills making steel rails were concentrated in the Northeast and Midwest.

As molten metal passed through the egg-shaped converter, it met a stream of air from below. The combustion that resulted removed carbon and other impure elements from the metal. The strong steel produced by this process was used for railroad rail, skyscrapers, pipes, and metal plates for new naval vessels.

BESSEMER CONVERTER IN OPERATION

Steel Prices, 1870–1890 (dollars per gross ton)

$106.75 — 1870
$67.50 — 1880
$31.75 — 1890

Steelworks and Steelworkers (1869–1899)

The use of the Bessemer process vastly increased production within three decades.

= 50 persons   = thous. of tons $ = $50,000

	1869	1879	1889	1899
Wage Earners (no. of persons)				
Product (thous. of tons)				
Capital Investment (thous. of dollars)				

Steel Production by Bessemer Process 1869–1899

(THOUSANDS GROSS TONS)

7000
6000
5000
4000
3000
2000
1000

1869 1879 1889 1899

This chart shows the expansion of the workforce engaged in the steel making, the increased output, and, most dramatic of all, the resources needed to build and equip the mills.

vigorously promoted railroad construction with land grants from the public domain. Eventually, railroads received lands one and a half times the size of Texas. Local governments gave everything from land for stations to tax breaks.

With such incentives, the first transcontinental railroad was finished in 1869. Four additional transcontinental lines and miles of feeder and branch roads were laid down in the 1870s and 1880s. By 1890, trains rumbled across 165,000 miles of tracks. Telegraph lines arose alongside them.

Railroads, the pioneers of big business, were a great modernizing force. After the Civil War, railroad companies expanded in size and complexity. The costs of construction required unprecedented amounts of capital, while the numbers of workers and the operation of the business demanded new management techniques. No single person could finance a railroad, supervise its vast operations, or resolve the questions such a large enterprise raised. How should the operations and employees be organized? What were long- and short-term needs? What were proper rates? What share of the profits did workers deserve?

Unlike small businesses, railroads' high costs and heavy indebtedness encouraged aggressive business practices. When several lines competed, railroads often offered lower rates or secret rebates (cheaper fares in exchange for all of a company's business). Rate wars caused freight rates to drop steadily but could also plunge a railroad into bankruptcy. Instability plagued the industry.

In the 1870s, railroad leaders sought to eliminate this ruinous competition. They established "pools"—informal agreements that set uniform rates or divided up the traffic. Yet these deals never completely succeeded. Too often, companies broke them, especially during business downturns.

Railroad leaders often tried to control costs and counter late-nineteenth-century falling prices by slashing wages. Owners justified this by reasoning that they had taken all the risks. As a result, railroads faced powerful worker unrest.

The huge scale and complexity of railroads called for innovative management techniques. In 1854, the Erie Railroad hired engineer and inventor Daniel McCallum to discover how to make managers and employees more accountable. McCallum pointed out that large organizations needed to be handled differently than small ones. He worked out a system that divided responsibilities and ensured a regular flow of information. It attracted widespread interest. Other large-scale businesses copied the new procedures that effectively distributed work and separated management from operations. They also

learned lessons from the railroads' competitiveness, their efforts to underprice one another, and their drive to cut workers' wages.

Growth in Other Industries

By the last quarter of the century, the textile, metal, and machinery industries equaled the railroads in size. In 1870, the typical iron and steel firm employed under 100 workers. Thirty years later, the average workforce was four times as large. By 1900, more than 1,000 American factories had giant labor forces ranging between 500 and 1,000 workers. Almost 450 others employed more than 1,000 workers. Big business had come of age.

Business expansion was accomplished in one of two ways (or a combination of both). Some owners, like steel magnate Andrew Carnegie, integrated their businesses vertically. Vertical integration meant adding operations either before or after the production process. Even though he had introduced the most up-to-date innovations in his steel mills, Carnegie realized he needed his own sources of pig iron, coal, and coke. This was "backward" integration, away from the consumer, to avoid dependence on suppliers. When Carnegie acquired steamships and railroads to transport his finished products, he was integrating "forward," toward the consumer. Companies that integrated vertically frequently achieved economies of scale through more efficient management techniques.

Other companies copied the railroads and integrated horizontally by combining similar businesses. They did not intend to control the various stages of production, as was the case with vertical integration, but rather to gain a monopoly of the market to eliminate competition and to stabilize prices. Horizontal integration sometimes, though not always, brought economies and thus greater profits. But by controlling prices, monopolies did boost earnings.

John D. Rockefeller used the strategy of horizontal integration to gain control of the oil market. By a combination of astute and ruthless techniques, Rockefeller bought or drove out competitors of his Standard Oil of New Jersey. Although the company never achieved a complete monopoly, by 1898 it was refining 84 percent of the nation's oil. Rockefeller reflected, "The day of individual competition [in the oil business] . . . is past and gone."

Rockefeller accurately characterized the new economic climate. As giant businesses competed intensely, often cutting wages and prices, they absorbed or eliminated smaller and weaker producers. Business ownership became increasingly concentrated. In 1870, some 808 American iron and steel firms competed in the marketplace. By 1900, fewer than 70 were left.

Like the railroads, many big businesses saw the wisdom of incorporation. Corporations had many advantages. By selling stock, they could raise funds for large-scale operations. Limited liability protected investors' personal assets while the corporation's legal identity allowed it to survive the death of original and subsequent shareholders. Longevity suggested a measure of stability that made corporations attractive to investors.

Financing Postwar Growth

Such changes demanded huge amounts of capital along with the willingness to accept financial risks. The creation of the railroad system alone cost over $1 billion by 1859 (the canal system's modest price tag was less than $2 million). The completion of the national railroad network required another $10 billion. British, French, and German investors saw American railroads as a good investment; ultimately, foreigners contributed one-third of the sum needed to complete the system. Americans also eagerly supported new ventures and began to devote an increasing percentage of the national income to investment rather than consumption.

Although savings and commercial banks continued to invest their depositors' capital, investment banking houses like Morgan & Co. played a new and significant role in transferring resources to economic enterprises. Investment bankers marketed investment opportunities. They bought up blocks of corporate bonds (which offered set interest rates and eventually the repayment of principal) at a discount for interested investors and also sold stocks (which paid dividends only if the company made a profit). Because stocks were riskier investments than bonds, buyers were cautious at first. But when John Pierpont Morgan, a respected investment banker, began to market stocks, they became more popular. The market for industrial securities expanded rapidly in the 1880s and 1890s. Although some Americans feared the power of investment bankers and distrusted the financial market, both were integral to the economic expansion of the late nineteenth century.

American Industry and the World

The industrialization of the late nineteenth century represented the second stage of the great transformation that began in Great Britain in the eighteenth century. By reorganizing production, often through the use of machinery, early manufacturers were able to turn out more and cheaper goods than at any time in human history. Innovation created the tex-

Recipients of European Migration, 1846–1932

While most migration from Europe was headed toward the United States, immigrants flocked to South America, Canada, and Australia and New Zealand as well. In Argentina, Italian immigrants made up a larger percentage of the population than they did in the United States and thus influenced Argentinean culture more profoundly than they affected American culture. **Reflecting on the Past** What does this chart suggest about the push-pull factors in the process of migration?

(Estimates in millions)

United States	34.2
Argentina and Uruguay	7.1
Canada	5.2
Brazil	4.4
Australia and New Zealand	3.5
Cuba	.9

tile, mining, and metal industries and stimulated changes in transportation and communications. From Britain, industrialization spread to other countries in Europe as well as to the United States.

The second stage of the industrial revolution was marked by the application of science and technology to manufacturing and by the creation of new ways to mass-produce goods. The United States was the leader in developing techniques of mass production, while Germany excelled in using science and technology to reshape production. Technological innovations transformed German industry. As in the United States, giant firms turned out goods (especially heavy machinery and chemicals) for ever lower prices. Along with Great Britain, Germany and the United States produced two-thirds of the world's manufactured products between 1870 and 1930.

Great Britain, the world's most powerful nation during the nineteenth century, had long been its economic leader. But now the balance of power began to shift as German and American businesses developed large new enterprises, introduced new ways of organizing and efficiently managing them, invested heavily in equipment, and promoted research. Great Britain lost ground, preferring traditional ways of organizing businesses rather than the new corporate structure. British manufacturing continued to be centered in older industries like textiles, while British investors channeled their capital away from domestic industries towards investment opportunities abroad. American railroads and subways were constructed partly with the assistance of British investors.

The full impact of the changed position of the United States in the world triggered by its industrial might only became fully apparent in the twentieth century. But the importance of connections with other nations was obvious. Standard Oil sent two-thirds of the kerosene it refined to overseas markets. Firms manufacturing sewing machines and a range of office machines like typewriters and those producing farm machinery came to dominate the world market. Singer Sewing Machine had a factory in Scotland in the 1880s and two decades later manufactured over 400,000 machines in Moscow, employing 2,500 workers and 300 managers. American locomotives were exported to South America, parts of Africa and Europe, the Middle East, and Asia. The Baldwin Locomotive Works of Philadelphia produced as many engines as any other locomotive company in the world. These connections between American business and other nations meant that events elsewhere in the world could affect the American economy. Furthermore, they suggested the intricate ties binding American business to other parts of the world. American industrial pro-

duction contributed to the economic development of other countries around the globe, while American business also competed with foreign producers. John D. Rockefeller told a Congressional committee that Standard Oil "spared no expense in forcing its products into the markets of the world among people civilized and uncivilized," and that the company was "holding its market against the competition of Russia and all the many countries which are producers of oil and competitors against American oil."

An Erratic Global Economy

Affected by national and worldwide economic trends, the transformation of the American economy was neither smooth nor steady. Rockefeller, describing his years in the oil business as "hazardous," confessed that he did not know "how we came through them."

Two depressions, one from 1873 to 1879 and the other from 1893 to 1897, surpassed the severity of economic downturns before the Civil War. Collapsing land values, unsound banking practices, and changes in the supply of money had

European and American Industrial Investment, 1900

Here we can see the broad impact that industrialized countries had on the rest of the world. Although industrialization was initially centered in western Europe and the United States, its influence was global. Industrial countries sought new markets, new sources of raw material, and new places for investment and development. **Reflecting on the Past** In what places was the United States most interested? Where did individual European countries invest heavily? How would you compare the global impact of the United States to major European countries?

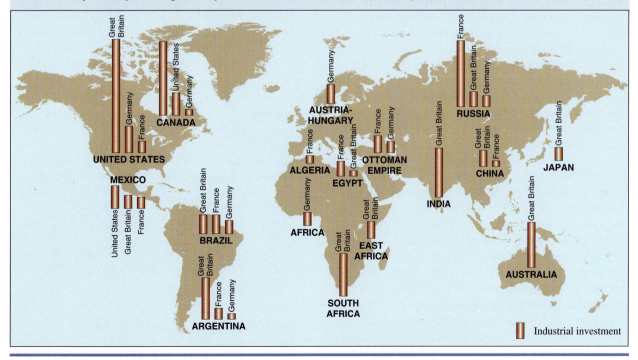

World's Industrial Output

This table shows the changing pattern of industrial production among the world's most significant manufacturing nations. **Reflecting on the Past** In which period did American industry makes its greatest gains? What lies behind these rapid gains? What economic impact does the chart suggest World War I had on the three countries? How might the patterns of the 1920s shape the three countries' experiences during the 1930s?

	Great Britain	United States	Germany
1870	32	23	13
1896–1900	20	30	17
1913	14	36	16
1926–1929	9	42	12

caused antebellum depressions. The depressions of the late nineteenth century, when the economy was larger and more interdependent, were industrial, intense, and accompanied by widespread unemployment, a phenomenon new to American life. They were also related to economic declines in European industrial nations.

During expansionary years, manufacturers flooded markets with goods. The global pattern of falling prices that characterized the postwar period and fierce competition between producers combined to encourage overproduction. When the market was finally saturated, sales and profits declined, and the economy spiraled downward. Owners slowed production and laid off workers. Industrial workers, now an increasing percentage of the American workforce, depended solely on wages for their livelihood. As they economized and bought less food, farm prices also plummeted. Farmers, like wage workers, cut back on purchases. Business and trade stagnated, and the railroads were finally affected. Eventually, the cycle bottomed out, but in the meantime, millions of workers lost employment, thousands of businesses went bankrupt, and many Americans suffered deprivation and hardship.

Pollution

Widespread pollution, another by-product of the industrial age, worried most Americans less than the vagaries of the economic cycle. But industrial processes everywhere adversely affected the environment. In the iron and steel city of Birmingham, Alabama, for example, the coke ovens poured smoke, soot, and ashes into the air. Coal tar, a by-product of the coking process, was dumped, making the soil so acid that nothing would grow on it.

When industrial, human, and animal wastes were channeled into rivers, they killed fish and other forms of marine life and plants that were part of that ecosystem. By the late nineteenth century, major pollution of eastern and midwestern rivers as well as lakes had become pronounced.

The intellectual rationale stressed growth, development, and the rapid exploitation of the country's resources—not conservation. As the last chapter pointed out, small steps were taken toward protecting the environment. Presidents Grover Cleveland and Benjamin Harrison both set aside forest reserves, and there was growing interest in creating national parks. But such activities were limited in scope and did not begin to touch the problems created by the rise of heavy industry and the rapid urban expansion that it stimulated.

URBAN EXPANSION IN THE INDUSTRIAL AGE

Before the Civil War, manufacturers had relied on water power and had chosen rural sites for their factories. Now as they shifted to steam power, most favored urban locations that provided workers, specialized services, local markets, and railroad links to materials and distant markets. Although technological innovations like electric lights (invented in 1879) and telephones (1876) were still not widespread, they further increased the desirability of urban sites. Industry, rather than commerce or finance, fueled urban expansion between 1870 and 1900.

Increase in Size of Industries, 1860–1900

This table highlights the dramatic changes in the workplace over a 40-year period. Think about what the figures suggest about the experience of work.

Industry	Average Number of Workers per Establishment	
	1860	1900
Cotton goods	112	287
Glass	81	149
Iron and steel	65	333
Hosiery and knit goods	46	91
Silk and silk goods	39	135
Woollen goods	33	67
Carpets and rugs	31	213
Tobacco	30	67
Slaughtering and meatpacking	20	61
Paper and wood pulp	15	65
Shipbuilding	15	42
Agricultural implements	8	65
Leather	5	40
Malt liquors	5	26

Source: U.S. Bureau of the Census.

Cities of all sizes grew. The population of New York and Philadelphia doubled and tripled. Smaller cities, especially those in the industrial Midwest like Omaha, Duluth, and Minneapolis, boasted impressive growth rates. Southern cities, as we saw in Chapter 17, also shared in the dramatic growth. Far western cities grew most rapidly of all. In 1870, some 25 percent of Americans lived in cities, but in California, 37 percent did. By 1900, fully 40 percent of Americans were urban dwellers.

A Growing Population

The American population as a whole was growing at a rate of about 2 percent a year, but cities were expanding far more rapidly. What accounted for the dramatic increase in the urban population? This increase certainly was not the result of a high birthrate. Although more people were born than died in American cities, births contributed only modestly to the urban population explosion. The general pattern of declining family size that had emerged before the Civil War continued. By 1900, the average woman bore only 3.6 children, in contrast to 5.2 children in 1860. Urban families, moreover, tended to have fewer children than their rural counterparts. And urban children faced a host of health hazards like tuberculosis, diarrhea, and diphtheria. All city residents were vulnerable, but children were especially so. The death rate for infants was twice as high in cities as in the countryside. In the 1880s, half the children born in Chicago did not live to celebrate their fifth birthday.

The real cause of urban growth was the special ability of cities to attract newcomers from the nation's small towns and farms and from abroad. For foreigners and Americans alike, a combination of pressures, some encouraging them to abandon their original homes, others attracting them to the urban environment, prompted the decision to relocate. For rural Americans, the "push" came from the modernization of agricultural life. Factories poured out farm machines that replaced human hands. By 1896, one man with machinery could harvest 18 times as much wheat as a farmer working with hand tools could in 1830.

The City's Appeal

Work in the industrial city was the prime attraction. Although urban jobs were often dirty, dangerous, and exhausting, so was farmwork. Moreover, by 1890, manufacturing workers were earning hundreds of dollars more a year than farm laborers. Some industrial workers, like miners in the Far West, earned even more. Part of the difference between

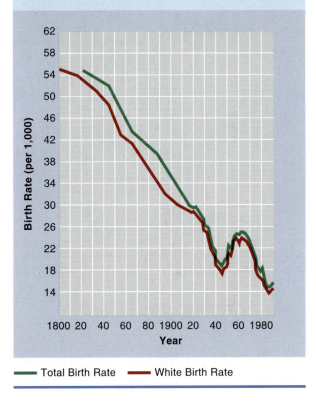

Falling Birthrates

This chart shows the falling birthrate over the course of almost 200 years. By 1860, the average size of an American family was 5.3 members as compared to 5.8 in 1800. While the American birthrate was falling, it was higher than in Europe. By 1860, due to natural increase and immigration, the American population as a whole was larger than the British population. It was not long before the United States was also larger than Germany and France.

—— Total Birth Rate   —— White Birth Rate

rural and urban wages was eaten up by the higher cost of living in the city, but not all of it.

An intangible but important lure was the glitter of city life. Rural life was often monotonous. The shops, theaters, restaurants, churches, department stores, newspapers, ball games, and the urban throng all amazed and attracted young men and women from farms and small towns.

Southern blacks, often single and young, also fed the migratory stream into the cities. In the West and the North, African Americans constituted only a tiny part of the population: 3 percent in Denver in the 1880s and 1890s, 2 percent in Boston. In southern cities, however, they were more numerous. About 44 percent of Atlanta's and 38 percent of Nashville's residents in the late nineteenth century were African American.

This 1896 picture of Chicago shows how the appearance of cities changed when structural steel became available for skyscrapers. Once the national rail system was complete, steelmakers turned to new urban markets to maintain profits. *(Chicago Historical Society)*

The New Immigration, 1880–1900

Sadie Frowne was born in a small Polish village, where her mother ran a small grocery store and her father farmed. After her father died, times were hard, and mother and daughter came by steerage to New York, where they had relatives. Although she was only 13 years old, Sadie first worked as a domestic servant and then labored in a sweatshop. Her mother found a job in an underwear factory. Mother and daughter were part of a mass migration from Europe that sent 40 million to the United States between 1815 and 1915 and another 20 million to Canada and Latin America. Like the Frownes, three-quarters of the newcomers arriving in the United States in the last quarter century stayed in the Northeast. Many of the rest settled in cities across the nation, where they soon outnumbered native-born whites.

Over the course of the century, the major sources of immigration to the United States changed. Until 1880, three-quarters of those coming to the United States, often called the "old immigrants," hailed from the British Isles, Germany, and Scandinavia. Irish and Germans were the largest groups. By 1890,

however, these nationalities composed only 60 percent of the total number of newcomers. "New immigrants" like the Frownes from southern and eastern Europe (Italy, Poland, Russia, Austria-Hungary, Greece, Turkey, and Syria) made up most of the rest. Italian Catholics were by far the most numerous (8 million came between 1876 and 1915), followed by eastern European Jews and then Slavs (Russians and Poles).

The large numbers were the result of cheaper, faster, and better transportation. Trains reached far into eastern and southern Europe. On transatlantic vessels, even steerage passengers could now expect a bed with blankets, cooked meals, and a communal washroom. But dissatisfaction with life at home was basic to the decision to migrate. Overpopulation, famine, and disease drove people to leave. "We could have eaten each other had we stayed," explained one Italian immigrant.

Efforts to modernize European economies also stimulated immigration. New agricultural techniques led landlords to consolidate their land, evicting longtime tenants. Younger European farmers traveled in increasingly wide circles searching for work. Some emigrated to cities elsewhere in Europe, others to Canada or South America. The largest share went to the United States. Similarly, artisans and craftsmen whose skills were made obsolete by the introduction of machinery pulled up stakes and headed for the United States and other destinations.

Government policies pushed others to leave. Up until 1881, most Jews coming to the United States were Germans who had integrated successfully into American society. Many became Reform Jews, which they considered a "distinctively American" form of Judaism, quite different from "the boneless Orthodoxy of the old World." After 1881, however, Orthodox Jews fled to the United States from Russia, Lithuania, and Poland. Following the assassination of the Russian tsar in 1881, a harsh policy toward Jews was implemented. Jews were barred from most occupations, forced to relocate their homes, and restricted in the practice of their religion. Vicious persecution threatened life itself as the following eyewitness account makes clear: "From their hiding places in cellars and garrets the Jews were dragged forth and tortured to death. . . . Babies were thrown from the higher stories to the street pavement. . . . The local bishop drove in a carriage and passed through the crowd, giving them his blessing as he passed." In the first 10 years of persecution, 150,000 Jews left Russia, the vast majority headed for the United States. By 1914, 2 million had made the journey.

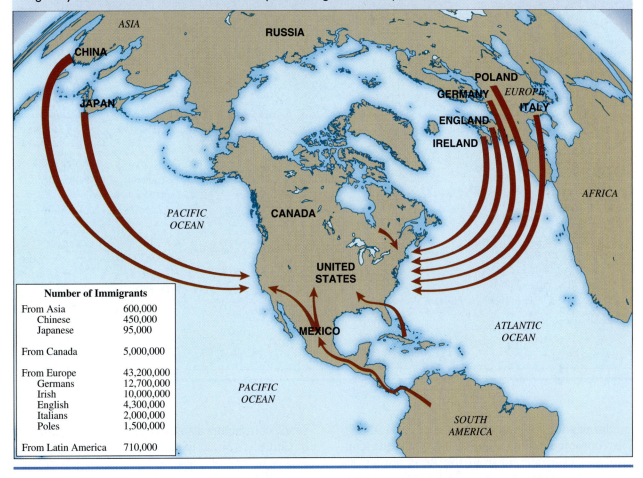

Migration to the United States, 1860–1910

This map makes clear the many parts of the world that sent population to the United States. Many of those who came were dislodged by economic changes in their home countries. **Reflecting on the Past** What were the most important short-term consequences of these migratory streams? What have been the most important long-term consequences?

Number of Immigrants	
From Asia	600,000
Chinese	450,000
Japanese	95,000
From Canada	5,000,000
From Europe	43,200,000
Germans	12,700,000
Irish	10,000,000
English	4,300,000
Italians	2,000,000
Poles	1,500,000
From Latin America	710,000

Opportunity also lured thousands to American shores. State commissioners of immigration and American railroad and steamship companies, eager for workers and customers, wooed potential immigrants. Friends and relatives wrote letters describing favorable living and working conditions and promising to help newcomers find work. American cities were great places for "blast frnises and Rolen milles," explained one unskilled worker. Often passage money or pictures of friends in alluringly fashionable clothes were slipped between the pages. The phenomenon of immigrants being recruited through the reports and efforts of their predecessors has come to be known as "chain migration."

Like rural and small-town Americans, Europeans came primarily to work. Most were young, single men who, in contrast to pre–Civil War immigrants, had few skills. Jews, however, came most often in family groups, and women predominated among the Irish. When times were good and American industry needed large numbers of unskilled laborers, migration was heavy. When times were bad and letters warned that "work is dull all over . . . no work to be got except by chance or influence," numbers fell off. Many immigrants hoped to earn enough money in America to realize their ambitions at home. Italians were particularly likely to return to Italy. Between 20 and 30 percent did. But others, like the Jews, had little interest in going back to their former homelands.

Although the greatest influx of Mexicans would come in the twentieth century, Mexican laborers added to the stream of migrants. Like many European countries, Mexico was in the throes of

Foreign Immigration, 1880–1920

This map shows how immigrants favored industrial areas as well as the West and areas along American borders. As you can see, the South did not attract large numbers of foreigners. What factors deferred immigration to the South and Southern Great Plains?

More than 20% Foreign born in 1881

Major industrial areas, 1900

State capitals

New York   20 largest cities

modernization. Overpopulation and new land policies uprooted many inhabitants, while the construction of a railroad from the Texas border 900 miles into Mexico in 1895 facilitated migration. Many Mexicans ended up in the Southwest and West, working for the railroads and in mines.

Writing to his son in the United States, a Chinese father pointed out, "Men go abroad so that they might make money for support of their families, but you have sent neither money nor a letter since you left." Overpopulation, depressed conditions, unemployment, and crop failures drove 264,000 Chinese to the United States between 1860 and 1900. Most stayed on the West Coast, where they constituted a significant minority. As unskilled male contract laborers who planned to work for a number of years and then return to their wives and families at home, they performed some of the hardest, dirtiest, and least desirable jobs in the West. They worked in mining and agriculture, on railroad and levee construction, and labored in factory and laundry work. To serve these men, often away from their wives for

years, contractors also brought in a limited number of Chinese women to serve as prostitutes. Virtually enslaved, few of these women could pay off the costs of their passage or escape from brothel life.

The importance of migration from Europe, Mexico, and Asia can hardly be overestimated. Immigrants contributed to the country's rapid urbanization and provided much of the labor needed to accomplish the economic transformation of the late nineteenth century. Their presence also helped transform American society. The American population became far more heterogeneous in terms of ethnicity and religion than any other industrial nation. Since most immigrants were workers, they altered the character of the laboring class. Differences between immigrant groups and between immigrants and American workers weakened immigrants' ability to respond to employers with one voice. The presence of those who spoke little or no English and had values and experiences very different from those of native-born Americans challenged American ideals, beliefs, and practices.

Although not one of the largest immigrant groups in the late nineteenth century, Chinese made up a sizable proportion of foreign workers in California. The overwhelming male nature of this immigration is apparent in this photograph. Because many of the Chinese women coming to the United States were prostitutes, Congress passed a law in 1873 curtailing Asian female immigration on moral grounds. *(Asian American Studies Library, University of California, Berkeley)*

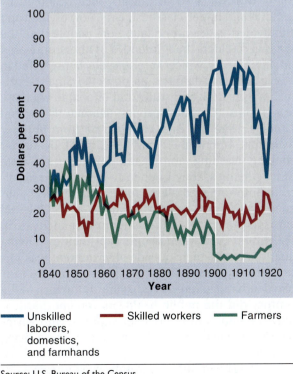

Working-Class Immigration, 1840–1920

The large numbers of unskilled workers coming to the United States were responding to the need for unskilled labor during the second Industrial Revolution.

Dollars per cent (y-axis: 0–100)

Year (x-axis: 1840 1850 1860 1870 1880 1890 1900 1910 1920)

— Unskilled laborers, domestics, and farmhands
— Skilled workers
— Farmers

Source: U.S. Bureau of the Census.

THE INDUSTRIAL CITY, 1880–1900

The late-nineteenth-century industrial city had new physical and social arrangements that attracted widespread comment. Slums, not new, seemed disturbing because so many lived in them. Yet cities also contained grand mansions, handsome business and industrial buildings, grandiose civic monuments, parks, and acres of substantial middle-class homes.

By the last quarter of the nineteenth century, the antebellum "walking city," whose size and configuration had been limited by the necessity of walking to work, disappeared. Where once substantial houses, businesses, and small artisan dwellings had stood side by side, central business districts emerged. Here were banks, shops, theaters, professional firms, and businesses. Few people lived downtown, although many worked or shopped there. Surrounding the business center were areas of light manufacturing and wholesale activity with housing for workers. Beyond these working-class neighborhoods stretched middle-class residential areas. Then came the suburbs, with "pure air, peacefulness," and "natural scenery." Scattered throughout the city were pockets of industrial activity surrounded by crowded working-class housing.

This new pattern, with the poorest city residents clustered near the center, reversed the early nineteenth-century urban form in which much of the most desirable housing was in the heart of the city. New living arrangements were also more segregated by race and class than those in the preindustrial

Downtown New York City in 1890 hosted a mixture of horse-drawn vehicles and the new "horseless carriages." The non-residential character of the central business district gave a special character to the late-nineteenth-century city. *(Brown Brothers)*

walking city. Homogeneous social and economic neighborhoods emerged, and it became more unusual than before for a poor, working-class family to live near a middle- or upper-class family.

Transportation improvements enormously affected the development of American cities. The revolution started modestly in the 1820s and 1830s with slow, horse-drawn "omnibuses" accommodating only 10 to 12 passengers. Expensive fares meant most people still walked to work. In the 1850s, many cities introduced faster and bigger horse railways, allowing the city to expand outward about four miles. The cost of a fare, however, limited ridership to the prosperous classes. Cable cars, trolleys, and subways after 1880 further extended city boundaries, enabling the middle class to escape grimy industrial districts.

Neighborhoods and Neighborhood Life

Working-class neighborhoods clustered near the center of most industrial cities. Here lived newcomers from the American countryside and, because most immigrants settled in cities, crowds of foreigners as well.

Ethnic groups frequently gathered in particular neighborhoods, often located near industries requiring their labor. In Detroit in 1880, for example, 37 percent of the city's native-born families lived in one area, whereas 40 percent of the Irish inhabited the "Irish West Side." Over half the Germans and almost three-quarters of the Poles settled on the city's east side. Although such neighborhoods often had an ethnic flavor, with small specialty shops and foreign-language signs, they were not ethnic ghettos.

Immigrants and native-born Americans often lived in the same neighborhoods, on the same streets, and even in the same houses. The Chinatowns that sprang up in western cities and in places like New York were exceptions to this pattern. Hostility from whites kept most Chinese secluded in Chinatowns where they felt safe among their countrymen.

Working-class neighborhoods were often what would be called slums today. They were crowded and unsanitary with inadequate public services. Many workers lived in houses once occupied by middle- and upper-class residents, now divided and subdivided to accommodate more people than the original builders had intended. Others squeezed into tenements, which were specially constructed to house as many families as possible. Small apartments were dark and stuffy and often had windowless rooms. Outdoor privies, shared by several families, were the rule. Water came from outdoor hydrants, and women had to carry it inside for cooking, washing, and cleaning. When there were indoor fixtures, they frequently emptied waste directly into unpaved alleys and courts served by inadequate sewage systems or none at all. Piles of garbage and waste stank in the summer and froze in the winter. Even when people kept their own living quarters clean, their outside environment was unsanitary and unhealthy. It was no surprise that urban death rates were so high. Only at the turn of the century did the public health movement, particularly the efforts to treat water supplies with germ-killing chemicals, begin to ameliorate these living conditions.

Not every working-class family lived in abject circumstances. Skilled workers might rent comfortable

Here we see a village street in Russia in the late nineteenth century. Notice that the street is not paved, that there are no signs of any utilities, and that the children are barefoot. The impoverished conditions that many immigrants left behind made them less discontented with what they experienced in the United States. *(Keystone-Mast Collection, URL/California Museum of Photography, University of California, Riverside)*

quarters, and a few even owned their own homes. A study of working-class families in Massachusetts found the family of one skilled worker living "in a tenement of five rooms in a pleasant and healthy locality, with good surroundings. The apartments are well furnished and [the] parlor carpeted." The family even had a sewing machine. But the unskilled and semiskilled workers were not so fortunate. The Massachusetts survey describes the family of an unskilled ironworker crammed into a tenement of four rooms,

> in an overcrowded block, to which belong only two privies for about fifty people. When this place was visited the vault had overflowed in the yard and the sink-water was also running in the same place, and created a stench that was really frightful. . . . The house inside, was badly furnished and dirty, and a disgrace to Worcester.

Drab as their neighborhoods usually were, working families created a community life that helped alleviate some of their dreary physical surroundings. The expense of moving around the city helped encourage a neighborhood and family focus. Long working hours meant that precious free time was apt to be spent close to home.

The wide range of institutions and associations that came to life in urban neighborhoods demonstrates that working-class men and women were not just victims of their environment. Frequently rooted in religious and ethnic identities, these organizations helped residents feel at home in the city. But they also could separate ethnic groups from one another and from native-born Americans. A Lithuanian worker in Chicago found companionship in a Lithuanian Concertina Club and a Lithuanian society that gave two picnics and two balls each year. Irish collective life focused around the Roman Catholic parish church, Irish nationalist organizations, ward politics, and Irish saloons. Jews gathered in their synagogues, Hebrew schools, and Hebrew- and Yiddish-speaking literary groups. Germans had their family saloons and educational and singing societies. Various Chinese organizations provided benefits, including education, health, and religious services. Although such activities may have slowed assimilation into American society and discouraged intergroup contact, they provided companionship, a social network, spiritual consolation, and a bridge between life in the "old country" and life in America.

African Americans faced the most wretched living conditions of any group in the city. In the North, they often lived in segregated black neighborhoods. In southern cities, they gathered in back alleys and small streets. Many could afford only rented rooms. However, a rich religious and associational life tempered the suffering. African-American churches enjoyed phenomenal growth. Black members of mainline Protestant denominations separated from their white counterparts to establish autonomy and self-respect. The African Methodist Episcopal Church, with a membership of 20,000 in 1856, founded churches in every city and sizable town, and by 1900 claimed more than 400,000 members. African-American worship continued to express the emotional exuberance that had characterized slave religion. Energetic preaching and expressive music helped make churchgoing a fulfilling spiritual experience. Often associated with churches were mutual-aid and benevolent societies that helped needy members of the community. Outreach activities also included support for missionaries in Africa.

Some urban African Americans in the late nineteenth century rose into the middle class. In spite of the heavy odds against them, they created the nucleus of professional life. Ministers, businessmen, doctors, and lawyers became leaders of their communities.

Beyond working-class neighborhoods and pockets of black housing lay streets of middle-class houses. Here lived the urban lower middle class: clerks, shopkeepers, bookkeepers, salesmen, and small tradesmen. Their salaries allowed them to buy or rent houses with some privacy and comfort. Separate spaces for cooking and laundry work kept hot and often odorous housekeeping tasks away from other living areas. Many houses boasted up-to-date gas lighting and bathrooms. Outside, the neighborhoods were cleaner and more attractive than in the inner city. Residents could pay for garbage collection, gaslights, and other improvements.

Streetcar Suburbs

On the fringes of the city were houses for the substantial middle class and the rich, who made their money in business, commerce, and the professions or inherited family fortunes. Public transportation sped them downtown to their offices and then home. For example, Robert Work, a modestly successful cap and hat merchant, moved his family to a $5,500 house in West Philadelphia in 1865 and commuted more than four miles to work.

The 1880 census revealed the Work family's comfortable lifestyle. The household contained two servants, two boarders, Robert's wife, and their eldest son, who was still in school. The Works' house had running hot and cold water, indoor bathrooms, central heating, and other modern conveniences of the age. Elaborately carved furniture, rugs, draperies, and lace curtains probably graced the downstairs, where the family entertained and gathered for meals. Upstairs, comfortable bedrooms provided a maximum of privacy for family members. The live-in servants, who did most of the housework, shared little of this space or privacy, however. They were restricted to the kitchen, the pantry, and bedrooms in the attic.

This photograph of a middle-class house in River Forest, Illinois, suggests the comfort available to those who could afford it and the ways suburban life shielded the middle class from the squalor and ugliness of industrial life. *(Culver Pictures)*

The Social Geography of the Cities

In industrial cities of this era, people were sorted by class, income, occupation, and race. Their circumstances not only dictated who would live comfortably with access to some of the conveniences and improvements that industrial development had made possible but also affected family size and domestic life. Although the size of the middle-class family was shrinking over the course of the century, working-class and immigrant families remained large. For example, in Buffalo, New York, in 1900, middle-class families had 3.5 children, while laboring families had 5.7 children. Because working-class children went out to work, large families made economic sense and represented one means of improving a family's well-being.

Upper- and middle-class neighborhoods and working-class neighborhoods were physically separated, so city dwellers often had little firsthand knowledge of people different from themselves. Ignorance led to distorted views and social disapproval. Reformers criticized working-class families for encouraging their children to leave school and work. Middle-class newspapers unsympathetically described laboring men as "loafing" and criticized the "crowds of idlers, who, day and night, infect Main Street." Yet those "idlers" were often men who could not find employment. The comments of a working-class woman to her temperance visitors in 1874 suggest the critical view from the bottom of society up: "When the rich stopped drinking, it would be time to speak to the poor about it."

THE LIFE OF THE MIDDLE CLASS

The sharp comments made by different classes of Americans suggest the economic and social polarization that late-nineteenth-century industrialization spawned. Middle-class Americans found much to value in the new age: job and education opportunities, material comforts, and leisure time. Between 1865 and 1890, the average middle-class income had risen about 30 percent. Although the cost of living rose even faster than income, the difference was met by more family members holding jobs and by taking in lodgers. By 1900, fully 36 percent of urban families owned their homes.

The expansion of American industry raised living standards for increasing numbers of Americans, who were better able to purchase consumer products manufactured, packaged, and promoted in an explosion of technological inventions and shrewd marketing techniques. Among the still familiar products and brands invented or mass-produced for the first time in the 1890s were Del Monte canned fruits and vegetables, National Biscuit Company (Nabisco) crackers, Van Camp's pork and beans, Wesson oil, the Hershey bar, Jell-O, Coca-Cola, Pepsi-Cola, and Michelob beer. Cooked chopped meat put between two pieces of bread was first sold (for 7 cents) and called a "hamburger" in 1899.

More time for recreation like bicycling or watching professional baseball and greater access to consumer goods signaled the power of industrialism to transform the lives of middle-class Americans. Middle-class women became agents of the rise in consumer spending, indulging in shopping for home furnishings, clothes, and other items in the new department stores that began to appear in central business districts in the 1870s. A plentiful supply of immigrant servant girls relieved urban middle-class wives of many housekeeping chores, and smaller families reduced the burdens of motherhood.

New Freedoms for Middle-Class Women

At the same time that many middle-class women enjoyed more leisure time and purchasing power, they won new freedoms. Several states granted women more property rights in marriage, adding to their growing sense of independence. Women, moreover, finally cast off confining crinolines and bustles. The new dress, a shirtwaist blouse and ankle-length skirt, was more comfortable for working, school, and sports. The *Ladies' Home Journal* recommended bicycling, tennis, golf, gymnastics—even having fewer babies—to women in the early 1890s. This "new woman," celebrated as *Life* magazine's active, healthy, slightly rebellious "Gibson girl," differed dramatically from the frail ideals of beauty admired earlier in the century.

Using their new freedom, women joined organizations of all kinds. Literary societies, charity groups, and reform clubs like the Women's Christian Temperance Union gave women organizational experience, awareness of their talents, and contact with people and problems away from their traditional family roles. The General Federation of Women's Clubs, founded in 1890, boasted 1 million members by 1920. The depression of 1893 stimulated many women to become socially active, investigating slum and factory conditions, but some began this work even earlier. Jane Addams told her graduating classmates at the Rockford, Illinois, Female Seminary in 1881 to lead lives "filled with good works and honest toil." She eventually founded Hull House, a social settlement that did more than its share of good works.

Job opportunities for these educated, middle-class women were generally limited to the social services and teaching. Still regarded as a suitable female occupation, teaching was a highly demanding job as urban schools expanded under the pressure of a burgeoning population. Women teachers, frequently hired because they accepted lower pay than men, often faced classes of 40 to 50 children in poorly equipped rooms. In Poughkeepsie, New York, teachers earned the same salaries as school janitors. Moving up to high-status jobs proved difficult.

After the Civil War, educational opportunities for women expanded. New women's colleges such as Smith, Vassar, Bryn Mawr, and Goucher offered programs similar to those at competitive men's colleges, while state schools in the Midwest and the West dropped prohibitions against women. The number of women attending college rose. In 1890, some 13 percent of all college graduates were women; by 1900, this number had increased to nearly 20 percent.

Higher education prepared middle-class women for conventional female roles as well as for work and public service. A few courageous graduates succeeded in joining the professions, but they had to overcome barriers. Many medical schools refused to accept women students. As a Harvard doctor explained in 1875, a woman's monthly period "unfits her from taking those responsibilities which are to control questions often of life and death." Despite the obstacles, 2,500 women managed to become physicians and surgeons by 1880 (constituting 2.8 percent of the total). Women were less successful at breaking into the legal world. In 1880, fewer than 50 female lawyers practiced in the entire country, and as late as 1920, only 1.4 percent of the nation's lawyers and judges were women. George Washington University did not admit women to law school because mixed classes would be an "injurious diversion of attention of the students." Despite such resistance, by the early twentieth century, the number of women professionals (including teachers) was increasing at three times the rate for men.

One reason for the greater independence of American middle-class women, especially those who were educated, is that they were having fewer children. Advances in birth control technology (the modern diaphragm was developed in 1880) in addition to older devices like condoms, abortion, and the use of abstinence helped make new patterns possible. Between 1850 and 1900, the number of live children born to white women fell from 5.42 to 3.56. In 1900, nearly one married woman in five was childless. Decreasing family size and an increase in the divorce rate (one out of 12 marriages ended in divorce in 1905) fueled men's fears that the new woman threatened the family, traditional gender roles, and social order. Theodore Roosevelt called this "race suicide," arguing that the falling white birthrate endangered national self-interest.

Arguments against the new woman intensified as many men reaffirmed Victorian stereotypes of the "woman's sphere." Magazine editors and ministers borrowed from biology, sociology, and theology to find "scientific" proof that a woman's place was at home. One male orator in 1896 attacked the new woman's public role because "a woman's brain involves emotions rather than intellect." This fact "painfully disqualifies her for the sterner duties to be performed by the intellectual faculties. The best wife and mother and sister would make the worst legislator, judge and police."

Many men worried about female independence because it threatened their own masculinity. Male campaigns against prostitution and for sex hygiene, as well as efforts to reinforce traditional gender roles, reflected their deeper fears that female passions might weaken male vigor. The intensity of men's opposition to the new woman put limits on her emerging freedom.

Male Mobility and the Success Ethic

As middle-class women's lives were changing, so were men's. As the postwar economy expanded and the structure of American business changed, many new job opportunities opened up for middle-class men. The growing complexity of census classifications attests to some of them. Where once the census taker had noted only the occupation of "clerk," now "accountant," "salesman," and "shipping clerk" were listed. As the lower ranks of the white-collar world became more specialized, the number of middle-class jobs increased.

To prepare for these new careers, Americans required more education. The number of public high schools in the United States increased from 160 in 1870 to 6,000 in 1900. By 1900, a majority of states and territories had compulsory school-attendance laws.

Higher education also expanded in this period. The number of students in colleges and universities nearly doubled, from 53,000 in 1870 to 101,000 in 1900. Charles Eliot, president of Harvard from 1869 to 1909, led that university through a period of dynamic growth, introducing reforms such as higher faculty salaries and sabbatical leaves as well as the elective system of course selection for students. Harvard's growth reflected the rise of the university to a new stature in American life. As the land-grant state universities (made possible by the Morrill Act of 1862) continued to expand, generous gifts from wealthy businessmen helped found leading research universities such as Stanford, Johns Hopkins, and the University of Chicago.

These developments led to greater specialization and professionalism in education, medicine, law, and business. Before the Civil War, a Swedish pioneer in Wisconsin described a young mason who "laid aside the trowel, got himself some medical books, and assumed the title of doctor." But by the 1890s, with government licensing and the rise of professional schools, the word *career* began to take on its modern meaning. No longer were tradesmen likely to read up on medicine and become doctors. In this period, organizations like the American Medical Association and the American Bar Association were regulating and professionalizing membership. The number of law schools doubled in the last quarter of the century, and 86 new medical schools were founded in the same period. Dental schools increased from 9 to 56 between 1875 and 1900.

The need for lawyers, bankers, architects, and insurance agents to serve business and industry expanded career opportunities. Between 1870 and 1900, the number of engineers, chemists, metallurgists, and architects grew rapidly. As large companies formed and became bureaucratized, business required many more managerial positions. As the public sector expanded, new careers in social services and government opened up as well. Young professional experts with graduate training in the social sciences filled many of them. The professional disciplines of history, economics, sociology, psychology, and political science all date from the last 20 years of the nineteenth century.

The social ethic of the age stressed that economic rewards were available to anyone who fervently sought them. Many people argued that, unlike in Europe, where family background and social class determined social rank, in America, few barriers held back those of good character and diligent work habits. Anyone doubting this opportunity needed only be reminded of the rise of two giants of industry. John D. Rockefeller had worked for a neighboring farmer and raised turkeys as a boy. Andrew Carnegie's mother was a washerwoman, and his father had worked himself to death in the mills within five years of reaching the United States. Both had risen spectacularly through their own efforts. Writers, lecturers, clergymen, and politicians zealously propagated the rags-to-riches tradition of upward mobility. Self-help manuals that outlined the steps to success for self-made men became widely available.

The best-known popularizer of the myth of the self-made man was Horatio Alger, Jr. Millions of boys read his 119 novels, with titles like *Strive and Succeed* and *Bound to Rise*. In a typical Alger novel *Ragged Dick,* the story opens with the hero leading the low life of a shoeshine boy in the streets. Dressed in rags, he sleeps in packing crates and unwisely spends his money on tobacco, liquor, gambling, and the theater. A chance opportunity to foil an attempt to cheat a gentleman results in the reward of a new suit of clothes for Dick. Before long, Dick aspires to become an office boy, "learn the business and grow up 'spectable." As he begins the process of becoming respectable, good fortune intervenes again. Dick rescues a child who tumbles into the icy waters of the harbor. Her father completes the hero's transformation from Ragged Dick to Richard Hunter, Esq., by offering him a job as a clerk in his counting house. Although moralists pointed to virtuous habits as crucial in Alger's heroes, success often depended as much on luck as on pluck.

Unlimited and equal opportunity for upward advancement in America has never been as easy as the "bootstraps" ethic maintains. But the persistence of the success myth owes something to the fact that many Americans, particularly those who began well, did rise rapidly. Native-born, middle-class whites tended to have the skills, resources, and connections that opened up the most desirable jobs. Financier Jay Gould overstated the case in maintaining that "nearly every one that occupies a prominent position has come up from the ranks." In fact, the typical big businessman was a white, Anglo-Saxon Protestant from a middle- or upperclass family whose father was most likely in business, banking, or commerce.

INDUSTRIAL WORK AND THE LABORING CLASS

David Lawlor, an Irish immigrant who came to the United States in 1872, might have agreed with Jay Gould on the opportunities for mobility. As a child, he worked in the Fall River textile mills and read Horatio Alger in his free time. Like Alger's heroes, he went to night school and rose in the business world, eventually becoming an advertising executive.

But Lawlor's success was exceptional. Most working-class Americans labored long hours on dangerous factory floors, in cramped sweatshops, or in steamy basement kitchens for meager wages. As industrialization transformed the nature of work and the composition of the workforce, traditional opportunities for mobility and even for a secure livelihood slipped from the grasp of many working-class Americans.

The Impact of Ethnic Diversity

Immigrants made up a sizable portion of the urban working class in the late nineteenth century. They formed 20 percent of the labor force and over 40 percent of laborers in the manufacturing and extractive industries. In cities, where they tended to settle, they accounted for more than half the working-class population.

Industrial work, urban life, labor protest, and local politics were influenced by the fact that more than half the urban industrial class was foreign, unskilled, perhaps illiterate, and often possessed only a limited command of the English language. Eager for the unskilled positions rapidly being created as mechanization and mass production took hold, immigrants often shared little with nativeborn workers or even with one another. Because of immigration, American working-class society was a mosaic of nationalities, cultures, religions, and interests.

The ethnic diversity of the industrial workforce helps explain its occupational patterns. Generally occupation was related to ethnic background and experience. At the top of the working-class hierarchy, native-born Protestant whites held a disproportionate share of well-paying skilled jobs. They were the aristocrats of the working class. Their jobs demanded expertise and training, as had been true of skilled industrial workers in the pre–Civil War period. But their occupations bore the mark of latenineteenth-century industrialism. They were machinists, iron puddlers and rollers, engineers, foremen, mechanics, and printers.

Skilled northern European immigrants filled most of the middle-rank positions. Often they had held similar jobs in their homeland. The Germans found work as tailors, bakers, brewers, and shoemakers, while Cornish and Irish miners secured skilled jobs in midwestern and western mines. The Jews, who had tailoring experience in their homelands, became the backbone of the garment industry (where they faced little competition from American male workers, who considered it unmanly to work on women's clothes).

But most of the "new immigrants" from southern and central Europe had no urban industrial experience. They labored in the unskilled, dirty jobs near the bottom of the occupational ladder. They relined blast furnaces in steel mills, carried raw materials or finished products from place to place, or cleaned up

The picture of a puddler at work makes clear the physical demands of his job and the harsh environment of his workplace. While we might be dismayed by the nature of the puddler's job, puddling was an occupation that demanded skill and paid well. *(Courtesy of Rivers of Steel Archives)*

Labor Force Distribution, 1890

Whereas a majority of Americans in the twentieth century defined themselves as middle class, in the nineteenth century, most Americans held working-class jobs.

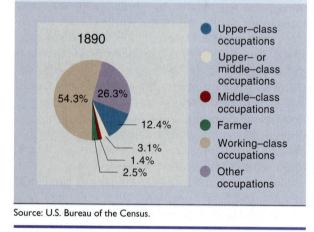

1890

54.3%   26.3%
12.4%
3.1%
1.4%
2.5%

- Upper–class occupations
- Upper– or middle–class occupations
- Middle–class occupations
- Farmer
- Working–class occupations
- Other occupations

Source: U.S. Bureau of the Census.

after skilled workers. Often, they were carmen or day laborers on the docks, ditchdiggers, or construction workers. Hiring was often on a daily basis, arranged through middlemen like the Italian padrone. Unskilled work provided little in the way of either job stability or income.

At the bottom, blacks occupied the most marginal positions as janitors, servants, porters, and laborers. Racial discrimination generally excluded them from industrial jobs, even though their occupational background differed little from that of rural white immigrants. There were always plenty of whites eager to work, so it was not necessary to hire blacks except occasionally as scabs during a labor strike. "It is an exceptional case where you find any colored labor in the factories, except as porters," observed one white. "Neither colored female . . . nor male laborer is engaged in the mechanical arts."

The Changing Nature of Work

The rise of big business, characterized by mechanization and mass production, changed the size and shape of the workforce and the nature of work itself. More and more Americans became wage earners. The number of manufacturing workers doubled between 1880 and 1900, with the fastest expansion in the unskilled and semiskilled ranks.

But the need for skilled workers remained. New positions, as in steam fitting and structural ironwork, appeared as industries expanded and changed. Increasingly, older skills became obsolete, however. And all skilled workers faced the possibility that technical advances would eliminate their favored jobs or that employers would hire unskilled helpers to take over parts of their jobs. In industries as different as shoemaking, cigar making, and iron puddling, new methods of production and organization undermined the position of skilled workers.

Work Settings and Experiences

The workplace could be a dock or cluttered factory yard, a multistoried textile mill, a huge, barnlike steel mill with all the latest machinery, or a mine tunnel hundreds of feet underground. A majority of

American manufacturing workers now labored in factories, and the numbers of those working in large plants dominated by the unceasing rhythms of machinery increased steadily.

Some Americans, however, still toiled in small shops and sweatshops tucked away in basements, lofts, or immigrant apartments. Even in these smaller settings, the pressure to produce was relentless, for volume, not hours, determined pay. When contractors cut wages, workers had to speed up to earn the same pay.

The organization of work divided workers. Those paid by the piece competed against the speed, agility, and output of other workers. It was hard to feel bonds with unknown and unseen competitors. In large factories, workers separated into small work groups and mingled only rarely with the rest of the workforce. The clustering of ethnic groups in certain types of work also undermined working-class solidarity.

All workers had a very long working day in common. Although the factory day had fallen from the 12 hours expected before the Civil War, people still spent over half their waking hours on the job—usually ten hours a day, six days a week. Different occupations had specific demands. Bakers worked 65 hours a week; canners worked 77. Sweatshop workers might labor far into the night, long after factory workers had gone home.

Work was usually unhealthy, dangerous, and comfortless. Although a few states passed laws to regulate work conditions, enforcement was spotty.

Factory work was usually uncomfortable and hazardous. Here workers in the Stetson hat factory, none of them with proper back support, cut fur hats to be sewn together by hand. The division of labor by gender is clear in the picture. (*Philadelphia Commercial Museum, Pennsylvania State Archives*)

Few owners observed regulations about toilets, drinking facilities, or washing areas. Nor did they concern themselves with the health or safety of their employees. Women, bent over sewing machines, developed digestive illnesses and curved spines. Poorly ventilated mines stank of human waste and spoiled garbage, with temperatures sometimes rising to over 120 degrees. Miners worked with dynamite and all too often died in cave-ins caused by inadequate timber supports in the mine shafts. When new drilling machinery was introduced into western mines, it produced tiny stone particles that caused lung disease.

Accident rates in the United States far exceeded those of Europe's industrial nations. Each year, 35,000 workers died from industrial mishaps. Iron and steel mills were the big killers, although the railroads alone accounted for 6,000 fatalities a year during the 1890s. Nationwide, nearly one-quarter of the men reaching the age of 20 in 1880 would not live to see 44 (compared with 7 percent today). American business owners had little legal responsibility—and some felt none—for employees' safety or health. The law placed the burden of avoiding accidents on the workers, who were expected to quit if they thought conditions were unsafe.

Industrial workers labored at jobs that were also increasingly specialized and monotonous. The size of many firms allowed a kind of specialization that was impossible in a small enterprise. Even skilled workers did not produce a complete product, and the range of their skills was narrowing. "A man never learns the machinist's trade now," one New Yorker grumbled. "The different branches of the trade are divided and subdivided so that one man may make just a particular part of a machine and may not know anything whatever about another part of the same machine." Cabinetmakers found themselves not crafting cabinets but putting together and finishing pieces made by others. In such circumstances, many skilled workers complained that they were being reduced to drudges and wage slaves.

Still, industrial work provided some personal benefits. New arrangements helped humanize the workplace. Workers who obtained jobs through family and friends labored alongside them. In most industries, the foreman controlled day-to-day activities. He chose workers from the crowds at the gate, fired those who proved unsatisfactory, selected appropriate materials and equipment, and determined the order and pace of production. Because the foreman was himself a member of the working class who had climbed his way up, he might sympathize with subordinates. Yet the foreman could also be authoritarian and harsh, especially if the workers he supervised were unskilled or belonged to another ethnic group.

The Worker's Share in Industrial Progress

The huge fortunes accumulated by famous industrialists like Andrew Carnegie and John D. Rockefeller during the late nineteenth century dramatized the pattern of wealth concentration that had begun in the early period of industrialization. In 1890, the top 1 percent of American families possessed over a quarter of the wealth, whereas the share held by the top 10 percent was about 73 percent. Economic growth still benefited people who influenced its path, and they claimed the lion's share of the rewards.

But what of the workers who tended the machines that lay at the base of industrial wealth? Working-class Americans made up the largest segment of the labor force (more than 50 percent), so their experience reveals important facets of the American social and economic systems and American values.

Statistics of increasing production, of ever more goods, tell part of the story. Figures on real wages also reveal something important. Industry still needed skilled workers and paid them well. Average real wages rose over 50 percent between 1860 and 1900. Skilled manufacturing workers, about one-tenth of the nonagricultural working class in the late nineteenth century, saw their wages rise by about 74 percent. But wages for the unskilled increased by only 31 percent. The differential was substantial and widened as the century drew to a close.

Taken as a whole, the working class accrued substantial benefits in the late nineteenth century, even if its share of the total wealth did not increase. American workers had more material comforts than their European counterparts. But the general picture conceals the realities of working-class economic life. A U.S. Bureau of Labor study of working-class families in 1889 revealed great disparities of income: a young girl in a silk mill made $130 a year; a laborer earned $384 a year; a carpenter took home $686. The carpenter's family lived in a four-room house. Their breakfast usually included meat or eggs, hotcakes, butter, cake, and coffee. The silk worker and the laborer, by contrast, ate bread and butter as the main portion of two of their three daily meals. Their yearly income fell far short of the $600 to $800 that was necessary for a family to survive in any comfort.

For workers without steady employment, rising real wages were meaningless. Workers, especially those who were unskilled, often found work only

---

Two Nineteenth-Century Budgets

The differences between these two family budgets capture different standards of living and different consumption choices. In 2001 dollars, the laborer took home $448 a month while the accountant earned about $1,259 a month. The laborer spent about $530 on his monthly expenses while the accountant's budgeted expenses came to about $817.

	Monthly budget of a laborer, his wife, and one child in 1891; his income is $23.67	Monthly budget of a married bank accountant with no children in 1892; his income is about $66.50
Food	$6.51	$13.22
Rent	9.02	9.88
Furniture	3.61	0.30
Taxes and insurance	3.32	7.11
Utilities	2.94	4.99
Sundries	1.09	2.10
Liquor and tobacco	0.66	0.42
Medicine	0.29	0.27
Clothes	0.21	0.19
Dry goods	0.16	2.45
Postage	0.10	—
Transportation	0.08	1.71
Reading material	—	0.53
	$27.99	$43.17

Source: Olivier Zunz, *The Changing Face of Inequality* (1982).

sporadically. When times were slow or conditions depressed, as they were between 1873 and 1879 and 1893 and 1897, employers, especially in small firms, laid off both skilled and unskilled workers and reduced wages. Even in a good year like 1890, one out of every five men outside of agriculture had been unemployed at least a month. One-quarter lost four months or more.

Unemployment insurance did not exist, so workers had no cushion against losing their jobs. One woman grimly recalled, "If the factory shuts down without warning, as it did last year for six weeks, we have a growing expense with nothing to counterbalance." Older workers who had no social security or those who had accidents on the job but no disability insurance had severely reduced incomes. Occasionally, kindhearted employers offered assistance in hard times, but it was rarely enough. The Lawrence Manufacturing Company compensated one of its workers $50 for the loss of a hand and awarded another $66.71 for a severed arm.

Although nineteenth-century ideology pictured men as breadwinners, many working-class married men could not earn enough to support their families alone. A working-class family's standard of living thus often depended on its number of workers. Today, two-income families are common. But in the nineteenth century, married women did not usually take outside employment, although they contributed to family income by taking in sewing, laundry, and boarders. In 1890, only 3.3 percent of married women were to be found in the paid labor force.

The Family Economy

If married women did not work for pay outside their homes, their children did. The laborer whose annual earnings amounted to only $384 depended on his 13-year-old son, not his wife, to go out and earn an extra $196, critical to the family's welfare. Sending children into the labor market was an essential survival strategy for many working-class Americans. In 1880, one-fifth of the nation's children between the ages of 10 and 14 held jobs.

Child labor was closely linked to a father's income, which in turn depended on skill, ethnic background, and occupation. Immigrant families more frequently sent their young children out to work (and also had more children) than native-born families. Middle-class reformers who sentimentalized childhood disapproved of parents who put their children to work. As one investigator of working-class life reported, "Father never attended school, and thinks his children will have sufficient schooling before they reach their tenth year, thinks no advantage will be gained from longer attendance at school, so children will be put to work as soon as able." Reformers believed that such fathers condemned their children to future destitution by denying them education. Actually, sending children

Children and young adults worked, although the pattern of employment differed based on gender, ethnic background, and economic circumstances. Here three boys enter the Hill Manufacturing Company in Lewiston, Maine. The boys' workday began at 5:30 A.M. How old would you estimate the different boys are? (*Library of Congress [LC-USZ62-91570]*)

Congressional Hearings

Students of history can discover fascinating materials on nineteenth-century life by exploring the published records of the American political system. Privately published from 1833 to 1873, the *Congressional Globe* details the proceedings of the Senate and the House, revealing the nature of congressional deliberations in an era when debate, such as that over the Compromise of 1850 in the Senate, was the focus of the national political process. After 1873, the government published these proceedings in the *Congressional Record*. The *Record* is not a literal transcription of debate, for members can edit their remarks, insert speeches, and add supporting materials. Still, it gives a good sense of the proceedings of both the Senate and the House.

Much of the serious work of government, past and present, takes place in congressional committees. One foreign observer called Congress "not so much a legislative assembly as a huge panel from which committees are selected." The committee system is almost as old as the constitutional system itself and is rooted in the Constitution's granting of the lawmaking power to Congress. From the start, Congress divided into assorted committees to gather information, enabling members to evaluate legislative proposals intelligently.

Two kinds of committees existed in the House and Senate. Standing committees had permanent responsibility for reviewing legislative proposals on a host of financial, judicial, foreign, and other affairs. By 1892, the Senate had 44 standing committees, and the House had 50. Select committees were temporary, often charged with investigating specific problems. In the late nineteenth century, congressional committees investigated such problems as Ku Klux Klan terrorism, the sweatshop system, tenement house conditions, and relations between labor and capital. In each case, extensive hearings were held.

Congressional hearings have become increasingly important sources of historical evidence in recent years. They show the Senate and the House of Representatives in action as they seek to translate popular sentiment into law. But they also reveal public attitudes as they record the voices of Americans testifying in committee halls. Because one function of legislative hearings is to enable diverse groups to express their frustrations and desires, they often contain the testimony of witnesses drawn from many different social and economic backgrounds. Included here is the partial testimony of a Massachusetts laborer who appeared before the Senate Committee on Education and Labor in 1883. Because working-class witnesses like this man usually left no other record of their experiences or thoughts, committee reports and hearings provide valuable insight into the lives and attitudes of ordinary people.

Hearings also reveal the attitudes and social values of committee members. Hence, caution is needed in the use of hearings. Witnesses often have vested interests and are frequently coached and cautious in what they communicate on the stand. Rather than seeking to illuminate issues, committee members often speak and explore questions for other—usually political—reasons.

Despite these limitations, committee hearings are rich sources of information. In this excerpt, what can you learn about the life of the witness testifying before the committee? In what way are the values of the committee members in conflict with those of the witness? Why is the chairman so harsh toward the witness? Is he entirely unsympathetic? Why do you think the questioner overemphasizes the relationship between moral beliefs and economic realities? What kind of social tensions does the passage reveal?

Reflecting on the Past   Have you observed any recent hearings of congressional investigating committees on television? Are moral behavior and hunger still topics of concern for Americans? How is the interaction between modern "haves" and "have-nots" similar to and different from the interaction between this laborer and the committee members in 1883? Do ethical beliefs and economic realities still separate social classes?

Hearings on the Relations Between Labor and Capital

Q. You get a dollar a day, wages?—A. That is the average pay that men receive. The rents, especially in Somerville, are so high that it is almost impossible for the working men to live in a house.

Q. What rent do you pay?—A. For the last year I have been paying $10 a month, and most of the men out there have to pay about that amount for a house—$10 a month for rooms.

Q. For a full house, or for rooms only?—A. For rooms in a house.

Q. How many rooms?—A. Four or five.

Q. How much of your time have you been out of work, or idle, for the last full year, say?—A. I have not been out of work more than three weeks altogether, because I have been making a dollar or two peddling or doing something, when I was out of work, in the currying line.

Q. Making about the same that you made at your trade?—A. Well, I have made at my trade a little more than that, but that is the average.

Q. Are you a common drunkard?—A. No, sir.

Q. Do you smoke a great deal?—A. Well, yes, sir; I smoke as much as any man.

The CHAIRMAN. I want to know how much you have got together in the course of a year, and what you have spent your money for, so that folks can see whether you have had pay enough to get rich on.

The WITNESS. A good idea.

The CHAIRMAN. That is precisely the sort of idea that people ought to know. How much money do you think you have earned during this last year; has it averaged a dollar a day for three hundred days?

The WITNESS. I have averaged more than that; I have averaged $350 or $400. I will say, for the year.

Q. You pay $10 a month rent; that makes $120 a year?—A. Yes, sir.

The CHAIRMAN. I have asked you these questions in this abrupt way because I want to find out whether you have spent much for practices that might have been dispensed with. You say you smoke?

The WITNESS. Yes, sir.

Q. How much a week do you spend for that?—A. I get 20 cents worth of tobacco a week.

Q. That is $10.40 a year?—A. Yes, sir.

Q. And you say you are not a common drunkard?—A. No, sir.

Q. Do you imagine that you have spent as much more for any form of beer, or ale, or anything of that kind, that you could have got along without?—A. No, sir.

Q. How much do you think has gone in that way?—A. About $1 or $2.

Q. During the whole year?—A. Yes, sir.

Q. That would make $11.40 or $12.40—we will call it $12—gone for wickedness. Now, what else, besides your living, besides the support of your wife and children?—A. Well, I don't know as there is anything else.

Q. Can you not think of anything else that was wrong?—A. No, sir.

Q. Twelve dollars have gone for sin and iniquity; and $120 for rent; that makes $132?—A. Yes.

Q. How many children have you?—A. Two.

Q. Your family consists of yourself, your wife, and two children?—A. Yes.

Q. One hundred and thirty-two dollars from $400 leaves you $268, does it not?—A. Yes, sir.

Q. And with that amount you have furnished your family?—A. Yes, sir.

Q. You have been as economical as you could, I suppose?—A. Yes.

Q. How much money have you left?—A. Sixty dollars in debt.

Q. How did you do that?—A. I don't know, sir.

Q. Can you not think of something more that you have wasted?—A. No, sir.

Q. Have you been as careful as you could?—A. Yes, sir.

Q. And you have come out at the end of the year $60 in debt?—A. Yes, sir.

Q. Have you been extravagant in your family expenses?—A. No, sir; a man can't be very extravagant on that much money. . . .

Q. And there are four of you in the family?—A. Yes, sir.

Q. How many pounds of beefsteak have you had in your family, that you bought for your own home consumption within this year that we have been speaking of?—A. I don't think there has been five pounds of beefsteak.

Q. You have had a little pork steak?—A. We had a half a pound of pork steak yesterday; I don't know when we had any before.

Q. What other kinds of meat have you had within a year?—A. Well, we have had corn beef twice I think that I can remember this year—on Sunday, for dinner.

Q. Twice is all that you can remember within a year?—A. Yes—and some cabbage.

Q. What have you eaten?—A. Well, bread mostly, when we could get it; we sometimes couldn't make out to get that, and have had to go without a meal.

Q. Has there been any day in the year that you have had to go without anything to eat?—A. Yes, sir, several days.

Q. More than one day at a time?—A. No.

Q. How about the children and your wife—did they go without anything to eat too?—A. My wife went out this morning and went to a neighbor's and got a loaf of bread and fetched it home, and when she got home the children were crying for something to eat.

Q. Have the children had anything to eat to-day except that, do you think?—A. They had that loaf of bread—I don't know what they have had since then, if they have had anything.

Q. Did you leave any money at home?—A. No, sir.

Q. If that loaf is gone, is there anything in the house?—A. No, sir; unless my wife goes out and gets something; and I don't know who would mind the children while she goes out.

Number of Women Employed in Selected Industries, 1870–1910

This chart shows the growth of women workers in several key industries. Although far fewer women had paid jobs than men, they were never absent from the workplace.

Year	Industry					
	Chemical	Electrical	Paper	Printing	Food	Metal
1870	403	—	6,242	4,397	2,460	5,217
1880	862	—	14,126	9,322	4,503	7,668
1890	2,140	—	22,444	24,640	10,169	15,232
1900	3,427	—	27,261	32,938	19,713	21,335
1910	15,198	12,093	33,419	47,640	48,099	56,208

Source: U.S. Department of Labor, Women's Bureau, *Women's Occupations through Seven Decades*, Bulletin no. 218 (Washington, D.C.: Government Printing Office, 1947), pp. 95, 120, 121, 123, 130, 133.

to work was a means of coping with the immediate threat of poverty, financing the education of one of the children, or paying off the mortgage.

Many more young people over the age of 14 were working for wages than was the case for children. Half of all Philadelphia's students had quit school by that age. Daughters as well as sons were expected to take positions, although young women from immigrant families were more likely to work than young American women. As *Arthur's Home Magazine* for women pointed out, a girl's earnings would help "to relieve her hard-working father of the burden of her support, to supply home with comforts and refinements, to educate a younger brother." By 1900, nearly 20 percent of American women were in the labor force.

Employed women earned far less than men. An experienced female factory worker might be paid between $5 and $6 a week, whereas an unskilled male laborer could make about $8. Discrimination, present from women's earliest days in the workforce, persisted. Still, factory jobs were desirable because they often paid better than other kinds of work open to women.

By the 1890s, new forms of employment in office work, nursing, and clerking in department stores offered some young women attractive opportunities. In San Francisco, the number of clerical jobs doubled between 1852 and 1880. But most women faced limited employment options, and ethnic taboos and cultural traditions helped shape choices. About a quarter of working women secured factory jobs. Italian and Jewish women (whose cultural backgrounds virtually forbade their going into domestic service) clustered in the garment industry, and Poles and Slavs went into textiles, food processing, and meatpacking. In some industries, like textiles and tobacco, women composed an important segment of the workforce. But about 40 percent of

them, especially those from Irish, Scandinavian, and black families, took jobs as maids, cooks, laundresses, and nurses.

Domestic service was arduous, with few machines to lighten the labor. A Minneapolis housemaid described an exhausting routine. "I used to get up at four o'clock every morning and work till ten P.M. every day of the week. Mondays and Tuesdays, when the washing and ironing was to be done, I used to get up at two o'clock and wash or iron until breakfast time." Nor could domestics count on much sympathy from their employers. "Do not think it necessary to give a hired girl as good a room as that used by members of the family," said one lady of the house. "She should sleep near the kitchen and not go up the front stairs or through the front hall to reach her room." Live-in servants received room and board plus $2 to $5 a week. The fact that so many women took domestic work despite the job's disadvantages speaks clearly of their limited opportunities.

The dismal situation facing working women drove some, like Rose Haggerty, into prostitution. Burdened with a widowed and sickly mother and four young brothers and sisters, Rose was only 14 years old when she started work at a New York paper bag factory. She earned $10 a month, with $6 going for rent. Her fortunes improved when a friend helped her buy a sewing machine. Rose then sewed shirts at home, often working as long as 14 hours a day, to support her family. Suddenly, the piecework rate for shirts was slashed in half. In desperation, Rose contemplated suicide. But when a sailor offered her money for spending the night with him, she realized she had an alternative. Prostitution meant food, rent, and heat for her family. "Let God Almighty judge who's to blame most," the 20-year-old Rose reflected, "I that was driven, or them that drove me to the pass I'm in."

Wearing their best clothes, these domestics pose with the symbol of their work in what appears to be the parlor. Although there is no way to ascertain the background of these young women, a majority of domestic servants were Irish or Irish American. Domestic work was often exhausting and provided little privacy or free time, but many women were attracted by the opportunity to live in a middle-class home and have regular meals. In addition, domestic work often paid better than factory work. Still, some young women avoided service, explaining that "it's freedom that we want when the day's work is done." *(State Historical Society of Wisconsin, neg. #WHi [V22] 1387)*

Prostitution appears to have increased in the late nineteenth century, although there is no way of knowing the actual numbers of women involved. Probably most single women accepted the respectable jobs open to them. They tolerated discrimination and low wages because their families depended on their contributions. They also knew that when they married, they would probably leave the paid workforce forever.

Marriage hardly ended women's work, however. Like colonial families, late-nineteenth-century working-class families operated as cooperative economic units. The unpaid domestic labor of working-class wives was critical to family survival. With husbands away for 10 to 11 hours a day, women bore the burden of child care and the domestic chores. Because working-class families could not afford labor-saving conveniences, housework was time-consuming and arduous. Without an ice box, a working-class woman spent part of each day shopping for food (more expensive in small quantities). Doing laundry entailed carrying water from outside pumps, heating it on the stove, washing the clothes, rinsing them with fresh water, and hanging them up to dry. Ironing was a hot and unpleasant job in small and stuffy quarters. Keeping an apartment or house clean when the atmosphere was grimy and unpaved roads were littered with refuse and horse dung was a challenge.

As managers of family resources, married women bore important responsibilities. What American families had once produced for themselves now had to be bought. It was up to the working-class wife to scour secondhand shops to find cheap clothes for her family. Domestic economies were vital to survival. "In summer and winter alike," one woman explained, "I must try to buy the food that will sustain us the greatest number of meals at the lowest price."

Women also supplemented family income by taking in work. Jewish and Italian women frequently did piecework and sewing at home. In the Northeast and the Midwest, between 10 and 40 percent of all working-class families kept boarders. Immigrant families in particular often made ends meet by taking single, young countrymen into their homes. Having borders meant providing meals and clean laundry, juggling different work schedules, and sacrificing privacy. But the advantages of extra income far outweighed the disadvantages for many working-class families.

Black women's working lives reflected the obstacles African Americans faced in late-nineteenth-century cities. Although only about 7 percent of married white women worked outside the home, African-American women did so both before and after marriage. In southern cities in 1880, about three-quarters of single black women and one-third of married women worked outside the home. Because industrial employers would not hire African-American women, most of them had to work as domestics or laundresses. The high percentage of married black women in the labor force reflected the marginal wages their husbands earned. But it may also be explained in part by the lesson learned during slavery that children could thrive without the constant attention of their mothers.

CAPITAL VERSUS LABOR

Class conflict characterized late-nineteenth-century industrial life. Although workers welcomed the progress that factories made possible, many rejected their employers' values, which emphasized individual gain at the expense of collective good. While owners reaped most of the profits, workers were turning into wage slaves. Fashioning their arguments from their republican legacy, workers claimed that the degradation of the country's citizen laborers threatened to undermine the republic itself.

On-the-Job Protests

Workers and employers engaged in a struggle over who would control the workplace. Many workers staunchly resisted unsatisfactory working conditions and the tendency of bosses to treat them "like any other piece of machinery, to be made to do the maximum amount of work with the minimum expenditure of fuel." Skilled workers, like iron puddlers and glassblowers, had indispensable knowledge about the production process as well as practical experience and were in a key position to direct on-the-job actions. Sometimes they struggled to retain control over critical work decisions. Detroit printers, for example, tried to retain the right to distribute headlines and white space (the "fat") rather than letting their bosses hand out the fat as a special reward and means of increasing competition among workers. Others hoped to humanize work. Cigar makers clung to their custom of having one worker read to others as they performed their tedious chores.

Workers sought to control the pace of production. Too many goods meant an inhuman pace of work and might result in overproduction, massive layoffs, and a reduction in the prices paid for piecework. So an experienced worker might whisper to a new hand, "See here, young fellow, you're working too fast. You'll spoil our job for us if you don't go slower."

A newspaper account of a glassblower's strike in 1884 illustrates the clash between capital and labor. With an eye toward bigger profits, the boss tried to increase output. "He knew if the limit was taken off, the men could work ten or twelve hours every day in the week; that in their thirst for the mighty dollar they would kill themselves with labor; they would 'black sheep' their fellows by doing

the labor of two men." But his employees resisted his proposal, refusing to drive themselves to exhaustion for a few dollars more. "They thundered out no. They even offered to take a reduction that would average ten percent all around, but they said, 'We will keep the forty-eight box limit.' Threats and curses would not move them." For these workers, a decent pace of work and a respectable wage was more important than promises of extra money.

In attempting to protect themselves and the dignity of their labor, workers devised ways of combating employer attempts to speed up the production process. Denouncing fellow workers who refused to honor production codes as "hogs," "runners," "chasers," and "job wreckers," they ostracized and even injured them. As the banner of the Detroit Coopers' Union proudly proclaimed at a parade in 1880: "Each for himself is the bosses' plea / [but] Union for all will make you free."

Absenteeism, drunkenness at work, and general inefficiency were other widespread worker practices that contained elements of protest. In three industrial firms in the late nineteenth century, one-quarter of the workers stayed home at least one day a week. Some of these lost days were due to layoffs, but not all. The efforts of employers to impose stiff fines on absent workers suggested their frustration with uncooperative workers.

To a surprising extent, workers made the final protest by quitting their jobs altogether. Most employers responded by penalizing workers who left without giving sufficient notice—but to little avail. A Massachusetts labor study in 1878 found that although two-thirds of the workers surveyed had been in the same occupation for more than 10 years, only 15 percent of them were in the same job. A similar rate of turnover occurred in the industrial workforce in the early twentieth century. Workers unmistakably and clearly voted with their feet.

Strike Activity After 1876

The most direct and strenuous attempts to change conditions in the workplace came in the form of thousands of strikes punctuating the late nineteenth century. In 1877, railroad workers staged the first and most violent nationwide industrial strike of the nineteenth century. The immediate cause of the disturbance was the railroad owners' decision to reduce wages. But the rapid spread of the strike from Baltimore to Pittsburgh and then to cities as distant as San Francisco, Chicago, and Omaha, as well as the violence of the strikers, who destroyed railroad property and kept trains idle, indicated more fundamental discontent.

An erratic economy, high unemployment rates, and the lack of job security all contributed to the conflagration. Over 100 people died before federal troops ended the strike. The frenzied response of the properted class, which saw the strike as the beginning of revolution and favored the intervention of the military, forecast the pattern of later conflicts. Time and time again, middle- and upper-class Americans would turn to the power of the state to crush labor activism.

A wave of confrontations followed the strike of 1877. Between 1881 and 1905, a total of 36,757 strikes erupted, involving over 6 million workers—three times the strike activity in France.

These numbers indicate that far more than the "poorest part" of the workers were involved. Many investigations of this era found evidence of widespread working-class discontent. When Samuel M. Hotchkiss, commissioner of the Connecticut Bureau of Labor Statistics, informally surveyed the state's workers in 1887, he was shocked by the "feeling of bitterness," the "distrust of employers," and the "discontent and unrest." These sentiments exploded into strikes, sabotage, and violence, most often linked to demands for higher wages and shorter hours.

Nineteenth-century strike activity underwent important changes, however, as the consciousness of American workers expanded. In the period of early industrialization, discontented laborers rioted in their neighborhoods rather than at their workplaces. Between 1845 and the Civil War, however, strikes at the workplace began to replace neighborhood riots. Although workers showed their anger against their employers by turning out and often calling for higher wages, they had only a murky sense that the strike could be a weapon to force employers to improve working conditions.

As industrialization transformed work and an increasing percentage of the workforce entered factories, collective actions at the workplace spread. Local and national unions played a more important role in organizing protest, conducting 60 percent of the strikes between 1881 and 1905. As working-class leaders realized more clearly the importance of collective action and perceived that transportation had knit the nation together, they worked to coordinate local and national efforts. By 1891, more than one-tenth of the strikes called by unionized workers were sympathy strikes. Coordination among strikers employed by different companies improved as workers made similar wage demands. Finally, pay among the most highly unionized workers became less of an issue. Workers sought more humane conditions. Some attempted to end subcontracting and

the degradation of skills. Others, like the glassblowers, struggled to enforce work rules. Indeed, by the early 1890s, over one-fifth of strikes involved the rules governing the workplace.

Labor Organizing, 1865–1900

The Civil War experience colored labor organizing in the postwar years. As one working-class song pointed out, workers had borne the brunt of that struggle.

You gave your son to the war
The rich man loaned his gold
And the rich man's son is happy to-day,
And yours is under the mold.

Now workers who had fought to save the Union argued that wartime sacrifices justified efforts to gain justice and equality in the workplace.

Labor leaders quickly realized the need for national as well as local organizations to protect the laboring class against "despotic employers." In 1866, several craft unions and reform groups formed the National Labor Union (NLU). Claiming 300,000 members by the early 1870s, the organization supported a range of causes, including temperance, women's rights, and the establishment of cooperatives to bring the "wealth of the land" into "the hands of those who produce it," thus ending "wage slavery."

The call for an eight-hour day reveals some of the basic assumptions of the organized labor movement. Few workers saw employers as a hostile class or felt it necessary to overturn the economic system. But they did believe bosses were tyrants whose time demands threatened to turn citizens into slaves. The eight-hour day would curb the power of owners and allow workers the time to cultivate the qualities necessary for republican citizenship.

Many of the NLU's specific goals survived, although the organization did not. An unsuccessful attempt to create a political party and the depression of 1873 decimated the NLU and many local unions as well. Survival and the search for a job took precedence over union causes.

The Knights of Labor and the AFL

As the depression wound down, a new mass organization, the Noble and Holy Order of the Knights of Labor, rose to national importance. Founded as a secret society in 1869, the order became public and national when Terence V. Powderly, an Irish American, was elected Grand Master Workman in 1879. The Knights of Labor sought "to secure to the workers the full enjoyment of the wealth they create." Because the industrial system denied workers

This depiction of working-class unrest appeared in *Harper's Weekly* in 1894. Note the prominence of the destruction wrought by the enraged workers and the artist's decision to place the National Guardsmen in the foreground. Contrast the individualized guardsmen with the faceless mob in the background. The artist's choices convey his sympathy with the forces of order. *(The Granger Collection, New York)*

their fair share as producers, the Knights of Labor proposed to mount a cooperative system of production alongside the existing system. "There is no reason," Powderly believed, "why labor cannot, through cooperation, own and operate mines, factories and railroads." Cooperative efforts would give workers the economic independence necessary for citizenship, and an eight-hour day would provide them with the leisure for moral, intellectual, and political pursuits.

The Knights of Labor opened its ranks to all American "producers," defined as all contributing members of society—skilled and unskilled, black and white, men and women. Only the idle and the corrupt (bankers, speculators, lawyers, saloonkeepers, and gamblers) were to be excluded. Membership was even open to sympathetic merchants and manufacturers. In fact, many shopkeepers joined the order and advertised their loyalty as "friend of the workingman."

This inclusive membership policy meant that the Knights potentially had the power of great numbers. The organization grew in spurts, attracting miners between 1874 and 1879 and skilled urban tradesmen between 1879 and 1885. Masses of unskilled workers joined thereafter.

Although Powderly frowned on using the strike as a labor weapon, the organization reaped the benefits of grassroots strike activity. Local struggles proliferated after 1883. In 1884, unorganized workers of the Union Pacific Railroad walked off the job when management announced a wage cut. Within two days, the company caved in, and the men joined the Knights of Labor. The next year, a successful strike against the Missouri Pacific Railroad brought in another wave of members. Then, in 1886, the Haymarket Riot in Chicago led to such a growth in labor militancy that in that single year, the membership of the Knights of Labor ballooned from 100,000 to 700,000.

The "riot" at Haymarket was, in fact, a peaceful protest meeting connected with a lockout at the McCormick Reaper Works. When the Chicago police arrived to disperse the crowd, a bomb exploded, killing seven policemen. Although no one knows who planted the bomb, eight anarchists were tried and convicted. Four were executed, one committed suicide, and the others served prison terms.

Labor agitation and turbulence spilled over into politics. In 1884 and 1885, the Knights of Labor lobbied to secure a national contract labor law that would demand work contracts and state laws outlawing the use of convict labor. The organization also pressed successfully for the creation of a federal Department of Labor. As new members poured in, however, direct political action became increasingly attractive. Between 1885 and 1888, the Knights of Labor sponsored candidates in 200 towns and cities in 34 states and 4 territories. They achieved many electoral victories. In Waterloo, Iowa, a bank janitor ousted a successful attorney to become the town's mayor. Despite local successes, no national labor party emerged. But in the 1890s, the Knights cooperated with the Populists in their attempt to reshape American politics and society. (See Chapter 19.)

Despite the dramatic surge in membership, the Knights of Labor lost their momentum as the voice for the American laboring people. Employers, alerted by the Haymarket riot, were determined to break the power of the organization. A strike against Jay Gould's southwestern railroad system in 1886 failed, tarnishing the Knights' reputation. Consumer and producer cooperatives fizzled; the policy of accepting both black and white workers led to strife and discord in the South. The two major parties proved adept at co-opting labor politicians. As labor politicians became respectable, they left the rank and file to fend for themselves.

The failure of national leaders paralleled the failure of local leadership. Powderly was never able to unify or direct his diverse following. His concern with general reform issues and political action dissatisfied members wanting better wages and work conditions. Nor could Powderly control the militants opposing him. Local, unauthorized strike actions were often ill-considered and violent. Lawlessness helped neither the organization nor its members. By 1890, the membership had dropped to 100,000, although the Knights continued to play a role well into the 1890s.

In the 1890s, the American Federation of Labor (AFL), founded in 1886, replaced the Knights of Labor as the nation's dominant union. The history of the Knights pointed up the problems of a national union that admitted all who worked for wages but officially rejected strike action in favor of the ballot box and arbitration. The leader of the AFL, Samuel Gompers, had a different notion of an effective worker organization. Gompers's experience as head of the Cigarmakers' Union in the 1870s and as a founder of the Federation of Organized Trades and Labor Unions in 1881 convinced him that skilled workers should put their specific occupational interests before the interests of workers as a whole. By so doing, they could control the supply of skilled labor and keep wages up.

Gompers organized the AFL as a federation of skilled trades—cigar makers, iron molders, ironworkers, carpenters, and others—each one autonomous, yet linked through an executive council to work together for prolabor national legislation and mutual support during boycott and strike actions. Gompers was a practical man. He repudiated the notion of a cooperative commonwealth and dreams of ending the wage system, accepting the fact that workers "are a distinct and practically permanent class of modern society." Thus, he focused on immediate, realizable "bread and butter" issues, particularly higher wages, shorter hours, industrial safety, and the right to organize.

Although Gompers rejected direct political action as a means of obtaining labor's goals, he did believe in the value of the strike. He told a congressional hearing in 1899 that unless working people had "the power to enter upon a strike, the improvements will all go to the employer and all the injuries to the employees." A shrewd organizer, he knew from bitter experience the importance of dues high enough to sustain a strike fund through a long, tough fight.

Under Gompers's leadership, the AFL grew from 140,000 members in 1886 to nearly 1 million by 1900. Although his notion of a labor organization was elitist, he succeeded in steering his union through a series of crises, fending off challenges from socialists on his left and corporate opposition to strikes from his right. But there was no room in his organization for the unskilled or for blacks, in whom he claimed to see an "abandoned and reckless disposition."

The AFL made a brief and halfhearted attempt to unionize women in 1892. Hostile male attitudes constituted a major barrier against organizing women. Men resented women as coworkers and preferred for them to stay in the home. The AFL stood firmly for the principle that "the man is the provider" and that women who work in factories "bring forth weak children." The Boston Central Labor Union declared in 1897 "the demand for female labor an insidious assault upon the home. . . . It is the knife of the assassin, aimed at the family circle." Change was slow in coming. In 1900, the International Ladies' Garment Workers Union (ILGWU) was established. Although women were the backbone of the organization, men dominated the leadership.

Working-Class Setbacks

Despite the growth of working-class organizations, workers lost many of their battles with management. Some of the more spectacular clashes reveal why working-class activism often ended in defeat and why so many workers lived precariously on the edge of poverty.

In 1892, silver miners in Coeur d'Alene, Idaho, struck when their employers installed machine drills in the mines, reduced skilled workers to shovelmen, and announced a wage cut of a dollar a day. The owners, supported by state militiamen and the federal government, successfully broke the strike by using scabs, but not without armed fighting. Several hundred union men were arrested, herded into huge bull pens, and eventually tried and found guilty of a wide variety of charges. Out of the defeat emerged the Western Federation of Miners (WFM), whose chief political goal was an eight-hour law for miners. The pattern of struggle in Coeur d'Alene was followed in many subsequent strikes.

Determined mine owners characteristically met strikes by shutting off credit to union men, hiring strikebreakers and armed guards, and paying spies to infiltrate unions. Violence was frequent, and confrontations usually ended with the arrival of state militia, the erection of bull pens, incarceration or intimidation of strikers and their local sympathizers, legal action, and elaborate blacklisting systems. In spite of this, the WFM won as many strikes as it lost.

The Homestead and Pullman Strikes of 1892 and 1894

The most serious setback to labor occurred in 1892 at the Homestead steel mills near Pittsburgh, Pennsylvania. Andrew Carnegie had recently purchased the Homestead plant and put Henry Clay Frick in charge. Together, they wanted to eliminate the Amalgamated Association of Iron, Steel, and Tin Workers, which threatened to increase its organization of the steel industry. After three months of stalemated negotiations over a new wage contract, Frick issued an ultimatum. Unless the union accepted wage decreases, he would lock them out and replace them. As the deadline passed, Frick erected a formidable wood and barbed wire fence around the entire plant, with searchlight and sentry stands on it, and hired 300 armed Pinkerton agents to guard the factory. As the Pinkertons arrived on July 6, they engaged armed steelworkers in a daylong gun battle. Several men on both sides were killed, and the Pinkertons retreated.

Frick telegraphed Pennsylvania's governor, who sent 8,000 troops to crush both the strike and the union. Two and a half weeks later, Alexander Berkman, a New York anarchist sympathetic to the plight of the oppressed Homestead workers, attempted to assassinate Frick. The events at Homestead dramatized the lengths to which both labor and capital would go to achieve their ends.

Observing these events, Eugene Victor Debs of Terre Haute, Indiana, for many years an ardent organizer of railroad workers, wrote, "If the year 1892 taught the workingmen any lesson worthy of heed, it was that the capitalist class, like a devilfish, had grasped them with its tentacles and was dragging

In this 1892 engraving of the Homestead strikers surrendering, done for *Harper's Weekly*, the sympathy of the artist lies with the detectives in the foreground. The strikers appear as an unruly crowd in the distance, whereas the detectives' kindly faces are highlighted. *(Library of Congress)*

them down to fathomless depths of degradation." Debs saw 1893 as the year in which organized labor would "escape the prehensile clutch of these monsters." But 1893 brought a new depression and even worse challenges and setbacks for labor. Undaunted, Debs succeeded in combining several of the separate railroad brotherhoods into a united American Railway Union (ARU). Within a year, over 150,000 railroadmen joined the ARU, and Debs won a strike against the Great Northern Railroad, which had attempted to slash workers' wages.

Debs faced his toughest crisis at the Pullman Palace Car Company in Chicago. Pullman was a model company town, where management controlled all aspects of workers' lives. "We are born in a Pullman house, fed from the Pullman shop, taught in the Pullman school, catechized in the Pullman church, and when we die we shall be buried in the Pullman cemetery and go to the Pullman hell," said one worker wryly.

Late in 1893, as the depression worsened, Pullman cut wages by one-third and laid off many workers but did not reduce rents or prices in the town stores. Families struggled to survive the winter. Some parents kept their children home from school because they had no shoes or coats and could keep warm only in bed. Those still working suffered speedups, intimidating threats, and further wage cuts. Desperate and "without hope," the Pullman workers joined the ARU in the spring of 1894 and went out on strike.

In late June, after Pullman refused to submit the dispute to arbitration, Debs led the ARU into a sympathy strike in support of the striking Pullman workers. Remembering the ill-fated railroad strike of 1877, Debs advised his lieutenants to "use no violence" and "stop no trains." Rather, he sought to boycott trains handling Pullman cars throughout the West. As the boycott spread, the General Managers Association, which ran the 24 railroads centered in Chicago, came to Pullman's support, convinced that "we have got to wipe him [Debs] out." After hiring some 2,500 strikebreakers, the GMA appealed to the state and federal governments for military and judicial support in stopping the strike.

Governor Richard Altgeld of Illinois, sympathizing with the workers and believing that local law enforcement was sufficient, opposed the use of federal troops. But Richard Olney, a former railroad lawyer and U.S. attorney general, persuaded President Cleveland that only federal troops could restore law and order. On July 2, Olney obtained a court injunction to end the strike as a "conspiracy in restraint of trade." Two days later, Cleveland ordered in federal troops to support the injunction and crush the strikers.

Violence now escalated rapidly. Local and federal officials hired armed guards, and the railroads paid them to help the troops. Within two days, strikers and guards were fighting bitterly, freight cars were burned, and over $340,000 worth of railroad property was destroyed. The press reported "Unparalleled Scenes of Riot, Terror and Pillage." As troops poured into Chicago, the violence worsened, leaving scores of workers dead.

Debs's resources were near an end unless he could enlist wider labor support. "Capital has combined to enslave labor," he warned other labor groups. "We must all stand together or go down in hopeless defeat." When Samuel Gompers refused his support, the strike collapsed. Debs and several other leaders were arrested for the contempt of the court injunction of July 2 and found guilty. A lifelong Democrat, Debs soon became a confirmed socialist. His arrest and the defeat of the Pullman strike provided a deathblow to the American Railway Union. In 1895, the Supreme Court upheld the legality of using an injunction to stop a strike and provided

management with a powerful weapon to use against unions in subsequent years. Most unions survived the difficult days of the 1890s, but the labor movement emerged with distinct disadvantages in its conflicts with organized capital.

The failures of the American labor movement are apparent when compared to union actions in European industrialized nations. There, the working class, more homogeneous than its American counterpart, gained the vote as their countries experienced the second industrial revolution. Working class and political consciousness developed together, and labor and socialist political parties emerged. Labor parties gave workers and their concerns a voice in the political forum and strengthened the hands of trade unions.

But in the United States, most labor conflicts ran up against the widespread middle- and upper-class conviction that unions and their demands were un-American. Many people claimed to accept the idea of worker organizations, but they would not concede that unions should participate in making economic or work decisions. Most employers violently resisted union demands as infringements of their rights to make production decisions, hire and fire, lock workers out, hire scabs, or reduce wages in times of depression. The sharp competition of the late nineteenth century, combined with a pattern of falling prices, stiffened employers' resistance to workers' demands. State and local governments and the courts frequently supported them in their battles to curb worker activism.

The severe depressions of the 1870s and 1890s also undermined working-class activism. Workers could not focus on union issues when survival itself was in question. They could not afford union dues or turn down offers of work, even at wages below union standards. Many unions collapsed during hard times. Of the 30 national unions in 1873, fewer than one-third managed to survive the depression.

A far more serious problem was the reluctance of most workers to organize even in favorable times. In 1870, less than one-tenth of the industrial workforce belonged to unions, about the same as on the eve of the Civil War. Thirty years later, despite the expansion of the workforce, only 8.4 percent (mostly skilled workers) were union members. This percentage was far lower than in Europe.

Why were American workers so slow to join unions? Certainly, diverse work settings and ethnic differences made it difficult for workers to recognize common bonds. Moreover, many unskilled workers sensed that labor aristocrats did not have their interests at heart. Said one Cleveland Pole, "The [union] committee gets the money, 'Bricky' Flannigan [a prominent Irish striker] gets the whiskey, and the Polack gets nothing."

Moreover, many native-born Americans still clung to the tradition of individualism. "The sooner working-people get rid of the idea that somebody or something is going to help them," one Massachusetts shoemaker declared, "the better it will be for them." Others dreamt of escaping from the working class and entering the ranks of the middle class. The number of workers who started their own small businesses attests to the power of that ideal, which prevented an identification with working-class causes.

The comments of an Irish woman highlight another important point. "There should be a law . . . to give a job to every decent man that's out of work," she declared, "and another law to keep all them I-talians from comin' in and takin' the bread out of the mouths of honest people." The ethnic and religious diversity of the workforce made it difficult to forge a common front. No other industrial country depended so heavily on immigrants for its manufacturing labor force. The lack of common cultural traditions, goals, and a common language created friction and misunderstandings. In addition, immigrants clustered in certain jobs and were insulated from other workers, both foreign-born and American. When Italian women working in New York canneries wanted to strike, their Syrian and

Polish workers, who were satisfied with their pay, refused. American workers supported the owners rather than "Eyetalians." Skill differences related to ethnic group membership also clouded common class concerns.

The perspective of immigrant workers contributed to their indifference to unions and to tension with native-born Americans. Many foreigners planned to return to their homeland and had limited interest in changing conditions in the United States. Moreover, because their goal was to work, they took jobs as scabs. Much of the violence that accompanied working-class actions erupted when owners brought in strikebreakers. Some Americans blamed immigrants for both low wages and failed worker actions. Divisions among workers were often as bitter as those between strikers and employers. When workers divided, employers benefited.

The tension within laboring ranks appeared most dramatically in the anti-Chinese campaign of the 1870s and 1880s as white workers in the West began to blame the Chinese for economic hardships. The Chinese were particularly vulnerable because, unlike European immigrants, they could not be naturalized. A meeting of San Francisco workers in 1877 in favor of the eight-hour day exploded into a rampage against the Chinese. In the following years, angry mobs killed Chinese workers in Tacoma, Seattle, Denver, and Rock Springs, Wyoming. "The

This 1898 photograph shows a crowded street in San Francisco's Chinatown. Violent outbreaks against Chinese immigrants must have made some of them wary of leaving Chinatown. The fact that there are only men on the street highlights the male character of Chinese immigration to the United States. *(Library of Congress [LC-USZ62-41901])*

Chinese must go! They are stealing our jobs!" became a rallying cry for American workers. When one Chinese immigrant arrived in San Francisco in 1900, he reported that "some white boys came up and starting throwing rocks" at the carriage in which he was sitting.

Hostility was also expressed at the national level with the Chinese Exclusion Act of 1882. The law, which enjoyed support from the Knights of Labor in the West, prohibited the immigration of both skilled and unskilled Chinese workers for a 10-year period. It was extended in 1892 and made permanent in 1902. It paved the way for further restriction of immigration in the 1920s. Although both middle- and working-class Americans supported sporadic efforts to cut off immigration, working-class antipathy exacerbated the deep divisions that undermined worker unity.

At the same time, many immigrants, especially those who were skilled, did support unions and cooperate with native-born Americans. Irish Americans played important roles in the Knights of Labor and the AFL. British and Germans also helped build up the unions. Often ethnic bonds served labor causes by tying members to one another and to the community. For example, in the 1860s and 1870s, as the Molders' Union in Troy, New York, battled with manufacturers, its Irish membership won sympathy and support from the Irish-dominated police force, the Roman Catholic Church, fraternal orders, and public officials.

The importance of workers' organizations lay not so much in their successful struggles and protests as in the implicit criticism they offered of American society. Using the language of republicanism, many workers lashed out at an economic order that robbed them of their dignity and humanity. As producers of wealth, they protested that so little of it was theirs. As members of the working class, they rejected the middle-class belief in individualism and social mobility.

The Balance Sheet

Except for skilled workers, most laboring people found it impossible to earn much of a share in the material bounty that industrialization created. Newly arrived immigrants especially suffered from low pay and economic uncertainty. Long hours on the job and the necessity of walking to and from work left workers with little free time. Family budgets could include, at best, only small amounts for recreation. Even a baseball game ticket was a luxury.

Yet this view of the harshness of working-class life partly grows out of our own standards of what is acceptable today. Because so few working-class men or women recorded their thoughts and reactions, it is hard to know just what they expected or how they viewed their experiences. But culture and background influenced their perspectives. The family tenement, one Polish immigrant remarked, "seemed quite advanced when compared with our home" in Poland. A Lithuanian agreed. "Even though the toilet was in the hall, and the whole floor used it, yet it was a toilet. There was no such thing in Lithuania." A 10-hour job in the steel mill might be an improvement over dawn-to-dusk farmwork that brought no wages.

Studies of several cities show that nineteenth-century workers achieved some occupational mobility. One worker in five in Los Angeles and Atlanta during the 1890s, for example, managed to climb into the middle class. Most immigrant workers were stuck in ill-paid, insecure jobs, but their children ended up doing better. The son of an unskilled laborer might move on to become a semiskilled or skilled worker as new immigrants took the jobs at the bottom. Second-generation Irish made progress, especially in the West and the Midwest. Even in Boston, 40 percent of the children of Irish immigrants obtained white-collar jobs.

Mobility, like occupation, was related to background. Native-born whites, Jews, and Germans rose more swiftly and fell less often than Irish, Italians, or Poles. Cultural attitudes, family size, education, and group leadership all contributed to different ethnic mobility patterns. Jews, for example, valued education and sacrificed to keep children in school. By 1915, Jews represented 85 percent of the free City College student body in New York City, 20 percent of New York University's student body, and one-sixth of those studying at Columbia University. With an education, they moved upward. The Slavs, however, who valued a steady income over mobility and education, took their children out of school and sent them to work at an early age. They believed that this course of action not only helped the family but gave the child a head start in securing reliable, stable employment. The southern Italian proverb "Do not make your child better than you are" suggests the value Italians placed on family rather than individual success. Differing attitudes and values led to different aspirations and career patterns.

Two groups enjoyed little mobility: African Americans and Hispanic Americans. African Americans were largely excluded from the industrial occupational structure and were restricted to unskilled jobs. Unlike immigrant industrial workers, they did not have the opportunity to move to better jobs as new, unskilled workers took the positions at the bottom. A study in Los Angeles suggests that Hispanic residents made minimal gains. Their experiences elsewhere may have been much the same.

Although immigrants' occupational mobility was limited, other kinds of rewards often compensated for the lack of success at the workplace. Home ownership loomed important for groups like the Irish, for in their homeland, home ownership had been all but impossible. Ownership of a home also allowed a family to earn extra income by taking in boarders and provided some protection against the uncertainties of industrial life and the coming of old age. The Irish also proved adept politicians and came to dominate big-city government in the late nineteenth century. Their political success opened up city jobs, particularly in the police force. In 1886, one-third of Chicago's police force was Irish-born; many more were second-generation Irish Americans. The Irish were also successful in the construction industry and dominated the hierarchy of the Catholic church. Irish who did not share this upward mobility could nevertheless benefit from ethnic connections and take pride in their group's achievements.

Likewise, participation in social clubs and fraternal orders compensated in part for lack of advancement at work. Ethnic associations, parades, and holidays provided a sense of identity and security that offset the limitations of the job world.

Moreover, a few rags-to-riches stories always encouraged the masses who struggled. For example, the family of John Kearney in Poughkeepsie, New York, achieved modest success. After 20 years as a laborer, John started his own business as a junk dealer and even bought a simple house. His sons started off in better jobs than their father. One became a grocery store clerk and then later a baker, a policeman, and, finally, at the age of 40, an inspector at the waterworks. Another was an iron molder, and the third son was a post office worker and eventually the superintendent of city streets. If this success paled next to that of industrial giants like Andrew Carnegie and John D. Rockefeller, it was still enough to keep the American dream alive.

Timeline	
1843–1884	"Old immigration"
1844	Telegraph invented
1850s	Steam power widely used in manufacturing
1859	Value of U.S. industrial production exceeds value of agricultural production
1866	National Labor Union founded
1869	Transcontinental railroad completed Knights of Labor organized
1870	Standard Oil of Ohio formed
1870s–1880s	Consolidation of continental railroad network
1873	Bethlehem Steel begins using Bessemer process
1873–1879	Depression
1876	Alexander G. Bell invents telephone Thomas Edison establishes his "invention factory" at Menlo Park, New Jersey
1877	Railroad workers hold first nationwide industrial strike
1879	Thomas Edison invents incandescent light
1882	Chinese Exclusion Act
1885–1914	"New immigration"
1886	American Federation of Labor founded Haymarket Riot in Chicago
1887	Interstate Commerce Act
1890	Sherman Anti-Trust Act
1892	Standard Oil of New Jersey formed Coeur d'Alene strike Homestead steelworkers strike
1893	Chicago World's Fair
1893–1897	Depression
1894	Pullman railroad workers strike
1900	International Ladies' Garment Workers Union founded Corporations responsible for two-thirds of U.S. manufacturing

✦ Conclusion

THE COMPLEXITY OF INDUSTRIAL CAPITALISM

The rapid growth of the late nineteenth century made the United States one of the world's industrial giants. Many factors contributed to the "wonderful accomplishments" of the age. They ranged from sympathetic government policies to the rise of big business and the emergence of a cheap industrial workforce. But it was also a turbulent period. Many Americans benefited only marginally from the new wealth. Some of them protested by joining unions, walking out on strike, or initiating on-the-job actions. Most lived their lives more quietly and never had the opportunity that Thomas O'Donnell did of telling their story to others. But middle-class Americans began to wonder about the O'Donnells of the country. It is to their concerns, worries, and aspirations that we now turn.

◆ Recommended Reading

The Texture of Industrial Progress

Alfred D. Chandler, Jr., *The Visible Hand: The Managerial Revolution in American Business* (1977); Robert L. Heilbroner, *The Economic Transformation of America* (1977); Thomas P. Hughes, *American Genius* (1989); Thomas J. Misa, *A Nation of Steel* (1995); James D. Norris, *Advertising and the Transformation of American Society, 1865–1920* (1990); William G. Roy, *Socializing Capitalism: The Rise of the Large Industrial Corporation in America* (1997); Douglas Steeples, *Democracy in Desperation: The Depression of 1893* (1998); Olivier Zunz, *Making America Corporate, 1870–1929* (1990).

Urban Expansion in the Industrial Age

James Borchert, *Alley Life in Washington: Family, Community, Religion, and Folklife in the City, 1850–1970* (1980); Yong Chen, *Chinese San Francisco, 1850–1943* (2000); William E. Montgomery, *Under Their Own Fig Tree: The African-American Church in the South, 1865–1900* (1993); David Nasaw, *Going Out: The Rise and Fall of Public Amusements* (1993); Carl Smith, *Urban Disorder and the Shape of Belief: The Great Chicago Fire, the Haymarket Bomb, and the Model Town of Pullman* (1993).

The Industrial City, 1880–1900

William Cronon, *Nature's Metropolis: Chicago and the Great West* (1991); David Goldfield, *Cotton Fields and Sky Scrapers: Southern City and Region* (1989); Sam Bass Warner, Jr., *Streetcar Suburbs: The Process of Growth in Boston, 1870–1900* (1962).

The Life of the Middle Class

Gunther Barth, *The Rise of Modern City Culture in Nineteenth-Century America* (1980); Sven Beckert, *The Monied Metropolis: New York City and the Consolidation of the American Bourgeoisie, 1850–1896* (2000); Anne Ruggles Geere, *Intimate Practices: Literacy and Cultural Work in U.S. Women's Clubs, 1880–1992* (1997); Thomas Goebel, *The Children of Athena: Chicago Professionals and the Creation of a Credentialing Society* (1996); Judy Hilkey, *Character in Capital: Success Manuals and Manhood in Gilded Age America* (1997).

Industrial Work and the Laboring Class

Thomas J. Archdeacon, *Becoming American: An Ethnic History* (1983); David M. Gordon, Richard Edwards, and Michael Reich, *Segmented Work, Divided Workers: The Historical Transformation of Labor in the United States* (1982); Herbert G. Gutman, *Work, Culture, and Society in Industrializing America* (1976); Christiane Harrig et al.,

Peasant Maids—City Women: From the European Countryside to Urban America (1997); David M. Katzman, *Seven Days a Week: Women and Domestic Service in Industrializing America* (1978); Alice Kessler-Harris, *Out to Work: A History of Wage-Earning Women in the United States* (1982); Kerby A. Miller, *Emigrants and Exiles: Ireland and the Irish Exodus to North America* (1985); Gunther Peck, *Reinventing Free Labor: Padrones and Immigrant Workers in the North American West, 1880–1930* (2000); Madelon Powers, *Faces along the Bar: Lore and Order in the Working-Man's Saloon, 1870–1920* (1998).

Capital Versus Labor

Leon Fink, *Workingmen's Democracy: The Knights of Labor and American Politics* (1983); David Montgomery, *Workers' Control in America: Studies in the History of Work, Technology, and Labor Struggles* (1970) and *The Fall of the House of Labor: The Workplace, the State, and American Labor Activism, 1865–1925* (1987); Craig Phelan, *Grand Master Workman: Terence Powderly and the Knights of Labor* (2000); Ronald Takaki, *A Different Mirror: A History of Multicultural America* (1993); Daniel J. Walkowitz, *Worker City, Company Town: Iron and Cotton-Worker Protest in Troy and Cohoes, New York, 1855–84* (1978); Robert E. Weit, *Beyond Labor's Veil: The Culture of the Knights of Labor* (1996); James Whiteside, *Regulating Danger: The Struggle for Mine Safety in the Rocky Mountain Coal Industry* (1990).

Fiction and Film

In *Sister Carrie* (1900), Theodore Dreiser tells the story of a young rural woman who comes to Chicago and violates its social norms to acquire some of the city's offerings. Stephen Crane's novel *Maggie: A Girl of the Streets* (1893) gives a grim picture of life in the urban slums. Thomas Bell follows several generations of the same immigrant family whose American life is entwined with steel in *Out of This Furnace* (1976 ed.). *The Richest Man in the World: Andrew Carnegie,* a 1997 film made for PBS, analyzes the personal and professional life of Carnegie and makes good use of interviews with business and labor historians. It offers extended treatment of the Homestead strike, for which the film holds Carnegie largely responsible. *The Age of Innocence,* which takes place in 1870s New York, offers a splendid picture of the sumptuous lives of the rich and the norms and values to which they were supposed to adhere. This 1993 Martin Scorsese film is based on the novel of the same name by Edith Wharton.

♦ Discovering U.S. History Online

Andrew Carnegie

www.pbs.org/wgbh/pages/amex/carnegie/

The online companion to the PBS film *The Richest Man in the World: Andrew Carnegie*, this Web site provides an outline of the film, a biography, a photo gallery, and information about the Homestead Strike.

The Rockefellers

www.pbs.org/wgbh/amex/rockefellers/index.html

Companion to the PBS film of the same title, the site presents audio clips from historians, illustrated essays, maps, and images about this famous industrialist.

John D. Rockefeller and the Standard Oil Company

www.micheloud.com/FXM/SC

This study, with accompanying images, tells of the rise of Rockefeller's mammoth company.

Enarco

www.enarco.com/home.htm

This positive history of the company reflects the industrial changes of late-nineteenth-century America.

Angel Island: The Pacific Gateway

www.internationalchannel.com/education/angelisland.

Angel Island was the principal gateway for Chinese immigrants. This site documents and illustrates the experiences of these immigrants as they entered the United States.

The Great Chicago Fire

www.chicagohs.org/fire/index.html

This site examines the Chicago fire from contemporary accounts and photographs as well as from personal artifacts and memories. Since Chicago was emblematic of the urban industrialization of the country, the story of its great fire and reconstruction provide a window on the nature of cities of this era.

Lower East Side Tenement Museum

www.thirteen.org/tenement/index.html

The goal of this museum is "to preserve and interpret the history of the immigrant experience on the Lower East Side." This site presents digital exhibits from the museum.

Ellis Island

www.ellisisland.com/indexHistory.html

This official museum site presents a timeline and an overview of the Ellis Island immigration experience.

Nineteenth-Century American Children and What They Read

www.merrycoz.org/kids.htm

The author of this site presents text and author information from several nineteenth-century contemporary children's books and magazines, giving an insight to the culture of the times.

Jane Addams

www.hullhouse.org/website

This site presents a biography of Jane Addams as well as the history of the association as "the direct descendent of the settlement house founded by Jane Addams in 1889."

Anarchism

www.Pitzer.edu/~dward/Anarchist_Archives/archivehome.html

This site offers classic anarchist texts, including information and graphics for the Haymarket Riot.

Haymarket

www.chicagohistory.org/dramas

This illustrated site, drawing extensively from the "Haymarket Affair Digital Collection," thoroughly examines the Haymarket bombing in seven sections: a Prologue, five "Acts," and the Epilogue. The material examines the national as well as the local political context of the incident.

American Labor History

www.geocities.com/CollegePark/Quad/6460/AmLabHist/

This site provides a general chronological survey of the history of labor in America. The author also has included with each section an extensive list of Internet references on labor history.

The Samuel Gompers Papers: A Documentary History of the American Working Class

www.inform.umd.edu/EdRes/Colleges/ARHU/Depts/History/Gompers/web 1.html

This site includes information about the papers project and also has a photo gallery, selected documents, and a brief history of the first president of the American Federation of Labor (AFL).

The Strike at Homestead, 1892

www.history.ohio-state.edu/projects/HomesteadStrike1892/

Drawing from the contemporary sources, this site provides an overview of the town and the strike. A photographic essay is also included.

19 Politics and Reform

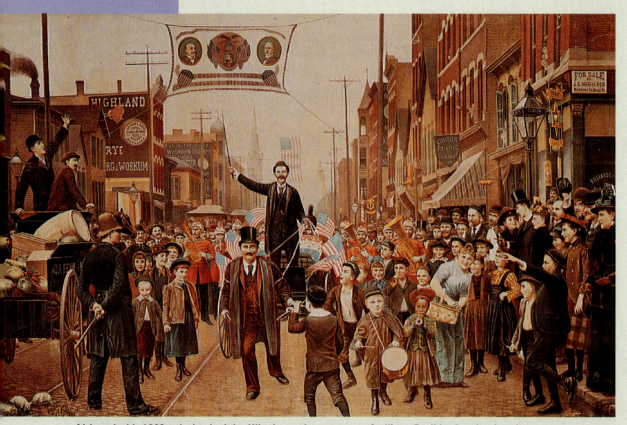

Although this 1892 painting by John Klir shows the outcome of a "Lost Bet" in the election that year, note the ethnic, racial, and class diversity of the street crowds, momentarily united in the enjoyment of watching the humiliated loser pulling his victorious opponent (and a wagon full of American flags). Will a more diverse America hold together? *(Library of Congress)*

◆ *American Stories*

A UTOPIAN NOVELIST WARNS OF TWO AMERICAS

At the start of his best-seller *Looking Backward* (1888), Edward Bellamy likened the American society of his day to a huge stagecoach. Dragging the coach along sandy roads and over steep hills were the "masses of humanity." While they strained desperately "under the pitiless lashing of hunger" to pull the coach, at the top sat the favored few, riding in breezy comfort but still fearful that they might fall from their seats and have to pull the coach themselves.

Bellamy's famous coach allegory began a utopian novel in which the class divisions and pitiless competition of the nineteenth century were replaced by a classless, caring, cooperative new society. Economic anxieties and hardships were supplanted by satisfying labor and leisure. In place of the coach, all citizens in the year 2000 walked together and shopped in equal comfort and security under a huge umbrella (not unlike modern malls) over the sidewalks of the city.

The novel opens in 1887. The hero, a wealthy Bostonian, falls asleep worrying about the effect local labor struggles might have on his upcoming wedding. When he wakes up, it is the year 2000. Utopia has been achieved peacefully through the development of one gigantic trust, owned and operated by the national government. All citizens between the ages of 21 and 45 work in an industrial army with equalized pay and work difficulty. Retirement after age 45 is devoted to hobbies, reading, culture, and the minimal leadership necessary in a society without crime, corruption, poverty, or war.

Bellamy's treatment of the role of women reflected his era's struggle with changing gender relationships. Women in 2000 were relieved of housework by labor-saving gadgets, married for love, and worked in the industrial army, albeit in "lighter occupations" in a women's division. But they did not participate in government, and their primary role was still to supervise domestic affairs, nurture the young, and beautify culture.

Bellamy's book was popular with educated middle-class Americans, who were attracted by his vision of a society in which humans were both morally good and materially well off. But his book also had an enormous appeal because the core values of the 1880s survived intact, including individual taste and incentive, private property, and rags-to-riches presidents; in addition, he filled the novel with futuristic technological wonders, such as television and credit cards, a double-dream surprise ending, and a love story.

Like most middle-class Americans of his day, Bellamy disapproved of European socialism. Although some features of his utopia were socialistic, he and his admirers called his system "nationalism." This appealed to a new generation of Americans who had put aside Civil War antagonisms to embrace the greatness of a growing, if now economically divided, nation. In the early 1890s, with Americans buying nearly 10,000 copies of *Looking Backward* every week, over 160 Nationalist clubs were formed to crusade for the adoption of Bellamy's ideas.

The inequalities of wealth described in Bellamy's coach scene reflected a political life in which many participated but only a few benefited. The wealthiest 10 percent, who rode high on the coach, dominated national politics, while untutored bosses held sway in governing cities. Except for token expressions of support, national political leaders ignored the cries of factory workers, immigrants, farmers, African Americans, Native Americans, and other victims of the vast transformation of American industrial, urban, and agrarian life in the late nineteenth century. But as the century closed, middle-class Americans like Bellamy, as well as labor, agrarian, and ethnic leaders themselves, proposed various reforms. Their concern was never more appropriate than during the depression of the mid-1890s, a real-life social upheaval that mirrored the worst features and fears of Bellamy's fictional coach.

In this chapter, we will examine American politics at the national and local level from the end of Reconstruction to the 1890s, a period that in the United States as well as in Europe bolstered the rich and neglected the corrosive human problems of urban industrial life. Then we will look at the growing social and political involvement of educated middle-class reformers who, despite their distaste for mass politics, now acted to effect change both locally and nationally. We will conclude with an account of the pivotal importance of the 1890s, highlighted by the Populist revolt, the depression of 1893–1897, and the election of 1896. In an age of strong national identity and pride, the events of the 1890s shook many comfortable citizens out of their apathy and began the reshaping of American politics.

POLITICS IN THE GILDED AGE

Co-authoring a satirical book in 1873, Mark Twain coined the expression "Gilded Age" to describe Grant's corrupt presidency. The phrase, with its suggestion of shallow glitter, has come to characterize social and political life in the last quarter of the nineteenth century. Although politics was marred by corruption and politicians avoided fundamental issues in favor of the politics of mass entertainment—pomp, parades, pennants and penny beer—voter participation in national elections between 1876 and 1896 hovered at an all-time high of 73 to 82 percent of all registered voters.

Behind the glitter of Gilded Age politics, two gradual changes occurred that would greatly affect twentieth-century politics. First was the development of a professional bureaucracy. In congressional committees and executive branch offices, elite specialists and experts emerged as a counterfoil to the perceived dangers of majority rule represented by high voter participation, especially by new immigrants. How else, New England poet James Russell Lowell wondered, could the culturally "better" classes temper the excesses of equality "when . . . applied politically by millions of newcomers alien to our traditions?" Second, after a period of close elections and Republican-Democratic party stalemate, new issues, concerns, and parties fostered a political realignment in the 1890s.

Politics, Parties, Patronage, and Presidents

American government in the 1870s and 1880s clearly supported the interests of riders atop Bellamy's coach. Few nineteenth-century Americans would have agreed that the national government should tackle problems of poverty, unemployment, and trusts. They mistrusted organized power and believed that all would benefit from an economic life free of government interference. After the traumas of the Civil War era, when a strong centralized state pursued high moral causes, late-nineteenth-century political leaders favored a period of government passivity, permitting the free pursuit of industrial

expansion and wealth. As Republican leader Roscoe Conkling explained, the primary role of government was "to clear the way of impediments and dangers, and leave every class and every individual free and safe in the exertions and pursuits of life."

The Gilded Age, Henry Adams observed, was the most "thoroughly ordinary" period ever in American politics. "One might search the whole list of Congress, Judiciary, and Executive during the twenty-five years 1870–95 and find little but damaged reputation." Few eras of American government were so corrupt, and Adams was especially sensitive to the low quality of democratic politics compared to the exalted morality of his grandfather John Quincy Adams and great-grandfather John Adams.

During the weak Johnson and Grant presidencies, Congress emerged as the dominant branch of government with power in the committee system. Senators James G. Blaine (Maine) and Roscoe Conkling (New York) typified the moral quality of legislative leadership. Despite lying about having been paid off by favors to railroads, Blaine was probably the most popular Republican politician of the era. Charming, intelligent, witty, and able, he served twice as secretary of state and was a serious contender for the presidency in every election from 1876 to 1892.

Conkling was even more typical, described by the *New York Times* as "a man by whose career and character the future will judge of the political standards of the present." A stalwart Republican who dispensed lucrative jobs at the New York customhouse, Conkling spent most of his career bickering over patronage. He opposed liberal Republican civil service reformers, who wanted government jobs based on merit rather than party loyalty. Conkling could imagine no other purpose of politics than rewarding the faithful, and he accused reformers of wanting the jobs for themselves. "Their real object is office and plunder." His career ended fittingly when he resigned from the Senate in a patronage dispute. Though Conkling served in Congress for over two decades, he never drafted a bill.

Legislation was not Congress's primary purpose. In 1879, a disgusted student of legislative politics,

Woodrow Wilson, described the degradation of Gilded Age politics: "No leaders, no principles; no principles, no parties." The two parties diverged mostly over patronage rather than principles. At stake in elections were not laws but thousands of government jobs. A British observer, Lord Bryce, concluded that the most cohesive force in American politics was the "desire for office and for office as a means of gain." The two parties, like two bottles of liquor, Bryce said, bore different labels, yet "each was empty."

Yet these characterizations were not entirely accurate. There were differences, which party professionals emphasized to solidify their popular base. Party affiliation generally reflected interest in both economic and in cultural, religious, and ethnic questions. Republican votes came from northeastern Yankee industrial interests along with New England and Scandinavian Lutheran farming migrants across the Upper Midwest. Democrats depended on southern whites, northern workers, and urban immigrants. Because the Republican Party had proved its willingness in the past to mobilize the power of the state to reshape society, people who wished to regulate moral as well as economic power were attracted to it. White southerners and Irish and German Catholics preferred the Democratic party because it opposed government efforts to regulate morals. Said one Chicago Democrat, "A Republican is a man who wants you t' go t' church every Sunday. A Democrat says if a man want t' have a glass of beer on Sunday he can have it."

For a few years, Civil War and Reconstruction issues generated party differences. But after 1876, the two parties were evenly matched, and they avoided controversial stands on national issues. In three of the five presidential elections between 1876 and 1892, a mere 1 percent of the vote separated the two major candidates. In 1880, James Garfield won by only 7,018 votes; in 1884, Grover Cleveland squeaked past Blaine by a popular vote margin of 48.5 to 48.2 percent. In two elections (1876 and 1888), the electoral vote winner had fewer popular votes. Further evidence of political stalemate was that only twice, each time for only two years, did one party control the White House and both houses of Congress. Although all the presidents in the era except Cleveland were Republicans, the Democrats controlled the House of Representatives in eight of the ten sessions of Congress between 1875 and 1895.

Gilded Age presidents were undistinguished and, like Washington, D.C., itself, played a minor role in national life. None of them—Hayes (1877–1881), Garfield (1881), Chester A. Arthur (1881–1885), Cleveland (1885–1889 and 1893–1897), and Benjamin Harrison (1889–1893)—served two consecutive

Presidential Elections, 1872–1892

A British observer of American politics, James Bryce, said in 1888 that "the American usually votes with his party, right or wrong, and the fact that there is little distinction of view between the parties makes it easier to stick to your old friends." To what extent does this chart show that American voters stuck to their party? How close were the elections? What was the usual percent difference? In which two elections did the popular vote winner, as in 2000, lose the election? Are parties today more alike or unalike those from the late nineteenth century?

Year	Candidate	Party	Popular Vote	Electoral Vote
1872	ULYSSES S. GRANT	Republican	3,596,745 (56%)	286
	Horace Greeley*	Democrat	2,843,446 (44%)	0*
1876	Samuel J. Tilden	Democrat	4,284,020 (51%)	184
	RUTHERFORD B. HAYES	Republican	4,036,572 (48%)	185
1880	JAMES A. GARFIELD	Republican	4,449,053 (48.5%)	214
	Winfield S. Hancock	Democrat	4,442,035 (48.1%)	155
	James B. Weaver	Greenback-Labor	308,578	0
1884	GROVER CLEVELAND	Democrat	4,911,017 (48.5%)	219
	James G. Blaine	Republican	4,848,334 (48.2%)	182
	Minor parties		325,739 (03.3%)	0
1888	Grover Cleveland	Democrat	5,540,050 (48.6%)	168
	BENJAMIN HARRISON	Republican	5,444,337 (47.9%)	233
	Minor parties		396,441 (03.5%)	0
1892	GROVER CLEVELAND	Democrat	5,554,414 (46%)	277
	Benjamin Harrison	Republican	5,190,802 (43%)	145
	James B. Weaver	Populist	1,027,329 (9%)	22

*Greeley died before the electoral college met.

Note: Winners names are in capital letters.

terms. None was strongly identified with any particular issue. None has been highly regarded by historians. Garfield is remembered primarily for being shot by a disappointed office seeker and by hanging on for two and a half months before he died. Although he was the only Democrat in the group, Cleveland differed little from the Republicans. Upon Cleveland's election in 1884, financier Jay Gould sent him a telegram stating that "the vast business interests of the country will be entirely safe in your hands." When Cleveland threatened that image by calling for a lower tariff in 1887, Congress did nothing, and voters turned him out of office a year later.

National Issues

Four issues were important at the national level in the Gilded Age: the tariff, money, civil service, and government regulation of railroads. In confronting these issues, legislators tried to serve both their own self-interest and the national interest of an efficient, productive, growing economy.

The tariff was one issue where party, as well as regional attitudes toward the use of government power, made some difference. Republicans wanted government to support business interests; they stood for a high tariff to protect businessmen, wage earners, and farmers from foreign competition. Democrats demanded a low tariff because "the government is best which governs least." But politicians accommodated local interests when it came to tariffs. Democratic senator Daniel Vorhees of Indiana explained, "I am a protectionist for every interest which I am sent here by my constituents to protect."

Tariff revisions were bewilderingly complex as legislators catered to many special interests that one senator described as "not far from disgusting." Most tariffs included a mixture of higher and lower rates that defied understanding. The federal government depended on tariffs and excise taxes (primarily on tobacco and liquor) for most of its revenue, so there was little chance that the tariff would be abolished or substantially lowered. Moreover, surpluses produced by the tariff during the Gilded Age helped the parties finance patronage jobs and government programs.

The money question was even more complicated. During the Civil War, the federal government had circulated paper money (greenbacks) that could not be exchanged for gold or silver (specie). In the late 1860s and 1870s, politicians debated whether the United States should return to a metallic standard, which would allow paper money to be exchanged for specie. "Hard-money" advocates supported either withdrawing all paper money from circulation or making it convertible to specie. They

opposed increasing the volume of money, fearing inflation. "Soft money" Greenbackers argued that there was not enough currency in circulation for an expanding economy and urged increasing the supply of paper money in order to raise farm prices and cut interest rates.

Hard-money interests had more clout. In 1873, Congress demonetized silver. In 1875, it passed the Specie Resumption Act, gradually retiring greenbacks from circulation and putting the nation firmly on the gold standard. But as large supplies of silver were mined in the West, pressure resumed for increasing the money supply by coining silver. Soft-money advocates pushed for the unlimited coinage of silver in addition to gold. In an 1878 compromise, the Treasury was required to buy between $2 million and $4 million of silver each month and to coin it as silver dollars. Despite this increase in the money supply, the period was not inflationary. Prices fell, disappointing supporters of soft money. They pushed for more silver, continuing the controversy into the 1890s.

As Henry Adams observed, the issue of civil service reform was a "subject almost as dangerous in political conversation in Washington as slavery itself in the old days before the war." The worst feature of the spoils system was that parties financed themselves by assessing holders of patronage jobs often as much as 1 percent of their annual salaries. Reformers, mostly genteel, native-born, white Protestants, demanded competitive examinations to create an honest and professional civil service—but also one that would bar immigrants and their urban political machine bosses from the spoils of office.

Although patronage was an expected part of national politics, when Garfield was assassinated by a crazed office-seeker, even a Republican politician (who knew the vice president's connection with the Conkling machine) couldn't help exclaiming, "My God! Chet Arthur in the White House!" But Arthur surprised doubters by being a capable and dignified president who was responsive to growing demands for civil service reform. Congress found itself forced into passing the Pendleton Act of 1883, mandating merit examinations for about one-tenth of federal offices. Gradually, more bureaucrats fell under its coverage, but parties became no more honest. As campaign contributions from government employees dried up, parties turned to huge corporate contributions that in 1888 helped elect Benjamin Harrison.

The Lure of Local Politics

The fact that the major parties did not disagree substantially on issues like money and civil service does not mean that nineteenth-century Americans

Although the tariff protectionist Harrison defeated Cleveland in 1888 (the results were reversed in 1892), all Gilded Age presidents were essentially "preservers" rather than innovators. None had approached the greatness of Washington, Lincoln, and the other Republican presidents hovering over Harrison and Morton in this illustration. *(Library of Congress)* In a second image from 1888, titled *The Presidential B.B. Club*, politics and business are merged in a tobacco advertisement, which shows Cleveland the fielder tagging out Harrison the batter—true enough for the election of 1892 but not for 1888, which Harrison won. *(From the collection of David J. and Janice L. Frent)*

found politics dull. Far more eligible voters turned out in the late nineteenth century than at any time since. The 78.5 percent average turnout to vote for president in the 1880s contrasts sharply with the near–50 percent of eligible Americans who voted in 1996 and 2000.

American men were drawn to the polls in part by the hoopla of party parades, buttons, and banners, but also by local issues. Voters expressed strong interest in emotional issues of race, religion, nationality, and alcohol, which often overrode economic self-interest. Iowa farmers favored curbing the power of the railroads to set high grain-shipping rates, but they also turned out to vote for temperance and compulsory education laws. Irish Catholics in New York wanted support for parochial schools, while third-generation, middle-class American Protestants from Illinois and Connecticut voted for laws compelling attendance at public schools. Nashville whites supported laws that established segregated railroad cars and other public facilities. Ohio and Indiana Protestants urged laws against drinking to protect social order and morality against hard-drinking Catholics, while German-Catholic Milwaukee brewery workers, cherishing

both their jobs and their beer, voted against local temperance laws.

The new urban immigrants played a large role in stimulating political participation. As traditional native-born elites left local government for more lucrative and higher-status business careers, urban bosses stepped in. Their control rested on their ability to deliver the immigrant vote, which they secured by operating informal welfare systems. Bosses like "Big Tim" Sullivan of New York and "Hinky Dink" Kenna of Chicago handed out jobs and money for rent, fuel, and bail. Sullivan gave birthday shoes to poor children in his district and turkeys to poor families at Thanksgiving. Thus, party bosses provided a personal touch in a strange and forbidding environment. As one explained, "I think that there's got to be in every ward somebody that any bloke can come to—no matter what he's done—and get help."

New York City's Tammany Hall boss, George Washington Plunkitt, perfected the relationship of mutual self-interest with his constituents. The favors he provided in return for votes ranged from attending weddings and funerals to influencing police and the courts. His clients not only included Jewish brides, Italian mourners, and burned-out tenants

Women, often targets of drunken male violence, campaigned for temperance as well as for equal rights. Here Victoria Claflin Woodhull reads a suffrage proposal to the House Judiciary Committee in 1871. If denied the vote, she vowed that women "mean secession, and on a thousand times grander scale than was that of the South. We are plotting a revolution; we will overthrow this bogus Republic and plant a government of righteousness in its stead." *(Library of Congress)*

but also job seekers, store owners, saloon keepers, and madams, all of whom needed favors.

Party leaders also won votes by making politics exciting. The parades, rallies, buttons, songs, and oratory of late-nineteenth-century campaigns generated excitement even when substantive issues were not at stake. In the election of 1884, for example, emotions ran high over the moral lapses of the opposition candidate. The Democrats made much of Blaine's record of dishonesty, chanting in election eve parades and rallies: "Blaine! Blaine! James G. Blaine! / Continental liar from the state of Maine!" Republicans mocked Cleveland's illegitimate child with their own chant: "Ma! Ma! Where's my pa? / Gone to the White House, Ha! Ha! Ha!" Cleveland won in part because an unwise Republican clergyman called the Democrats the party of "rum, Romanism, and rebellion" on election eve in New York. The remark backfired, and the Republicans lost both New York, which should have been a safe state, and the election.

Race, religion, and class often played a strong role in local politics. New Mexico, for example, was marked for 20 years by the corrupt land grabs of the Santa Fe ring, a small group of Anglo-Protestant Republican bankers, lawyers, and politicians who exploited anti-Mexican and anti-Catholic sentiments. The ring controlled judges, legislators, and the business interests of the state, as well as many Spanish-speaking voters. In the late 1880s, desperate Mexican-American tenant farmers turned to violence, which the ring manipulated to dispossess

Mexican Americans, Indians, and even white squatters from enormous tracts of land.

The New Mexico events showed the power of race and religion in local politics. Prohibition also provoked spirited local contests. Many Americans considered drinking a serious social problem. Annual consumption of brewery beer had risen from 2.7 gallons per capita in 1850 to 17.9 in 1880. In one city, saloons outnumbered churches 31 to 1. Such statistics shocked those who believed that drinking would destroy character, corrupt politics, and cause poverty, crime, and unrestrained sexual-

Grover Cleveland's hypocrisy as "Grover the Good" is lampooned by this cartoon from the election of 1884 showing a tearful mother with Cleveland's "illegitimate" child. The people elected him anyway. *(The Granger Collection, New York)*

ity. Because they were often the targets of violent, drunken men, women especially supported temperance. Rather than try to persuade individuals to give up drink, as the pre–Civil War temperance movement had done, many now sought to stop drinking by making it illegal.

The battle in San Jose, California, illustrates the strong passions such efforts aroused. In the 1870s, temperance reformers put on the ballot a local option referendum to ban the sale of liquor in San Jose. Women, using their influence as guardians of morality, erected a temperance tent, where they held conspicuous daily meetings. Despite denunciations from clergymen and heckling from some local drinkers, the women refused to retreat to their homes. On election eve, a large crowd appeared at the temperance tent, but a larger one turned up at a pro-liquor rally. In the morning, women roamed the streets, urging men to adopt the referendum. Children marched to the polls and saloons, singing, "Father, dear father, come home with me now." By afternoon, the mood grew ugly; the women were harassed and threatened by drunken men, and the proposal lost by a vote of 1,430 to 918.

Emotional conflicts in the 1880s also boiled at the state level over issues like education. As Catholics in Boston and New York sought political support for parochial schools, Protestant Republicans in Iowa, Illinois, and Wisconsin sponsored laws mandating that children attend "some public or private day school" where instruction was in English, an early (but not the last) movement for English-only education. These laws aimed to undermine parochial schools, which taught in the language of the immigrants. In Iowa, where a state prohibition law also passed, the Republican slogan was "A schoolhouse on every hill, and no saloon in the valley." Local Republicans bragged that "Iowa will go Democratic when hell goes Methodist," and indeed they won. But in Wisconsin, a law for compulsory school attendance was so strongly anti-Catholic that it backfired. Many voters, disillusioned with pious Republican moralisms, began shifting to the Democratic party.

MIDDLE-CLASS REFORM

Most middle-class Americans avoided reformist politics. But urban corruption, poverty, and labor violence frightened many out of their aversion to politics. They worried that their absence from political discourse was having a negative effect on the morality of American life.

Frances Willard and the Women's Christian Temperance Union (WCTU) is an example. As president of the WCTU from 1879 until 1898, Willard headed the largest women's organization in the country. Most WCTU members were churchgoing, white, Protestant women who believed drunkenness caused poverty and family violence. But after 1886, the WCTU reversed its position, attributing drunkenness to poverty, unemployment, and bad labor conditions. Willard joined the Knights of Labor in 1887 and by the 1890s had influenced the WCTU to extend its programs to alleviate the problems of workers, particularly women and children.

The Gospel of Wealth and Social Darwinism

Willard called herself a Christian socialist because she believed in applying the ethical principles of Jesus to economic life. For her and many other educated, middle-class reformers, Christianity called for a cooperative social order that would reduce inequalities of wealth. But for most Gilded Age Americans, Christianity was seen to support the competitive individualistic ethic. Leading ministers preached sermons and wrote treatises justifying class divisions and the moral superiority of the wealthy. Episcopal Bishop William Lawrence wrote that it was "God's will that some men should attain great wealth." Philadelphia Baptist preacher Russell Conwell's famous sermon "Acres of Diamonds," delivered 6,000 times to an estimated 13 million listeners, praised riches as a sure sign of "godliness" and stressed the power of money to "do good."

Industrialist Andrew Carnegie expressed the ethic most clearly. In the article "The Gospel of Wealth" (1889), Carnegie celebrated competition for producing better goods at lower prices. The concentration of wealth in a few hands, he concluded, was "not only beneficial but essential to the future of the race." The fittest would bring order and efficiency out of the chaos of rapid industrialization. Carnegie's defense of the new economic order in his book *Triumphant Democracy* (1886) found as many supporters as Bellamy's *Looking Backward*, partly because Carnegie insisted that the rich must spend some of their wealth to benefit their "poorer brethren." Carnegie built hundreds of libraries, many still operating in large and small towns throughout the United States, and in later years turned his philanthropic attentions to world peace.

Carnegie's ideas about wealth were drawn from an ideology known as social Darwinism, based on the work of English naturalist Charles Darwin, whose *Origin of Species* was published in 1859. Darwin had concluded that plant and animal

The luxury of a fashionable bedroom with a chandelier, elegant furniture, and fancy curtains was accessible to anyone who worked hard, according to advocates of the gospel of wealth and social Darwinism. The successful elite, illustrated here by the bedroom in Alexander Stewart's Fifth Avenue mansion, represented society's "fittest" element. *(Brown Brothers)* This contrasted with poor immigrants forced to live in crowded, filthy, unhealthy, one-room tenements on New York's Lower East Side. *(International Museum of Photography/George Eastman House)*

species evolved through natural selection. In the struggle for existence, some species managed to adapt to their environment and survived; others failed to adapt and perished. Herbert Spencer, an English social philosopher, applied this "survival of the fittest" notion to human society. Progress, Spencer said, resulted from relentless competition in which the weak were eliminated and the strong climbed to the top, as in Bellamy's coach. Spencer warned against any interference in the economic world by tampering with the natural laws of selection: "The whole effort of nature is to get rid of such as are unfit, to clear the world of them, and make room for better."

When Spencer visited the United States in 1882, leading men of business, science, religion, and politics thronged to honor him with a lavish banquet in New York City. Here was the man whose theories justified their amassed fortunes as men of "superior ability, foresight, and adaptability," and they praised him as the founder not only of a new sociology but also of a new religion. Spencer's American followers, like Carnegie and Yale political economist William Graham Sumner, insisted that poverty resulted from the struggle for existence and that attempts to end it were pointless, if not immoral. To take power or money away from millionaires, Sumner scoffed, was

"like killing off our generals in war." It was "absurd," he wrote, to pass laws permitting society's "worst members" to survive, or to "sit down with a slate and pencil to plan out a new social world."

The scientific vocabulary of social Darwinism injected scientific rationality into what often seemed a baffling economic order. Sumner and Spencer argued that underlying laws of political economy, like those of the natural world, dictated economic affairs. Social Darwinists also believed in the superiority of the Anglo-Saxon race, which they maintained had reached the highest stage of evolution. Their theories were used to justify race supremacy and imperialism (see Chapter 20), as well as the monopolistic efforts of American businessmen. "The growth of a large business," John D. Rockefeller, Jr., told a YMCA class in Cleveland, like the growth of "the American beauty rose," happens "only by sacrificing the early buds which grow up around it." This was, he said, "merely the working out of a law of nature and a law of God."

Reform Darwinism and Pragmatism

Others questioned social Darwinism. Brooks Adams, Henry's brother, wrote that social philosophers like Spencer and Sumner were "hired by the comfortable classes to prove that everything was all right."

Fading aristocrats like the Adams family, increasingly displaced by a new industrial elite, may have felt a touch of envy for the new rich. They succeeded, however, in suggesting that possibilities for social change were not as closed as the social Darwinists claimed.

Intellectual reformers directly challenged the gloomy social Darwinian notion that nothing could be done to alleviate poverty and injustice. With roots in antebellum abolitionism, women's rights, and other crusades for social justice, men like Wendell Phillips, Frederick Douglass, and Franklin Sanborn and women like Elizabeth Cady Stanton and Susan B. Anthony transferred their reform fervor to post-bellum issues. Sanborn, for example, an Emersonian Transcendentalist, founded the American Social Science Association in 1865 to "treat wisely the great social problems of the day." As an early advocate of serious social scientific research as well as the Massachusetts inspector of charities in the 1880s, Sanborn became known as the "leading social worker of his day."

Reformer Henry George, who was not a social scientist, nevertheless observed that wherever the highest degree of "material progress" had been realized, "we find the deepest poverty." George's book *Progress and Poverty* (1879) dramatically showed the contradictions of American life. Along with Bellamy's *Looking Backward*, it was the most influential book of the age, selling 2 million copies by 1905. George admitted that economic growth had produced wonders, but he pointed out the social costs and the loss of Christian values. His remedy was to break up land-holding monopolists who profited from the increasing value of their land, which they rented to those who actually did the work. He proposed a "single tax" on the unearned increases in land value received by landlords.

George's solution may seem simplistic, but his religious tone and optimistic faith in the capacity of humans to effect change appealed to many middle-class intellectuals. Some went further, developing social scientific models to justify reform. Sociologist Lester Frank Ward and economist Richard T. Ely both found examples of cooperation in nature and demonstrated that competition and laissez-faire had proved both wasteful and inhumane. Reform Darwinists urged an economic order marked by cooperation and regulation.

Two pragmatists, John Dewey and William James, established a philosophical foundation for reform. James, a Harvard professor, argued that while environment was important, so was human will. People could influence the course of human events. "What is the 'cash value' of a thought, idea, or belief?"

James asked. What was its result? "The ultimate test for us of what a truth means," he suggested, was in the "consequences" of a particular idea and what kind of moral "conduct it dictates." He argued that expressions of human sympathy and opposition to international wars were appropriate examples of conduct with ethical consequences.

James and young social scientists like Ward and Ely gathered statistics documenting social wrongs and rejected the social determinism of Spencer and Sumner. They argued that the application of intelligence and human agency could change the "survival of the fittest" into the "fitting of as many as possible to survive." Their position encouraged educators, economists, and reformers of every stripe, giving them an intellectual justification to struggle against misery and inequalities of wealth.

Settlements and Social Gospel

Jane Addams saw the gap between progress and poverty in the streets of Chicago in the winter of 1893. "The stream of laboring people goes past you," she wrote, and "your heart sinks with a sudden sense of futility." Addams had long been aware that life in big cities for working-class families was bitter and hard. Born in rural Illinois, she founded Hull House in Chicago in 1889 "to aid in the solution of the social and industrial problems which are engendered by the modern conditions of life in a great city." Wellesley literature professor Vida Scudder also "felt the agitating and painful vibrations" of urban poverty. Influenced by British reformers who were agitating for urban housing and health reforms, she committed her life to easing the suffering of the poor. In 1889, Scudder and six other Smith College graduates formed an organization of college women to work in settlement houses.

Middle-class activists like Addams and Scudder worried about social conditions, particularly the degradation of life and labor in America's cities, factories, and farms. They were influenced by middle-class English socialists; by European social prophets like Karl Marx, Leo Tolstoy, and Victor Hugo; by Americans such as Emerson, Whitman, George, and Bellamy; and by the ethical teachings of Jesus. Their message was highly idealistic, ethical, and Christian. They preferred a society marked by cooperation rather than competition—where, as they liked to say, people were guided by the "golden rule rather than the rule of gold." Like Frances Willard, they meant to apply the ethics of Jesus to industrial and urban life in order to bring about the kingdom of heaven on earth. Some preferred to put their goals in more secular terms; they spoke of radically transforming American society. Most, however,

In the settlement houses, immigrant women learned English along with proper cooking, hygiene, child care, and other American domestic practices. *(U.S. Government Education Bureau of the National Geographic Image Collection)* The settlements also included public health clinics, like this one at Vida Scudder's Denison House in Boston. Settlement house work, Scudder wrote, fulfilled "a biting curiosity about the way the Other Half lived, and a strange hunger for fellowship with them." *(Schlesinger Library, Radcliffe Institute, Harvard University)*

worked within existing institutions. As middle-class intellectuals and professionals, they tended to stress an educational approach to problems. But they were also practical, seeking tangible improvements by crusading for tenement-house and factory-conditions legislation, mediating labor disputes, and living among the poor people they helped.

The settlement house movement typified 1890s middle-class reformers' blend of idealism and practicality. Addams's Hull House in Chicago, Scudder's Denison House in Boston, and Lillian Wald's "house on Henry Street" in New York were the models. The primary purpose of settlement houses was to help immigrant families, especially women, adapt Old World rural styles of childbearing, child care, and housekeeping to American urban life. They launched day nurseries, kindergartens, and boarding rooms for immigrant working women; they offered classes in sewing, cooking, nutrition, health care, and English; and they tried to keep young people out of saloons by organizing sports clubs and coffeehouses.

A second purpose of the settlement house movement was to give college-educated women meaningful work at a time when they faced professional barriers and to allow them to preserve the strong feelings of sacrifice and sisterhood they had experienced at college. As Scudder explained, settlement house workers were like "early Christians" in their renunciation of worldly goods and dedication to a life of service. A third goal was to gather data exposing social misery in order to spur legislative action—developing city building codes for tenements, abolishing child labor, and improving factory safety. Hull

House, Addams said, was intended in part "to investigate and improve the conditions in the industrial districts of Chicago."

The settlement house movement, with its dual emphasis on the scientific gathering of facts and spiritual commitment, nourished the new discipline of sociology, which was first taught in divinity schools. Many organizations were founded to blend Christian belief and academic study in an attempt to change society along Christian collectivist lines. One was the American Institute of Christian Sociology, founded in 1893 by Josiah Strong, a Congregational minister, and economist Richard T. Ely. Influenced by British models, they formed organizations like the Christian Social Union, the Church Association for the Advancement of the Interests of Labor, and the Society of Christian Socialists.

Dwight Moody preached a more traditional Christianity in American cities, where he led hundreds of urban revivals in the 1870s. Discovering his mission while in England for the YMCA, Moody mastered the art of the folksy sermon filled with Bible and family stories, the easy path from sin to salvation by filling out a decision card, and the importance of music in making converts. The revivals appealed to lower-class, rural folk who had been forced to the city by economic ruin. Supported by businessmen who felt that religion would make workers and immigrants more docile, Moody's revivalist "passion for souls" provided a safe community in the midst of urban confusion. Revivalism helped to nearly double evangelical Protestant church membership in the last two decades of the century. Although some urban workers drifted into secular faiths like social-ism, most embraced the old-time religion.

Many Protestant ministers preferred the Social Gospel movement of the 1890s, which tied salvation to social betterment. Like settlement house workers, these religious leaders sought to make Christianity relevant to urban problems. Congregational minister Washington Gladden advocated collective bargaining and corporate profit sharing in books such as *Working Men and Their Employers, Social Salvation,* and *Applied Christianity.* Walter Rauschenbusch, a young Baptist minister in the notorious Hell's Kitchen area of New York City, raised an even louder voice. Often called on to conduct funeral services for children killed by the airless, diseased tenements and sweatshops, Rauschenbusch scathingly attacked capitalism and church ignorance of socioeconomic issues. His progressive ideas for social justice and a welfare state were later published in two landmark books: *Christianity and the Social Crisis* (1907) and *Christianizing the Social Order* (1912).

Perhaps the most influential book promoting social Christianity was the best-selling novel *In His Steps,* published in 1896 by Charles Sheldon. The novel portrayed the dramatic changes made possible by a few community leaders who resolved to base all their actions on a single question: "What would Jesus do?" For a minister, this meant seeking to "bridge the chasm between the church and labor." For the idle rich, it meant settlement house work and reforming prostitutes. For landlords and factory owners, it meant improving the living and working conditions of tenants and laborers. A city election pitting these middle-class reformers against seedy saloon interests and corrupt urban political machines was the crucial event in the novel. Although filled with naive sentimentality characteristic of much of the Social Gospel, *In His Steps* prepared thousands of influential, middle-class Americans for progressive civic leadership.

Reforming the City

No late-nineteenth-century institution needed reforming more than urban government, called by the president of Cornell "the worst in Christendom—the most expensive, the most inefficient, and the most corrupt." A Philadelphia committee pointed to years of "inefficiency, waste, badly paved and filthy streets, unwholesome and offensive water, and slovenly and costly management." New York and Chicago, where cholera and typhoid epidemics resulted from raw sewage poured into Lake Michigan, were even worse, rivaling the appalling sewage, wa-ter, and health conditions in European cities like London, Frankfort, and Rome.

Creating a "city beautiful" through environmental remedies was one approach to cleaning up dirty cities. Urban planners and landscape architects attempted to counteract pollution and reshape the urban environment by putting in water mains and sewers, planting trees along broadened boulevards, expanding city parks, and erecting monumental public buildings—libraries, museums, theaters, and music halls. Cities could become centers of culture. Boston filled in over 500 acres of tidal flats in the Back Bay and elsewhere around the core of the city and created an elegant upper-class neighborhood along tree-lined Commonwealth Avenue.

Such environmental transformations of urban space, however beautiful, rarely reached the squalid sections of the city inhabited by the urban masses, who lived in crowded tenement house districts on narrow, dirty streets filled with people, garbage, and animals pulling streetcars and food and clothing carts. Although the "city beautiful" movement was intended to benefit poor as well as rich, it hardly touched these slums, which looked worse by contrast, especially as the influx of rural transplants and European immigrants increased.

Rapid urban growth swamped city leaders with new demands for service. Flush toilets, thirsty horses pulling street railways, and industrial users of water, for example, all exhausted the capacity of municipal waterworks built for an earlier age. As city governments struggled, they raised taxes and incurred vast debts, which bred graft and the rise of the boss. Urban bosses dispensed patronage jobs in return for votes and contributions to the party machine. They awarded street railway, gas line, and other utility franchises and construction contracts to local businesses in return for kickbacks and other favors. They tipped off friendly real estate men about the location of projected city improvements, and they received favors from the owners of saloons, brothels, and gambling clubs in return for help with police protection, bail, and influence with the judges. These institutions were vital to the urban economy and played an important role in easing the immigrants' way into American life. For many young women, prostitution was a means of economic survival. For men, the saloon was the center of social life and a source of cheap meals and job leads.

Bossism deeply offended middle-class urban reformers, unkindly dubbed "goo-goos" for their advocacy of good government. They opposed not only graft and vice but also the perversion of democracy

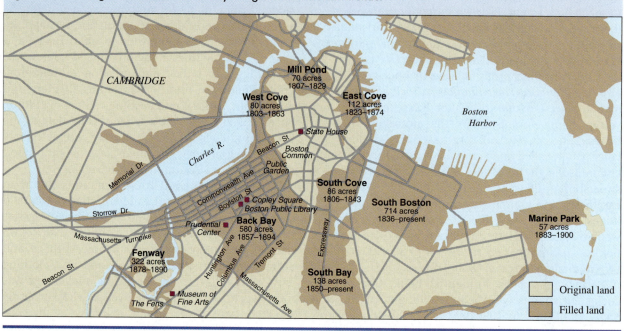

The City Beautiful: Enlarging Boston

As part of the "city beautiful" movement, Boston filled in coastal, swampy lowlands with gravel, thus adding the fashionable Back Bay along Commonwealth Avenue.

by the exploitation of ignorant immigrants. The immigrants, said one, "follow blindly leaders of their own race, are not moved by discussion, and exercise no judgment of their own"—and so were "not fit for the suffrage."

Urban reformers' programs were similar in most cities. They not only advocated the "Americanization" of immigrants in public schools (and opposed parochial schooling) but also formed clubs and voters' leagues to discuss the failings of municipal government. They delighted in making spectacular exposures of electoral irregularities and large-scale graft. These discoveries led to strident calls for replacing the mayor, often an Irish Catholic, with an Anglo-Saxon Protestant reformer.

Politics colored every reform issue. Many Anglo-Saxon men favored prohibition partly to remove ethnic saloon-owner influence from politics and supported woman suffrage partly to gain a middle-class political advantage against male immigrant voters. Most urban reformers could barely hide their distaste for the "city proletariat mob," as one put it. They proposed replacing the bosses with expert city managers, who would bring honest professionalism to city government. They hoped to make government cheaper and thereby lower taxes, which ironically ended up cutting services to the poor. Another unexpected consequence was to disfranchise work-

ing-class and ethnic groups, whose political participation depended on the old ward-boss system.

Not all urban reformers were elitist. Toledo mayor Samuel Jones, for example, opposed bossism and passionately advocated political participation by urban immigrants. He had begun as a poor Welsh immigrant in the Pennsylvania oil fields and, in the rags-to-riches tradition, had worked his way up to the ownership of several oil fields and a factory in Toledo. Once successful, however, Jones espoused a different ethic from Carnegie's "Gospel of Wealth." Influenced by a combination of firsthand contact with the "piteous appeals" of unemployed workers and by his reading of Emerson, Whitman, Tolstoy, and the New Testament, Jones called himself "the Golden Rule man."

In 1894, Jones resolved that he would "apply the Golden Rule as a rule of conduct" in his factory. He instituted an eight-hour day, a $2 minimum daily wage (50 to 75 cents higher than the local average for ten hours), a cooperative insurance program, and an annual 5 percent Christmas dividend. Plastering the Golden Rule over his factory walls, Jones hired former criminals and social outcasts. He anticipated twentieth-century industrial reforms by creating a company cafeteria offering a hot lunch for 15 cents, a Golden Rule Park for workers and their families, employee music groups, and a

As critically portrayed in many cartoons by Thomas Nast, William "Boss" Tweed was head of New York City's corrupt Democratic party organization, Tammany Hall. Tweed typified bossism in its cynical disregard for morality, truth, and accurate ballot counting. Here he is saying: "As long as I count the Votes, what are you going to do about it? say?" Well, Nast did a lot about it in his cartoons. (Harper's Weekly, *September 5, 1868*)

Golden Rule Hall, where he invited social visionaries to speak.

In 1897, he was elected to the first of an unprecedented four terms as mayor. A maverick Republican, Jones antagonized prominent citizens and was adored by ordinary people. He advocated municipal ownership of utilities; public works jobs and housing for the unemployed; more civic parks and playgrounds with free pools, skating rinks, and sleigh rides; and vocational education and kindergartens. Although few of these reforms were implemented, as a pacifist mayor, he took away policemen's sidearms and heavy clubs. In police court, he regularly dismissed most cases of petty theft and drunkenness on grounds that the accused were victims of social injustice, and he usually released prostitutes after fining every man in the room 10 cents—and himself a dollar—for condoning prostitution. Crime in notoriously sinful Toledo fell during his term. When "Golden Rule" Jones died in 1904, nearly 55,000 people, "tears streaming down their faces," filed past his coffin.

The Struggle for Woman Suffrage

Women served, in Jane Addams's phrase, as "urban housekeepers" in the settlement house and good government movements, which reflected the tension many women felt between their public and private lives, that is, between their obligations to self, family, and society. This tension was seldom expressed openly. A few women writers, however, began to vent the frustrations of middle-class domestic life. In her novel *The Awakening* (1899), Kate Chopin told the story of a young woman who, in awakening to her own sexuality and life's possibilities beyond being a "mother-woman," defied conventional expectations of a woman's role. Her sexual affair and eventual suicide prompted a St. Louis newspaper to label the novel "poison."

Some middle-class women (for example, Addams and Scudder) avoided marriage, preferring the nurturing relationships found in the female settlement house community. "Married life looks to me . . . terribly impoverished for women," a Smith College graduate observed, adding, "most of my deeper friendships have been with women." A few women boldly advocated free love or, less openly, formed lesbian relationships. Although most preferred traditional marriages and chose not to work outside the home, the generation of women that came of age in the 1890s married less—and later—than any other in American history.

Many women reconciled the conflicting pressures between their private and public lives and deflected male criticism by seeing their work as maternal. Addams called Hull House the "great mother breast of our common humanity." Frances Willard told Susan B. Anthony in 1898 that "government is only housekeeping on the broadest scale," a job men had botched, requiring women's saving participation. A leading labor organizer was "Mother" Jones, and the fiery feminist anarchist Emma Goldman titled her monthly journal *Mother Earth.* By using nurturing language to describe their work, women furthered the very arguments used against them. Many remained economically dependent on men, and all women still lacked the essential rights of citizenship. How could they be municipal housekeepers if they could not yet even vote?

After the Seneca Falls Convention in 1848, women's civil and political rights advanced very slowly. Although several western states gave women the right to vote in municipal and school board elections, before 1890 only the territory of Wyoming (1869) granted full political equality. Colorado, Utah, and Idaho enfranchised women in the 1890s, but no other states granted suffrage until 1910. This slow pace resulted in part from an anti-suffrage

The young Jane Addams was one of the college-educated women who chose to remain unmarried and pursue a career as an "urban housekeeper" and social reformer, serving immigrant families in the Chicago neighborhood near her Hull House. *(Jane Addams Memorial Collection, [JAMC neg. 21], Special Collections, University Library, University of Illinois at Chicago)*

movement led by an odd combination of ministers, saloon interests, and men threatened in various ways by women's voting rights. "Equal suffrage," said a Texas senator, "is a repudiation of manhood."

In the 1890s, leading suffragists reexamined the situation. The two wings of the women's rights movement, split since 1869, combined in 1890 as the National American Woman Suffrage Association (NAWSA). Although Elizabeth Cady Stanton and Susan B. Anthony continued to head the association, both were in their seventies. Stanton's *Woman's Bible* (1895), a devastating attack on the religious argument against woman suffrage, embarrassed many younger women. At the NAWSA convention in 1896, despite the pleas of Anthony not to "sit in judgment" on her good friend, a resolution renouncing any NAWSA connection with Stanton's book passed by a vote of 53 to 41. That vote signaled the passage of leadership to younger, more moderate women who, unlike Stanton and Anthony, concentrated on the single issue of the vote.

Changing leadership meant a shift in the arguments for the suffrage. Since 1848, suffragists had argued primarily from the principle of "our republican idea, individual citizenship," as Stanton put it in 1892. But as Stanton's leadership waned, younger leaders shifted to three expedient arguments. The first was that women needed the vote to pass self-protection laws to guard against rapists and unsafe industrial work. The second argument, Addams's notion of urban housekeeping, pointed out that political enfranchisement would further women's role in cleaning up immoral cities and corrupt politics.

The third expedient argument reflected urban middle-class reformers' prejudice against non-Protestant immigrants. Machine bosses saw to it that immigrant men got to vote, sometimes several times in a day. Suffragists argued that educated, native-born American women should get the vote to counteract the undesirable influence of illiterate male immigrants. In an speech in Iowa in 1894, Carrie Chapman Catt, who would succeed Anthony as president of NAWSA in 1900, argued that the "Government is menaced with great danger . . . in the votes possessed by the males in the slums of the cities," a danger that could be averted only by cutting off that vote and giving it to women. In the new century, under the leadership of women like Catt, suffrage would finally be secured.

POLITICS IN THE PIVOTAL 1890s

Americans mistakenly think of the last decade of the nineteenth century as the "gay nineties," symbolized by mustached baseball players, sporty Gibson girls, and the opulent dinners of rich entrepreneurs. The 1890s was, indeed, a decade of sports and leisure, urban electrification, and the enormous wealth of the few. But for many more Americans, it was also a decade of dark tenements, grinding work, desperate unemployment, and poverty. The early 1890s, as seen in Chapters 17 and 18, saw protesting farmers; Wounded Knee and the "second great removal" of Native Americans; lynchings, disfranchisement, and segregation of blacks; and the "new immigration," a changing workplace, and devastating labor defeats at Coeur d'Alene, Homestead, and Pullman.

The 1890s, far from gay, were years of contrasts and crises. The obvious contrast, as Bellamy had anticipated, was between the rich and the poor. Supreme Court Justice John Harlan saw a "deep feeling of unrest" everywhere among people worrying that the nation was in "real danger from . . . the slavery that would result from aggregations of capital in the hands of a few." Populist "Sockless" Jerry Simpson simply saw a struggle between "the robbers and the robbed." On one side, Simpson saw "the allied hosts of monopolies, the money power, [and] great trusts . . . who seek the enactment of laws to benefit them and impoverish the people." On the other side, he put those "who produce wealth and bear the burdens of taxation. Between these two there is no middle ground."

Although Simpson was wrong about the absence of a middle ground, the gap was indeed huge between Kansas orator Mary E. Lease, who in 1890 said, "What you farmers need to do is to raise less corn, and more Hell," and the wealthy Indianapolis woman who told her husband, "I'm going to Europe and spend my money before these crazy people take it." The pivotal nature of the 1890s hinged on this feeling of polarizing unrest and upheaval as the nation underwent the traumas of change from a rural to an urban society. The new immigration from Europe and the internal migrations of African Americans and farmers added to the "great danger" against which Carrie Catt warned. The depression of 1893 widened the gap between rich and poor, accelerating demands for reform. The federal bureaucracy slowly began to adapt to the needs of governing a complex specialized society, and Congress purposefully moved to confront national problems.

Republican Legislation in the Early 1890s

Harrison's election in 1888 was accompanied by Republican control of both houses of Congress. As the English and Germans were enacting national health, housing, and social insurance laws,

The contrasts between rich and poor and the threat of social upheaval are dramatically illustrated in this turn-of-the-century work called *From the Depths. (Culver Pictures)*

American legislators in 1890 focused on five areas: Civil War veterans' pensions, trusts, tariffs, the money question, and rights for blacks. On the first issue, a bill providing generous support of $160 million a year for Union veterans and their dependents sailed through Congress.

The Sherman Anti-Trust Act passed with only one nay vote. It declared illegal "every contract, combination . . . or conspiracy in restraint of trade or commerce." Although the Sherman Act was vague and not really intended to break up big corporations, it was an initial attempt to restrain large business combinations. But in *United States* v. *E. C. Knight* (1895), the Supreme Court ruled that the American Sugar Refining Company, which controlled more than 90 percent of the nation's sugar-refining capacity, was not in violation of the Sherman Act.

A tariff bill, introduced in 1890 by Ohio Republican William McKinley, proposed raising tariffs higher than ever and stirred more controversy. As European nations moved away from a commitment to free trade and experienced heightened feelings of nationalism, they put in place protective measures that affected American interests. Despite heated opposition from agrarian interests, whose products were generally not protected, McKinley's bill passed the House and, after nearly 500 amendments, also the Senate.

Silver was trickier. Recognizing the appeal of free silver to agrarian debtors and organized farmers, Republican leaders feared that the issue might hurt their party. Senator Sherman proposed a compromise that momentarily satisfied almost everyone. The Sherman Silver Purchase Act ordered the Treasury to buy 4.5 million ounces of silver monthly and to issue Treasury notes for it. Silverites were pleased by the proposed increase in the money supply. Opponents felt they had averted the worst—free coinage of silver. The gold standard remained secure.

Republicans were also prepared to confront violations of the voting rights of southern blacks in 1890. As usual, political considerations paralleled moral ones. Since 1877, the South had become a Democratic stronghold, where party victories could be traced to fraud and intimidation of black Republican voters. "To be a Republican . . . in the South," one Georgian noted, "is to be a foolish martyr." Republican legislation, then, was intended to honor old commitments to freed male voters and improve party fortunes in the South. An elections bill proposed by Massachusetts Senator Henry Cabot Lodge sought to ensure African-American voter registration and fair elections. But a storm of Democratic disapproval arose, branding Lodge's measure the "Force Bill." Former president Cleveland called it a "dark blow at the freedom of the ballot," and the Mobile *Daily Register* claimed that it "would deluge the South in blood." Senate Democrats delayed action with a filibuster.

Meanwhile, in order to secure passage of the McKinley Tariff, Republican leaders bargained away the elections bill, ending major-party efforts to protect African-American voting rights in the South until the 1960s. In a second setback for black southerners, the Senate, fearful of giving the federal government a role in education, defeated a bill to provide federal aid to black schools in the South that received a disproportionately small share of local and state funds. These two failed measures signaled the end of the Republican party's commitment to the idealistic goals of Reconstruction. "The plain truth is," said the New York *Herald*, "the North has got tired of the negro," foreshadowing a similar retreat from civil rights legislation 100 years later.

The legislative efforts of the summer of 1890, impressive by nineteenth-century standards, fell far short of solving the nation's problems. Trusts grew more rapidly after the Sherman Act than before.

Union veterans were pleased with their pensions, but southerners were incensed that Confederate veterans were left out. Others, seeing the pension measure as extravagant, labeled the 51st Congress the "billion-dollar Congress." Despite efforts to please farmers, many still viewed tariff protection as a benefit primarily for eastern manufacturers. Farm prices continued to slide, and gold and silver advocates were only momentarily silenced. African-American rights were put off to another time. Polarizing inequalities of wealth remained. Nor did Republican legislative activism lead the Republicans to a "permanent tenure of power," as party leaders had hoped. Voters abandoned the GOP in droves in the 1890 congressional elections, dropping the Republican contingent in the House from 168 to 88.

Two years later, Cleveland won a presidential rematch with Harrison. "The lessons of paternalism ought to be unlearned," he said in his inaugural address, "and the better lesson taught that while the people should . . . support their government, its functions do not include the support of the people."

Formation of the People's Party, 1892

Farmers knew all too well that government did not support them. In February 1892, the People's, or Populist, party was established with Leonidas Polk, president of the National Farmers Alliance, as its presidential candidate. "The time has arrived," he thundered, "for the great West, the great South, and the great Northwest, to link their hands and hearts together and march to the ballot box and take possession of the government . . . and run it in the interest of the people." But by July, at the party convention in Omaha, Polk had died. Reflecting its Midwestern and southern alliance roots, the party nominated James B. Weaver, Union army veteran from Iowa, as its standard bearer and James G. Field, a former Confederate soldier, for vice president.

The platform preamble, which was written by Ignatius Donnelly, a Minnesota farmer, author, and politician, blazed with the urgent spirit of the agrarian protest movement:

> We meet in the midst of a nation brought to the verge of moral, political and material ruin. Corruption dominates the ballot box, the legislatures, the Congress, and touches even the ermine of the bench. The people are demoralized. . . . The fruits of the toil of millions are boldly stolen to build up colossal fortunes . . . we breed two great classes—paupers and millionaires.

To heal that divide, the charge was clear—to end "the controlling influences dominating the old political parties."

Major Legislative Activity of the Gilded Age

In the table, notice the kinds of issues dealt with at the national level as opposed to state and local. What does this suggest about the interests of the American people and how federalism worked in the late nineteenth century? Do you think the apparent division of governmental responsibilities made sense? How is it the same or different today?

Date	National
1871	National Civil Service Commission created
1873	Coinage Act demonetizes silver
	"Salary Grab" Act (increased salaries of Congress and top federal officials) partly repealed
1875	Specie Resumption Act retires greenback dollars
1878	Bland-Allison Act permits partial coining of silver
1882	Chinese Exclusion Act
	Federal Immigration Law restricts certain categories of immigrants and requires head tax of all immigrants
1883	Standard time (four time zones) established for the entire country
	Pendleton Civil Service Act
1887	Interstate Commerce Act sets up Interstate Commerce Commission
	Dawes Act divides Indian tribal lands into individual allotments
1890	Dependent Pension Act grants pensions to Union army veterans
	Sherman Anti-Trust Act
	Sherman Silver Purchase Act has government buy more silver
	McKinley Tariff sets high protective tariff
	Federal elections bill to protect black voting rights in South fails in Senate
	Blair bill to provide support for education defeated
1891	Immigration law gives federal government control of overseas immigration
1893	Sherman Silver Purchase Act repealed
1894	Wilson-Gorman Tariff lowers duties slightly
1900	Currency Act puts United States on gold standard

Date	State and Local
1850s–1880s	State and local laws intended to restrict or prohibit consumption of alcoholic beverages
1871	Illinois Railroad Act sets up railroad commission to fix rates and prohibit discrimination
1874	Railroad regulatory laws in Wisconsin and Iowa
1881	Kansas adopts statewide prohibition
1882	Iowa passes state prohibition amendment
1880s	Massachusetts, Connecticut, Rhode Island, Montana, Michigan, Ohio, and Missouri all pass local laws prohibiting consumption of alcohol
	Santa Fe ring dominates New Mexico politics and land grabbing
1889	New Jersey repeals a county-option prohibition law of 1888
	Laws in Wisconsin and Illinois mandate compulsory attendance of children at schools in which instruction is in English
	Kansas, Maine, Michigan, and Tennessee pass antitrust laws
1889–1890	Massachusetts debates bill on compulsory schooling in English
1890–1910	Eleven former Confederate states pass segregation laws
1891	Nebraska passes eight-hour workday law
1893	Colorado adopts woman suffrage
1894–1896	Woman suffrage referenda defeated in Kansas and California
1899–1902	Eleven former Confederate states amend state constitutions and pass statutes restricting the voting rights of blacks

The Omaha demands, drawn from the Ocala platform of 1890, were greatly expanded. They included more direct democracy (popular election of senators, direct primaries, the initiative and referendum, and the secret ballot) and several planks intended to enlist the support of urban labor (the eight-hour day, immigration restriction, and condemnation of the use of Pinkerton agents as an "army of mercenaries . . . a menace to our liberties"). The new party also endorsed a graduated income tax, the free and unlimited coinage of silver at a ratio of 16 to 1 (meaning that the U.S. Mint would have to buy silver for coinage at one-sixteenth the current, official price of the equivalent amount of gold), and government ownership of railroads, telephone, and telegraph. "The time has come," the platform said, "when the railroad corporations will either own the people or the people must own the railroads."

Populists attempted to widen political debate by promoting a new vision of government activism to resolve farmers' problems. But the obstacles they faced were monumental: weaning the South from the Democrats, encouraging southern whites to work with blacks, and persuading voters of both parties to abandon familiar political ties. Since many Alliance members were reluctant to follow their leaders into the third party, the Populists had to create the political machinery for a major electoral campaign.

The new party pressed ahead. Unlike the major-party candidates in 1892, Weaver campaigned actively. In the South, he faced egg- and rock-throwing Democrats, who raised the cry of "nigger rule" and fanned racial fears in opposing his efforts to include blacks in the People's party. Despite hostile opposition, Weaver won over 1 million popular votes (the first third-party candidate to do so), and he carried four states (Kansas, Colorado, Idaho, and Nevada) and parts of two others (Oregon and North Dakota), for a total of 22 electoral votes.

The Populists' support was substantial but regional, coming from western miners and mine owners who favored the demand for silver coinage and from rural Americans from the Great Plains. But the People's party failed to break the Democratic stranglehold on the South, nor did it appeal to city workers of the Northeast who were suspicious of the party's anti-urban tone and its desire for higher agricultural prices (which meant higher food prices). Perhaps most damaging, the Populists made little inroads on Midwestern farmers, who owed fewer debts and were relatively more prosperous than farmers elsewhere and saw little value in the Omaha platform. Farmers who were better integrated into their world tended to believe they could work through existing political parties. Although the Populists were not yet finished, most discontented farmers in 1892 voted for Cleveland and the Democrats, not for the Populists.

The Depression of 1893

Though winning the election, Cleveland soon faced a difficult test. No sooner had he taken office than began one of the worst depressions ever to grip the American economy, lasting from 1893 to 1897. Its severity was heightened by the growth of a national economy and global economic interdependence. The depression started in Europe and spread to the United States as overseas buyers cut back on their purchases of American products. Shrinking markets abroad soon crippled American manufacturing.

Foreign investors, worried about the stability of American currency after passage of the Sherman Silver Purchase Act, dumped some $300 million of their securities in the United States. As gold left the country to pay for these securities, the nation's money supply declined. At the same time, falling prices hurt farmers, many of whom discovered that it cost more to raise their crops and livestock than they could make in the market. Workers fared no better: wages fell faster than the price of food and rent.

The collapse in 1893 was also caused by an overextension of the domestic economy, especially in railroad construction. Farmers, troubled by falling prices, planted more, hoping the market would pick up. As the realization of overextension spread, confidence faltered, then gave way to financial panic. When Wall Street crashed early in 1893, investors frantically sold their shares, companies plunged into bankruptcy, and disaster spread. People rushed to exchange paper notes for gold, further reducing gold reserves and confidence in the economy. Banks called in loans, which by the end of the year led to 16,000 business bankruptcies and 500 bank failures.

The capital crunch and diminished buying power of rural and small-town Americans (still half the population) forced massive factory closings. Within a year, an estimated 3 million Americans—20 percent of the workforce—lost their jobs. People fearfully watched tramps wandering from city to city looking for work. "There are thousands of homeless and starving men in the streets," one young man reported from Chicago, indicating that he had seen "more misery in this last week than I ever saw in my life before."

As in Bellamy's coach image, the misery of the many was not shared by the few, which only increased discontent. While unemployed men foraged in garbage dumps for food, the wealthy gave lavish parties, sometimes costing $100,000. At one such affair, diners ate their meal while seated on horses; at another, many guests proudly proclaimed that they had spent over $10,000 on their attire. While poor families shivered in poorly heated tenements, the very rich built million-dollar summer resorts at Newport, Rhode Island, or grand mansions on New York's Fifth Avenue and Chicago's Gold Coast. While Lithuanian immigrants walked or rode packed streetcars to work, wealthy men luxuriated on huge pleasure yachts. J. P. Morgan owned three, one with a crew of 85 sailors.

Nowhere were these inequalities more apparent than in Chicago during the World's Columbian Exposition, which opened on May 1, 1893, five days before a plummeting stock market began the de-

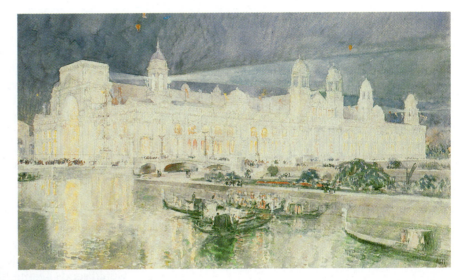

The depression of 1893 accentuated contrasts between rich and poor. While middle-class Americans enjoyed visiting the Palace of Electricity and boating on the lagoons of the Chicago World's Columbian Exposition (above) *(Corbis/Bettmann)*, slum children played in filthy streets nearby, with Jane Addams's Hull House less than a mile away (left). *(Library of Congress)*

pression. As President Cleveland said in an opening-day speech, the Chicago World's Fair showcased the "stupendous results of American enterprise." When he pressed an ivory telegraph key, he started electric current that unfurled flags, spouted water through gigantic fountains, lit 10,000 electric lights, and powered huge steam engines. For six months, some 27 million visitors strolled around the White City, admiring its wide lagoons, its neoclassical white plaster buildings, and its exhibit halls filled with inventions. Built at a cost of $31 million, the fair celebrated the marvelous mechanical accomplishments of American enterprise and of the "city beautiful" movement to make cities more livable.

But as fairgoers celebrated by sipping pink champagne, Americans in immigrant wards less than a mile away drank contaminated water, crowded into packed tenements, and looked in vain for jobs. The area around Hull House was especially disreputable, with saloons, gambling halls, brothels, and pawnshops dotting the neighborhood. "If Christ came to Chicago," British journalist W. T. Stead wrote in a book of that title in 1894, this would be "one of the last precincts into which we should care to take Him." Stead's book showed readers the "ugly sight" of corruption, poverty, and wasted lives in a city with 200 millionaires and 200,000 unemployed men.

Despite the magnitude of despair during the depression, national politicians and leaders were reluctant to respond. Mass demonstrations forced some city authorities to provide soup kitchens and places for the homeless to sleep. But when an army of unemployed led by Jacob Coxey marched on Washington in the spring of 1894 to press for public work relief, its leaders were arrested for stepping on the Capitol grass. Cleveland's reputation for callousness worsened later that summer when he sent federal troops to Chicago to crush the Pullman strike.

The president focused on tariff reform and repeal of the Silver Purchase Act, which he blamed for the depression. Although repeal was ultimately necessary to reestablish business confidence, in the short run, Cleveland only worsened the financial crisis, highlighted the silver panacea, and hurt conservative Democrats. With workers, farmers, and wealthy silver miners alienated, voters abandoned the Democrats in droves in the midterm elections of 1894, giving both Populists and Republicans high hopes for 1896.

The Crucial Election of 1896

The 1896 presidential campaign, waged during a depression and featuring a climactic battle over the currency, was one of the most critical in American history. Although Cleveland was in disgrace for ignoring depression woes, few leaders in either major party thought the federal government was responsible for alleviating the suffering of the people. But unemployed Polish meatpackers in Chicago, railway firemen in Terre Haute, unskilled Slavic workers in Pennsylvania blast furnaces, Italian immigrant women in New Haven tenements, and desperate white and black tenant farmers in Georgia all wondered where relief might be found. Would either major party respond to the pressing human needs of the depression? Would the People's party set a new national agenda for politics? Or would the established order prevail? These questions were raised and largely resolved in the election of 1896.

As the election approached, Populist leaders emphasized the silver issue and debated whether to fuse with one of the major parties by agreeing on a joint ticket, which meant abandoning much of the Populist platform. Influenced by silver mine owners, many Populists became convinced that they must make a single-issue commitment to the free and unlimited coinage of silver at the ratio of 16 to 1. Populist candidate James Weaver expected both parties to nominate gold candidates, which he thought would send silverites to the Populist standard.

In the throes of the depression in the mid-1890s, silver took on enormous importance as the symbol of the many grievances of downtrodden Americans. Popular literature captured the rural, moral dimensions of the silver movement. L. Frank Baum's *Wonderful Wizard of Oz* (1900) was a free-silver moral allegory of rural values (Kansas, Auntie Em, the uneducated but wise scarecrow, and the good-hearted tin woodsman) and Populist attitudes and policies (the wicked witch of the East, and the magical silver shoes in harmony with the yellow brick road, in "Oz"—ounces).

The Republicans nominated William McKinley. As a congressman and twice governor of Ohio, McKinley

William Jennings Bryan, a surprise nominee at the 1896 Democratic Convention, was a vigorous proponent of the "cause of humanity." His nomination threw the country into a frenzy of fear and the Populist party into a fatal decision over "fusion." *(Library of Congress)*

was happily identified with the high protective tariff that bore his name. Citing the familiar argument that prosperity depended on the gold standard and protection, Republicans blamed the depression on Cleveland's attempt to lower the tariff.

The excitement of the Democratic convention in July contrasted with the staid, smoothly organized Republican gathering. With Cleveland already repudiated by his party, state after state elected delegates pledged to silver. Gold Democrats, however, had enough power to wage a close battle for the platform plank on money. Leading the silver forces was an ardent young silverite, William Jennings Bryan, a 36-year-old former congressman from Nebraska. Few saw him as presidential material, but Bryan arranged to give the closing argument for a silver plank himself. His dramatic speech swept the convention for silver and ensured his own nomination. "I come to speak to you," Bryan cried out, "in defense of a cause as holy as the cause of liberty—the cause of humanity." Concluding one of the most famous political speeches in American history, Bryan attacked the "goldbugs":

> Having behind us the producing masses of this nation . . . and toilers everywhere, we will answer their demand for a gold standard by saying to them: "You shall not press down upon the brow of labor this crown of thorns, you shall not crucify mankind upon a cross of gold."

Bryan stretched out his arms as if on a cross, and the convention exploded with applause.

Populist strategy lay in shambles when the Democrats named a silver candidate. Some party leaders favored fusion with the Democratic ticket (whose vice-presidential candidate was a goldbug), but anti-fusionists were outraged. Unwisely, the Populists also nominated Bryan, with Georgia Populist Tom Watson for vice president. Running on competing silver slates damaged Bryan's chances.

During the campaign, McKinley stayed at his home in Canton, Ohio, where some 750,000 admirers came to visit him, brought by low excursion rates offered by the railroads. The Republicans made an unprecedented effort to reach voters through a highly sophisticated media campaign, heavily financed by such major corporations as Standard Oil and the railroads. Party leaders hired thousands of speakers to support McKinley and distributed more than 200 million pamphlets in 14 languages to a voting population of 15 million, all advertising McKinley as the "advance agent of prosperity."

From his front porch in Canton, McKinley appealed not only to the business classes but also to unemployed workers, to whom he promised a "full dinner pail." He also spoke about the money issue, declaring that "our currency today is . . . as good as gold." Free silver, he warned, would cause inflation and more economic disaster. Recovery depended not on money, but on tariff reform to stimulate industry and provide jobs—"not open mints for the unlimited coinage of the silver of the world," he said, "but open mills for the full and unrestricted labor of American workingmen."

Bryan took his case to the people. Three million Americans in 27 states heard him speak as he traveled over 18,000 miles, giving as many as 30 speeches a day. Bryan's message was simple: prosperity required free coinage of silver. Government policies should attend to the needs of the producing classes rather than the vested interests. But the rhetoric favored rural toilers. "The great cities rest upon our broad and fertile prairies," he said in the "Cross of Gold" speech. "Burn down your cities and leave our farms, and your cities will spring up again as if by magic; but destroy our farms and the grass will grow in the streets of every city in the country." Urban workers were not inspired by this rhetoric, nor were immigrants influenced by Bryan's prairie moralizing.

To influential easterners, the brash young Nebraskan represented a threat. Theodore Roosevelt wrote, "This silver craze surpasses belief. Bryan's election would be a great calamity." A Brooklyn minister declared that the Democratic platform was "made in Hell." One newspaper editor said of Bryan that he was just like Nebraska's Platte River: "six inches deep and six miles wide at the mouth." Others branded him a "madman" and an "anarchist." The New York *Mail* wrote, "No wild-eyed and rattle-brained horde of the red flag ever proclaimed a fiercer defiance of law, precedent, order, and government."

With such intense interest in the election, voters turned out in record numbers. In key states like Illinois, Indiana, and Ohio, 95 percent of those eligible to vote went to the polls. McKinley won with 271 electoral votes to Bryan's 176 and with the largest popular majority since Grant trounced Greeley in 1872. Millionaire Mark Hanna jubilantly wired McKinley: "God's in his heaven, all's right with the world."

Although Bryan won over 6 million votes (47 percent of the total), more than any previous Democratic winner, he failed to carry the Midwest or the urban middle classes and industrial masses, who had little confidence that the Democrats could stimulate economic growth or cope with industrialism. McKinley's promise of a "full dinner pail" was more convincing than the untested formula for free silver. Northern laborers feared that inflation would

Political Campaign Artifacts: Buttons and Posters

Historians recover the past in printed sources such as books, diaries, magazines, and government documents as well as in visual records such as paintings, photographs, and the artifacts of material culture. Throughout American history, presidential political campaigns have produced, in addition to the streams of speeches, words, and sound bites, mountains of material objects: buttons, badges, banners, bumper stickers, yard signs, posters, cartoons, and other campaign paraphernalia to persuade voters to support one candidate or another.

The election of 1896 was no exception and, in fact, produced a plethora of political campaign artifacts on behalf of William McKinley and William Jennings Bryan. The fervor of that pivotal political contest led to the production of thousands and thousands of lapel pins, buttons, ribbons, bandanas, shirts, teacups, paper cutout and soap dolls, posters, and other articles intended to influence American voters to cast their ballot for Bryan or McKinley. Although some of it seems silly, symbolic imagery was important. The examination of just two kinds of material paraphernalia—buttons and posters—reveals a great deal about the issues, values, symbolism, and style of the election of 1896.

Reflecting on the Past Examine the buttons pictured here (as well as the "goldbug" and other stickpins). What issues are voters reminded of, and how complex is the message? How many different ways is the message, reinforced by recurring symbols, repeated on these buttons? Now compare the buttons and pins with the two posters. Do not worry that you cannot read most of the words; focus instead on the visual imagery and such words as you can make out. How do the posters reinforce key symbols, slogans, and substantive issues associated with each candidate? What visual images do the posters add? What audience do you think these campaign artifacts had in mind? What summary statements would you make about the 1896 campaign on the basis of these material items? Do these artifacts suggest that voters were more or less involved with political issues and party identification than they are today? What artifacts would best reflect an early twenty-first century presidential campaign, and what would future historians learn from them?

Artifacts from the McKinley and Bryan campaigns. *(left: Courtesy Michael Kelly; right: © David J. and Janice L. Frent Collection/Corbis)*

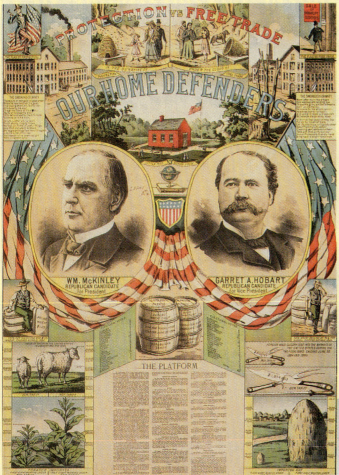

Campaign poster showing William McKinley and his running mate, Garret Hobart. *(Library of Congress)*

Campaign poster showing William Jennings Bryan, his wife and children, and the text of the "Cross of Gold" speech. *(The Granger Collection, New York)*

The Presidential Election of 1896

In his sweep of the densely populated urban Northeast and Midwest, McKinley beat Bryan by the largest popular-vote margin since 1872. In his cabled congratulations (the first ever by a loser), Bryan, ever the "democrat," said: "We have submitted the issues to the American people and their will is law." Note that California's nine electoral votes (few compared with today) were split. As was then legal, one elector, from the Imperial Valley bordering the Arizona Territory, voted for Bryan and the Democrats.

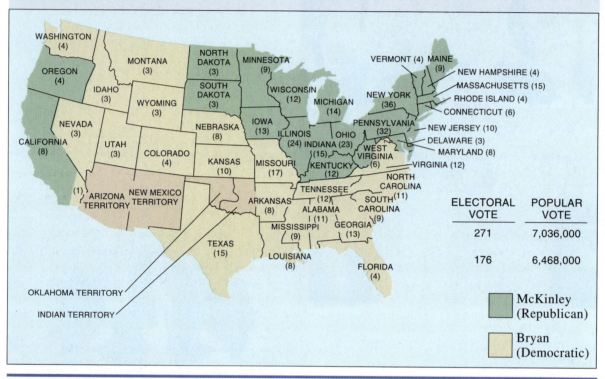

ELECTORAL VOTE	POPULAR VOTE
271	7,036,000
176	6,468,000

McKinley (Republican)

Bryan (Democratic)

leave them even poorer—that prices and rents would rise faster than their wages. Catholic immigrants distrusted Populist Protestantism. In the Great Lakes states, prosperous farmers felt less discontent than farmers elsewhere. But the realities of an increasingly global network of production, prices, and markets also played a part in Bryan's defeat. Bad wheat harvests in India, Australia, and Argentina drove up world grain prices, and many of the complaints of American farmers evaporated with a better price for their crops.

The New Shape of American Politics

The landslide Republican victory broke the stalemate in post–Civil War American politics. Republicans dropped their identification with the politics of piety and strengthened their image as the party of prosperity and national greatness, which gave them a party dominance that lasted until the 1930s. The Democrats, under Bryan's leadership until 1912, put on the mantle of Populist moralism, but were largely reduced to a sectional party, reflecting

southern views on money, race, and national power. The 1896 election demonstrated that the Northeast and Great Lakes states had acquired so many immigrants that they now controlled the nation's political destiny. The demoralized Populists disappeared, yet within the next 20 years, many Populist issues (e.g., direct election of senators, direct primaries, graduated income tax, woman suffrage, and others) were adopted by the two major parties.

Another result of the election of 1896 was a change in the pattern of political participation. Because the Republicans were so dominant outside of the South, and Democrats were so powerful in the South, few states had vigorous two-party political battles and therefore had less reason to mobilize large numbers of voters. With results so often a foregone conclusion, voters had little motivation to cast a ballot. Many black voters in the South, moreover, were disfranchised, and middle-class good government reformers were not as effective as party bosses in turning out urban voters. The tremendous rate of political participation that had characterized the nineteenth

Timeline

1873	Congress demonetizes silver
1875	Specie Resumption Act
1877	Rutherford B. Hayes becomes president
1878	Bland-Allison Act
1879	Henry George, *Progress and Poverty*
1880	James A. Garfield elected president
1881	Garfield assassinated Chester A. Arthur succeeds to presidency
1883	Pendleton Civil Service Act
1884	Grover Cleveland elected president W. D. Howells, *The Rise of Silas Lapham*
1887	College Settlement House Association founded
1888	Edward Bellamy, *Looking Backward* Benjamin Harrison elected president
1889	Jane Addams establishes Hull House Andrew Carnegie promulgates "The Gospel of Wealth"
1890	General Federation of Women's Clubs founded Sherman Anti-Trust Act Sherman Silver Purchase Act McKinley Tariff Elections bill defeated
1890s	Wyoming, Colorado, Utah, and Idaho grant woman suffrage
1892	Cleveland elected president for the second time Populist party wins over 1 million votes Homestead steel strike
1893	World's Columbian Exposition, Chicago
1893–1897	Financial panic and depression
1894	Pullman strike Coxey's march on Washington
1895	*United States v. E. C. Knight*
1896	Charles Sheldon, *In His Steps* Populist party fuses with Democrats William McKinley elected president
1897	"Golden Rule" Jones elected mayor of Toledo, Ohio Economic recovery begins

century since the Jackson era gradually declined. In the twentieth century, political involvement among poorer Americans lessened considerably, a phenomenon unique among western democracies.

McKinley had promised that Republican rule meant prosperity, and as soon as he took office, the economy recovered. Discoveries of gold in the Yukon and the Alaskan Klondike increased the money supply, ending the silver mania until the next great depression in the early 1930s. Industrial production returned to full capacity. Touring the Midwest in 1898, McKinley spoke to cheering crowds about the hopeful shift from "industrial depression to industrial activity."

McKinley's election marked not only the return of economic health but also the emergence of the executive as the preeminent focus of the American political system. Just as McKinley's campaign set the pattern for the extravagant efforts to win office that have dominated modern times, his conduct as president foreshadowed the twentieth-century presidency. McKinley rejected traditional views of the president as the passive executor of laws, instead playing an active role in dealing with Congress and the press. His frequent trips away from Washington showed an increasing regard for public opinion. Some historians see McKinley as the first modern president in his emphasis on the role of the chief executive in contributing to industrial growth and national power. As we shall see in Chapter 20, McKinley began the transformation of the presidency into a potent force, not only in domestic life, but in world affairs as well.

◆ *Conclusion*

LOOKING FORWARD

This chapter began with Edward Bellamy's imaginary look backward from the year 2000 at the grim economic realities and unresponsive politics of American life in the late nineteenth century. McKinley's triumph in 1896 indicated that in a decade marked by depression, Populist revolt, and cries for action to close the inequalities of wealth—represented by Bellamy's coach—the established order remained intact. Calls for change did not necessarily lead to change. But in the areas of personal action and the philosophical bases for social change, intellectual middle-class reformers like Edward Bellamy, Henry George, Frances Willard, Jane Addams, "Golden Rule" Jones, and many others were showing the way to progressive reforms in the new century. More Americans were able to look forward to the kind of cooperative, caring, and cleaner world envisioned in Bellamy's utopian novel.

As 1900 approached, people took a predictably intense interest in what the new century would be like. Henry Adams, still the pessimist, saw an ominous future; he predicted the explosive and ultimately destructive energy of unrestrained industrial development, symbolized by the "dynamo" and other engines of American and European power. Such forces, he warned, would overwhelm the gentler, moral forces represented by art, woman, and religious symbols like the Virgin. But others were more optimistic, preferring to place their confidence in America's self-image as an exemplary nation, demonstrating to the world the moral superiority of its economic system, democratic institutions, and middle-class Protestant values. Surely the new century, most thought, would see not only the continued perfection of these values and institutions but also the spread of American influence throughout the world. Such confidence resulted in foreign expansion by the American people even before the old century had ended. We turn to that next.

◆ Recommended Reading

Politics in the Gilded Age

John Allswang, *Bosses, Machines, and Urban Voters* (1977); Charles W. Calhoun, ed., *The Gilded Age: Essays on the Origins of Modern America* (1996); Sean Dennis Cashman, *America and the Gilded Age: From the Death of Lincoln to the Rise of Theodore Roosevelt* (1984); Morton Keller, *Affairs of State: Public Life in Late Nineteenth-Century America* (1977); Paul Kleppner, *The Third Electoral System, 1853–1892: Parties, Voters, and Political Cultures* (1979); H. Wayne Morgan, *From Hayes to McKinley: National Party Politics, 1877–1896* (1969); William Riordon, *Plunkitt of Tammany Hall* (1963); Gretchen Ritter, *Goldbugs and Greenbacks* (1997); Mark Wahlgren Summers, *Rum, Romanism and Rebellion: The Making of a President, 1884* (2000); R. Hal Williams, *Years of Decision: American Politics in the 1890s* (1978).

Middle-Class Reform

Jane Addams, *Twenty Years at Hull House* (1910); Ruth Bordin, *Frances Willard: A Biography* (1986) and *Women and Temperance: The Quest for Power and Liberty, 1873–1900* (1981); Mina Carson, *Settlement Folk: Social Thought and the American Settlement Movement, 1885–1930* (1990); Susan Curtis, *A Consuming Faith: The Social Gospel and Modern American Culture* (1991); Allen F. Davis, *American Heroine: The Life and Legend of Jane Addams* (1973) and *Spearheads for Reform: The Social Settlements and the Progressive Movement, 1890–1914* (1967); Richard Digby-Junger, *The Journalist as Reformer: Henry Demarest Lloyd and Wealth Against Commonwealth* (1996); John P. Diggins, *The Promise of Pragmatism* (1994); Mona Dowash, *Invented Cities: The Creation of Landscape in Nineteenth Century New York & Boston* (1996); Peter J. Frederick, *Knights of the Golden Rule: The Intellectual as Christian Reformer in the 1890s* (1976); Marnie Jones, *Holy Toledo: Religion and Politics in the Life of "Golden Rule" Jones* (1998); Paulette D. Kilmer, *The Fear of Sinking: The American Success Formula in the Gilded Age* (1996); Carol Mattingly, *Well-Tempered Women: Nineteenth-Century Temperance Rhetoric* (1998); Kathryn Kish Sklar, *Florence Kelley and the Nation's Work: The Rise of Women's Political Culture, 1830–1900* (1995);

Eleanor J. Stebner, *The Women of Hull House: A Study in Spirituality, Vocation, and Friendship* (1997); Marjorie Spruill Wheeler, ed., *One Woman, One Vote: Rediscovering the Woman Suffrage Movement* (1995).

Politics in the Pivotal 1890s

Peter H. Argersinger, *The Limits of Agrarian Radicalism: Western Populism and American Politics* (1995); Gene Clanton, *Populism: The Humane Preference in America, 1890–1900* (1991) and *Congressional Populism and the Crisis of the 1890s* (1999); Robert F. Durden, *The Climax of Populism: The Election of 1896* (1965); Paul Glad, *McKinley, Bryan and the People* (1964); Lawrence Goodwyn, *Democratic Promise: The Populist Movement in America* (1976); Charles Hoffman, *The Depression of the Nineties: An Economic History* (1970); Michael Kazin, *The Populist Persuasion* (1994); Elizabeth Sanders, *Roots of Reform: Farmers, Workers, and the American State, 1877–1917* (1999); Douglas Steeples and David O. Whitten, *Democracy in Desperation: The Depression of 1893* (1998).

Fiction and Film

Mark Twain and Charles D. Warner's *The Gilded Age* (1873) spares no one in its satirical critique of the social, political, and economic life of late-nineteenth-century America. Henry Adams's *Democracy: An American Novel* (1880) uses an ironic title to capture the elitist nature of politics and life in Washington in the Gilded Age. Two novels by William Dean Howells, *A Hazard of New Fortunes* (1889) and *The Rise of Silas Lapham* (1885), portray the social life of the new rich in the 1880s. Edward Bellamy's *Looking Backward* (1888) is the utopian novel that began this chapter and that stimulated much late-nineteenth-century reform, rivaled only by Charles Sheldon's social gospel novel *In His Steps* (1896). Kate Chopin's *The Awakening* (1899), set in New Orleans in the 1890s, tells the story of a woman's discovery of self. Theodore Dreiser's *Sister Carrie* (1900), influenced by social Darwinian determinism and set in Chicago and New York, shows the life of a young farm girl who rises to fame and fortune in the city. Frank

Norris's immense novel *The Octopus* (1901), set in the San Joaquin Valley of California, shows struggles not only between ranchers and railroads but also between rich and poor, city and country, commercial wheat farmers and sheep herders, and native-born and immigrant Americans. Anzia Yezierska's *Bread Givers* (1925) reveals the struggles between an Old World Jewish father and his Americanized daughter. *Hester Street* (1975) is a wonderfully teachable video about Jewish immigrants in New York City and, like the *Bread Givers,* the process of Americanization. Edgar L. Doctorow's *Ragtime* (1975) is an innovative novel that plays fast and loose with the history and historical figures of turn-of-the-century America; it was also made into a Broadway play. Upper-class life in the late nineteenth century is portrayed in the Hollywood film *The Bostonians* (1998), based on a novel by Henry James. Gore Vidal's *1876: A Novel* (1976) takes a playful, imaginative look at America in its centennial year.

✦ Discovering U.S. History Online

Gilded Age Presidents

www.potus.com/rbhayes.html
www.potus.com/jagarfield.html
www.potus.com/caarthur.html
www.potus.com/gcleveland.html
www.potus.com/bharrison.html

These sites contain basic factual data about Gilded Age presidents Hayes, Garfield, Arthur, Cleveland, and Harrison, including speeches and online biographies.

Late Nineteenth-Century Articles

www.boondocksnet.com

This site includes several exhibitions with links to contemporary articles, art, and cartoons about the late nineteenth century and early twentieth century, including "World's Fairs and Expositions: Defining America and the World, 1876–1916" and "Mark Twain on War and Imperialism."

Edward Bellamy

www.vineyard.net/vineyear/history/pdgech3.htm

This site contains text on Bellamy's life and on the influence of *Looking Backward* on reform movements in the early 1890s.

The Gilded Age

www.wm.edu/~srnels/gilded.html

This site offers links to Gilded Age documents and sources, especially literature.

The Rich During the Gilded Age

www.newportmansions.org

This site presents a virtual tour of Newport mansions along with background information.

The Life of William Jennings Bryan

www.mission.lib.tx.us/exhibits/bryan/bryan.htm

An online presentation of Hidalgo County Historical Museum's Exhibit on William Jennings Bryan as well as digitized sources on his life and campaign for president.

The Election of 1896

www.iath.virginia.edu/seminar/unit8/home.htm

This fine University of Virginia site contains biographical information, images, great cartoons, and related links about the pivotal election of 1896.

1896: The Presidential Campaign: Cartoons and Commentary

www.iberia.vassar.edu/1896/

The site contains several sections: "Cartoons," "Parties and Platforms," "Leaders," "Campaign Themes," and "Special Features" as well as background on the depression of 1893.

Coal Mining During the Gilded Age and Progressive Era

www.history.ohio-state.edu/projects/Lessons_US/Gilded_Age/Coal_Mining/default.htm

Primary-source documents examine the development of the coal industry, including the sometimes violent labor–management conflict.

20 Becoming a World Power

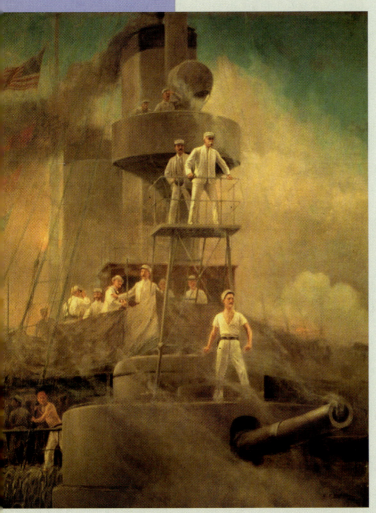

Dewey at Manila Bay, May 1, 1898 (painting by Rufus Zogbaum): **American Expansionism Triumphant.** *(Courtesy of The Vermont State House)*

◆ *American Stories*

PRIVATE GRAYSON KILLS A SOLDIER IN THE PHILIPPINES

In January 1899, the United States Senate was locked in a dramatic debate over whether to ratify the Treaty of Paris concluding the recent war with Spain over Cuban independence. At the same time, American soldiers uneasily faced Filipino rebels across a neutral zone around the outskirts of Manila, the capital of the Philippines. Until recent weeks, the Americans and Filipinos had been allies, together defeating the Spanish to liberate the Philippines. The American fleet under Admiral George Dewey had destroyed the Spanish naval squadron in Manila Bay on May 1, 1898. Three weeks later, an American ship brought from exile the native Filipino insurrectionary leader Emilio Aguinaldo to lead rebel forces on land, while U.S. gunboats patrolled the seas.

At first, the Filipinos looked on the Americans as liberators. Although the intentions of the United States were never clear, Aguinaldo believed that, as in Cuba, the Americans had no territorial ambitions. They would simply drive the Spanish out and then leave. In June, therefore, Aguinaldo declared the independence of the Philippines and began setting up a constitutional government. American officials pointedly ignored the independence ceremonies. When an armistice ended the war in August, American troops denied Aguinaldo's Filipino soldiers an opportunity to liberate their own capital city and shunted them off to the suburbs. The armistice agreement recognized American rights to the "harbor, city, and bay of Manila," while the proposed Treaty of Paris gave the United States the entire Philippine Islands archipelago.

Consequently, tension mounted in the streets of Manila and along 14 miles of trenches separating American and Filipino soldiers. Taunts, obscenities, and racial epithets were shouted across the neutral zone. Barroom skirmishes and knifings filled the nights; American soldiers searched houses without warrants and looted stores. Their behavior was not unlike that of English soldiers in Boston in the 1770s.

On the night of February 4, 1899, Privates William Grayson and David Miller of Company B, 1st Nebraska Volunteers, were on patrol in Santa Mesa, a Manila suburb surrounded on three sides by insurgent trenches. The Americans had orders to shoot any Filipino soldiers who were in the neutral area. As the two Americans cautiously worked their way to a bridge over the San Juan River, they heard a Filipino signal whistle, answered by another. Then a red lantern flashed from a nearby blockhouse. The two froze as four Filipinos emerged from the darkness on the road ahead. "Halt!" Grayson shouted. The native lieutenant in charge answered, "Halto!"—either mockingly or because he had similar orders. Standing less than 15 feet apart, the two men repeated their commands. After a moment's hesitation, Grayson fired, killing his opponent with one bullet. As the other Filipinos jumped out at them, Grayson and Miller shot two more. Then they turned and ran back to their own lines shouting warnings of attack. A full-scale battle followed.

The next day, Commodore Dewey cabled Washington that the "insurgents have inaugurated general engagement" and promised a hasty suppression of the insurrection. The outbreak of hostilities ended the Senate debates. On February 6, the Senate ratified the Treaty of Paris, thus formally annexing the Philippines and sparking a war between the United States and Aguinaldo's Filipino revolutionaries who represented a small percentage of the population.

In a guerrilla war similar to those fought later in the twentieth century in Eastern Asia, Filipino nationalists tried to undermine the American will by hit-and-run attacks. American soldiers, meanwhile, remained in heavily garrisoned cities and undertook search-and-destroy missions to root out rebels and pacify the countryside. The Filipino-American War lasted until July 1902, three years longer than the Spanish-American War that caused it and involving far more troops, casualties, and monetary and moral costs.

How did all this happen? What brought Private Grayson to "shoot my first nigger," as he put it, halfway around the world? For the first time in history, regular American soldiers found themselves fighting outside North America. The "champion of oppressed nations," as Aguinaldo said, had turned into an oppressor nation itself, imposing the American way of life and American institutions on faraway peoples against their will.

The war in the Philippines marked a critical transformation of America's role in the world. Within a few years at the turn of the century, the United States acquired an empire, however small by European standards, and established itself as a world power. In this chapter, we will review the historical dilemmas of America's role in the world in the late nineteenth century when expansionism was increasing worldwide. In this global context, we will examine the motivations for intensified expansionism by the United States in the 1890s and how they were manifested in Cuba, the Philippines, and elsewhere. Finally, we will look at how the fundamental patterns of American foreign policy to this day were established for Latin America, Eastern Asia, and Europe in the early twentieth century. Throughout, we will see that the tension between idealism and self-interest that has permeated America's domestic history has also guided its foreign policy.

STEPS TOWARD EMPIRE

The circumstances that brought Privates Grayson and Miller from Nebraska to the Philippines originated deep in American history. As early as the seventeenth-century Puritan migration, Americans worried about how to do good in a world that does wrong. John Winthrop sought to set up a "city on a hill" in the New World, a model community of righteous living for the rest of the world to imitate. "Let the eyes of the world be upon us," Winthrop had said. That wish, reaffirmed during the American Revolution, became a permanent goal of American policy toward the outside world.

America as a Model Society

Nineteenth-century Americans, like Russians, French, the English and others, continued to believe in their nation's special mission in the world. But only the United States claimed a mission of democratic representative government. The Monroe Doctrine in 1823, pointing out the differences between autocratic Europe and republican America, warned Europe's monarchies to keep out of the New World and not to interfere with the emerging Latin American republics as they declared their independence from Spain. Distinguished European visitors throughout the century came to observe the "great social revolution" in the Americas, especially in the United States. They found widespread democracy, representative and responsive political and legal institutions, a religious commitment to human perfectibility, unlimited energy, and an ability to apply unregulated economic activity and inventive genius to stupendous achievements of production.

In an evil world, Americans believed that they stood as a transforming force for good. But how could a nation committed to isolationism—to avoiding entanglements with European nations—do the transforming? One way was to encourage other countries to observe and imitate the good example set by the United States. But this required patience and passivity, two traits not characteristic of Americans. Moreover, other nations often preferred their own sense of distinctiveness or were attracted to competing models of modernization, which tested American patience. Therefore, throughout its history, the American people have proudly proclaimed and sometimes forcefully imposed their ideas and institutions on others. Motivated by a mixture of idealism and self-interest, these international crusades have been well-intentioned if not always well-received, as in recent years in Somalia, Kosovo, and Afghanistan. Hence, the effort to spread the American model to an imperfect world has been both a blessing and a burden—for others as well as for the American people.

Early Expansionism

Persistent expansionism marked the first century of American independence. Jefferson's purchase of Louisiana in 1803, the conquering of Indian lands during the War of 1812, and the mid-century pursuit of "Manifest Destiny" spread the United States across North America. In the 1850s, Americans began to look beyond their own continent as Commodore Perry in 1853 "opened" Japan, and southerners sought more cotton lands in the Caribbean. Although generally not entangled with European affairs for most of the century (as Washington and Jefferson had advised), the American people and government were very much entangled elsewhere. To the Mexicans, and to the Cherokee, Creek, Iroquois, Shawnee, Lakota, Navajo, and other Indian nations, the United

When the United States went to war against Spain in 1898, partly to help the Cubans win their independence from imperial Spanish rule, no one could have imagined the ironic outcome. Within a year, Americans would impose imperial rule over the Philippines, marching through and burning villages (as the 20th Kansas Volunteers are doing here) and waging war against civilians in a faraway Asian land. *(Above: Courtesy of The Newberry Library, Chicago; right: Keystone-Mast Collection [24039], URL/California Museum of Photography, University of California at Riverside)*

States was far from isolationist, a concept that referred only to Europe.

After the Civil War, Secretary of State William Seward spoke of an America that would hold a "commanding sway in the world," destined to exert commercial domination "on the Pacific ocean, and its islands and continents." He purchased Alaska from Russia in 1867 for $7.2 million and acquired a coaling station in the Midway Islands near Hawaii, where missionaries and merchants were already active. He advocated annexing Cuba and other Caribbean islands, tried to negotiate a treaty for an American-built canal through Panama, and dreamed of "possession" of the entire North and Central American continent and ultimately "control of the world."

In 1870, foreshadowing the Philippines debates 30 years later, supporters of President Grant tried to persuade the Senate to annex Santo Domingo on the island of Hispaniola, arguing the strategic importance of the Caribbean and the economic value of Santo Domingo. Opponents responded that annexation violated American principles of self-determination and government by consent. They also argued that native peoples of the Caribbean were brown-skinned, non-English-speaking, and therefore unassimilable. Expansionism, moreover, might involve foreign entanglements, a large and expensive navy, bigger government, and higher taxes. The Senate rejected annexation.

Although reluctant to add territory outright, Americans eagerly sought commercial dominance in Latin America and Asia, with a canal through Central America to facilitate inter-ocean traffic. But talk by England and the United States of jointly building a canal across Nicaragua produced only Nicaraguan suspicions. In 1881, Secretary of State James G. Blaine sought to convene a conference of American nations to promote hemispheric peace and trade. Latin Americans may have wondered what Blaine intended, for in 1881 he intervened in three separate border disputes in Central and South America, in each case at the cost of goodwill. Things worsened in 1889. A barroom brawl in Chile resulted in the death of two American sailors, and President Harrison threatened war, demanding "prompt and full reparation." After Chile complied, Blaine succeeded in holding the first Pan-American Conference to improve economic ties among the nations of the Americas.

American economic influence spread to the Pacific. In the mid-1870s, American sugar-growing interests in the Hawaiian Islands were strong enough to put whites in positions of influence over the monarchy. In 1875, they obtained a treaty admitting Hawaiian sugar duty-free to the United States, and in 1887, the United States also won exclusive rights to build a naval base at Pearl Harbor.

Attracted to sugar and the mid-Pacific location of the Hawaiian Islands, American imperial interests sought to tie Hawaii more closely to the far-away U.S. mainland. The Iolani Palace, former home of Queen Liliuokalani, was the scene of annexation ceremonies in 1898, when Hawaii became a U.S. territory. "We need Hawaii just as much as and a good deal more than we did California," President McKinley said. "It is manifest destiny." *(Library of Congress)*

Native Hawaiians resented the influence of American sugar interests, especially as they brought in Japanese to replace native people in the sugarcane fields, with some 200,000 arriving between 1885 and 1924.

In 1891, the nationalistic queen Liliuokalani assumed the throne and pursued a policy of "Hawaii for the Hawaiians." Two years later, white planters, fearful that the queen might turn to Japan for support, staged a coup with the help of U.S. gunboats and marines, and imprisoned the queen. With the success of their bloodless coup, called by one journalist a revolution "of sugar, by sugar, for sugar," the whites sought formal annexation by the friendly Harrison administration. But when Grover Cleveland, who opposed imperial expansion, returned to the presidency for his second term, he stopped the move. The sugar growers waited patiently for a more desirable time for annexation, which came during the war in 1898.

American Expansionism in Global Context

American forays into the Pacific and Latin America brought the United States increasingly into contact and conflict with European nations. The nineteenth century was marked by European imperial expansionism throughout much of the world. In southern and southeastern Asia, the British were in India, Burma, and Malaya; the French in Cambodia, Vietnam, and Laos; the Dutch in Singapore and the East Indies; and the Spanish in the Philippines. These and other colonial powers divided China, its Manchu dynasty weakened by the opium trade, internal conflicts, and European pressure, into spheres of economic influence. A China newspaper editorial complained that other nations "all want to satisfy their ambitions to nibble at China and swallow it." The Russians wrested away Manchuria, and Japan took Korea after intervention in a Korean peasant rebellion in 1894. In addition, China was forced to cede Taiwan and southern Manchuria to Japanese influence and control.

In Africa, Europeans scrambled to gain control of both coastal and interior areas, with England, France, Germany, Portugal, and Belgium grabbing the most land and exploiting African peoples. There were only two independent African nations in the whole continent in the late nineteenth century: Liberia, founded by Americans to resettle free blacks in 1822, and the fragmented kingdom of Ethiopia, which thrashed the Italians when they invaded in 1896 and preserved its autonomy. With nearly all of Africa divided amongst them, the only way imperial powers could acquire more land was

to fight each other. Thus, in 1899, war broke out in southern Africa between the British and the Boers, descendants of Dutch settlers—a war waged with a savagery Europeans usually reserved for black indigenous peoples. The Boers were outraged that the English "looted our property, wantonly killed our cattle and devastated our farms," and drove civilians into concentration camps where an estimated 20,000 women and children perished from starvation and malnutrition. The British won, but at a horrific cost.

Africa was not then of interest to the United States. But in the Pacific and the Caribbean, it was inevitable that the United States, a late arrival to imperialism, would bump into European rivals. Moving outward from Hawaii closer to the markets of Eastern Asia, the United States acquired a naval and coaling station in the Samoan Islands in 1878, sharing the port with Great Britain and Germany. American and German naval forces almost fought each other there in 1889—before a typhoon ended the crisis by wiping out both navies. Troubles in the Pacific also occurred in the late 1880s over the American seizure of several Canadian ships in fur seal and fishing disputes in the Bering Sea. The issue was settled only by the threat of British naval action and an international arbitration commission ruling, which ordered the United States to pay damages.

Closer to home, the United States sought to replace Great Britain as the most influential nation in Central and South America. In 1895, a boundary dispute between Venezuela and British Guyana threatened to bring British intervention against the Venezuelans. President Cleveland, needing a popular political issue amid the depression, asked Secretary of State Richard Olney to send a message to Great Britain. Invoking the Monroe Doctrine, Olney's note (stronger than Cleveland intended) called the United States "practically sovereign on this continent" and demanded international arbitration to settle the dispute. The British ignored the note, and war loomed. Both sides realized that war between two English-speaking nations would be an "absurdity," and the dispute was settled when they agreed to an impartial commission to settle the boundary.

These encounters showed that by 1895 the United States had neither the means nor a consistent policy for enlarging its role in the world. The diplomatic service was small and unprofessional. No U.S. embassy official in Beijing spoke Chinese. The U.S. Army, with about 28,000 men, was smaller than Bulgaria's. The navy, dismantled after the Civil War and partly rebuilt under President Arthur, ranked no higher than tenth and included dangerously obsolete ships. But by 1898, things would change.

EXPANSIONISM IN THE 1890s

In 1893, historian Frederick Jackson Turner wrote that for three centuries "the dominant fact in American life has been expansion." The "extension of American influence to outlying islands and adjoining countries," he thought, indicated still more expansionism. Turner struck a responsive chord in a country that had always been restless and optimistic. With the western frontier declared closed, Americans would surely look for new frontiers, for mobility and markets as well as for morality and missionary activity. The motivations for the expansionist impulse of the late 1890s resembled those that had prompted Europeans to settle the New World in the first place: greed, glory, and God. We will examine expansionism as a reflection of profits, patriotism, piety, and politics.

Profits: Searching for Overseas Markets

Senator Albert Beveridge of Indiana bragged in 1898 that "American factories are making more than the American people can use; American soil is producing more than they can consume. Fate has written our policy for us; the trade of the world must and shall be ours." Americans like Beveridge revived older dreams of an American commercial empire in the Caribbean Sea and the Pacific Ocean. American businessmen saw huge profits beckoning in heavily populated Latin America and Asia, and they wanted to get their share of these markets, as well as access to the sugar, coffee, fruits, oil, rubber, and minerals that were abundant in these lands.

Understanding that commercial expansion required a stronger navy and coaling stations and colonies, business interests began to shape diplomatic and military strategy. Senator Orville Platt of Connecticut said in 1893: "A policy of isolationism did well enough when we were an embryo nation, but today things are different." By 1901, the economic adviser for the State Department described overseas commercial expansion as a "natural law of economic and race development." But not all businessmen in the 1890s liked commercial expansion or a vigorous foreign policy. Some preferred traditional trade with Canada and Europe rather than risky new ventures in Asia and Latin America. Taking colonies and developing faraway markets not only was expensive but might involve the United States in wars in distant places. Many thought it more important to recover from the depression than to annex islands.

But the drop in domestic consumption during the depression also encouraged businessmen to expand into new markets to sell surplus goods. The tremendous growth of American production in the post–Civil War years made expansionism more attractive than drowning in overproduction, cutting prices, or laying off workers, which would increase social unrest. The newly formed National Association of Manufacturers, which led the way, proclaimed in 1896 that "the trade centers of Central and South America are natural markets for American products."

Despite the 1890s depression, products spewed from American factories at a staggering rate. The United States moved from fourth place in the world in manufacturing in 1870 to first place in 1900, doubling the number of factories and tripling the value of farm output—mainly cotton, corn, and wheat. The United States led the world in railroad construction and mass-produced technological products such as agricultural machinery, sewing machines, electrical implements, telephones, cash registers, elevators, and cameras. Manufactured

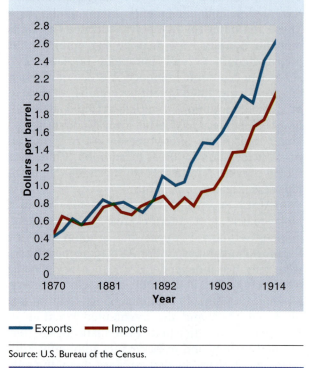

American Foreign Trade, 1870–1914

After a rather gradual increase in trade through the boom-and-bust cycles of the 1870s and 1880s and an actual dip during the depression of 1893–1895, American foreign trade saw spectacular increases during the Republican era of Presidents McKinley, Roosevelt, and Taft.

Exports   Imports

Source: U.S. Bureau of the Census.

goods grew nearly fivefold between 1895 and 1914. The total value of American exports tripled, from $434 million in 1866 to nearly $1.5 billion in 1900. By 1914, exports had risen to $2.5 billion, a 67 percent increase over 1900.

The increased trade continued to go mainly to Europe rather than Asia. In 1900, for example, only 3 to 4 percent of U.S. exports went to China and Japan, though it would increase astronomically by the 1920s. The number of American firms in China grew from 50 to 550 between 1870 and 1930, and interest in Asian markets grew, especially as agricultural output continued to increase and prices stayed low.

Investments followed a similar pattern. American direct investments abroad increased from about $634 million to $2.6 billion between 1897 and 1914. Although the greatest activity was in Britain, Canada, and Mexico, most attention focused on actual and potential investment in Latin America and Eastern Asia. Central American investment increased from $21 million in 1897 to $93 million by 1914, mainly in mines, railroads, and banana and coffee plantations. At the turn of the century came the formation and growth of America's biggest multinational corporations: the United Fruit Company, Alcoa Aluminum, Du Pont, American Tobacco, and others. Although slow to respond to investment and market opportunities abroad, these companies soon supported an aggressive foreign policy.

Patriotism: Asserting National Power

American interest in global investments, markets, and raw materials reflected a determination to join the international competition for spheres of influence and colonies in Eastern Asia and Latin America. In 1898, a State Department memorandum stated that "we can no longer afford to disregard international rivalries now that we ourselves have become a competitor in the world-wide struggle for trade." The national state, then, should support commercial interests.

More Americans, however, saw expansion in terms of national glory and greatness. In the late 1890s, Assistant Secretary of the Navy Theodore Roosevelt and Massachusetts Senator Henry Cabot Lodge emerged as highly influential leaders of a changing American foreign policy. Along with a group of other intensely nationalistic young men, they shifted official policy to what Lodge called the "large policy." Roosevelt agreed that economic interests should take second place to questions of what he called "national honor." And by 1899, a State Department official wrote that the United

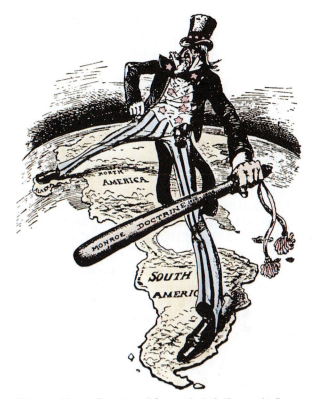

Citing the Monroe Doctrine and Senator Lodge's "large policy" as justification, U.S. imperial interests at the turn of the century spread American economic, political, and military influence from Alaska across the Caribbean to South America and into the islands of the Pacific Ocean. Note Uncle Sam's determined gaze westward. *(Bettmann/Corbis)*

States had become "a world power. . . . Where formerly we had only commercial interests, now we have territorial and political interests as well."

Naval strategist Alfred Thayer Mahan greatly influenced the new foreign policy elite. Mahan's many books on the importance of sea power to national greatness argued that in a world of Darwinian struggle for survival, national power depended on naval supremacy, control of sea lanes, and vigorous development of domestic resources and foreign markets. He advocated colonies in both the Caribbean and the Pacific, linked by a canal built and controlled by the United States. Mahan believed that in a world of constant "strife," where "everywhere nation is arrayed against nation," it was imperative that Americans begin "to look outward." National pride and glory would surely follow.

Piety: The Missionary Impulse

As Mahan and Roosevelt's statements suggest, a strong sense of duty and the missionary ideal of doing good for others also motivated expansionism—and sometimes rationalized the exploitation and oppression of weaker peoples. Americans like Roosevelt, Lodge, and Mahan all would have agreed with the following summary of expansionist arguments:

> Certain nations are more civilized than others, especially those peopled by English-speaking, white, Protestant Anglo-Saxons. They enjoy free enterprise and republican political institutions, which means representative government, distributive power, and the rule of law. Further evidence of the civilized nature of such nations includes their advanced technological and industrial development, large middle classes, and a high degree of education and literacy. The prime examples in the world are England, Germany, and the United States.
>
> In the natural struggle for existence, those races and nations that survive and prosper prove their fitness and superiority. The United States, as a matter of history, geographic location, and political genius, is so favored and fit that God has chosen it to uplift less favored peoples. This responsibility cannot be avoided. It is a national duty, or burden—the "white man's burden"—that civilized nations undertake to bring peace, progressive values, and ordered liberty to the world.

The argument begins with principles of modernization and ends in statements of America's pious sense of itself as morally exceptional. In 1885, a missionary put it more concisely—and crudely: "The Christian nations are subduing the world in order to make mankind free." Richard Olney agreed, saying in 1898, "The mission of this country is . . . to forego no fitting opportunity to further the progress of civilization."

Josiah Strong, a Congregationalist minister, was perhaps the most ardent advocate of American missionary expansionism. In a book titled *Our Country* (1885), he argued that in the struggle for survival among nations, the United States had emerged as the center of Anglo-Saxonism and was "divinely commissioned" to spread political liberty, Protestant Christianity, and civilized values over the earth. "This powerful race," he wrote, "will move down upon Mexico, down upon Central and South America, out upon the islands of the sea, over upon Africa and beyond." In a cruder statement of the same idea, Indiana Senator Albert Beveridge said in 1899 that God had prepared English-speaking Anglo-Saxons to become "the master organizers of the world to establish and administer governments among savages and senile peoples."

Missionaries carried Western values to non-Christian lands around the world, especially China. The number of American Protestant missionaries in China increased from 436 in 1874 to 5,462 in 1914, and the estimated number of Christian converts in China jumped from 5,000 in 1870 to nearly 100,000 in 1900. Although this number was much less than missionaries hoped, this tiny fraction of the Chinese population included many young reformist intellectuals who, absorbing Western ideas, in 1912 helped overthrow the Manchu dynasty. Economic relations between China and the United States increased at approximately the same rate as missionary activity.

Politics: Manipulating Public Opinion

Although less significant than the other factors, politics also played a role. For the first time in American history, public opinion on international issues helped shape presidential politics. The psychological tensions and economic hardships of the 1890s depression jarred national self-confidence. Foreign adventures then, as now, provided an emotional release from domestic turmoil and promised to restore patriotic pride and win votes.

This process was helped by the growth of a highly competitive popular press, the penny daily newspapers, which brought international issues before a mass readership. When New York City newspapers, notably William Randolph Hearst's *Journal* and Joseph Pulitzer's *World*, competed in stirring up public support for the Cuban rebels against Spain, politicians dared not ignore the outcry. Daily reports of Spanish atrocities in 1896 and 1897 kept public moral outrage constantly before President McKinley. His Democratic opponent, William Jennings Bryan, entered the fray, advocating American intervention in Cuba on moral grounds of a holy war to help the oppressed. He even raised a regiment of Nebraska volunteers to go to war, but the Republican administration kept him far from battle and therefore far from the headlines.

Politics, then, joined profits, patriotism, and piety in motivating the expansionism of the 1890s. These four impulses interacted to produce the Spanish-American War, the annexation of the Philippine Islands and subsequent war, and the energetic foreign policy of President Theodore Roosevelt.

WAR IN CUBA AND THE PHILIPPINES

Lying 90 miles off Florida, Cuba had been the object of intense American interest for a half century. Spain could not halt the continuing struggle of the Cuban people for a measure of autonomy and relief from exploitive labor in the sugar plantations, even after slavery itself ended. An uprising lasting from 1868 to 1878 raised tensions between Spain and the

United States, just as it whetted the Cuban appetite for complete independence.

The Road to War

When the Cuban revolt flared up anew in 1895, the Madrid government again failed to implement reforms. Instead, it sent General Weyler, dubbed the "butcher" by the American press, with 50,000 troops to quell the disturbance. When Weyler began herding rural Cubans into reconcentration camps, Americans were outraged. An outpouring of sympathy swept the nation, especially as sensationalist reports of horrible suffering and the deaths of thousands in the camps filled American newspapers. "The old, the young, the weak, the crippled," wrote the New York *World*, "all are butchered without mercy."

The Cuban struggle appealed to a country convinced of its role as protector of the weak and defender of the right of self-determination. One editorial deplored Spanish "injustice, oppression, extortion, and demoralization," while describing the Cubans as heroic freedom fighters "largely inspired by our glorious example of beneficent free institutions and successful self-government." Motivated in part by genuine humanitarian concern and a sense of duty, many Americans held rallies to raise money and food for famine relief, called for land reform and, for some, armed intervention. But neither Cleveland nor McKinley wanted war.

Self-interest also played a role. For many years, Americans had noted the profitable resources and strategic location of the island. American companies had invested extensively in Cuban sugar plantations. By 1897, appeals for reform had much to do with ensuring a stable environment for further investments and trade ($27 million in 1897), as well as for protecting the sugar fields against the ravages of civil war.

The election of 1896 only temporarily diverted attention from Cuba to the silver issue. A new government in Madrid recalled Weyler and made half-hearted concessions. But conditions worsened in

U.S. Territorial Expansion to 1900

Compare this map with the one on U.S. territorial expansion to 1860 on page 447 (represented in miniature in the U.S. portion of this map). What obvious differences do you see? Can you explain how each new territory was acquired? Do you see any patterns?

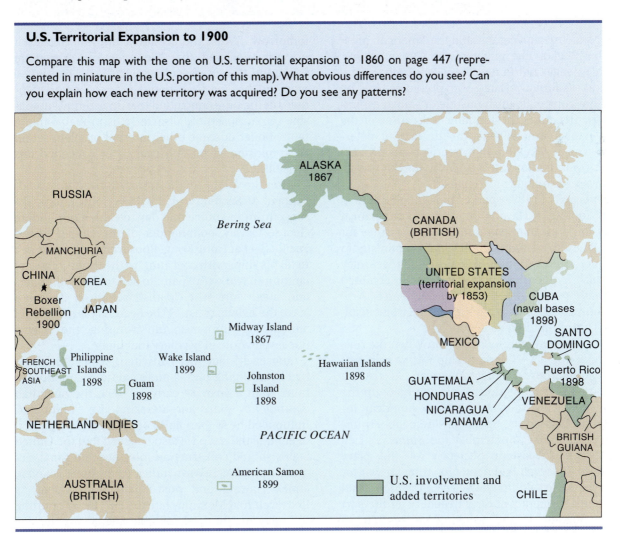

The artist has captured here the horror of the sinking of the *Maine*, with scenes before and after the explosion. Secretary of the Navy John Long, on returning to his office to discover that Assistant Secretary Roosevelt had cabled Admiral Dewey to prepare for war in the aftermath of the *Maine* explosion, wrote in his diary, "I find that Roosevelt has come very near causing more of an explosion than happened to the *Maine*." *(Chicago Historical Society [ICHi-08428])*

the reconcentration camps, and the American press kept harping on the plight of the Cuban people. McKinley, eager not to upset recovery from the depression, skillfully resisted war pressures. But he could not control Spanish misrule or Cuban aspirations for freedom. The fundamental causes of the war—Spanish intransigence in the face of determined Cuban rebellion and American sugar interests in combination with sympathy for the underdog—were seemingly unstoppable.

Events early in 1898 sparked the outbreak of hostilities. Rioting in Havana intensified both Spanish repression and American outrage. As pressures for war increased, a letter from the Spanish minister to the United States, Dupuy de Lôme, calling McKinley a "weak," hypocritical politician, was intercepted and made public. Americans fumed. Hearst's New York *Journal* called de Lôme's letter "the worst insult to the United States in its history."

A second event was more serious. When the rioting broke out, the U.S. battleship *Maine* was sent to Havana harbor to protect American citizens. On February 15, a tremendous explosion blew up the *Maine,* killing 262 men. Advocates of American intervention blamed the Spanish. Newspapers trumpeted slogans like "Remember the *Maine!* To hell with Spain!" Assistant Secretary of the Navy Theodore Roosevelt had been preparing for war for many years. He said that he believed the *Maine* had been sunk "by an act of dirty treachery on the part of the Spaniards" and would "give anything if President McKinley would order the fleet to Havana

tomorrow." When the president did not, Roosevelt privately declared that McKinley had "no more backbone than a chocolate éclair" and continued readying the navy for action. Although a board of inquiry at the time concluded that an external submarine mine caused the disaster, it is probable that a faulty boiler or some other internal problem set off the explosion. Even Roosevelt later conceded this possibility.

After the sinking of the *Maine,* Roosevelt took advantage of Secretary of the Navy John Long's absence from the office one day to cable Commodore George Dewey, commander of the United States' Pacific fleet at Hong Kong. Roosevelt ordered Dewey to fill his ships with coal and, "in the event" of a declaration of war with Spain, to sail to the Philippines and make sure "the Spanish squadron does not leave the Asiatic coast." "The Secretary is away and I am having immense fun running the Navy," Roosevelt wrote in his diary that night.

Roosevelt's act was consistent with policies he had been urging on his more cautious superior for more than a year. As early as 1895, the navy had contingency plans for attacking the Philippines. Influenced by Mahan and Lodge, Roosevelt wanted to enlarge the navy. He also believed that the United States should construct an inter-oceanic canal, acquire the Danish West Indies (the Virgin Islands), annex Hawaii, and oust Spain from Cuba. As Roosevelt told McKinley late in 1897, he was putting the navy in "the best possible shape" for the day "when war began."

The public outcry over the *Maine* drowned out McKinley's efforts to avoid war. With midterm elections in the fall and a presidential race only two years away, the issues had become highly politicized. Lodge warned McKinley, "If war in Cuba drags on through the summer with nothing done we shall go down to the greatest [political] defeat ever known." McKinley pressured the Madrid government to make further concessions, which it did. But the Spanish refused to grant full independence to the Cubans, and McKinley finally acted.

On April 11, 1898, the president sent an ambiguous message to Congress that seemed to call for war. Two weeks later, Congress authorized using troops against Spain and recognized Cuban independence, actions amounting to a declaration of war. In an additional resolution, the Teller Amendment, Congress stated that the United States had no intention of annexing Cuba. Massachusetts Senator George Hoar, who later assailed the United States for its war against the Filipinos, declared that intervention in Cuba would be "the most honorable single war in all history," undertaken without "the slightest thought or desire of foreign conquest or of national gain." A Cuban revolutionary general was more realistic, saying, "I expect nothing from the Americans. We should trust everything to our efforts. It is better to rise or fall without help than to contract debts of gratitude with such a powerful neighbor."

"A Splendid Little War": Various Views

The outbreak of war between Spain and the United States did not go unnoticed in Europe. German Kaiser Wilhelm II declared with sarcasm, "It is high time that we other monarchs . . . agree jointly to offer our help to the Queen in case the American-British Society for International Theft and Warmongering looks as if it seriously intends to snatch Cuba from Spain." But Spain was left to face the United States alone, fully expecting a defeat. As soon as war broke out, a Madrid newspaper boldly predicted, "in reality, Cuba is lost to Spain." A Spanish Rear Admiral said that the ruptured relations with the United States "would surely be fatal."

The celebrated charge of "Teddy's Rough Riders" up Kettle Hill, shown in this heroic picture (left), was made possible (and safe) because Spanish resistance was neutralized by African American troops like these from the 9th U.S. Cavalry (above). *(The Granger Collection, New York)*

Indeed, the war was short and relatively easy for the Americans, and "fatal" for the Spanish, who at the war's conclusion were left with "only two major combat vessels." The Americans won naval battles almost without return fire. At both major engagements, Manila Bay and Santiago Bay in Cuba, only two Americans died, one of them from heat prostration while stoking coal. Guam and Puerto Rico were taken virtually without a shot. Only 385 men died from Spanish bullets, but more than 5,000 succumbed to tropical diseases. As the four-month war neared its end in August, Secretary of State John Hay wrote Roosevelt that "it has been a splendid little war; begun with the highest motives, carried on with magnificent intelligence and spirit."

The Spanish-American War seemed splendid in other ways, as letters from American soldiers suggest. One young man wrote that his comrades were all "in good spirits" because oranges and coconuts were plentiful and "every trooper has his canteen full of lemonade all the time." Another wrote his mother that he found Cuba better than Texas because "our money is worth twice as much as Spanish money," and still another told his brother that he was having "a lot of fun chasing Spaniards."

But the war was not much fun for other soldiers. One said, "Words are inadequate to express the feeling of pain and sickness when one has the fever. For about a week every bone in my body ached and I

did not care much whether I lived or not." Another described "a man shot while loading his gun," noting that "the Spanish Mauser bullet struck the magazine of his carbine and split, a part of it going through his scalp and a part through his neck. . . . He was a mass of blood."

Nor was the war splendid for African-American soldiers, who fought in segregated units and noted stark differences between how they were treated in the American South and in the Caribbean islands, where they were warmly greeted. One commented while traveling to Tampa, the embarkation port for Cuba, "We were not treated with much courtesy while coming through the South." African Americans were especially sympathetic to the Cuban people's struggle against unjust treatment. One wrote in his journal, "Oh God! At last we have taken up the sword to enforce the divine rights of a people who have been unjustly treated," an understandable sentiment during a decade marked by the restricting of rights for African Americans by southern state legislatures.

For Colonel Roosevelt, who resigned from the Navy Department to lead a cavalry unit as soon as war was declared, the war was excitement and political opportunity. After a close brush with death in Cuba, Roosevelt declared with delight that he felt "the wolf rise in the heart" during "the power of joy in battle." But ironically, he needed help from African-

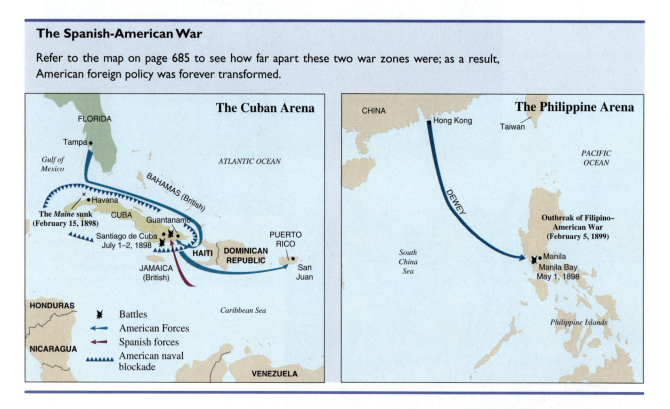

The Spanish-American War

Refer to the map on page 685 to see how far apart these two war zones were; as a result, American foreign policy was forever transformed.

The Cuban Arena

FLORIDA
Tampa
Gulf of Mexico
ATLANTIC OCEAN
BAHAMAS (British)
Havana
The *Maine* sunk (February 15, 1898)
CUBA
Guantánamo
Santiago de Cuba July 1–2, 1898
HAITI
DOMINICAN REPUBLIC
PUERTO RICO
San Juan
JAMAICA (British)
HONDURAS
Caribbean Sea
NICARAGUA
VENEZUELA

Battles
American Forces
Spanish forces
American naval blockade

The Philippine Arena

CHINA
Hong Kong
Taiwan
PACIFIC OCEAN
DEWEY
Outbreak of Filipino–American War (February 5, 1899)
South China Sea
Manila
Manila Bay May 1, 1898
Philippine Islands

American soldiers to achieve his goals. His celebrated charge up Kettle Hill near Santiago was made possible by black troops first clearing the hill and then protecting his flank. The "charge" made three-inch headlines and propelled him toward the New York governor's mansion. "I would rather have led that charge," he said later, "than served three terms in the U. S. Senate." More than anyone, Roosevelt used the war to advance not only his political career but also the glory of national expansionism.

The Philippines Debates and War

When Roosevelt ordered Dewey to Manila, he initiated a chain of events that led to the annexation of the Philippines. The most crucial battle of the Spanish-American War occurred on May 1, 1898, when Dewey destroyed the Spanish fleet in Manila Bay and cabled McKinley for additional troops. Although the president admitted later that he was uncertain "within two thousand miles" where "those darned islands were," he sent twice as many troops as Dewey had asked for. McKinley immediately began shaping American public opinion to accept the "political, commercial [and] humanitarian" reasons for annexing all 7,000 of the Philippines islands. The Treaty of Paris gave the United States all of the islands in exchange for a $20 million payment to Spain.

The treaty went to the Senate for ratification during the winter of 1898–1899. Senators hurled arguments across the floor of the Senate as American soldiers hurled oaths and taunts across the neutral zone at Aguinaldo's insurgents near Manila. Private Grayson's encounter, as we have seen, led to the passage of the treaty in a close Senate vote—and began the Filipino-American War and the debates over what to do with the Philippines.

The entire nation joined the argument. At stake were two very different views of foreign policy and of America's vision of itself. After several months of quietly seeking advice and listening to public opinion, McKinley finally recommended annexation on the grounds of international politics, commercial advantage, Filipino incapacity for self-rule, and the American responsibility for Christian, civilized order.

Fellow Republicans confirmed McKinley's arguments for annexation, and many Democrats supported the president out of fear of being labeled disloyal. Americans of both parties added arguments reflecting the openly racist thought that flourished in the United States. Filipinos were described as childlike, dirty, and backward; they were compared to blacks and Indians. "The country won't be paci-

fied," a Kansas veteran of the Sioux wars told a reporter, "until the niggers are killed off like the Indians." Roosevelt called Aguinaldo a "renegade Pawnee" and said that the Filipinos had no right "to administer the country which they happen to be occupying."

A small but prominent and vocal Anti-Imperialist League vigorously opposed war and annexation. These dignitaries included ex-presidents Harrison and Cleveland, Samuel Gompers and Andrew Carnegie, Jane Addams, and Mark Twain. The anti-imperialists argued that imperialism in general and annexation in particular contradicted American ideals. First, the annexation of territory without immediate or planned steps toward statehood was unprecedented and unconstitutional. Second, to occupy and govern a foreign people without their consent violated the ideals of the Declaration of Independence. Third, social reforms needed at home demanded American energies and money before foreign expansionism. "Before we attempt to teach house-keeping to the world," one writer put it, we needed "to set our own house in order."

Not all anti-imperialist arguments were so noble. A racist position alleged that Filipinos were non-white, Catholic, inferior in size and intelligence, and therefore unassimilable. Annexation would lead to miscegenation and contamination of Anglo-Saxon blood. South Carolina Senator Ben Tillman opposed "incorporating any more colored men into the body politic." A practical argument suggested that once in possession of the Philippines, the United States would have to defend them, possibly even acquiring more territories—in turn requiring higher taxes and bigger government, and perhaps demanding that American troops fight distant Asian wars.

The last argument became fact when Private Grayson's encounter started the Filipino-American War. Before it ended in 1902, some 126,500 American troops served in the Philippines, 4,234 died there, and 2,800 more were wounded. The cost was $400 million. Filipino casualties were much worse. In addition to 18,000 killed in combat, an estimated 200,000 Filipinos died of famine and disease as American soldiers burned villages and destroyed crops and livestock to deny the rebels their food supply. General Jacob H. Smith told his troops that "the more you kill and burn, the better you will please me." Insurgent ineptness, Aguinaldo's inability to extend the fight across ethnic boundaries, and atrocities on both sides increased the frustrations of a lengthening war. The American "water cure" and other tortures were especially brutal.

RECOVERING THE PAST

Political Cartoons

One of the most enjoyable ways of recovering the values and attitudes of the past is through political cartoons. Ralph Waldo Emerson once said, "Caricatures are often the truest history of the times." A deft drawing of a popular or unpopular politician can freeze ideas and events in time, conveying more effectively than columns of print the central issues—and especially the hypocrisies and misbehaviors of an era. Cartoonists are often at their best when they are critical, exaggerating a physical feature of a political figure, or capturing public sentiment against the government.

The history of political cartoons in the United States goes back to Benjamin Franklin's "Join or Die" cartoon calling for colonial cooperation against the French in 1754. But political cartoons were rare until Andrew Jackson's presidency. Even after such cartoons as "King Andrew the First" in the 1830s, they did not gain notoriety until the advent of Thomas Nast's cartoons in *Harper's Weekly* in the 1870s. Nast drew scathing cartoons exposing the corruption of William "Boss" Tweed's Tammany Hall, depicting Tweed and his men as vultures and smiling deceivers. "Stop them damn pictures," Tweed ordered. "I don't care so much what the papers write about me. My constituents can't read. But, damn it, they can see pictures." Tweed sent some of his men to Nast with an offer of $100,000 to "study art" in Europe. The $5,000-a-year artist negotiated up to a half million dollars before refusing Tweed's offer. "I made up my mind not long ago to put some of those fellows behind bars," Nast said, "and I'm going to put them there." His cartoons helped to drive Tweed out of office.

The emergence of the United States as a world power and the rise of Theodore Roosevelt gave cartoonists plenty to draw about. At the same time, the rise of cheap newspapers such as William Randolph Hearst's *Journal* and Joseph Pulitzer's *World* provided a rich opportunity for cartoonists, whose clever images attracted more readers. When the Spanish-American War broke out, newspapers whipped up public sentiment by having artists draw fake pictures of fierce Spaniards stripping American women at sea and killing helpless Cubans. Hearst used these tactics to increase his paper's daily circulation to 1 million copies.

By the time of the debates over Philippine annexation, many cartoonists took an anti-imperialist

"The Spanish Brute Adds Mutilation to Murder" by Grant Hamilton in *Judge*, July 9, 1898. *(Culver Pictures)*

stance, pointing out American hypocrisy. Within a year, cartoonists shifted from depicting "The Spanish Brute Adds Mutilation to Murder" (1898) to "Liberty Halts American Butchery in the Philippines" (1899), both included here. Note the similarities in that both cartoons condemn the "butchery" of native peoples. But the villain has changed. Although Uncle Sam as a killer is not nearly as menacing as the figure of Spain as an ugly gorilla, both cartoons share a similarity of stance, blood-covered swords, and a trail of bodies behind.

Theodore Roosevelt's rise to the presidency and his broad grin, eyeglasses, and walrus mustache gave cartoonists a perfect target for caricature, as did his energetic style and such distinctive aspects as the "big stick" symbol and the "rough rider" image. To understand and appreciate the meaning of any cartoon, certain facts must be ascertained, such as the date, artist, and source of the cartoon; the particular historical characters, events, and context depicted in it; the significance of the caption; and the master symbols employed by the cartoonist. The Roosevelt cartoons "Panama or Bust" (1903) and "For President!" (1904), filled with symbols and images, were both printed in American daily newspapers.

Reflecting on the Past What symbols and images do you see in these two cartoons? How many can you identify, and how are they used? Who is the

"Liberty Halts American Butchery in the Philippines" from *Life,* 1899. *(TimePix, Inc.)*

woman figure, and what does she represent? How would you explain the change of bloodied sword-bearer? What is the attitude of the Roosevelt cartoonists toward the president? In addition to these cartoons, look at the others in this chapter, most with variations of a long stride reflecting the widening reach of American expanisionism. How do the images and symbols used in these reflect the cartoonist's point of view? How are various nationalities depicted in the cartoons? Check some recent newspapers: Who is criticized and stereotyped today, and how do cartoonists reveal their attitudes and political positions? What do contemporary cartoons reveal about American attitudes?

L. C. Gregg in the Atlanta Constitution.

FOR PRESIDENT!

"Panama or Bust," from the *New York Times,* 1903 (above). "For President!" by L. C. Gregg, in the *Atlanta Constitution,* 1904 (right).

Compare the photograph with the cartoon from 1898–99. The photo shows American soldiers standing guard over captured Filipino guerrillas in 1899. The cartoon, by Charles L. (Bart) Batholomew of the *Minneapolis Journal* (July 2, 1898), presents a happier, if stereotyped view of three new Americans, including one labeled "Philippines" on the skirt to the right. Or are they happier? What is the cartoonist's message? What similarities and differences do you see in these two visual images? *(Photo: Library of Congress)*

As U.S. treatment of the Filipinos became more and more like Spanish treatment of the Cubans, the hypocrisy of American behavior became even more evident. This was especially true for black American soldiers who fought in the Philippines. They identified with the dark-skinned insurgents, whom they saw as tied to the land, burdened by debt and pressed by poverty like themselves. "I feel sorry for these people," a sergeant in the 24th Infantry wrote. "You have no idea the way these people are treated by the Americans here."

The war starkly exposed the hypocrisies of shouldering the white man's burden. After the war,

Aguinaldo wrote that Americans made "vague verbal offers of friendship and aid and then fairly drowned them out with the boom of cannons and the rattle of Gatling guns." On reading a report that 8,000 Filipinos had been killed in the first year of the war, Carnegie wrote a letter, dripping with sarcasm, congratulating McKinley for "civilizing the Filipinos. . . . About 8,000 of them have been completely civilized and sent to Heaven. I hope you like it." Another writer penned a devastating one-liner: "Dewey took Manila with the loss of one man—and all our institutions." An ardent anti-imperialist, poet Ernest Howard Crosby penned a parody of Rudyard

Kipling's "White Man's Burden," which he titled "The Real 'White Man's Burden'":

Take up the White Man's burden.
Send forth your sturdy kin,
And load them down with Bibles
And cannon-balls and gin.
Throw in a few diseases
To spread the tropic climes,
For there the healthy niggers
Are quite behind the times.
They need our labor question too.
And politics and fraud—
We've made a pretty mess at home,
Let's make a mess abroad.

The anti-imperialists failed either to prevent annexation or to interfere with the war effort. However prestigious and sincere, they had little or no political power. An older elite, they were out of tune with the period of exuberant expansionist national pride, prosperity, and promise.

Expansionism Triumphant

By 1900, Americans had ample reason to be patriotic. Within a year, the United States had acquired several island territories in the Pacific and Caribbean. But several questions arose over what to do with the new territories. What was their status? Were they colonies? Would they be granted statehood, or would they develop gradually from colonies to constitutional parts of the United States? Did the indigenous peoples of Hawaii, Puerto Rico, Guam, and the Philippines have the same rights as mainland American citizens? Were they protected by the U.S. Constitution?

Although slightly different governing systems were worked out for each new territory, the solution in each case was to define its status as somewhere between a colony and a candidate for statehood. The indigenous people were usually allowed to elect their own legislature for domestic law-making, but governors and other judicial and administrative officials were appointed by the American president. The first full governor of the Philippines, McKinley appointee William Howard Taft, effectively moved the Filipinos toward self-government. Final independence did not come until 1946.

The question of constitutional rights was resolved by deciding that Hawaiians and Puerto Ricans, for example, would be treated differently from Texans and Oregonians. In the "insular cases" of 1901, the Supreme Court ruled that these people would achieve citizenship and constitutional rights only when Congress said they were ready. To the question, "Does the Constitution follow the flag?" the answer, as Secretary of State Elihu Root put it, was "Ye-es, as near as I can make out the Constitution follows the flag—but doesn't quite catch up with it."

In the election of 1900, Bryan was again the Democratic nominee and tried to make imperialism the "paramount issue" of the campaign. He failed, in part because the country strongly favored annexation and the popular war in the Philippines. In the closing weeks of the campaign, Bryan shied away from imperialism and focused on domestic issues— trusts, the labor question, and free silver.

That did Bryan no good either. Prosperity returned with the discovery of gold in Alaska, and cries for reform fell on deaf ears. The McKinley forces rightly claimed that four years of Republican rule had brought more money, jobs, thriving factories, and manufactured goods, as well as the tremendous growth in American prestige abroad. Spain had been kicked out of Cuba, and the American flag flew in many places around the globe. As Tom Watson put it, noting the end of the Populist revolt with the war fervor over Cuba, "The blare of the bugle drowned out the voice of the reformer."

He was more right than he knew. Within one year, expansionist Theodore Roosevelt rose from assistant secretary of the navy to colonel of the Rough Riders to governor of New York. For some Republican politicos, who thought he was too vigorous and independent, this quick rise as McKinley's potential rival came too fast. One way to eliminate Roosevelt politically, or at least slow him down, was to make him vice president, which they did in 1900. But six months into McKinley's second term, an anarchist killed him; this was the third presidential assassination in less than 40 years. "Now look," exclaimed party boss Mark Hanna, who had opposed putting Roosevelt on the ticket, "that damned cowboy is President of the United States!"

THEODORE ROOSEVELT'S ENERGETIC DIPLOMACY

At a White House dinner party in 1905, a guest told a story about visiting the Roosevelt home when "Teedie" was a baby. "You were in your bassinet, making a good deal of fuss and noise," the guest reported, "and your father lifted you out and asked me to hold you." Secretary of State Elihu Root looked up and asked, "Was he hard to hold?" Whether true or not, the story reveals much about President Roosevelt's principles and policies on foreign affairs. As president from 1901 to 1909, and as the most

This 1900 campaign poster for McKinley makes a compelling case that four years of Republican party leadership had brought prosperity and humanity both at home and abroad. Note not only that McKinley and Roosevelt have wrapped themselves in the American flag but also the dramatic contrasts after four years of Republican rule compared with the condition of the United States and Cuba when the Democrats left office in 1896. *(From the collection of David J. and Janice L. Frent)*

dominating American personality for the 15 years between 1897 and 1912, Roosevelt made much fuss and noise about the activist role he thought the United States should play in the world. As he implemented his policies, he often seemed "hard to hold." Yet Roosevelt's energetic foreign policy in Latin America, Eastern Asia, and Europe paved the way for the vital role as a world power that the United States would play for the next century.

Foreign Policy as Darwinian Struggle

Roosevelt advocated both individual physical fitness and collective national strength. An undersized boy, he had pursued a rigorous body-building program, and as a young man on his North Dakota ranch, he learned to value the "strenuous life." Reading Darwin taught him that life was a constant struggle for survival. As president, his ideal was a "nation of men, not weaklings." To be militarily prepared and to fight well were tests of racial superiority and national greatness. "All the great masterful races," he said, "have been fighting races." Although

he believed in Anglo-Saxon superiority, he admired—and feared—Japanese military prowess. Roosevelt believed that powerful nations, like individuals, had a duty to cultivate vigor, strength, courage, and moral commitment to civilized values. In practical terms, this meant developing natural resources, building large navies, and being ever-prepared to fight.

Although famous for saying "speak softly and carry a big stick," Roosevelt often not only wielded a large stick but spoke loudly as well. In a speech in 1897, he used the word *war* 62 times, saying, "no triumph of peace is quite so great as the supreme triumphs of war." But despite his bluster, Roosevelt was usually restrained in exercising force. He won the Nobel Peace Prize in 1906 for helping end the Russo-Japanese War. The big stick and the loud talk were meant to preserve order and peace.

Roosevelt divided the world into civilized and uncivilized nations, the former usually defined as Anglo-Saxon and English-speaking. Civilized nations had a responsibility to "police" the uncivilized,

The "big stick" became a memorable image in American diplomacy as Teddy Roosevelt sought to make the United States a policeman not only of the Caribbean basin but also of the whole world. "As our modern life goes on," Roosevelt said, "and the nations are drawn closer together for good and for evil, and this nation grows in comparison with friends and rivals, it is impossible to adhere to the policy of isolation." (Puck, 1901)

not only maintaining order but also spreading superior values and institutions. Taking on the "white man's burden," civilized nations sometimes had to wage war on the uncivilized, as the British did against the Boers and the Americans did in the Philippines. These wars were justified because the victors bestowed the blessings of culture and racial superiority on the vanquished.

But a war between two civilized nations (for example, Germany and Great Britain) would be foolish. Above all, Roosevelt believed in the balance of power. Strong, advanced nations like the United States had a duty to use their power to preserve order and peace. The United States had "no choice," Roosevelt said, but to "play a great part in the world." With a 1900 population of 75 million, more than Great Britain, Germany, or France, Americans could no longer "avoid responsibilities" that followed from "the fact that on the east and west we look across the waters at Europe and Asia."

As Roosevelt looked across the oceans, he developed a highly personal style of diplomacy. Bypassing the State Department, he preferred face-to-face contact and personal exchanges of letters with foreign diplomats and heads of state. He made foreign policy while horseback riding with the German ambassador and while discussing history with a French minister. A British emissary observed that Roosevelt had a "powerful personality" and a commanding knowledge of the world. Ministries from London to Tokyo respected both the president and the power of the United States.

When threats failed to accomplish his goals, Roosevelt used direct personal intervention. "In a crisis the duty of a leader is to lead," he said, noting that Congress was too slow. When he wanted Panama, Roosevelt bragged later, "I took the Canal Zone" rather than submitting a long "dignified State Paper" for congressional debate. And while Congress debated, the building of the canal began. Roosevelt's energetic executive activism in foreign policy set a pattern for nearly every twentieth-century president.

Taking the Panama Canal

To justify the intervention of 2,600 American troops in Honduras and Nicaragua in 1906, Philander Knox, later a secretary of state, said, "because of the Monroe Doctrine" the United States is "held responsible for the order of Central America." The closeness of the Canal, he said, "makes the preservation of peace in that neighborhood particularly necessary." The Panama Canal was not yet finished when Knox spoke, but it had already become a cornerstone of United States policy.

Three problems had to be surmounted in order to dig an inter-oceanic connection. First, an 1850 treaty bound the United States to build a canal jointly with Great Britain, a problem resolved in 1901 when the British canceled the treaty in exchange for an American guarantee that the canal would be open to

(Above) In 1903, despite protests from the Panamanian government, the United States acquired the right to begin the enormous engineering feat of building the Panama Canal. *(The Granger Collection)* (Left) A year later, a cartoonist showed the American eagle celebrating "his 128th birthday" with wings spanning the globe from Panama to the Philippines. In a prophetic anticipation of American overexpansion in the twentieth century, the eagle says, "Gee, but this is an awful stretch." *(The Granger Collection, New York)*

all nations. A second problem was where to dig it. American engineers rejected a long route through Nicaragua in favor of a shorter, more rugged path across Panama, where a French firm had already begun work. This raised the third problem: Panama was a province of Colombia, which rejected the terms the United States offered. This angered Roosevelt, who called the Colombians "Dagoes" who tried to "hold us up" like highway robbers.

Aware of Roosevelt's fury, encouraged by hints of American support, and eager for the economic benefits that a canal would bring, Panamanian nationalists in 1903 staged a revolution led by several rich families and Philippe Bunau-Varilla of the French canal company. An American warship deterred Colombian intervention, and local troops were separated from their officers, who were bought off. A bloodless revolution occurred on November 3; the next day, Panama declared its independence, and on November 6, the United States recognized it.

Although Roosevelt did not directly encourage the revolution, it would not have occurred without American help.

On November 18, Hay and Bunau-Varilla signed a treaty establishing the American right to build and operate a canal through Panama and to exercise "titular sovereignty" over the 10-mile-wide Canal Zone. The Panamanian government protested, and a later government called it the "treaty that no Panamanian signed." Roosevelt, in his later boast that he "took the canal," claimed that his diplomatic and engineering achievement, completed in 1914, would "rank . . . with the Louisiana Purchase and the acquisition of Texas."

Policing the Caribbean

As late as 1901, the Monroe Doctrine was still regarded, according to Roosevelt, as the "equivalent to an open door in South America." To the United

States, this meant that although no nation had a right "to get territorial possessions," all nations had equal commercial rights in the Western Hemisphere south of the Rio Grande. But as American investments poured into Central America and the Caribbean, the policy changed to one of asserting U.S. dominance in the Caribbean basin.

This change was demonstrated in 1902 when Germany and Great Britain blockaded Venezuela's ports to force the government to pay defaulted debts. Roosevelt was especially worried that German influence would replace the British. He insisted that the European powers accept arbitration and threatened to "move Dewey's ships" to the Venezuelan coast. The crisis passed, largely for other reasons, but Roosevelt's threat of force made very clear the paramount presence and self-interest of the United States in the Caribbean.

After kicking the Spanish out of Cuba, the United States supervised the land under Military Governor Leonard Wood until 1902, when the Cubans elected a congress and president. The United States honored Cuban independence, as it had promised to do in the Teller Amendment. But through the Platt Amendment, which Cubans reluctantly added to their constitution in 1901, the United States obtained many economic rights in Cuba, a naval base at Guantanamo Bay, and the right to intervene if Cuban sovereignty were ever threatened. Newspapers in Havana assailed this violation of their newfound independence. A cartoon titled "The Cuban Calvary" showed a figure representing "the Cuban people" crucified between two thieves, Wood and McKinley.

American policy intended to make Cuba a model of how a newly independent nation could achieve orderly self-government with only minimal guidance. Cuban self-government, however, was shaky. When in 1906 a political crisis threatened to spiral into civil war, Roosevelt expressed his fury with "that infernal little Cuban republic." He sent warships to patrol the coastline and special commissioners and troops "to restore order and peace and public confidence." As he left office in 1909, Roosevelt proudly proclaimed, "we have done our best to put Cuba on the road to stable and orderly government." The road was paved with sugar, as U.S. trade with Cuba increased from $27 to $43 million in the decade following 1898. Along with economic development, which mostly benefited American companies, American political and even military involvement in Cuban affairs would continue throughout the century.

The pattern was repeated throughout the Caribbean. The Dominican Republic, for example, suffered from unstable governments and great poverty. In 1904, as a revolt erupted, European creditors pressured the Dominican government for payment of $40 million in defaulted bonds. Sending its warships to discourage European intervention, the United States took over the collection of customs in the republic. Two years later, the United States intervened in Guatemala and Nicaragua, where American bankers controlled nearly 50 percent of all trade, the first of several twentieth-century interventions in those countries.

Roosevelt clarified his policy that civilized nations should "insist on the proper policing of the world" in his annual message to Congress in 1904. The goal of the United States, he said, was to have "stable, orderly and prosperous neighbors." A country that paid its debts and kept order "need fear no interference from the United States." But "chronic wrong-doing" would require the United States to intervene as an "international police power." This policing policy became known as the Roosevelt Corollary to the Monroe Doctrine. Whereas the Monroe Doctrine had warned European nations not to intervene in the Western Hemisphere, Roosevelt's corollary justified American intervention. Starting with a desire to protect property, loans, and investments, the United States wound up supporting the tyrannical regimes of elites who owned most of the land, suppressed the poor, blocked reforms, and acted as American surrogates.

After 1904, the Roosevelt Corollary was invoked in several Caribbean countries. Intervention usually required the landing of U.S. Marines to counter a threat to American property. Occupying the capital and major seaports, Marines, bankers, and customs officials usually remained for several years, until they were satisfied that stability had been reestablished. Roosevelt's successors, William Howard Taft and Woodrow Wilson, pursued the same interventionist policy. So would late-twentieth-century presidents: Ronald Reagan (Grenada and Nicaragua), George Bush (Panama), and Bill Clinton (Haiti).

Opening Doors to China and Closing Doors to America

Throughout the nineteenth century, American relations with China were restricted to a small but profitable trade. The British, in competition with France, Germany, and Russia, took advantage of the crumbling Manchu dynasty to force treaties on China, creating "treaty ports" and granting exclusive trading privileges in various parts of the country. After 1898, Americans with dreams of exploiting the seemingly unlimited markets of China wanted to join the competition and enlarge their share. Those with moral interests, however, including many missionaries, reminded Americans of their revolutionary tradition against European imperialism. They opposed U.S. commercial exploitation of a weak nation and supported the preservation of China's political integrity as the other imperial powers moved toward partitioning the country.

American attitudes toward the Chinese people reflected this confusion of motives. Although some admired China's ancient culture, the dominant American attitude viewed the Chinese as heathen, exotic, and backward. Workers' riots against the competition of Chinese workers in the 1870s and 1880s and the Chinese Exclusion Act of 1882 barring further immigration to the United States reflected this negative stereotype. The Chinese, in turn, regarded the United States with a mixture of admiration, curiosity, resentment, suspicion, and disdain.

The annexation of Hawaii and the Philippines in 1898 and 1899 convinced Secretary of State Hay that the United States should announce a China policy. He did so in the Open Door notes of 1899–1900, which became the cornerstone of U.S. policy in eastern Asia for half a century. The first note demanded an open door for American trade by declaring the principle of equal access to commercial rights in China by all nations. The second note, addressing Russian movement into Manchuria, called on all countries to respect the "territorial and administrative integrity" of China. This second principle announced a larger American role in Asia, offering China protection and preserving an east Asian balance of power.

An early test of this new role came during the Boxer Rebellion in 1900. The Boxers were a society of young traditionalist Chinese in revolt against both the Manchu dynasty and the growing Western presence in China. During the summer of 1900, Boxers killed some 242 missionaries and other foreigners and besieged the western quarter of Beijing. Eventually an international military force of 19,000 troops, including some 3,000 Americans sent from the Philippines, marched on Beijing to end the siege.

The relationship with China was plagued by the exclusionist immigration policy of the United States and by laws inhibiting Chinese in America from becoming naturalized citizens. Educated at Yale, Yung Wing had been living in the United States since the 1850s and headed the Chinese Educational Mission to bring Chinese students to the United States. Unfortunately, while visiting China in 1898, his American citizenship was revoked and he was allowed to reenter the country only as an alien. Wing denounced American discriminatory laws, pointing out "how far this Republic has departed from its high ideal." Others banded together in a Chinese American Citizens Alliance in protest. Despite unjust laws, barriers, and riots, Chinese workers and students kept coming to the United States, entering illegally through Mexico and British Columbia. Meanwhile, in 1905, Chinese nationalists at home boycotted American goods to protest exclusion and the discrimination of Chinese workers. President Roosevelt, contemptuous of what he called "backward" Chinese, sent troops to the Philippines as a threat. Halfheartedly, he also asked Congress for a modified immigration bill, but nothing came of it.

Despite exclusion and insults, the idea that the United States had a unique guardian relationship with China persisted into the twentieth century. Japan had ambitions in China, which created a rivalry between Japan and the United States, testing the American commitment to the Open Door in China and the balance of power in eastern Asia. Economic motives, however, proved to be less significant. Investments there developed very slowly, as did the dream of the "great China market" for American grains and textiles. The China trade always remained larger in imagination than in reality.

Balancing Japan in the Pacific from California to Manchuria

Population pressures, war, and a quest for economic opportunities caused Japanese immigration to the United States to increase dramatically around the turn of the century. Some came from Hawaii, where they had "worked like machines" in the sugarcane fields, many dying from overwork and white diseases. "Hawaii, Hawaii," a sorrowful poet wrote: "Like a dream / So I came / But my tears / Are flowing now / In the canefields." Pursuing "huge dreams of fortune . . . across the ocean," some 200,000 went directly to the West Coast of the United States, coming first to work on railroads and in West Coast canneries, mines, and logging camps. Others worked on farms in the valleys of Oregon and California, many successfully rising to own their own lands and turning marginal farmlands into productive agricultural businesses.

One such story is that of Kinji Ushijima, who rose from a potato picker to a labor contractor, eventually developing 10,000 acres of potato lands worth $500,000 in the fertile deltas between Stockton and Sacramento. By 1912, known then as George Shima, the "Potato King," he was praised as a model by the *San Francisco Chronicle*. But when Shima moved to

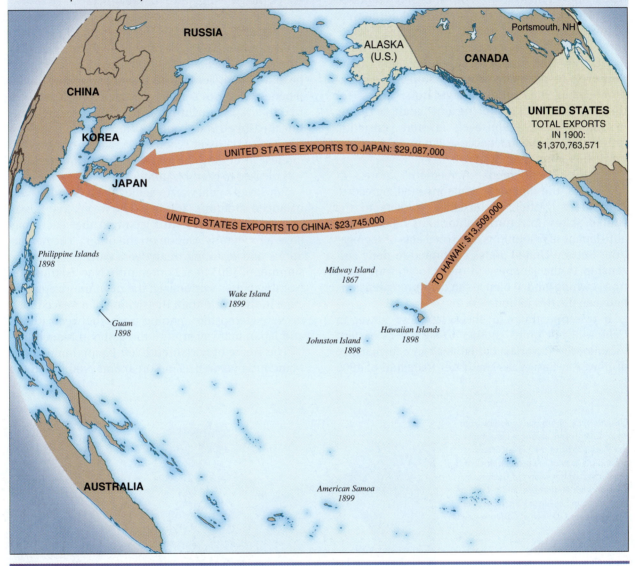

U.S. Involvement in the Pacific and Eastern Asia, 1898–1909

By 1898, the United States expanded far into eastern Asia and the Pacific. **Reflecting on the Past** Which motivations do you think were most important for U.S. involvement in the Pacific and eastern Asia at the turn of the twentieth century: profits, patriotism, piety, or politics? What major twentieth-century events followed the acquisition of territories in the Pacific and the development of greater trade with eastern Asian countries? Where is there a strong American presence today?

RUSSIA

Portsmouth, NH

ALASKA (U.S.)

CANADA

CHINA

KOREA

UNITED STATES EXPORTS TO JAPAN: $29,087,000

JAPAN

UNITED STATES
TOTAL EXPORTS
IN 1900:
$1,370,763,571

UNITED STATES EXPORTS TO CHINA: $23,745,000

TO HAWAII: $13,509,000

Philippine Islands
1898

Midway Island
1867

Wake Island
1899

Guam
1898

Hawaiian Islands
1898

Johnston Island
1898

AUSTRALIA

American Samoa
1899

a well-to-do neighborhood in Berkeley, local newspapers and protesters led by a classics professor complained of the "Yellow Peril in College Town." Shima refused to move. Another success story was Abiko Kyutaro, who built several successful service businesses and in 1906 founded a model Japanese farming community in the San Joaquin Valley, with 42 families turning desert land into bountiful or-

chards, grape vineyards, and alfalfa fields. In discussing the Yamato (or "new Japan") Colony, Kyutaro proclaimed, "The Japanese must settle permanently with their countrymen on large pieces of land if they are to succeed in America." Men like Shima and Kyutaro contributed to a huge jump in the acreage owned by Japanese farmers, which increased from 4,698 acres in 1900 to 194,742 by 1910, when Japanese-owned farms produced 70 percent of the California strawberry crop.

Threatened by this competitive success, native white Californians sought ways to exclude Japanese immigrants, discriminate against them, and limit their ability to own or lease land. Japanese workers were barred from factory jobs and shunted off to agricultural labor in California fields and orchards. In 1906, the San Francisco school board, claiming that Japanese children were "crowding the whites out of the schools," segregated them into separate schools. Californians passed an anti-Japanese resolution and asked Roosevelt to persuade Japan to stop the emigration. Calling the California legislators "idiots" for their actions and denouncing anti-Japanese rioting in San Francisco, Roosevelt favored restriction rather than exclusion because Japan was a more powerful nation than China.

In the "Gentlemen's Agreement" notes of 1907–1908, the Japanese, while insulted, agreed to limit the migration of unskilled workers to the United States. In return, Californians repealed the anti-Japanese resolutions and some acts of segregation. But the United States continued to deny citizenship to the Japanese in order to prevent them from owning land, which led to continuing tensions between the two nations.

It was one thing to check Japanese power in California but quite another to stop it in eastern Asia. Roosevelt worked hard to maintain the balance of power in East Asia. The Boxer Rebellion of 1900

left Russia with 50,000 troops in Manchuria, making it the strongest regional power. Roosevelt's admiration for the Japanese as a "fighting" people and valuable factor in the "civilization of the future" contrasted with his low respect for the Russians, whom he described as "corrupt," "treacherous," and "incompetent." As Japan moved into Korea and Russia into Manchuria, Roosevelt hoped that each would check the growing power of the other.

Roosevelt welcomed news in 1904 that Japan had successfully mounted a surprise attack on Port Arthur in Manchuria, beginning the Russo-Japanese War. He was "well pleased with the Japanese victory," he told his son, "for Japan is playing our game." But as Japanese victories continued, many Americans worried that Japan might play the game too well, shutting the United States out of Asian markets. Roosevelt tilted toward Russia. When the Japanese expressed an interest in ending the war, the American president was pleased to exert his influence.

Roosevelt's goal was to achieve peace and leave a balanced situation. "It is best," he wrote, that Russia be left "face to face with Japan so that each may have a moderative action on the other." The negotiations and resulting treaty were carried out in the summer of 1905 near Portsmouth, New Hampshire. Nothing better-symbolized the new American presence in the world than the signing of a peace treaty in New Hampshire, ending a war between Russia and Japan halfway around the globe in Manchuria.

The Treaty of Portsmouth left Japan dominant in Manchuria (as well as in Korea) and established the

Despite facing enormous prejudice from white Californians, Japanese immigrants to the West Coast of the United States around the turn of the century worked hard, irrigated the valleys of California, Oregon, and Washington, and became independent and highly productive farmers. *(Pat Hathaway Collection of California Views)*

United States as the major balance to Japan's power. Almost immediately, the Japanese developed a naval base at Port Arthur, built railroads, and sought exclusive rights of investment and control in the Chinese province. In the Root-Takahira Agreement of 1908, in return for recognizing these developments, Roosevelt got Japan's promise to honor U.S. control in the Philippines and to make no further encroachments into China.

The agreement barely papered over Japanese-American tensions. Some Japanese blamed Roosevelt that the Treaty of Portsmouth had not given them indemnities from Russia. American insensitivity on the immigration issue left bad feelings. In Manchuria, the U.S. consul general aggressively pushed an anti-Japanese program of financing capital-investment projects in banking and railroads. Like the pursuit of markets, this policy (known as "dollar diplomacy" under Roosevelt's successor, William Howard Taft) was larger in prospect than results. Nevertheless, the United States was in Japan's way, and rumors of war circulated.

It was clearly a moment for Roosevelt's "big stick." In 1907, he told Secretary of State Root that he was "more concerned over the Japanese situation than almost any other. Thank Heaven we have the navy in good shape." Although the naval buildup had begun over a decade earlier, under Roosevelt the U.S. Navy developed into a formidable force. From 1900 to 1905, outlays to the navy rose from $56 to $117 million, a naval binge unprecedented in peacetime. In 1907, to make it clear that "the Pacific was as much our home waters as the Atlantic," Roosevelt sent his new, modernized "Great White Fleet" on a goodwill world tour. The first stop was Yokohama. Although American sailors were greeted warmly, the act may have stimulated navalism in Japan, which came back to haunt the United States in 1941. But for the time being, the balance of power in eastern Asia was preserved.

Preventing War in Europe

The United States had stretched the Monroe Doctrine to justify sending Marines and engineers to Latin America and the navy and dollars to eastern Asia. Treaties, agreements, and the protection of territories and interests entangled the United States with foreign nations from Panama and Nicaragua to the Philippines and Japan. Toward European nations, however, traditional neutrality continued.

Roosevelt believed—and for good reason—that the most serious threats to world peace and civilized order lay in the relationships among Germany, Great Britain, and France. Those powers were competing amongst themselves for colonies in Asia and Africa and building large, threatening, modern navies. Tensions increased in Europe as the major countries sought to construct alliances with other nations to protect themselves in the eventuality of war.

Roosevelt established two fundamental policies toward Europe that would define the U.S. role throughout the century. The first was to make friendship with Great Britain the cornerstone of U.S. policy, telling King Edward VII in 1905, "In the long run the English people are more apt to be friendly to us than any other." Second, the goal of a neutral power like the United States was to prevent a general war in Europe among strong nations. Toward this end, Roosevelt depended on his personal negotiating skills and began the twentieth-century practice of a kind of summit diplomacy with leaders of major nations.

The Venezuelan crisis of 1895 shocked the United States and Britain into an awareness of their mutual interests. Both nations appreciated the neutrality of the other in their respective colonial wars in the Philippines and South Africa. Roosevelt supported British imperialism because he favored the dominance of the "English-speaking race" and believed that Britain was "fighting the battle of civilization." Furthermore, both nations worried about growing German power around the world. As German naval power increased, Britain had to bring its fleet closer to home. Friendly allies were needed to police parts of the world formerly patrolled by the British navy. The United Kingdom therefore concluded a mutual-protection treaty with Japan in 1902 and willingly let the Americans police Central America and the Caribbean Sea.

Language, cultural traditions, and strategic self-interest drew the two countries together. Roosevelt, moreover, was unashamedly pro-British, and his most intimate circle of friends included many Englishmen. As Roosevelt wrote to Lodge in 1901, he knew that the United States had "not the least particle of danger to fear" from Britain and that German ambitions and militarism represented the major threat to peace in Europe. As Roosevelt left the presidency in 1909, one of his final acts was to proclaim the special American friendship with Great Britain.

German Kaiser Wilhelm II underestimated the Anglo-American friendship and thought that Roosevelt was really pro-German. Roosevelt cultivated the Kaiser's illusion, and Wilhelm sought his support on several diplomatic issues between 1905 and 1909. In each case, Roosevelt flattered the Kaiser while politely rejecting his overtures. The relationship gave Roosevelt a unique advantage in trying to prevent war in Europe, most notably

Global Imperial Activities, 1893–1904

Reflecting on the Past Note the increasing presence of the United States and the world-wide nature of imperialism. Can you locate on a map, or globe, the many places mentioned in this chart? What is the racial composition of the "where" and the "who"? What conclusions do you draw?

Year	Where	Who	What
1893	Hawaii	United States	U.S.-backed annexationists overthrow Hawaiian queen.
1893	Laos	France	Laos becomes a French protectorate.
1893	French Guyana; Ivory Coast	France	France establishes two colonies on two continents.
1894–1895	China	Japan	Japan starts and wins war with China. Japan acquires Taiwan and gets an indemnity for war costs.
1895	South Africa	Britain	British annex Tongaland.
1895	Venezuela	United States; Britain	Tensions over boundary dispute with British Guyana.
1896	Ethiopia	Italy	Italy invades Ethiopia and is defeated by the Ethiopian army.
1896	Rhodesia (Zimbabwe)	Britain	A revolt begins in Rhodesia and is suppressed.
1896–1897	Madagascar	France	French claim Madagascar and depose the queen.
1896–1898	Sudan	Britain	British reconquer Sudan.
1897	Madagascar	France	The Queen of Madagascar is deposed.
1897–1898	Hawaii	United States	United States annexes Hawaii.
1897	China	Germany	Germans occupy Shandong Province.
1898–1899	Philippines	Spain; United States	Annexed by United States after Spanish-American War.
1898–1902	Guam; Puerto Rico; Cuba	Spain; United States	Those islands become U.S. territories or protectorates after Spanish-American War.
1899	China	United States	United States establishes Open Door policy.
1899–1902	South Africa; Philippines	Britain; Boers; United States; Philippines	Wars pass control of indigenous peoples to British and Americans.
1899	Ghana	Britain	Ashanti rebellion suppressed.
1900–1901	China	United States; Japan; Britain; Germany and others	Boxer Rebellion suppressed.
1902	Venezuela	United States; Britain; Germany	Blockade ports and compete with each other over Venezuelan debt crisis.
1903	Colombia/Panama	United States	United States backs Panamanian revolutionaries for independence from Colombia.
1904	Manchuria	Japan; Russia	Japan attacks Port Arthur, starting the Russo-Japanese War.

during the Moroccan crisis in 1905 and 1906. When Germany and France threatened to go to war over the control of Morocco, Roosevelt intervened at the Kaiser's bidding and arranged a conference in Algeciras, Spain, to head off conflict. The treaty signed in 1906 peacefully settled the Moroccan issue, though favorably for the French.

Roosevelt continued to successfully counter meddlesome German policies. At the Hague conference on disarmament in 1907, the Kaiser sought an agreement to reduce British naval supremacy, a superiority Roosevelt thought "quite proper." The German emperor also tried to promote a German-Chinese-American entente to balance the Anglo-Japanese Treaty in Asia. Roosevelt rebuffed all these efforts. Touring Europe in 1910, the ex-president was warmly entertained by Wilhelm, who continued to misunderstand him. Roosevelt, meanwhile, kept urging his English friends to

counter the German naval buildup in order to maintain peace in Europe.

In 1911, Roosevelt wrote that there would be nothing worse than that "Germany should ever overthrow England and establish the supremacy in Europe she aims at." A German attempt "to try her hand in America," he thought, would surely follow. To avert it, Roosevelt's policy for Europe included cementing friendship with England and, while maintaining official neutrality, using diplomacy to prevent hostilities among European powers. The relationship between Great Britain and Germany continued to deteriorate, however, and by 1914, a new American president, Woodrow Wilson, would face the terrible reality that Roosevelt had skillfully sought to prevent. When World War I finally broke out, no American was more eager to fight on the British side against the Germans than the leader of the Rough Riders.

Timeline

1823	Monroe Doctrine
1857	Trade opens with Japan
1867	Alaska purchased from Russia
1870	Failure to annex Santo Domingo (Hispaniola)
1875	Sugar reciprocity treaty with Hawaii
1877	United States acquires naval base at Pearl Harbor
1878	United States acquires naval station in Samoa
1882	Chinese Exclusion Act
1889	First Pan-American Conference
1890	Alfred Mahan publishes *Influence of Sea Power upon History*
1893	Hawaiian coup by American sugar growers
1895	Cuban revolt against Spanish Venezuelan boundary dispute
1896	Weyler's reconcentration policy in Cuba McKinley-Bryan presidential campaign
1897	Roosevelt's speech at Naval War College
1898	Sinking of the *Maine* Spanish-American War Teller Amendment Dewey takes Manila Bay Annexation of Hawaiian Islands Americans liberate Manila; War ends Treaty of Paris; Annexation of the Philippines
1899	Senate ratifies Treaty of Paris Filipino-American War begins American Samoa acquired

1899–1900	Open Door notes
1900	Boxer Rebellion in China William McKinley reelected president
1901	Supreme Court insular cases McKinley assassinated; Theodore Roosevelt becomes president
1902	Filipino-American War ends U.S. military occupation of Cuba ends Platt Amendment Venezuela debt crisis
1903	Panamanian revolt and independence Hay-Bunau-Varilla Treaty
1904	Roosevelt Corollary
1904–1905	Russo-Japanese War ended by treaty signed at Portsmouth, New Hampshire
1904–1906	United States intervenes in Nicaragua, Guatemala, and Cuba
1905–1906	Moroccan crisis
1906	Roosevelt receives Nobel Peace Prize
1907	Gentleman's agreement with Japan
1908	Root-Takahira Agreement
1909	U.S. Navy ("Great White Fleet") sails around the world
1911	United States intervenes in Nicaragua
1914	Opening of the Panama Canal World War I begins
1916	Partial home rule granted to the Philippines

✦ *Conclusion*

THE RESPONSIBILITIES OF POWER

Since the earliest settlements in Massachusetts, Americans had struggled with the dilemma of how to do good in a world that did wrong. The realities of power in the 1890s brought increasing international responsibilities. Roosevelt said in 1910 that because of "strength and geographical situation," the United States had itself become "more and more, the balance of power of the whole world." This ominous responsibility was also an opportunity to extend American economic, political, and moral influence around the globe even while insulting new and would-be immigrants at home.

As president in the first decade of the twentieth century, Roosevelt established aggressive American policies toward the rest of the world. The United States dominated and policed Central America and the Caribbean Sea to maintain order and protect its investments and other economic interests. In eastern Asia, Americans marched through Hay's Open Door with treaties, troops, navies, missionaries and dollars to protect the newly annexed Philippine Islands, to develop markets and investments, and to preserve the balance of power. In Europe, the United States sought to remain neutral and uninvolved in European affairs and at the same time to cement Anglo-American friendship and prevent "civilized" nations from going to war.

How well these policies worked would be seen later in the twentieth century. Whatever the particular judgment, the fundamental ambivalence of America's sense of itself as a model "city on a hill," an example to others, remained. As questionable actions around the world—Private Grayson's and others' in the Filipino-American War, for example—painfully demonstrated, it was increasingly difficult for the United States to be both responsible and good, both powerful and loved. The American people thus learned to experience both the satisfactions and burdens, both the profits and costs, of the missionary role, as they still are 100 years later.

◆ Recommended Reading

Steps Toward Empire and Expansionism in the 1890s
Robert Beisner, *From the Old Diplomacy to the New, 1865–1900* (1975); John Dobson, *Reticent Expansionism: The Foreign Policy of William McKinley* (1988); Ada Ferrer, *Insurgent Cuba: Race, Nation, and Revolution, 1868–1898* (1999); David Healy, *U.S. Expansion: Imperialist Urge in the 1890s* (1970); Walter LaFeber, *The Cambridge History of Foreign Relations: The Search for Opportunity, 1865–1913* (1993); H. Wayne Morgan, *America's Road to Empire: The War with Spain and Overseas Expansion* (1965); Frank Ninkovich, *The United States and Imperialism* (2001); Milton Plesur, *America's Outward Thrust, 1865–1890* (1971).

War in Cuba and the Philippines
Robert Beisner, *Twelve Against Empire: The Anti-Imperialists, 1898–1900* (1968); James E. Bradford, ed., *Crucible of Empire: The Spanish-American War and Its Aftermath* (1993); Willard Gatewood, Jr., *Black Americans and the White Man's Burden* (1975); Kristen L. Hoganson, *Fighting for American Manhood: How Gender Politics Provoked the Spanish-American and Philippine-American Wars* (1998); Brian Linn, *The Philippine War: 1899–1902* (2000); Stuart Creighton Miller, *"Benevolent Assimilation": The American Conquest of the Philippines, 1899–1903* (1982); Ivan Musicant, *Empire by Default: The Spanish-American War and the Dawn of the American Century* (1998); John L. Offner, *An Unwanted War: The Diplomacy of the United States and Spain over Cuba, 1895–1898* (1992); Louis A. Perez, Jr., *The War of 1898: The United States and Cuba in History and Historiography* (1998); Angel Smith and Emma Davila-Cox, eds., *The Crisis of 1898: Colonial Redistribution and Nationalist Mobilization* (1999); David Trask, *The War with Spain in 1898* (1981); David Traxel, *1898: The Birth of the American Century* (1998); Richard Welch, *Response to Imperialism: The United States and the Philippine-American War, 1899–1902* (1979).

Theodore Roosevelt's Energetic Diplomacy
Howard Beale, *Theodore Roosevelt and the Rise of America to World Power* (1956); Richard H. Collin, *Theodore Roosevelt's Caribbean: The Panama Canal, the Monroe Doctrine, and the Latin American Context* (1990); Roger Daniels, *Asian Americans: Chinese and Japanese in the United States Since 1850* (1988); Walter La Feber, *Inevitable Revolutions: The United States in Central America* (1983); Frederick Marks III, *Velvet on Iron: The Diplomacy of Theodore Roosevelt* (1979); David McCollough, *The Path Between the Seas: The Creation of the Panama Canal, 1870–1914* (1977); Edmund Morris, *The Rise of Theodore Roosevelt* (1979) and *Theodore Rex* (2001); Ronald Takaki, *A Different Mirror* (1993) and *Strangers from a Different Shore: A History of Asian Americans* (1989); Scott Wong and Sucheng Chan, eds., *Claiming America: Constructing Chinese American Identities during the Exclusion Era* (1998); Marilyn B. Young, *The Rhetoric of Empire: American China Policy, 1895–1901* (1968).

Fiction and Film
Ernest Howard Crosby's *Captain Jinks, Hero* (1902), a delight if you can find it, is an anti-imperialist novel set in the Philippines. James Michener's *Hawaii* (1959) is an immense saga of the multicultural history of the islands annexed by the United States in 1898. *The Woman Warrior* by Maxine Hong Kingston (1975) faithfully reflects Chinese culture in the coming-of-age story of a young Chinese-American woman in California. Frank Chinn's *Donald Duk* (1911) is a fanciful story of San Francisco's Chinatown, with flashbacks to the history of Chinese railroad workers in the late nineteenth century. The PBS video *Crucible of Empire: The Spanish-American War* (1999) uses rare archival materials, photos, motion pictures, newspapers, and popular songs to recreate the war. Two PBS videos from *The American Experience* series depict the history of the era: *Hawaii's Last Queen* (1997) describes the clash between native Hawaiians and U.S. business interests and Marines, and *America, 1900* (1998) focuses on the year 1900, including the second presidential race between McKinley and Bryan. *In Our Image*, a history of America in the Philippines from 1898 to 1946, is a video produced to accompany Stanley Karnow's *In Our Image: America's Empire in the Philippines* (1989). The first tape covers the Filipino-American war.

◆ Discovering U.S. History Online

Alaska Purchase

www.library.state.ak.us./hist/cent/home.html

"An interesting array of portraits of persons important in Alaska's history, photographs of communities, transportation, gold rush views and more."

Imperialism in the Making of America

www.boondocksnet.com

This site has nineteenth-century articles indexed by author about imperialism from archival sites at the University of Michigan and Cornell University.

Anti-Imperialism in the United States, 1898–1935

www.boondocksnet.com/ai

An extensive collection of primary and present-day documents about anti-imperialism in America.

The Age of Imperialism

www.smplanet.com/imperialism/toc.html

An online history of U.S. imperialism with teaching resources and links.

Images from the Philippine-United States War

www.historicaltextarchive.com/USA/twenty/filipino.html

An archive of historical photos from the war.

William McKinley

www.history.ohio-state.edu/projects/McKinley

The Ohio State University site contains a collection of essays and photos about McKinley through different political periods, the Mexican War, and in political cartoons.

The Panama Canal

www.pancanal.com/eng

The English version of the official Panama Canal site. The site includes a colorful, interactive section on the history of the canal.

America, 1900

www.pbs.org/wgbh/amex/1900

A companion to the film, this site contains information on more than 20 key figures from the period and many key events from the early 1990s.

21

The Progressives Confront Industrial Capitalism

George Bellows, *Cliff Dwellers,* 1913. Bellows was one of many talented artists who migrated from the Midwest to New York early in the century. In this painting, he captures some of the life and excitement in a tenement district on a hot summer night. To Bellows, this was romantic; to the progressive reformers, it was a problem to be solved. *(Los Angeles County Museum of Art, Los Angeles County Funds)*

◆ *American Stories*

A PROFESSIONAL WOMAN JOINS THE PROGRESSIVE CRUSADE

Frances Kellor, a young woman who grew up in Ohio and Michigan, received her law degree in 1897 from Cornell University and became one of the small but growing group of professionally trained women in the United States. Deciding that she was more interested in solving the nation's social problems than in practicing law, she moved to Chicago, studied sociology, and trained herself as a social reformer. Kellor believed passionately that poverty and inequality could be eliminated in America. She also had the progressive faith that if Americans could only hear the truth about the millions of people living in urban slums, they would rise up and make changes. She was one of the experts who provided the evidence to document what was wrong in industrial America.

Like many progressives, Kellor believed that environment was more important than heredity in determining ability, prosperity, and happiness. Better schools and better housing, she thought, would produce better citizens. While a small group of progressives advocated the sterilization of criminals and the so-called "mentally defective," Kellor argued that even criminals were victims of their environment. Kellor demonstrated that poor health and deprived childhoods explained the only differences between criminals and college students. If it were impossible to define a criminal type, then it must be possible to reduce crime by improving the environment.

Kellor was an efficient professional. Like the majority of the professional women of her generation, she never married but devoted her life to social research and social reform. She lived for a time at Hull House in Chicago and at the College Settlement in New York, centers not only of social research and reform but also of lively community. For many young people, the settlement, with its sense of commitment and its exciting conversation around the dinner table, provided an alternative to the nuclear family or the single apartment.

While staying at the College Settlement, Kellor researched and wrote a muckraking study of employment agencies, published in 1904 as *Out of Work*. She revealed how employment agencies exploited immigrants, blacks, and other recent arrivals in the city. Kellor's book, like the writing of most progressives, spilled over with moral outrage. But Kellor went beyond moralism to suggest corrective legislation at the state and national levels. She became one of the leaders of the movement to Americanize the immigrants pouring into the country in unprecedented numbers. Between 1899 and 1920, over 8 million people came to the United States, most from southern and eastern Europe. Many Americans feared that this flood of immigrants threatened the very basis of American democracy. Kellor and her coworkers represented the side of progressivism that sought state and federal laws to protect the new arrivals from exploitation and to establish agencies and facilities to educate and Americanize them. Another group of progressives, often allied with organized labor, tried to pass laws to restrict immigration. Kellor did not entirely escape the ethnocentrism that was a part of her generation's worldview, and like most progressives she tried to teach middle-class values to the new arrivals, but she did believe that all immigrants could be made into useful citizens.

Convinced of the need for a national movement to promote reform legislation, Kellor helped to found the National Committee for Immigrants in America, which tried to promote a national policy "to make all these people Americans," and a federal bureau to organize the campaign. Eventually, she helped establish the Division of Immigrant Education within the Department of Labor. But political movement led by Theodore Roosevelt excited her most. More than almost any other single person, Kellor had been responsible for alerting Roosevelt to the problems the immigrants faced in American cities. When Roosevelt formed the new Progressive party in 1912, she was one of the many social workers and social researchers who joined him. She campaigned for Roosevelt and directed the Progressive Service Organization, intended to educate voters in all areas of social justice and welfare after the election. After Roosevelt's defeat and the collapse of the Progressive party in 1914, Kellor continued to work for Americanization. She spent the rest of her life promoting justice, order, and efficiency as well as trying to find ways of resolving industrial and international disputes.

While no one person can represent all facets of a complex movement, Frances Kellor's life illustrates two important aspects of progressivism, the first nationwide reform movement of the modern era: first, a commitment to promote social justice, ensure equal opportunity, and preserve democracy; and second, a search for order and efficiency in a world complicated by rapid industrialization, immigration, and spectacular urban growth. Like many progressive leaders, she was a part of a global movement to confront these problems, and she was influenced by writers and reformers in England and Germany as well as

those in the United States. Progressivism reached a climax in the years from 1900 to 1914. Like most American reform movements, the progressive movement did not plot to overthrow the government; rather, it sought to use the government to reform the system to ensure the survival of the American way of life.

This chapter traces the important aspects of progressivism. It examines the social justice movement, which sought to promote reform among the poor and to improve life for those who had fallen victim to an urban and industrial civilization. It surveys life among workers, a group the reformers sometimes helped but often misunderstood. Then it traces the reform movements in the cities and states, where countless officials and experts tried to reduce chaos and promote order and democracy. Finally, it examines progressivism at the national level during the administrations of Theodore Roosevelt and Woodrow Wilson, the first thoroughly modern presidents.

THE SOCIAL JUSTICE MOVEMENT

Historians write of a "progressive movement," but actually there were a number of movements, some of them contradictory, but all focusing on the problems created by a rapidly expanding urban and industrial world. Some reformers, often from the middle class, sought to humanize the modern city. They hoped to improve housing and schools and to provide a better life for the poor and recent immigrants. Others were concerned with the conditions of work and the rights of labor. Still others pressed for changes in the political system to make it more responsive to their interests. Progressivism had roots in the 1890s, when many reformers were shocked by the devastation caused by the depression of 1893, and they read Henry George's *Progress and Poverty* (1879) and Edward Bellamy's *Looking Backward* (1888). They were also influenced by John Ruskin, the strange and eccentric British reformer and art historian, who hated the industrial city. Like the British, they were appalled by a pamphlet, entitled *The Bitter Cry of Outcast London*, which revealed the horrors of the slums of East London. They were also influenced by the British and American Social Gospel movement, which sought to build the kingdom of God on earth by eliminating poverty and promoting equality (see Chapter 19).

The Progressive Movement in Global Context

Most progressives saw their movement in a global context with a particular focus on an Atlantic world. Many had studied at European universities. They attended conferences on urban and industrial problems held at the Paris Exposition of 1900, and belonged to organizations like the International Association for Labor Legislation, which tried to promote legislation to aid workers. They read the latest sociological studies from Britain, France, and Germany. Many were introduced to the problems of the modern industrial city by walking through the streets of East London or the slums of Berlin. Others were inspired by visiting Toynbee Hall, the pioneer social settlement in London, and by observing the municipal housing and government-owned streetcar lines in Glasgow, Scotland, and Dresden, Germany. John R. Commons, the economist from the University of Wisconsin who trained many progressive experts, kept a chart of labor legislation from around the world on the wall of his seminar room as a constant reminder of the global reform network. At the same time, European reformers visited American cities and took part in American conferences.

The United States lagged behind much of the industrialized world when it came to the passage of

John Sloan (1871–1951) was one of the leading members of the "ash can school," a group of artists who experimented with new techniques and painted ordinary scenes of urban life, such as this 1912 painting titled *Sunday, Women Drying Their Hair*. His paintings offended many because he flouted genteel codes of propriety and decorum, and he showed working-class women in ways that were just as shocking as progressive era reports on child labor and prostitution. *(© Addison Gallery of American Art, Phillips Academy, Andover, Massachusetts. All Rights Reserved.)*

social legislation. Many European countries, along with Australia, New Zealand, and Brazil, passed laws regulating hours and wages and creating pensions for the elderly. Germany enacted sickness, accident, and disability insurance in the 1880s, and Denmark followed in the 1890s. Great Britain had workmen's compensation by the late 1890s, and old age, sickness, and unemployment insurance by 1911, all paid for with public funds. But despite all the global connections, the progressive movement in America was different. American cities, unlike those in Europe, were filled with immigrants from a dozen countries who had cultural adjustments and a language barrier to overcome. The United States also lacked the strong labor and socialist movements present in most European countries. The American federal system meant that most reform battles had to be fought first at the local and state levels before they could reach the national level. The United States had "the feeblest, least accessible and most inefficient central government in the world," one British critic decided. In addition, the progressive movement, despite its international connections, was made up of a particular American mix of religion, politics, and moral outrage.

The Progressive Worldview

Intellectually, the progressives were influenced by the Darwinian revolution. They believed that the world was in flux, and they rebelled against the fixed and the formal in every field. One of the philosophers of the movement, John Dewey, wrote that ideas could become instruments for change. In his philosophy of pragmatism, William James tried to explain all ideas in terms of their consequences. Most of the progressives were environmentalists who were convinced that environment was much more important than heredity in forming character. Thus, if one could build better schools and houses, one could make better people and a more perfect society. Yet even the more advanced reformers thought in racial and ethnic categories. They believed that some groups could be molded and changed more easily than others. Thus, progressivism did not usually mean progress for blacks.

In many ways, progressivism was the first modern reform movement. It sought to bring order and efficiency to a world that had been transformed by rapid growth and new technology. Yet elements of nostalgia infected the movement as reformers tried to preserve the handicrafts of a preindustrial age and to promote small-town and farm values in the city. The progressive leaders were almost always middle class, and they quite consciously tried to teach their middle-class values to the immigrants and the working class. Often, the progressives seemed more interested in control than in reform; frequently, they betrayed a sense of paternalism toward those they tried to help.

The progressives were part of a statistics-minded, realistic generation, and here they followed their

European colleagues. They conducted surveys, gathered facts, wrote reports about every conceivable problem, and usually had faith that their reports would lead to change. Their urge to document and record came out in haunting photographs of young workers taken by Lewis Hine, in the stark and beautiful city paintings by John Sloan, and in the realist novels of Theodore Dreiser and William Dean Howells.

The progressives were optimistic about human nature, and they believed that change was possible. In retrospect, they may seem naive or bigoted, but they wrestled with many social questions, some of them old but fraught with new urgency in an industrialized society. What is the proper relation of government to society? In a world of large corporations, huge cities, and massive transportation systems, how much should the government regulate and control? How much responsibility does society have to care for the poor and needy? The progressives could not agree on the answers, but they struggled with the questions.

The Muckrakers

Writers who exposed corruption and other social evils were labeled "muckrakers" by Theodore Roosevelt. Not all muckrakers were reformers—some just wrote for the money—but reformers learned from their techniques of exposé. In part, the muckrakers were a product of a journalistic revolution in the 1890s. The older magazines often had elite audiences and few illustrations. The new magazines had slick formats, more advertising, and wide sales. Competing for readers, editors eagerly published articles telling the public what was wrong in America.

Lincoln Steffens, a young California journalist, wrote articles exposing the connections between respectable businessmen and corrupt politicians. When published as a book in 1904, *The Shame of the Cities* became a battle cry for people determined to clean up city government. Ida Tarbell, a teacher turned journalist, revealed the ruthlessness of John D. Rockefeller's Standard Oil Company. David Graham Phillips uncovered the alliance of politics and business in *The Treason of the Senate* (1906). Robert Hunter, a young settlement worker, shocked Americans in 1904 with his book *Poverty*. In his compelling novel *The Octopus,* Frank Norris dramatized the railroads' stranglehold on the farmers, while Upton Sinclair's novel *The Jungle* (1906) described the horrors of the Chicago meatpacking industry.

Child Labor

Nothing disturbed the social justice progressives more than the sight of children, sometimes as young as eight or ten, working long hours in dangerous and depressing factories. Young people had worked in factories since the beginning of the Industrial Revolution, but that did not make the practice any less repugnant to the reformers. "Children are put into industry very much as we put in raw material," Jane Addams objected, "and the product we look for is not better men and women, but better manufactured goods."

Florence Kelley was one of the most important leaders in the crusade against child labor. Kelley had grown up in an upper-class Philadelphia family and graduated from Cornell in 1882—like Addams and Kellor she was a member of the first generation of college women in the United States. When the University of Pennsylvania refused her admission as a graduate student because she was a woman, she went to the University of Zurich in Switzerland. Her European experience was crucial in her development. It transformed her from an upper-class dilettante into a committed reformer. She married a Polish-Russian scholar and became a socialist. The marriage failed, and some years later, Kelley moved to Chicago with her children, became a Hull House resident, and poured her considerable energies into the campaign against child labor. A friend described her as "explosive, hot-tempered, determined . . . a smoking volcano that at any moment would burst into flames." When she could find no attorney in Chicago to argue child labor cases against some of the prominent corporations, she went to law school, passed the bar exam, and argued the cases herself.

Although Kelley and the other child labor reformers won a few cases, they quickly recognized the need for state laws if they were going to have any real influence. Child labor was an emotional issue. Many businesses made large profits by employing children, and many legislators and government officials, remembering their own rural childhoods, argued that it was good for the children's character to work hard and take responsibility. Reformers, marshaling their evidence about the tragic effects on growing children of working long hours in dark and damp factories, pressured the Illinois state legislature into passing an anti–child labor law. A few years later, however, the state supreme court declared the law unconstitutional.

Judicial opposition was one factor that led reformers to the national level in the first decade of the twentieth century. Florence Kelley again led the charge. In 1899, she became secretary of the National Consumers League, the first organization to enlist consumers in a campaign to lobby elected officials and corporations to ensure that products were produced under safe and sanitary conditions.

Nothing tugged at the heartstrings of the reformers more than the sight of little children, sullen and stunted, working long hours in factory, farm, and mine. These children, breaker boys who spent all day sorting coal in western Pennsylvania, were carefully posed by documentary photographer Lewis Hine while he worked for the National Child Labor Committee in 1911. *(Records of the Children's Bureau, The National Archives, Office of the Chief Signal Officer)*

It was not Kelley, however, but Edgar Gardner Murphy, an Alabama clergyman, who suggested the formation of the National Child Labor Committee. Like many other Social Gospel ministers, Murphy believed that the church should reform society as well as save souls. He was appalled by the number of young children working in southern textile mills, where they were exposed to great danger and condemned to "compulsory ignorance" (because they dropped out of school).

The National Child Labor Committee, headquartered in New York, drew up a model state child labor law, encouraged state and city campaigns, and coordinated the movement around the country. Although two-thirds of the states passed some form of child labor law between 1905 and 1907, many had loopholes that exempted a large number of children, including newsboys and youngsters who worked in the theater. The committee also supported a national bill introduced in Congress by Indiana Senator Albert Beveridge in 1906 "to prevent the employment of children in factories and mines." The bill went down to defeat. However, the child labor reformers convinced Congress in 1912 to establish a children's bureau in the Department of Labor. Despite these efforts, compulsory school attendance laws did more to reduce the number of children who worked than federal and state laws, which proved difficult to pass and even more difficult to enforce. The American child labor reformers borrowed their tactics and research methods from European reformers. But the movement to restrict the labor of children was much more successful in Europe. With more centralized government and stronger labor unions, the European reformers did not face the obstacles their American friends confronted. And in most European countries, legislation quickly restricted the hours of all workers including men. This did not happen consistently in the United States until the 1930s.

The crusade against child labor was a typical social justice reform effort. Its origins lay in the moral indignation of middle-class reformers. But reform went beyond moral outrage as reformers gathered statistics, took photographs documenting the abuse of children, and used their evidence to push for legislation first on the local level, then in the states, and eventually in Washington.

Like other progressive reform efforts, the battle against child labor was only partly successful. Too many businessmen, both small and large, were profiting from employing children at low wages. Too many politicians and judges were reluctant to regulate the work of children or adults because work seemed such an individual and personal matter. And some parents, who often desperately needed the money their children earned in the factories, opposed the reformers and even broke the law to allow their children to work.

The reformers also worried over the young people who got into trouble with the law, often for pranks that in rural areas would have seemed harmless. They feared for young people tried by adult courts and thrown into jail with hardened criminals. Almost simultaneously in Denver and Chicago, reformers organized juvenile courts, where judges had the authority to put delinquent youths on probation, take them from their families and make them wards of the state, or assign them to an institution. A uniquely American invention, the juvenile court often helped prevent young delinquents from adopting a life of crime. Yet the juvenile offender was frequently deprived of all rights of due process, a fact that the Supreme Court finally recognized in 1967, when it ruled that children were entitled to procedural rights when accused of a crime.

Working Women

Closely connected with the anti–child labor movement was the effort to limit the hours of women's work. In all their briefs and articles, the reformers cited examples from around the world, especially from Great Britain and Germany. The most important court case on women's work came before the U.S. Supreme Court in 1908. Josephine Goldmark, a friend and coworker of Kelley's at the Consumers League, wrote the brief for *Muller* v. *Oregon* that her brother-in-law, Louis Brandeis, used when he argued the case. The Court upheld the Oregon ten-hour law largely because Goldmark's sociological argument detailed the danger and disease that factory women faced. Brandeis opposed laissez-faire legal concepts, arguing that the government had a special interest in protecting the health of its citizens. Most states fell into line with the Supreme Court decision and passed protective legislation for women, though many companies found ways to circumvent the laws. Even the work permitted by the law seemed too long to some women. "I think ten hours is too much for a woman," one factory worker stated. "I have four children and have to work hard at home. Make me awful tired. I would like nine hours. I get up at 5:30. When I wash, I have to stay up till one or two o'clock."

By contending that "women are fundamentally weaker than men in all that makes for endurance: in muscular strength, in nervous energy, in the powers of persistent attention and application," the reformers won some protection for women workers. But their arguments that women were weaker than men would eventually be used to reinforce gender segregation of the workforce for the next half century.

In addition to working for protective legislation for working women, the social justice progressives also campaigned for woman suffrage. The early battles for the right of women to vote were fought at the state level with the greatest success coming in the West. Wyoming (1869), Utah (1870), Colorado (1893), Idaho (1896), Washington (1910), California (1911), Arizona and Oregon (1912), and Montana and Nevada (1914) gave women the right to vote in at least some elections. But this did not mean that the western states were more enlightened on gender issues. In the East and Midwest, both with large immigrant populations, suffrage and prohibition were often tied closely together. Many men believed that women, if given the vote, would support prohibition. Utah, on the other hand, passed woman suffrage in order to defend the Mormon way of life. The campaign to win the vote for women was a global movement, and the suffrage leaders in the United States were in constant touch with women in other countries. They often met their foreign counterparts at meetings of the International Woman Suffrage Alliance. Ironically, despite the country's democratic traditions, the United States lagged behind several other countries in granting female suffrage. Women in New Zealand won the vote in 1893, Australia in 1902, Finland in 1906, Norway in 1913, Denmark and Iceland in 1915, and Canada in 1918. Women in Great Britain were allowed to vote in 1918, but it was not until 1938 that they could vote on an equal basis with men.

The political process that eventually led to woman suffrage in the United States was slowed by the difficulty of amending the Constitution and the need to fight the battle one state at a time. But the progressives pressed on. They worked with Carrie Chapman Catt and the National Woman Suffrage Association (see Chapter 19), but unlike some suffrage advocates who argued that middle-class women would offset the votes of ignorant and corrupt immigrant men, many progressives supported votes for all women. Jane Addams argued that urban women not only could vote intelligently but also needed the vote to protect, clothe, and feed their families. Women in an urban age, she suggested, needed to be municipal housekeepers. Through the suffrage, they would ensure that elected officials provided adequate services—pure water, uncontaminated food, proper sanitation, and police protection. The progressive insistence that all women needed the vote helped to push woman suffrage toward the victory that would come after World War I.

Much more controversial than either votes for women or protective legislation was the movement for birth control. Even many advanced progressives could not imagine themselves teaching immigrant women how to prevent conception, especially because the Comstock Law of 1873 made it illegal to promote or even write about contraceptive devices.

Margaret Sanger, a nurse who had watched poor women suffer from too many births and even die from dangerous, illegal abortions, was one of the founders of the modern American birth-control movement. Middle-class Americans had limited family size in the nineteenth century through abstinence, withdrawal, and abortion, as well as through the use of primitive birth control devices, but much ignorance and misinformation remained, even among middle-class women. Sanger obtained the latest medical and scientific European studies and in 1914 explained in her magazine, *The Woman Rebel*, and in a pamphlet, *Family Limitation*, that women could separate sex from procreation. She was promptly indicted for violation of the postal code and fled to Europe to avoid arrest.

Birth control remained controversial, and in most states illegal, for many years. Yet Sanger helped to bring the topic of sexuality and contraception out into the open. When she returned to the United States in 1921, she founded the American Birth Control League, which became the Planned Parenthood Federation in 1942.

Home and School

The reformers believed that better housing and education could transform the lives of the poor and create a better world. Books such as Jacob Riis's *How the Other Half Lives* (1890) horrified them. With vivid language and haunting photographs, Riis had documented the misery of New York's slums.

In the first decade of the twentieth century, the progressives took a new approach toward housing problems. They collected statistics, conducted surveys, organized committees, and constructed exhibits to demonstrate the effect of urban overcrowding. Then they set out to pass tenement house laws in several cities. These laws set fire codes and regulated the number of windows, bathrooms, and the size of apartments, but the laws were often evaded or modified. In 1910, the progressives organized the National Housing Association, and some of them looked ahead to federal laws and even to government-subsidized housing. American housing reformers were inspired by the model working-class dwellings in London, the municipal housing in Glasgow, and by various experiments in government-constructed housing in France, Belgium, and Germany, but they realized that in the United States, they had to start with regulation at the local level.

The housing reformers combined a moral sense of what needed to be done to create a more just society with practical ability to organize public opinion and get laws passed. They also took a paternalistic view toward the poor. Many reformers disapproved of the clutter and lack of privacy in immigrant tenements. But often immigrant family ideals and values differed from those of the middle-class reformers. The immigrants actually did not mind the clutter and lack of privacy. Despite the reformers' efforts to separate life's functions into separate rooms, most immigrants still crowded into the kitchen and hung religious objects rather than "good pictures" on the walls.

Ironically, many middle-class women reformers who tried to teach working-class families how to live

While the poor lived in overcrowded tenements, the middle and upper classes surrounded themselves with overstuffed abundance. The piano became a symbol of middle-class status for many, and the draped, cluttered interiors were a sign of success. The elegantly clad wife and daughter, who had the leisure time to play the piano, were additional ornaments in the crowded decor. Many progressive reformers rebelled against this opulent style and urged a leaner, arts and crafts look. (Museum of The City of New York)

RECOVERING THE PAST

Documentary Photographs

As we saw in Chapter 15, photographs are a revealing way of recovering the past visually. But when looking at a photograph, especially an old one, it is easy to assume that it is an accurate representation of the past. However, much like novelists and historians, photographers have a point of view. They take their pictures for a reason—often to prove a point. As one photographer remarked, "Photographs don't lie, but liars take photographs."

To document the need for reform in the cities, progressives collected statistics, made surveys, described settlement house life, and even wrote novels. But they discovered that the photograph was often more effective than words. Jacob Riis, the Danish-born author of *How the Other Half Lives* (1890), a devastating exposure of conditions in New York City tenement house slums, was also a pioneer in urban photography. Others had taken pictures of dank alleys and street urchins before, but Riis was the first to photograph slum conditions with the express purpose of promoting reform. At first he hired photographers, but then he bought a camera and taught himself how to use it. He even tried a new German flash powder to illuminate dark alleys and tenement rooms to record the horror of slum life.

Riis made many of his photographs into lantern slides and used them to illustrate his lectures on the need for housing reform. Although he was a creative and innovative photographer, his pictures were often far from objective. His equipment was awkward, his film slow. He had to set up and prepare carefully before snapping the shutter. His views of tenement ghetto streets and poor children now seem like clichés, but they were designed to make Americans angry and to arouse them to reform.

Another important progressive photographer was Lewis Hine. Although trained as a sociologist, he taught himself photography. Hine used his camera to illustrate his lectures at the Ethical Culture School in New York. In 1908, he was hired as a full-time investigator by the National Child Labor Committee. His haunting photographs of children in factories helped convince many Americans of the need to abolish child labor. Hine's children were appealing human beings. He showed them eating, running, working, and staring wistfully out factory windows. His photographs avoided the pathos that

Lewis Hine, *Carolina Cotton Mill, 1908.* (George Eastman House)

Riis was so fond of recording, but just as surely they documented the need for reform.

Another technique that the reform photographer used was the before-and-after shot. The two photographs shown opposite of a one-room apartment in Philadelphia early in the century illustrate how progressive reformers tried to teach immigrants to imitate middle-class manners. The "before" photograph shows a room cluttered with washtubs, laundry, cooking utensils, clothes, tools, even an old Christmas decoration. In the "after" picture, much of the clutter has been cleaned up. A window has been installed to let in light and fresh air. The wallpaper, presumably a haven for hidden bugs and germs, has been torn off. The cooking utensils and laundry have been put away. The woodwork has been stained, and some ceremonial objects have been gathered on a shelf.

What else can you find that has been changed? How well do you think the message of the photographic combinations like this one worked? Would the immigrant family be happy with the new look and condition of their room? Could anyone live in one room and keep it so neat?

Reflecting on the Past   As you look at these, or any photographs, ask yourself: What is the photographer's purpose and point of view? Why was this particular angle chosen for the picture? And why center on these particular people or objects? What does the photographer reveal about his or her purpose? What does the photographer reveal unintentionally? How have fast film and new camera styles changed photography? On what subjects do reform-minded photographers train their cameras today?

The reality of one-room tenement apartments (above) contrasted with the tidiness that reformers saw as the ideal (right). *(Urban Archives, Temple University, Philadelphia, PA)*

in their tenement flats had never organized their own homes. Often they lived in settlement houses, where they ate in a dining hall and never had to worry about cleaning, cooking, or doing laundry. Some of them, however, began to realize that the domestic tasks expected of women of all classes kept many of them from taking their full place in society. Charlotte Perkins Gilman, author of *Women and Economics* (1898), dismantled the traditional view of "woman's sphere" and sketched an alternative. Suggesting that entrepreneurs ought to build apartment houses designed to allow women to combine motherhood with careers, she advocated shared kitchen facilities and a common dining room, a laundry run by efficient workers, and a roof-garden day nursery with a professional teacher.

Gilman, who criticized private homes as "bloated buildings, filled with a thousand superfluities," was joined by a few radicals in promoting new living arrangements. However, most Americans of all political persuasions continued to view the home as sacred space where the mother ruled supreme and created an atmosphere of domestic tranquillity for the husband and children.

Next to better housing, the progressives stressed better schools as a way to produce better citizens. Public school systems were often rigid and corrupt. Far from producing citizens who would help transform society, the schools seemed to reinforce the conservative habits that blocked change. A reporter who traveled around the country in 1892 discovered mindless teachers who drilled pupils through repe-

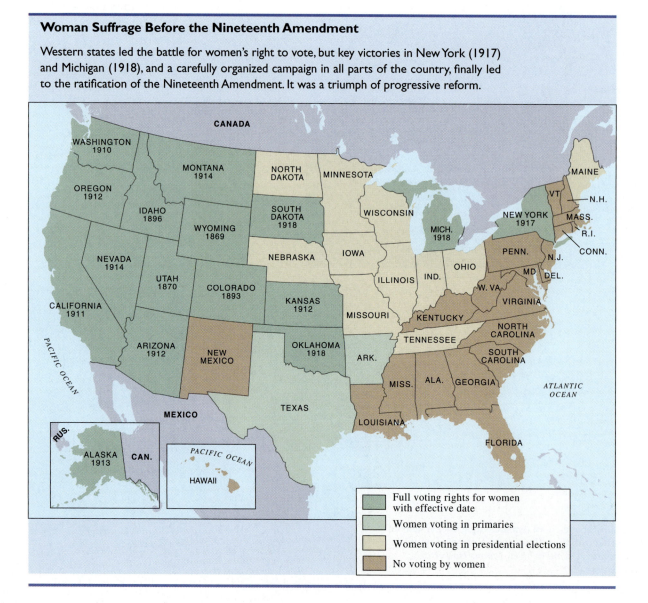

Woman Suffrage Before the Nineteenth Amendment

Western states led the battle for women's right to vote, but key victories in New York (1917) and Michigan (1918), and a carefully organized campaign in all parts of the country, finally led to the ratification of the Nineteenth Amendment. It was a triumph of progressive reform.

Legend:
- Full voting rights for women with effective date
- Women voting in primaries
- Women voting in presidential elections
- No voting by women

titious rote learning. A Chicago teacher advised her students, "Don't stop to think; tell me what you know." When asked why the students were not allowed to move their heads, a New York teacher replied, "Why should they look behind when the teacher is in front of them?"

Progressive education, like many other aspects of progressivism, opposed the rigid and the formal in favor of flexibility and change. John Dewey was the key philosopher of progressive education. In his laboratory school at the University of Chicago, he experimented with new educational methods. He replaced the school desks, which were bolted down and always faced the front, with seats that could be moved into circles and arranged in small groups. The movable seat, in fact, became one of the symbols of the progressive education movement.

Dewey insisted that the schools be child-centered, not subject-oriented. Teachers should teach children rather than teach history or mathematics. Dewey did not mean that history and math should not be taught but that those subjects should be related to the students' experience. Students should learn by doing. They should actually build a house, not just study how others constructed houses. Students should not just learn about democracy; the school itself should operate like a democracy.

Dewey also maintained that the schools should become instruments for social reform. But like most progressives, Dewey was never quite clear whether he wanted the schools to help the students adjust to the existing society or to turn out graduates who would change the world. Although he wavered on that point, the spirit of progressive education, like the spirit of progressivism in general, was optimistic. The schools could create more flexible, better-educated adults who would go out to improve society. Dewey's progressive education, which sought to educate all Americans, stood in sharp contrast to European models, where educating the intellectual and social elite took precedence over schooling the masses.

Crusades Against Saloons, Brothels, and Movie Houses

Progressives often displayed a moral outrage when it came to the behavior of the working class that surprised and confused European observers. American attitudes toward prostitution and prohibition especially baffled many Europeans. Most social justice progressives opposed the sale of alcohol. Some came from Protestant homes where the consumption of liquor was considered a sin, but most favored

prohibition for the same reasons they opposed child labor and favored housing reform. They saw eliminating the sale of alcohol as part of the process of reforming the city and conserving human resources, but they were also appalled by the drinking culture they observed in the cities.

Americans did drink great quantities of beer, wine, and hard liquor, and the amount they consumed rose rapidly after 1900, peaking between 1911 and 1915. An earlier temperance movement had achieved some success in the 1840s and 1850s (see Chapter 12), but only three states still had prohibition laws in force. The modern antiliquor movement was spearheaded in the 1880s and 1890s by the Women's Christian Temperance Union and after 1900 by the Anti-Saloon League and a coalition of religious leaders and social reformers. During the progressive era, temperance forces had considerable success in influencing legislation. Seven states passed temperance laws between 1906 and 1912.

The reformers were appalled to see young children going into saloons to bring home a pail of beer for the family and horrified by tales of alcoholic fathers beating wives and children. But most often progressives focused on the saloon and its social life. Drug traffic, prostitution, and political corruption all seemed linked to the saloon. Although they never quite understood the role alcoholic drinks played in the social life of many ethnic groups, Jane Addams and other settlement workers appreciated the saloon's importance as a neighborhood social center. Addams started a coffeehouse at Hull House in an attempt to lure the neighbors away from the evils of the saloon. The progressives never found an adequate substitute for the saloon, but they set to work to pass local and state prohibition laws. As in many other progressive efforts, they joined forces with diverse groups to push for change. Their combined efforts led to victory on December 22, 1917, when Congress sent to the states for ratification a constitutional amendment prohibiting the sale, manufacture, and import of intoxicating liquor within the United States. The spirit of sacrifice for the war effort facilitated its rapid ratification. In addition to the saloon, the progressives saw the urban dance hall and the movie theater as threats to the morals and well-being of young people, especially young women. The motion picture, invented in 1889, developed as an important form of entertainment only during the first decade of the twentieth century. At first, the "nickelodeons," as the early movie theaters were called, appealed mainly to a lower-class and largely ethnic audience. In 1902, New York City had

State Prohibition by 1919

Temperance reform had achieved considerable success before the adoption of the Eighteenth Amendment in 1919. Some states like Maine, Kansas, and North Dakota had voted dry since the middle of the nineteenth century, while other states joined the anti-liquor crusade during the progressive era. Anti-German hysteria during World War I helped to close breweries (most with German names), setting the stage for national prohibition in 1919.

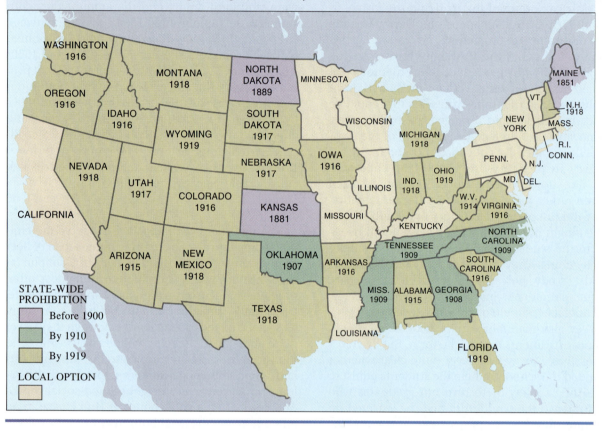

50 theaters; by 1908, there were more than 400 showing 30-minute dramas and romances.

Not until World War I, when D. W. Griffith produced long feature films, did the movies begin to attract a middle-class audience. The most popular of these early films was Griffith's *Birth of a Nation* (1915), a blatantly racist and distorted epic of black debauchery during Reconstruction. Many early films were imported from France, Italy, and Germany; because they were silent, it was easy to use subtitles in any language. But one did not need to know the language, or even be able to read, to enjoy the action. That was part of the attraction of the early films. Some of the films stressed slapstick humor or romance and adventure; others bordered on pornography. The reformers objected not only to the plots and content of the films but also to the location of the theaters (near saloons and burlesque houses) and to their dark interiors. But for young

immigrant women, who made up the bulk of the audience at most urban movie theaters, the films provided rare exciting moments in their lives. One daughter of strict Italian parents remarked, "The one place I was allowed to go by myself was the movies. I went to the movies for fun. My parents wouldn't let me go anywhere else, even when I was twenty-four."

Saloons, dance halls, and movie theaters all seemed dangerous to progressives interested in improving life in the city, because all appeared to be somehow connected with the worst evil of all, prostitution. Campaigns against prostitution had been waged since the early nineteenth century, but they were nothing compared with the progressives' crusade to wipe out what they called the "social evil." All major cities and many smaller ones appointed vice commissions and made elaborate studies of prostitution. The reports, which often ran to several

Lillian Gish was one of the stars of the silent film *The Musketeers of Pig Alley* (1912), which was directed by D. W. Griffith three years before he made *Birth of a Nation*. The film shows Gish and other characters trapped in a ghetto but at the same time enjoying the pleasures of the saloons and dance halls—hardly the message that the progressive reformers were trying to get across. *(Photofest)*

thick volumes, were typical progressive documents. Compiled by experts, they were filled with elaborate statistical studies and laced with moral outrage.

The progressive antivice crusade attracted many kinds of people, for often contradictory reasons. Racists and immigration restrictionists maintained that inferior people—blacks and recent immigrants, especially those from southern and eastern Europe—became prostitutes and pimps. Others had a variety of motives. Most progressives, however, stressed the environmental causes of vice. They viewed prostitution, along with child labor and poor housing, as evils that education and reform could eliminate.

Most progressive antivice reformers stressed the economic causes of prostitution. "Is it any wonder," the Chicago Vice Commission asked, "that a tempted girl who receives only six dollars per week working with her hands sells her body for twenty-five dollars per week when she learns there is a demand for it and men are willing to pay the price?" "Do you suppose I am going back to earn five or six dollars a week in a factory," one prostitute asked an investigator, "when I can earn that amount any night and often much more?"

Despite all their reports and all the publicity, the progressives failed to end prostitution and did virtually nothing to address its roots in poverty. They wiped out a few red-light districts, closed a number of brothels, and managed to push a bill through Congress (the Mann Act of 1910) that prohibited the interstate transport of women for immoral pur-

poses. Perhaps more important, in several states they got the age of consent for women raised, and in 20 states they made the Wassermann test for syphilis mandatory for both men and women before a marriage license could be issued.

THE WORKER IN THE PROGRESSIVE ERA

Progressive reformers sympathized with industrial workers who struggled to earn a living for themselves and their families. The progressives sought protective legislation (particularly for women and children), unemployment insurance, and workers' compensation. But often they had little understanding of what it was really like to sell one's strength by the hour. For example, they supported labor's right to organize at a time when labor had few friends, yet they often opposed the strike as a weapon against management. And neither organized labor nor the reformers, individually or in shaky partnership, had power over industry. Control was in the hands of the owners and managers, and they were determined to strengthen their grip on the workplace as the nature of industrial work was being transformed.

Immigrants and Industrial Labor

John Mekras arrived in New York from Greece in 1912 and traveled immediately to Manchester, New Hampshire, where he found a job in the giant Amoskeag textile mill. He did not speak a word of English. "The man who hands out the jobs sent me to the spinning room," he later remembered. "There I don't know anything about the spinning. I'm a farmer. . . . I don't know what the boss is talking about." Mekras didn't last long at the mill. He was one of the many industrial workers who had difficulty adjusting to factory work in the early twentieth century.

Many workers—whether they were from Greece, eastern Europe, rural Vermont, or Michigan—confronted a bewildering world based on order and routine. Unlike farm or craft work, factory life was dominated by the clock, the bell tower, and the boss. The workers continued to resist the routine and pace of factory work, and they subtly sabotaged the employers' efforts to control the workplace, as they had done in earlier periods (see Chapters 10 and 18). They stayed at home on holidays when they were supposed to work, took unauthorized breaks, and set their own informal productivity schedules. Often they were fired or quit. In the woollen industry, for example, the annual turnover of workers between 1907 and 1910 was more than 100 percent. In New York needleworker shops in 1912 and 1913, the turnover rate was over 250 percent. Overall in American industry, one-third of the workers stayed at their jobs less than a year.

This industrial workforce, still composed largely of immigrants, had a fluid character. Many migrants, especially those from southern and eastern Europe, expected to stay for only a short time and then return to their homeland. Many men came alone—70 percent in some years. They saved money by living in boardinghouses. In 1910, two-thirds of the workers in Pittsburgh made less than $12 a week, but by lodging in boarding houses and paying $2.50 a month for a bed, they could save perhaps one-third of their pay. "Here in America one must work for three horses," one immigrant wrote home. "The work is very heavy, but I don't mind it," another wrote; "let it be heavy, but may it last without interruption." The work could also be dangerous. In the mining town of Butte, Montana, in June 1917, a fire in a mine shaft (caused by the owners lack of attention to safety) killed 164 young workers, most of them recent Irish immigrants.

All immigrants faced some prejudice but none more than Asians. Immigration was blocked by the Chinese Exclusion Act of 1882 and by the Gentleman's Agreement notes of 1907–1908 with Japan. Asian immigrants and their children, unlike some other immigrant groups, could not go home, and they became trapped in ethnic enclaves, which were largely male. They were pushed out of jobs in manufacturing and transportation. Chinatowns in San Francisco and New York as well as in Seattle, Portland, Boston, and other cities housed much of the Chinese population, and by 1920, nearly one-third of those employed worked in laundries. Most of the Japanese were concentrated in California, where they worked as agricultural laborers. But many owned their own land and operated small business, which created further prejudice and caused the California legislature to prohibit Japanese ownership of land in 1913. Prejudice limited Asian economic opportunities in America, but ethnic solidarity and hard work allowed some Asian Americans to achieve a measure of success.

The nature of work continued to change in the early twentieth century as industrialists extended late-nineteenth-century efforts to make their factories and their workforces more efficient, productive, and profitable. In some industries, the introduction of new machines revolutionized work and eliminated highly paid, skilled jobs. For example, glass-blowing machines (invented about 1900) replaced thousands of glassblowers or reduced them from craftsmen to workers. Power-driven machines, better-organized operations, and, finally, the moving assembly line, perfected by Henry Ford, transformed the nature of work and turned many laborers into unskilled tenders of machines.

More than machines changed the nature of industrial work. The principles of scientific management, which set out new rules for organizing work, were just as important. The key figure was Frederick Taylor, the son of a prominent Philadelphia family. After Taylor had a nervous breakdown while at a private school, his physicians prescribed manual labor as a cure, and he went to work as a laborer at the

Immigrants from Eastern and Southern Europe came to the United States in great numbers from 1890 to 1914. The women were often employed in textile factories and the men in construction. They provided the labor that drove the American economy. This photograph by Lewis Hine captures the moment of arrival of an immigrant family. *(Courtesy George Eastman House)*

Midvale Steel Company in Philadelphia. Working his way up rapidly while studying engineering at night, he became chief engineer at the factory in the 1880s. Later he used this experience to rethink the organization of industry.

Taylor was obsessed with efficiency. He emphasized centralized planning, systematic analysis, and detailed instructions. Most of all, he studied all kinds of workers and timed the various components of their jobs with a stopwatch. "The work of every workman is fully planned out by the management at least one day in advance," Taylor wrote in 1898, "and each man receives in most cases complete written instructions, describing in detail the task which he is to accomplish, as well as the means to be used in doing the work." Many owners enthusiastically adopted Taylor's concepts of scientific management, seeing an opportunity to increase their profits and shift control of the workplace from the skilled workers to the managers. Not surprisingly, many workers resented the drive for efficiency and control. "We don't want to work as fast as we are able to," one machinist remarked. "We want to work as fast as we think it comfortable for us to work."

Union Organizing

The progressive reformers, who often tried to promote efficiency, probably had little understanding of Taylor's schemes or of the revolution going on in the factory. Samuel Gompers, head of the American Federation of Labor, however, was quick to recognize that Taylorism would reduce workers to "mere machines." Under his guidance, the AFL prospered during the progressive era. Between 1897 and 1904, union membership grew from 447,000 to over 2 million, with three out of every four union members claimed by the AFL. By 1914, the AFL alone had over 2 million members. Gompers's "pure and simple unionism" was most successful among coal miners, railroad workers, and the building trades. As we saw in Chapter 18, Gompers ignored the growing army of unskilled and immigrant workers and concentrated on raising the wages and improving the working conditions of the skilled craftsmen who were members of unions affiliated with the AFL.

For a time, Gompers's strategy seemed to work. Several industries negotiated with the AFL as a way of avoiding disruptive strikes. But cooperation was short-lived. Labor unions were defeated in a number of disastrous strikes, and the National Association of Manufacturers (NAM) launched an aggressive counterattack. NAM and other employer associations provided strikebreakers, used industrial spies, and blacklisted union members to prevent them from obtaining other jobs.

The Supreme Court came down squarely on management's side, ruling in the Danbury Hatters case (*Loewe* v. *Lawler,* 1908) that secondary boycotts were illegal under the Sherman Anti-Trust Act. The secondary boycott had been a valuable tool for workers, enabling them to picket and pressure companies doing business with their employers during a strike. Early in the century, courts at all levels sided overwhelmingly with employers. They often declared strikes illegal and were quick to issue restraining orders, making it impossible for workers to interfere with the operation of a business.

Although many social justice progressives sympathized with the working class, they spent more time promoting protective legislation than strengthening organized labor. Often cast in the role of mediators during industrial disputes, they found it difficult to comprehend what life was really like for people who had to work six days a week.

Working women and their problems aroused more sympathy among progressive reformers than the plight of working men. The number of women working outside the home increased steadily during the progressive era, from over 5 million in 1900 to nearly 8.5 million in 1920. But few belonged to unions—only a little over 3 percent in 1900—and the percentage declined by 50 percent by 1910 before increasing a little after that date because of aggressive organizing in the textile and clothing trades.

Many upper-class women reformers tried to help these working women in a variety of ways. The settlement houses organized day-care centers, clubs, and classes, and many reformers tried to pass protective legislation. Tension and misunderstanding often cropped up between the reformers and the working women, but one organization in which there was genuine cooperation was the Women's Trade Union League. Founded in 1903, the league was organized by Mary Kenney and William English Walling, a socialist and reformer, but it also drew local leaders from the working class, such as Rose Schneiderman, a Jewish immigrant cap maker, and Leonora O'Reilly, a collar maker. The league established branches in most large eastern and midwestern cities and served for more than a decade as an important force in helping to organize women into unions. The league forced the AFL to pay more attention to women, helped out in time of strikes, put up bail money for the arrested, and publicized the plight of working women.

Garment Workers and the Triangle Fire

Thousands of young women, most of them Jewish and Italian, were employed in the garment industry in New York City. Most were between the ages of 16

The Triangle fire shocked the nation, and dramatic photographs, such as this candid shot showing bodies and bystanders waiting for more young women to jump, helped stimulate the investigation that followed. *(Brown Brothers)*

and 25; some lived with their families, and others lived alone or with a roommate. They worked a 56-hour, 6-day week and made about $6 for their efforts. New York was the center of the garment industry, with over 600 shirtwaist (blouse) and dress factories employing more than 30,000 workers.

Like other industries, garment manufacturing had changed in the first decade of the twentieth century. Once conducted in thousands of dark and dingy tenement rooms, now all the operations were centralized in large loft buildings in lower Manhattan. These buildings were an improvement over the sweating labor of the tenements, but many were overcrowded, and they had few fire escapes or safety features. In addition, the owners applied scientific management techniques to increase their profits, making life miserable for the workers. Most of the women had to rent their sewing machines and even had to pay for the electricity they used. They were penalized for mistakes or for talking too loudly. They were usually supervised by a male contractor who badgered and sometimes even sexually harassed them. Partly because of stronger labor unions, workplace regulation and maximum hour laws had passed more quickly in Great Britain, France, and Germany. American reformers were aware of these laws but were helpless to pass similar legislation in the United States.

In 1909, some of the women went out on strike to protest the working conditions. The International Ladies' Garment Workers Union (ILGWU) and the Women's Trade Union League supported them. But strikers were beaten and sometimes arrested by unsympathetic policemen and by strikebreakers on the picket lines. At a mass meeting held at Cooper Union in New York on November 22, 1909, Clara Lemlich, a young shirtwaist worker who had been injured on the picket line and was angered by the long speeches and lack of action, rose and in an emotional speech in Yiddish demanded a general strike. The entire audience pledged its agreement. The next day, all over the city, the shirtwaist workers went out on strike.

"The uprising of the twenty thousand," as the strike was called, startled the nation. One young worker wrote in her diary, "It is a good thing, that strike is. It makes you feel like a grown-up person." The Jews learned a little Italian and the Italians a little Yiddish so that they could communicate. Many social reformers, ministers, priests, and rabbis urged the strikers on. Mary Dreier, an upper-class reformer and president of the New York branch of the Women's Trade Union League, was arrested for marching with the strikers. A young state legislator, Fiorello La Guardia, later to become a congressman and mayor of New York, was one of the many public officials to aid the strikers.

The shirtwaist workers won, and in part, the success of the strike made the garment union one of the most powerful in the AFL. But the victory was limited. Over 300 companies accepted the union's terms, but others refused to go along. The young women went back to work amid still oppressive and unsafe conditions. That became dramatically obvious on Saturday, March 25, 1911, when a fire broke out on the eighth floor of the 10-story loft building housing the Triangle Shirtwaist Company near Washington Square in New York. There had been several small fires in the factory in previous weeks, so no one thought much about another one. But this fire was different. Within minutes, the top three floors of the factory were ablaze. The owners had locked most of the exit doors. The elevators broke down. There were no fire escapes. Forty-six women jumped to their deaths, some of them in groups of three and four holding hands. Over 100 died in the flames.

Shocked by the Triangle fire, the state legislature appointed a commission to investigate working conditions in the state. One investigator for the commission was a young social worker named Frances Perkins, who in the 1930s would become secretary of labor. She led the politicians through the dark lofts, filthy tenements, and unsafe factories around the state to show them the conditions under which young women worked. The result was state legislation limiting the work of women to 54 hours a week, prohibiting labor by children under the age of 14, and improving safety regulations in factories. One supporter of the bills in Albany was a young state senator named Franklin Delano Roosevelt.

The investigative commission was a favorite progressive tactic. When there was a problem, reformers often got a city council, a state legislature, or the federal government to appoint a commission. If they could not find a government body to give them a mandate, they made their own studies. They brought in experts, compiled statistics, and published reports. While many had learned their research techniques by studying at European universities and often patterned their studies after German and British articles, others were American trained.

The federal Industrial Relations Commission, created in 1912 to study the causes of industrial unrest and violence, conducted one of the most important investigations. As it turned out, the commission spent most of its time exploring a dramatic and tragic incident of labor–management conflict in Colorado known as the Ludlow Massacre. A strike broke out in the fall of 1913 in the vast mineral-rich area of southern Colorado, much of it controlled by the Colorado Fuel and Iron Industry, a company largely owned by the Rockefeller family. It was a paternalistic empire where workers lived in company towns and sometimes in tent colonies. They were paid in company scrip and forced to shop at the company store. When the workers, supported by the United Mine Workers, went on strike demanding an eight-hour day, better safety precautions, and the removal of armed guards, the company refused to negotiate. The strike turned violent, and in the spring of 1914, strikebreakers and national guardsmen fired on the

workers. Eleven children and two women were killed in an attack on a tent city near Ludlow, Colorado.

The Industrial Relations Commission called John D. Rockefeller, Jr., to testify and implied that he was personally guilty of the murders. The commission decided in its report that violent class conflict could be avoided only by limiting the use of armed guards and detectives, by restricting monopoly, by protecting the right of the workers to organize, and, most dramatically, by redistributing wealth through taxation. The commission's report, not surprisingly, fell on deaf ears. Most progressives, like most Americans, denied the commission's conclusion that class conflict was inevitable.

Radical Labor

Not everyone accepted the progressives' faith in investigations and protective labor legislation. Nor did everyone approve of Samuel Gompers's conservative tactics or his emphasis on getting better pay for skilled workers. A group of about 200 radicals met in Chicago in 1905 to form a new union as an alternative to the AFL. They called it the Industrial Workers of the World (IWW) and talked of one big union. Like the Knights of Labor in the 1880s, the IWW would welcome all workers: the unskilled, and even the unemployed, women, African Americans, Asians, and all other ethnic groups.

Daniel De Leon of the Socialist Labor Party attended the organizational meeting, and so did Eugene Debs. Debs, who had been converted to socialism after the Pullman strike of 1894, had already emerged by 1905 as one of the outstanding radical leaders in the country. Also attending was Mary Harris Jones, who dressed like a society matron but attacked labor leaders "who sit on velvet chairs in conferences with labor's oppressors." In her sixties at the time, everyone called her "Mother" Jones. She had been a dressmaker, a Populist, and a member of the Knights of Labor. During the 1890s, she had marched with miners' wives on the picket line in western Pennsylvania. She was imprisoned and denounced, and by 1905 she was already a legend.

Presiding at the Chicago meeting was "Big Bill" Haywood, the president of the Western Federation of Miners. He had been a cowboy, a miner, and a prospector. Somewhere along the way, he had lost an eye and mangled a hand, but he had a booming voice and a passionate commitment to the workers. Denouncing Gompers and the AFL, he talked of class conflict. "The purpose of the IWW," he proclaimed, "is to bring the workers of this country into the possession of the full value of the product of

The way art and politics sometimes combined in the progressive era is illustrated by this poster for a performance by a group of political radicals at Madison Square Garden in New York. They reenacted the IWW-supported silk workers' strike, which was then going on in Paterson, New Jersey. Many of the actual strikers took part in the performance. But the play lost money, and the strike ultimately failed. Still, this impressively designed program cover recalls a time when radical artists and labor leaders sought to transform the world. *(The Tamiment Institute Library, New York University)*

their toil." De Leon was influenced by European socialism, but most of the other radicals, including Debs, were home grown.

The IWW remained a small organization, troubled by internal squabbles and disagreements. Debs and De Leon left after a few years. Haywood dominated the movement, which played an important role in organizing the militant strike of textile workers in Lawrence, Massachusetts, in 1912 and the following year in Paterson, New Jersey, and Akron, Ohio. The IWW had its greatest success organizing itinerant lumbermen and migratory workers in the Northwest. But in other places, especially in times of high unemployment, the Wobblies (as they were called) helped unskilled workers vent their anger against their employers.

Most American workers did not feel, as European workers did, that they were involved in a perpetual class struggle with their capitalist employers, but that did not mean that they were docile and passive. Many American workers engaged their managers in a constant struggle over who controlled the workplace, and they occasionally went on strike to win better wages and working conditions. Some immigrant workers, intent on earning enough money to go back home, had no time to join the conflict. Most of those who stayed in the United States were consoled by the promises of the American dream. Thinking they might secure a better job or move up into the middle class, they avoided organized labor militancy. They knew that even if they failed, their sons and daughters would profit from the American way. The AFL, not the IWW, became the dominant American labor movement. But for a few, the IWW represented a dream of what might have been. For others, its presence, though small and largely ineffective, meant that perhaps someday a European-style labor movement might develop in America.

REFORM IN THE CITIES AND STATES

The reform movements of the progressive era usually started at the local level, then moved to the state, and finally to the nation's capital. Progressivism in the cities and states had roots in the depression and discontent of the 1890s. The reform banners called for more democracy, more power for the people, and legislation regulating railroads and other businesses. Yet often the professional and business classes were the movement's leaders. They intended to bring order out of chaos and to modernize the city and the state during a time of rapid growth.

Municipal Reformers

American cities grew rapidly in the last part of the nineteenth and the first part of the twentieth centuries. New York, which had a population of 1.2 million in 1880, grew to 3.4 million by 1900 and 5.6 million in 1920. Chicago expanded even more dramatically, from 500,000 in 1880 to 1.7 million in 1900 and 2.7 million in 1920. Los Angeles was a town of 11,000 in 1880 but multiplied ten times by 1900, and then increased another five times, to more than a half million, by 1920.

The spectacular and continuing growth of the cities caused problems and created a need for housing, transportation, and municipal services. But it was the kind of people who were moving into the cities that worried many observers. Americans from the small towns and farms continued to throng to the urban centers, as they had throughout the nineteenth century, but immigration produced the greatest surge in population. Fully 40 percent of New York's population and 36 percent of Chicago's was foreign-born in 1910; if one included the children of the immigrants, the percentage approached 80 percent in some cities. To many Protestant Americans, the new immigrants seemed to threaten the American way of life and the very tenets of democracy.

The presence of large immigrant populations was the most important difference between American and European cities, and it made attempts to reform the city different in the United States. The twentieth-century reformers, mostly middle-class citizens like those in the nineteenth century, wanted to regulate and control the sprawling metropolis, restore democracy, reduce corruption, and limit the power of the political bosses and their immigrant allies. When these reformers talked of restoring power to the people, they usually meant ensuring control for people like themselves. The chief aim of municipal reform was to make the city more organized and efficient for the business and professional classes who were to control its workings.

Municipal reform movements varied from city to city, but everywhere the reformers tried to limit the power of the city bosses who they saw as corrupt and anti-democratic. In Boston, the reformers tried to strengthen the power of the mayor, break the hold of the city council, and eliminate council corruption. They succeeded in removing all party designations from city election ballots, and they extended the term of the mayor from two to four years. But to their chagrin, in the election of 1910, John Fitzgerald, grandfather of John F. Kennedy and foe of reform, defeated their candidate. In other cities, the reformers used different tactics, but they almost always conducted elaborate studies and campaigned to reduce corruption.

The most dramatic innovation was the replacement of both mayor and council with a nonpartisan commission of administrators. This scheme began quite accidentally when a hurricane devastated Galveston, Texas, in September 1900. In one of the worst natural disasters in the nation's history, over 6,000 people died. The existing government was helpless to deal with the crisis, so the state legislature appointed five commissioners to run the city during the emergency.

The idea spread to Houston, Dallas, and Austin and to Oakland, Denver, Buffalo, as well as to cities

Cities grew so rapidly that they often ceased to work. This 1909 photograph shows Dearborn Street looking south from Randolph Street in Chicago. Horse-drawn vehicles, streetcars, pedestrians, and even a few early autos clogged the intersection and created the urban inefficiency that angered municipal reformers. *(Chicago Historical Society)*

in other states. It proved most popular in small to medium-sized cities in the Midwest and the Pacific Northwest. By World War I, more than 400 cities had adopted the commission form. Dayton, Ohio, went one step further: after a disastrous flood in 1913, the city hired a manager to run the city and to report to the elected council. The city manager was appointed not elected and he was more a businessman or technician than a politician. Government by experts was the perfect symbol of what most municipal reformers had in mind.

The commission and the expert manager did not replace the mayor in most large cities. One of the most flamboyant and successful of the progressive mayors was Tom Johnson of Cleveland. Johnson had made a fortune by investing in utility and railroad franchises before he was 40. But Henry George's *Progress and Poverty* so influenced him that he began a second career as a reformer. After serving in Congress, he was elected mayor of Cleveland in 1901. During his two terms in city hall, he managed to reduce transit fares and to build parks and municipal bath houses throughout the city. Johnson also broke the connection between the police and prostitution in the city by promising the madams and the brothel owners that he would not bother them if they would be orderly and not steal from their customers or pay off the police.

His most controversial move, however, was to advocate city ownership of the street railroads and utilities. Like many American urban reformers, Johnson had always admired the municipally owned transportation systems in European cities. "Only through municipal ownership," he argued, "can the gulf which divides the community into a small dominant class on one side and the unorganized people on the other be bridged." Johnson was defeated in 1909 in part because he alienated many powerful business interests, but one of his lieutenants, Newton D. Baker, was elected mayor in 1911 and carried on many of his programs. Cleveland was one of many cities that began to regulate municipal utilities or to take them over from the private owners.

The way much of municipal reform and the progressive social justice movement was closely tied to religion, especially to the Protestant Social Gospel movement, can be illustrated by the Men and Religion Forward Movement. Led by the YMCA, the Federal Council of Churches, and a coalition of Protestant agencies, the Men and Religion Forward Movement conducted a whirlwind campaign in 1911–1912, not only to reform the cities but also to

bring men back into the churches. Believing that religion, like much of American life, had become too effeminate, too dominated by women, the leaders of the movement tried to bring "3,000,000 missing men" back to Christianity. Teams of men consisting of Social Gospel ministers and lay experts fanned out across the country, stopping for a week in each city. They held rallies and revival meetings; and they met with clergy, labor leaders, and urban reformers. They tried to stimulate an interest in the churches and at the same time to wipe out child labor, slum housing, gambling dens, and houses of prostitution. They also tried to promote cleaner streets and better government. One of the leaders of the movement, Raymond Robins, had been a settlement worker and a coworker with Jane Addams in many reform crusades in Chicago. When the Men and Religion Forward campaign was finished, he moved directly to work for Theodore Roosevelt and the Progressive party. The movement failed to bring a great many men back to religion, and it did not appreciably improve the cities, but it does suggest how religion and politics became intertwined during the progressive era in a distinctly American way.

City Beautiful

In Cleveland, both Tom Johnson and Newton Baker promoted the arts, music, and adult education. They also supervised the construction of a civic center, a library, and a museum. Most other American cities during the progressive era set out to bring culture and beauty to their centers. They were influenced at least in part by the great, classical White City constructed for the Chicago World's Fair of 1893, but even more by the grand European boulevards, especially the Champs-Élysées in Paris.

The architects of the "city beautiful" movement, strongly influenced by European city planners, preferred the impressive and ceremonial architecture of Rome or the Renaissance for libraries, museums, railroad stations, and other public buildings. The huge Pennsylvania Station in New York (now replaced by Madison Square Garden) was modeled after the imperial Roman baths of Caracalla, and the Free Library in Philadelphia was an almost exact copy of a building in Paris. The city beautiful leaders tried to make the city more attractive and meaningful for the middle and upper classes. The museums and the libraries were closed on Sundays, the only day the working class could possibly visit them.

The social justice progressives, especially those connected with the social settlements, were more concerned with neighborhood parks and play-

The Global Adoption of the Telephone

The United States and Europe led the way in adopting the telephone during the progressive era. But the small towns and the farms lagged behind the cities everywhere in the world. **Reflecting on the Past** How did the telephone change business and personal habits for those who could afford the new device?

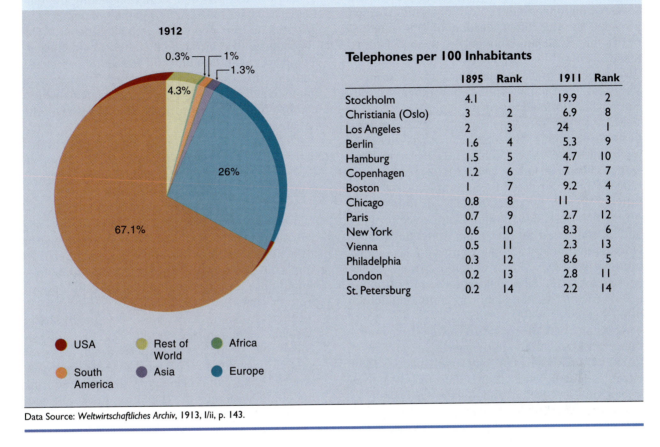

1912

0.3% — 1%
1.3%
4.3%
26%
67.1%

USA
Rest of World
Africa
South America
Asia
Europe

Telephones per 100 Inhabitants

	1895	Rank	1911	Rank
Stockholm	4.1	1	19.9	2
Christiania (Oslo)	3	2	6.9	8
Los Angeles	2	3	24	1
Berlin	1.6	4	5.3	9
Hamburg	1.5	5	4.7	10
Copenhagen	1.2	6	7	7
Boston	1	7	9.2	4
Chicago	0.8	8	11	3
Paris	0.7	9	2.7	12
New York	0.6	10	8.3	6
Vienna	0.5	11	2.3	13
Philadelphia	0.3	12	8.6	5
London	0.2	13	2.8	11
St. Petersburg	0.2	14	2.2	14

Data Source: *Weltwirtschaftliches Archiv*, 1913, I/ii, p. 143.

grounds than with the ceremonial boulevards and grand buildings. Hull House established the first public playground in Chicago. Jacob Riis, the housing reformer, and Lillian Wald of the Henry Street Settlement campaigned in New York for small parks and for the opening of schoolyards on weekends. Some progressives looked back nostalgically to their rural childhoods and desperately tried to get urban children out of the city in the summertime to attend rural camps. But they also tried to make the city more livable as well as more beautiful.

Most progressives had an ambivalent attitude toward the city. They feared it, and they loved it. Some saw the great urban areas filled with immigrants as a threat to American democracy, but one of Tom Johnson's young assistants, Frederic C. Howe, who had traveled and studied in Europe, wrote a book called *The City: The Hope of Democracy* (1905). Hope

or threat, the progressives realized that the United States had become an urban nation and that the problems of the city had to be faced.

Reform in the States

The progressive movements in the states had many roots and took many forms, but because of the American federal system, the states took on an importance that confused observers from other parts of the world. In some states, especially in the West, progressive attempts to regulate railroads and utilities were simply an extension of Populism. In other states, the reform drive bubbled up from reform efforts in the cities. Most states passed laws during the progressive era designed to extend democracy and give more authority to the people. Initiative and referendum laws allowed citizens to originate legislation and to overturn laws passed by the legislature, and recall laws gave the people a way to remove elected officials. Oregon was one of the leaders in this kind of legislation and, like other Western states, the progressives in Oregon tried to limit the power of the public utilities and the railroads. One important success for progressive reform was finally achieved in 1913 with the ratification of the Seventeenth Amendment to the Constitution, which provided for the direct election of U.S. senators rather than their appointment by the legislatures. Most of these "democratic" laws worked better in theory than in practice, but their passage in many states did represent a genuine effort to remove special privilege from government.

Much progressive state legislation promoted order and efficiency, but many states passed social justice measures as well. Maryland enacted the first workers' compensation law in 1902, paying employees for days missed because of job-related injuries. By 1917, 37 states (almost all outside the south) had passed workmen's compensation laws and 28 states had set maximum hours for women working in industry. Illinois approved a law aiding mothers with dependent children. Several states passed anti–child labor bills, and Oregon's 10-hour law restricting women's labor became a model for other states.

The states with the most successful reform movements elected strong and aggressive governors: Charles Evans Hughes in New York, Hoke Smith in Georgia, Hiram Johnson in California, Woodrow Wilson in New Jersey, and Robert La Follette in Wisconsin. After Wilson, La Follette was the most famous and in many ways the model progressive governor. Born in a small town in Wisconsin, he graduated from the University of Wisconsin in 1879 and was admitted to the bar. Practicing law during the 1890s in Madison, the state capital, he received a large retainer from the Milwaukee Railroad and defended the railroad against both riders and laborers who sued the company.

The depression of 1893 hit Wisconsin hard. More than one-third of the state's citizens were out of work, farmers lost their farms, and many small businesses went bankrupt. At the same time, the rich seemed to be getting richer. As grassroots discontent spread, a group of Milwaukee reformers attacked the giant corporations and the street railways. Several newspapers joined the battle and denounced special privilege and corruption. Everyone could agree on the need for tax reform, railroad regulation, and more participation of the people in government.

La Follette, who had had little interest in reform, took advantage of the general mood of discontent to win the governorship in 1901. It seemed ironic that La Follette, who had once taken a retainer from a railroad, owed his victory to his attack on the railroads. But La Follette was a shrewd politician. He used professors from the University of Wisconsin (in the capital) to prepare reports and do statistical studies. Then he worked with the legislature to pass a state primary law and an act regulating the railroads. "Go back to the first principles of democracy; go back to the people" was his battle cry. The "Wisconsin idea" attracted the attention of journalists like Lincoln Steffens and Ray Stannard Baker, and they helped to popularize the "laboratory of democracy" around the country. La Follette became a national figure and was elected to the Senate in 1906.

The progressive movement did improve government and made it more responsible to the people in states like Wisconsin. For example, the railroads were brought under the control of a railroad commission. But by 1910, the railroads no longer complained about the new taxes and restrictions. They had discovered that it was to their advantage to make their operations more efficient, and often they were able to convince the commission that they should raise rates or abandon the operation of unprofitable lines.

Progressivism in the states, like progressivism everywhere, had mixed results. But the spirit of reform that swept the country was real, and progressive movements on the local level did eventually have an impact on Washington, especially during the administrations of Theodore Roosevelt and Woodrow Wilson.

THEODORE ROOSEVELT AND THE SQUARE DEAL

President William McKinley was shot in Buffalo, New York, on September 6, 1901, by Leon Czolgosz, an anarchist. McKinley died eight days later, making Theodore Roosevelt, at the age of 42, the youngest man ever to become president. The nation mourned its fallen leader, and in many cities, anarchists and other radicals were rounded up for questioning.

No one knew what to expect from Roosevelt. Some politicians thought he was too radical, but a few social justice progressives remembered his suggestion that the soldiers fire on the strikers during the 1894 Pullman strike. Nonetheless, under his leadership, progressivism reshaped the national political agenda. Although early progressive reformers had attacked problems that they saw in their own communities, they gradually understood that some problems could not be solved at the state or local level. The emergence of a national industrial economy had spawned conditions that demanded national solutions. Roosevelt began the process that would continue, sometimes with setbacks, throughout the twentieth century—a process that would regulate business, move beyond the states, and promote reform.

Progressives at the national level turned their attention to the workings of the economic system. They scrutinized the operation and organization of the railroads and other large corporations. They examined the threats to the natural environment. They reviewed the quality of the products of American industry. As they fashioned legislation to remedy the flaws in the economic system, they vastly expanded the power of the national government.

A Strong and Controversial President

Roosevelt came to the presidency with considerable experience. He had run unsuccessfully for mayor of New York, served a term in the New York state assembly, spent four years as a U.S. civil service commissioner, and served two years as the police commissioner of New York City. His exploits in the Spanish-American War brought him to the public's attention, but he had also been an effective assistant secretary of the navy and a reform governor of New York. While police commissioner and governor, he had been influenced by a number of progressives. But no one was sure how he would act as pres-

ident. He came from an upper-class family, had traveled widely in Europe, and had associated with the important and the powerful all over the world. He had written a number of books and was one of the most intellectual and cosmopolitan presidents since Thomas Jefferson. But none of these things ensured that he would be a progressive in office.

Roosevelt loved being president. He called the office a "bully pulpit," and he enjoyed talking to the people and the press. His appealing personality and sense of humor made him a good subject for the new mass-market newspapers and magazines. The American people quickly adopted him as their favorite. They called him "Teddy" and named a stuffed bear after him. Sometimes his exuberance got a little out of hand. On one occasion, he took a foreign diplomat on a nude swim in the Potomac River. You have to understand, another observer remarked, that "the president is really only six years old."

Roosevelt was much more than an exuberant six year old. He was the strongest president since Lincoln. By revitalizing the executive branch, reorganizing the army command structure, and modernizing the consular service, he made many aspects of the federal government more efficient. He established the Bureau of Corporations, appointed independent commissions staffed with experts, and enlisted talented and well-trained men to work for the government. "TR," as he became known, called a White House conference on the care of dependent

Theodore Roosevelt was a dynamic public speaker who used his position to influence public opinion. Despite his high-pitched voice, he could be heard at the back of the crowd in the days before microphones. Note the row of reporters decked out in their summer straw hats writing their stories as the president speaks. (Brown Brothers)

Key Progressive Legislation

National Reclamations Act (Newlands Act), 1902

Used proceeds from sale of public lands in the western states to finance construction and maintenance of irrigation projects.

Elkins Act, 1903

Strengthened the Interstate Commerce Commission Act primarily by eliminating rebates to selected corporations.

Hepburn Act, 1906

Strengthened the Interstate Commerce Commission by giving it power to fix rates and broadening its jurisdiction to include express companies, oil pipelines, terminals, and bridges.

Pure Food and Drug Act, 1906

Prohibited the manufacture, sale, or transportation of adulterated or fraudulently labeled foods or drugs in interstate commerce.

Meat Inspection Act, 1906

Provide for federal inspection of all companies selling meat in interstate commerce.

Mann-Elkins Act, 1910

Put telephone, telegraph, cable, and wireless companies under the jurisdiction of the Interstate Commerce Commission.

Mann Act, 1910

Prohibited interstate transportation of women for immoral purposes.

Sixteenth Amendment to the Constitution, 1913 (proposed in 1909)

Gave Congress the power to impose a federal tax on income from all sources. An inheritance tax was added in 1916.

Federal Child Labor Law (Keatings-Owen Act), 1916

Barred products of child labor from interstate commerce; declared unconstitutional in 1918. Another act passed in 1919; declared unconstitutional in 1920. 1924 child labor amendment to the Constitution submitted to the states, but was never ratified.

Adamson Act, 1916

Provided for an eight-hour day and time and a half for overtime on interstate railroads.

Federal Farm Loan Act, 1916

Provided farmers with long-term credit.

Eighteenth Amendment to the Constitution, 1919 (proposed in 1917)

Prohibited the manufacture, sale, or transportation of intoxicating beverages. Repealed by the Twenty-First Amendment in 1933.

Nineteenth Amendment to the Constitution, 1920 (proposed in 1919)

Provided that the right of citizens of the United States to vote should not be denied or abridged by the United States or any state on account of sex.

children, and in 1905, he even summoned college presidents and football coaches to the White House to discuss ways to limit violence in football. But he angered many social justice progressives by not going far enough. In fact, on one occasion, Florence Kelley was so furious with him that she walked out of the Oval Office and slammed the door. But he was the first president to listen to the pleas of the progressives and to invite them to the White House. Learning from experts like Frances Kellor, he became more concerned with social justice as time went on. In 1904, running on a platform of a "Square Deal" for the American people, he was reelected by an overwhelming margin.

Dealing with the Trusts

One of Roosevelt's first actions as president was to attempt to control the large industrial corporations. He took office in the middle of an unprecedented wave of business consolidation. Between 1897 and 1904, some 4,227 companies combined to form 257 large corporations. U.S. Steel, the first billion-dollar corporation, was formed in 1901 by joining Carnegie Steel with its eight main competitors. The new company controlled two-thirds of the market, and J. P. Morgan made $7 million on the deal.

The Sherman Anti-Trust Act of 1890 had been virtually useless in controlling the trusts, but a new outcry from muckrakers and progressives called for regulation. Some even demanded the return to the age of small business. Roosevelt opposed neither bigness nor the right of businessmen to make money. "We draw the line against misconduct, not against wealth," he said.

To the shock of much of the business community, he directed his attorney general to file suit to dissolve the Northern Securities Company, a giant railroad monopoly put together by James J. Hill and financier J. P. Morgan. Morgan came to the White House to tell Roosevelt, "If we have done anything wrong, send your man to my man and they can fix it up." A furious Roosevelt let Morgan and other businessmen know that they could not deal with the president of the United States as just another

Landmark Social Legislation in the States

1902   Maryland passed the first state workmen's compensation law.

1903   Oregon adopted a law limiting women's work to ten hours a day in factories (upheld by the United States Supreme Court in *Muller v. Oregon*, 1908).

1911   Illinois enacted the first state law providing public assistance to mothers with dependent children.

1912   Massachusetts passed the first minimum-wage law. A commission fixed wage rates for women and children. This and other similar state laws were overturned by the United States Supreme Court in *Atkins v. Children's Hospital*, 1923.

tycoon. The government won its case and proceeded to prosecute some of the largest corporations, including Standard Oil of New Jersey and the American Tobacco Company.

Roosevelt's antitrust policy did not end the power of the giant corporations or even alter their methods of doing business, nor did it force down the price of kerosene, cigars, or railroad tickets. But it did breathe some life into the Sherman Anti-Trust Act, and it increased the role of the federal government as regulator. It also caused large firms such as U.S. Steel to diversify to avoid antitrust suits.

Roosevelt sought to strengthen the regulatory powers of the federal government in other ways. He steered the Elkins Act through Congress in 1903 and the Hepburn Act in 1906, which together increased the power of the Interstate Commerce Commission (ICC). The first act eliminated the use of rebates by railroads, a method that many large corporations had used to get favored treatment. The second act broadened the power of the ICC and gave it the right to investigate and enforce rates. Opponents in Congress weakened both bills, however, and the legislation neither ended abuses nor satisfied the farmers and small businessmen who had always been the railroads' chief critics.

Roosevelt firmly believed in corporate capitalism. He detested socialism and felt much more comfortable around business executives than labor leaders. Yet he saw his role as mediator and regulator. His view of the power of the presidency was illustrated in 1902 during the anthracite coal strike. Led by John Mitchell of the United Mine Workers, the coal miners went on strike to protest low wages, long hours, and unsafe working conditions. In 1901, a total of 513 coal miners had died in industrial accidents. The mine owners refused to talk to the miners. They hired strikebreakers and used private security forces to threaten and intimidate the workers.

Roosevelt had no particular sympathy for labor, but in the fall of 1902, schools began closing for lack of coal, and it looked like many citizens would suffer through the winter. Coal, which usually sold for $5 a ton, rose to $14. Roosevelt called the owners and representatives of the union to the White House even though the businessmen protested that they would not deal with "outlaws." Finally, the president appointed a commission that included representatives of the union as well as the community. Within weeks, the miners went back to work with a 10 percent raise, back pay, and a nine hour day. But the agreement failed to recognize the union. Neither side was entirely happy with the agreement. Roosevelt often compromised and sought the middle ground; in fact, one of his critics called him " a man on two horsebacks."

Meat Inspection and Pure Food and Drugs

Roosevelt's first major legislative reform began almost accidentally in 1904 when Upton Sinclair, a 26-year-old muckraking journalist, started research on the Chicago stockyards. Born in Baltimore, Sinclair had grown up in New York, where he wrote dime novels to pay his tuition at City College. He was converted to socialism, but it was more a romantic, Christian socialism than a Marxist-style European radicalism. Like Eugene Debs, Sinclair was a home-grown radical. Though he knew little about Chicago, he wanted to expose the exploitation of the poor and oppressed in America. He boarded at the University of Chicago Settlement while he did research, conducted interviews, and wrote the story that would be published in 1906 as *The Jungle*. Sinclair documented exploitation in his fictional account, but his description of contaminated meat drew more attention. He described spoiled hams treated with formaldehyde and sausages made from rotten meat scraps, rats, and other refuse. Hoping to convert his readers to socialism, Sinclair instead turned their stomachs and caused a public outcry for better regulation of the meatpacking industry.

Roosevelt ordered a study of the meatpacking industry and then used the report to pressure Congress and the meatpackers to accept a bill introduced by Albert Beveridge, the progressive senator from Indiana. In the end, the Meat Inspection Act of 1906 was a compromise. It enforced some federal inspection and mandated sanitary conditions in all companies selling meat in interstate commerce. The meatpackers defeated a provision that would have required the dating of all meat. Some of the large companies supported the compromise bill because it gave them an advantage in their battle with the smaller firms. But the bill was a beginning. It illustrates how muckrakers, social justice progressives, and public outcry eventually led to reform legislation. It also shows how Roosevelt used the public mood and manipulated the political process to get a bill through Congress. Many of the progressive reformers were disappointed with the final result, but Roosevelt was always willing to settle for half a loaf rather than none at all. Ironically, the Meat Inspection Act restored the public's confidence in the meat industry and helped the industry increase its profits.

Taking advantage of the publicity that circulated around *The Jungle,* a group of reformers, writers, and government officials supported legislation to regulate the sale of food and drugs. Americans consumed an enormous quantity of patent medicines, which they purchased through the mail, from traveling salesmen, and from local stores.. Many packaged and canned foods contained dangerous chemicals and impurities. One popular remedy, Hosteter's Stomach Bitters, was revealed on analysis to contain 44 percent alcohol. Coca-Cola, a popular soft drink, contained a small amount of cocaine, and many medicines were laced with opium. Many people, including women and children, became alcoholics or drug addicts in their quest to feel better. The Pure Food and Drug Act, which passed Congress on the same day in 1906 as the Meat Inspection Act, was not a perfect bill, but it corrected some of the worst abuses, including eliminating the cocaine from Coca-Cola.

Conservation

Although Roosevelt was pleased with the new legislation for regulating the food and drug industries, he always considered his conservation program his most important domestic achievement. An outdoorsman, hunter, and amateur naturalist since his youth, he announced soon after he became president that the planned protection of the nation's forests and water resources would be one of his most vital concerns. Using his executive authority, he more than tripled the land set aside for national forests, bringing the total to more than 150 million acres.

Because he had traveled widely in the West, Roosevelt understood, as few easterners did, the problems created by limited water in the western states. In 1902, with his enthusiastic support, Congress passed the Newlands Act, named after Francis Newlands, its most ardent advocate from the arid state of Nevada. The National Reclamation Act (as it was officially called) set aside the proceeds from the sale of public land in 16 western states to

pay for the construction of irrigation projects in those states. Although it tended to help big farmers more than small producers, the Newlands Act federalized irrigation for the first time.

More important than the conservation bills passed during Roosevelt's presidency, however, were his efforts to raise the public consciousness about the need to save the nation's natural resources. He convened a White House Conservation Conference in 1908 that included among its delegates most of the governors and representatives of 70 national organizations. A direct result of the conference was Roosevelt's appointment of a National Conservation Commission charged with making an inventory of the natural resources in the entire country. To chair the commission, Roosevelt appointed Gifford Pinchot, probably the most important conservation advocate in the country.

A graduate of Yale, Pinchot had studied scientific forestry management in Germany and France before becoming the forest manager of the Vanderbilt's Biltmore estate in North Carolina. In 1898, he was appointed chief of the U.S. Division of Forestry, and in 1900, he became the head of the Bureau of Forestry in the Department of Agriculture. An advocate of selective logging, fire control, and limited grazing on public lands, he became a friend and adviser to Roosevelt.

Pinchot's conservation policies pleased many in the timber and cattle industries; at the same time, they angered those who simply wanted to exploit the land. But his policies were denounced by the followers of John Muir, who believed passionately in preserving the land in a wilderness state. Muir had founded the Sierra Club in 1862 and had led a successful campaign to create Yosemite National Park in California. With his shaggy gray beard, his rough blue work clothes, and his black slouch hat, Muir seemed like an eccentric to many, but thousands agreed with him when he argued that to preserve the American wilderness was a spiritual and psychological necessity for overcivilized and overstimulated urban dwellers. Muir was one of the leaders in a "back to nature" movement at the turn of the century. Many middle-class Americans took up hiking, camping, and other outdoor activities, and children joined the Boy Scouts (founded in 1910) and the Camp Fire Girls (1912). The "back to nature movement" was not strictly American. The Boy Scouts were patterned after the British Boy Scouts, and hiking and mountain climbing were popular activities in many countries early in the twentieth century.

The conflicting conservation philosophies of Pinchot and Muir were most dramatically demonstrated by the controversy over Hetch-Hetchy, a re-

National Parks and Forests

Yellowstone, Yosemite, and a few other national parks were established before Theodore Roosevelt became president, but his passionate interest in conservation led to a movement to set aside and preserve thousands of acres of the public domain. Despite disagreements over the proper goals for the management of federal land, the movement continues to this day.

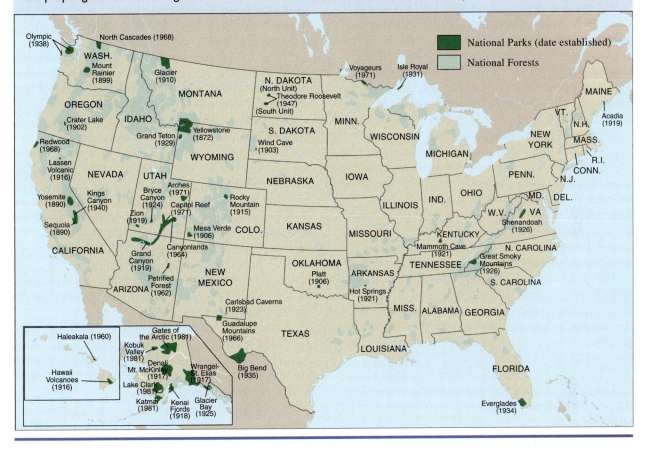

mote valley deep within Yosemite National Park. It was a pristine wilderness area, and Muir and his followers wanted to keep it that way. But in 1901, the mayor of San Francisco decided the valley would make a perfect place for a dam and reservoir to supply his growing city with water for decades to come. Muir argued that wilderness soon would be scarcer than water and more important for the moral strength of the nation. Pinchot, on the other hand, maintained that it was foolish to pander to the aesthetic enjoyment of a tiny group of people when the comfort and welfare of the great majority were at stake.

The Hetch-Hetchy affair was fought out in the newspapers and magazines as well as in the halls of Congress, but in the end, the conservationists won out over those who wanted only to preserve the wilderness. Roosevelt and Congress sided with Pinchot and eventually the dam was built, turning the valley into a lake. But the debate over how to use

the nation's land and water would continue throughout the twentieth century.

Progressivism for Whites Only

Like most of his generation, Roosevelt thought in stereotyped racial terms. He called Indians "savages" and once remarked that blacks were "wholly unfit for the suffrage." He believed that blacks, Asians, and Native Americans were inferior, and he feared that massive migrations from southern and eastern Europe threatened the United States. This kind of racism was supported by scientific theories accepted by many experts in the universities. In 1916, Madison Grant summarized these theories in his book *The Passing of the Great Race,* in which he argued against the dangers of "mongrelization" and urged the protection of the purity of the Anglo-Saxon race. A few who believed in eugenics even advocated the forced sterilization of criminals, mental patients, and other undesirable types. Roosevelt was influenced by these theories, but he was first of all a politician, so he made gestures of goodwill to most groups. He even invited Booker T. Washington to the White House in 1901, though many southerners viciously attacked the president for his breach of etiquette. Roosevelt also appointed several qualified blacks to minor federal posts, notably Dr. William D. Crum to head the Charleston, South Carolina, customs house in 1905.

At other times, however, Roosevelt seemed insensitive to the needs and feelings of black Americans. This was especially true in his handling of the Brownsville, Texas, riot of 1906. Members of a black army unit stationed there, angered by discrimination against them, rioted one hot August night. Exactly what happened no one was sure, but one white man was killed and several wounded. Waiting until after the midterm elections of 1906, Roosevelt ordered all 167 members of three companies dishonorably discharged. It was an unjust punishment for an unproven crime, and 66 years later, the secretary of the army granted honorable discharges to the men, although most of them were by that time dead.

The progressive era coincided with the years of greatest segregation in the South, and in southern states, progressivism meant not only regulation of the railroads, but also keeping blacks outside the political process. Even the most advanced progressives seldom included blacks in their reform schemes. Like most social settlements, Hull House was segregated, although Jane Addams (more than most progressives) struggled to overcome the racist attitudes of her day. She helped found a settlement that served a black neighborhood in Chicago, and she spoke out repeatedly against lynching. Addams also supported the founding of the National Association for the Advancement of Colored People (NAACP) in 1909, the most important organization of the progressive era aimed at promoting equality and justice for blacks.

The founding of the NAACP is the story of cooperation between a group of white social justice progressives and a number of courageous black leaders. Even in the age of segregation and lynching, blacks in all parts of the country—through churches, clubs, and schools—sought to promote a better life for themselves. In Boston, William Monroe Trotter used his newspaper to oppose Washington's policy of accommodation. In Chicago, Ida B. Wells, a large woman with flashing eyes, launched a one-woman crusade against lynching, organized a women's club for blacks, and founded the Negro Fellowship League to help black migrants. The most important black leader who argued for equality and opportunity for his people was W. E. B.

Du Bois. He differed dramatically from Booker T. Washington on the proper position of blacks in American life (see Chapter 17.) Whereas Washington advocated vocational education, Du Bois argued for the best education possible for the most talented tenth of the black population. Whereas Washington preached compromise and accommodation to the dominant white society, Du Bois increasingly urged aggressive action to ensure equality.

Denouncing Washington for accepting the "alleged inferiority of the Negro," Du Bois called a meeting of young and militant blacks in 1905. They met in Canada, not far from Niagara Falls, and issued an angry statement. "We want to pull down nothing but we don't propose to be pulled down," the platform announced. "We believe in taking what we can get but we don't believe in being satisfied with it and in permitting anybody for a moment to imagine we're satisfied." The Niagara movement, as it came to be called, was small, but it was soon augmented by a group of white liberals concerned with violence against blacks and race riots in Atlanta and even in Springfield, Illinois, the home of Abraham Lincoln. Jane Addams joined the new organization, as did Oswald Garrison Villard, grandson of abolitionist William Lloyd Garrison.

In 1910, the Niagara movement combined with the NAACP, and Du Bois became editor of its journal, *The Crisis*. He toned down his rhetoric, but he tried to promote equality for all blacks. The NAACP was a typical progressive organization, seeking to work within the American system to promote reform. But to Roosevelt and many others who called themselves progressives, the NAACP seemed dangerously radical.

William Howard Taft

After two terms as president, Roosevelt decided to step down. But he soon regretted his decision. Only 50 years old, he was at the peak of his popularity and power. Because the U.S. system of government provides little creative function for former presidents, Roosevelt decided to travel and to go big-game hunting in Africa. But before he left, he personally selected his successor.

William Howard Taft, Roosevelt's personal choice for the Republican nomination in 1908, was a distinguished lawyer, federal judge, and public servant. Born in Cincinnati, he had been the first civil governor of the Philippines and Roosevelt's secretary of war. After defeating William Jennings Bryan for the presidency in 1908, he quickly ran into difficulties. In some ways, he seemed more progressive than Roosevelt. His administration instituted more suits against monopolies in one term than Roosevelt had

Tuskegee Institute followed Booker T. Washington's philosophy of black advancement through accommodation to the white status quo. Here students study white American history, but most of their time was spent on more practical subjects. This photo was taken in 1902 by Frances Benjamin Johnson, a pioneer woman photographer. *(Library of Congress)*

in two. He supported the eight-hour workday and legislation to make mining safer, and he urged the passage of the Mann-Elkins Act in 1910, which strengthened the ICC by giving it more power to set railroad rates and extending its jurisdiction over telephone and telegraph companies. Taft and Congress also authorized the first tax on corporate profits. He also encouraged the process that eventually led to the passage of the federal income tax, which was authorized under the Sixteenth Amendment, ratified in 1913. That probably did more to transform the relationship of the government to the people than all other progressive measures combined.

Taft's biggest problem was his style. He was a huge man, weighing over 300 pounds. (Rumors circulated that he had to have a special, oversize bathtub installed in the White House.) Easily made fun of, the president wrote ponderous prose and spoke uninspiringly. He also lacked Roosevelt's political skills and angered many of the progressives in the Republican party, especially the midwestern insurgents led by Senator Robert La Follette of Wisconsin. Many progressives were annoyed when he signed

the Payne-Aldrich Tariff, which Midwesterners thought left rates on cotton and wool cloth and other items too high and played into the hands of the eastern industrial interests.

Even Roosevelt was infuriated when his successor reversed many of his conservation policies and fired Chief Forester Gifford Pinchot, who had attacked Secretary of the Interior Richard A. Ballinger for giving away rich coal lands in Alaska to mining interests. Roosevelt broke with Taft, letting it be known that he was willing to run again for president. This set up one of the most exciting and significant elections in American history.

The Election of 1912

Woodrow Wilson won the Democratic nomination for president in 1912. Born two years before Roosevelt, Wilson came from a very different background and would be cast in opposition to the former president during most of his political career. Wilson was the son and grandson of Presbyterian ministers. Growing up in a comfortable and intellectual southern household, he very early seemed more interested in politics than in religion. After graduating from Princeton University in 1879, he studied law at the University of Virginia and practiced law briefly before entering graduate school at the Johns Hopkins University in Baltimore. Soon after receiving his Ph.D., he published a book, *Congressional Government* (1885), that established his reputation as a shrewd analyst of American politics. He taught history briefly at Bryn Mawr College near Philadelphia and at Wesleyan in Connecticut before moving to Princeton. Less flamboyant than Roosevelt, he was an excellent public speaker, possessing the power to convince people with his words. In 1902, Wilson was elected president of Princeton University, and during the next few years, he established a national reputation as an educational leader. Wilson had never lost interest in politics, however, so when offered a chance by the Democratic machine to run for governor of New Jersey, he took it eagerly. In his two years as governor, he showed courage as he quickly alienated some of the conservatives who had helped to elect him. Building a coalition of reformers, he worked with them to pass a direct primary law and a workers' compensation law. He also created a commission to regulate transportation and public utility companies. By 1912, Wilson not only was an expert on government and politics but had also acquired the reputation of a progressive.

Roosevelt, who had been speaking out on a variety of issues since 1910, competed with Taft for the Republican nomination, but Taft, as the incumbent president and party leader, was able to win it. Roosevelt then startled the nation by walking out of the convention and forming a new political party, the Progressive party. The new party would not have been formed without Roosevelt, but it was always more than Roosevelt. It appealed to progressives from all over the country who had become frustrated with the conservative leadership in both major parties.

Many social workers and social justice progressives supported the Progressive party because of its platform, which contained provisions they had been advocating for years. The Progressives supported an eight-hour day, a six-day week, the abolition of child labor under age 16, and a federal system of accident, old age, and unemployment insurance. Unlike the Democrats, the Progressives also endorsed woman suffrage.

Most supporters of the Progressives in 1912 did not realistically think they could win, but they were convinced that they could organize a new political movement that would replace the Republican party, just as the Republicans had replaced the Whigs after 1856. To this end, Progressive leaders led by Frances Kellor set up the Progressive Service, designed to apply the principles of social research to educating voters between elections.

The Progressive convention in Chicago seemed to many observers more like a religious revival meeting or a social work conference than a political gathering. The delegates sang "Onward Christian Soldiers," "The Battle Hymn of the Republic," and "Roosevelt, Oh Roosevelt" (to the tune of "Maryland, My Maryland"). They waved their bandannas, and when Jane Addams rose to second Roosevelt's nomination, a large group of women marched around the auditorium with a banner that read "Votes for Women."

The enthusiasm for Roosevelt and the Progressive party was misleading, for behind the unified facade lurked many disagreements. Roosevelt had become more progressive on many issues since leaving the presidency. He even attacked the financiers "to whom the acquisition of untold millions is the supreme goal of life, and who are too often utterly indifferent as to how these millions are obtained." But he was not as committed to social reform as some of the delegates. Perhaps the most divisive issue was the controversy over seating black delegates from several southern states. A number of social justice progressives fought hard to include a plank in the platform supporting equality for blacks and for seating the black delegation. Roosevelt, however, thought he had a realistic chance to carry several southern states, and he was not convinced that black equality was an important progressive issue. In the end, no blacks sat with the southern delegates, and the platform made no mention of black equality.

The political campaign in 1912 became a contest primarily between Roosevelt and Wilson; Taft, the Republican candidate and incumbent, was ignored by most reporters who covered the campaign. On one level, the campaign became a debate over political philosophy. What is the proper relationship of government to society in a modern industrial age? Roosevelt borrowed some of his ideas from the book *The Promise of American Life* (1909), written by Herbert Croly, a young journalist. But he had also been working out his own philosophy of government. He spoke of the "new nationalism." In a modern industrial society, he argued, large corporations were "inevitable and necessary." What was needed was not the breakup of the trusts but a strong president and increased power in the hands of the federal government to regulate business and industry and to ensure the rights of labor, women and children, and other groups. The government should be

The Armory Show held in New York in 1913 introduced modern art to the American public. It was a cultural moment of great importance during the progressive era. Marcel Duchamp's *Nude Descending Staircase* illustrates the impact of technology on painting as well as the beginning of cubism and abstract construction. It was denounced by many critics as "an explosion in a shingle factory" and as "a rude descending a staircase." But it was one of the most popular paintings in the show, and it has remained a symbol of modernism in America. *(Marcel Duchamp.* Nude Descending Staircase, No. 2. *1912. Oil on canvas, 58" × 35". Philadelphia Museum of Art: The Louise and Walter Annenberg Collection/© 2003 Artists Rights Society [ARS], New York/ADAGP, Paris/Succession Marcel Duchamp)*

the "steward of the public welfare." He argued for using Hamiltonian means to ensure Jeffersonian ends, for using strong central government to guarantee the rights of the people.

Wilson responded with a slogan and a program of his own. Using the writings of Louis Brandeis, he talked of the "new freedom." He emphasized the need for the Jeffersonian tradition of limited government with open competition. He spoke of the "curse of bigness" and argued against too much federal power.

The level of debate during the campaign was impressive, making this one of the few elections in

American history in which important ideas were actually discussed. It also marked a watershed for political thought for liberals who rejected Jefferson's distrust of a strong central government. It is easy to exaggerate the differences between Roosevelt and Wilson. There was some truth in the charge of William Allen White, the editor of the Emporia *Gazette* in Kansas, when he remarked, "Between the New Nationalism and the New Freedom was that fantastic imaginary gulf that always had existed between Tweedle-dum and Tweedle-dee." Certainly, in the end, the things that Roosevelt and Wilson could agree on were more important than the issues that divided them. Both Roosevelt and Wilson urged reform within the American system. Both defended corporate capitalism, and both opposed socialism and radical labor organizations such as the IWW. Both wanted to promote more democracy and to strengthen conservative labor unions. And both were very different in style and substance from the fourth candidate, Eugene Debs, who ran on the Socialist party ticket in 1912.

In 1912, Debs was the most important socialist leader in the country. Socialism has always been a minority movement in the United States. It never had the impact it had in several European countries in large part because the American two-party system gave little influence to minor parties. Socialism also had less appeal to the working class than in Europe, but socialism had its greatest success in the United States in the first decade of the twentieth century. Thirty-three cities, including Milwaukee, Wisconsin; Reading, Pennsylvania; Butte, Montana; Jackson, Michigan; and Berkeley, California, chose socialist mayors. Socialists Victor Berger from Wisconsin and Meyer London from New York were elected to Congress. The most important socialist periodical, *Appeal to Reason*, published in Girard, Kansas, increased its circulation from about 30,000 in 1900 to nearly 300,000 in 1906. Socialism appealed to a diverse group. In the cities, some who called themselves socialists merely favored municipal ownership of street railways. Some reformers, such as Florence Kelley and William English Walling, joined the party because of their frustration with the slow progress of reform. The party also attracted many recent immigrants, who brought with them a European sense of class and loyalty to socialism.

A tremendously appealing figure and a great orator, Debs had run for president in 1900, 1904, and 1908, but in 1912 he reached much wider audiences in more parts of the country. His message differed radically from that of Wilson or Roosevelt. Unlike the progressives, socialists argued for fundamental change in the American system. Debs polled almost 900,000 votes in 1912 (6 percent of the popular vote), the best showing ever for a socialist in the United States. Wilson received 6.3 million votes; Roosevelt, a little more than 4 million; and Taft, 3.5 million. Wilson garnered 435 electoral votes; Roosevelt, 88; and Taft, only 8.

WOODROW WILSON AND THE NEW FREEDOM

Wilson was elected largely because Roosevelt and the Progressive party split the Republican vote. But once elected, Wilson became a vigorous and aggressive chief executive who set out to translate his ideas about progressive government into legislation. Wilson was the first southerner elected president since the Civil War, but Wilson, like Roosevelt, had to work within his party, and that restricted how progressive he could be. But he was also constrained by his own background and inclinations. Still, like Roosevelt, Wilson became more progressive during his presidency.

Tariff and Banking Reform

Wilson was not as charismatic as Roosevelt. He had a more difficult time relating to people in small groups, but he was an excellent public speaker who dominated through the force of his intellect. He probably had an exaggerated belief in his ability to persuade and a tendency to trust his own intuition too much. Ironically, his early success in getting his legislative agenda through Congress contributed to the overconfidence that would get him into difficulty later in foreign affairs. But his ability to push his legislative program through Congress during his first two years in office was matched only by Franklin Roosevelt during the first months of the New Deal and by Lyndon Johnson in 1965.

Within a month of his inauguration, Wilson went before a joint session of Congress to outline his legislative program. He recommended reducing the tariff to eliminate favoritism, freeing the banking system from Wall Street control, and restoring competition in industry. By appearing in person before Congress, he broke a precedent established by Thomas Jefferson. First on Wilson's agenda was tariff reform. The Underwood Tariff, passed in 1913, was not a free-trade bill, but it did reduce the schedule for the first time in many years.

Attached to the Underwood bill was a provision for a small and slightly graduated income tax, which had been made possible by the passage of the Sixteenth Amendment. It imposed a modest rate of 1 percent on income over $4,000 (thus exempting a large portion of the population), with a surtax rising to 6 percent on high incomes. The income tax was enacted to replace the money lost from lowering the tariff. Wilson seemed to have no interest in using it to redistribute wealth in America.

The next item on Wilson's agenda was reform of the banking system. A financial panic in 1907 had revealed the need for a central bank, but few people could agree on the exact nature of the reforms. The progressive faction of the Democratic party, armed with the findings of the Pujo Committee's investiga-

Year	Candidate	Party	Popular Vote	Electoral Vote
1900	WILLIAM MCKINLEY	Republican	7,218,039 (51.7%)	292
	William Jennings Bryan	Democratic, Populist	6,358,345 (45.5%)	155
1904	THEODORE ROOSEVELT	Republican	7,628,834 (56.4%)	336
	Alton B. Parker	Democratic	5,084,401 (37.6%)	140
	Eugene V. Debs	Socialist	402,460 (3.0%)	0
1908	WILLIAM H. TAFT	Republican	7,679,006 (51.6%)	321
	William J. Bryan	Democratic	6,409,106 (43.1%)	162
	Eugene V. Debs	Socialist	420,820 (2.8%)	0
1912	WOODROW WILSON	Democratic	6,296,547 (41.9%)	435
	Theodore Roosevelt	Progressive	4,118,571 (27.4%)	88
	William H. Taft	Republican	3,486,720 (23.2%)	8
	Eugene V. Debs	Socialist	897,011 (6.0%)	0
1916	WOODROW WILSON	Democratic	9,129,606 (49.4%)	277
	Charles E. Hughes	Republican	8,538,221 (46.2%)	254
	Allan L. Benson	Socialist	585,113 (3.2%)	0

Presidential Elections of the Progressive Era

Note: Winners' names appear in capital letters.

Many men opposed suffrage for women because they feared the vote would change gender roles and destroy women's feminine ways. They also believed that women with the vote would support prohibition and other dangerous reforms. They often argued that women had no place in the masculine and corrupt world of politics. Many women also opposed suffrage because they believed their husbands and fathers or because they feared change. *(Library of Congress [LC-USZ62-25338])*

tion of the money trust, argued for a banking system and a currency controlled by the federal government. The congressional committee, led by Arsène Pujo of Louisiana, had revealed a massive consolidation of banks and trust companies and a system of interlocking directorates and informal arrangements that concentrated resources and power in the hands of a few firms, such as the J. P. Morgan Company. But talk of banking reform raised the specter among conservative Democrats and the business community of socialism, populism, and the monetary ideas of William Jennings Bryan.

The bill that passed Congress was a compromise. In creating the Federal Reserve System, it was the first reorganization of the banking system since the Civil War. The bill provided for 12 Federal Reserve banks and a Federal Reserve Board appointed by the president. The bill also created a flexible currency, based on Federal Reserve notes, that could be expanded or contracted as the situation required. The Federal Reserve System was not without its flaws, as later developments would show, and it did not end the power of the large eastern banks; but it was an improvement, and it appealed to the part of the progressive movement that sought order and efficiency.

Despite these reform measures, Wilson was not very progressive in some of his actions during his first two years in office. In the spring of 1914, he failed to support a bill that would have provided long-term rural credit financed by the federal government. He opposed a woman suffrage amend-

ment, arguing that the states should decide who could vote. He also failed to support an anti–child labor bill after it had passed the House. Most distressing to some progressives, he ordered the segregation of blacks in several federal departments.

Booker T. Washington had remarked on Wilson's election, "Mr. Wilson is in favor of the things which tend toward the uplift, improvement, and advancement of my people, and at his hands we have nothing to fear." But when southern Democrats, suddenly in control in many departments, began dismissing black federal officeholders, especially those "who boss white girls," Wilson did nothing. When the NAACP complained that the shops, offices, rest rooms, and lunchrooms of the post office and treasury departments and the Bureau of Engraving were segregated, Wilson replied, "I sincerely believe it to be in their [the blacks'] best interest." When the president endorsed the blatantly racist movie *Birth of a Nation*, others doubted that he believed in justice for the African-American people. "Have you a 'new freedom' for white Americans and a new slavery for your African-American fellow citizens?" William Monroe Trotter, a Boston journalist, asked.

Moving Closer to a New Nationalism

How to control the great corporations in America was a question Wilson and Roosevelt debated extensively during the campaign. Wilson's solution was the Clayton Act, submitted to Congress in 1914. The bill prohibited a number of unfair trading practices, outlawed the interlocking directorate, and made it illegal for corporations to purchase stock in other corporations if this tended to reduce competition. It was not clear how the government would enforce these provisions and ensure the competition that Wilson's New Freedom doctrine called for, but the bill became controversial for another reason.

Labor leaders protested that the bill had no provision exempting labor organizations from prosecution under the Sherman Anti-Trust Act. When a section was added exempting both labor and agricultural organizations, Samuel Gompers hailed it as labor's Magna Carta. It was hardly that, because the courts interpreted the provision so that labor unions remained subject to court injunctions during strikes despite the Clayton Act.

More important than the Clayton Act, which both supporters and opponents realized was too vague to be enforced, was the creation of the Federal Trade Commission (FTC), modeled after the ICC, with enough power to move directly against corporations accused of restricting competition. The FTC was the idea of Louis Brandeis, but Wilson accepted it even though it seemed to move him more toward the philosophy of New Nationalism.

The Federal Trade Commission and the Clayton Act did not end monopoly, and the courts in the next two decades did not increase the government's power to regulate business. The success of Wilson's reform agenda appeared minimal in 1914, but the outbreak of war in Europe and the need to win the election of 1916 would influence him in becoming more progressive in the next years (see Chapter 22).

Neither Wilson nor Roosevelt satisfied the demands of the advanced progressives. Most of the efforts of the two progressive presidents were spent trying to regulate economic power rather than to promote social justice. Yet the most important legacy of these two fascinating and powerful politicians was their attempts to strengthen the office of president and the executive branch of the federal government. The nineteenth-century American presidents after Lincoln had been relatively weak, and much of the federal power had resided with Congress. The progressive presidents reasserted presidential authority, modernized the executive branch, and began the creation of the federal bureaucracy, which had had a major impact on the lives of Americans in the twentieth century.

Both Wilson and Roosevelt used the presidency as a bully pulpit to make pronouncements, create news, and influence policy. For example, both presidents called White House conferences and appointed committees and commissions. Roosevelt

strengthened the Interstate Commerce Commission and Wilson created the Federal Trade Commission, both of which were the forerunners of many other federal regulatory bodies. And by breaking precedent and actually delivering his annual message in person before a joint session of Congress, Wilson symbolized the new power of the presidency.

Timeline

1901	McKinley assassinated; Theodore Roosevelt becomes president
	Robert La Follette elected governor of Wisconsin
	Tom Johnson elected mayor of Cleveland
	Model tenement house bill passed in New York
	U.S. Steel formed
1902	Anthracite coal strike
1903	Women's Trade Union League founded
	Elkins Act
1904	Roosevelt reelected
	Lincoln Steffens writes *The Shame of the Cities*
1905	Frederic C. Howe writes *The City: The Hope of Democracy*
	Industrial Workers of the World formed
1906	Upton Sinclair writes *The Jungle*
	Hepburn Act
	Meat Inspection Act
	Pure Food and Drug Act
1907	Financial panic
1908	*Muller* v. *Oregon*
	Danbury Hatters case
	William Howard Taft elected president
1909	Herbert Croly writes *The Promise of American Life*
	NAACP founded
1910	Ballinger–Pinchot controversy
	Mann Act
1911	Frederick Taylor writes *The Principles of Scientific Management*
	Triangle Shirtwaist Company fire
1912	Progressive party founded by Theodore Roosevelt
	Woodrow Wilson elected president
	Children's Bureau established
	Industrial Relations Commission founded
1913	Sixteenth Amendment (income tax) ratified
	Underwood Tariff
	Federal Reserve System established
	Seventeenth Amendment (direct election of senators) passed
1914	Clayton Act
	Federal Trade Commission Act
	AFL has over 2 million members
	Ludlow Massacre in Colorado

The nature of politics was changed by more than just the increased power of the executive branch. The new bureaus, committees, and commissions brought to Washington a new kind of expert, trained in the universities, at the state and local level, and in voluntary organizations. Julia Lathrop, a coworker of Jane Addams at Hull House, was one such expert. Appointed by President Taft in 1912 to become chief of the newly created Children's Bureau, she was the first woman ever appointed to such a position. She used her post not only to work for better child labor laws but also to train a new generation of women experts who would take their positions in state, federal, and private agencies in the 1920s and 1930s. Other experts emerged in Washington during the progressive era to influence policy in subtle and important ways. The expert, the commission, the statistical survey, and the increased power of the executive branch were all legacies of the progressive era.

✦ Conclusion

THE LIMITS OF PROGRESSIVISM

The progressive era was a time when many Americans set out to promote reform because they saw poverty, despair, and disorder in the country transformed by immigration, urbanism, and industrialism. But unlike the socialists, the progressives saw nothing fundamentally wrong with the American system. Progressivism, part of a global movement to regulate and control rampaging industrialism, was largely a middle-class movement that sought to help the poor, the immigrants, and the working class. Yet the poor were rarely consulted about policy, and many groups, especially African Americans, were almost entirely left out of reform plans. Progressives had an optimistic view of human nature and an exaggerated faith in statistics, commissions, and committees. They talked of the need for more democracy, but they often succeeded in promoting bureaucracy and a government run by experts. They believed there was a need to regulate business, promote efficiency, and spread social justice, but these were often contradictory goals. In the end, their regulatory laws tended to aid business and strengthen corporate capitalism, while social justice and equal opportunity remained difficult to achieve. By contrast, most of the industrialized nations of western Europe, especially Germany, Denmark, and Great Britain, passed legislation during this period providing for old-age pensions and health and unemployment insurance.

Progressivism was a broad, diverse, and sometimes contradictory movement that had its roots in the 1890s and reached a climax in the early twentieth century. It began with many local movements and voluntary efforts to deal with the problems created by urban industrialism and then moved to the state and finally the national level. Women played important roles in organizing reform, and many became experts at gathering statistics and writing reports. Eventually, they began to fill positions in the new agencies in the state capitals and in Washington. Frances Kellor was one of those professional women who devoted her life to reform and to helping the immigrants. Neither Theodore Roosevelt nor Woodrow Wilson was an advanced progressive, but during both their administrations, progressivism achieved some success. Both presidents strengthened the power of the presidency, and both promoted the idea that the federal government had the responsibility to regulate and control and to promote social justice. Progressivism would be altered by World War I, but it survived, with its strengths and weaknesses, to affect American society through most of the twentieth century.

✦ Recommended Reading

The Social Justice Movement
Jean H. Baker, ed., *Votes for Women: The Struggle for Suffrage Revisited* (2002); Paul Boyer, *Urban Masses and Moral Order in America, 1820–1920* (1978); Mark Connelly, *The Response to Prostitution in the Progressive Era* (1980); Robert Crunden, *Ministers of Reform* (1982); Susan Curtis, *Consuming Faith: The Social Gospel and Modern American Culture* (1991); Allen F. Davis, *Spearheads For Reform: The Social Settlements and the Progressive Movement* (1967); Steven J. Diner, *A Very Different Age: America in the Progressive Era* (1998); David Kennedy, *Birth Control in America* (1970); Aileen Kraditor, *The Ideas of the Woman Suffrage Movement* (1965); Daniel Levine, *Poverty and Society: The Growth of the American Welfare State in International Perspective* (1988); Gary Gerstle, *American Crucible: Race and Nation*

in the Twentieth Century (2001); Robin Muncy, *Creating a Female Dominion in American Reform* (1991); Clifford Putney, *Muscular Christianity: Manhood and Sports in Protestant America, 1880–1920* (2001); Daniel T. Rodgers, *Atlantic Crossings: Social Politics in a Progressive Age* (1998); Ruth Rosen, *The Lost Sisterhood: Prostitutes in America: 1900–1918* (1982); Kathryn Kish Sklar, *Florence Kelley and the Nation's Work: The Rise of Women's Political Culture* (1995); James H. Timberlake, *Prohibition and the Progressive Movement* (1963); Robert C. Westbrook, *John Dewey and American Democracy* (1989).

The Worker in the Progressive Era

David Brody, *Workers in Industrial America* (1980); Elliot J. Gorn, *Mother Jones: The Most Dangerous Woman in America* (2001); Julie Green, *Pure and Simple Politics: The American Federation of Labor and Political Activism* (1998); Herbert Gutman, *Work, Culture and Society in Industrializing America* (1976); Alice Kessler-Harris, *Out to Work: A History of Wage-Earning Women in America* (1982); Lary May, *Screening Out the Past: The Birth of Mass Culture and the Motion Picture Industry* (1980); David Montgomery, *Workers Control in America* (1979); Kathy Peiss, *Cheap Amusements: Working Women and Leisure at Turn of the Century New York* (1986); Leo Stein, *The Triangle Fire* (1962).

Reform in the Cities and States

John D. Buenker, *Urban Liberalism and Progressive Reform* (1973); James J. Connolly, *The Triumph of Ethnic Progressivism* (1998); Dewey Grantham, *Southern Progressivism* (1983); Melvin G. Holli, *Reform in Detroit: Hazen Pingree and Urban Politics* (1969); Marnie Jones, *Holy Toledo: Religion and Politics in the Life of "Golden Rule" Jones* (1998); David P. Thelen, *Robert M. LaFollette and the Insurgent Spirit* (1976); Robert Wiebe, *The Search for Order, 1877–1920* (1967).

Theodore Roosevelt and the Square Deal

John Morton Blum, *The Progressive Presidents* (1980); John Milton Cooper Jr., *The Warrior and the Priest* (1983); Kathleen Dalton, *Theodore Roosevelt: A Strenuous Life* (2002); Edmund Morris, *Theodore Rex* (2001); George Mowry, *The Era of Theodore Roosevelt* (1958); Lewis L. Gould, *The Presidency of Theodore Roosevelt* (1991); James Penick Jr., *Progressive Politics and Conservation: The Ballinger-Pinchot Affair* (1968).

Woodrow Wilson and the New Freedom

John Morton Blum, *Woodrow Wilson and the Politics of Morality* (1956); Kendrick A. Clements, *The Presidency of Woodrow Wilson* (1992); Paolo E. Coletta, *The Presidency of William Howard Taft* (1973); Arthur Link, *Woodrow Wilson and the Progressive Era* (1954); Nick Salvatore, *Eugene V. Debs* (1982).

Fiction and Film

Three books written in the early 1900s help readers understand what life was like during the progressive era. Theodore Dreiser's *Sister Carrie* (1900) is a classic of social realism that was controversial at the time it was published. Upton Sinclair's *The Jungle* (1906) is about the meatpacking industry and the failure of the American dream. *Susan Lenox* (1917), written by David Graham Phillips, is an epic of slum life and political corruption. *Birth of a Nation* (1915) is an important film not only because of its innovative technique but also because it is a mirror of the racism of the progressive era. *Hester Street* (1975), a later film, creates a realistic picture of the immigrant experience and the conflict between husbands and wives created by assimilation. According to some critics, *Citizen Kane* (1941) is the best American film ever made. Based loosely on the life of newspaper magnate William Randoph Hearst, the film deals with much of the history of the early twentieth century.

✦ Discovering U.S. History Online

How the Other Half Lives: Studies Among the Tenements of New York

www.cis.yale.edu/amstud/inforev/riis/title.html

This site presents the full text, including illustrations, of this classic text.

Turn-of-the-Century America, 1880–1920

http://lcweb2.loc.gov/ammem/detroit/dethome.htm

This Library of Congress collection has thousands of photographs from turn-of-the-century America.

American Sweatshops

www.americanhistory.si.edu/sweatshops/

This site presents a history of American Sweatshops from 1820–1997 through images and text.

The Triangle Factory Fire

www.ilr.cornell.edu/trianglefire/

The Kheel Center has put together this site composed of oral histories, cartoons, images, and essays about the shirtwaist factory fire of March 1911.

The Westinghouse World

http://memory.loc.gov/ammem/papr/west/westgorg.html

Part of the Westinghouse Works Collection, this special exhibition presents an overview of this turn of-the-century factory, the working conditions, projects, and a brief biography of the founder.

The Trial of Bill Haywood

www.law.umkc.edu/faculty/projects/ftrials/haywood/haywood.htm

Bill Haywood was a labor radical accused of ordering the assassination of former governor of Idaho Frank Steunenberg in 1907. This site contains images, chronology, and court and official documents.

Memories of the Industrial Workers of the World (IWW)

www.geocities.com/CapitolHill/5202/rebelgirl.html

Elizabeth Gurley Flynn gave this speech presenting her memoirs of IWW two years before her death.

IWW Historical Reclamation Project

http://parsons.iww.org/~iw/info/books/

A cooperative effort of present union members to preserve the history of IWW, this site presents a collection of pamphlets, writings, Web references, etc.

Arts and Crafts Archives

www.arts-crafts.com/archive/archive.shtml

This site serves as a guide to materials on the arts and crafts movement, which lasted roughly from 1890 to 1929.

The Evolution of the Conservation Movement, 1850–1920

http://memory.loc.gov/ammem/amrvhtml/conshome.html

This Library of Congress site brings together scores of primary sources and photographs about "the historical formation and cultural foundations of the movement to conserve and protect America's natural heritage."

America 1900

www.pbs.org/wgbh/pages/amex/1900

This is the companion site to the PBS documentary "America 1900." It includes audio clips of respected historians on the economics, politics, and culture of 1900; a primary-source database; a timeline of the year; downloadable software to compile your family tree; and other materials.

Chicago in 1900

www.chipublib.org/004chicago/1900/intro.html

This site presents a sketch of Chicago in 1900, including its architecture, commerce, crime, education, family, economics, amusements, geography, government, health, population, and transportation.

The Anthracite Coal Strike, 1902

www.history.ohio-state.edu/projects/coal/1902anthracitestrike/

As an example of turn-of-the-century strikes, this site presents the anthracite strike of 1902, including a chronology of the strike, primary documents, a description of the issues, and political cartoons.

The Wright Brothers in Photographs

www.libraries.wright.edu/special/wright_brothers/dmc.html

This image database "provides thorough coverage of the Wrights' early inventive period documenting their experimental gliders and flight testing in both North Carolina and Ohio."

Theodore Roosevelt Association

www.theodoreroosevelt.org/

Chartered by Congress in 1920 to "preserve the memory and ideals of the 26th President of the United States," the Theodore Roosevelt Association presents a thorough site containing much biographical and research information.

Theodore Roosevelt

http://www.potus.com/troosevelt.html

This site contains basic factual data about Roosevelt's election and presidency, speeches, and online biographies.

William Howard Taft

http://www.potus.com/whtaft.html

This site contains basic factual data about Taft's election and presidency, speeches, and online biographies.

Woodrow Wilson

http://www.potus.com/wwilson.html

This site contains basic factual data about Wilson's election and presidency, speeches, and online biographies.

22 The Great War

A 1918 painting of German and American wounded and exhausted soldiers after the Meuse-Argonne offensive captures some of the horror and pathos of war. *(Harvey Dunn, Argonne, 1918/Smithsonian Institution)*

✦ *American Stories*

A YOUNG MAN ENLISTS IN THE GREAT ADVENTURE

On April 7, 1917, the day after the United States officially declared war on Germany, Edmund P. Arpin, Jr., a young man of 22 from Grand Rapids, Wisconsin, decided to enlist in the army. The war seemed to provide a solution for his aimless drifting. It was not patriotism that led him to join the army but his craving for adventure and excitement. A month later, he was at Fort Sheridan, Illinois, along with hundreds of other eager young men, preparing to become an army officer. He felt a certain pride and sense of purpose, and especially a feeling of comradeship with the other men, but the war was a long way off.

Arpin finally arrived with his unit in Liverpool on December 23, 1917, aboard the *Leviathan*, a German luxury liner that the United States had interned when war was declared and then pressed into service as a troop transport. In England, he discovered that American troops were not greeted as saviors. Hostility against the Americans simmered partly because of the previous unit's drunken brawls. Despite the efforts of the U.S. government to protect its soldiers from the sins of Europe, drinking seems to have been a preoccupation of the soldiers in Arpin's outfit. Arpin also learned something about French wine and women, but he spent most of the endless waiting time learning to play contract bridge.

Arpin saw some of the horror of war when he went to the front with a French regiment as an observer, but his own unit did not engage in combat until October 1918, when the war was almost over. He took part in the bloody Meuse-Argonne offensive, which helped end the war. But he discovered that war was not the heroic struggle of carefully planned campaigns that newspapers and books described. War was filled with misfired weapons, mix-ups, and erroneous attacks. Wounded in the leg in an assault on an unnamed hill and awarded a Distinguished Service Cross for his bravery, Arpin later learned that the order to attack had been recalled, but word had not reached him in time.

When the armistice came, Arpin was recovering in a field hospital. He was disappointed that the war had ended so soon, but he was well enough to go to Paris to take part in the victory celebration and to explore some of the famous Paris restaurants and nightclubs. In many ways, the highlight of his war experiences was not a battle or his medal but his adventure after the war was over. With a friend, he went absent without leave and set out to explore Germany. They avoided the military police, traveled on a train illegally, and had many narrow escapes, but they made it back to the hospital without being arrested.

Edmund Arpin was in the army for two years. He was one of 4,791,172 Americans who served in the army, navy, and marines. He was one of the 2 million who went overseas and one of the 230,074 who were wounded. Some of his friends were among the 48,909 who were killed. When he was mustered out of the army in March 1919, he felt lost and confused. Being a civilian was not nearly as exciting as being in the army and visiting new and exotic places.

In time, Arpin settled down. He became a successful businessman, married, and raised a family. A member of the American Legion, he periodically went to conventions and reminisced with men from his division about their escapades in France. Although the war changed their lives in many ways, most would never again feel the same sense of common purpose and adventure. "I don't suppose any of us felt, before or since, so necessary to God and man," one veteran recalled.

For Edmund P. Arpin, Jr., the Great War was the most important event of a lifetime. Just as war changed his life, so, too, did it alter the lives of most Americans. Trends begun during the progressive era accelerated. The power and influence of the federal government increased. Not only did the war promote woman suffrage, prohibition, and public housing, but it also helped to create an administrative bureaucracy that blurred the lines between public and private, between government and business—a trend that would continue throughout the twentieth century.

In this chapter, we examine the complicated circumstances that led the United States into the war and share the wartime experiences of American men and women overseas and at home. We will study not only military actions but also the impact of the war on domestic policies and on the lives of ordinary Americans, including the migration of African Americans into northern cities. The war left a legacy of prejudice and hate and raised the basic question: could the tenets of American democracy, such as freedom of speech, survive participation in a major war? The chapter concludes with a look at the idealistic efforts to promote peace at the end of the war and the disillusion that followed. The Great War was global war in every sense, and it thrust the United States into the role of leadership on the world scene, but many Americans were reluctant to accept that role. But whether they liked it or not, the world was a different place in 1919 than it had been in 1914 and that would have a profound influence on American lives.

THE EARLY WAR YEARS

Few Americans expected the Great War that erupted in Europe in the summer of 1914 to affect their lives or alter their comfortable world. When a Serbian student terrorist assassinated Archduke Franz Ferdinand of Austria-Hungary in Sarajevo, the capital of the province of Bosnia, a place most Americans had never heard of, it precipitated a series of events leading to the most destructive war the world had ever known.

The Causes of War

The Great War, as everyone called it at the time, seemed to begin accidentally, but its root causes reached back many years and involved intense rivalry over trade, empire, and military strength. The Great War, which would cost at least 10 million lives and have a profound influence on every aspect of culture and society, did not seem inevitable in 1914. There had been wars throughout the nineteenth century, including the Boer War, the Franco-Prussian War, and the American Civil War, but these wars, though bloody, were mostly local. There had not been a major global conflict since the end of the Napoleonic Wars in 1815. In fact, there were many signs of international cooperation, with agreements on telegraphs in 1865, postage in 1875, and copyright in 1880. Most nations in the world had even agreed on international time zones by the 1890s. An international conference at the Hague in the Netherlands in 1899 had set up a World Court to settle disputes before they led to war. Peace advocates and politicians alike promoted disarmament conferences and predicted that better technology and improved communication would lead to permanent peace. "It looks as though we are going to be the age of treaties rather than the age of wars, the century of reason rather than the century of force," a leader of the American peace movement announced.

However, the same forces of improved technology and communication that seemed to be bringing nations closer together also helped to create a rising tide of nationalism—a pride in being French, or English, or German. This new nationalism was fanned by a popular press, much the way Hearst's *Journal* and Pulitzer's *World* had increased American patriotism before the Spanish-American War (see Chapter 20.) There was also a growing European rivalry over trade, colonies, and spheres of influence in Africa and Asia. Theodore Roosevelt had tried to arbitrate differences between Germany, France, and Great Britain over trade in Morocco in 1905 and 1906, but the tension and disagreements remained. At the same time, Austria and Russia clashed over territory and influence in the Balkans, where there was a rising sense of Slavic nationalism. Modern Germany, which was created from a number of small states in 1871, emerged as a powerful industrial giant. About 1900, Germany began to build a navy large enough to compete with the British Fleet, the most powerful in the world. This caused Great Britain to build even more battleships. As European nations armed, they drew up a complex series of treaties. Austria-Hungary and Germany (the Central Powers) became military allies, and Britain, France, and Russia (the Allied Powers) agreed to assist one another in case of attack. Despite peace conferences and international agreements, many promoted by the United States, the European balance of power rested precariously on layers of treaties that barely obscured years of jealousy and distrust.

The incident in Sarajevo destroyed that balance. The leaders of Austria-Hungary determined to punish Serbia for the assassination. Russia mobilized to aid Serbia. Germany, supporting Austria-Hungary, declared war on Russia and France. England hesitated, but when Germany invaded Belgium to attack France, England declared war on Germany. Within a few months, the Ottoman Empire (Turkey) and Bulgaria joined the Central Powers. Italy joined the Allies after being secretly promised additional territory after the war. Japan declared war on Germany not because of an interest in the European struggle but in order to acquire German rights in China's Shantung province and a number of Pacific Islands. Spain, Switzerland, the Netherlands, Denmark,

Norway, Sweden, and initially the United States, remained neutral. In August 1914, as Europe rushed toward war, British Foreign Secretary Sir Edward Grey remarked: "The lamps are going out all over Europe. We shall not see them lit again in our lifetime." His prediction proved to be deadly accurate.

When news of the German invasion of Belgium and reports of the first bloody battles began to reach the United States in late summer, it seemed to most Americans that madness had replaced reason.

Europeans "have reverted to the condition of savage tribes roaming the forests and falling upon each other in a fury of blood and carnage," the *New York Times* announced. The American sense that the nation would never succumb to the barbarism of war, combined with the knowledge that the Atlantic Ocean separated Europe from the United States, contributed to a great sense of relief after the first shock of the war began to wear off. Woodrow Wilson's official proclamation of neutrality on

European Empires in 1914

In 1914, European countries had colonies or "spheres of influence" in all parts of the world. Although the United States got into the imperialism game late, it also had an empire and an interest in global trade. European imperialism and competition over trade was very much a factor in the origins of World War I. The war would alter the economic and political map of the world. **Reflecting on the Past** Which European nations were most powerful in Asia and Africa in 1914? How has this map changed today?

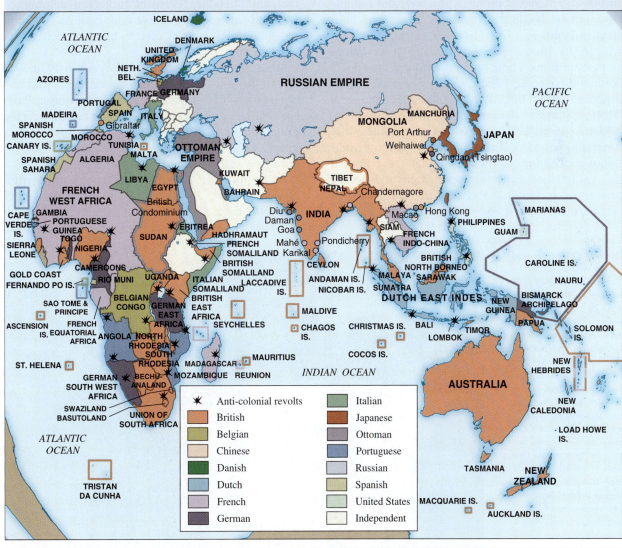

August 4, 1914, reinforced the belief that the United States had no major stake in the outcome of the war and would stay uninvolved. The president was preoccupied with his own personal tragedy. His wife, Ellen Axson Wilson, died of Bright's disease the day after his proclamation. Two weeks later, still engulfed by his own grief, he urged all Americans to "be neutral in fact as well as in name, . . . impartial in thought as well as in action." The United States, he argued, must preserve itself "fit and free" to do what "is honest and disinterested . . . for the peace of the world." But it was obvious that it was going to be difficult to stay uninvolved, at least emotionally, with the battlefields of Europe.

American Reactions

Many social reformers despaired when they heard the news from Europe. Even during its first months, the war seemed to deflect energy away from reform. "We are three thousand miles away from the smoke and flames of combat, and have not a single regiment or battleship involved," remarked John Haynes Holmes, a liberal New York minister. "Yet who in the United States is thinking of recreation centers, improved housing or the minimum wage?" Settlement worker Lillian Wald responded to the threat of war by helping to lead 1,500 women in a "woman's peace" parade down Fifth Avenue. Jane Addams of Hull House helped to organize the American Woman's Peace party. Drawing on traditional conceptions of female character, she argued that women had a special responsibility to work for peace and to speak out against the blasphemy of war because women and children suffered most in

any war, especially in a modern war where civilians as well as soldiers became targets.

Although many people worked to promote an international plan to end the war through mediation, others could hardly wait to take part in the great adventure. Hundreds of young American men, most of them students or recent college graduates, volunteered to join ambulance units in order to take part in the war effort without actually fighting. Among the most famous of these men were Ernest Hemingway, John Dos Passos, and e. e. cummings, who later turned their wartime adventures into literary masterpieces. Others volunteered for service with the French Foreign Legion or joined the Lafayette Escadrille, a unit of pilots made up of well-to-do American volunteers attached to the French army. Many of these young men were inspired by an older generation who pictured war as a romantic and manly adventure. One college president talked of the chastening and purifying effect of armed conflict, and Theodore Roosevelt projected an image of war that was something like a football game where red-blooded American men could test their idealism and manhood.

Alan Seeger, a graduate of Harvard in 1910, was one of those who believed in the romantic and noble purpose of the war. He had been living in Paris since 1912, and when the war broke out, he quickly joined the French Foreign Legion. For the next two years, he wrote sentimental poetry, articles, and letters describing his adventures. "You have no idea how beautiful it is to see the troops undulating along the road . . . with the captains and lieutenants on horse back at the head of the companies," he

Part of the American delegation to the International Congress of Women at The Hague, The Netherlands, April 28–May 1, 1915. The American women braved submarine-infested waters to join women from the neutral countries and from those at war to try to stop the war through mediation. Jane Addams (behind the peace banner, facing right) was elected president of the congress. The women were ridiculed by the press on both sides of the Atlantic, but they represented an important part of an idealistic American peace movement. *(The Swarthmore College Peace Collection)*

wrote his mother. When Seeger was killed in 1916, he became an instant hero. Some called him "America's Rupert Brooke," after the gallant British poet who died early in the war.

Many Americans visualized war as a romantic struggle for honor and glory because the only conflict they remembered was the "splendid little war" of 1898. For them, war meant Theodore Roosevelt leading the charge in Cuba and Commodore Dewey destroying the Spanish fleet in Manila harbor without the loss of an American life. Many older Americans recalled the Civil War, but the horrors of those years had faded, leaving only the memory of heroic triumphs. As Oliver Wendell Holmes, the Supreme Court justice who had been wounded in the Civil War, remarked, "War, when you are at it, is horrible and dull. It is only when time has passed that you see that its message was divine."

The reports from the battlefields, even during the first months of the war, should have indicated that the message was anything but divine. This would be a modern war in which men died by the thousands, cut down by an improved and efficient technology of killing.

The New Military Technology

Military planners had not anticipated the stalemate that quickly developed. The German Schlieffen plan called for a rapid strike through Belgium to attack Paris and the French army from the rear. However, the French stopped the German advance at the Battle of the Marne in September 1914, and the fighting soon bogged down in a costly and bloody routine. Soldiers on both sides dug miles of trenches and strung out barbed wire to protect them. Thousands died in battles that gained only a few yards or nothing at all. At the Battle of the Somme in the summer of 1916, the German casualties were 600,000 men killed or wounded. The British lost 419,00 and the French 194,00, and the battle did not change the course of the war. Rapid-firing rifles, improved explosives, incendiary shells, and tracer bullets all added to the destruction. Most devastating of all, however, was the improved artillery, sometimes mounted on trucks and directed by spotters using wireless radios, that could fire over the horizon and hit targets many miles behind the lines. The technology of defense, especially the machine gun, neutralized the frontal assault, the most popular military tactic since the American Civil War. As one writer explained: "Three men and a machine gun can stop a battalion of heroes." But the generals on both sides continued to order their men to charge to their almost certain deaths.

The war was both a traditional and a revolutionary struggle. It was the last war in which cavalry was used and the first to employ a new generation of military technologies. By 1918, airplanes, initially used only for observation, were creating terror below with their bombs. Tanks made their first tentative appearance in 1916, but it was not until the last days of the war that this new offensive weapon began to neutralize the machine gun. Trucks hauled men and equipment, but hundreds of thousands of horses were also used on the battlefields; for some soldiers, the sight of great numbers of dead horses on the battlefields was more depressing than the presence of dead men. Wireless radio and the telephone were indispensable, but carrier pigeons sometimes provided the only link between the front line and the command post in the rear. In the spring of 1915, the Germans introduced a terrible new weapon—poison gas. Chlorine gas blinded its victims, caused acid burns on the skin, and consumed the lungs. Gas masks provided some protection but were never entirely effective. Poison gas attacks, used by both sides after 1915, were one of the most terrifying aspects of trench warfare.

For most Americans, the western front, which stretched from Belgium through France, was the most important battleground of the war. But along the eastern front, Russian troops engaged German and Austrian armies in bitter fighting. After Italy joined the conflict in 1915, a third front developed along the Northern Italian and Austrian border, while submarines and battleships carried the fight around the world.

The Great War was truly a global struggle. Soldiers from the British Empire, New Zealand, Australia, Canada, and India fought on the western front alongside French-speaking black Africans. The British and the French battled in Africa to capture the German-African colonies, and the struggle continued until 1918, especially in East Africa. The British, who initially thought they were only going to support the French on the western front, found themselves in the Middle East, in Mesopotamia (Iraq), and fighting Turks in the Dardanelles between the Aegean and the Black Sea. In one of the great disasters of the war, the British attacked Gallipoli, first with battleships and then with hundreds of thousands of men. After losing one-third of their fleet and more than a quarter of a million men, many of them Australians and New Zealanders, the British withdrew. Reports of carnage, on and off the battlefield, poured in. After they entered the war, the Turks systematically massacred an estimated 800,000 Armenians, in one of the worst acts of genocide in the world's history. Yet the United States and the European countries stood by and did nothing.

The Great War in Europe and the Middle East

The Great War had an impact not only on Europe but also on North Africa and the Middle East. Even the countries that remained neutral felt the influence of global war.   **Reflecting on the Past**   For most Americans, the war was in France on the western front. Where else were major battles fought?

But some Americans could hardly wait to join the fighting. Theodore Roosevelt and his friend Leonard Wood, the army chief of staff, led a movement to prepare American men for war. Wood was determined that upper-class and college-educated men be ready to lead the nation into battle. In 1913, he established a camp for college men at Plattsburgh, New York, to give them some experience with mili-

tary life, order, discipline, and command. By 1915, thousands had crowded into the camp; even the mayor of New York enrolled. The young men learned to shoot rifles and to endure long marches and field exercises. But most of all, they associated with one another. Gathered around the campfire at night, they heard Wood and other veterans tell of winning glory and honor on the battlefield. In their minds at least, they were already leading a bayonet charge against the enemy, and the enemy was Germany.

Difficulties of Neutrality

Not all Americans were so eager to enter the fray, but many sympathized with one side or the other. Some Americans favored the Central Powers. About 8 million Austrian Americans and German Americans lived in the United States. Some supported their homeland. They viewed Kaiser Wilhelm II's Germany as a progressive parliamentary democracy. The anti-British sentiment of some Irish Americans led them to take sides not so much for Germany as against England. A few Swedish Americans distrusted Russia so vehemently that they had difficulty supporting the Allies. A number of American scholars, physicians, and intellectuals fondly remembered studying in Germany. To them, Germany meant great universities and cathedrals, music and culture. It also represented social planning, health insurance, unemployment compensation, and many programs for which the progressives had been fighting.

Despite Wilson's efforts to promote neutrality, for most Americans, the ties of language and culture tipped the balance toward the Allies. After all, did not the English-speaking people of the world have special bonds and special responsibilities to promote civilization and ensure justice in the world? American connections with the French were not so close, but they were even more sentimental. The French, everyone remembered, had supported the American Revolution, and the French people had given the Statue of Liberty, the very symbol of American opportunity and democracy, to the United States.

Other reasons made real neutrality nearly impossible. The fact that export and import trade with the Allies was much more important than with the Central Powers favored the Allies. Wilson's advisers, especially Robert Lansing and Edward House, openly supported the French and the British. Most newspaper owners and editors had close ethnic, cultural, and sometimes economic ties to the British and the French. The newspapers were quick to picture the Germans as barbaric Huns and to accept and embellish the atrocity stories that came from the front, some of them planted by British propaganda experts. Gradually for Wilson, and probably for most Americans, the perception that England and France were fighting to preserve civilization from the forces of Prussian evil replaced the idea that all Europeans were barbaric and deca-

dent. But the American people were not yet willing to go to war to save civilization. Let France and England do that.

Woodrow Wilson also sympathized with the Allies for practical and idealistic reasons. He wanted to keep the United States out of the war, but he did not object to using force to promote diplomatic ends. "When men take up arms to set other men free, there is something sacred and holy in the warfare," he had written. Moreover, Wilson believed that by keeping the United States out of the war, he might control the peace. The war, he hoped, would show the futility of imperialism and would usher in a world of free trade in products and ideas. The United States had a special role to play in this new world and in leading toward an orderly international society. "We are the mediating nation of the world [and] we are therefore able to understand all nations."

Remaining neutral while maintaining trade with the belligerents became increasingly difficult. Remaining neutral while speaking out about the peace eventually became impossible. The need to trade and the desire to control the peace finally led the United States into the Great War.

World Trade and Neutrality Rights

The United States was part of an international economic community in 1914 in a way that it had not been a hundred years earlier during the Napoleonic Wars, the last world conflict. The outbreak of war in the summer of 1914 caused an immediate economic panic in the United States. On July 31, 1914, the Wilson administration closed the stock exchange to prevent the unloading of European securities and panic selling. It also adopted a policy discouraging loans by American banks to belligerent nations. Most difficult was the matter of neutral trade. Wilson insisted on the rights of Americans to trade with both the Allies and the Central Powers, but Great Britain instituted an illegal naval blockade, mined the North Sea, and began seizing American ships, even those carrying food and raw materials to Italy, the Netherlands, and other neutral nations. The first crisis that Wilson faced was whether to accept the illicit British blockade. To do so would be to surrender one of the rights he supported most ardently, the right of free trade.

Wilson eventually backed down and accepted British control of the sea. His conviction that the destinies of the United States and Great Britain were intertwined outweighed his idealistic belief in free trade and caused him to react more harshly to German violations of international law than he did to British violators. Consequently, American trade with the Central Powers declined between 1914 and 1916 from $169 million to just over $1 million, whereas with the Allies it increased during the same period from $825 million to over $3 billion. At the same time, the U.S. government eased restrictions on private loans to belligerents. In March 1915, the House of Morgan loaned the French government $50 million, and in the fall of 1915, the French and British obtained an unsecured loan of $500 million from American banks. With dollars as well as sentiments, the United States gradually ceased to be neutral.

Germany retaliated against British control of the seas with submarine warfare. The new weapon, the U-boat (*Unterseeboot*), created unprecedented problems. Nineteenth-century international law obligated a belligerent warship to warn a passenger or merchant ship before attacking, but the chief advantage of the submarine was surprise. Rising to the surface to issue a warning would have meant being blown out of the water by an armed merchant ship.

On February 4, 1915, Germany announced a submarine blockade of the British Isles. Until Britain gave up its campaign to starve the German population, the Germans would sink even neutral ships. Wilson warned Germany that it would be held to "strict accountability" for illegal destruction of American ships or lives.

In March 1915, a German U-boat sank a British liner en route to Africa, killing 103 people, including one American. How should the United States respond? Wilson's advisers could not agree. Robert Lansing, a legal counsel at the State Department, urged the president to issue a strong protest, charging a breach of international law. William Jennings Bryan, the secretary of state, argued that an American traveling on a British ship was guilty of "contributory negligence" and urged Wilson to prohibit Americans from traveling on belligerent ships in the war zone. Wilson never did settle the dispute, for on May 7, 1915, a greater crisis erupted. A German U-boat torpedoed the British luxury liner *Lusitania* off the Irish coast. The liner, which was not armed but was carrying war supplies, sank in 18 minutes. Nearly 1,200 people, including many women and children, drowned. Among the dead were 128 Americans. Suddenly Americans confronted the horror of total war fought with modern weapons, a war that killed civilians, including women and children, just as easily as it killed soldiers.

The tragedy horrified most Americans. Despite earlier warnings by the Germans in American newspapers that it was dangerous to travel in war zones, the same newspapers denounced the act as "mass murder." Some called for a declaration of war. Wilson and most Americans had no idea of going to war in the spring of 1915, but the president refused to take Bryan's advice and prevent further loss of American lives by simply prohibiting all Americans from traveling on belligerent ships. Instead, he sent

A German U-boat sinking a fishing ship somewhere in the Atlantic. The German submarine revolutionized the war at sea, and the sinking of the British ocean liner *Lusitania* and various American ships led directly to the United States entering the war. At first the submarines had the advantage, but by 1918, anti-submarine technology had been developed to enable the United States and Great Britain to win the battle of the Atlantic. Germany lost 178 submarines with 5,400 men. *(Erich Lessing/Art Resource, NY)*

a series of protest notes demanding reparation for the loss of American lives and a pledge from Germany that it would cease attacking ocean liners without warning.

Bryan resigned as secretary of state over the tone of the notes and charged that the United States was not being truly neutral. Some denounced Bryan as a traitor, but others charged that if the United States really wanted to stay out of the war, Bryan's position was more logical, consistent, and humane than Wilson's. The president replaced Bryan with Robert Lansing, who was much more eager than Bryan to oppose Germany, even at the risk of war.

The tense situation eased late in 1915. After a German U-boat sank the British steamer *Arabic,* which claimed two American lives, the German ambassador promised that Germany would not attack ocean liners without warning (the *Arabic* pledge). But the *Lusitania* crisis caused an outpouring of books and articles urging the nation to prepare for war. The National Security League, the most effective of the preparedness groups, called for a bigger army and navy, a system of universal military training, and "patriotic education and national sentiment and service among the people of the United States."

Organizing on the other side was a group of progressive reformers who formed the American Union Against Militarism. They feared that those urging preparedness were deliberately setting out to destroy liberal social reform at home and to promote imperialism abroad.

Wilson sympathized with the preparedness groups to the extent of asking Congress on November 4, 1915, for an enlarged and reorganized army. The bill met with great opposition, especially from southern and western congressmen, but the Army Reorganization Bill that Wilson signed in June 1916 increased the regular army to just over 200,000 and integrated the National Guard into the defense structure. Few Americans, however, expected those young men to go to war. One of the most popular songs of 1916 was "I Didn't Raise My Boy to Be a Soldier." Even before American soldiers arrived in France, however, Wilson used the army and the marines in Mexico and Central America.

Intervening in Mexico and Central America

Wilson envisioned a world purged of imperialism, a world of free trade, but a world where American ideas and products would find their way. Combining the zeal of a Christian missionary with the conviction of a college professor, he spoke of "releasing the intelligence of America for the service of mankind."

Along with his secretary of state, William Jennings Bryan, Wilson denounced the "big stick" and "dollar diplomacy" of the Roosevelt and Taft years. Yet Wilson's administration used force more systematically than did his predecessors. The rhetoric was different, yet just as much as Roosevelt, Wilson tried to maintain stability in the countries to the south in order to promote American economic and strategic interests.

At first, Wilson's foreign policy seemed to reverse some of the most callous aspects of dollar diplomacy in Central America. Bryan signed a treaty with Colombia in 1913 that agreed to pay $5 million for the loss of Panama and virtually apologized for the Roosevelt administration's treatment of Colombia. The Senate, not so willing to admit that the United States had been wrong, refused to ratify the treaty.

The change in spirit proved illusory. After a disastrous civil war in the Dominican Republic, the United States offered in 1915 to take over the country's finances and police force. When the Dominican leaders rejected a treaty making their country virtually a protectorate of the United States, Wilson ordered in the marines. They took control of the government in May 1916. Although Americans built roads, schools, and hospitals, people resented their presence. The United States also intervened in Haiti with similar results. In Nicaragua, the Wilson administration kept the marines sent by Taft in 1912 to prop up a pro-American regime and acquired the right, through treaty, to intervene at any time to preserve order and protect American property. Except for a brief period in the mid-1920s, the marines remained until 1933.

Wilson's policy of intervention ran into the greatest difficulty in Mexico, a country that had been ruled by dictator Porfirio Díaz, who had long welcomed American investors. By 1910, more than 40,000 American citizens lived in Mexico, and more than $1 billion of American money was invested there. In 1911, however, Francisco Madero, a reformer who wanted to destroy the privileges of the upper classes, overthrew Díaz. Two years later, Madero was deposed and murdered by order of Victoriano Huerta, the head of the army.

To the shock of many diplomats and businessmen, Wilson refused to recognize the Huerta government. Everyone admitted that Huerta was a ruthless dictator, but diplomatic recognition, the exchange of ambassadors, and the regulation of trade and communication had never meant approval. In the world of business and diplomacy, it merely meant that a particular government was in power. But Wilson set out to remove what he called a "government of butchers."

Pancho Villa on horseback leading the rebel Mexican army that clashed with the American army in Mexico in 1916. President Wilson sent American forces over 300 miles into Mexico to arrest Villa, who allegedly had murdered a number of Americans, but the Americans were not able to catch him. *(Brown Brothers)*

At first, Wilson applied diplomatic pressure. Then, using a minor incident as an excuse, he asked Congress for power to involve American troops if necessary. Few Mexicans liked Huerta, but they liked the idea of North American interference even less, and they rallied around the dictator. The United States landed troops at Veracruz, Mexico. Angry Mexican mobs destroyed American property wherever they could find it. Wilson's action outraged many Europeans and Latin Americans as well as Americans.

Wilson's military intervention drove Huerta out of office, but a civil war between forces led by Venustiano Carranza and those led by General Francisco "Pancho" Villa ensued. The United States sent arms to Carranza, who was considered less radical than Villa, and Carranza's soldiers defeated Villa's. When an angry Villa led what was left of his army in a raid on Columbus, New Mexico, in March 1916, Wilson sent an expedition commanded by Brigadier General John Pershing to track down Villa and his men. The strange and comic scene developed of an American army charging 300 miles into Mexico unable to catch the retreating villain. The Mexicans feared that Pershing's army was planning to occupy northern Mexico. Carranza shot off a bitter note to Wilson, accusing him of threatening war, but Wilson refused to withdraw the troops. Tensions rose. An American patrol attacked a Mexican garrison, with loss of life on both sides. Just as war seemed inevitable, Wilson agreed to recall the troops and to recognize the Carranza government. But this was in January 1917, and if it had not been for the growing crisis in Europe, it is likely that war would have resulted.

THE UNITED STATES ENTERS THE WAR

A significant minority of Americans opposed going to war in 1917, and that decision would remain controversial when it was reexamined in the 1930s. But once involved, the government and the American people made the war into a patriotic crusade that influenced all aspects of American life.

The Election of 1916

American political campaigns do not stop even in times of international crisis. As 1915 turned to 1916, Wilson had to think of reelection as well as of preparedness, submarine warfare, and the Mexican campaign. At first glance, the president's chances of reelection seemed poor. He had won in 1912 only because Theodore Roosevelt and the Progressive party had split the Republican vote. If supporters of the Progressives in 1912 returned to the Republican fold, Wilson's chances were slim indeed. Because the Progressive party had done very badly in the 1914 congressional elections, Roosevelt seemed ready to seek the Republican nomination.

Wilson was aware that he had to win over voters who had favored Roosevelt in 1912. In January 1916, he appointed Louis D. Brandeis to the Supreme Court. The first Jew ever to sit on the Court, Brandeis was confirmed over the strong opposition of many legal organizations. His appointment pleased the social justice progressives because he had always championed reform causes. They made it clear to Wilson that the real test for them was whether he supported the anti–child labor and workers' compensation bills pending in Congress.

In August, Wilson put heavy pressure on Congress and obtained passage of the Workmen's Compensation Bill, which gave some protection to federal employees, and the Keatings-Owen Child Labor Bill, which prohibited the shipment in interstate commerce of goods produced by children under the age of 14 and in some cases under 16. This bill, later declared unconstitutional, was a far-reaching proposal that for the first time used federal control over interstate commerce to dictate the conditions under which businesspeople could manufacture products.

To attract farm support, Wilson pushed for passage of the Federal Farm Loan Act, which created 12 Federal Farm Loan banks to extend long-term credit to farmers. Urged on by organized labor as well as by many progressives, he supported the Adamson Act, which established an eight-hour day for all interstate railway workers. Within a few months, Wilson reversed the New Freedom doctrines he had earlier supported and brought the force of the federal government into play on the side of reform. The flurry of legislation early in 1916 provided one climax to the progressive movement. The strategy seemed to work, for progressives of all kinds enthusiastically endorsed the president.

The election of 1916, however, turned as much on foreign affairs as on domestic policy. The Republicans ignored Theodore Roosevelt and nominated instead the staid and respectable Charles Evans Hughes, a former governor of New York and future Supreme Court justice. Their platform called for "straight and honest neutrality" and "adequate preparedness." In a bitter campaign, Hughes attacked Wilson for not promoting American rights in Mexico more vigorously and for giving in to the unreasonable demands of labor. Wilson, on his part, implied that electing Hughes would guarantee war with both Mexico and Germany and that his opponents were somehow not "100 percent Americans." As the campaign progressed, the peace issue became more and more important, and the cry "He kept us out of war"

echoed through every Democratic rally. It was a slogan that would soon seem strangely ironic.

The election was extremely close. In fact, Wilson went to bed on election night thinking he had lost the presidency. The election was not finally decided until the Democrats carried California (by fewer than 4,000 votes). Wilson won by carrying the West as well as the South.

Deciding for War

Wilson's victory in 1916 seemed to be a mandate for staying out of the European war. But the campaign rhetoric made the president nervous. He had tried to emphasize Americanism, not neutrality. As he told one of his advisers, "I can't keep the country out of war. They talk of me as though I were a god. Any little German lieutenant can put us into war at any time by some calculated outrage."

People who supported Wilson as a peace candidate applauded in January 1917 when he went before the Senate to clarify the American position on a negotiated settlement of the war. The German government had earlier indicated that it might be willing to go to the conference table. Wilson outlined a plan for a negotiated settlement before either side had achieved victory. It would be a peace among equals, "a peace without victory," a peace without indemnities and annexations. The peace agreement Wilson outlined contained his idealistic vision of the postwar world as an open marketplace, and it could have worked only if Germany and the Allies were willing to settle for a draw. But neither side was interested in such a conclusion after years of bitter and costly conflict.

The German government refused to accept a peace without victory, probably because early in 1917, the German leaders thought they could win. On January 31, 1917, the Germans announced that they would sink on sight any ship, belligerent or neutral, sailing toward England or France. A few days later, in retaliation, the United States broke diplomatic relations with Germany. But Wilson—and probably most Americans—still hoped to avert war without shutting off American trade. As goods began to pile up in warehouses and American ships stayed idly in port, however, pressure mounted to arm American merchant ships. An intercepted telegram from the German foreign secretary, Arthur Zimmermann, to the German minister in Mexico increased anti-German feeling. If war broke out, the German minister was to offer Mexico the territory it had lost in Texas, New Mexico, and Arizona in 1848. In return, Mexico would join Germany in a war against the United States. When the Zimmermann note was released to the press on March 1, 1917, many Americans demanded war against Germany. Wilson still hesitated.

As the country waited on the brink of war, news of revolution in Russia reached Washington. That event would prove as important as the war itself. The March 1917 revolution in Russia was a spontaneous uprising of the workers, housewives, and soldiers against the government of Tsar Nicholas II and its conduct of the war. The army had suffered staggering losses at the front. The civilian population was in desperate condition. Food was scarce, and the railroads and industry had nearly collapsed. At first, Wilson and other Americans were enthusiastic about the new republic led by Alexander Kerensky. The overthrow of the feudal aristocracy seemed in the spirit of the American Revolution. Kerensky promised to continue the struggle against Germany. But on November 6, 1917, the revolution took a more extreme turn. Vladimir Ilyich Ulyanov, known as Lenin, returned from exile in Switzerland and led the radical Bolsheviks to victory over the Kerensky regime. He immediately signed an armistice with Germany that released thousands of German troops, who had been fighting the Russians, to join the battle against the Allies on the western front.

Lenin, a brilliant lawyer and revolutionary tactician, was a follower of Karl Marx (1818–1883). Marx was a German intellectual and radical philosopher who had described the alienation of the working class under capitalism and predicted a growing split between the proletariat (the unpropertied workers) and the capitalists. Lenin extended Marx's ideas and argued that capitalist nations eventually would be forced to go to war over raw materials and markets. Believing that capitalism and imperialism went hand in hand, Lenin, unlike Wilson, argued that the only way to end imperialism was to end capitalism. The new Soviet Union, not the United States, was the model for the rest of the world to follow; communism, Lenin predicted, would eventually dominate the globe. The Russian Revolution posed a threat to Wilson's vision of the world and to his plan to bring the United States into the war "to make the world safe for democracy."

More disturbing than the first news of revolution in Russia, however, was the situation in the North Atlantic, where German U-boats sank five American ships between March 12 and March 21, 1917. Wilson no longer hesitated. On April 2, he urged Congress to declare war. His words conveyed a sense of mission about the country's entry into the war, but Wilson's voice was low and somber. "It is a fearful thing," he concluded, "to lead this great, peaceful people into war, into the most terrible and disastrous of all wars." The war resolution swept the Senate 82 to 6 and the House of Representatives 373 to 50.

Once war was declared, most Americans forgot their doubts. Young men rushed to enlist; women volunteered to become nurses or to serve in other ways. Towns were united by patriotism.

A Patriotic Crusade

Not all Americans applauded the declaration of war. Some pacifists and socialists opposed the war, and a black newspaper, *The Messenger,* decried the conflict. "The real enemy is War rather than Imperial Germany," wrote Randolph Bourne, a young New York intellectual. "We are for peace," Morris Hillquit, a socialist leader, announced. "We are unalterably opposed to the killing of our manhood and the draining of our resources in . . . a pursuit which begins by suppressing the freedom of speech and press and public assemblage, and by stifling legitimate political criticism." "To whom does war bring prosperity?" Senator George Norris of Nebraska asked on the Senate floor. He continued:

> Not to the soldier, . . . not to the broken hearted widow, . . . not to the mother who weeps at the death of her brave boy. . . . War brings no prosperity to the great mass of common patriotic citizens. We are going into war upon the command of gold. . . . I feel that we are about to put the dollar sign on the American flag.

For most Americans in the spring of 1917, the war seemed remote. A few days after the war was declared, a Senate committee listened to a member of the War Department staff list the vast quantities of materials needed to supply an American army in France. One of the senators, jolted awake, exclaimed, "Good Lord! You're not going to send soldiers over there, are you?"

To convince senators and citizens alike that the war was real and that American participation was just, Wilson appointed a Committee on Public Information, headed by George Creel, a muckraking journalist from Denver. The Creel Committee launched a gigantic propaganda campaign to persuade the American public that the United States had gone to war to promote the cause of freedom and democracy and to prevent the barbarous hordes from overrunning Europe and eventually the Western Hemisphere.

The patriotic crusade soon became stridently anti-German and anti-immigrant. Most school districts banned the teaching of German, a "language that disseminates the ideals of autocracy, brutality and hatred." Anything German became suspect.

Sauerkraut was renamed "liberty cabbage," and German measles became "liberty measles." Many families Americanized their German surnames. Several cities banned music by German composers from symphony concerts. South Dakota prohibited the use of German on the telephone, and in Iowa, a state official announced, "If their language is disloyal, they should be imprisoned. If their acts are disloyal, they should be shot." Occasionally, the patriotic fever led to violence. The most notorious incident occurred in East St. Louis, Illinois, which had a large German population. A mob seized Robert Prager, a young German American, in April 1918, stripped off his clothes, dressed him in an American flag, marched him through the streets, and lynched him. The eventual trial led to the acquittal of the ringleaders on the grounds that the lynching was a "patriotic murder."

The Wilson administration did not condone domestic violence and murder, but heated patriotism led to irrational hatreds and fears. Suspect were not only German Americans but also radicals, pacifists, and anyone who raised doubts about the American war efforts or the government's policies. In New York, the black editors of *The Messenger* were given two-and-a-half-year jail sentences for the paper's article "Pro-Germanism Among Negroes." The Los Angeles police ignored complaints that Mexicans were being harassed, because after learning of the Zimmermann telegram they believed that all Mexicans were pro-German. In Wisconsin, Senator Robert La Follette, who had voted against the war resolution, was burned in effigy and censured by the faculty of the University of Wisconsin. At a number of universities, professors were dismissed, sometimes for as little as questioning the morality or the necessity of America's participation in the war.

On June 15, 1917, Congress, at Wilson's behest, passed the Espionage Act, which provided imprisonment of up to 20 years or a fine of up to $10,000, or both, for people who aided the enemy or who "willfully cause . . . insubordination, disloyalty, mutiny or refusal of duty in the military . . . forces of the United States." The act also authorized the postmaster general to prohibit from the mails any matter he thought advocated treason or forcible resistance to U.S. laws. The act was used to stamp out dissent, even to discipline anyone who questioned the administration's policies. Using the act, Postmaster General Albert S. Burleson banned the magazines *American Socialist* and *The Masses* from the mails.

Congress later added the Trading with the Enemy Act and a Sedition Act. The latter prohibited disloyal, profane, scurrilous, and abusive remarks about the form of government, flag, or uniform of the United States. It even prohibited citizens from opposing the purchase of war bonds. In the most famous case tried under the act, Eugene Debs was sentenced to 10 years in prison for opposing the war. In 1919, the Supreme Court upheld the conviction, even though Debs had not explicitly urged the violation of the draft laws. Not all Americans agreed with the decision, for while still in prison, Debs polled close to 1 million votes in the presidential election of 1920. Ultimately, the government prosecuted 2,168 people under the Espionage and Sedition Acts and convicted about half of them. But these figures do not include the thousands who were informally persecuted and deprived of their liberties and their right of free speech.

A group of amateur loyalty enforcers, called the American Protective League, cooperated with the Justice Department. League members often reported nonconformists and anyone who did not appear 100 percent loyal. One woman was sentenced to prison for writing, "I am for the people

Recruiting posters helped to create a sense of purpose and patriotism and often used pictures of attractive women to make their point. To be a soldier was to be a real man; to avoid service was to be something less than a man. *(The Granger Collection, New York)*

Many women joined the "great adventure" by serving overseas as nurses with the Red Cross or as volunteers with the Salvation Army, but they could not join the army or navy as women did in World War II. This woman is serving coffee to soldiers behind the lines in France. *(Culver Pictures, Inc.)*

and the government is for the profiteers." Ricardo Flores Magon, a leading Mexican-American labor organizer and radical in the Southwest, was sentenced to 20 years in prison for criticizing Wilson's Mexican policy and violating the Neutrality Acts. In Cincinnati, a pacifist minister, Herbert S. Bigelow, was dragged from the stage where he was about to give a speech, taken to a wooded area by a mob, bound and gagged, and whipped. In Bisbee, Arizona, where wartime demand for copper had increased the population to 20,000, the miners went on strike in June 1917 to protest low wages and unsafe conditions in the mines. The owners blamed the strike on the IWW, who they claimed was controlled by the Germans. The IWW had little to do with the strike, but the local sheriff led a posse of men into the miners' homes where they rounded up 1,200 "undesirables" and shipped them in boxcars into Mexico. The mine owners then quickly hired strikebreakers so the production of copper to support the war effort could continue.

The Civil Liberties Bureau, an outgrowth of the American Union Against Militarism, protested the blatant abridgment of freedom of speech during the war, but the protests fell on deaf ears at the Justice Department and in the White House. Rights and freedoms have been reduced or suspended during all wars, but the massive disregard for basic rights was greater during World War I than during the Civil War. This was ironic because Wilson had often written and spoken of the need to preserve freedom of speech and civil liberties. During the war, however, he tolerated the vigilante tactics of his own Justice Department, offering no more than feeble protest. Wilson was so convinced his cause was just that he ignored the rights of those who opposed him.

Raising an Army

The debate over a volunteer army versus the draft had been going on for several years before the United States entered the war. People who favored some form of universal military service argued that college graduates, farmers, and young men from the slums of eastern cities could learn from one another as they trained together. The opponents of a draft pointed out that people making such claims were most often the college graduates, who assumed they would command the boys from the slums. The draft was not democratic, they argued, but the tool of an imperialist power bent on ending dissent. "Back of the cry that America must have compulsory service or perish," one opponent charged, "is a clearly thought out and heavily backed project to mold the United States into an efficient, orderly nation, economically and politically controlled by those who know what is good for the people." Memories of massive draft riots during the Civil War also led some to fear a draft.

Wilson and his secretary of war, Newton Baker, both initially opposed the draft. In the end, both concluded that it was the most efficient way to organize military manpower. Ironically, it was Theodore Roosevelt who tipped Wilson in favor of the draft. Even though his health was failing and he was blind in one eye, the old Rough Rider was determined to recruit a volunteer division and lead it personally against the Germans. The thought of his old enemy Theodore Roosevelt blustering about Europe so frightened Wilson that he supported the Selective Service Act in part, at least, to prevent such volunteer outfits as Roosevelt planned. Yet controversy filled Congress over the bill, and the House finally insisted that the minimum age for draftees should be 21, not 18. On June 5, 1917, some 9.5 million men between the ages of 21 and 31 registered, with little protest. In August 1918, Congress extended the act to men between the ages of 18 and 45. In all, over 24 million men registered and over 2.8 million were inducted, making up over 75 percent of soldiers who served in the war.

The draft worked well, but it was not quite the perfect system that Wilson claimed. Most Americans took seriously their obligation of "service" during time of war. But because local draft boards had so much control, favoritism and political influence allowed some to stay at home. Draft protests erupted in a few places, the largest in Oklahoma, where a group of tenant farmers planned a march on Washington to take over the government and end the "rich man's war." But the Green Corn Rebellion, as it came to be called, died before it got started. A local posse arrested about 900 rebels and took them off to jail.

Some men escaped the draft. Some were deferred because of war-related jobs, and others resisted by claiming exemption for reasons of conscience. The Selective Service Act did exempt men who belonged to religious groups that forbade members from engaging in war, but religious motivation was often difficult to define, and nonreligious conscientious objection was even more complicated. Thousands of conscientious objectors were inducted. Some served in noncombat positions; others went to prison. Roger Baldwin, a leading pacifist, was jailed for refusing military service. But Norman Thomas, a socialist, urged young men to register for the draft and to express their dissent within the democratic process.

THE MILITARY EXPERIENCE

Family albums in millions of American homes contain photographs of those who were drafted or volunteered: young men in uniform, some of them stiff and formal, some of them candid shots of soldiers on leave in Paris or Washington or Chicago. These photographs testify to the importance of the war to a generation of Americans. For years afterward, the men and women who lived through the war sang "Tipperary," "There's a Long, Long Trail," and "Pack Up Your Troubles" and remembered rather sentimentally what the war had meant to them. For some, the war was a tragic event, as they saw the horrors of the battlefield firsthand. For others, it was a liberating experience and the most exciting period in their lives.

The American Soldier

The typical soldier, according to the U.S. Medical Department, stood 5 feet 7½ inches tall, weighed 141½ pounds, and was about 22 years old. He took a physical exam, an intelligence test, and a psychological test, and he probably watched a movie called *Fit to Fight,* which warned him about the dangers of venereal disease. The majority of the American soldiers had not attended high school. The median level of education for native whites was 6.9 years and for immigrants was 4.7 years but was only 2.6 years for southern blacks. As many as 31 percent of the recruits were declared illiterate, but the tests

Army Medical Examiner: "At last a perfect soldier!"

"At Last a Perfect Soldier," an anti-war, anti-military cartoon from the American radical magazine *The Masses* in July 1916. *The Masses* was an irreverent journal that for a few years published important articles and illustrations by leading artists. It was shut down as subversive during the war by the United States government. (The Masses 8, *July 1916, [back cover]/The Tamiment Institute Library, New York University*)

Government Propaganda

All governments produce propaganda. Especially in time of war, governments try to convince their citizens that the cause is important and worthwhile even if it means sacrifice. Before the United States entered the war, both Great Britain and Germany presented their side of the conflict through stories planted in newspapers, photographs, and other devices. Some historians argue that the British propaganda depicting the Germans as barbaric Huns who killed little boys and Catholic nuns played a large role in convincing Americans of the righteousness of the Allied cause.

When the United States entered the war, a special committee under the direction of George Creel did its best to persuade Americans that the war was a crusade against evil. The committee organized a national network of "four-minute men," local citizens with the proper political views who could be used to whip up a crowd into a patriotic frenzy. These local rallies, enlivened by bands and parades, urged people of all ages to support the war effort and buy war bonds. The Creel Committee also produced literature for the schools, much of it prepared by college professors who volunteered their services. One pamphlet, titled *Why America Fights Germany,* described in lurid detail a possible German invasion of the United States. The committee also used the new technology of motion pictures, which proved to be the most effective propaganda device of all.

There is a narrow line between education and propaganda. As early as 1910, Thomas Edison made films instructing the public about the dangers of tuberculosis, and others produced movies that demonstrated how to avoid everything from typhoid to tooth decay. However, during the war, the government quickly realized the power of the new medium and adopted it to train soldiers, instill patriotism, and help the troops avoid the temptations of alcohol and sex.

After the United States entered World War I, the Commission of Training Camp Activities made a film called *Fit to Fight* that was shown to almost all male servicemen. It was an hour-long drama following the careers of five young recruits. Four of them, by associating with the wrong people and through lack of willpower, caught venereal disease. The film interspersed a simplistic plot with

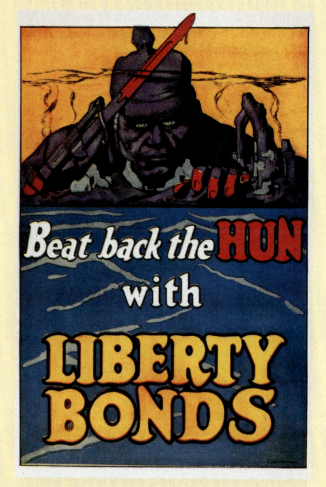

Liberty Bond propaganda. *(The Granger Collection, New York)*

grotesque shots of men with various kinds of venereal disease. The film also glorified athletics, especially football and boxing, as a substitute for sex. It emphasized the importance of patriotism and purity for America's fighting force. In one scene, Bill Hale, the only soldier in the film to remain pure, breaks up a peace rally and beats up the speaker. "It serves you right," the pacifist's sister remarks, "I'm glad Billy punched you."

Fit to Fight was so successful that the government commissioned another film, *The End of the Road,* to be shown to women who lived near military bases. The film is the story of Vera and Mary. Although still reflecting progressive attitudes, the film's message is somewhat different from that of *Fit to Fight.* Vera's strict mother tells her daughter that sex is dirty, leaving Vera to pick up "distorted and obscene" information about sex on the street. She falls victim to the first man who comes along and contracts a venereal disease. Mary, in contrast, has an enlightened mother who explains where babies come from. When Mary grows up, she rejects marriage and becomes a professional woman, a nurse. In the end, she falls in love with a doctor and gets married. *The End of the Road* has a number of subplots and many frightening shots of syphilitic sores. Several illustrations show the dangers of indiscriminate sex. Among other things, the film preached the importance of science and sex education and the need for self-control.

Reflecting on the Past   What do the anti-VD films tell us about the attitudes, ideas, and prejudices of the World War I period? What images do they project about men, women, and gender roles? Would you find the same kind of moralism, patriotism, and fear of VD today? How have attitudes toward sex changed? Were you shown sex education films in school? Were they like these? Who sponsored them? What can historians learn from such films? Does the government produce propaganda today?

Anti-VD poster issued by the U.S. Commission on Training Camp Activities. *(Army Educational Commission)*

Scene from *Fit to Fight*. *(War Department, Commission on Training Camps)*

were so primitive that they probably tested social class more than anything else. More than half the recent immigrants from eastern Europe ranked in the "inferior" category. Fully 29 percent of the recruits were rejected as physically unfit for service, which shocked the health experts.

Most World War I soldiers were ill-educated and unsophisticated young men, quite different from Ernest Hemingway's heroes or even from Edmund Arpin. They came from farms, small towns, and urban neighborhoods. They came from all social classes and ethnic groups, yet most were transformed into soldiers. In the beginning, however, they didn't look the part, because uniforms and equipment were in short supply. Many men had to wear their civilian clothes for months, and they often wore out their shoes before they were issued army boots. "It was about two months or so before I looked really like a soldier," one recruit remembered.

The military experience changed the lives and often the attitudes of many young men and some women. Women contributed to the war effort as telephone operators and clerk typists in the navy and the marines. Some went overseas as army and navy nurses. Others volunteered for a tour of duty with the Red Cross, the Salvation Army, or the YMCA. Yet the military experience in World War I was predominantly male. Even going to training camp was a new and often frightening experience. A leave in Paris or London, or even in New York or New Orleans, was an adventure to remember for a lifetime. Even those who never got overseas or who never saw a battle experienced subtle changes. Many soldiers saw their first movie in the army or had their first contact with trucks and cars. Military service changed the shaving habits of a generation because the new safety razor was standard issue. The war also led to the growing popularity of the cigarette rather than the pipe or cigar because a pack of cigarettes fit comfortably into a shirt pocket and a cigarette could be smoked during a short break. The war experience also caused many men to abandon the pocket watch for the more convenient wristwatch, which had been considered effeminate before the war.

The Black Recruit

Blacks had served in all American wars, and many fought valiantly in the Civil War and the Spanish-American War. Yet black soldiers had most often performed menial work and belonged to segregated units. Most black leaders supported American participation in the war. An exception was William Monroe Trotter, a Boston editor, who argued that German atrocities were no worse than the lynching of black men in America. Instead of making the world safe for democracy, he suggested, the government should make "the South safe for Negroes " But W. E. B. Du Bois, the editor of *The Crisis,* urged blacks to close ranks and support the war. He predicted that the war experience would cause the "walls of prejudice" to crumble gradually before the "onslaught of common sense." But the walls did not crumble, and the black soldier never received equal or fair treatment during the war.

The Selective Service Act made no mention of race, and African Americans in most cases registered without protest. Many whites, especially in the South, feared having too many blacks trained in the use of arms. In some areas, draft boards exempted single white men but drafted black fathers. The most notorious situation existed in Atlanta, where one draft board inducted 97 percent of the African Americans registered but exempted 85 percent of the whites. Still, most southern whites found it difficult to imagine a black man in the uniform of the U.S. Army.

White attitudes toward African Americans sometimes led to conflict. In August 1917, violence erupted in Houston, Texas, involving soldiers from the regular army's all-black 24th Infantry Division. Harassed by the Jim Crow laws, which had been tightened for their benefit, a group of soldiers went on a rampage, killing 17 white civilians. Over 100 soldiers were court-martialed; 13 were condemned to death. Those convicted were hanged three days later before any appeals could be filed.

This violence, coming only a month after the race riot in East St. Louis, Illinois, brought on in part by the migration of southern blacks to the area, caused great concern about the handling of African-American soldiers. Secretary of War Baker made it clear that the army had no intention of upsetting the status quo. The basic government policy was of complete segregation and careful distribution of black units throughout the country.

African Americans were prohibited from joining the marines and restricted to menial jobs in the navy. A great many black nurses volunteered to go to France, but only six actually went—and they were assigned to black units. In 1918, official policy and American prejudice would not allow black women to care for white men. While some African Americans were trained as junior officers in the army, they were assigned to the all-black 92nd Division, where the high-ranking officers were white. But few black officers or enlisted men would see action. A staff report decided that "the mass of colored drafted men cannot be used for combatant troops." Most of the black soldiers, including about

Assigned to segregated units, black soldiers were also excluded from white recreation facilities. Here black women from Newark, New Jersey, aided by white social workers, entertain black servicemen. *(National Archives)*

80 percent of those sent to France, worked as stevedores and common laborers under the supervision of white, noncommissioned officers. "Everyone who has handled colored labor knows that the gang bosses must be white if any work is to be done," remarked Lieutenant Colonel U. S. Grant, the grandson of the Civil War general. Other black soldiers acted as servants, drivers, and porters for the white officers. It was a demeaning and ironic policy for a government that advertised itself as standing for justice, honor, and democracy.

Over There

The conflict that Wilson called the war "to make the world safe for democracy" had become a contest of stalemate and slaughter. Hundreds of thousands had died on both sides, but victory remained elusive. To this ghastly war, Americans made important contributions. In fact, without their help, the Allies might have lost. But the American contribution was most significant only in the war's final months.

When the United States entered the conflict in the spring of 1917, the fighting had dragged on for nearly three years. After a few rapid advances and retreats, the war in western Europe had settled down to a tactical and bloody stalemate. The human costs of trench warfare were horrifying. In one battle in 1916, a total of 60,000 British soldiers were killed or wounded in a single day, yet the battle lines did not move an inch. By the spring of 1917, the

British and French armies were down to their last reserves. Italy's army had nearly collapsed. In the East, the Russians were engaged in a bitter internal struggle, and in November, the Bolshevik Revolution would cause them to sue for a separate peace, freeing the German divisions on the eastern front to join in one final assault in the West. The Allies desperately needed fresh American troops, but those troops had to be trained, equipped, and transported to the front. That took time.

A few token American regiments arrived in France in the summer of 1917 under the command of General John J. "Black Jack" Pershing, a tall, serious, Missouri-born graduate of West Point. He had fought in the Spanish-American War and led the Mexican expedition in 1916. When the first troops marched in a parade in Paris on July 4, 1917, the emotional French crowd shouted, *"Vive les Américains"* and showered them with flowers, hugs, and kisses. But the American commanders worried that many of their soldiers were so inexperienced they did not even know how to march, let alone fight. The first Americans saw action near Verdun in October 1917. By March 1918, over 300,000 American soldiers had reached France, and by November 1918, more than 2 million.

One reason that the United States forces were slow to see actual combat was Pershing's insistence that they be kept separate from the French and British divisions. An exception was made for four

Western Front of the Great War, 1918

For more than three years, the war settled down to a bloody stalemate on the western front. But in 1918, American soldiers played important roles in the Allied offensive that finally ended the war.

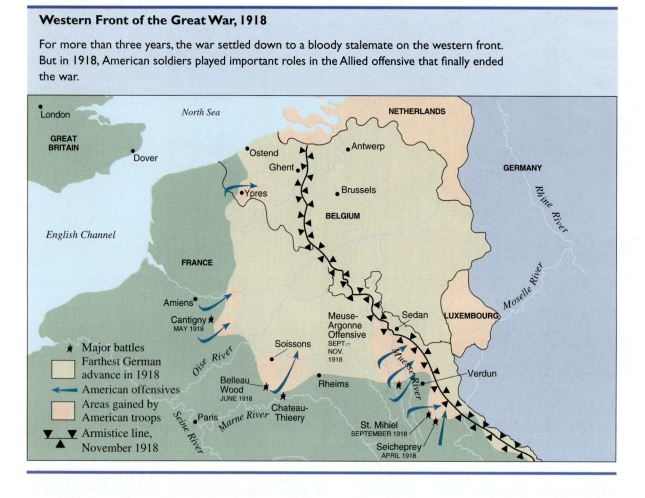

regiments of black soldiers who were assigned to the French army. Despite the American warning to the French not to "spoil the Negroes" by allowing them to mix with the French civilian population, these soldiers fought so well that the French later awarded three of the regiments the Croix de Guerre, their highest unit citation.

In the spring of 1918, with Russia out of the war and the British blockade becoming more and more effective, the Germans launched an all-out, desperate offensive to win the war before full American military and industrial power became a factor in the contest. By late May, the Germans had pushed to within 50 miles of Paris. American troops were thrown into the line and helped stem the German advance at Château-Thierry, Belleau Wood, and Cantigny, place names that proud survivors would later endow with almost sacred significance. Americans also took part in the Allied offensive led by General Ferdinand Foch of France in the summer of 1918.

In September, over one-half million American troops fought near St. Mihiel; this was the first battle in which large numbers of Americans were pressed into action. One enlisted man remembered that he "saw a sight which I shall never forget. It was zero hour and in one instant the entire front as far as the eye could reach in either direction was a sheet of flame, while the heavy artillery made the earth quake." The Americans suffered over 7,000 casualties, but they captured more than 16,000 German soldiers. The victory, even if it came against exhausted and retreating German troops, seemed to vindicate Pershing's insistence on a separate American army. The British and French commanders were critical of what they considered the disorganized, inexperienced, and ill-equipped American forces. They especially denounced the quality of the American high-ranking officers. One French report in the summer of 1918 suggested that it would take at least a year before the American army could become a "serious fighting force."

In the fall of 1918, the combined British, French, and American armies drove the Germans back. Faced with low morale among the German soldiers and finally the mutiny of the German fleet and the surrender of Austria, Kaiser Wilhelm II abdicated on November 8, and the armistice was signed on

November 11. More than 1 million American soldiers took part in the final Allied offensive near the Meuse River and the Argonne forest. It was in this battle that Edmund Arpin was wounded. Many of the men were inexperienced, and some, who had been rushed through training as "90-day wonders," had never handled a rifle before arriving in France. There were many disastrous mistakes and bungled situations. The most famous blunder was the "lost battalion." An American unit advanced beyond its support and was cut off and surrounded. The battalion suffered 70 percent casualties before being rescued.

The performance of the all-black 92nd Division was also controversial. The 92nd had been deliberately dispersed around the United States and had never trained as a unit. Its higher officers were white, and they repeatedly asked to be transferred. Many of its men were only partly trained and poorly equipped, and they were continually being called away from their military duties to work as stevedores and common laborers. At the last minute during the Meuse-Argonne offensive, the 92nd was assigned to a particularly difficult position on the line. They had no maps and no wire-cutting equipment. Battalion commanders lost contact with their men, and on several occasions, the men broke and ran in the face of enemy fire. The division was withdrawn in disgrace, and for years politicians and military

leaders used this incident to point out that black soldiers would never make good fighting men, ignoring the difficulties under which the 92nd fought and the valor shown by black troops assigned to the French army.

The war produced a few American heroes. Joseph Oklahombie, a Choctaw, overran several German machine gun nests and captured more than 100 German soldiers. Sergeant Alvin York, a former conscientious objector from Tennessee, single-handedly killed or captured 160 Germans using only his rifle and pistol. The press made him a celebrity, but his heroics were not typical. Artillery, machine guns, and, near the end, tanks, trucks, and airplanes won the war. "To be shelled when you are in the open is one of the most terrible of human experiences," one American soldier wrote. "You hear this rushing, tearing sound as the thing comes toward you, and then the huge explosion as it strikes, and infinitely worse, you see its hideous work as men stagger, fall, struggle, or lie quiet and unrecognizable."

With few exceptions, the Americans fought hard and well. Although the French and British criticized American inexperience and disarray, they admired their exuberance, their "pep," and their ability to move large numbers of men and equipment efficiently. One British officer, surveying the abundance

New technology made the Great War more horrible in some ways than past wars. British soldiers wearing primitive gas masks operate a Vickers machine gun. The machine gun effectively neutralized the tactic of massive infantry charges, while poison gas attacks increased the number of soldiers with "shell shock" or mental illness. *(Imperial War Museum, London)*

of American men and supplies, remarked, "For any particular work they seem to have about five times as much of both as we do." Sometimes it seemed that Americans simply overwhelmed the enemy with their numbers. They suffered over 120,000 casualties in the Meuse-Argonne campaign alone. One officer estimated that he lost 10 soldiers for every German his men killed in the final offensive.

The United States entered the war late but still lost more than 48,000 service personnel and had many more wounded. Disease claimed 15 of every 1,000 soldiers each year (compared with 65 per 1,000 in the Civil War). But American losses were tiny compared to those suffered by the European armies. The British lost 900,000 men, the French 1.4 million, and the Russians 1.7 million. Nor was the financial burden so costly for the United States as it was for its Allies. American units fired French artillery pieces; American soldiers were usually transported in British ships and wore helmets and other equipment modeled after the British. The United States purchased clothing and blankets, even horses, in Europe. American fliers, including heroes like Eddie Rickenbacker, flew French and British planes. The United States contributed huge amounts of men and supplies in the last months of the war, and that finally tipped the balance. But it had entered late and sacrificed little compared with France and England. That would influence the peace settlement.

A Global Pandemic

The end of the Great War brought relief and joy to many, but in the fall of 1918 an influenza pandemic swept around the world, killing at least 40 million people, with 675,000 deaths in the United States in a little more than a year. The Spanish Flu, as it was called (although there is no evidence that it originated in Spain), seems to have started at about the same time in Europe, Asia, America, and even in remote Eskimo villages. The flu started with a cough and sore throat, then developed into pneumonia; its victims were often dead within a few days. Only a small percentage of those who caught the disease died from it, but, unlike most epidemics, it hit hardest among young adults. Over 43,000 American servicemen died from the flu (almost as many as died on the battlefield). Early in the epidemic, rumors blamed German germ warfare for the disease, but the German army was infected as well. There were no antibiotics or shots that could prevent or cure the disease, and the surgical masks required in some cities did no good. Even President Wilson came near death from the disease in the spring of 1919. The flu of 1918–1919 killed more people in a

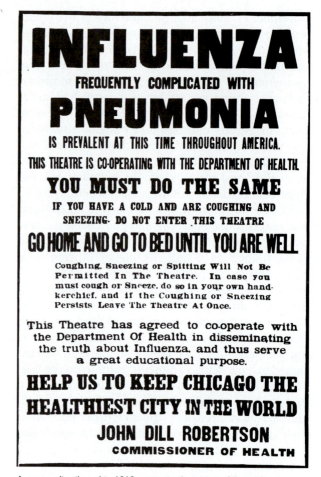

A poster distributed in 1918 to movie theaters in Chicago by the Commissioner of Health. The language of the poster reveals the fear and near panic that many Americans felt in the face of the deadly flu epidemic. *(National Library of Medicine)*

short time than any event in human history, perhaps 20 million world wide. The speed with which the disease spread around the world was another reminder of how the modern world was interconnected and isolation was impossible. The virus that caused the outbreak has never been identified.

DOMESTIC IMPACT OF THE WAR

For at least 30 years before the United States entered the Great War, a debate raged over the proper role of the federal government in regulating industry and protecting people who could not protect themselves. Controversy also centered on the question of how much power the federal government should have to tax and control individuals and corporations and the proper relation of the federal government to state and local governments. Even within the Wilson administration, advisers disagreed on the proper role of the federal government. In fact, Wilson had only recently moved away from what he defined in 1912 as the New Freedom—limited government and open competition. But the war and the problems it raised increased the power of the federal government in a variety of ways. The wartime experience did not end the debate, but the United States emerged from the war a more modern nation, with more power residing in Washington. At the same time, the federal government with its huge expenditures provided immense economic advantage to businesses engaged in war production and to the cities where those businesses were located.

Financing the War

The war, by one calculation, cost the United States over $33 billion. Interest and veterans' benefits bring the total to nearly $112 billion. Early on, when an economist suggested that the war might cost the United States $10 billion, everyone laughed. Yet many in the Wilson administration knew the war was going to be expensive, and they set out to raise the money by borrowing and by increasing taxes.

Secretary of the Treasury William McAdoo, who, like Wilson, had moved from the South to the North because of the lure of greater economic opportunities, shouldered the task of financing the war. Studying the policies that Treasury Secretary Salmon Chase had followed during the Civil War, he decided that Chase had made a mistake in not appealing to the emotions of the people. A war must be a "kind of crusade," he remarked. He also learned from the British, French, and German propaganda campaigns. They used modern graphics and advertising techniques to promote patriotism and support for the war. McAdoo's campaign to sell liberty bonds to ordinary American citizens at a very low interest rate appealed to American loyalty. "Lick a Stamp and Lick the Kaiser," one poster urged. Celebrities such as film stars Mary Pickford and Douglas Fairbanks promoted the bonds, and McAdoo employed the Boy Scouts to sell them. "Every Scout to Save a Soldier" was the slogan. He even implied that people who did not buy bonds were traitors. "A man who can't lend his government $1.25 per week at the rate of 4% interest is not entitled to be an American citizen," he announced. A banner flew over the main street in Gary, Indiana, that made the point of the campaign clear: "ARE YOU WORTHY TO BE FOUGHT AND DIED FOR? BUY LIBERTY BONDS."

The public responded enthusiastically, but they discovered after the war that their bonds had dropped to about 80 percent of face value. Because the interest on the bonds was tax exempt, well-to-do citizens profited more from buying the bonds than did ordinary men, women, and children. But the wealthy were not as pleased with McAdoo's

other plan to finance the war: raising taxes. The War Revenue Act of 1917 boosted the tax rate sharply, levied a tax on excess profits, and increased estate taxes. The next year, another bill raised the tax on the largest incomes to 77 percent. The wealthy protested, but a number of progressives were just as unhappy with the bill, for they wanted to confiscate all income over $100,000 a year. Despite taxes and liberty bonds, however, World War I, like the Civil War, was financed in large part by inflation. Food prices, for example, nearly doubled between 1917 and 1919.

Increasing Federal Power

The major wars of the twentieth century made huge demands on the nations that fought them and helped to transform their governments. The United States was no exception. At first, Wilson tried to work through a variety of state agencies to mobilize the nation's resources. The need for more central control and authority soon led Wilson to create a series of federal agencies to deal with the war emergency. The first crisis was food. Poor grain crops for two years and an increasing demand for American food in Europe caused shortages. Wilson appointed Herbert Hoover, a young engineer who had won great prestige as head of the Commission for Relief of Belgium, to direct the Food Administration. Hoover set out to meet the crisis not so much through government regulation as through an appeal to the patriotism of farmers and consumers alike. He instituted a series of "wheatless" and "meatless" days and urged housewives to cooperate. In Philadelphia, a large sign announced, "FOOD WILL WIN THE WAR; DON'T WASTE IT." Women emerged during the war as the most important group of consumers. The government urged them to save, just as later it would urge them to buy.

The Wilson administration used the authority of the federal government to organize resources for the war effort. The National Research Council and the National Advisory Committee on Aeronautics helped mobilize scientists in industry and the universities to produce strategic materials formerly imported from Germany, especially optical glass and chemicals to combat poison-gas warfare. American companies also tried to reproduce German color lithography that had dominated the market for postcards, posters, and magazine illustrations before the war. Perhaps most valuable were the efforts of scientists in industry to improve radio, airplanes, and instruments to predict the weather and detect submarines. The war stimulated research and development and made the United States less dependent on European science and technology.

The War Industries Board, led by Bernard Baruch, a shrewd Wall Street broker, used the power of the government to control scarce materials and, on occasion, to set prices and priorities. But cooperation among government, business, and university scientists to promote research and develop new products was one legacy of the war. The government itself went into the shipbuilding business. The largest shipyard, at Hog Island, near Philadelphia, employed as many as 35,000 workers but did not launch its first ship until the late summer of 1918. San Francisco and Seattle also became major shipbuilding centers, while San Diego owed its rapid growth to the presence of a major naval base.

The government also got into the business of running the railroads. When a severe winter and a lack of coordination brought the rail system near collapse in December 1917, Wilson put all the nation's railroads under the control of the United Railway Administration. The government spent more than $500 million to improve the rails and equipment, and in 1918, the railroads did run more efficiently than they had under private control. Some businessmen complained of "war socialism" and resented the way government agencies forced them to comply with rules and regulations. But most came to agree with Baruch that a close working relationship with government could improve the quality of their products, promote efficiency, and increase profits.

War Workers

The Wilson administration sought to protect and extend the rights of organized labor during the war, while mobilizing the workers necessary to keep the factories running. The National War Labor Board insisted on adequate wages and reduced hours, and it tried to prevent the exploitation of women and children working under government contracts. On one occasion, when a munitions plant refused to accept the War Labor Board's decision, the government simply took over the factory. When workers threatened to strike for better wages or hours or for greater control over the workplace, the board often ruled that they either work or be drafted into the army.

The Wilson administration favored the conservative labor movement of Samuel Gompers and the AFL, and the Justice Department put the radical Industrial Workers of the World "out of business." Beginning in September 1917, federal agents conducted massive raids on IWW offices and arrested most of the leaders.

Samuel Gompers took advantage of the crisis to strengthen the AFL's position to speak for labor. He lent his approval to administration policies by making it clear that he opposed the IWW as well as socialists and communists. Convincing Wilson that it was important to protect the rights of organized labor during wartime, he announced that "no other policy is compatible with the spirit and methods of democracy." As the AFL won a voice in home-front policy, its membership increased from 2.7 million in 1916 to over 4 million in 1917. Organized labor's wartime gains, however, would prove only temporary.

The war opened up industrial employment opportunities for black men. With 4 million men in the armed forces and the flow of immigrants interrupted by the war, American manufacturers for the first time hired African Americans in large numbers. In Chicago before the war, only 3,000 black men held factory jobs; in 1920, more than 15,000 did.

Northern labor agents and the railroads actively recruited southern blacks, but the news of jobs in northern cities spread by word of mouth as well. By 1920, more than 300,000 blacks had joined the "great migration" north. This massive movement of people, which continued into the 1920s, had a permanent impact on the South as well as on the northern cities. Like African Americans, thousands of Mexicans headed north into the United States, as immigration officials relaxed the regulations because of the need for labor in the farms and factories of the Southwest.

The war also created new employment opportunities for women. Posters and patriotic speeches urged women to do their duty for the war effort. One poster showed a woman at her typewriter, the shadow of a soldier in the background, with the message: "STENOGRAPHERS, WASHINGTON NEEDS YOU." Women responded to these appeals out of patriotism, as well as out of a need to increase their earnings and to make up for inflation, which diminished real wages. Women went into every kind of industry. They labored in brickyards and in heavy industry, became conductors on the railroad, and turned out shells in munitions plants. They even organized the Woman's Land Army to mobilize female labor for the farms. They demonstrated that women could do any kind of job, whatever the physical or intellectual demands. "It was not until our men were called overseas," one woman banking executive reported, "that we made any real onslaught on the realm of finance, and became tellers, managers of departments, and junior and senior officers." One black woman who gave up her position as a live-in servant to work in a paperbox factory declared:

I'll never work in nobody's kitchen but my own any more. No indeed, that's the one thing that makes me

African-American Migration, 1910–1920

This map makes graphic the massive migration of African Americans from the South to the North during the Great War. Most moved to find better jobs, but in the process they changed the dynamics of race relations in the country.

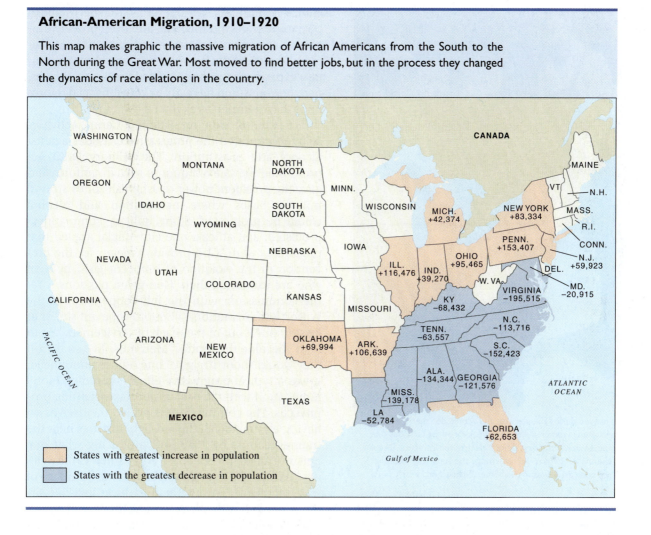

MICH. +42,374
NEW YORK +83,334
PENN. +153,407
OHIO +95,465
ILL. +116,476
IND. +39,270
N.J. +59,923
W. VA.
VIRGINIA −195,515
MD. −20,915
KY −68,432
OKLAHOMA +69,994
ARK. +106,639
TENN. −63,557
N.C. −113,716
S.C. −152,423
ALA. −134,344
GEORGIA −121,576
MISS. −139,178
LA −52,784
FLORIDA +62,653

■ States with greatest increase in population
■ States with the greatest decrease in population

stick to this job, but when you're working in anybody's kitchen, well you out of luck. You almost have to eat on the run; you never get any time off.

As black women moved out of domestic service, they took jobs in textile mills or even in the stockyards. However, racial discrimination, even in the North, prevented them from moving too far up the occupational ladder.

Even though women demonstrated that they could take over jobs once thought suitable only for men, their progress during the war proved temporary. Only about 5 percent of the women employed during the war were new to the workforce, and almost all of them were unmarried. For most, it meant a shift of occupations or a move up to a better-paying position. Moreover, the war accelerated trends already underway. It increased the need for telephone operators, sales personnel, secretaries, and other white-collar workers, and in these occupations, women soon became a majority. Telephone

operator, for example, became an almost exclusively female job. There were 15,000 operators in 1900 but 80,000 in 1910, and by 1917, women represented 99 percent of all operators as the telephone network spanned the nation.

In the end, the war did provide limited opportunities for some women, but it did not change the dominant perception that a woman's place was in the home. After the war was over, the men returned, and the gains made by women almost disappeared. There were 8 million women in the workforce in 1910 but only 8.5 million in 1920.

The Climax of Progressivism

Many progressives, especially the social justice progressives, opposed the U.S. entry into the war until a few months before the nation declared war. But after April 1917, many began to see the "social possibilities of war." They deplored the death and destruction, the abridgment of freedom of speech, and

Women proved during the war that they could do "men's work." These two young women deliver ice, a backbreaking task, but one that was necessary in the days before electric refrigerators. Despite women like these, the war did not change the American ideal that women's proper place was in the home. *(National Archives)*

the patriotic spirit that accompanied the war. But they praised the social planning the conflict stimulated. They approved of the Wilson administration's support of collective bargaining, the eight-hour day, and protection for women and children in industry. They applauded Secretary of War Baker when he announced, "We cannot afford, when we are losing boys in France, to lose children in the United States at the same time." They welcomed the experiments with government-owned housing projects, woman suffrage, and prohibition. Many endorsed the government takeover of the railroads and control of business during the war.

One of the best examples of the progressives' influence on wartime activities was the Commission on Training Camp Activities, set up early in the war to solve the problem of mobilizing, entertaining, and protecting American servicemen at home and abroad. This experiment was a uniquely American effort; no other country tried anything like it. The chairman of the commission was Raymond Fosdick, a former settlement worker. He appointed a number of experts from the Playground Association, the YMCA, and social work agencies. They set out to or-

ganize community singing and baseball, establish post exchanges and theaters, and even provide university extension lectures to educate the servicemen. The overriding assumption was that the military experience would help produce better citizens, people who would be ready to vote for social reform once they returned to civilian life.

The Commission on Training Camp Activities also incorporated the progressive crusades against alcohol and prostitution. The Military Draft Act prohibited the sale of liquor to men in uniform and gave the president power to establish zones around military bases where prostitution and alcohol would be prohibited. Some military commanders protested, and at least one city official argued that prostitutes were "God-provided means for the prevention of the violation of innocent girls, by men who are exercising their 'God-given passions.'" Yet the commission, with the full cooperation of the Wilson administration, set out to wipe out sin, or at least to put it out of the reach of servicemen. "Fit to fight" became the motto. "Men must live straight if they would shoot straight," one official announced. It was a typical progressive effort combining moral indignation with the use of the latest scientific prophylaxis. The commissioners prided themselves on having eliminated all the red-light districts near the training camps by 1918 and producing what one person called "the cleanest army since Cromwell's day." When the boys go to France, the secretary of war remarked, "I want them to have invisible armour to take with them. I want them to have armour made up of a set of social habits replacing those of their homes and communities."

France tested the "invisible armour." The government, despite hundreds of letters of protest from American mothers, decided that it could not prevent the soldiers from drinking wine in France, but it could forbid them to buy or accept as gifts anything but light wine and beer. If Arpin's outfit is typical, the soldiers often ignored the rules.

Sex was even more difficult to regulate in France than liquor. Both the British and the French armies had tried to solve the problem of venereal disease by licensing and inspecting prostitutes. Clemenceau, the French premier, found the American attitude toward prostitution difficult to comprehend. On one occasion, he accused the Americans of spreading disease throughout the French civilian population and graciously offered to provide the Americans with licensed prostitutes. General Pershing considered the letter containing the offer "too hot to handle." So he gave it to Fosdick, who showed it to Baker, who remarked, "For God's sake, Raymond, don't show this to the President or he'll stop the war." The Americans never accepted Clemenceau's offer, and he continued to be baffled by the American progressive mentality.

Suffrage for Women

In the fall of 1918, while American soldiers were mobilizing for the final offensive in France and hundreds of thousands of women were working in factories and serving as Red Cross and Salvation Army volunteers near the army bases, Woodrow Wilson spoke before the Senate to ask its support for the vote for women. He argued that woman suffrage was "vital to the winning of the war." Wilson had earlier opposed the vote for women. His positive statement at this late date was not important, but his voice was a welcome addition to a rising chorus of support for an amendment to the Constitution that would permit the female half of the population to vote.

Many still opposed woman suffrage. Some still argued that the vote would make women less feminine, more worldly, and less able to perform their primary tasks as wives and mothers. The National Association Opposed to Woman Suffrage argued that it was only radicals who wanted the vote and declared that woman suffrage, socialism, and feminism were "three branches of the same Social Revolution."

Carrie Chapman Catt, an efficient administrator and tireless organizer, devised the strategy that finally secured the vote for women. Catt, who grew up in Iowa, joined the Iowa Woman Suffrage Association at age 28 shortly after her first husband died. Before remarrying, she insisted on a legal agreement giving her four months a year away from her husband to work for the suffrage cause. In 1915, she became president of the National American Woman Suffrage Association (NAWSA), the organization founded in 1890 and based in part on the society organized by Elizabeth Cady Stanton and Susan B. Anthony in 1869.

Catt coordinated the state campaigns with the office in Washington, directing a growing army of dedicated workers. The Washington headquarters sent precise information to the states on ways to pressure congressmen in local districts. In Washington, they maintained a file on each congressman and senator. "There were facts supplied by our members in the states about his personal, political, business and religious affiliations; there were reports of interviews; . . . there was everything that could be discovered about his stand on woman suffrage."

The careful planning began to produce results, but a group of more militant reformers, impatient with the slow progress, broke off from NAWSA to form the National Women's Party (NWP) in 1916.

This group was led by Alice Paul, a Quaker from New Jersey, who had participated in some of the suffrage battles in England. Paul and her group, using tactics borrowed from the British militant suffragettes, picketed the White House, chained themselves to the fence, and blocked the streets. They carried banners that asked, "MR. PRESIDENT, HOW LONG MUST WOMEN WAIT FOR LIBERTY?" In the summer of 1917, the government arrested more than 200 women and charged them with "obstructing the sidewalk." It was just the kind of publicity the militant group sought, and it made the most of it. Wilson, fearing even more embarrassment, began to cooperate with the more moderate reformers.

The careful organizing of NAWSA and the more militant tactics of the NWP both contributed to the final success of the woman suffrage crusade. The militant tactics of Alice Paul and her group seemed to make the moderate suffrage advocates more acceptable to Wilson. The war did not cause the passage of the Nineteenth Amendment, but it did accelerate the process. Fourteen state legislatures petitioned Congress in 1917 and twenty-six in 1919, urging the enactment of the amendment. Early in 1919, the House of Representatives passed the suffrage amendment 304 to 90, and the Senate approved by a vote of 56 to 25. Fourteen months later, the required 36 states had ratified the amendment, and women at last had the vote. "We are no longer petitioners," Catt announced in celebration. "We are not wards of the nation, but free and equal citizens." But the achievement of votes for women would not prove the triumph of feminism, nor the signal for the beginning of a new reform movement, that the women leaders believed at the time.

PLANNING FOR PEACE

Woodrow Wilson turned U.S. participation in the war into a religious crusade to change the nature of international relations. It was a war to make the world safe for democracy—and more. On January 8, 1918, in part to counteract the Bolshevik charge that the war was merely a struggle among imperialist powers, he announced his plan to organize the peace. Called the Fourteen Points, it argued for "open covenants of peace openly arrived at," freedom of the seas, equality of trade, and the self-determination of all peoples. But his most important point, the fourteenth, called for an international organization, a "league of nations," to preserve peace. The victorious Allies, who had suffered grievously in the conflict, had less idealistic goals than did Wilson for peacemaking.

The Versailles Peace Conference

Late in 1918, Wilson announced that he would head the American delegation at Versailles, near Paris, symbolizing his belief that he alone could overcome the forces of greed and imperialism in Europe and bring peace to the world. Wilson and his entourage of college professors, technical experts, and advisers set sail for Paris on the *George Washington* on December 4, 1918. Secretary of State Lansing, Edward House, and a number of other advisers were there; conspicuously missing, however, was Henry Cabot Lodge, the most powerful man in the Senate, or any other Republican senator.

This would prove a serious blunder, for the Republican-controlled Senate would have to approve any treaty negotiated in Paris. It is difficult to explain Wilson's lack of political insight, except that he disliked Lodge intensely and hated political bargaining and compromise. Preferring to announce great principles, he had supreme confidence in his ability to persuade and to get his way by appealing to the people.

Wilson's self-confidence grew during a triumphant tour through Europe before the conference. The ordinary people greeted him like a savior who had ended the tragic war. But the American president had greater difficulty convincing the political leaders at the peace conference of his genius or his special grace. In Paris, he faced the reality of European power politics and ambitions and the personalities of David Lloyd George of Great Britain, Vittorio Orlando of Italy, and Georges Clemenceau of France.

Though Wilson was more naive and idealistic than his European counterparts, he was a clever negotiator who won many concessions at the peace table, sometimes by threatening to go home if his counterparts would not compromise. The European leaders were determined to punish Germany and enlarge their empires. Wilson, however, pressed for a new kind of international relations based on his Fourteen Points. He achieved limited acceptance of the idea of self-determination, his dream that each national group could have its own country and that the people should decide in what country they wanted to live.

From what had been the Austro-Hungarian empire, the peacemakers carved the new countries of Austria, Hungary, and Yugoslavia. In addition, they created Poland, Czechoslovakia, Finland, Estonia, Latvia, and Lithuania, in part to help contain the threat of bolshevism in eastern Europe. France was to occupy the industrial Saar region of Germany for 15 years with a plebiscite at the end of that time to determine whether the people wanted to become a part of Germany or France. Italy gained the port city of Trieste, but not the neighboring city of Fiume, with its largely Italian-speaking population. Dividing up the map of Europe was difficult at best, but perhaps the biggest mistake that Wilson and other major leaders made was to give the small nations little power at the negotiating table and to exclude Soviet Russia entirely.

While Wilson won some points at the peace negotiations, he also had to make major concessions. He was forced to give in to the Allied demand that Germany pay reparations (later set at $56 billion), lose much of its oil- and coal-rich territory, and admit to its war guilt. He accepted a mandate system, to be supervised by the League of Nations, that allowed France and Britain to take over portions of the Middle East and Japan to occupy Germany's colonies in the Pacific as well as China's Shantung province. And he acquiesced when the Allies turned Germany's African colonies into "mandate possessions" because they did not want to allow the self-determination of blacks in areas they had colonized.

Although Wilson yielded to the Allies on the fate of Germany's former colonies in Africa, he did not envision a reordering of global race relations. He opposed and finally defeated a measure introduced by Japan to include a clause in the League covenant to support racial equality in all parts of the world. W. E. B. Du Bois, who was in Paris as part of the American delegation at the first Pan-African Congress, supported the Japanese resolution for

World War I Losses

The total cost of the war was estimated at over $330 billion. The cost in human life was even more horrible. The number of known dead was placed at about 10 million men and the wounded at about 20 million, distributed among chief combatants as follows (round numbers).
Reflecting on the Past Which countries bore the brunt of dead and wounded? How did this influence the peace settlement?

	Dead	Wounded	Prisoner
Great Britain	947,000	2,122,000	192,000
France	1,385,000	3,044,000	446,000
Russia	1,700,000	4,950,000	500,000
Italy	460,000	947,000	530,000
United States	115,000	206,000	4,500
Germany	1,808,000	4,247,000	618,000
Austria-Hungary	1,200,000	3,620,000	200,000
Turkey	325,000	400,000	

Europe and the Near East After World War I

Led in part by President Wilson's goal to promote the self-determination of people and in part by a desire to block the expansion of Germany and the Soviet Union, the diplomats meeting at Versailles reconfigured the map of Europe and the Near East. Redrawing the map, however, was easier than solving the problems of nationalism and ethnic conflict.

Legend:
- To Great Britain
- To France
- To Belgium
- To Denmark
- To Romania
- To Greece
- To Italy
- Became independent
- New states as of 1921
- Border of German Empire in 1914
- Border of Austrian-Hungarian Empire in 1914
- Border of Russian Empire in 1914
- Border of Ottoman Empire in 1914
- New boundaries as a result of postwar treaties
- Boundaries as of 1914

racial equality. He also spoke against colonialism and criticized "white civilization" for subjugating blacks in various parts of the world. He hoped that the Pan-African movement would become a global effort to unite people of color around the world. But Wilson and the other leaders at Versailles ignored Du Bois.

The Versailles treaty did not represent "peace without victory." The German people felt betrayed. Japan, which had expected to play a larger role in the peace conference, felt slighted. The Italians were angry because they received less territory than they expected. These resentments would later have grave consequences. Wilson also did not win approval for freedom of the seas or the abolition of trade barriers, but he did gain endorsement for the League of Nations, the organization he hoped would prevent all future wars. The league consisted of a council of the five great powers, elected delegates from the smaller countries, and a World Court to settle disputes. But the key to collective security was contained in Article 10 of the league covenant, which pledged all members "to respect and preserve against external aggression the territorial integrity" of all other members.

Women's Vision of Peace

While the statesmen met at Versailles to sign the peace treaty hammered out in Paris and to divide up Europe, a group of prominent and successful women—lawyers, physicians, administrators, and writers from all over the world, including many from the Central Powers—met in Zurich, Switzerland. Jane Addams led the American delegation that included Florence Kelley of the National Consumers League; Alice Hamilton, a professor at Harvard Medical School; and Jeannette Rankin, a congresswoman from Montana (one of the few states where women could vote). They met amid the devastation of war to promote a peace that would last. At their conference, they formed the Women's International League for Peace and Freedom. Electing Addams president of the new organization, they denounced

the harsh peace terms, which called for disarmament of only one side and exacted great economic penalties against the Central Powers. Prophetically, they predicted that the peace treaty would result in the spread of hatred and anarchy and "create all over Europe discords and animosities which can only lead to future wars."

Hate and intolerance were legacies of the war. They were present at the Versailles peace conference, where Clemenceau especially wanted to humiliate Germany for the destruction of French lives and property. Also hanging over the conference was the Bolshevik success in Russia. Lenin's vision of a communist world order, led by workers, conflicted sharply with Wilson's dream of an anti-imperialist, free-trade, capitalist world. The threat of revolution seemed so great that Wilson and the Allies sent American and Japanese troops into Siberia in 1919 to attempt to defeat the Bolsheviks and create a moderate republic. But by 1920, the troops had failed in their mission. They withdrew, but Russians never forgot American intervention and the threat of Bolshevism remained.

Wilson's Failed Dream

Most Americans supported the concept of the League of Nations in the summer of 1919. A few, like former senator Albert Beveridge of Indiana, an ardent nationalist, denounced the league as the work

The Big Four in December 1919: Italy's Orlando, Britain's Lloyd George, France's Clemenceau, and the United States' Wilson. *(The Granger Collection, New York)*

of "amiable old male grannies who, over their afternoon tea, are planning to denationalize America and denationalize the nation's manhood." But 33 governors endorsed the plan. Yet in the end, the Senate refused to accept American membership in the league. The League of Nations treaty, one commentator has suggested, was killed by its friends and not by its enemies.

First there was Lodge, who had earlier endorsed the idea of some kind of international peacekeeping organization but who objected to Article 10, which obligated all members to come to the defense of the others in case of attack. He claimed that it would force Americans to fight the wars of foreigners. Chairman of the Senate Foreign Relations Committee, Lodge, like Wilson, was a lawyer and a scholar as well as a politician. But in background and personality, he was very different from Wilson. A Republican senator since 1893, he had great faith in the power and prestige of the Senate. He disliked all Democrats, especially Wilson, whose idealism and missionary zeal infuriated him.

Then there was Wilson, whose only hope of passage of the treaty in the Senate was a compromise to bring moderate senators to his side. But Wilson refused to compromise or to modify Article 10 to allow Congress the opportunity to decide whether the United States would support the league in time of crisis. Angry at his opponents, who were exploiting the disagreement for political advantage, he stumped the country to convince the American people of the rightness of his plan. The people did not need to be convinced. They greeted Wilson much the way the people of France had. Traveling by train, he gave 37 speeches in 29 cities in the space of three weeks. When he described the graves of American soldiers in France and announced that American boys would never again die in a foreign war, the people responded with applause.

After one dramatic speech in Pueblo, Colorado, Wilson collapsed. His health had been failing for some months, and the strain of the trip was too much. He was rushed back to Washington, where a few days later he suffered a massive stroke. For the next year and a half, the president was incapable of running the government. Protected by his second wife and his closest advisers, Wilson was partially paralyzed, depressed, and unable to lead a fight for the league. For a year and a half, the country limped along without a president.

After many votes and much maneuvering, the Senate finally killed the league treaty in March 1920. Had the United States joined the League of Nations, it probably would have made little difference in the

Timeline

1914	Archduke Ferdinand assassinated; World War I begins
	United States declares neutrality
	American troops invade Mexico and occupy Veracruz
1915	Germany announces submarine blockade of Great Britain
	Lusitania sunk
	Arabic pledge
	Marines land in Haiti
1916	Army Reorganization Bill
	Expedition into Mexico
	Wilson reelected
	Workmen's Compensation Bill
	Keatings-Owen Child Labor Bill
	Federal Farm Loan Act
	National Women's Party founded
1917	Germany resumes unrestricted submarine warfare
	United States breaks relations with Germany
	Zimmermann telegram
	Russian Revolution
	United States declares war on Germany
	War Revenue Act
	Espionage Act
	Committee on Public Information established
	Trading with the Enemy Act
	Selective Service Act
	War Industries Board formed
1918	Sedition Act
	Flu epidemic sweeps nation
	Wilson's Fourteen Points
	American troops intervene in Russian Revolution
1919	Paris peace conference
	Eighteenth Amendment prohibits alcoholic beverages
	Senate rejects Treaty of Versailles
1920	Nineteenth Amendment grants suffrage for women

international events of the 1920s and 1930s. Nor would American participation have prevented World War II. The United States did not resign from the world of diplomacy or trade, nor did the United States with that single act become isolated from the rest of the world. But the rejection of the league treaty was symbolic of the refusal of many Americans to admit that the world and America's place in it had changed dramatically since 1914. The United States was now one of the world's most powerful countries, but the American people had not yet integrated that reality into their sense of themselves as a people and a nation.

✦ *Conclusion*

THE DIVIDED LEGACY OF THE GREAT WAR

For Edmund Arpin and many of his friends, who left small towns and urban neighborhoods to join the military forces, the war was a great adventure. For the next decades at American Legion conventions and Armistice Day parades, they continued to celebrate their days of glory. For others who served, the war's results were more tragic. Many died. Some came home injured, disabled by poison gas, or unable to cope with the complex world that had opened up to them.

In a larger sense, the war was both a triumph and a tragedy for the American people. The war created opportunities for blacks who migrated to the North, for women who found more rewarding jobs, and for farmers who suddenly discovered a demand for their products. But much of the promise and the hope proved temporary.

The war provided a certain climax to the progressive movement. The passage of the woman suffrage amendment and the use of federal power in a variety of ways to promote justice and order pleased reformers, who had been working toward these ends for many decades. But the results were often disappointing. Once the war ended, much federal legislation was dismantled or reduced in effectiveness and votes for women had little initial impact on social legislation. Yet the power of the federal government did increase during the war in a variety of ways. From taking control of the railroads to building ships and public housing, to regulating the economy, the government took an active role. Much of that role would diminish in the next decade, but a strong, active government during the war would become a model during the 1930s for those who tried to solve the problem of a major depression.

The Great War marked the coming of age of the United States as a world power. At the end of the war, the United States had become the world's largest creditor and an important factor in international trade and diplomacy. But the country seemed reluctant to accept the new responsibility. The war and the settlement were at least in part responsible for the global depression of the 1930s, and the problems created by the war led directly to another global war causing the next generation to rename the conflict, World War I. The war stimulated patriotism and pride in the country, but it also increased intolerance. With this mixed legacy from the war, the country entered the new era of the 1920s.

✦ Recommended Reading

The Early War Years
C. C. Clemenden, *The United States and Pancho Villa* (1961); Nial Ferguson, *The Pity of War* (1998); Paul Fussell, *The Great War and Modern Memory* (1975); Martin Gilbert, *The First World War: A Complete Account* (1994); John Keegan, *An Illustrated History of the First World War* (2001); C. Roland Marchand, *The American Peace Movement and Social Reform* (1973); Thomas F. O'Brien, *The Revolutionary Mission: American Enterprise in Latin America, 1900–1945* (1996); James Toll, *The Origins of the First World War* (1984); Barbara Tuchman, *The Guns of August* (1962).

The United States Enters the War
C. C. Adams, *The Great Adventure: Male Desire and the Coming of World War I* (1990); Robert H. Ferrell, *Woodrow Wilson and World War I* (1985); Ellis W. Hawley, *The Great War and the Search for Modern Order* (1979); N. Gordon Levin Jr., *Woodrow Wilson and World Politics* (1968); Ernest R. May, *The World War and American Isolation* (1966); Daniel M. Smith, *The Great Departure: The United States and World War I* (1965).

The Military Experience
Arthur D. Barbeau and Florette Henri, *The Unknown Soldiers: Black American Troops in World War I* (1974); Edward M. Coffman, *The War to End All Wars: The American Military Experience in World War I* (1968); John Ellis, *The Social History of the Machine Gun* (1975); Byron Farwell, *Over There: The United States in the Great War* (1999); Herbert M. Mason, Jr., *The Lafayette Escadrille* (1964); Lawrence Stallings, *The Doughboys: The Story of the A. E. F., 1917–1918* (1963); Russell Weigley, *The American Way of War* (1973).

Domestic Impact of the War
Nancy K. Bristow, *Making Men Moral: Social Engineering During the Great War* (1996); Alfred W. Crosby, *America's Forgotten Pandemic: The Influenza of 1918* (1989); Eric Foner, *The Story of American Freedom* (1998); Lettie Gavin, *American Women in World War I* (1997); Maurine Greenwald, *Women, War and Work* (1980); Florette Henri, *Black Migration: The Movement Northward, 1900–1920* (1975); Donald Johnson, *The Challenge of American Freedoms: World War I and the*

Rise of the American Civil Liberties Union (1963); David M. Kennedy, *Over Here: The First World War and American Society* (1980); Gina Kolata, *Flu: The Story of the Great Influenza Pandemic of 1918 and the Search for the Virus that Caused It* (1999); Ronald Schaffer, *America in the Great War: The Rise of the War Welfare State* (1991).

Planning for Peace

John Morton Blum, *Woodrow Wilson and the Politics of Morality* (1956); John Milton Cooper Jr., *Breaking the Heart of the World: Woodrow Wilson and the Fight for the League of Nations* (2001); Peter Filene, *America and the Soviet Experiment* (1967); Lloyd C. Gardner, *Safe for Democracy: The Anglo-American Response to Revolution, 1913–1923* (1984); Warren Kuehl, *Seeking World Order* (1969); Phyllis Lee Levin, *Edith and Woodrow: The Wilson White House* (2001); Charles L. Mee, Jr., *The End of Order: Versailles, 1919* (1980).

Fiction and Film

Erich Maria Remarque highlights the horror of the war in his classic *All Quiet on the Western Front* (1929), which is told from the German point of view; John Dos Passos describes the war as a bitter experience in *Three Soldiers* (1921); and Ernest Hemingway portrays its futility in *A Farewell to Arms* (1929). *All Quiet on the Western Front* was made into a powerful movie (1930) from Remarque's novel. Told from the German point of view, it became an antiwar classic in the 1930s. *Reds* (1981) is a Hollywood film about socialists, feminists, and communists. It tells the story of John Reed, Louise Bryant, and their radical friends in Greenwich Village before the war and their support of the Russian Revolution after 1917. *Lawrence of Arabia* (1962) is the epic story of how British writer, soldier, and eccentric T. E. Lawrence enlisted the desert tribes of Africa to fight against the Turks during World War I.

✦ Discovering U.S. History Online

The World War I Document Archive

www.lib.byu.edu/~rdh/wwi/

This archive contains sources about World War I in general, not just America's involvement.

Lusitania Online

www.lusitania.net/

This site presents a background of the luxury liner, information about its crew and its passengers, as well as accounts of its sinking by a German submarine.

Letters of World War I

www.news.bbc.co.uk/1/hi/special_report/1998/10/98/world_war_1/197437.stm

A special collection of illustrated articles on World War I including "The War to End All Wars," "War Revolution in Russia," "The Christmas Truce," and many others. Several collections of letters home are included as well.

Great War Series

www.wtj.com/wars/greatwar

This online journal has a collection of World War I archives and several World War I articles including "The Western Front" and "The Eastern Front."

The Balkan Causes of World War I

www.firstworldwar.com/features/balkan_causes.htm

This illustrated essay on the role of the Balkan events in precipitating World War I also includes links to a year-by-year timeline of the war.

World War I Trenches

www.worldwar1.com

Presented and maintained by a WWI enthusiast, this site provides information on armory, war maps, photos, documents, timelines, and other data concerning the prosecution of the world's first global war.

Election of 1916

www.presidency.ucsb.edu/site/elections/1916.htm

Along with the official counts, this site has several sections: "Mandates," "president's party in House elections," "voter turnout," "financing," and "popularity."

Influenza, 1918

www.pbs.org/wgbh/pages/amex/influenza

Companion to the PBS film of the same title, this site reveals the impact of the great flu epidemic of 1918.

Art of the First World War

www.art-ww1.com/gb/index2.html

A cooperative effort of major history museums, this site presents over 100 paintings depicting scenes from World War I.

Women's Suffrage

www.rochester.edu/SBA/history.html

This site includes a chronology, important texts relating to woman suffrage, biographical information on Susan B. Anthony and Elizabeth Cady Stanton.

The Versailles Treaty

http://history.acusd.edu/gen/text/versaillestreaty/vercontents.html

The complete treaty is presented on the site along with links to relevant maps, photos, and political cartoons.

23

Affluence and Anxiety

The movies, illegal liquor, the stock market, and the new jazz dances all appear in Thomas Hart Benton's painting of the pleasures of urban life in the 1920s. *(City Activities with Dance Hall, 1930, Courtesy Maurice Segoura Gallery, New York)*

✦ *American Stories*

A BLACK SHARECROPPER AND HIS FAMILY MOVE NORTH

John and Lizzie Parker were black sharecroppers who lived in a "stubborn, ageless hut squatted on a little hill" in central Alabama. They had two daughters—one age six, the other already married. The whole family worked hard in the cotton fields, but they had little to show for their labor. One day in 1917, Lizzie straightened her shoulders and declared, "I'm through. I've picked my last sack of cotton. I've cleared my last field." Like many southern African Americans, the Parkers sought opportunity and a better life in the North. World War I cut off the flow of immigrants from Europe, and suddenly there was a shortage of workers. Some companies sent special trains into the South to recruit African Americans. John Parker signed up with a mining company in West Virginia. The company offered free transportation for his family. "You will be allowed to get your food at the company store and there are houses awaiting for you," the agent promised.

The sound of the train whistle seemed to promise better days ahead for her family as Lizzie gathered her possessions and headed north. But it turned out that the houses in the company town in West Virginia were little better than those they left in Alabama. After deducting for rent and for supplies from the company store, almost no money was left at the end of the week. John hated the dirty and dangerous work in the mine and realized that he would never get ahead by staying there. But instead of venting his anger on his white boss, he ran away, leaving his family in West Virginia.

John drifted to Detroit, where he got a job with the American Car and Foundry Company. It was 1918, and the pay was good, more than he had ever made before. After a few weeks, he rented an apartment and sent for his family. For the first time, Lizzie had a gas stove and an indoor toilet, and Sally, who was now seven, started school. It seemed as if their dream had come true. John had always believed that if he worked hard and treated his fellow man fairly, he would succeed.

Detroit was not quite the dream, however. It was crowded with all kinds of migrants, many attracted by the wartime jobs at the Ford Motor Company and other factories. The new arrivals increased the racial tension already present in the city. Sally was beaten up by a gang of white youths at school. Even in their neighborhood, which had been solidly Jewish before their arrival, the shopkeeper and the old residents made it clear that they did not like blacks moving into their community. The Ku Klux Klan, which gained many new members in Detroit, also made life uncomfortable for the blacks who had moved north to seek jobs and opportunity. Suddenly the war ended, and almost immediately John lost his job. Then the landlord raised the rent, and the Parkers were forced to leave their apartment for housing in a section just outside the city near Eight Mile Road. The surrounding suburbs had paved streets, wide lawns, and elegant houses, but this black ghetto had dirt streets and shacks that reminded the Parkers of the company town where they had lived in West Virginia. Lizzie had to get along without her bathroom, for here there was no indoor plumbing and no electricity, only a pump in the yard and an outhouse.

The recession winter of 1921–1922 was particularly difficult. The auto industry and other companies laid off most of their workers. John could find only part-time employment, while Lizzie worked as a domestic servant for white families. Because no bus route connected the black community to surrounding suburbs, she often had to trek miles through the snow. The shack they called home was freezing cold, and it was cramped because their married daughter and her husband had joined them in Detroit.

Lizzie did not give up her dream, however. With strength, determination, and a sense of humor, she kept the family together. In 1924, Sally entered high school. By the end of the decade, Sally had graduated from high school, and the Parkers finally had electricity and indoor plumbing in the house, though the streets were still unpaved. Those unpaved streets stood as a symbol of their unfulfilled dream. The Parkers, like most of the African Americans who moved north in the decade after World War I, had improved their lot, but they still lived outside Detroit—and, in many ways, outside America.

Like most Americans in the 1920s, the Parkers pursued the American dream of success. For them, a comfortable house and a steady job, a new bathroom, and an education for their younger daughter constituted that dream. For others during the decade, the symbol of success was a new automobile, a new suburban house, or perhaps making a killing on the stock market. The Parkers, like all Americans, whether they realized it or not, were influenced by a global market beyond their control. The 1920s, the decade between the end of World War I and the stock market crash, has often been referred to as the "jazz age," a time when the American people had one long party complete with flappers, speakeasies, illegal bathtub gin, and young people doing the Charleston long into the night. This frivolous interpretation has some basis in fact, but most Americans did not share in the party, for they were too busy struggling to make a living.

In this chapter, we will explore some of the conflicting trends of an exciting decade. First, we will examine the currents of intolerance that influenced almost all the events and social movements of the time. We will also look at some developments in technology, especially the automobile, which changed life for almost everyone during the 1920s and created the illusion of prosperity for all. We will then focus on groups—women, blacks, industrial workers, and farmers—who had their hopes raised but not always fulfilled during the decade. We will conclude by looking at the way business, politics, and foreign policy were intertwined during the age of Harding, Coolidge, and Hoover.

POSTWAR PROBLEMS

The enthusiasm for social progress that marked the war years evaporated in 1919. Public housing, social insurance, government ownership of the railroads, and many other experiments quickly ended. The sense of progress and purpose that the war had fostered withered. The year following the end of the war was marked by strikes and violence and by fear that Bolsheviks, blacks, foreigners, and others were destroying the American way of life. Some of the fear and intolerance resulted from wartime patriotism, while some arose from the postwar economic and political turmoil that forced Americans to deal with new and immensely troubling situations.

Red Scare

Americans have often feared radicals and other groups that seem to be conspiring to overthrow the American way of life. In the 1840s, the 1890s, and at other times in the past, Catholics, Mormons, Populists, immigrants, and holders of many political views have all been attacked as dangerous and "un-American." But before 1917, anarchists seemed to pose the worst threat. The Russian Revolution changed that. *Bolshevik* suddenly became the most dangerous and devious radical, while *Communist* was transformed from a member of a utopian community to a dreaded, threatening subversive. For some Americans, Bolshevik and German became somehow mixed together, especially after the Treaty of Brest-Litovsk in 1918 removed the new Soviet state from the war. In the spring of 1919, with the Russian announcement of a policy of worldwide revolution and with Communist uprisings in Hungary

and Bavaria, many Americans feared that the Communists planned to take over the United States. There were a few American Communists, but they never really threatened the United States or the American way of life.

Some idealists, like John Reed, found developments in Russia inspiring. Reed, the son of a wealthy businessman, was born in Oregon and went east to a private school and then to Harvard. After graduation, he drifted to New York's Greenwich Village, where he joined his classmate Walter Lippmann as well as Max Eastman, Mabel Dodge, and other intellectuals and radicals. This group converted Reed to socialism and made him understand that "my happiness is built on the misery of others."

In Europe shortly after the war began, Reed was appalled by the carnage in what he considered a capitalistic war. The news of the Russian tsar's abdication in 1917 brought him to Russia just in time to witness the bloody Bolshevik takeover. His eyewitness account, *Ten Days That Shook the World*, optimistically predicted a worldwide revolution. However, when he saw how little hope there was for that revolution in postwar America, he returned to the Soviet Union. By the time he died from typhus in 1920, the authoritarian nature of the new Russian regime caused him to become disillusioned.

The "Red Menace" and the Palmer Raids

Reed was one of the romantic American intellectuals who saw great hope for the future in the Russian Revolution. His mentor Lincoln Steffens, the muckraking journalist, remarked after a visit to the Soviet

Union a few years later, "I have been over into the future and it works." But relatively few Americans, even among those who had been Socialists, and fewer still among the workers, joined the Communist party. Perhaps in all there were 25,000 to 40,000 party members, and those were split into two groups: the American Communist party and the Communist Labor party. The threat to the American system of government was very slight. But in 1919, the Communists seemed to be a threat, particularly as a series of devastating strikes erupted across the country. Workers in the United States had suffered from wartime inflation, which had almost doubled prices between 1914 and 1919, while most wages remained the same. During 1919, more than 4 million workers took part in 4,000 strikes. Few wanted to overthrow the government; rather, they demanded higher wages, shorter hours, and in some cases more control over the workplace.

On January 21, 1919, some 35,000 shipyard workers went on strike in Seattle, Washington. Within a few days, a general strike paralyzed the city; transportation and business stopped. The mayor of Seattle called for federal troops. Within five days, using strong-arm tactics, the mayor put down the strike and was hailed across the country as a "red-blooded patriot."

Yet the strikes continued elsewhere. In September 1919, all 343,000 employees of U.S. Steel walked out in an attempt to win an eight-hour day and an "American living wage." The average workweek in the steel industry in 1919 was 68.7 hours; the unskilled worker averaged $1,400 per year, while the minimum subsistence for a family of five that same year was estimated at $1,575. Within days, the strike spread to Bethlehem Steel.

From the beginning, the owners blamed the strikes on the Bolsheviks. They put ads in the newspapers urging workers to "Stand by America, Show Up the Red Agitator." They also imported strikebreakers, provoked riots, broke up union meetings, and finally used police and soldiers to end the strike. Eighteen strikers were killed. Because most people believed that the Communists had inspired the strike, the issue of long hours and poor pay got lost, and eventually the union surrendered.

While the steel strike was still in progress, the police in Boston went on strike. Like most other workers, the police were struggling to survive on prewar salaries in inflationary times. The Boston newspapers blamed the strike on Communist influence, but one writer warned that the protest could not succeed because "behind Boston in this skirmish with Bolshevism stands Massachusetts and behind Massachusetts stands America." College students

and army veterans volunteered to replace the police and prevent looting in the city. The president of Harvard assured the students that their grades would not suffer. The government quickly broke the strike and fired the policemen. When Samuel Gompers urged Governor Calvin Coolidge to ask the Boston authorities to reinstate them, Coolidge responded with the laconic statement that made him famous and eventually helped him win the presidency: "There is no right to strike against the public safety by anybody, anywhere, anytime."

To many Americans, strikes were bad enough, especially strikes that dangerous radicals seemingly inspired, but bombs were even worse. The "bomb-throwing radical" was almost a cliché, probably stemming from the hysteria over the Haymarket Riot of 1886. On April 28, 1919, a bomb was discovered in a small package delivered to the home of the mayor of Seattle. The next day, the maid of a former senator from Georgia opened a package, and a bomb blew her hands off. Other bombings occurred in June, including one that shattered the front of Attorney General A. Mitchell Palmer's home in Washington. The bombings seem to have been the work of misguided radicals who thought they might spark a genuine revolution in America. But their effect was to provide substantial evidence that revolution was around the corner, even though most American workers wanted only shorter hours, better working conditions, and a chance to realize the American dream.

The strikes and bombs, combined with the general postwar mood of distrust and suspicion, persuaded many people of a real and immediate threat to the nation. No one was more convinced than A. Mitchell Palmer. From a Quaker family in a small Pennsylvania town, the attorney general had graduated from Swarthmore College and had been admitted to the Pennsylvania bar in 1893 at the age of 21. After serving three terms as a congressman, he helped swing the Pennsylvania delegation to Wilson at the 1912 convention.

Wilson offered him the post of secretary of war, but Palmer's pacifism led him to refuse. He did support the United States' entry into the war, however, and served as alien property custodian, a job created by the Trading with the Enemy Act. This position apparently convinced him of the danger of radical subversive activities in America. The bombing of his home intensified his fears, and in the summer of 1919, he determined to find and destroy the Red network. He organized a special anti-radical division within the Justice Department and put a young man named J. Edgar Hoover in charge of coordinating information on domestic radical activities.

Obsessed with the "Red Menace," Palmer instituted a series of raids, beginning in November 1919. Simultaneously, in several cities, his men rounded up 250 members of the Union of Russian Workers, many of whom were beaten and roughed up in the process. In December, 249 aliens, including the famous anarchist Emma Goldman, were deported, although very few were Communists and even fewer had any desire to overthrow the government of the United States. Palmer's men arrested 500 people in Detroit and 800 in Boston.

The Palmer raids, one of the most massive violations of civil liberties in American history to this date, found few dangerous radicals but did fan the flames of fear and intolerance in the country. In Indiana, a jury quickly acquitted a man who had killed an alien for yelling, "To hell with the United States." Billy Sunday, a Christian evangelist, suggested that the best solution was to shoot aliens rather than to deport them.

Palmer became a national hero for ferreting out Communists, but Assistant Secretary of State Louis Post insisted that the arrested aliens be given legal rights, and in the end, only about 600 were deported out of the more than 5,000 arrested. The worst of the "Red Scare" was over by the end of 1920, but the fear of radicals and the emotional patriotism survived throughout the decade to color almost every aspect of politics, daily life, and social legislation.

The Red Scare promoted many patriotic organizations and societies determined to eliminate Communism from American life. The best known was the American Legion, but there were also the American Defense Society, the Sentinels of the Republic (whose motto was "Every Citizen a Sentinel, Every Home a Sentry Box"), the United States Flag Association, and the Daughters of the American Revolution. Such groups provided a sense of purpose and a feeling of belonging in a rapidly changing America. But often what united their efforts was an obsessive fear of Communists and radicals.

Some organizations targeted women social reformers. One group attacked the "Hot-House, Hull House Variety of Parlor Bolshevists" and during the 1920s circulated a number of "spider-web charts" that purported to connect liberals and progressives, especially progressive women, to Communist organizations. In one such chart, even the Needlework Guild and the Sunshine Society were accused of being influenced by Communists. The connections were made only through the use of half-truths, innuendo, and outright lies. To protest their charges did little good, for the accusers knew the truth and

would not be deflected from their purpose of exterminating dangerous radicals.

Ku Klux Klan

Among the superpatriotic organizations claiming to protect the American way of life, the Ku Klux Klan was the most extreme. The Klan was organized in Georgia by William J. Simmons, a lay preacher, salesman, and member of many fraternal organizations. He adopted the name and white-sheet uniform of the old antiblack Reconstruction organization that was glorified in 1915 in the immensely popular but racist feature film *Birth of a Nation.* Simmons appointed himself head ("Imperial Wizard") of the new Klan.

Unlike the original organization, which took almost anyone who was white, the new Klan was thoroughly Protestant and explicitly anti-foreign, anti-Semitic, and anti-Catholic. As an increasing number of second- and third-generation American Catholics began to achieve some success, even winning elections at the state and municipal level, many Protestants began to worry. The Klan declared that "America is Protestant and so it must remain." It opposed the teaching of evolution; glorified old-time religion; supported immigration restriction; denounced short skirts, petting, and "demon rum"; and upheld patriotism and the purity of women. The Klan was also militantly anti-black and its members took as their special mission the task of keeping blacks in their "proper place." They often used peaceful measures to accomplish their aim, but if those failed, they resorted to violence, kidnapping, and lynching.

The Klan grew slowly until after the war. In some places, returning veterans could join the Klan and the American Legion at the same table. The Klan added over 100,000 new members in 1920 alone. It grew rapidly because of aggressive recruiting but also because of the fear and confusion of the postwar period. A great many women joined the Klan. In some states Women of the Ku Klux Klan (WKKK) made up more than half the membership. Although women shared the ideology of their male counterparts, they also campaigned for women's rights and for equal treatment of all white, Protestant women. For both men and women, the Klan served as a social club—a club that kept out all who were different and dangerous.

The Klan flourished in small towns and rural areas in the South, where it set out to keep the returning black soldiers in their "proper place," but it soon spread throughout the country; at least half the members came from urban areas. The Klan was

The Klan, with its elaborate rituals and white uniforms, exploited the fear of blacks, Jews, liberals, and Catholics while preaching "traditional" American values. The appeal of the Klan was not limited to the South. This is a photo of a Klan initiation ceremony. *(FPG International)*

especially strong in the working-class neighborhoods of Detroit, Indianapolis, Atlanta, and Chicago, where the migration of African Americans and other ethnic groups increased fear of everything "un-American." At the peak of its power, the Klan had several million members, many of them from the middle class. In some states, especially Indiana, Colorado, Oregon, Oklahoma, Louisiana, and Texas, it influenced politics and determined some elections. The Klan's power declined after 1925 because of a series of internal power struggles and several scandals. The Klan survived in some areas into the 1930s, but it had all but disappeared by the outbreak of World War II. Yet the end of the Klan did not mean the end of prejudice.

The Sacco-Vanzetti Case

One result of the Red Scare and the unreasoned fear of foreigners and radicals, which dragged on through much of the decade, was the conviction and sentencing of two Italian anarchists, Nicola Sacco and Bartolomeo Vanzetti. Arrested in 1920 for allegedly murdering a guard during a robbery of the shoe factory in South Braintree, Massachusetts, the two were convicted and sentenced to die in the

summer of 1921 on what many liberals considered circumstantial and flimsy evidence. Indeed, it seemed to many that the two Italians, who spoke in broken English and were admitted anarchists, were punished because of their radicalism and their foreign appearance.

Even now, it is not clear whether Sacco and Vanzetti were guilty, but the case took on symbolic significance as many intellectuals in Europe and America rallied to their defense and to the defense of civil liberties. Appeal after appeal failed, but finally the governor of Massachusetts appointed a commission to reexamine the evidence in the case. The commission reaffirmed the verdict, and the two were executed in the electric chair on August 23, 1927, despite massive protests and midnight vigils around the country. But the case and the cause would not die. On the fiftieth anniversary of their deaths in 1977, Governor Michael Dukakis of Massachusetts exonerated Sacco and Vanzetti and cleared their names.

Religious Intolerance

The KKK and well-publicized cases like Sacco-Vanzetti touched a relatively small number of people, but a general spirit of intolerance permeated the decade and influenced the lives of millions. In Dearborn, Michigan, Henry Ford published anti-Semitic diatribes in the *Dearborn Independent,* and many country clubs and resort hotels prohibited Jews from even entering the doors. Unable to frequent the fashionable resorts, Jews built their own in the Catskills in New York State, Long Branch in New Jersey, and other areas. Many colleges, private academies, and medical schools had Jewish quotas, some openly and others informally, and many suburbs explicitly limited residents to "Christians." Catholics, too, were prohibited from many fashionable and fraternal organizations as well as many country clubs, but unlike Jews, Catholics created their own schools and colleges. Few Catholics even tried to enroll in the elite colleges where bias against Catholics and Catholicism remained. There had always been a great deal of prejudice and intolerance in the United States, but during the decade of the 1920s, much of that intolerance was made more fixed and formal.

A PROSPERING ECONOMY

Although the decade after World War I was a time of intolerance and anxiety, it was also a time of industrial expansion and widespread prosperity. After recovering from a postwar depression in 1921 and 1922, the economy took off. Fueled by new technology, more efficient planning and management, and innovative advertising, industrial production almost doubled during the decade, and the gross national product rose by an astonishing 40 percent. A construction boom created new suburbs around American cities, and a new generation of skyscrapers transformed the cities themselves. However, the benefits of this prosperity fell unevenly on the many social groups that formed American society.

While the American economy boomed, much of the rest of the world suffered in the aftermath of the war. Germany, wracked by inflation so great that it took millions of marks to buy a loaf of bread, sunk into depression and was unable to make reparation payments. Great Britain and France recovered slowly from the war's devastation. Although it was not clear at the time, it became obvious later that the United States was part of a global economy and eventually would be affected by the economic difficulties of the rest of the world.

The Rising Standard of Living

Signs of the new prosperity appeared in many forms. Millions of sturdy homes and apartments were built and equipped with the latest conveniences. The number of telephones installed nearly

A German woman in 1923 uses the devalued mark to light a fire because it was cheaper to use paper currency than to purchase kindling wood or even a newspaper. Women used baby carriages to carry enough money to buy a loaf of bread. A postage stamp cost a million marks. Most European countries faced inflation in the postwar years, but it was the worst in Germany. In 1918, a mark was worth about a dollar. By January 1923, it took 7,000 marks to buy a dollar; by February, 18,000; by July, 160,000; by August, 1 million; and by December, 4 trillion marks to equal a dollar. The hyperinflation, caused by the war and by the harsh peace settlement, wiped out the savings of the middle class, led to depression, and contributed directly to the rise of Hitler.

doubled between 1915 and 1930. Plastics, rayon, and cellophane altered the habits of millions of Americans, and new products, such as cigarette lighters, reinforced concrete, dry ice, and Pyrex glass created new demands unheard of a decade before.

Perhaps the most tangible sign of the new prosperity was the modern American bathroom. For years, the various functions we associate with the bathroom were separated. There was an outhouse or privy, a portable tin bathtub filled with water heated on the kitchen stove, and a pitcher and washbasin in the bedroom. Hotels and the urban upper class began to install cast-iron bathtubs and primitive flush toilets in the late nineteenth century, but not until the early 1920s did the enameled tub, toilet, and washbasin become standard. By 1925, American factories turned out 5 million enameled bathroom fixtures annually. The bathroom, with unlimited hot water, privacy, and clean white fixtures, symbolized American affluence.

In sharp contrast to people in European countries, middle-class Americans had more leisure time, a shorter work week, and more vacations with pay. The American diet also improved during the decade. Health improved and life expectancy increased. Educational opportunities also expanded. In 1900, only one in ten young people of high-school age remained in school; by 1930, that number had increased to six in ten, and much of the improvement came in the 1920s. In 1900, only one college-age person in 33 attended an institution of higher learning; by 1930, the ratio was one in seven, and over a million people were enrolled in the nation's colleges.

The Rise of the Modern Corporation

The structure and practice of American business were transformed in the 1920s. After a crisis created by the economic downturn of 1920–1922, business boomed until the crash of 1929. Mergers increased during the decade at a rate greater than at any time since the end of the 1890s—there were more than 1,200 mergers in 1929 alone—creating such giants as General Electric, General Motors, Sears Roebuck, Du Pont, and U.S. Rubber. These were not monopolies but oligopolies (industry domination spread among a few large firms). By 1930, the 200 largest corporations controlled almost half the corporate wealth in the country.

Perhaps the most important business trend of the decade was the emergence of a new kind of manager. No longer did family entrepreneurs make decisions relating to prices, wages, and output. Alfred P. Sloan, Jr., an engineer who reorganized General Motors, was a prototype of the new kind of manager. He divided the company into components, freeing the top managers to concentrate on planning new products, controlling inventory, and integrating the whole operation. Marketing and advertising became as important as production, and many businesses began to spend more money on research. The new manager often had a large staff but owned no part of the company. He was usually an expert at cost accounting and analyzing data. Increasingly, he was a graduate of one of the new business colleges.

Continuing and extending the trends started by Frederick Taylor before World War I, the new managers tried to keep employees working efficiently, but they used more than the stopwatch and the assembly line. They introduced pensions, recreation facilities, cafeterias, and, in some cases, paid vacations and profit-sharing plans. But the managers were not being altruistic; rather, "welfare capitalism" was designed to reduce worker discontent and to discourage labor unions.

Planning was the key to the new corporate structure, and planning often meant a continuation of the business–government cooperation that had developed during World War I. Experts from philanthropic foundations, the National Bureau of Economic Research, and the U.S. Department of Commerce worked together, hoping that they could provide a middle ground between collectivism and laissez-faire economy. All the planning and the new managerial authority failed to prevent the economic collapse of 1929, but the modern corporation survived the depression to exert a growing influence on American life in the 1930s and after.

Electrification

The 1920s also marked the climax of the "second Industrial Revolution," which was powered by electricity—a form of energy that rapidly replaced steam power after 1900. In the previous two decades, inventors such as Thomas A. Edison and George Westinghouse had developed generators for producing electric current and methods for transmitting it and using it to drive machinery. Edison's illuminating company opened the first commercial power station in New York in 1882; by the end of the century, more than 3,000 stations were supplying businesses and homes with electricity. Meanwhile, Edison's most famous invention, the electric lightbulb, was rapidly replacing gas lanterns in homes and on streets.

Between 1900 and 1920, the replacement of steam power by electricity worked as profound a change as had the substitution of steam power for water power after the Civil War. In 1902, electricity supplied a mere 2 percent of all industrial power; by 1929, fully 80 percent was derived from electrical generators. Less than one out of every ten American homes was supplied with electricity in 1907, but more than two-thirds were by 1929. Powered by electricity, American industries reached new heights of productivity. By 1929, the workforce was turning out twice as many goods as a similarly sized workforce had ten years before.

Electricity brought dozens of gadgets and labor-saving devices into the home. Washing machines and electric irons gradually reduced the drudgery of wash day for women, and vacuum cleaners, electric toasters, and sewing machines lightened housework. But the new machines still needed human direction and did not reduce the time the average housewife spent doing housework. For many

Advertising

Have you ever noticed that television commercials can often be more interesting and creative than the programs? One authority has suggested that the best way for a foreign visitor to understand the American character and popular culture is to study television commercials. Television advertising, the thesis goes, appeals to basic cultural assumptions. The nature of advertising not only reveals for historians the prejudices, fears, values, and aspirations of a people but also makes an impact on historical development itself, influencing patterns of taste and purchasing habits. One modern critic calls advertising a "peculiarly American force that now compares with such long-standing institutions as the school and church in the magnitude of its social impact."

As long as manufacturing was local and limited, there was no need to advertise. Before the Civil War, for example, the local area could usually absorb all that was produced; therefore, a simple announcement in a local paper was sufficient to let people know that a particular product was available. But when factories began producing more than the local market could ordinarily consume, advertising came into play to create a larger demand.

Although national advertising began with the emergence of "name brands" in the late nineteenth century, it did not achieve the importance it now holds until the 1920s. In 1918, the total gross advertising revenue in magazines was $58.5 million. By 1920, it had more than doubled to $129.5 million, and by 1929, it was nearly $200 million. These figures should not be surprising in a decade that often equated advertising with religion. The biblical Moses was called the "ad-writer for the Deity," and in a best-selling book, Bruce Barton, a Madison Avenue advertiser, reinterpreted Jesus, the "man nobody knows," as a master salesman. Wrote Barton: "He would be a national advertiser today."

The designers of ads began to study psychology to determine what motives, conscious or unconscious, influenced consumers. One psychologist concluded that the appeal to the human instinct for "gaining social prestige" would sell the most goods. Another way to sell products, many learned, was to create anxiety in the mind of the consumer over body odor, bad breath, oily hair, dandruff, pimples, and other embarrassing ailments. In 1921, the

"...and Jane, dear... Jack just raved about my teeth."

"I just smiled my prettiest smile ... and let him rave. I could have said 'Of course I have beautiful teeth ... I've used Colgate's all my life'. But I didn't want Jack to think I was a living advertisement for Colgate's tooth paste."

* * * *

Beautiful teeth glisten gloriously. They compel the admiration of all who see them. And there is health as well as beauty in gleaming teeth, for when they are scrupulously kept clean, germs and poisons of decay can't lurk and breed around them.

Remove Those Causes of Decay

Save yourself the embarrassment so often caused by poor teeth. Fight the germs of tooth decay.

Colgate's will keep your teeth scrupulously clean. It reaches all the hard-to-get-at places between the teeth and around the edges of the gums, and so removes causes of tooth decay. It is the dependable tooth paste for you to use.

Washes — Polishes — Protects

The principal ingredients of Colgate's are mild soap and fine chalk, the two

things that dental authorities say a safe dental cream should contain. The combined action of these ingredients washes, polishes and protects the delicate enamel of your teeth.

Use Colgate's Regularly

Just remember that beautiful, healthy teeth are more a matter of good care than of good luck. Use Colgate's after meals and at bedtime. It will keep your teeth clean and gloriously attractive.

And you'll like its taste ... even children love to use it regularly.

Priced right too! Large tube 25c.

Colgate & Co.
Established 1806

COLGATE'S RIBBON DENTAL CREAM

Toothpaste advertisement. *(Courtesy of Colgate-Palmolive)*

Lambert Company used the term *halitosis* for bad breath in an ad for Listerine. Within six years, sales of Listerine had increased from a little over 100,000 bottles a year to more than 4 million.

The appeal to sex also sold products, advertisers soon found, as did the desire for the latest style or invention. But perhaps the most important thing advertisers marketed was youth. "We are going to sell every artificial thing there is," a cosmetic salesman wrote in 1926, "and above all it is going to be young-young-young! We make women feel young."

A great portion of the ads were aimed at women. As one trade journal announced: "The proper study of mankind is man . . . , but the proper study of markets is woman."

Reflecting on the Past   Look at the accompanying advertisements carefully. What do they tell you about American culture in the 1920s? What do they suggest about attitudes toward women? Do they reveal any special anxieties? How are they similar to and different from advertising today?

Automobile advertisement (1929). *(Corbis-Bettmann)*

For Clean-up King I Nominate . . .
by LOU GEHRIG
New York Yankees' Clean-up Ace Makes Novel Choice for All-Time Honor

I DON'T need to tell baseball fans how important the "clean-up" (number four) man is in the batting line-up. With three reliable hitters batting ahead of him, it is his wallops that bring in the runs.

In my thirteen years of big league baseball I have watched some of the most famous "clean-up" men in the history of the game. But the other day in Boston I had the pleasure of seeing the "clean-up" king that gets my vote for the "all-time" honors. Strangely enough, this "clean-up" king isn't a slugger at all. Instead of cleaning up the bases, this one's specialty is cleaning up faces.

Here's how it happened. While in Boston playing the Red Sox, I made an inspection trip through the Gillette Safety Razor factory. There I discovered that what is true of baseball is also true of Gillette Blades. In baseball, the pick of the raw material is tried out, tested, and trained for the big league teams. At the Gillette factory I found that they buy only the finest steel, and put it through gruelling tests before it is made into Gillette Blades.

For instance, like a rookie baseball player, Gillette Blade steel has to be hardened and tempered.

To do this, Gillette uses electric furnaces, each one controlled by a device which can tell in an instant if the steel passing through the furnaces requires more heat or less heat. Faster than a speedball, the signal is flashed from the box to a great battery of switches, and the heat is raised or lowered accordingly. Then to make doubly sure that there is no possibility of error, they X-ray the steel with an electro-magnetic tester to detect hidden flaws.

A good ball player has to have precision and accuracy, too . . . and that's where Gillette chalks up a winning score. Grinding machines, adjustable to 1/10,000 of an inch give Gillette Blades shaving edges so keen you can't see them, even with the most powerful microscope.

These are some of the reasons why I nominate the Gillette Blade for all-time Clean-up King. For when it comes to cleaning up on stubborn bristles—with the greatest of ease and comfort—Gillette hits a home run with the bases loaded. Yes, Sir!—if baseball could only train players as accurately and efficiently as Gillette makes razor blades, we'd all find it easy to bat 1000.

With these important facts before you, why let anyone deprive you of shaving comfort by selling you a substitute! Ask for Gillette Blades and be sure to get them.

GILLETTE SAFETY RAZOR COMPANY, BOSTON, MASS.

Razor blade advertisement. *(R. Kravette, Jericho, New York)* poor urban and rural women, the traditional female tasks of carrying, pushing, pulling, and lifting went on as they had for centuries. In many ways, the success of the electric revolution increased the contrast in American life. The "great white ways" of the cities symbolized progress, but they also made the darkness of slums and hamlets seem even more forbidding.

A Global Automobile Culture

Automobile manufacturing, like electrification, underwent spectacular growth in the 1920s, and the United States led the way. The automobile was one major factor in the postwar economic boom. It stimulated and transformed the petroleum, steel, and rubber industries. The auto forced the construction and improvement of streets and highways and caused the spending of millions of dollars on labor and concrete. In 1925, the secretary of agriculture approved the first uniform numbering system for the nation's highways, but it was still an adventure to drive from one city to another.

The best known transcontinental road was the Lincoln Highway. It started in New York, continued to Philadelphia, Pittsburgh, Fort Wayne, and Joliet, and then roughly traced the route of the first transcontinental railroad to Omaha, Cheyenne, Salt Lake City, Reno, and San Francisco (paralleling today's Route 80.) The Lincoln Highway was marked using existing roads in 1913, but large sections were barely passable until well into the 1920s. Beginning in 1916, with the Federal Highway Act, the government began to aid road building. The federal government matched state funds on a one-to-one basis for some roads. Another Highway Act in 1921 increased federal funding, but the great majority of roads remained under state or local control. In Europe, where the national governments built the roads, the highways were superior in the 1920s, but there were far fewer cars in Europe and the distance between cities much less than in the United States.

The auto created new suburbs and allowed families to live many miles from their work. The filling station, the diner, and the tourist court became familiar and eventually standardized objects on the American scene. Traffic lights, stop signs, billboards, and parking lots appeared. Hitching posts and watering troughs became rarer, and gradually the garage replaced the livery stable. The auto changed the look of the American landscape and threatened the environment as well. Oil and gasoline contaminated streams, and piles of old tires and rusting hulks of discarded cars became a familiar sight along the highways. At the same time, the emissions from thousands and then millions of internal combustion engines polluted the air. The increasing use of nonrenewable fossil fuels was already apparent in the 1920s, and it was a trend that would continue. In 1916, American oil refineries produced 50 million barrels of gasoline; in 1929, production had increased to 425 million barrels. But there was no turning back. The age of the auto had replaced the age of the horse.

The auto changed American life in other ways. It led to the decline of the small crossroads store as well as many small churches because the rural family could now drive to the larger city or town. The tractor changed methods of farming. Trucks replaced the horse and wagon and altered the marketing of farm products. Buses began to eliminate the one-room school, because it was now possible to transport students to larger schools. The automobile allowed young people for the first time to escape the chaperoning of parents. It was hardly the "house of prostitution on wheels" that one judge called it, but it did change courting habits in all parts of the country.

Gradually, as the decade progressed, the automobile became not just transportation but a sign of status. Advertising helped create the impression that it was the symbol of the good life, of sex, freedom, and speed. The auto in turn transformed advertising and design. It even altered the way products were purchased. By 1926, three-fourths of the cars sold were bought on some kind of deferred-payment plan. Installment credit, first tried by a group of businessmen in Toledo, Ohio, in 1915 to sell more autos, was soon used to promote sewing machines, refrigerators, and other consumer products. "Buy now, pay later" became the American way.

The United States had a love affair with the auto from the beginning. There were 8,000 motor vehicles registered in the country in 1900, and nearly a million in 1912. But only in the 1920s did the auto come within the reach of middle-class consumers. In 1929, Americans purchased 4.5 million cars, and by the end of that year, nearly 27 million were registered. In p rt because of Henry Ford and the development of the inexpensive car, and because the United States had a much larger middle class who could afford a car, the ownership of automobiles expanded much more rapidly in the United States. Most European autos were custom-made. Morris Motors, the most important British company, did not adopt the assembly line until 1934. France, Germany, and England all subsidized auto manufacture for military purposes, further delaying the development of an inexpensive car. But because of their strong central governments, European countries adopted safety standards and required national

ANALYZING HISTORY

THE IMPACT OF THE AUTOMOBILE

With the introduction of the automobile, the isolation of rural life gradually disappeared. The construction and improvement of roads and highways meant that Americans were logging more miles for both leisure travel and the transportation of goods and materials. However, coupled with the increase in autos was the number of auto-related deaths.

Reflecting on the Past In what ways did the automobile contribute to the postwar economic boom? What do you think accounted for the decrease in auto deaths between 1940 and 1943, even as the number of motor vehicles on the road continued to increase? Why were auto factories concentrated in the Midwest? What other impact did the auto have on American lives that is not explored in these charts?

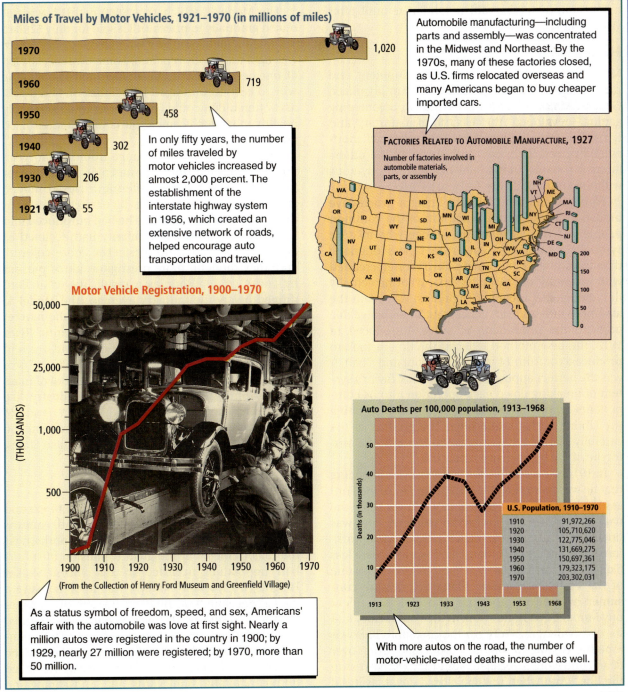

Miles of Travel by Motor Vehicles, 1921–1970 (in millions of miles)

1970 — 1,020
1960 — 719
1950 — 458
1940 — 302
1930 — 206
1921 — 55

In only fifty years, the number of miles traveled by motor vehicles increased by almost 2,000 percent. The establishment of the interstate highway system in 1956, which created an extensive network of roads, helped encourage auto transportation and travel.

Automobile manufacturing—including parts and assembly—was concentrated in the Midwest and Northeast. By the 1970s, many of these factories closed, as U.S. firms relocated overseas and many Americans began to buy cheaper imported cars.

FACTORIES RELATED TO AUTOMOBILE MANUFACTURE, 1927
Number of factories involved in automobile materials, parts, or assembly

Motor Vehicle Registration, 1900–1970

(From the Collection of Henry Ford Museum and Greenfield Village)

As a status symbol of freedom, speed, and sex, Americans' affair with the automobile was love at first sight. Nearly a million autos were registered in the country in 1900; by 1929, nearly 27 million were registered; by 1970, more than 50 million.

Auto Deaths per 100,000 population, 1913–1968

U.S. Population, 1910–1970	
1910	91,972,266
1920	105,710,620
1930	122,775,046
1940	131,669,275
1950	150,697,361
1960	179,323,175
1970	203,302,031

With more autos on the road, the number of motor-vehicle-related deaths increased as well.

licenses for vehicles and drivers before such rules were adopted in the United States. In America, the states created the rules, and in the beginning it was assumed that anyone could drive a car. The world agreed on time zones, postage regulations, and other things, but not on which side of the road to drive on. In Great Britain, Australia, Japan, and a few other countries, cars were driven on the left side, while in the United States and most of Europe, driving on the right side was the proper thing to do. Eventually most of the world, following the American lead, was transformed by automobile culture, but in many countries, that did not happen until after World War II.

Henry Ford

Many men contributed to the development and production of the auto—William Durant organized General Motors; Charles Kettering, an engineering genius, developed the electric self-starter; and Ransom E. Olds built the first mass-produced, moderately priced, light car. And above all the others loomed a name that would become synonymous with the automobile itself—Henry Ford.

Ford had the reputation of being a progressive industrial leader and a champion of the common people. As with all men and women who take on symbolic significance, the truth is less dramatic than the stories. For example, Ford is often credited with inventing the assembly line. What he actually did (along with a team of engineers) was adapt the assembly line and the concept of interchangeable parts to the production of autos. Introduced in 1913, the new method reduced the time it took to produce a car from 14 hours to an hour and a half. It was the perfect application of Frederick Taylor's system of breaking down each operation into its components, applying careful timing, and integrating the laborer with the machine. The product of the carefully planned system was the Model T, the prototype of the inexpensive family car.

In 1914, Ford startled the country by announcing that he was increasing the minimum pay of the Ford assembly-line worker to $5 a day (almost twice the national average pay for factory workers). Ford was not a humanitarian. He wanted a dependable workforce and understood that skilled workers were less likely to quit if they received good pay. Ford was one of the first to appreciate that workers were consumers as well as producers and that they might buy Model T Fords. But work in the Ford factory had its disadvantages. Work on the assembly line was repetitive and numbing. "You could drop over dead" one worker recalled, "and they wouldn't stop the line." And when the line closed down, as it did

periodically, the workers were released without compensation.

Henry Ford was not an easy man for whom to work. One newspaper account in 1928 called him "an industrial fascist—the Mussolini of Detroit." He ruthlessly pressured his dealers and used them to bail him out of difficult financial situations. Instead of borrowing money from a bank, he forced dealers to buy extra cars, trucks, and tractors. He used spies on the assembly lines and fired workers and executives at the least provocation. But he did produce a car that transformed America.

The Model T, which cost $600 in 1912, was reduced gradually in price until it sold for only $290 in 1924. The "Tin Lizzie," as it was affectionately called, was light and easily repaired. Some owners claimed all one needed were a pair of pliers and some baling wire to keep it running. If it got stuck on bad roads, as it often did, it could be lifted out by a reasonably healthy man. Replacement parts were standardized and widely available.

The Model T did not change from year to year, nor did it deviate from its one color, black. Except for adding a self-starter, offering a closed model, and making a few minor face-lift changes, Ford kept the Model T in 1927 much as he had introduced it in 1909. By that time, its popularity had declined as many people traded up to sleeker, more colorful, and, they thought, more prestigious autos put out by Ford's competitors; as a result, wages at Ford dipped below the industry average. The Model A, introduced in 1927, did not dominate the market as the Model T had done, but the gigantic River Rouge factory, spreading over a thousand acres in Dearborn, Michigan, was built especially to produce the new model. It became the symbol of mass production in the new era. The auto industry, like most American business, went through a period of consolidation in the 1920s. In 1908, more than 250 companies were producing cars in the United States. By 1929, only 44 remained.

The Exploding Metropolis

The automobile caused American cities to expand into the countryside. In the late nineteenth century, railroads and streetcars had created suburbs near the major cities, but the great expansion of suburban population occurred in the 1920s. Shaker Heights, a Cleveland suburb, was in some ways a typical development. Built on the site of a former Shaker community, the new suburb was planned and developed by two businessmen. They controlled the size and style of the homes and restricted buyers. No blacks were allowed. Curving roads led off the main auto boulevards, and landscaping and

Ten Largest Cities in 1900 and 1930*

1900		1930	
1. New York	4,023,000	1. New York	9,423,000
2. Chicago	1,768,000	2. Chicago	3,870,000
3. Philadelphia	1,458,000	3. Philadelphia	2,399,000
4. Boston	905,000	4. Detroit	1,837,000
5. Pittsburgh	622,000	5. Los Angeles	1,778,000
6. St. Louis	612,000	6. Boston	1,545,000
7. Baltimore	543,000	7. Pittsburgh	1,312,000
8. San Francisco	444,000	8. San Francisco	1,104,000
9. Cincinnati	414,000	9. St. Louis	1,094,000
10. Cleveland	402,000	10. Cleveland	1,048,000

*Figures are for the entire metropolitan areas, including suburbs.

Source: U.S. Bureau of the Census.

natural areas contributed to a parklike atmosphere. The suburb increased in population from 1,700 in 1919 to over 15,000 in 1929, and the price of lots multiplied by ten during the decade.

Other suburbs grew in an equally spectacular manner. Beverly Hills, near Los Angeles, increased in population by 2,485 percent during the decade. Grosse Point Park, near Detroit, grew by 725 percent, and Elmwood Park, near Chicago, increased by 716 percent. The automobile also allowed industry to move to the suburbs. Employees in manufacturing establishments in the suburbs of the 11 largest cities increased from 365,000 in 1919 to 1.2 million in 1937.

The biggest land boom of all occurred in Florida, where the city of Miami mushroomed from 30,000 in 1920 to 75,000 in 1925. One plot of land in West Palm Beach sold for $800,000 in 1923; two years later, it was worth $4 million. A hurricane in 1926 ended the Florida land boom temporarily, but most cities and their suburbs continued to grow during the decade.

The census of 1920 indicated that for the first time, more than half the population of the United States lived in "urban areas" of more than 2,500. The census designation of an urban area was a little misleading because a town of 5,000 could still be more rural than urban. A more significant concept was the metropolitan area of at least 100,000 people. There were only 52 of these areas in 1900, but in 1930 there were 115.

The automobile transformed the city and led to the gradual decline of the street car and the interurban trolly. The most spectacular growth of all took place in two cities that the auto virtually created. Detroit grew from 300,000 in 1900 to 1,837,000 in 1930, and Los Angeles expanded from 114,000 in 1900 to 1,778,000 in 1930. With sprawling subdivi-

sions connected by a growing network of roads, Los Angeles was the city of the future.

Cities expanded horizontally during the 1920s, sprawling into the countryside, but city centers grew vertically. A building boom that peaked near the end of the decade created new skylines for most urban centers. Even cities such as Tulsa, Dallas, Kansas City, Memphis, and Syracuse built skyscrapers. By 1929, there were 377 buildings of over 20 stories in American cities. Many were started just before the stock market crash ended the building boom, and the empty offices stood as a stark reminder of the limits of expansion. The most famous skyscraper of all, the Empire State Building in New York, which towers 102 stories in the air, was finished in 1931 but not completely occupied until after World War II.

A Communications Revolution

Changing communications altered the way many Americans lived as well as the way they conducted business. The telephone was first demonstrated in 1876. By 1899, more than 1 million phones were in operation. During the 1920s, the number of homes with phones increased from 9 to 13 million. Still, by the end of the decade, more than half of American homes were without phones.

Even more than the telephone, the radio symbolized the technological and communicational changes of the 1920s. Department stores quickly began to stock radios, or crystal sets as they were called, but many Americans in the 1920s built their own receivers. The first station to begin commercial broadcasting was WWJ in Detroit in the summer of 1920. When WWJ and KDKA in Pittsburgh broadcast the election returns in 1920, they ushered in a new era in politics. The next year, WJZ of Newark, New Jersey, broadcast the World Series, beginning a

Radio's Reach

The radio spread rapidly throughout the 1920s and 1930s in the United States. By the end of the 1930s, almost all Americans could tune in to their favorite programs, although in some rural areas, especially in the West, reception was possible only at night. Static caused by storms made the signal fade in and out everywhere.

process that would transform baseball and eventually football and basketball as well. Five hundred stations took to the airwaves in 1922 alone, many of them sponsored by department stores and others by newspapers and colleges. In the same year, a radio station in New York broadcast the first commercial, an indication that the airways would be used to increase the demand for the goods the factories were producing.

Much early broadcasting consisted of classical music, but soon came news analysis and coverage of presidential inaugurals and important events. Some stations produced live dramas, but it was the serials such as "Amos 'n' Andy" that more than any other programs made radio a national medium. Millions of people scattered across the country could sit in their living rooms (and after 1927, in their cars) listening to the same program. The record industry grew just as rapidly. By the end of the decade, people in all sections of the country were humming the same popular songs. Actors and announcers became celebrities. The music, voice, and sound of the radio, even more than the sound of

the automobile, marked the end of silence and, to a certain extent, the end of privacy.

Even more dramatic was the phenomenon of the movies. Forty million viewers a week went to the movies in 1922, and by 1929 that number had increased to over 100 million. Early movies were made in New York, Chicago, and a few other cities, but by the mid-1920s, the village of Hollywood, near Los Angeles, had become the movie capital of the world. Giant firms like Metro-Goldwyn-Mayer, created in 1924, dominated the industry, which ranked first among all industries in California. Men, women, and children flocked to small theaters in the towns and to movie palaces in the cities, where they could dream of romance or adventure. Charlie Chaplin, Rudolph Valentino, Lillian Gish, and Greta Garbo were more famous and more important to millions of Americans than were most government officials. The motion pictures, which before the war had attracted mostly the working class, now seemed to appeal across class, regional, and generational lines.

The movies had the power to influence attitudes and ideas. In the 1920s, many parents feared that

Opening night, October 6, 1927, at a theater in Times Square, New York. *The Jazz Singer* with Al Jolson, the first commercially successful film with sound, attracted large audiences. The silent film continued to survive for a few years, but gradually the sound film took over, forcing theaters to buy new equipment and actors to change their style. Some silent-film stars with unattractive voices were forced to retire. *(The Museum of Modern Art, New York, Film Stills Archive)*

the movies would dictate ideas about sex and life. One young college woman remembered, "One day I went to see Viola Dana in *The Five Dollar Baby*. The scenes which showed her as a baby fascinated me so that I stayed to see it over four times. I forgot home, dinner and everything. About eight o'clock mother came after me." She also admitted that the movies taught her how to smoke, and in some of the movies "there were some lovely scenes which just got me all hot 'n' bothered."

Not only movie stars became celebrities in the 1920s. Sports figures such as Babe Ruth, Bobby Jones, Jack Dempsey, and Red Grange were just as famous. The great spectator sports of the decade owed much to the increase in leisure time and to the automobile, the radio, and the mass-circulation newspaper. Thousands drove autos to college towns to watch football heroes perform. Millions listened for scores or read about the results the next day. One writer in 1924 called this era "the age of play." He might better have called it "the age of the spectator." The popularity of sports, like the movies and radio, was in part the product of technology.

The year 1927 seemed to mark the beginning of the new age of mechanization and progress. That was the year Henry Ford produced his 15 millionth car and introduced the Model A. During that year, radio-telephone service was established between San Francisco and Manila. The first radio network was organized (CBS), and the first talking movie was released (*The Jazz Singer*). In 1927, the Holland Tunnel, the first underwater vehicular roadway, connected New York and New Jersey. It was also the year that Charles Lindbergh flew from New York to Paris in his single-engine plane in 33 ½ hours. Lindbergh was not the first to fly the Atlantic, but he was the first to fly it alone, an accomplishment that won him $25,000 in prize money and captured the world's imagination. He was young and handsome, and his feat seemed to represent not only the triumph of an individual but also the triumph of the machine. Lindbergh never talked of his accomplishments in the first person; he always said "we," meaning his airplane as well. He was greeted by 4 million people when he returned to New York for a triumphant ticker-tape parade. Like many movie stars and sports heroes, he had become an instant celebrity. When Americans cheered Lindbergh, they were reaffirming their belief in the American dream and their faith in individual initiative as well as in technology.

HOPES RAISED, PROMISES DEFERRED

The 1920s was a time when all kinds of hopes seemed realizable. "Don't envy successful salesmen—be one!" one advertisement screamed. Buy a car. Build a house. Start a career. Invest in land. Invest in stocks. Make a fortune.

Not all Americans, of course, were intent on making a stock-market killing or expected to win a huge fortune. Some merely wished to retain traditional values in a society that seemed to question them. Others wanted a steady job and a little respect. Still others hungered for the new appliances so alluringly described in ads and on the radio. Many discovered, however, that no matter how modest their hopes might be, they lay tantalizingly out of reach.

Clash of Values

During the 1920s, radio, movies, advertising, and mass-circulation magazines promoted a national, secular culture. But this new culture, which emphasized consumption, pleasure, upward mobility, and even sex, clashed with the traditional values of hard work, thrift, church, family, and home. Although it would be easy to see these cultural differences as a reflection of an urban–rural conflict, in fact, many people clinging to the old ways had moved into the cities. Still, many Americans feared that new cultural values, scientific breakthroughs, and new ideas like bolshevism, relativism, Freudianism, and Biblical criticism threatened their familiar way of life. A trial over the teaching of evolutionary ideas in high school in the little town of Dayton, Tennessee, symbolized, even as it exaggerated, the clash of the old versus the new, the traditional versus the modern, the city versus the country.

The scientific community and most educated people had long accepted the basic concepts of evolution, if not all the details of Charles Darwin's theories. But many Christians, especially those from Protestant evangelical churches, accepted the Bible as the literal truth. They believed that faith in the Gospel message was crucial to living a virtuous life on earth and, more important, going to heaven. Many of these faithful saw a major spiritual crisis in the dramatic changes of the 1920s. Resistance to the concept of evolution resulted in legislative efforts in several states to forbid its teaching. The Tennessee law enacted in 1925 became the most famous, for it made it illegal

> for any teacher in any of the universities, normal and all other public schools of the state to teach any theory that denies the story of the divine creation of man as taught in the Bible and to teach instead that man has descended from a lower order of animals.

John Scopes, a young biology teacher, broke the law by teaching evolutionary theory to his class, and the state of Tennessee brought him to trial. The American Civil Liberties Union hired Clarence Darrow, perhaps the country's most famous defense lawyer, to defend Scopes; the World Christian Fundamentalist Association engaged William Jennings Bryan, former presidential candidate and secretary of state, to assist the prosecution. Bryan was old and tired (he died only a few days after the trial), but he was still an eloquent and deeply religious man. In cross-examination, Darrow reduced Bryan's statements to intellectual rubble and also revealed that Bryan was at a loss to explain much of the Bible. He could not explain how Eve was created from Adam's rib or where Cain got his wife. Nevertheless, the jury declared Scopes guilty, for he had clearly broken the law.

The press from all over the country covered the trial and upheld science and academic freedom. Journalists like H. L. Mencken had a field day poking fun at Bryan and the fundamentalists. "Heave an egg out a Pullman window," Mencken wrote, "and you will hit a Fundamentalist almost anywhere in the United States today. . . . They are everywhere where learning is too heavy a burden for mortal minds to carry."

Religious Fundamentalism

Some observers, including Mencken, thought that the Scopes trial ended what one writer in 1926 called "the fundamentalist menace." Yet religious fundamentalism continued to survive in a world fast becoming urban, modern, and sophisticated. Fundamentalism cut across many denominations and covered over many differences, but all fundamentalists believed in the literal interpretation and the infallibility of the Bible and that Jesus Christ was the only road to salvation. They rejected secularism, liberal theology, pluralism, the Social Gospel, and any sense that reform on earth could lead to perfection. They had a strong and unshakable belief in what they knew was the truth, and they were willing to stand up and fight for their belief.

Throughout the 1920s and the 1930s, attendance at Christian colleges and the circulation of fundamentalist periodicals and newspapers increased dramatically, and evangelical ministers reached large audiences. One of the most popular and flamboyant of the ministers was Billy Sunday, a former baseball player who jumped about the stage as he pitched his brand of Christianity. For Sunday, Christianity and patriotism were synonymous. Another popular preacher was Aimee Semple McPherson, a faith healer who founded her own church, the International Church of the Four Square Gospel, in Los Angeles in 1927. Dressed as a University of Southern California football player, she ran across the stage "carrying the ball for

John Steuart Curry was one of the 1920s regionalist painters who found inspiration in the American heartland. In *Baptism in Kansas*, he depicts a religious ritual that underscores the conflict between rural and urban values. *(John Steuart Curry, [1897–1946], Baptism in Kansas, 1928. Oil on canvas, 40 × 50 in. [101.6 × 127 cm]. Gift of Gertrude Vanderbilt Whitney © 1996 Whitney Museum of American Art, New York [31.159])*

Christ"; wielding a pitchfork, she drove the devil out of the auditorium.

Sunday and McPherson may have been flamboyant performers, but it was the radio that extended the reach of the fundamentalist preachers even more dramatically. McPherson was the first woman to hold a radio license, and she had the second most popular radio show in Los Angeles in the late 1920s. In the 1930s, "The Old Fashioned Revival Hour" was carried on 356 stations and reached an audience of over 20 million people, more than any other prime-time broadcast. For many, the period between the wars was a time when people drifted away from organized religion, an age of technological marvels, and modernism in all fields, but for many others, it was a time when fundamentalist religion and old-fashioned values not only survived but also prospered. Yet many fundamentalist sects succeeded in winning numerous converts because their leaders were skilled at using modern technology.

Immigration and Migration

Immigrants and anyone else perceived as "un-American" seemed to threaten the old ways. A movement to restrict immigration had existed for decades. An act passed in 1882 prohibited the entry of criminals, paupers, and the insane, and special agreements between 1880 and 1908 restricted both Chinese and Japanese immigration. But it was the fear and intolerance of the war years and the period right after the war that resulted in major restrictive legislation.

The first strongly restrictive immigration law passed in 1917 over President Wilson's veto. It required a literacy test for the first time (an immigrant had to read a passage in one of a number of languages). The bill also prohibited the immigration of certain political radicals. However, the literacy test did not stop the more than 1 million immigrants who poured into the country in 1920 and 1921.

In 1921, Congress limited European immigration in any one year to 3 percent of the number of each nationality present in the country in 1910. Congress changed the quota in 1924 to 2 percent of those in the country in 1890; this was done in order to limit immigration from southern and eastern Europe and to ban all immigration from Asia. The National Origins Act of 1927 set an overall limit of 150,000 European immigrants a year, with more than 60 percent coming from Great Britain and Germany, but fewer than 4 percent from Italy.

Ethnicity increasingly became a factor in political alignments during the 1920s. Restrictive immigration laws, sponsored by Republicans, helped attract American Jews, Italians, and Poles to the Democratic party. By 1924, the Democratic party was so evenly divided between northern urban

Catholics and southern rural Protestants that the party voted, by a very small margin, to condemn the Ku Klux Klan.

The immigration acts of 1921, 1924, and 1927 sharply limited European immigration and virtually banned Asian immigrants. The 1924 law contained a provision prohibiting the entry of aliens ineligible for citizenship. This provision was aimed directly at the Japanese, for the Chinese had already been excluded; but even without this provision, only a small number could have immigrated. " We try hard to be American," one California resident remarked, "But Americans always say you always Japanese." Denied both citizenship and the right to own land, the first generation Issei placed all of their hope in the children, but the second generation Nisei often felt trapped between the land of their parents and the America they lived in, and they still were treated like second-class citizens. A California politician called the Japanese a "non-assimilable people" who threatened to make California a "Japanese Plantation."

The immigration laws of the 1920s cut off the streams of cheap labor that had provided muscle for an industrializing country since the early nineteenth century. At the same time, by exempting immigrants from the Western Hemisphere, the new laws opened the country to Mexican laborers who were eager to escape poverty in their own land and to work in the fields and farms of California and the Southwest. Though they never matched the flood of eastern and southern Europeans who entered the country before World War I, Mexican immigrants soon became the country's largest first-generation immigrant group. Nearly one-half million arrived in the 1920s, in contrast to only 31,000 in the first decade of the century. Mexican farm workers often lived in primitive camps, where conditions were unsanitary and health care was nonexistent. "When they have finished harvesting my crops I will kick them out on the country road," one employer announced. "My obligation is ended."

Mexicans also migrated to industrial cities such as Detroit, St. Louis, and Kansas City. Northern companies recruited them and paid their transportation. The Bethlehem Steel Corporation brought 1,000 Mexicans into its Pennsylvania plant in 1923, and U.S. Steel imported 1,500 as strikebreakers to Lorain, Ohio, about the same time. During the 1920s, the population of El Paso, Texas, became more than 50 percent Mexican, and that of San Antonio, a little less than 50 percent Mexican. In California, the Mexican population reached 368,000 in 1929, and in Los Angeles, the population was about 20 percent Mexican. Like African Americans,

the Mexicans found opportunity by migrating, but they did not escape prejudice or hardship.

African Americans migrated north in great numbers from 1915 to 1920. Reduced European immigration and industrial growth caused many northern companies to recruit southern blacks. Trains stopped at the depots in small southern towns, sometimes picking up hundreds of blacks in a single day. Lured by editorials and advertisements placed by industries in northern black newspapers such as the Chicago *Defender* and driven out of the South by an agricultural depression, many African Americans eagerly headed north.

One young black man wrote to the Chicago *Defender* from Texas that he would prefer to go to Chicago or Philadelphia, but "I don't care where so long as I go where a man is a man." It was the young who tended to move. "Young folks just aren't satisfied to see so little and stay around on the farm all their lives like old folks did," one older man from South Carolina pointed out. Most black migrants were unskilled. They found work in the huge meatpacking plants of Chicago, East St. Louis, Omaha, and Kansas City and in the shipyards and steel mills. Only 50 African Americans worked for the Ford Motor Company in 1916, but there were 2,500 working there in 1920 and 10,000 in 1926. The black population of Chicago increased from 44,000 in 1910 to 234,000 by 1930. Cleveland's black population grew eightfold between 1910 and 1930.

African Americans unquestionably improved their lives by moving north. But most were like the Parkers (see pages 778–779)—their dreams were only partly fulfilled. Most crowded into segregated housing and faced prejudice and hate. "Black men stay South," the *Chicago Tribune* advised, and it offered to pay the transportation for any who would return. In one section of Chicago, a group of white residents, fearing the encroachment of blacks, stretched across the street a banner that read: THEY SHALL NOT PASS.

Often the young black men moved first, and only later brought their wives and children, putting great pressure on many black families. Some young men, like John Parker, restrained their anger, but others, like Richard Wright's fictional Bigger Thomas, portrayed movingly in *Native Son* (1940), struck out violently against white society. The presence of more African Americans in the industrial cities of the North led to the development of black ghettos and increased the racial tension that occasionally flared into violence.

One of the worst race riots took place in Chicago in 1919. The riot began at a beach on a hot July day.

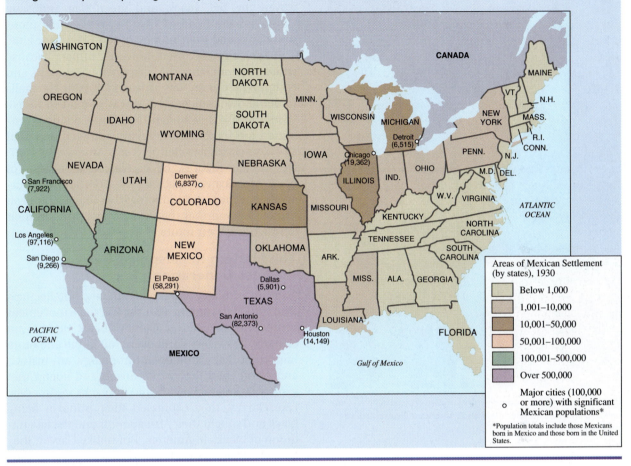

Mexican Population, 1930

Mexicans migrated across the border in great numbers in the 1920s; by 1930, they constituted a significant Spanish-speaking minority, especially in Texas, California, and Arizona.

Areas of Mexican Settlement (by states), 1930

- Below 1,000
- 1,001–10,000
- 10,001–50,000
- 50,001–100,000
- 100,001–500,000
- Over 500,000

○ Major cities (100,000 or more) with significant Mexican populations*

*Population totals include those Mexicans born in Mexico and those born in the United States.

A black youth drowned in a white swimming area. Blacks claimed he had been hit by stones, but the police refused to arrest any of the white men. A group of African Americans attacked the police, and the riot was on. It lasted four days. White youths drove through the black sections of the city, shooting blacks from car windows. Blacks returned the fire. Several dozen were killed, and hundreds were wounded. The tension between the races did not die when the riot was over.

Race riots broke out in other places as well. In the early 1920s, few cities escaped racial tension and violence. Riots exploded in Knoxville, Tennessee; Omaha, Nebraska; and Tulsa, Oklahoma. Racial conflict in Elaine, Arkansas, demonstrated that not even the rural South was immune.

The wave of violence and racism angered and disillusioned W. E. B. Du Bois, who had urged African Americans to close ranks and support the American cause during the war. In an angry editorial for *The Crisis,* he called on blacks to

> fight a sterner, longer, more unbending battle against the forces of hell in our own land. We return. We return from fighting. We return fighting. Make way for Democracy; we saved it in France, and by the Great Jehovah, we will save it in the United States of America, or know the reason why.

Marcus Garvey: Black Messiah

Du Bois was not the only militant black leader in the postwar years. A flamboyant Jamaican fed a growing sense of black pride during that time. Marcus Garvey arrived in New York at the age of 29. Largely self-taught, he was an admirer of Booker T. Washington. Although he never abandoned Washington's philosophy of self-help, he thoroughly transformed it. Washington focused on

Marcus Garvey (second from the right), shown dressed in his favorite uniform, became a hero for many black Americans. *(Hulton Archive/ Getty Images)*

economic betterment through self-help; Garvey saw self-help as a means of political empowerment by which African peoples would reclaim their homelands from European powers.

In Jamaica, Garvey had founded the Universal Negro Improvement Association. By 1919, he had established 30 branches in the United States and the Caribbean. He also set up the newspaper *The Negro World,* the Black Cross Nurses, and a chain of grocery stores, millinery shops, and restaurants. His biggest project was the Black Star Line, a steamship company that was to be owned and operated by African Americans. Advocating the return of blacks to Africa, he declared himself the "provisional president of Africa," a title he adopted from Eamon De Valera, the first "provisional president of Ireland." Garvey glorified the African past and preached that God and Jesus were black.

Garvey won converts, mostly among lower-middle-class blacks, through the force of his oratory and the power of his personality, but especially through his message that blacks should be proud of being

black. "Up you mighty race, you can accomplish what you will," Garvey thundered. Thousands of blacks cheered as his Universal African Legions, dressed in blue and red uniforms, marched by. They waved the red, black, and green flag and sang "Ethiopia, the Land of Our Fathers," while thousands invested their money in the Black Star Line. The line soon collapsed, however, in part because white entrepreneurs sold Garvey inferior ships and equipment. Garvey was arrested for using the mails to defraud shareholders and was sentenced to five years in prison. Although President Coolidge commuted the sentence, Garvey was ordered deported as an undesirable alien and left America in 1927. Despite his failures, he convinced thousands of black Americans, especially the poor and discouraged, that they could join together and accomplish something and that they should feel pride in their heritage and their future.

The Harlem Renaissance and the Lost Generation

A group of black writers, artists, and intellectuals who settled in Harlem after the war led a movement related in some ways to Garvey's black nationalism crusade. It was less flamboyant but in the end more important. They studied anthropology, art, history, and music, and they wrote novels and poetry that explored the ambivalent role of blacks in America. Like Garvey, they expressed their pride in being black and sought their African roots and the folk tradition of blacks in America. But unlike Garvey, they had no desire to go back to Africa; instead, they sought a way to be both black and American.

Alain Locke, the first black Rhodes scholar and a dapper professor of philosophy at Howard University, was in one sense the father of the renaissance. His collection of essays and art, *The New Negro* (1925), announced the movement to the outside world and outlined black contributions to American culture and civilization. Langston Hughes, a poet and novelist born in Missouri, went to high school in Cleveland, lived in Mexico, and traveled in Europe and Africa before settling in Harlem. He wrote bitter but laughing poems, using black vernacular to describe the pathos and the pride of African Americans. In *Weary Blues*, he adapted the rhythm and beat of black jazz and the blues to his poetry.

Jazz was an important force in Harlem in the 1920s, and many prosperous whites came from downtown to listen to Louis Armstrong, Fletcher Henderson, Duke Ellington, and other black musicians. The promise of expressing primitive emotions, the erotic atmosphere, the music, and the illegal sex, drugs, and liquor made Harlem an in-

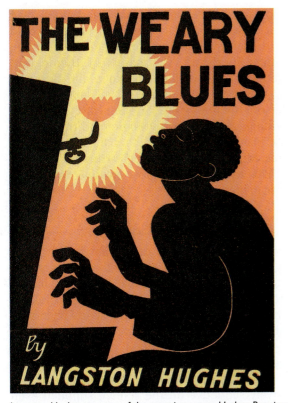

Langston Hughes was one of the most important Harlem Renaissance writers. Like many other African-American writers, he sought out his African roots. But he later wrote: "I was only an American Negro who loved the surface of Africa and the rhythms of Africa, but I was not Africa. I was Chicago and Kansas City and Broadway and Harlem." *(Fales Library/Special Collections, New York University)*

triguing place for many brought up in Victorian white America.

Harlem jazz was also exported to Europe, especially to Paris. Returning black servicemen reported that African Americans were treated without prejudice in France, and black musicians began to drift to the Montmartre section of Paris where American jazz and jazz singers like the seductive Josephine Baker, star of *Revue Nègre*, became the toast of the town. Ironically, many American tourists in the 1920s first heard an African-American jazz band in Paris. Many Europeans criticized the United States for its materialism and for its innocent exuberance. They were not impressed with American literature or American art, but they loved American jazz. It was the beginning of the export of American popular culture that would impress most of the rest of the world in the decades after World War II.

The Jamaican Claude McKay, who came to Harlem by way of Tuskegee and Kansas, wrote about the underside of life in Harlem in *Home to Harlem* (1925), one of the most popular of the "new Negro" novels. McKay portrayed two black men—one, named Jake, who has deserted the white man's army

and finds a life of simple and erotic pleasure in Harlem's cabarets, the other an intellectual who is unable to make such an easy choice. "My damned white education has robbed me of much of the primitive vitality, the pure stamina, the simple unwaggering strength of the Jakes of the negro race," he laments.

This was the dilemma of many of the Harlem writers: how to be both black and intellectual. They worried that they depended on white patrons, who introduced them to writers and artists in Greenwich Village and made contacts for them at New York publishing houses. Many of the white patrons pressured the black writers to conform to the white elite idea of black authenticity. The black writers resented this intrusion, but it was their only hope to be recognized. Jean Toomer, more self-consciously avant-garde than many of the other black writers, wrote haunting poems trying to explore the difficulty of black identity; in the novel *Cane* (1923), he sketched maladjusted, almost grotesque characters who expressed some of the alienation that many writers felt in the 1920s.

Many African-American writers felt alienated from American society. They tried living in Paris or in Greenwich Village, but most felt drawn to Harlem, which in the 1920s was rapidly becoming the center of black population in New York City. More than 117,000 white people left the neighborhood during the decade, while over 87,000 blacks moved in. Countee Cullen, the only writer in the group actually born in New York, remarked, "In spite of myself I find that I am activated by a strong sense of race consciousness." So, too, was Zora Neale Hurston activated—born in Florida, she went to New York to study at Barnard College, earned an advanced degree in anthropology from Columbia University, and used her interest in folklore to write stories of robust and passionate rural blacks. Much of the work of the Harlem writers was read by very small numbers, but another generation of young black intellectuals in the 1960s still struggling with the dilemma of how to be both black and American would rediscover it.

One did not need to be black to be disillusioned with society. Many white intellectuals, writers, and artists also felt alienated from what they perceived as the materialism, conformity, and provincial prejudice that dominated American life. Many writers, including F. Scott Fitzgerald, Ernest Hemingway, e. e. cummings, and T. S. Eliot, moved to Europe. They wanted to divorce themselves from the country they pretended to detest, but cheap rents and inexpensive food in Paris also influenced their decisions. Many of those who gathered at European cafés, drinking the wine that was illegal in the United States, wrote novels, plays, and poems about America. Like so many

American intellectuals in all periods, they had a love–hate relationship with their country.

For many writers, the disillusionment began with the war itself. Hemingway eagerly volunteered to go to Europe as an ambulance driver. But when he was wounded on the Italian front, he reevaluated the purpose of the war and the meaning of all the slaughter. His novel *The Sun Also Rises* (1926) is the story of the purposeless European wanderings of a group of Americans. But it is also the story of Jake Barnes, who was made impotent by a war injury. His "unreasonable wound" is a symbol of the futility of life in the postwar period. F. Scott Fitzgerald, who loved to frequent the cafés and parties in Paris, became a celebrity during the 1920s. He was sometimes confused, even in his own mind, with the dashing heroes about whom he wrote. He epitomized some of the despair of his generation, which had "grown up to find all Gods dead, all wars fought, all faiths in man shaken." His best novel, *The Great Gatsby* (1925), was a critique of the American success myth. The book describes the elaborate parties given by a mysterious businessman, who, it turns out, has made his money illegally as a bootlegger. Gatsby hopes to win back a beautiful woman who has forsaken him for another man. But wealth does not buy happiness, and Gatsby's life ends tragically, as so many lives seemed to end in the novels written during this decade.

Paris was the place to which many American writers flocked, but it was not necessary to live in France to criticize American society. Sherwood Anderson, born in Camden, Ohio, created a fictional, midwestern town in *Winesburg, Ohio* (1919) as a way to describe the dull, narrow, warped lives that seemed to provide a metaphor for American culture. Sinclair Lewis, another midwesterner, created scathing parodies of middle-class, small-town life in *Main Street* (1920) and *Babbitt* (1922). The "hero" of the latter novel is a salesman from the town of Zenith. He is a "he-man," a "regular guy" who distrusts "red professors," foreign-born people, and anyone from New York. He lives in a world of gadgets and booster clubs and seems to be the worst product of a standardized civilization.

But no one had more fun laughing at the American middle class than H. L. Mencken, who edited the *American Mercury* in Baltimore and denounced what he called the "booboisie." He labeled Woodrow Wilson a "self-bamboozled Presbyterian" and poked fun at Warren Harding's prose, which he said reminded him of "a string of wet sponges, . . . of stale bean soup, of college yells, of dogs barking idiotically through endless nights."

Ironically, while intellectuals despaired over American society and complained that art could not survive in a business-dominated civilization, literature flourished. The novels of Hemingway, Fitzgerald, Lewis, William Faulkner, and Gertrude Stein; the plays of Eugene O'Neill and Maxwell Anderson; the poetry of T. S. Eliot, Hart Crane, e. e. cummings, and Marianne Moore; and the work of many black writers, such as Langston Hughes, Claude McKay, and Zora Neale Hurston, marked the 1920s as one of the most creative decades in American literature.

Women Struggle for Equality

Any mention of the role of women in the 1920s brings to mind the image of the flapper—a young woman with a short skirt, bobbed hair, and a boyish figure doing the Charleston, smoking, drinking, and being very casual about sex. F. Scott Fitzgerald's heroines in novels like *This Side of Paradise* (1920) and *The Great Gatsby* (1925) provided the role models for young people to imitate, and movie stars such as Clara Bow and Gloria Swanson, aggressively seductive on the screen, supplied even more dramatic examples of flirtatious and provocative behavior.

The revolution created by electricity remained out of reach for many rural and working-class women, who continued to use the scrub board rather than the washing machine. *(Culver Pictures)*

Without question, women acquired more sexual freedom in the 1920s. "None of the Victorian mothers had any idea how casually their daughters were accustomed to being kissed," F. Scott Fitzgerald wrote. However, it is difficult, if not impossible, to know how accustomed those daughters (and their mothers) were to kissing and enjoying other sexual activity. Contraceptives, especially the diaphragm, became more readily available during the decade, and Margaret Sanger, who had been indicted for sending birth control information through the mail in 1914, organized the first American birth control conference in 1921. Still, most states made the selling or prescribing of birth control devices illegal, and federal laws prohibited sending literature discussing birth control through the mail.

Family size declined during the decade (from 3.6 children in 1900 to 2.5 in 1930), and young people were apparently more inclined to marry for love than for security. More women expected sexual satisfaction in marriage (nearly 60 percent in one poll) and felt that divorce was the best solution for an unhappy marriage. In another poll, nearly 85 percent approved of sexual intercourse as an expression of love and affection and not simply for procreation. But the polls were hardly scientific and tended to be biased toward the attitudes of the urban middle class. Despite more freedom for women, the double standard persisted. "When lovely woman stoops to folly, she can always find someone to stoop with her," one male writer announced, "but not always someone to lift her up again to the level where she belongs."

Women's lives were shaped by other innovations of the 1920s. Electricity, running water, washing machines, vacuum cleaners, and other labor-saving devices made housework easier for the middle class. Yet these developments did not touch large numbers of rural and urban working-class women. Even middle-class women discovered that new appliances did not reduce time spent doing housework. Standards of cleanliness rose, and women were urged to make their houses more spotless than any nineteenth-century housekeeper would have felt necessary. At the same time, magazines and newspapers bombarded women with advertising urging them to buy products to make themselves better housekeepers yet still be beautiful. It must have been frustrating for those who could not afford the magic new products or whose hands and teeth and skin failed to look youthful despite all their efforts. The ads also promoted new dress styles, shorter skirts, and no corsets. The young adopted them quickly, and they also learned to swim (and to dis-

Although the flapper look of short skirts and bobbed hair appeared in the workplace in the 1920s, for most working women of the era, employed in low-paying jobs as file clerks, typists, and telephone operators, the flapper lifestyle of freedom and equality was more illusion than reality. *(Corbis-Bettmann)*

play more of their bodies on the beach), to play tennis (but only if they belonged to a tennis club), and to ride a bicycle.

More women worked outside the home. Whereas in 1890, only 17 percent of women were employed, by 1933, some 22 percent were. But their share of manufacturing jobs fell from 19 to 16 percent between 1900 and 1930. The greatest expansion of jobs was in white-collar occupations that were being feminized—for example, secretary, bookkeeper, clerk, and telephone operator. In 1930, fully 96 percent of stenographers were women. Although more married women had jobs (an increase of 25 percent during the decade), most of them held low-paying jobs, and most single women assumed that marriage would terminate their employment.

For some working women—secretaries and teachers, for example—marriage often led to dismissal. "A married woman's attitude toward men who come to the office is not the same as that of an unmarried woman," one employment agency decided. Married women are "very unstable in their work; their first claim is to home and children," concluded a businessman. Although women might not be able to work after their weddings (in one poll of college men, only one in nine said he would allow his wife to work after marriage), a job as a secretary could be good preparation for marriage. A business office was a good place to meet eligible men, but more than that, a secretary learned endurance, self-effacement, and obedience, traits that would make her a good wife. Considering these attitudes, it is not surprising that the disparity between male and female wages widened during the decade. By 1930, women earned only 57 percent of what men were paid.

The image of the flapper in the 1920s promised more freedom and equality for women than they actually achieved. The flapper was young, white, slender, and upper class (Fitzgerald fixed her ideal age at 19), and most women did not fit those categories. The flapper was frivolous and daring, not professional and competent. Although the proportion of women lawyers and bankers increased slightly during the decade, the rate of growth declined, and the number of women doctors and scientists dropped. In the 1920s, women acquired some sexual freedom and a limited amount of opportunity outside the home, but the promise of the prewar feminist movement and the hopes that accompanied the suffrage amendment remained unfulfilled.

Winning the vote for women did not ensure equality. In most states, a woman's service belonged to her husband. Women could vote, but often they could not serve on juries. In some states, women could not hold office, own a business, or sign a contract without their husbands' permission. Women were usually held responsible for an illegitimate birth, and divorce laws almost always favored men. Many women leaders were disappointed in the small turnout of women in the presidential election of 1920. To educate women in the reality of politics, they organized the National League of Women Voters to "finish the fight." A nonpartisan organization, it became an important educational organization for middle-class women, but it did little to eliminate inequality.

Alice Paul, who had led the militant National Women's Party in 1916, chained herself to the White House fence once again to promote an equal rights amendment to the Constitution. The amendment got support in Wisconsin and in several other states, but many women opposed it on the grounds that such an amendment would cancel the special legislation to protect women in industry that had taken so long to enact in the two decades before. Feminists disagreed in the 1920s on the proper way to promote equality and rights for women, but the political and social climate was not conducive to feminist causes.

Rural America in the 1920s

Most farmers did not share in the prosperity of the 1920s. Responding to worldwide demands and rising prices for wheat, cotton, and other products, many farmers invested in additional land, tractors, and farm equipment during the war. Then prices tumbled. By 1921, the price of wheat had dropped 40 percent, corn 32 percent, and hogs 50 percent.

Total farm income fell from $10 million to $4 million in the postwar depression. Many farmers could not make payments on their tractors. Because the value of land fell, they often lost both mortgage and land and still owed the bank money. One Iowa farmer remembered, "We gave the land back to the mortgage holder, and then we're sued for the remainder—the deficiency judgment—which we have to pay."

The changing nature of farming was part of the problem. The use of chemical fertilizers and new hybrid seeds, some developed by government experiment stations and land-grant colleges, increased the yield per acre. By 1930, some 920,000 tractors and 900,000 trucks were in use on American farms. They not only made farming more efficient, but they also released for cash crops land formerly used to raise feed for horses and mules. Production increased at the very time that worldwide demand for American farm products declined. In 1929, the United States shipped abroad only one-third the wheat it had exported in 1919, and only one-ninth the meat. Farmers, especially in North America and Europe, had prospered during the war because of the great demand for food. Expecting the demand to continue, many farmers borrowed to purchase new equipment and to increase the number of acres they cultivated. But the demand for produce did not last leading to a world-wide decline in prices, making debts difficult to repay. American farmers were victims of the global marketplace.

Not all farmers suffered. During the 1920s, the farming class separated into those who were getting by barely or not at all and those who earned large profits. Large commercial operations, using mechanized equipment, produced most of the cash crops. At the same time, many small farmers found themselves unable to compete with agribusiness. Some of them, along with many farm laborers, solved the problem of declining rural profitability by leaving the farms. In 1900, fully 40 percent of the labor force worked on farms; by 1930, only 21 percent earned their living from the land.

Few farmers could afford the products of the new technology. Although many middle-class urban families were more prosperous than they had ever been—buying new cars, radios, and bathrooms—only one farm family in ten had electricity in the 1920s. The lot of the farm wife had not changed for centuries. She ran a domestic factory, did all the household chores, and helped on the farm as well.

As they had done in the nineteenth century, farmers tried to act collectively. They sought to influence legislation in the state capital and in Washington. Most of their efforts went into the McNary-Haugen Farm Relief Bill, which would have provided government price support for key agricultural products. The bill was introduced a number of times between 1924 and 1928 without success, but farm organizations in all parts of the country learned how to work together to influence Congress. That would have important ramifications for the future.

Farmers were especially vulnerable to the power and unpredictability of nature; that became apparent in the spring of 1927, when the worst flood in the nation's history devastated the Mississippi River valley. Despite efforts to improve the levies, over 27,000 miles of land were flooded. Nearly a million people were made homeless. There was over a billion dollars in property damage, and 246 people died. The black sharecroppers, who often lived near the river, bore the brunt of the disaster. President Coolidge appointed Secretary of Commerce Herbert Hoover to coordinate flood relief. Hoover, who believed in voluntary efforts, enlisted the help of the Red Cross, the American Legion, and other groups, but the relief efforts remained inadequate. The next year Coolidge signed a flood control bill that for the first time committed the federal government to build levies to control the Mississippi River. But the debate continued about the best way to control nature and how to solve the farmer's problems.

The Workers' Share of Prosperity

Hundreds of thousands of workers improved their standard of living in the 1920s, yet inequality grew. Real wages increased 21 percent between 1923 and 1929, but corporate dividends went up by nearly two-thirds in the same period. The workers did not profit from the increased production they helped to create, and that boded ill for the future. The richest 5 percent of the population increased their share of the wealth from a quarter to a third, and the wealthiest 1 percent controlled a whopping 19 percent of all income.

Even among workers there was great disparity. Those employed on the auto assembly lines or in the new factories producing radios saw their wages go up, and many saw their hours decline. Yet the majority of American working-class families did not earn enough to move them much beyond subsistence level. One study suggested that a family needed $2,000 to $2,400 in 1924 to maintain an "American standard of living." But in that year, 16 million families earned under $2,000. For the chambermaids in New York hotels who worked seven days a week or the itinerant Mexican migrant laborers in the Southwest, labor was so exhausting that at the end of the day, it was impossible to take advantage of new consumer products and modern lifestyles, even if they had the money.

Although some workers prospered in the 1920s, organized labor fell on hard times. Labor union membership fell from about 5 million in 1921 to less than 3.5 million in 1929. Although a majority of American workers had never supported unions, unions now faced competition from employers' new policies. A number of large employers lured workers away from unions with promises that seemed to equal union benefits: profit-sharing plans, pensions, and their own company unions. The National Association of Manufacturers and individual businesses carried on a vigorous campaign to restore the open shop. The leadership of the AFL became increasingly conservative during the decade and had little interest in launching movements to organize the large industries.

The more aggressive unions like the United Mine Workers, led by the flamboyant John L. Lewis, also encountered difficulties. The union's attempt to organize the mines in West Virginia had led to violent clashes between union members and imported guards. President Harding called out troops in 1921 to put down an "army organized by the strikers." The next year, Lewis called the greatest coal strike

Women in the Labor Force, 1900–1930

Year	Women in Labor Force	Percentage of Women in Total Labor Force	Percentage of Total Women of Working Age	Percentage of Women in Labor Force		
				Single	Married	Widowed
1900	4,997,000	18.1	20.6	66.2	15.4	18.4
1910*	7,640,000	NA	25.4	60.2	24.7	15.0
1920	8,347,000	20.4	23.7	77.0†	23.0	—†
1930	10,632,000	21.9	24.8	53.9	28.9	17.2

*Data not comparable with other censuses due to a difference in the basis of enumeration.

†Single includes widowed and divorced.

Source: U.S. Bureau of the Census.

in history and further violence erupted, especially in Williamson County, Illinois. Internal strife also weakened the union, and Lewis had to accept wage reductions in the negotiations of 1927.

Organized labor, like so many other groups, struggled desperately during the decade to take advantage of the prosperity. It won some victories, and it made some progress. But American affluence was beyond the reach of many groups during the decade. Eventually, the inequality would lead to disaster.

THE BUSINESS OF POLITICS

"Among the nations of the earth today America stands for one idea: *Business*," a popular writer announced in 1921. "Through business, properly conceived, managed and conducted, the human race is finally to be redeemed." Bruce Barton, the head of the largest advertising firm in the country, was the author of one of the most popular nonfiction books of the decade. In *The Man Nobody Knows* (1925), he depicted Christ as "the founder of modern business." He took 12 men from the bottom ranks of society and forged them into a successful organization. "All work is worship; all useful service prayer," Barton argued. If the businessman would just copy Christ, he could become a supersalesman.

Business, especially big business, prospered in the 1920s, and the image of businessmen, enhanced by their important role in World War I, rose further. The government reduced regulation, lowered taxes, and cooperated to aid business expansion at home and abroad. Business and politics, always intertwined, were especially allied during the decade. Wealthy financiers such as Andrew Mellon and Charles Dawes played important roles in formulating both domestic and foreign policy. Even more significant, a new kind of businessman was elected president in 1928. Herbert Hoover, international engineer and efficiency expert, was the very symbol of the modern techniques and practices that many people confidently expected to transform the United States and the world. Business leaders wielded power in other countries, but in no country were business and politics so closely intertwined as in the United States.

Harding and Coolidge

The Republicans, almost assured of victory in 1920 because of bitter reaction against Woodrow Wilson, might have preferred nominating their old standard-bearer, Theodore Roosevelt, but he had died the year before. Warren G. Harding, a former newspaper editor from Ohio, captured the nomination after meeting late at night with some of the party's most powerful men in a hotel room in Chicago. No one ever discovered what Harding promised, but the meeting in the "smoke-filled room" became legendary. To balance the ticket, the Republicans chose as their vice presidential candidate Calvin Coolidge of Massachusetts, who had gained attention by his firm stand during the Boston police strike. The Democrats seemed equally unimaginative. After 44 roll calls, they finally nominated Governor James Cox of Ohio and picked Franklin D. Roosevelt, a young politician from New York, to run as vice president. Roosevelt had been the assistant secretary of the navy but otherwise had not distinguished himself.

Harding won in a landslide. His 60.4 percent of the vote was the widest margin yet recorded in a presidential election. More significant, fewer than 50 percent of the eligible voters went to the polls. The newly enfranchised women, especially in working-class neighborhoods, stayed away from the voting booths. So did large numbers of men. To many people, it did not seem to matter who was president.

In contrast to the reform-minded presidents Roosevelt and Wilson, Harding reflected the conservatism of the 1920s. He was a jovial man who brought many Ohio friends to Washington and placed them in positions of power. A visitor to the White House described Harding and his cohorts discussing the problems of the day, with "the air heavy with tobacco smoke, trays with bottles containing every imaginable brand of whiskey" near at hand.

At a little house a few blocks from the White House on K Street, Harry Daugherty, Harding's attorney general and longtime associate, held forth with a group of friends. Amid bootleg liquor and the atmosphere of a brothel, they did a brisk business in selling favors, taking bribes, and organizing illegal schemes. Harding, however, was not personally corrupt, and the nation's leading businessmen approved of his policies of higher tariffs and lower taxes. Nor did Harding spend all his time drinking with his cronies. He called a conference on disarmament and another to deal with the problems of unemployment, and he pardoned Eugene Debs, who had been in prison since the war. Harding once remarked that he could never be considered one of the great presidents, but he thought perhaps he might be "one of the best loved." He was probably right. When he died suddenly in August 1923, the American people genuinely mourned him.

Only after Calvin Coolidge became president did the full extent of the corruption and scandals of the Harding administration come to light. A Senate committee discovered that the secretary of the interior, Albert Fall, had illegally leased government-owned oil reserves in the Teapot Dome section of Wyoming to private business interests in return for over $300,000 in bribes. Illegal activities were also discovered in the Veterans Administration and elsewhere in government. Harding's attorney general resigned in disgrace, the secretary of the Navy barely avoided prison, two of Harding's advisers committed suicide, and the secretary of the interior was sentenced to jail.

Though dour and taciturn, Coolidge was honest. No hint of scandal infected his administration or his personal life. Born in a little town in Vermont, he was sworn in as president by his father, a justice of the peace, in a ceremony conducted by the light of kerosene lamps at his ancestral home. To many, Coolidge represented old-fashioned rural values, simple religious faith, and personal integrity—a world fast disappearing in the 1920s. In reality, Coolidge was uncomfortable playing the rural yokel. He was ill at ease posing for photographers holding a pitchfork or sitting on a hay rig; he was much more comfortable around corporate executives.

Coolidge ran for reelection in 1924 with the financier Charles Dawes as his running mate. There was little question that he would win. The Democrats were so equally divided between northern urban Catholics and southern rural Protestants that it took 103 ballots before they nominated John Davis, an affable corporate lawyer with little national following.

A group of dissidents, mostly representing the farmers and the laborers dissatisfied with both nominees, formed a new Progressive party. They adopted the name, but little else, from Theodore Roosevelt's party of 1912. Nominating Robert La Follette of Wisconsin for president, they drafted a platform calling for government ownership of railroads and ratification of the child labor amendment. La Follette attacked the "control of government and industry by private monopoly." He received nearly 5 million votes, only 3.5 million short of Davis's total. But Coolidge and prosperity won easily.

Like Harding, Coolidge was a popular president. Symbolizing his administration was his wealthy secretary of the treasury, Andrew Mellon, who set out to lower individual and corporate taxes. In 1922, Congress, with Mellon's endorsement, repealed the wartime excess profits tax. Although it raised some taxes slightly, it exempted most families from any tax at all by giving everyone a $2,500 exemption, plus $400 for each dependent. In 1926, the rate was lowered to 5 percent and the maximum surtax to 40 percent. Only families with incomes above $3,500

paid any taxes at all. In 1928, Congress reduced taxes further, removed most excise taxes, and lowered the corporate tax rate. The 200 largest corporations increased their assets during the decade from $43 to $81 billion.

"The chief business of the American people is business," Coolidge announced. "The man who builds a factory builds a temple. . . . The man who works there worships there." Coolidge's idea of the proper role of the federal government was to have as little as possible to do with the functioning of business and the lives of the people. Not everyone approved of his policies, or his personality. "No other president in my time slept so much," a White House usher remembered. But most Americans approved of his inactivity.

Herbert Hoover

One bright light in the lackluster Harding and Coolidge administrations was Herbert Hoover. Born in Iowa, raised in Oregon, and educated in California, he served as secretary of commerce under both presidents. Hoover had made a fortune as an international mining engineer before 1914 and then earned the reputation as a great humanitarian for his work managing the Belgian Relief Committee and directing the Food Administration during World War I. He was mentioned as a candidate for president in 1920, when he had the support of such progressives as Jane Addams, Louis Brandeis, and Walter Lippmann.

Hoover was a dynamo of energy and efficiency. He expanded his department to control and regulate the airlines, radio, and other new industries. By directing the Bureau of Standards to work with the trade associations and with individual businesses, Hoover managed to standardize the size of almost everything manufactured in the United States, from nuts and bolts and bottles to automobile tires, mattresses, and electric fixtures. He supported zoning codes, the eight-hour day in major industries, better nutrition for children, and the conservation of national resources. He pushed through the Pollution Act of 1924, which represented the first attempt to control oil pollution along the American coastline.

While secretary of commerce, Hoover used the force of the federal government to regulate, stimulate, and promote, but he believed first of all in American free enterprise and local volunteer action to solve problems. In 1921, he convinced Harding of the need to do something about unemployment during the postwar recession. The president's conference on unemployment, convened in September 1921, marked the first time the national government had admitted any responsibility to the unemployed.

Presidential Elections, 1920–1928

Year	Candidate	Party	Popular Vote	Electoral Vote
1920	WARREN G. HARDING	Republican	16,152,200 (60.4%)	404
	James M. Cox	Democratic	9,147,353 (34.2%)	127
	Eugene V. Debs	Socialist	919,799 (3.4%)	0
1924	CALVIN COOLIDGE	Republican	15,725,016 (54.0%)	382
	John W. Davis	Democratic	8,385,586 (28.8%)	136
	Robert M. La Follette	Progressive	4,822,856 (16.6%)	13
1928	HERBERT C. HOOVER	Republican	21,392,190 (58.2%)	444
	Alfred E. Smith	Democratic	15,016,443 (40.9%)	87

Note: Winners' names appear in capital letters.

The result of the conference (the first of many on a variety of topics that Hoover was to organize) was a flood of publicity, pamphlets, and advice from experts. Most of all, the conference urged state and local governments and businesses to cooperate on a volunteer basis to solve the problem. The primary responsibility of the federal government, Hoover believed, was to educate and promote. With all his activity and his organizing, Hoover got the reputation during the Harding and Coolidge years as an efficient and progressive administrator and as a humanitarian who could organize flood relief. He became one of the most popular figures in government service.

Global Expansion

The decade of the 1920s is often remembered as a time of isolation, when the United States rejected the League of Nations treaty and turned its back on the rest of the world. It is true that many Americans had little interest in what was going on in Paris, Moscow, or Rio de Janeiro, and it is also true that a bloc of congressmen was determined that the United States would never again enter another European war. But the United States remained involved—indeed, increased its involvement—in international affairs during the decade. Although the United States never joined the League of Nations, and a few dedicated isolationists, led by Senator William Borah, blocked membership in the World Court, the United States cooperated with many league agencies and conferences and took the lead in trying to reduce naval armaments and to solve the problems of international finance caused in part by the war.

Looking back from the vantage point of World War II, the decade of the 1920s seemed happy, productive, and normal in most parts of the world. But there were ominous clouds on the horizon. Great Britain and France recovered slowly from the war, while Germany was mired in economic and political chaos. Japan and Italy were unhappy with the peace settlement. Germany's African colonies had been split between France and Great Britain, but imperialism and colonial empires had not diminished. Fascism was establishing a foothold in Spain and Italy, while Soviet communism was becoming more firmly entrenched in Russia. The collapse of the Ottoman Empire had led to the establishment of a new Turkish republic, but the rest of the Middle East was fragmented both economically and politically and presented problems that would persist for the rest of the twentieth century and beyond.

Business, trade, and finance marked the decade as one of international expansion for the United States. With American corporate investments overseas growing sevenfold during the decade, the United States was transformed from a debtor to a creditor nation. The continued involvement of the United States in the affairs of South and Central American countries also indicated that the country had little interest in hiding behind its national boundaries. But it was not just trade and investment that increased during the decade. The United States increased its international position in cable communication, wireless telegraphy, news services, and motion pictures. In most cases, the British had controlled international communication, but by the end of the decade, the United States government had positioned itself to compete in global communications by supporting private companies; in fact, in some areas, such as film, the United States led the world. In 1925, 95 percent of the films shown in Great Britain and Canada and 70 percent of those shown in France were American made. In addition, American organizations such as the YMCA, Rotary International, and the Rockefeller Foundation increased their activities around the world during the decade.

Despite growing global expansion in many areas, the United States government took up its role of international power reluctantly and with a number of contradictory and disastrous results."We seek no part in directing the destiny of the world," Harding announced in his inaugural address, but even Harding discovered that international problems would not disappear. One that required immediate attention was the naval arms race. Since the late nineteenth century, the battleship had become the symbol of national power and pride. Although the aircraft carrier would be more important than the battleship in World War II, the battleship retained its prestige between the wars. A navy was important for protecting trade and empire, but the race to built battleships was caused by something more than practical economics.

Although moderates in Japan and Great Britain wanted to restrict the production of battleships, it was the United States, encouraged by men like William Borah, that took the lead and called the first international conference to discuss disarmament. At the Washington Conference on Naval Disarmament, which convened in November 1921, Secretary of State Charles Evans Hughes startled the delegates by proposing a 10-year "holiday" on the construction of warships and by offering to sink or scrap 845,000 tons of American ships, including 30 battleships. He urged Britain and Japan to do the same. The delegates greeted Hughes's speech with enthusiastic cheering and applause, and they set about the task of sinking more ships than the admirals of all their countries had managed to do in a century.

The conference participants ultimately agreed to fix the tonnage of capital ships at a ratio of the United States and Great Britain, 5; Japan, 3; and France and Italy, 1.67. Japan agreed only reluctantly, but when the United States promised not to fortify its Pacific Island possessions, Japan yielded. In light of what happened in 1941, the Washington Naval Conference has often been criticized, but in 1921, it was appropriately hailed as the first time in history that the major nations of the world had agreed to disarm. The conference did not cause World War II; neither, as it turned out, did it prevent it. But it was a creative start to reducing tensions and to meeting the challenges of the modern arms race. And it was the United States that took the lead by offering to be the first to scrap its battleships.

American foreign policy in the 1920s tried to reduce the risk of international conflict, resist revolution, and make the world safe for trade and investment. Nobody in the Republican administrations even suggested that the United States should remain isolated from Latin America. American diplomats argued for an open door to trade in China and in Latin America, but the United States had always assumed a special and distinct role. Throughout the decade, American investment in agriculture, minerals, petroleum, and manufacturing increased in the countries to the south. The United States bought nearly 60 percent of Latin America's exports and sold the region nearly 50 percent of its imports. "We are seeking to establish a Pax Americana maintained not by arms but by mutual agreement and good will," Hughes maintained.

Still, the United States continued the process of intervention that was begun earlier. By the end of the decade, the United States controlled the financial affairs of 10 Latin American nations. The marines were withdrawn from the Dominican Republic in 1924, but that country remained a virtual protectorate of the United States until 1941. The government ordered the marines from Nicaragua in 1925 but sent them back the next year when a liberal insurrection threatened the conservative government. But the U.S. Marines, and the Nicaraguan troops they had trained, had a difficult time containing a guerrilla band led by Augusto Sandino, a charismatic leader and one of Latin America's greatest heroes. The Sandinistas, supported by the great majority of peasants, came out of the hills to attack the politicians and their American supporters. One American coffee planter decided in 1931 that the American intervention had been a disaster. "Today we are hated and despised," he announced. "This feeling has been created by employing American Marines to hunt down and kill Nicaraguans in their own country." In 1934, Sandino was murdered by General Anastasio Somoza, a ruthless leader supported by the United States. For more than 40 years, Somoza and his two sons ruled Nicaragua as a private fiefdom, a legacy not yet resolved in that strife-torn country.

Mexico frightened American businessmen in the mid-1920s by beginning to nationalize foreign holdings in oil and mineral rights. Fearing that further military activity would "injure American interests," businessmen and bankers urged Coolidge not to send marines but to negotiate instead. Coolidge appointed Dwight W. Morrow of the J. P. Morgan Company as ambassador, and his conciliatory attitude led to agreements protecting American investments. Throughout the decade, the goal of U.S. policy toward Central and South America, whether in the form of negotiations or intervention, was to maintain a special sphere of influence.

The U.S. policy of promoting peace, stability, and trade was not always consistent or carefully thought out, and this was especially true in its relationships with Europe. At the end of the war, European countries owed the United States over $10 billion, with Great Britain and France responsible for about three-fourths of that amount. Both countries, mired in postwar economic problems, suggested that the United States forgive the debts, arguing that they had paid for the war in lives and property destroyed. But the United States, although adjusting the interest and the payment schedule, refused to forget the debt. "They hired the money, didn't they?" Coolidge supposedly remarked.

International debt was not the same as money borrowed at the neighborhood bank; it influenced trade and investment, which the United States wanted to promote. Practically the only way European nations could repay the United States was by exporting products, but in a series of tariff acts, especially the Fordney-McCumber Tariff of 1922, Congress erected a protective barrier to trade. This act also gave the president power to lower or raise individual rates; in almost every case, both Harding and Coolidge used the power to raise them. Finally, in 1930, the Hawley-Smoot Tariff raised rates even further, despite the protests of many economists. American policy of high tariffs (a counterproductive policy for a creditor nation) caused retaliation and restrictions on American trade, which American corporations were trying to increase.

The inability of the European countries to export products to the United States and to repay their loans was intertwined with the reparation agreement made with Germany. Germany's economy was in disarray after the war, with inflation raging and its industrial plant throttled by the peace treaty. By 1921, Germany was defaulting on its payments. The United States, which believed a healthy Germany important to the stability of Europe and of world trade, instituted a plan engineered by Charles Dawes whereby the German debt would be renegotiated and spread over a longer period. In the meantime, American bankers and the American government lent Germany hundreds of millions of dollars. In the end, the United States lent money to Germany so it could make payments to Britain and France so that those countries could continue their payments to the United States. The United States was not only trying to help Germany, but also was using the old idea of dollar diplomacy long-practiced in Central and South America. Private loans extended by American banks helped to extend American influence abroad.

The United States had replaced Great Britain as the dominant force in international finance, but the nation in the 1920s was a reluctant and inconsistent world leader. The United States had stayed out of the League of Nations and was hesitant to get involved in multinational agreements. However, some agreements seemed proper to sign; the most idealistic of all was the Kellogg-Briand pact to outlaw war. The French foreign minister, Aristide Briand, suggested a treaty between the United States and France in large part to commemorate long years of friendship between the two countries, but Secretary of State Frank B. Kellogg in 1928 expanded the idea to a multinational treaty to outlaw war. Fourteen nations agreed to sign the treaty, and eventually 62 nations signed, but the only power behind the treaty was moral force rather than economic or military sanctions.

The Survival of Progressivism

The decade of the 1920s was a time of reaction against reform, but progressivism did not simply die. It survived in many forms through the period that Jane Addams called a time of "political and social sag." Progressives who sought efficiency and order were perhaps happier during the 1920s than those who tried to promote social justice, but even the fight against poverty and for better housing and the various campaigns to protect children persisted. In a sense, the reformers went underground, but they did not disappear or give up the fight. Child labor reformers worked through the Women's Trade Union League, the Consumers League, and other organizations to promote a child labor amendment to the Constitution after the 1919 law was declared unconstitutional in 1922.

The greatest success of the social justice movement was the 1921 Sheppard-Towner Maternity Act, one of the first pieces of federal social welfare legislation and the product of long progressive agitation. A study conducted by the Children's Bureau discovered that more than 3,000 mothers died in childbirth in 1918 and that more than 250,000 infants also died. The United States ranked eighteenth out of 20 countries in maternal mortality and eleventh in infant deaths. The low rank of the United States was caused in part by the poor conditions in urban slums and by rural poverty, especially among southern blacks. But it was also the result of the lack of government intervention to improve health care while many European countries had health insurance and government supported medical clinics. Sara Josephine Baker, the pioneer physician and founder of the American Child Health Association, was not being ironic when she remarked, "It's six times safer to be a soldier in the trenches in France than to be born a baby in the United States."

The maternity bill called for 1 million dollars a year to assist the states in providing medical aid, consultation centers, and visiting nurses to teach expectant mothers how to care for themselves and their babies. The bill was controversial from the beginning. The American Medical Association, which had supported pure food and drug legislation and laws to protect against health quacks and to enforce standards for medical schools, attacked this bill as leading to socialism and interfering with the relationship between doctor and patient and with the "fee for service" system. Others, especially those who had opposed woman suffrage, argued that it was put forward by extreme feminists, that it was "inspired by foreign experiments in Communism and backed by radical forces in the country," that it "strikes at the heart of American Civilization," and that it would lead to socializing medicine and radicalizing the children.

Despite the opposition, the bill passed Congress and was signed by President Harding in 1921. The appropriation for the bill was for only six years, and the opposition, again raising the specter of a feminist-Socialist-Communist plot, succeeded in repealing the law in 1929. Yet the Sheppard-Towner Act, promoted and fought for by a group of progressive women, indicated that concern for social justice was not dead in the age of Harding and Coolidge.

Temperance Triumphant

For one large group of progressives, prohibition, like child labor reform and maternity benefits, was an important effort to conserve human resources. By 1918, over three-fourths of the people in the country lived in dry states or counties, but it was the war that allowed the antisaloon advocates to associate prohibition with patriotism. "We have German enemies across the water," one prohibitionist announced. "We have German enemies in this country too. And the worst of all our German enemies, the most treacherous, the most menacing are Pabst, Schlitz, Blatz and Miller." In 1919, Congress passed the Volstead Act, banning the brewing and selling of beverages containing more than one-half percent alcohol. The thirty-sixth state ratified the Eighteenth Amendment in June 1919, but the country had, for all practical purposes, been dry since 1917.

The prohibition experiment probably did reduce the total consumption of alcohol in the country, especially in rural areas and urban working-class neighborhoods. Fewer arrests for drunkenness occurred, and deaths from alcoholism declined. But the legislation showed the difficulty of using law to promote moral reform. Most people who wanted to drink during the "noble experiment" found a way. Speakeasies replaced saloons, and people consumed bathtub gin, home brew, and many strange and dangerous concoctions. Bartenders invented the cocktail to disguise the poor quality of liquor, and women, at least middle- and upper-class women, began to drink in public for the first time.

Prohibition also created great bootlegging rings, which were tied to organized crime in many cities. Al Capone of Chicago was the most famous underworld figure whose power and wealth were based on the sale of illegal alcohol. His organization alone is believed to have grossed over $60 million in 1927; ironically, most of the profit came from distributing beer. Many supporters of prohibition slowly came to favor its repeal, some because it reduced the power of the states, others because it stimulated too much illegal activity and because it did not seem to be worth the social and political costs.

The Election of 1928

On August 2, 1927, President Coolidge announced simply, "I do not choose to run for President in 1928." Hoover immediately became the logical Republican candidate. Hoover and Coolidge were not especially close. Coolidge resented what he considered Hoover's spendthrift ways. "That man has offered me unsolicited advice for six years, all of it bad," Coolidge once remarked. Though lacking an enthusiastic endorsement from the president and opposed by some Republicans who thought him to be too progressive, Hoover easily won the nomination. In a year when the country was buoyant with optimism and when prosperity seemed as if it would go on forever, few doubted that Hoover would be elected.

The Democrats nominated Alfred Smith, a Catholic Irish American from New York. With his New York accent, his opposition to prohibition, and his flamboyant style, he contrasted sharply with the more sedate Hoover. On one level, it was a bitter contest between Catholic "wets" and Protestant "drys," between the urban, ethnic Tammany politician and former governor of New York against the rural-born but sophisticated secretary of commerce. Religious prejudice, especially a persistent anti-Catholicism, played an important role in the campaign. But looked at more closely, the two candidates differed little. Both were self-made men, both were "progressives." Social justice reformers campaigned for each candidate. Both candidates tried to attract women voters, both were favorable to organized labor, both defended capitalism, and both had millionaires and corporate executives among their advisers.

Hoover won in a landslide, 444 electoral votes to 76 for Smith, who carried only Massachusetts and Rhode Island outside the Deep South. But the 1928 campaign revitalized the Democratic party. Smith polled nearly twice as many votes as the Democratic candidate in 1924, and for the first time, the Democrats carried the 12 largest cities.

Timeline

1900–1930	Electricity powers the "second Industrial Revolution"
1917	Race riot in East Saint Louis, Illinois
1918	World War I ends
1919	Treaty of Versailles
	Strikes in Seattle, Boston, and elsewhere
	Red Scare and Palmer raids
	Race riots in Chicago and other cities
	Marcus Garvey's Universal Negro Improvement Association spreads
1920	Warren Harding elected president
	Women vote in national elections
	First commercial radio broadcast
	Sacco and Vanzetti arrested
	Sinclair Lewis, *Main Street*
1921	Immigration Quota Law
	Naval Disarmament Conference
	First birth-control conference
	Sheppard-Towner Maternity Act
1921–1922	Postwar depression
1922	Fordney-McCumber Tariff
	Sinclair Lewis, *Babbitt*
1923	Harding dies; Calvin Coolidge becomes president
	Teapot Dome scandal
1924	Coolidge reelected president
	Peak of Ku Klux Klan activity
	Immigration Quota Law
1925	Scopes trial in Dayton, Tennessee
	F. Scott Fitzgerald, *The Great Gatsby*
	Bruce Barton, *The Man Nobody Knows*
	Alain Locke, *The New Negro*
	Claude McKay, *Home to Harlem*
	Five million enameled bathroom fixtures produced
1926	Ernest Hemingway, *The Sun Also Rises*
1927	National Origins Act
	McNary-Haugen Farm Relief Bill
	Sacco and Vanzetti executed
	Lindbergh flies solo from New York to Paris
	First talking movie, *The Jazz Singer*
	Henry Ford produces 15 millionth car
1928	Herbert Hoover elected president
	Kellogg-Briand Treaty
	Stock market soars
1929	27 million registered autos in country
	10 million households own radios
	100 million people attend movies
	Stock market crash

Stock Market Crash

Hoover, as it turned out, had only six months to apply his progressive and efficient methods to running the country; in the fall of 1929, the prosperity that seemed endless suddenly came to a halt. In 1928 and 1929, rampant speculation made the stock market boom. Money could be made everywhere—in real estate and business ventures, but especially in the stock market. "Everybody ought to be Rich," Al Smith's campaign manager argued in an article in the *Ladies' Home Journal* early in 1929. Just save $15 a month and buy good common stock with it, and that money would turn into $80,000 in 20 years (a considerable fortune in 1929). Good common stock seemed to be easy to find in 1929.

Only a small percentage of the American people invested in the stock market, for many had no way of saving even $15 a month. But a large number got into the game in the late 1920s because it seemed a safe and sure way to make money. For many, the stock market came to represent the American economy, and the economy was booming. The *New York Times* index of 25 industrial stocks reached 100 in 1924, moved up to 181 in 1925, dropped a bit in 1926, and rose again to 245 by the end of 1927.

Then the orgy started. During 1928, the market rose to 331. Many investors and speculators began to buy on margin (borrowing to invest). Businessmen and others began to invest money in the market that would ordinarily have gone into houses, cars, and other goods. Yet even at the peak of the boom, probably only about 1.5 million Americans owned stock.

In early September 1929, the *New York Times* index peaked at 452 and then began to drift downward. On October 23, the market lost 31 points. The next day ("Black Thursday"), it first seemed that everyone was trying to sell, but at the end of the day, the panic appeared to be over. It was not. By mid-November, the market had plummeted to 224, about half what it had been two months before. This represented a loss on paper of over $26 billion. Still, a month later, the chairman of the board of Bethlehem Steel could announce, "Never before has American business been as firmly entrenched for prosperity as it is today." Some businessmen even got back into the market, thinking that it had reached its low point. But it continued to go down. Tens of thousands of investors lost everything. Those who had bought on margin had to keep coming up with money to pay off their loans as the value of their holdings declined. There was panic and despair, but the legendary stories of executives jumping out of windows were grossly exaggerated.

Cars, mounted policemen, frantic bankers, worried stock brokers, and investors on Wall Street on October 24, 1929—"Black Thursday." The stock market crash in the United States would have a global impact. It revealed weaknesses in the world economy and helped to trigger a global depression. *(Corbis)*

The stock market crash was more symptom than cause of the economic collapse. Weak banking systems in both Europe and America, the rise of protectionism, the drop in farm prices, and the decline of purchasing power all foreshadowed the economic disaster that would follow the stock market debacle.

✦ *Conclusion*

A NEW ERA OF PROSPERITY AND PROBLEMS

The stock market crash ended the decade of prosperity. The crash did not cause the Depression, but the stock market debacle revealed the weakness of the economy. The fruits of economic expansion had been unevenly distributed. Not enough people could afford to buy the autos, refrigerators, and other products pouring from American factories. Prosperity had been built on a shaky foundation. When that foundation crumbled in 1929, the nation slid into a major depression. But the Depression was related to global financial trends and to economic problems created by World War I and the peace settlement. High tariffs and reparations that wrecked the Germany economy and a weakened banking system all contributed to the economic collapse. Looking back from the vantage point of the 1930s or later, the 1920s seemed a golden era—an age of flappers, bootleg gin, constant parties, literary masterpieces, sports heroes, and easy wealth. The truth is much more complicated. More than most decades, the 1920s was a time of paradox and contradictions.

The 1920s was a time of prosperity, yet a great many people, including farmers, blacks, and other ordinary Americans, did not prosper. The Parkers, the black sharecropper family we met at the beginning of this chapter, made some progress during the decade but they did not really profit from the economic boom. The 1920s was a time of modernization, but only about 10 percent of rural families had electricity. It was a time when women achieved more sexual freedom, but the feminist movement declined. It was a time of prohibition, but many Americans increased their consumption of alcohol. It was a time of reaction against reform, yet progressivism survived. It was a time when intellectuals felt disillusioned with America, yet it was one of the most creative and innovative periods for American writers. It was a time of flamboyant heroes, yet the American people elected the lackluster Harding and Coolidge as their presidents. It was a time of progress, when almost every year saw a new technological breakthrough, but it was also a decade of hate and intolerance. The complex and contradictory legacy of the 1920s continues to fascinate and to influence our time.

✦ Recommended Reading

Postwar Problems

Kathleen M. Blee, *Women of the Klan: Racism and Gender in the 1920s* (1991); Roberta Strauss Feurlicht, *Justice Crucified: The Story of Sacco and Vanzetti* (1977); Robert L. Friedheim, *The Seattle General Strike* (1965); David J. Goldberg, *Discontented America: The United States in the 1920s* (1998); Kenneth Jackson, *The Ku Klux Klan in the City* (1967); Nancy Maclean, *Behind the Mask of Chivalry: The Making of the Second Ku Klux Klan* (1994); Robert K. Murray, *Red Scare* (1965).

A Prospering Economy

Erik Barnouw, *A Tower of Babel: A History of American Radio to 1933* (1966); Lendal Calder, *Financing the American Dream: A Cultural History of Consumer Credit* (1999); Lizabeth Cohen, *Making a New Deal: Industrial Workers in Chicago, 1919–1939* (1990); Robert M. Crunden, *Body and Soul: The Making of American Modernism* (2000); Susan J. Douglas, *Listening In: Radio and the American Imagination* (1999); David Farber, *Sloan Rules: Alfred Sloan and the Triumph of General Motors* (2002); James J. Flink, *The Car Culture* (1975); Daniel Horowitz, *The Morality of Spending: Attitudes Toward the Consumer Society in America* (1985); William Leuchtenburg, *The Perils of Prosperity, 1919–1932* (1970); Tom Lewis, *Empire of the Air: The Men who Made Radio* (1991); Zane Miller, *The Urbanization of America* (1973); David Nye, *Electrifying America* (1991); Roland Marchand, *Advertising the American Dream* (1985); Susan Strasser, *Satisfaction Guaranteed: The Making of the American Mass Market* (1989); Jules Tygiel, *Past Time: Baseball as History* (2000).

Hopes Raised, Promises Deferred

Neil Baldwin, *Henry Ford and the Jews: The Mass Production of Hate* (2001); William H. Chafe, *The American Woman: Her Changing Social and Political Worlds* (1992); George Chauncey, *Gay New York: Gender, Urban Culture and the Meaning of the Gay World* (1994); Ellen Chesler, *Woman of Valor: Margaret Sanger and the Birth Control Movement* (1992); Nancy F. Cott, *The Grounding of Modern Feminism* (1987); Lynn Dumenil, *Modern Temper: American Culture and Society in the 1920s* (1995); Paula Fass, *The Damned and the Beautiful: American Youth in the 1920s* (1977); John Higham, *Strangers in the Land: Patterns of American Nativism,* *1860–1925* (1955); Frederick Hoffman, *The Twenties* (1949); Alice Kessler-Harris, *Out to Work: A History of Wage Earning Women in America* (1982); Edward Larson, *Summer for the Gods: The Scopes Trial and America's Continuing Debate Over Science and Religion* (1997); David Levering Lewis, *When Harlem Was in Vogue* (1981); George M. Marsden, *Fundamentalism and American Culture* (1980); Vicki L. Ruiz, *From Out of the Shadows: Mexican Women in Twentieth Century America* (1998); Mark Robert Schneider, *"We Return Fighting": The Civil Rights Movement in the Jazz Age* (2002); William A. Shack, *Harlem in Montmartre* (2001); Susan Strasser, *Never Done: A History of American Housework* (1982); Ronald Takaki, *Strangers From a Distant Shore: A History of Asian Americans* (1989); Theodore Vincent, *Black Power and the Garvey Movement* (1979).

The Business of Politics

David Burner, *The Politics of Provincialism* (1967); Warren I. Cohen, *Empire Without Tears* (1987); Robert H. Ferrell, *The Presidency of Calvin Coolidge* (1998); John Kenneth Galbraith, *The Great Crash* (1954); Oscar Handlin, *Al Smith and His America* (1958); K. Austin Kerr, *Organized for Prohibition* (1985); Emily S. Rosenberg, *Financial Missionaries to the World: The Politics and Culture of Dollar Diplomacy, 1900–1930* (1999); David Wilson, *The Presidency of Warren G. Harding* (1977); William Appleman Williams, *The Tragedy of American Diplomacy* (1962); Joan Hoff Wilson, *Herbert Hoover: Forgotten Progressive* (1975).

Fiction and Film

Sinclair Lewis's novel *Babbitt* (1922) depicts the narrowness of small-town life in the Midwest. F. Scott Fitzgerald describes the reckless lives of the very rich in *The Great Gatsby* (1925). Claude McKay's novel *Home to Harlem* (1928) is one of the best fictional works to come out of the Harlem Renaissance. *Front Page* (1931) is a movie that depicts the world of corrupt politicians and cynical newspapermen in Chicago during the roaring twenties. The 1974 film version of *The Great Gatsby* is not entirely faithful to the novel, but it still captures some of the opulence and pathos of the lives of the very rich in the 1920s. To appreciate two of the great actors and comics of the silent film era, check out Charles Chaplin in *City Lights* (1931) and Buster Keaton in *The General* (1927).

✦ Discovering U.S. History Online

Red Scare (1918–1921)

www.newman.baruch.cuny.edu/digital/redscare/default.htm

The site presents an extensive database of post–World War I images, mostly taken from *Literary Digest,* a weekly compendium of news from various newspapers and magazines contemporary to the period.

The Trial of Sacco and Vanzetti

www.courttv.com/greatesttrials/sacco.vanzetti/

An illustrated summary of the trial, commentary by experts, and video clips from the companion film.

Automotive History

www.mel.lib.mi.us/business/autos-history.html

This site, from the Michigan Electronic Library, has several links to sites about automotive history in America.

Emergence of Advertising in America
http://scriptorium.lib.duke.edu/eaa
The images presented in this exhibit "illustrate the rise of consumer culture, especially after the American Civil War, and the birth of a professionalized advertising industry in the United States."

Chicago: Destination for the Great Migration
www.loc.gov/exhibits/african/afam011.html
This Library of Congress site looks at the black experience of the great migration through the lens of one prominent destination.

Titanic
www.nationalgeographic.com/society/ngo/explorer/titanic/movie.html
This site offers historical perspective via photos from the wreckage of the *Titanic,* a first-person account from a survivor, and a discussion forum.

Ernest Hemingway
www.npg.si.edu/exh/hemingway/
This site presents a biography of author Ernest Hemingway, illustrated with various paintings.

Tennessee vs. John Scopes
www.law.umkc.edu/faculty/projects/ftrials/scopes/scopes.htm
This site contains images, chronology, and court and official documents of the so-called Monkey Trial of 1925.

The 1920s
www.louisville.edu/~kprayb01/1920s.html
This site is divided into three sections: a descriptive timeline, essays and biographies, and an opinion essay.

The Marcus Garvey and Universal Negro Improvement Association Papers Project
www.isop.ucla.edu/mgpp
This site presents a biography of Garvey, sample documents from the volumes of his papers, and photo and sound archives.

Harlem 1900–1940: An African-American Community
www.si.umich.edu/CHICO/Harlem
A timeline of the Harlem Renaissance along with an exhibit that covers such topics as the "Schomburg Center itself, political movements, education, sports, social organizations, religion, the Harlem Hospital theater, business and music."

Photographs from the Golden Age of Jazz
http://lcweb2.loc.gov/ammem/wghtml/wghome.html
A searchable database of Gottlieb's photographs of jazz pioneers, audio commentary on some of the photographs, and scanned articles from the 1940s in which his photographs appeared.

Negro League Baseball
www.negroleaguebaseball.com
This site has articles about desegregation, baseball, and Jim Crow, as well as images of teams and players.

Urban Leisure
www.suba.com/~scottn/explore/mainmenu.htm
An exploration of the jazz culture in Chicago and its influence on the multi-ethnic commercial culture in that city, the "groundwork for the spread of mass culture across the nation during the twentieth century."

The Harlem Renaissance
www.nku.edu/~diesmanj/harlem_intro.html
This site provides an overview of writing and painting from the Harlem Renaissance, with a gallery of paintings by Loïs Mailou, William H. Johnson, and Palmer Hayden and the full text of several poems and short stories by various authors.

Temperance and Prohibition
http://prohibition.history.ohio-state.edu
This site looks at the temperance movement over time and contains many information links.

The Coolidge Era and the Consumer Economy, 1921–1929
http://lcweb2.loc.gov/ammem/coolhtml/ccpres00.html
This site "assembles a wide array of Library of Congress source materials from the 1920s that document the widespread prosperity of the Coolidge years, the nation's transition to a mass consumer economy, and the role of government in this transition."

Calvin Coolidge
http://www.potus.com/ccoolidge.html
This site contains basic factual data about Coolidge's election and presidency, speeches, and online biographies.

Herbert C. Hoover
http://www.potus.com/hhoover.html
This site contains basic factual data about Hoover's election and presidency, speeches, and online biographies.

October 24, 1929
www.arts.unimelb.edu.au/amu/ucr/student/1997/Yee/ny.html
An overview of "Black Thursday" and the events leading up to it by way of headlines that appeared in the *New York Times.*

The Great Depression and the New Deal

The WPA (Works Progress Administration) hired artists from 1935 to 1943 to create murals for public buildings. The assumption was not only that "artists need to eat too," as Harry Hopkins announced, but also that art was an important part of culture and should be supported by the federal government. Here Moses Soyer, a Philadelphia artist, depicts WPA artists creating a mural. *(Moses Soyer,* Artists on WPA, *1935/National Museum of American Art, Smithsonian Institution, Gift of Mr. and Mrs. Moses Soyer/Art Resource, New York)*

✦ *American Stories*

A "SOUTHERN BELLE" SUFFERS DURING THE DEPRESSION

Diana Morgan grew up in a small North Carolina town, the daughter of a prosperous cotton merchant. She lived the life of a "southern belle," oblivious to the country's social and political problems, but the Great Depression changed that. She came home from college for Christmas vacation during her junior year to discover that the telephone had been disconnected. Her world suddenly fell apart. Her father's business had failed, her family didn't have a cook or a cleaning woman anymore, and their house was being sold for back taxes. Confused and embarrassed, she sometimes felt it was the little things that were the hardest. Friends would come from out of town, and there would be no ice because her family did not own an electric refrigerator and they could not afford to buy ice. "There were those frantic arrangements of running out to the drugstore to get Coca-Cola with crushed ice, and there'd be this embarrassing delay, and I can remember how hot my face was."

Like many Americans, Diana Morgan and her family blamed themselves for what happened during the Great Depression. Americans had been taught to believe that if they worked hard, saved their money, and lived upright and moral lives, they could succeed. Success was an individual matter for Americans. When so many failed during the Depression, they blamed themselves rather than society or larger forces for their plight. The shame and the guilt affected people at all levels of society. The businessman who lost his business, the farmer who watched his farm being sold at auction, and the worker who was suddenly unemployed and felt his manhood stripped away because he could not provide for his family were all devastated by the Depression.

Diana Morgan had never intended to get a job; she expected to get married and let her husband support her. But the failure of her father's business forced her to join the growing number of women who worked outside the home in the 1930s. She finally found a position with the Civil Works Administration, a New Deal agency. As part of her job, she had to ask humiliating questions of the people applying for assistance to make sure they were destitute. "Do you own a car?" "Does anyone in the family work?" Diana was appalled at the conditions she saw when she traveled around the county to corroborate their stories. She found dilapidated houses, a dirty, "almost paralyzed-looking mother," and a drunken father, together with malnourished children. She felt helpless that she could do nothing more than write out a food order. One day, a woman who had formerly cooked for her family came in to apply for help. Each was embarrassed to see the other in changed circumstances.

Diana had to defend the New Deal programs to many of her friends, who accused her of being sentimental and told her that the poor, especially poor blacks, did not know any better than to live in squalor. "If you give them coal, they'd put it in the bathtub," was a charge she often heard. But she knew "they didn't have bathtubs to put coal in. So how did anybody know that's what they'd do with coal if they had it?"

Diana Morgan's experience working for a New Deal agency influenced her life and her attitudes; it made her more of a social activist. Her Depression experience gave her a greater appreciation for the struggles of the country's poor and unlucky. Although she prospered in the years after the Depression, the sense of guilt and the fear that the telephone might again be cut off never left her.

The Great Depression changed the lives of all Americans, separating that generation from the one that followed. An exaggerated need for security, the fear of failure, a nagging sense of guilt, and a real sense that it might happen all over again divided the Depression generation from everyone born after 1940. Like Diana Morgan, most Americans were victims of the global marketplace and the world-wide economic collapse. And like Diana Morgan, they never forgot those bleak years.

This chapter explores the causes and consequences of the Great Depression. We will look at Herbert Hoover and his efforts to combat the Depression and then turn to Franklin Roosevelt, the dominant personality of the 1930s. We will examine the New Deal and Roosevelt's program to bring relief, recovery, and reform to the nation. But we will not ignore the other side of the 1930s, for the decade did not consist only of crippling unemployment and New Deal agencies. It was also a time of great strides in technology, when innovative developments in radio, movies, and the automobile affected the lives of most Americans.

THE GREAT DEPRESSION

There had been recessions and depressions in American history, notably in the 1830s, 1870s, and 1890s, but nothing compared with the devastating economic collapse of the 1930s. The Great Depression was all the more shocking because it came after a decade of unprecedented prosperity, when most experts assumed that the United States was immune to a downturn in the business cycle. The Great Depression had an impact on all areas of American life; perhaps most important, it destroyed American confidence in the future.

The Depression Begins

Few people anticipated the stock market crash in the fall of 1929. But even after the collapse of the stock market, few expected the entire economy to go into a tailspin. General Electric stock, selling for 396 in 1929, fell to 34 in 1932; U.S. Steel declined from 261 to 21. By 1932, the median income had plunged to half of what it had been in 1929. Construction spending fell to one-sixth of the 1929 level. By 1932, at least one of every four American breadwinners was out of work, and industrial production had almost ground to a halt.

Why did the nation sink deeper and deeper into depression? After all, only about 2 percent of the population owned stock of any kind. The answer is complex, but it appears in retrospect that the prosperity of the 1920s was superficial. Farmers and coal and textile workers had suffered all through the 1920s from low prices, and the farmers were the first group in the 1930s to plunge into depression. But other aspects of the economy also lurched out of balance. Two percent of the population received about 28 percent of the national income, but the lower 60 percent got only 24 percent. Businesses increased profits while holding down wages and the prices of raw materials. This pattern depressed consumer purchasing power. American workers, like American farmers, did not have the money to buy the goods they helped to produce. There was a relative decline in purchasing power in the late 1920s, unemployment was high in some industries, and the housing and automobile industries were already beginning to slacken before the crash.

Well-to-do Americans were speculating a significant portion of their money in the stock market. Their illusion of permanent prosperity helped fire the boom of the 1920s, just as their pessimism and lack of confidence helped exaggerate the Depression in 1931 and 1932.

Other factors were also involved. The stock market crash revealed serious structural weaknesses in the financial and banking systems (7,000 banks had failed during the 1920s). The Federal Reserve Board, fearing inflation, tightened credit—exactly the opposite of the action it should have taken to fight a slowdown in purchasing. But the Depression was also caused by global economic problems created by World War I and the peace settlement. Large reparations exacted against Germany had led to the collapse of the German economy, and high tariffs had reduced international trade. When American investment in Europe slowed in 1928 and 1929, European economies declined. Americans purchased fewer European goods, and Europeans got along without American products. As the European financial situation worsened, the American economy spiraled downward.

The federal government might have prevented the stock market crash and the Depression by more careful regulation of business and the stock market. Central planning might have ensured a more equitable distribution of income. But that kind of policy would have taken more foresight than most people had in the 1920s. It certainly would have required different people to be in power, and it is unlikely that the Democrats, had they been in control, would have altered the government's policies in fundamental ways.

Hoover and the Great Depression

Initial business and government reactions to the stock market crash were optimistic. "All the evidence indicates that the worst effects of the crash upon unemployment will have been passed during the next sixty days," Herbert Hoover reported. Hoover, the great planner and progressive efficiency expert, did not sit idly by and watch the country drift toward disorder. His upbeat first statements were calculated to prevent further panic.

The Agricultural Marketing Act of 1929 set up a $500 million revolving fund to help farmers organize cooperative marketing associations and to establish minimum prices. But as agricultural prices plummeted and banks foreclosed on farm mortgages, the available funds proved inadequate. The Farm Board was helpless to aid the farmer who could not meet mortgage payments because the price of grain had fallen so rapidly, largely because of global overproduction. Nor could it help the Arkansas woman who stood weeping in the window as her possessions, including the cows (which all had names), were sold one by one.

Hoover acted aggressively to stem the economic collapse. More than any president before him, he used the power of the federal government and the office of the president to deal with an economic crisis. Nobody called it a depression for the first year at least, for the economic problems seemed very much like earlier cyclic recessions. Hoover called conferences of businessmen and labor leaders. He met with mayors and governors and encouraged them to speed up public works projects. He created agencies and boards, such as the National Credit Corporation and the Emergency Committee for Employment, to obtain voluntary action to solve the problem. Hoover even supported a tax cut, which Congress enacted in December 1929, but it did little to stimulate spending. Hoover also went on the radio in his effort to convince the American people that the fundamental structure of the economy was sound.

ECONOMIC DECLINE

Voluntary action and psychological campaigns could not stop the Depression. The stock market, after appearing to bottom out in the winter of 1930–1931, continued its decline, responding in part to the European economic collapse that undermined international finance and trade. Of course, not everyone lost money in the market. William Danforth, founder of Ralston Purina, and Joseph Kennedy, film magnate, entrepreneur, and the father of a future president, were among those who made millions of dollars by selling short as the market went down.

More than a collapsing market afflicted the economy. More than 1,300 additional banks failed in 1930. Despite Hoover's pleas, many factories cut back on production, and some simply closed. U.S. Steel announced a 10 percent wage cut in 1931. As the auto industry laid off workers, the unemployment rate rose to over 40 percent in Detroit. More than 4 million Americans were out of work in 1930, and at least 12 million were unemployed by 1932. Foreclosures and evictions created thousands of personal tragedies. There were 200,000 evictions in New York City alone in 1930. While the middle class watched in horror as their life savings and their dreams disappeared, the rich were increasingly concerned as the price of government bonds (the symbol of safety and security) dropped. They began to hoard gold and fear revolution.

There was never any real danger of revolution. Some farmers organized to dump their milk to protest low prices, and when a neighbor's farm was sold, they gathered to hold a penny auction, bidding only a few cents for equipment and returning it to their dispossessed neighbor. But everywhere, people despaired as the Depression deepened in 1931 and 1932. For unemployed blacks and for many tenant farmers, the Depression had little immediate ef-

fect because their lives were already so depressed. Most Americans (the 98 percent who did not own stock) hardly noticed the stock market crash; for them, the Depression meant the loss of a job or a bank foreclosure. For Diana Morgan, it was the discovery that the telephone had been cut off; for some farmers, it was burning corn rather than coal because the price of corn had fallen so low that it was not worth marketing.

For some in the cities, the Depression meant not having enough money to feed the children. In Chicago, children fought with men and women over the garbage dumped by the city trucks. In Toledo, when municipal and private charity funds were drying up (as they did in all cities), those granted assistance were given only 2.14 cents per meal per person. In another city, a social worker noticed that the children were playing a game called "Eviction." "Sometimes they play 'Relief,'" she remarked, "but 'Eviction' has more action and all of them know how to play."

Not everyone went hungry, stood in bread lines, or lost jobs during the Depression, but almost everyone was affected, and many victims tended to blame themselves. A businessman who lost his job and had to stand in a relief line remembered years

Unemployment Rate, 1929–1940

Although the unemployment rate declined during the New Deal years, the number still unemployed remained tragically high until World War II brought full employment.

Source: U.S. Bureau of the Census.

later how he would bend his head low so nobody would recognize him. A 28-year-old teacher in New Orleans was released because of a cut in funds, and in desperation she took a job as a domestic servant. "If with all the advantages I've had," she remarked, "I can't make a living, I'm just no good, I guess. I've given up ever amounting to anything. It's no use."

The Depression probably disrupted women's lives less than men's. "When hard times hit, it didn't seem to bother mother as much as it did father," one woman remembered. There were many exceptions, of course, but when men lost their jobs, their identity and sense of purpose as the family breadwinner were shattered. Some helped out with family chores, but usually with bitterness and resentment. For women, however, even when money was short, there was still cooking, cleaning, and mending, and women were still in command of their households. Yet many women were forced to do extra work. They took in laundry, found room for a boarder, and made the clothes they formerly would have bought. Women also bore the psychological burden of unemployed husbands, hungry children, and unpaid bills. The Depression altered patterns of family life, and many families were forced to move in with relatives. The marriage rate, the divorce rate, and the birthrate all dropped during the decade. Many of these changes created tension that statistics cannot capture.

A Global Depression

Hoover reacted to growing despair by urging more voluntary action. "We are going through a period," he announced in February 1931, "when character and courage are on trial, and where the very faith that is within us is under test." He insisted on maintaining the gold standard, believing it to be the only responsible currency, and a balanced budget, but so did almost everyone else. Congress was nearly unanimous in supporting those ideals, and Governor Franklin Roosevelt of New York accused Hoover of endangering the country by spending too much. Hoover increasingly blamed the Depression on international economic problems, and he was at least partly right The legacy of the war and the global economic policies of the 1920s had been one cause of the economic downturn in the United States, and as the United States sunk into depression, the world followed. In May 1931, the leading Austrian bank collapsed; by June, the German financial system, which had gone from hyperinflation to false stability, was in chaos. In September, England abandoned the gold standard, precipitating a decline in international lending and trade.

Soon most of the industrialized world, including Argentina, Brazil, and Japan, were caught in the Great Depression. In some countries, the social safety net of health and unemployment insurance helped, but there were hungry and unemployed people in much of the world. That a stock market crash in the United States triggered a world-wide Depression indicated that by 1930 the United States was an economic world power, but that was little solace as the global Depression exaggerated and extended the Depression at home.

Despite the world-wide Depression, Americans began to blame Hoover for some of the disaster. The president became isolated and bitter. The shanties that grew near all the large cities were called "Hoovervilles," and the privies "Hoover villas." Unable to admit mistakes and to take a new tack, he could not communicate personal empathy for the poor and the unemployed.

Hoover did try innovative schemes. More public works projects were built during his administration than in the previous 30 years. In the summer of 1931, he attempted to organize a pool of private money to rescue banks and businesses that were near failure. When the private effort failed, he turned reluctantly to Congress, which passed a bill early in 1932 authorizing the Reconstruction Finance Corporation. The RFC was capitalized at $500 million, but a short time later that was increased to $3 billion. It was authorized to make loans to banks, insurance companies, farm mortgage companies, and railroads. Some critics charged that it was simply another trickle-down measure whereby businessmen and bankers would be given aid while the unemployed were ignored. Hoover, however, correctly understood the immense costs to individuals and to communities when a bank or mortgage company failed. The RFC did help shore up a number of shaky financial institutions and remained the major government finance agency until World War II. But it became much more effective under Roosevelt because it lent directly to industry.

Hoover also asked Congress for a Home Financing Corporation to make mortgages more readily available. The Federal Home Loan Bank Act of 1932 became the basis for the Federal Housing Administration of the New Deal years. He supported the passage of the Glass-Steagall Banking Act of 1932, which expanded credit to make more loans available to businesses and individuals. But Hoover rejected calls for the federal government to restrict production in hopes of raising farm prices—that, he believed, was too much federal intervention. He

The worst result of the Depression was hopelessness and despair. Those emotions are captured in this painting by Isaac Soyer of an unemployment office. *(Isaac Soyer, Employment Agency, 1937, Oil on canvas, 34¼ × 45 in. [87 × 114.3 cm]. Collection of Whitney Museum of American Art, Purchase, 37.44, Photograph © 2000: Whitney Museum of American Art)*

maintained that the federal government should promote cooperation and even create public works. But he firmly believed in loans, not direct subsidies, and he thought it was the responsibility of state and local governments, as well as of private charity, to provide direct relief to the unemployed and the needy.

The Bonus Army

Many World War I veterans lost their jobs during the Great Depression, and beginning in 1930, they lobbied for the payment of their veterans' bonuses, which were not due until 1945. A bill passed Congress in 1931, over Hoover's veto, allowing them to borrow up to 50 percent of the bonus due them, but this concession did not satisfy the destitute veterans. In May 1932, about 17,000 veterans marched on Washington. Some took up residence in a shantytown called Bonus City that was located in the Anacostia flats outside the city.

In mid-June, the Senate defeated the bonus bill, and most of the veterans, disappointed but resigned, accepted a free railroad ticket home. Several thousand remained, however, along with some wives and children, in the unsanitary shacks during the steaming summer heat. Among them were a small group of committed communists and other radicals. Hoover, who exaggerated the subversive elements among those still camped out in Washington, refused to talk to the leaders and finally called out the U.S. Army.

General Douglas MacArthur, the army chief of staff, ordered the army to disperse the veterans. He described the Bonus marchers as a "mob . . . animated by the essence of revolution." With tanks, guns, and tear gas, the army routed veterans who 15 years before had worn the same uniform as their attackers. Two Bonus marchers were killed, and several others were injured. "What a pitiful spectacle is that of the great American Government, mightiest in the world, chasing unarmed men, women and children with Army tanks," commented a Washington newspaper. "If the Army must be called out to make war on unarmed citizens, this is no longer America." The army was not attacking revolutionaries in the streets of Washington but was routing bewildered, confused, unemployed men who had seen their American dream collapse.

The Bonus army fiasco, bread lines, and Hoovervilles became the symbols of Hoover's presidency. He deserved better because he tried to use the power of the federal government to solve growing and increasingly complex economic problems. But in the end, his personality and background limited him. He could not understand why army veterans marched on Washington to ask for a handout

U.S. soldiers burn the Bonus army shacks within sight of the Capitol in the summer of 1932. This image of the failure of the American dream was published widely around the world. *(National Archives)*

when he thought they should all be back home working hard, practicing self-reliance, and cooperating "to avert the terrible situation in which we are today." He believed that the greatest problem besetting Americans was a lack of confidence. Yet he could not communicate with these people or inspire their confidence. Willing to use the federal government to support business, he could not accept federal aid for the unemployed. He feared an unbalanced budget and a large federal bureaucracy that would interfere with the "American way." Ironically, his actions and his inactions led in the next years to a massive increase in federal power and in the federal bureaucracy.

ROOSEVELT AND THE FIRST NEW DEAL

The first New Deal, lasting from 1933 to early 1935, focused mainly on recovery from the Depression and relief for the poor and unemployed. Congress passed legislation to aid business, the farmers, and labor and authorized public works projects and massive spending to put Americans back to work. Some of the programs were borrowed from the Hoover administration, and some had their origin in the progressive period. Others were inspired by the nation's experiences in mobilizing for World War I. No single ideological position united all the programs, for Roosevelt was a pragmatist who was willing to try a variety of programs. More than Hoover, however, he believed in economic planning and in government spending to help the poor.

Roosevelt's caution and conservatism shaped the first New Deal. He did not promote socialism or suggest nationalizing the banks. He was even careful in authorizing public works projects to stimulate the economy. The New Deal was based on the assumption that it was possible to create a just society by superimposing a welfare state on the capitalistic system, leaving the profit motive undisturbed. While the progressives believed in voluntary action, and only reluctantly came to the conclusion that the federal government needed to intervene to promote a just society, the New Dealers, from the beginning, believed in an active role for the government. During the first New Deal, Roosevelt believed he would achieve his goals through cooperation with the business community. Later he would move more toward reform, but at first his primary concern was simply relief and recovery. Roosevelt was a controversial president who could be devious and maddening, but he believed in experimentation and was not afraid to change his mind. Perhaps even more remarkable, during a time of economic crisis when dictators were taking over in Italy, Germany, Spain, and the Soviet Union, democracy survived in America in large part because of Roosevelt and the New Deal.

The Election of 1932

The Republicans nominated Herbert Hoover for a second term, but in the summer of 1932, the Depression and Hoover's unpopularity opened the way for the Democrats. After a shrewd campaign, Franklin D. Roosevelt, governor of New York, emerged from the pack and won the nomination. Journalist Walter Lippmann's comment during the campaign that Roosevelt was a "pleasant man who, without any important qualifications for office, would like very much to be President" was exaggerated at the time and seemed absurd later. Roosevelt, distantly related to Theodore Roosevelt, had served as an assistant secretary of the navy during World War I and had been the Democratic vice presidential candidate in 1920. Crippled by infantile paralysis not long after, he had recovered enough to serve as governor of New York for two terms, although he was not especially well-known by the general public in 1932.

Governor Roosevelt had promoted cheaper electric power, conservation, and old-age pensions. Urged on by advisers Frances Perkins and Harry Hopkins, he became the first governor to support state aid for the unemployed, "not as a matter of charity, but as a matter of social duty." But it was difficult to tell during the presidential campaign exactly what he stood for. He did announce that the government must do something for the "forgotten man at the bottom of the economic pyramid," and he struck out at the small group of men who "make huge profits from lending money and the marketing of securities." Yet he also mentioned the need for balancing the budget and maintaining the gold standard. Ambiguity was probably the best strategy in 1932, but the truth was that Roosevelt did not have a master plan to save the country. Yet he won the election overwhelmingly, carrying more than 57 percent of the popular vote.

During the campaign, Roosevelt had promised a "new deal for the American people." But after his victory, the New Deal had to wait for four months because the Constitution provided that the new president be inaugurated on March 4 (this was changed to January 20 by the Twentieth Amendment, ratified in 1933). During the long interregnum, the state of the nation deteriorated badly. The banking system seemed near collapse, and the hardship increased. Despite his bitter defeat, Hoover tried to cooperate with the president-elect and with a hostile Congress, but he could accomplish little. Everyone waited for the new president to take office and to act.

In his inaugural address, Roosevelt announced confidently, "The only thing we have to fear is fear itself." This, of course, was not true, for the country faced the worst crisis since the Civil War, but Roosevelt's confidence and his ability to communicate with ordinary Americans were obvious early in his presidency. He had clever speech writers, a sense of pace and rhythm in his speeches, and an ability, when he spoke on the radio, to convince listeners that he was speaking directly to them. Recognizing the possibilities of the new media, he instituted a series of radio "fireside chats" to explain to the American people what he was doing to solve the nation's problems. When he said "my friends," millions believed that he meant it, and they wrote letters to him in unprecedented numbers to explain their needs.

Roosevelt's Advisers

During the interregnum, Roosevelt surrounded himself with intelligent and innovative advisers. Some, like James A. Farley, a former New York State boxing commissioner with a genius for remembering names, and Louis Howe, Roosevelt's secretary and confidant since 1912, had helped plan his successful campaign. His cabinet was made up of a mixture of people from different backgrounds who often did not agree with one another. Harold Ickes, the secretary of the interior, was a Republican lawyer from Chicago and a one-time supporter of Theodore Roosevelt. Another Republican, Henry Wallace of Iowa, a plant geneticist and agricultural statistician, became the secretary of agriculture.

This is a rare photograph of Franklin Roosevelt in his wheelchair taken in a private moment with his dog, Fala, and a young friend. Usually FDR's advisers carefully arranged to have the president photographed only when he was seated or propped up behind a podium. Despite being paralyzed from the waist down, the president gave the impression of health and vitality until near the end of his life. *(Margaret Suckley Collection, Franklin Delano Roosevelt Library)*

Frances Perkins, the first woman ever appointed to a cabinet post, became the secretary of labor. A disciple of Jane Addams and Florence Kelley, she had been a settlement resident, secretary of the New York Consumers League, and an adviser to Al Smith.

In addition to the formal cabinet, Roosevelt appointed an informal "Brain Trust," including Adolph Berle, Jr., a young expert on corporation law, and Rexford Tugwell, a Columbia University authority on agricultural economics and a committed national planner. Roosevelt also appointed Raymond Moley, another Columbia professor, who later became one of the president's severest critics, and Harry Hopkins, a nervous, energetic man who loved to bet on horse races and had left Iowa to be a social worker in New York. Hopkins's passionate concern for the poor and unemployed would play a large role in the formulation of New Deal policy.

Eleanor Roosevelt, the president's wife, was a controversial first lady. She wrote a newspaper column and made a great many speeches and radio broadcasts. She traveled widely and was constantly listening to the concerns of women, minorities, and ordinary Americans. Attacked by critics who thought she had too much power and mocked for her protruding front teeth, her awkward ways, and her upper-class accent, she courageously took stands on issues of social justice and civil rights. She helped push the president toward social reform.

Roosevelt proved to be an adept politician. He was not well read, especially on economic matters, but he had the ability to learn from his advisers and yet not be dominated by them. He took ideas, plans, and suggestions from conflicting sources and combined them. He had a "flypaper mind," one of his advisers decided. There was no overall plan, no master strategy. An improviser and a pragmatist who once likened himself to a football quarterback who called one play and if it did not work called a different one, Roosevelt was an optimist by nature. And he believed in action.

ONE HUNDRED DAYS

Because Roosevelt took office in the middle of a major crisis, a cooperative Congress was willing to pass almost any legislation that he put before it. Not since Woodrow Wilson's first term had a president orchestrated Congress so effectively. In three months, a bewildering number of bills was rushed through. Some of them were hastily drafted and not well thought out, and some contradicted other legislation. But many of the laws passed during Roosevelt's first 100 days would have far-reaching implications for the relationship of government to society. Roosevelt was

an opportunist, but unlike Hoover, he was willing to use direct government action to solve the problems of depression and unemployment. As it turned out, none of the bills passed during the first 100 days cured the Depression, but taken together, the legislation constituted one of the most innovative periods in American political history.

The Banking Crisis

The most immediate problem Roosevelt faced was the condition of the banks. Many had closed, and American citizens, no longer trusting the financial institutions, were hoarding money and putting their assets into gold. Roosevelt immediately declared a four-day bank holiday. Three days later, an emergency session of Congress approved his action and within hours passed the Emergency Banking Relief Act. The bill gave the president broad powers over financial transactions, prohibited the hoarding of gold, and allowed for the reopening of sound banks, sometimes with loans from the Reconstruction Finance Corporation.

Within the next few years, Congress passed additional legislation that gave the federal government more regulatory power over the stock market and over the process by which corporations issued stock. It also passed the Banking Act of 1933, which strengthened the Federal Reserve System, established the Federal Deposit Insurance Corporation (FDIC), and insured individual deposits up to $5,000. Although the American Bankers Association opposed the plan as "unsound, unscientific, unjust and dangerous," banks were soon attracting depositors by advertising that they were protected by government insurance.

The Democratic platform in 1932 called for reduced government spending and an end to prohibition. Roosevelt moved quickly on both. The Economy Act, which passed Congress easily, called for a 15 percent reduction in government salaries as well as a reorganization of federal agencies to save money. The bill also cut veterans' pensions, despite their protests. However, the Economy Act's small savings were dwarfed by other bills passed the same week, which called for increased spending. The Beer-Wine Revenue Act legalized 3.2 beer and light wines and levied a tax on both. The Twenty-first Amendment, ratified on December 5, 1933, repealed the Eighteenth Amendment and ended the prohibition experiment. The veterans and the antiliquor forces, two of the strongest lobbying groups in the nation, were both overwhelmed by a Congress that seemed ready to give the president free rein.

Congress granted Roosevelt great power to devalue the dollar and to manipulate inflation. Some members argued for the old Populist solution of free and unlimited coinage of silver, while others called for issuing billions of dollars in paper currency. Bankers and businessmen feared inflation, but farmers and debtors favored an inflationary policy as a way to raise prices and put more money in their pockets. "I have always favored sound money," Roosevelt announced, "and I do now, but it is 'too darned sound' when it takes so much of farm products to buy a dollar." He rejected the more extreme inflationary plans supported by many congressmen from the agricultural states, but he did take the country off the gold standard. No longer would paper currency be redeemable in gold. The action terrified some conservative businessmen, who argued that it would lead to "uncontrolled inflation and complete chaos." Even Roosevelt's director of the budget announced solemnly that going off the gold standard "meant the end of Western Civilization."

Devaluation did not end Western civilization, but neither did it lead to instant recovery. After experimenting with pushing the price of gold up by buying it in the open market, Roosevelt and his advisers fixed the price at $35 an ounce in January 1934 (against the old price of $20.63). This inflated the dollar by about 40 percent. Roosevelt also tried briefly to induce inflation through the purchase of silver, but soon the country settled down to a slightly inflated currency and a dollar based on both gold and silver. Some experts still believed that gold represented fiscal responsibility, even morality, and others still cried for more inflation.

Relief Measures

Roosevelt believed in economy in government and in a balanced budget, but he also wanted to help the unemployed and the homeless. One survey estimated in 1933 that 1.5 million Americans were homeless. One man with a wife and six children from Latrobe, Pennsylvania, who was being evicted wrote, "I have 10 days to get another house, no job, no means of paying rent, can you advise me as to which would be the most humane way to dispose of myself and family, as this is about the only thing that I see left to do."

Roosevelt's answer was the Federal Emergency Relief Administration (FERA), which Congress authorized with an appropriation of $500 million in direct grants to cities and states. A few months later, Roosevelt created a Civil Works Administration (CWA) to put more than 4 million people to work on various state, municipal, and federal projects. Hopkins, who ran both agencies, had experimented with work relief programs in New York. Like most social workers, he believed it was much better to pay people to work than to give them charity. A woman with two daughters from Houston, Texas, wrote and asked, "Why don't they give us materials and let us make our children's clothes . . . you've no idea how children hate wearing relief clothes." An

Margaret Bourke-White, one of the outstanding documentary photographers of the 1930s, captured the disjunction between the ideal and the real in the Depression era. This photograph, depicting African-American flood victims lining up for food in Louisville, Kentucky, underneath a propaganda billboard erected by the National Association of Manufacturers, contrasts the American Dream with the reality of racism and poverty. *(Photograph Copyright © 1966: Whitney Museum of American Art, New York, Gift of Sean Callahan)*

accountant working on a road project said, "I'd rather stay out here in that ditch the rest of my life than take one cent of direct relief."

The CWA was not always effective, but in just over a year, the agency built or restored a half-million miles of roads and constructed 40,000 schools and 1,000 airports. It hired 50,000 teachers to keep rural schools open and others to teach adult education courses in the cities. The CWA helped millions of people get through the bitterly cold winter of 1933–1934. It also put over a billion dollars of purchasing power into the economy. Roosevelt, who later would be accused of deficit spending, feared that the program was costing too much and might create a permanent class of relief recipients. In the spring of 1934, he ordered the CWA closed down.

The Public Works Administration (PWA), directed by Harold Ickes, in some respects overlapped the work of the CWA, but it lasted longer. Between 1933 and 1939, the PWA built hospitals, courthouses, and school buildings. It helped construct structures as diverse as the port of Brownsville, Texas, a bridge that linked Key West to the Florida mainland, and the library at the University of New Mexico. It built the aircraft carriers *Yorktown* and *Enterprise*, planes for the Army Air Corps, and low-cost housing for slum dwellers.

One purpose of the PWA was economic pump priming—the stimulation of the economy and consumer spending through the investment of government funds. Afraid that there might be scandals in the agency, Ickes spent money slowly and carefully. Thus, during the first years, PWA projects, worthwhile as most of them were, did little to stimulate the economy.

Agricultural Adjustment Act

In 1933, most farmers were desperate, as mounting surpluses and falling prices drastically cut their incomes. Some in the Midwest talked of open rebellion, even of revolution. But most observers saw only hopelessness and despair in farmers who had worked hard but were still losing their farms.

Congress passed a number of bills in 1933 and 1934 to deal with the agricultural crisis. But the New Deal's principal solution to the farm problem was the Agricultural Adjustment Act (AAA), which sought to control the overproduction of basic commodities so that farmers might regain the purchasing power they had enjoyed before World War I. To guarantee these "parity prices" (the average prices in the years 1909–1914), the production of major agricultural staples—wheat, cotton, corn, hogs, rice, tobacco, and milk—would be controlled by paying the farmers to reduce their acreage under cultiva-

tion. The AAA levied a tax at the processing stage to pay for the program.

The act aroused great disagreement among farm leaders and economists, but the controversy was nothing compared with the outcry from the public over the initial action of the AAA in the summer of 1933. To prevent a glut on the cotton and pork markets, the agency ordered 10 million acres of cotton plowed up and 6 million young pigs slaughtered. It seemed unnatural, even immoral, to kill pigs and plow up cotton when millions of people were underfed and in need of clothes. The story circulated that in the South, mules trained for many years to walk between the rows of cotton now refused to walk on the cotton plants. Some suggested that those mules were more intelligent than the government bureaucrats who had ordered the action.

The Agricultural Adjustment Act did raise the prices of some agricultural products. But it helped the larger farmers more than the small operators, and it was often disastrous for the tenant farmers and sharecroppers, whom crop reduction made expendable. Landowners often discharged tenant families when they reduced the acres under cultivation. There were provisions in the act to help marginal farmers, but little trickled down to them. Many were simply cast out on the road with a few possessions and nowhere to go. As for large farmers, they cultivated their fewer acres more intensely, so that the total crop was little reduced. In the end, the prolonged drought that hit the Southwest in 1934 did more than the AAA to limit production and raise agricultural prices. But the long-range significance of the AAA, which was later declared unconstitutional, was the establishment of the idea that the government should subsidize farmers for limiting production.

Industrial Recovery

The legislation during the first days of the Roosevelt administration contained something for almost every group. The National Industrial Recovery Act (NIRA) was designed to help business, raise prices, control production, and put people back to work. The act established the National Recovery Administration (NRA), with the power to set fair competition codes in all industries. For a time, everyone forgot about antitrust laws and talked of cooperation and planning rather than competition.

To run the NRA, Roosevelt appointed Hugh Johnson, who had helped organize the World War I draft and served on the War Industries Board. Johnson used his wartime experiences and the enthusiasm of the bond drives to rally the country around the NRA and, implicitly, around all New

Deal measures. There were parades and rallies, even a postage stamp, and industries that cooperated could display a blue eagle, the symbol of the NRA, designed to symbolize patriotic cooperation. "We Do Our Part," the posters and banners proclaimed, but the results were somewhat less than the promise.

Section 7a of the NIRA, included at the insistence of organized labor, guaranteed labor's right to organize and to bargain collectively and established the National Labor Board to see that their rights were respected. But the board, usually dominated by businessmen, often interpreted the labor provisions of the contracts loosely. In addition, small businessmen complained that the NIRA was unfair to their interests. Any attempt to set prices led to controversy.

Many consumers suspected that the codes and contracts were raising prices, while others feared the return of monopoly in some industries. One woman wrote the president that she was taking down her blue eagle because she had lost her job; another wrote from Tennessee to denounce the NIRA as a joke because it helped only the chain stores. Johnson's booster campaign backfired in the end because anyone with a complaint about a New Deal agency seemed to take it out on the symbol of the blue eagle. When the Supreme Court declared the NIRA unconstitutional in 1935, few people complained. Still, the NIRA was an ambitious attempt to bring some order into a confused business situa-

tion, and the labor provisions of the act were picked up later by the National Labor Relations Act.

Civilian Conservation Corps

One of the most popular and successful of the New Deal programs, the Civilian Conservation Corps (CCC), combined work relief with the preservation of natural resources. It put young unemployed white men between the ages of 18 and 25 to work on reforestation, road and park construction, flood control, and other projects. There were a few, carefully segregated black units. The men lived in work camps (there were over 1,500 camps in all) and earned $30 a month, $25 of which had to be sent home to their families. Some complained that the CCC camps, run by the U.S. Army, were too military, and one woman wrote from Minnesota to point out that all the best young men were at CCC camps when they ought to be home looking for real jobs and finding brides. Others complained that the CCC did nothing for unemployed young women, so a few special camps were organized for them, but only 8,000 women took part in a program that by 1941 had included 2.5 million men participants. Overall, the CCC was one of the most successful and least controversial of all the New Deal programs.

Tennessee Valley Authority

Franklin Roosevelt, like his distant Republican relative Theodore, believed in conservation. He promoted flood-control projects and added millions of

A Civilian Conservation Corps recruit planting a tree near Spartanburg, South Carolina, in September 1941. The CCC built trails, planted trees, and in other ways tried to improve the environment. But they also tried to build better bodies. The recruits, often only 17 years old, did calisthenics, military drills, and were provided with healthy food. The CCC was ended shortly after this photo was taken. With a war on, there was no longer a need to create work for young men. (*National Archives [111SC-10-392(WW2)]*)

The Tennessee Valley Authority

The TVA transformed the way the Tennessee valley looked; it replaced a wild river with a series of flood-control and hydroelectric dams and created a series of lakes behind the dams. It stopped short of the coordinated regional planning that some people wanted, but it was one of the most important New Deal projects.

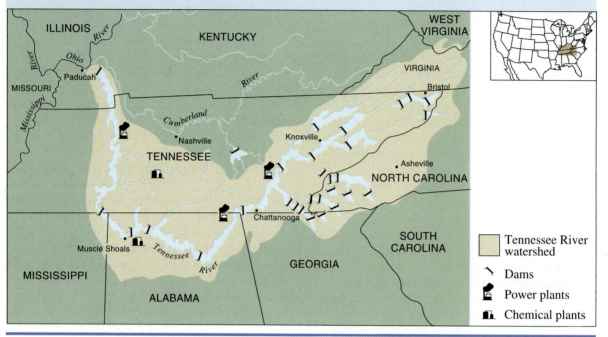

acres to the country's national forests, wildlife refuges, and fish and game sanctuaries. But the most important New Deal conservation project, the Tennessee Valley Authority (TVA), owed more to Republican George Norris, a progressive senator from Nebraska, than to Roosevelt.

During World War I, the federal government had built a hydroelectric plant and two munitions factories at Muscle Shoals, on the Tennessee River in Alabama. The government tried unsuccessfully to sell these facilities to private industry, but all through the 1920s, Norris campaigned to have the federal government operate them for the benefit of the valley's residents. Twice Republican presidents vetoed bills that would have allowed federal operation, but Roosevelt endorsed Norris's idea and expanded it into a regional development plan.

Congress authorized the TVA as an independent public corporation with the power to sell electricity and fertilizer and to promote flood control and land reclamation. The TVA built nine major dams and many minor ones between 1933 and 1944, affecting parts of Virginia, North Carolina, Georgia, Alabama, Mississippi, Tennessee, and Kentucky. Some private utility companies claimed that the TVA offered unfair competition to private industry, but it was an imaginative experiment in regional planning. It promoted everything from flood control to library bookmobiles. For residents of the valley, it meant cheaper electricity and changed lifestyles. The TVA meant radios, electric irons, washing machines, and other appliances for the first time. The largest federal construction project ever launched, it also created jobs for many thousands who helped build the dams. But government officials and businessmen who feared that the experiment would lead to socialism always curbed the regional planning possibilities of the TVA.

Critics of the New Deal

The furious legislative activity during the first 100 days of the New Deal helped alleviate the pessimism and despair hanging over the country. Stock market prices rose slightly, and industrial production was up 11 percent at the end of 1933. Still, the country remained locked in depression, and nearly 12 million Americans were without jobs. Yet Roosevelt captured the imagination of ordinary Americans everywhere. But conservatives were not so sure that Roosevelt was a savior; in fact, many businessmen, after being impressed with Roosevelt's early economy measures and approving programs such as the NIRA, began to fear that the president was leading the country toward socialism. Appalled by work relief programs, regional planning such as the TVA, and the abandonment of the gold standard, many businessmen were also annoyed by the style of the president, whom they called "that man in the White House."

The conservative revolt against Roosevelt surfaced in the summer of 1934 as the congressional elections approached. A group of disgruntled politicians and businessmen formed the Liberty League. The league supported conservative or at least anti–New Deal candidates for Congress, but it had little influence. In the election of 1934, the Democrats increased their majority from 310 to 319 in the House and from 60 to 69 in the Senate (only the second time in the twentieth century that the party in power had increased its control of Congress in the midterm election). A few people were learning to hate Roosevelt, but it was obvious that most Americans approved of what he was doing.

While some thought the New Deal was too radical, others maintained that the government had not done enough to help the poor. One source of criticism was the Communist party. Attracting supporters from all walks of life during a time when capitalism seemed to have failed, the Communist party increased its membership from 7,500 in 1930 to 75,000 in 1938. The Communists organized protest marches and tried to reach out to the oppressed and unemployed. While a majority who joined the party came from the working class, communism had a special appeal to writers, intellectuals, and some college students during a decade when the American dream had turned into a nightmare.

A larger number of Americans, however, was influenced by other movements promising easy solutions to poverty and unemployment. In Minnesota, Governor Floyd Olson, elected on a Farm-Labor ticket, accused capitalism of causing the Depression and startled some listeners when he thundered, "I hope the present system of government goes right to hell." In California, Upton Sinclair, the muckraking socialist and author of *The Jungle,* ran for governor on the platform "End Poverty in California." He promised to pay everyone over 60 years of age a pension of $50 a month using higher income and inheritance taxes to finance the program. He won in the primary but lost the election, and his program collapsed.

California also produced Dr. Francis E. Townsend, who claimed he had a national following of over 5 million people. His supporters backed the Townsend Old Age Revolving Pension Plan, which promised

Father Charles E. Coughlin from Royal Oak, Michigan, was a flamboyant Catholic priest who was just as much the master of the radio as the president himself. A first he supported Roosevelt, but then in 1935, he became one of FDR's most caustic critics. His impassioned anti-Semitic remarks finally caused the Catholic church to take him off the air. *(Library of Congress [LC-USZ6-2-111027])*

$200 a month to all unemployed citizens over the age of 60 on the condition that they spend it in the same month they received it. Economists laughed at the utopian scheme, but followers organized thousands of Townsend Pension Clubs across the country. As one Minnesota woman wrote to Eleanor Roosevelt, "The old folks who have paid taxes all their lives and built this country up will live in comfort." The plan "will banish crime, give the young a chance to work, pay off the national debt which is mounting every day."

More threatening to Roosevelt and the New Deal were the protest movements led by Father Charles E. Coughlin and Senator Huey P. Long. Father Coughlin, a Roman Catholic priest from a Detroit suburb, attracted an audience of 30 to 45 million to his national radio show. At first, he supported Roosevelt's policies, but later he savagely attacked the New Deal as excessively probusiness. Mixing religious commentary with visions of a society operating without bankers and big businessmen, he roused his audience with blatantly anti-Semitic appeals. Most often the "evil" bankers he described were Jewish—the Rothschilds, Warburgs, and Kuhn-Loebs. Anti-Semitism reached a peak in the 1930s, so Jews bore the brunt of nativist fury.

Huey Long, like Coughlin, had a charisma that won support from the millions still trying to survive in a country where the continuing depression made day-to-day existence a struggle. Elected governor of

Louisiana in 1928, Long promoted a "Share the Wealth" program. He taxed the oil refineries and built hospitals, schools, and thousands of miles of new highways. By 1934, he was the virtual dictator of his state, personally controlling the police and the courts. Long talked about a guaranteed $2,000 to $3,000 income for all American families (18.3 million families earned less than $1,000 per year in 1936) and promised pensions for the elderly and college educations for the young. He would pay for these programs by taxing the rich and liquidating the great fortunes. Had not an assassin's bullet cut Long down in September 1935, he might have mounted a third-party challenge to Roosevelt.

THE SECOND NEW DEAL

Responding in part to the discontent of the lower middle class but also to the threat of various utopian schemes, Roosevelt moved his programs in 1935 toward the goals of social reform and social justice. At the same time, he departed from attempts to cooperate with the business community. "We find our population suffering from old inequalities," Roosevelt announced in his annual message to Congress in January 1935. "In spite of our efforts and in spite of our talk, we have not weeded out the overprivileged and we have not effectively lifted up the underprivileged."

Work Relief and Social Security

The Works Progress Administration (WPA), authorized by Congress in April 1935, was the first massive attempt to deal with unemployment and its demoralizing effect on millions of Americans. The WPA employed about 3 million people a year on a variety of socially useful projects. The WPA workers, who earned wages lower than private industry paid, built bridges, airports, libraries, roads, and golf courses. Nearly 85 percent of the funds went directly into salaries and wages.

A minor but important part of the WPA funding supported writers, artists, actors, and musicians. Richard Wright, Jack Conroy, and Saul Bellow were among the 10,000 writers who were paid less than $100 a month. Experimental theater, innovative and well-written guides to all the states, murals painted in municipal and state buildings, and the Historical Records Survey were among the long-lasting results of these projects.

Only one member of a family could qualify for a WPA job, and first choice always went to the man. A

The WPA (which some wags said stood for "We Putter Around") employed many people for a great variety of jobs. This is an unusual photograph because it is in color. A few photographers who worked for government agencies were beginning to experiment with color film, but most of the photographs that survive from the 1930s are black and white. *(Corbis-Bettmann)*

woman could qualify only if she headed the household. But eventually more than 13 percent of the people who worked for the WPA were women, although their most common employment was in the sewing room, where old clothes were made over. "For unskilled men we have the shovel. For unskilled women we have only the needle," one official remarked.

The WPA was controversial from the beginning. Critics charged that the agency had hired Communists to paint murals or work on the state guides. For others, a "lazy good-for-nothing" leaning on a shovel symbolized the WPA. The initials WPA, some wags charged, stood for "We Pay for All" or "We Putter Around." Yet for all the criticism, the WPA did useful work; the program built nearly 6,000 schools, more than 2,500 hospitals, and 13,000 playgrounds. More important, it restored the morale of millions of unemployed Americans.

The National Youth Administration (NYA) supplemented the work of the WPA and assisted young men and women between the ages of 16 and 25, many of them students. A young law student named Richard Nixon earned 35 cents an hour working for the NYA while he was at Duke University, and Lyndon Johnson began his political career as director of the Texas NYA.

By far the most enduring reform came with the passage of the Social Security Act of 1935. Since the progressive period, social workers and reformers had argued for a national system of health insurance, old-age pensions, and unemployment insurance. By the 1930s, the United States remained the only major industrial country without such programs. Within the Roosevelt circle, Frances Perkins argued most strongly for social insurance, but the popularity of the Townsend Plan and other schemes to aid the elderly helped convince Roosevelt of the need to act. The number of people over the age of 65 in the country increased from 5.7 million in 1925 to 7.8 million in 1935, and that group demanded action.

The Social Security Act of 1935 was a compromise. Congress quickly dropped a plan for federal health insurance because of opposition from the medical profession. The most important provision of the act was old-age and survivor insurance to be paid for by a tax of 1 percent on both employers and employees. It was never intended as a traditional pension plan, but rather it was a social contract where one generation helped to pay for the previous generation's retirement. The benefits initially ranged from $10 to $85 a month. The act also established a cooperative federal–state system of unemployment

compensation. Other provisions authorized federal grants to the states to assist in caring for the disabled and the blind. Finally, the Social Security Act provided some aid to dependent children. This provision would eventually expand to become the largest federal welfare program.

The National Association of Manufacturers denounced social security as a program that would regiment the people and destroy individual self-reliance. Yet in no other country was social insurance paid for in part by a regressive tax on the workers' wages. "We put those payroll contributions there so as to give the contributors a legal, moral, and political right to collect their pensions and unemployment benefits," Roosevelt later explained. "With those taxes in there, no damn politician can ever scrap my social security program." It was never intended as a traditional pension program, but rather as a social contract whereby one generation helped to pay for the previous generation's retirement. But the law also excluded many people, including those who needed it the most, such as farm laborers and domestic servants. It discriminated against married women who were wage earners, and it failed to protect against sickness. Yet for all its weaknesses, it was one of the most important New Deal measures. A landmark in American social legislation, it marked the beginning of the welfare state that would expand significantly after World War II.

Aiding the Farmers

The Social Security Act and the Works Progress Administration were only two signs of Roosevelt's greater concern for social reform. The flurry of legislation in 1935 and early 1936, often called the "second New Deal," also included an effort to help American farmers. Over 1.7 million farm families had incomes of under $500 annually in 1935, and 42 percent of all those who lived on farms were tenants. The Resettlement Administration (RA), motivated in part by a Jeffersonian ideal of yeoman farmers working their own land, set out to relocate tenant farmers on land purchased by the government. Lack of funds and fears that the Roosevelt administration was trying to establish Soviet-style collective farms limited the effectiveness of the RA program.

Much more important in improving the lives of farm families was the Rural Electrification Administration (REA), which was authorized in 1935 to lend money to cooperatives to generate and distribute electricity in isolated rural areas not served by private utilities. Only 10 percent of the nation's farms had electricity in 1936. When the REA's lines were finally attached, they dramatically changed the lives of millions of farm families who had been able only to dream about the radios, washing machines, and farm equipment advertised in magazines.

In the hill country west of Austin, Texas, for example, there was no electricity until the end of the 1930s. Life went on in small towns and on ranches much as it had for decades. Houses were illuminated by kerosene lamps, whose wicks had to be trimmed just right or the lamp smoked or went out, but even with perfect adjustment, it was difficult to read by them. There were no bathrooms, because bathrooms required running water, and running water depended on an electric pump. "Yes, we had running water," one woman remembered. "I always said we had running water because I grabbed those two buckets up and ran the two hundred yards to the house with them."

Women and children hauled water constantly—for infrequent baths, for continuous canning (because without a refrigerator, fruits and vegetables had to be put up almost immediately or they spoiled), and for wash day. Wash day, always Monday, meant scrubbing clothes by hand with harsh soap on a washboard; it meant boiling clothes in a large copper vat over a woodstove and stirring them with a wooden fork. It was a hot, backbreaking job, especially in summer. Next, the women had to lift the hot, heavy clothes into a rinsing tub. After the clothes were thoroughly mixed with bluing (to make them white), they had to be wrung out by hand and then carried to the lines, where they were hung to dry. Tuesday was for ironing, and even in summer, a wood fire was needed to heat the irons. When irons got dirty on the stove, as could easily happen, dirt got on a white shirt or blouse and it had to be washed all over again.

It was memory of life in the hill country and personal knowledge of how hard his mother and grandmother toiled that inspired a young congressman from Texas, Lyndon Johnson, to work to bring rural electrification to the area. In November 1939, the lights finally came on in the hill country, plugging the area into the twentieth century.

The Dust Bowl: An Ecological Disaster

Those who tried to farm on the Great Plains fell victim to years of drought and dust storms. Record heat waves and below-average rainfall in the 1930s turned an area from the Oklahoma panhandle to western Kansas into a giant dust bowl. A single storm on May 11, 1934, removed 300 million tons of topsoil and turned day into night. Between 1932

The Dust Bowl

This map depicts the wide extent of damage caused by high winds and drought, the worst in the history of the country, according to the U.S. Weather Bureau.

Areas of Wind Erosion 1935–1940
- Severe
- Severest

and 1939, there was an average of 50 storms a year. Cities kept their street lights on for 24 hours a day. Dust covered everything from food to bedspreads and piled up in dunes in city streets and barnyards. Thousands died of "dust pneumonia." One woman remembered what it was like at night: "A trip for water to rinse the grit from our lips, and then back to bed with washcloths over our noses, we try to lie still, because every turn stirs the dust on the blankets."

A 1936 survey of 20 counties in the heart of the dust bowl concluded that 97.6 percent of the land suffered from erosion and more than 50 percent was seriously damaged. By the end of the decade, 10,000 farm homes were abandoned to the elements, and 9 million acres of farmland were reduced to a wasteland. By the end of the decade, 3.5 million people had abandoned their farms and joined a massive migration to find better lives.

Not all were forced out by the dust storms; some fell victim to large-scale agriculture, and many tenant farmers and hired hands were expendable during the Depression. In most cases, they not only lost their jobs, but they also were evicted from their houses. More than 350,000 left Oklahoma

Thousands of families fled the dust bowl in old cars and headed for California. With no place to sleep, they used sheets and blankets to turn their cars into tents. John Steinbeck wrote about these migrants in *Grapes of Wrath*. *(Courtesy Franklin D. Roosevelt Library [53227(575)])*

during the decade and moved to California, a place that seemed to many like the promised land. But the name *Okie* came to mean any farm migrant. The plight of these wayfarers was immortalized by John Steinbeck in his novel about the Joad family, *The Grapes of Wrath* (1939). The next year, John Ford made a powerful movie based on the book, starring Henry Fonda as Tom Joad. Many Americans sympathized with the plight of the embattled farm family trying to escape the dust bowl and find a better life in California; others interpreted their defeat as a symbol of the failure of the American dream.

The dust bowl was a natural disaster, but it was aided and exaggerated by human actions and inactions. The semiarid plains west of the 98th meridian were not suitable for intensive agriculture. Overgrazing, too much plowing, and indiscriminate planting over a period of 60 years exposed the thin soil to the elements. When the winds came in the 1930s, much of the land simply blew away. In the end, it was a matter of too little government planning and regulation and too many farmers using new technology to exploit natural resources for their own gain.

The Roosevelt administration did try to deal with the problem. The Taylor Grazing Act of 1934 restricted the use of the public range in an attempt to prevent overgrazing, and it ended an era of unregulated use of natural resources in the West. Before 1934, anyone could use public land, but the 1934 act required a permit and a fee. The Taylor Act established the principle that the remaining public domain was under federal control and not for sale. The Civilian Conservation Corps and other New Deal agencies planted trees, and the Soil Conservation Service promoted drought-resistant crops and contour plowing, but it was too little and too late. Even worse, according to some authorities, government measures applied after the disaster of 1930 encouraged farmers to return to raising wheat and other inappropriate crops, leading to more dust bowl crises in the 1950s and 1970s.

The New Deal and the West

The New Deal probably aided the West more than any other region. The CCC, AAA, drought relief measures, and various federal agencies helped the region to an extent that was out of proportion to the people who lived there. In fact, the top 14 states in per capita expenditure by federal agencies during the 1930s were all in the West. Most important were the large-scale water projects. The Boulder Dam (later renamed the Hoover Dam) on the Colorado River not only provided massive amounts of hydroelectric power but, with the construction of a 259-mile aqueduct, also provided the water that caused the city of Los Angeles to boom.

The largest power project of all was the Grand Coulee Dam on the Columbia River northwest of Spokane, Washington. Employing tens of thousands

Taylor Grazing Act, 1934

The Taylor Grazing Act of 1934 marked the end of an era when the federal government transferred public land to private ownership. The federal ownership or control of vast amounts of land in the West set up a conflict between rugged individualism and government planning and management.

30% or more Bureau of Land Management control
Bureau of Indian Affairs control
Department of Defense control
National Forest Service control
National Park Service control

of men and pouring millions of dollars into the economy, the dam, finally completed in 1941, provided cheap electricity for the Pacific Northwest and eventually irrigated over a million acres of arid land.

Despite all the federal aid to the region, many westerners, holding fast to the myth of frontier individualism, bitterly criticized the regulation and the bureaucracy that went with the grants. The cattlemen in Wyoming, Colorado, and Montana desperately needed the help of the federal government, but even as they accepted the aid, they denounced Roosevelt and the New Deal.

Controlling Corporate Power and Taxing the Wealthy

In the summer of 1935, Roosevelt also moved to control the large corporations, and he even toyed with radical plans to tax the well-to-do heavily and redistribute wealth in the United States. The Public Utility Holding Company Act, passed in 1935, attempted to restrict the power of the giant utility companies, the 12 largest of which controlled more than half the country's power. The act gave various government commissions the authority to regulate and control the power companies and included a "death sentence" clause that gave each company five years to demonstrate that its services were efficient. If it could not demonstrate this, the government could dissolve the company. This was one of the most radical attempts to control corporate power in American history.

In his message to Congress in 1935, Roosevelt also pointed out that the federal revenue laws had "done little to prevent an unjust concentration of wealth and economic power." He suggested steeper income taxes for wealthy groups and a much larger inheritance tax. When Congress dropped the inheritance tax provision, however, Roosevelt did not fight to have it restored. Even the weakened bill, increasing estate and gift taxes and raising the income tax rates at the top, angered many in the business community who thought that Roosevelt had sold out to Huey Long's "Share the Wealth" scheme.

The New Deal for Labor

Like many progressive reformers, Roosevelt was more interested in improving the lot of working people by passing social legislation than by strengthening the bargaining position of organized labor. Yet he saw labor as an important balance to the power of industry, and he listened to his advisers, especially Frances Perkins and Senator Robert Wagner of New York, who persistently brought up the needs of organized labor.

After strikes in San Francisco, Minneapolis, and Toledo, Roosevelt supported the Wagner Act, officially called the National Labor Relations Act, which outlawed blacklisting and a number of other practices and reasserted labor's right to organize and to bargain collectively. The act also established a Labor Relations Board with the power to certify a properly elected bargaining unit. The act did not require workers to join unions, but it made the federal government a regulator, or at least a neutral force, in management–labor relations. That alone made the National Labor Relations Act one of the most important New Deal reform measures.

The Roosevelt administration's friendly attitude toward organized labor helped increase union membership from under 3 million in 1933 to 4.5 million by 1935. Many groups, however, were left out, including farm laborers, unskilled workers, and women. Only about 3 percent of working women belonged to unions, and women earned only about 60 percent of wages paid to men for equivalent work.

Still, many people resented that women were employed at all. The Brotherhood of Railway and Steamship Clerks ruled that no married woman whose husband could support her was eligible for a job. One writer had a perfect solution for the unemployment problem: "Simply fire the women, who shouldn't be working anyway, and hire the men."

The American Federation of Labor (AFL) had little interest in organizing unskilled workers, but a new group of committed and militant labor leaders emerged in the 1930s to take up that task. John L. Lewis, the eloquent head of the United Mine Workers, was the most aggressive. He was joined by David Dubinsky of the International Ladies' Garment Workers and Sidney Hillman, president of the Amalgamated Clothing Workers. Both were socialists who believed in economic planning, but both had worked closely with social justice progressives. These new progressive labor leaders formed the Committee of Industrial Organization (CIO) within the AFL and set out to organize workers in the steel, auto, and rubber industries. Rather than separating workers by skill or craft as the AFL preferred, they organized everyone into an industry-wide union much as the Knights of Labor had done in the 1880s. They also used new and aggressive tactics. When a foreman tried to increase production or enforce discipline, the union leaders would simply pull the switch and declare a spontaneous strike. This "brass knuckle unionism" worked especially well in the auto and rubber industries.

In 1936, the workers at three rubber plants in Akron, Ohio, went on unauthorized strikes. Instead of picketing outside the factory, they occupied the buildings and took them over, preventing the owners from running the factory with non-union workers. The "sit-down strike" became a new protest technique. Sometimes the workers occupied a factory for a week or more. Wives and children brought food and water. And the whole spectacle attracted the press and the newsreel cameras and created favorable publicity for the workers. After sit-down strikes against General Motors plants in Atlanta, Georgia, and Flint, Michigan, General Motors finally accepted the United Auto Workers (UAW) as their employees' bargaining agent. The General Motors strike was the most important event in a

Distribution of Income, 1935–1936

Roosevelt and the New Deal never sought consistently to redistribute wealth in America, and a great disparity in income and assets remained.

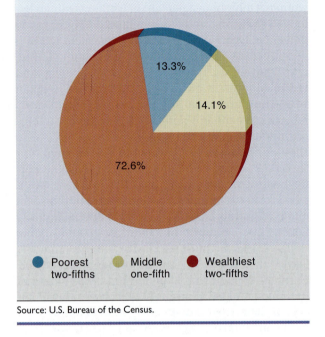

13.3%

14.1%

72.6%

● Poorest two-fifths
● Middle one-fifth
● Wealthiest two-fifths

Source: U.S. Bureau of the Census.

critical period of labor upheaval. Labor's voice now began to be heard in the decision-making process in major industries where labor had long been denied any role. They also helped raise the status of organized labor in the eyes of many Americans.

Violence spread along with the sit-down strike. Chrysler capitulated, but the Ford Motor Company used hired gunmen to discourage the strikers. A bloody struggle ensued before Ford agreed to accept the UAW as the bargaining agent. Even U.S. Steel, which had been militantly anti-union, signed an agreement with the Steel Workers Organizing Committee calling for a 40-hour week and an eight-hour day. But other steel companies refused to go along. In Chicago on Memorial Day in 1937, a confrontation between the police and peaceful pickets at the Republic Steel plant resulted in 10 deaths. In the "Memorial Day Massacre," as it came to be called, the police fired without provocation into a crowd of workers and their families, who had gathered near the plant in a holiday mood. All 10 of the dead were shot in the back.

The CIO's aggressive tactics gained many new members, to the horror of AFL leaders. They expelled the CIO leaders from the AFL, only to see them form a separate Congress of Industrial Organization (the initials stayed the same). By the end of the decade, the CIO had infused the labor movement with a new spirit. Accepting unskilled workers, African Americans, and others who had never belonged to a union before, the CIO won increased pay, better working conditions, and the right to bargain collectively in most of the basic American industries.

America's Minorities in the 1930s

One-half million African Americans joined unions through the CIO during the 1930s, and many blacks were aided by various New Deal agencies. Yet the familiar pattern of discrimination, low-paying jobs, and intimidation through violence persisted. Lynchings in the South actually increased in the New Deal years, rising from 8 in 1932 to 28 in 1933 and 20 in 1935.

One particular case came to symbolize and dramatize discrimination against African Americans in the 1930s. On March 25, 1931, in Scottsboro, Alabama, two young white women accused nine black men of raping them in a railroad boxcar as they all hitched a free ride. A jury of white men found all nine blacks guilty, and the court sentenced eight to die. The U.S. Supreme Court ordered new trials in 1933, on the grounds that the accused rapists had not received proper legal counsel. The case garnered much publicity in the United States and abroad. The youth of the defendants, their quick trial, and the harsh sentences made the "Scottsboro boys" a popular cause for many northern liberals and especially the Communist party.

For many southerners, however, it was a matter of defending the honor of white women. As one observer remarked of one of the accusers, she "might be a fallen woman, but by God she is a white woman." However, evidence supporting the alleged rapes was never presented, and eventually one of the women recanted. Yet the case dragged on. In new trials, five of the young men were convicted and given long prison terms. Charges against the other four were dropped in 1937. Four of the remaining five were paroled by 1946, and the fifth escaped to Michigan.

African Americans did not have to be accused of rape to want to flee to the North, however, and the migration of blacks to northern cities, which had accelerated during World War I, continued during the 1930s. The collapse of cotton prices forced black farmers and farm laborers to flee north for survival. But since most were poorly educated, they soon became trapped in northern ghettos, where they were eligible for only the most menial jobs. The black unemployment rate was triple that of whites, and blacks often received less per person in welfare payments.

Black leaders attacked the Roosevelt administration for supporting or allowing segregation in government-sponsored facilities. The TVA model town of Norris, Tennessee, was off limits for blacks, and AAA policies actually drove blacks off the land in the South. The CCC segregated black and white workers, and the PWA financed segregated housing projects. Some charged that NRA stood for "Negroes Rarely Allowed." Many African Americans wrote to the president or the first lady to protest discrimination in New Deal agencies. As one woman from Georgia put it, "I can't sign my name, Mr. President, they will beat me up and run me away from here and this is my home." Blacks ought to realize, a writer in the NAACP journal *The Crisis* warned in 1935, "that the powers-that-be in the Roosevelt administration have nothing for them."

Roosevelt, fearing that he might antagonize southern congressmen whose backing he needed, refused to support the two major civil rights bills of the era, an antilynching bill and a bill to abolish the poll tax. Yet Harold Ickes and Harry Hopkins worked to ensure that blacks were given opportunities in New Deal agencies. By 1941, black federal employees totaled 150,000, more than three times the number during the Hoover administration. Most worked in the lower ranks, but some were lawyers, architects, office managers, and engineers.

Partly responsible for the presence of more black employees was the "black cabinet," a group of more than 50 young blacks who had appointments in vari-

ous New Deal agencies and were led by Mary McLeod Bethune, the daughter of a sharecropper. She had founded a black primary school in Florida and then transformed it into Bethune-Cookman College. In the 1920s, she had organized the National Council of Negro Women. In 1934, Harry Hopkins, following the advice of Eleanor Roosevelt, appointed her to the advisory committee of the National Youth Administration. Bethune had some impact on New Deal policy and on the black cabinet. She spoke out forcefully, she picketed and protested, and she intervened shrewdly to obtain civil rights and more jobs for African Americans, but in the end the gains for blacks during the New Deal were very limited.

W. E. B. Du Bois, in the meantime, had become increasingly discouraged with token appointments and the reform of race relations through integration with white society. In the 1920s, he supported a series of pan-African conferences designed to unite black people from around the world. He resigned from the NAACP and from his position as editor of *The Crisis* in 1934 and devoted his time to promoting "voluntary segregation" and a "Negro Nation within a nation." Eventually, he joined the Communist party and moved to Ghana, where he died in 1963.

Although Roosevelt appointed a number of blacks to government positions, he was never particularly committed to civil rights. That was not true of Eleanor Roosevelt, who was educated in part by Mary McLeod Bethune. In 1939, when the Daughters of the American Revolution refused to allow Marian Anderson, a black concert singer, to use their stage, Mrs. Roosevelt publicly protested and

Eleanor Roosevelt meeting in 1937 with the National Youth Administration's executive director, Aubrey Williams, and its director of Negro activities, Mary McLeod Bethune. Eleanor Roosevelt, considered the most visible and active of first ladies, was both praised and attacked for her activities. *(Bettmann/Corbis)*

resigned her membership in the DAR. She also arranged for Anderson to sing from the steps of the Lincoln Memorial, where 75,000 people gathered to listen and to support civil rights for all black citizens.

Hundreds of thousands of Mexicans, brought to the Unites States to work in the 1920s, lost their jobs in the Depression. Drifting to the Southwest or settling in the urban *barrios* and the small towns and farms in the Southwest, they met signs such as "Only White Labor Employed" and "No Niggers, Mexicans, or Dogs Allowed." Some New Deal agencies helped destitute Mexicans. A few worked for the CCC and the WPA, but to be employed, an applicant had to qualify for state relief, and that eliminated most migrants. The primary solution was not to provide aid for Mexicans but to ship them back to Mexico. In Los Angeles and other cities, the police and immigration authorities rounded up aliens and held them illegally. A trainload of repatriates left Los Angeles every month during 1933, and officials deported thousands from other cities. One estimate placed the number sent back in 1932 at 200,000, including some American citizens.

Not all the Mexicans were repatriated, however, and some who remained adopted militant tactics to obtain fair treatment. Mexican strawberry pickers went on strike in El Monte, California, and 18,000 cotton pickers walked away from their jobs in the San Joaquin valley in 1933. On August 31, 1939, during a record-breaking heat wave, nearly all of the 430 workers, most of them Mexican-American women, staged a massive walkout at one of the largest food processing plants in Los Angeles. In Gallup, New Mexico, several thousand Mexican coal miners walked out on strike. They constructed a village of shacks and planned to wait out the strike. The miners, who were aided by writers and artists from Santa Fe and Taos, were evicted from their village by the city authorities. Federal agents arrested their leader, Jesus Pallares, and deported him to Mexico.

Asians (Chinese, Japanese, and a smaller number of Koreans and Asian Indians) also suffered during the Depression. Most lived in ethnic enclaves, lost their jobs, and were treated as foreigners—not quite black, but not white either. Asians, especially the second generation who were automatically citizens if they were born in the United States, were troubled by a "twoness." They were both Chinese or Japanese and American At least their parents wanted them to retain ties to the old country and the old culture. One young Chinese student from San Francisco had to go to Chinese school after her regular school. "We never became proficient in reading or writing Chinese, " she recalled, "probably because we never thought of ourselves as needing Chinese. After all, weren't we Americans?" A Japanese Nisei remembered the "queer mixture of Occident and the Orient. I sat down to American breakfast and Japanese lunch. My palate developed a fondness for rice along with corned beef and cabbage. I became equally adept with knife and fork and with chopsticks. I said grace at mealtime in Japanese, and recited the Lord's prayer in English." But one Japanese father told his son to learn Japanese because there was no future for him in the United States. Most American failed to appreciate the sense of "twoness" that the Asians suffered with; indeed, they treated all Asians as

Mexican farm workers, eagerly recruited in the 1920s, often found themselves deported back to Mexico in the 1930s. The fact that even the migrants drove cars and trucks, though old and repaired, shocked foreign observers. In much of the rest of the world, autos were owned only by the wealthy. *(Library of Congress)*

aliens, and they had great difficulty distinguishing a Chinese from a Japanese from a Korean.

Native Americans also experienced alienation, disease, and despair during the Depression, and their plight was compounded by years of exploitation. Since the Dawes Act of 1887 (described in Chapter 17), government policy had sought to make the Indian into a property-owning farmer and to limit tribal rights. Native Americans lost over 60 percent of the 138 million acres granted them in 1887. The government declared some of the land surplus and encouraged individuals to settle on 160 acres and adopt the "habits of civilized life." Few Native Americans profited from this system, but many whites did.

Just as other progressives sought the quick assimilation of immigrants, the progressive era Indian commissioners sped up the allotment process to increase Indian detribalization. But many Native Americans who remained on the reservations were not even citizens. Finally, in 1924, Congress granted citizenship to all Indians born in the United States. The original Americans became U.S. citizens, but that did not end their suffering.

Franklin Roosevelt brought a new spirit to Indian policy by appointing John Collier as commissioner of Indian affairs. Collier was primarily responsible for the passage of the Indian Reorganization Act of 1934, which sought to restore the political independence of the tribes and to end the allotment policy of the Dawes Act. "Even where a tribal group is split into factions, where leadership has broken down, where Indians clamor to distribute the tribal property, even there deep forces of cohesion persist and can be evoked," Collier wrote. The bill also sought to promote the "study of Indian civilization" and to "preserve and develop the special cultural contributions and achievements of such civilization, including Indian arts, crafts, skills and traditions." Not all Indians agreed with the new policies. Some chose to become members of the dominant culture, and the Navajos voted to reject the Reorganization Act. Some Americans charged that the act was inspired by communism. Others argued that its principal result would be to increase government bureaucracy, while missionaries claimed that the government was promoting paganism by allowing the Indians to practice their native religions.

The paradox and contradictions of U.S. policy toward the Indians can be illustrated by Collier's attempt to solve the Navajo problem. Genuinely sympathetic to Native Americans, he was also a modern man who believed in soil conservation, science, and progress. The Navajo lands, like most of the West, were overgrazed, and soil erosion threatened to fill the new lake behind the Hoover Dam with silt. By supporting a policy of reducing the herds of sheep and goats on Indian land and by promoting soil conservation, Collier contributed to the change in the Navajo lifestyle and to the end of their self-sufficiency, something he wanted to support.

Women and the New Deal

Women made some gains during the 1930s, and more women occupied high government positions than in any previous administration. Besides Frances Perkins, the secretary of labor, there was Molly Dewson, a social worker with the Massachusetts Girls Parole Department and the National Consumers League before becoming head of the Women's Division of the Democratic Committee and then an adviser to Roosevelt. Working closely with Eleanor Roosevelt to promote women's causes, she helped achieve a number of firsts: two women appointed ambassadors, a judge on the U.S. Court of Appeals, the director of the mint, and many women in government agencies. Katharine Lenroot, director of the Children's Bureau, and Mary Anderson, head of the Women's Bureau, selected many other women to serve in their agencies. Some of these women had collaborated as social workers and now joined government bureaus to continue the fight for social justice. But they were usually in offices where they did not threaten male prerogatives. Despite some gains, the early New Deal programs did nothing for an estimated 140,000 homeless women, or the 2 to 4 million unemployed women. Married women often were fired from their jobs on the grounds that they should be home caring for their families rather than depriving men of employment. Single, divorced, and widowed women were usually ignored. Eleanor Roosevelt was genuinely concerned over the plight of poor women. She sponsored a White House Conference in November 1933 on the Emergency Needs of Women. She also advocated including more women in the CCC, the WPA, and other programs, but in the end the New Deal did little for poor women.

THE LAST YEARS OF THE NEW DEAL

The New Deal was not a consistent or well-organized effort to end the Depression and restructure society. Roosevelt was a politician and a pragmatist, unconcerned about ideological or programmatic consistency. The first New Deal in 1933 and 1934 concentrated on relief and recovery, while the legislation passed in 1935 and 1936 was more involved with social reform. In many ways, the election of 1936 marked the high point of Roosevelt's power and influence. After 1937, in part because of the growing threat of war but also because of increasing opposition in Congress, the pace of social legislation slowed. Yet several measures passed in 1937 and 1938 had such far-reaching significance that some historians refer to a third New Deal. Among the new measures were bills that provided for a minimum wage and for housing reform.

The Election of 1936

The Republicans in 1936 nominated a moderate, Governor Alfred Landon of Kansas. Although he attacked the New Deal, charging that new government programs were wasteful and created a dangerous federal bureaucracy, Landon only promised to do the same thing more cheaply and efficiently. Two-thirds of the newspapers in the country supported him, and the *Literary Digest* predicted his victory on the basis of a "scientific" telephone poll.

Roosevelt, helped by signs that the economy was recovering and supported by a coalition of the Democratic South, organized labor, farmers, and urban voters, won easily. A majority of African Americans for the first time deserted the party of Lincoln, not because of Roosevelt's interest in civil rights for blacks but because New Deal relief programs assisted many poor blacks. A viable candidate to the left of the New Deal failed to materialize. In fact, the Socialist party candidate, Norman Thomas, polled fewer than 200,000 votes. Roosevelt won by over 10 million votes, carrying every state except Maine and Vermont. Even the traditionally Republican states of Pennsylvania, Delaware, and Connecticut, which had voted Republican in almost every election since 1856, went for Roosevelt. As he announced in his acceptance speech, "To some generations much is given, of other generations much is expected. This generation has a rendezvous with destiny." Now he had a mandate to continue his New Deal social and economic reforms.

The Battle of the Supreme Court

"I see one-third of a nation ill-housed, ill-clad, ill-nourished," Roosevelt declared in his second inaugural address, and he vowed to alter that situation. But the president's first action in 1937 did not call for legislation to alleviate poverty. Instead, he announced a plan to reform the Supreme Court and the judicial system. The Court had invalidated not only a number of New Deal measures—including the NIRA and the first version of the AAA—but other measures as well.

Increasingly angry at the "nine old men" who seemed to be destroying New Deal initiatives and defying Congress's will, Roosevelt determined to create a more sympathetic Court. He hoped to gain power to appoint an extra justice for each justice over 70 years of age, of whom there were six. His plan also called for modernizing the court system at all levels, but that plan got lost in the public outcry over the Court-packing scheme.

Roosevelt's plan to nullify the influence of the older and more reactionary justices foundered. Republicans accused him of being a dictator and of subverting the Constitution. Many congressmen from his own party refused to support him. Led by Vice President John Nance Garner of Texas, a number of southern Democrats broke with the president and formed a coalition with conservative Republicans that lasted for more than 30 years. After months

FDR's Successful Presidential Campaigns, 1932–1944

Year	Candidate	Party	Popular Vote	Electoral Vote
1932	FRANKLIN D. ROOSEVELT	Democratic	22,809,638 (57.4%)	472
	Herbert C. Hoover	Republican	15,758,901 (39.7%)	59
	Norman Thomas	Socialist	881,951 (2.2%)	0
1936	FRANKLIN D. ROOSEVELT	Democratic	27,751,612 (60.8%)	523
	Alfred M. Landon	Republican	16,681,913 (36.5%)	8
	William Lemke	Union	891,858 (1.9%)	0
1940	FRANKLIN D. ROOSEVELT	Democratic	27,243,466 (54.8%)	449
	Wendell L. Willkie	Republican	22,304,755 (44.8%)	82
1944	FRANKLIN D. ROOSEVELT	Democratic	25,602,505 (53.5%)	432
	Thomas E. Dewey	Republican	22,006,278 (46.0%)	99

Note: Winners' names appear in capital letters.

of controversy, Roosevelt withdrew the legislation and admitted defeat. He had perhaps misunderstood his mandate, and he certainly underestimated the respect, even the reverence, that most Americans felt for the Supreme Court. Even in times of economic catastrophe, Americans proved themselves fundamentally conservative toward their institutions, in stark contrast to Europeans, who experimented radically with their governments.

Ironically, though he lost the battle of the Supreme Court, Roosevelt won the war. By the spring of 1937, the Court began to reverse its position and in a 5–4 decision upheld the National Labor Relations Act. When Justice Willis Van Devanter retired, Roosevelt was able to make his first Supreme Court appointment, thus ensuring at least a shaky liberal majority on the Court. But Roosevelt triumphed at great cost. His attempt to reorganize the Court dissipated energy and slowed the momentum of his legislative program. Seen as the most unpopular action he took as president, it made him vulnerable to criticism from opponents of the New Deal, and even some of his supporters were dismayed by what they regarded as an attack on the principle of separation of powers.

The economy improved in late 1936 and early 1937, but in August, the fragile prosperity collapsed. Unemployment shot back up, industrial production fell, and the stock market plummeted. Facing an embarrassing economic slump that evoked charges that the New Deal had failed, Roosevelt resorted to "deficit spending," as recommended by John Maynard Keynes, the British economist. Keynes argued that to get out of a depression, the government must spend massive amounts of money on goods and services to increase demand and revive production. The economy responded slowly but never fully recovered until wartime expenditures, beginning in 1940, stimulated it, reduced unemployment, and ended the Depression.

Completing the New Deal

Despite increasing hostility, Congress passed a number of important bills in 1937 and 1938 that completed the New Deal reform legislation. The Bankhead-Jones Farm Tenancy Act of 1937 created the Farm Security Administration (FSA) to aid tenant farmers, sharecroppers, and farm owners who had lost their farms. The FSA, which provided loans to grain collectives, also set up camps for migratory workers. Some people saw such policies as the first step toward communist collectives, but the

FSA in fact never had enough money to make a real difference.

Congress passed a new Agricultural Adjustment Act in 1938 that tried to solve the problem of farm surpluses, which persisted even after hundreds of thousands of farmers had lost their farms. The new act replaced the processing tax (which the Supreme Court had declared unconstitutional) with direct payments from the federal treasury to farmers; added a soil conservation program; and provided for the marketing of surplus crops. Like its predecessor, the new act tried to stabilize farm prices by controlling production. But only the outbreak of World War II would end the problem of farm surplus, and then only temporarily.

In the cities, housing continued to be a problem. Progressive reformers had dreamed of providing better housing for the urban poor. They had campaigned for city ordinances and state laws and had built model tenements, but the first experiment with federal housing occurred during World War I. That brief experience encouraged a number of social reformers, who later became advisers to Roosevelt. They convinced him that federal low-cost housing should be part of New Deal reform.

The Reconstruction Finance Corporation made low-interest loans to housing projects, and the Public Works Administration constructed some apartment buildings. But not until the National Housing Act of 1937 did Roosevelt and his advisers try to develop a comprehensive housing policy for the poor. The act provided federal funds for slum clearance projects and for the construction of low-cost housing. By 1939, however, only 117,000 units had been built. Most of these housing projects were bleak and boxlike, and many of them soon became problems rather than solutions. Though it made the first effort, the New Deal did not meet the challenge of providing decent housing for millions of American citizens.

In the long run, New Deal housing legislation had a greater impact on middle-class housing policies and patterns. During the first 100 days of the New Deal, at Roosevelt's urging, Congress passed a bill creating the Home Owners Loan Corporation (HOLC), which over the next two years made more than $3 billion in low-interest loans and helped over a million people save their homes from foreclosure. The HOLC also had a strong impact on housing policy by introducing the first long-term, fixed-rate mortgages. Formerly, all mortgages were for periods of no more than five years and were subject to frequent renegotiation.

The HOLC also introduced a uniform system of real estate appraisal that tended to undervalue urban property, especially in neighborhoods that were old, crowded, and ethnically mixed. The system gave the highest ratings to suburban developments where, according to the HOLC, there had been no "infiltration of Jews" or other undesirable groups. This was the beginning of the practice later called "redlining," where lending agencies drew lines around neighborhoods and made it nearly impossible for prospective home buyers of certain ethnic or racial backgrounds to obtain a mortgage.

The Federal Housing Administration (FHA), created in 1934 by the National Housing Act, expanded and extended many of these HOLC policies. The FHA insured mortgages, many of them for 25 or 30 years, reduced the down payment required from 30 percent to under 10 percent, and allowed over 11 million families to buy homes between 1934 and 1972. The system, however, tended to favor purchasing new suburban homes rather than repairing older urban residences. New Deal housing policies helped make the suburban home with the long FHA mortgage part of the American way of life, but the policies also contributed to the decline of many urban neighborhoods.

Just as important as housing legislation was the Fair Labor Standards Act, which Congress passed in June 1938. Roosevelt's bill proposed for all industries engaged in interstate commerce a minimum wage of 25 cents an hour, to rise in two years to 40 cents an hour, and a maximum workweek of 44 hours, to be reduced to 40 hours. Congress amended the legislation and exempted many groups, including farm laborers and domestic servants. The act covered only 20 percent of the labor force and only 14 percent of working women. Nevertheless, when it went into effect, 750,000 workers immediately received raises, and by 1940, some 12 million had received pay increases. The law also prohibited child labor in interstate commerce, making it the first permanent federal law to prohibit youngsters under the age of 16 from working. And without emphasizing the matter, the law made no distinction between men and women, thus diminishing, if not completely ending, the need for special legislation for women. The passage of the bill widened the split between Roosevelt and conservative southern Democrats, because it was in the South where nearly 20 percent of industrial workers earned below the minimum wage. "Cheap wages mean low buying power," Roosevelt announced. "And let us remember that buying power means many other kinds of better things, better schools, better health, better hospitals, better highways."

The Fair Labor Standards Act was the last New Deal measure passed. The New Deal had many weaknesses, but it did dramatically increase government support for the needy. In 1913, local, state, and federal governments spent $21 million on public assistance. By 1932, that had risen to $218 million; by 1939, it was $4.9 billion.

THE OTHER SIDE OF THE 1930s

The Great Depression and the New Deal so dominate the history of the 1930s that it is easy to conclude that nothing else happened, that there were only bread lines and relief agencies. But there is another side of the decade, for a communications revolution changed the lives of middle-class Americans. The sale of radios and attendance at movies increased during the 1930s, and literature flourished. Americans were fascinated by technology, especially automobiles. Many people traveled during the decade; they stayed in motor courts and looked ahead to a brighter future dominated by streamlined appliances and gadgets that would mean an easier life.

Taking to the Road

"People give up everything in the world but their car," a banker in Muncie, Indiana, remarked during the Depression, and that seems to have been true all over the country. Although automobile production dropped off after 1929 and did not recover until the end of the 1930s, the number of motor vehicles registered, which declined from 26.7 million in 1930 to just over 24 million in 1933, increased to over 32 million by 1940. People who could not afford new cars drove used ones. Even the "Okies" fleeing the dust bowl of the Southwest traveled in cars. They were secondhand, run-down cars to be sure, but the fact that even many poor Americans owned cars shocked visitors from Europe, where automobiles were still only for the rich.

The American middle class traveled at an increasing rate after the low point of 1932 and 1933. In 1938, the tourist industry was the third largest in the United States, behind only steel and automobile production. Over 4 million Americans traveled every year, and four out of five went by car. Many dragged a trailer for sleeping or stopped at the growing number of tourist courts and overnight cabins. In these predecessors of the motel, there were no doormen, no bellhops, no register to sign. The tourist court was much more informal than the hotel, and you could park your car next to your cabin.

The Electric Home

If the 1920s was the age of the bathroom, the 1930s was the era of the modern kitchen. The sale of electrical appliances increased throughout the decade, with refrigerators leading the way. In 1930, the number of refrigerators produced exceeded the number of iceboxes for the first time. Refrigerator production continued to rise throughout the decade, reaching a peak of 2.3 million in 1937. At first, the refrigerator was boxy and looked very much like an icebox with a motor sitting on top. In 1935, however, the refrigerator, like most other appliances, became streamlined. Sears, Roebuck advertised "The New 1935 Super Six Coldspot ... Stunning in Its Streamlined Beauty." The Coldspot, which quickly influenced the look of all other models, was designed by Raymond Loewy, one of a group of industrial designers who emphasized sweeping horizontal lines, rounded corners, and a slick modern look. They hoped modern design would stimulate an optimistic attitude and, of course, increase sales.

Replacing an icebox with an electrical refrigerator, as many middle-class families did in the 1930s, altered more than the appearance of the kitchen. It also changed habits and lifestyles, especially for women. An icebox was part of a culture that included icemen, ice wagons (or ice trucks), picks, tongs, and a pan that had to be emptied continually. The refrigerator required no attention beyond occasional defrosting the freezer compartment. Like the streamlined automobile, the sleek refrigerator became a symbol of progress and modern civilization in the 1930s. At the end of the decade, in 1939, the World's Fair in New York glorified the theme of a streamlined future, carefully planned and based on new technology.

This reverence for technological progress contrasted with the economic despair in the 1930s, but people adapted to it selectively. For example, the electric washing machine and electric iron revolutionized wash day. Yet even with labor-saving machines, most women continued to do their wash on Monday and their ironing on Tuesday. Packaged and canned goods became more widely available during the decade, and many women discovered that it was easier, and in some cases cheaper, to serve Kellogg's Corn Flakes or Nabisco Shredded Wheat than to make oatmeal, to heat Van Camp's pork and beans or Heinz spaghetti from a can than to prepare a meal, or to use commercially baked bread than to bake their own.

Ironically, despite these new conveniences, a great many middle-class families maintained their standard of living during the 1930s only because the women in the family learned to stretch and save and make do, and most wives spent as much time on housework as before. Some also took jobs outside the home to maintain their level of consumption. The number of married women who worked increased substantially during the decade. At the same time, many rural women, like those in the hill country of Texas and other remote areas, and many wives of the unemployed simply made do. They continued to cook, clean, and sew as their ancestors had for generations.

The Age of Leisure

During the Depression, many middle-class people found themselves with time on their hands and sought out ways of spending it. The 1920s was a time of spectator sports, of football and baseball heroes, of huge crowds that turned out to see boxing matches. Those sports continued during the Depression decade, although attendance suffered. Softball and miniature golf, which were cheap forms of entertainment and did not require expensive travel, also became popular. But leisure in the 1930s actually grew to be a problem, and professionals published some 450 new books on the subject. Leisure was mechanized; millions put their nickels

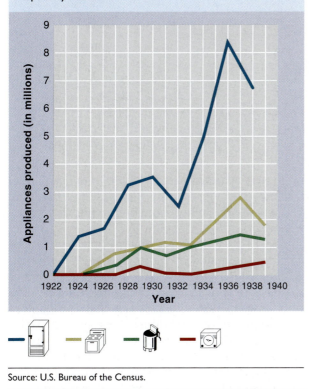

Household Appliance Production, 1922–1939

Electric appliances altered the lives of many American middle-class families during the 1930s. The replacement of the icebox with the electric refrigerator was especially dramatic.

Source: U.S. Bureau of the Census.

Although the washing machine dates from the mid-nineteenth century, it did not end the drudgery of wash day; even the introduction of electric washers did not eliminate the constant wringing and rinsing that made wash day (usually Monday) a day to dread. The first automatic washing machines were introduced in the late 1930s but did not become commonplace until after World War II. This advertisement promotes the convenience of a machine that will spin dry as well as wash. Notice the gender roles in the advertisement. The husband appreciates the saving but apparently does not put the clothes in the machine. "The Bendix" was a great improvement, but it was not until the 1950s that electric and gas dryers finally ended the task of hanging clothes on the line. *(Bendix Home Appliances, Inc.)*

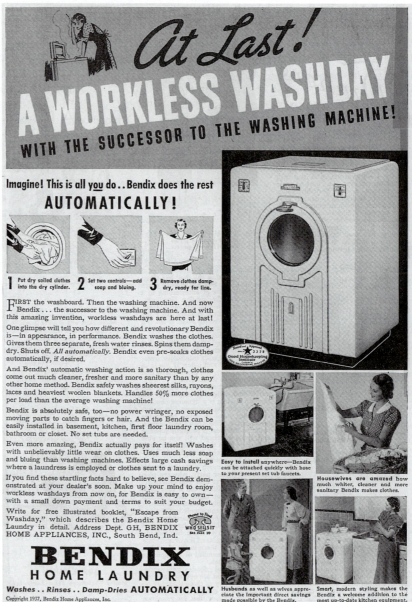

in a slot and listened to a record played on a jukebox. Millions more played a pinball machine, a mechanized device that had no practical use other than entertainment and could end the game with one word: "Tilt."

Many popular games of the period had elaborate rules and directions. Contract bridge swept the country during the decade, and Monopoly was the most popular game of all. Produced by Parker Brothers, Monopoly was a fantasy of real estate speculation in which chance, luck, and the roll of the dice determined the winner. But one still had to obey the rules: "Go Directly to Jail. Do Not Pass Go. Do Not Collect $200." During a depression brought on in part by frenzied speculation, Americans were fascinated by a game whose purpose was to obtain real estate and utility monopolies and drive one's opponents into bankruptcy.

The 1930s was also a time of fads and instant celebrities, created by radio, newsreels, and businessmen ready to turn almost anything to commercial advantage. The leading box office attraction between 1935 and 1938 was Shirley Temple, a blond and adorable child star. She inspired dolls, dishes, books, and clothes. Even stranger was the excitement created by the birth of five girl babies to a couple in northern Ontario in 1934. The Dionne quintuplets appeared on dozens of magazine covers and endorsed every imaginable product. Millions of people waited eagerly for the latest news about the babies, and over 3 million traveled to see their home in Canada. The crazes over Shirley Temple and the Dionne quintuplets were products of the new technology, especially radio and the movies.

Literary Reflections of the 1930s

Though much of the literature of the 1930s reflected the decade's troubled currents, reading continued to be a popular and cheap entertainment. John Steinbeck, whose later novel *The Grapes of Wrath* (1939) followed the fortunes of the Joad family, described the plight of Mexican migrant workers in *Tortilla Flat* (1935). His novels expressed his belief that there was in American life a "crime . . . that goes beyond denunciation." He warned that "In the eyes of the hungry there is a growing wrath."

Other writers also questioned the American dream. John Dos Passos's trilogy *U.S.A.* (1930–1936) conveyed a deep pessimism about American capitalism that many other intellectuals shared. Less political were the novels of Thomas Wolfe and William Faulkner, who more sympathetically portrayed Americans caught up in the web of local life and facing the complex problems of the modern era. Faulkner's fictional Yoknapatawpha County, brought to life in *The Sound and the Fury, As I Lay Dying, Sanctuary,* and *Light in August* (1929–1932), documented the South's racial problems and its poverty as well as its stubborn pride. But the book about the South that became one of the decade's best-sellers was far more optimistic and far less complex than Faulkner's work—Margaret Mitchell's *Gone with the Wind* (1936). Its success suggested that many Americans read to escape, not to explore their problems.

Radio's Finest Hour

The number of radios purchased increased steadily during the decade. In 1929, slightly more than 10 million households owned radios; by 1939, more than 27.5 million households had radios. Not just a source of music and news, the radio was a focal point of the living room. In many homes, the top of the radio became the symbolic mantel where cherished photos were displayed. Families gathered around the radio at night to listen to and laugh at Jack Benny or Edgar Bergen and Charlie McCarthy or to try to solve a murder mystery with Mr. and Mrs. North. "The Lone Ranger," another popular program, had 20 million listeners by 1939.

The radio played an important role in the 1930s. Here a family crowds around a typical floor model to listen to the latest news or a favorite program. *(UPI/Corbis-Bettmann)*

During the day there were soap operas. "Between thick slices of advertising," wrote James Thurber, "spread twelve minutes of dialogue, add predicament, villainy, and female suffering in equal measure, throw in a dash of nobility, sprinkle with tears, season with organ music, cover with a rich announcer sauce and serve five times a week." After school, teenagers and younger children argued over whether to listen to "Jack Armstrong, the All-American Boy" and "Captain Midnight" or "Stella Dallas" and "The Young Widder Brown."

Most families had only one radio, but everyone could join in the contests or send for magic rings or secret decoders. In Chicago's working-class neighborhoods in 1930, there was one radio for every two or three households, but often families and friends gathered to listen to favorite programs. The reception was sometimes poor, especially in rural areas and small towns. Voices faded in and out and disappeared during storms. But the magic of radio allowed many people to feel connected to distant places and to believe they knew the radio performers personally. Radio was also responsible for one of the most widespread episodes of mass hysteria of all time. On October 31, 1938, Orson Welles broadcast "The War of the Worlds" so realistically that thousands of listeners really believed that

The Movies

Just as some historians have used fiction to help define the cultural history of a decade, others in the twentieth century have turned to film to describe the "spirit of an age." On an elementary level, the movies help us appreciate changing styles in dress, furniture, and automobiles. We can even get some sense of how a particular time defined a beautiful woman or a handsome man, and we can learn about ethnic and racial stereotypes and assumptions about gender and class.

The decade of the 1930s is sometimes called the "golden age of the movies." Careful selection among the 500 or so feature films Hollywood produced each year during the decade—ranging from gangster and cowboy movies to Marx Brothers comedies, from historical romances to Busby Berkeley musical extravaganzas—could support a number of interpretations about the special myths and assumptions of the era. But one historian has argued that, especially after 1934, "not only did the movies amuse and entertain the nation through its most severe economic and social disorder, holding it together by their capacity to create unifying myths and dreams, but movie culture in the 1930s became

a dominant culture for many Americans, providing new values and social ideals to replace shattered old traditions."

The year 1934 was a dividing line for two reasons. The motion picture industry, like all other industries, had suffered during the Depression; 1933 marked the low point in attendance, with more than one-third of the theaters in the country shut down. The next year, however, attendance picked up, heralding a revival that lasted until 1946. Also in 1934, the movie industry adopted a code for which the Catholic Legion of Decency and other religious groups had lobbied. The new code prohibited the depiction of "sex perversion, interracial sex, abortion, incest, drugs and profanity." Even married couples could not be shown together in a double bed. Although a movie could depict immoral behavior, sin always had to be punished. "Evil and good should never be confused," the code announced.

Before the code, Hollywood had indeed produced graphic films, such as *The Public Enemy* (1931) and *Scarface* (1932), with a considerable amount of violence; musicals, such as *Gold Diggers of 1933,* filled with scantily clad young women; films featuring prostitutes, such as Jean Harlow in *Red Dust* (1932) and Marlene Dietrich in *Blond Venus* (1930); and

A scene from *It Happened One Night,* **1934.** *(The Museum of Modern Art Film Stills Archive)*

A scene from *Drums Along the Mohawk*, 1939. *(The Museum of Modern Art Film Stills Archive)*

other films that confronted the problems of real life. But after 1934, Hollywood concentrated on movies that created a mythical world where evil was always punished, family moral values won out in the end, and patriotism and American democracy were never questioned. Although the code was modified from time to time, it was not abandoned until 1966, when it was replaced by a rating system.

It Happened One Night (1934) and *Drums Along the Mohawk* (1939), two films out of thousands, illustrate some of the myths the movies created and sustained. Frank Capra, one of Hollywood's masters at entertaining without disturbing, directed *It Happened One Night,* a comedy-romance. A rich girl (played by Claudette Colbert) dives from her father's yacht off the coast of Florida and takes a bus for New York. She meets a newspaper reporter (Clark Gable), and they have a series of madcap adventures and fall in love. But mix-ups and misunderstandings make it appear that she will marry her old boyfriend. In the end, however, they are reunited and marry in an elaborate outdoor ceremony. Afterward, they presumably live happily ever after. The movie is funny and entertaining and presents a variation on the poor-boy-marries-rich-girl theme. Like so many movies of the time, this one suggests that life is fulfilled for a woman only if she can find the right man to marry.

Claudette Colbert also stars in *Drums Along the Mohawk,* this time with Henry Fonda. Based on a 1936 novel by Walter Edmonds, *Drums* is a sentimental story about a man who builds a house in the wilderness, marries a pretty girl, fights off the Indians, and works with the simple country folk to create a satisfying life in the very year the American colonies rebel against Great Britain. *Drums* was one of a number of films based on historical themes that Hollywood released just before World War II. *The Howards of Virginia* (1940), *Northwest Passage* (1939), and, most popular of all, *Gone with the Wind* (1939) were others in the same genre. Historical themes had been popular before, but with the world on the brink of war, the story of men and women in the wilderness struggling for family and country against the Indians (stereotyped as savages) proved comforting as well as entertaining.

Reflecting on the Past   Can a historian use movies to describe the values and myths of a particular time, or are the complexities and exaggerations too great? Are the most popular or most critically acclaimed films more useful than others in getting at the "spirit of an age"? Which films that are popular today tell us the most about our time and culture? Is there too much sex and violence in movies today? Should the government control the language, themes, and values depicted in movies? Are movies as important today as they were in the 1930s in defining and influencing the country's myths and values?

Key 1930s Reform Legislation

Year	Legislation	Provisions
1932	Reconstruction Finance Corporation (RFC)	Granted emergency loans to banks, life insurance companies, and railroads (passed during Hoover administration)
1933	Civilian Conservation Corps (CCC)	Employed young men (and a few women) in reforestation, road construction, and flood control projects
1933	Agricultural Adjustment Act (AAA)	Granted farmers direct payments for reducing production of certain products; funds for payments provided by a processing tax, which was later declared unconstitutional
1933	Tennessee Valley Authority (TVA)	Created independent public corporation to construct dams and power projects and to develop the economy of a nine-state area in the Tennessee River valley
1933	National Industrial Recovery Act (NIRA)	Sought to revive business through a series of fair-competition codes; Section 7a guaranteed labor's right to organize (later declared unconstitutional)
1933	Public Works Administration (PWA)	Sought to increase employment and business activity through construction of roads, buildings, and other projects
1934	National Housing Act—created Federal Housing Administration (FHA)	Insured loans made by banks for construction of new homes and repair of old homes
1935	Emergency Relief Appropriation Act—created Works Progress Administration (WPA)	Employed over 8 million people to repair roads, build bridges, and work on other projects; also hired artists and writers
1935	Social Security Act	Established unemployment compensation and old-age and survivors' insurance paid for by a joint tax on employers and employees
1935	National Labor Relations Act (Wagner-Connery Act)	Recognized the right of employees to join labor unions and to bargain collectively; created a National Labor Relations Board to supervise elections and to prevent unfair labor practices
1935	Public Utility Holding Act	Outlawed pyramiding of gas and electric companies through the use of holding companies and restricted these companies to activity in one area; a "death sentence" clause gave companies five years to prove local, useful, and efficient operation or be dissolved
1937	National Housing Act (Wagner-Steagall Act)	Authorized low-rent public housing projects
1938	Agricultural Adjustment Act (AAA)	Continued price supports and payments to farmers to limit production, as in 1933 act, but replaced processing tax with direct federal payment
1938	Fair Labor Standards Act	Established minimum wage of 40 cents an hour and maximum workweek of 40 hours in enterprises engaged in interstate commerce

Martians had landed in New Jersey. If anyone needed proof, that single program demonstrated the power of the radio.

The Silver Screen

The 1930s were the golden decade of the movies. Between 60 and 90 million Americans went to the movies every week. The medium was not entirely Depression-proof, but talking films had replaced the silent variety in the late 1920s, and attendance soared. Though it fell off slightly in the early 1930s, by 1934 movie viewing was climbing again. For many families, even in the depth of the Depression, movie money was almost as important as food money.

In the cities, one could go to an elaborate movie palace and live in a fantasy world far removed from the reality of Depression America. In small towns across the country, for 25 cents (10 cents for those under age 12) one could go to at least four movies during the week. There was a Sunday–Monday feature film (except in communities where the churches had prevented Sunday movies), a different feature of somewhat lesser prominence on Tuesday–Wednesday, and another on Thursday–Friday. On Saturday, there was a cowboy or detective movie. Sometimes a double-feature played, and there were always short subjects, a cartoon, and a newsreel. On Saturday, there was usually a serial that left the heroine or hero in

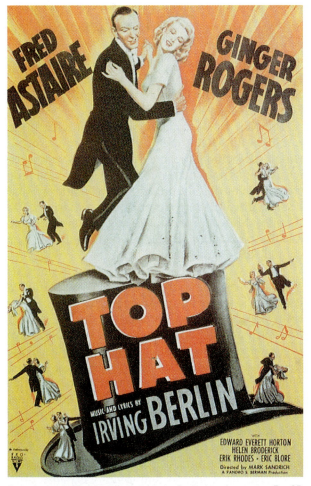

Even during the Depression, Americans flocked to the movies. For 25 cents (10 cents for children), they could see a double feature as well as a cartoon and a newsreel. Among the most popular films were elaborate musical fantasies, and among the most popular stars were the dance team of Fred Astaire and Ginger Rogers. *(Corbis)*

Timeline

1929	Stock market crashes Agricultural Marketing Act
1930	Depression worsens Hawley-Smoot Tariff
1932	Reconstruction Finance Corporation established Federal Home Loan Bank Act Glass-Steagall Banking Act Federal Emergency Relief Act Bonus march on Washington Franklin D. Roosevelt elected president
1933	Emergency Banking Relief Act Home Owners Loan Corporation Twenty-first Amendment repeals Eighteenth Amendment, ending prohibition Agricultural Adjustment Act National Industrial Recovery Act Civilian Conservation Corps Tennessee Valley Authority established Public Works Administration established
1934	Unemployment peaks Federal Housing Administration established Indian Reorganization Act
1935	Second New Deal begins Works Progress Administration established Social Security Act Rural Electrification Act National Labor Relations Act Public Utility Holding Company Act Committee of Industrial Organization (CIO) formed
1936	United Auto Workers hold sit-down strikes against General Motors Roosevelt reelected president Economy begins to rebound
1937	Attempt to expand the Supreme Court Economic collapse Farm Security Administration established National Housing Act
1938	Fair Labor Standards Act Agricultural Adjustment Act
1939	John Steinbeck, *The Grapes of Wrath* Margaret Mitchell, *Gone with the Wind*

such a dire predicament that one just had to come back the next week to see how she or he survived.

The movies were a place to take a date, to go with friends, or to go as a family. Movies would be talked about for days. Young women tried to speak like Greta Garbo and to hold a cigarette like Joan Crawford. Jean Harlow and Mae West so popularized blonde hair that sales of peroxide shot up. Young men tried to emulate Clark Gable and Cary Grant, and one young man admitted that it was "directly through the movies that I learned to kiss a girl on her ears, neck, and cheeks, as well as on the mouth." The animated cartoons of Walt Disney, one of the true geniuses of the movie industry, were so popular that Mickey Mouse was more famous and familiar than most human celebrities. In May 1933, halfway into Roosevelt's first 100 days, Disney released *The Three Little Pigs,* whose theme

song "Who's Afraid of the Big Bad Wolf?" became a national hit overnight. Some people felt it boosted the nation's morale as much as New Deal legislation. One critic suggested that the moral of the story, as retold by Disney, was that the little pig survived because he was conservative, diligent, and hard-working; others felt that it was the pig who used modern tools and planned ahead who won out.

✦ *Conclusion*

THE MIXED LEGACY OF THE GREAT DEPRESSION AND THE NEW DEAL

The New Deal, despite its great variety of legislation, did not end the Depression, nor did it solve the problem of unemployment. For many Americans looking back on the decade of the 1930s, the most vivid memory was the shame and guilt of being unemployed, the despair and fear that came from losing a business or being evicted from a home or an apartment. For Diane Morgan's generation, the experience of the Depression would influence their lives and their attitude toward money for the rest of their lives. Parents who lived through the decade urged their children to find a secure job, to get married, and to settle down. "Every time I've encountered the Depression it has been used as a barrier and a club," one daughter of Depression parents remembered; "older people use it to explain to me that I can't understand anything: I didn't live through the Depression."

New Deal legislation did not solve the country's problems, but it did strengthen the federal government, especially the executive branch. Federal agencies like the Federal Deposit Insurance Corporation and programs like social security influenced the daily lives of most Americans, and rural electrification, the WPA, and the CCC changed the lives of millions. The New Deal also established the principle of federal responsibility for the health of the economy, initiated the concept of the welfare state, and dramatically increased government spending to help the poor. Federally subsidized housing, minimum-wage laws, and a policy for paying farmers to limit production, all aspects of these principles, had far-

reaching implications. The shift of responsibility for the nation's welfare to Washington marked the New Deal as a landmark in the continuing story of the relationship of government to society.

The New Deal was as important for what it did not do as for what it did. It did not promote socialism or redistribute income or property. It promoted social justice and social reform, but it provided little for people at the bottom of American society, and less for African Americans and other minorities. The New Deal did not prevent business consolidation, and, in the end, it probably strengthened corporate capitalism.

Roosevelt, with his colorful personality and his dramatic response to the nation's crisis, dominated his times in a way few presidents have done. Yet for some people who lived through the decade, neither Roosevelt nor bread lines but a new streamlined refrigerator or a Walt Disney movie symbolized the Depression decade. It is easy to study the United States in the 1930s without reference to what was going on in the rest of the world. But the United States was influenced by international economic and political trends during the decade. The Depression was global in its impact, and it was at least in part responsible for the rise of Hitler in Germany, for economic and military expansionism in Japan, and for encouraging Mussolini to undertake foreign adventures. Great Britain, France, the United States, and other countries, faced with economic disaster, passed high tariffs which in turn increased international tensions and led to aggressive nationalism. These global trends would eventually involve the United States in World War II.

✦ Recommended Reading

The Great Depression

John Kenneth Galbraith, *The Great Crash* (1954); Charles P. Kindleberger, *The World in Depression, 1929–1939* (1973); David M. Kennedy, *Freedom From Fear: The American People in Depression and War* (1999); Robert S. McElvain, *The Great Depression* (1984); William Mullins, *The Depression and the Urban West Coast* (1991); Arthur M. Schlesinger, Jr., *The Crisis of the Old Order* (1957); Charles J. Shinto, *Dust Bowl Migrants in the American Imagination* (1997); Kevin Starr, *Endangered Dream: The Great Depression in California* (1996); Studs Terkel, *Hard Times* (1970); T. H. Watkins, *The Hungry Years* (1999); Joan Hoff Wilson, *Herbert Hoover: Forgotten Progressive* (1975); Donald Worster, *Dust Bowl* (1979).

Roosevelt and the First New Deal

James MacGregor Burns, *Roosevelt: The Lion and the Fox* (1956); Paul Conkin, *The New Deal* (1967); Blanche Wiesen Cook, *Eleanor Roosevelt*, Vol. 2 (1999); Frank Freidel, *Launching the New Deal* (1973); James J. Patterson, *America's Struggle Against Poverty, 1900–1980* (1981); Eliot Rosen, *Hoover, Roosevelt and the Brains Trust* (1977).

One Hundred Days

Anthony Badger, *The New Deal* (1989), Alan Brinkley, *Voices of Protest: Huey Long, Father Coughlin and the Great Depression* (1982); Thomas K. McGraw, *TVA and the Power Fight* (1970); Arthur M. Schlesinger, Jr., *The Coming of the New Deal* (1958).

The Second New Deal

Irving Bernstein, *The Turbulent Years: A History of the American Worker, 1933–1941* (1970); Dan T. Carter, *Scottsboro* (1969); Lizabeth Cohen, *Making a New Deal: Industrial Workers in Chicago, 1919–1939* (1990); Abraham Hoffman, *Unwanted: Mexican Americans and the Great Depression* (1974); Alice Kessler-Harris, *In Pursuit of Equity: Women, Men and the Quest for Economic Citizenship in the 20th Century* (2001); Nelson Lichtenstein, *State of the Union: A Century of American Labor* (2002); Richard Lowitt, *The New Deal and the West* (1984); Roy Lubove, *The Struggle for Social Security* (1968); Gerald D. Nash, *The Federal Landscape: An Economic History of the Twentieth Century West* (1999); Richard Pells, *Radical Visions and American Dreams* (1973); Kenneth R. Philip, *John Collier's Crusade for Indian Reform* (1977); Vicki L. Ruiz, *From Out of the Shadows: Mexican Women in Twentieth Century America* (1998); Jordan A. Schwartz, *The New Dealers: Power Politics in the Age of Roosevelt* (1993); Harvard Sitkoff, *A New Deal for Blacks* (1978); Susan Ware, *Holding Their Own: American Women in the 1930s* (1982); David K. Yoo, *Growing Up Nisei: Race, Generation and Culture Among Japanese Americans of California, 1924–1949* (2000); Richard White, *The Roots of Dependency: Subsistence, Environment and Social Change Among the Choctaws, Pawnees, and Navajos* (1983).

The Last Years of the New Deal

Alan Brinkley, *The End of Reform: New Deal Liberalism in Recession and War* (1995); Barry Cushman, *Rethinking the New Deal Court* (1998); Steve Fraser and Gary Gertstle, eds., *The Rise and Fall of the New Deal Order* (1989); William E. Leuchtenburg, *The Supreme Court Reborn: The Constitutional Revolution in the Age of Roosevelt* (1995); James T. Patterson, *The New Deal and the States* (1969); G. Edward White, *The Constitution and the New Deal* (2000).

The Other Side of the 1930s

Andrew Bergman, *We're in the Money: Depression America and Its Films* (1971); Terry A. Cooney, *Balancing Acts: American Thought and Culture in the 1930s* (1995); David Gelernter, *1939: The Lost World of the Fair* (1995); Jerre Mangione, *The Dream and the Deal* (1972); Lary May, *The Big Tomorrow: Hollywood and the Politics of the American Way* (2000); Jeffrey L. Meikle, *Twentieth Century Limited: Industrial Design in America, 1925–1939* (1979); Robert Sklar, *Movie Made America* (1975); William Stott, *Documentary Expression in Thirties America* (1973); Warren Susman, *Culture as History* (1984).

Fiction and Film

James Farrell describes growing up in Depression Chicago in *Studs Lonigan* (1932–1935). John Steinbeck shows Oklahomans trying to escape the dust bowl in his novel *The Grapes of Wrath* (1939). Richard Wright details the trials of a young black man in *Native Son* (1940). *Modern Times* (1936) is a classic film that features Charlie Chaplin at his best as he depicts the impersonality of industrial civilization, where machines dominate people. *The Grapes of Wrath* (1940) is another classic film. Although it doesn't exhibit the despair and anger of the book, it is still a powerful depiction of the human cost of the dust bowl and the Depression. To appreciate how people in the 1930s were entertained by the movies, check out *Gone With the Wind* (1939), Fred Astaire and Ginger Rogers in *Top Hat* (1935) and *Swing Time* (1936) as well as *The Wizard of Oz* (1939). To see the genius of Walt Disney, watch *Snow White and the Seven Dwarfs* (1937).

✦ Discovering U.S. History Online

Riding the Rails

www.pbs.org/wgbh/amex/rails

"At the height of the Great Depression, more than 250,000 teenagers were living on the road in America." This site, a companion to the PBS film, includes stories from real "hobos" and an examination of racial factors in the hobo lifestyle, hobo songs, a timeline, and maps.

Americans React to the Great Depression

http://lcweb2.loc.gov/ammem/ndlpedu/features/timeline/deprwwii/depress.depress.html

Documents and photographs illustrate after-effects of the Great Depression, including a pushcart peddlar's colony, a photo collage of Hoovervilles, and photos of protests and demonstrations during this time period.

The Hoover Dam

http://xroads.virginia.edu/~MA98/haven/hoover

The site describes the construction of Hoover Dam in the context of the Great Depression.

Hooverville

www.realchangenews.org/pastarticles/features/articles/fea_hooverville1.html
www.realchangenews.org/pastarticles/features/articles/fea_hooverville2.html
www.realchangenews.org/pastarticles/features/articles/fea_hooverville3.html

These sites present illustrated articles on Seattle's Hooverville.

Migrant Labor Camps

www.lib.utexas.edu/photodraw/sanchez/migrant_camps.html

Annotated photographs document the conditions in Texas migrant camps during the 1930s.

New Deal

www.newdeal.feri.org/

This database includes photographs, political cartoons, and texts—including speeches, letters, and other historic documents—from the New Deal period.

A New Deal for the Arts

www.archives.gov/exhibit_hall/new_deal_for_the_arts/index.html

Artwork, documents, and photographs recount the federal government's efforts to fund artists in the 1930s in this National Archives site.

Franklin D. Roosevelt Library and Digital Archives

www.fdrlibrary.marist.edu.

The library presents over 13,000 digitized documents in an effort to fulfill "Franklin Roosevelt's dream of making the records of the past available" to the general public.

A Short History of the Tennessee Valley Authority

www.tva.gov/abouttva/history.htm

This official history of the agency includes the complete text of the act that founded it.

One Hundred Days

www.nps.gov/fdrm/home.htm

This illustrated site presents information on Roosevelt's presidency, including the "one hundred days," arranged in "rooms."

Franklin Delano Roosevelt

http://www.potus.com/fdroosevelt.html

This site contains basic factual data about Roosevelt's election and presidency, speeches, and online biographies.

Voices from the Dust Bowl

www.memory.loc.gov/ammem/afctshtml/tshome.html

Farm Security Administration (FSA) studies of migrant work camps in central California in 1940 and 1941 compose the bulk of this site. The collection includes audio recordings, photographs, manuscript materials, and publications.

Weedpatch Camp

www.weedpatchcamp.com/

History and personal reminiscences of life at the real-life migrant labor camp, Arvin Federal Government Camp, portrayed as "Weedpatch Camp" in a John Steinbeck novel.

Taxation in War and Depression, 1933–1946

www.tax.org/THP/Civilization/Default.htm

This site is an online tax information resource. It includes thousands of searchable pages of documents and analysis on tax issues during the Depression and World War II and is part of a larger site that contains a cartoon gallery and World War II–era posters.

America from the Great Depression to World War II

http://lcweb2.loc.gov/ammem/fsahtml/fahome.html

This extensive, searchable database includes special collections "Documenting America: Photographers on Assignment" and "Selected FSA Images: Popular Requests and Staff Selections."

Los Angeles at Work, 1920–1939

www.lapl.org/photo/laatwork

This archive contains promotional photographs created by the Los Angeles Chamber of Commerce during the "economic heyday" of the 1920s along with follow-up photos that were taken of business innovations during the Depression years.

America in the 1930s

www.xroads.virginia.edu/~1930s/home_1.html

A timeline of the 1930s along with a cultural overview of the decade in film, print, on radio, and by other displays.

World
War II

Reading Right to Left—FIRST ROW: Britain, Canada, Australia, New Zealand. SECOND ROW: Southern Rhodesia, Newfoundland, South Africa. THIRD ROW: India. FOURTH ROW: The Colonial Empire.

Reading Left to Right—FIRST ROW: U.S.A., China, U.S.S.R., Yugoslavia. SECOND ROW: Holland, France, Poland, Czechoslovakia. THIRD ROW: Greece, Norway, Belgium.

FREEDOM SHALL PREVAIL!

PRINTED IN ENGLAND BY FOSH & CROSS LTD, LONDON.

A World War II poster depicting the many nations united in the fight against the Axis powers.
In reality there were often disagreements. Notice to the right, the American sailor is marching
next to Chinese and Soviet soldiers. Within a few years after victory, they would be enemies.
(From the poster collection of The American Legion, Indianapolis, Indiana)

◆ *American Stories*

A NATIVE-AMERICAN BOY PLAYS AT WAR

N. Scott Momaday, a Kiowa Indian born in Lawton, Oklahoma, in 1934, grew
up on Navajo, Apache, and Pueblo reservations. He was only 11 years old
when World War II ended, yet the war had changed his life. Shortly after the
United States entered the war, Momaday's parents moved to New Mexico,
where his father got a job with an oil company and his mother worked in the
civilian personnel office at an army air force base. Like many couples, they
had struggled through the hard times of the Depression. The war meant jobs.

Momaday's best friend was Billy Don Johnson, a "reddish, robust boy of great good humor and intense loyalty." Together they played war, digging trenches and dragging themselves through imaginary minefields. They hurled grenades and fired endless rounds from their imaginary machine guns, pausing only to drink Kool-Aid from their canteens. At school, they were taught history and math and also how to hate the enemy and be proud of America. They recited the Pledge of Allegiance to the flag and sang "God Bless America," "The Star-Spangled Banner," and "Remember Pearl Harbor." Like most Americans, they believed that World War II was a good war fought against evil empires. The United States was always right, the enemy always wrong. It was an attitude that would influence Momaday and his generation for the rest of their lives.

Momaday's only difficulty was that his Native-American face was often mistaken for that of an Asian. Almost every day on the playground, someone would yell, "Hi ya, Jap," and a fight was on. Billy Don always came to his friend's defense, but it was disconcerting to be taken for the enemy. His father read old Kiowa tales to Momaday, who was proud to be an Indian but prouder still to be an American. On Saturday, he and his friends would go to the local theater to cheer as they watched a Japanese Zero or a German ME-109 go down in flames. They pretended that they were P-40 pilots. "The whole field of vision shuddered with our fire: the 50-caliber tracers curved out, fixing brilliant arcs upon the span, and struck; then there was a black burst of smoke, and the target went spinning down to death."

Near the end of the war, his family moved again, as so many families did, so that his father might get a better job. This time they lived right next door to an air force base, and Momaday fell in love with the B-17 "Flying Fortress," the bomber that military strategists thought would win the war in the Pacific and in Europe. He felt a real sense of resentment and loss when the B-17 was replaced by the larger but not nearly so glamorous B-29.

Looking back on his early years, Momaday reflected on the importance of the war in his growing up. "I see now that one experiences easily the ordinary things of life," he decided, "the things which cast familiar shadows upon the sheer, transparent panels of time, and he perceives his experience in the only way he can, according to his age." Though Momaday's life during the war differed from the lives of boys old enough to join the armed forces, the war was no less real for him. Though his youth was affected by the fact that he was male, was an Indian, and lived in the Southwest, the most important influence was that he was an American growing up during the war. Ironically, his parents had been made U.S. citizens by an act of Congress in 1924, but like all Native Americans living in Arizona and New Mexico, they were denied the right to vote by state law.

The Momadays fared better than most Native Americans, who found prejudice against them undiminished and jobs, even in wartime, hard to find. Native-American servicemen returning from the war discovered that they were still treated like "Indians." They were prohibited from buying liquor in many states, and those who returned to the reservations learned that they were ineligible for veterans' benefits. Still, Momaday thought of himself not so much as an Indian as an American, and that too was a product of his generation. But as he grew to maturity, he became a successful writer and spokesman for his people. In 1969, he won the Pulitzer Prize for his novel *House Made of Dawn*. He also recorded his experiences and memories in a book called *The Names* (1976). In his writing, he stresses the Indian's close identification with the land. Writing about his grandmother, he says: "The immense landscape of the continental interior lay like memory in her blood."

Momaday was just a child during World War II, but it had a profound effect on his life as it did on all of those who remembered the conflict. His generation would judge the global events of the rest of the twentieth century in terms of their sense of patriotism and valor acquired during the war. Although no American cities were bombed and the country was never invaded, World War II influenced almost every aspect of American life. The war ended the Depression. Industrial jobs were plentiful, and even though prejudice and discrimination did not disappear, blacks, Hispanics, women, and other minorities had new opportunities. Like World War I, the second war expanded cooperation between government and industry and increased the influence of government in all areas of American life. The war also ended the last remnants of American isolationism. The United States emerged from the war in 1945 as the most powerful and prosperous nation in the world.

This chapter traces the gradual involvement of the United States in the international events during the 1930s that finally led to participation in the most devastating war the world had seen. It recounts the diplomatic and military struggles of the war and the search for a secure peace. It also seeks to explain the impact of the war on ordinary people and on American attitudes about the world, as well as its effect on patriotism and the American way of life. The war brought prosperity to some as it brought death to others. It left the American people the most affluent in the world and the United States the most powerful nation.

THE TWISTING ROAD TO WAR

Looking back on the events between 1933 and 1941 that eventually led to American involvement in World War II, it is easy either to be critical of decisions made or actions not taken or to see everything that happened during the period as inevitable. Historical events are never inevitable, and leaders who must make decisions never have the advantage of retrospective vision; they have to deal with situations as they find them, and they never have all the facts.

Foreign Policy in a Global Age

In March 1933, Roosevelt faced not only overwhelming domestic difficulties but also international crisis. The worldwide depression had caused near financial disaster in Europe. Germany had defaulted on its reparations installments, and most European countries were unable to keep up the payments on their debts to the United States.

Roosevelt had no master plan in foreign policy, just as he had none in the domestic sphere. In the first days of his administration, he gave conflicting signals as he groped to respond to the international situation. At first, it seemed that the president would cooperate in some kind of international economic agreement on tariffs and currency. But then he undercut the American delegation in London by refusing to go along with any international agreement. Solving the American domestic economic crisis seemed more important to Roosevelt in 1933 than international economic cooperation. His actions signaled a decision to go it alone in foreign policy in the 1930s.

Roosevelt did, however, alter some of the foreign policy decisions of previous administrations. For example, he recognized the Soviet government, hoping to gain a market for surplus American grain. Although the expected trade bonanza never materialized, the Soviet Union agreed to pay the old debts and to extend rights to American citizens living in the Soviet Union. Diplomatic recognition opened communications between the two emerging world powers.

Led by Secretary of State Cordell Hull, Roosevelt's administration also reversed the earlier policy of intervention in South America. The United States continued to support dictators, especially in Central America, because they promised to promote stability and preserve American economic interests. But Roosevelt, extending the Good Neighbor policy that Hoover had initiated, completed the removal of American military forces from Haiti and Nicaragua in 1934, and, in a series of pan-American conferences, he joined in pledging that no country in the hemisphere would intervene in the "internal or external affairs" of any other. The United States still had economic and trade interests in Latin America, however, and with many of the Latin American economies in disarray because of the Depression, pressures mounted to resume the policy of military intervention.

The first test case came in Cuba, where a revolution threatened American investments of more than 1 billion dollars. But the United States did not send troops. Instead, Roosevelt dispatched special envoys to work out a conciliatory agreement with the revolutionary government. A short time later, when a coup led by Fulgencio Batista overthrew the revolutionary government, the United States not only recognized the Batista government but also offered a large loan and agreed to abrogate the Platt Amendment (which made Cuba a virtual protectorate of the United States) in return for the rights to a naval base.

The Trade Agreements Act of 1934 gave the president power to lower tariff rates by as much as 50 percent and took the tariff away from the pressure of special-interest groups in Congress. Using this act, the Roosevelt administration negotiated a series of agreements that improved trade. By 1935, half of American cotton exports and a large proportion of other products were going to Latin America. So the Good Neighbor policy was also good business for the United States. But increased trade did not solve the economic problems for either the United States or Latin America.

Another test for Latin American policy came in 1938 when Mexico nationalized the property of a number of American oil companies. Instead of intervening, as many businessmen urged, the State Department patiently worked out an agreement that included some compensation for the companies. The American government might have acted differently, however, if the threat of war in Europe in 1938 had not created a fear that all the Western Hemisphere nations would have to cooperate to resist the growing power of Germany and Italy. At a pan-American conference held that year, the United States and most Latin American countries agreed to resist all foreign intervention in the hemisphere.

Europe on the Brink of War

Around the time that Roosevelt was first elected president, Adolf Hitler came to power in Germany. Born in Austria in 1889, Hitler had served as a corporal in the German army during World War I. Like many other Germans, he was angered by the Treaty of Versailles, and he blamed Germany's defeat on the Communists and the Jews. World War II in Europe was caused by World War I and by Germany's attempt to reverse the peace settlement.

Hitler had a checkered life after the war. He became the leader of the National Socialist party of the German workers (*Nazi* is short for *National*), and in 1923, after leading an unsuccessful coup, he was sentenced to prison. While in jail he wrote *Mein Kampf* ("My Struggle"), a long, rambling book spelling out his theories of racial purity, his hopes for Germany, and his venomous hatred of the Jews.

After his release from prison, Hitler's following grew. He had a charismatic style and a plan. On January 30, 1933, he became chancellor of Germany, and within months the Reichstag (parliament) suspended the constitution, making Hitler Fuehrer (leader) and dictator. His Fascist regime concentrated political and economic power in a centralized state. He intended to conquer Europe and to make the German Third Reich (empire) the center of a new civilization. Under Hitler's leadership, Germany prospered and recovered from the Depression faster than any country except Japan. Economic recovery was caused in part by military spending, but Hitler also provided money for public works, autobahns (superhighways), and the development of the Volkswagen (or people's car). He raised the quality of worker's lives and provided free recreational facilities and better health care. Many Germans were so grateful for restored prosperity and national pride that they failed to notice the dark side of his regime, which included concentration camps and virulent anti-Semitism.

In 1934, Hitler announced a program of German rearmament, violating the Versailles Treaty of 1919. Meanwhile, in Italy, the Fascist dictator Benito Mussolini was building a powerful military force; in 1934, he threatened to invade the East African country of Ethiopia. These ominous rumblings in Europe frightened Americans at the very time they were reexamining American entry into the Great War and vowing that they would never again get involved in a European conflict.

Senator Gerald P. Nye of North Dakota, a conscientious and determined man who had helped expose the Teapot Dome scandal in 1924, turned to an investigation of the connection between corporate profits and American participation in World War I. His committee's public hearings revealed that many American businessmen had close relationships with the War Department. Businesses producing war materials had made huge profits. Though the committee failed to prove a conspiracy, it was easy to conclude that the United States had been tricked into going to war by the people who profited the most from it.

On many college campuses, students demonstrated against war. On April 13, 1934, a day of protest around the country, students at Smith College placed white crosses on the campus as a memorial to the people killed in the Great War and those who would die in the next one. The next year, even more students went on strike for a day. Students joined organizations like Veterans of Future Wars and Future Gold Star Mothers and protested the presence of the Reserve Officers Training Corps on their campuses. One college president, who supported the peace movement, announced, "We will be called cowards . . . [but] I say that war must be banished from civilized society if democratic civilization and culture are to be perpetuated." Not all students supported the peace movement, but in the mid-1930s, many young people as well as adults joined peace societies such as the Fellowship of Reconciliation and the Women's International League for Peace and Freedom. They were determined never again to support a foreign war. But in Europe, Asia, and Africa, there were already rumblings of another great international conflict.

Ethiopia and Spain

In May 1935, Italy invaded Ethiopia after rejecting the League of Nations' offer to mediate the difficulties between the two countries. Italian dive bombers and machine guns made quick work of the small and poorly equipped Ethiopian army. The Ethiopian war, remote as it seemed, frightened Congress, which passed a Neutrality Act authorizing the president to prohibit all arms shipments to nations at war and to advise all U.S. citizens not to travel on belligerents' ships except at their own risk. Remembering the process that led the United States into World War I, Congress was determined that it would not happen again.

Though he would have preferred a more flexible bill, Roosevelt used the authority of the Neutrality

Act of 1935 to impose an arms embargo. The League of Nations condemned Italy as the aggressor in the war, and Great Britain moved its fleet to the Mediterranean. But, in the midst of depression, neither Britain nor the United States wanted to stop shipments of oil to Italy or to commit its own soldiers to the fight. The embargo on arms had little impact on Italy, but it was disastrous for the poor African nation. Italy quickly defeated Ethiopia. Many African Americans were disappointed and angry as they watched Europe and the United States fail to intervene to stop the invasion of Ethiopia, which symbolized black African freedom and independence to many. In 1936, Mussolini joined forces with Germany to form the Rome-Berlin Axis.

"We shun political commitments which might entangle us in foreign war," Roosevelt announced in 1936. "We are not isolationist except in so far as we seek to isolate ourselves completely from war." But isolation became more difficult when a civil war broke out in Spain in 1936. General Francisco Franco, supported by the Catholic church and large landowners, revolted against the republican government. Germany and Italy aided Franco, sending planes and other weapons, while the Soviet Union came to the support of the anti-Franco Loyalists. On April 26, 1937, German airplanes supporting Franco's soldiers bombed and machine gunned the historic Basque capital city of Guernica, killing over 1,600 people and foreshadowing the massive de-

On April 26, 1937, German airplanes supporting Franco's soldiers bombed and machine gunned the historic Basque capital city of Guenica, killing over 1,600 people and foreshadowing the massive destruction of civilians during World War II. Pablo Picasso, probably the most famous artist of the twentieth century, painted this black and white mural to denounce the attack. After the defeat of the Republican forces in Spain, Picasso refused to allow the painting to be displayed in the country. Only in 1975, after the end of the Franco regime, did the painting return to Madrid. What kind of symbols and images can you find in the painting? (Art Resource, NY/© 2002 The Estate of Pablo Picasso/Artists Rights Society [ARS], New York)

struction of cities and the death of hundreds of thousands of civilians during World War II.

The war in Spain polarized the United States. Most Catholics and many anti-Communists sided with Franco. But many American radicals, even those opposed to all war a few months before, found the Loyalist cause worth fighting and dying for. Over 3,000 Americans joined the Abraham Lincoln Brigade, and hundreds were killed fighting fascism in Spain. "If this were a Spanish matter, I'd let it alone," Sam Levenger, a student at Ohio State, wrote. "But the rebellion would not last a week if it weren't for the Germans and the Italians. And if Hitler and Mussolini can send troops to Spain to attack the government elected by the people, why can't they do so in France? And after France?" Levenger was killed in Spain in 1937 at the age of 20.

Not everyone agreed that the moral issues in Spain were worth dying for. The U.S. government tried to stay neutral and to ship arms and equipment to neither side. The Neutrality Act, extended in 1936, technically did not apply to civil wars, but the State Department imposed a moral embargo. However, when an American businessman disregarded it and attempted to send 400 used airplane engines to the Loyalists, Roosevelt asked Congress to extend the arms embargo to Spain. While the United States, along with Britain and France, carefully protected its neutrality, Franco consolidated his dictatorship with the active aid of Germany and Italy. Meanwhile, Congress in 1937 passed another Neutrality Act, this time making it illegal for American citizens to travel on belligerents' ships. The act extended the embargo on arms and made even nonmilitary items available to belligerents only on a cash-and-carry basis.

In a variety of ways, the United States tried to avoid repeating the mistakes that had led it into World War I. Unfortunately, World War II, which moved closer each day, would be a different kind of war, and the lessons of the first war would be of little use.

War in Europe

Roosevelt had no carefully planned strategy to deal with the rising tide of war in Europe in the late 1930s. He was by no means an isolationist, but he wanted to keep the United States out of the European conflagration. When he announced, "I hate war," he was expressing a deep personal belief that wars solve few problems. Unlike his distant cousin Theodore Roosevelt, he did not view war as a test of one's manhood. In foreign policy, just as in domestic affairs, he responded to events, but he moved reluctantly (and with agonizing slowness, from the point

of view of many of his critics) toward more and more American involvement in the war.

In March 1938, Hitler's Germany annexed Austria and then in September, as a result of the Munich Conference, occupied the Sudetenland, a part of Czechoslovakia. Within six months, Hitler's armies had overrun the rest of Czechoslovakia. Little protest came from the United States. Most Americans sympathized with the victims of Hitler's aggression, and eventually some were horrified at rumors of the murder of hundreds of thousands of Jews. But because newspapers avoided intensive coverage of the well-documented but unpleasant stories, many Americans did not learn of the Holocaust of the early 1940s until near the end of the war.

At first, almost everyone hoped that compromises could be worked out and that Europe could settle its own problems. But that notion was destroyed on August 23, 1939, by the news of a Nazi–Soviet pact. Fascism and communism were political philosophies supposedly in deadly opposition. Many Americans had secretly hoped that Nazi Germany and Soviet Russia would fight it out, neutralizing each other. Now they had signed a nonaggression pact. A week later, Hitler's army attacked Poland, marking the official beginning of World War II. Britain and France honored their treaties and came to Poland's defense. "This nation will remain a neutral nation," Roosevelt announced, "but I cannot ask that every American remain neutral in thought as well."

Roosevelt asked for a repeal of the embargo section of the Neutrality Act and for the approval of the sale of arms on a cash-and-carry basis to France and Britain. The United States would help the countries struggling against Hitler, but not at the risk of entering the war or even at the threat of disrupting the civilian economy. Yet Roosevelt did take some secret risks. In August 1939, Albert Einstein, a Jewish refugee from Nazi Germany, and other distinguished scientists warned the president that German researchers were at work on an atomic bomb. Fearing the consequences of a powerful new weapon in Hitler's hands, Roosevelt authorized funds for a top-secret project to build an American bomb first. Only a few advisers and key members of Congress knew of the project, which was officially organized in 1941 and would ultimately change the course of human history.

The war in Poland ended quickly. With Germany attacking from the west and the Soviet Union from the east, the Poles were overwhelmed in a month. The fall of Poland in September 1939 brought a lull in the fighting. A number of Americans, including the American ambassador to Great Britain, Joseph

Kennedy, who feared communist Russia more than fascist Germany, urged the United States to take the lead in negotiating a peace settlement that would recognize the German and Russian occupation of Poland. The British and French, however, were not interested in such a solution, and neither was Roosevelt.

Great Britain sent several divisions to aid the French against the expected German attack, but for months nothing happened. This interlude, sometimes called the "phony war," dramatically ended on April 9, 1940, when Germany attacked Norway and Denmark with a furious air and sea assault. A few weeks later, using armored vehicles supported by massive air strikes, the German *Blitzkrieg* ("lightning war") swept through Belgium, Luxembourg, and the Netherlands. A week later, the Germans stormed into France.

The famed Maginot line, a series of fortifications designed to repulse a German invasion, was useless, as German mechanized forces swept around the end of the line and attacked from the rear. The French guns, solidly fixed in concrete and pointing toward Germany, were never fired. The Maginot line, which would have been an effective defensive weapon in World War I, was ineffective in the new mechanized and mobile war of the 1940s. France surrendered in June as the British army fled back across the English Channel from Dunkirk.

How should the United States respond to the new and desperate situation in Europe? William Allen White, journalist and editor, and other concerned Americans organized the Committee to Defend America by Aiding the Allies, but others, including Charles Lindbergh, the hero of the 1920s, supported a group called America First. They argued that the United States should forget about England and concentrate on defending America. Roosevelt steered a cautious course. He approved the shipment to Britain of 50 overage American destroyers. In return, the United States received the right to establish naval and air bases on British territory from Newfoundland to Bermuda and British Guiana.

Winston Churchill, prime minister of Great Britain, asked for much more, but Roosevelt hesitated. In July 1940, the president did sign a measure authorizing $4 billion to increase the number of American naval warships. In September, Congress passed the Selective Service Act, which provided for the first peacetime draft in the history of the United States. Over a million men were to serve in the army for one year, but only in the Western Hemisphere. As the war in Europe reached a crisis in the fall of 1940, the American people were still undecided about the proper response.

The Election of 1940

Part of Roosevelt's reluctance to aid Great Britain more energetically came from his genuine desire to keep the United States out of the war, but it was also related to the presidential campaign waged during the crisis months of the summer and fall of 1940. Roosevelt broke a long tradition by seeking a third term. He marked the increasing support he was drawing from the liberal wing of the Democratic party by selecting liberal farm economist Henry Wallace of Iowa as his running mate.

The Republicans nominated Wendell Willkie of Indiana. Despite his big-business ties, Willkie approved of most New Deal legislation and supported aid to Great Britain. Energetic and attractive, Willkie was the most persuasive and exciting Republican candidate since Theodore Roosevelt, and he appealed to many people who distrusted or disliked Roosevelt. Yet in an atmosphere of international crisis, most voters chose to stay with Roosevelt. He won, 27 million to 22 million, and carried 38 of 48 states.

Lend-Lease

After the election, Roosevelt invented a scheme for sending aid to Britain without demanding payment. He called it "lend-lease." He compared the situation to lending a garden hose to a neighbor whose house was on fire. Senator Robert Taft of Ohio, however, thought the idea of lending military equipment and expecting it back was absurd. He decided it was more like lending chewing gum to a friend: "Once it had been used you did not want it back." Others were even more critical. Senator Burton K. Wheeler, an extreme isolationist, branded lend-lease "Roosevelt's triple A foreign policy" (after the Agricultural Adjustment Act) because it was designed to "plow under every fourth American boy."

The Lend-Lease Act, which Congress passed in March 1941, destroyed the fiction of neutrality. By that time, German submarines were sinking one-half million tons of shipping each month in the Atlantic. In June, Roosevelt proclaimed a national emergency and ordered the closing of German and Italian consulates in the United States. On June 22, Germany suddenly attacked the Soviet Union. It was one of Hitler's biggest blunders of the war, for now his armies had to fight on two fronts.

The surprise attack created a dilemma for the United States. Suddenly the great communist "enemy" had become America's friend and ally. When Roosevelt extended lend-lease aid to Russia in November 1941, many Americans were shocked. But most made a quick transition from viewing the Soviet Union as an enemy to treating it like a friend.

By the autumn of 1941, the United States was virtually at war with Germany in the Atlantic. On September 11, Roosevelt issued a "shoot on sight" order for all American ships operating in the Atlantic, and on October 30, a German submarine sank an American destroyer off the coast of Newfoundland. The war in the Atlantic, however, was undeclared, and many Americans opposed it. Eventually, the sinking of enough American ships or another crisis would probably have provided the excuse for a formal declaration of war against Germany. It was not Germany, however, but Japan that catapulted the United States into World War II.

The Path to Pearl Harbor

Japan, controlled by ambitious military leaders, was the aggressor in the Far East as Hitler's Germany was in Europe. Intent on becoming a major world power yet desperately needing natural resources, especially oil, Japan was willing to risk war with China, the Soviet Union, and even the United States to get those resources. Japan invaded Manchuria in 1931 and launched an all-out assault on China in 1937. This was the beginning of what the Japanese would call "the Pacific War." The Japanese leaders assumed that at some point the United States would go to war if Japan tried to take the Philippines, but the Japanese attempted to delay that moment as long as possible by diplomatic means. For its part, the United States feared the possibility of a two-front war and was willing to delay the confrontation with Japan until it had dealt with the German threat. Thus, between 1938 and 1941, the United States and Japan engaged in a kind of diplomatic shadow boxing.

The United States did exert economic pressure on Japan. In July 1939, the United States gave the required six months' notice regarding cancellation of the 1911 commercial agreement between the two countries. In September 1940, the Roosevelt administration forbade the shipment of airplane fuel and scrap metal to Japan. Other items were added to the embargo until by the spring of 1941, the United States allowed only oil to be shipped to Japan, hoping that the threat of cutting off the important resource would lead to negotiations and avert a crisis. Japan did open negotiations with the United States, but there was little to discuss. Japan would not withdraw from China as the United States demanded. Indeed, Japan, taking advantage of the situation in Europe, occupied French Indochina in 1940 and 1941. In July 1941, Roosevelt froze all Japanese assets in the United States, effectively embargoing trade with Japan.

Roosevelt had an advantage in the negotiations with Japan, for the United States had broken the Japanese secret diplomatic code. But Japanese intentions were hard to decipher from the intercepted messages. The American leaders knew that Japan planned to attack, but they didn't know where. In September 1941, the Japanese decided to strike sometime after November unless the United States offered real concessions. The strike came not in the Philippines but at Pearl Harbor, the main American Pacific naval base, in Hawaii.

On the morning of December 7, 1941, Japanese airplanes launched from aircraft carriers attacked the U.S. fleet at Pearl Harbor. The surprise attack destroyed or disabled 19 ships (including 5 battleships) and 150 planes and killed 2,335 soldiers and sailors and 68 civilians. On the same day, the Japanese launched attacks on the Philippines, Guam, and the Midway Islands, as well as on the British colonies of Hong Kong and Malaya. The next day, with only one dissenting vote, Congress declared war on Japan. Jeannette Rankin, a member of Congress from Montana who had voted against the war resolution in 1917, voted no again in 1941. She recalled that in 1917, after a week of tense debate, 50 voted against going to war. "This time I stood alone."

Corporal John J. "Ted" Kohl, a 25-year-old from Springfield, Ohio, was standing guard that Sunday morning near an ammunition warehouse at Hickam Field, near Pearl Harbor. He had joined the army two years before when his marriage failed and he could not find work. A Japanese bomb hit nearby, and Ted Kohl blew up with the warehouse. It was not until Wednesday evening, December 10, that the telegram arrived in Springfield. "The Secretary of War desires to express his deep regrets that your son Cpl. John J. Kohl was killed in action in defense of his country." Ted's younger brothers cried when they heard the news. There would be hundreds of thousands of telegrams and even more tears before the war was over.

December 7, 1941, was a day that "would live in infamy," in the words of Franklin Roosevelt. It was also a day that would have far-reaching implications for American foreign policy and for American attitudes toward the world. The surprise attack united the country as nothing else could have. Even isolationists and America First advocates quickly rallied behind the war effort.

After the shock and anger subsided, Americans searched for a villain. Someone must have blundered, someone must have betrayed the country to have allowed the "inferior" Japanese to have carried out such a successful and devastating attack. A myth persists to this day that the villain was

An exploding American destroyer at Pearl Harbor, December 7, 1941. The attack on Pearl Harbor united the country and came to symbolize Japanese treachery and American lack of preparedness. Photographs such as this were published throughout the war to inspire Americans to work harder. *(Superstock, Inc.)*

Roosevelt, who, the story goes, knew of the Japanese attack but failed to warn the military commanders so that the American people might unite behind the war effort against Germany. But Roosevelt did not know. There was no specific warning that the attack was coming against Pearl Harbor, and the American ability to read the Japanese coded messages was of no help because the fleet kept radio silence.

The irony was that the Americans, partly because of racial prejudice against the Japanese, underestimated their ability. They ignored many warning signals because they did not believe that the Japanese could launch an attack on a target as far away as Hawaii. Most of the experts, including Roosevelt, expected the Japanese to attack the Philippines or perhaps Thailand. Many people blundered, but there was no conspiracy on the part of Roosevelt and his advisers to get the United States into the war.

Even more important in the long run than the way the attack on Pearl Harbor united the American people was its effect on a generation of military and political leaders. Pearl Harbor became the symbol of unpreparedness. For a generation that experienced the anger and frustration of the attack on Pearl Harbor by an unscrupulous enemy, the lesson was to be prepared and ready to stop an aggressor before it had a chance to strike at the United States. The smoldering remains of the sinking battleships at Pearl Harbor on the morning of December 7, 1941, and the history lesson learned there would influence American policy not only during World War II but also in Korea, Vietnam, and the international confrontations thereafter.

THE HOME FRONT

Too often wars are described in terms of presidents and generals, emperors and kings, in terms of grand strategy and elaborate campaigns. But wars affect the lives of all people—the soldiers who fight and the women and children and men who stay home. World War II especially had an impact on all aspects of society—the economy, the movies and radio, even attitudes toward women and blacks. For many people, the war represented opportunity and the end of the Depression. For others, the excitement of faraway places meant that they could never return home again. For still others, the war left lasting scars.

Mobilizing for War

Converting American industry to war production was a complex task. Many corporate executives refused to admit that an emergency existed. Shortly after Pearl Harbor, Roosevelt created the War Production Board (WPB) and appointed Donald Nelson, executive vice president of Sears, Roebuck, to mobilize the nation's resources for an all-out war effort. The WPB offered businesses cost-plus contracts, guaranteeing a fixed and generous profit. Often the government also financed new plants and

Military Expenditures and the National Debt, 1929–1945

Increased taxes, the sale of war bonds, and price controls kept inflation under relative control during the war. Still, the war industry not only stimulated the economy but also increased the national debt.

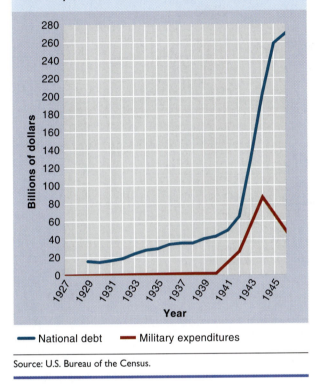

National debt ■ **Military expenditures**

Source: U.S. Bureau of the Census.

industry, and the government would lay the groundwork for massive projects in the postwar years.

The Roosevelt administration tried in a variety of ways to gain the cooperation of businessmen. The president appointed many business executives to key positions, some of whom, like Nelson, served for a dollar a year. He also abandoned antitrust actions in all industries that were remotely war-related. The policy worked. Both industrial production and net corporate profits nearly doubled during the war.

Large commercial farmers also profited. The war years accelerated the mechanization of the farm. Between 1940 and 1945, a million tractors joined those already in use. At the same time, the farm population declined by 17 percent. The consolidation of small farms into large ones and the dramatic increase in the use of fertilizer made farms more productive and farming more profitable for the large operators.

Many government agencies in addition to the War Production Board helped run the war effort efficiently. The Office of Price Administration (OPA) set prices on thousands of items to control inflation. The OPA also rationed scarce products. Because the OPA's decisions affected what people wore and ate and whether they had gasoline, many regarded it as oppressive. The National War Labor Board (NWLB) had the authority to set wages and hours and to monitor working conditions and could, under the president's wartime emergency powers, seize industrial plants whose owners refused to cooperate.

Membership in labor unions grew rapidly during the war, from a total of 10.5 million in 1941 to 14.7 million in 1945. In return for a "no-strike pledge," the NWLB allowed agreements that required workers to retain their union membership through the life of a contract. Labor leaders, however, complained about increased government regulations and argued that wage controls coupled with wartime inflation were unfair. The NWLB finally allowed a 15 percent cost-of-living increase on some contracts, but that did not apply to overtime pay, which helped drive up wages in some industries during the war by about 70 percent.

In addition to wage and price controls and rationing, the government tried to reduce inflation by selling war bonds and by increasing taxes. The Revenue Act of 1942 raised tax rates, broadened the tax base, increased corporate taxes to 40 percent, and raised the excess-profits tax to 90 percent. In addition, the government initiated a payroll deduction for income taxes. The war made the income tax a reality for most Americans for the first time.

equipment. Secretary of War Henry Stimson explained: "If you . . . go to war . . . in a capitalist country, you have to let business make money out of the process or business won't work." Roosevelt seemed to agree.

Even before the United States entered the war, Roosevelt had created a National Defense Research Committee to organize scientists to help in the war effort. Later he set up the Office of Scientific Research and Development (OSRD) to perfect new weapons and other products. The most important science and technology project carried on during the war was the development of the atomic bomb, but OSRD also improved radar and developed high-altitude bomb sights, jet engines, pressurized cabins for airplanes, and penicillin and other miracle drugs. Scientists under contract to the government also developed DDT and other effective insecticides, but none of the scientists recognized the dangerous side effects that DDT would have on the environment. The wartime collaboration of science,

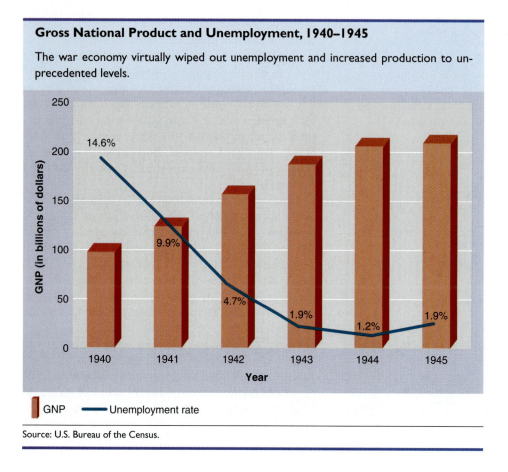

Gross National Product and Unemployment, 1940–1945

The war economy virtually wiped out unemployment and increased production to unprecedented levels.

GNP (in billions of dollars)

14.6%

9.9%

4.7%

1.9%

1.2%

1.9%

1940   1941   1942   1943   1944   1945

Year

GNP ▬▬ Unemployment rate

Source: U.S. Bureau of the Census.

Despite some unfairness and much confusion, the American economy responded to the wartime crisis and produced the equipment and supplies that eventually won the war. American industries built 300,000 airplanes, 88,140 tanks, and 3,000 merchant ships. In 1944 alone, American factories produced 800,000 tons of synthetic rubber to replace the supply of natural rubber captured by the Japanese. Although the national debt grew from about $143 billion in 1943 to $260 billion in 1945, the government policy of taxation paid for about 40 percent of the war's cost. At the same time, full employment and the increase in two-income families, together with forced savings, helped provide capital for postwar expansion. In a limited way, the tax policy also tended to redistribute wealth, which the New Deal had failed to do. The top 5 percent income bracket, which controlled 23 percent of the disposable income in 1939, accounted for only 17 percent in 1945.

The war stimulated the growth of the federal bureaucracy and accelerated the trend, begun during World War I and extended in the 1920s and 1930s, toward the government's central role in the economy. The war also increased the cooperation between industry and government, creating what would later be called a military-industrial complex. But for most Americans, despite anger at the OPA and the income tax, the war meant the end of the Depression.

Patriotic Fervor

The war, so horrible elsewhere, was remote in the United States—except for the families that received the official telegram informing them that a loved one had been killed. The government tried to keep the conflict alive in the minds of Americans and to keep the country united behind the war effort. The Office of War Information, staffed by writers and advertising executives, controlled the news the American public received about the war. It promoted patriotism and presented the American war effort in the best possible light. The government also sold war bonds, not only to help pay for the war and reduce inflation but also to sell the war to the American people. As had been true during World War I, movie stars and other celebrities appeared at war bond rallies. Dorothy Lamour, one of Hollywood's most glamorous actresses, took credit for selling $350 million worth of bonds. Schoolchildren purchased war stamps and faithfully pasted them in an album until they had accumulated stamps worth $18.75, enough to buy a $25 bond (redeemable 10 years later). Their bonds, they were told, would purchase bullets or a part for an airplane to kill "Japs" and Germans and defend the American way of life. "For Freedom's Sake, Buy War Bonds," one poster announced. Working men and women purchased bonds through payroll deduction plans and looked forward to spending the money on consumer goods after the war. In the end, the government sold over $135 billion in war bonds. While the bond drives did help control inflation, they were most important in making millions of Americans feel that they were contributing to the war effort.

Those too old or too young to join the armed forces served in other ways. Thousands became air raid wardens or civilian defense and Red Cross volunteers. They raised victory gardens and took part in scrap drives. Even small children could join the war effort by collecting old rubber, wastepaper, and kitchen fats. Some items, including gasoline, sugar, butter, and meat, were rationed, but few people complained. Even horsemeat hamburgers seemed edible if they helped win the war. Newspaper and magazine advertising characterized ordinary actions as either speeding victory or impeding the war effort. "Hoarders are the same as spies," one ad announced. "Every time you decide not to buy something you help win the war."

Internment of Japanese Americans

Wartime campaigns not only stimulated patriotism but also promoted hatred for the enemy. The Nazis, especially Hitler and his Gestapo, had become synonymous with evil even before 1941. But at the beginning of the war, there was little animosity toward the German people. But before long, most Americans ceased to make distinctions. All Germans seemed evil, although the anti-German hysteria that had swept the country during World War I never developed. The Japanese were easier to hate than the Germans. The attack on Pearl Harbor created a special animosity toward the Japanese, but the depiction of the Japanese as warlike and subhuman owed something to a long tradition of fear of the so-called yellow peril and a distrust of all Asians. The movies, magazine articles, cartoons, and posters added to the image of the Japanese soldier or pilot with a toothy grin murdering innocent women and children or shooting down helpless Americans. Two weeks after Pearl Harbor, *Time* magazine explained to Americans how they could distinguish our Asian friends the Chinese "from the

Japanese-American children on their way to a "relocation center." For many Japanese Americans, but especially for the children, the nightmare of the relocation camp experience would stay with them all their lives. *(Library of Congress)*

Japs." "Virtually all Japanese are short, Japanese are seldom fat; they often dry up with age," *Time* declared. "Most Chinese avoid horn-rimmed spectacles. Japanese walk stiffly erect, hard-heeled. Chinese, more relaxed, have an easy gait. The Chinese expression is likely to be more kindly, placid, open; the Japanese more positive, dogmatic, arrogant." But Americans were not very good at distinguishing one Asian face from another. The Chinese and the Koreans tried to help by putting up signs which read, "We Are Not Japs," or "This is a Chinese Shop."

The racial stereotype of the Japanese played a role in the treatment of Japanese Americans during the war. Some prejudice was shown against German and Italian Americans, but Japanese Americans were the only group confined in internment camps, in the greatest mass abridgment of civil liberties in American history.

At the time of Pearl Harbor, about 127,000 Japanese Americans lived in the United States, most on the West Coast. About 80,000 were nisei

Relocation Camps

Early in 1942, responding to the hysterical fear that Japanese Americans living on the West Coast might engage in sabotage, the government ordered over 100,000 Japanese Americans (many of them citizens) into relocation camps. A larger group of Japanese Americans living in Hawaii did not have their lives disrupted or their property confiscated.

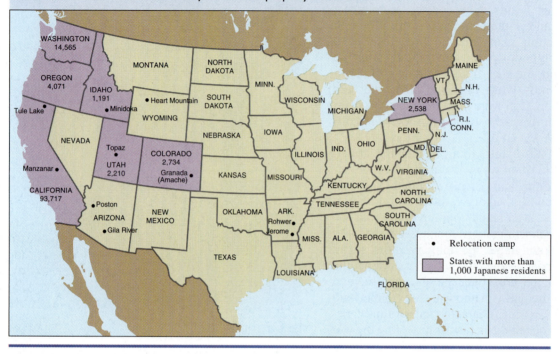

(Japanese born in the United States and holding American citizenship) and sansei (the sons and daughters of nisei); the rest were issei (aliens born in Japan who were ineligible for U.S. citizenship). The Japanese had long suffered from racial discrimination and prejudice in the United States. They were barred from intermarriage with other groups and excluded from many clubs, restaurants, and recreation facilities. Many worked as tenant farmers, fishermen, and small businessmen. Others made up a small professional class of lawyers, teachers, and doctors and a large number of land-owning farmers.

Although many retained cultural and linguistic ties to Japan, they posed no more threat to the country than did the much larger groups of Italian Americans and German Americans. But their physical characteristics made them stand out as the others did not. After Pearl Harbor, an anti-Japanese panic seized the West Coast. A Los Angeles newspaper reported that armed Japanese were in Baja, California, ready to attack. Rumors suggested that Japanese fishermen were preparing to sow mines in the harbor, blow up tunnels, and poison the water supply.

West Coast politicians and ordinary citizens urged the War Department and the president to evacuate the Japanese. The president capitulated and issued Executive Order 9066 authorizing the evacuation in February 1942. "The continued pressure of a largely unassimilated, tightly knit racial group, bound to an enemy nation by strong ties of race, culture, custom and religion, constituted a menace which had to be dealt with," General John De Witt argued, justifying the removal on military grounds. But racial fear and animosity, not military necessity, stood behind the order.

Eventually, the government built the "relocation centers" in remote, often arid, sections of the West. "The Japs live like rats, breed like rats, and act like rats. We don't want them," the governor of Idaho announced. The camps were primitive and unattractive. "When I first entered our room, I became sick to my stomach," a Japanese-American woman remembered. "There were seven beds in the room and no furniture nor any partitions to separate the males and the females of the family. I just sat on the bed, staring at the bare wall."

The government evacuated about 110,000 Japanese, including about 60,000 American citizens. Those who were forced to leave their homes, farms, and businesses lost almost all their property and possessions. Farmers left their crops to be harvested by their American neighbors. Store owners sold out for a small percentage of what their goods were worth. No personal items or household goods could be transported. The Japanese Americans lost their worldly possessions, and something more—their pride and respect. One six-year-old kept asking his mother to "take him back to America." He thought his relocation center was in Japan.

The evacuation of the Japanese Americans appears in retrospect to have been unjustified. Even in Hawaii, where a much larger Japanese population existed, the government evacuated only a few (in part because the Japanese were so vital to the economy of the Islands), and no sabotage and little disloyalty occurred. The government allowed Japanese-American men to volunteer for military service, and many served bravely in the European theater. The 442nd Infantry Combat Team, made up entirely of nisei, became the most decorated unit in all the military service—another indication of the loyalty and patriotism of most Japanese Americans. After January 1944, the United States government began drafting nisei men who were being retained in the relocation centers, but a few, as many as 10 percent in some camps, refused and became draft resisters and were sent to prison. They appreciated the irony and the injustice of being asked to register for the draft as citizens while being deprived of the rights of citizenship in relocation centers. At the same time that Japanese-American citizens were confined to relocation centers, more than 400,000 German prisoners were confined to prison camps, usually in small towns across America. In some cases, they were treated better than Japanese-American citizens. In 1988, Congress belatedly voted limited compensation for the Japanese Americans relocated during World War II.

Asian, African, and Hispanic Americans at War

The Pacific War made China an ally of the United States, but Congress did not repeal the Chinese Exclusion Act until 1943, and then only 105 Chinese a year were allowed to enter the United States legally. Despite this affront, the Chinese communities joined the war effort enthusiastically. They bought war bonds, collected scrap metal, and in other ways tried to show that they were loyal citizens. Almost 13,500 Chinese men enlisted or were drafted into the army. Many others took jobs in war industry. Formerly restricted to jobs in laundries or restaurants, they eagerly sought employment in factories. In fact, so many waiters left their jobs that four restaurants in New York's Chinatown had to close in 1942.

The Korean, Filipino, and Asian-Indian population also contributed to the war effort. In California, 16,000 Filipinos registered for the first draft, and many served behind enemy lines in the battle to recapture the Philippine Islands. As members of the United States Armed Forces, they were allowed to become citizens, but the Koreans were classified as enemy aliens. Still, many served in the army and proved valuable because they often could speak Japanese. Although the Asian-Indian population had been denied citizenship by a 1923 Supreme Court decision, this was altered during the war in part because the United States needed India as an ally in the Pacific War. Despite increased acceptance during the war, Asians still faced prejudice and were often denied service in restaurants or refused admittance to theaters. Many Americans hated the Japanese; to them, all Asians looked like the enemy.

Even in much of the North, the United States remained a segregated society in 1941. African Americans could not live, eat, travel, work, or go to school with the same freedom that whites enjoyed. Black Americans profited little from the revival of prosperity and the expansion of jobs early in the war. Those who joined the military were usually assigned to menial jobs as cooks or laborers and were always assigned to segregated units with whites as the high-ranking officers. The myth that black soldiers had failed to perform well in World War I persisted. "Leadership is not embedded in the negro race yet," Secretary of War Henry Stimson wrote, "and to try to make commissioned officers . . . lead men into battle—colored men—is only to work a disaster to both."

Some black leaders found it especially ironic that as the country prepared to fight Hitler and his racist policies, the United States persisted in its own brand of racism. "A jim crow Army cannot fight for a free world," announced *The Crisis*, the journal of the NAACP. A. Philip Randolph decided to act rather than talk. The son of a Methodist minister, Randolph had worked with the first wave of African Americans migrating from the South to the northern cities during and just after World War I. He spent years trying "to carry the gospel of unionism to the colored world." He organized and led the Brotherhood of Sleeping Car Porters, and in 1937, he finally won grudging recognition of the union from the Pullman Company.

Respected and admired by black leaders of all political persuasions, Randolph convinced many of them in 1941 to join him in a march on Washington to demand equal rights. "Dear fellow Negro Americans," Randolph wrote, "be not dismayed in these terrible times. You possess power, great power. Our problem is to harness and hitch it up for action on the broadest, daring and most gigantic scale."

The threat of as many as 100,000 African Americans marching in protest in the nation's capital alarmed Roosevelt. At first, he sent his assistants, including his wife, Eleanor (who was greatly admired in the black community), to dissuade Randolph from such drastic action. Finally, he talked to Randolph in person on June 18, 1941. Randolph and Roosevelt struck a bargain. Roosevelt refused to desegregate the armed forces, but in return for Randolph's calling off the march, the president issued Executive Order 8802, which stated that it was the policy of the United States that "there shall be no discrimination in the employment of workers in defense industries or government because of race, creed, color or national origin." He also established the Fair Employment Practices Commission (FEPC) to enforce the order.

By threatening militant action, the black leaders wrested a major concession from the president. But the executive order did not end prejudice, and the FEPC, which its chairman described as the "most hated agency in Washington," had limited success in erasing the color line. Many black soldiers were angered and humiliated throughout the war by being made to sit in the back of buses and being barred from hotels and restaurants. Years later, one former black soldier recalled being refused service in a restaurant in Salina, Kansas, while the same restaurant served German prisoners from a camp nearby. "We continued to stare," he recalled. "This was really happening. . . . The people of Salina would serve these enemy soldiers and turn away black American G.I.'s."

Many African Americans improved their economic conditions during the war by taking jobs in war industries. Continuing the migration that had begun during World War I, 750,000 southern blacks moved to northern and western cities in search of economic opportunity. Some became skilled workers and a few became professionals, but they did not escape racial prejudice. In Detroit, where a major race riot broke out in the summer of 1943, Polish Americans had protested a public housing development that promised to bring blacks into their neighborhood. In one year, more than 50,000 blacks moved into that city, already overcrowded with many others seeking wartime jobs. The new arrivals increased the pressure on housing and other facilities, and the war accentuated the tension among the various groups.

The riot broke out on a hot, steamy day at a municipal park after a series of incidents led to fights between black and white young people and then to looting in the black community. Before federal and state troops restored order, 34 had been killed (25 blacks and 9 whites) and rioters had destroyed more than $2 million worth of property. Groups of whites roamed the city attacking blacks, overturning cars, setting fires, and sometimes killing wantonly. Other riots broke out in Mobile, Los Angeles, New York, and Beaumont, Texas. In all these cities, and in many others where the tension did not lead to open

Even before the United States entered the war, black families like this one moved north to look for work and a better life. This massive migration would change the racial mix in northern cities. *(Library of Congress)*

violence, the legacy of bitterness and hate lasted long after the war.

Mexican Americans, like most minority groups, profited during the war from the increased job opportunities provided by wartime industry, but they, too, faced racial prejudice. In California and in many parts of the Southwest, Mexicans could not use public swimming pools. Often lumped together with blacks, they were excluded from certain restaurants. Usually they were limited to menial jobs and were constantly harassed by the police, picked up for minor offenses, and jailed on the smallest excuse. In Los Angeles, the anti-Mexican prejudice flared into violence. The increased migration of Mexicans into the city as well as old hatreds created a volatile situation. Most of the hostility and anger focused on Mexican gang members, or *pachuchos*, especially those wearing zoot suits. The suits consisted of long, loose coats with padded shoulders, ballooned pants pegged at the ankles, and a wide-brimmed hat. A watch chain and a ducktail haircut completed the uniform. The zoot suit had originated in the black sections of northern cities and became a national craze during the war. It was a look some teenage males adopted to call attention to themselves and shock conventional society.

The zoot-suiters especially angered soldiers and sailors who were stationed or on leave in Los Angeles. After a number of provocative incidents, violence broke out between the Mexican-American youths and the servicemen in the spring of 1943. The violence reached a peak on June 7, when gangs of servicemen, often in taxicabs, combed the city, attacking all the young zoot-suiters they could find or anyone who looked Mexican. The servicemen, joined by others, beat up the Mexicans, stripped them of their offensive clothes, and then gave them haircuts. The police, both civilian and military, looked the other way, and when they did move in, they arrested the victims rather than their attackers.

SOCIAL IMPACT OF THE WAR

Modern wars have been incredibly destructive of human lives and property, but they have social results as well. The Civil War ended slavery and ensured the triumph of the industrial North for years to come; in so doing, it left a legacy of bitterness and transformed the race question from a sectional to a national problem. World War I ensured the success of woman suffrage and prohibition, caused a migration of blacks to northern cities, and ushered in a time of intolerance. World War II also had many social results. It altered patterns of work, leisure, edu-

cation, and family life; caused a massive migration of people; created jobs; and changed lifestyles. It is difficult to overemphasize the impact of the war on the generation that lived through it.

Wartime Opportunities

More than 15 million American civilians moved during the war. Like the Momadays, many left home to find better jobs. In fact, for many Native Americans, wartime opportunities led to a migration from the rural areas and the reservations into the cities. Americans moved off the farms and away from the small towns, flocking to cities, where defense jobs were readily available. They moved west: California alone gained more than 2 million people during the war. But they also moved out of the South into the northern cities, while a smaller number moved from the North to the South. Late in the war, when a shortage of farm labor developed, some reversed the trend and moved back onto the farms. But a great many people moved somewhere. One observer, noticing the heavily packed cars heading west, decided that it was just like *The Grapes of Wrath*, without the poverty and the hopelessness.

The World War II migrants poured into industrial centers; 200,000 came to the Detroit area, nearly one-half million to Los Angeles, and about 100,000 to Mobile, Alabama. They put pressure on the schools, housing, and other services. Often they had to live in new Hoovervilles, trailer parks, or temporary housing. In San Pablo, California, a family of four adults and seven children lived in an 8-by-10-foot shack. Bill Mauldin, the war cartoonist, showed a young couple with a child buying tickets for a movie with the caption: "Matinee, heck—we want to register for a week."

Nowhere was the change more dramatic than in the West, and especially in California, where the wartime boom transformed the region more dramatically than any development since the nineteenth-century economic revolution created by the railroads and mining. The federal government spent over $70 billion in the state (one-tenth of the total for the entire country) to build army bases, shipyards, supply depots, and testing sites. In addition, private industry constructed so many facilities that the region became the center of a growing military-industrial complex. San Diego, for example, was transformed from a sleepy port and naval base into a sprawling metropolis. The population grew by 147 percent between 1941 and 1945, from 202,000 to 380,000. Vallejo, a small city near Oakland, grew from 20,000 to over 100,000 in just two years. The U.S. Navy's Mare Island Shipyard, which was nearby, increased its workforce from 5,000 to 45,000. Vanport, just north of Portland, Oregon, was an empty mud flat in 1940; three years later, it was a bustling city of more than 40,000. Almost everyone in the new town worked for the Kaiser Ship Yards.

This spectacular growth created problems. There was a housing shortage, schools were overcrowded, and hospitals and municipal services could not keep up with the demand. Crime and prostitution increased as did racial tensions. Some migrants had never lived in a city and were homesick. On one occasion in a Willow Grove, Michigan, school, the children were all instructed to sing "Michigan, My Michigan"; no one knew the words because they all came from other states.

For the first time in years, many families had money to spend, but they had nothing to spend it on. The last new car rolled off the assembly line in February 1942. There were no washing machines, refrigerators, or radios in the stores, no gasoline and no tires to permit weekend trips. Even when people had time off, they tended to stay at home or in the neighborhood. Some of the new housing developments had the atmosphere of a mining camp, complete with drinking, prostitution, and barroom brawls.

The war required major adjustments in American family life. With several million men in the service

The war caused many quick romances, but also many tearful good-byes. *(Alfred Eisenstadt/LIFE Magazine © Time Inc.)*

and others far away working at defense jobs, the number of households headed by a woman increased dramatically. The number of marriages also rose sharply. Early in the war, a young man could be deferred if he had a dependent, and a wife qualified as a dependent. Later, many servicemen got married, often to women they barely knew, because they wanted a little excitement and perhaps someone to come home to. The birthrate also began to rise in 1940, as young couples started a family as fast as they could. Some children were "good-bye babies," conceived just before the husband left to join the military or go overseas. The illegitimacy rate also went up, and from the outset of the war, the divorce rate began to climb sharply. Yet most of the wartime marriages survived, and many of the women left at home looked ahead to a time after the war when they could settle down to a normal life.

Women Workers for Victory

Thousands of women took jobs in heavy industry that formerly would have been considered unladylike. They built tanks, airplanes, and ships, but they still earned less than men. At first, women were rarely taken on because as the war in Europe pulled American industry out of its long slump, unemployed men snapped up the newly available positions. In the face of this male labor pool, one government official remarked that we should "give the women something to do to keep their hands busy as we did in the last war, then maybe they won't bother us."

But by 1943, with many men drafted and male unemployment virtually nonexistent, the government was quick to suggest that it was women's patriotic duty to take their place on the assembly line. A government poster showed a woman worker and her uniformed husband standing in front of an American flag with the caption: "I'm proud . . . my husband wants me to do my part." The government tried to convince women that if they could run a vacuum cleaner or a sewing machine or drive a car, they could operate power machinery in a factory. Advertisers in women's magazines joined the campaign by showing fashion models in work clothes. A popular song was "Rosie the Riveter," who was "making history working for victory." She also helped her marine boyfriend by "working overtime on the riveting machine."

At the end of the war, the labor force included 19.5 million women, but three-fourths of them had been working before the conflict, and some of the additional ones might have sought work in normal times. The new women war workers tended to be

SAVE FREEDOM OF SPEECH

NORMAN ROCKWELL

BUY WAR BONDS

Norman Rockwell, a popular illustrator, created four paintings to illustrate the Four Freedoms that President Roosevelt mentioned in his 1941 address to spell out what the United States was fighting for: Freedom of Worship, Freedom of Speech, Freedom from Fear, and Freedom from Want. Commissioned by the *Saturday Evening Post,* these paintings were turned into posters and used to support the sale of war bonds. *(National Archives [208-PMP-44])*

older, and they were more often married than single. Some worked for patriotic reasons. "Every time I test a batch of rubber, I know it's going to help bring my three sons home quicker," a woman worker in a rubber plant remarked. But others worked for the money or to have something useful to do. Yet in 1944, women's weekly wages averaged $31.21, compared with $54.65 for men, reflecting women's more menial tasks and their low seniority as well as outright discrimination. Still, many women enjoyed factory work. "Boy have the men been getting away with murder all these years," exclaimed a Pittsburgh housewife. "Why I worked twice as hard selling in a department store and got half the pay."

Black women faced the most difficult situation during the war, and often when they applied for work, they were told, "We have not yet installed sep- arate toilet facilities" or "We can't put a Negro in the front office." Not until 1944 did the telephone com- pany in New York City hire a black telephone opera- tor. Still, some black women moved during the war from domestic jobs to higher-paying factory work. Married women with young children also found it difficult to obtain work. There were few day-care facilities, and the women were often informed that they should be home with their children.

Women workers often had to endure catcalls, whistles, and more overt sexual harassment on the job. Still, most persisted, and they tried to look femi- nine despite the heavy work clothes. In one Boston factory, a woman was hooted at for carrying a lunch box. Only men, it seemed, carried lunch boxes; women brought their lunch in a paper bag.

Many women war workers quickly left their jobs after the war ended. Some left by choice, but dis- missals ran twice as high for women as for men. The war had barely shaken the notion that a woman's place was at home. Some women who learned what an extra paycheck meant for the family's standard of living would have preferred to keep working. But most women, and an even larger percentage of men, agreed at the end of the war that women did not de- serve an "equal chance with men" for jobs. For most Americans, a woman's place was still in the home.

Entertaining the People

According to one survey, Americans listened to the radio an average of 4½ hours a day during the war. The major networks increased their news programs from less than 4 percent to nearly 30 percent of broadcasting time. Americans heard Edward R. Murrow broadcasting from London during the German air blitz with the sound of the air raid sirens in the background. They listened to Eric Sevareid cover the battle of Burma and describe the sensa- tion of jumping out of an airplane. Often the signal faded out and the static made listening difficult, but the live broadcasts had drama and authenticity never before possible.

Even more than the reporters, the commentators became celebrities on whom the American people depended to explain what was going on around the world. Millions listened to the clipped, authorita- tive voice of H. V. Kaltenborn or to Gabriel Heatter, whose trademark was "Ah, there's good news tonight." But the war also intruded on almost all other programming. Even the advertising, which took up more and more air time, reminded listeners of the war. Lucky Strike cigarettes, which changed the color of its package from green to white, presum- ably because there was a shortage of green pigment, made "Lucky Strike Green Has Gone to War" almost as famous as "Remember Pearl Harbor."

Music, which took up a large proportion of radio programming, also conveyed a war theme. There were "Goodbye, Mama (I'm Off to Yokohama)" and "Praise the Lord and Pass the Ammunition," but more numerous were songs of romance and love, songs about separation and hope for a better time after the war. The danceable tunes of Glenn Miller and Tommy Dorsey became just as much a part of wartime memories as ration books and far-off battlefields.

For many Americans, the motion picture became the most important leisure activity and a part of their fantasy life during the war. Attendance at the movies averaged about 100 million viewers a week. There might not be gasoline for weekend trips or Sunday drives, but the whole family could go to the movies. Even those in the military service could watch American movies on board ship or at a remote outpost. "Pinup" photographs of Hollywood stars decorated the barracks and even tanks and planes wherever American troops were stationed.

Musical comedies, cowboy movies, and historical romances remained popular during the war, but the conflict intruded even on Hollywood. Newsreels that offered a visual synopsis of the war news, always with an upbeat message and a touch of human interest, preceded most movies. Their theme was that the Americans were winning the war, even if early in the conflict there was little evidence to that effect. Many feature films also had a wartime theme, picturing the war in the Pacific complete with grinning, vicious Japanese villains (usually played by Chinese or Korean character actors). In the beginning of these films, the Japanese were always victorious, but in the end, they always got "what they deserved."

The movies set in Europe differed from those depicting the Far Eastern war. British and Americans, sometimes spies, sometimes downed airmen, could dress up like Germans and get away with it. They outwitted the Germans at every turn, sabotaging important installations and made daring escapes from prison camps. Many wartime movies featured a multicultural platoon led by a veteran sergeant with a Protestant, a Catholic, a Jew, a black, a farmer, and a city resident. In several movies, the army was integrated, but in the real army, blacks served in segregated platoons.

Religion in Time of War

One of the four freedoms threatened by German and Japanese aggression was the "freedom to worship," and Roosevelt continually emphasized that the enemy was opposed to all religion. According to one estimate in 1940, 65 million Americans belonged to 250,000 churches and other religious institutions. There were about 23 million Catholics, 5 million Jews, and the rest were of one Protestant denomination or another. Most Americans thought of the United States as a Christian nation, and by that they usually meant a Protestant nation. While the war did lead to a measure of religious tolerance, anti-Semitism and anti-Catholicism did not disappear. According to one poll, although 18 percent of Americans never went to church, more than 30 percent said that the war had strengthened their religious faith.

Those who joined the armed forces were given three choices under religion: They were asked to check either Protestant, Catholic, or Jew, and appropriate symbols were marked on their "dog tags." There was no room for Hindu, Buddhist, Muslim, or atheist. Some men refused to fight on religious grounds. During World War I, only members of the traditional peace churches (Quaker, Bretheren, and Mennonite) were deferred from military service as conscientious objectors. In World War II, the criteria was broadened to include those who opposed war because of "religious training and belief." More than 70,000 claimed exemption on those grounds, and the government honored about half those claims. Twenty-five thousand were assigned to noncombat military service, and 12,000 were appointed to alternative civilian service.

A few clergymen remained pacifists and opposed the war, but far fewer than in World War I. A great many more volunteered to serve as chaplains, and like the men, they were categorized as Protestant, Catholic, or Jew. One of the most influential of the ministers who supported the use of force to combat evil was Reinhold Niebuhr. In a series of books including *Moral Man and Immoral Society* (1932) and *Children of Light and Children of Darkness* (1944), he struck out against what he saw as a naïve faith in the goodness of men, a faith that permeated the Social Gospel movement, the Progressive movement, and the New Deal. In a world gone mad, he interpreted all men as sinful, and he stressed the "evil that good men do." He argued for the use of force against evil. Neibhur's Christian Realism had little impact on most Americans, but he influenced the continuing debate in the 1930s, 1940s, and 1950s over the proper American response to evil around the world.

The GIs' War

GI, the abbreviation for *government issue,* became the affectionate designation for the ordinary soldier in World War II. The GIs came from every background and ethnic group. Some served reluctantly, some eagerly. A few became genuine heroes. All were turned into heroes by the press and the public, who seemed to believe that one American could easily defeat at least 20 Japanese or Germans. Ernie Pyle, one of the war correspondents who chronicled the authentic story of the ordinary GI, wrote of soldiers "just toiling from day to day in a world full of insecurity, discomfort, homesickness, and a dulled sense of danger."

Bill Mauldin, another correspondent, told the story of the ordinary soldier in a series of cartoons featuring two tired and resigned infantrymen, Willie and Joe. Joe tries to explain what the war is about, "when they run we try to ketch 'em, when we ketch 'em we try to make 'em run." In another cartoon, Willie says, "Joe, yestiddy ya saved my life an' I swore I'd pay you back. Here's my last pair of dry socks." For the soldier in the front line, the big strategies were irrelevant. The war seemed a constant mix-up; much more important were the little comforts and staying alive.

In the midst of battle, the war was no fun, but only one soldier in eight who served ever saw combat, and even for many of those, the war was a great adventure (just as World War I had been). "When World War II broke out I was delighted," Mario Puzo, author of *The Godfather,* remembered. "There is no other word, terrible as it may sound. My country called. I was delivered from my mother, my family, the girl I was loving passionately but did not love. And delivered *without guilt.* Heroically my country called, ordered me to defend it." World War II catapulted young men and women out of their small towns and urban neighborhoods into exotic places, where they met new people and did new things.

The war was important for Mexican Americans, who were drafted and volunteered in great numbers. One-third of a million served in all branches of the military, a larger percentage than for many other ethnic groups. Although they encountered prejudice, they probably found less in the armed forces than they had at home, and many returned to civilian life with new ambitions and a new sense of self-esteem.

Many Native Americans also served. In fact, many were recruited for special service in the Marine Signal Corps. One group of Navajos completely befuddled the Japanese with a code based on their native language. But the Navajo code talkers and all other Native Americans who chose to return to the reservations after the war were ineligible for veterans' loans, hospitalization, and other benefits. They lived on federal land, and that, according to the law, canceled all the advantages that other veterans enjoyed after the war.

Over 300,000 American servicemen died during the war, but the government tried to protect the American people from learning the real cost of the battles. This photograph, published in 1943, was the first to show dead American soldiers. *(George Strock/LIFE Magazine © 1943 Time Inc.)*

For African Americans, who served throughout the war in segregated units and faced prejudice wherever they went, the military experience also had much to teach. Fewer blacks were sent overseas (about 79,000 of 504,000 blacks in the service in 1943), and fewer were in combat outfits, so the percentage of black soldiers killed and wounded was low. Many illiterate blacks, especially from the South, learned to read and write in the service. Blacks who went overseas began to realize that not everyone viewed them as inferior. One black army officer said, "What the hell do we want to fight the Japs for anyhow? They couldn't possibly treat us any worse than these 'crackers' right here at home." Most realized the paradox of fighting for freedom when they themselves had little freedom; they hoped things would improve after the war.

Because the war lasted longer than World War I, its impact was greater. In all, over 16 million men and women served in some branch of the military service. About 322,000 were killed in the war, and more than 800,000 were wounded. The 12,000 listed as missing just disappeared. The war claimed many more lives than World War I and was the nation's costliest after the Civil War. But because of penicillin, blood plasma, sulfa drugs, and rapid battlefield evacuation, the wounded in World War II were twice as likely to survive as those wounded in World War I. Penicillin also minimized the threat of venereal disease, but all men who served saw an anti-VD film, just as their predecessors had in World War I.

Women in Uniform

Women had served in all wars as nurses and cooks and in other support capacities, and during World War II many continued in these traditional roles. A few nurses landed in France just days after the Normandy invasion. Nurses served with the army and the marines in the Pacific. They dug their own foxholes and treated men under enemy fire. Sixty-six nurses spent the entire war in the Philippines as prisoners of the Japanese. Most nurses, however, served far behind the lines tending the sick and wounded. Army nurses who were given officer rank were forbidden to date enlisted men. "Not permitting nurses and enlisted men to be seen together is certainly not American," one soldier decided.

Though nobody objected to women's serving as nurses, not until April 1943 did women physicians win the right to join the Army and Navy Medical Corps. Some people questioned whether it was right for women to serve in other capacities, but Congress authorized full military participation for women (except for combat) because of the military emergency and the argument that women could free men for combat duty. World War II thus became the first war in which women were given regular military status. About 350,000 women joined up, most in the Women's Army Corps (WACS) and the women's branch of the Navy (WAVES), but others served in the coast guard and the marines. Over 1,000 women trained as pilots. As members of Women's Airforce Service Pilots (WAFS), they flew bombers from the factories to landing fields in Great Britain.

Many recruiting posters suggested that the services needed women "for the precision work at which women are so adept" or for work in hospitals to comfort and attend to the wounded "as only women can do." Most women served in traditional female roles, doing office work, cooking, and cleaning. But others were engineers and pilots. Still, men and women were not treated equally. Women were explicitly kept out of combat situations and were often underused by male officers who found it difficult to view women in nontraditional roles.

Men were informed about contraceptives and encouraged to use them, but information about birth control was explicitly prohibited for women. Rumors charged many servicewomen with sexual promiscuity. On one occasion, the secretary of war defended the morality and the loyalty of the women in the service, but the rumors continued, spread apparently by men made uncomfortable by women's invasion of the male military domain. One cause for immediate discharge was pregnancy; yet the pregnancy rate for both married and unmarried women remained low.

Thus, despite difficulties, women played important roles during the war, and when they left the service (unlike the women who had served in other wars), they had the same rights and privileges as the male veterans. The women in the service did not permanently alter the military or the public's perception of women's proper role, but they did change a few minds, and many of the women who served had their lives changed and their horizons broadened.

A WAR OF DIPLOMATS AND GENERALS

Pearl Harbor catapulted the country into war with Japan, and on December 11, 1941, Hitler declared war on the United States. Why he did so has never been fully explained; he was perhaps impressed by the apparent weakness of America that was demonstrated at Pearl Harbor. He was not required by his treaty with Japan to go to war with the United States, and without his declaration, the United States might have concentrated on the war against Japan. But Hitler forced the United States into the war against the Axis powers in both Europe and Asia.

War Aims

Why was the United States fighting the war? What did it hope to accomplish in a peace settlement once the war was over? Roosevelt and the other American leaders never really decided. In a speech before Congress in January 1941, Roosevelt had mentioned the four freedoms: freedom of speech and expression, freedom of worship, freedom from want, and freedom from fear. For many Americans, especially after Norman Rockwell expressed those freedoms in four sentimental paintings, this was what they were fighting for. Roosevelt spoke vaguely of the need to extend democracy and to establish a peacekeeping organization, but in direct contrast to

Woodrow Wilson's Fourteen Points, he never spelled out in any detail the political purposes for fighting. There were some other implied reasons for going to war. Henry Luce, the editor of *Life Magazine,* made those reasons explicit in an editorial written nine months before Pearl Harbor. He called his essay "The American Century," and he argued that the United States had the responsibility to spread the American way of life around the world. In 1943, Wendell Willkie, the Republican presidential candidate in 1940, wrote a best-selling plea for internationalism called *One World.* Like Luce, he argued that the world should adopt the American system of free enterprise. But first the war had to be ended as quickly as possible.

Roosevelt and his advisers, realizing that it would be impossible to mount an all-out war against both Japan and Germany, decided to fight a holding action in the Pacific while concentrating efforts against Hitler in Europe, where the immediate danger seemed greater. But the United States was not fighting alone. It joined the Soviet Union and Great Britain in what became a difficult, but ultimately effective alliance to defeat Nazi Germany. Churchill and Roosevelt got along well, although they often disagreed on strategy and tactics. Roosevelt's relationship with Stalin was much more strained, but he often agreed with the Russian leader about the way to fight the war. Stalin, a ruthless leader who had maintained his position of power only after eliminating hundreds of thousands of opponents, distrusted both the British and the Americans, but he needed them, just as they depended on him. Without the tremendous sacrifices of the Russian army and the Russian people in 1941 and 1942, Germany would have won the war before the vast American military and industrial might could be mobilized.

Year of Disaster, 1942

The first half of 1942 was disastrous for the Allied cause. In the Pacific, the Japanese captured the Dutch East Indies with their vast riches in rubber, oil, and other resources. They swept into Burma, took Wake Island and Guam, and invaded the Aleutian Islands of Alaska. They pushed the American garrison on the Philippines onto the Bataan peninsula and finally onto the tiny island of Corregidor, where U.S. General Jonathan Wainwright surrendered more than 11,000 men to the Japanese. American reporters tried to play down the disasters, concentrating their stories on the few American victories and on tales of American heroism against overwhelming odds. One of the soldiers on a Pacific island picked up an American broadcast one night. "The news commentators in the States had us all winning the war," he discovered, "their buoyant cheerful voices talking of victory. We were out here where we would see these victories. They were all Japanese."

In Europe, the Germans pushed deep into Russia, threatening to capture all the industrial centers and the valuable oil fields. For a time, it appeared that they would even take Moscow. In North Africa, General Erwin Rommel and his mechanized divisions, the Afrika Korps, drove the British forces almost to Cairo in Egypt and threatened the Suez Canal. In contrast to World War I, which had been a war of stalemate, the opening phase of World War II was marked by air strikes and troops supported by trucks and tanks covering many miles each day. In the Atlantic, German submarines sank British and American ships more rapidly than they could be replaced. For a few dark months in 1942, it seemed that the Berlin–Tokyo Axis would win the war before the United States got itself ready to fight.

The Allies could not agree on the proper military strategy in Europe. Churchill advocated tightening the ring around Germany, using bombing raids to weaken the enemy, and encouraging resistance among the occupied countries but avoiding any direct assault on the continent until success was ensured. Remembering the vast loss of British lives during World War I, he was determined to avoid similar casualties in this conflict. Stalin demanded a second front, an invasion of Europe in 1942, to relieve the pressure on the Russian army, which faced 200 German divisions along a 2,000-mile front. Roosevelt agreed to an offensive in 1942. But in the end, the invasion in 1942 came not in France but in North Africa. The decision was probably right from a military point of view; it would have been impossible to launch an invasion of France in 1942, and landing in Morocco helped to relieve the pressure on the British Army that was fighting desperately to keep Cairo and the Suez Canal out of German hands. But Stalin never forgave Churchill and Roosevelt for not coming to the aid of the beleaguered Soviet troops.

Attacking in North Africa in November 1942, American and British troops tried to link up with a beleaguered British army. The American army, enthusiastic but inexperienced, met little resistance in the beginning, but at Kasserine Pass in Tunisia, the Germans counterattacked and destroyed a large American force, inflicting 5,000 casualties. Roosevelt, who launched the invasion in part to give the

World War II: Pacific Theater

After the surprise attack on Pearl Harbor, the Japanese extended their control in the Pacific from Burma to the Aleutian Islands and almost to Australia. But after American naval and air victories at Coral Sea and Midway in 1942, the Japanese were increasingly on the defensive. **Reflecting on the Past** How did the great distances in the Pacific influence military plans for both sides? Why was the aircraft carrier more important than the battleship in the Pacific War? Was there any alternative to the American strategy of moving slowly from one Japanese-occupied island to another? Why did China play such a crucial role in the war against Japan?

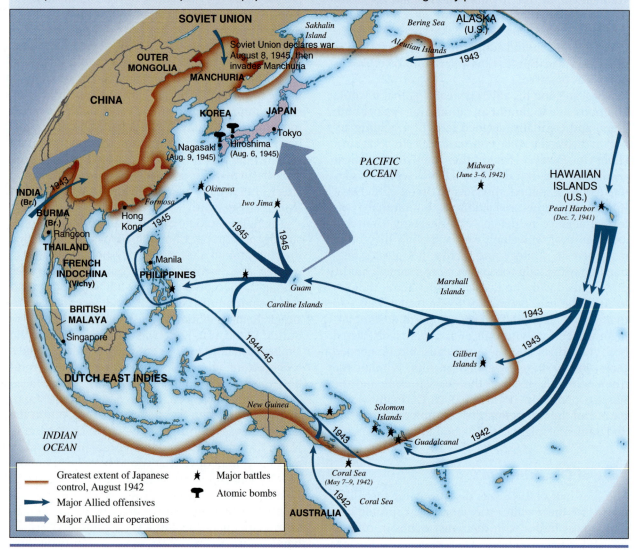

American people a victory to relieve the dreary news from the Far East, learned that victories often came with long casualty lists.

He also learned the necessity of political compromise. To gain a ceasefire in conquered French territory in North Africa, the United States recognized Admiral Jean Darlan as head of its provisional government. Darlan persecuted the Jews, exploited the Arabs, imprisoned his opponents, and collaborated with the Nazis. He seemed diametrically opposed to the principles the Americans said they were fighting for. Did the Darlan deal mean the United States would negotiate with Mussolini? Or with Hitler? The Darlan compromise reinforced Soviet distrust of the Americans and angered many Americans as well.

Roosevelt never compromised or made a deal with Hitler, but he did aid General Francisco Franco, the Fascist dictator in Spain, in return for safe passage of American shipping into the Mediterranean. But the United States did not aid only right-wing

World War II: European and North African Theaters

The German war machine swept across Europe and North Africa and almost captured Cairo and Moscow, but after major defeats at Stalingrad and El Alamein in 1943, the Axis powers were in retreat. Many lives were lost on both sides before the Allied victory in 1945. **Reflecting on the Past** How was the African campaign important to the Allies' strategy to defeat Germany and Italy? Why was the invasion of France necessary even after the capture of North Africa and a portion of Italy? Why was the Soviet Union crucial to the war in Europe? Why was the war in Europe very different from the war in the Pacific?

▨ Allied powers	▬ Farthest extent of Axis control, 1942
▨ Axis powers	➜ Allied advances
☐ Neutral nations	➜ Allied air operations, 1942–1945

dictators. It also supplied arms to the left-wing resistance in France, to the Communist Tito in Yugoslavia, and to Ho Chi Minh, the anti-French resistance leader in Indochina. Roosevelt also authorized large-scale, lend-lease aid to the Soviet Union. Although liberals criticized his support of dictators, Roosevelt was willing to do almost anything to win the war. Military expediency often dictated his political decisions.

Even on one of the most sensitive issues of the war, the plight of the Jews in occupied Europe, Roosevelt's solution was to win the war as quickly as possible. By November 1942, confirmed information had reached the United States that the Nazis were systematically exterminating Jews. Yet the Roosevelt administration did nothing for more than a year, and even then it did scandalously little to rescue European Jews from the gas chambers. Only

Only at the end of the war did most Americans learn about the horrors of Nazi concentration camps and gas chambers. Senator Alben Barkley of Kentucky looks in disbelief at dead Jews stacked like wood at Buchenwald, April 24, 1945. *(National Archives [RG-111-SC-204745, Box 63])*

21,000 refugees were allowed to enter the United States over a period of 3½ years, just 10 percent of those who could have been admitted under immigration quotas. The U.S. War Department rejected suggestions that the Auschwitz gas chambers be bombed, and government officials turned down many rescue schemes. Widespread anti-Semitic feelings in the United States in the 1940s and the fear of massive Jewish immigration help explain the failure of the Roosevelt administration to act. The fact that the mass media, Christian leaders, and even American Jews failed to mount effective pressure on the government does not excuse the president for his indifference to the systematic murder of millions of people. Roosevelt could not have prevented the Holocaust, but vigorous action on his part could have saved many thousands of lives during the war. Roosevelt was not always right, nor was he even consistent, but people who assumed he had a master strategy or a fixed ideological position misunderstood the American president.

A Strategy for Ending the War

The commanding general of the Allied armies in the North African campaign emerged as a genuine leader. Born in Texas, Dwight D. Eisenhower spent his boyhood in Abilene, Kansas. His small-town background made it easy for biographers and newspaper reporters to make him into an American hero.

Eisenhower, however, had not come to hero status easily. In World War I, he trained soldiers in Texas and never got to France. He was only a lieutenant colonel when World War II erupted. George Marshall, the Army's top General, had discovered Eisenhower's talents even before the war began. Eisenhower was quickly promoted to general and achieved a reputation as an expert planner and organizer. Gregarious and outgoing, he had a broad smile that made most people like him instantly. He was not a brilliant field commander and made many mistakes in the African campaign, but he had the ability to get diverse people to work together, which was crucial in situations where British and American units had to cooperate.

The American army moved slowly across North Africa, linked up with the British, invaded Sicily in July 1943, and finally stormed ashore in Italy in September. The Italian campaign proved long and bitter. Although the Italians overthrew Mussolini and surrendered in September 1943, the Germans occupied the peninsula and gave ground only after bloody fighting. The whole American army seemed to be bogged down for months. The Allies did not reach Rome until June 1944, and they never controlled all of Italy.

Despite the decision to make the war in Europe the first priority, American ships and planes halted the Japanese advance in the spring of 1942. In the Battle of Coral Sea in May 1942, American carrier-based planes inflicted heavy damage on the Japanese fleet and prevented the invasion of the southern tip of New Guinea and probably of Australia as well. It was the first naval battle in history in which no guns were fired from one surface ship against another; airplanes caused all the damage. In World War II, the aircraft carrier proved more important than the battleship. A month later, at the Battle of Midway, American planes sank four Japanese aircraft carriers and destroyed nearly 300 planes. This was the first major Japanese defeat; it restored some balance of power in the Pacific and ended the threat to Hawaii.

In 1943, the American sea and land forces leapfrogged from island to island, gradually retaking territory from the Japanese and building bases to attack the Philippines and eventually Japan itself. Progress often had terrible costs, however. In November 1943, about 5,000 marines landed on the coral beaches of the tiny island of Tarawa. Despite heavy naval bombardment and the support of hundreds of planes, the marines met heavy opposition. The four-day battle left more than 1,000 Americans dead and over 3,000 wounded. One marine general thought it was all wasted effort and believed that the island should have been bypassed. Others disagreed. And no one asked the marines who stormed the beaches; less than half of the first wave survived.

The Pacific War was often brutal and dehumanizing. American soldiers often collected Japanese ears, skulls, and other body parts as souvenirs, something unheard of on the European battlegrounds. "In Europe we felt that our enemies, horrible and deadly as they were, were still people," Ernie Pyle, the American war correspondent, remarked. "But out here I soon gathered that the Japanese were looked upon as something subhuman or repulsive, the way some people feel about cockroaches or mice."

The Invasion of France

Operation Overlord, the code name for the largest amphibious invasion in history, the invasion Stalin had wanted in 1942, began only on June 6, 1944. It was, according to Churchill, "the most difficult and complicated operation that has ever taken place." The initial assault along a 60-mile stretch of the Normandy coast was conducted with 175,000 men supported by 600 warships and 11,000 planes. Within a month, over a million troops and more than 170,000 vehicles had landed. Such an invasion would have been impossible during World War I.

Eisenhower, now bearing the title Supreme Commander of the Allied Expeditionary Force in Western Europe, coordinated and planned the operation. British and American forces, with some units from other countries, worked together, but Overlord was made possible by American industry, which, by the war's end, was turning out an astonishing 50 percent of all the world's goods. During the first few hours of the invasion, there seemed to be too many supplies. "Everything was confusing," one soldier remembered. It cost 2,245 killed and 1,670 wounded to secure the beachhead. "It was much lighter than anybody expected," one observer remarked. "But if you saw faces instead of numbers on the casualty list, it wasn't light at all."

For months before the invasion, American and British planes had bombed German transportation lines, industrial plants, and even cities. In all, over 1.5 million tons of bombs were dropped on Europe. The massive bombing raids helped make the invasion a success, but evidence gathered after the war suggests that the bombs did not disrupt German war production as seriously as Allied strategists believed at the time. Often a factory or a rail center would be back in operation within a matter of days, sometimes within hours, after an attack. In the end, the bombing of the cities, rather than destroying morale, may have strengthened the resolve of the German people to fight to the bitter end. And the destruction of German cities did not come cheaply. German fighters and antiaircraft guns shot down 22 of 60 B-17s on June 23, 1943, and in July 1943, 100 planes and 1,000 airmen were lost and an additional 75 men had mental breakdowns.

The most destructive bombing raid of the war, carried out against Dresden on the nights of February 13 and 14, 1945, had no strategic purpose. It was launched by the British and Americans to help demonstrate to Stalin that they were aiding the Russian offensive. Dresden, a city of 630,000, was a communications center. Three waves of 1,200 planes dropped more than 4,000 tons of bombs, causing a firestorm that swept over eight square miles, destroyed everything in its path, and killed an estimated 100,000 civilians. One of the American pilots remarked, "For the first time I felt sorry for the population below." The fire bombing of Tokyo on March 9, 1945, also killed an estimated 100,000 people. The massive "strategic" bombing of European and Asian cities for the purpose of breaking the morale of the civilian population introduced terror as a strategy and eventually made the decision to drop the atomic bomb on two Japanese cities easier.

With the dashing and eccentric General George Patton leading the charge and the more staid General Omar Bradley in command, the American army broke out of the Normandy beachhead in July 1944. Led by the tank battalions, it swept across France.

American productive capacity and the ability to supply a mobile and motorized army eventually brought victory. But not all American equipment was superior. The American fighter plane, the P-40, could not compete early in the war with the German ME-109. The United States was also far behind Germany in the development of rockets, but that was not as important in the actual fighting as was the inability of the United States, until the end of the war, to develop a tank that could compete in armament or firepower with the German tanks. But the American army made up for the deficiency of its tanks in part by having superior artillery. Perhaps even more important, most of the American soldiers had grown up tinkering with cars and radios. Children of the machine age, they managed to make repairs and to keep tanks, trucks, and guns functioning under difficult circumstances. They helped give the American army the superior mobility that eventually led to the defeat of Germany.

By late 1944, the American and British armies had swept across France, while the Russians had pushed the German forces out of much of eastern Europe. The war seemed nearly over. However, just before Christmas in 1944, the Germans launched a massive counterattack along an 80-mile front, much of it held by thinly dispersed and inexperienced American troops. The Germans drove 50 miles inside the American lines before they were checked. During the Battle of the Bulge, as it was called, Eisenhower was so desperate for additional infantry that he offered to pardon any military prisoners in Europe who would take up a rifle and go into battle. Most of the prisoners, who were serving short sentences, declined the opportunity to clear their record. Eisenhower also promised any black soldiers in the service and supply outfits an opportunity to become infantrymen in the white units, though usually with a lower rank. However, Walter Bedell Smith, his chief of staff, pointed out that this was against War Department regulations and was the "most dangerous thing I have seen in regard to race relations." Eisenhower recanted, not wishing to start a social revolution. Black soldiers who did volunteer to join the battle fought in segregated platoons commanded by white officers.

The Politics of Victory

As the American and British armies raced across France into Germany in the winter and spring of 1945, the political and diplomatic aspects of the war began to overshadow military concerns. It became a matter not only of defeating Germany but also of determining who was going to control Germany and the rest of Europe once Hitler fell. The relationship between the Soviet Union and the other Allies had been badly strained during the war; with victory in sight, the tension became even greater. Although the American press pictured Stalin as a wise and democratic leader and the Russian people as quaint and heroic, a number of high-level American diplomats and presidential advisers distrusted the Russians and looked ahead to a confrontation with Soviet communism after the war. These men urged Roosevelt to make military decisions with the postwar political situation in mind.

The main issue in the spring of 1945 concerned who would capture Berlin. The British wanted to beat the Russians to the capital city. Eisenhower, however, fearing that the Germans might barricade themselves in the Austrian Alps and hold out indefinitely, ordered the armies south rather than toward Berlin. He also wanted to avoid unnecessary American casualties, and he planned to meet the Russian army at an easily marked spot to avoid any unfortunate incidents. The British and American forces could probably not have arrived in Berlin before the Russians in any case, but Eisenhower's decision generated controversy after the war. Russian and American troops met on April 25, 1945, at the Elbe River. On May 2, the Russians took Berlin. Hitler committed suicide. The long war in Europe finally came to an end on May 8, 1945, but political problems remained.

In 1944, the United States continued to tighten the noose on Japan. American long-range B-29 bombers began sustained strikes on the Japanese mainland in June 1944. In a series of naval and air engagements, especially at the Battle of Leyte Gulf, American planes destroyed most of the remaining Japanese navy. By the end of 1944, an American victory in the Pacific was all but ensured. American forces recaptured the Philippines early the next year, yet it might take years to conquer the Japanese on their home islands.

While the military campaigns reached a critical stage in both Europe and the Pacific, Roosevelt took time off to run for an unprecedented fourth term. To appease members of his own party, he agreed to drop Vice President Henry Wallace from the ticket because some thought him too radical and impetuous. To replace him, the Democratic convention selected a relatively unknown senator from Missouri. Harry S Truman, a World War I veteran, had been a judge in Kansas City before being elected to the Senate in 1934. His only fame came when, as chairman of the Senate Committee to Investigate the National Defense Program, he had insisted on honesty and efficiency in war contracts. He got some publicity for saving the taxpayers' dollars.

The Republicans nominated Thomas Dewey, the colorless and politically moderate governor of New York, who had a difficult time criticizing Roosevelt without appearing unpatriotic. Roosevelt seemed haggard and ill during much of the campaign, but he won the election easily. He would need all his strength to deal with the difficult political problems of ending the war and constructing a peace settlement.

The Big Three at Yalta

Roosevelt, Churchill, and Stalin, together with many of their advisers, met at Yalta in the Crimea in February 1945 to discuss the problems of the peace settlements. Most of the agreements reached at Yalta were secret, and in the atmosphere of the subsequent Cold War, many would become controversial. Roosevelt wanted the help of the Soviet Union in ending the war in the Pacific to avoid the needless slaughter of American men in an invasion of the Japanese mainland. In return for a promise to enter the war within three months after the war in Europe was over, the Soviet Union was granted the Kurile Islands, the southern half of Sakhalin, and railroads and port facilities in North Korea, Manchuria, and Outer Mongolia. Later that seemed like a heavy price to pay for the promise, but realistically the Soviet Union controlled most of this territory and could not have been dislodged short of going to war.

When the provisions of the secret treaties were revealed much later, many people would accuse Roosevelt of trusting the Russians too much. But Roosevelt wanted to retain a working relationship with the Soviet Union. If the peace was to be preserved, the major powers of the Grand Alliance would have to work together. Moreover, Roosevelt hoped to get the Soviet Union's agreement to cooperate with a new peace-preserving United Nations organization after the war.

The European section of the Yalta agreement proved even more controversial. The diplomats decided to partition Germany and to divide the city of Berlin. The Polish agreements were even more difficult to swallow, in part because the invasion of Poland in 1939 had precipitated the war. The Polish government in exile in London was militantly anti-Communist and looked forward to returning to Poland after the war. Stalin demanded that the eastern half of Poland be given to the Soviet Union. Churchill and Roosevelt finally agreed to the Russian demands with the proviso that Poland be compen-

Churchill, Truman, and Stalin at the Potsdam Conference, July 25, 1945. It was at Potsdam that the "Big Three" demanded the "unconditional surrender" of Japan. Truman already had word that the atomic bomb had been successfully tested in the New Mexico desert. The three world leaders seem jovial here, but Churchill will soon be replaced after he loses an election, and difficulties that will soon lead to the Cold War have already emerged between the United States and the Soviet Union. (Harry S. Truman Library [NRE-338-FTL(EF)-7215(5)])

sated with German territory on its western border. Stalin also agreed to include some members of the London–based Polish group in the new Polish government. He also promised to carry out "free and unfettered elections as soon as possible."

The Polish settlement would prove divisive after the war, and it quickly became clear that what the British and Americans wanted in eastern Europe contrasted with what the Soviet Union intended. Yet at the time it seemed imperative that Russia enter the war in the Pacific, and the reality was that in 1945 the Soviet army occupied most of eastern Europe.

The most potentially valuable accomplishment at Yalta was Stalin's agreement to join Roosevelt and Churchill in calling a conference in San Francisco in April 1945 to draft a United Nations charter. The charter gave primary responsibility for keeping global peace to the Security Council, composed of five permanent members (the United States, the Soviet Union, Great Britian, France, and China) and six other nations elected for two-year terms. Perhaps just as important as Yalta for structuring the postwar world was the Bretton Woods Conference held at a resort hotel in the White

History, Memory, and Monuments

In recent years, historians have been studying collective memory—the stories people tell about the past. Collective memory is closely related to national regional identity and is often associated with patriotism and war. But memory is usually selective and often contested. The generation that lived through World War II is getting older, and often these people fear that few remember or care about their war. One veteran of the Italian campaign recently remarked: "Today they don't even know what Anzio was. Most people aren't interested." The collective memory of World War II may include letters, photos, old uniforms, stories told to grandchildren (oral history), but the collective memory of war often includes monuments as well.

Almost every small town and city in the Northeast, the Midwest, and the South has monuments to the soldiers who fought and died in the Civil War; often it is a statue of a common soldier with rifle at rest. In the South, a statue of Robert E. Lee on horseback came to symbolize the "Lost Cause." Usually monuments to war symbolize triumph or fighting for a just cause, even in defeat.

There is not yet a major monument on the mall in Washington, D.C., to honor those who fought in World War II, though a controversial monument on the mall has recently been approved. There have been many other attempts to honor the World War II generation. The Air and Space Museum of the Smithsonian Institution in Washington, D.C., planned a major exhibit for 1995 to commemorate the fiftieth anniversary of the dropping of the first atomic bomb on Hiroshima and the end of World War II. The *Enola Gay,* the B-29 that dropped the bomb, was to be the centerpiece of the exhibit, but the historians and curators who organized the exhibit also planned to raise a number of questions that historians had been debating for years. Would the war have ended in days or weeks without the bomb? How was the decision to drop the bomb made? Was there a racial component to the decision? Would the United States have dropped the bomb on Germany? Was the bomb dropped more to impress the Soviet Union than to force the Japanese to surrender? What was the impact of the bomb on the ground? What implications did dropping the bomb have on the world after 1945?

The exhibit (except in greatly modified form) never took place. Many veterans of World War II and other Americans denounced it as traitorous and un-American. For these critics the decision to drop the bomb was not something to debate. For them, World War II was a contest between good and evil, and the bomb was simply a way to defeat the evil empire and save American lives. The controversy

Dedication of the Iwo Jima Memorial Monument in Washington, D.C., November 10, 1954. *(National Archives)*

over the *Enola Gay* exhibit demonstrated that 50 years later, memory and history were at odds and that the memory of the war was still contested. The main reason the exhibit did not satisfy those who remembered the war was that it did not commemorate triumph but instead seemed to question the motives of those who fought and died.

The Vietnam Veterans Memorial erected in Washington in 1982 was initially controversial for similar reasons. Designed by Maya Lin, a young artist and sculptor, it consists of a wall of polished granite inscribed with the names of 58,000 dead. There are no soldiers on horseback; in fact, there are no figures at all, not even a flag. Critics called it a "black gash of shame." Even the addition of a sculpture of three "fighting men" did not satisfy many. But to almost everyone's surprise, hundreds of thousands of veterans and friends of veterans found the monument deeply moving, and they left photos, flowers, poems, and other objects. For them, the memorial successfully represented collective memory. Still the critics were dissatisfied; they wanted something more like the Iwo Jima monument.

Iwo Jima was a tiny, desolate island 640 miles from Tokyo, important only because it was a base for Japanese fighters to attack American bombers on their way to the Japanese mainland. The 4th and 5th Marine Divisions invaded the island on February 17, 1945. After bitter fighting, the marines captured Mt. Suribachi, the highest point on the island, on February 23 and completed the conquest of the island on March 17. But it was a costly victory—there were 4,189 Americans killed, 15,000 wounded, and 419 missing.

Associated Press photographer Joe Rosenthal was one of several journalists who went ashore with the marines and one of three photographers assigned to record the raising of the American flag on top of Mt. Suribachi. A group of marines raised the flag twice so the photographers could get their pictures. It was Rosenthal's photograph of the second flag raising that became famous. On February 25, 1945, his photograph of the five marines and a navy corpsman raising the flag was on the front page of Sunday newspapers across the country. "Stars and Stripes on Iwo," "Old Glory over Volcano," the captions read. Within months, the image of the flag raising appeared on a War Bond poster with the caption: "Now All Together" and also on a postage stamp. Three of the six flag raisers were killed in the battle for Iwo Jima, but those who survived became heroes, and their images were used to sell war bonds. Clearly, the flag-raising image had touched American emotions and quickly became part of the

Official poster for the 1945 war bond drive using the image of the Iwo Jima flag raising. *(Courtesy of the Virginia War Museum)*

collective memory of the war, a symbol of the country pulling together to defeat the enemy.

In November 1954, a giant statue of the flag raising, designed by Felix De Weldon, was dedicated as a memorial to the U.S. Marine Corps on the edge of Arlington National Cemetery. Vice President Richard Nixon, speaking at the dedication, said that the statue symbolized "the hopes and dreams of the American people and the real purpose of our foreign policy." The flag-raising image played an important role in two movies, *The Sands of Iwo Jima* (1949), starring John Wayne, and *The Outsider* (1960), starring Tony Curtis. During the 1988 presidential campaign, George H. W. Bush chose to make a speech urging a constitutional amendment to ban the desecration of the flag in front of the marine monument. The image of the flag raising in photograph, drawing, film, and cartoon remains part of the collective memory of World War II.

Reflecting on the Past   Why did the Iwo Jima monument mean so much to the World War II generation? Was the monument more important than the photograph? What makes a monument meaningful? Is it the size? The accuracy? The ability to arouse emotion? Why do some monuments and symbols become part of collective memory, while others become controversial or forgotten? There are over 15,000 outdoor sculptures and monuments in the country, most created since the Civil War. What monuments can you locate in your community? What collective memory do they symbolize?

Mountains of New Hampshire in the summer of 1944 and attended by delegates from 44 nations (the Soviet Union refused to participate). The economists and politicians established a Bank for Reconstruction and Development (The World Bank) and the International Monetary Fund. They also decided on a fixed rate of exchange among the world's currencies using the dollar rather than the pound as the standard. The Bretton Woods agreement lasted for 25 years and established that the United States, not Great Britain, would be the dominant economic power in the postwar world.

The Atomic Age Begins

Two months after Yalta, on April 12, 1945, as the United Nations charter was being drafted, Roosevelt died suddenly of a massive cerebral hemorrhage. Hated and loved to the end, he was replaced by Harry Truman, who was both more difficult to hate and harder to love. In the beginning, Truman seemed tentative and unsure of himself. Yet it fell to the new president to make some of the most difficult decisions of all time. The most momentous of all was the decision to drop the atomic bomb.

The Manhattan Project, first organized in 1941, was one of the best-kept secrets of the war, even though thousands were employed at the machine shops and nuclear reactors in Hanford, Washington, to produce plutonium, and others worked at Oak Ridge Tennessee to produce uranium 235. The task of the distinguished group of scientists whose work on the project was centered in Los Alamos, New Mexico (which grew to a city of 7,000), was to manufacture an atomic bomb before Germany did. But by the time the bomb was successfully tested in the New Mexico desert on July 16, 1945, the war in Europe had ended.

The scientists working on the bomb assumed that they were perfecting a military weapon. Yet when they saw the ghastly power of that first bomb, J. Robert Oppenheimer, a leading scientist on the project, remembered that "some wept, a few cheered. Most stood silently." Some opposed the military use of the bomb. They realized its revolutionary power and worried about the future reputation of the United States if it unleashed this new force. But a presidential committee made up of scientists, military leaders, and politicians recommended that it be used on a military target in Japan as soon as possible.

"The final decision of where and when to use the atomic bomb was up to me," Truman later remembered. "Let there be no doubt about it. I regarded the bomb as a military weapon and never had any doubt that it should be used." But the decision had both military and political ramifications. Even

Even before the destruction of Hiroshima and Nagasaki by atomic bombs, American fire-bombing raids destroyed many Japanese cities. A raid on Tokyo on March 9, 1945 (shown here a few days later) killed at least 100,000 people and left over a million homeless. Was this kind of destruction of civilians justifiable even in a brutal war? (*National Archives [80-G-490421]*)

Timeline

1931–1932	Japan seizes Manchuria
1933	Hitler becomes German chancellor
	United States recognizes the Soviet Union
	Roosevelt extends Good Neighbor policy
1934	Germany begins rearmament
1935	Italy invades Ethiopia
	First Neutrality Act
1936	Spanish civil war begins
	Second Neutrality Act
	Roosevelt reelected
1937	Third Neutrality Act
1938	Hitler annexes Austria, occupies Sudetenland
	German persecution of Jews intensifies
1939	Nazi–Soviet Pact
	German invasion of Poland; World War II begins
1940	Roosevelt elected for a third term
	Selective Service Act
1941	FDR's "Four Freedoms" speech
	Proposed black march on Washington
	Executive order outlaws discrimination in
	defense industries
	Lend-Lease Act
	Germany attacks Russia
	Japanese assets in United States frozen
	Japanese attack Pearl Harbor; United States
	declares war on Japan
	Germany declares war on United States
1942	Internment of Japanese Americans
	Second Allied front in Africa launched
1943	Invasion of Sicily
	Italian campaign; Italy surrenders
	United Mine Workers strike
	Race riots in Detroit and other cities
1944	Normandy invasion (Operation Overlord)
	Congress passes GI Bill
	Roosevelt elected for a fourth term
1945	Yalta Conference
	Roosevelt dies; Harry Truman becomes president
	Germany surrenders
	Successful test of atomic bomb
	Hiroshima and Nagasaki bombed; Japan
	surrenders

though Japan had lost most of its empire by the summer of 1945, it still had a military force of several million men and thousands of kamikaze planes that had already wreaked havoc on the American fleet. The kamikaze pilots gave up their own lives to make sure that their planes, heavily laden with bombs, crashed on American ships. In the Battle of Okinawa, kamikaze pilots destroyed or disabled 28 American ships and killed 5,000 American sailors. There was little defense against such fanaticism.

Even with the Russian promise to enter the war, it appeared that an amphibious landing on the Japanese mainland would be necessary to end the war. The month-long battle for Iwo Jima, only 750 miles from Tokyo, had resulted in over 4,000 American dead and 15,000 wounded, and the battle for Okinawa was even more costly. An invasion of the Japanese mainland would presumably be even more expensive in human lives. The bomb, many thought, could end the war without an invasion. But some people involved in the decision wanted to retaliate for Pearl Harbor, and still others needed to justify spending over $2 billion on the project in the first place. The timing of the first bomb, however, indicates to some that the decision was intended to impress the Russians and ensure that they had little to do with the peace settlement in the Far East. One British scientist later charged that the decision to drop the bomb on Hiroshima was the "first major operation of the cold diplomatic war with Russia."

Historians still debate whether the use of the atomic bomb on the Japanese cities was necessary to end the war, but for the hundreds of thousands of American troops waiting on board ships and on island bases (even in Europe) to invade the Japanese mainland, there was no question about the rightness of the decision. They believed that the bombs ended the war and saved their lives. On August 6, 1945, two days before the Soviet Union had promised to enter the war against Japan, a B-29 bomber, the "Enola Gay," dropped a single atomic bomb over Hiroshima. It killed or severely wounded 160,000 civilians and destroyed four square miles of the city. One of the men on the plane saw the thick cloud of smoke and thought that they had missed their target. "It looked like it had landed on a forest. I didn't see any sign of the city." The Soviet Union entered the war on August 8. When Japan refused to surrender, a bomb was dropped on Nagasaki on August 9. The Japanese surrendered five days later. The war was finally over, but the problems of the atomic age and the postwar world were just beginning.

✦ Conclusion

PEACE, PROSPERITY, AND INTERNATIONAL RESPONSIBILITIES

The United States emerged from World War II with an enhanced reputation as the world's most powerful industrial and military nation. The war had finally ended the Great Depression and brought prosperity to most Americans. The war had also increased the power of the federal government. The payroll deduction of federal income taxes, begun during the war, symbolized the growth of a federal bureaucracy that affected the lives of all Americans. Ironically the war to preserve liberty and freedom was fought with a segregated armed forces, and some American citizens, including many Japanese Americans, were deprived of their freedom. The war had also ended American isolationism and made the United States into the dominant global power. Of all the nations that fought in the war, the United States had suffered the least. No bombs were dropped on American factories, and no cities were destroyed. Although more than 300,000 Americans lost their lives, even this carnage seemed minimal when compared with more than 20 million Russian soldiers and civilians who died or the 6 million Jews and millions of others systematically exterminated by Hitler.

Americans greeted the end of the war with joy and relief. But those who lived through the war years, even those too young to fight, recalled the war as a time when all Americans were united to achieve victory. It was a memory that would influence their judgment of global events for the remainder of the century. They looked forward to the peace and prosperity for which they had fought. Yet within two years, the peace would be jeopardized by the Cold War, and the United States would be rearming its former enemies, Japan and Germany, to oppose its former friend, the Soviet Union. The irony of that situation reduced the joy of the hard-won peace and made the American people more suspicious of their government and its foreign policy.

✦ Recommended Reading

The Twisting Road to War
A. Russell Buchanan, *The United States in World War II,* 2 vols. (1964); Robert Dalleck, *Franklin Roosevelt and American Foreign Policy, 1932–1945* (1979); Waldo Heinrichs, *Threshold of War* (1988); Akira Iriye, *The Origins of the Second World War in Asia and the Pacific* (1988); Walter LaFeber, *Inevitable Revolutions: The United States and Central America* (1983); Gordon W. Prange, *At Dawn We Slept* (1981); Gerhard Weinberg, *A Global History of World War II* (1994).

The Home Front
Amy Bentley, *Eating for Victory: Food Rationing and the Politics of Domesticity* (1997); Alison Bernstein, *American Indians and World War II* (1991); John Morton Blum, *V Was for Victory* (1976); Roger Daniels, *Concentration Camp, USA* (1971); Lewis A. Erenberg and Susan E. Hirsch, eds., *The War in American Culture* (1996); John W. Jeffries, *Wartime America: The World War II Home Front* (1996); Doris Kearns Goodwin, *No Ordinary Time: Franklin and Eleanor Roosevelt, the Home Front in World War II* (1994); Bill Gilbert, *They Also Served: Baseball and the Home Front* (1992); Daniel Kryder, *Divided Arsenal: Race and the American State During World War II* (2000); Nicholas Lemann, *The Promised Land: The Great Black Migration and How It Changed America* (1991); Eric L. Muller, *Free to Die for Their Country: The Story of the Japanese-American Draft Resisters in World War II* (2001); Richard Polenberg, *War and Society* (1972); Ronald Takaki, *Double Victory: A Multicultural History of America in World War II* (2000); Kevin Starr, *Embattled Dreams: California in War and Peace, 1940–1950* (2002); William Tuttle, *"Daddy's Gone to War"* (1993).

Social Impact of the War
D'Ann Campbell, *Women at War with America* (1984); Richard Dalfiume, *Desegregation of the U.S. Armed Forces* (1975); Sherna B. Gluck, *Rosie the Riveter Revisited* (1987); Susan Hartmann, *The Home Front and Beyond: American Women in the 1940s* (1982); David M. Kennedy, *Freedom from Fear: The American People in Depression and War* (1999); Ruth Milkman, *Gender at Work* (1987); Gerald D. Nash, *The American West Transformed: The Impact of the Second World War* (1985); George H. Roseder, *The Censored War: American Visual Experience During World War II* (1993); Alan M. Winkler, *The Politics of Propaganda: The Office of War Information* (1978); Neil A. Wynn, *The Afro-American and the Second World War* (1976).

A War of Diplomats and Generals
Gar Alperovitz, *Atomic Diplomacy* (1965); Stephen Ambrose, *Citizen Soldiers* (1997) and *D-Day* (1994); John Dower, *War Without Mercy* (1986); Paul Fussell, *Wartime* (1989); Suburo Ienaga, *The Pacific War, 1931–1945* (1978); John Keegan, *The Battle for History: Re-Fighting World War II* (1995); Walter LaFeber, *The Clash: U.S. Japanese Relations Throughout History* (1997); Gerald F. Linderman, *The World Within War: America's Combat*

Experience in World War II (1997); Karal Ann Marling, *Iwo Jima: Monuments, Memories, and the American Hero* (1991); Williamson Murray and Allan R. Millett, *A War to Be Won: Fighting the Second World War* (2000); Joseph E. Persico, *Roosevelt's Secret War: FDR and World War II Espionage* (2001); Richard Rhodes, *The Making of the Atomic Bomb* (1986); Ronald Schaffer, *Wings of Judgement: American Bombing in World War II* (1985); Gaddis Smith, *American Diplomacy During the Second World War* (1964); Robert Smith Thompson, *World War II and the Struggle For Mastering of Asia* (2001); Russell Weigley, *Eisenhower's Lieutenants: The Campaign of France and Germany, 1944–1945* (1981); David S. Wyman, *The Abandonment of the Jews: America and the Holocaust, 1941–1945* (1984).

Fiction and Film

In *The Dollmaker* (1954), Harriette Arnow tells the fictionalized story of a young woman from Kentucky who finds herself in wartime Detroit. Two powerful novels that tell the story of the battlefield experience are Norman Mailer's *The Naked and the Dead* (1948) and Irwin Shaw's *The Young Lions* (1948). *Pearl Harbor* (2001) is a blockbuster film worth seeing for the special effects, but more interesting is *Tora! Tora! Tora!* (1970), a film that tells the story of the attack on Pearl Harbor from both the American and the Japanese points of view. It is compelling even as it oversimplifies history. *Saving Private Ryan* (1998), a film about one platoon's adventures on D-Day and after, is sentimental and romantic in spots but contains some graphic and violent scenes of the invasion of Normandy. *Memphis Belle* (1990) tells the story of one bomber crew. *Schindler's List* (1993) uses the Holocaust as background and subject. It is important to sample some of the movies produced during the war even though they are often filled with propaganda. *Bataan* (1943) was the first movie featuring an ethnic platoon. *Casablanca* (1943) and *Lifeboat* (1944) are classics.

✦ Discovering U.S. History Online

World War II Timeline
http://history.acusd.edu/gen/WW2Timeline/start.html
This interactive timeline includes the years prior to American involvement in World War II.

Resource Listing for World War II
www.sunsite.unc.edu/pha/index.html
This site presents an extensive, categorized listing of World War II primary documents available on the Web.

World War II Museum
www.thedropzone.org
A virtual museum of World War II, this site covers the European and Pacific theaters, training, Axis accounts, and an innovative collection of oral histories.

Remembering Pearl Harbor
www.nationalgeographic.com/pearlharbor/
This site includes a detailed account of the attack, illustrated with maps and photographs, as well as a searchable archive of survivors' stories.

A People at War
www.archives.gov/exhibit_hall/a_people_at_war/
a_people_at_war.html
This National Archives exhibit takes a close look at the contributions that millions of Americans made to the war effort.

Poster Art of World War II
www.archives.gov/exhibit_hall/powers_of_persuasion/
powers_of_persuasion_home.html
These powerful posters at the National Archives were part of the battle for the hearts and minds of the American people during World War II.

Fighters on the Farm Front
http://arcweb.sos.state.or.us/osu/osuhomepage.html
An illustrated presentation of the efforts to replace the labor force lost by men going into military service.

Tuskegee Airmen
www.wpafb.af.mil/museum/history/prewwii/ta.htm
The Air Force Museum at Wright-Patterson Air Force Base maintains this site about the African-American pilots of World War II.

African Americans in World War II
www.coax.net/people/lwf/ww2.htm
This site presents an extensive compilation of links to essays, some internal and some external to the site, which detail the experience of African Americans during World War II.

A. Philip Randolph
www.georgemeany.org/archives/apr.html
A biography of Randolph, emphasizing his beliefs and his work in civil and labor rights.

Japanese Americans
www.lib.washington.edu/exhibits/harmony
This site deals with all aspects of the Japanese wartime internment, relocation centers, and the human stories behind the massive removal of Japanese Americans from the West Coast.

Japanese Relocation Sites
www.cr.nps.gov/history/online_books/anthropology74/
This book describes every relocation site used during the war and includes photographs, architectural drawings, and personal accounts. The full text is presented online.

Japanese American Relocation Photographs
www.usc.edu/isd/archives/arc/digarchives/jarda
This site presents a searchable archive of photos taken from the *Los Angeles Examiner*. The photos document "the relocation of Japanese Americans in California principally during the period 1941–1946. Many of the photographs show daily life in the camps."

Latinos and Latinas & World War II

www.utexas.edu/projects/latinoarchives

This site presents a background of Hispanic involvement in World War II as well as reprints of its publication, *Narratives,* with individual accounts of Hispanic services in the war and on the homefront.

An Oral History of Rhode Island Women During World War II

www.stg.brown.edu/projects/WWII_Women/tocCS.html

This site presents oral histories by students in the Honors English Program at South Kingstown High School as well as an explanation of oral history, essays on women and the war, and a timeline of World War II.

"Flygirls"

www.pbs.org/wgbh/amex/flygirls

This site presents the "largely unknown story of the Women Airforce Service Pilots (WASP)" with photos, sound clips, essays, profiles, a timeline, and a transcript of the companion film with a teacher's guide.

United States Holocaust Memorial Museum

www.ushmm.org

This official Web site of the Holocaust Museum in Washington, D.C., includes over 15 online exhibitions.

A-Bomb

http://www.csi.ad.jp/ABOMB

This site offers information about the impact of the first atomic bomb as well as the background and context of weapons of total destruction.

Fifty Years from Trinity

http://seattletimes.nwsource.com/trinity/

A complete reprint of an anniversary special section of the newspaper that "detailed the history, impacts and future of atomic weapons and nuclear power." The site also includes teaching and discussion materials.

The U.S. Army Campaigns of World War II: Normandy

www.army.mil/cmh-pg/brochures/normandy/nor-pam.htm

An online version of a 45-page brochure covering the assault including maps and photographs.

26 Postwar America at Home, 1945–1960

The post–World War II years saw tremendous suburban development, which reflected the more general economic growth and economic prosperity of the period. *(Robert Bechtle, '58 Rambler/Sloan Collection, Valparaiso University Museum of Art, gift of Mrs. McCauley Conner in memory of her father, Barklie McK. Henry)*

◆ *American Stories*

AN ENTREPRENEUR FRANCHISES THE AMERICAN DREAM

Ray Kroc, an ambitious salesman, headed toward San Bernardino, California, on a business trip in 1954. For more than a decade he had been selling "multimixers"—stainless steel machines that could make six milkshakes at once—to restaurants and soda shops around the United States. On this trip, he was particularly interested in checking out a hamburger stand run by Richard and Maurice McDonald, who had bought eight of his "contraptions" and could therefore make 48 shakes at the same time.

Always eager to increase sales, Kroc wanted to see the McDonalds' operation for himself. The 52-year-old son of Bohemian parents had sold everything from real estate to radio time to paper cups before peddling the multimixers but had enjoyed no stunning success. Yet he was still on the alert for the key to the fortune that was part of the American dream. As he watched the lines of people at the San Bernardino McDonald's, the answer seemed at hand.

The McDonald brothers sold only standard hamburgers, french fries, and milkshakes, but they had developed a system that was fast, efficient, and clean. It drew on the automobile traffic that moved along Route 66. And it was profitable indeed. Sensing the possibilities, Kroc proposed that the two owners open other establishments as well. When they balked, he negotiated a 99-year contract that allowed him to sell the fast-food idea and the name—and their golden arches design—wherever he could.

On April 15, 1955, Kroc opened his first McDonald's in Des Plaines, a suburb of Chicago. Three months later, he sold his first franchise in Fresno, California. Others soon followed. Kroc scouted out new locations, almost always on highway "strips," persuaded people to put up the capital, and provided them with specifications guaranteed to ensure future success. For his efforts, he received a percentage of the gross take.

From the start, Kroc insisted on standardization. Every McDonald's was the same—from the two functional arches supporting the glass enclosure that housed the kitchen and take-out window to the single arch near the road bearing a sign indicating how many 15-cent hamburgers had already been sold. All menus and prices were exactly the same, and Kroc demanded that everything from hamburger size to cooking time be constant. He insisted, too, that the establishments be clean. No pinball games or cigarette machines were permitted; the premium was on a good, inexpensive hamburger, quickly served, at a nice place.

McDonald's, of course, was an enormous success. In 1962, total sales exceeded $76 million. In 1964, before the company had been in operation for 10 years, it had sold over 400 million hamburgers and 120 million pounds of french fries. By the end of the next year, there were 710 McDonald's stands in 44 states. In 1974, only 20 years after Kroc's vision of the hamburger's future, McDonald's did $2 billion worth of business. When Kroc died in 1984, a total of 45 billion burgers had been sold at 7,500 outlets in 32 countries. Ronald McDonald, the clown who came to represent the company, became known to children around the globe after his Washington, D.C., debut in November 1963. When McDonald's began to advertise, it became the country's first restaurant to buy television time. Musical slogans like "You deserve a break today" and "We do it all for you" became better known than some popular songs.

The success of McDonald's provides an example of the development of new trends in the United States in the post–World War II years. Kroc capitalized on the changes of the automobile age. He understood that a restaurant had a better chance of success not in the city but along the highways, where it could draw on heavier traffic. The drive-in design, catering to a new and ever-growing clientele, soon became common.

He understood, too, that the franchise notion provided the key to rapid growth. Not prepared to open up thousands of stands himself, he sold the idea to eager entrepreneurs who stood to make sizable profits as long as they remained a part of the larger whole. In numerous other product areas as well as the hamburger business, the franchise method helped create a nationwide web of firms.

Finally, Kroc sensed the importance of standardization and uniformity. He understood the mood of the time—the quiet conformity of Americans searching for success. The McDonald's image may have been monotonous, but that was part of its appeal.

Customers always knew what they would get wherever they found the golden arches. If the atmosphere was "bland," that too was deliberate. As Kroc said, "Our theme is kind of synonymous with Sunday school, the Girl Scouts and the YMCA. McDonald's is clean and wholesome." It was a symbol of the age.

This chapter describes the structural and political changes in American society in the 25 years following World War II. Even as the nation became involved in the Cold War with the Soviet Union (a story taken up in Chapter 27), Americans were preoccupied with the shifts in social and economic patterns that were taking place. This chapter examines how economic growth, spurred by technological advances, transformed the patterns of work and daily life in the United States. Self-interest triumphed over idealism, as most people gained a level of material comfort previously unknown. Working-class Americans shared in the gains, as the union movement pressed its claims more successfully than it had ever done in the past, and workers entered into a new equilibrium with the world of management. Life for most Americans was more comfortable than it had ever been before. For many, this period appeared to promise the possibility of living the American dream.

The political world reflected the prosperity and affluence that followed years of depression and war. Building on the impact of the New Deal and the American role as the "arsenal of democracy" in World War II, government was larger and more involved in people's lives than ever before, despite Republican resistance in the 1950s. Political commitments in the decade and a half after the war laid the groundwork for the welfare state that emerged in the 1960s.

But even as the nation prospered, it experienced serious social and economic divisions. This chapter also shows the enormous gaps that existed between rich and poor, even in the best of times. It shows the continuing presence of what one critic eloquently called "the other America" and documents the considerable income disparity and persistent prejudice African Americans (like members of other minority groups) encountered in their efforts to share in the postwar prosperity. The frustrations they experienced highlighted the limits of the postwar American dream and led to the reform movements that changed American society.

ECONOMIC BOOM

Most Americans were optimistic after 1945. As servicemen returned home from fighting in World War II, their very presence caused a change in family patterns. A baby boom brought unprecedented population growth. The simultaneous and unexpected economic boom had an even greater impact. Large corporations increasingly dominated the business world, but unions grew as well, and most workers improved their lives. Technology appeared triumphant, with new products flooding the market and finding their way into most American homes. Prosperity convinced the growing middle class that all was well in the United States.

The Thriving Peacetime Economy

The wartime return of prosperity after the Great Depression continued in the postwar years, relieving fears of another depression. The next several decades saw one of the longest sustained economic expansions the country had ever known, as the United States solidified its position as the richest nation in the world. Other nations struggled with the aftereffects of World War II (see next section). Yet in the United States, prosperity was the norm.

The statistical evidence of economic success was impressive. The gross national product (GNP) jumped dramatically between 1945 and 1960 (see graph on next page), while per capita personal income likewise rose—from $1,087 in 1945 to $2,026 in 1960. Almost 60 percent of all families in the country were now part of the middle class, a dramatic change from the class structure in the nineteenth and early twentieth centuries.

Personal resources fueled economic growth. During World War II, American consumers had been unable to spend all they earned because factories were producing for war. With accumulated savings of $140 billion at the end of the struggle, consumers were ready to buy whatever they could. Equally important was the 22 percent rise in real purchasing power between 1946 and 1960. Families now had far more discretionary income—money to satisfy wants as well as needs—than before. At the end of the Great Depression, fewer than one-quarter of all households had any discretionary income; in 1960, three of every five did.

The United States, which produced half the world's goods, was providing new products that average Americans, unlike their parents, could afford. Higher real wages allowed people across social

Increase in GNP, 1945–1960

Gross National Product (GNP) rose steadily in the decade and a half after World War II as the United States enjoyed an unprecedented period of prosperity.

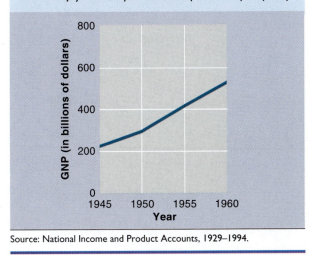

Source: National Income and Product Accounts, 1929–1994.

The automobile industry played a key part in the boom. Just as cars and roads transformed America in the 1920s when mass production came of age, so they contributed to the equally great transformation three decades later. Limited to the production of military vehicles during World War II, the auto industry expanded dramatically in the postwar period. Seventy thousand cars were made in 1945; 8 million were manufactured in 1955; and not quite 7 million were produced in 1960. Customers now chose from a wide variety of engines, colors, and optional accessories. Fancy grills and tail fins distinguished each year's models.

The development of a massive interstate highway system also stimulated auto production and so contributed to prosperity. Rather than encourage the growth of a mass transit system, through the Interstate Highway Act of 1956, the Eisenhower administration poured $26 billion, the largest public works expenditure in American history, into building over 40,000 miles of federal highways, linking all parts of the United States. Federal officials claimed the system would make evacuation quicker in the event of nuclear attack. President Eisenhower boasted that "the amount of concrete poured to form these roadways would build . . . six sidewalks to the moon. . . . More than any single action by the government since the end of the war, this one would change the face of America." Significantly, this massive effort helped create a nation dependent on oil.

A housing boom also fed economic growth as home-ownership rates rose from 53 percent in 1945

classes to buy consumer goods, and that consumer power, in contrast to the underconsumption of the 1920s and 1930s, spurred the economy. Most homes now had an automobile, a television set, a refrigerator, a washing machine, and a vacuum cleaner. But consumers could also indulge themselves with electric can openers, electric pencil sharpeners, electric toothbrushes, aerosol cans, and automatic transmissions for their cars.

McDonald's provided a model for other franchisers in the 1950s and the years that followed. The golden arches, shown here in an early version, were virtually the same wherever they appeared. Initially found along highways around the country, they were later built within cities and towns as well. (*Courtesy McDonald's Corporation*)

U.S. Interstate Highway System

The interstate highway system, established by legislative action in 1956, created an extensive network of roads that changed the landscape and living patterns of people throughout the United States. While the network was most extensive in the East, it extended throughout the entire country.

to 62 percent in 1960. Much of the stimulus came from the GI Bill of 1944. In addition to giving returning servicemen priority for many jobs and providing educational benefits, it offered low-interest home mortgages. Millions of former servicemen from all social classes eagerly purchased their share of the American dream.

The government's increasingly active economic role both stimulated and sustained the expansion. Businesses were allowed to buy almost 80 percent of the factories built by the government during the war

for much less than they cost. Even more important was the dramatic rise in defense spending as the Cold War escalated. In 1947, Congress passed the National Security Act creating the Department of Defense and authorized an initial budget of $13 billion. With the onset of the Korean War, the defense budget rose to $22 billion in 1951 and to about $47 billion in 1953. Approximately half of the total federal budget went to the armed forces. This spending, in turn, helped stimulate the aircraft and electronic industries. The government underwrote 90 percent of aviation and space research, 65 percent of electricity and electronics work, and 42 percent of scientific instrument development. Meanwhile, the close business–government ties of World War II grew stronger.

Most citizens welcomed the huge expenditures, not only because they supported the American stance in the struggle against communism (see Chapter 27) but also because they understood the economic impact of military spending. Columnist David Lawrence noted in 1950, "Government planners figure they have found the magic formula for almost endless good times. Cold war is an automatic pump primer. Turn a spigot, and the public clamors for more arms spending."

Postwar American growth avoided some of the major problems that often bedevil periods of economic expansion—inflation and the enrichment of a few at the expense of the many. Inflation, a problem in the immediate postwar period, slowed from an average of 7 percent per year in the 1940s to a gentle 2 to 3 percent per year in the 1950s. And though the concentration of income remained the same—the bottom half of the population still earned less than the top tenth—the ranks of middle-class Americans grew.

American products were sold around the world. People in other countries had developed a taste for Coca-Cola during the war. Now numerous other goods became available overseas. Other soft drinks became more popular. American books and magazines could be purchased in other countries. American movies and records promoted the spread of American culture and provided still more profits for American entrepreneurs.

A major economic transformation had occurred in the United States. Peaceful, prosperous, and productive, the nation had became what economist John Kenneth Galbraith called the "affluent society."

Postwar Growth Around the World

Elsewhere in the world, postwar reconstruction began but affluence took longer to arrive. Both European and Asian countries had suffered greater casualties than the United States, and some nations, even those on the winning side, had to deal with the enormous devastation that had taken place.

Great Britain was ravaged by the war. German bombs had fallen on downtown London, and residents had used the underground—the extensive subway system—to take shelter from the attacks. Rationing in England, necessary to provide the eq-

uitable distribution of scarce resources, lasted until the early 1950s. British factories, which had been the first to industrialize, were now inefficient and outdated. Home of the Industrial Revolution, England now failed to keep up with the rapid pace of technological innovation. The British automobile industry, for example, yielded part of its share of the world market to other nations, like Germany, which introduced the inexpensive and reliable Volkswagen Beetle that was soon sold around the world. Meanwhile, Britain lagged behind other European nations in developing a modern superhighway system that could spur industrial development.

In the general election of 1945, British voters ousted Winston Churchill and the Conservative party in favor of the Labour party, which was committed to social change. It took over the coal and railroad industries and began to nationalize the steel industry. While owners were compensated, some critics argued that the government's actions stifled industrial progress. Nevertheless, Great Britain began an economic and social recovery. It even provided a system of socialized medicine far in advance of anything in the United States.

While France was on the winning side of the war, it had suffered the indignity of occupation. It, too, experienced recovery, thanks in part to a rising birthrate, which was also occurring in the United States. At the same time, France, like Britain, was struggling with the demands of its colonial empire to be free. Brutal struggles in Indochina and Algeria caused financial instability and helped undermine economic development until France pulled out of both areas in the 1950s.

Defeated nations showed the most dramatic development of all. As the United States decided that a strong West Germany was necessary as a buffer against the Soviet Union, it helped cause what came to be known as "the German miracle." Because much of German industrial capacity had been destroyed by the war, new factories could be built with the newest technological equipment. The Allied High Commission, responsible for governing Germany, provided economic aid, scaled down German debts, and eliminated controls over German industry. In the early 1950s, the West German rate of growth reached 10 percent a year, while the gross national product rose from $23 billion in 1950 to $103 billion in 1964.

Japan likewise revived quickly. Like Germany, it suffered tremendous wartime destruction, due to both conventional bombing and to the new atomic bombs that devastated Hiroshima and Nagasaki in 1945. Under the direction of General Douglas

MacArthur, the United States directed the reconstruction effort. A new constitution created a democratic framework and led to the signing of a peace treaty in 1952. As political change occurred, the economy grew rapidly, and Japan overtook France and West Germany, soon ranking third in the world behind the United States and the Soviet Union.

So too did the Soviet Union rebuild. Reparations from West Germany and industrial extractions from eastern Europe helped promote the reconstruction effort. The totalitarian structure of the Soviet state eliminated public debate about the allocation of resources, and the nation embarked upon a series of initiatives that led to the development of a Soviet atomic bomb and the increase in the size of collective farms.

The Corporate Impact on American Life

After 1945, the major corporations in the United States tightened their hold on the American economy. Government policy in World War II had produced tremendous industrial concentration. The government suspended antitrust actions that might impede the war effort, while government contracts spurred expansion of the big corporations at the expense of smaller firms.

Industrial concentration continued after the war, making oligopoly—domination of a given industry by a few firms—a feature of American capitalism. Several waves of mergers had taken place in the past, including one in the 1890s and another in the 1920s. Still another occurred in the 1950s. At the same time, the booming economy encouraged the development of conglomerates—firms with holdings in a variety of industries in order to protect themselves against instability in one particular area. It also led to the further development of finance capitalism to help put the deals together, just as the demands of consolidation in the late nineteenth century had opened the way for bankers like J. P. Morgan (see Chapter 18).

Expansion took other forms as well. Even as the major corporations grew, so did smaller franchise operations like McDonald's, Kentucky Fried Chicken, and Burger King. Ray Kroc, introduced at the start of this chapter, provided a widely imitated pattern.

While expanding at home, large corporations also moved increasingly into foreign markets, as they had in the 1890s. But at the same time, they began to build plants overseas, where labor costs were cheaper. In the decade after 1957, General Electric built 61 plants abroad, and numerous other firms did the same. Corporate planning, meanwhile, developed rapidly, as firms sought managers who could assess information, weigh marketing trends, and make rational decisions to maximize profit.

Changing Work Patterns

As corporations changed, so did the world of work. Reversing a 150-year trend after World War II, the United States became less a goods producer and more a service provider. Between 1947 and 1957, the number of factory workers fell by 4 percent, while the number of clerical workers increased 23 percent and the number of salaried, middle-class employees rose 61 percent. By 1956, a majority of American workers held white-collar jobs, and the percentage rose in the years that followed. These new white-collar workers, paid by salary rather than by the hour, served as corporate managers, office workers, salespeople, and teachers.

People lived comfortably, enjoying leisure time. Experts predicted that a four-day work week beckoned and some worried how people would deal with even more spare time.

Yet white-collar employees paid a price for comfort. Work in the huge corporations became ever more impersonal and bureaucratic, and white-collar employees seemed to dress, think, and act the same (as depicted in a popular novel and film of the 1950s, *The Man in the Gray Flannel Suit*). Corporations, preaching that teamwork was all-important, indoctrinated employees with the appropriate standards of conduct. RCA issued company neckties. IBM had training programs to teach employees the company line. Some large firms even set up training programs to show wives how their own behavior could help their husbands' careers. William H. Whyte, an analyst of organizational behavior, vividly described the lives of young executives whose ultimate goal was "belongingness." Social critic C. Wright Mills observed, "When white-collar people get jobs, they sell not only their time and energy but their personalities as well."

But not all Americans held white-collar jobs. Many were still blue-collar assembly-line workers, who made the goods others enjoyed. They too dreamed of owning a suburban home and several cars and providing more for their children than they had enjoyed while growing up. Their lives were now more comfortable than ever before, as the union movement brought substantial gains (see the next section). These were the more fortunate members of the working class. Millions of others, perhaps totaling 40 percent of the workforce, held less appealing and less well-paying positions. More and more worked as taxi drivers, farm laborers, or dime-store sales clerks. For them, jobs were less stable, less secure, and less interesting. Casual employment had involved manual labor in the past; now it consisted of service work, and much of this was done by minorities, teenagers, and women who were gradually returning to the labor force.

The Union Movement at High Tide

The union movement had come of age during the New Deal (see Chapter 24), and the end of World War II found it even stronger. There were more union members—14.5 million—than ever before. Ten million belonged to the American Federation of Labor (AFL); the other 4.5 million belonged to the Congress of Industrial Organizations (CIO). Having taken a wartime no-strike pledge and given their full support to the war effort, they now looked forward to better pay and a greater voice in workplace management.

The immediate postwar period was difficult. Cancellation of defense orders laid off war workers and prompted fears of a depression, like the one that had followed World War I. Even workers who held their jobs lost the overtime pay they had enjoyed during the war. Many responded by striking. In 1946 alone, 4.6 million workers went out on strike—more than ever before in U.S. history. There were work stoppages in the automobile, coal, steel, and electrical industries and a threatened strike by railway workers. These disruptions alienated middle-class Americans and outraged conservative Republicans who felt that unionization had gone too far.

In the late 1940s, a new equilibrium emerged. In many industries, big business at last recognized the basic rights of industrial workers, and union leaders and members in turn acknowledged the prerogatives of management and accepted the principle of fair profit. Corporations in the same industry agreed to cooperate rather than compete with one another over labor costs. This meant that once a leading firm reached agreement with the union, the other firms in that area adopted similar terms, and the costs of the new contract would be met by a general increase in prices.

At the same time, companies made material concessions to workers—for example, adjusting their pay to protect them against inflation. In 1948, General Motors offered the United Automobile Workers a contract that included a cost-of-living adjustment (COLA) and a 2 percent "annual improvement factor" wage increase intended to share GM's productivity gains with workers. In 1950, GM again took the lead, this time with a five-year agreement providing pensions along with a cost-of-living

adjustment and wage increase. Five years later, automobile workers won a guaranteed annual wage. The merger of the AFL and CIO in 1955 ratified the changes that had occurred in the labor movement, as the new organization, led by building trade unionist George Meany, represented more than 90 percent of the country's now larger group of 17.5 million union members. By the end of the 1950s, the COLA principle was built into most union contracts.

Union gains, like middle-class affluence, came at a price. With higher, more predictable incomes, workers were more willing to limit strikes and avoid challenging management. Co-opted by the materialistic benefits big business provided, workers fell increasingly under the control of middle-level managers and watched anxiously as companies automated at home or expanded abroad, where labor was cheaper. But the agreements they had reached often precluded any response. The anti-Communist crusade, described in the next chapter, also undermined union radicalism. And throughout the period, in unions, as in other institutions, women and blacks faced continued discrimination.

Agricultural Workers in Trouble

The agricultural world changed even more than the industrial world in the postwar United States. On the eve of World War II, agriculture had supported one of every five Americans. Now, in one generation, mechanization and consolidation forced that figure down to one of every twenty. Altogether, some 15 million rural jobs disappeared.

New technology revolutionized farming. Improved planting and harvesting machines and better fertilizers and pesticides brought massive gains in productivity. Increasing profitability led to agricultural consolidation. In the 25 years after 1945, average farm size almost doubled. Farms specialized more in cash crops, like corn or soybeans, that were more profitable than hay or oats used to feed animals. Demanding large-scale investment, farming became a big business—often called "agribusiness." Family farms found it difficult to compete with the technologically superior corporations and watched their share of the market fall.

In response, farmers left the land in increasing numbers. Some were midwestern whites who generally found jobs in offices and factories. In the South, the upheaval was more disruptive. Many of the uprooted agricultural workers were African Americans, who became part of the huge migration north that had been going on since World War I. Overall, from 1910 to 1970, more than 6.5 million African Americans left the South; of these, 5 million

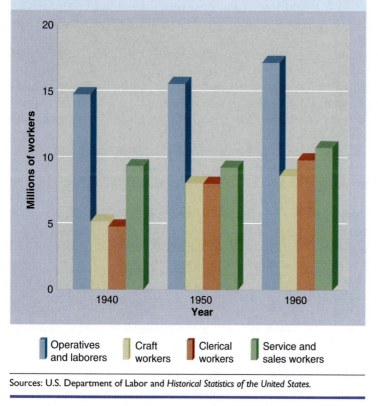

Occupational Distribution, 1940–1960

In the postwar years, the size of the workforce increased considerably. In this graph, observe how all categories grew, particularly the number of clerical workers and service and sales workers in the decades after 1950.

Operatives and laborers · Craft workers · Clerical workers · Service and sales workers

Sources: U.S. Department of Labor and *Historical Statistics of the United States.*

moved north after 1940. Most of them gravitated to cities, where they faced difficulties described later in this chapter. The agricultural life, as it had been known for decades, even centuries, was over.

DEMOGRAPHIC AND TECHNOLOGICAL SHIFTS

The postwar economic boom was intertwined with a series of demographic changes. The population grew dramatically and continued to move west, while at the same time, millions of white Americans left the cities for the suburbs that began to grow exponentially in the postwar years. New patterns, revolving around television and other gadgets provided by the advances of technology, came to characterize the consumer culture that dominated suburban life.

Population Growth

In post–World War II America, a growing population testified to prosperity's return. During the Great Depression, the birthrate had dropped to an all-time low of 19 births per 1,000, as hard times obliged people to delay marriage and parenthood. As the Second World War boosted the economy, the birthrate began to rise again.

The birthrate soared in the postwar years as millions of Americans began families. The "baby boom" peaked in 1957, with a rate of more than 25 births per 1,000. In that year, 4.3 million babies were born, one every seven seconds. While the population growth of 19 million in the 1940s was double the rise of the decade before, that increase paled against the increase in the 1950s, which totaled 29 million.

The rising birthrate was the dominant factor affecting population growth, but the death rate was also declining. Miracle drugs made a difference. Federal sponsorship of medical research during World War II had spurred the development of penicillin and streptomycin, now widely available. They helped cure strep throat and other bacterial infections, intestinal ailments, and more serious illnesses such as tuberculosis. A polio vaccine introduced a

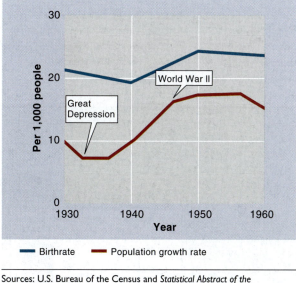

Birth and Population Rates, 1900–1960

Both birth and population rates increased dramatically after the difficult years of the Great Depression. Note the baby boom that began at the end of World War II and continued for the next decade.

— Birthrate   — Population growth rate

Sources: U.S. Bureau of the Census and *Statistical Abstract of the United States.*

decade after the war virtually eliminated that dreaded disease. Life expectancy rose: midway through the 1950s, the average was 70 years for whites and 64 for blacks, compared with 55 for whites and 45 for blacks in 1920.

The baby boom shaped family and social patterns. Many women who had taken jobs during the war now left the workforce to rear their children and care for their homes. Their lives changed considerably as they substituted housework for paid work. Demand grew for diaper services and baby foods. Entering school, the baby-boom generation strained the educational system. Between 1946 and 1956, enrollment in grades 1 through 8 soared from 20 million to 30 million. Since school construction had slowed during the Depression and had virtually halted during the Second World War, classrooms were needed. Teachers, too, were in short supply.

Movement West

As the population grew, Americans became more mobile, and much of the movement was westward. For many generations, working-class Americans had been the most likely to move; now geographic mobility spread to the middle class. Each year in the 1950s, over a million farmers left their farms in search of new employment. Other Americans picked up stakes

and headed on as well, some moving to look for better jobs, others simply wandering for a while after returning home from the war and then settling down.

Wartime mobility encouraged the development of the West. Although the scarcity of water in the western states required massive water projects to support population growth, war workers and their families streamed to western cities where shipyards, airplane factories, and other industrial plants were located. After the war, this migration pattern persisted. The Sun Belt—the region stretching along the southern tier of the United States from Florida to California—attracted numerous new arrivals. Cities like Houston, Albuquerque, Tucson, and Phoenix expanded phenomenally. The population of Phoenix soared from 65,000 in 1940 to 439,000 in 1960. In the 1950s, Los Angeles pulled ahead of Philadelphia as the third-largest city in the United States.

Los Angeles relied on a high-speed freeway system that led to increased automobile use. A state measure started the process in 1947 by using gasoline taxes and registration fees to build roads, and then the federal Interstate Highway Act of 1956 further subsidized the process. By 1960, the city had 250 miles of freeways.

One-fifth of all the growth in the period took place in California. Even baseball teams—the Brooklyn Dodgers and the New York Giants—left the East Coast for western shores. By 1963, in a dramatic illustration of the importance of the West, California passed New York as the nation's most populous state.

The migration west resulted from a number of reasons. Servicemen who had been stationed in the West liked the scenery, climate, and pace of life. Many returned with their families after the war. With funds from the Federal Housing Administration or Veterans Administration, they could afford to borrow money and buy new homes. That spending, in turn, helped fuel the region's economic growth.

Meanwhile, as noted earlier in this chapter, Cold War spending promoted economic development, and much of that expansion occurred in the West.

Population Changes in Selected Sun Belt Cities, 1940–1960 (in thousands)

	1940	1950	1960
Los Angeles, California	1,504	1,970	2,479
Miami, Florida	172	249	292
Atlanta, Georgia	302	331	487
Dallas, Texas	295	434	680
Phoenix, Arizona	65	107	439

Source: U.S. Bureau of the Census.

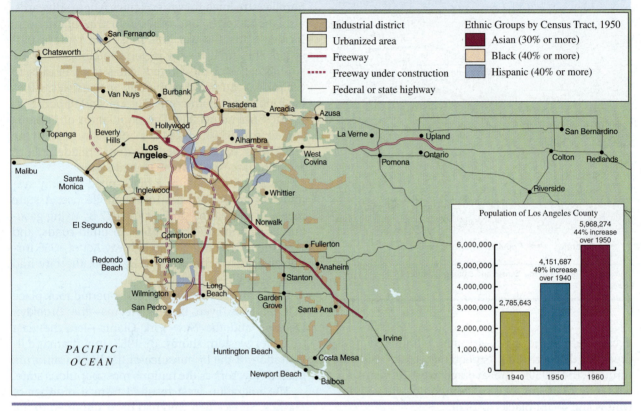

The Greater Los Angeles Area in the 1950s

In the years after World War II, the population of the greater Los Angeles area increased dramatically. Like other western cities, Los Angeles built an extensive freeway system in the metropolitan area that allowed people to live throughout the region. While the population of the city itself increased 31 percent between 1940 and 1950 and another 26 percent between 1950 and 1960, the population of the county, shown in the insert chart, grew even more.

Once the Korean War sparked increased military expenditures, California's economic growth outpaced that of the country as a whole. Aircraft production in the state accounted for more than 40 percent of the total increase in manufacturing employment there between 1949 and 1953. In the 1950s, rocket research further stimulated the aerospace industry. In 1959, California had nearly one-quarter of all prime military contracts in the nation. By 1962, the Pacific Coast as a whole held almost half of all Defense Department research and development contracts.

The West also benefited from the boom in the service economy. Many western workers in postwar America were part of the growing service sector. The percentage of workers in such jobs was higher in virtually all western states than in eastern counterparts. Denver became a major regional center of the federal bureaucracy in the postwar years. From 14,000 people on the payroll in 1951, the number rose to 23,000 in 1961. Albuquerque likewise gained

numerous federal offices and became known as "little Washington." The old West of cowboys, farmers, and miners was turning into a new West of bureaucrats, lawyers, and clerks.

The New Suburbs

As the population shifted westward after World War II, another form of movement was taking place. Millions of white Americans fled the inner city to suburban fringes, intensifying a movement that had begun before the war. Fourteen of the nation's largest cities, including New York, Boston, Chicago, Philadelphia, and Detroit, actually lost population in the 1950s. As central cities became places where poor nonwhites clustered, new urban and racial problems emerged.

For people of means, cities were places to work in but then to leave at five o'clock. In Manhattan, south of the New York borough's City Hall, the noontime population of 1.5 million dropped to

Population Shifts, 1940–1950

This map reveals the huge growth of population in the West and the sizable, though less extensive, increase in the Northeast and Southeast between 1940 and 1950.

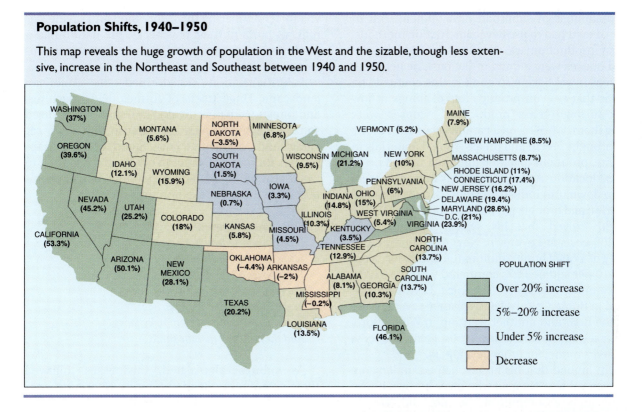

WASHINGTON (37%)
OREGON (39.6%)
IDAHO (12.1%)
NEVADA (45.2%)
CALIFORNIA (53.3%)
ARIZONA (50.1%)
MONTANA (5.6%)
WYOMING (15.9%)
UTAH (25.2%)
NEW MEXICO (28.1%)
NORTH DAKOTA (−3.5%)
SOUTH DAKOTA (1.5%)
COLORADO (18%)
TEXAS (20.2%)
MINNESOTA (6.8%)
NEBRASKA (0.7%)
KANSAS (5.8%)
OKLAHOMA (−4.4%)
IOWA (3.3%)
MISSOURI (4.5%)
ARKANSAS (−2%)
LOUISIANA (13.5%)
WISCONSIN (9.5%)
ILLINOIS (10.3%)
MISSISSIPPI (−0.2%)
MICHIGAN (21.2%)
INDIANA (14.8%)
KENTUCKY (3.5%)
TENNESSEE (12.9%)
ALABAMA (8.1%)
GEORGIA (10.3%)
OHIO (15%)
WEST VIRGINIA (5.4%)
VERMONT (5.2%)
NEW YORK (10%)
PENNSYLVANIA (6%)
VIRGINIA (23.9%)
NORTH CAROLINA (13.7%)
SOUTH CAROLINA (13.7%)
FLORIDA (46.1%)
MAINE (7.9%)
NEW HAMPSHIRE (8.5%)
MASSACHUSETTS (8.7%)
RHODE ISLAND (11%)
CONNECTICUT (17.4%)
NEW JERSEY (16.2%)
DELAWARE (19.4%)
MARYLAND (28.6%)
D.C. (21%)

POPULATION SHIFT
Over 20% increase
5%–20% increase
Under 5% increase
Decrease

2,000 overnight. "It was becoming a part-time city," according to writer John Brooks, "tidally swamped with bustling humanity every weekday morning when the cars and commuter trains arrived, and abandoned again at nightfall when the wave sucked back—left pretty much to thieves, policemen, and rats."

As the cities declined, new suburbs blossomed. If the decade after World War I had witnessed a rural-to-urban shift, the decades after World War II saw a reverse shift to the regions outside the central cities, usually accessible only by car. By the end of the 1950s, one-third of all Americans resided in suburbs.

Americans moved to the suburbs to buy homes that could accommodate their larger families. Often rapidly constructed, suburban tract houses provided the appearance of comfort and space and the chance to have at least one part of the American dream—a place of one's own. They seemed protected from city problems, insulated from the troubles of the world outside.

The pioneer of the postwar suburbanization movement was William J. Levitt, a builder eager to gamble and reap the rewards of a growing demand. Levitt had recognized the advantages of mass production during World War II, when his firm constructed housing for war workers. Aware that the GI Bill made mortgage money readily available, he saw

Step-by-step mass production, with units completed in assembly-line fashion, was the key to William Levitt's approach to housing. But the suburban developments he and others created were marked by street after street of houses that all looked the same. The Levittown in this picture was built on 1,200 acres of potato fields on Long Island in New York. *(Cornell Capa/Magnum Photos, Inc.)*

the possibilities of suburban development. But to cash in, Levitt had to use new construction methods.

Mass production was the key. Individually designed houses were a thing of the past, he believed. "The reason we have it so good in this country," he said, "is that we can produce lots of things at low prices through mass production." Houses were among them. Working on a careful schedule, Levitt's team brought precut and preassembled materials to each site, put them together, and then moved on to the next location. As on an assembly line, tasks were broken down into individual steps. Groups of workers performed a single job on each tract.

Levitt proved that his system worked. Construction costs at Levittown, New York, a new community of 17,000 homes built in the late 1940s, were only $10 per square foot, compared with the $12 to $15 common elsewhere. The next Levittown appeared in Bucks County, Pennsylvania, several years after the first, and another went up in Willingboro, New Jersey, at the end of the 1950s. Levitt's success provided a model for other developers.

Levitt argued that his homes helped underscore American values. "No man who owns his own house and lot can be a Communist," he once said. "He has too much to do." Levitt also helped perpetuate segregation by refusing to sell homes to blacks. "We can solve a housing problem, or we can try to solve a racial problem but we cannot combine the two," he declared in the early 1950s.

Government-insured mortgages, especially for veterans, fueled the housing boom. So did fairly low postwar interest rates. With many American families vividly remembering the Depression and saving significant parts of their paychecks, the nation had a pool of savings large enough to keep mortgage interest rates in the affordable 5 percent range.

Suburbanization transformed the American landscape. Huge tracts of former fields, pastures, and forests were now divided into tiny standardized squares, each bearing a small house with a two-car garage and a manicured lawn. Stands of trees disappeared, for it was cheaper to cut them down than to work around them. Folksinger Malvina Reynolds described the new developments she saw:

> Little boxes on the hillside
> Little boxes made of ticky tacky
> Little boxes on the hillside
> Little boxes all the same.
> There's a green one and a pink one
> And a blue one and a yellow one
> And they're all made out of ticky tacky
> And they all look just the same.

As suburbs flourished, businesses followed their customers out of the cities. Shopping centers led the way. At the end of World War II, there were eight, but the number multiplied rapidly in the 1950s. In a single three-month period in 1957, 17 new centers opened; by 1960, there were 3,840 in the United States. Developers like Don M. Casto, who built the Miracle Mile near Columbus, Ohio, understood the importance of location as Americans moved out of the cities. "People have path-habits," he said, "like ants."

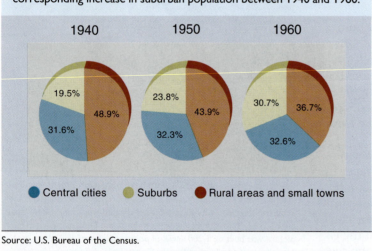

Shifts in Population Distribution, 1940–1960

This graph shows the progressive decline in rural population and the corresponding increase in suburban population between 1940 and 1960.

1940 | 1950 | 1960

1940: 19.5%, 48.9%, 31.6%
1950: 23.8%, 43.9%, 32.3%
1960: 30.7%, 36.7%, 32.6%

● Central cities ● Suburbs ● Rural areas and small towns

Source: U.S. Bureau of the Census.

Shopping centers catered to the suburban clientele and transformed consumer patterns. They allowed shoppers to avoid the cities entirely and further eroded urban health.

The Environmental Impact

Suburbanization had environmental consequences. Rapid expansion often took place without extensive planning and encroached on some of the nation's most attractive rural areas. Before long, virtually every American city was ringed by an ugly highway sporting garish neon signs. Billboard advertisements filled whatever space was not yet developed.

Responding to the increasingly cluttered terrain, architect Peter Blake ruthlessly attacked the practices of the 1950s in his muckraking book *God's Own Junkyard: The Planned Deterioration of America's Landscape*, published in 1964. He condemned the careless attitudes toward the environment that led to the "uglification" of a once lovely land. After describing breathtaking natural resources, Blake deplored the unconscionable desecration of the American landscape:

> Our suburbs are interminable wastelands dotted with millions of monotonous little houses on monotonous little lots and crisscrossed by highways lined with billboards, jazzed-up diners, used-car lots, drive-in movies, beflagged gas stations, and garish motels. Even the relatively unspoiled countryside beyond these suburban fringes has begun to sprout more telephone poles than trees, more trailer camps than national parks.

Despite occasional accounts like Blake's, there was little real consciousness of environmental issues in the early post–World War II years. The term *environment* itself was hardly used prior to the war. Americans had been concerned with conservation earlier in the century and had first focused on efficient use and development of water and forests. Later, they turned their attention to the preservation of grasslands, soils, and game.

Yet the very prosperity that created the dismal highway strips in the late 1940s and 1950s was leading more and more Americans to appreciate natural environments as treasured parts of their rising standard of living. The shorter workweek provided more free time, and many Americans now had the means for longer vacations. They began to explore mountains and rivers and ocean shores and to ponder how to protect them. In 1958, Congress established the National Outdoor Recreation Review Commission, a first step toward consideration of environmental issues that became far more common in the next decade. Americans also began to recognize the need for open space in their communities in order to compensate for the urban overdevelopment.

Technology Supreme

A technological revolution transformed postwar America. Some developments—the use of atomic energy, for example—flowed directly from war research. Federal support for scientific activity increased dramatically, as the pattern of wartime collaboration continued. The government established the National Institutes of Health in 1948 to coordinate medical research and the National Science Foundation in 1950 to fund basic scientific research. Scientists who had created the atomic bomb now found themselves in demand with both politicians and the public. They frequently spoke out about new developments and their impact on American life. Ties with Europe continued as the refugee scientists who had fled the Nazi regime were joined by others uprooted by the war, and men like the German Wernher von Braun played a major role in the development of American rockets.

The advent of the Cold War led to ever-greater government involvement. The Atomic Energy Commission, created in 1946, and the Department of Defense, established in 1949, provided rapidly increasing funding for research and development. Support for the Los Alamos Scientific Laboratory, where the atomic bomb had been assembled, continued, while the government contracted with the University of California to open the new Livermore Laboratory near San Francisco. Money went to other large research universities as well and fueled their growth. Scientists engaged in both basic and applied research and helped develop nuclear weapons, jet planes, satellites, and consumer goods that were often the side products of military research. At the same time, other innovations came from the research and development activities sponsored by big business.

Computers both reflected and assisted the process of technological development. Prior to World War II, Vannevar Bush, an electrical engineer at the Massachusetts Institute of Technology, had built a machine filled with gears and shafts, along with electronic tubes in place of some mechanical parts, to solve differential equations. Wartime advances brought large but workable calculators, such as the Mark I electromechanical computer developed by engineer Howard Aiken and installed by IBM at Harvard in 1944. It was huge—55 feet long and 8 feet high—and had a million components.

Even more complicated was the Electronic Numerical Integrator and Calculator, called ENIAC, built in 1946 at the University of Pennsylvania. Like

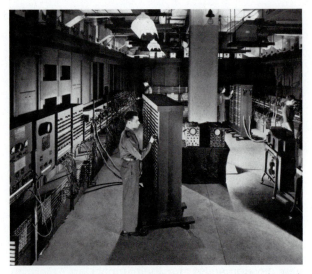

The ENIAC computer, first used in 1946, was a huge machine that took up an entire room. Yet it was far slower and far less powerful than the tiny desktop computers that became popular several decades later. *(Used by permission of the University of Pennsylvania's School of Engineering and Applied Sciences)*

the Mark I, it was large, containing 18,000 electronic tubes and requiring tremendous amounts of electricity and special cooling procedures. It also needed to be "debugged" to remove insects attracted to the heat and light, giving rise to the term still used today by computer scientists for solving software glitches. In a widely publicized test conducted soon after installation, operators set out to multiply 97,367 by itself 5,000 times. A reporter pushed the necessary button, and the task was completed in less than half a second. In the years that followed, new machines with their own internal instructions and memories were developed.

A key breakthrough in making computers faster and more reliable was the development of the transistor by three scientists at Bell Laboratories in 1948. Computers transformed American society as surely as industrialization had changed it a century before. Airlines, hotels, and other businesses computerized their reservation systems. Business accounting and inventory control began to depend on computers. Computer programmers and operators were in increasing demand as computers contributed dramatically to the centralization and interdependence of American life.

Computers were essential for space exploration. They helped scientists to perform the mathematical calculations that let astronauts venture beyond the confines of the earth itself. In the postwar years, increasingly sophisticated forms of space flight became possible. Rocketry had developed during World War II but came of age after the war. Rockets could deliver nuclear weapons but could also launch satellites and provide the means to venture millions of miles into outer space.

Tiny transistors powered not only computers but also a wide variety of new appliances and gadgets designed for personal use. A transistorized miniature hearing aid, for example, could fit into the frame of a pair of eyeglasses. Stereophonic high fidelity systems, using new transistor components, provided better sound.

An ominous technological trend related to computerization was the advent of automation. Mechanization was not new, but now it became far more widespread, threatening both skilled and unskilled workers. In 1952, the Ford Motor Company began using automatic drilling machines in an engine plant and found that 41 workers could do a job that 117 workers had done before. The implications of falling purchasing power as machines replaced workers were serious for an economy dependent on consumer demand.

The Consumer Culture

Americans were excited by everything they could buy. Television, developed in the 1930s, became a major influence on American life after World War II. In 1946, there were fewer than 17,000 television sets, but by 1960, three-quarters of all American families owned at least one set. In 1955, the average American family tuned in four to five hours each day. Some studies predicted that an American student, upon graduating from high school, would have spent 11,000 hours in class and 15,000 hours before the "tube." Young Americans grew up to the strains of "Winky Dink and You," "The Mickey Mouse Club," and "Howdy Doody Time" in the 1950s. Older viewers watched situation comedies like "I Love Lucy" and "Father Knows Best" and live dramas such as "Playhouse 90."

Television highlighted the rock and roll music that developed in the 1950s. Americans watched Elvis Presley play his guitar and sing, gyrating his hips in a sexually suggestive way that terrified parents, who worried about the influence of this new music, based on black rhythm and blues songs, on their children. Young people eagerly watched their counterparts dance to the music of Bill Haley and the Comets, Little Richard, Chuck Berry, and Elvis himself on "American Bandstand" every afternoon.

Americans maintained an ardent love affair with the appliances and gadgets produced by modern technology. By the end of the 1950s, most families had at least one automobile, as well as the staple appliances they had begun to purchase earlier—refrigerator, washing machine, television, and vacuum cleaner. Dozens of less essential items also became popular. There were electric can openers, electric pencil sharpeners, and electric toothbrushes, as well as push-button phones and aerosol bombs, and automatic transmissions to eliminate the manual shifting of car gears.

Consumption, increasingly a pillar of the American economy, required a vast expansion of consumer credit. Installment plans facilitated buying a new car, while credit cards encouraged the purchase of smaller items such as television sets and household appliances. Eating out became easier when meals could be charged on a card. The first of the consumer credit cards—the Diner's Club card—appeared in 1950, followed at the end of the decade by the American Express card and the BankAmericard (later renamed VISA). By the end of the 1960s, there were about 50 million credit cards of all kinds in use in the United States. Consumer credit—total private indebtedness—increased from $8.4 billion in 1946 to nearly $45 billion in 1958.

Households Owning Radios and Televisions, 1940–1960

Radio became increasingly popular in the postwar years, but observe the astronomical increase in the number of households owning television sets in the decade after 1950.

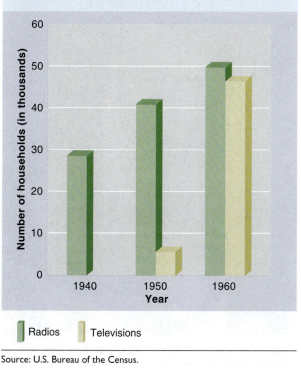

Source: U.S. Bureau of the Census.

"The Mickey Mouse Club" was a popular daily feature on television in the 1950s. Millions of American children were glued to their television sets each day after school, as they shared a common experience and absorbed the values promoted by the television networks. *(Photofest)*

For consumers momentarily unsure about new purchases, a revitalized advertising industry was ready to convince them to go ahead and buy. Advertising had come of age in the 1920s, as businesses persuaded customers that buying new products brought status and satisfaction. It had faltered when the economy collapsed in the 1930s but began to revive during the war, as firms kept the public aware of consumer goods, even those in short supply. With the postwar boom, advertisers again began to hawk their wares, this time even more aggressively than before.

Motivational research discovered new ways of persuading people to buy. Television played an important part in conveying the spirit of consumption to millions of Americans. Advertisements featuring the luxury items needed for the good life bombarded television viewers. Programs such as "The Price Is Right" stressed consumption in direct ways: contestants won goods for quoting the correct retail price.

If the appeal often seemed overdone, advertisers had their defenders, too. Vance Packard argued in 1957 in his best-selling book *The Hidden Persuaders* that advertisers "fill an important and constructive role in our society. Advertising, for example, not only plays a vital role in promoting our economic growth but [serves] as a colorful, diverting aspect of

American life, and many of the creations of admen are tasteful, honest works of artistry." That may have been true of some ads, but others were garish and reflected material wealth run amok.

Having weathered the poverty and unemployment of the 1930s and made sacrifices during a long war, Americans now regarded abundance and leisure as their due, sometimes neglecting to look beyond the immediate objects of their desire. As journalist William Shannon wrote, the decade was one of "self-satisfaction and gross materialism. . . . The loudest sound in the land has been the oink and grunt of private hoggishness. . . . It has been the age of the slob."

CONSENSUS AND CONFORMITY

As the economy expanded, an increasing sense of sameness pervaded American society. Third- and fourth-generation ethnic Americans became much more alike. As immigration slowed to a trickle after 1924, ties to Europe weakened, assimilation speeded up, and inter-ethnic marriage skyrocketed. Television gave young and old a shared, visually seductive experience. Escaping the homogenizing tendencies was difficult. Sociologist David Riesman pointed out that in the classic nursery rhyme "This Little Pig Went to Market," each pig went his own way. "Today, however, all little pigs go to market; none stay home; all have roast beef, if any do; and all say 'we-we.'"

Contours of Religious Life

Postwar Americans discovered a shared religious sense and returned to their churches in record numbers. By the end of the 1950s, fully 95 percent of all Americans identified with some religious denomination.

Ecumenical activities—worldwide efforts on the part of different Christian churches—promoted greater religious involvement. A first World Council of Churches meeting in 1948 in Amsterdam, The Netherlands, helped draw attention to the place of religion in modern life. Evangelical revivalism, led by Southern Baptist Billy Graham and others, became increasingly popular.

At the same time, Catholicism sought to broaden its appeal. This effort succeeded as Pope John XXIII convened the Vatican Ecumenical Council in 1962 to make the Catholic church's traditions and practices more accessible—for example, substituting modern languages for Latin in the liturgy.

Judaism likewise broadened its appeal. As assimilation occurred, quotas that had kept many out of more exclusive universities and other institutions

began to disappear. Jews, like others, relied on the G.I. Bill to move to the suburbs, where they bought new homes and built new synagogues, most of which followed the more casual patterns of Reform or Conservative, rather than Orthodox, Judaism.

The religious revival drew in part on the power of suggestion that led Americans to do what others did. Religion could reinforce the importance of family life, for, according to one slogan, "The family that prays together stays together." The renewal of interest in religion also offered an acceptable means of escape from the anxieties of a middle-class executive's life. In the 1950s, the Full Gospel Businessmen's Fellowship not only provided religious camaraderie but also enjoyed access to the White House. In 1953, President Dwight D. Eisenhower began the tradition of opening the inaugural ceremony with a prayer.

Eisenhower reflected the national mood when he observed that "our government makes no sense unless it is founded in a deeply felt religious faith—and I don't care what it is." In 1954, Congress added the words "under God" to the pledge to the flag and the next year voted to require the phrase "In God We Trust" on all U.S. currency. Yet the revival sometimes seemed to rest on a shallow base of religious knowledge. In one public opinion poll, 80 percent of the

Evangelist Billy Graham preached a fiery message to millions of Americans in the 1950s. On the radio, on television, and in huge revivals, he urged sinners to embrace God and so save their nation from the perils of the Communist threat. *(UPI/Corbis-Bettmann)*

respondents indicated that the Bible was God's revealed word, but only 35 percent were able to name the four Gospels and over half were unable to name even one.

A challenge to religious conformity came from members of the so-called "Beat Generation" (see the section in this chapter on "Cultural Rebels") who embraced Buddhism. They helped promote the Buddhist vogue that emerged in the 1950s and 1960s, with Zen centers opening in Los Angeles in 1956, San Francisco in 1959, and New York in 1966. Zen stressed Buddha's emphasis on meditation that led to his enlightenment. In the next decade, the counterculture reached out to a variety of alternative religions, including some related to Buddhism (see Chapter 28).

Traditional Roles for Men and Women

World War II had interrupted traditional patterns of behavior for both men and women. As servicemen went overseas, women left their homes to work. After 1945, there was a period of adjustment as the men returned, and government offices and employers told many working women that they were no longer needed in their jobs. In the 1950s, women faced tremendous pressure to conform to accepted prewar gender patterns, even though, paradoxically, more women entered the workforce than ever before.

Men and women had different postwar expectations. Most men expected to go to school and then find jobs to support their families. Viewing themselves as the primary breadwinners, they wanted their jobs waiting for them after the war. For women, the situation was more complex. While they wanted to resume patterns of family life that had been disrupted by the war, many had enjoyed working in the military plants and were reluctant to retreat to the home, despite pressure to do so.

In 1947, *Life* magazine ran a long photo essay called "The American Woman's Dilemma" that summed up the problem. The essay observed that women were caught in a conflict between the traditional expectation to stay home and the desire to have a paid job. A 1946 *Fortune* magazine poll also captured the discontent of some women. Asked whether they would prefer to be born again as men or as women, 25 percent of the women interviewed said they would prefer to be men. That dissatisfaction was strongest among white, well-educated, middle-class women, which was understandable, since family economic circumstances usually required black and lower-class white women to continue working outside the home.

By the 1950s, middle-class doubts and questions had largely receded. The baby boom increased average family size and made the decision to remain home easier. The flight to the suburbs gave women more to do, and they settled into the routines of redecorating their homes and gardens and transporting children to and from activities and schools.

In 1956, when *Life* produced a special issue on women, the message differed strikingly from that of nine years before. Profiling Marjorie Sutton, the magazine spoke of the "Busy Wife's Achievements" as "Home Manager, Mother, Hostess, and Useful Civic Worker." Married at the age of 16, Marjorie was now involved with the PTA, Campfire Girls, and charity causes. She cooked and sewed for her family of four children, supported her husband by entertaining 1,500 guests a year, and worked out on the trampoline "to keep her size 12 figure."

Marjorie Sutton reflected the widespread social emphasis on marriage and home. Many women went to college to find husbands—and dropped out if they succeeded. Almost two-thirds of the women in college, but less than half the men, left before completing a degree. Women were expected to marry young, have children early, and encourage their husbands' careers. An article in *Esquire* magazine in 1954 called working wives a "menace."

Adlai Stevenson, Democratic presidential candidate in 1952 and 1956, defined the female role in politics. "The assignment for you, as wives and mothers," he told a group of women, "you can do in the living room with a baby in your lap or in the kitchen with a can opener in your hand." As in much of the nineteenth century, a woman was "to influence man and boy" in her "humble role of housewife" and mother.

Pediatrician Benjamin Spock agreed. In 1946 he published *Baby and Child Care*, the book most responsible for the child-rearing patterns of the postwar generation. In it, he advised mothers to stay at home if they wanted to raise stable and secure youngsters. Working outside the home might jeopardize their children's mental and emotional health.

Popular culture highlighted the stereotype of the woman concerned only about marriage and family. Author Betty Friedan described these patterns in her explosive 1963 critique *The Feminine Mystique*. Shifting her attention away from the working-class and union issues that had concerned her before, she now profiled women in the 1950s and early 1960s. They "could desire no greater destiny than to glory in their own femininity. . . . All they had to do was to devote their lives from earliest girlhood to finding a husband and bearing children." Their role was clear. "It was unquestioned gospel," she wrote, "that women could identify with *nothing* beyond the home—not politics, not art, not science, not events

Clothing

Clothing can be an important source of information about the past. The clothes people wear often announce their age, gender, and class and frequently transmit some sense of their origin, occupation, and even their politics. The vocabulary of dress includes more than garments alone: hairstyles, jewelry, and makeup all contribute to the way people choose to present themselves. Clothing can signal strong emotions; a torn, unbuttoned shirt, for example, can indicate that a person who seldom dresses that way is really upset. Bright colors can demonstrate a daring sense and a willingness to make a strong statement. By examining clothing styles in a number of different decades, we can begin to understand something of the changing patterns of people's lives.

In the 1920s, flappers and other women often dressed like children, with loose dresses usually in pastel colors ending just below the knee. Large trimmings, like huge artificial flowers, accentuated the effect. A "boyish" figure was considered most attractive. The clothes conveyed a feeling of playfulness and a willingness to embrace the freedom of the young. Men's suits in the same period were now made out of lighter materials and looked less padded

Harlem women in the 1920s. *(Photographs and Prints Division, Schomburg Center for Research in Black Culture, The New York Public Library, Astor, Lenox, and Tilden Foundations)*

906

Frances Perkins with laborers in the 1930s. *(Brown Brothers)*

than before. As the tall, stiff collar of an earlier age disappeared and trousers became more high-waisted, men too had a more youthful look.

The Great Depression of the 1930s brought a change in style. Flappers now looked silly, especially as millions of people were starving. Advertisements and films promoted a new maturity and sophistication, more appropriate to hard times. Men's suits became heavier and darker, as if symbolically to provide protection in a bread line. Trousers were wider, and jackets were frequently double-breasted. Overcoats became longer. Women's clothes were likewise made out of heavier fabrics and used darker colors. Skirts fell almost to the ankles on occasion and were covered by longer coats. Clothes indicated that there was no place for the playfulness of the decade before.

As conditions improved during and after World War II, styles changed once more. In the 1940s, young teenage girls frequently wore bobby socks rolled down to their ankles. Working women wore overalls, but with their own adornments to maintain their femininity. Rosie the Riveter, drawn by noted artist Norman Rockwell, wore her overalls proudly as she sat with a riveting gun in her lap and an attractive scarf around her hair. In the postwar years, the "Man in the Gray Flannel Suit" looked serious, sober, and well-tailored, ready to go work for

World War II women at work. *(Oregon Historical Society, Portland)*

A woman and child in the 1950s. *(© The Dorothea Lange Collection, The Oakland Museum of California, City of Oakland, Gift of Paul S. Taylor)*

corporate America. His female partner wanted to look equally worldly and sophisticated and wore carefully tailored adult clothing, with the waist drawn in (often by a girdle) and heels as tall as three inches, when going out. The fashion industry helped define the decorative role women were supposed to play in supporting men as they advanced their business careers.

Then came the 1960s and an entirely new look. Casual clothing became a kind of uniform. The counterculture was a movement of the young, and clothing took on an increasingly youthful look. Skirts rose above the knee in 1963 and a few years later climbed to mid-thigh. Women began to wear pants and trouser suits. Men and women both favored jeans and informal shirts and let their hair grow longer. Men broke away from the gray suits of the preceding decade and indulged themselves in bright colors in what has been called the "peacock revolution."

Reflecting on the Past Look carefully at the pictures on these pages. They show fashions from different periods and can tell us a good deal about how these people defined themselves. Examine first the photo of the three black women from the 1920s. What kinds of adornments do you notice? What impression do these women convey?

Look at the photograph of Frances Perkins, secretary of labor in the 1930s. What kind of dress is she wearing? How do her clothes differ from those of the women in the 1920s? In the picture, she is talking to a number of working men. What do their clothes tell you about the kind of work they might be doing?

In the picture of two drill press operators during World War II, the women are dressed to handle the heavy machinery. Are their clothes different from those of the laborers in the preceding picture? How have the women accommodated themselves to their work, while still maintaining their individuality?

Now look at the picture of a woman in the 1950s. What kind of work might she do? What kind of flexibility do these clothes give her? What do the stylistic touches convey?

Finally, examine the photograph of the man and woman at an outdoor music festival in the 1960s. What does their clothing remind you of? Where might it come from? What impression are these people trying to create by their dress?

Countercultural dress in the 1960s. *(Ken Heyman/Woodfin Camp & Associates)*

Film star Doris Day was enormously popular in the 1950s. She was pert and pretty, with a winning smile and a captivating charm, and she looked like the special girl next door many men dreamed of marrying. *(Hulton Archive/Getty Images)*

large or small, war or peace, in the United States or the world, unless it could be approached through female experience as a wife or mother or translated into domestic detail."

Movies reinforced conventional images. Doris Day, charming and wholesome, was a favorite heroine. In film after film, she showed how an attractive woman who played her cards right could land her man.

The family was all important in this scenario. Fewer than 10 percent of all Americans felt that an unmarried person could be happy. A popular advice book declared: "The family is the center of your living. If it isn't, you've gone far astray." In a pattern endlessly reiterated by popular television programs, the family was meant to provide all satisfaction and contentment. The single-story ranch house that became so popular in this period reflected the focus on the family as the source of recreation and fun. No longer were kitchen and den private, as they had been earlier in a reflection of the notion of separate spheres. Now houses, with far more shared and open space, stressed livability and family comfort.

Sexuality was a troublesome if compelling post-war concern. In 1948, Alfred C. Kinsey published *Sexual Behavior in the Human Male.* Kinsey was an Indiana University zoologist who had previously studied the gall wasp. When asked to teach a course

on marriage problems, he found little published material about human sexual activity and decided to collect his own. He compiled case histories of 5,300 white males and recorded patterns of sexual behavior.

Kinsey shocked the country with his statistics on premarital, extramarital, and otherwise illicit sexual acts. Among males who went to college, he concluded, 67 percent had engaged in sexual intercourse before marriage as had 84 percent of those who went to high school but not beyond. Thirty-seven percent of the total male population had experienced some kind of overt homosexual activity. Five years later, Kinsey published a companion volume, *Sexual Behavior in the Human Female,* which detailed many of the same sexual patterns. Although critics denounced Kinsey for what they considered his unscientific methodology and challenged his results, both books sold widely, for they opened the door to a subject previously considered taboo.

Interest in sexuality was reflected in the fascination with sex goddesses like Marilyn Monroe. With her blonde hair, breathy voice, and raw sexuality, she personified the forbidden side of the good life and became one of Hollywood's most popular stars. The images of such film goddesses corresponded to male fantasies of women, visible in *Playboy* magazine, which first appeared in 1953 and soon achieved a huge readership. As for men's wives, they were expected to manage their suburban homes and to be cheerful and willing objects of their husbands' desire.

Despite reaffirming the old ideology that a woman's place was in the home, the 1950s were years of unnoticed but important change. Because the supply of single women workers fell as a result of the low birthrate of the Depression years and increased schooling and early marriage, older married women continued the pattern begun during the war and entered the labor force in larger numbers than before. In 1940, only 15 percent of American wives had jobs. By 1950, 21 percent were employed, and 10 years later, the figure had risen to 30 percent. Moreover, more than half of all working women were married, a dramatic reversal of pre–World War II patterns. Although the media hailed those women who primarily tended to their families, some magazine articles, in fact, did stress the achievements of women outside the home.

While many working women were poor, divorced, or widowed, many others worked to acquire the desirable new products that were badges of middle-class status. They stepped into the new jobs created by economic expansion, clustering in office,

Sex goddess Marilyn Monroe—shown here in a widely distributed promotional photo for *The Seven Year Itch*—stirred the fantasies of American males in the 1950s. Despite the family orientation of suburban America, millions were captivated by her seductive appeal. *(Matthew Zimmerman/AP/World Wide Photos)*

sales, and service positions, occupations already defined as female. They and their employers considered their work subordinate to their primary role as wives and mothers. The conviction that women's main role was homemaking justified low wages and the denial of promotions. Comparatively few women entered professions where they would have challenged traditional notions of a woman's place.

African-American women worked as always but often lost the jobs they had held during the war. For example, as the percentage of women in the Detroit automobile industry dropped from 25 to 7.5 in the immediate postwar period, black women who had held some of the jobs were the first to go. Bernice McCannon, an African-American employee at a Virginia military base, observed, "I have always done domestic work for families. When war came, I made the same move many domestics did. I took a higher paying job in a government cafeteria as a junior baker. If domestic work offers a good living, I see no reason why most of us will not return to our old jobs. We will have no alternative." These jobs, however, did not pay well at all. In the 1950s, the employment picture improved somewhat. African-American women succeeded both in moving into white-collar

positions and in increasing their income. By 1960, more than one-third of all black women held clerical, sales, service, or professional jobs. The income gap between white women and black women holding similar jobs dropped from about 50 percent in 1940 to about 30 percent in 1960.

Cultural Rebels

Not all Americans fit the 1950s stereotypes. Some were alienated from the culture and rebelled against its values. As young people struggled to meet the standards and expectations of their peers, they were intrigued by Holden Caulfield, the main figure in J. D. Salinger's popular novel *The Catcher in the Rye* (1951). Holden, a boarding-school misfit, rebelled against the "phonies" around him who threatened his individuality and independence. Holden's ill-fated effort to preserve his own integrity in the face of pressures to conform aroused readers' sympathy and struck a resonant chord.

Writers of the "Beat Generation" espoused unconventional values in their stories and poems. Challenging the apathy and conformity of the period, they stressed spontaneity and spirituality and claimed that intuition was more important than reason, Eastern mysticism (with its Buddhist influence) more valuable than Western faith. The "Beats" deliberately outraged respectability by sneering at materialism, flaunting unconventional sex lives, and smoking marijuana.

Their literary work reflected their approach to life. Finding conventional academic forms confining, they rejected them. Jack Kerouac typed his best-selling novel *On the Road* (1957), describing free-wheeling trips across country, on a 250-foot roll of paper. Dispensing with conventional punctuation and paragraphing, the book was a song of praise to the free lifestyle the "Beats" espoused.

Poet Allen Ginsberg, who, like Kerouac, was a Columbia University dropout, became equally well known for his poem "Howl." Written during a wild weekend in 1955, the poem was a scathing critique of modern, mechanized culture. The poem, which began with the line "I saw the best minds of my generation destroyed by madness, starving hysterical naked," became a cult piece, particularly after the police seized it on the grounds that it was obscene. When the work survived a court test, national acclaim followed for Ginsberg. He and the other "Beats" furnished a model for rebellion in the 1960s.

The popularity of Salinger, Kerouac, and Ginsberg owed much to a revolution in book publishing and to the democratization of education that

knives, and sticks to apply paint, glass shards, sand, and other materials in wild explosions of color. Known as abstract expressionists, these painters regarded the unconscious as the source of their artistic creations. "I am not aware of what is taking place [as I paint]," Pollock explained; "it is only after that I see what I have done." Like much of the literature of rebellion, abstract expressionism reflected the artist's alienation from a world filled with nuclear threats, computerization, and materialism.

ORIGINS OF THE WELFARE STATE

The modern American welfare state originated in the New Deal. Franklin D. Roosevelt's efforts to deal with the ravages of the Great Depression and protect Americans from the problems stemming from industrial capitalism (see Chapter 24) provided the basis for subsequent efforts to commit the government to help those who could not help themselves, even in prosperous times. Harry Truman's Fair Deal built squarely on Roosevelt's New Deal. His Republican

Allen Ginsberg was one of the most influential "Beats" who went out of his way to protest what he considered the stultifying patterns of American life. His poetry challenged more conventional norms. *(W. S. Burroughs/Allen Ginsberg Trust)*

accompanied the program of GI educational benefits. More Americans than ever before acquired a taste for literature, and they found huge numbers of inexpensive books available because of the "paperback revolution." The paperback, introduced in 1939, dominated the book market after World War II.

The signs of cultural rebellion also appeared in popular music. Parents recoiled as their children flocked to hear a young Tennessee singer named Elvis Presley belt out rock and roll songs. Presley's sexy voice, gyrating hips, and other techniques borrowed from black singers made him the undisputed "king of rock and roll." A multimedia blitz of movies, television, and radio helped make songs like "Heartbreak Hotel," "Don't Be Cruel," and "Hound Dog" smash singles. Eighteen Presley hits sold more than a million copies in the last four years of the 1950s. His black leather jacket and ducktail haircut became standard dress for rebellious male teenagers.

American painters, shucking off European influences that had shaped American artists for two centuries, also became a part of the cultural rebellion. Led by Jackson Pollock and the "New York school," some artists discarded the easel, laid gigantic canvases on the floor, and then used trowels, putty

Elvis Presley, a truck driver from Memphis, Tennessee, turned rock and roll into a kind of teenage religion. He was wildly popular whenever he performed and helped a new youth culture develop. *(Robert Kelley/TimePix)*

Jackson Pollock often stood over the canvas and flung the paint around him as he moved across the painting in progress. Here he is shown in 1951 dripping the paint on the work that became *Autumn Rhythm.* (Photo by Hans Namuth/Courtesy, Center for Creative Photography, The University of Arizona. © 1991 Hans Namuth Estate)

successor, Dwight Eisenhower, sought to scale down spending but made no effort to roll back the most important initiatives of the welfare state.

Harry S Truman

Harry S Truman, America's first postwar president, was an unpretentious man who took a straightforward approach to public affairs. He was, however, ill-prepared for the office he assumed in the final months of World War II. His three months as vice president had done little to school him in the complexity of postwar issues. Nor had Franklin Roosevelt confided in Truman. It was no wonder that the new president felt insecure. To a former colleague in the Senate, he groaned, "I'm not big enough for this job." Critics agreed.

Yet Truman matured rapidly. A sign on the president's White House desk read "The Buck Stops Here," and he was willing to make quick decisions on issues, even if associates sometimes wondered if he understood all the implications.

Truman took the same feisty approach to public policy that characterized his conduct of foreign af-

fairs (see Chapter 27). He stated his position clearly and simply, often in black-and-white terms. Believing in plain speaking, he seldom hesitated to let others know exactly where he stood. He attacked his political enemies vigorously when they resisted his initiatives and often took his case to the American people. He was, in many ways, an old-style Democratic politician, who hoped to use his authority to benefit the middle-class and working-class Americans who made up his political base.

Truman's Struggles with a Conservative Congress

Like Roosevelt, Harry Truman believed that the federal government had the responsibility for ensuring the social welfare of all Americans. He shared his predecessor's commitment to assisting less prosperous inhabitants of the country in a systematic, rational way. Truman wanted his administration to embrace and act upon a series of carefully defined social and economic goals to extend New Deal initiatives even further.

Immediate problems of reconversion—demands for the return of servicemen, fears of inflation, and labor unrest—had to be resolved first. But even as he worked (not always successfully) to handle these issues, Truman outlined his larger vision of the welfare state.

Less than a week after the end of World War II, Truman called on Congress to pass a 21-point program. He wanted housing assistance, a higher minimum wage, more unemployment compensation, and a national commitment to maintaining full-employment. During the next 10 weeks, Truman sent blueprints of further proposals to Congress, including health insurance and atomic energy legislation. But this liberal program soon ran into fierce political opposition.

The debate surrounding the Employment Act of 1946 hinted at the fate of Truman's proposals. This measure was a deliberate effort to apply the theory of English economist John Maynard Keynes to preserve economic equilibrium and prevent depression. Keynes had argued a decade earlier that massive spending was necessary to extricate a nation from depression (see Chapter 24). The money spent during World War II caused the economy to respond precisely as Keynes had predicted. Now economists wanted to institutionalize his ideas to forestall further problems. The initial bill, which enjoyed the strong support of labor, committed the government to maintaining full employment by monitoring the economy and taking remedial action in case of decline. Responses to a downturn included tax cuts and spending programs to stimulate the economy and reduce unemployment.

While liberals and labor leaders hailed the measure, business groups such as the National Association of Manufacturers condemned it. They claimed that government intervention would undermine free enterprise and promote socialism. Responding to the business community, Congress cut the proposal to bits. As finally passed, the act created a Council of Economic Advisers to make recommendations to the president, who was to report annually to Congress and the nation on the state of the economy. But it stopped short of committing the government to using fiscal tools to maintain full employment when economic indicators turned downward.

As the midterm elections of 1946 approached, Truman knew he was vulnerable. He often appeared to be a petty, bungling administrator who became the butt of countless political jokes. Opponents observed, "You just sort of forget about Harry until he makes another mistake." As more and more people questioned his competence as president, his support dropped from 87 percent of those polled after he assumed the office to 32 percent in November 1946. Gleeful Republicans asked the voters, "Had enough?"

They had. Republicans won majorities in both houses of Congress for the first time since the 1928 elections and gained a majority of the governorships as well. In Atlantic City, New Jersey, even a Republican candidate for justice of the peace who had died a week before the election was victorious.

After the 1946 elections, Truman faced an unsympathetic 80th Congress. Republicans and conservative Democrats, dominating both houses, planned to reverse the liberal policies of the Roosevelt years. Hoping to reestablish congressional authority and cut the power of the executive branch, they insisted on less government intervention in business and private affairs. They also demanded tax cuts and curtailment of the privileged position they felt labor had come to enjoy.

When the new Congress met, it slashed federal spending and taxes. Robert A. Taft, one of the Republican leaders in the Senate, believed that $5 to $6 billion could be cut to bring the overall budget down to $30 billion. In 1947, Congress twice passed tax-cut measures, which Truman vetoed. In 1948, another election year, Congress overrode the veto.

Congress also struck at Democratic labor policies. Angry at the gains won by labor in the 1930s and 1940s, Republicans wanted to check unions and to circumscribe their right to engage in the kind of disruptive strikes that had occurred immediately after the war, when more workers than ever before in the nation's history stayed away from their jobs. Early in Truman's presidency, Congress had passed a bill requiring notice for strikes as well as a cooling-off period if a strike occurred. Truman vetoed it. But in 1947, commanding more votes, the Republicans passed the Taft-Hartley Act, which sought to limit the power of unions by restricting the weapons they could employ. It spelled out unfair labor practices (such as preventing nonunion workers from working if they wished) and outlawed the closed shop, whereby an employee had to join a union before getting a job. The law likewise allowed states to prohibit the union shop, which forced workers to join the union after they had been hired. It gave the president the right to call for an 80-day cooling-off period in strikes affecting national security and required union officials to sign non-Communist oaths.

Union leaders and members were furious. They called the measure a "slave-labor law" and argued vigorously that it eliminated many of their hard-won rights and left labor–management relations the way they had been in pre–New Deal days. Vetoing the measure, Truman claimed that it was unworkable and unfair and went on nationwide radio to seek public approval. This regained him some of the support he had lost earlier when he had sought to force strikers to go back to work immediately after the war. Congress, however, passed the Taft-Hartley measure over Truman's veto.

The Fair Deal and Its Fate

In 1948, Truman wanted a chance to consolidate a liberal program and decided to seek the presidency in his own right. Aware that he was an accidental occupant of the White House, he won what most people thought was a worthless nomination. Not only was his own popularity waning, but the Democratic party itself seemed to be falling apart.

The civil rights issue (see the last section of this chapter) split the Democrats. When liberals defeated a moderate platform proposal and pressed for a stronger commitment to African-American rights, angry delegates from Mississippi and Alabama stormed out of the convention. They later formed the States' Rights, or Dixiecrat, party. At their own convention, delegates from 13 states nominated Governor J. Strom Thurmond of South Carolina as their presidential candidate and affirmed their support for continued racial segregation.

Meanwhile, Henry A. Wallace, first secretary of agriculture, then vice president during Roosevelt's third term, and finally secretary of commerce, mounted his own challenge. Truman had fired

In one of the nation's most extraordinary political upsets, Harry Truman beat Thomas E. Dewey in 1948. Here an exuberant Truman holds a newspaper headline printed while he slept, before the vote turned his way. *(Corbis-Bettmann)*

Wallace from his cabinet for supporting a more temperate approach to the Soviet Union. Now Wallace became the presidential candidate of the Progressive party. Initially, he attracted widespread liberal interest because of his moderate position on Soviet–American affairs, his promotion of desegregation, and his promise to nationalize the railroads and major industries, but then support dropped off.

In that fragmented state, the Democrats took on the Republicans, who coveted the White House after 16 years out of power. Once again, the GOP nominated New York Governor Thomas E. Dewey, the unsuccessful candidate in 1944. Even though he was stiff and egocentric, the polls uniformly picked the Republicans to win. Dewey saw little value in brawling with his opponent and campaigned, in the words of one commentator, "with the humorless calculation of a Certified Public Accountant in pursuit of the Holy Grail."

Truman, as the underdog, conducted a two-fisted campaign. He appealed to ordinary Americans as an unpretentious man engaged in an uphill fight. Believing that everyone was against him but the people, he addressed Americans in familiar language. He called the Republicans a "bunch of old mossbacks" out to destroy the New Deal as he attacked the "do nothing" 80th Congress. Speaking informally in his choppy, aggressive style, he appealed to crowds which yelled, "Give 'em hell, Harry!" He did.

The pollsters predicting a Republican victory were wrong. On election day, disproving the bold headline "Dewey Defeats Truman" in the *Chicago Daily Tribune,* the incumbent president scored one of the most unexpected political upsets in American history, winning 303–189 in the Electoral College. Democrats also swept both houses of Congress.

Truman won primarily because he was able to revive the major elements of the Democratic coalition that Franklin Roosevelt had constructed more than a decade before. Despite the rocky days of 1946, Truman managed to hold on to labor, farm, and black votes. Labor's support was crucial. Working men and women had been irritated by his response to the strikes in the immediate postwar period but had been buoyed by his veto, even though unsuccessful, of the Taft-Hartley Act. In the end, worried about Wallace, they backed Truman.

The fragmentation of the Democratic party, which had threatened to hurt the president severely, helped him instead. The splinter parties drew off some votes but allowed Truman to make a more aggressive, direct appeal to the center.

With the election behind him, Truman pursued his liberal program. In his 1949 State of the Union message, he declared, "Every segment of our population and every individual has a right to expect from our Government a fair deal." The Fair Deal became the name for his domestic program, which included the measures he had proposed since 1945.

Parts of Truman's Fair Deal worked; others did not. Lawmakers raised the minimum wage and expanded social security programs. A housing program brought modest gains but did not really meet housing needs. A farm program, aimed at providing income support to farmers if prices fell, never made it through Congress. Although he desegregated the military, other parts of his civil rights program failed to win congressional support (see the last section of this chapter). The American Medical Association undermined the effort to provide national health insurance, and Congress rejected a measure to provide federal aid to education.

The mixed record was not entirely Truman's fault. Conservative legislators were largely responsible for sabotaging his efforts. At the same time, critics charged correctly that Truman was often unpragmatic and shrill in his struggles with an unsympathetic Congress. They argued that he sometimes seemed to provoke the confrontations that became a hallmark of his presidency. They also claimed that he was most concerned with foreign policy as he strove to secure bipartisan support for Cold War initiatives (see Chapter 27) and allowed his domestic program to suffer. Rising defense expenditures meant less money for projects at home.

Still, Truman kept the liberal vision alive. The Fair Deal ratified many of the initiatives begun during the New Deal and led Americans to take programs like social security for granted. Truman had not achieved everything he wanted—he had not even come close—but the nation had taken another step toward endorsing liberal goals.

The Election of Ike

Acceptance of the liberal state continued in the 1950s, even as the Republicans took control. By 1952, Truman's popularity had plummeted to 23 percent of the American people, and all indicators pointed to a political shift. The Democrats nominated Adlai Stevenson, Illinois's articulate and moderately liberal governor. The Republicans turned to Dwight Eisenhower, the World War II hero known as Ike.

Stevenson approached political issues in intellectual terms. "Let's talk sense to the American people," he said. "Let's tell them the truth." While liberals loved his approach, Stevenson himself anticipated the probable outcome. How, he wondered, could a man named Adlai beat a soldier called Ike?

The Republicans focused on communism, corruption, and Korea as major issues. They called the Democrats "soft on communism" and demanded a more aggressive approach at home and abroad. They criticized scandals involving Truman's cronies

Dwight Eisenhower provided a reassuring presence in the White House in the 1950s. His wide smile made Americans feel good about themselves and their country and conveyed the message that everything was going to be all right. *(Hulton Archive/Getty Images)*

and friends. The Republicans also promised to end the unpopular Korean War (see Chapter 27).

Eisenhower proved to be a highly effective campaigner. He had a natural talent for taking his case to the American people, speaking in simple, reassuring terms they could understand. He struck a grandfatherly pose, unified the various wings of his party, and went on to victory at the polls. He received 55 percent of the vote and carried 41 states. The new president took office with a Republican Congress as well and had little difficulty gaining a second term.

Dwight D. Eisenhower

Eisenhower stood in stark contrast to Truman. His easy manner and warm smile made him widely popular. As British Field Marshall Bernard Montgomery observed, "He has the power of drawing the hearts of men towards him as a magnet attracts bits of metal."

Eisenhower had not taken the typical route to the presidency. After World War II, he served successively as army chief of staff, president of Columbia University, and head of the North Atlantic Treaty Organization (NATO). Despite his lack of formal political background, he had a real ability to get people to compromise and work together.

Ike's limited experience with everyday politics conditioned his sense of the presidential role. Whereas Truman loved political infighting and wanted to take charge, Eisenhower was more restrained. The presidency for him was no "bully pulpit," as it had been for Theodore Roosevelt and even FDR. "I am not one of those desk-pounding types that likes to stick out his jaw and look like he is bossing the show," he said. "You do not lead by hitting people over the head. Any damn fool can do that, but it's usually called 'assault'—not 'leadership.' "

"Modern Republicanism"

Eisenhower wanted to limit the presidential role. He was uncomfortable with the growth of the executive office over the past 20 years. Like the Republicans in Congress with whom Truman had tangled, he wanted to restore the balance between the branches of government and to reduce the authority of the national government. He recognized, however, that it was impossible to scale back federal power to the limited levels of the 1920s, and he wanted to preserve social gains that even Republicans now accepted. Eisenhower sometimes termed his approach "dynamic conservatism" or "modern Republicanism," which, he explained, meant "conservative when it comes to money, liberal when it comes to human beings." Liberals quipped that his approach meant endorsing social projects and then failing to authorize the funds.

Economic concerns dominated the Eisenhower years. The president and his chief aides wanted desperately to preserve the value of the dollar, pare down levels of funding, cut taxes, and balance the budget after years of deficit spending. To achieve those aims, the president appointed George Humphrey, a fiscal conservative, as secretary of the treasury. Humphrey declared, "We have to cut one-third out of the budget and you can't do that just by eliminating waste. This means, whenever necessary, using a meat axe." In times of economic stagnation, Republican leaders were willing to risk unemployment to control inflation. The business orientation became obvious when Defense Secretary Charles E. Wilson, former president of General Motors, declared at his confirmation hearing, "What is good for our country is good for General Motors, and vice versa."

Eisenhower fulfilled his promise to reduce government's economic role. After Republicans received financial support from oil companies during the campaign, the new Congress, with a strong endorsement from the president, passed the Submerged Lands Act in 1953, transferring control of about $40 billion worth of oil lands from the federal government to the states. The *New York Times* called it "one of the greatest and surely the most unjustified give-away programs in all the history of the United States."

The administration also sought to reduce federal activity in the electric power field. Eisenhower favored private rather than public development of power, and once said about the Tennessee Valley Authority (TVA), the extensive public power and development project begun during the New Deal, "I'd like to see us sell the whole thing, but I suppose we can't go that far." He opposed a TVA proposal for expansion to provide power to the Atomic Energy Commission and instead authorized a private group, the Dixon–Yates syndicate, to build a plant in Arkansas for that purpose. Later, when charges of scandal arose, the administration canceled the agreement, but the basic preference for private development remained.

Committed to supporting business interests, the administration sometimes saw its program backfire. As a result of its reluctance to stimulate the economy too much, the annual rate of economic growth declined from 4.3 percent between 1947 and 1952 to 2.5 percent between 1953 and 1960. The economy was still growing, but more slowly than before. The country also suffered three recessions—in 1953–1954, 1957–1958, and 1960–1961—in Eisenhower's eight years. During the slumps, tax revenues fell and the deficits that Eisenhower so wanted to avoid increased.

Eisenhower's understated approach led to a legislative stalemate, particularly when the Democrats

Presidential Elections, 1948–1956

Year	Candidate	Party	Popular Vote	Electoral Vote
1948	HARRY S TRUMAN	Democratic	24,105,812 (49.5%)	303
	Thomas E. Dewey	Republican	21,970,065 (45.1%)	189
	J. Strom Thurmond	States' Rights	1,169,063 (12.4%)	39
	Henry A. Wallace	Progressive	1,157,172 (12.4%)	0
1952	DWIGHT D. EISENHOWER	Republican	33,936,234 (55.1%)	442
	Adlai E. Stevenson	Democratic	27,314,992 (44.4%)	89
1956	DWIGHT D. EISENHOWER	Republican	35,590,472 (57.4%)	457
	Adlai E. Stevenson	Democratic	26,022,752 (42.0%)	73

Note: Winners' names appear in capital letters.

regained control of Congress in 1954. Opponents gibed at Ike's restrained stance and laughed about limited White House leadership. One observed that Eisenhower proved that the country did not "need" a president. Another spoke of the Eisenhower doll— you wound it up and it did nothing for eight years.

Yet Eisenhower understood just what he was doing; he had a better grasp of public policy than his critics realized. Beneath his casual approach lay real shrewdness. "Don't worry," he once assured his aides as they briefed him for a press conference. "If that question comes up, I'll just confuse them." He worked quietly to create the consensus that he believed was necessary for legislative progress and practiced what later observers called a "hidden hand" presidency, unobtrusively orchestrating support for his own ends.

Even more important was his role in ratifying the welfare state. By 1960, the government had become a major factor in ordinary people's lives. It had grown enormously, employing close to 2.5 million people throughout the 1950s. Federal expenditures, which had stood at $3.5 billion in 1927, rose to $97 billion in 1960. The White House now took the lead in initiating legislation and in steering bills through Congress. Individuals had come to expect old-age pensions, unemployment payments, and a minimum wage. By accepting the fundamental features of the national state that the Democrats had created, Eisenhower ensured its survival.

For all the jokes at his expense, Eisenhower remained popular with the voters. He accomplished most of his goals, and he was one of the few presidents to leave office as highly regarded by the people as when he entered it. He was the kind of leader Americans wanted in prosperous times.

THE OTHER AMERICA

Not all Americans shared postwar middle-class affluence. Although most white Americans were barely conscious of poverty, it clearly existed in inner cities and rural areas. African Americans, uprooted from rural roots and transplanted into urban slums, were among the hardest hit. But members of other minority groups, as well as less fortunate whites, suffered similar dislocations, unknown to the middle class.

Poverty Amid Affluence

Many people in the "affluent society" lived in poverty. Economic growth favored the upper and middle classes. Although the popular "trickle-down" theory argued that economic expansion benefited

all classes, little wealth, in fact, reached the citizens at the bottom. In 1960, according to the Federal Bureau of Labor Statistics, a yearly subsistence-level income for a family of four was $3,000 and for a family of six was $4,000. The bureau reported that 40 million people (almost one-quarter of the population) lived below those levels, with nearly the same number only marginally above the line. Two million migrant workers labored long hours for a subsistence wage. Many less mobile people were hardly better off. According to the 1960 census, 27 percent of the residential units in the United States were substandard.

Michael Harrington, socialist author and critic, shocked the country with his 1962 study *The Other America*. The poor, Harrington showed, were everywhere. He described New York City's "economic underworld," where "Puerto Ricans and Negroes, alcoholics, drifters, and disturbed people" haunted employment agencies for temporary positions as "dishwashers and day workers, the fly-by-night jobs." In the afternoon, he continued, "the jobs have all been handed out, yet the people still mill around. Some of them sit on benches in the larger offices. There is no real point to their waiting, yet they have nothing else to do."

Harrington also described the conditions faced by the rural poor. Despite the prosperity that surrounded them, the mountain folk of Appalachia, the tenant farmers of Mississippi, and the migrant farmers of Florida, Texas, and California were all caught in poverty's relentless cycle.

Hard Times for African Americans

African Americans were among the postwar nation's least prosperous citizens. In the South, agricultural workers continued to experience the transformation, mentioned earlier in this chapter, that had been underway for decades. New Deal farm legislation, the popularity of synthetic fabrics, and foreign competition robbed "King Cotton" of world markets. Mechanized cotton picking, first introduced in Mississippi in 1944, wiped out jobs in the Delta. As cotton farmers turned to less labor-intensive crops like soybeans and peanuts, they ousted their tenants, most of whom were African Americans.

The southern agricultural population declined dramatically, as millions of blacks moved to southern cities, where they found better jobs, better schooling, and freedom from landlords. Some achieved middle-class status; many more did not. They remained poor, with even less of a support system than they had known before.

Millions of African Americans also headed for northern cities after 1940. In the 1950s, Detroit's black population increased from 16 to 29 percent, and Chicago's went from 14 to 23 percent. At one point in this decade, Chicago's black population rose by more than 2,200 people each week. The new arrivals congregated in urban slums, where the growth of social services failed to keep pace with population growth.

The black ghetto that had begun to develop earlier in the twentieth century became a permanent fixture in the post–World War II years. African Americans attempting to move elsewhere often found the way blocked. In 1951, a black couple purchasing a home in Cicero, Illinois, was driven away when an angry crowd broke the house's windows, defaced the walls, and shouted vile insults. This pattern was repeated around the country—in Birmingham, Chicago, Detroit, and countless other cities.

The experiences of African Americans in the cities often proved different from what they had expected. As author Claude Brown recalled, blacks were told that in the North, "Negroes lived in houses with bathrooms, electricity, running water, and indoor toilets. To them, this was the 'promised land' that Mammy had been singing about in the cotton fields for many years." But no one had told them "about one of the most important aspects of the promised land: it was a slum ghetto. . . . There were too many people full of hate and bitterness crowded into a dirty, stinky, uncared-for closet-size section of a great city."

Novelist and essayist James Baldwin likewise described slum conditions and their corrosive effect on American blacks in his 1961 book *Nobody Knows My Name:*

> They work in the white man's world all day and come home in the evening to this fetid block. They struggle to instill in their children some private sense of honor or dignity, which will help the child to survive. This means, of course, that they must struggle, stolidly, incessantly, to keep this sense alive in themselves, in spite of the insults, the indifference, and the cruelty they are certain to encounter in their working day. They patiently browbeat the landlord into fixing the heat, the plaster, the plumbing; this demands prodigious patience, nor is patience usually enough. . . . Such frustration, so long endured, is driving many strong and admirable men and women whose only crime is color to the very gates of paranoia.

Such conditions, and the constant slights that accompanied segregation in both the North and the South, took a toll. African Americans learned how, in the words of a turn-of-the-century poem by Paul Laurence Dunbar, to "wear the mask."

Still, the black community remained intact. Chicago's South Side neighborhood was a vibrant place, replacing New York's Harlem as black America's cultural capital in the 1950s. This section of the city included such figures as boxing champion Joe Louis, gospel singer Mahalia Jackson, and Representative William Dawson, one of the few African-American members of Congress.

Here and elsewhere, the black church played an important role in sustaining African-American life. Blacks moving into the cities retained churchgoing habits and a commitment to religious institutions from their rural days. Older, established churches assisted newcomers in the transition to urban America, while new religious groups began to form. The churches offered more than religious sustenance alone. Many provided day-care facilities, ran Boy Scout and Girl Scout troops, and sponsored a variety of other social services.

The growth of the black urban population fostered the increased growth of businesses catering to the African-American community. Black newspapers now provided a more regional, rather than a national, focus, but magazines such as *Jet*, a pocket-size weekly with a large, countrywide circulation, filled the void. Black-owned and black-operated banks and other financial institutions increased in number.

Yet most African Americans remained second-class citizens. Escape from the slums was difficult for many and impossible for most. Persistent poverty remained a dismal fact of life.

African-American Gains

African Americans had made significant gains during World War II (see Chapter 25). Black servicemen returning from the war vowed to reject second-class citizenship and helped mobilize a grassroots movement to counter discrimination. In the postwar years, African struggles for independence, such as the Kenyan Mau Mau revolt against the British, inspired African-American leaders who now saw the quest for black equality in a broader context. They took enormous pride in the achievement of independence by a number of African nations (see map on next page) and demanded comparable change at home. As Adam Clayton Powell, a Harlem preacher (and later congressman), warned, the black man "is ready to throw himself into the struggle to make the dream of America become flesh and blood, bread and butter, freedom and equality. He walks conscious of the fact that he is no longer alone—no longer a minority."

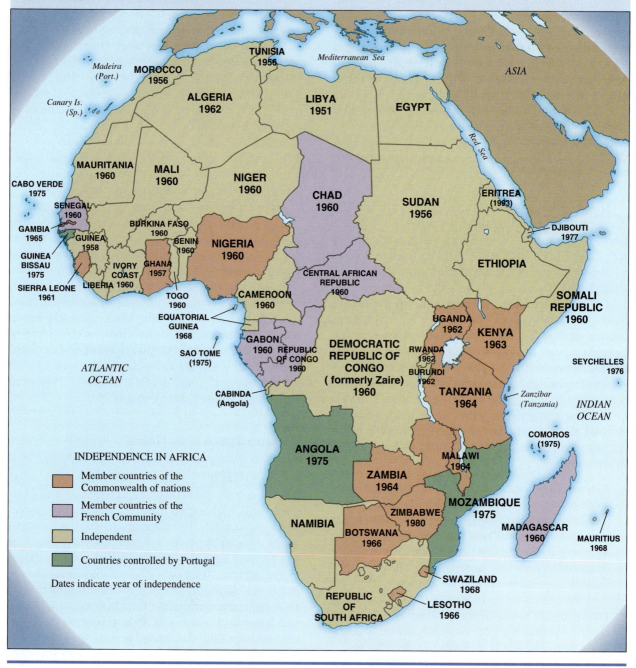

Independence in Africa

In the 1950s and 1960s, most African nations threw off their colonial rulers and achieved independence. **Reflecting on the Past** During which decade did more nations become free? How did attaining independence change social and economic patterns in the African nations? What effect did it have on the patterns of the Cold War? What effect did it have on the civil rights struggle in the United States?

Jackie Robinson's electrifying play as the first African American in the major leagues led to acceptance of the integration of baseball. A spectacular rookie season in 1947 opened the way for other African Americans who had earlier been limited to the Negro leagues. In this photo, taken at Ebbets Field in Brooklyn during the 1957 World Series, Robinson is about to steal home. *(Ralph Morse/TimePix)*

The racial question was dramatized in 1947 when Jackie Robinson broke the color line and began playing major league baseball with the Brooklyn Dodgers. Sometimes teammates were hostile, sometimes opponents crashed into him with spikes high, but Robinson kept his frustrations to himself. A splendid first season helped ease the way and resulted in his selection as Rookie of the Year. African Americans flocked to the ballpark and followed his exploits on the radio. As Charles Jones of Charlotte, North Carolina, noted, "Robinson was knocking a ball everywhere on a *white man's* baseball field. . . . I mean the entire community would be glued to listening, and inevitably Jackie would steal a base or knock a home run, and we'd be rooting." After Robinson's trailblazing effort, other blacks, formerly confined to the old Negro leagues, moved into the major leagues in baseball and then into other sports.

Some Americans were embarrassed as racial discrimination became entangled with Cold War poli-

tics. The appeal for support in Africa and Asia seemed hollow with segregation at home.

Somewhat reluctantly, Truman supported the civil rights movement. A moderate on questions of race, who believed in political, not social, equality, he responded to the growing strength of the African-American vote. In 1946, he appointed a Committee on Civil Rights to investigate the problem of lynching and other brutalities against blacks and recommend remedies. The committee's report, released in October 1947, showed that black Americans remained second-class citizens in every area of American life and called for change.

Though Truman hedged at first, in February 1948, he sent a 10-point civil rights program to Congress, the first presidential civil rights plan since Reconstruction. When the southern wing of the Democratic party bolted later that year, he moved forward even more aggressively. First he issued an executive order barring discrimination in the federal establishment. Then he ordered equality of treatment in the military services. Manpower needs in the Korean War broke down the last restrictions, particularly when the army found that integrated units performed well.

Elsewhere, the administration pushed other reforms. The Justice Department, not previously supportive of litigation from the National Association for the Advancement of Colored People (NAACP) on behalf of equal rights for African Americans, now entered the battle against segregation and filed briefs challenging the constitutionality of restrictions in housing, education, and interstate transportation. These actions helped build the pressure for change that influenced the Supreme Court. Congress, however, took little action.

As the civil rights struggle gained momentum during the 1950s, the judicial system played a crucial role. The NAACP was determined to overturn the 1896 Supreme Court decision *Plessy* v. *Ferguson,* in which the Court had declared that segregation of the black and white races was constitutional if the facilities used by each were "separate but equal." The decree had been used for generations to sanction rigid segregation, primarily in the South, even though separate facilities were seldom, if ever, equal.

A direct challenge came in 1951. Oliver Brown, the father of eight-year-old Linda Brown, sued the school board of Topeka, Kansas, to allow his daughter to attend a school for white children that she passed as she walked to the bus that carried her to a black school farther away. The case reached the Supreme Court, which grouped several school segregation cases together.

On May 17, 1954, the Supreme Court released its bombshell ruling in *Brown* v. *Board of Education.* For more than a decade, Supreme Court decisions had gradually expanded black civil rights. Now the Court unanimously decreed that "separate facilities are inherently unequal" and concluded that the "separate but equal" doctrine had no place in public education. African Americans were elated. "The Supreme Court decision is the greatest victory for the Negro people since the Emancipation Proclamation," Harlem's *Amsterdam News* proclaimed. Author Ralph Ellison observed, "What a wonderful world of possibilities are unfolded for the children." A year later, the Court turned to the question of implementation and declared that local school boards, acting with the guidance of lower courts, should move "with all deliberate speed" to desegregate their facilities.

President Eisenhower had the ultimate responsibility for executing the law. Doubting that simple changes in the law could improve race relations, he once observed, "I don't believe you can change the hearts of men with laws or decisions." While he thought privately that the *Brown* ruling was wrong, he knew that it was his constitutional duty to see that the decision was carried out. Even while urging sympathy for the South in its period of transition, he acted immediately to desegregate the Washington, D.C., schools as a model for the rest of the country. He also ordered desegregation in navy yards and veterans' hospitals.

The South resisted. The crucial confrontation came in Little Rock, Arkansas, in 1957. A desegregation plan, beginning with the token admission of a few black students to Central High School, was ready to go into effect. Just before the school year began, Governor Orval Faubus declared on television that it would not be possible to maintain order if integration took place. National Guardsmen, posted by the governor to keep the peace and armed with bayonets, turned away nine black students as they tried to enter the school. After three weeks, a federal court ordered the troops to leave. When the black children entered the building, the white students, spurred on by their elders, belligerently opposed them, chanting such slogans as "Two, four, six, eight, we ain't gonna integrate." In the face of hostile mobs, the black children left the school.

With the lines drawn, Ike knew that such resistance could not be tolerated, and he finally took the

National Guardsmen, under federal command, escorted African-American students into Central High School in Little Rock, Arkansas, in 1957. Observe the number of students and the number of soldiers as forcible integration began. *(Burt Glinn/Magnum Photos)*

one action he had earlier called unthinkable. For the first time since the end of Reconstruction, an American president called out federal troops to protect the rights of black citizens. Eisenhower ordered paratroopers to Little Rock and placed National Guardsmen under federal command. The black children entered the school and attended classes with the military protecting their rights. Thus desegregation began.

Meanwhile, African Americans, encouraged by their churches, began organizing themselves to take direct action, and their efforts significantly advanced the civil rights movement. In the 1930s and 1940s, some had joined demonstrations protesting job discrimination and segregation. Now they were ready for an even more dramatic confrontation.

The crucial event occurred in Montgomery, Alabama, in December 1955. Rosa Parks, a 42-year-old black seamstress who was also secretary of the Alabama NAACP, sat down in the front of a bus in a section reserved by custom for whites. When ordered to move back, the longtime activist refused to budge. The bus driver called the police at the next stop, and Parks was arrested and ordered to stand trial for violating the segregation laws.

That episode had an enormous impact. "Somewhere in the universe, a gear in the machinery shifted," black activist Eldridge Cleaver observed, as African-American civil rights officials seized the issue. E. D. Nixon, state NAACP president, told Parks, "This is the case we've been looking for. We can break this situation on the bus with your case." Fifty black leaders met to discuss the case and decided to organize a massive boycott of the bus system.

Martin Luther King, Jr., the 27-year-old minister of the Baptist church where the meeting was held, soon emerged as the preeminent spokesman of the protest. King was an impressive figure and an inspiring speaker. "There comes a time when people get tired . . . of being kicked about by the brutal feet of oppression," he declared. It was time to be more assertive, to cease being "patient with anything less than freedom and justice."

Although King, like others, was arrested on the trumped-up charge of speeding and jailed, grassroots support bubbled up. In Montgomery, 50,000 African Americans walked or formed car pools to avoid the transit system. Their actions cut gross revenue on city buses by 65 percent. Almost a year later, the Supreme Court ruled that bus segregation, like school segregation, violated the Constitution, and the boycott ended. But the mood it fostered

Baptist minister Martin Luther King, Jr., emerged as the black spokesman in the Montgomery, Alabama, bus boycott and soon became the most eloquent African-American leader of the entire civil rights movement. He was often jailed for his efforts, as shown in this picture of him sharing a cell with Ralph Abernathy, another civil rights leader. *(Corbis)*

continued, as ordinary black men and women challenged the racial status quo and forced both white and black leaders to respond.

Meanwhile, a concerted effort developed to guarantee black voting rights. The provisions of the Fifteenth Amendment notwithstanding, many states had circumvented the law for decades (see Chapter 16). Some states required a poll tax or a literacy test or an examination of constitutional understanding. Blacks often found themselves excluded from the polls.

Largely because of the legislative genius of Senate majority leader Lyndon B. Johnson of Texas, a civil rights bill, the first since Reconstruction, moved toward passage. Paring the bill down to the provisions he felt would pass, Johnson pushed the measure through.

The Civil Rights Act of 1957 created a Civil Rights Commission and empowered the Justice Department to go to court in cases where blacks were denied the right to vote. The bill was a compromise measure, yet it was the first successful effort to protect civil rights in 82 years.

Again led by Johnson, Congress passed the Civil Rights Act of 1960. This new measure set stiffer penalties for people who interfered with the right to vote but again stopped short of authorizing federal registrars to register blacks to vote and so, like its predecessor, was generally ineffective.

Latinos on the Fringe

Latinos, like other groups, had similar difficulties in the postwar United States. Latino immigrants from Cuba, Puerto Rico, Mexico, and Central America, often unskilled and illiterate, followed other less fortunate Americans to the cities. The conditions they encountered there were similar to those faced by blacks. Author Piri Thomas, born of Puerto Rican and Cuban parents in New York City's Spanish Harlem, described his neighborhood in his memoir *Down These Mean Streets:*

> Man! How many times have I stood on the rooftop of my broken-down building at night and watched the bulb-lit world below.
> Like somehow it's different at night, this my Harlem.
> There ain't no bright sunlight to reveal the stark naked truth of garbage-lepered streets.
> Gone is the drabness and hurt, covered by a friendly night.
> It makes clean the dirty-faced kids.

In the face of recurring discrimination, Spanish-speaking groups maintained a strong sense of group identity. The urban *barrios* where they settled preserved a sense of community and close-knit cohesive culture, even in the midst of pervasive poverty. The ties fostered in these communities provided a strong base for a growing political consciousness.

Chicanos, or Mexican Americans, were the most numerous of the newcomers and faced peculiar difficulties. During World War II, as the country experienced a labor shortage at home, American farmers sought Mexican *braceros* (helping hands) to harvest their crops. A program to encourage the seasonal immigration of farm workers continued after the war when the government signed a Migratory Labor Agreement with Mexico. Between 1948 and 1964, some 4.5 million Mexicans were brought to the United States for temporary work. *Braceros* were expected to return to Mexico at the end of their labor contract, but often they stayed. Joining them were millions more who entered the country illegally.

Conditions were harsh for the *braceros* in the best of times, but in periods of economic difficulty, troubles worsened. During a serious recession in 1953–1954, the government mounted Operation Wetback to deport illegal entrants and *braceros* who had remained in the country illegally and expelled 1.1 million. As immigration officials searched out illegal workers, all Chicanos found themselves vulnerable.

Operation Wetback did not end the reliance on poor Mexican farm laborers. A coalition of southern Democrats and conservative Republicans, mostly representing farm states, extended the Migratory Labor Agreement with Mexico, for the legislators wanted to continue to take advantage of the cheap labor. Two years after the massive deportations of 1954, a record 445,000 *braceros* crossed the border.

Puerto Ricans were numerous in other parts of the country. A steady stream of immigrants had been coming to New York from Puerto Rico since the 1920s. As the island's sugarcane economy became more mechanized, nearly 40 percent of the inhabitants left their homes. By the end of the 1960s, New York City had more Puerto Ricans than San Juan, the island's capital. El Barrio, in East Harlem, became the center of Puerto Rican activity, the home of *salsa* music and small *bodegas,* grocery stores that served the neighborhood. Author Guillermo Cotto-Thorner described the place fondly in his autobiographical novel, *Trópico en Manhattan,* through the words of Antonio, an older resident.

> This . . . is our neighborhood, El Barrio. . . . It's said that we Latins run things here. And that's how we see ourselves. While the American take most of the money that circulates around here, we consider this part of the city to be ours. . . . The stores, barbershops, restaurants, butcher shops, churches, funeral parlors, greasy spoons, pool halls, everything is all Latino. Every now and then you see a business run by a Jew or an Irishman or an Italian, but you'll also see that even these people know a little Spanish.

Puerto Ricans, like many other immigrants, hoped to earn money in America and then return home. Some did; others stayed. Like countless Latinos, most failed to enjoy the promise of the American dream.

Like African Americans, Latinos fought for their own rights. The roots of the Latino struggle dated back to the World War II years. Chicanos established the American GI Forum because a Texas funeral home refused to bury a Mexican-American casualty of World War II. When the group's protest led to a

Mexicans who entered the United States illegally were often arrested and deported. The men in this picture, waiting in a border patrol jail at Calexico, California, in 1951, walked 50 miles across the desert without adequate food and water, only to be apprehended and sent back. *(Loomis Dean/TimePix)*

burial in Arlington National Cemetery, the possibilities of concerted action became clear. In the waning months of the war, a court case challenged Mexican-American segregation in the schools. Gonzalo Méndez, an asparagus grower and a U.S. citizen who had lived in Orange County, California, for 25 years, filed suit to permit his children to attend the school reserved for Anglo-Americans, which was far more attractive than the Mexican one to which they had been assigned. A federal district court upheld his claim in the spring of 1945, and two years later, the circuit court affirmed the original ruling. With the favorable decision, other communities filed similar suits and began to press for integration of their schools. Meanwhile, Mexican-American veterans chafed under continuing discrimination at home.

New organizations arose to struggle for equal rights. The Community Service Organization mobilized Chicanos against discrimination, as did the more radical Associación Nacional México-Americana. And the League of United Latin American Citizens continued reform efforts.

Confrontations continued. Los Angeles, with its large number of Chicanos, was the scene of numerous unsavory racial episodes. In mid-1951, on receiving a complaint about a loud record player, police officers raided a baptismal gathering at the home of Simon Fuentes. Breaking into the house without a warrant, they assaulted the members of the party. In the "Bloody Christmas" case at the end

of the year, officers removed seven Mexican Americans from jail cells and beat them severely.

Chicano activism in the 1950s was fragmented. Some Mexican Americans considered their situation hopeless. More effective mobilization had to await another day.

The Native-American Struggle

Native Americans likewise remained outsiders in the postwar years. Years of persistent discrimination made it even harder to cope with the changes they faced. As power lines reached their reservations, Indians purchased televisions, refrigerators, washing machines, and automobiles. As they partook of the consumer culture, old patterns inevitably changed. Reservation life lost its cohesiveness, and alcohol became a major problem. With good jobs unavailable on the reservations, more and more Indians gravitated to the cities. Bennie Bearskin, a Winnebago, left home for Chicago in 1947, explaining: "The most important reason was that I could at least feel confident that [I could get] perhaps fifty paychecks a year here. ... Even though it might be more pleasant to be back home, for instance, Nebraska." But Indians who moved to the cities often had difficulty adjusting to urban life and frequently faced hostility from white Americans.

Native Americans, like Latinos, began their own struggle for equality. They achieved an important

After returning home at the end of World War II, many Indian veterans found it difficult to fit into either Indian or white society. Alcoholism—which sometimes led to confrontations with the law— became a problem, as reflected in this sketch by Indian artist Aaron Yava, who drew what he saw in what he called the "border towns of the Navajo Nation." *(Aaron Yava/Courtesy of the family of Aaron Yava)*

victory just after the end of World War II when Congress established the Indian Claims Commission. Hundreds of tribal suits charging that ancestral lands had been illegally seized could now be filed against the government in federal courts. Many of them led to large settlements of cash—a form of reparation for past injustices—and sometimes the return of long-lost lands.

In the 1950s, federal Indian policy shifted course. As part of its effort to limit the role of the national government, the Eisenhower administration turned away from the New Deal policy of government support for tribal autonomy. In the Indian Reorganization Act of 1934, the government had stepped in to restore lands to tribal ownership and end their loss or sale to outsiders. In 1953, instead of trying to encourage Native-American self-government, the administration adopted a new approach, known as "termination." The government proposed settling all outstanding claims and eliminating reservations as legitimate political entities. To encourage their assimilation into mainstream society, families who would leave the reservations and move to cities were offered small subsidies by the government.

The new policy infuriated American Indians. Earl Old Person, a Blackfoot elder, declared: "It is important to note that in our Indian language the only translation for termination is to 'wipe out' or

'kill off' . . . How can we plan our future when the Indian Bureau threatens to wipe us out as a race? It is like trying to cook a meal in your tipi when someone is standing outside trying to burn the tipi down." With their lands no longer federally protected and their members deprived of treaty rights, many tribes became unwitting victims of people who wanted to seize their land. Though promising more freedom, the new policy caused great disruption as the government terminated tribes like the Klamath in Oregon, the Menominee in Wisconsin, the Alabama and Coushatta in Texas, and bands of Paiute in Utah.

The policy increased Indian activism. The National Congress of American Indians mobilized opposition to the federal program. A Seminole petition to the president in 1954 summed up a general view:

> We do not say that we are superior or inferior to the White Man and we do not say that the White Man is superior or inferior to us. We do say that we are not White Men but Indians, do not wish to become White Men but wish to remain Indians, and have an outlook on all things different from the outlook of the White Man.

Not only did the termination policy foster a sense of Indian identity, but it also sparked a dawning awareness among whites of the Indians' right to maintain their heritage. In 1958, the Eisenhower administration changed the policy of termination so that it required a tribe's consent. The policy continued to have the force of law, but implementation ceased.

Asian-American Advances

For Asian Americans, conditions improved somewhat in the aftermath of World War II. The war against Nazism eroded the racism that proclaimed a commitment to white superiority. Japanese Americans, ravaged by their devastating internment during the war, fought back after the struggle. In 1946, a measure supporting a wartime law confiscating Japanese-American property appeared on the ballot in California. But a spirited campaign by the Japanese American Citizens League reminding voters of the contributions of Japanese-American soldiers during the war led to the measure's overwhelming defeat. Two years later, the Supreme Court, noting that the law was "nothing more than outright racial discrimination," declared it unconstitutional.

In 1952, the Immigration and Nationality Act, also known as the McCarran-Walter Act, eased im-

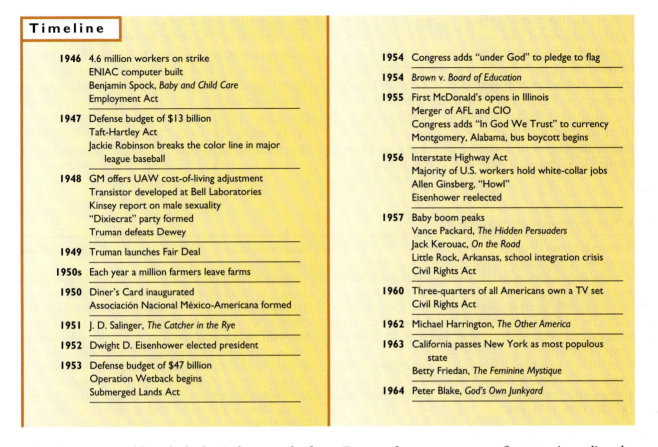

Timeline

1946	4.6 million workers on strike ENIAC computer built Benjamin Spock, *Baby and Child Care* Employment Act
1947	Defense budget of $13 billion Taft-Hartley Act Jackie Robinson breaks the color line in major league baseball
1948	GM offers UAW cost-of-living adjustment Transistor developed at Bell Laboratories Kinsey report on male sexuality "Dixiecrat" party formed Truman defeats Dewey
1949	Truman launches Fair Deal
1950s	Each year a million farmers leave farms
1950	Diner's Card inaugurated Associación Nacional México-Americana formed
1951	J. D. Salinger, *The Catcher in the Rye*
1952	Dwight D. Eisenhower elected president
1953	Defense budget of $47 billion Operation Wetback begins Submerged Lands Act
1954	Congress adds "under God" to pledge to flag
1954	*Brown v. Board of Education*
1955	First McDonald's opens in Illinois Merger of AFL and CIO Congress adds "In God We Trust" to currency Montgomery, Alabama, bus boycott begins
1956	Interstate Highway Act Majority of U.S. workers hold white-collar jobs Allen Ginsberg, "Howl" Eisenhower reelected
1957	Baby boom peaks Vance Packard, *The Hidden Persuaders* Jack Kerouac, *On the Road* Little Rock, Arkansas, school integration crisis Civil Rights Act
1960	Three-quarters of all Americans own a TV set Civil Rights Act
1962	Michael Harrington, *The Other America*
1963	California passes New York as most populous state Betty Friedan, *The Feminine Mystique*
1964	Peter Blake, *God's Own Junkyard*

migration quotas. Although the basic framework of the National Origins Act of 1924 remained intact, it removed the longstanding ban on Japanese immigration and made first-generation Japanese immigrants eligible for citizenship. It also established a quota of 100 immigrants a year from each Asian country. While that number was tiny compared to those admitted annually from northern and western Europe, the measure was a first step in ending the discriminatory exclusion of the past.

By the 1950s, many second and third generation Chinese, Japanese, and Koreans had moved into white-collar work. Promoting education for their children, they became part of the growing middle class, hoping like others to enjoy the benefits of the American dream.

✦ *Conclusion*

QUALMS AMID AFFLUENCE

In general, the United States during the decade and a half after World War II was stable and secure. Structural adjustments caused occasional moments of friction but were seldom visible in prosperous times. Recessions occurred periodically, but the economy righted itself after short downturns. For the most part, business boomed. The standard of living for many of the nation's citizens reached new heights, especially compared with standards in other parts of the world. Millions of middle-class Americans joined the ranks of suburban property owners, enjoying the benefits of shopping centers, fast-food establishments, and other material manifestations of what they considered the good life. Workers found themselves savoring the materialistic advantages of the era. The political world reflected prosperous times.

Some Americans did not share in the prosperity, but they were not visible in the affluent suburbs. Many African Americans and members of other minority groups were seriously disadvantaged, although they still believed they could share in the American dream and remained confident that deeply rooted patterns of discrimination could be changed. Even when they began to mobilize, their protest was peaceful at first.

Beneath the calm surface, though, there were signs of discontent. The seeds for the protest movements of the 1960s had already been sown. Disquieting signs were likewise evident on other fronts. The divorce rate increased, as one-third of all marriages in the 1950s broke apart. Americans increasingly used newly developed tranquilizers in an effort to cope with problems in their lives. Some Americans began to criticize the materialism that seemed to undermine American efforts in the Cold War. Such criticisms in turn legitimized challenges by other groups, in the continuing struggle to make the realities of American life match the nation's ideals.

Criticisms and anxieties notwithstanding, the United States—for most whites and some people of color—continued to develop according to Ray Kroc's dreams as he first envisioned McDonald's establishments across the land. Healthy and comfortable, upper- and middle-class Americans expected prosperity and growth to continue in the years ahead.

✦ Recommended Reading

Economic Boom

American Social History Project, *Who Built America? Working People & the Nation's Economy, Politics, Culture, and Society* (1992); David Brody, *Workers in Industrial America* (1980); James R. Green, *The World of the Worker* (1980); Jacqueline Jones, *American Work: Four Centuries of Black and White Labor* (1998); James T. Patterson, *Grand Expectations: Postwar America, 1945–1974* (1996); Juliet B. Schor, *The Overworked American: The Unexpected Decline of Leisure* (1991); Robert H. Zieger, *American Workers, American Unions,* 2nd ed. (1994) and *The CIO, 1935–1955* (1995).

Demographic and Technological Shifts

Peter Blake, *God's Own Junkyard: The Planned Deterioration of America's Landscape* (1964); Paul A. Carter, *Another Part of the Fifties* (1983); David Halberstam, *The Fifties* (1993); Samuel P. Hays, *Beauty, Health, and Permanence: Environmental Politics in the United States, 1955–1985* (1987); Daniel Horowitz, ed., *American Social Classes in the 1950s: Selections from Vance Packard's* The Status Seekers (1995); Kenneth T. Jackson, *Crabgrass Frontier: The Suburbanization of the United States* (1985); Patricia Nelson Limerick, *Something in the Soil: Legacies and Reckonings in the New West* (2000); Zane L. Miller, *The Urbanization of Modern America* (1973); Richard Polenberg, *One Nation Divisible: Class, Race, and Ethnicity in the United States Since 1938* (1980); Richard White, *"It's Your Misfortune and None of My Own": A History of the American West* (1991).

Consensus and Conformity

Erik Barnouw, *Tube of Plenty: The Evolution of American Television* (1975); James L. Baughman, *The Republic of Mass Culture* (1992); Joel Foreman, ed., *The Other Fifties: Interrogating Midcentury American Icons* (1997); James Howard Jones, *Alfred C. Kinsey: A Public/Private Life* (1997); W.T. Lhamon, Jr., *Deliberate Speed: The Origins of a Cultural Style in the American 1950s* (1990); Alison Lurie, *The Language of Clothes* (1981); C. Wright Mills, *White Collar: The American Middle Classes* (1951); David Riesman, *The Lonely Crowd: A Study of the Changing American Character* (1950); Cecelia Tichi, *Electronic Hearth; Creating an American Television Culture* (1991).

David Chidester, *Patterns of Power: Religion and Politics in American Culture* (1988); Erling Jorstad, *Holding Fast/Pressing On: Religion in America in the 1980s* (1990); Charles H. Lippy, *Pluralism Comes of Age: American Religious Culture in the Twentieth Century* (2001); R. Laurence Moore, *Selling God: American Religion in the Marketplace of Culture* (1994); Peter W. Williams, *Popular Religion in America: Symbolic Change and the Modernization Process in Historical Perspective* (1980); Garry Wills, *Under God: Religion and American Politics* (1990).

Beth L. Bailey, *From Front Porch to Back Seat: Courtship in Twentieth-Century America* (1988); William H. Chafe, *The American Woman: Her Changing Social, Economic, and Political Roles, 1920–1970* (1972); Stephanie Coontz, *The Way We Never Were: American Families and the Nostalgia Trap* (1992); John D'Emilio and Estelle B. Freedman, *Intimate Matters: A History of Sexuality in America* (1988); Sara Evans, *Born for Liberty: A History of Women in America* (1989); Betty Friedan, *The Feminine Mystique* (1963); Susan M. Hartmann, *The Home Front and Beyond: American Women in the 1940s* (1982); Judith A. Hennessee, *Betty Friedan: Her Life* (1999); Daniel Horowitz, *Betty Friedan and the Making of* The Feminine Mystique: *The American Left, the Cold War and Modern Feminism* (1998); Eugenia Kaledin, *Mothers and More: American Women in the 1950s* (1984); Elaine Tyler May, *Homeward Bound: American Families in the Cold War Era* (1988); Joanne Meyerowitz, ed., *Not June Cleaver: Women and Gender in Postwar America, 1945–1960* (1994); Gloria Steinem, *Outrageous Acts and Everyday Rebellions,* 2nd ed. (1995).

Origins of the Welfare State

Edward D. Berkowitz and Kim McQuaid, *Creating the Welfare State: The Political Economy of 20th Century Reform* (1994); Jacqueline Jones, *The Dispossessed: America's Underclasses from the Civil War to the Present* (1992); Michael B. Katz, *In the Shadow of the Poorhouse: A Social History of Welfare in America,* 10th anniv. ed. (1997); Charles Murray, *Losing Ground: American Social Policy, 1950–1980,* 10th anniv. ed. (1995); Frances F.

Piven and Richard A. Cloward, eds., *Regulating the Poor: The Functions of Public Welfare*, 2nd ed. (1993); Margaret Weir, Ann Shola Orloff, and Theda Skocpol, *The Politics of Social Policy in the United States* (1988).

Robert J. Donovan, *Conflict and Crisis: The Presidency of Harry S Truman, 1945–1948* (1977) and *Tumultuous Years: The Presidency of Harry S Truman* (1982); Robert H. Ferrell, *Harry S. Truman and the Modern American Presidency* (1998); Alonzo L. Hamby, *Man of the People: A Life of Harry S. Truman* (1995); David McCullough, *Truman* (1992); Harry S Truman, *Memoirs*, 2 vols. (1955, 1956).

Craig Allen, *Eisenhower and the Mass Media: Peace, Prosperity, and Prime-Time TV* (1993); Stephen E. Ambrose, *Eisenhower: The President* (1984) and *Eisenhower: Soldier and President* (1990); Blanche Wiesen Cook, *The Declassified Eisenhower: A Divided Legacy* (1981); Dwight D. Eisenhower, *Mandate for Change, 1953–1956* (1963) and *Waging Peace* (1965); Fred I. Greenstein, *The Hidden-Hand Presidency: Eisenhower as Leader* (1982); Chester J. Pach, Jr., and Elmo Richardson, *The Presidency of Dwight D. Eisenhower* (1991).

The Other America

Michael Harrington, *The Other America: Poverty in the United States* (1962); James T. Patterson, *America's Struggle Against Poverty, 1900–1994* (1994).

James Baldwin, *Nobody Knows My Name* (1961) and *The Fire Next Time* (1962); Claude Brown, *Manchild in the Promised Land* (1965); William H. Chafe, Raymond Gavins, and Robert Korstad, eds., *Remembering Jim Crow: African Americans Tell about Life in the Segregated South* (2001); Darlene Clark Hine and Kathleen Thompson, *A Shining Thread of Hope: The History of Black Women in America* (1998); Jacqueline Jones, *Labor of Love, Labor of Sorrow: Black Women, Work, and the Family from Slavery to the Present* (1985); Robin D.G. Kelley and Earl Lewis, eds., *To Make Our World Anew: A History of African Americans* (2000); Nicholas Lemann, *The Promised Land: The Great Black Migration and How It Changed America* (1991); Carole Marks, *Farewell, We're Good and Gone: The Great Black Migration* (1989).

Thomas Borstelmann, *The Cold War and the Color Line: American Race Relations in the Global Arena* (2001); Taylor Branch, *Parting the Waters: America in the King Years, 1954–1963* (1988); Douglas Brinkley, *Rosa Parks* (2000); John C. Chalberg, *Rickey and Robinson: The Preacher, the Player, and America's Game* (2000); Mary L. Dudziak, *Cold War Civil Rights: Race and the Image of American Democracy* (2000); Eric Foner, *The Story of American Freedom* (1998); David J. Garrow, *Bearing the Cross: Martin Luther King, Jr., and the Southern Christian Leadership Conference* (1986); Martin Luther King, Jr., *Why We Can't Wait*, reissue ed. (1991); Arnold Rampersad, *Jackie Robinson: A Biography* (1997); James T. Patterson, *Brown v. Board of Education: A Civil Rights Milestone and Its Troubled Legacy* (2001); Harvard Sitkoff, *The Struggle for Black Equality, 1954–1992*,

revised ed. (1993); Jules Tygiel, *Baseball's Great Experiment: Jackie Robinson and His Legacy* (1983).

Rodolfo Acuña, *Occupied America: A History of Chicanos*, 4th ed. (2000); Neil Foley, *The White Scourge: Mexicans, Blacks, and Poor Whites in Texas Cotton Culture* (1997); Ed Ludwig and James Santibañez, eds., *The Chicanos: Mexican American Voices* (1971); George J. Sánchez, *Becoming Mexican American: Ethnicity, Culture and Identity in Chicano Los Angeles, 1900–1945* (1993); Peter Skerry, *Mexican Americans: The Ambivalent Minority* (1993); Ronald Takaki, *A Different Mirror: A History of Multicultural America* (1993) and *A Larger Memory: A History of Our Diversity, with Voices* (1998); Piri Thomas, *Down These Mean Streets* (1967).

Frederick E. Hoxie, ed., *Indians in American History* (1988); Frederick E. Hoxie, Peter C. Mancall, and James Merrell, eds., *Encounters in Indian Country: 1850 to the Present* (2000); Peter Iverson, *"We Are Still Here": American Indians in the Twentieth Century* (1998); Alvin M. Josephy, Jr., *Now That the Buffalo's Gone* (1982); James S. Olson and Raymond Wilson, *Native Americans in the Twentieth Century* (1986); Roger Daniels, *Coming to America: A History of Immigration and Ethnicity in American Life*, revised edition (2002); Reed Ueeda, *Postwar Immigrant America: A Social History* (1994).

Fiction and Film

Guillermo Cotto-Thorner, *Trópico en Manhattan* (1967) is an autobiographical novel about the Puerto Rican community in New York City; Allen Drury, *Advise and Consent* (1959) is a novel about Washington politics, complete with blackmail and demagoguery; Ralph Ellison's *Invisible Man* (1952) is a powerful fictional account of an African American's journey through the 1950s; Allen Ginsberg, *Howl and Other Poems* (1956) is a collection of iconoclastic poetry challenging the materialism of contemporary life; Jack Kerouac, *On the Road* (1957) is a stream-of-consciousness novel that questions the values of the 1950s; Arthur Miller's *Death of a Salesman* (1949) is the Pulitzer Prize–winning play about the shallow values of postwar American culture; J. D. Salinger, *Catcher in the Rye* (1951) is the story of Holden Caulfield, a troubled adolescent who is overwhelmed by the phoniness of contemporary life; Sloan Wilson, *The Man in the Gray Flannel Suit* (1955) is a novel challenging the conformity of corporate America in the 1950s.

The Best Years of Our Lives (1946), the Academy Award–winning story of three servicemen returning home after World War II, captures the values of the immediate postwar era; *The Seven Year Itch* (1955) features Marilyn Monroe as the beautiful and enticing girl next door; *To Kill a Mockingbird* (1962) is a film based on Harper Lee's novel by the same title about children learning about racism—and about how to deal with it—in the South. *The Man in the Gray Flannel Suit* (1956), the film made from the novel of the same name, critiques the lifestyle of corporate America in the 1950s. *No Down Payment* (1957) deals with life in the suburbs, as does the much more recent *Pleasantville* (1998), as it looks back at an earlier era.

✦ Discovering U.S. History Online

The Postwar Economic Boom

www.aflcio.org/cse/mod3/mod_3_11.htm

Several aspects of the postwar economy are described in essays.

The Postwar United States

http://lcweb2.loc.gov/ammem/ndlpedu/features/
timeline/postwar/postwar.html

By way of primary documents, interviews, and artifacts, this site presents two sections: Arts and Entertainment: 1945–1968 and The Presidential Election of 1960.

Creating the Interstate System

www.tfhrc.gov/pubrds/summer96/p96su10.htm

An illustrated article from the U.S. Department of Transportation, Federal Highway Administration "Public Roads Website."

Levittown: Documents of an Ideal American Suburb

www.uic.edu/~pbhales/Levittown/

The postwar boom in housing made suburban living the cultural norm in America and shaped a generation. The story of the classic suburb, Levittown, is told on this site in pictures and text.

Computer History Museum

www.cyberstreet.com/hcs/museum/museum/htm

Choose from an interactive timeline, an image gallery, a video gallery, and a "guided" tour of the exhibits to explore the history of computers.

Candace Rich, Fifties Website Home Page

www.fiftiesweb.com

This is an entertaining personal site that tells about and samples music and television from the 1950s. It also includes a related links page.

American Cultural History: 1950–1959

www.nhmccd.edu/contracts/lrc/kc/decade50.html

This site present facts about the decade and a comprehensive overview of several cultural subtopics.

Religion in Post World War II America

http://www.nhc.rtp.nc.us:8080/tserve/twenty/tkeyinfo/
trelww2.htm

An essay on religion along with links to online resources.

Rachel Carson

www.rachelcarson.org.

An illustrated biography and bibliography of this pioneering ecologist.

Harry S Truman

www.ipl.org/ref/POTUS/hstruman.html

This site contains basic factual data about Truman's election and presidency, speeches, and online biographies.

Harry S Truman Library and Museum

www.trumanlibrary.org

This presidential library site has numerous photos and various important primary documents relating to Truman.

Dwight David Eisenhower

www.ipl.org/ref/POTUS/ddeisenhower.html

This site contains basic factual data about Eisenhower's election and presidency, including speeches and other materials.

The Dwight D. Eisenhower Library and Museum

www.eisenhower.utexas.edu

This site contains mainly photos of the president.

The Central High Crisis, Little Rock 1957

www.ardemgaz.com/prev/central/

Using articles and photographs from Arkansas newspapers, the site explores the 1957 Little Rock events.

Massive Resistance

www.vcdh.virginia.edu/vahistory/massive.resistance/
index.html

This site documents Virginia's resistance to segregation of schools with photographs, interview clips, documents, and a timeline of events.

Civil Rights

www.museum.tv/education/unit1.shtml

This site includes three online video documentaries. "As We See It: Little Rock Central High School" is a remarkable story of growth at the once infamous Little Rock Central High School as seen through the eyes of three sets of students from each period of change: the late 1950s; the late 1960s; and the late 1970s. This show was narrated and produced by the class of 1979 at Central High (1979, Color/B&W). In "Corner of the Carpet," Frank McGee examines the economic and moral cost of slums in Montgomery, Alabama (1956, B&W). And "Malcolm X: City Desk" is an interview featuring Malcolm X that centers on civil rights and the Black Muslim movement (1963, Color).

27 Chills and Fever During the Cold War, 1945–1960

The Cold War created a climate of confrontation between East and West and led to wars in Korea and Vietnam that left millions of people injured or dead. *(Edward Keinholz,* O'er the Ramparts We Watched Fascinated/*Courtesy of L.A. Louver Gallery, Venice, CA)*

✦ *American Stories*

A GOVERNMENT EMPLOYEE CONFRONTS THE ANTI-COMMUNIST CRUSADE

Val Lorwin was in France in November 1950 when he learned of the charges against him. A State Department employee on leave of absence after 16 years of government service, he was in Paris working on a book. Now he had to return to the United States to defend himself against the accusation that he was a member of the Communist party and thus a loyalty and security risk. It seemed to him a tasteless joke. Yet communism was no laughing matter in the United States. Suspicions of the Soviet Union had escalated after 1945, and a wave of paranoia swept through the United States.

Lorwin was an unlikely candidate to be caught up in the fallout of the Cold War. He had begun to work for the government in 1935, serving in a number of New Deal agencies, then in the Labor Department and on the War Production Board before he was drafted during World War II. While in the army, he was assigned to the Office of Strategic Services, an early intelligence agency, and he was frequently granted security clearances in the United States and abroad.

Lorwin, however, did have a left-wing past as an active Socialist in the 1930s. His social life then had revolved around Socialist party causes, particularly the unionization of southern tenant farmers and the provision of aid to the unemployed. He and his wife, Madge, drafted statements and stuffed envelopes to support their goals. But that activity was wholly open and legal, and Lorwin had from the start been aggressively anti-Communist in political affairs.

Suddenly, Lorwin, like others in the period, faced a nightmare. Despite his spotless record, Lorwin was told that an unnamed accuser had identified him as a Communist. The burden of proof was entirely on him, and the chance of clearing his name was slim. He was entitled to a hearing if he chose, or he could resign.

Lorwin requested a hearing, and one was held late in 1950. Still struck by the absurdity of the situation, he refuted all accusations but made little effort to cite his own positive achievements. At the conclusion, he was informed that the government no longer doubted his loyalty but considered him a security risk, likewise grounds for dismissal from his job.

When he appealed the judgment, Lorwin was again denied access to the identity of his accuser. This time, however, he thoroughly prepared his defense. At the hearing, a total of 97 witnesses either spoke under oath on Lorwin's behalf or left sworn written depositions testifying to his good character and meritorious service.

The issues in the hearings might have been considered comic in view of Lorwin's record, had not a man's reputation been at stake. The accuser had once lived with the Lorwins in Washington, D.C. Fifteen years later, he claimed that in 1935 Lorwin had revealed that he was holding a Communist party meeting in his home and had even shown him a party card.

Lorwin proved all the charges groundless. He also showed that in 1935 the Socialist party card was red, the color the accuser reported seeing, while the Communist party card was black. In March 1952, Lorwin was finally cleared for both loyalty and security.

Lorwin's troubles were not yet over. His name appeared on one of the lists produced by Senator Joseph McCarthy of Wisconsin, the most aggressive anti-Communist of the era, and Lorwin was again victimized. The next year, he was indicted for making false statements to the State Department Loyalty-Security Board. The charges this time proved as specious as before. Finally, in May 1954, admitting that its special prosecutor had deliberately lied to the grand jury and had no legitimate case, the Justice Department asked for dismissal of the indictment. Cleared at last, Lorwin went on to become a distinguished labor historian.

Lorwin was more fortunate than some victims of the anti-Communist crusade. People rallied around him and gave him valuable support. Despite considerable emotional cost, he survived the witch-hunt of the early 1950s, but his case still reflected vividly the ugly domestic consequences of the breakdown in relations between the Soviet Union and the United States.

The Cold War, which unfolded soon after the end of World War II and lasted for nearly 50 years, powerfully affected all aspects of American life. Rejecting for good the isolationist impulse that had governed foreign policy in the 1920s and 1930s, the United States began to play a major role in the world in the postwar years. Doubts about intervention in other lands faded as the nation acknowledged its dominant international position and resolved to do whatever was necessary to maintain it. The same sense of mission that had infused the United States in the Spanish-American War, World War I, and World War II now committed most Americans to the struggle against communism at home and abroad.

This chapter explores that continuing sense of mission and its consequences. It examines the roots of the Cold War both in the idealistic aim to keep the world safe for democracy and in the pursuit of economic self-interest that had long fueled American capitalism. It records how the de-termination to prevent the spread of communism led American policymakers to consider vast parts of the world as pivotal to American security and to act accordingly, par-ticularly in Korea and Vietnam. It notes the impact on eco-nomic development, particularly in the West, where the mighty defense industry flourished. And it considers the tragic consequences of the effort to promote ideological unity within the United States, where excesses threatened the principles of democracy itself.

ORIGINS OF THE COLD WAR

The Cold War developed by degrees. It stemmed from divergent views about the shape of the post–World War II world as the colonial empires in Asia, Africa, and the Middle East began to crumble. The United States, strong and secure, was intent on spreading its vision of freedom and free trade around the world to maintain its economic hege-mony. The Soviet Union, concerned about security after a devastating war, demanded politically sym-pathetic neighbors on its borders to preserve its own autonomy. Suppressed during World War II, these differences now surfaced in a Soviet–American con-frontation. As tensions rose, the two nations be-haved, according to Senator J. William Fulbright, "like two big dogs, chewing on a bone."

The American Stance

The United States emerged from World War II more powerful than any nation ever before, and it sought to use that might to achieve a world order that could sustain American aims. American policymakers, fol-lowing in Woodrow Wilson's footsteps, hoped to spread the values—liberty, equality, and democ-racy—underpinning the American dream. They as-sumed that they could furnish the stability that postwar reconstruction required. They did not al-ways recognize that what they considered universal truths were rooted in specific historical circum-stances in their own country and might not flourish elsewhere.

At the same time, American leaders sought a world where economic enterprise could thrive. Recollections of the Great Depression haunted lead-ers. With the American economy operating at full speed as a result of the war, world markets were needed once the fighting stopped. Government offi-cials wanted to eliminate trade barriers—imposed by the Soviet Union and other nations—to provide outlets for industrial products and for surplus farm commodities such as wheat, cotton, and tobacco. As the largest source of goods for world markets, with exports totaling $14 billion in 1947, the United States required open channels for growth to con-tinue. Americans assumed that their prosperity would benefit the rest of the world, even when other nations disagreed.

Soviet Aims

The Soviet Union formulated its own goals after World War II. Russia had usually been governed in the past by a strongly centralized, sometimes auto-cratic, government, and that tradition—as much as Communist ideology, with its stress on class strug-gle and the inevitable triumph of a proletarian state—guided Soviet policy.

During the war, the Russians had played down talk of world revolution, which they knew their allies found threatening, and had mobilized domestic support with nationalistic appeals. As the struggle drew to a close, the Soviets still said little about world conquest, emphasizing socialism within the nation itself.

Rebuilding was the first priority. Devastated by the war, Soviet agriculture and industry lay in sham-bles. But revival required internal security. At the same time, the Russians felt vulnerable along their western flank. Such anxieties had a historical basis, for in the early nineteenth century, Napoleon had reached the gates of Moscow. Twice in the twentieth century, invasions had come from the west, most re-cently when Hitler had attacked in 1941. Haunted by fears of a quick German recovery, the Soviets de-manded defensible borders and neighboring regimes sympathetic to Russian aims. They insisted on military and political stability in the regions closest to them.

Early Cold War Leadership

Both the United States and the Soviet Union had strong leadership in the early years of the Cold War. On the American side, presidents Harry Truman and Dwight Eisenhower accepted the centralization of authority Franklin Roosevelt had begun, as the executive branch became increasingly powerful in guiding foreign policy. In the Soviet Union, first Joseph Stalin, then Nikita Khrushchev provided equally forceful direction.

Truman and Eisenhower, both introduced in Chapter 26, paid close attention to the Cold War struggle with the Soviet Union. Though their personal styles differed, both subscribed to traditional American attitudes about self-determination and the superiority of American political institutions and values. Both were determined to stand firm in the face of the Soviet threat. If accommodation was not possible, they were willing to take whatever steps were necessary to achieve American diplomatic aims.

As World War II drew to an end, Truman grew increasingly hostile to Soviet actions. Viewing collaboration as a wartime necessity, he was uncomfortable with what he felt were Soviet designs in Eastern Europe and Asia as the struggle wound down. It was now time, he said, "to stand up to the Russians" before they solidified positions in various parts of the world.

Like Truman, Eisenhower saw communism as a monolithic force struggling for world supremacy and agreed that the Kremlin in Moscow was orchestrating subversive activity around the globe. Like Truman, he saw issues in black and white terms and regarded the Soviet system as a "tyranny that has brought thousands, millions of people into slave camps and is attempting to make all mankind its chattel." Yet Eisenhower was more willing than Truman to practice accommodation when it served his ends.

Joseph Stalin, the Soviet leader at war's end, possessed almost absolute powers. He looked, in the words of one American diplomat, like "an old battle-scarred tiger." Though quiet and unassuming in appearance, he had presided over ruthless purges against his opponents in the 1930s. Now he was determined to do whatever was necessary to rebuild Soviet society, if possible with Western assistance, and to keep Eastern Europe within the Russian sphere of influence.

Stalin's death in March 1953 left a power vacuum in Soviet political affairs that was eventually filled by Nikita Khrushchev, who by 1958 held the offices of both prime minister and party secretary. A crude man, Khrushchev once used his shoe to pound a table at the United Nations while the British prime minister was speaking. During Krushchev's regime, the Cold War continued, but for brief periods of time Soviet–American relations became less hostile.

Disillusionment with the USSR

American support for the Soviet Union faded quickly after the war. In September 1945, 54 percent of a national sample trusted the Russians to cooperate with the Americans in the postwar years. Two months later, the figure dropped to 44 percent, and by February 1946, to 35 percent.

As Americans soured on Russia, they began to equate the Nazi and Soviet systems. Just as they had in the 1930s, authors, journalists, and public officials pointed to similarities, some of them legitimate, between the regimes. Both states, they contended, maintained total control over communications and could eliminate political opposition whenever they chose. Both states used terror to silence dissidents, and Stalin's labor camps in Siberia could be compared with Hitler's concentration camps. After the U.S. publication in 1949 of George Orwell's frightening novel *1984*, *Life* magazine noted in an editorial that the ominous figure Big Brother was but a "mating" of Hitler and Stalin. Truman spoke for many Americans when he said in 1950 that "there isn't any difference between the totalitarian Russian government and the Hitler government. . . . They are all alike. They are . . . police state governments."

The lingering sense that the nation had not been quick enough to resist totalitarian aggression in the 1930s heightened American fears. Had the United States stopped the Germans, Italians, or Japanese when those nations first caused international trouble, it might have prevented the long, devastating war. The free world had not responded quickly enough before and was determined never to repeat the same mistake.

The Troublesome Polish Question

The first clash between East and West came, even before the war ended, over Poland. Soviet demands for a government willing to accept Russian influence clashed with American hopes for a more representative structure patterned after the Western model. The Yalta Conference of February 1945 attempted to resolve the issue (see Chapter 25) with a loosely worded and correspondingly imprecise agreement. When Truman assumed office, the Polish situation remained unresolved. Averell Harriman,

Joseph Stalin's autocratic approach to foreign and domestic affairs affronted American sensibilities. Here, in this Soviet propaganda poster, the Russian caption reads: "Under the Leadership of the Great Stalin—Forward to Communism!" *(Hoover Institution Archives, Stanford, CA Russian & Soviet Poster Collection)*

the U.S. ambassador to the Soviet Union, warned that the United States faced a "barbarian invasion of Europe" unless the Soviets could be checked and Western-style democracies established. The president agreed.

Truman's unbending stance was clear in an April 1945 meeting with Soviet foreign minister Vyacheslav Molotov on the question of Poland. Concerned that the Russians were breaking the Yalta agreements, imprecise as they were, the American leader demanded a new democratic government there. Though Molotov appeared conciliatory,

Truman insisted on Russian acquiescence. Truman later recalled that when Molotov protested, "I have never been talked to like that in my life," he himself retorted bluntly, "Carry out your agreements and you won't get talked to like that." Such bluntness contributed to the deterioration of Soviet–American relations.

Truman and Stalin met face-to-face for the first (and last) time at the Potsdam Conference in July 1945, the final wartime Big Three meeting of the United States, the Soviet Union, and Great Britain. There, outside of devastated Berlin, the two leaders

Soviet leader Nikita Khrushchev was an aggressive leader who sometimes spoke out belligerently in defense of his country's interests. Here he appears at the podium at the United Nations delivering a speech. *(Hulton Archive/Getty Images)*

Conflicting Aims During the Cold War

United States	Soviet Union
Spread ideological values of liberty, equality, and democracy	Spread ideological values of class struggle, triumph of the proletariat
Extend the tradition of representative government	Extend the tradition of strong centralized government
Maintain stability around the world	Support revolutionary movements around the world
Fill vacuum created by the end of imperialism with regimes sympathetic to Western ideals	Support regimes sympathetic to the Soviet Union, particularly to avoid attack on its western flank
Maintain a world free for economic enterprise by eliminating trade barriers and providing markets for American exports	Rebuild the devastated Soviet economy by creating preferential trading arrangements in the region of Soviet dominance

sized each other up as they considered the Russian–Polish boundary, the fate of Germany, and the American desire to obtain an unconditional surrender from Japan. It was Truman's first exposure to international diplomacy at the highest level, and it left him confident of his abilities. When he learned during the meeting of the first successful atomic bomb test in New Mexico, he became even more determined to insist that the Soviets behave in the ways he wished.

Economic Pressure on the USSR

One major source of controversy in the last stages of World War II was the question of U.S. aid to its allies. Responding to congressional pressure at home to limit foreign assistance as hostilities ended, Truman acted impulsively. Six days after V-E Day signaled the end of the European war in May 1945, he issued an executive order cutting off lend-lease supplies to the Allies. Ships heading for allied ports had to turn back in the middle of the ocean. Though the policy affected all nations receiving aid, it hurt the Soviet Union most of all and caused serious resentment.

The United States intended to use economic pressure in other ways as well. The USSR desperately needed financial assistance to rebuild after the war and, in January 1945, had requested a $6 billion loan. Roosevelt hedged, hoping to win concessions in return. In August, four months after FDR's death, the Russians renewed their application, but this time for only $1 billion. Truman, like his predecessor, dragged his heels, seeking to use the loan as a lever to gain access to markets in areas traditionally dominated by the Soviet Union. The United States first claimed to have lost the Soviet request, then in March 1946 indicated a willingness to consider the matter—but only if Russia pledged "nondiscrimination in world commerce." Stalin refused the offer and launched his own five-year plan instead.

Declaring the Cold War

As Soviet–American relations deteriorated, both sides stepped up their rhetorical attacks. In 1946, Stalin spoke out first, arguing that capitalism and communism were on a collision course, that a series of cataclysmic disturbances would tear the capitalist world apart, and that the Soviet system would inevitably triumph. Though the Soviet Union lost millions of people in World War II, victory, he declared, meant that "our Soviet social system has won, that the Soviet social system has successfully stood the test in the fire of war and has proved its complete vitality," and victory in the struggle ahead was likewise assured. Stalin's speech was a stark and ominous statement that worried the West. Supreme Court Justice William O. Douglas called it the "declaration of World War III."

The response to Stalin's speech came not from an American but from England's former prime minister, Winston Churchill, long suspicious of the Soviet state. Speaking in Fulton, Missouri, in 1946, with Truman on the platform during the address, Churchill declared that "from Stettin in the Baltic to Trieste in the Adriatic, an iron curtain has descended across the Continent." To counter the threat, he urged that a vigilant association of English-speaking peoples work to contain Soviet designs. Such a coalition was the only way the Soviet Union could be stopped.

CONTAINING THE SOVIET UNION

Containment formed the basis of postwar American policy. While the fledgling United Nations, established in 1945, might have provided a forum to ease tensions, both the United States and the Soviet Union acted unilaterally, and with the aid of allies, in pursuit of their own ends. Within the United States, both Democrats and Republicans were determined to check Soviet expansion wherever threats appeared. In an increasingly contentious world, the American government formulated rigid anti-Soviet policies to prevent the spread of communism. The Soviet Union responded in an equally uncompromising way.

Containment Defined

George F. Kennan, chargé d'affaires at the American embassy in the Soviet Union and an expert on Soviet matters, was primarily responsible for defining the new policy of containment. After Stalin's speech in February 1946, Kennan sent an 8,000-word telegram to the State Department. In it he argued that Soviet hostility stemmed from the "Kremlin's neurotic view of world affairs," which in turn came from the "traditional and instinctive Russian sense of insecurity." The stiff Soviet stance was not so much a response to American actions as a reflection of the Russian leaders' own efforts to maintain their autocratic rule. Russian fanaticism would not soften, regardless of how accommodating American policy became. Therefore, it had to be opposed at every turn.

Kennan's "long telegram" struck a resonant chord in Washington. It made his diplomatic reputation and brought him into an influential position in the State Department. Soon he published an extended analysis, under the pseudonym "Mr. X," in the prominent journal *Foreign Affairs.* "The whole Soviet governmental machine, including the mechanism of diplomacy," he wrote, "moves inexorably along the prescribed path, like a persistent toy automobile wound up and headed in a given direction, stopping only when it meets with some unanswerable force." Many Americans agreed with Kennan that Soviet pressure had to "be contained by the adroit and vigilant application of counter-force at a series of constantly shifting geographical and political points."

The concept of containment provided the philosophical justification for the hard-line stance that Americans, both in and out of government, adopted. Containment created the framework for military and economic assistance to countries that seemed threatened by the perceived Communist menace around the globe.

The First Step: The Truman Doctrine

The Truman Doctrine represented the first major application of containment policy. The new policy was devised to respond to conditions in the eastern Mediterranean, an area that Americans had never before considered vital to their national security. The Soviet Union was pressuring Turkey for joint control of the Dardanelles, the passage between the Black Sea and the Mediterranean. Meanwhile, a civil war in Greece pitted Communist elements against the ruling English-aided right-wing monarchy. Revolutionary pressures threatened to topple the government.

In February 1947, the British ambassador to the United States informed the State Department that his exhausted country could no longer give Greece and Turkey economic and military aid. Still reeling from the devastation of the war, Britain also faced serious challenges to its empire and had to focus on those challenges. Would the United States now move into the void in Greece and Turkey?

Administration officials, who were willing to move forward, knew they needed bipartisan support to accomplish such a major policy shift. A conservative Congress wanted smaller budgets and lower taxes rather than massive and expensive aid programs. Senator Arthur Vandenberg of Michigan, a key Republican, aware of the need for bipartisanship, told top policymakers that they had to begin "scaring hell out of the country" if they wanted support for a bold new containment policy.

Undersecretary of State Dean Acheson took the lead. Meeting with congressional leaders, he declared that "like apples in a barrel infected by one

Harry Truman relied heavily on Dean Acheson, pictured here on the right, who served first as undersecretary of state and then from 1949 on as secretary of state. Together Truman and Acheson helped develop the outlines of the containment policy that sought to limit the advances of the Soviet Union. *(Harry S. Truman Library)*

Americans in the early postwar years were afraid that communism was a contagious disease spreading around the globe. In this picture from the spring of 1946, *Time* magazine pictured the relentless spread of an infection that would need to be contained. (© 1946 Time, Inc. Reprinted by permission.)

rotten one, the corruption of Greece would infect Iran and all to the east." He warned ominously that a Communist victory would "open three continents to Soviet penetration." The major powers were now "met at Armageddon," as the Soviet Union pressed forward. Only the United States had the power to resist.

Truman likewise played on the Soviet threat. On March 12, 1947, he told Congress, in a statement that came to be known as the Truman Doctrine, "I believe that it must be the policy of the United States to support free peoples who are resisting subjugation by armed minorities or by outside pressures." Unless the United States acted, the free world might not survive. "If we falter in our leadership," Truman said, "we may endanger the peace of the world—and we shall surely endanger the welfare of our own nation." To avert that calamity, he urged Congress to appropriate $400 million for military and economic aid to Turkey and Greece.

Not everyone approved of Truman's request or of his overblown description of the situation. Autocratic regimes controlled Greece and Turkey, some observers pointed out. And where was the proof that Stalin had a hand in the Greek conflict? Others warned that the United States could not by itself stop encroachment in all parts of the world. Nonetheless, Congress passed Truman's foreign aid bill.

In assuming that Americans could police the globe, the Truman Doctrine was a major step in the advent of the Cold War. Truman's address, observed financier Bernard Baruch, "was tantamount to a declaration of . . . an ideological or religious war." Journalist Walter Lippmann was more critical. He termed the new containment policy a "strategic monstrosity" that could embroil the United States

in disputes around the world. In the two succeeding decades, Lippmann proved correct.

The Next Steps: The Marshall Plan, NATO, and NSC-68

The next step for American policymakers involved sending extensive economic aid for postwar recovery in Western Europe. At the war's end, most of Europe was economically and politically unstable, thereby offering opportunities to the Communist movement. In France and Italy, large Communist parties grew stronger and refused to cooperate with established governments. In such circumstances, administration officials believed, the Soviet Union might easily intervene. Decisive action was needed, for as the new secretary of state, George Marshall, declared, "The patient is sinking while the doctors deliberate." Another motive for action was to bolster the European economy to provide markets for American goods. Excellent customers earlier, Western Europeans in the aftermath of the war were able to purchase less at a time when the United States was producing more.

Marshall revealed the administration's willingness to assist European recovery in a Harvard University commencement address in June 1947. He asked all troubled European nations to draw up an aid program that the United States could support, a program "directed not against any country or doctrine but against hunger, poverty, desperation, and chaos." Soviet-bloc countries were welcome to participate, Marshall announced, aware that their involvement was unlikely since they would have to disclose economic records to join, and Communist nations maintained rigorous secrecy about their internal affairs.

The proposed program would assist the ravaged nations, provide the United States with needed markets, and advance the nation's ideological aims. American aid, Marshall pointed out, would permit the "emergence of political and social conditions in which free institutions can exist." The Marshall Plan and the Truman Doctrine, Truman noted, were "two halves of the same walnut."

Responding quickly to Marshall's invitation, the Western European nations worked out the details of massive requests. In early 1948, Congress committed $13 billion over a period of four years to 16 co-operating nations. But not all Americans supported the Marshall Plan. Henry A. Wallace, former vice president and secretary of agriculture, who had broken with the administration over his effort to be more accommodating to the Soviet Union, called the scheme the "Martial Plan" and argued that it was another step toward war. Some members of Congress feared spreading American resources too thin. But most legislators approved, and the containment policy moved forward another step.

Closely related to the Marshall Plan was a concerted Western effort to integrate a rebuilt Germany into a reviving Europe. At Yalta, after debate over the past year about how to deal with Germany at the end of the war, Allied leaders had agreed to divide the defeated Nazi nation into four occupation zones (Soviet, American, British, and French), and at Potsdam they had resolved to treat Germany as a single economic unit and to require payment of reparations. At the same time, the capital city of Berlin, located in the Soviet zone, was divided into four sectors.

Allied leaders intended the division of both Germany and Berlin to be temporary, until a permanent peace treaty could be signed, but the lines of demarcation became rigid. A year after the end of the war, the balance of power in Europe had shifted. With the onset of the Cold War and the growing Soviet domination of Eastern Europe, the West became worried and moved to fill the vacuum in Central Europe to counter the Russian threat. In late 1946, the Americans and British merged their zones for economic purposes and began assigning administrative duties to Germans. By mid-1947, the process of rebuilding German industry in the combined Western sector was underway. Meanwhile, the same increasingly rigid separation into two separate cities occurred in Berlin.

Despite French fears, the United States sought to make Germany strong enough to anchor Europe. Secretary Marshall cautiously laid out the connections for Congress:

> The restoration of Europe involves the restoration of Germany. Without a revival of German production there can be no revival of Europe's economy. But we must be very careful to see that a revived Germany cannot again threaten the European community.

The Soviet Union was furious at what it regarded as a violation of the wartime agreement to act to-

An American and British airlift in 1948 brought badly needed supplies to West Berliners isolated by a Soviet blockade of the city. By refusing to allow the Western powers to reach the city, located within the Soviet zone, the Russians hoped to drive them from Berlin, but the airlift broke the blockade. *(Corbis-Bettmann)*

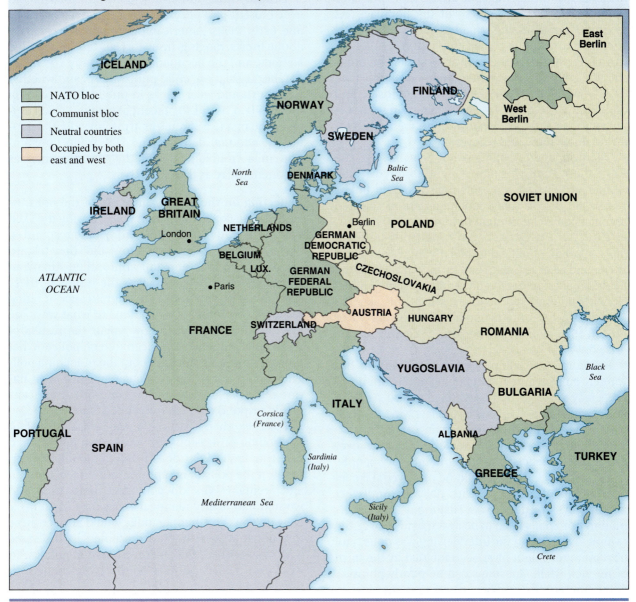

Cold War Europe in 1950

This map shows the rigid demarcation between East and West during the Cold War. Although there were a number of neutral countries in Europe, the other nations found themselves in a standoff, as each side tried to contain the possible advances of the other. The small insert map in the upper-right-hand corner shows the division of Berlin that paralleled the division of Germany itself after World War II. **Reflecting on the Past** How widespread was the policy of neutrality in Cold War Europe? How powerful was the NATO bloc? How easily could one side move against the other in divided Europe?

gether. In mid-1948, the Soviets became irritated at an effort to introduce a new currency for the combined Western zones, a first step toward the creation of a separate West German nation, that would include the western part of divided Berlin, located within the Soviet-controlled eastern part of Germany. A crisis erupted when the Soviets attempted to force the Western powers out of Berlin by refusing to allow them land access to their part of the city and banning all shipments through eastern Germany. What became known as the Berlin blockade threatened to create severe shortages,

Public Opinion Polls

In recent years, historians have used a new source of evidence: the public opinion poll. People have always been concerned with what others think, and leaders have often sought to frame their behavior according to the preferences of the populace. As techniques of assessing the mind of the public have become more sophisticated, the poll has emerged as an integral part of the analysis of social and political life. Polls now measure opinion on many questions—social, cultural, intellectual, political, and diplomatic. Because of polls' increasing importance, it is useful to know how to use them in an effort to understand and recover the past.

The principle of polling is not new. In 1824, the *Harrisburg Pennsylvanian* sought to predict the winner of that year's presidential race, and in the 1880s, the *Boston Globe* sent reporters to selected precincts on election night to forecast final returns. In 1916, *Literary Digest* began conducting postcard polls to predict political results. By the 1930s, Elmo Roper and George Gallup had further developed the field of market research and public opinion polling. Notwithstanding an embarrassing mistake by *Literary Digest* in predicting a Landon victory over FDR in 1936, polling had become a scientific enterprise by World War II.

According to Gallup, a poll is not magic but "merely an instrument for gauging public opinion," especially the views of those often unheard. As Elmo Roper said, the poll is "one of the few ways through which the so-called common man can be articulate." Polling, therefore, is a valuable way to recover the attitudes, beliefs, and voices of ordinary people.

Yet certain cautions should be observed. Like all instruments of human activity, polls are imperfect and may even be dangerous. Historians using information from polls need to be aware of how large the samples were, when the interviewing was done, and how opinions might have been molded by the form of the poll itself. Questions can be poorly phrased. Some hint at the desirable answer or plant ideas in the minds of those interviewed. Polls sometimes provide ambiguous responses that can be interpreted many ways. More seriously, some critics worry that human freedom itself is threatened by the pollsters' manipulative and increasingly accurate predictive techniques.

Despite these limitations, polls have become an ever-present part of American life. In the late 1940s and early 1950s, Americans were polled frequently about topics ranging from foreign aid, the United Nations, and the occupation of Germany and Japan to labor legislation, child punishment, and whether women should wear slacks in public (39 percent of men said no, as did 49 percent of women). Such topics as the first use of nuclear arms, presidential popularity, national defense, and U.S. troop intervention in a troubled area of the world remain as pertinent today as they were then.

Reflecting on the Past   A number of the polls included here deal with foreign policy during the Cold War in the early 1950s. How did people respond to Soviet nuclear capability? How did they regard Russian intentions and the appropriate American response? How do you analyze the results of these polls? What do you think is the significance of rating responses by levels of education? In what ways are the questions "loaded"? How might the results of these polls influence American foreign policy? What do you think is significant about the Indochina poll? These polls show the challenge-and-response nature of the Cold War. How do you think Americans would respond today to these questions?

Polls also shed light on domestic issues. Consider the poll on professions for young men and women taken in 1950. What does it tell us about the attitudes of the pollster on appropriate careers for men and women? Why do you think both men and women had nearly identical views on this subject? How do you think people today would answer these questions? Would they be presented in the same way? Also observe the poll on women in politics. To what extent have attitudes on this issue changed in the intervening years?

Foreign Policy Polls

December 2, 1949—Atom Bomb

Now that Russia has the atom bomb, do you think another war is more likely or less likely?

More likely	45%
Less likely	28%
Will make no difference	17%
No opinion	10%

BY EDUCATION
College

More likely	36%	Will make no difference	23%
Less likely	35%	No opinion	6%

High School

More likely	44%	Will make no difference	19%
Less likely	28%	No opinion	9%

Grade School

More likely	50%	Will make no difference	12%
Less likely	26%	No opinion	12%

May 1, 1950—National Defense

Do you think United States Government spending on national defense should be increased, decreased, or remain about the same?

Increased	63%
Same	24%
Decreased	7%
No opinion	6%

September 18, 1953—Indochina

The United States is now sending war materials to help the French fight the Communists in Indochina. Would you approve or disapprove of sending United States soldiers to take part in the fighting there?

Approve	8%
Disapprove	85%
No opinion	7%

January 11, 1950—Russia

As you hear and read about Russia these days, do you believe Russia is trying to build herself up to be the ruling power of the world—or is Russia just building up protection against being attacked in another war?

Rule the world	70%
Protect herself	18%
No opinion	12%

BY EDUCATION
College

Rule the world	73%
Protect herself	21%
No opinion	6%

High School

Rule the world	72%
Protect herself	18%
No opinion	10%

Grade School

Rule the world	67%
Protect herself	17%
No opinion	16%

February 12, 1951—Atomic Warfare

If the United States gets into an all-out war with Russia, do you think we should drop atom bombs on Russia first—or do you think we should use the atom bomb only if it is used on us?

Drop A-bomb first	66%
Only if used on us	19%
No opinion	15%

The greatest difference was between men and women—72% of the men questioned favored our dropping the bomb first, compared to 61% of the women.

Source: George H. Gallup, *The Gallup Poll: Public Opinion, 1935–1971*, vol. 2 (New York: Random House, 1972). © American Institute of Public Opinion.

Domestic Policy Polls

October 29, 1949—Women in Politics

If the party whose candidate you most often support nominated a woman for President of the United States, would you vote for her if she seemed qualified for the job?

Yes	48%
No	48%
No opinion	4%

BY SEX
Men

Yes	45%
No	50%
No opinion	5%

Women

Yes	51%
No	46%
No opinion	3%

BY POLITICAL AFFILIATION
Democrats

Yes	50%
No	48%
No opinion	2%

Republicans

Yes	46%
No	50%
No opinion	4%

Would you vote for a woman for Vice President of the United States if she seemed qualified for the job?

Yes	53%
No	43%
No opinion	4%

May 5, 1950—Most Important Problem

What do you think is the most important problem facing the entire country today?

War, threat of war	40%
Atomic bomb control	6%
Economic problems, living costs, inflation, taxes	15%
Strikes and labor troubles	4%
Corruption in government	3%
Unemployment	10%
Housing	3%
Communism	8%
Others	11%

July 12, 1950—Professions

Suppose a young man came to you and asked your advice about taking up a profession. Assuming that he was qualified to enter any of these professions, which one of them would you first recommend to him?

Doctor of medicine	29%
Government worker	6%
Engineer, builder	16%
Professor, teacher	5%
Business executive	8%
Banker	4%
Clergyman	8%
Dentist	4%
Lawyer	8%
Veterinarian	3%
None, don't know	9%

July 15, 1950—Professions

Suppose a young girl came to you and asked your advice about taking up a profession. Assuming that she was qualified to enter any of these professions, which one of them would you first recommend?

CHOICE OF WOMEN

Nurse	33%
Teacher	15%
Secretary	8%
Social service worker	8%
Dietitian	7%
Dressmaker	4%
Beautician	4%
Airline stewardess	3%
Actress	3%
Journalist	2%
Musician	2%
Model	2%
Librarian	2%
Medical, dental technician	1%
Others	2%
Don't know	4%

The views of men on this subject were nearly identical with those of women.

Source: George H. Gallup, *The Gallup Poll: Public Opinion, 1935–1971*, vol. 2 (New York: Random House, 1972). © American Institute of Public Opinion.

and even starvation, for the 2.5 million people in West Berlin.

An airlift launched by the United States and the British Royal Air Force flew supplies to the beleaguered Berliners. Over the next year, more than 200,000 flights provided 13,000 tons daily of food, fuel, and other necessary materials. The fliers called the effort "Operation Vittles," and it broke the Russian blockade. "Operation Little Vittles" provided bags of candy for Berlin children at the same time. "The difficult we do immediately," one American involved in the airlift proclaimed. "The impossible takes a little longer." The airlift proved to be a public relations disaster for the Soviet Union, a triumph for the West. The Soviets finally ended the blockade, but Berlin remained a focal point of conflict, and there were now two separate German states: the Federal Republic of Germany, or West Germany, and the German Democratic Republic, or East Germany. The episode also highlighted for the Western powers the need for a more cohesive way of working together to meet the Soviet threat.

The next major link in the containment strategy was the creation of a military alliance in Europe in 1949 to complement the economic program. After the Soviets tightened their control of Hungary and Czechoslovakia, the United States took the lead in establishing the North Atlantic Treaty Organization (NATO). Twelve nations formed the alliance, vowing that an attack against any one member would be considered an attack against all, to be met by appropriate armed force.

The Senate, long opposed to such military pacts, approved this time. In his presidential farewell address in 1796, George Washington had warned against "entangling alliances," and the United States had long heeded his warning. Now the nation established its first military treaty ties with Europe since the American Revolution. Congress also voted military aid for its NATO allies. The Cold War had softened longstanding American reluctance to become closely involved in European affairs.

Two dramatic events in 1949—the Communist victory in the Chinese civil war and the Russian detonation of an atomic device—shocked the United States. While the fall of China (described in the next section) was frightening, the erosion of the American atomic monopoly was horrifying. Although American scientists had understood that the Soviets could create a bomb of their own in several years, once the secret of the atom had been unlocked, many top policy makers believed it would take the less technologically advanced Russians at least a decade and a half. President Truman thought they might never be able to accomplish such a feat at all. Over the Labor Day weekend in 1949, an air force reconnaissance plane picked up air samples with a radioactivity content that revealed the Soviets had tested their own bomb, just four years after the United States had ushered in the atomic age. Now a nuclear arms race beckoned. As physical chemist Harold Urey observed on hearing the news: "There is only one thing worse than one nation having the atomic bomb—that's two nations having it."

The Chinese Communist victory and the Soviet bomb led the United States to define its aims still more specifically. Responding to Truman's request for a full-fledged review of U.S. foreign and defense policy, the National Security Council, organized in 1947 to provide policy coordination, produced a document called NSC-68, which shaped U.S. policy for the next 20 years.

NSC-68 built on the Cold War rhetoric of the Truman Doctrine, describing challenges facing the United States in cataclysmic terms. "The issues that face us are momentous," the paper said, "involving the fulfillment or destruction not only of this Republic but of civilization itself." Conflict between East and West, the document assumed, was unavoidable, for amoral Soviet objectives ran totally counter to U.S. aims. Negotiation was useless, for the Soviets could never be trusted to bargain in good faith.

NSC-68 then argued that if the United States hoped to meet the Russian challenge, it must increase defense spending from the $13 billion set for 1950 to as much as $50 billion per year and increase the percentage of its budget allotted to defense from 5 to 20 percent. The costs were huge but necessary if the free world was to survive. "In summary," the document declared, "we must . . . wrest the initiative from the Soviet Union, [and] confront it with convincing evidence of the determination and ability of the free world to frustrate the Kremlin design of a world dominated by its will."

Containment in the 1950s

Containment, the keystone of American policy throughout the Truman years, was the rationale for the Truman Doctrine, the Marshall Plan, NATO, and NSC-68. Because this policy required detailed and up-to-date information about Communist moves, the government relied increasingly on the Central Intelligence Agency (CIA). Established by the National Security Act of 1947, which had also created the National Security Council, the CIA conducted espionage in foreign lands, some of it aboveboard and visible, some of it secret and seldom seen. During the Eisenhower administration, Allen Dulles, brother of the secretary of state, headed the agency and provided close foreign policy coordination. With the president's approval, the CIA rearranged its priorities so that by 1957, 80 percent of its budget went toward covert activities. More and more, Eisenhower relied on clandestine CIA actions to undermine foreign governments, subsidize friendly newspapers in distant lands, and assist those who supported the American stance in the Cold War.

The civil rights movement that was gaining momentum in the 1950s had an impact on Cold War policy. American policymakers were aware of the impact of stories about racial discrimination in other nations, particularly nations moving toward independence in sub-Saharan Africa. Leaders sought to portray the struggle in the best possible light in propaganda aimed abroad.

At the same time, the administration reassessed the impact of the containment policy itself, especially in light of criticism that it was too cautious to counter the threat of communism. For most of Eisenhower's two terms, John Foster Dulles was secretary of state. A devout Presbyterian who hated

Secretary of State John Foster Dulles viewed the Cold War as a moral struggle between good and evil. Opposed to "godless Communism," he often appeared as a religious crusader for measures he believed were necessary for the survival of the free world. *(Corbis-Bettmann)*

atheistic communism, he sought to move beyond containment. Eager to counter the "Godless terrorism" of communism, Dulles wanted to commit the nation to a holy crusade to promote democracy and to free the countries under Soviet domination. Instead of advocating containment, the United States should make it "publicly known that it wants and expects liberation to occur." Dulles also advocated immediate retaliation in the face of hostile Soviet ventures: "There is one solution and only one: that is for the free world to develop the will and organize the means to retaliate instantly against open aggression by Red armies, so that, if it occurred anywhere, we could and would strike back where it hurts, by means of our own choosing."

Eisenhower's own rhetoric was equally strong. In his 1953 inaugural address, he declared, "Forces of good and evil are massed and armed and opposed as rarely before in history. Freedom is pitted against slavery, lightness against dark." Yet Eisenhower was more conciliatory, cautious, and realistic than Dulles and recognized the impossibility of changing the governments of the USSR's satellites. In mid-1953, when East Germans mounted anti-Soviet demonstrations, in a challenge that foreshadowed the revolt against communism three and a half decades later, the United States maintained its distance. In 1956, when Hungarian "freedom fighters" rose up against Russian domination, the United States again stood back as Soviet forces smashed the rebels and kept control of their satellite. Because Western action could have precipitated a more general conflict, Eisenhower refused to translate rhetoric into action. Throughout the 1950s, the policy of containment, largely as it had been defined earlier, remained in effect.

CONTAINMENT IN ASIA, THE MIDDLE EAST, AND LATIN AMERICA

In a dramatic departure from its history of noninvolvement, the United States extended the policy of containment to meet challenges around the globe. Colonial empires were disintegrating, and countries seeking and attaining their independence now found themselves caught in the middle of the superpower struggle. Decolonization became even more complicated as it became intertwined with the Cold War. Although the containment initiative had resulted from the effort to promote European stability, it now became worldwide. In Asia, the Middle East, and Latin America, the United States discovered the tremendous appeal of communism as a social and political system in emerging nations and found that ever greater efforts were required to advance American aims.

The Shock of the Chinese Revolution

The U.S. commitment to global containment became stronger with the Communist victory in the Chinese civil war in 1949. An ally during World War II, China had struggled against the Japanese, while simultaneously fighting a bitter civil war deeply rooted in the Chinese past—in widespread poverty, disease, oppression by the landlord class, and national humiliation at the hands of foreign powers. Mao Zedong (Mao Tse-tung)*, founder of a branch of the Communist party, gathered followers who wished to reshape China in a distinctive Marxist mold. Opposing the Communists were the Nationalists, led by Jiang Jieshi (Chiang Kai-shek) who wanted to preserve their power and governmental leadership. By the early 1940s, Jiang Jieshi's regime was exhausted, inefficient, and corrupt. Mao's movement, meanwhile, grew stronger during the Second World War as he opposed the Japanese invaders and won the loyalty of the peasantry. Mao finally prevailed, as Jiang fled in 1949 to the island of Taiwan (Formosa), where he nursed the improbable belief that he was still the rightful ruler of all China and would one day return.

The United States failed to understand issues that were part of the long internal conflict in China or the immense popular support Mao had garnered. As the Communist army moved toward victory, the *New York Times* termed Mao's party as a "nauseous force," a "compact little oligarchy dominated by Moscow's nominees." Mao's proclamation of the People's Republic of China on October 1, 1949, fanned fears of Russian domination, for he had already announced his regime's support for the Soviet Union against the "imperialist" United States.

Events in China caused near hysteria in America. Even before Mao's victory, the State Department issued a 1,000-page document entitled *The China White Paper*, which outlined the background of the struggle and argued that the United States was powerless to alter the results. "The unfortunate but inescapable fact is that the ominous result of the civil war in China was beyond the control of the government of the Untied States," the *White Paper* declared. Nothing that this country did or could have

Mao Zedong, chairman of the Chinese Communist party, was a powerful and popular leader who drove Jiang Jieshi from power in 1949 and established a stronghold over the People's Republic of China he created at that time. *(Corbis-Bettmann)*

done within the reasonable limits of its capabilities could have changed that result; nothing that was left undone by this country has contributed to it." Staunch anti-Communists responded by arguing that Truman and the United States were to blame for Jiang's defeat because they failed to provide him with sufficient support. Four senators called the *White Paper* a "whitewash of a wishful, do-nothing policy which has succeeded only in placing Asia in danger of Soviet conquest with its ultimate threat to the peace of the world and our own national security." Secretary of State Dean Acheson briefly considered granting diplomatic recognition to the new government but backed off after the Communists seized American property, harassed American citizens, and openly allied China with the USSR. Like other Americans, Acheson mistakenly viewed the Chinese as Soviet puppets.

Tension with China increased during the Korean War (1950–1953) and again in 1954 when Mao's government began shelling Nationalist positions on the offshore islands of Quemoy and Matsu. Eisenhower, now president, was committed to defending the Nationalists on Taiwan from a Communist attack, but he was unwilling to risk war over the islands.

---

* Chinese names are rendered in their modern *pinyin* spelling. At first occurrence, the older but perhaps more familiar spelling (usually Wade-Giles) is given in parentheses.

Again he showed an understanding of the need to proceed with caution.

Stalemate in the Korean War

The Korean War, on the other hand, highlighted growing U.S. intervention in Asia. Concern about China and determination to contain communism led the United States into a bloody foreign struggle. But American objectives were not always clear and were largely unrealized after three years of war.

The conflict in Korea stemmed from tensions lingering after World War II. Korea, long under Japanese control, hoped for independence after Japan's defeat. But the Allies temporarily divided Korea along the 38th parallel to expedite the transition to peace

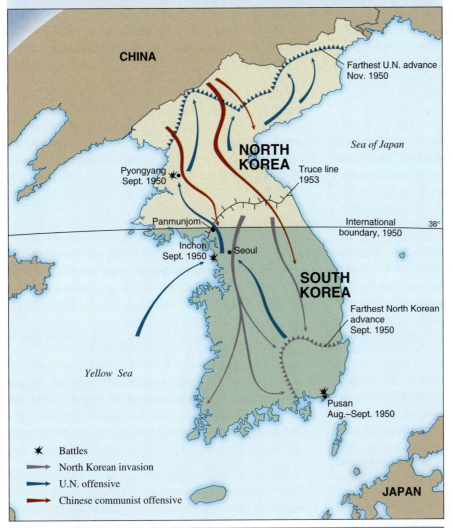

 The Korean War

This map shows the ebb and flow of the Korean War. North Korea crossed the 38th parallel first, then the UN offensive drove the North Koreans close to the Chinese border, and finally the Chinese Communists entered the war and drove the UN forces back below the 38th parallel. The armistice signed at Panmunjom in 1953 provided a dividing line very close to the prewar line. **Reflecting on the Past** How far did both North Korea and South Korea penetrate into the territory of the other nation? What role did China play in the Korean War?

with the rapid end to the Pacific struggle after the atomic bombs dropped on Japan. The arrangement allowed Soviet troops to accept Japanese surrender in the north while American forces did the same in the south. The Soviet–American line, initially intended as a matter of military convenience, hardened after 1945, just as a similar division became rigid in Germany. In time, the Soviets set up one Korean government in the north and the Americans another government in the south. Though the major powers left Korea by the end of the decade, they continued to support the regimes they had created. Each Korean government hoped to reunify the country on its own terms.

North Korea moved first. On June 25, 1950, North Korean forces crossed the 38th parallel and invaded South Korea. While the North Koreans followed Soviet-built tanks, they operated on their own initiative. Kim Il Sung, the North Korean leader, had visited Moscow earlier and gained Soviet acquiescence in the idea of an attack, but both the planning and the implementation occurred in Korea.

North Korea's action took the United States by surprise. Earlier, the nation had seemed reluctant to defend South Korea, but the Communist victory in China had changed the balance of power in Asia. Certain that Russia had masterminded the North Korean offensive and was testing the American policy of containment, Truman responded by telling the public that "the attack upon Korea makes it plain beyond all doubt that communism has passed beyond the use of subversion to conquer independent nations and will now use armed invasion and war." He later reflected in his memoirs: "In my generation, this was not the first occasion when the strong had attacked the weak . . . Communism was acting in Korea just as Hitler, Mussolini, and the Japanese had acted ten, fifteen, and twenty years earlier. . . . If this was allowed to go unchallenged it would mean a third world war, just as similar incidents had brought on the second world war."

Truman readied American naval and air forces and directed General Douglas MacArthur, head of the American occupation in Japan, to supply South Korea. The United States also went to the United Nations Security Council. With the Soviet Union absent in protest of the UN's refusal to admit the People's Republic of China, despite its victory in the Chinese civil war, the United States secured a unanimous resolution branding North Korea an aggressor, then another resolution calling on members of the organization to assist South Korea in repelling aggression and restoring peace. This was the largest UN operation to date, and MacArthur became leader of all UN forces. While the United States and South Korea provided over 90 percent of the manpower, 15 other nations were involved in the UN effort.

Air and naval forces, then ground forces, went into battle south of the 38th parallel. Following a daring amphibious invasion that pushed the North Koreans back to the former boundary line, UN troops crossed the 38th parallel, hoping to reunify Korea under an American-backed government. Despite Chinese signals that this movement toward their border threatened their security, the UN troops pressed on. In October, Chinese troops appeared briefly in battle, then disappeared. The next month, the Chinese mounted a full-fledged counterattack, which pushed the UN forces back below the dividing line.

The resulting stalemate provoked a bitter struggle between MacArthur and his civilian commander in chief. The brilliant but arrogant general called for retaliatory air strikes against China. He faced opposition from General Omar Bradley, chairman of the Joint Chiefs of Staff, who declared, "Frankly, in the opinion of the Joint Chiefs of Staff, this strategy would involve us in the wrong war, at the wrong place, at the wrong time, with the wrong enemy," and from President Truman, who remained committed to conducting a limited war. MacArthur's statements, issued from the field, finally went too far. In April 1951, he argued that the American approach in Korea was wrong and asserted publicly that "there is no substitute for victory." Truman had no choice but to relieve the general for insubordination and to replace him with General Matthew Ridgeway as head of both the American military effort and the UN command. The decision outraged many Americans. After the stunning victories of World War II, limited war was frustrating and difficult to understand.

The Korean War dragged on into Eisenhower's presidency. Campaigning in 1952, Ike promised to go to Korea, and three weeks after his election, he did so. When UN truce talks bogged down in May 1953, the fighting intensified. Anthony Ebron, a marine corporal, noted that "those last few days were pretty brutal." In a final assault, "we shot off so much artillery the ground shook." Meanwhile, the new administration privately threatened the Chinese with the use of atomic weapons. This brought about renewed UN negotiations, and on July 27, 1953, an armistice was signed. The Republican administration had succeeded where the preceding Democratic administration had failed: after three long years, the unpopular war had ended.

American involvement carried a heavy price: over 33,000 Americans killed in action and more than 142,000 American casualties in all. The other 15 UN nations involved in the struggle accounted for another 17,000 casualties. But those figures

General Douglas MacArthur was a superb tactician but a supremely egotistical commander of UN forces in Korea, where this picture was taken in the first year of the Korean War. Eventually his arrogance led him to challenge Truman's policy, whereupon the president relieved him of his command. *(Carl Mydans/TimePix)*

part of all military units. Their successful performance led to acceptance of military integration.

The Korean War years also saw military expenditures soar from $13 billion in 1950 to about $47 billion three years later, as defense spending followed the guidelines proposed in NSC-68. In the process, the United States accepted the demands of permanent mobilization. Whereas the military absorbed less than one-third of the federal budget in 1950, a decade later, it took half. More than a million military personnel were stationed around the world. At home, an increasingly powerful military establishment became closely tied to corporate and scientific communities and created a military–industrial complex that employed 3.5 million Americans by 1960.

The Korean War had important political effects as well. It led the United States to sign a peace treaty with Japan in September 1951 and to rely on that nation to maintain the balance of power in the Pacific. At the same time, the struggle poisoned relations with the People's Republic of China, which remained unrecognized by the United States, and ensured a diplomatic standoff that lasted more than 20 years.

paled beside as many as 2 million Koreans dead and countless others wounded and maimed.

Some of the casualties came from the use of napalm, a highly flammable explosive even more widely used in the war in Vietnam (see next section). A BBC journalist described napalm's effects:

> In front of us a curious figure was standing, a little crouched, legs straddled, arms held out from his sides. He had no eyes, and the whole of his body, nearly all of which was visible through tatters of burnt rags, was covered with a hard black crust speckled with yellow pus. . . . He had to stand because he was no longer covered with a skin, but with a crust-like crackling which broke easily.

The war significantly changed American attitudes and institutions. For the first time, American forces fought in racially integrated units. As commander in chief, Truman had ordered the integration of the armed forces in 1948, over the opposition of many generals, and African Americans became

The Korean War disrupted numerous families in both the north and south and led them to leave their homes. Here fleeing Korean civilians, with the belongings they could carry with them, pass U.S. soldiers as the bitter struggle dragged on. *(UPI/Corbis-Bettmann)*

Vietnam: The Roots of Conflict

The commitment to stopping the spread of communism led to the massive U.S. involvement in Vietnam. That struggle tore the United States apart, wrought enormous damage in Southeast Asia, and finally forced a reevaluation of America's Cold War policies.

The roots of the war extended far back in the past. Indochina—the part of Southeast Asia that included Vietnam, Laos, and Cambodia—had been a French colony since the mid-nineteenth century. During World War II, Japan occupied the region but allowed French collaborators to administer internal affairs. An independence movement, led by the Communist organizer and revolutionary Ho Chi Minh, sought to expel the Japanese conquerors from Vietnam. In 1945, the Allied powers faced the decision of how to deal with Ho and his nationalist movement.

Franklin Roosevelt, like Woodrow Wilson, believed in self-determination and wanted to end colonialism. But France was determined to regain its colony as a way of preserving its status as a great power, and by the time of his death, Roosevelt had backed down. Meanwhile, Ho Chi Minh established the Democratic Republic of Vietnam in 1945. The new government's Declaration of Independence hearkened back to its American counterpart. It declared: "All men are created equal. They are endowed by their Creator with certain inalienable rights, among these are Life, Liberty and the pursuit of Happiness." Although the new government enjoyed widespread popular support, the United States refused to recognize it.

A long, bitter struggle broke out between French and Vietnamese forces, which became entangled with the larger Cold War. President Truman was less concerned about ending colonialism than with checking Soviet power. He needed France to balance the Soviets in Europe, where he wanted French support for America's policy in Germany and as a member of NATO, and that meant cooperating with France in Vietnam.

Although Ho did not have close ties to the Soviet Union and was committed to his independent nationalist crusade, Truman and his advisers, who saw communism as a monolithic force, assumed wrongly that Ho took orders from Moscow. Hence, in 1950, the United States formally recognized the French puppet government in Vietnam, and by 1954, the United States was paying over three-quarters of the cost of France's Indochina war.

After Eisenhower took office, France's position in Southeast Asia deteriorated. Secretary of State Dulles was eager to assist the French, and the chairman of the Joint Chiefs of Staff even contemplated using nuclear weapons, but Eisenhower refused to intervene directly. He understood the lack of American support for intervention in that far-off land. Senator John F. Kennedy spoke for many of his congressional colleagues when he declared in 1954: "I am frankly of the belief that no amount of American military assistance in Indochina can conquer an enemy which is everywhere and at the same time nowhere, 'an enemy of the people' which has the sympathy and covert support of the people." As a French fortress at Dien Bien Phu in the north of Vietnam finally fell to Ho's forces, an international conference in Geneva sought to prevent Ho Chi Minh from gaining control of the entire country. The final declaration of the conference divided Vietnam along the 17th parallel, with elections promised in 1956 to unify the country and determine its political fate.

Two separate Vietnamese states emerged. Ho Chi Minh held power in the north, while in the south, Ngo Dinh Diem, a fierce anti-Communist who had

Ho Chi Minh waged a long struggle first against France, then Japan, and finally the United States for the independence of Vietnam. He is pictured with children to convey the impression that he is the father of his country. *(Library of Congress [LC-USZ62-126864])*

been in exile in the United States, returned to form a government. Diem, a Vietnamese nationalist who had served in the colonial bureaucracy earlier, had proclaimed his support for Vietnamese independence while in America. Now he enjoyed the full support of the United States, which saw him as a way of securing stability in Southeast Asia and avoiding further communist incursions. When he decided not to hold the elections mandated in the Geneva accord, the United States backed him in that decision. In the next few years, American aid increased and military advisers—675 by the time Eisenhower left office—began to assist the South Vietnamese. The United States had taken its first steps toward direct involvement in a ruinous war halfway around the world that would escalate out of control.

The Creation of Israel and Its Impact on the Middle East

The creation of the state of Israel became intertwined with larger Cold War issues. Jews had longed for a homeland for years, and the Zionist movement had sought a place in Palestine, in the Middle East, since the latter part of the nineteenth century. Jewish settlers who began to gravitate to Palestine were not welcomed by the Turks, who dominated the region, or by the British, who exercised control after World War I.

Then the Holocaust—and the slaughter of 6 million Jews—during World War II created new pressure for a Jewish state. The unwillingness—and inability—of the Western powers to intervene in time to stop the Nazi genocide created a groundswell of support, particularly among American Jews, for a Jewish homeland in the Arab-dominated Middle East.

In 1948, the fledgling United Nations attempted to partition Palestine into an Arab state and a Jewish state. Truman officially recognized the new state of Israel 15 minutes after it was proclaimed. But American recognition could not end bitter animosities between Arabs, who believed they had been robbed of their territory, and Jews, who felt they had finally regained a homeland after the horrors of the Holocaust. As Americans looked on, Arab forces from Egypt, Trans-Jordan, Syria, Lebanon, and Iraq invaded Israel, in the first of a continuing series of conflicts that dominated the Middle East in the second half of the twentieth century. The Israelis, fighting for the survival of the new nation, won the war and added territory to what the UN had given them. But other struggles, in 1967, and then again in 1973, remained to be fought with adversaries who did not recognize Israel's right to exist.

While sympathetic to Israel, the United States tried at the same time to maintain stability in the rest of the region. The Middle East had tremendous strategic importance as the supplier of oil for industrialized nations. In 1953, the CIA helped the Iranian army overthrow the government of Mohammed Mossadegh, which had nationalized oil wells formerly under British control, and placed the shah of Iran securely on the throne. After the coup, British and American companies regained command of the wells, and thereafter the U.S. government provided military assistance to the shah.

As it cultivated close ties with Israel, the United States also tried to maintain the friendship of oil-rich Arab states or, at the very least, to prevent them from falling into the Soviet orbit of influence. In Egypt, the policy ran into trouble when Arab nationalist General Gamal Abdel Nasser planned a huge dam on the Nile River to produce electric power. Nasser hoped to follow a middle course by proclaiming his country's neutrality in the Cold War. Although Dulles offered U.S. financial support for the Aswan Dam project, Nasser also began discussions with the Soviet Union. Furious, the secretary of state, who believed that neutralism was immoral, withdrew the American offer. Left without funds for the dam, in July 1956, Nasser seized and nationalized the British-controlled Suez Canal and closed it to Israeli ships. Now Great Britain was enraged. All of Europe feared that Nasser would disrupt the flow of oil from the Middle East.

In the fall, Israeli, British, and French military forces invaded Egypt. Eisenhower, who had not been consulted, was irate. He was especially angry at British Prime Minister Anthony Eden, whom he had known since World War II. "Bombs, by God," he roared. "What does Anthony think he's doing?" When told that paratroopers were about to land near the canal, he said, "I think it's the biggest error of our time, outside of losing China." Realizing that the attack might push Nasser into Moscow's arms, the United States sponsored a UN resolution condemning the attack and Dulles persuaded other nations not to send petroleum to England and France as long as they remained in Egypt. These actions convinced the invaders to withdraw.

Before long, the United States again intervened in the Middle East. Concerned about the region's stability, the president declared in 1957, in what came to be called the Eisenhower Doctrine, that "the existing vacuum in the Middle East must be filled by the United States before it is filled by Russia." A year later, in line with a congressional resolution that committed the United States to stop suspected Communist aggression, he authorized

The Middle East in 1949

This map shows the extensive oil reserves that made the Middle East such an important region; it also shows the shifting boundaries of Israel as a result of the war following its independence in 1948. Notice how Israel's size increased after its victory in the first of a series of Middle Eastern conflicts. **Reflecting on the Past** Why was Middle Eastern oil such an important commodity to the rest of the world? How secure was Israel as it confronted the other Middle Eastern nations? How much territory did Israel gain in the conflict after the partition in 1948?

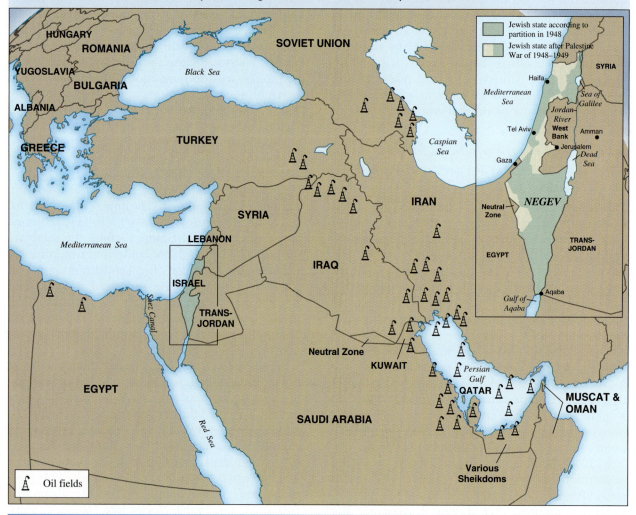

the landing of 14,000 soldiers in Lebanon to prop up a right-wing government challenged from within.

Restricting Revolt in Latin America

The Cold War also led to intervention in Latin America, the United States' traditional sphere of influence. In 1954, Dulles sniffed Communist activity in Guatemala, and Eisenhower ordered CIA support for a coup aimed at ousting the elected government of reform-minded Colonel Jacobo Arbenz Guzmán. It trained and equipped Guatemalans to overthrow the legitimate regime, which had appropriated property of the American-owned United Fruit

Company. The right-wing takeover succeeded, established a military dictatorship that responded to U.S. wishes, and restored the property of the United Fruit Company. These actions demonstrated again the shortsighted American commitment to stability and private investment, whatever the internal effect or ultimate cost. The interference in Guatemala fed anti-American feeling throughout Latin America.

In 1959, when Fidel Castro overthrew the dictatorship of Fulgencio Batista in Cuba, the shortsightedness of American policy became even clearer. Nationalism and the thrust for social reform were powerful forces in Latin America, as in the rest of the Third World formerly dominated by European powers. As Milton Eisenhower, Ike's brother and adviser, pointed out: "Revolution is inevitable in Latin America. The people are angry. They are shackled to the past with bonds of ignorance, injustice, and poverty. And they no longer accept as universal or inevitable the oppressive prevailing order." But when Castro confiscated American property in Cuba, the Eisenhower administration cut off exports and severed diplomatic ties. In response, Cuba turned to the Soviet Union for support.

ATOMIC WEAPONS AND THE COLD WAR

Throughout the Cold War, the atomic bomb was a crucial factor that hung over all diplomatic discussions and military initiatives. Atomic weapons were destructive enough, but when the United States and the Soviet Union both developed hydrogen bombs, an age of overkill began.

Sharing the Secret of the Bomb

The United States, with British aid, had built the first atomic bomb and attempted to conceal the project from its wartime ally, the Soviet Union. Soviet spies,

however, discovered that the Americans were working on the bomb, and, even before the war was over, the Soviets had initiated a program to create a bomb of their own.

The question of sharing the atomic secret was considered in the immediate postwar years. Just before he retired, Secretary of War Henry L. Stimson favored cooperating with the Soviet Union rather than acting unilaterally. Recognizing the futility of trying to cajole the Russians while "having this weapon ostentatiously on our hip," he warned that "their suspicions and their distrust of our purposes and motives will increase." Only mutual accommodation could bring international cooperation.

For a time, the administration contemplated a system of international arms control. Realizing by early 1946 that mere possession of the bomb by the United States did not make the Russians more malleable, Truman decided to offer the United Nations a proposal for an international agency to control atomic energy. When the Russians balked at a plan they argued favored the United States, negotiations collapsed.

The United States gave up on the process of sharing atomic secrets. Intent on retaining the technological advantage until the creation of a "foolproof method of control," Truman endorsed the Atomic Energy Act, passed by Congress in 1946. It established the Atomic Energy Commission (AEC) to supervise all atomic energy development in the United States and, under the tightest security, to authorize all nuclear activity in the nation at large. It also opened the way to a nuclear arms race once Russia developed its own bomb.

Nuclear Proliferation

As the atomic bomb found its way into popular culture, Americans at first showed more excitement than fear. In Los Angeles, the "Atombomb Dancers" wiggled at the Burbank Burlesque Theater. In 1946, the Buchanan Brothers released a record called "Atomic Power," noting the brimstone fire from heaven that was "given by the mighty hand of God." David E. Lilienthal, first chairman of the Atomic Energy Commission, recalled that the atom "had us bewitched. It was so gigantic, so terrible, so beyond the power of the imagination to embrace, that it seemed to be the ultimate fact. It would either destroy us all or it would bring about the millennium."

Anxiety lurked beneath the exuberance, though it did not surface dramatically as long as the United States held a nuclear monopoly. Then, in September 1949, when Americans learned that the Soviet Union had tested its own bomb, the

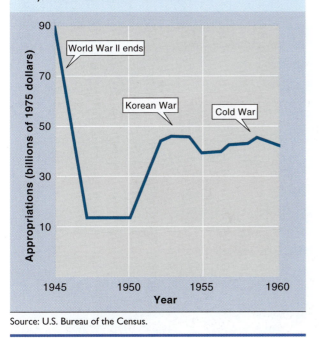

Defense Expenditures, 1945–1960

Defense spending plummeted after World War II, only to quadruple with the onset of the Korean War. After that increase, spending levels never dropped dramatically, even after the end of the war.

Source: U.S. Bureau of the Census.

American public was shocked. Suddenly the security of being the world's only atomic power had vanished. People wondered whether the Soviet test foreshadowed a nuclear attack and speculated when it might come. At the Capitol in Washington, D.C., members of the Joint Committee on Atomic Energy struggled to make sense of the announcement of the Soviet bomb. When a thunderclap startled them, someone in the room said, "My God, that must be Number Two!" The editors of the *Bulletin of the Atomic Scientists,* the nation's foremost publication dealing with nuclear affairs, moved the minute hand of the "doomsday clock" on the cover of the journal from seven minutes before midnight to three minutes before midnight to reflect their fear of proliferation.

In early 1950, Truman authorized the development of a new hydrogen superbomb, potentially far more devastating than the atomic bomb. Edward Teller, a physicist on the Manhattan Project, was intrigued with the novelty of the puzzle. During the war, as other scientists struggled with the problem of fission—splitting the atom apart—he had contemplated the possibility that fusion—joining atoms together in a reaction like that on the surface of the sun—might release energy in even greater amounts. Now he had his chance to prove whether it would work.

By 1953, both the United States and the Soviet Union had unlocked the secret of the hydrogen bomb. A far more powerful reaction, sparked by an ordinary atomic bomb, could now do far more damage than ever before. As kilotons gave way to mega-

tons, the stakes rose higher and higher. The government remained quiet about MIKE, the first test of a hydrogen device in the Pacific Ocean in 1952, but rumors circulated that it had created a hole in the ocean floor 175 feet deep and a mile wide. Later, after the 1954 BRAVO test, Lewis Strauss, Atomic Energy Commission chairman, admitted that "an H-bomb can be made . . . large enough to take out a city," even New York. Then, in 1957, shortly after the news that the Soviets had successfully tested their first intercontinental ballistic missile (ICBM), Americans learned that the Soviets had lifted the first satellite, *Sputnik*, into outer space—with a rocket that could also deliver a hydrogen bomb.

The discovery of radioactive fallout added another dimension to the nuclear dilemma. Fallout became publicly known after the BRAVO blast in 1954 showered Japanese fishermen on a ship called the *Lucky Dragon* 85 miles away with radioactive dust. They became ill with radiation sickness, and several months later, one of the seamen died. The Japanese, who had been the first to experience the effects of atomic weapons, were outraged and alarmed to be the first victims of the hydrogen bomb. Despite the contention of Atomic Energy Commission chairman Lewis Strauss that the *Lucky Dragon* was not a fishing boat but a "Red spy outfit" monitoring the test, the American ambassador to Japan apologized to the Japanese and the United States eventually provided financial compensation. But the damage was done. Everywhere people began to realize the terrible consequences of the new weapons. Fallout had become a serious interna-

The spectacular mushroom cloud resulting from an atomic blast became a familiar sight as it accompanied hundreds of nuclear tests in the postwar years. This picture shows the hydrogen blast at Eniwetok in the Pacific in 1952. While the cloud was beautiful, it also filled the atmosphere with fallout that contaminated people, plants, and animals below. *(National Archives)*

The Cold War moved into space when the Soviet Union launched the first artificial satellite, known as *Sputnik* (fellow traveler). The satellite, weighing 184 pounds, traveled in an elliptical orbit, ranging from about 140 to 560 miles above the earth. Americans, who prided themselves on their technological expertise, were stunned. *(NASA)*

tional problem—in the words of physicist Ralph Lapp, "a peril to humanity."

Authors in both the scientific and the popular press focused attention on radioactive fallout. Radiation, Lapp observed, "cannot be felt and possesses all the terror of the unknown. It is something which evokes revulsion and helplessness—like a bubonic plague." Nevil Shute's best-selling 1957 novel *On the Beach,* and the film that followed, also sparked public awareness and fear. The story described a war that released so much radioactive waste that all life in the Northern Hemisphere disappeared, while the Southern Hemisphere awaited the same deadly fate. Worried about public opinion around the world, the Eisenhower administration sought to counter the film's pessimistic message both at home and abroad. The assumption that a war would wipe out all life was untrue, officials argued, as was the image of people simply passively awaiting death. In 1959, when *Consumer Reports,* the popular magazine that tested and compared various products, warned of the contamination of milk with the radioactive isotope strontium-90, the public grew even more alarmed.

The discovery of fallout provoked a shelter craze. Bob Russell, a Michigan sheriff, declared that "to build a new home in this day and age without including such an obvious necessity as a fallout shelter would be like leaving out the bathroom 20 years ago." *Good Housekeeping* magazine carried a full-page editorial in November 1958 urging the construction of family shelters. More and more companies advertised ready-made shelters. A firm in Miami reported numerous inquiries about shelters costing between $1,795 and $3,895, depending on capacity, and planned 900 franchises. *Life* magazine

in 1955 featured an "H-Bomb Hideaway" for $3,000. By late 1960, the Office of Civil and Defense Mobilization estimated that a million family shelters had been built.

The Nuclear West

The bomb stimulated more than just shelter building. It sparked an enormous increase in defense spending and created a huge nuclear industry, particularly in the West. Contractors liked the region because of its antiunion attitudes; labor stability, they argued, would make it easier to meet government deadlines.

During World War II, a number of the Manhattan Project's major centers were located in the West. The plant at Hanford, Washington, was one of the most important producers of fissionable material, and the first atomic weapon had been produced at Los Alamos, New Mexico. Development in this area expanded after the war. Hanford continued to produce plutonium, a facility outside Denver made plutonium triggers for thermonuclear bombs, the new Sandia National Laboratory in Albuquerque provided the production engineering of nuclear bombs, and the Los Alamos laboratory remained a major atomic research center. In 1951, the United States opened the Nevada Test Site, 65 miles north of Las Vegas, to try out nuclear weapons, and the facility had a major impact on the city. The 1,350 square-mile tract of uninhabited land (larger than the state of Rhode Island) was the site of approximately 100 above-ground tests that generated extensive attention. The Chamber of Commerce offered schedules of test shots, and the mushroom cloud became the logo for the Southern Nevada telephone directory. Utah residents often rose early

Americans sought protection from fallout in shelters that civil defense authorities told them would be just like home. Here a typical family in 1955 practices in the Kiddie Kokoon, which has beds and supplies of food and water to last for several weeks. (*J. Edward Bailey/TimePix*)

to watch atomic flashes and years later recalled "the beautiful mushroom as it'd come up, [and] change colors." Californians could sometimes see the light.

Songwriter Tom Lehrer highlighted the West in the song "The Wild West is Where I Want to Be" in his first album in 1953. The first verse went:

> *Along the trail you'll find me lopin'*
> *Where the spaces are wide open,*
> *In the land of the old A.E.C.*
> *Where the scenery's attractive,*
> *And the air is radioactive,*
> *Oh, the wild west is where I want to be.*

Defense spending promoted other development as well. Naval commands had headquarters in Seattle, San Francisco, San Diego, and Honolulu. Radar sites, aimed at tracking incoming missiles, stretched all the way up to Alaska. The Boeing Company, located in Seattle, stimulated tremendous development in that city as it produced B-47 and B-52 airplanes that were the U.S. Air Force's main delivery vehicles for nuclear bombs.

"Massive Retaliation"

As Americans grappled with the implications of nuclear weapons, government policy came to depend increasingly on an atomic shield. The Soviet success in building its own bomb encouraged the conviction that America had to beef up its atomic forces. Truman authorized the development of a nuclear arsenal but also stressed conventional forms of defense. Eisenhower, however, found the effort fragmented and wasteful. Concerned with controlling the budget and cutting taxes, his ad-

ministration decided to rely on atomic weapons rather than combat forces as the key to American defense.

Secretary of State Dulles developed the policy of threatening "massive retaliation." The United States, he declared, was willing and ready to use nuclear weapons against Communist aggression on whatever targets it chose. The policy allowed troop cutbacks and promised to be cost-effective by giving "more bang for the buck."

Massive retaliation provided for an all-or-nothing response, leaving no middle course, no alternatives between nuclear war and retreat. Still, it reflected Dulles's willingness to threaten direct retaliation to deter Soviet challenges around the world. "The ability to get to the verge without getting into war is the necessary art," he said. "If you cannot master it you inevitably get into war." Critics called the policy "brinkmanship" and wondered what would happen if the line was crossed in the new atomic age. Eisenhower himself was horrified when he saw reports indicating that a coordinated atomic attack could leave a nation "a smoking, radiating ruin at the end of two hours." With characteristic caution, he did his best to ensure that the rhetoric of massive retaliation did not lead to war.

Atomic Protest

As the arms race spiraled, critics demanded that it end. In 1956, Democratic presidential candidate Adlai Stevenson pointed to "the danger of poisoning the atmosphere" and called for a halt to nuclear tests. Eisenhower did not respond, but Vice President Richard Nixon called Stevenson's suggestion "catastrophic nonsense," while Dulles minimized the hazards of radiation by arguing, "From a health standpoint, there is greater danger from wearing a wrist watch with a luminous dial."

In 1957, activists organized SANE, the National Committee for a Sane Nuclear Policy. One of its most effective advertisements featured internationally known pediatrician Benjamin Spock, looking down at a little girl with a frown on his face. "Dr. Spock is worried," the caption read, and the text below amplified on his concern. "I *am* worried," he said, "not so much about the effect of past tests but at the prospect of endless future ones. As the tests multiply, so will the damage to children—here and around the world."

Several years later, women who had worked with SANE took the protest movement a step further. As one activist later recalled, "This movement was inspired and motivated by mothers' love for children. . . . When they were putting their breakfasts on the table, they saw not only Wheaties and milk, but they also saw Strontium 90 and Iodine 131." To challenge continued testing, which dropped such

lethal elements on all inhabitants of the globe, the protesters called on women throughout the country to suspend normal activities for a day and strike for peace. An estimated 50,000 women marched in 60 communities around the nation. Their slogans included "Let the Children Grow" and "End the Arms Race—Not the Human Race."

Pressure from many groups produced a political breakthrough and sustained it for a time. The superpowers began a voluntary moratorium on testing in the fall of 1958. It lasted until the Soviet Union resumed testing in September 1961 and the United States began again the following March.

THE COLD WAR AT HOME

The Cold War also affected domestic affairs and led to the creation of an internal loyalty program that seriously violated civil liberties. Americans had feared radical subversion before and after the Russian Revolution (see Chapters 16, 21, and 22). Now the Soviet Union appeared ever more ominous in confrontations around the globe. Maps (such as the one on page 937) showed half the world colored red to dramatize the spread of the monolithic Communist system. As Americans began to suspect Communist infiltration at home, some determined to root out all traces of communism inside the United States.

Truman's Loyalty Program

When the Truman administration mobilized support for its containment program in the immediate postwar years, its rhetoric became increasingly shrill. Spokesmen contrasted American virtues with diabolical Russian designs. For Truman, the issue confronting the world was one of "tyranny or freedom." Attorney General J. Howard McGrath spoke of "many Communists in America," each bearing the "germ of death for society."

When administration officials perceived an internal threat to security after the discovery of classified documents in the offices of the allegedly pro-Communist *Amerasia* magazine, Truman appointed a Temporary Commission on Employee Loyalty. Republican gains in the midterm elections of 1946 led him to try to head off a congressional loyalty probe that could be used for partisan ends, especially since Republicans had accused the Democrats of being "soft on communism."

On the basis of the report from his temporary commission, Truman established a new Federal Employee Loyalty Program by executive decree in 1947. In the same week that he announced his containment policy, Truman ordered the FBI to check its

SANE tried to get the United States, and the rest of the world, to stop testing nuclear weapons and dumping huge amounts of fallout in the atmosphere. This newspaper advertisement, which appeared in 1962, was part of the larger effort to make the world a safer place. *(The Peace Collection, Swarthmore College, PA)*

files for evidence of subversive activity and to bring suspects before a new Civil Service Commission Loyalty Review Board. Initially, the program included safeguards and assumed that a challenged employee was innocent until proven guilty. But as the Loyalty Review Board assumed more power, it ignored individual rights. Employees about whom there was any doubt, regardless of proof, found themselves under attack, with little chance to fight back. Val Lorwin, whose story was told at the start of the chapter, was just one of many victims.

The Truman loyalty program examined several million employees and found grounds for dismissing only several hundred. Nonetheless, it bred the unwarranted fear of subversion, led to the assumption that absolute loyalty could be achieved, and legitimated investigatory tactics that were used irresponsibly to harm innocent individuals.

The Congressional Loyalty Program

While Truman's loyalty probe investigated government employees, Congress launched its own program. In the early years of the Cold War, the law became increasingly explicit about what was illegal in the United States. The Smith Act of 1940 made it a crime to advocate or teach the forcible overthrow of the U.S. government. The McCarran Internal Security Act of 1950, passed over Truman's veto, further circumscribed Communist activity by declaring that it was illegal to conspire to act in a way that would "substantially contribute" to establishing a totalitarian dictatorship in America and by requiring members of Communist organizations to register with the attorney general. The American Communist party, which had never been large, even in the Depression, declined still further. Membership, numbering about 80,000 in 1947, fell to 55,000 in 1950 and to 25,000 in 1954.

The investigations of the House Un-American Activities Committee (HUAC) contributed to that decline. Intent on rooting out subversion, HUAC probed the motion picture industry in 1947, claiming that left-wing sympathies of writers, actors, directors, and producers were corrupting the American public. A frequent refrain in congressional hearings was "Are you now or have you ever been a member of the Communist Party?" Altogether, HUAC called 19 Hollywood figures to testify. When 10 of them—including noted writers Ring Lardner, Jr., and Dalton Trumbo—refused to answer such accusatory questions by invoking their constitutional right to remain silent, Congress issued contempt citations, and they went to prison and served sentences ranging from six months to

one year. At that point, Hollywood knuckled under and blacklisted anyone with even a marginally questionable past. Hollywood executives issued a statement that declared: "We will not knowingly employ a Communist nor a member of any party or groups which advocates the overthrow Government of the United States by force or by illegal or unconstitutional means." No one so accused could find jobs at the studios anymore.

Congress made a greater splash with the Hiss-Chambers case. Whittaker Chambers, a former Communist who had broken with the party in 1938 and had become a successful editor of *Time* magazine, charged that Alger Hiss had been a Communist in the 1930s. Hiss was a distinguished New Dealer who had served in the Agriculture Department before becoming assistant secretary of state. Now out of the government, he was president of the Carnegie Endowment for International Peace. He denied Chambers's charge, and the matter might have died there had not freshman congressman Richard Nixon taken up the case. Nixon finally extracted from Hiss an admission that he had once known Chambers, though by a different name. Outside the hearing room, Hiss sued Chambers for libel, whereupon Chambers changed his story and charged that Hiss was a Soviet spy. Dramatically, he produced a number of rolls of microfilm that had been hidden in a hollowed-out pumpkin on his farm. Some of the documents on microfilm were State Department documents typed on a typewriter Hiss had once owned.

Hiss was indicted for perjury for lying under oath about his former relationship with Chambers, for the statute of limitations prevented prosecution for espionage. The case made front-page news around the nation. Millions of Americans read about the case at around the same time they learned of Russia's first atomic explosion and the final victory of the Communist revolution in China. Chambers appeared unstable and changed his story several times. Yet Hiss, too, seemed contradictory in his testimony and never adequately explained how he had such close ties with members of the Communist party or how some copies of stolen State Department documents had been typed on his typewriter. The first trial ended in a hung jury; the second trial, in January 1950, sent Hiss to prison for almost four years.

For years, Americans debated whether or not Hiss was guilty as charged. He continued to assert his innocence for the remainder of his life, although evidence made available much later makes his involvement clear.

For many Americans, the Hiss case proved that a Communist threat indeed existed in the United

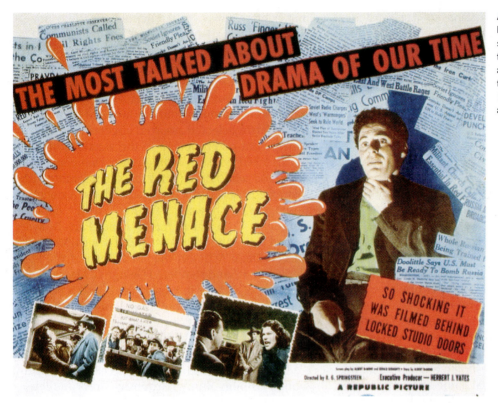

As Hollywood implemented its blacklist of anyone deemed sympathetic to communism, filmmakers also began to make a number of anti-Communist films, such as *The Red Menace* in 1949, to show their own loyalty. *(Michael Barson Collection)*

As Whittaker Chambers (sitting on the left) confronted Alger Hiss, members of Congress as well as other Americans wondered which one of them was lying and which one was telling the truth. Newspaper headlines dramatized the confrontation, as the public followed the case with rapt attention. *(Library of Congress [LC-USZ62-126777])*

States. It "forcibly demonstrated to the American people that domestic Communism was a real and present danger to the security of the nation," Richard Nixon declared after using the case to win a Senate seat from California and then the Republican vice presidential nomination in 1952. The case also led people to question the Democratic approach to the problem. Critics attacked Secretary of State Dean Acheson for supporting Hiss, who was his friend. They likewise questioned Truman's own commitment to protect the nation from internal subversion. The dramatic Hiss case helped justify the even worse witch-hunts that followed.

Congress also charged that homosexuals posed a security risk. The issue surfaced in February 1950, when Under Secretary of State John Peurifoy mentioned in testimony before the Senate Appropriations Committee that most of the 91 employees the State Department had dismissed for reasons of "moral turpitude" were homosexuals. This led to a press campaign against "sexual perverts." Then, in December, the Senate released a report that painted a threatening picture of the problems of homosexuals in the civil service. They lacked moral and emotional stability, the report suggested, and were therefore likely candidates for blackmail, which threatened national security:

Those charged with the responsibility of operating the agencies of Government must insist that Government employees meet acceptable standards of personal conduct. In the opinion of this subcommittee homosexuals and other sex perverts are not proper persons to be employed in Government for two reasons; first, they are generally unsuitable, and second, they constitute security risks.

No one was safe from the intrusions of the Cold War crusade.

Senator Joe McCarthy

The key anti-Communist warrior in the 1950s was Joseph R. McCarthy. He capitalized on the fear sparked by congressional and executive investigations and made the entire country cognizant of the Communist threat.

McCarthy came to the Communist issue almost accidentally. Elected to the Senate from Wisconsin in 1946, McCarthy had an undistinguished career for much of his first term. As he began to contemplate reelection two years hence, he was worried, for Truman had carried Wisconsin in 1948. McCarthy saw in the Communist question a way of mobilizing Republican support. He first gained national attention with a speech before the Wheeling, West Virginia, Women's Club in February 1950, not long after the conviction of Alger Hiss. In that address, McCarthy brandished in his hand what he said was a list of 205 known Communists in the State Department. Pressed for details, McCarthy first said that he would release his list only to the president, then reduced the number of names to 57.

Early reactions to McCarthy were mixed. A subcommittee of the Senate Foreign Relations Committee, after investigating, called his charge a "fraud and a hoax." Even other Republicans like Robert Taft and Richard Nixon questioned his effectiveness. As his support grew, however, Republicans realized his partisan value and egged him on. Senator John Bricker of Ohio allegedly told him, "Joe, you're a dirty s.o.b., but there are times when you've got to have an s.o.b. around, and this is one of them."

McCarthy selected assorted targets in his crusade to wipe out communism. In the elections of 1950, he attacked Millard Tydings, the Democrat from Maryland who had chaired the subcommittee that dismissed McCarthy's first accusations. A doctored photograph showing Tydings with deposed American Communist party head Earl Browder helped bring about the defeat of Tydings. McCarthy blasted Dean Acheson the "Red Dean of the State Department" and slandered George C. Marshall, the architect of victory in World War II and a powerful figure in formulating both Far Eastern policy and the Marshall Plan for European recovery, as a "man steeped in falsehood . . . who has recourse to the lie whenever it suits his convenience."

A demagogue throughout his career, McCarthy gained visibility through extensive press and television coverage. He knew how to issue press releases just before newspaper deadlines and to provide reporters with leaks that became the basis for stories. Playing on his tough reputation, he did not mind appearing disheveled, unshaven, and half sober. He used obscenity and vulgarity freely as he lashed out against his "vile and scurrilous" enemies as part of his effort to appeal for popular support by appearing as an ordinary man of the people.

McCarthy's tactics worked because of public alarm about the Communist threat. The Korean War

Senator Joseph McCarthy's spurious charges inflamed anti-Communist sentiment in the 1950s. Here he uses a chart of Communist party organization in the United States to suggest that the nation would be at risk unless subversives were rooted out.
(Corbis-Bettmann)

revealed the aggressiveness of Communists in Asia. The arrest in 1950 of Julius and Ethel Rosenberg fed fears of internal subversion. The Rosenbergs, a seemingly ordinary American couple with two small children, were charged with stealing and transmitting atomic secrets to the Russians. To many Americans, it was inconceivable that the Soviets could have developed the bomb on their own. Treachery helped explain the Soviet explosion of an atomic device.

The next year, the Rosenbergs were found guilty of espionage. Judge Irving Kaufman expressed the rage of an insecure nation as he sentenced them to death. "I consider your crime worse than murder," he said. "Your conduct in putting into the hands of the Russians the A-bomb years before our best scientists predicted Russia would perfect the bomb has already caused, in my opinion, the Communist aggression in Korea, . . . and who knows but that millions more of innocent people may pay the price of your treason." Their execution in the electric chair after numerous appeals were turned down reflected a national commitment to respond to the Communist threat. For years, supporters of the Rosenbergs claimed that they were innocent victims of the anti-Communist crusade. More recent evidence indicates that Julius was guilty. Ethel, cognizant of his activities but not involved herself, was arrested, convicted, and executed in a futile government attempt to make Julius talk. Their deaths underscored the intensity of anti-Communist feeling in the United States.

When the Republicans won control of the Senate in 1952, McCarthy's power grew. He became chairman of the Government Operations Committee and head of its Permanent Investigations Subcommittee. He now had a stronger base and two dedicated assistants, Roy Cohn and G. David Schine, who helped keep attention focused on the ostensible Communist threat. They assisted him in his domestic investigations and even traveled abroad, ripping books off the shelves of American embassy libraries that they deemed subversive. The lists of suspects, including Val Lorwin (introduced at the start of this chapter), grew ever larger.

As McCarthy's anti-Communist witch-hunt continued, Eisenhower became uneasy. He disliked the senator but, recognizing his popularity, was reluctant to challenge him. At the height of his influence, polls showed that McCarthy had half the public behind him. With the country so inclined, Eisenhower compromised by voicing his disapproval quietly and privately.

Some allies of the United States were likewise concerned. The British, for example, had faced their own spy scandals in recent years but had dealt with disclosures of espionage more quietly and grace-

Julius and Ethel Rosenberg proclaimed their innocence when charged with passing on secrets about the atomic bomb, but were found guilty and executed. Here they are going back to prison in a patrol car after hearing the verdict. *(Bettmann/Corbis)*

fully. They were uncomfortable with the hysterical American anti-Communist crusade.

With the help of Cohn and Schine, McCarthy pushed on, but finally he pushed too hard. In 1953, the army drafted Schine and then refused to allow the preferential treatment that Cohn insisted his colleague deserved. Angered, McCarthy began to investigate army security and even top-level army leaders. When the army charged that McCarthy was going too far, the Senate investigated the complaint.

The Army–McCarthy hearings began in April 1954 and lasted 36 days. Beamed to a fascinated nationwide audience, they demonstrated the power of television to shape people's opinions. Americans saw McCarthy's savage tactics on screen. He came across to viewers as irresponsible and destructive, particularly in contrast to Boston lawyer Joseph Welch, who argued the army's case with quiet eloquence and showed McCarthy as the demagogue he was. At one point in the hearings, when McCarthy accused a member of Welch's staff of being involved with an organization sympathetic to the Communist party, despite an earlier agreement not to raise the issue, Welch exploded. "Little did I dream you could be so reckless and so cruel as to do an injury to that lad," he said with a carefully controlled fury. "Have you no sense of decency, sir, at long last? Have you left no sense of decency?"

The hearings shattered McCarthy's mystical appeal. In broad daylight, before a national television audience, his ruthless tactics offended millions. The Senate, which had earlier backed off confronting

Major Events of the Cold War

Year	Event	Effect
1946	Winston Churchill's "Iron Curtain" speech	First Western "declaration" of the Cold War
	George F. Kennan's long telegram	Spoke of Soviet insecurity and the need for containment
1947	George F. Kennan's article signed "Mr. X"	Elaborated on arguments in the telegram
	Truman Doctrine	Provided economic and military aid to Greece and Turkey
	Federal Employee Loyalty Program	Sought to root out subversion in the U.S. government
	HUAC investigation of the motion picture industry	Sought to expose Communist influences in the movies
1948	Marshall Plan	Provided massive American economic aid in rebuilding postwar Europe
	Berlin airlift	Brought in supplies when USSR closed off land access to the divided city
1949	NATO	Created a military alliance to withstand a possible Soviet attack
	First Soviet atomic bomb	Ended the American nuclear monopoly
	Communist victory in China	Made Americans fear the worldwide spread of communism
1950	Conviction of Alger Hiss	Seemed to bear out Communist danger at home
	Joseph McCarthy's first charges	Launched aggressive anti-Communist campaign in the United States
	NSC-68	Called for vigilance and increased military spending to counter the Communist threat
	Outbreak of the Korean War	North Korean invasion of South Korea viewed as part of Soviet conspiracy
1953	Armistice in Korea	Brought little change after years of bitter fighting
1954	Vietnamese victory over French at Dien Bien Phu	Early triumph for nationalism in Southeast Asia
	Army–McCarthy hearings	Brought downfall of Joseph McCarthy

McCarthy, finally summoned the courage to condemn him for his conduct. Even conservatives turned against McCarthy because he was no longer limiting his venom to Democrats and liberals. Although McCarthy remained in office, his influence disappeared. Three years later, at the age of 48, he died a broken man.

Yet for a time he had exerted a powerful hold in the United States. "To many Americans," radio commentator Fulton Lewis, Jr., said, "McCarthyism is Americanism." Seizing upon the frustrations and anxieties of the Cold War, McCarthy struck a resonant chord. As his appeal grew, he put together a following that included both lower-class ethnic groups, who responded to the charges against established elites, and conservative midwestern Republicans. But his real power base was the Senate, where, particularly after 1952, conservative Republicans saw McCarthy as a means of reasserting their own authority. Their support encouraged the vicious crusade.

The Casualties of Fear

The anti-Communist campaign kindled pervasive suspicion in American society. In the late 1940s and early 1950s, dissent no longer seemed safe. Civil servants, government workers, academics, and actors all came under attack and found that the right of due process often evaporated amid the Cold War Red Scare. Seasoned China experts lost their positions in the diplomatic service, and social justice legislation faltered.

This paranoia affected American life in countless ways. In New York, subway workers were fired when they refused to answer questions about their own political actions and beliefs. In Seattle, a fire department officer who denied current membership in the Communist party but refused to speak of his past was dismissed just 40 days before he reached the 25 years of service that would have qualified him for retirement benefits. Navajos in Arizona and New Mexico, facing starvation in the bitter winter of 1947–1948, were denied government relief because of charges that their communal way of life was communistic and therefore un-American. Racism became intertwined with the anti-Communist crusade when African-American actor Paul Robeson was accused of Communist leanings for criticizing American foreign policy and denied opportunities to perform. Subsequently the State Department revoked his passport. Black author W. E. B. Du Bois, who actually joined the Communist party, faced even more virulent attacks and likewise lost his passport. Hispanic laborers faced deportation for membership in unions with left-wing sympathies. In 1949, the Congress of Industrial Organizations (CIO) expelled 11 unions with a total membership

Timeline

1945	Yalta Conference
	Roosevelt dies; Harry Truman becomes president
	Potsdam Conference
1946	American plan for control of atomic energy fails
	Atomic Energy Act
	Iran crisis in which U.S. forces USSR to leave
	Churchill's "Iron Curtain" speech
1947	Truman Doctrine
	Federal Employee Loyalty Program
	House Un-American Activities Committee (HUAC) investigates the movie industry
1948	Marshall Plan launched
	Berlin airlift
	Israel created by the United Nations
	Hiss–Chambers case
	Truman elected president
1949	Soviet Union tests atomic bomb
	North Atlantic Treaty Organization (NATO) established
	George Orwell, *1984*
	Mao Zedong's forces win Chinese civil war; Jiang Jieshi flees to Taiwan
1950	Truman authorizes development of the hydrogen bomb
	Alger Hiss convicted
	Joseph McCarthy's Wheeling (W. Va.) speech on subversion
	NSC-68
	McCarran Internal Security Act
1950–1953	Korean War
1951	Japanese–American treaty
1952	Dwight D. Eisenhower elected president
	McCarthy heads Senate Permanent Investigations Subcommittee
1953	Stalin dies; Khrushchev consolidates power
	East Germans stage anti-Soviet demonstrations
	Shah of Iran returns to power in CIA-supported coup
1954	Fall of Dien Bien Phu ends French control of Indochina
	Geneva Conference on Vietnam
	Guatemalan government overthrown with CIA help
	Mao's forces shell Quemoy and Matsu
	Army–McCarthy hearings
1956	Suez incident
	Hungarian "freedom fighters" suppressed
	Eisenhower reelected
1957	Russians launch *Sputnik* satellite
1958	U.S. troops sent to support Lebanese government
1959	Castro deposes Batista in Cuba

of more than 1 million for alleged domination by Communists. Val Lorwin weathered the storm of malicious accusations and was finally vindicated, but others were less lucky. They were the unfortunate victims as the United States became consumed by the passions of the Cold War.

✦ *Conclusion*

THE COLD WAR IN PERSPECTIVE

The Cold War dominated international relations in the post–World War II years. Tensions grew after 1945 as the United States and the Soviet Union found themselves engaged in a bitter standoff that affected all diplomatic exchanges, encouraged an expensive arms race, and limited the resources available for reform at home. For the United States, it was a first experience with the fiercely competitive international relations that had long plagued the nations of Europe. And while there was seldom actual shooting, the struggle required war-like measures and imposed costs on all countries involved.

What caused the Cold War? Historians have long argued over the question of where responsibility should be placed. In the early years after the Second

World War, policymakers and commentators who supported their actions justified the American stance as a bold and courageous effort to meet the Communist threat. Later, particularly in the 1960s, as the war in Vietnam eroded confidence in American foreign policy, revisionist historians began to argue that American actions were misguided, insensitive to Soviet needs, and at least partially responsible for escalating friction. As with most historical questions, there are no easy answers, but both sides must be weighed.

The Cold War stemmed from a competition for international influence between the two great world powers. After World War II, the U.S. goal was to exercise economic and political leadership in the world and thus to establish capitalist economies and democratic political institutions throughout Europe and in nations emerging from colonial rule. But these goals put the United States on a collision course with nations such as the Soviet Union that had a different vision of what the postwar world should be like and with anticolonial movements in emerging countries around the globe. Perceiving threats from the Soviet Union, China, and other Communist countries, the United States clung to its deep-rooted sense of mission and embarked on an increasingly aggressive effort at containment, based on its reading of the lessons of the past. American efforts culminated in the ill-fated war in Vietnam (that we will see unfold in Chapter 29) as the Communist nations of the world defended their own interests with equal force. The Cold War, with its profound effects at home and abroad, was the unfortunate result.

✦ Recommended Reading

Origins of the Cold War
Stephen E. Ambrose and Douglas G. Brinkley, *Rise to Globalism: American Foreign Policy Since 1938*, 8th rev. ed. (1997); H.W. Brands, *The Devil We Knew: Americans and the Cold War* (1993); John Lewis Gaddis, *The Long Peace: Inquiries into the History of the Cold War* (1987), *The United States and the Origins of the Cold War, 1941–1947* (1972), and *We Now Know: Rethinking Cold War History* (1997); Walter LaFeber, *America, Russia, and the Cold War, 1945–1996*, 8th ed. (1996); Ralph B. Levering, *The Cold War: A Post-Cold War History* (1994); Thomas J. McCormick, *America's Half Century: United States Foreign Policy in the Cold War* (1992); Ronald A. Powaski, *The Cold War: The United States and the Soviet Union, 1917–1991* (1997); Allan M. Winkler, *The Cold War: A History in Documents* (2000); Daniel Yergin, *Shattered Peace: The Origins of the Cold War and the National Security State* (1977).

Containing the Soviet Union
Thomas Borstelman, *The Cold War and the Color Line: American Race Relations in the Global Arena* (2001); H. W. Brands, Jr., *Cold Warriors: Eisenhower's Generation and American Foreign Policy* (1988); Robert A. Divine, *Eisenhower and the Cold War* (1981) and *The Sputnik Challenge: Eisenhower's Response to the Soviet Satellite* (1993); Mary L. Dudziak, *Cold War Civil Rights: Race and the Image of American Democracy* (2000); Michael J. Hogan, *The Marshall Plan: America, Britain, and the Reconstruction of Western Europe* (1987) and *A Cross of Iron: Harry S Truman and the Origins of the National Security State, 1945–1954* (1998); Townsend Hoopes, *The Devil and John Foster Dulles* (1973); Melvyn P. Leffler, *A Preponderance of Power: National Security, the Truman Administration, and the Cold War* (1992); Thomas G. Patterson, *Meeting the Communist Threat: Truman to Reagan* (1988).

Containment in Asia, the Middle East, and Latin America
Frances FitzGerald, *Fire in the Lake: The Vietnamese and the Americans in Vietnam* (1972); Joseph C. Goulden, *Korea: The Untold Story of the War* (1982); David Halberstam, *The Best and the Brightest* (1972); George C. Herring, *America's Longest War: The United States and Vietnam, 1950–1975*, 3rd ed. (1996); Chaim Herzog, *The Arab-Israeli Wars: War and Peace in the Middle East,* rev. ed. (1984); Stanley Karnow, *Vietnam: A History: The First Complete Account of Vietnam at War* (1983); Burton I. Kaufman, *The Korean War: Challenges in Crisis, Credibility, and Command* (1986); Walter LaFeber, *Inevitable Revolutions: The United States in Central America*, 2nd ed. (1993); Steven Hugh Lee, *The Korean War* (2001).

Atomic Weapons and the Cold War
Paul Boyer, *By the Bomb's Early Light: American Thought and Culture at the Dawn of the Atomic Age* (1985); McGeorge Bundy, *Danger and Survival: Choices About the Bomb in the First Fifty Years* (1988); Gregg Herken, *Counsels of War* (1985); Bruce Hevly and John M. Findlay, eds., *The Atomic West* (1998); Richard G. Hewlett and Francis Duncan, *Atomic Shield: Volume II: A History of the United States Atomic Energy Commission, 1947–1952* (1972); Richard G. Hewlett and Jack M. Holl, *Atoms for Peace and War: Eisenhower and the Atomic Energy Commission, 1953–1961* (1989); John Newhouse, *War and Peace in the Nuclear Age* (1989); Jessica Wang, *American Science in an Age of Anxiety: Scientists, Anti-Communism, and the Cold War* (1999); Spencer R. Weart, *Nuclear Fear: A History of Images* (1988); Allan M. Winkler, *Life Under a Cloud: American Anxiety About the Atom* (1993).

The Cold War at Home
John D'Emilio, "The Homosexual Menace: The Politics of Sexuality in Cold War America," *Making Trouble: Essays on Gay History, Politics, and the University* (1992); Robert Griffith, *The Politics of Fear: Joseph R. McCarthy and the Senate* (1970); John Earl Haynes and Harvey Klehr, *Venona: Decoding Soviet Espionage in America* (1999); David M. Oshinsky, *A Conspiracy So Immense: The World of Joe McCarthy* (1983); Ronald Radash and Joyce Milton, *The Rosenberg File: A Search for Truth* (1984); Thomas C. Reeves, *The Life and Times of Joe McCarthy: A Biography* (1982); Sam Roberts, *The Brother: The Untold Story of Atomic Spy David Greenglass and How He Sent His Sister, Ethel Rosenberg, to the Electric Chair* (2001); Lisle A. Rose, *The Cold War Comes to Main Street: America in 1950* (1999); Richard H. Rovere, *Senator Joe McCarthy* (1960); Ellen W. Schrecker, *No Ivory Tower: McCarthyism and the Universities* (1986), *The Age of McCarthyism: A Brief History with Documents* (1994), and *Many Are the Crimes: McCarthyism in America* (1998); Allen Weinstein,

Perjury: The Hiss-Chambers Case, rev. ed. (1997); Allen Weinstein and Alexander Vassiliev, *The Haunted Wood: Soviet Espionage in America—The Stalin Era* (1999).

Fiction and Film

Fail-Safe by Eugene Burdick and Harvey Wheeler (1962) is a novel about an accidental nuclear war. *The Bridges at Toko-ri* (1953) by James A. Michener is a novel about the frustrations of fighting the Korean War when people at home do not seem to care. Walter M. Miller, Jr.'s *A Canticle for Leibowitz* (1959) is about the devastation following a nuclear war that reduces civilization to a primitive state. Nevil Shute's *On the Beach* (1957) is a novel about a nuclear war that wiped out most life and created a radioactive cloud that is killing the rest.

Dr. Strangelove or: How I Learned to Stop Worrying and Love the Bomb (1964) is a movie made by Stanley Kubrick about the absurdity of nuclear war. *Fail-Safe* (1964) is the film from the novel of the same name about an accidental nuclear war that destroyed both Moscow and New York. *High Noon* (1952) is a Western dramatizing the need to stand up to outlaws and reflecting the need to resist the excesses of the anti-Communist crusade. *On the Beach* (1959) is the film from the novel of the same name about a nuclear war that ended all life on earth.

✦ Discovering U.S. History Online

Cold War

www.learningcurve.pro.gov.uk/coldwar/default.htm
www.cnn.com/SPECIALS/cold.war

This site from the United Kingdom uses primary sources from the United States and Europe to examine such questions as "Did the Cold War really start in 1919–39?" "Who caused the Cold War?" and "How Did the Cold War Work?" The second is the companion site to the CNN series on the Cold War. It contains a good deal of information about a wide variety of issues.

The Marshall Plan

www.lcweb.loc.gov/exhibits/marshall

This site examines the Marshall Plan speech, reactions to the speech, and implementation of the European Recovery Program during the next 50 years. The site includes a photo exhibit of reconstruction projects at midpoint.

NATO

www.cnn.com/SPECIALS/1999/nato/

This site from CNN has an excellent timeline and images telling the history of the North Atlantic Treaty Organization.

The Truman Doctrine

www.trumanlibrary.org/whistlestop/study_collections/
doctrine/large/doctrine.htm

Part of the Truman presidential library Web site, this site offers images of primary sources dealing with what came to be known as "The Truman Doctrine."

Korean War

www.trumanlibrary.org/korea/index.html
www.koreanwar.org

A joint project of two presidential libraries, this site presents many of the archival resources (documents and photographs) from the two administrations involved in the Korean War. The second site has information about the Korean War and is a guide to resources on the struggle.

Vietnam War

http://vietnam.vassar.edu
www.pbs.org/wgbh/amex/vietnam/

The overview section of this site gives a good background to the Vietnam War and the origins of American involvement under Eisenhower. The second site contains a detailed, interactive timeline of the war, interpretive essays, and autobiographical reflections.

Atomic Weapons

www.atomicarchive.com/index.shtml

A companion to a CD-ROM of the same name, this site offers biographies, documents, treaties, an atomic timeline, and more.

Nuclear Age Peace Foundation

www.nuclearfiles.org/

The stated aim of this site is to create an "informed citizenry" regarding nuclear power and weapons. To achieve this goal, the site presents an interactive timeline, an image and audio archive, a database of nuclear treaties, various other primary documents, and a collection of essays.

Oak Ridge National Laboratory

www.ornl.gov/timeline/index.html

An interactive and illustrated timeline explains the projects of this governmental laboratory, from the first nuclear reactor (1940) to electron microscope images of the silicon crystal (1999).

Alger Hiss

www.homepages.nyu.edu/~th/5

Funded by grants from The Alger Hiss Research and Publication Project of the Nation Institute and from a Donor Advised Fund at the Community Foundation for Southern Arizona, this site seeks vindication for Hiss and also provides an array of information and sources on this key episode in the Cold War on the home front.

Senator Joe McCarthy

www.webcorp.com/mccarthy/mccarthypage.htm

This site includes audio and visual clips of McCarthy's speeches.

Reform and Rebellion in the Turbulent Sixties, 1960–1969

The United States was comfortable and confident as the 1960s began. There was a basic consensus about the responsibility of the government to help those who could not help themselves. Then that consensus eroded in the turbulence that accompanied the Vietnam War. *(© Kay Brown)*

✦ *American Stories*

A YOUNG LIBERAL QUESTIONS THE WELFARE STATE

Paul Cowan was an idealist in the 1960s. Like many students who came of age in these years, he believed in the possibility of social change and plunged into the struggle for liberal reform. He shared the hopes and dreams of other members of his generation, who felt that their government could make a difference in people's lives.

Cowan's commitment had developed slowly. He was a child of the 1950s, when most Americans were caught up in the consumer culture and paid little attention to the problems of people less fortunate than themselves. His grandfather had sold used cement bags in Chicago, but his father had become an executive at CBS television, and Cowan grew up in comfortable surroundings. He graduated from the Choate School (where John Kennedy had gone) in 1958, and then from Harvard University (where Kennedy had also been a student) in 1963.

When he entered college, Cowan was interested in politically conscious writers like John Dos Passos, John Steinbeck, and James Agee and folk singers like Pete Seeger and Woody Guthrie. They offered him entrance, he later recalled, into a "nation that seemed to be filled with energy and decency," one that lurked "beneath the dull, conformist facade of the Eisenhower years." While at Harvard, he was excited by antinuclear campaigns in New England and civil rights demonstrations in the South.

After college, he made good on his commitment to civil rights by going to Mississippi to work in the Freedom Summer Project of 1964. He was inspired by the example of John Kennedy, the liberal president whose administration promised "a new kind of politics" that could make the nation, and the world, a better place. During that summer, he wrote, "it was possible to believe that by changing ourselves we could change, and redeem, our America."

The Peace Corps came next. Paul and his wife, Rachel, were convinced that this organization, the idea of the young president, "really was a unique government agency, permanently protected by the lingering magic of John F. Kennedy's name." They were assigned to the city of Guayaquil, in Ecuador, in South America. Their task was to serve as mediators between administrators of the city hall and residents of the slums. They wanted to try to raise the standard of living by encouraging local governments to provide basic services such as garbage disposal and clean water.

But the work proved more frustrating than they had imagined. They bristled at the restrictions imposed by the Peace Corps bureaucracy. They despaired at the inadequate resources local government officials had to accomplish their aims. They wondered if they were simply new imperialists, trying to impose their values on others who had priorities of their own. "From the day we moved into the *barrio*," Cowan later recalled, "the question we were most frequently asked by the people we were supposed to be organizing was whether we would leave them our clothes when we returned to the States."

Cowan came home disillusioned. "I saw that even the liberals I had wanted to emulate, men who seemed to be devoting their lives to fighting injustice, were unable to accept people from alien cultures on any terms but their own." He called his account of his own odyssey *The Making of an Un-American.*

Paul Cowan's passage through the 1960s mirrored the passage of American society as a whole. Millions of Americans shared his views as the period began. Mostly comfortable and confident, they supported the liberal agenda advanced by the Democratic party of John Kennedy and Lyndon Johnson. They endorsed the proposition that the government had responsibility for the welfare of all its citizens and accepted the need for a more active government role to help those who were unable to help themselves. That commitment lay behind the legislative achievements of the "Great

Society," the last wave of twentieth-century reform that built upon the gains of the Progressive era and the New Deal years before.

Then political reaction set in as the nation was torn apart by the ravages of the Vietnam War. The escalation of the war, and the involvement of more than one-half million American soldiers in a far-off land, led to a protest movement that ripped apart the United States. Young Americans challenged the priorities of their parents. At the same time, they paraded their sexuality more openly and enjoyed readily available drugs. In the end, their challenges helped reverse the course of the war. But in the process, liberal assumptions eroded, as conservatives argued that an activist approach was responsible for the chaos that consumed the country.

This chapter describes both the climax of twentieth-century liberalism and the turbulence that led to its decline. It focuses on the effort of the government, begun in the New Deal of Franklin Roosevelt, to help those caught short by the advances of industrial capitalism. It first examines the initiatives in the 1960s to provide necessary assistance to the less fortunate members of American society and then describes the turmoil that undermined the possibility of such aid. In pondering the possibilities of reform, this chapter outlines the various attempts to devise an effective political response to the major structural changes in the post–World War II economy described in Chapter 26. And then it shows how the Cold War assumptions outlined in Chapter 27 led to the rifts that ripped the nation apart.

JOHN F. KENNEDY: THE CAMELOT YEARS

The commitment to an American welfare state reached its high-water point in the 1960s. As the left-wing Labour Party in Great Britain played a more and more influential role and occasionally assumed power, and social democratic coalitions were equally active in other European nations, Americans took note. Democrats wanted to follow their example and broaden the role of government even further than Franklin D. Roosevelt and Harry S Truman had done in the 1930s and 1940s, in an effort to address the problems of poverty, unemployment, and racism. John F. Kennedy, a senator from Massachusetts, demanded that the United States move in the direction of what he called a "New Frontier."

The Election of 1960

In the 1960 presidential campaign, Kennedy argued that the government in general, and the president in particular, had to play an even more active role than they had in the Eisenhower years. He charged that the country had become lazy as it reveled in the

prosperity of the 1950s. There were, in fact, serious problems that needed to be solved.

Kennedy ran against Vice President Richard Nixon, who had served as second-in-command to Eisenhower for eight years. When Ike had been ill with a heart attack, a stroke, and serious intestinal difficulty, Nixon had taken his place. He clearly had more executive experience than Kennedy.

The two candidates squared off against one another in the first televised presidential debates. Seventy million Americans tuned in to watch the two men in the first contest. Kennedy appeared tanned and rested. Nixon, who had recently been hospitalized with an infection, looked tired and gaunt. Even worse, the make-up he applied to hide his heavy beard growth only accentuated it and gave him a swarthy complexion on screen. The debates made a major difference in the campaign (see the "Recovering the Past" section of this chapter). Kennedy himself admitted, "It was TV more than anything else that turned the tide." From this point on, television would play a major role in the political process and reshape its character.

Kennedy overcame seemingly insuperable odds to become the first Catholic in the White House. Al

Presidential Election of 1960			
Candidate	Party	Popular Vote	Electoral Vote
JOHN F. KENNEDY	Democratic	34,227,096	303
Richard M. Nixon	Republican	34,108,546	219
Harry F. Byrd	Independent	501,643	15

Note: The winner's name appears in capital letters.

Smith had gained the Democratic nomination in 1928 but had then lost to Herbert Hoover, and the conventional wisdom held that a Catholic could not be elected. Yet Kennedy's victory was razor-thin. The electoral margin of 303 to 219 concealed the close popular tally, in which he triumphed by fewer than 120,000 of 68 million votes cast. If only a few thousand people had voted differently in Illinois and Texas, the election would have gone to Nixon. While Kennedy had Democratic majorities in Congress, many members of his party came from the South and were less sympathetic to liberal causes.

JFK

John Kennedy served as a symbol of the early 1960s. He was far younger than his predecessor; at the age of 43, he was the youngest man ever elected to the presidency. He came from an Irish Catholic family from Massachusetts that saw politics as a means of acceptance in Protestant America. Raised in comfort, he graduated from Harvard University and went on to serve heroically in the navy during World War II, saving the lives of a number of his men when his boat—PT 109—was hit. When his brother was killed during the war, he inherited his family's political hopes. He was elected first to the House of Representatives in 1946, then to the Senate in 1952, and was reelected six years later by the largest majority in the history of the state.

The new president had a charismatic public presence. He was able to voice his aims in eloquent yet understandable language that motivated his followers. During the campaign, he pointed to "uncharted areas of science and space, unsolved problems of peace and war, unconquered pockets of ignorance and prejudice, unanswered questions of poverty and surplus" that Americans must confront, for "the New Frontier is here whether we seek it or not." He made the same point even more movingly in his inaugural address: "The torch has been passed to a new generation of Americans—born in this century, tempered by war, disciplined by a hard and bitter peace, proud of our ancient heritage." Many Americans, like Paul Cowan, whom we met at the start of the chapter, were inspired by Kennedy's concluding call to action: "And so, my fellow Americans: Ask not what your country can do for you—ask what you can do for your country."

For Kennedy, strong leadership was all-important. The president, he believed, "must serve as a catalyst, an energizer." He must be able and willing to perform "in the very thick of the fight." Viewing himself as "tough-minded" and "hard-nosed," he was determined to provide firm direction and play a

John Kennedy's energy and enthusiasm captured the imagination of Americans and people around the world, though few were aware of the physical ailments that affected him. He was fond of using this rocking chair in the White House, which he found comfortable for his ailing back. *(Corbis-Bettmann)*

leading role in creating the national agenda, just as Franklin Roosevelt had done.

Kennedy surrounded himself with talented assistants. On his staff were 15 Rhodes scholars and several famous authors. The secretary of state was Dean Rusk, a former member of the State Department who had then served as president of the Rockefeller Foundation. The secretary of defense was Robert S. McNamara, the highly successful president of the Ford Motor Company, who had proved creative in mobilizing talented assistants—"whiz kids"—and in using computer analysis to turn the company around.

Further contributing to Kennedy's attractive image were his glamorous wife, Jacqueline, and the glittering social occasions the couple hosted. Nobel Prize winners, musicians, and artists attended White House dinners. The Kennedys and their friends played touch football on the White House lawn and charged off on 50-mile hikes. Energy, exuberance, and excitement filled the air. The administration seemed like the Camelot of King Arthur's day, popularized in a Broadway musical in 1960.

Television

In the last 50 years, television has played an increasingly important part in American life, providing historians with another source of evidence about American culture and society in the recent past.

Television's popularity by the 1950s was the result of decades of experimentation dating back to the nineteenth century. In the 1930s, NBC installed a television station in the new Empire State Building in New York. Wearing green makeup and purple lipstick to provide better visual contrast, actors began to perform before live cameras in studios. At the end of the decade, "Amos 'n' Andy," a popular radio show, was telecast, and as the 1940s began, Franklin D. Roosevelt became the first president to appear on television. World War II interrupted the development of television, and Americans relied on radio to bring them news. After the war, however, the commercial development of television quickly resumed. Assembly lines that had made electronic implements of war were now converted to consumer production, and thousands of new sets appeared on the market. The opening of Congress could be seen live in 1947; baseball coverage improved that same year owing to the zoom lens; children's shows like "Howdy Doody" made their debut; and "Meet the Press," a radio interview program, made the transition to television.

Although sports programs, variety shows hosted by Ed Sullivan and Milton Berle, TV dramas, and episodic series ("I Love Lucy" and "Gunsmoke," for example) dominated TV broadcasting in the 1950s, television soon became entwined with politics and public affairs. Americans saw Senator Joseph McCarthy for themselves in the televised Army–McCarthy hearings in 1954; his malevolent behavior on camera contributed to his downfall. The 1948 presidential nominating conventions were the first to be televised, but the use of TV to enhance the public image of politicians was most thoroughly developed by the fatherly Dwight D. Eisenhower and the charismatic John F. Kennedy.

In November 1963, people throughout the United States shared the tragedy of John Kennedy's assassination, sitting stunned before their sets trying to understand the events of his fateful Texas trip. The shock and sorrow of the American people was repeated in the spring of 1968 as they gazed in disbelief at the funerals of Martin Luther King, Jr., and Robert Kennedy. A year later, a quarter of the world's population watched as Neil Armstrong became the first man to set foot on the moon. In that same era, television played an important part in shaping impressions of the war in Vietnam. More and more

The candidates squaring off in their debate. *(AP/Wide World Photos)*

Americans began to understand the nature and impact of the conflict from what they saw on TV.

This combination of visual entertainment and enlightenment made owning a television set virtually a necessity. By 1970, fully 95 percent of American households owned a TV set, a staggering increase from the 9 percent only 20 years earlier. In fact, fewer families owned refrigerators or indoor toilets.

Reflecting on the Past The implications of the impact of television on American society are of obvious interest to historians. How has television affected other communications and entertainment industries, such as radio, newspapers, and movies? Look at the "Television Tonight" listings shown here. What does the content of TV programming tell us about the values, interests, and tastes of the American people?

Perhaps most significant, what impact has TV had on the course of historical events like presidential campaigns, human relations, and wars? The pictures shown here are from the Kennedy–Nixon debates in the presidential campaign of 1960. The first picture shows the two candidates in the studio. The second picture shows a relaxed and energetic Kennedy staring directly into the TV camera. The third picture shows a taut and tense Nixon challenging the points made by his opponent. Which candidate seems to be speaking directly to the American people? Which candidate makes the better impression? Why? Polls of radio listeners taken after the first debate showed Nixon the winner; surveys of television viewers placed Kennedy in front. How do you account for this discrepancy?

John Kennedy (above) and Richard Nixon (right). *(AP/Wide World Photos)*

Television Tonight

6:00—WTTV 4: Leave It to Beaver. Beaver tries to help a friend who has run away from home. Repeat.

6:30—WLTW-I 13: Cheyenne has a Laramie adventure in which Slim, Jess, and Jonesy work on a cattle drive. Repeat.

7:30—WTTV 4: The Untouchables. Eliot Ness tries to deal with a late gangster's niece who has a record of the murdered hood's career. Repeat.

7:30—WLW-I 13: Voyage to the Bottom of the Sea presents "Mutiny," in which Admiral Nelson shows signs of a mental breakdown during the search for a giant jellyfish which supposedly consumed a submarine.

7:30—WFBM-TV 6: Members of the Indianapolis Rotary Club discuss the 1965 business outlook with former U.S. Sen. Homer Capehart.

8:00—WFBM-TV 6: The Man from UNCLE is in at a new time and night. Thrush agents try to recapture one of their leaders before Napoleon Solo can deliver him to the Central Intelligence Agency. Ralph Taeger is guest star.

8:00—WISH-TV 8: I've Got a Secret welcomes the panel from To Tell the Truth: Tom Poston, Peggy Cass, Kitty Carlisle, and Orson Bean.

8:30—WLW-I 13: Basketball, I.U. vs. Iowa.

8:30—WISH-TV 8: Andy Griffith's comedy involves Goober's attempts to fill in at the sheriff's office.

9:00—WFBM-TV 6: Andy Williams is visited by composer Henry Mancini, Bobby Darin, and Vic Damone. Musical selections include "Charade," "Hello Dolly," and "Moon River."

9:00—WTTV 4: Lloyd Thaxton welcomes vocal group, Herman's Hermits.

9:30—WISH-TV 8: Many Happy Returns. Walter's plan for currying favor with the store's boss hits a snag.

10:00—WFBM-TV 6: Alfred Hitchcock presents Margaret Leighton as a spinster who goes mad when she cannot cope with the strain of rearing an orphaned niece in "Where the Woodbine Twineth."

10:00—WLW-I 13: Ben Casey gets help in diagnosing a boy's illness from an Australian veterinarian with terminal leukemia. The vet's knowledge of bats provides the key.

10:00—WISH-TV 8: "Viet Nam: How We Got In—Can We Get Out?" is the topic of CBS Reports.

Source: Indianapolis News, January 11, 1965.

The New Frontier in Action

In office, Kennedy was committed to extending the welfare state. He sought to maintain an expanding economic system and to enlarge social welfare programs. As he told one of his advisers in 1962, "I want to go beyond the things that have already been accomplished. Give me facts and figures on things we still have to do." On the economic front, he tried to end the lingering recession that began in Eisenhower's last year by working with the business community while controlling price inflation.

These two goals conflicted when, in the spring of 1962, the large steel companies decided on a major price increase after steel unions had accepted a modest wage package. The angry president termed the price increases unjustifiable and on television charged that the firms pursued "private power and profit" rather than the public interest. Determined to force the steel companies to their knees, Kennedy pressed for executive and congressional action. In the end, the large companies capitulated, but they disliked Kennedy's heavy-handed approach and decided that this Democratic administration, like all the others, was hostile to business. In late May, six weeks after the steel crisis, the stock market plunged in the greatest drop since the Great Crash of 1929. Kennedy received the blame. "When Eisenhower had a heart attack," Wall Street analysts joked, "the market broke. If Kennedy would have a heart attack, the market would go up."

It now seemed doubly urgent to end the recession. Earlier a proponent of a balanced budget, Kennedy began to listen to his liberal advisers who proposed a Keynesian approach to economic growth. Budget deficits had promoted prosperity during the Second World War and might work in the same way in peacetime, too. A tax cut could put money in people's pockets, and their spending could stimulate the economy. By the summer of 1962, the president was convinced. In early 1963, he called for a $13.5 billion cut in corporate taxes over the next three years. While that cut would cause a large deficit, it would also provide capital that business leaders could spend to revive the economy and ultimately increase tax revenues.

Opposition mounted. Conservatives refused to accept the basic premise that deficits would stimulate economic growth and argued, in Eisenhower's words, that "no family, no business, no nation can spend itself into prosperity." Some liberals claimed that it would be better to stimulate the economy by spending money to improve society rather than by cutting taxes and putting money in people's pockets. What good would it do, economist John Kenneth Galbraith wondered, to have "a few more dollars to spend if the air is too dirty to breathe, the water is too polluted to drink, the commuters are losing out in the struggle to get in and out of cities, the streets are filthy, and the schools are so bad that the young, perhaps wisely, stay away?" In Congress, where Democrats had thin majorities but still had to contend with conservative Southerners within the party, opponents pigeonholed the proposal in committee, and there it remained.

On other issues on the liberal agenda, Kennedy met similar resistance. Though he proposed legislation increasing the minimum wage and providing for federal aid for education, medical care for the elderly, housing subsidies, and urban renewal, the results were meager. His new minimum-wage measure passed Congress in pared-down form, but Kennedy did not have the votes in Congress to achieve most of his legislative program.

His inability to win necessary congressional support was most evident in the struggle to aid public education. Soon after taking office, Kennedy proposed a $2.3 billion program of grants to the states over a three-year period to help build schools and raise teachers' salaries. Immediately, a series of prickly questions emerged. Was it appropriate to spend large sums of money for social goals? Would federal aid bring federal control of school policies and curriculum? Should assistance go to segregated schools? Should it go to parochial schools? The administration proved willing to allow assistance to segregated schools, thereby easing white southern minds. On the Catholic question, however, it stumbled to a halt. Kennedy at first insisted, as he had throughout the campaign, that he would not allow his religion to influence his actions, and he opposed aid for parochial schools. But as Catholic pressure mounted and the administration realized that Catholic votes were necessary for passage, Kennedy began to reconsider. In the end, compromise proved impossible and the school aid measure died in committee.

Kennedy was more successful in securing funding for the exploration of space. The space program was caught up in the competition of the Cold War, and with the Soviet launching of *Sputnik* and then shots with first dogs, then astronauts, the USSR clearly had the lead. Finally, the American space program got off the ground. As first Alan Shepard and then John Glenn flew in space, Kennedy proposed that the United States commit itself to landing a man on the moon and returning him to earth before the end of the decade. Congress, caught up in the glamour of the proposal and worried about

Soviet space achievements, assented and increased funding of the National Aeronautics and Space Administration (NASA).

Kennedy also established the Peace Corps, which sent young men and women overseas to assist developing countries. American diplomats sometimes faced resentment in developing nations, especially when they appeared out of touch with local needs. According to Kennedy aide Arthur M. Schlesinger, Jr., the Peace Corps was an effort "to replace protocol-minded, striped-pants officials by reform-minded missionaries of democracy who mixed with the people, spoke the native dialects, ate the food, and involved themselves in local struggles against ignorance and want." Paul Cowan, introduced at the start of this chapter, was one of thousands of volunteers who hoped to share their liberal dreams.

If Kennedy's successes were modest, he had at least made commitments that could be broadened later. He had reaffirmed the importance of executive leadership in the effort to extend the boundaries of the welfare state. And he had committed himself to using modern economics to maintain fiscal stability. The nation was poised to achieve liberal goals.

Civil Rights and Kennedy's Response

So it was with civil rights. The pressures that had mounted in the decade and a half after World War II had brought significant change in eliminating segregation in American society. As the effort continued, a spectrum of organizations, some old, some new, carried the fight forward. The NAACP, founded in 1910, remained committed to overturning the legal bases for segregation in the aftermath of its victory in the *Brown* v. *Board of Education* case of 1954 (see Chapter 26). The Congress of Racial Equality (CORE), an interracial group established in 1942, promoted change through peaceful confrontation. In 1957, after their victory in the bus boycott in Montgomery, Alabama, Martin Luther King, Jr., and others formed the Southern Christian Leadership Conference (SCLC), an organization of southern black clergy. Far more militant was the Student Nonviolent Coordinating Committee (SNCC, pronounced "snick"), which began to operate in 1960 and recruited young Americans who had not been involved in the civil rights struggle.

Confrontations continued in the 1960s. On January 31, 1960, four black college students from the Agricultural and Technical College in Greensboro, North Carolina, protested continuing patterns of segregation, despite the Supreme Court's important rulings. Frustrated that they were permitted to shop but not to eat at a Woolworth's, part of a department store chain specializing in household goods, they sat down at the lunch counter in the store and deliberately violated southern segregation laws by refusing to leave. When a reporter inquired how long they had been planning the protest, the students responded, "All our lives!" While they left at the end of the day, the next day more students showed up, and the following day still more. The sit-ins, which spread to other cities, captured media attention and

In violation of southern law, black college students refused to leave a lunch counter, launching a new campaign in the struggle for civil rights. Here the students wait patiently for service, or forcible eviction, as a way of dramatizing their determination to end segregation. *(Bruce Roberts/Photo Researchers)*

eventually included as many as 70,000 participants. Those protesting often met with a brutal response. John Lewis, an African-American activist who participated in a sit-in in Nashville, Tennessee, described his experience:

> A group of young white men came in and they started pulling and beating primarily the young women. They put lighted cigarettes down their backs, in their hair, and they were really beating people. In a short time police officials came in and placed all of us under arrest, and not a single member of the white group, the people that were opposing our sit-in, was arrested.

The following year, sit-ins gave rise to freedom rides, aimed at testing southern transportation facilities that recently had been desegregated by a Supreme Court decision. Organized initially by CORE and aided by SNCC, the program sent groups of blacks and whites together on buses heading south and stopping at terminals along the way. The riders, peaceful themselves, anticipated confrontations that would publicize their cause and generate political support. In Anniston, Alabama, CORE leader James Farmer depicted the confrontation that occurred as a mob of white men attacked a bus that was preparing to leave:

> Before the bus pulled out . . . members of the mob took their sharp instruments and slashed tires. The bus got to the outskirts of Anniston and the tires blew out and the bus ground to a halt. Members of the mob had boarded cars and followed the bus, and now with the disabled bus standing there, the members of the mob surrounded it, held the door closed, and a member of the mob threw a firebomb into the bus, breaking a window to do so.

In Birmingham, police made an agreement with the Ku Klux Klan to give Klansmen 15 minutes alone to beat the Freedom Riders. Although the FBI knew about the plan, the federal agency did nothing to stop it.

In the North and South alike, consciousness of the need to combat racial discrimination grew. The civil rights movement became the most powerful moral campaign since the abolitionist crusade before the Civil War. Often working together closely, blacks and whites vowed to eliminate racial barriers.

Anne Moody, who grew up in a small town in Mississippi, personified the awakening of black consciousness. As a child, she had watched the murder of friends and acquaintances who had somehow transgressed the limits set for blacks. Overcoming the hardships of growing up poor and black in the rural South, Moody became the first

member of her family to go to college, enrolling at Tougaloo College, near Jackson, Mississippi. Once there, she found her own place in the civil rights movement. She joined the NAACP and became involved in the activities of SNCC and CORE. Slowly, she noted, "I could feel myself beginning to change. For the first time I began to think something would be done about whites killing, beating, and misusing Negroes. I knew I was going to be a part of whatever happened." Participating in sit-ins, where she was thrashed and jailed for her activities, she remained deeply involved in the movement.

Moody was but one of countless black women participating in the struggle. As African-American activist Ella Baker observed, "When demonstrations took place and when the community acted, usually it was some woman who came to the fore."

Many whites also joined the movement in the South. Mimi Feingold, a white student at Swarthmore College in Pennsylvania, helped picket the Woolworth's in Chester, Pennsylvania, and worked to unionize Swarthmore's black dining-hall workers. In 1961, after her sophomore year, she headed south to join the freedom rides sponsored by CORE. Like

James Meredith refused to be driven from the University of Mississippi, despite the opposition of the governor and a campus riot. His perseverance paid off, as he ultimately earned his degree. *(UPI/Corbis-Bettmann)*

In Birmingham, city officials responded to peaceful demonstrators with brutal force. Here city police use trained dogs to drive marchers back. Televised nationally, the police response appalled the American public. As newsman Eric Sevareid observed, "A newspaper or television picture of a snarling police dog set upon a human being is recorded on the permanent photoelectric file of every human brain." *(Charles Moore/Black Star)*

many others, Feingold found herself in the midst of often-violent confrontations and went to jail as an act of conscience. In Jackson, Mississippi, she spent a month behind bars.

In 1962, the civil rights movement accelerated. James Meredith, a black air force veteran and student at Jackson State College, applied to the all-white University of Mississippi, only to be rejected on racial grounds. Suing to gain admission, he carried his case to the Supreme Court, where Justice Hugo Black affirmed his claim. But then Governor Ross Barnett, an adamant racist, announced defiantly that Meredith would not be admitted, whatever the Court decision, and on one occasion personally blocked the way. A major riot followed; tear gas covered the university grounds; and by the riot's end, two men lay dead and hundreds were hurt.

Other governors were equally aggressive. In his 1963 inaugural address, George C. Wallace of Alabama declared boldly, "Segregation now! Segregation tomorrow! Segregation forever!" as he voiced his opposition to integration.

Alabama became a national focus that year as a violent confrontation unfolded in Birmingham. Local black leaders encouraged Martin Luther King, Jr., to launch another attack on southern segregation in the city, 40 percent black, which remained rigidly segregated along racial and class lines. "We believed

that while a campaign in Birmingham would surely be the toughest fight of our civil rights careers," King later explained, "it could, if successful, break the back of segregation all over the nation."

Though the demonstrations were nonviolent, the responses were not. City officials declared that protest marches violated city regulations against parading without a license, and, over a five-week period, they arrested 2,200 blacks, some of them schoolchildren. Police Commissioner Eugene "Bull" Connor used high-pressure fire hoses, electric cattle prods, and trained police dogs to force the protesters back. As the media recorded the events, Americans watching television and reading newspapers were horrified. The images of violence created mass sympathy for black Americans' civil rights struggle.

Kennedy claimed to be sickened by the pictures from Birmingham but insisted that he could do nothing, even though he had sought and won black support in 1960. The narrowness of his electoral victory made him reluctant to press white southerners on civil rights when he needed their votes on other issues. Kennedy initially failed to propose any civil rights legislation and likewise ignored a campaign promise to end housing discrimination by presidential order. Not until November 1962, after the midterm elections, did he take a modest action—an executive order ending segregation in federally financed housing.

Events finally forced Kennedy to act more boldly. In the James Meredith confrontation, the president, like his predecessor in the Little Rock crisis, had to send federal troops to restore control and to guarantee Meredith's right to attend the university. The administration also forced the desegregation of the University of Alabama and helped arrange a compromise providing for desegregation of Birmingham's municipal facilities, implementation of more equitable hiring practices, and formation of a biracial committee. And when white bombings aimed at eliminating black leaders in Birmingham caused thousands of blacks to abandon nonviolence and rampage through the streets, Kennedy readied federal troops to intervene.

He also spoke out more forcefully than before. In a nationally televised address, he called the quest for equal rights a "moral issue" and asked, "Are we to say to the world, and, much more importantly, to each other that this is a land of the free except for the Negroes." Just hours after the president spoke, assassins killed Medgar Evers, a black NAACP official, in his own driveway in Jackson, Mississippi.

Kennedy sent Congress a new and stronger civil rights bill, outlawing segregation in public places, banning discrimination wherever federal money was involved, and advancing the process of school integration. Polls showed that 63 percent of the nation supported his stand.

To lobby for passage of this measure, civil rights leaders, pressed from below by black activists, arranged a massive march on Washington in August 1963. More than 200,000 people gathered from across the country and demonstrated enthusiastically. Celebrities present included diplomat Ralph Bunche, writer James Baldwin, entertainers Sammy Davis, Jr., Harry Belafonte, and Lena Horne, and former baseball player Jackie Robinson. The folk music artists of the early 1960s were there as well. Joan Baez, Bob Dylan, and Peter, Paul and Mary led the crowd in songs associated with the movement, such as "Blowin' in the Wind" and "We Shall Overcome."

The high point of the day was the address by Martin Luther King, Jr., the nation's preeminent spokesman for civil rights and proponent of nonviolent protest. King proclaimed his faith in the decency of his fellow citizens and in their ability to extend the promises of the Constitution and the Declaration of Independence to every American. With all the power of a southern preacher, he implored his audience to share his faith.

The 1963 march on Washington was a high point in the civil rights movement. Several hundred thousand demonstrators lined the reflecting pool leading out from the Washington Monument and heard Martin Luther King, Jr., shown here, and other black leaders eloquently plead for racial equality. *(AP/Wide World Photos)*

"I have a dream," King declared, "that one day this nation will rise up and live out the true meaning of its creed: 'We hold these truths to be self-evident, that all men are created equal.' I have a dream that one day on the red hills of Georgia, the sons of former slaves and the sons of former slave-owners will be able to sit together at the table of brotherhood." It was a fervent appeal, and one to which the crowd responded. Each time King used the refrain "I have a dream," thousands of blacks and whites roared together. King concluded by quoting from an old hymn: "Free at last! Free at last! Thank God almighty, we are free at last!"

Not all were moved. Anne Moody, who had come up from her activist work in Mississippi to attend the event, sat on the grass by the Lincoln Memorial as the speaker's words rang out. "Martin Luther King went on and on talking about his dream," she said. "I sat there thinking that . . . we never had time to sleep, much less dream." Nor was the Congress prompted to do much. Despite large Democratic majorities, strong white southern resistance to the cause of civil rights continued, and the bill was bottled up in committee.

LYNDON B. JOHNSON AND THE GREAT SOCIETY

Kennedy knew he faced a difficult reelection battle in 1964. He wanted not only to win the presidency for a second term but also to increase liberal Democratic strength in Congress. Instead, an assassin's attack took his life and brought a new leader to the helm.

Change of Command

In November 1963, Kennedy traveled to Texas, where he hoped to unite the state's Democratic party for the upcoming election. Dallas, one of the stops on the trip, was reputed to be hostile to the administration. Four weeks before, a conservative mob had abused Adlai Stevenson, ambassador to the United Nations. Now, on November 22, Kennedy had a chance to feel the pulse of the city for himself. Arriving at the airport, Henry González, a congressman accompanying the president in Texas, remarked jokingly, "Well, I'm taking my risks. I haven't got my steel vest yet." As the party entered the city in an open car, the president encountered friendly crowds. Suddenly shots rang out, and Kennedy slumped forward as bullets ripped through his head and throat. Mortally wounded, he died a short time later at a Dallas hospital. Lee Harvey Oswald, the accused assassin, was shot and killed a few days later by a minor underworld figure as he was being moved within the jail.

Americans were stunned. For days, people stayed at home and watched endless television replays of the assassination and its aftermath. The images of the handsome president felled by bullets, the funeral cortege, and the president's young son saluting his father's casket as it rolled by on the way to final burial at Arlington National Cemetery were all imprinted on people's minds. United around the event, members of an entire generation remembered where they had been when Kennedy was shot, just as an earlier generation recalled Pearl Harbor.

Vice President Lyndon Johnson succeeded Kennedy as president. Though less polished, Johnson was a more effective political leader than Kennedy and brought his own special skills and vision to the presidency.

LBJ

Johnson had taken a different road to the White House. He came from a far more humble background than Kennedy. After finishing college in his home state of Texas, he had worked as a teacher for a while. He had begun his public career as a legislative assistant in the House of Representatives in Washington, D.C., then served as a New Deal official

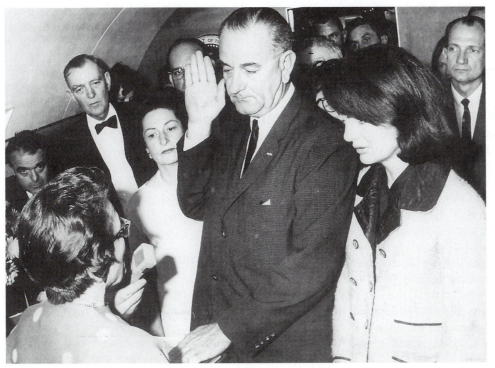

Kennedy's assassination thrust Lyndon Johnson into the presidency in an atmosphere of shocked grief and loss. Here, with Jacqueline Kennedy by his side, he takes the oath of office as he flew back from Dallas to Washington on the presidential plane. *(Corbis-Bettmann)*

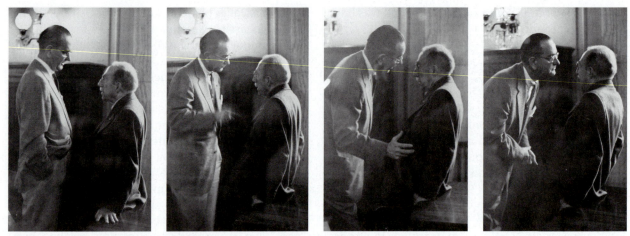

Lyndon Johnson kept tight control of the Senate in the 1950s and was known for his ability to get his way. Here he is shown giving the famous "Johnson treatment" to Senator Theodore Francis Green in 1957. Note the way Green is bending backwards in an unsuccessful effort to keep his distance from LBJ. *(George Tames/The New York Times)*

in Texas. Entering the political world himself, he won election first to the House in 1937 and then to the Senate in 1948. Eager to be president, he accepted the vice presidential nomination when it became clear in 1960 that Kennedy was going to win.

Johnson was a man of elemental force. Always manipulative, he reminded people of a riverboat gambler, according to one White House aide. Though he desperately wanted to be loved, he was, former secretary of state Dean Acheson once told him, "not a very likable man." There was a streak of vulgarity that contributed to his earthy appeal but offended some of his associates. Asked once why he had not responded more sympathetically to a suggestion from Richard Nixon, he said to his friends in Congress, "Boys, I may not know much, but I know the difference between chicken shit and chicken salad."

Those qualities notwithstanding, he was successful in the passion of his life—politics. Schooled in Congress and influenced by FDR, Johnson was the most able legislator of the postwar years. As Senate majority leader, he became famous for his ability to get things done. Ceaseless in his search for information, tireless in his attention to detail, he knew the strengths and weaknesses of everyone he faced. When he approached someone in the hall, one senator remarked, he was like a "great overpowering thunderstorm that consumed you as it closed in on you." He could flatter and cajole, and became famous for what came to be called the "Johnson treatment." According to columnists Rowland Evans, Jr., and Robert Novak, he zeroed in, "his face a scant millimeter from his target, his eyes widening and narrowing, his eyebrows rising and falling." He grabbed people by the lapels, made them listen, and

usually got his way (see the series of illustrations on this page).

Johnson ran the Senate with tight control and established a credible record for himself and his party during the Eisenhower years. He was the Democrat most responsible for keeping liberal goals alive in a conservative time, as he tried to broaden his own appeal in his quest for the presidency. When that proved unsuccessful, he helped Kennedy win the election by serving in the second slot on the ticket, then went into a state of eclipse as vice president. He felt uncomfortable with the Kennedy crowd, useless and stifled in his new role. He told friends that he agreed with John Nance Garner, a vice president under FDR, who once observed that the vice presidency "wasn't worth a pitcher of warm spit."

Despite his own ambivalence about Kennedy, Johnson sensed the profound shock that gripped the United States after the assassination and was determined to utilize Kennedy's memory to achieve legislative success. Even more than Kennedy, he was willing to wield presidential power aggressively and to use the media to shape public opinion in pursuit of his vision of a society in which the comforts of life would be more widely shared and poverty would be eliminated once and for all.

The Great Society in Action

Lyndon Johnson had an expansive vision of the possibilities of reform. Using his considerable political skills, he succeeded in pushing through Congress the most extensive reform program in American history. "Is a new world coming?" the president asked. "We welcome it, and we will bend it to the hopes of man."

Johnson began to develop the support he needed the day he took office. In his first public address, delivered to Congress and televised nationwide, he sought to dispel the image of impostor as he embraced Kennedy's liberal program. He began, in a measured tone, with the words, "All I have, I would have given gladly not to be standing here today." He asked members of Congress to work with him, and he underscored the theme "Let us continue" throughout his speech.

As a first step, Johnson resolved to secure the measures Kennedy had been unable to extract from Congress. Bills to reduce taxes and ensure civil rights were his first and most pressing priorities, but he was interested too in aiding public education, providing medical care for the aged, and eliminating poverty. By the spring of 1964, he began to use the phrase "Great Society" to describe his expansive reform program.

Successful even before the election of 1964, his landslide victory over conservative Republican challenger Barry Goldwater of Arizona validated his approach. This was the first time in recent history that a conservative had gained the Republican nomination. Goldwater, however, frightened even members of his own party by proclaiming that "extremism in the defense of liberty is no vice," and by speaking out against such popular programs as social security. LBJ received 61 percent of the popular vote and an electoral tally of 486 to 52 and gained Democratic congressional majorities of 68–32 in the Senate and 295–140 in the House. Despite his defeat, Goldwater's candidacy reflected the growing power of conservatism within the Republican party and the ability of a grassroots group to organize a successful campaign in party primaries. It also drove moderate Republicans to vote for the Democratic party this time and gave Johnson a far more impressive mandate than Kennedy had ever enjoyed.

Johnson knew how to get laws passed. He appointed task forces that included legislators to study problems and suggest solutions, worked with them to draft bills, and maintained close contact with congressional leaders through a sophisticated liaison staff. Not since the FDR years had there been such a coordinated effort.

Civil rights reform was LBJ's first legislative priority and an integral part of the Great Society program (see next section), but other measures were equally important. Following Kennedy's lead, Johnson pressed for a tax cut. He accepted the Keynesian theory that deficits, properly managed, could promote prosperity. If people had more money to spend, then their purchases could stimulate the economy. Soon the tax bill passed.

With the tax cut in hand, the president pressed for the antipoverty program that Kennedy had begun to plan. Such an effort was bold and unprecedented in the United States, even though social democracy had a long history in European nations and other countries around the world. During the Progressive era at the turn of the century, some legislation had attempted to alleviate conditions associated with poverty. During the New Deal, Franklin Roosevelt had proposed programs to assist the one-third of the nation that could not help itself. Now Johnson took a step that no president had taken before; in his 1964 State of the Union message, he declared an "unconditional war on poverty in America."

The center of this utopian effort to eradicate poverty was the Economic Opportunity Act of 1964. It created an Office of Economic Opportunity (OEO) to provide education and training through programs such as the Job Corps for unskilled young people trapped in the poverty cycle. VISTA (Volunteers in Service to America), patterned after the Peace Corps, offered assistance to the poor at home, while Head Start tried to give disadvantaged children a chance to succeed in school. Assorted community action programs gave the poor a voice in improving housing, health, and education in their own neighborhoods. Two agencies responded to Native American pressure by allowing Indians to devise programs and budgets and then administer programs themselves.

Aware of the escalating costs of medical care, Johnson also proposed a medical assistance plan. Both Truman and Kennedy had supported such an initiative but had failed to win congressional approval. Johnson succeeded. To head off conservative attacks, the administration tied the Medicare measure to the social security system and limited

Presidential Election of 1964			
Candidate	**Party**	**Popular Vote**	**Electoral Vote**
LYNDON B. JOHNSON	Democratic	43,126,584 (61.1%)	486
Barry M. Goldwater	Republican	27,177,838 (38.5%)	52

Note: The winner's name appears in capital letters.

Federal Aid to Education in the 1960s

Passage of a bill to provide federal aid to education in 1965 led to rapidly increasing government support at all levels for the remainder of the decade.

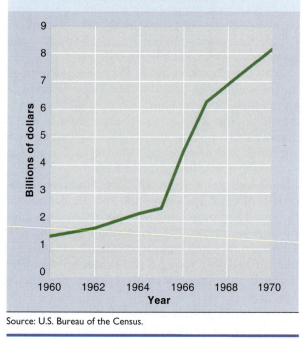

Source: U.S. Bureau of the Census.

it themselves. It moved further in funding higher education, including colleges and universities in its financial grants. Congress also provided artists and scholars with assistance through the National Endowments for the Arts and Humanities, created in 1965. Not since the Works Progress Administration in the New Deal had such groups been granted government aid.

At the same time, Johnson's administration provided much-needed immigration reform. It replaced the restrictive immigration policy, in place since 1924 (which had limited immigration severely and favored northern and western Europeans), with a measure that vastly increased the ceiling on immigration and opened the door to immigrants from Asia and Latin America. The Immigration Act of 1965 also exempted from the quotas family members of U.S. citizens and political refugees, including at first Cuban and later Indochinese immigrants. By the late 1960s, some 350,000 immigrants were entering the United States annually, compared to the average of 47,000 per year between 1931 and 1945. This new stream of immigration—largely from Asia and Latin America—created a population more diverse than it had been since the early decades of the twentieth century. The consequences of this new diversity were far-ranging and affected many areas of American life, from politics, radio programming, and consumer products to street signs and public school classrooms.

The Great Society also reflected the stirring of the environmental movement. In 1962, naturalist Rachel Carson alerted the public to the dangers of pesticide poisoning and environmental pollution in her book *Silent Spring*. She took aim at chemical pesticides, especially DDT, which had increased crop yields but had brought disastrous side effects:

> The most alarming of all man's assaults upon the environment is the contamination of air, earth, rivers, and sea with dangerous and even lethal materials. This pollution is for the most part irrecoverable; the chain of evil it initiates not only in the world that must support life but in living tissues is for the most part irreversible. In this now universal contamination of the environment, chemicals are the sinister and little-recognized partners of radiation in changing the very nature of the world—the very nature of its life.

Chemicals entered the food chain and caused a cycle of poisoning and death. Though the chemical industry fought Carson and argued that she left readers "unable to sort fact from fancy," a special presidential advisory committee warned against widespread pesticide use. As Americans learned of the pollutants surrounding them, they became in-

the program to the elderly. The new Medicaid program met the needs of those on welfare and certain other groups who could not afford private insurance. The Medicare–Medicaid initiative was the most important extension of federally directed social benefits since the Social Security Act of 1935. By the middle of the next decade, the two programs were paying for the medical costs of 20 percent of the American people.

Johnson was similarly successful in his effort to provide aid for elementary and secondary schools. Kennedy had met defeat when Catholics had insisted on assistance to parochial schools. Johnson, a Protestant, was able to deal with the ticklish religious question without charges of favoritism. His legislation allocated education money to the states based on the number of children from low-income families. Those funds would then be distributed to assist deprived children in public as well as private schools.

In LBJ's expansive vision, the federal government would ensure that everyone shared in the promise of American life. Under his prodding, Congress passed a new housing act to give rent supplements to the poor and created a Cabinet Department of Housing and Urban Development. The federal government provided new forms of aid, such as legal assistance for those who could not afford to pay for creasingly worried, not just about pesticides, but about motor vehicle exhaust and industrial wastes that filled the air, earth, and water.

Johnson was determined to deal with caustic fumes in the air, lethal sludge in rivers and streams, and the steady disappearance of wildlife. The National Wilderness Preservation Act of 1964 set aside 9.1 million acres of wilderness, and Congress passed other measures to limit air and water pollution. In addition, Lady Bird Johnson, the president's wife, led a beautification campaign to eliminate unsightly billboards and junkyards along the nation's highways.

Achievements and Challenges in Civil Rights

Lyndon Johnson was enormously successful in advancing the cause of civil rights. Seizing the opportunity provided by Kennedy's assassination, Johnson told Congress, "No memorial oration or eulogy could more eloquently honor President Kennedy's memory than the earliest possible passage of the civil rights bill." He pushed the bill through Congress, heading off a Senate filibuster by persuading his old colleague, minority leader Everett Dirksen of Illinois, to work for cloture—a two-thirds vote to cut off debate.

The Civil Rights Act of 1964 outlawed racial discrimination in all public accommodations and authorized the Justice Department to act with greater authority in school and voting matters. In addition, an equal-opportunity provision prohibited discriminatory hiring on grounds of race, gender, religion, or national origin in firms with more than 25 employees.

Although the law was one of the great achievements of the 1960s, Johnson realized that it was only a starting point, for widespread discrimination still existed in American society. Even with the voting rights measures of 1957 and 1960, African Americans in large areas of the South still found it difficult to vote. Freedom Summer, sponsored by SNCC and other civil rights groups in 1964, focused attention on the problem by sending black and white students to Mississippi to work for black rights. Early in the summer, two whites, Michael Schwerner and Andrew Goodman, and one black, James Chaney, were murdered. By the end of the summer, 80 workers had been beaten, 1,000 arrests had been made, and 37 churches had been bombed.

Early in 1965, another confrontation made national headlines. Alabama police clubbed and teargassed demonstrators in an aborted march from Selma to the state capital at Montgomery. President Johnson sent the National Guard to protect another march to Montgomery and then asked Congress for a voting bill that would close the loopholes of the previous two acts.

The Voting Rights Act of 1965, perhaps the most important law of the decade, singled out the South

Roots of Selected Great Society Programs

Progressive Period	New Deal	Great Society
Settlement house activity of Jane Addams and others	Relief efforts to ease unemployment (FERA, WPA)	Poverty programs (OEO)
Efforts to clean up slums (tenement house laws)	Housing program	Rehabilitation of slums through Model Cities program
Progressive party platform calling for federal accident, old-age, and unemployment insurance	Social security system providing unemployment compensation and old-age pensions	Medical care for the aged through social security (Medicare)
Activity to break up monopolies and regulate business	Regulation of utility companies	Regulation of highway safety and transportation
Efforts to regulate working conditions and benefits	Establishment of standards for working conditions and minimum wage	Raising of minimum wage
Efforts to increase literacy and spread education at all levels	Efforts to keep college students in school through NYA	Assistance to elementary, secondary, and higher education
Theodore Roosevelt's efforts at wilderness preservation	Conservation efforts (CCC, TVA planning)	Safeguarding of wilderness lands
Establishment of federal income tax	Tax reform to close loopholes and increase taxes for the wealthy	Tax cut to stimulate business activity
Theodore Roosevelt's overtures to Booker T. Washington	Discussion (but not passage) of antilynching legislation	Civil rights measures to ban discrimination in public accommodations and to guarantee right to vote

for its restrictive practices and authorized the U.S. attorney general to appoint federal examiners to register voters where local officials were obstructing the registration of blacks. In the year after passage of the act, 400,000 blacks registered to vote in the Deep South; by 1968, the number reached 1 million.

Despite passage of the Civil Rights Act of 1964 and the Voting Rights Act of 1965, racial discrimination remained throughout the country. Still-segregated schools, wretched housing, and inadequate job opportunities were continuing problems. As the struggle for civil rights moved north, dramatic divisions within the movement emerged.

Initially, the civil rights campaign had been integrated and nonviolent. Its acknowledged leader was Martin Luther King, Jr. But now tensions between blacks and whites flared within organizations, and younger black leaders began to challenge King's nonviolent approach. They were tired of beatings, jailings, church bombings, and the slow pace of change when dependent on white liberal support and government action. Anne Moody, the stalwart activist in Mississippi, voiced the doubts so many blacks harbored about the possibility of real change. Discouraged after months of struggle, she boarded a bus taking civil rights workers north to testify about the abuses that still remained. As she listened to the others singing the movement's songs, she was overwhelmed by the suffering she had so often seen. "We Shall Overcome" reverberated around her, but all she could think was, "I wonder. I really wonder."

One episode that contributed to many blacks' suspicion of white liberals occurred at the Democratic national convention of 1964 in Atlantic City. SNCC, active in the Freedom Summer project in

Fannie Lou Hamer, pictured here, provided eloquent testimony about the discrimination that kept many southern blacks from voting as she lobbied unsuccessfully for seating the delegates of the Mississippi Freedom Democratic party at the Democratic national convention of 1964. *(AP/Wide World Photos)*

Mississippi, had founded the Freedom Democratic party as an alternative to the all-white delegation that was to represent the state. Testifying before the credentials committee, black activist Fannie Lou Hamer reported that she had been beaten, jailed, and denied the right to vote. Yet the committee's final compromise, pressed by President Johnson, who worried about losing southern support in the coming election, was that the white delegation would still be seated, with two members of the protest organization offered seats at large. That response hardly satisfied those who had risked their lives and families to try to vote in Mississippi. As civil rights leader James Forman observed, "Atlantic City was a powerful lesson, not only for the black people from Mississippi, but for all of SNCC. . . . No longer was there any hope . . . that the federal government would change the situation in the Deep South." SNCC, once a religious, integrated organization, began to change into an all-black cadre that could mobilize poor blacks for militant action. "Liberation" replaced civil rights as a goal.

Increasingly, angry blacks argued that the nation must no longer withhold the rights pledged in its founding credo. Black author James Baldwin wrote in one of his eloquent essays that unless change came soon, the worst could be expected: "If we do not now dare everything, the fulfillment of that prophecy, recreated from the Bible in song by a slave, is upon us: God gave Noah the rainbow sign, No more water, the fire next time!"

Even more responsible for channeling black frustration into a new set of goals and tactics was Malcolm X. Born Malcolm Little and reared in ghettos from Detroit to New York, he hustled numbers and prostitutes in the big cities. Arrested and imprisoned, he became a convert to the Nation of Islam and a disciple of black leader Elijah Muhammad. He began to preach that the white man was responsible for the black man's condition and that blacks had to help themselves.

Malcolm was impatient with the moderate civil rights movement. He grew tired of hearing "all of this non-violent, begging-the-white-man kind of dying . . . all of this sitting-in, sliding-in, wading-in, eating-in, diving-in, and all the rest." Espousing black separatism and black nationalism for most of his public career, he argued for black control of black communities, preached an international perspective embracing African peoples in diaspora, and appealed to blacks to fight racism "by any means necessary."

Malcolm X became the most dynamic spokesman for poor northern blacks since Marcus Garvey in the 1920s. Though he was assassinated by black

"The day of nonviolence is over," Malcolm X proclaimed, as many African Americans listened enthusiastically. A compelling speaker, Malcolm made a powerful case for a more aggressive campaign for black rights. *(UPI/Corbis-Bettmann)*

antagonists in 1965, his African-centered, uncompromising perspective helped shape the struggle against racism.

One man influenced by Malcolm's message was Stokely Carmichael. Born in Trinidad, he came to the United States at the age of 11, where he grew up with an interest in political affairs and black protest. While at Howard University, he participated in pickets and demonstrations and was beaten and jailed. Frustrated with the strategy of civil disobedience as he became active in SNCC, he urged fieldworkers to carry weapons for self-defense. It was time for blacks to cease depending on whites, he argued, and to make SNCC into a black organization. His election as head of the student group reflected SNCC's growing radicalism.

The split in the black movement was dramatized in June 1966 when Carmichael's followers challenged those of Martin Luther King, Jr., during a march in Mississippi. King still adhered to nonviolence and interracial cooperation. Just out of jail after being arrested for his protest activities, Carmichael jumped onto a flatbed truck to address the group. "This is the twenty-seventh time I have been arrested—and I ain't going to jail no more!" he

shouted. "The only way we gonna stop them white men from whippin' us is to take over. We been saying freedom for six years and we ain't got nothing. What we gonna start saying now is Black Power!" Carmichael had the audience in his hand as he repeated, and the crowd shouted back, "We . . . want . . . Black . . . Power!"

Black Power was a call for a broad-based campaign to build independent institutions in the African-American community. It drew on growing demands for an end to the physical and sexual abuse of black women. When Malcolm X heard about a vicious beating Fannie Lou Hamer had received in Winona, Mississippi, he cried, "I ask myself how in the world we can expect to be respected as *men* when we will allow something like this to be done to our women, and we do nothing about it." Black Power fostered a powerful sense of black pride. The movement included a wide variety of different figures: cultural nationalists such as Maulana Ron Karenga, an activist scholar and early authority on Black Studies; advocates of black capitalism such as Nathan Wright, Jr., chairman of the 1967 and 1968 National and International Conferences on Black Power; and revolutionary nationalists such as Huey P. Newton, a proponent of aggressive liberation measures. Its most enduring legacy was political and cultural mobilization at the grassroots level, even if it only partially realized its goals.

Black Power led to demands for more drastic action. The Black Panthers, radical activists who organized first in Oakland, California, and then in other cities, formed a militant organization that vowed to eradicate not only racial discrimination but capitalism as well. H. Rap Brown, who succeeded Carmichael as head of SNCC, became known for his statement that "violence is as American as cherry pie."

Violence accompanied the more militant calls for reform and showed that racial injustice was not a southern problem but an American one. Riots erupted in Rochester, New York City, and several New Jersey cities in 1964. In 1965, in the Watts neighborhood of Los Angeles, a massive uprising lasting five days left 34 dead, more than 1,000 injured, and hundreds of structures burned to the ground. Violence broke out again in other cities in 1966, 1967, and 1968.

A Sympathetic Supreme Court

With the addition of four new liberal justices appointed by Kennedy and Johnson, the Supreme Court supported and promoted the liberal agenda. Under the leadership of Chief Justice Earl Warren, the Court followed the lead it had taken in *Brown* v. *Board of Education* outlawing school segregation. Several decisions reaffirmed the Court's support of black rights by moving against Jim Crow practices in other public establishments.

The Court also supported civil liberties. Where earlier judicial decisions had affirmed restrictions on members of the Communist party and radical groups, now the Court began to protect the rights of individuals with radical political views. Similarly, the Court sought to protect accused suspects from police harassment. In *Gideon* v. *Wainwright* (1963), the justices decided that poor defendants in serious cases had the right to free legal counsel. In *Escobedo* v. *Illinois* (1964), they ruled that a suspect had to be given access to an attorney during questioning. In *Miranda* v. *Arizona* (1966), they argued that offenders had to be warned that statements extracted by the police could be used against them and that they could remain silent.

Other decisions similarly broke new ground. *Baker* v. *Carr* (1962) opened the way to reapportionment of state legislative bodies according to the standard, defined a year later in Justice William O. Douglas's words, of "one person, one vote." This crucial ruling helped break the political control of lightly populated rural districts in many state assemblies and similarly made the U.S. House of Representatives much more responsive to urban and suburban issues. Meanwhile, the Court outraged conservatives by ruling that prayer could not be required in the public schools and that obscenity laws could no longer restrict allegedly pornographic material that might have some "redeeming social value."

The Great Society Under Attack

Supported by healthy economic growth, the Great Society worked for a few years as Johnson had hoped. The tax cut proved effective, and the consumer and business spending that it promoted led to a steady increase in gross national product (GNP) of 7.1 percent in 1964, 8.1 percent in 1965, and 9.5 percent in 1966. As the economy improved, the budget deficit dropped just as predicted. Unemployment fell, and inflation remained under control. Medical programs provided basic security for the old and the poor. Education flourished as schools were built, and teachers' salaries increased as a result of the influx of federal aid.

Yet Johnson's dream of the Great Society proved illusory. Some programs, like the effort to eliminate poverty, promised too much, and the administra-

tion's rhetorical oversell led to disillusionment when problems failed to disappear. Other programs, planned in haste, were simply ill-conceived and did not work. Massive sums were not allocated to these programs, although some argued that the money was necessary to make them successful.

Factionalism also plagued the Great Society. Lyndon Johnson had reconstituted the old Democratic coalition in his triumph in 1964, with urban Catholics and southern whites joining organized labor, the black electorate, and the middle class. But diverse interests within the coalition soon clashed. Conservative white southerners and blue-collar white northerners felt threatened by the government's support of civil rights. Local urban bosses, long the backbone of the Democratic party, objected to grassroots participation of the urban poor, which threatened their own political control.

Criticisms of the Great Society and its liberal underpinnings came from across the political spectrum. There had never been widespread popular enthusiasm for much of the effort. Conservatives disliked the centralization of authority and the government's increased role in defining the national welfare. They also questioned involving the poor in reform programs, arguing that poor people lacked a broad vision of the nation's needs. Even middle-class Americans, generally supportive of liberal goals, sometimes grumbled that the government was paying too much attention to the underprivileged and thereby neglecting the needs of the middle class.

Radicals attacked the Great Society as a warmed-over version of the New Deal. The same middle-class liberal orientation remained, they claimed, with the real intent of programs to provide the working-class poor with middle-class values. "The welfare state is more machinery than substance," activist Tom Hayden declared. Furthermore, radicals charged, the assumption of Great Society programs that the American system was basically sound and that economic growth would finance benefits of the American dream for all meant that no real effort was being made to redistribute income. Only the redistribution of wealth, in their view, could transform American life.

The Vietnam War (discussed later in this chapter) dealt the Great Society a fatal blow. LBJ wanted to maintain both the war and his treasured domestic reform programs, but his effort to pursue these goals simultaneously produced serious inflation. The economy was already booming as a result of the tax cut and the spending for reform. As military expenditures increased, the productive system of the country could not keep up with demand. When

Johnson refused to raise taxes, in an effort to hide the costs of the war, inflation spiraled out of control. Congress finally got into the act and slashed Great Society programs. As hard economic choices became increasingly necessary, many decided the country could no longer afford social reform on the scale that Johnson had proposed.

CONTINUING CONFRONTATIONS WITH COMMUNISTS

The Cold War continued throughout the 1960s. Presidents John F. Kennedy and Lyndon B. Johnson were both aggressive cold warriors who subscribed to the policies of their predecessors. Their commitment to stopping the spread of communism kept the nation locked in the same bitter conflict that had dominated foreign policy in the 1950s and led to continuing global confrontations that sometimes threatened the stability of the entire world.

The Bay of Pigs Fiasco and Its Consequences

Kennedy was intensely interested in foreign affairs. In his ringing inaugural address, his major focus was on diplomacy, and he barely mentioned domestic issues. In the midst of the Cold War, he was determined to stand firm in the face of Russian power. During the campaign, he had declared: "The enemy is the communist system itself—implacable, insatiable, unceasing in its drive for world domination." In his inaugural address, he eloquently described the dangers and challenges the United States faced. "In the long history of the world," he cried out, "only a few generations have been granted the role of defending freedom in its hour of maximum danger." The United States would "pay any price, bear any burden, meet any hardship, support any friend, oppose any foe, to assure the survival and success of liberty."

Kennedy perceived direct challenges from the Soviet Union almost from the beginning of his presidency. The first came at the Bay of Pigs in Cuba in the spring of 1961. Cuban–American relations had been strained since Fidel Castro's revolutionary army had seized power in 1959. A radical regime in Cuba, leaning toward the Soviet Union, could provide a model for upheaval elsewhere in Latin America and threaten the venerable Monroe Doctrine. One initiative to counter the Communist threat was the Alliance for Progress, which provided social and economic assistance to the less-developed nations of the hemisphere. But other, more aggressive, responses were deemed necessary as well.

Just before Kennedy assumed office, the United States broke diplomatic relations with Cuba. The CIA, meanwhile, was covertly training anti-Castro exiles to storm the Cuban coast at the Bay of Pigs. The American planners assumed the invasion would lead to an uprising of the Cuban people against Castro.

Some top officials resisted the scheme. Senator J. William Fulbright, on learning of the plan, declared that "to give this activity even covert support is of a piece with the hypocrisy and cynicism for which the United States is constantly denouncing the Soviet Union." The situation, he observed, was not desperate: "The Castro regime is a thorn in the flesh; but it is not a dagger in the heart." Marine Commandant David Shoup had other objections. He argued that Cuba was larger than commonly thought and would not be taken with ease. It would be better to calculate the consequences before making such a commitment. Nonetheless, Kennedy approved the plan.

The invasion, which took place on April 17, 1961, was an unmitigated disaster. When an early air strike failed to destroy Cuban air power, Castro was able to hold off the troops coming ashore. Urged to use American planes for air cover, Kennedy refused, for by that time failure was clear. Rather than supporting the exiles, the Cubans had followed Castro instead, and the popular uprising that was predicted never materialized. The United States stood exposed to the world, attempting to overthrow a sovereign government. It had broken agreements not to interfere in the internal affairs of hemispheric neighbors and had intervened clumsily and unsuccessfully.

Although chastened by the debacle at the Bay of Pigs, Kennedy remained determined to deal sternly with the perceived Communist threat. Germany became the next battleground. For more than a decade, the nation had been divided (see Chapter 27). The Western powers had promoted the industrial development of West Germany, which was prospering and which stood in stark contrast to the drab, Soviet-controlled East Germany. Berlin, likewise divided, remained an irritant to the Russians, particularly since some 2.6 million East Germans had fled to West Germany, many of them making their escape through the city. Following a hostile meeting with Soviet leader Nikita Khrushchev in Vienna in June 1961 (where discussion centered on the question of a permanent settlement for the bifurcated city of Berlin to prevent the flow of East

The Berlin Wall

The Berlin Wall effectively sealed West Berlin off both from the eastern sector of the city and from East Germany itself. Now people could only enter and exit West Berlin through a number of carefully monitored checkpoints.   **Reflecting on the Past** Why was it so important for East Germany to prevent people from going into West Berlin? Why would people in West Berlin have wanted to go into East Berlin? How effective do you think such a wall might be in keeping people in or out?

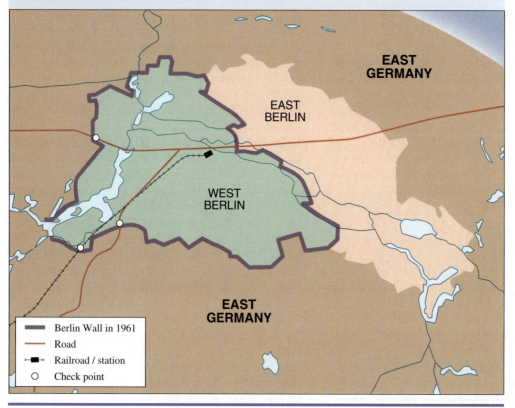

EAST
GERMANY

EAST
BERLIN

WEST
BERLIN

EAST
GERMANY

	Berlin Wall in 1961
	Road
	Railroad / station
○	Check point

The wall built by the Soviet Union bifurcated Berlin. Here West Berliners looked over the wall to the East. East Berliners likewise gazed at the West, where even larger and glitzier buildings were constructed. Later the wall became even higher than it appears here. *(© 2001 Collection Heiko Burkhardt, Dailysoft.com)*

Germany refugees), Kennedy reacted aggressively. He asked Congress for $3 billion more in defense appropriations, for more men in the armed forces, and for funds for a civil defense fallout-shelter program, explicitly warning of the threat of nuclear war. The USSR responded in August by erecting a wall in Berlin to seal off its section entirely. The concrete structure, topped by barbed wife, was 96 miles long and an average of 11.8 feet high. Menacing machine-gun emplacements made escape difficult. People who were caught scaling the wall were shot. Families were separated (and only allowed to cross to the other side to visit relatives and friends on special occasions) as the wall became a dramatic symbol of the division between East and West.

The Cuban Missile Face-Off

The next year, a new crisis arose. Understandably fearful of the American threat to Cuban independence after the Bay of Pigs invasion, Fidel Castro sought and secured Soviet assistance. American aerial photographs taken in October 1962 revealed that the USSR had begun to place what Kennedy considered offensive missiles on Cuban soil, although Cuba insisted they were defensive. The missiles did not change the strategic balance significantly, for the Soviets could still wreak untold damage on American targets from more distant bases. But with Russian weapons installed just 90 miles from American shores, appearance was more important than reality.

This time Kennedy was determined to win a confrontation with the Soviet Union over Cuba.

Top administration officials quickly convened and examined various alternatives. Some members of the Executive Committee of the National Security Council wanted an air strike to knock out the sites. Robert Kennedy opposed such a move by recalling the Japanese attack on Pearl Harbor in 1941 and declaring that his brother would not be the Tojo of his day. Still, the United States moved to a state of full alert. Bombers and missiles were armed with nuclear weapons and readied to go. The fleet prepared to move toward Cuba, and troops geared up to invade the island.

Kennedy went on nationwide television to tell the American people about the missiles and to demand their removal. He declared that the United States would not shrink from the risk of nuclear war and announced what he had decided to do: impose a naval "quarantine"—not a blockade, which would have been an act of war—around Cuba to prevent Soviet ships from bringing in additional missiles.

As the Soviet ships steamed toward the blockade and the nations stood "eyeball to eyeball" at the brink, the world held its breath. After several days, the tension broke, but only because Khrushchev called the Soviet ships back. Khrushchev then sent a long letter, transmitted by teletype, to Kennedy pledging to remove the missiles if the United States lifted the quarantine and promised to stay out of

Aerial photographs in the fall of 1962 showed the Soviet missile sites in Cuba, and this evidence led President Kennedy to insist on removal of the weapons. The Cuban missile crisis threatened to engulf the world in a nuclear war. (UPI/Corbis-Bettmann)

Israeli Conquests in 1967

The Six Day War of 1967 ended in huge Israeli territorial gains, both in the Sinai and on the West Bank of the Jordan River.   **Reflecting on the Past**   How did the new territory compare with the size of the state of Israel prior to 1967? What effect did the Israeli victory have on the stability of the Middle East? How would the Arab nations have responded to the defeat?

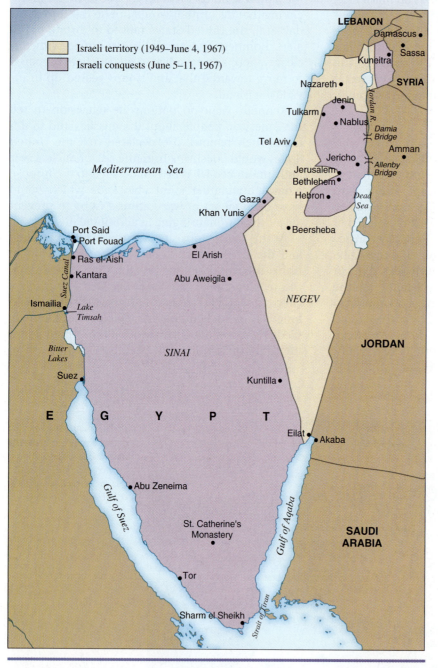

Israeli territory (1949–June 4, 1967)

Israeli conquests (June 5–11, 1967)

Cuba altogether. A second letter demanded that America remove its missiles from Turkey as well. The United States agreed to the first letter, ignored the second, and said nothing about its intention, al-ready voiced, of removing its own missiles from Turkey. With that, the crisis ended. Secretary of State Dean Rusk observed, "We have won a considerable victory. You and I are still alive."

The Cuban missile crisis was the most terrifying confrontation of the Cold War. The world was closer than it had ever been to nuclear war. Yet the president emerged from it as a hero who had stood firm. His reputation was enhanced, and his party benefited a few weeks later in the congressional elections. As the relief began to fade, however, critics charged that what Kennedy saw as his finest hour was in fact an unnecessary crisis. One consequence of the affair was the installation of a Soviet–American hot line to avoid similar episodes in the future. Another consequence was the USSR's determination to increase its nuclear arsenal so that it would never again be exposed as inferior to the United States. Despite the Limited Test Ban Treaty of 1963, which prohibited atmospheric testing, the nuclear arms race continued.

Confrontation and Containment Under Johnson

Johnson shared many of Kennedy's assumptions about the threat of communism. His understanding of the onset of World War II led him to believe that aggressors had to be stopped before they committed more aggression, for "if you let a bully come into your front yard one day, the next day he'll be up on your porch and the day after that he'll rape your wife in your own bed." Like Eisenhower and Kennedy, Johnson believed in the domino theory: if one country in a region fell, others were bound to follow. He was determined to preserve American power and contain the Communist menace. He assumed he could treat foreign adversaries just as he treated political opponents in the United States, and he was frustrated with what he called "piddly little piss-ant" countries that caused trouble.

In 1965, Johnson dispatched over 20,000 troops to the Dominican Republic in the West Indies, believing that "Castro-type elements" might win in a civil war there. In fact, the group Johnson called Communist was led by the former president, Juan Bosch, who had been overthrown by a military junta. Bosch ruefully pointed out that "this was a democratic revolution smashed by the leading democracy of the world." Johnson's credibility suffered badly from the episode.

In the Middle East, the United States sought to use its influence to temper the violence that erupted in the area. In 1967, Israeli forces defeated the Egyptian army in the Six Day War and seized the West Bank and Jerusalem, the Golan Heights, and the Sinai Peninsula. Americans pressed for a quick end to the fighting to maintain regional equilibrium and uninterrupted supplies of oil.

WAR IN VIETNAM AND TURMOIL AT HOME

The commitment to stopping the spread of communism led to the massive U.S. involvement in Vietnam. The roots of the conflict, described in Chapter 26, extended back to the early post–World War II years, but American participation remained relatively limited until Kennedy took office. Then the United States became more and more engaged in a major effort to resist a Communist takeover. That struggle wrought enormous damage in Southeast Asia, tore the United States apart, and finally forced a full-fledged reevaluation of America's Cold War policies.

Escalation in Vietnam

John Kennedy's commitment to Cold War victory led him to expand the American role in Vietnam, the country he once called the "cornerstone of the free world in Southeast Asia." Now resolved to resist the spread of communism, Kennedy and his closest associates were confident of success. As Secretary of Defense Robert McNamara observed, "North Vietnam will never beat us. They can't even make ice cubes." During the Kennedy administration, the number of advisers rose from 675 to more than 16,000, and American soldiers were already losing their lives.

Despite American backing, South Vietnamese leader Diem, a Catholic, was rapidly losing support in his own country. Buddhist priests burned themselves alive in the capital of Saigon to protest the corruption and arbitrariness of Diem's regime, which required everyone to obey Catholic religious laws. After receiving assurances that the United States would not object to an internal coup, South Vietnamese military leaders assassinated Diem and seized the government. Kennedy understood the importance of popular support for the South Vietnamese government if that country was to maintain its independence. But he was reluctant to withdraw and let the Vietnamese solve their own problems.

Lyndon Johnson shared the same reservations. After an early briefing, he said he felt like a catfish that had "grabbed a big juicy worm with a right sharp hook in the middle of it." Soon after assuming the presidency, Johnson made a fundamental decision that guided policy for the next four years. South Vietnam was more unstable than ever after the assassination of Diem. Guerrillas, known as Viet Cong, challenged the regime, sometimes covertly and sometimes through the National Liberation Front,

The Vietnam War

This map shows the major campaigns of the Vietnam War. The North Vietnamese Tet offensive of early 1968, pictured with red arrows, turned the tide against U.S. participation in the war and led to peace talks. The U.S. invasion of Cambodia in 1970, pictured with blue arrows, provoked serious opposition. **Reflecting on the Past** What role did North Vietnam play in the war? How far did American air power penetrate? Why did the United States and South Vietnam attack neighboring nations, such as Cambodia?

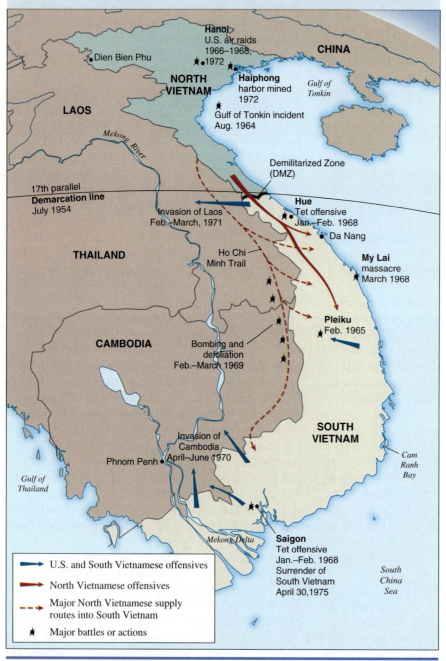

their political arm. Aided by Ho Chi Minh and the North Vietnamese, the insurgent Viet Cong slowly gained ground. Henry Cabot Lodge, the American ambassador to South Vietnam, was on his way home to brief Kennedy at the time of the assassination. He told the new president that if he wanted to save that country he had to stand firm. "I am not going to lose Vietnam," Johnson replied. "I am not going to be the President who saw Southeast Asia go the way China went."

In the election campaign of 1964, Johnson posed as a man of peace. "We don't want our American boys to do the fighting for Asian boys," he declared. "We are not going to send American boys nine or ten thousand miles away from home to do what Asian boys ought to be doing for themselves." He criticized those who suggested moving in with American bombs. But secretly he was planning to escalate the American role.

In August 1964, Johnson cleverly obtained congressional authorization for the war by announcing that North Vietnamese torpedo boats had made unprovoked attacks on American destroyers in the international waters of the Gulf of Tonkin, 30 miles from North Vietnam. Only later did it become clear that the American ships had violated the territorial waters of North Vietnam by assisting

South Vietnamese commando raids in offshore combat zones. With the details of the attack still unclear, Johnson used the episode to obtain from Congress a resolution giving him authority to "take all necessary measures to repel any armed attack against the forces of the United States and to prevent further aggression." The Gulf of Tonkin resolution gave Johnson the leverage he sought. As he noted, it was "like grandma's nightshirt—it covered everything."

Military escalation began in earnest in February 1965, after Johnson's landslide electoral victory, when Viet Cong forces killed 7 Americans and wounded 109 in an attack on an American base at Pleiku. Johnson responded by authorizing retaliatory bombing of North Vietnam to cut off the flow of supplies and to ease pressure on South Vietnam. He personally authorized every raid, boasting that the air force "can't even bomb an outhouse without my approval." A few months later, the president sent American ground troops into action. This marked the crucial turning point in the Americanization of the Vietnam War. Only 25,000 American soldiers were in Vietnam at the start of 1965; by the end of the year, there were 184,000. The number swelled to 385,000 in 1966, to 485,000 in 1967, and to 543,000 in 1968.

In 1963, Buddhist priests in Vietnam burned themselves to death in Saigon to dramatize their opposition to the Diem government. Photographs in American newspapers horrified readers and created suspicion that South Vietnam was led by a corrupt and autocratic leader. *(UPI/Corbis-Bettmann)*

Napalm, a jellylike chemical dropped by American planes, stuck to people as it burned. In this picture, widely circulated throughout the world, a small girl whose skin was seared off by napalm tries unsuccessfully to escape the ravages of war. *(AP/Wide World Photos)*

As escalation occurred, Johnson recognized his dilemma. He understood that the war was probably unwinnable, but he feared the loss of both American power and personal prestige if he pulled out. "Vietnam is getting worse every day," he told his wife in mid-1965. "It's like being in an airplane and I have to choose between crashing the plane or jumping out. I do not have a parachute."

And so American forces became direct participants in the fight to prop up a dictatorial regime in faraway South Vietnam. Although a somewhat more effective government headed by Nguyen Van Thieu and Nguyen Cao Ky was finally established, the level of violence increased. Saturation bombing of North Vietnam continued. Fragmentation bombs, killing and maiming countless civilians, and napalm, which seared off human flesh, were used extensively. Similar destruction wracked South Vietnam. And still, despite the repeatedly expressed contention of military commander William Westmoreland that there was "light at the end of the tunnel," the violence continued without pause.

Student Activism and Antiwar Protest

Americans began to protest their involvement in the war. But their protest had roots in a deeper disaffection, based in large part on post–World War II demographic patterns. Members of the baby boom generation came of age in the 1960s, and many of them, especially from the large middle class, moved on to some form of higher education. Between 1950 and 1964, the number of students in college more than doubled. By the end of the 1960s, college enrollment was more than four times what it had been in the 1940s. College served as a training ground for industry and corporate life; more important, it gave students time to experiment and grow before they had to make a living. In college, some students joined the struggle for civil rights. Hopeful at first, they gradually became discouraged by the gap between Kennedy's New Frontier rhetoric and the government's actual commitment.

Out of that disillusionment arose the radical spirit of the New Left. Civil rights activists were among those who in 1960 organized Students for a Democratic Society (SDS). In 1962, SDS issued a manifesto, the Port Huron Statement, written largely by Tom Hayden of the University of Michigan. "We are people of this generation, bred in at least modest comfort, housed now in universities, looking uncomfortably at the world we inherit," it began. It went on to deplore the vast social and economic distances separating people from each other and to condemn the isolation and estrangement of modern life. The document called for a better system, a "democracy of individual participation."

ANALYZING HISTORY

THE VIETNAM WAR

The war in Vietnam consumed both soldiers and resources. The rapid escalation was accompanied by a mounting protest movement back in the United States that peaked when the troop involvement was greatest. Meanwhile, American planes and helicopters did devastating damage to the rice paddies and palm groves of this far-away land.

Reflecting on the Past   Why did the rapid buildup cause such intense protest at home? What effects did the bombs have on the Vietnamese? Why did the number of troops diminish after 1968?

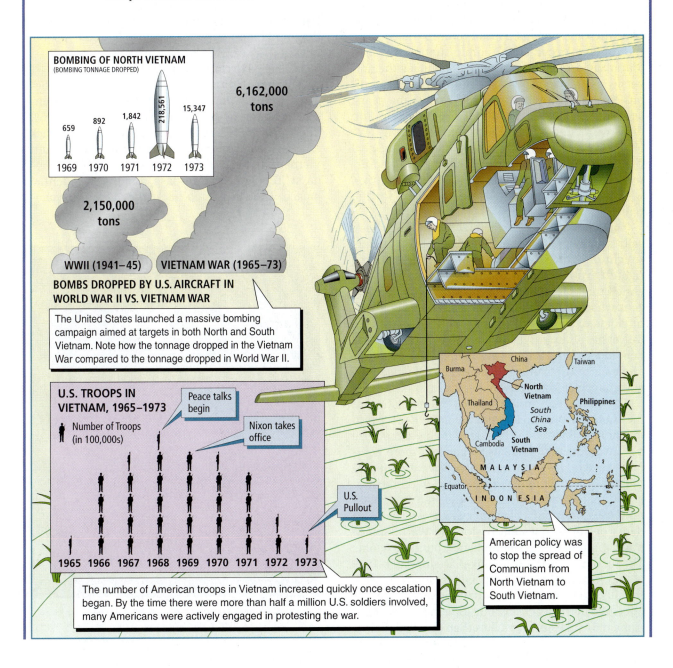

BOMBING OF NORTH VIETNAM
(BOMBING TONNAGE DROPPED)

659 — 1969
892 — 1970
1,842 — 1971
218,561 — 1972
15,347 — 1973

6,162,000 tons

2,150,000 tons

WWII (1941–45)   VIETNAM WAR (1965–73)

BOMBS DROPPED BY U.S. AIRCRAFT IN WORLD WAR II VS. VIETNAM WAR

The United States launched a massive bombing campaign aimed at targets in both North and South Vietnam. Note how the tonnage dropped in the Vietnam War compared to the tonnage dropped in World War II.

U.S. TROOPS IN VIETNAM, 1965–1973

Number of Troops (in 100,000s)

Peace talks begin

Nixon takes office

U.S. Pullout

1965 1966 1967 1968 1969 1970 1971 1972 1973

The number of American troops in Vietnam increased quickly once escalation began. By the time there were more than half a million U.S. soldiers involved, many Americans were actively engaged in protesting the war.

China   Taiwan
Burma
North Vietnam
Thailand   South China Sea   Philippines
Cambodia   South Vietnam
MALAYSIA
Equator
INDONESIA

American policy was to stop the spread of Communism from North Vietnam to South Vietnam.

The first blow of the growing student rebellion came at the University of California in Berkeley. There, civil rights activists became involved in a confrontation soon known as the Free Speech Movement. It began in September 1964 when the university refused to allow students to distribute protest material outside the main campus gate. The students, many of whom had worked in the movement in the South, argued that their tables were off campus and therefore not subject to university restrictions on political activity. When police arrested one of the leaders, students surrounded the police car and kept it from moving all night. The university regents brought charges against the student leaders, and when the regents refused to drop the charges, the students occupied the administration building. Mario Savio, one of the leaders, denounced the university as an impersonal machine: "It becomes odious, so we must put our bodies against the gears, against the wheels . . . and make the machine stop until we're free." Folksinger Joan Baez sang "We Shall Overcome," the marching song of the civil rights movement. Then police stormed in and arrested the students in the building. A student strike, with faculty aid, mobilized wider support for the right to free speech.

The Free Speech Movement at Berkeley was basically a plea for traditional liberal reform. Students sought only the reaffirmation of the long-standing right to express themselves as they chose, and they aimed their attacks at the university, not at society as a whole. Later, in other institutions, the attack broadened. Students sought greater involvement in university affairs, argued for curricular reform, and demanded admission of more minority students. Their success in gaining their demands changed the governance of American higher education.

The mounting protest against the escalation of the Vietnam War fueled and refocused the youth movement. SDS, which had been trying to mobilize both workers and students to create a more equitable society at home, now turned its attention to the war. As escalation began, 82 percent of the public felt that American forces should stay in Vietnam until the Communist elements withdrew. Then students began to question basic Cold War assumptions about battling communism around the globe. The first antiwar teach-in took place in March 1965 at the University of Michigan. Others soon followed. Initially, both supporters and opponents of the war appeared at the teach-ins, but soon the sessions became more like antiwar rallies than instructional affairs. Boxer Muhammad Ali legitimated draft resistance when he declared, "I ain't got no quarrel with them Viet Cong" and refused military induction.

Working through Students for a Democratic Society (SDS) and other organizations, radical activists campaigned against the draft, attacked ROTC units on campus, and sought to discredit firms that produced the destructive tools of war. "Make love, not war," students proclaimed.

The antiwar movement expanded. Women Strike for Peace, the most forceful women's antiwar organization, mobilized support by saying, "Stop! Don't drench the jungles of Asia with the blood of our sons. Don't force our sons to kill women and children whose only crime is to live in a country ripped by civil war." Students became even more shrill. "Hey, hey, LBJ. How many kids did you kill today?" they chanted. In 1967, some 300,000 people marched in New York City. In Washington, D.C., 100,000 tried to close down the Pentagon.

Working-class and middle-class Americans began to sour on the war at the time of the Tet offensive, celebrating the lunar new year in early 1968. The North Vietnamese mounted a massive attack on provincial capitals and district towns in South Vietnam. In Saigon, they struck the American embassy, Tan Son Nhut air base, and the presidential palace. Though beaten back, they won a psycho-

Muhammad Ali, one of the best boxers in history, liked to say he could "float like a butterfly, sting like a bee." When he refused army induction on the basis of his religious beliefs, the case eventually reached the Supreme Court, which decided in his favor. Allowed to box again, he regained his heavyweight title and served as a model to many African Americans. (© Gordon Parks)

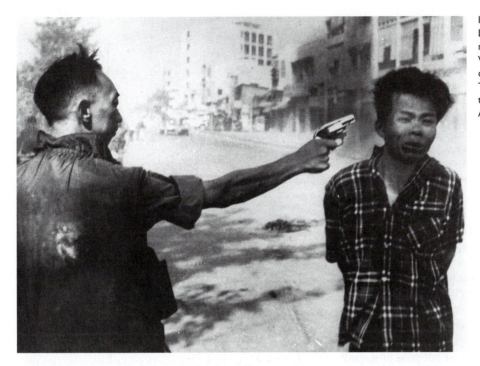

In this picture, General Nguyen Ngoc Loan, the chief of the South Vietnamese National Police, looks at a Viet Cong prisoner, lifts his gun, and calmly blows out the captive's brains. This prizewinning photograph captured the horror of the war for many Americans. *(AP/Wide World Photos)*

logical victory. American audiences watched the fighting on television, as they had for several years, seeing images of burning huts and wounded soldiers each evening as they ate dinner. During the Tet offensive, American television networks showed scenes of a kind never screened before. One such clip, from NBC News, appears here in still photograph form. Viewers who watched the television clip saw the corpse drop to the ground, blood spouting from his head. Gazing at such graphic representations of death and destruction, many Americans wondered about their nation's purposes and actions—indeed, about whether the war could be won.

Protest became a way of life. Between January 1 and June 15, 1968, hundreds of thousands of students staged 221 major demonstrations at more than 100 educational institutions.

One of the most dramatic episodes came in April 1968 at Columbia University, where the issues of civil rights and war were tightly intertwined. A strong SDS chapter urged the university to break ties with the Institute of Defense Analysis, which specialized in military research. The Students' Afro-American Society tried to stop the building of a new gymnasium, which it claimed encroached on the Harlem community and disrupted life there. Whites occupied one building, blacks another. Finally, the president of the university called in the police. Hundreds of students were arrested; many were hurt. A student sympathy strike followed, and Columbia closed for the summer several weeks early.

The student protests in the United States were part of a worldwide wave of student activism. French students demonstrated in the streets of Paris. In Germany, young radicals like Rudi Dutschke and Ulrike Meinhof were equally vocal in challenging conventional norms. In Japan, students waged armed battles with police.

The Counterculture

Cultural change accompanied political upheaval. In the 1960s, many Americans, particularly young people, lost faith in the sanctity of the American system. "There was," observed Joseph Heller, the irreverent author of *Catch-22* (1961), "a general feeling that the platitudes of Americanism were horseshit." The protests exposed the emptiness of some of the old patterns, and many Americans— some politically active, some not—found new ways to assert their individuality and independence. As in the political sphere, the young led the way, often drawing on the example of the Beats of the 1950s as they sought new means of self-gratification and self-expression.

Surface appearances were most visible and, to older Americans, most troubling. The "hippies" of the 1960s carried themselves in different ways. Men let their hair grow and sprouted beards; men and women both donned jeans, muslin shirts, and other simple garments. Stressing spontaneity above all else, some rejected traditional marital customs and gravitated to communal living groups. Their example, shocking to some, soon found its way into the culture at large, both in the United States and among young people around the world.

Sexual norms underwent a revolution as more people separated sex from its traditional ties to family life. A generation of young women came of age with access to "the pill"—an oral contraceptive that was effortless to use and freed sexual experimentation from the threat of pregnancy. In 1960, the Food and Drug Administration approved Enovid, the first oral contraceptive available on the market. Within three years of its introduction, more than 2 million women were on the pill, and as the cost dropped, millions more began to use it. In 1961, 14 percent of new patients at Planned Parenthood clinics chose oral contraception. In 1963, the figure jumped to 42 percent, and in 1964, it soared to 62 percent.

Americans of all social classes became more open to exploring, and enjoying, their sexuality. Scholarly findings supported natural inclinations. In 1966, William H. Masters and Virginia E. Johnson published *Human Sexual Response,* based on intensive laboratory observation of couples engaged in sexual activities. Describing the kinds of response that women, as well as men, could experience, they destroyed the myth of the sexually passive woman.

Author and editor Nora Ephron summed up the sexual changes in the 1960s as she reflected on her own experiences. Initially she had "a hangover from the whole Fifties virgin thing," she recalled. "The first man I went to bed with, I was in love with and wanted to marry. The second one I was in love with, but I didn't have to marry him. With the third one, I thought I might fall in love."

The arts reflected the sexual revolution. Federal courts ruled that books like D. H. Lawrence's *Lady Chatterley's Lover,* earlier considered obscene, could not be banned. Many suppressed works, long available in Europe, now began to appear. Nudity became more common on stage and screen. In *Hair,* a rock musical, one scene featured the disrobing of performers of both genders in the course of an erotic celebration.

Paintings reflected both the mood of dissent and the urge to innovate, apparent in the larger society. "Op" artists painted sharply defined geometric figures in clear, vibrant colors, starkly different from the flowing, chaotic work of the abstract expressionists. "Pop" artists such as Andy Warhol, Roy Lichtenstein, and Jasper Johns broke with formalistic artistic conventions as they made ironic comments on American materialism and taste with their representations of everyday objects like soup cans, comic strips, and pictures of Marilyn Monroe.

Andy Warhol's painting of a Campbell's soup can was one of the best-known examples of "pop" art in the 1960s. Warhol and other artists drew on advertising images, comic strips, and other elements of popular culture in their painting and sculpture. (© *SuperStock, Inc./© 2003 Andy Warhol Foundation for the Visual Arts/Artists Rights Society (ARS), New York.)*

Hallucinogenic drugs also became a part of the counterculture. One prophet of the drug scene was Timothy Leary, a scientific researcher experimenting with LSD at Harvard University. Fired for violating a pledge not to use undergraduates as subjects, Leary aggressively asserted that drugs were necessary to free the mind. Working through his group, the League for Spiritual Discovery, he dressed in long robes and preached his message, "Tune in, turn on, drop out."

Another apostle of life with drugs was Ken Kesey. While writing his first novel, *One Flew Over the Cuckoo's Nest,* he began participating in medical experiments at a hospital where he was introduced to LSD. With the profits from his novel, Kesey established a commune of "Merry Pranksters" near Palo Alto, California. In 1964, the group headed east in a converted school bus painted in psychedelic Day-Glo colors, wired for sound, and stocked with enough orange juice and "acid" (LSD) to sustain the Pranksters across the continent.

Drug use was no longer confined to urban subcultures of musicians, artists, and the streetwise. Soldiers brought experience with drugs back from Vietnam. Young professionals began experimenting with cocaine as a stimulant. Taking a "tab" of LSD became part of the coming-of-age ritual for many middle-class college students. Marijuana became phenomenally popular in the 1960s. "Joints" of "grass" were passed around at high school, neighborhood, and college parties as readily as cans of beer had been in the previous generation.

Music became intimately connected with these cultural changes. The rock and roll of the 1950s and the gentle strains of folk music gave way to a new kind of rock that swept the country—and the world (see the "Recovering the Past" section of Chapter 29 for a discussion of the music of the 1960s).

Rock festivals became popular throughout the 1960s. Held all over the country, the most dramatic such event occurred at the end of the decade. On an August weekend in 1969, some 400,000 people gathered in a large pasture in upstate New York for the Woodstock rock festival. This exuberant celebration, which featured ear-splitting, around-the-clock entertainment and endlessly available marijuana, went off without a hitch and seemed to the young to herald a new era. Another festival four months later at a stock car raceway in Altamont, California, was less fortunate. The Rolling Stones—one of the world's best known rock groups—hired members of the Hell's Angels motorcycle gang to serve as security guards at the concert. They beat to death one man who ventured on stage, and they attacked others whose actions they found offensive. At final count, four people were dead.

The underside of the counterculture was most visible in the Haight-Ashbury section of San Francisco, where runaway "flower children" mingled with "burned-out" drug users and radical activists. For all the spontaneity and exuberance, the counterculture's darker side could not be ignored.

An Age of Assassination

In 1968, American society seemed to be tearing apart. The generation gap caused major rifts between parents and children. Political protest was growing increasingly violent. And yet there was still a basic confidence that the democratic process could bring meaningful change. John Kennedy had fallen to an assassin's bullet five years before and the nation had survived that trauma. Then two more killings of highly prominent figures undermined any sense of hope.

Martin Luther King, Jr., was the most visible spokesman for African Americans in the years after 1955 (see Chapter 26). By the mid-1960s, he had broadened his crusade to attack poverty and economic justice and had also begun to speak out against the war in Vietnam, which included a dis-

proportionate number of black soldiers serving in combat roles and losing their lives.

King knew he was a target. He had been hounded for years by J. Edgar Hoover and the FBI, who accused him unreasonably of Communist ties. On April 3, 1968, he spoke eloquently at a church service, making reference to threats on his life. "We've got some difficult days ahead," he said. "But it doesn't matter with me now, because I've been to the mountain top . . . and I've seen the promised land."

The next day, as King stood on the balcony of his motel in Memphis, Tennessee, a bullet from a high-powered rifle ripped through his jaw and killed him.

King's assassination sparked a wave of violence throughout the United States. In a spontaneous outburst of rage, African Americans in 124 cities rioted, setting fires and looting stores. For all Americans, King's death eroded faith in the possibility of nonviolent change.

Several months later, Robert F. Kennedy likewise lost his life. Bobby, who had served his brother—the president—as attorney general, then won election to the Senate from New York after John Kennedy's death, was running for the Democratic presidential nomination. Kennedy had spoken out eloquently to the poor and had persuaded antiwar activists that he could bring the conflict to an end. In June, he won an important victory in the California primary. That evening, after giving his victory speech, he too was shot by an assassin. Civil rights leader John Lewis, working on Kennedy's campaign, said, "Something was taken from us. The type of leadership that we had in a sense invested in, that we had helped to make and to nourish, was taken from us." Kennedy's death ended many people's hopes for reconciliation or reform.

The Chaotic Election of 1968

The turbulent Democratic convention undermined any hopes the party had for victory. Chicago mayor Richard Daley was outraged that radicals, peace activists, and hippies were coming to his city to protest the war and ordered police to clear out demonstrators from public areas along Lake Michigan. As the convention prepared to nominate Vice President Hubert Humphrey (Lyndon Johnson had announced earlier in the face of the mounting protest movement that he would not run again), police began attacking demonstrators on the street. Much of the violence took place in front of television cameras as crowds chanted, "The whole world

Policemen attacked demonstrators and bystanders alike at the turbulent Democratic convention of 1968. The senseless violence, pictured in graphic detail on national television, revealed serious rifts in the Democratic party and underscored the inability of political leaders to bridge the gaps. The horrifying chaos destroyed support for Democratic candidates and helped Nixon win the election. *(UPI/Corbis-Bettmann)*

is watching." Humphrey gained what most people viewed as a worthless nomination.

Humphrey faced former Vice President Richard Nixon, who had long dreamed of the nation's highest office. He had failed in his first bid in 1960 and then two years later lost a race for governor of California. His political career seemed over, as he told the press in 1962, "You won't have Nixon to kick around any more because, gentlemen, this is my last press conference." Written off by most politicians, he staged a comeback after the Goldwater disaster of 1964, and by 1968, he seemed to have a good shot at the presidency again.

Governor George C. Wallace of Alabama, a third-party candidate, exploited social and racial tensions in his campaign. Appealing to northern working-class voters as well as southern whites, Wallace characterized those who wanted to reform American life as "left-wing theoreticians, briefcase-totin' bureaucrats, ivory-tower guideline writers, bearded anarchists, smart-aleck editorial writers and pointy-headed professors." He hoped to ride into office on

blue-collar resentment of social disorder and liberal aims.

Nixon addressed the same constituency, calling it the "silent majority." Capitalizing on the dismay these Americans felt over campus disruptions and inner-city riots and appealing to latent racism, he promised law and order if elected. He also called the Great Society a costly mistake, declaring that it was "time to quit pouring billions of dollars into programs that have failed." Heeding the advice of public-relations advisers, Nixon took the high ground and avoided shrill criticism himself. He gave Governor Spiro Agnew of Maryland, his vice presidential running mate, the task of leading the attack, just as he had done for Eisenhower in 1952. Agnew, much like the Nixon of old, responded aggressively, calling Hubert Humphrey "squishy soft on communism" and declaring that "if you've seen one city slum, you've seen them all."

Nixon received 43 percent of the popular vote, not quite 1 percent more than Humphrey, with Wallace capturing the rest. But it was enough to give

Presidential Election of 1968

Candidate	Party	Popular Vote	Electoral Vote
RICHARD M. NIXON	Republican	31,783,783 (43.4%)	301
Hubert M. Humphrey	Democratic	31,271,839 (42.7%)	191
George C. Wallace	American Independent	9,899,557 (13.5%)	46

Note: The winner's name appears in capital letters.

the Republicans a majority in the Electoral College and Nixon the presidency at last. Sixty-two percent of all white voters (but only 12 percent of black voters) had cast their votes for either Nixon or Wallace, suggesting that the covert racial appeal had worked. Because many Americans split their tickets, the Democrats won both houses of Congress.

Continuing Protest

Meanwhile, protests continued. The next year, in October 1969, the Weathermen, a militant fringe group of SDS, sought to show that the revolution had arrived with a frontal attack on Chicago, scene of the violent Democratic convention of 1968. The Weathermen, taking their name from a line in a Bob Dylan song—"You don't need a weatherman to know which way the wind blows"—came from all over the country. Dressed in hard hats, jackboots, work gloves, and other padding, they rampaged through the streets with clubs, pipes, chains, and rocks. They ran into the police, as they had expected and hoped, and continued the attack. Some were arrested, others were shot, and the rest withdrew to regroup. For the next two days, they plotted strategy, engaged in minor skirmishes, and prepared for a final thrust. It came on the fourth day, once again pitting aggressive Weathermen against hostile police.

Why had the Weathermen launched their attack? "The status quo meant to us war, poverty, inequality, ignorance, famine and disease in most of the world," Bo Burlingham, a participant from Ohio, reflected. "To accept it was to condone and help perpetuate it. We felt like miners trapped in a terrible poisonous shaft with no light to guide us out. We resolved to destroy the tunnel even if we risked destroying ourselves in the process." The rationale of the Chicago "national action" may have been clear to the participants, but it convinced few other Americans. Citizens around the country were infuriated at what they saw.

Timeline

1960	John F. Kennedy elected president
	Birth control pill becomes available
	Sit-ins begin
	Students for a Democratic Society (SDS) founded
1961	Freedom rides
	Joseph Heller, *Catch-22*
	Ken Kesey, *One Flew Over the Cuckoo's Nest*
	Bay of Pigs invasion fails
	Khrushchev and Kennedy meet in Berlin
	Berlin Wall constructed
	JFK confronts steel companies
1962	Cuban missile crisis
	James Meredith crisis at the University of Mississippi
	SDS's Port Huron Statement
	Rachel Carson, *Silent Spring*
1963	Buddhist demonstrations in Vietnam
	Birmingham demonstration
	Civil rights march on Washington
	Kennedy assassinated; Lyndon B. Johnson becomes president
	Betty Friedan, *The Feminine Mystique*
1964	Economic Opportunity Act initiates War on Poverty
	Gulf of Tonkin resolution
	Johnson reelected president
	Civil Rights Act
	Free speech movement, Berkeley
1965	Department of Housing and Urban Development established
	Elementary and Secondary Education Act
	Medicare established
	Martin Luther King, Jr., leads march from Selma to Montgomery
	Voting Rights Act
	United Farm Workers grape boycott
	Malcolm X assassinated
	Riot in Watts section of Los Angeles
	Ralph Nader, *Unsafe at Any Speed*
	Vietnam conflict escalates
	Marines sent to Dominican Republic
1966	Stokely Carmichael becomes head of SNCC and calls for "black power"
	Black Panthers founded
	Masters and Johnson, *Human Sexual Response*
1967	Urban riots in 22 cities
1967–1968	Antiwar demonstrations
1968	Student demonstrations at Columbia University and elsewhere
	Tet offensive in Vietnam
	Martin Luther King, Jr., assassinated
	Robert F. Kennedy assassinated
	Police and protesters clash at Democratic national convention
	Richard Nixon elected president
1969	Woodstock and Altamont rock festivals
	Weathermen's "Days of Rage" in Chicago

◆ *Conclusion*

POLITICAL AND SOCIAL UPHEAVAL

The 1960s were turbulent years. In the first part of the decade, the United States was relatively calm. Liberal Democrats went even further than Franklin Roosevelt and Harry Truman as they pressed for large-scale government intervention to meet the social and economic problems that accompanied the modern industrial age. They were inspired by John Kennedy's rhetoric and saw the triumph of their approach in Lyndon Johnson's Great Society, as the nation strengthened its commitment to a capitalist welfare state. Then the Democratic party became impaled on the Vietnam War, and opposition to the conflict created more turbulence than the nation had known since the Civil War.

American society was in a state of upheaval. Young radicals challenged basic assumptions about how the government worked. They railed against social injustice at home, and they protested a foreign policy that they regarded as wrong. Their efforts faltered at first but then succeeded when they seized on the war in Vietnam as a primary focus and began to attack the Cold War policy that led to massive American military involvement in that faraway land. Student leaders, who often came from politically active families, soon found hundreds of thousands of followers who joined in the marches and demonstrations that finally forced the nation to reconsider its aims. Meanwhile, members of the counterculture promoted their own more fluid values, challenged the patterns of conformity so important in the 1950s, and led millions of other Americans, some politically active, some not, to dress and act differently than in the past. The two strands of political activism and countercultural action were independent but intertwined, and they left the nation at the end of the decade very different than it had been before.

Most Americans, like Paul Cowan (introduced at the start of this chapter), embraced the message of John Kennedy and the New Frontier in the early 1960s and endorsed the liberal approach. But over time, they began to question the tenets of liberalism as the economy faltered, as hard economic choices had to be made, and as the country became mired in an unwinnable war in Vietnam. Conservatives deplored the chaos, while disillusioned liberals like Paul Cowan wondered if their approach could ever succeed.

◆ Recommended Reading

John F. Kennedy: The Camelot Years
Carl M. Brauer, *John F. Kennedy and the Second Reconstruction* (1977); Paul Cowan, *The Making of an Un-American: A Dialogue with Experience* (1970); James N. Giglio, *The Presidency of John F. Kennedy* (1991); Nigel Hamilton, *JFK: Reckless Youth* (1992); Seymour M. Hersh, *The Dark Side of Camelot* (1997); Diane McWhorter, *Carry Me Home: Birmingham, Alabama: The Climactic Battle of the Civil Rights Revolution* (2001); Herbert S. Parmet, *Jack: The Struggles of John F. Kennedy* (1980) and *JFK: The Presidency of John F. Kennedy* (1983); Geoffrey Perret, *Jack: A Life Like No Other* (2001); Richard Reeves, *President Kennedy: Profile of Power* (1993); Thomas C. Reeves, *A Question of Character: A Life of John F. Kennedy* (1991); Arthur M. Schlesinger, Jr., *A Thousand Days: John F. Kennedy in the White House* (1965); Theodore C. Sorensen, *Kennedy* (1965); Mark J. White, ed., *Kennedy: The New Frontier Revisited* (1998).

Lyndon B. Johnson and the Great Society
Michael R. Bechloss, ed., *Taking Charge: The Johnson White House Tapes, 1963–1964* (1997) and *Reaching for Glory: Lyndon Johnson's Secret White House Tapes, 1964–1965* (2001); Taylor Branch, *Parting the Waters: America in the King Years, 1954–1963* (1988) and *Pillar of Fire: America in the King Years, 1963–1965* (1998); Robert A. Caro, *Master of the Senate: The Years of Lyndon Johnson (2002);* Robert Dallek, *Lone Star Rising: Lyndon Johnson and His Times* (1990) and *Flawed Giant: Lyndon Johnson and His Times, 1961–1973* (1998); Robert A. Divine, ed., *Exploring the Johnson Years* (1981), *The Johnson Years, Volume Two: Vietnam, the Environment, and Science* (1984), and *The Johnson Years: LBJ at Home and Abroad* (1994); Lyndon Johnson, *The Vantage Point: Perspectives of the Presidency* (1971); Allen J. Matusow, *The Unraveling of America: A History of Liberalism in the 1960s* (1984); Rick Perlstein, *Before the Storm: Barry Goldwater and the Unmaking of the American Consensus* (2001).

Continuing Confrontations with Communists
Laurence Chang and Peter Kornbluh, eds., *The Cuban Missile Crisis, 1962: A National Security Archive Documents Reader* (1998); Aleksandr Fursenko and Timothy Naftali, *One Hell of a Gamble: Khrushchev, Castro, and Kennedy* (1997); Ernest R. May and Philip D. Zelikow, eds., *The Kennedy Tapes: Inside the White House During the Cuban Missile Crisis* (1997); Richard J. Walton, *Cold War and Counterrevolution: The Foreign Policy of John F. Kennedy* (1972); Mark J. White, *Missiles*

in Cuba: Kennedy, Khrushchev, Castro, and the 1962 Crisis (1997).

War in Vietnam and Turmoil at Home

Christian G. Appy, *Working-Class War: American Combat Soldiers and Vietnam* (1993); Michael Bechloss, ed., *Reaching for Glory: Lyndon Johnson's Secret White House Tapes, 1964–1965* (2001); Frances FitzGerald, *Fire in the Lake: The Vietnamese and the Americans in Vietnam* (1972); David Halberstam, *The Best and the Brightest* (1972); Le Ly Hayslip, *When Heaven and Earth Changed Places* (1989); George C. Herring, *America's Longest War: The United States and Vietnam, 1950–1975*, 3rd ed. (1996) and *LBJ and Vietnam: A Different Kind of War* (1994); Stanley Karnow, *Vietnam: A History: The First Complete Account of Vietnam at War* (1983); Jeffrey P. Kimball, *Nixon's Vietnam War* (1998); Ron Kovic, *Born on the Fourth of July* (1976); Guenter Lewy, *America in Vietnam* (1978); Robert S. McNamara, *In Retrospect* (1995); George Donelson Moss, *Vietnam: An American Ordeal*, 3rd ed., (1997); Tim Page, ed. by Doug Niven and Chris Riley, *Another Vietnam: Pictures of the War from the Other Side* (2002); Al Santoli, *Everything We Had: An Oral History of the Vietnam War by Thirty-three American Soldiers Who Fought It* (1981); Neil Sheehan, *A Bright Shining Lie: John Paul Vann and America in Vietnam* (1988); Jon Swain, *River of Time* (1995).

Terry H. Anderson, *The Movement and the Sixties: Protest in America from Greensboro to Wounded Knee* (1995) and *The Sixties* (1999); Alexander Bloom, ed., *Long Time Gone: Sixties America Then and Now* (2001); David Burner, *Making Peace with the Sixties* (1996); David Chalmers, *And the Crooked Places Made Straight: The Struggle for Social Change in the 1960s* (1991); Barbara Epstein, *Political Protest and Cultural Revolution: Nonviolent Direct Action in the 1970s and 1980s* (1991); David Farber, *The Age of Great Dreams: America in the 1960s* (1994); David Farber and Beth Bailey, eds., *The Columbia Guide to America in the 1960s* (2001); James J. Farrell, *The Spirit of the Sixties: The Making of Postwar Radicalism* (1997); Todd Gitlin, *The Sixties: Years of Hope, Days of Rage* (1987); Godfrey Hodgson, *America in Our Time* (1976); Maurice Isserman and Michael Kazin, *America Divided: The Civil War of the 1960s* (2000); W. J. Rorabaugh, *Berkeley at War: The 1960s* (1989); Jules Witcover, *The Year the Dream Died: Revisiting 1968 in America* (1998).

David Allyn, *Make Love, Not War: The Sexual Revolution: An Unfettered History* (2000); Beth L. Bailey,

Sex in the Heartland (1999); Peter Braunstein and Michael William Doyle, eds., *Imagine Nation: The American Counterculture of the 1960s and '70s* (2001); John D'Emilio and Estelle B. Freedman, *Intimate Matters: A History of Sexuality in America* (1988); Joan Didion, *Slouching Towards Bethlehem* (1968); Neil A. Hamilton, *The ABC-CLIO Companion to the 1960s Counterculture in America* (1997); Charles A. Reich, *The Greening of America* (1978); Theodore Roszak, *The Making of a Counter Culture* (1969); Tom Wolfe, *The Electric Kool-Aid Acid Test* (1968).

Fiction and Film

Richard Fariña's *Been Down So Long It Looks Like Up to Me* (1966) is a novel about hallucinatory life in the 1960s. Barbara Garson's *MacBird* (1966), a play patterned loosely after *Macbeth*, pokes fun at the overarching ambitions of Lyndon Johnson. Vaughn Meader's two record albums about *The First Family* (1962 and 1963—reissued on CD) provide a fictional glimpse at the Kennedy family. Bao Ninh's *The Sorrow of War* (1991) is a North Vietnamese novel (English version by Frank Palmos, from the original translation by Phan Thanh Hao) about the impact of the war; Tim O'Brien's *Going after Cacciato* (1978) is a novel about Vietnam in which one soldier simply decides to lay down his gun and walk home. O'Brien's *The Things They Carried* (1990) is a collection of short stories about the war. Robert Stone's *Dog Soldiers* (1974) is an older novel about the military side of the war in Vietnam.

Born on the Fourth of July (1989) is a film that tells Ron Kovic's story about being wounded in Vietnam and then returning home; Oliver Stone's film *The Doors* (1991) deals with Jim Morrison and his rock group in the 1960s. *Eyes on the Prize* (1987) is a superb, multi-part documentary about the civil rights movement. *The Graduate* (1967) became a cult film as it challenged the values of the 1950s and mocked the priorities of the world in which "plastics" were most important. *JFK* (1991) is Oliver Stone's film about the Kennedy assassination, in which he suggests a conspiracy killed the president. *Malcolm X* (1992) is Spike Lee's movie about the dramatic and outspoken black rights spokesman. *Mississippi Burning* (1988) is a film about three civil rights volunteers killed in Mississippi in 1964. Oliver Stone's movie *Platoon* (1986) deals with soldiers in the field in the war in Vietnam. *Thirteen Days* (2001) is a feature film about the Cuban Missile Crisis.

✦ Discovering U.S. History Online

John Fitzgerald Kennedy
www.ipl.org/ref/POTUS/jfkennedy.html
This site contains basic factual data about Kennedy's election and presidency, speeches, and online biographies.

The Kennedy Assassination
http://mcadams.posc.mu.edu/home.htm
This well-organized site has images, essays, and photos on the assassination.

Lyndon Baines Johnson

www.ipl.org/ref/POTUS/lbjohnson.html

This site contains basic factual data about Johnson's election and presidency, speeches, and online biographies.

Voices of the Civil Rights Era

www.webcorp.com/civilrights/index.htm

This site provides audio clips about the civil rights movement from Martin Luther King, Jr., and Malcolm X.

Martin Luther King, Jr., Papers Project

www.stanford.edu/group/king/

This site has links and selected digital documents by and about Martin Luther King, Jr.

Timeline of the American Civil Rights Movement

www.wmich.edu/politics/mlk/

This site contains a timeline of events in the 1950s and 1960s with pictures and documents.

Cold War Policies

http://history.acusd.edu/gen/20th/coldwar0.html

This site is an illustrated and annotated outline of the Cold War through the Johnson and Kennedy years.

The Cuban Missile Crisis

www.gwu.edu/~nsarchiv/nsa/cuba_mis_cri/

Declassified intelligence reports, photographs, audio, and essays shed new light on the Cuban missile crisis.

CIA and the Vietnam Policymakers: 1962–1968

www.odci.gov/csi/books/vietnam/index.html

Based on now-declassified material, this site offers a detailed account of CIA intelligence assessments during the Vietnam War and how U.S. policymakers used these assessments.

Battlefield Vietnam

www.pbs.org/battlefieldvietnam

This site presents an overview of the history of the Vietnam War; battle methods used, including guerrilla tactics and the air war; and the story of the Khe Sanh base.

Free Speech Movement: Student Protest—U.C. Berkeley, 1964–65

http://bancroft.berkeley.edu/FSM/

This site describes student protest through oral histories, documents, and a chronology.

The Sixties Project

http://lists.village.virginia.edu/sixties

This site has extensive exhibits, documents, and personal narratives from the 1960s.

The Digger Archives

www.diggers.org

This site provides information about the San Francisco Diggers, who became one of the legendary anarchist guerilla street theater groups in Haight-Ashbury during the years 1966–1968.

1969 Woodstock Festival and Concert

www.woodstock69.com/index.htm

This site provides pictures and lists of songs from the famous rock festival.

29 Disorder and Discontent, 1969–1980

Latinos, like women and members of other groups, worked to mobilize their communities behind the campaign for equal rights. This mural in an East Los Angeles housing project helped foster a sense of **Chicano** pride. *(Craig Aurness/Woodfin Camp & Associates)*

◆ *American Stories*

AN OLDER WOMAN RETURNS TO SCHOOL

Ann Clarke—as she chooses to call herself now—always wanted to go to college. But girls from Italian families rarely did when she was growing up. Her mother, a Sicilian immigrant and widow, asked her brother for advice: "Should Antonina go to college?" "What's the point?" he replied. "She's just going to get married."

Life had not been easy for Antonina Rose Rumore. As a child in the 1920s, her Italian-speaking grandmother cared for her while her mother worked to support the family, first in the sweatshops, then as a seamstress. Even as she dreamed about the future, Ann accommodated her culture's demands for dutiful daughters. Responsive to family needs, Ann finished the high school commercial course in three years. She struggled with ethnic prejudice as a legal secretary on Wall Street but still believed in the American dream and the Puritan work ethic. She was proud of her ability to bring money home to her family.

When World War II began, Ann wanted to join the WACS. "Better you should be a prostitute," her mother said. Ann went off to California instead, where she worked at a number of resorts. When she left California, she vowed to return to that land of freedom and opportunity.

After the war, Ann married Gerard Clarke, a college man with an English background. Her children would grow up accepted with Anglo-Saxon names. Over the next 15 years, Ann devoted herself to her family. She was a mother first and foremost, and that took all her time. But she still waited for her own chance. "I had this hunger to learn, this curiosity," she later recalled. By the early 1960s, her three children were all in school. Promising her husband to have dinner on the table every night at six, she enrolled at Pasadena City College. It was not easy, for family still came first, but Ann proved creative in finding time to study. When doing dishes or cleaning house, she memorized lists of dates, historical events, and other material for school. Holidays, however, complicated her efforts to complete assignments. Ann occasionally felt compelled to give everything up "to make Christmas." Forgetting about a whole semester's work two weeks before finals one year, she sewed nightgowns instead of writing her art history paper.

Her conflict over her studies was intensified by her position as one of the first older women to go back to college. "Sometimes I felt like I wanted to hide in the woodwork," she admitted. Often her teachers were younger than she was. It took four years to complete the two-year program. But she was not yet done, for she really wanted a bachelor's degree. Back she went, this time to California State College at Los Angeles.

As the years passed and the credits piled up, Ann became an honors student. Her children, now in college themselves, were proud and supportive; dinners became arguments over Faulkner and foreign policy. Even so, Ann still felt caught between her world at home and the world outside. Since she was at the top of her class, graduation should have been a special occasion. But she was only embarrassed when a letter from the school invited her parents to attend the final ceremonies. Ann could not bring herself to go.

With a college degree in hand, Ann returned to school for a teaching credential. Receiving her certificate at age 50, she faced the irony of social change. Once denied opportunities, Italians had assimilated into American society. Now she was just another Anglo in Los Angeles, caught in a changing immigration wave; now the city sought Latinos and other minorities to teach in the schools. Jobs in education were scarce, and she was close to retirement age, so she became a substitute teacher in Mexican-American areas for the next 10 years, specializing in bilingual education.

Meanwhile, Ann was troubled by the Vietnam War. "For every boy that died, one of us should lie down," she told fellow workers. She was not an activist, but rather one of the millions of quieter Americans who ultimately helped bring about change. The social adjustments caused by the war affected her. Her son grew long hair and a beard and attended protest rallies. She worried that he would antagonize the ladies in Pasadena. Her daughter came home from college in boots and a leather miniskirt designed to shock. Ann accepted her children's changes as relatively superficial, confident in their fundamental values; "they were good kids," she knew. She trusted them, even as she worried about them.

Ann Clarke's experience paralleled that of millions of women in the post–World War II years. Caught up in traditional patterns of family life, these women began to recognize their need for something more against a backdrop of continuing political turbulence. They worried about the consequences of the war in Vietnam and the constitutional issues in the Watergate scandal that brought President Richard Nixon down. Meanwhile, American women, like blacks, Latinos, Native Americans, and members of other groups, struggled to transform the conditions of their lives and the rights they enjoyed within American society. In the process, they changed the nation itself.

This chapter describes the continuing upheaval that shook American society in the 1970s. It shows the Nixon administration's effort to extricate American soldiers from the devastating struggle in Vietnam, while widening the war at the same time and creating further chaos in the United States. It chronicles the most serious political scandal in American history that led the president to resign. And it describes the ongoing effort to provide liberty and equality in racial, gender, and social relations. While political challenges came from middle-class activists, social complaints came from often marginalized Americans who finally spoke out in an attempt to make the nation live up to its professed values. This chapter highlights the voices of political and social protest that continued to echo throughout the 1970s in a heated debate about the distribution of power in the United States.

THE DECLINE OF LIBERALISM

After eight years of Democratic rule, many Americans were frustrated with the liberal approach. They questioned the liberal agenda and the government's ability to solve social problems. As the war in Vietnam polarized the country, critics argued that the government was trying to do too much. Capitalizing on the alienation sparked by the war, the Republican administration of Richard Nixon resolved to scale down the commitment to social change. Like Dwight Eisenhower a decade and a half before, Nixon accepted some social programs as necessary for the well-being of modern America but still wanted to cut spending and trim the federal bureaucracy. Furthermore, he and his political colleagues were determined to pay more attention to the needs of white, middle-class Americans who disliked the social disorder they saw as a consequence of rapid social change and resented the government's perceived favoritism toward the poor and dispossessed.

Richard Nixon and His Team

In and out of office, Nixon was a complex, remote man, who carefully concealed his private self. Born poor, he was determined to be successful and accomplished that aim in the political sphere. Yet the setbacks he suffered hurt him, and he constantly appeared to be scheming to right himself again. There was, one of his aides noted, "a mean side to his nature" that he sought to keep from public view. Nixon embraced political life, but never with the exuberance of Lyndon Johnson. Physically awkward and humorless, he was most comfortable alone or with a few wealthy friends. Even at work he insu-

lated himself, preferring written contacts to personal ones, and he often retreated to a small room in the executive office building to be alone.

Nixon was keenly aware of the psychology of politics in the electronic age. He believed that "in the modern presidency, concern for image must rank with concern for substance." Thus, he posed in public as the defender of American morality, though in private he was frequently coarse and profane. Earlier in his career he had been labeled "Tricky Dick" for his apparent willingness to do anything to advance his career. In subsequent years, he had tried to create the appearance of a "new Nixon," but to many he still appeared to be a mechanical man, always calculating his next step. As author and columnist Garry Wills pointed out, "He is the least 'authentic' man alive, the late mover, tester of responses, submissive to 'the disciple of consent.' A survivor. There is one Nixon only, though there seem to be new ones all the time—he will try to be what people want."

Philosophically, Nixon disagreed with the liberal faith in federal planning and wanted to decentralize social policy. But he agreed with his liberal predecessors that the presidency ought to be the engine of the political system. Faced with a Congress dominated by Democrats and their allocations of money for programs he opposed, he simply impounded (refused to spend) funds authorized by Congress. Later commentators saw the Nixon years as the height of what they came to call the "imperial presidency."

Nixon's cabinet appointees, sworn in with NBC "Today" cameras relaying the ceremony directly to television viewers, were white, male Republicans. For the most part, however, the president worked around his cabinet, relying on other White House

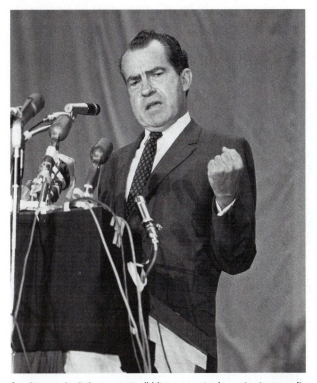

Speaking to the "silent majority," Nixon promised to reinstitute traditional values and restore law and order. A private man, Nixon tried to insulate himself from the public and present a carefully crafted image through the national media. *(Hiroji Kubota/Magnum Photos)*

staff members. In domestic affairs, Arthur Burns, a former chairman of the Council of Economic Advisers, and Daniel Patrick Moynihan, a Harvard professor of government (and a Democrat) were the most important. In foreign affairs, the talented and ambitious Henry A. Kissinger, another Harvard government professor, directed the National Security Council staff and later became secretary of state.

Another tier of White House officials—none with public-policy experience but all intensely loyal—insulated the president from the outside world and carried out his commands. Advertising executive H. R. Haldeman, a tireless Nixon campaigner, became chief of staff. Of his relationship with the president, Haldeman remarked, "I get done what he wants done and I take the heat instead of him." Working with Haldeman was lawyer John Ehrlichman. Starting as a legal counselor, he rose to the post of chief domestic adviser. Haldeman and Ehrlichman framed issues and narrowed options for Nixon. They came to be called the "Berlin Wall" for the way they guarded the president's privacy. John Mitchell was known as "El Supremo" by the staff, as the "Big Enchilada" by Ehrlichman. A tough, successful bond lawyer from Nixon's New York law office, he became a fast friend and managed the 1968 campaign. In the new administration,

he became attorney general and gave the president daily advice.

The Republican Agenda at Home

Although Nixon had come to political maturity in Republican circles, he understood that it was impossible to roll back the government's expanded role altogether. Accepting the basic contours of the welfare state, as other countries around the world did, he sought instead to systematize and scale back its programs. He was particularly determined "to reverse the flow of power and resources" away from the federal government and channel them to state and local governments, where he believed they belonged.

Despite initial reservations, Nixon proved willing to use economic tools to maintain stability. The economy was faltering when he assumed office. Inflation had risen from 2.2 percent in 1965 to 4.5 percent in 1968, largely as a result of the Vietnam War. Nixon responded by reducing government spending and pressing the Federal Reserve Board to raise interest rates. Although parts of the conservative plan worked, a mild recession occurred in 1969–1970, and inflation continued to rise. Realizing the political dangers of pursuing this policy, Nixon shifted course, imposed wage and price controls to stop inflation, and used monetary and fiscal policies to stimulate the economy. After his reelection in 1972, however, he lifted wage and price controls, and inflation resumed.

A number of factors besides the Vietnam War contributed to the troubling price spiral. Eager to court the farm vote, the administration made a large wheat sale to Russia in 1972. The sale proved to be a major miscalculation. With insufficient wheat left for the American market, grain prices shot up. Twenty-five years of grain surpluses suddenly vanished, and shortages occurred. Other agricultural setbacks like corn blight compounded the problem. Between 1971 and 1974, farm prices rose 66 percent, as agricultural inflation accompanied industrial inflation.

The most critical factor in disrupting the economy, though, was the Arab oil embargo. American economic expansion had rested on cheap energy just as American patterns of life had depended on inexpensive gasoline. Turbulence in the Middle East intruded on the economic stability of the Western world.

The Six Day War in 1967 made it clear that the Middle East was still a battleground. In 1967, anticipating an attack and launching a preemptive strike, Israeli forces defeated the Egyptian army and seized the West Bank and the Golan Heights, as well as the Arab sector of Jerusalem, which was now reunited

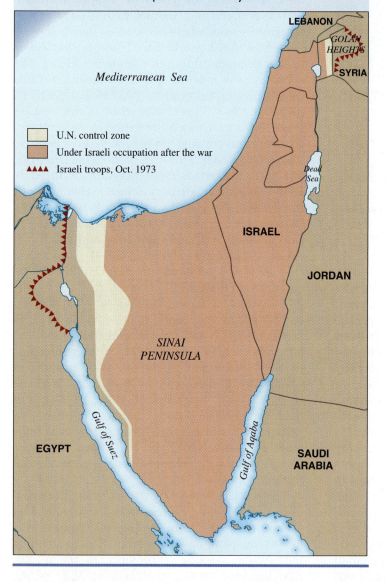

🌐 The Yom Kippur War of 1973

The Arab attack during the Yom Kippur holiday took Israel by surprise. Initially, Egypt and Syria regained some of their lost territory, but then the Israeli counterattack cut back many of the gains. In the end, United Nations troops were stationed on borders of the Sinai Peninsula and Golan Heights to help stabilize those regions. **Reflecting on the Past** How had the map of the Middle East changed in the years after the establishment of the state of Israel in 1948? Who was the victor in the 1973 Yom Kippur War? Why could United Nations forces help maintain stability?

with the Israeli part of the city for the first time since 1948.

In the aftermath of the Six Day War, the Organization of Petroleum Exporting Countries (OPEC) slowly raised oil prices in the early 1970s. Then another Arab-Israeli war in 1973 further disrupted the region. This conflict—the Yom Kippur War—came as Jews celebrated their holiest holiday—the Day of Atonement—and took them by surprise. The war pitted Israel against Egypt, Syria, Iraq, and Jordan. Initially Egypt, in the Sinai peninsula, and Syria, in the Golan Heights, were successful, but then the Israelis fought back. In the end, after several weeks of fighting, cease fires went into effect, leaving Egypt and Syria with modest gains but the Israelis largely in control.

Meanwhile, in the midst of the fighting, Saudi Arabia, an economic leader of the Arab nations, imposed an embargo on oil shipped to Israel's ally, the United States. Other OPEC nations continued to supply oil but quadrupled their prices. Dependent on imports for one-third of their energy needs, Americans faced shortages and skyrocketing prices. When the embargo ended in 1974, prices remained high. Even though oil prices around the world increased, the United States was hardest hit because of the huge amounts of oil it used.

The oil crisis affected all aspects of American economic life. Manufacturers, farmers, homeowners—all were touched by high energy prices. A loaf of bread that had cost 28 cents in the early 1970s jumped to 89 cents, and automobiles cost 72 percent more in 1978 than they had in 1973. Accustomed to filling up their cars' tanks for only a few dollars, Americans were shocked at paying 65 cents a gallon. In 1974, inflation reached 11 percent. But then, as higher energy prices encouraged consumers to cut back on their purchases, the nation entered a recession as well. Unemployment climbed to 9 percent for several months in 1975, the highest level since the 1930s.

The United States faced fierce economic competition from abroad. The auto industry provided a good example. Large American cars, which gobbled up gasoline, now were challenged by smaller Japanese imports that were far more fuel-efficient. The tiny German Volkswagen Beetle was already popular with cost-conscious drivers. Now they had their choice of smaller cars from Honda, Datsun (later called Nissan), and Toyota, too.

As economic growth and stability eluded the nation, Nixon also tried to reorganize rapidly expanding and expensive welfare programs. Changes in welfare during the years of the Great Society had led the government to spend considerably more in this area. Critics claimed that welfare was inefficient and that benefits discouraged people from seeking work. Nixon faced a political dilemma. He recognized the conservative tide growing in the Sun Belt regions of the country from Florida to Texas to California, where many voters wanted cutbacks in what they viewed as excessive government programs. At the same time, he wanted to create a new Republican coalition by winning over traditionally Democratic blue-collar workers with reassurances that the Republicans would not dismantle the parts of the welfare state on which they relied.

Urged by domestic adviser Daniel Moynihan, Nixon endorsed an expensive but feasible new program. The Family Assistance Plan would have guaranteed a minimum yearly stipend of $1,600 to a family of four, with food stamps providing about $800 more. The program, aiming to cut "welfare cheaters" who took unfair advantage of the system and to encourage recipients to work, required all participants to register for job training and to accept employment when found. Proponents, who doubtless exaggerated the number of cheaters, wanted to make it more profitable to work than to subsist on the public rolls. Though promising, the program was attacked by both liberals, who felt it was too limited, and conservatives, who claimed it tried to do too much. It died in the Senate.

As he struggled with the economy and with what many called the "welfare mess," Nixon irritated liberals still further in his effort to restore "law and order." Political protest, rising crime rates, increased drug use, and more permissive attitudes toward sex all created a growing backlash among working-class and many middle-class Americans. Nixon decided to use government power to silence disruption and thereby strengthen his conservative political constituency.

Part of the administration's campaign involved denouncing disruptive elements. Nixon lashed out at demonstrators, at one point calling student activists "bums." More and more, however, he relied on his vice president to play the part of hatchet man. As he had demonstrated during the 1968 campaign, Spiro Agnew had a gift for jugular attack. He branded opposition elements, students in particular, as "ideological eunuchs" who made up an "effete corps of impudent snobs." At the same time, Nixon and Agnew appealed for support to blue-collar youth, whom they described as patriotic supporters of the Vietnam War.

Another part of Nixon's effort to circumscribe the liberal approach involved attacking the communications industry. Although Nixon himself was well aware of the power of the press and used both television and radio effectively, he believed the media represented the opinions of the "Eastern establishment" and viewed him with hostility. After commentators responded negatively to a major address in 1969, he decided to challenge the television networks. Again Agnew spearheaded the pointed attack.

The third and strongest part of Nixon's plan was Attorney General John Mitchell's effort to demonstrate that the administration supported the values of citizens upset by domestic upheavals. Mitchell sought enhanced powers for a campaign on crime, sometimes at the expense of individuals' constitutional rights. He intended to send a message to the

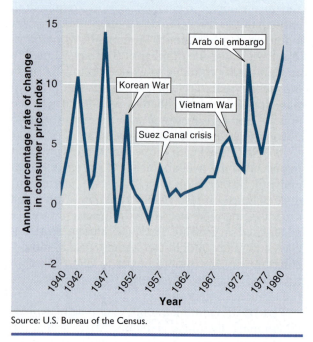

Rate of Inflation, 1940–1980

Inflation often accompanied military spending in the postwar years. In the early 1970s, the Arab oil embargo contributed to an even higher rate.

Source: U.S. Bureau of the Census.

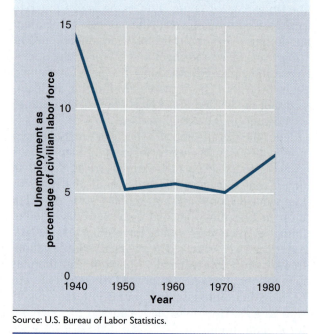

Unemployment Rate, 1940–1980

The unemployment rate fell dramatically during World War II, remained relatively constant from 1950–1969, and rose as inflation increased in the 1970s.

Source: U.S. Bureau of Labor Statistics.

entire country that the new team in the White House would not tolerate certain actions, even if they were protected by the right to free speech.

Mitchell's plan included reshaping the Supreme Court, which had rendered increasingly liberal decisions on the rights of defendants in the past decade and a half. That shift, Republican leaders argued, had resulted in moral and ethical laxity. During his first term, Nixon had the opportunity to name four judges to the Court, and he nominated men who shared his views. His first choice was Warren E. Burger as chief justice to replace the liberal Earl Warren, who was retiring. Burger, a moderate, was confirmed quickly. Other appointments, however, were more partisan and reflected Nixon's aggressively conservative approach. Intent on appealing to white southerners, he first selected Clement Haynesworth of South Carolina, then G. Harold Carswell of Florida. Both men on examination showed such racial biases or limitations that the Senate refused to confirm them. Nixon then appointed Harry Blackmun, Lewis F. Powell, Jr., and William Rehnquist, all able and qualified, and all inclined to tilt the Court in a more conservative direction.

Not surprisingly, the Court gradually shifted to the right. It narrowed defendants' rights in an attempt to ease the burden of the prosecution in its cases and slowed liberalizing of pornography laws. It supported Nixon's assault on the media by ruling that journalists did not have the right to refuse to answer questions for a grand jury, even if they had promised sources confidentiality. On other questions, however, the Court did not always act as the president had hoped. In the controversial 1973 *Roe* v. *Wade* decision, the Court legalized abortion, stating that women's rights included the right to control their own bodies. This decision was one that feminists, a group hardly supported by the president, had ardently sought.

Continuing Confrontations in Civil Rights

Richard Nixon, elected president in 1968, was less sympathetic to the cause of civil rights than his predecessors. The roots of what came to be called the "Southern strategy" lay in a speech Republican Senator Barry Goldwater made in 1961, three years before he received his party's presidential nomination; he declared, "We're not going to get the Negro vote as a bloc in 1964 and 1968, so we ought to go hunting where the ducks are." In 1968, the Republicans in fact won only 12 percent of the black vote, leading Nixon to conclude that any effort to

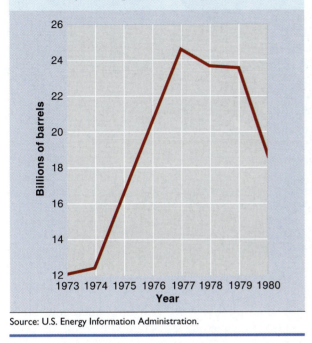

Oil Imports, 1973–1980

American reliance on foreign oil increased in the mid-1970s, until the United States tried to respond to price increases by reducing reliance on imports.

Source: U.S. Energy Information Administration.

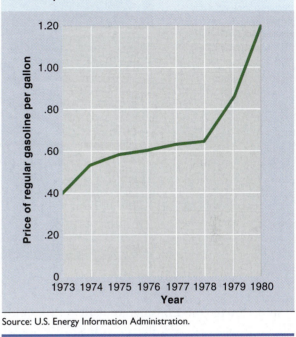

Gasoline Prices, 1973–1980

Gasoline prices rose steadily in the years following the Arab oil embargo and affected the entire American economy.

Source: U.S. Energy Information Administration.

woo the black electorate would endanger his attempt to obtain white southern support.

From the start, the Nixon administration sought to scale back the federal commitment to civil rights. It first moved to reduce appropriations for fair-housing enforcement, then tried to block an extension of the Voting Rights Act of 1965. Although Congress approved the extension, the administration's position on racial issues was clear. When South Carolina Senator Strom Thurmond and others tried to suspend federal school desegregation guidelines, the Justice Department lent support by urging a delay in meeting desegregation deadlines in 33 of Mississippi's school districts. While a unanimous Supreme Court rebuffed the effort, the president disagreed publicly with the decision.

Nixon also faced the growing controversy over busing as a means of desegregation, a highly charged issue in the 1970s. Transporting students from one area to another to attend school was nothing new. By 1970, over 18 million students, almost 40 percent of those in the United States, rode buses to school. Yet when busing became tangled with the question of integration, it inflamed passions.

In the South, before the Supreme Court endorsed integration, busing had long been used to maintain segregated schools. Some black students in Selma,

Alabama, for example, traveled 50 miles by bus to an entirely black trade school in Montgomery, even though a similar school for whites stood nearby. Now, however, busing was a means of breaking down racial barriers.

The issue came to a head in North Carolina, in the Charlotte-Mecklenburg school system. A desegregation plan involving voluntary transfer was in effect, but many blacks still attended largely segregated schools. A federal judge ruled that the district was not in compliance with the latest Supreme Court decisions, and in 1971, the Supreme Court ruled that district courts had broad authority to order the desegregation of school systems—by busing, if necessary.

Earlier, Nixon had opposed such busing. Now he proposed a moratorium or even a restriction on busing and went on television to denounce it. Although Congress did not accede to his request, southerners knew where the president stood. So did northerners, for the issue became a national one. Many of the nation's largest northern cities had school segregation as rigid as in the South, largely because of residential patterns. This segregation was called *de facto* to differentiate it from the *de jure,* or legal, segregation that had existed in the South. Mississippi senator John C. Stennis, a bitter foe of busing, hoped to stir up the North by making

When busing was mandated to end de facto school segregation in the North, the order frequently prompted fierce resistance. This photograph shows a bitter antibusing demonstration unfolding in Boston in 1976. *(Stanley J. Forman, Pulitzer Prize 1977, "The Soiling of Old Glory")*

it subject to the same busing standards as the South. He proposed requiring the government to enforce federal desegregation guidelines uniformly throughout the country or not use them at all. Court decisions subsequently ordered many northern cities to desegregate their schools.

Northern resistance to integration was fiercest in Boston, but the situation there was typical. In 1973, 85 percent of the blacks in the city attended schools that had a black majority. More than half of the African-American students were in schools that were 90 percent black. In June 1974, a federal judge ordered busing to begin. The first phase, involving 17,000 pupils, was to start in the fall of that year.

For many younger students, attendance at different elementary schools went smoothly. Reassigned high school students were less fortunate. A white boycott at South Boston High cut attendance from the anticipated 1,500 to fewer than 100 on the first day. Buses bringing in black students were stoned, and some children were injured. White, working-class South Bostonians felt that they were being asked to carry the burden of middle-class liberals' racial views. "They did it to me," screamed one white father, as he reacted to his son being transferred by bus from the white school he attended to a black one farther away. "They went and did it to me. . . . I told you they would. I told you there'd be no runnin from 'em. You lead your life perfect as a pane of glass, go to church, work 40 hours a week at

the same job—year in, year out—keep your complaints to yourself, and they still do it to you." Similar resentments triggered racial episodes elsewhere. In many cases, white families either enrolled their children in private schools or fled the city.

The Republicans managed to slow down the school desegregation movement. Nixon openly catered to his conservative constituents and demonstrated he was on their side. His successor, Gerald Ford, never came out squarely against civil rights, but his lukewarm approach to desegregation demonstrated a further weakening of the federal commitment.

The situation was less inflamed at the college level, but the same pattern held. Black Americans made significant progress until the Republican administrations in the late 1960s and 1970s slowed the movement for civil rights. Integration at the postsecondary level came easier as federal affirmative action guidelines seeking to provide opportunities for groups discriminated against in the past brought more blacks into colleges and universities. Black enrollment in colleges reached 9.3 percent of the college population in 1976, then dropped back slightly to 9.1 percent in 1980, just what it had been in 1973.

As blacks struggled on the educational and occupational fronts, some whites protested that gains came at their expense and amounted to "reverse discrimination." In 1973 and 1974, for example,

Ratio of Median Black-to-White Family Income, 1940–1980

This chart shows the substantial difference between family income for blacks and whites and reveals that the percentage has risen slowly since World War II. Observe, however, the downturn in the 1970s.

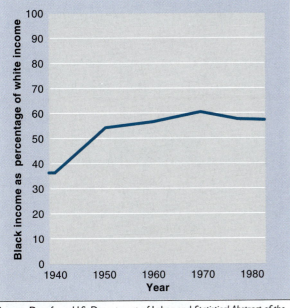

Source: Data from U.S. Department of Labor and *Statistical Abstract of the United States*, 1991.

Allan Bakke, a white, applied to the medical school at the University of California at Davis. Twice rejected, he sued on the grounds that a racial quota reserving 16 of 100 places for minority-group applicants was a form of reverse discrimination that violated the Civil Rights Act of 1964. In 1978, the Supreme Court ordered Bakke's admission to the medical school, but in a complex ruling including six separate opinions, the Court allowed "consideration" of race in admissions policies, but not quotas.

The civil rights movement underscored the democratic values on which the nation was based, but the gap between rhetoric and reality remained. In an era when industrial and farming employment shrank and rents rose at a highly inflationary rate, most black families remained poor. African-American income was substantially lower than white income, as the chart above shows. After early optimism in the years when the movement made its greatest strides, black Americans and sympathetic whites were troubled by the direction of public policy. Given a wavering national commitment to reform in the 1970s, only pressures from

reform groups kept the faltering civil rights movement alive.

THE ONGOING EFFORT IN VIETNAM

The war in Vietnam continued into the 1970s. When Nixon assumed office in 1969, he understood the need to heal the rifts that the struggle created in American society. During the campaign, he had spoken about a plan to end involvement in the war without specifying details. Once in office, he embarked on an effort to bring American troops home as a way of defusing opposition to the struggle. Unfortunately, his decision to try to avoid losing the war led to even further chaos at home.

Vietnamization—Bringing the Soldiers Home

A politician who had gained prominence as one of the nation's most aggressive anti-Communists, Nixon promised to bring the nation together. He gave top priority to extricating the United States from Vietnam while still seeking a way to win the war. To that end, he announced the Nixon Doctrine, which asserted that the United States would aid friends and allies but would not undertake the full burden of troop defense. The policy of Vietnamization entailed removing American forces and replacing them with Vietnamese troops. Between 1968 and 1972, American troop strength dropped from 543,000 to 39,000, and the reduction won political support for Nixon at home. Yet as the transition occurred, the South Vietnamese steadily lost ground to the Viet Cong.

At the same time, Americans launched ferocious air attacks on North Vietnam. "Let's blow the hell out of them," Nixon instructed the Joint Chiefs of Staff. Nixon used the bombing campaign to persuade his Vietnamese enemies that he would stop at nothing to achieve his ends. He later told Robert Haldeman, his trusted aide, what he was trying to do:

> I call it the madman theory, Bob. . . . I want the North Vietnamese to believe I've reached the point where I might do anything to stop the war. We'll just slip the word to them that, "For God's sakes, you know Nixon is obsessed about Communists. We can't restrain him when he's angry—and he has his hand on the nuclear button"—and Ho Chi Minh himself will be in Paris in two days begging for peace.

War protests multiplied in 1969 and 1970. In November 1969, as a massive protest demonstration took place in Washington, D.C., stories surfaced

Popular Music

One way to recover the past is through music. Popular songs not only provide insight into attitudes and beliefs but also quickly convey the mood and feelings of an era. Through their lyrics, songwriters express the hopes and fears of a people and the emotional tone of an age. Consider, for example, the powerful message conveyed in the Democratic party adoption of "Happy Days Are Here Again" as a campaign theme during the Great Depression. The decline of pop music and the rise of rock and roll in the 1950s tells historians a great deal about the mood of that period. Similarly, the popularity of both folk music and rock in the 1960s provides another way of following social change in that turbulent decade.

The music of the 1960s and 1970s moved beyond the syrupy ballads of the early 1950s and the rock and roll movement that Elvis Presley helped launch in the middle of the decade. As the United States confronted the challenges of the counterculture and the crosscurrents of political and social reform, new kinds of music began to be played.

Folk music took off at the start of the period. Building on a tradition launched by Woody Guthrie, Pete Seeger, and the Weavers, Joan Baez was one of the first folk singers to become popular. Accompanying herself on a guitar as she performed at coffee shops in Harvard Square and at the Newport Folk

Bob Dylan. *(AP/Wide World Photos)*

Festival, she soon overwhelmed audiences with her crystal-clear voice. She sang ballads, laments, and spirituals like "We Shall Overcome" and became caught up in the protest activities of the period.

Equally active was Bob Dylan, who grew up playing rock and roll in high school, then folk music in college at the University of Minnesota. Disheveled and gravelly voiced, he wrote remarkable songs like "Blowin' in the Wind" that were soon sung by other artists like Peter, Paul and Mary as well. His song "The Times They Are A-Changin'" (excerpted here) captured the inexorable force of the student protest movement best of all. Dylan, who alienated some of his folk music fans when he began playing the electric guitar, continued performing for decades.

The Times They Are A-Changin'
BY BOB DYLAN

Come mothers and fathers
Throughout the land
And don't criticize

Joan Baez *(John Launois/Black Star)*

What you can't understand
Your sons and your daughters
Are beyond your command
Your old road is
Rapidly agin'.
Please get out of the new one
If you can't lend your hand
For the times they are a-changin'.

But these years were marked by far more than folk music alone. In the early part of the decade, an English group from Liverpool began to build a following in Great Britain. At the start of 1964, the Beatles released "I Want to Hold Your Hand" in the United States and appeared on the popular Ed Sullivan television show. Within weeks, Beatles songs held the first, second, third, fourth, and fifth positions on the *Billboard* singles chart, and *Meet the Beatles* became the best-selling LP record to date. With the release of *Sergeant Pepper's Lonely Hearts Club Band* a few years later, the Beatles branched out in new musical directions and reflected the influence of the counterculture with songs like "Lucy in the Sky with Diamonds" (which some people said referred to the hallucinogenic drug LSD).

Mick Jagger and the Rolling Stones followed at the end of the 1960s. Another English group that changed the nature of American music, the Stones played a blues-based rock music that proclaimed a commitment to drugs, sex, and a decadent life of social upheaval. Jagger was an aggressive, some-

The Supremes *(Brown Brothers)*

times violent showman on stage, whose androgynous style showed his contempt for conventional sexual norms. Other artists, such as Jim Morrison of the Doors and Janis Joplin, reflected the same intensity of the new rock world, and both died from drug overdoses. This music too continued into the 1970s.

Meanwhile, other groups were setting off in different directions. On the pop scene, Motown Records in Detroit popularized a new kind of black rhythm and blues. By 1960, the gospel-pop-soul fusion was gaining followers. By the late 1960s, Motown Records was one of the largest black-owned companies in America and one of the most successful independent recording ventures in the business. Stevie Wonder, the Temptations, and the Supremes were among the groups who became enormously popular. The Supremes, led by Diana Ross, epitomized the Motown sound with such hits as "Where Did Our Love Go."

Reflecting on the Past   What songs come to your mind when you think of the 1960s and 1970s? How is the music different from that of the 1950s? What do the lyrics tell you about the period?

Look at the verse from "The Times They Are A-Changin'" that is reprinted here. What does it tell you about the turbulence of the time? What, if anything, do these lyrics imply can be done about the changes in the air? What other songs can you think of that give you a similar handle on these turbulent years?

The Beatles *(Hulton Archive/Getty Images)*

about a horrifying massacre of civilians in Vietnam the year before. My Lai, a small village in South Vietnam, was allegedly harboring 250 members of the Viet Cong. An American infantry company was helicoptered in to clear out the village. C Company had already taken heavy combat losses as it prepared to confront the enemy soldiers. Instead of troops, it found women, children, and old men. Perhaps hardened to the random destruction already wrought by the American military, perhaps concerned with the sometimes fuzzy distinction between combatants and civilians in a guerrilla war, the American forces lost control and mowed down the civilians in cold blood. Private Paul Meadlo, one of the soldiers involved, later recalled:

> We huddled them up. We made them squat down. . . . I poured about four clips into the group. . . . The mothers was hugging their children. . . . Well, we kept right on firing. They was waving their arms and begging. . . . I still dream about it. About the women and children in my sleep. Some days . . . some nights, I can't even sleep.

Stories of the massacre at My Lai underscored the senseless violence associated with the war and increased pressure for the United States to get out.

Widening the War

As much as Nixon wanted to defuse opposition to the war, he was determined not to lose the struggle either. Realizing that the Vietnamese relied on supplies funneled through Cambodia, Nixon announced in mid-1970 that American and Vietnamese troops were invading that country to clear out Communist enclaves there. The United States, he said, would not stand by as a "pitiful helpless giant" when there were actions it could take to stem the Communist advance.

Nixon's invasion of Cambodia brought renewed demonstrations on college campuses, some with tragic results. At Kent State University in Ohio, the antiwar response was fierce. The day after the president announced his moves, disgruntled students gathered downtown. Worried about the crowd, the local police called in sheriff's deputies to disperse the students. The next evening, groups of students collected on the college grounds. Assembling around the ROTC building, they began throwing firecrackers and rocks at the structure, which had become a hated symbol of the war. Then they set it on fire and watched it burn to the ground.

Governor James Rhodes of Ohio ordered the National Guard to the university. Tension grew, and finally the situation exploded. The Guardsmen watched as students gathered on campus. Though most were so far away they could not have reached

the troops, the soldiers reacted by firing without provocation on the students. When the shooting stopped, four students lay dead, nine wounded. Two of the dead had been demonstrators, who were more than 250 feet away when shot. The other two were innocent bystanders, almost 400 feet from the troops.

Students around the country, as well as other Americans, were outraged by the attack. Many were equally disturbed about a similar attack at Jackson State University in Mississippi. As students there returned to their dormitories one evening, they saw police officers and National Guardsmen responding to a bonfire. A few taunted the law officers. The troops responded without warning by firing 460 rounds of automatic weapon fire into a women's dormitory. When the gunfire ceased, two people were dead, more wounded. The dead, however, were black students at a black institution, and white America paid less attention to this attack.

In 1971, the Vietnam War made major headlines once more when the *New York Times* began publishing a secret Department of Defense account of American involvement. The so-called Pentagon Papers, leaked by Daniel Ellsberg, a defense analyst, gave Americans a firsthand look at the fabrications and faulty assumptions that had guided the steady expansion of the struggle. Even though the study stopped with the Johnson years, the Nixon administration was furious and tried, without success, to block publication.

The End of the War and Détente

Vietnam remained a political football as Nixon ran for reelection in 1972. Negotiations aimed at a settlement were underway, and just days before the election, Secretary of State Henry Kissinger announced, "Peace is at hand." When South Vietnam seemed to balk at the proposed settlement, however, the administration responded with the most intensive bombing campaign of the war. Hanoi, the capital of North Vietnam, was hit hard, and North Vietnamese harbors were mined. Only in the new year was a cease-fire finally signed.

The conflict in Vietnam lingered on into the spring of 1975. When at last the North Vietnamese consolidated their control over the entire country, Gerald Ford, Nixon's successor as president, called for another $1 billion in aid, even as the South Vietnamese were abandoning arms and supplies in chaotic retreat. But Congress refused, leaving South Vietnam's crumbling government to fend for itself. Republicans hailed Kissinger for having finally freed the United States from the Southeast Asian quagmire. Antiwar critics condemned him for remaining involved for so long. The *New Republic* wryly observed that Kissinger brought peace to Vietnam in the same way Napoleon brought peace to Europe: by losing.

The long conflict had enormous consequences. Disillusionment with the war undermined assumptions about America's role in world affairs. In the longest war in its history, the United States lost almost 58,000 men, with far more wounded or maimed. Blacks and Chicanos suffered more than whites, since they were disproportionately represented in combat units. Many minority men saw military service as a means of advancement. In 1965, 24 percent of all soldiers killed in Vietnam were African American—a figure far higher than their percentage of the population as a whole. Financially, the nation spent over $150 billion on the unsuccessful war. Domestic reform slowed, then stopped. Cynicism about the government increased, and American society was deeply divided. Only time would heal the wounds.

If the Republicans' Vietnam policy was a questionable success, accomplishments were impressive in other areas. Nixon, the consummate Red-baiter of the past, dealt imaginatively and successfully with the major Communist powers, reversing the direction of American policy since the Second World War.

Nixon's most dramatic step was establishing better relations with the People's Republic of China. In the two decades since Mao Zedong's victory in the Chinese revolution in 1949, the United States had refused to recognize the Communist government on the mainland, insisting that Jiang Jieshi's rump regime on Taiwan alone was the rightful government of the Chinese people. In 1971, with an eye on the upcoming elections, Nixon began softening his administration's rigid stance. After the Chinese invited an American table-tennis team to visit the mainland, the United States eased some trading restrictions. Then Nixon announced that he intended to visit China the following year. He suspected that he could use Chinese friendship as a bargaining chip when he dealt with the Soviet Union. He acknowledged what most nations already knew: Communism was not monolithic. He believed that he could open a dialogue with the Chinese Communists without political harm, for he had long ago established his anti-Communist credentials. Finally, he recognized that the press and television coverage of a dramatic trip could boost his image, as indeed it did.

Nixon went to China in February 1972. He met with Chinese leaders Mao Zedong and Zou Enlai (Chou En-lai), talked about international problems, exchanged toasts, and saw the Great Wall and other major sights. Wherever he went, American television cameras followed, helping introduce to the American public a nation about which it knew little. Though formal diplomatic relations were not yet restored, détente between the two countries had begun.

Seeking to play one Communist state against the other, Nixon also visited Russia, where he was likewise warmly welcomed. At a cordial summit meeting, the president and Soviet premier Leonid Brezhnev signed the first Strategic Arms Limitation Treaty (SALT I), which included a five-year agreement setting ceilings on intercontinental and other ballistic missiles, and an anti-ballistic missile treaty restricting the number of systems each nation could develop and deploy. At the same time, the two nations agreed to cooperate in space and to ease long-standing restrictions on trade. Business applauded the new approach, and most Americans approved of détente.

Nixon also recognized the need promote peace in the Middle East. Henry Kissinger engaged in shuttle diplomacy—moving from one nation to another—in an effort that helped arrange a ceasefire in the Yom Kippur War. In the aftermath of the struggle, recognizing the need for oil, Nixon and Kissinger worked to establish better relations with the Arab nations, even if that intruded on American support of Israel.

When Gerald Ford assumed office, he followed the policies begun under Nixon, although he ceased calling the approach détente. He continued the strategic arms limitation talks that provided hope for eventual nuclear disarmament, which culminated in the even more comprehensive SALT II agreement, signed but never ratified during Jimmy Carter's presidency.

CONSTITUTIONAL CONFLICT AND ITS CONSEQUENCES

As he dealt with chaos at home and abroad, Nixon worried about maintaining his political base. In his quest for reelection, he went too far and embroiled himself in a devastating political scandal that undermined his administration.

The Watergate Affair

Faced with a solidly Democratic Congress, the Nixon administration found many of its legislative initiatives blocked. Nixon was determined to end the stalemate by winning a second term and sweeping Republican majorities into both houses of Congress in 1972. His efforts to gain a decisive

Republican victory at the polls led to serious abuses of power.

Nixon's reelection campaign was even better organized than the effort four years earlier. His fiercely loyal aides were prepared to do anything to win. Special counsel Charles W. Colson described himself as a "flag-waving, kick-'em-in-the-nuts, anti-press, anti-liberal Nixon fanatic." He had earlier played an important part in developing an "enemies list" of prominent figures judged to be unsympathetic to the administration. White House counsel John Dean defined his task as finding a way to "use the available federal machinery to screw our political enemies." One way was by authorizing tax audits of political opponents. Active in carrying out commands were E. Howard Hunt, a former CIA agent and a specialist in "dirty tricks," and G. Gordon Liddy, a onetime member of the FBI, who prided himself on his willingness to do anything without flinching.

The Committee to Re-elect the President (CREEP), headed by John Mitchell, who resigned as attorney general, spared no expense in pursuit of its goal. It launched a massive fundraising drive, aimed at collecting as much money as it could before the reporting of contributions became necessary under a new campaign-finance law. That money could be used for any purpose, including payments for the performance of dirty tricks aimed at disrupting the opposition's campaign. Other funds financed an intelligence branch within CREEP that had Liddy at its head and included Hunt.

Early in 1972, Liddy and his lieutenants proposed an elaborate scheme to wiretap the phones of various Democrats and to disrupt their nominating convention. Twice Mitchell refused to go along, arguing that the proposal was too risky and expensive. Finally, he approved a modified version of the plan to tap the phones of the Democratic National Committee at its headquarters in the Watergate apartment complex in Washington, D.C. Mitchell, formerly the top justice official in the land, had authorized breaking the law.

The wiretapping attempt took place on the evening of June 16, 1972, and ended with the arrest of those involved. Their connection to the Republican party could incriminate the reelection campaign.

Top officials of the Nixon reelection team had to decide quickly what to do.

Reelection remained the most pressing priority, so Nixon's aides played down the matter and used federal resources to head off the investigation. When the FBI traced the money carried by the burglars to CREEP, the president authorized the CIA to call off the FBI on the grounds that national security was at stake. Though not involved in the planning of the break-in, the president was now party to the cover-up. In the succeeding months, he authorized payment of hush money to silence Hunt and others. Members of the administration, including Mitchell, perjured themselves in court to shield the top officials who were involved.

Nixon trounced Democrat George McGovern in the election of 1972, receiving 61 percent of the popular vote. In a clear indication of the collapse of the Democratic coalition, 70 percent of southern voters cast their ballots for Nixon. The president, however, failed to gain the congressional majorities he sought.

When the Watergate burglars were brought to trial, they pleaded guilty and were sentenced to jail, but the case refused to die. Judge John Sirica was not satisfied that justice had been done, asserting that the evidence indicated that others had played a part. Meanwhile, two zealous reporters, Bob Woodward and Carl Bernstein of the *Washington Post,* were following a trail of leads on their own. Slowly they recognized who else was involved. On one occasion, when they reached Mitchell and asked him about a story tying him to Watergate, he turned on them in fury. "All that crap you're putting in the paper?" he said. "It's all been denied."

Mitchell's irritation notwithstanding, the unraveling continued. The Senate Select Committee on Presidential Campaign Activities undertook an investigation, and one of the convicted burglars testified that the White House had been involved in the episode. Newspaper stories generated further leads, and the Senate hearings in turn provided new material for the press. Faced with rumors that the White House was actively involved, Nixon decided that he had to release Haldeman and Ehrlichman, his two closest aides, to save his own neck. On nationwide television he declared that he would take the ulti-

Presidential Election of 1972			
Candidate	Party	Popular Vote	Electoral Vote
RICHARD M. NIXON	Republican	45,767,218 (60.7%)	520
George S. McGovern	Democratic	28,357,668 (37.5%)	17

Note: The winner's name appears in capital letters.

DOONESBURY   by Garry Trudeau

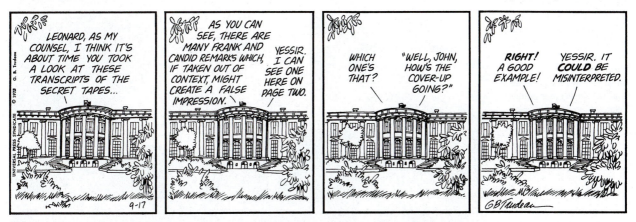

Although Nixon steadfastly denied his complicity in the Watergate affair, his tape recordings of White House conversations told a different story. In this classic "Doonesbury" cartoon from September 17, 1973, Garry Trudeau notes Nixon's efforts to head off the investigation. *(Doonesbury © 1973 G. B. Trudeau. Reprinted with permission of Universal Press Syndicate. All rights reserved.)*

mate responsibility for the mistakes of others, for "there can be no whitewash at the White House."

In May 1973, the Senate committee began televised public hearings, reminiscent of the McCarthy hearings of the 1950s. As millions of Americans watched, the drama built. John Dean, seeking to save himself, testified that Nixon knew about the cover-up, and other staffers revealed a host of illegal activities undertaken at the White House: money had been paid to the burglars to silence them; State Department documents had been forged to smear a previous administration; wiretaps had been used to prevent top-level leaks. The most electrifying moment was the disclosure by another aide that the president had installed a secret taping system in his office that recorded all conversations. Tapes could verify or disprove the growing rumors that Nixon had in fact been party to the cover-up all along.

To show his own honesty, Nixon appointed Harvard law professor Archibald Cox as a special prosecutor in the Department of Justice. But when Cox tried to gain access to the tapes, Nixon resisted and finally fired him. Nixon's own popularity plummeted, and even the appointment of another special prosecutor, Leon Jaworski, did not help. More and more Americans now believed that the president had played at least some part in the cover-up and should take responsibility for his acts. *Time* magazine ran an editorial headlined "The President Should Resign," and Congress considered impeachment.

The first steps, in accordance with constitutional mandate, took place in the House of Representatives. The House Judiciary Committee, made up of 21 Democrats and 17 Republicans, began to debate the impeachment case in late July 1974. By sizable tal-

lies, it voted to impeach the president on the grounds of obstruction of justice, abuse of power, and refusal to obey a congressional subpoena to turn over his tapes. A full House of Representatives vote still had to occur, and the Senate would have to preside over a trial before removal could take place. But for Nixon, the handwriting was on the wall.

After a brief delay, on August 5, Nixon obeyed a Supreme Court ruling and released the tapes. Despite a suspicious 18½ minute silence, they contained the "smoking gun"—clear evidence of his complicity in the cover-up. His ultimate resignation became but a matter of time. Four days later, on August 9, 1974, the extraordinary episode came to an end, as Nixon became the first American president ever to resign.

As other nations around the world watched the Watergate affair with interest, they did not always understand the stakes involved. In a parliamentary democracy, like the British system, a prime minister resigns whenever a vote of no confidence occurs. Scandals or simply serious political opposition can trigger this result. In the United States, however, a presidential resignation had never occurred in the nation's 200-year past, and so such a step loomed large.

The Watergate affair seemed disturbing evidence that the appropriate balance of power in the federal government had disappeared. As the scandal wound down, many began to question the centralization of power in the American political system and to cite the "imperial presidency" as the cause of recent abuses. Others simply lost faith in the presidency altogether. A 1974 survey showed that trust in the presidency had declined by 50 percent in a two-year period. Coming on the heels of Lyndon

The Watergate affair finally brought Nixon down. After resigning the presidency in 1974, Nixon took off for exile in California. Despite leaving Washington in disgrace, Nixon struck an incongruously triumphant pose as he boarded a helicopter on the White House lawn. *(Corbis)*

Johnson's lying to the American people about involvement in Vietnam, the Watergate affair contributed to the cumulative disillusionment with politics in Washington and to the steady decrease in political participation. Barely half of those eligible to vote bothered to go to the polls in the presidential elections of 1976, 1980, and 1984. Even fewer cast ballots in nonpresidential contests.

Gerald Ford: Caretaker President

When Nixon resigned in disgrace midway through his second term, he was succeeded by Gerald Ford. An unpretentious, middle-American Republican who believed in traditional virtues, Ford had been appointed vice president in 1973 when Spiro Agnew resigned in disgrace for accepting bribes. After the appointment, Richard Rovere, a noted journalist, wrote in the *New Yorker:* "That he is thoroughly equipped to serve as Vice President seems unarguable; the office requires only a warm body and occasionally a nimble tongue. However . . . neither Richard Nixon nor anyone else has come forward to explain Gerald Ford's qualifications to serve as Chief Executive." The new president acknowledged his own limitations, declaring, "I am a Ford, not a Lincoln."

More important than his limitations were his views about public policy. Throughout a long tenure in the House of Representatives, Ford had voted according to the Republican convictions he shared with his Michigan constituents. Over the years, he had opposed federal aid to education, the poverty program, and mass transit. He had voted for civil

Gerald Ford, a genial man, sought to reestablish confidence in the government after succeeding Nixon as president. Far different from his predecessor, he served just over two years, as his bid for election to the presidency in 1976 ended in defeat. *(UPI/Corbis-Bettmann)*

rights measures only when weaker substitutes he had favored had gone down to defeat. Like his predecessor, he was determined to stop the liberal advances promoted by the Democrats in the 1960s.

Ford faced a daunting task. After Watergate, Washington was in turmoil. Americans wondered whether any politician could be trusted to guide public affairs. The new president had to use his authority to restore national confidence at a time when the misuse of presidential power itself had precipitated the crisis.

Ford worked quickly to restore trust in the government. He emphasized conciliation and compromise, and he promised to cooperate both with Congress and with American citizens. The nation responded gratefully. *Time* magazine pointed to a "mood of good feeling and even exhilaration in Washington that the city had not experienced for many years."

The new feeling did not last long. Ford weakened his base of support by pardoning Richard Nixon barely a month after his resignation. Ford's decidedly conservative bent in domestic policy often threw him into confrontation with a Democratic Congress. Economic problems proved most pressing in 1974, as inflation, fueled by oil price increases, hit 11 percent, unemployment reached 6.6 percent at the end of the year, and GNP declined. Home construction slackened and interest rates rose, while stock prices fell. Nixon, preoccupied with the Watergate crisis, had been unable to curb rising inflation and unemployment. Not since Franklin Roosevelt took office in the depths of the Great Depression had a new president faced economic difficulties so severe.

Like Herbert Hoover 45 years before, the conservative Ford hoped to restore confidence and persuade the public that conditions would improve with patience and goodwill. But his campaign to cajole Americans to "Whip Inflation Now" voluntarily failed dismally. At last convinced of the need for strong government action, the administration introduced a tight-money policy as a means of curbing inflation. It led to the most severe recession since the Depression, with unemployment peaking at 9 percent in early 1975. In response, Congress pushed for an antirecession spending program. Recognizing political reality, Ford endorsed a multibillion-dollar tax cut coupled with higher unemployment benefits. The economy made a modest recovery, although inflation and unemployment remained high, and federal budget deficits soared.

Ford's dilemma was that his belief in limited presidential involvement set him against liberals who argued that strong executive leadership was necessary to make the welfare state work. When he failed to take the initiative, Congress intervened, and the two branches of government became embroiled in conflict. Ford vetoed numerous bills, including those creating a consumer protection agency and expanding programs in education, housing, and health. In response, Congress overrode a higher percentage of vetoes than at any time since the presidency of Franklin Pierce more than a century before.

The Carter Interlude

In the election of 1976, the nation's bicentennial year, Ford faced Jimmy Carter, former governor of Georgia. Carter, appealing to voters distrustful of political leadership, portrayed himself as an outsider. He stressed that he was not from Washington and observed that, unlike many of those mired in recent scandals, he was not a lawyer. Carter's quest for the Democratic nomination benefited from reforms that increased the significance of primary elections in selecting a presidential candidate and decreased the influence of party professionals. Assisted by public relations experts, he effectively utilized the media, especially television, which allowed him to bypass party machines and establish a direct electronic relationship with voters.

In the election, most elements of the old Democratic coalition came together once again, as the Democrats profited from the fallout of the Watergate affair. Carter won a 50 to 48 percent majority of the popular vote and a 297 to 240 tally in the Electoral College. He did well with members of the working class, African Americans, and Catholics. He won most of the South, heartening to the Democrats after Nixon's gains there. Racial voting differences continued, however, as Carter attracted less than half of all white voters but an overwhelming majority of black voters.

Carter stood in stark contrast to his recent predecessors in the White House. Rooted in the rural South, he was a peanut farmer who shared the values of the region. He was also a graduate of the Naval Academy, trained as a manager and an engineer. A modest man, he was uncomfortable with the pomp and incessant political activity in Washington.

Presidential Election of 1976

Candidate	Party	Popular Vote	Electoral Vote
JIMMY CARTER	Democratic	40,830,763 (50.0%)	297
Gerald R. Ford	Republican	39,147,793 (48.0%)	240

Note: The winner's name appears in capital letters.

Jimmy Carter holds hands with his wife, Rosalyn, as they walk to his inauguration in early 1977. As much as possible, Carter tried to avoid actions that reminded people of the "imperial presidency" of the Nixon years. (*Jimmy Carter Library, Atlanta, Georgia*)

He hoped to take a more restrained approach to the presidency and thereby defuse its imperial stamp.

Initially, voters saw Carter as a reform Democrat committed to his party's liberal goals. When he had accepted the Democratic nomination, he had called for an end to race and sex discrimination. He had challenged the "political and economic elite" in America and sought a new approach to providing for the poor, old, and weak.

But Carter was hardly the old-line liberal some Democrats had hoped for. Though he called himself a populist, his political philosophy and priorities were never clear. Critics charged that he had no legislative strategy. Rather, they said with some truth, he responded to problems in a haphazard way and failed to provide firm direction. His status as an outsider, touted during the campaign, led him to ignore traditional political channels when he assumed power. He also seemed to become mired in detail and to lose sight of larger issues. Like Herbert Hoover, he was a technocrat in the White House when liberals wanted a visionary to help them overcome hard times.

In economic affairs, Carter gave liberals some hope at first as he accepted deficit spending. When the Federal Reserve Board increased the money supply to help meet mounting deficits, which reached peacetime records in these years, inflation rose to about 10 percent a year. Seeking to reduce inflation in 1979, Carter slowed down the economy by reducing spending and cutting the deficit slightly. Contraction of the money supply led to greater unemployment—around 6 percent—and many small-business failures. Budget cuts fell largely on social programs and distanced Carter from reform-minded Democrats who had supported him three years before. Yet even that effort to arrest growing deficits was not enough. When the budget released in early 1980 still showed high spending levels, the financial community reacted strongly. Bond prices fell, and interest rates rose dramatically.

Similarly, Carter disappointed liberals by failing to construct an effective energy policy. OPEC's increase of oil prices led many Americans to resent their dependence on foreign oil—over 40 percent was being imported by the end of the decade—and to clamor for energy self-sufficiency. Carter responded in April 1977 with a comprehensive energy program, which he called the "moral equivalent of war." Critics seized on the acronym of that expression, MEOW, to ridicule the plan and had a field day attacking the president. Never an effective leader in working with the legislative branch, Carter watched his proposals bog down in Congress for 26 months. Eventually, the program committed the nation to move from oil dependence to reliance on coal, possibly even on sun and wind, and established a new synthetic-fuel corporation. Nuclear power, another alternative, seemed less attractive as costs rose and accidents occurred.

Carter further upset liberals by beginning deregulation—the removal of government controls in economic life. Arguing that certain restrictions established over the past century stifled competition and increased consumer costs, he supported decontrol of oil and natural gas prices to spur production. He also deregulated the railroad, trucking, and airline industries.

One of the high points in Carter's administration came with his involvement in the ever-turbulent Middle East. In the aftermath of the Yom Kippur War, Egyptian leader Anwar al-Sadat was disappointed in the ultimate failure of the struggle and was aware that his people needed relief from the incessant struggle. Dramatically, he flew to Israel and addressed the Knesset—the Israeli parliament—and committed himself to peace. At that point, Carter intervened and invited Sadat and Israeli leader Menachem Begin to come to a retreat at Camp David, in Maryland (not far from Washington, D.C.), where he helped the two leaders work out an accord in September 1978. It led to a formal peace treaty the next March. Egypt recognized Israel—and the

Israeli right to exist—for the first time, and the Israelis gave up part of the occupied Sinai Peninsula. The United States promised substantial military aid to both parties, which led to a closer relationship with Egypt that has continued ever since. As the United States superseded the Soviet Union as an ally of Egypt, the Russians countered by arming the radical Palestine Liberation Organization (PLO) and helped encourage leader Yasir Arafat in the ongoing guerrilla war.

Carter puzzled people overseas by his passionate commitment to human rights. It became a hallmark of his administration, especially when he ordered the United States to pull out of the Olympics in Moscow in 1980 in protest of a Soviet invasion of neighboring Afghanistan. Some Americans wondered how this commitment squared with the longstanding American approach of supporting dictators and overlooking human rights abuses in countries whose support the United States wanted in the Cold War.

Liberals were disappointed as the 1970s ended. Their hopes for a stronger commitment to a welfare state had been dashed, and conservatives had the upper hand. Despite a tenuous Democratic hold on the presidency at the end of the decade, liberalism was in trouble. And the turbulence that had marked the beginning of the decade had not disappeared.

THE CONTINUING QUEST FOR SOCIAL REFORM

A struggle for social reform was one more factor contributing to the turbulence of the 1970s. The black struggle for equality in the 1950s and 1960s helped spark a women's movement that soon developed a life of its own. This struggle, like the struggles of Latinos and Native Americans, employed the confrontational approach and the vocabulary of the civil rights movement to create pressure for change. In time, other groups appropriated the same strategies and kept reform efforts alive. While these movements had preexisting roots and usually began in the 1960s, they came of age in the 1970s, and in these years achieved their greatest gains.

Attacking the Feminine Mystique

Many white women joined the civil rights movement only to find that they were second-class activists. Men, black and white, held the policy positions and relegated women to menial chores when not actually involved in demonstrations or voter

drives. Many women also felt sexually exploited by male leaders. Stokely Carmichael's comment underscored their point. "The only position for women in SNCC," he said, "is prone."

Although the civil rights movement helped spark the women's movement, broad social changes provided the preconditions. During the 1950s and 1960s, increasing numbers of married women entered the labor force (see Chapter 26). Equally important, many more young women were attending college. By 1970, women earned 41 percent of all B.A. degrees awarded, in comparison with only 25 percent in 1950. These educated young women held high hopes for themselves, even if they still earned substantially less than men.

The women's movement, which came into its own in the 1970s, depended on reform legislation to help end gender discrimination. Title VII of the 1964 Civil Rights bill, as originally drafted, prohibited discrimination on the grounds of race. During legislative debate, conservatives opposed to black civil rights seized on an amendment to include discrimination on the basis of gender, in the hope of defeating the entire bill. But the amendment passed, and

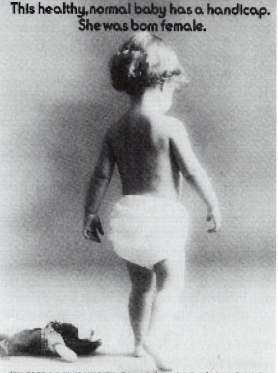

Awareness of racial discrimination led women to speak out against discrimination based on gender, as shown in this pointed advertisement sponsored by the National Organization for Women. *(NOW Legal Defense and Education Fund)*

Women in the Workforce, 1920–1980

This graph shows the dramatic increase in the number of women in the workforce over the years. Note particularly the rise in the number of working women 25–44 years old in the 1970s.

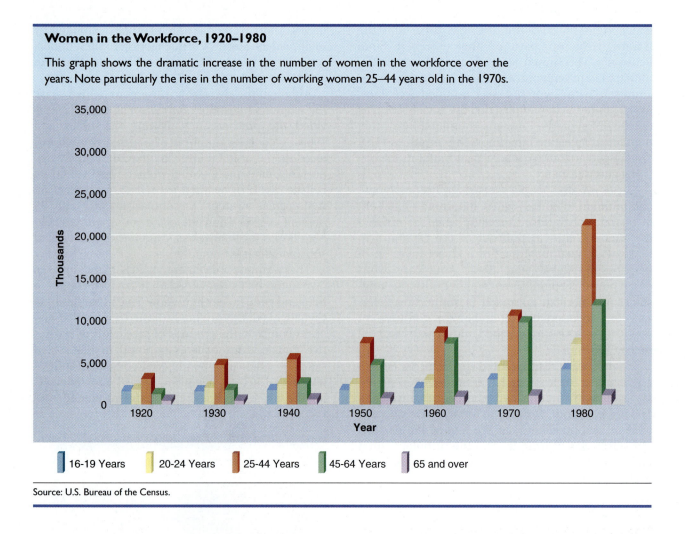

16-19 Years   20-24 Years   25-44 Years   45-64 Years   65 and over

Source: U.S. Bureau of the Census.

then the full measure was approved, giving women a legal tool for attacking discrimination. They discovered, however, that the Equal Employment Opportunities Commission regarded women's complaints of discrimination as far less important than those of blacks.

Women's organizations played an important role in bringing about change in the 1970s. In 1966, a group of 28 professional women, including author Betty Friedan, established the National Organization for Women (NOW) "to take action to bring American women into full participation in the mainstream of American society now." By full participation, the founders meant not only fair pay and equal opportunity but a new, more egalitarian form of marriage. NOW also attacked the "false image of women . . . in the media." By 1967, some 1,000 women had joined the organization, and four years later, its membership reached 15,000.

NOW was a pressure group that sought to reform American society by promoting equal opportunity

for women. To radical feminists, who had come up through the civil rights movement, NOW's agenda failed to confront adequately the problem of gender discrimination. Jo Freeman, a radical activist, observed, "Women's liberation does not mean equality with men . . . [because] equality in an unjust society is meaningless." These feminists wanted to educate millions of discontented but unpoliticized women about the oppression they faced. They tried, through the technique of consciousness raising, to help women understand the extent of their oppression and to analyze their experience as a political phenomenon. They wanted to demonstrate, in their phrase, that the personal was political.

The radicals gained mass-media attention at the Miss America pageant in Atlantic City, New Jersey, in September 1968. There, in the words of activist author Robin Morgan, they "announced our existence to the world." On the boardwalk, a hundred women nominated a sheep as their candidate for Miss America. They also set up a "freedom trash can" and placed in it "instruments of torture": bras, girdles, hair curlers, high heels, and copies of *Playboy* and *Cosmopolitan* magazines. In the pageant hall, they chanted "Freedom for women" and unfurled banners reading "Women's Liberation" in a public relations campaign that continued in the following years.

The women's movement hit its stride in the 1970s. In 1971, Helen Reddy expressed the energy of the movement in a song called "I Am Woman" that rose to the top of the charts:

I am woman, hear me roar
In numbers too big to ignore
And I know too much to go back and pretend
'Cause I've heard it all before
And I've been down there on the floor,
No one's ever gonna keep me down again.
Oh, yes, I am wise
But it's wisdom born of pain.
Yes, I've paid the price
But look how much I gained
If I have to
I can do anything.
I am strong,
I am invincible,
I am woman.

Reddy's song reflected a new militancy and sense of self-confidence among women.

Real changes were underway. A 1970 survey of first-year college students showed that men interested in such fields as business, medicine, engineering, and law outnumbered women eight to one; by 1975, the ratio had dropped to three to one. The proportion of women beginning law school quadrupled between 1969 and 1973. Women gained access to the military academies and entered senior officer ranks, although they were still restricted from combat command ranks. According to the Census Bureau, 45 percent of mothers with preschool children held jobs outside the home in 1980. That figure was four times greater than it had been 30 years before. To be sure, many employers systematically excluded women from certain positions, and women usually held "female" jobs in the clerical, sales, and service sectors, but the progress was still unmistakable.

Legal changes brought women more benefits and opportunities. Title IX of the Education Amendments of 1972 broadened the provisions of the Civil Rights Act of 1964. The new legislation, which barred gender bias in federally assisted educational activities and programs, made easier the admission

Women marched to mobilize support for ratification of the Equal Rights Amendment, but the campaign failed, as opponents aroused public fears and blocked support in a number of key states. A decade after passage, the ERA was dead. (*J. L. Atlan/Corbis Sygma*)

of women to colleges and changed the nature of intercollegiate athletics by requiring schools to fund sports teams for women. By 1980, fully 30 percent of the participants in intercollegiate sports were women, compared with 15 percent before Title IX became law.

A flurry of publications spread the principles of the women's movement. In 1972, journalist Gloria Steinem and several other women founded a new magazine, *Ms.,* which succeeded beyond their wildest dreams. By 1973, there were almost 200,000 subscribers. *The New Woman's Survival Catalogue* provided useful advice to women readers. *Our Bodies, Ourselves,* a handbook published by a women's health collective, encouraged women to understand and control their bodies; it sold 850,000 copies between 1971 and 1976.

These new books and magazines differed radically from older women's magazines like *Good Housekeeping* and *Ladies' Home Journal,* which focused on domestic interests and needs. *Ms.,* in

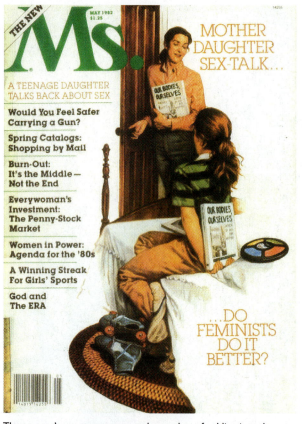

The women's movement spawned a number of publications that attempted to give women greater control over various aspects of their own lives. The book *Our Bodies, Ourselves* and *Ms.* magazine were two important sources in that effort. *(Reprinted by permission of Ms. Magazine, © 1982)*

dramatic contrast, dealt with abortion, employment, discrimination, and other feminist issues, such as the Equal Rights Amendment.

Women both in and out of NOW worked for congressional passage, then ratification, of the Equal Rights Amendment (ERA) to the Constitution. Passed by Congress in 1972, with ratification seemingly assured, it stated simply, "Equality of rights under the law shall not be denied or abridged by the United States or by any State on account of sex."

More radical feminists insisted that legal changes were not sufficient. Traditional gender and family roles would have to be discarded to end social exploitation. Socialist feminists claimed that it was not enough to strike out at male domination, for capitalist society itself was responsible for women's plight. Only through revolution could women be free.

Black women frequently viewed the women's movement with ambivalence. Some, like attorney Pauli Murray, became feminists. She worked closely with bureaucrats and legislators in Washington on legal measures to end gender discrimination. Others felt that the struggle for racial equality took precedence, and they were reluctant to divert en-

ergy and attention from it. Race, more than gender, was the source of their oppression. They were also suspicious of the middle-class orientation of many white feminists. Members of NOW and similar organizations, they claimed, "suffered little more than boredom, gentle repression, and dishpan hands" and were hardly confronting the most important issues when they burned their bras and insisted on using the title Ms. rather than Mrs. or Miss.

Not all women were feminists. Many felt the women's movement was contemptuous of women who stayed at home to perform traditional tasks. Marabel Morgan was one who still insisted that the woman had a place at home by her husband's side. The wife of a Florida attorney, she argued that "it is only when a woman surrenders her life to her husband, reveres and worships him, and is willing to serve him, that she becomes really beautiful to him." In her book *The Total Woman* (1973), she counseled others to follow the 4A approach: accept, admire, adapt, appreciate. As of 1975, some 500,000 copies of the hardcover volume had been sold.

In politics, Phyllis Schlafly headed a nationwide campaign to block ratification of the ERA. "It won't do anything to help women," she said, "and it will take away from women the rights they already have, such as the right of a wife to be supported by her husband, the right of a woman to be exempted from military combat, and the right, if you wanted it, to go to a single-sex college." The ERA, she predicted, would lead to the establishment of coed bathrooms, the elimination of alimony, and the legalization of homosexual marriage.

Schlafly and her allies had their way. Within a few years after passage of the ERA, 35 states had agreed to the measure, but then the momentum disappeared. Even with an extension in the deadline granted in 1979, the amendment could not win support of the necessary 38 states. By mid-1982, the ERA was dead.

Despite the counterattacks, the women's movement flourished in the late 1960s and 1970s. In the tenth anniversary issue of *Ms.* magazine in 1982, founding editor Gloria Steinem noted the differences a decade had made. "Now, we have words like 'sexual harassment' and 'battered women,'" she wrote. "Ten years ago, it was just called 'life.'" She also observed that "now, we are becoming the men we wanted to marry. Ten years ago, we were trained to marry a doctor, not be one."

Latino Mobilization

Latinos, like women, profited from the example of blacks in their struggle for equality that came of age in the 1970s. Long denied equal access to the American dream, they became more vocal and confrontational as their numbers increased dramatically in the postwar years. In 1970, some 9 million residents of the United States declared they were of Spanish origin; in 1980, the figure was 14.6 million. But median household income remained less than three-fourths that of Anglos, and inferior education and political weakness reinforced social and cultural separation. Latinos comprised Puerto Ricans in the Northeast, Cubans in Florida, and Chicanos—Mexican Americans—in the West and Southwest. Chicanos took the lead in the protest struggle, though all groups developed a heightened sense of solidarity and group pride as they began to assert their own rights.

In the 1960s and 1970s, Mexican Americans became more active politically. In 1960, Chicanos supported Kennedy, helping him win Texas, and began to see the benefits of such support. In 1961, Henry B. González was elected to Congress from San Antonio. Three years later, Elizo ("Kika") de la Garza of Texas won election to the House and Joseph Montoya of New Mexico went to the Senate. Chicanos were gaining a political voice.

More important than political representation, which came only slowly, was direct action, which triumphed in the 1970s. César Chávez, founder of the United Farm Workers, proved what could be done by organizing one of the most exploited and ignored groups of laboring people in the country, the migrant farm workers of the West. Chávez (who came from a family whose members were "the first ones to leave the fields if anyone shouted 'Huelga!'—which is Spanish for 'Strike!'") concentrated on migrant Mexican field hands, who worked long hours for meager pay. By 1965, his organization had recruited 1,700 people and was beginning to attract volunteer help.

Latina women played an important part in the organizing effort. Dolores Huerta, a third-generation Mexican American, who became vice president of the United Farm Workers, observed how entire families were involved:

> Excluding women, protecting them, keeping women at home, that's the middle-class way. Poor people's movements have always had whole families on the line, ready to move at a moment's notice, with more courage because that's all we had. It's a class not an ethnic thing.

Chávez's own wife, Helen, was equally involved in organizing, bookkeeping, and generating ideas in the movement.

Chávez first took on the grape growers of California. Calling the grape workers out on strike, the union demanded better pay and working conditions as well as recognition of the union. When the

César Chávez organized the United Farm Workers to give migrant Mexican workers representation in their struggle for better wages and working conditions. Here he works with laborers in his tireless campaign for their support. *(Bob Fitch/Take Stock/Black Star)*

growers did not concede, Chávez launched a nationwide consumer boycott of their products. Although the Schenley Corporation and several wine companies came to terms, others held out. In 1966, the DiGiorgio Corporation agreed to permit a union election but then rigged the results. When California governor Edmund G. Brown launched an investigation that resulted in another election, he became the first major political figure to support the long-powerless Chicano field hands. This time, the United Farm Workers won. Similar boycotts of lettuce and other products harvested by exploited labor also ended in success.

In 1975, César Chávez's long struggle for farmworkers won passage in California of a measure that required growers to bargain collectively with the elected representatives of the workers. Farmworkers had never been covered by the National Labor Relations Board. Now they had achieved the legal basis for representation that could help bring higher wages and improved working conditions. And Chávez had become a national figure.

Meanwhile, Mexican Americans pressed for reform in other areas. In the West and Southwest,

Mexican-American studies programs flourished. In 1969, at least 50 were available in California alone. Colleges and universities offered degrees, built library collections, and gave Chicanos access to their own past. The campuses also provided a network linking students together and mobilizing them for political action.

Beginning in 1968, Mexican-American students began to protest conditions in secondary schools. They pointed to overcrowded and run-down institutions and to the 50 percent dropout rate that came from expulsion, transfer, or failure because students had never been taught to read. In March 1968, some 10,000 Chicano students walked out of five high schools in Los Angeles. Their actions inspired other walkouts in Colorado, Texas, and other parts of California and led to successful demands for Latino teachers, counselors, and courses as well as better facilities.

At the same time, new organizations emerged. Young Citizens for Community Action, founded by teenager David Sánchez and four Chicanos in East Los Angeles, began as a service club to assist the neighborhood. Later, the organization adopted a paramilitary stance and evolved into a defensive patrol, now known as Young Chicanos for Community Action, which tried to protect local residents. Its members became identified as the Brown Berets and formed chapters throughout the Midwest and Southwest.

Other Latinos followed a more political path. In Texas, José Angel Gutiérrez formed a citizens' organization that developed into the La Raza Unida political party and successfully promoted Mexican-American candidates for political offices. Throughout the 1970s, it gained strength in the West and Southwest.

Among the new Chicano leaders was the charismatic Reies López Tijerina, or "El Tigre." A preacher, he became interested in land-grant issues and argued that the U.S. government had fraudulently deprived Chicanos of village lands. He formed an organization, La Alianza Federal de Mercedes (the Federal Alliance of Land Grants), which marched on the New Mexico state capital and occupied a number of national forests. Arrested, he stood trial and eventually served time in prison, where he became a symbol of political repression.

Rodolfo "Corky" Gonzáles was another such leader. A Golden Gloves boxing champion as a youth, he later served as a district captain for the Democratic party in Denver. He helped direct Denver poverty programs until he was fired for being overly zealous in his support of the Chicano community. Eloquently he described the despair many Chicanos felt:

> I am Joaquin,
> lost in a world of confusion,
> caught up in the whirl of a gringo society,
> confused by the rules,
> scorned by attitudes,
> suppressed by manipulation
> and destroyed by modern society.

Gonzáles founded the Crusade for Justice to advance the Chicano cause through community organization. Like Tijerina, he was arrested for his part in a demonstration but was subsequently acquitted.

Latinos made a particular point of protesting the Vietnam War. Because the draft drew most heavily from the poorer segments of society, the Latino casualty rate was far higher than that of the population at large. In 1969, the Brown Berets organized the National Chicano Moratorium Committee and demonstrated against what they argued was a racial war, with black and brown Americans being used against their Third World compatriots. Some of the rallies ended in confrontations with the police. News reporter Rubén Salazar, active in exposing questionable police activity, was killed in one such episode in 1970, and his death brought renewed charges of police brutality.

Aware of the growing numbers and growing demands of Latinos, the Nixon administration sought to defuse their anger and win their support. Cuban-American refugees, strongly opposed to communism, shifted toward the Republican party, which they assumed was more likely eventually to intervene against Fidel Castro. Meanwhile, Nixon courted Chicanos by dangling political positions, government jobs, and promises of better programs for Mexican Americans. The effort paid off; Nixon received 31 percent of the Latino vote in 1972. Rather than reward his Latino followers, however, the president moved to cut back the poverty program, begun under Johnson, that assisted many of them.

Despite occasional gains in the 1970s, Latinos from all groups faced continuing problems. Discrimination persisted in housing, education, and employment. Activists had laid the groundwork for a campaign for equal rights, but the struggle had just begun.

Native-American Protest

Like Latinos, Native Americans continued to suffer second-class status in the 1960s and 1970s. But, partly inspired by the confrontational tactics of other groups, they became more aggressive in their

Indian Reservations in the Mid-1970s

While Indian reservations occupied substantial areas in the West in the mid-1970s, they still included far less territory than in past years.

efforts to claim their rights and improve their living and working conditions. Their soaring numbers— the census put them at 550,000 in 1960 and 1,480,000 in 1980—gave them greater visibility and political clout.

In the 1960s, Native Americans had begun to assert themselves even more. Several hundred Indians meeting together in 1961 asked the government for the right to help make decisions about programs and budgets for the tribes. A group of college-educated Indians at the conference formed a National Indian Youth Council aimed at reestablishing Indian national pride. Over the next several decades, the council helped change the attitudes of tribal leaders, who were frequently called Uncle Tomahawks and "apples" (red outside, white inside) for their willingness to sacrifice their people's needs to white demands.

American Indians learned from the examples of protest they saw around them in rising Third World nationalism and, even more important, in the civil rights revolution. They too came to understand the place of interest-group politics in a diverse society. Finally, they were chastened by the excesses of the Vietnam War. They recognized a pattern of killing people of color that connected Indian–white relations to the excesses in the Philippines at the turn of the century and to atrocities in Korea and Vietnam.

Indians in the late 1960s and 1970s successfully promoted their own values and designs. Native-American fashions became more common, museums and galleries displayed Indian art, and Indian jewelry found a new market. The larger culture came to appreciate important work by Native Americans. In 1968, N. Scott Momaday won the Pulitzer Prize for his book *House Made of Dawn.*

Vine Deloria, Jr.'s *Custer Died for Your Sins* (1969) had even wider readership. Meanwhile, popular films such as *Little Big Man* (1970) provided sympathetic portrayals of Indian history. Indian-studies programs developed in colleges and universities. Organizations like the American Indian Historical Society protested traditional textbook treatment of Indians and demanded more honest portrayals.

At the same time, Native Americans became more confrontational. Like other groups, they worked through the courts when they could but also challenged authority more aggressively when necessary.

Led by a new generation of leaders, American Indians tried to protect what was left of their tribal lands. Elders reminded young people, "Once we owned all the land." For generations, federal and state governments had steadily encroached on Native-American territory. That intrusion had to cease. Indian activists echoed the words of D'Arcy McNickle, a Flathead anthropologist, who had declared in 1961, "Everything is tied to our homeland."

The protest spirit was apparent on the Seneca Nation's Allegany reservation in New York State. Although a 1794 treaty had established the Seneca's right to the land, the federal government had planned since 1928 to build a flood-control dam there. In 1956, after hearings to which the Indians were not invited and about which they were not informed, Congress appropriated funds for the project. Court appeals failed to block the scheme, and the dam was eventually built. The government belatedly passed a $15 million reparations bill, but money did not compensate for the loss of 10,000 acres of land that contained sacred sites, hunting and fishing grounds, and homes.

The Seneca did somewhat better in the 1970s. When New York State tried to condemn a section of Seneca land to build a superhighway to run through part of the Allegany reservation, the Indians again went to court. In 1981, the state finally agreed to an exchange: state land elsewhere in addition to a cash settlement in return for an easement through the reservation. That decision encouraged tribal efforts in Montana, Wyoming, Utah, New Mexico, and Arizona to resist similar incursions on reservation lands.

Native-American leaders found that lawsuits charging violations of treaty rights could give them powerful leverage. In 1967, in the first of many subsequent decisions upholding the Indian side, the U.S. Court of Claims ruled that the government in 1823 had forced the Seminole in Florida to cede their land for an unreasonably low price. The court directed the government to pay additional funds 144 years later. Legal assaults continued in the 1970s.

American Indians also vigorously protested a new assault on their long-abused water rights. On the northern plains, large conglomerates, responding to the international oil shortage, vastly extended their coal strip-mining operations. Fierce legal struggles over possession of limited water resources resulted. Litigating tribes gained some legal ammunition in a landmark case involving the water rights of the Paiute on the Nevada–California border; in 1973, a federal court ruled that the government must carry out its obligation as trustee to protect Indian property.

Another effort involved the reassertion of fishing rights. In various parts of the nation, the Nisqually, Puyallup, Muckleshoot, Chippewa, and other Indian tribes argued that they had treaty rights to fish where they chose, without worrying about the intrusive regulatory efforts of the states. Despite pressure from other fishermen, a series of court cases provided the tribes with some of the protection they claimed by ruling that nineteenth-century treaties allowing Indians fishing rights "in common with" whites meant that Indians could take up to 50 percent of allowable limits.

Urban Indian activism became highly visible in 1968 when George Mitchell and Dennis Banks, Chippewa living in Minneapolis, founded the activist American Indian Movement (AIM). AIM got Office of Economic Opportunity funds channeled to Indian-controlled organizations. It also established patrols to protect drunken Indians from harassment by the police. As its successes became known, chapters formed in other cities.

An incident in November 1969 dramatized Native-American militancy. A landing party of 78 Indians seized Alcatraz Island in San Francisco Bay in an effort to protest symbolically the inability of the Bureau of Indian Affairs to "deal practically" with questions of Indian welfare. The Indians converted the island, with its defunct federal prison, into a cultural and educational center. As author Vine Deloria, Jr., noted, "By making Alcatraz an experimental Indian center operated and planned by Indian people, we would be given a chance to see what we could do toward developing answers to modern social problems. . . . It just seems to a lot of Indians that this continent was a lot better off when we were running it." In 1971, federal officials removed the Indians from Alcatraz.

Similar protests followed. In 1972, militants launched the Broken Treaties Caravan to Washington. For six days, insurgents occupied the Bureau of

The American Indian movement's armed occupation of Wounded Knee, South Dakota, the site of a late-nineteenth-century massacre of the Sioux, resulted in bloodshed that dramatized unfair government treatment of Native Americans. *(AP/Wide World Photos)*

Indian Affairs. In 1973, AIM took over the South Dakota village of Wounded Knee, where in 1890 the U.S. 7th Cavalry had massacred the Sioux. The reservation surrounding the town was mired in poverty. Half the families were on welfare; alcoholism was widespread; and 81 percent of the student population had dropped out of school. The occupation was meant to dramatize these conditions and to draw attention to the 371 treaties AIM leaders claimed the government had broken. Federal officials responded by encircling the area and, when AIM tried to bring in supplies, killed one Indian and wounded another. The confrontation ended with a government agreement to reexamine the treaty rights of the Indians, although little of substance was subsequently done.

At the same time, Native Americans devoted increasing attention to providing education and de-

veloping legal skills. Because roughly half of the Indian population continued to live on reservations, many tribal communities founded their own colleges. In 1971, the Oglala Sioux established Oglala Lakota College on the Pine Ridge Reservation in South Dakota. The motto "Wa Wo Ici Ya" ("We can do it ourselves") revealed the college's goal. Nearby Sinte Gleska College on the Rosebud Reservation was the first to offer accredited four-year and graduate programs. The number of Indians in college increased from a few hundred in the early 1960s to tens of thousands by 1980.

Indians studied law and acted as legal advocates for their own people in the court cases they filed. In 1968, funding from the Office of Economic Opportunity helped the University of New Mexico Law School start a Native-American scholarship program. Since 1971, that program has graduated 35 to 40 Indian lawyers each year. They have worked for tribes directly and have successfully argued for tribal jurisdiction in conflicts between whites and Indians on the reservations.

Indian protest brought results. The outcry against termination in the 1950s (see Chapter 26) had led the Kennedy and Johnson administrations in the 1960s to steer a middle course, neither endorsing nor disavowing the policy. Instead, they tried to bolster reservation economies and raise standards of living by persuading private industries to locate on reservations and by promoting the leasing of reservation lands to energy and development corporations. In the 1970s, the Navajo, Northern Cheyenne, Crow, and other tribes tried to cancel or renegotiate such leases, fearing "termination by corporation." Meanwhile the Menominee of Wisconsin confronted the hated policy head-on. Activist Ada Deer became a major figure in the effort to restore reservation status. She and others organized new protest groups, secured political support from the state's senators, and in 1973 had the satisfaction of seeing President Richard Nixon sign the Menominee Restoration Act.

Other legislation likewise disavowed the termination policy. In 1975, Congress passed an Indian Self-Determination Act. Five years earlier, Richard Nixon had declared that self-determination had replaced termination as American policy. The self-determination measure was a largely rhetorical statement of that position. An Education Assistance Act that same year involved subcontracting federal services to tribal groups. Both laws reflected the government's decision to respond to Indian pressure and created a framework to guide federal policy in the decades ahead.

Gay and Lesbian Rights

Closely tied to the revolution in sexual norms that affected sexual relations, marriage, and family life was a fast-growing and increasingly militant gay liberation movement. There had always been people who accepted the "gay" lifestyle, but American society as a whole was unsympathetic, and many homosexuals kept their preferences to themselves. The climate of the 1970s encouraged gays to "come out of the closet." A nightlong riot in 1969, in response to a police raid on the Stonewall Inn, a homosexual bar in Greenwich Village in New York, helped spark a new consciousness and a movement for gay rights. Throughout the 1970s, homosexuals ended the most blatant forms of discrimination against them. In 1973, the American Psychiatric Association ruled that homosexuality should no longer be classified as a mental illness, and that decision was overwhelmingly supported in a vote by the membership the next year. In 1975, the U.S. Civil Service Commission lifted its ban on employment of homosexuals.

In this new climate of acceptance, many gay men who had hidden or suppressed their sexuality revealed their secret. Women, too, became more open about their sexual preferences and demanded not to be penalized for choosing other females as partners. A lesbian movement developed, sometimes involving women active in the more radical wing of the women's movement. But many Americans and some churches remained unsympathetic—occasionally vehemently so—to anyone who challenged traditional sexual norms.

Environmental and Consumer Agitation

Although many of the social movements of the 1960s and 1970s were defined by race, gender, and sexual preference, one cut across all boundaries. Emerging in the early 1960s but not flourishing until the 1970s, a powerful movement of Americans concerned with the environment began to revive issues raised in the Progressive era and to push them further. In the mid-1960s, a Gallup poll revealed that only 17 percent of the public considered air and water pollution to be one of the three major government problems. By 1970, that figure had risen to 53 percent.

The modern environmental movement stemmed in part from post–World War II yearnings for a better "quality of life." Many Americans began to recognize that clear air, unpolluted waters, and unspoiled wilderness were indispensable to a decent existence (see Chapter 26). They worried about threats to their natural surroundings, particularly after naturalist

Rachel Carson published her brilliant book *Silent Spring* in 1962 (see Chapter 28).

Public concern focused on a variety of targets. In 1969, Americans were troubled to learn how thermal pollution from nuclear power plants was killing fish in both eastern and western rivers. An article in *Sports Illustrated* aroused fishermen, sailors, and other recreational enthusiasts who had not been previously concerned. A massive oil spill off the coast of southern California turned white beaches black and wiped out much of the marine life in the immediate area. Concern about the deterioration of the environment increased as people learned more about substances they had once taken for granted. In 1978, the public became alarmed about the lethal effects of toxic chemicals dumped in the Love Canal neighborhood of Niagara Falls, New York. A few years later, attention focused on dioxin, one of the most deadly substances ever made, which sur-

The accident at the reactor on Three Mile Island helped spark opposition to nuclear power. For people around the world, the cooling towers pictured here came to represent the horrifying possibilities of a nuclear reaction out of control. *(UPI/Corbis-Bettmann)*

Antinuclear activists protested the proliferation of both atomic weapons and atomic power plants. Here members of the Clamshell Alliance agitate in 1977 against construction of a nuclear power plant in Seabrook, New Hampshire. *(AP/Wide World Photos)*

faced in the Love Canal and other areas in concentrated form.

Equally frightening was the potential environmental damage from a nuclear accident. Critics of nuclear power had warned for years that regulation of nuclear power was notoriously lax. The Atomic Energy Commission, the agency responsible for promoting the development of nuclear power, was the same agency responsible for regulating the power-producing reactors. Occasional mishaps in the 1960s and mid-1970s raised the specter of an even more serious accident in the future.

Such a calamity occurred at Three Mile Island near Harrisburg, Pennsylvania, in 1979. There, a faulty pressure-relief valve led to a loss of coolant. Initially, plant operators refused to believe indicators showing a serious malfunction. Part of the nuclear core became uncovered, part began to disintegrate, and the surrounding steam and water became highly radioactive. An explosion releasing radioactivity into the atmosphere appeared possible, and thousands of area residents fled. The scenario of nuclear disaster depicted in the film *The China Syndrome* (1979) seemed frighteningly real. *Mad* magazine's Alfred E. Newman posed in front of the now-famous cooling towers and said, "Yes, me worry!" The worst never occurred and the danger period passed, but the plant remained shut down, filled with radioactive debris, a monument to a form of energy that was once hailed as the wave of the future but now appeared more destructive than any ever known.

The threat of a nuclear catastrophe underscored the arguments of grassroots environmental activists. Groups like the Clamshell Alliance in New Hampshire and the Abalone Alliance in northern California campaigned aggressively against licensing new nuclear plants at Seabrook, New Hampshire, and Diablo Canyon, California. While activist tactics did not always succeed in their immediate goals, they mobilized opinion sufficiently so that no new plants were authorized after 1978. This pattern was at variance with the pattern in many other countries around the world, which continued to rely on nuclear power.

Western environmentalists were particularly worried about excessive use of water. The American West, one critic observed, had become "the greatest hydraulic society ever built in history." Massive irrigation systems had boosted the nation's use of water from 40 billion gallons a day in 1900 to 393 billion gallons by 1975, though the population had only tripled. Americans used three times as much water per capita as the world's average, and far more than other industrialized societies.

One serious source of concern was the Ogallala aquifer in the Great Plains. The drawing of enormous amounts of water in the 1950s and 1960s to make arid areas productive for farming had by the mid-1970s dramatically depleted the water stored in the aquifer. Conservation measures might delay, but not prevent, the day of reckoning.

The situation was similar in California. Because the state was naturally dry, its prosperity rested on massive irrigation projects, and in the late 1970s, it had 1,251 major reservoirs. Virtually every large river had at least one dam. Almost as much water was pumped from the ground, with little natural replenishment and even less regulation. Pointing to the destruction of the nation's rivers and streams and the severe lowering of the water table in many areas, environmentalists argued that something needed to be done before it was too late. Slowly, they made themselves heard. Critic Marc Reisner later noted, "Forty years ago, only a handful of heretics, howling at wilderness, challenged the notion that the West needed hundreds of new dams. Today they are almost vindicated."

Environmental agitation produced legislative results in the 1960s and 1970s. Lyndon Johnson, whose vision of the Great Society included an "environment that is pleasing to the senses and healthy to live in," won basic legislation to halt the depletion of the country's natural resources (see Chapter 28). In the next few years, environmentalists went further, pressuring legislative and administrative bodies to regulate polluters. During Richard Nixon's presidency, Congress passed the Clean Air Act, the Water Quality Improvement Act, and the Resource Recovery Act and mandated a new Environmental Protection Agency (EPA) to spearhead the effort to control abuses. Initially, these measures aimed at controlling the toxic by-products of the modern industrial order. In subsequent years, environmentalists broadened the effort to include occupational health and social justice issues.

One such effort developed into an extraordinarily bitter economic and ecological debate. The Endangered Species Act of 1973 prohibited the federal government from supporting any projects that might jeopardize species threatened with extinction. It ran into direct conflict with commercial imperatives in the Pacific Northwest. Loggers in the Olympic Peninsula had long exploited the land by clearcutting (cutting down all trees in a region, without leaving any standing). Environmentalists claimed that the forests they cut provided the last refuge for the spotted owl. Scientists and members of the U.S. Forest Service pushed to set aside timberland so that the owl could survive. Loggers protested that this action jeopardized their livelihood. As the issue wound its way through the courts, logging fell off drastically.

Another protest against regulation in the late 1970s and early 1980s came to be called the Sagebrush Rebellion. Critics argued that large federal landholdings in the West put that region at a disadvantage in economic competition with the East. They demanded that the national government cede the lands to states, which could sell or lease

Timeline	
1968	Richard Nixon elected president
1969	Native Americans seize Alcatraz
	La Raza Unida founded
1970	U.S. invasion of Cambodia
	Shootings at Kent State and Jackson State Universities
1971	*New York Times* publishes Pentagon Papers
1971–1975	School busing controversies in North and South
1972	Nixon visits People's Republic of China
	Nixon reelected
	SALT I Treaty on nuclear arms
	Ms. magazine founded
	Congress passes Equal Rights Amendment
1973	Vietnam cease-fire agreement
	Watergate hearings in Congress
	Spiro Agnew resigns as vice president
	AIM occupies Wounded Knee, South Dakota
1974	OPEC price increases
	Inflation hits 11 percent
	Nixon resigns; Gerald Ford becomes president
	Ford pardons Nixon
1975	South Vietnam falls to the Communists
	End of the Vietnam War
	Unemployment reaches 9 percent
	Farmworkers win right to bargain collectively with growers
	Indian Self-Determination and Education Assistance Acts
1976	Jimmy Carter elected president
1977	Carter energy program
1978	*Bakke v. Regents of the University of California*
1979	Accident at Three Mile Island nuclear power plant
	SALT II Treaty signed
1982	Ratification of ERA fails

them for local gain. Conservative state legislatures in the Rocky Mountain states supported the scheme. Ranchers applauded the notion. In the end, it went nowhere, though the agitation did persuade federal authorities to endorse a less restrictive policy on grazing.

Related to the environmental movement was a consumer movement. As Americans bought fashionable clothes, house furnishings, and electrical and electronic gadgets, they began to worry about unscrupulous sellers, just as they had earlier in the twentieth century. Over the years, Congress had established a variety of regulatory efforts as it started to safeguard citizens from marketplace abuse. In the 1970s, a stronger consumer movement developed, aimed at protecting the interests of the purchasing public and making business more responsible to consumers.

Ralph Nader led the movement. He had become interested in the issue of automobile safety while studying law at Harvard and had pursued that interest as a consultant to the Department of Labor. His book *Unsafe at Any Speed: The Designed-in Dangers of the American Automobile* (1965) argued that many cars were coffins on wheels. Head-on collisions, even at low speeds, could easily kill, for cosmetic bumpers could not withstand modest shocks. He termed the Chevrolet Corvair "one of the nastiest-handling cars ever built" because of its tendency to roll over in certain situations. His efforts paved

the way for the National Traffic and Motor Vehicle Safety Act of 1966, which set minimum safety standards for vehicles on public highways, provided for inspection to ensure compliance, and created a National Motor Vehicle Safety Advisory Council.

The consumer movement developed into a full-fledged campaign in the 1970s. Nader's efforts attracted scores of volunteers, called "Nader's Raiders." They turned out critiques and reports and, more important, inspired consumer activists at all levels of government—city, state, and national. Consumer protection offices began to monitor a flood of complaints as ordinary citizens became more vocal in defending their rights.

✦ *Conclusion*

SORTING OUT THE PIECES

The late 1960s and 1970s were turbulent years. The chaos that seemed to reach a peak in 1968 continued, even as American participation in the war in Vietnam wound down. Richard Nixon recognized that he could contain the protest movement by bringing American soldiers home. He understood too the growing frustration with liberal reform and the wish of some Americans to dispense with the excesses they attributed to the young. For a time, he managed to mute protest and to promote a measure of harmony by his policy of Vietnamization, which cut back on the number of Americans dying in battle. But his desire to avoid losing the war led him to expand the conflict into neighboring parts of Indochina, and that move sparked even greater opposition than before.

Meanwhile, his own overarching ambition and need for electoral support led to the worst political scandal in American history. At just the time that the nation was trying to pick up the pieces from the unpopular war, he found himself embroiled in the Watergate affair, which threatened the United States

with a real constitutional crisis that ended only when the president resigned.

During this entire time, disadvantaged groups demanded that the nation expand the meaning of equality. Building on the accomplishments of the civil rights movement in the 1950s and 1960s, women, like Ann Clarke, introduced at the start of the chapter, returned to school in ever-increasing numbers and found jobs and sometimes independence after years of being told that their place was at home. Native Americans and Latinos mobilized too and could see the stirrings of change. Gay rights activists made their voices heard. Environmentalists created a new awareness of the global dangers the nation and the world faced. Slowly, reformers succeeded in pressuring the government to help the nation fulfill its promise and ensure the realization of the ideals of American life.

But the course of change was ragged. Reform efforts suffered from the disillusionment with liberalism. Some movements were circumscribed by the changing political climate; others simply ran out of steam. Still, the various efforts left a legacy of ferment that could help spark further change in future years.

✦ Recommended Reading

The Decline of Liberalism
Stephen E. Ambrose, *Nixon: The Triumph of a Politician: 1962–1972* (1989); Mary C. Brennan, *Turning Right in the Sixties: The Conservative Capture of the GOP* (1995); Fawn M. Brodie, *Richard Nixon: The Shaping of His Career* (1981); William Bundy, *A Tangled Web: The Making of Foreign Policy in the Nixon Presidency* (1998); Rowland Evans, Jr., and Robert D. Novak, *Nixon in the White House* (1972); David Frum, *How We Got Here: The 70's: The Decade That Brought You Modern Life (For Better or*

Worse) (2000); Godfrey Hodgson, *The World Turned Right Side Up: A History of the Conservative Ascendency in America* (1996); Joan Hoff, *Nixon Reconsidered* (1994); Allen J. Matusow, *Nixon's Economy: Booms, Busts, Dollars, and Votes* (1998); Bruce Mazlish, *In Search of Nixon: A Psychohistorical Inquiry* (1972); Richard Nixon, *RN: The Memoirs of Richard Nixon* (1978); Richard Reeves, *President Nixon: Alone in the White House* (2001); Michael Schaller and George Rising, *The Republican Ascendancy: American Politics, 1968–2001* (2002); Melvin Small, *The*

Presidency of Richard Nixon (1999); Garry Wills, *Nixon Agonistes: The Crisis of the Self-Made Man* (1969).

The Ongoing Effort in Vietnam

Christian G. Appy, *Working-Class War: American Combat Soldiers and Vietnam* (1993); Larry Berman, *No Peace, No Honor: Nixon, Kissinger, and Betrayal in Vietnam* (2001); George C. Herring, *America's Longest War: The United States and Vietnam, 1950–1975*, 3rd ed. (1996); Stanley Karnow, *Vietnam: A History: The First Complete Account of Vietnam at War* (1983); Jeffrey P. Kimball, *Nixon's Vietnam War* (1998); Ron Kovic, *Born on the Fourth of July* (1976); Robert S. McNamara, *In Retrospect* (1995).

Constitutional Conflict and Its Consequences

Stanley I. Kutler, *The Wars of Watergate: The Last Crisis of Richard Nixon* (1990); Stanley I. Kutler, ed., *Abuse of Power: The New Nixon Tapes* (1997); J. Anthony Lukas, *Nightmare: The Underside of the Nixon Years* (1976); Bob Woodward and Carl Bernstein, *All the President's Men* (1974) and *The Final Days* (1976).

John Robert Greene, *The Limits of Power: The Nixon and Ford Administrations* (1992) and *The Presidency of Gerald R. Ford* (1995); John Hersey, *The President* (1975); Richard Reeves, *A Ford, Not a Lincoln* (1975).

Jimmy Carter, *Keeping Faith: Memories of a President* (1982); Gary M. Fink and Hugh Davis Graham, eds., *The Carter Presidency: Policy Choices in the Post-New Deal Era* (1998); Burton I. Kaufman, *The Presidency of James Earl Carter, Jr.* (1993); Kenneth A. Morris, *Jimmy Carter: American Moralist* (1996).

The Continuing Quest for Social Reform

Beth Bailey, *Sex in the Heartland* (1999); William H. Chafe, *The American Woman: Her Changing Social, Political, and Economic Roles, 1920–1970* (1972); Sara Evans, *Personal Politics: The Roots of Women's Liberation in the Civil Rights Movements and the New Left* (1979); Peter Gabriel Filene, *Him/Her/Self: Sex Roles in Modern America*, 2nd ed. (1986); Jacqueline Jones, *Labor of Love, Labor of Sorrow: Black Women, Work, and the Family from Slavery to the Present* (1985); Alice Kessler-Harris, *Out to Work: A History of Wage-earning Women in the United States* (1982).

Susan M. Hartmann, *The Other Feminists: Activists in the Liberal Establishment* (1998); Blanche Linden-Ward, *Changing the Future: American Women in the 1960s* (1993); Ruth Rosen, *The World Split Open: How the Modern Women's Movement Changed America* (2000); Gloria Steinem, *Outrageous Acts and Everyday Rebellions*, 2nd ed. (1995); Winifred D. Wandersee, *On the Move: American Women in the 1970s* (1988).

Rodolfo Acuña, *Occupied America: A History of Chicanos*, 4th ed. (2000); Richard Delgado and Jean Stefancic, *The Latino/a Condition: A Critical Reader* (1998); Richard Etulain, ed., *César Chávez: A Brief Biography with Documents* (2002); Mario T. García, *Memories of Chicano History: The Life and Narrative of Bert Corona* (1994) and *Mexican Americans: Leadership, Ideology, and Identity, 1930–1960* (1989); Ed Ludwig and James Santibañez, eds., *The Chicanos: Mexican American Voices* (1971); Beatrice Rodriguez Owsley, *The Hispanic-American Entrepreneur: An Oral History of the American Dream* (1992); Peter Skerry, *Mexican Americans: The Ambivalent Minority* (1993).

Dee Brown, *Bury My Heart at Wounded Knee: An Indian History of the American West* (1971); Stephen Cornell, *The Return of the Native: American Indian Political Resurgence* (1988); Vine Deloria, Jr., *Custer Died for Your Sins: An Indian Manifesto* (1969); Frederick E. Hoxie, ed., *Indians in American History* (1988); Peter Iverson, *"We Are Still Here": American Indians in the Twentieth Century* (1998); Alvin M. Josephy, Jr., *Now That the Buffalo's Gone* (1982); James S. Olson and Raymond Wilson, *Native Americans in the Twentieth Century* (1984).

Dudley Clendinen and Adam Nagourney, *Out for Good: The Struggle to Build a Gay Rights Movement in America* (1999); John D'Emilio, *Sexual Politics, Sexual Communities: The Making of a Homosexual Minority in the United States, 1940–1970* (1983); John Loughery, *The Other Side of Silence: Men's Lives and Gay Identities: A Twentieth Century History* (1998).

Rachel Carson, *Silent Spring* (1962); William Dietrich, *The Final Forest: The Battle for the Last Great Trees of the Pacific Northwest* (1992); Robert Gottlieb, *Forcing the Spring: The Transformation of the American Environmental Movement* (1993); Samuel P. Hays, *Beauty, Health, and Permanence: Environmental Politics in the United States, 1955–1985* (1987) and *A History of Environmental Politics since 1945* (2000); Patricia Nelson Limerick, *The Legacy of Conquest: The Unbroken Past of the American West* (1987); Marc Reisner, *Cadillac Desert: The American West and Its Disappearing Water*, revised and updated ed. (1993); Edmund Russell, *War and Nature: Fighting Humans and Insects with Chemicals from World War I to Silent Spring* (2001); Kirkpatrick Sale, *The Green Revolution: The American Environmental Movement, 1962–1992* (1993); Charles F. Wilkinson, *Crossing the Next Meridian: Land, Water, and the Future of the West* (1992); Donald Worster, *Rivers of Empire: Water, Aridity and the Growth of the American West* (1985).

Fiction and Film

Sara Davidson's *Loose Change* (1977) is a novel about the lives of three young women at the University of California at Berkeley. Marilyn French's *The Women's Room* (1977) is a novel about the impact of the women's movement on a circle of women. *House Made of Dawn* (1968) is N. Scott Momaday's Pulitzer Prize–winning novel about a young Indian living in both the white and Indian worlds. Alix Kates Shulman's *Memoirs of an Ex-Prom Queen* (1972) is the story of a young midwestern woman and her awakening during and after college.

All the President's Men (1976) is a film (based on the book of the same name) about the effort by *Washington Post* reporters Bob Woodward and Carl Bernstein to find the truth about the Watergate scandal. *Annie Hall* (1977) is Woody Allen's film about the problems of relationships. *The Times of Harvey Milk* (1984), which won the Academy Award for best documentary feature, tells the story of California's first openly gay politician, who was assassinated in 1978.

◆ Discovering U.S. History Online

Richard Milhous Nixon

www.ipl.org/ref/POTUS/rmnixon.html

This site contains basic factual data about Nixon's election and presidency, speeches, and online biographies.

Apollo 11

www.hq.nasa.gov/office/pao/History/ap11ann/introduction.htm

Galleries, timeline, biographies, documents, and astronaut comments about the Apollo 11 flight to the moon.

Moon Landing

www.wherewereyou.com

An Internet-based oral history, this site presents an on-going collection of individual memories of the moon landing.

Vietnam: Yesterday and Today

servercc.oakton.edu/~wittman

The author, a librarian, presents a thorough topical bibliography on the Vietnam War.

Reflections, Memories, and Images of Vietnam Past

www.vietvet.org/thepast.htm

This site presents a gallery of "imagery, stories, poems, songs, maps, and narratives from or about the Vietnam War era."

Vietnam, A Different War

www.nytimes.com/library/world/asia/vietnam-war-index.html

Drawing on its extensive coverage of the Vietnam War, this site offers both a contemporary perspective and a retrospective view of the events as a whole.

The Vietnam Veterans Memorial Wall Page

www.thewall-usa.com/

A memorial for Vietnam casualties, this site gives personal insights into the individual effects of the war. A photo gallery is also included.

The My Lai Courts Martial, 1970

www.law.umkc.edu/faculty/projects/ftrials/mylai/mylai.htm

This site contains chronology, images, and court documents describing the massacre of Vietnamese civilians at My Lai.

Watergate

www.washingtonpost.com/wp-srv/national/longterm/watergate/front.htm

From the newspaper that broke the story, this site features a chronology, images, searchable articles, and a good deal of background information about the burglary and its consequences.

Watergate and the Constitution

www.archives.gov/digital_classroom/lessons/watergate_and_constitution/watergate_and_constitution.html

From the National Archives teaching materials, this site has a good chronology of Watergate and documents describing the pros and cons of seeking an indictment against former president Richard Nixon.

Gerald Rudolph Ford

www.ipl.org/ref/POTUS/grford.html

This site contains basic factual data about Ford's presidency, speeches, and online biographies.

James Earl Carter, Jr.

www.ipl.org/ref/POTUS/jecarter.html

This site contains basic factual data about Carter's election and presidency, speeches, and online biographies.

Three Mile Island

www.pbs.org/wgbh/amex/three/

This site provides a chronology and description of the frightening nuclear accident that occurred in 1979.

The 1977 Women's Conference in Houston, Texas

www.lindagriffith.com/IWYcaptionsmain.html

A photographic history of this key national women's conference.

History of the Mexican-American Civil Rights Movement

www.chicano.nlcc.com

A companion site to a PBS video, this site has a timeline of the movement from 1840–1975 as well as biographies and photos.

The Revival of Conservatism, 1980–1992

REAGAN

FOR PRESIDENT
Let's make America great again.

Ronald Reagan appealed to millions of Americans with his vision of a heroic national past. His efforts, highlighted in this campaign poster, helped revive conservatism and created a new political consensus in the United States. (© David J. and Janice L. Frent Collection/Corbis)

◆ American Stories

A YOUNG WOMAN EMBRACES REPUBLICAN VALUES

Leslie Maeby, a Republican political staffer in New York State in the 1980s, came from an immigrant family that had long been sympathetic to the Democratic party. Her great-grandfather, Aleksander Obrycki, had come to

Baltimore from Poland in 1895. A common laborer who became a naturalized citizen in 1907, he worked for the Democratic party, meeting new immigrants on their arrival and introducing them to Democrats who could help them.

Leslie's grandfather Joe Obrycki became a numbers runner, collecting bets for local gamblers. More successful than his father, he survived the Great Depression of the 1930s with little difficulty. He too was a member of the Democratic party, a cog in the machine. As New Deal programs undermined machine rule, Joe, a ward heeler and professional gambler, ran for city council but lost. Defeat notwithstanding, he remained a loyal Democrat.

Leslie's mother, Vilma, was likewise a Democrat. Leslie's father, Jack Maeby, came from a working class background in Baltimore and was raised as a Democrat. But as his football exploits took him to college at Bucknell University in Pennsylvania, he began to see the possibility of upward mobility. His own father, a factory worker, counseled him to "use this," pointing to his head, "instead of these," looking at his hands. Turning down an offer to go to graduate school, he entered a management training program with Montgomery Ward. The Maebys moved to Chicago first, then to the Albany, New York area, where they settled in the suburb of Colonie. While Albany, like most big cities, voted Democratic, Colonie was Republican.

Leslie Maeby was raised in the 1950s in a home where her mother remained Democratic, though frustrated with the Albany machine, and her father was Republican. The suburb, in the midst of a housing boom, developed quickly, as whites fled the larger city—and its black population—and sought safety in the standardized tract houses that were going up everywhere. Nelson Rockefeller, the liberal Republican governor of New York, garnered the support of both of Leslie's parents and many of their neighbors. Yet besides voting, neither Jack nor Vilma was very active politically.

Leslie drifted into politics in 1968, at the age of 15, without thinking about it. A cheerleader, she was drafted into a congressional campaign by the wife of Fred Field, the Republican candidate, who wanted her to wave pom-poms for her husband and greet supporters. Like the other "Field Girls," she dressed in a blue felt skirt, a white blouse, and suspenders that were striped like the flag. Several nights a week, the group rang doorbells and passed out campaign literature to voters. Leslie often made the first overtures in a household, to be followed by the candidate himself. She found the experience intoxicating, even more so when Fred Field won.

Leslie had followed an increasingly common course into the Republican fold. In a second-grade classroom, she had supported Republican presidential candidate Richard Nixon in 1960. In a mock presidential debate in 1964, she had represented conservative Republican presidential nominee Barry Goldwater. And even though Leslie talked about current events with her mother, a liberal Democrat, she was also influenced by her increasingly conservative Republican father as well as by the Republican community in which she lived. She followed her father's political inclinations and became Republican, as she put it, "almost by default." Race riots, first in Detroit, later in Albany and other American cities, troubled her and others. The chaos in Vietnam led to the rifts in the nation that helped elect Richard Nixon—along with Fred Field—in 1968. By the time she went to the State University of New York at Albany in 1971, she was a solid Republican.

In college, she joined a sorority, where she found women of a similar personal and political bent. Her group drank beer, rather than smoking pot, and wore evening gowns to formal dances, rather than wearing tattered jeans to a rock concert. A sorority sister recommended her for a position as a page in the State Senate in Albany, and Leslie found herself immersed in the political world.

Leslie saw first hand the underside of politics, including the ways those in power manipulated issues to their own advantage. Yet she made a decision to set aside her idealism and to work within the system. She rose quickly, serving in 1974 on the state platform committee. She worked for John Dunne, a Republican state senator, after graduating from college in 1975, and attended the Republican National Convention as a delegate-at-large in 1976. When Dunne sought the office of executive of Nassau County, Leslie ran his campaign. He lost and Leslie left the United States and backpacked through Europe. Yet everywhere she went, she was interested in what she could find about American politics. She wanted to be part of the process as the United States—under the leadership of Ronald Reagan—moved away from the welfare state.

Returning to the United States, in 1984 Leslie took the job of salvaging the reelection campaign of a Republican state senator. She succeeded in that effort, served for four years as executive assistant to the Republican state comptroller, and in 1989, became finance director of the state Republican party.

Leslie was a rock-ribbed Republican, who, like many Americans, reacted with frustration to chaos in national life and moved right as the party moved right. "It's like if you decide to be a nurse when you're eighteen, and stay one for twenty years," she said. "It becomes who you are. How you read the paper. How you watch the news. Your whole outlook."

The experience of Leslie Maeby mirrored that of countless Americans in the 1980s who left the Democratic party and supported the Republican agenda instead. At a time when people were disturbed by continuing racial conflict, troubled by changes in the welfare state that seemed to help disadvantaged citizens at the expense of middle- and upper-class Americans, and upset at the chaos caused by the Vietnam War, the Republican party seized the initiative. In a process that began in the 1960s (as Jack Maeby left his Democratic roots and became a Republican), a new majority emerged in the United States. Millions of Americans voiced their frustration by voting Republican, some for the first time. They succeeded in transforming their vision into American policy, and in the 1980s and early 1990s, they watched the economy improve, though often to the benefit of the most affluent Americans. At the same time, members of minority groups continued to have difficulty finding jobs, the national debt skyrocketed, and finally, the stock market crashed. Meanwhile, harsh Cold War rhetoric led to fears that the continuing confrontation between the Soviet Union and the United States might end in nuclear war.

This chapter describes the enormous changes that occurred in the 1980s and early 1990s. It highlights the role of people like Leslie Maeby in bringing to power a new political force that altered the landscape of the United States. It describes the economic and technological shifts that affected the daily lives of millions of Americans, bringing unprecedented prosperity to people at the top of the economic pyramid but leaving millions of less fortunate Americans behind. It explores the efforts of the Republican administrations of Ronald Reagan and George Bush to redefine—and limit—the government's role in the economy, and it assesses the impact such constriction had on ordinary Americans. And finally, it examines how foreign policy initiatives brought a successful end to the Cold War.

THE CONSERVATIVE TRANSFORMATION

In the 1980s and early 1990s, the Republican party reestablished itself as the dominant force in national politics. The Republican ascendancy that had begun in the Nixon era was now largely complete. The liberal agenda that had governed national affairs ever since the New Deal of Franklin Roosevelt gave way to a new Republican coalition determined to scale back the welfare state and prevent what it perceived as the erosion of the nation's moral values.

Firmly in control of the presidency, sometimes in control of the Senate and later the whole Congress, the Republican party set the new national agenda.

The New Politics

Conservatism gained respect in the 1980s, not just in the United States but in other parts of the world as well. In Great Britain, for example, the Labour Party had gained power in the latter part of the 1960s, as the nation underscored its commitment to the welfare state. A national health plan provided medical care for all, and a comprehensive educational system opened up opportunities for people limited by the class-bound strictures of the past. But problems with both inflation and unemployment plagued Britain, like other nations, and in the 1980s, the Conservative Party was back in power, with Margaret Thatcher as prime minister. Elsewhere in the late 1980s, particularly as communism began to crumble in Eastern and Central Europe, Christian Democratic movements became increasingly popular. Founded in the early twentieth century to capture the middle ground of moderate conservatism, midway between the Left and the Right, they occasionally came to power, sometimes alone and sometimes in coalitions with other groups. Now, as socialism deteriorated, they seemed a more viable alternative.

In the United States, conservativism attracted countless new adherents after the turbulence of the 1960s and the backlash of the Vietnam War. Innovative advertising and fundraising techniques capitalized on national disaffection with liberal solutions to continuing social problems, even though welfare programs in the United States were far more limited than in many other parts of the world (Scandinavia, as just one example) and made the conservative movement almost unstoppable.

Conservatives seized on Thomas Jefferson's maxim: "That government is best which governs least." They argued that the United States in the 1980s had entered an era of limits, with international competition making resources scarcer. The dramatic economic growth of the 1960s and 1970s, they believed, left a legacy of rising inflation, falling productivity, enormous waste, and out-of-control entitlements. The liberal solution of "throwing money at social problems" no longer worked, conservatives argued. Therefore, they sought to downsize government, reduce taxes, and roll-back regulations they claimed hampered business competition. They wanted to restore the focus on individual initiative and private enterprise, which they believed had made the nation strong.

The conservative philosophy had tremendous appeal. It promised profitability to those who worked hard and showed initiative. It attracted middle-class Americans, who were troubled that they were being forgotten in the commitment to assist minorities and the poor. It also offered hope for the revival of basic social and religious values that many citizens worried had been eaten away by rising divorce rates, legalized abortion, homosexuality, and media preoccupation with violence and sex.

The new conservative coalition covered a broad spectrum. Some followers embraced the economic doctrines of University of Chicago economist Milton Friedman, who promoted the free play of market forces and a sharp restriction of governmental activism in regulating the economy. Others applauded the social and political conservatism of North Carolina Senator Jesse Helms, a tireless foe of anything he deemed pornographic and a fervent campaigner for a limited federal role. Still others flocked to the Republican fold because of their conviction that civil rights activists and "bleeding heart liberals" practiced "reverse racism" with affirmative action, job quotas, and busing to promote equal opportunity.

The conservative coalition also drew deeply from religious fundamentalists who advocated a literal interpretation of Scriptures. Millions—devout Catholics, orthodox Jews, evangelical Protestants—demanded a return to stricter standards of morality. Muslims, relying on the Koran, took an equally fundamentalist approach. All groups worried about sexual permissiveness and gay rights. They were disturbed at the increase in the number of women working outside the home, a practice they believed eroded family life. They were bothered by a sizable increase in crime. They were likewise troubled by spiraling drug use. Marijuana was not simply a youthful fad but a recreational drug for a broad segment of society. Cocaine use was increasingly common. In short, fundamentalists objected to what they viewed as the liberalizing tendencies they saw all around them and sought to refashion society by reaffirming scriptural morality and the centrality of religion in American life.

Many of these activists belonged to the so-called Moral Majority. The Reverend Jerry Falwell of Virginia and other television evangelists who focused on the concerns of religious fundamentalism attracted large followings in the 1980s. Emulating Father Charles E. Coughlin, the radio priest of the 1930s, they appealed to audiences who knew them only on the airwaves. Using electronic means to preach fiery sermons to enormous audiences, they focused their television congregations on specific political ends. They also used their fundraising ability to support candidates sympathetic to their cause. Moral Majority money began to fund politicians who demanded reinstituting school prayer, ending legalized abortion, and defeating the Equal Rights Amendment. Later a group calling itself the Christian Coalition became even more powerful in supporting—and electing—candidates who met its litmus test on conservative values.

In 1980, a group called Evangelicals for Social Action spelled out the need for religious involvement in political affairs. Echoing the pronouncements of the Reverend Billy Graham, who argued in

Islam became increasingly popular in the United States in the 1980s and 1990s. This picture shows girls at the Al Iman School in Queens, New York City, wearing the long, shapeless robes and head scarves traditional in the Muslim world. Boys and girls are separated, but all study Arabic and English and learn Muslim rituals and prayers. *(William Lopez/New York Times Picture Collection)*

the 1950s that Christians had a role to play in supporting American policy in the Cold War, they demanded active involvement in public policy. "Christ is Lord of the world as well as the church," the group proclaimed. "Our vote can become one of Christ's instruments for fostering the peace and justice he desires as Lord of the world." A religious framework was the best way to assess candidates running for office: "To proclaim Christ's lordship in politics means evaluating political candidates by their com-

The Reverend Jerry Falwell, founder of the Moral Majority, called for a crusade to revive moral values in the United States. His constituency was an important part of the new conservative movement. *(UPI/Corbis-Bettmann)*

mitment to biblical principles, rather than by their pragmatism, patriotism, or personality."

Conservatives from all camps capitalized on changing political techniques more successfully than their liberal opponents. They understood the importance of television in providing instant access to the American public. Politicians became increasingly adept at using "sound bytes," often lasting no more than 15 or 30 seconds, to state their views. They also relied on new electronic systems such as e-mail, fax machines, and the Internet to mobilize their followers.

Similarly, conservatives outdid liberals in using negative political advertising. Mudslinging has always been a part of the American political tradition, but now carefully crafted television ads concentrated not so much on conveying a positive image of a candidate's platform but on subtly attacking an opponent's character in order to create fundamental doubt in a voter's mind. That effort was visible in both presidential and congressional campaigns.

Conservatives likewise led the way in refining their appeal to voters. Polls, sometimes taken daily, showed which part of a candidate's image needed polishing or where an opponent was vulnerable. "Spin doctors" put the best possible gloss on what politicians said. It was small wonder that Americans became increasingly cynical about politics and avoided voting booths in record numbers.

Conservatives also were most successful in raising unprecedented sums of money for their campaigns. Richard Viguerie, the New Right mastermind, understood how to tap the huge conservative constituency for political ends. A young Houston activist who later moved to Washington, he developed direct-mail appeals that assisted conservative candidates around the country.

At the same time, conservatives understood the need to provide an intellectual grounding for their positions. Conservative scholars worked in "think tanks" and other research organizations such as the Hoover Institution at Stanford University or the American Enterprise Institute in Washington, D.C., that gave conservatism a solid institutional base. Their books, articles, and reports helped elect Ronald Reagan and other conservative politicians.

Conservative Leadership

More than any other Republican, Ronald Reagan was responsible for the success of the conservative cause. An actor turned politician, he had been a radio broadcaster in his native Midwest, then gravitated to California, where he began a movie career. Initially drawn to the Democratic party and impressed with the accomplishments of Franklin D. Roosevelt's New Deal, he was also sympathetic to union causes and served as president of the Screen Actor's Guild in Hollywood. But his success on the silver screen affected his political inclinations, and

he changed his affiliation from Democrat to Republican in the early 1960s. As his film career came to an end, he went to work as a public spokesman for General Electric, where his visibility and ability to articulate corporate values attracted the attention of conservatives who recognized his political potential and helped him win election as governor of California in 1966. He failed in his first bid for the presidency in 1976 but consolidated his strength over the next four years. By 1980, he had the firm support of the growing Right, which applauded his promise to reduce the size of the federal government but bolster military might.

Running against incumbent Jimmy Carter in 1980, Reagan scored a landslide victory, gaining a popular vote of 51 to 41 percent and a 489 to 49 Electoral College advantage. He also led the Republican party to control of the Senate for the first time since 1955. In 1984, he was reelected by an even larger margin. He received 59 percent of the popular vote and swamped Democratic candidate Walter Mondale in the Electoral College 525 to 13, losing only Minnesota, Mondale's home state, and the District of Columbia. The Democrats, however, netted two additional seats in the Senate and maintained superiority in the House of Representatives.

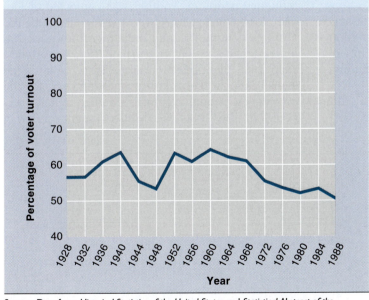

Voter Turnout, 1928–1988

Voter turnout was far lower in the twentieth century than it had been in the nineteenth century. The fact that barely 50 percent of the electorate voted in the 1980s reflects a pervasive sense of disillusionment with the political process.

Source: Data from *Historical Statistics of the United States* and *Statistical Abstract of the United States.*

Reagan had a pleasing manner and a special skill as a media communicator. Relying on his acting experience, he used television as Franklin D. Roosevelt had used radio in the 1930s. He was a gifted storyteller who loved using anecdotes or one-liners to make his point. In 1980, for example, he quibbled playfully with Carter over definitions of economic doldrums. "I'm talking in human terms and he is hiding behind a dictionary," Reagan said. "If he wants a definition, I'll give him one. A recession is when your neighbor loses his job. A depression is when you lose yours. A recovery is when Jimmy Carter loses his."

As president, Reagan managed to convey his sense of vision to the American people. He spoke of the United States as "the last best hope of man on earth," and, echoing John Winthrop's sermon to Puritans coming to the New World in 1630, he referred to America as a "shining city on a hill." He was fond of invoking images of Pilgrims coming ashore in New England, American prisoners of war returning from Vietnam, and astronauts landing on the moon, and he argued that history still had a place for the nation and its ideals. In response to those who spoke of a "national malaise," he retorted, "I find nothing wrong with the American people."

Throughout his eight years in office, Reagan enjoyed enormous popularity. People talked about a "Teflon" presidency, making a comparison with nonstick frying pans, for even serious criticisms failed to stick and disagreements over policy never diminished his personal-approval ratings. When he left the White House, an overwhelming 68 percent of the American public approved of his performance over the past eight years.

But Reagan had a number of liabilities that surfaced over time. As the oldest president the nation had ever had, his attention often drifted, and he occasionally fell asleep during meetings, including one with the pope. While he could speak eloquently with a script in front of him, he was frequently unsure about what was being asked in press confer-

Ronald Reagan drew on his experience in the movies to project an appealing, if old-fashioned, image. Though he was the nation's oldest president, he gave the appearance of vitality. Here he is pictured with his wife, Nancy, who was one of his most influential advisers. *(Diana Walker/Liaison Agency, Inc./Getty Images)*

ences. Uninterested in governing, he delegated a great deal of authority, even if that left him unclear about policy decisions.

Worst of all, he suffered from charges of "sleaze" in his administration. In a period of several months during his last year in office, one former aide was convicted of lying under oath to conceal episodes of influence peddling. Another was convicted of illegally lobbying former government colleagues. His attorney general escaped indictment but nonetheless resigned after severe criticism for improprieties.

In 1988, Republican George Bush, who served eight years as Reagan's vice president, ran for the presidency. Though a New Englander, he had prospered in the Texas oil industry, then served in

Presidential Elections, 1980–1988

Year	Candidate	Party	Popular Vote	Electoral Vote
1980	RONALD REAGAN	Republican	43,899,248 (50.8%)	489
	Jimmy Carter	Democratic	36,481,435 (41.0%)	49
	John B. Anderson	Independent	5,719,437 (6.6%)	0
1984	RONALD REAGAN	Republican	53,428,357 (58.7%)	525
	Walter F. Mondale	Democratic	36,930,923 (40.6%)	13
1988	GEORGE BUSH	Republican	47,946,422 (53.9%)	426
	Michael Dukakis	Democratic	41,016,429 (46.1%)	112

Note: Winners' names appear in capital letters.

George H.W. Bush capitalized on his position as vice president under Ronald Reagan and won a resounding victory in the election of 1988. Even so, he did not have the solid conservative mandate that Reagan enjoyed. *(Corbis Sygma)*

Congress, as top envoy to China, and as head of the CIA. Termed a preppy wimp by the press, he became a pit bull who ran a mudslinging campaign against his Democratic opponent, Governor Michael Dukakis of Massachusetts. On election day, Bush swamped Dukakis, winning a 54–46 percent popular-vote majority and carrying 40 states. But conservatives who admired Reagan were suspicious of Bush, and he did not have the kind of mandate Reagan had enjoyed in 1980 and again in 1984. Even worse from the Republican point of view, Democrats controlled both houses of Congress.

Bush quickly put his own imprint on the presidency. Despite his upper-crust background, he was an unpretentious man who made a point of trying to appear down-to-earth. He also maintained his own network of friends and political contacts through handwritten notes, telephone calls, and personal visits. More than a year and a half into his term, he was still on his political honeymoon, with a personal approval rating of 67 percent. Support grew even stronger as he presided over the Persian Gulf War in 1991. Then, as the economy faltered and the results of the war seemed suspect, approval lev-

els began to drop, and he failed in his bid for reelection in 1992 (see Chapter 31).

Republican Policies at Home

Republicans in the 1980s and early 1990s aimed to reverse the economic stagnation of the Carter years and to provide new opportunities for business to prosper. The United States, like industrialized nations around the world, had suffered from the Arab oil embargo of 1973 (see Chapter 29), which had vastly increased energy prices. As the cost of driving cars and heating homes skyrocketed, the entire economy was knocked out of kilter. In an increasingly globalized economy, where multinational firms had interests around the world, a downturn in one area—or one country—affected business efforts around the globe. Republicans wanted to provide American business interests with the ability to prosper at home and wherever else they operated.

To that end, Reagan proposed and implemented an economic recovery program that rested on the theory of supply-side economics. According to this much-criticized theory, reduction of taxes would encourage business expansion, which in turn would lead to a larger supply of goods to help stimulate the system as a whole. Even George Bush, during his brief run for the Republican nomination in 1980, was critical, charging that Reagan was promoting "voodoo economics." Despite such criticism, Republicans followed the president's lead and endorsed "Reaganomics," with its promise of a revitalized economy.

One early initiative involved tax reductions. A 5 percent cut in the tax rate was enacted to go into effect on October 1, 1981, followed by 10 percent cuts in 1982 and 1983. Although all taxpayers received some tax relief, the rich gained far more than middle- and lower-income Americans. Poverty-level Americans did not benefit at all. Tax cuts and enormous defense expenditures increased the budget deficit. From $74 billion in 1980, it jumped to $290 billion in 1992. Such massive deficits drove the gross federal debt—the total national indebtedness—upward from $909 billion in 1980 to $4.4 trillion in 1992. When Reagan assumed office, the per capita national debt was $4,035; 10 years later, in 1990, it was about $12,400.

Faced with the need to raise more money and rectify an increasingly skewed tax code, in 1986 Congress passed and Reagan signed the most sweeping tax reform since the federal income tax began in 1913. It lowered rates, consolidated brackets, and closed loopholes to expand the tax base. Though it ended up neither increasing nor decreasing the government's tax take, the measure

Federal Budget Deficits and the National Debt, 1970–1992

In the 1970s, 1980s, and early 1990s, the yearly federal budget deficit grew steadily larger, and the gross federal debt skyrocketed. In this economy, deficits and debt affected spending priorities.

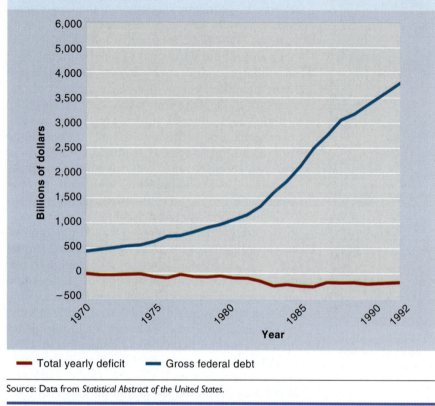

Total yearly deficit   Gross federal debt

Source: Data from *Statistical Abstract of the United States.*

was an important step toward treating low-income Americans more equitably. Still, most of the benefits went to the richest 5 percent of Americans.

At the same time, Reagan embarked on a major program of deregulation. In a campaign more comprehensive than Jimmy Carter's, he focused on agencies of the 1970s such as the Environmental Protection Agency, the Consumer Product Safety Commission, and the Occupational Safety and Health Administration. The Republican administration argued that regulations pertaining to the consumer, the workplace, and the environment were inefficient, paternalistic, and excessively expensive. They impeded business growth and needed to be eliminated.

The Federal Communications Commission (FCC), which had effectively regulated the airwaves in the past, now shifted course. The head of the agency under Reagan scoffed at the idea that television had a public-service role. "Television is just another ap-pliance," he declared. "It's just a toaster with pictures. . . . [It is] time to move away from thinking about broadcasters as trustees, [and to] treat them the way almost everyone else in society does—that is as business." Under new leadership, the FCC increased the amount of time allotted to commercials and eliminated the rule that some programming had to be in the area of public-service broadcasts.

Meanwhile, Reagan challenged the New Deal consensus that the federal government should monitor the economy and assist the least fortunate citizens. He had played by the rules of the system and had won fame and fortune. Others could do the same. He charged that government intruded too deeply into American life. It was time to eliminate "waste, fraud, and abuse" by cutting unnecessary programs.

Reagan needed to curtail social programs both because of sizable tax cuts and because of enormous military expenditures. Committed to a massive arms buildup, over a five-year period the administration sought an unprecedented military budget of $1.5 trillion. By 1985, with an allocation of $300 billion, the United States was spending half a million dollars a minute on defense and four times as much as at the height of the Vietnam War.

The huge cuts in social programs reversed the approach of liberals over the past 50 years. Republicans in the 1970s had begun to question the social policy goals of Lyndon Johnson's Great Society (see Chapter 28). In the 1980s, allied with conservative southern Democrats, they attacked those liberal aims head-on. They eliminated public service jobs and reduced other aid to the cities, where the poor congregated. They cut back unemployment compensation and required Medicare patients to pay more for treatment. They lowered welfare benefits and food stamp allocations. They slashed the Legal Services Corporation, which provided legal services for the poor. They replaced grants for college students with loans. Spending on human resources fell by $101 billion between 1980 and 1982. The process continued even after Reagan left office. Between 1981 and 1992, federal spending (adjusted for inflation) fell 82 percent for subsidized housing, 63 percent for job training and employment services, and 40 percent for community services. Middle-class Americans, benefiting from the tax cuts, were not hurt by the slashes in social programs. But for millions of the nation's poorest citizens, the administration's approach caused real suffering.

Ironically, despite the huge cuts, overall federal spending for social welfare rose from $313 billion in 1980 to $533 billion in 1988. The increase came about because of growth in the payments of entitlement programs, such as social security and Medicare, which provided benefits automatically to citizens in need. Even the most aggressive efforts of the Republicans could not wholly dismantle the welfare state.

As a political conservative distrustful of centralized government, Reagan wanted to place more power in the hands of state and local governments and to reduce the involvement of the federal government in people's lives. His "New Federalism" attempted to shift responsibilities from the federal to the state level. By eliminating federal funding and instead making grants to the states, which could spend the money as they saw fit, he hoped to fortify local initiative. Critics charged, with some justification, that the proposal was merely a backhanded way of moving programs from one place to another while eliminating federal funding. When a prolonged recession began in 1990, the administration's

policy contributed to the near-bankruptcy of a number of states and municipalities, which now bore responsibility for programs formerly funded in Washington.

Reagan took a conservative approach to social issues as well. Accepting the support of the New Right, he strongly endorsed conservative social goals. To avoid compromising his economic program, however, he provided only symbolic support at first. He spoke out for public prayer in the schools without expending political capital in Congress to support the issue. In the same way, he showed his opposition to abortion by making sure that the first nongovernmental group to receive an audience at the White House was an antiabortion March for Life contingent.

George Bush followed directly in his predecessor's footsteps. Having forsworn his objection to "voodoo economics" as soon as he received the vice-presidential nomination, Bush faithfully adhered to Reagan's general economic policy even after he became president. Running for president in 1988, he promised "no new taxes." Though he backed down from that pledge to join a bipartisan effort to bring the budget deficit under control, he later renounced his own agreement to modest tax increases when he went back on the campaign trail in 1992.

Like Reagan, Bush wanted deep cuts in social programs. Tireless in his criticism of the Democratic majorities in the Senate and House of Representatives, he vetoed measure after measure to assist those caught in the ravages of a troubling recession that sent unemployment rates up to 8 percent and left one of every four urban children living in poverty.

Bush was more outspoken than Reagan in his support of conservative social goals. At the start of the 1980s, conservatives had questioned Bush's commitment to their social agenda, and, indeed, Bush had been sympathetic to a woman's right to choice in the abortion issue. As president, however, he firmly opposed abortion, and his Supreme Court appointments, like Reagan's, guaranteed that the effort to roll back or overturn *Roe* v. *Wade* would continue.

The Republican philosophy under Reagan and Bush dramatically reversed the nation's domestic agenda. Liberalism in the 1960s had reached a high-water mark in a time of steady growth, when hard choices about where to spend money had been less necessary. As limits began to loom, decisions about social programs became more difficult, and millions of Americans like Leslie Maeby, introduced at the start of the chapter, came to believe

In 1988, and again in 1992, George Bush and the Republicans emphasized traditional family values as a way of healing the social ills of the nation. In this campaign picture, Bush poses with his family at their home in Maine as a way of showing that he was a good family man. *(Sipa Press)*

that most of the Great Society programs had failed to conquer poverty and in fact had created lifelong welfare dependency. Conservatism offered a more attractive answer, particularly to those Americans in the middle and upper classes who were already comfortable.

But the transformation was accompanied by a number of serious problems that emerged in the early 1990s. Bush faced a bankruptcy crisis in the long-mismanaged savings and loan industry. The Republican deregulation policy had allowed owners of savings and loan institutions to operate without previous restrictions. Many, paying themselves lavish salaries, made unwise, high-risk investments that proved profitable for a while but then produced tremendous losses. To protect depositors whose assets had been lost by these questionable lending practices, Congress approved a $166 billion rescue plan (that soon reached more than $250 billion) committing taxpayers to bail out the industry.

Republican policy also widened the gap between rich and poor. Tax breaks for the wealthy, deregulation initiatives, high interest rates for investors, permissiveness toward mergers, and an enormous growth in the salaries of top business executives all contributed to the disparity. So did more lenient antitrust enforcement and a general sympathy for speculative finance.

The 1980s, it became clear, produced "a decade of money fever," as author Tom Wolfe put it. Analyst Kevin Phillips called this period "the triumph of upper America," with "an ostentatious celebration of wealth, the political ascendancy of the rich and a glorification of capitalism, free markets and finance." The concentration of capital—an amassing of wealth at the top levels—produced dekamillion-aires, centmillionaires, half-billionaires, and billion-aires. "Garden-variety millionaires," Phillips noted, "had become so common that there were about 1.5 million of them by 1989." According to one study, the share of national wealth of the richest 1 percent of the nation rose from about 18 percent in 1976 to 36 percent in 1989. The net worth of the *Forbes* magazine 400 richest Americans nearly tripled between 1981 and 1989.

Meanwhile, less-fortunate Americans suffered more than they had since the Great Depression. Financial expert Felix Rohatyn decried the "huge transfer of wealth from lower-skilled, middle-class American workers to owners of capital assets and a new technological aristocracy." Meanwhile, in 1987, one out of every five American children lived in poverty, up 24 percent since 1979. And millions of people, ranging from foreclosed farmers to laid-off industrial workers, were struggling to make ends meet.

The Wealthiest Americans

During the 1980s, the percentage of national wealth held by the richest 1 percent of Americans reached the highest level since the 1930s.

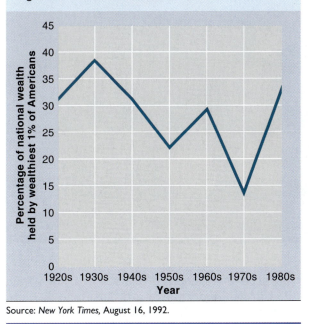

Source: *New York Times*, August 16, 1992.

AN END TO SOCIAL REFORM

The Republican attack on the welfare state included an effort to limit the commitment to social reform. Enough had been done already, conservatives argued, and gains for less fortunate Americans came at the expense of the middle class. It was time to end federal "intrusion" in this area.

Slowdown in the Struggle for Civil Rights

Republican policies slowed the civil rights movement. Reagan opposed busing to achieve racial balance, and his attorney general worked to dismantle affirmative action programs. Initially reluctant to support extension of the enormously successful Voting Rights Act of 1965, Reagan relented only under severe bipartisan criticism. He directed the Internal Revenue Service to cease banning tax exemptions for private schools that discriminated against blacks, only to see that move overturned by the Supreme Court in 1983. He also launched an assault on the Civil Rights Commission and hampered its effectiveness by appointing members who did not support its main goals.

The courts similarly weakened commitments to equal rights. As a result of Reagan's and Bush's judicial appointments, federal courts stopped pushing for school integration. The Supreme Court's *Freeman* v. *Pitts* decision in 1992 granted a suburban Atlanta school board relief from a desegregation order on the grounds that it was not possible to counteract massive demographic shifts.

Yet African Americans kept the struggle alive. The Reverend Jesse Jackson, a longtime civil rights activist, established what he called the Rainbow Coalition in 1984 and ran for the presidency. Though he lost in his bid for the Democratic nomination, he

Jesse Jackson demonstrated that an African American could attract a substantial level of support as he ran for president in 1984 and 1988. Here he is shown on the campaign trail in Chicago in 1988. *(Marc Pokempner)*

While many Americans prospered in the 1980s and early 1990s, others found themselves left behind. The riot in Los Angeles in 1992, following the acquittal of the police officers accused of beating black motorist Rodney King, reflected the pent-up frustrations that could no longer be ignored. *(Ed Carreon/Sipa Press)*

had the support of nearly 400 delegates, and in a nationally televised speech at the convention, he vowed not to forget his constituency of "the desperate, the damned, the disinherited, the disrespected, and the despised." All Americans, he went on, needed to work together for a common cause: "Our flag is red, white and blue, but our nation is a rainbow—red, yellow, brown, black and white—and we're all precious in God's sight." Four years later, in 1988, he sought the Democratic nomination again, this time with the support of 1,200 delegates at the convention, before falling short of his goal once more.

Despite significant progress in other areas of the electoral arena—where African Americans won mayoral elections in major cities and captured the governor's office in Virginia—black–white relations remained tense. As Joseph Lattimore, an African American from Chicago, observed, "As far as integrating with you—we have sang 'We Shall Overcome,' we have prayed at the courthouse steps, we have made all these gestures, and the door is not open." Sylvia Matthews, also from Chicago, noted, "Today it seems more acceptable to be racist. Just in the kinds of things you hear people say."

A riot in Los Angeles in 1992 revealed the continuing racial polarization. The year before, Americans had watched a videotaped, savage beating of black motorist Rodney King by white police officers, the most dramatic of a long string of incidents involving police brutality. When a California jury that did not include any African Americans acquitted the policemen, many people throughout the country became

convinced that people of color could not obtain equal justice under the law. In Los Angeles, thousands reacted with uncontrolled fury. As widespread arson and looting swept through many neighborhoods, the police proved unable to control the mayhem. Targets included supermarkets, drug stores, Korean businesses, restaurants, and mini-malls. Much of the chaos was orchestrated by gang members, but it also involved hundreds of ordinary citizens who acted irresponsibly, yet with a sense that the social contract had been broken by politicians and the rich who were unresponsive to their plight. Several days later, after the riot had run its course, 51 people (most of them black and Hispanic) lay dead, 2,000 were injured, and $1 billion in damage had been done to the city. It was the worst riot in decades, more deadly even than the Watts riot 27 years earlier. Political candidates from both parties scurried around trying to define an urban policy, as the upheaval served notice that racial injustice, social inequality, and poverty could no longer be ignored.

Obstacles to Women's Rights

Women had a similar experience in the 1980s and early 1990s. They, too, made significant electoral gains at the local, state, and national levels. In 1981, President Reagan named Sandra Day O'Connor as the first woman Supreme Court justice, and in 1984 Democrat Geraldine Ferraro became the first major-party female vice-presidential nominee.

Yet women still faced problems that were compounded by conservative social policies. Access to new positions did not change their concentration in lower-paying jobs. In 1985, most working women were still secretaries, cashiers, bookkeepers, registered nurses, and waitresses—the same jobs most frequently held 10 years before. Even when women moved into positions traditionally held by men, their progress often stopped at the lower and middle levels. Interruptions of work—to bear children or assume family responsibilities—impeded advancement. In virtually all areas, American women had less support juggling family, home, and work than women in many European countries. And for those who managed to do everything on their own, a "glass ceiling" seemed to prevent them from moving up.

Wage differentials between women and men continued to exist. In 1985, full-time working women still earned only 59 cents for every dollar earned by men. Comparable-worth arguments that women should receive equal pay for different jobs of similar value met conservative resistance.

Conservatives also waged a dedicated campaign against the right to legal abortion. Despite the 1973 Supreme Court decision legalizing abortion, the issue remained very much alive. The number of abortions increased dramatically in the decade after the

decision. In response, "pro-life" forces mobilized. Opponents lobbied to cut off federal funds that allowed the poor to obtain the abortions that the better-off could pay for themselves; they insisted that abortions should be performed in hospitals and not in less expensive clinics; and they worked to reverse the original decision itself.

Though the Supreme Court underscored its judgment in 1983, the pro-life movement was not deterred. In 1989, a solidifying conservative majority on the Court ruled in *Webster* v. *Reproductive Health Services* that while women's right to abortion remained intact, state legislatures could impose limitations if they chose. With that judgment, a major legislative debate over the issue began, and numerous states began to mandate restrictions.

In 1992, in *Planned Parenthood* v. *Casey,* the Supreme Court reaffirmed what it termed the essence of the right to abortion, while permitting further state restrictions. It declared that a 24-hour waiting period for women seeking abortions was acceptable and required teenage girls to secure the permission of a parent (or a judge) before ending a pregnancy. The ruling clearly gave states greater latitude in the overall restrictive effort and made an abortion harder to obtain, particularly for poor women and young women.

In response to a conservative backlash, the women's movement became more racially inclusive. Black women now found more common ground with white feminists. While black women in the early 1990s still earned less on a weekly basis than white men and white women, that situation began to improve.

Women and men became more sensitive to the issue of sexual harassment. The dramatic confrontation between Supreme Court nominee Clarence Thomas and lawyer Anita Hill during confirmation hearings in 1991 dramatized both racial questions and the problem of sexual harassment. After the retirement of Thurgood Marshall, the only African American on the Supreme Court, President Bush sought to replace him with the much more conservative Clarence Thomas, putting African Americans, who wanted one of their own on the court, in a political bind. Then, during nationally televised confirmation hearings, Anita Hill accused Thomas of harassing her when she had worked for him earlier. Thomas furiously countered with charges of a "high tech lynching." The Bush administration managed to garner the necessary votes for confirmation, and Thomas followed a conservative agenda in the years that followed. In the aftermath of the turbulent confirmation hearings, Americans in Congress, in the business community, and in the larger workplace all

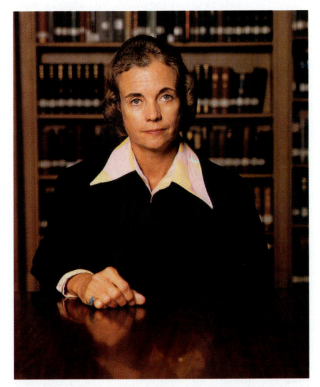

Sandra Day O'Connor became the first woman justice to sit on the U.S. Supreme Court. Her pre-Court career was similar to that of many other women, as she was denied numerous jobs when she emerged from law school. A decade later, Ruth Bader Ginsburg joined O'Connor on the nation's highest Court. *(Tom Zimberoff/Corbis Sygma)*

became more aware of inappropriate behavior that could no longer be tolerated.

The Limited Commitment to Latino Rights

Latinos likewise faced continuing concerns in the 1980s and early 1990s as the commitment to reform eroded. The Latino population increased substantially as a result of immigration reform during the Great Society of the 1960s (see Chapter 28). In the 1980s, 47 percent of all legal American immigration came from Mexico, the Caribbean, and Latin America. Many other immigrants arrived illegally. As the populations of Latin American nations soared and as economic conditions deteriorated, more and more people looked to the United States for relief. In the mid-1970s, Leonard Chapman, commissioner of the Immigration and Naturalization Service, estimated that there might be 12 million foreigners in the nation illegally. While official estimates were lower, Attorney General William French Smith declared in 1983, "Simply put, we've lost control of our own borders."

Many of the new arrivals were skilled workers or professionals, who still had to retool after arriving in the United States. But even more prevalent were laborers, service sector workers, and semiskilled employees, who needed the benefit of social services at just the time they were being cut back.

Spanish-speaking students often found it difficult to finish school. In 1987, 40 percent of all Latino high school students did not graduate, and only 31 percent of Latino seniors were enrolled in college-preparatory courses; those who were in such classes frequently received little help from guidance counselors. Anel Albarran, a Mexican immigrant who arrived in East Los Angeles when she was 11 years old, applied to UCLA when a special high school teacher encouraged her and made sure that she received help in choosing the necessary courses. By contrast, her regular counselor took little interest in her; he waited until only two months before graduation to ask her if she had considered going onto college. "All he had wanted to do during high school," Anel observed, "was give me my classes and get me out of the room."

Like other groups, Latinos slowly extended their political gains. In the 1980s, Henry Cisneros became mayor of San Antonio and Federico Peña was elected mayor of Denver. In New Mexico, Governor Toney Anaya called himself the nation's highest elected Hispanic. The number of Latinos holding elective offices nationwide increased 3.5 percent between 1986 and 1987, and the number of Latina women in such offices increased 20 percent in that time. The number of Latino public officials nationwide increased 73 percent between 1985 and 1994, and Lauro Cavazos became the first Latino Cabinet official when he was appointed secretary of education in 1988.

Latino workers, however, continued to have a hard time in the employment market. Even as the nation's overall unemployment rate dropped, the rate for the 12 million Latino workers barely budged—and worsened in relation to the rate for African Americans. Many found themselves suffering from outdated skills and weak educational backgrounds that limited economic opportunities.

Continuing Problems for Native Americans

Native Americans likewise experienced the waning commitment to reform, but they made some gains as a result of their own efforts. Some tribal communities developed business skills, although traditional Indian attitudes hardly fostered the capitalist perspective. As Dale Old Horn, an MIT graduate and department head at Little Big Horn College in Crow Agency, Montana, explained:

> The Crow Indian child is taught that he is part of a harmonious circle of kin relations, clans and nature. The white child is taught that he is the center of the circle. The Crow believe in sharing wealth, and whites believe in accumulating wealth.

Some Indian groups did adapt to the capitalist ethos. "Now we're beginning to realize that, if we want to be self-sufficient, we're going to have to become entrepreneurs ourselves," observed Iola Hayden, the Comanche executive director of Oklahomans for Indian Opportunity. The Choctaw in Mississippi were among the most successful. Before they began a drive toward self-sufficiency in 1979, their unemployment rate was 50 percent. By the middle of the 1980s, Choctaws owned all or part of three businesses on the reservation, employed 1,000 people, generated $30 million in work annually, and cut the unemployment rate in half. After Congress approved Native-American gambling in 1988, an increasing number of tribes became involved in this industry. The Pequots in Connecticut built a casino in the southeastern part of the state that became the most profitable one in the nation.

Despite entrepreneurial gains, Indians still remained (as the 1990 census showed) the nation's poorest group. As Ben Nighthorse Campbell, Republican senator from Colorado, noted in 1995, average Indian household income fell by 5 percent in the 1980s, while it rose for all other ethnic and racial groups. According to the 1990 census, median Indian household income was less than $20,000 a year.

Asian-American Gains

Asian Americans climbed the social and economic ladder one rung at a time. The Asian-American population increased dramatically with the influx of refugees at the end of the Vietnam War, with more than a half million arriving after 1975. In the 1980s, 37 percent of all immigrants to the United States came from Asia. In cities like Los Angeles, Samoans, Taiwanese, Koreans, Vietnamese, Filipinos, and Cambodians competed for jobs and apartments with Mexicans, African Americans, and Anglos, just as newcomers had contended with one another in New York City a century earlier.

Immigrants from India, the Philippines, China, and Korea often brought skills and professional expertise, although Southeast Asian refugees were frequently less well-off when they arrived. Many of these unskilled immigrants provided the labor for the rapidly expanding West Coast electronics industry, though Indians provided impressive engineering and scientific talent, to such a degree that it was sometimes noted that the dominant aroma in Silicon Valley (where many electronic and computer firms were located) was curry. The Asian immigrants, following a pattern established decades before, sought better and better opportunities for their children, and in California they became the largest group of entering students at a number of college campuses.

Sometimes the media highlighted the successes of Asian immigrants, particularly in contrast to the problems encountered by other groups. In 1986, *U.S. News & World Report* noted Asian-American advances in a cover story, while *Newsweek* ran a lead article on "Asian Americans: A 'Model Minority,'" and *Fortune* called them "America's Super Minority." Asian Americans were proud of the exposure but pointed out that many members of the working class still struggled for a foothold. In the Chinatowns of San Francisco and Los Angeles, 40 to 50 percent of the workers were employed in the ill-paid service sector or garment industry; in New York's Chinatown, the figure was close to 70 percent. Chinese immigrant women, in particular, often had little choice but to work as seamstresses, just as women from other nationalities had earlier in the century.

Each group, each family, had its own story. Nguyen Ninh and Nguyen Viet, two brothers who remained in Vietnam after the victory of the North Vietnamese in 1975, were among the many who finally fled their war-torn country by boat. The boat sank, but they were rescued, only to be shuttled to Kuwait, then Greece, and finally to the United States, where another brother had arrived a few years before. Though they spoke no English, they immediately began to look for work. One became a carpenter's helper; the other worked as an attendant at a valet parking firm. With the money they earned, they helped other members of their family emigrate. Slowly they learned English, obtained better jobs, and saved enough money to purchase a home.

Professionals from some countries had a hard time. One Vietnamese physician who resettled in Oklahoma noted, "When I come here, I am told that I must be a beginner again and serve like an

Asian workers often found themselves trapped in low-paying jobs with little hope of advancement. Here women work at sewing machines in a cluttered factory in Queens, New York, in conditions similar to those earlier in the twentieth century. *(Donna Binder/Impact Visuals)*

ANALYZING HISTORY

THE COMPUTER

The computer changed American life, just as the radio changed patterns in the 1920s and the television changed patterns in the 1950s. Dropping prices made computers increasingly accessible, and soon more and more Americans—and people around the world—began to use computers to work and play.

Reflecting on the Past   How has the computer changed American life? How has the increase in the number of computers changed relationships between America and the rest of the world? What different professions have been created by the growth of the computer?

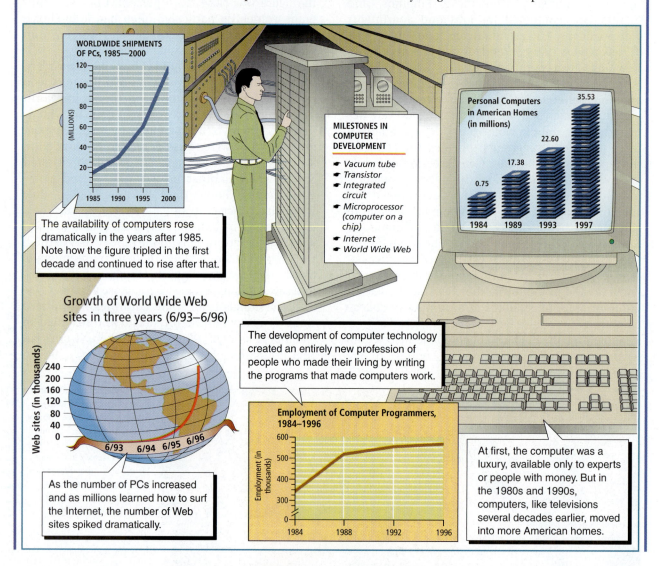

WORLDWIDE SHIPMENTS OF PCs, 1985—2000

(MILLIONS): 120, 100, 80, 60, 40, 20 — 1985 1990 1995 2000

The availability of computers rose dramatically in the years after 1985. Note how the figure tripled in the first decade and continued to rise after that.

MILESTONES IN COMPUTER DEVELOPMENT
- Vacuum tube
- Transistor
- Integrated circuit
- Microprocessor (computer on a chip)
- Internet
- World Wide Web

Personal Computers in American Homes (in millions)
0.75 (1984)   17.38 (1989)   22.60 (1993)   35.53 (1997)

Growth of World Wide Web sites in three years (6/93–6/96)

Web sites (in thousands): 240, 200, 160, 120, 80, 40, 0 — 6/93 6/94 6/95 6/96

As the number of PCs increased and as millions learned how to surf the Internet, the number of Web sites spiked dramatically.

The development of computer technology created an entirely new profession of people who made their living by writing the programs that made computers work.

Employment of Computer Programmers, 1984–1996
Employment (in thousands): 600, 500, 400, 300, 0 — 1984 1988 1992 1996

At first, the computer was a luxury, available only to experts or people with money. But in the 1980s and 1990s, computers, like televisions several decades earlier, moved into more American homes.

apprentice for two years. I have no choice, so I will do it, but I have been wronged to be asked to do this." Professionals from other nations, with programs recognized in the United States, made the transition more easily.

Violent episodes sometimes highlighted discrimination. In 1982, in Detroit, Chinese American Vincent Chin was about to get married. At a strip club with friends the week before his wedding, he encountered two auto workers who thought that Chin was Japanese, and they regarded Japan as responsible for the crisis in the American auto industry as Japanese cars flooded the market. They followed Chin out of the door and killed him with a baseball bat. In response to a guilty plea, both murderers received three years probation and $3,780 in fines. Detroit's Asian Americans were incensed but were reluctant to jeopardize what they considered their already vulnerable role in America.

Pressures on the Environmental Movement

Environmentalists, too, were discouraged by the direction of public policy in the 1980s and early 1990s. Activists found that they faced fierce opposition in the Republican years. Reagan systematically restrained the EPA in his avowed effort to promote economic growth. Under the leadership of James Watt of Colorado, the Department of the Interior opened forest lands, wilderness areas, and coastal waters to economic development, with no concern for preserving the natural environment. When asked whether he believed it was important to protect the environment for future generations, Watt, a devout Christian, responded that he did not know how many generations there were before the Second Coming. Bush initially proved more sympathetic to environmental causes and delighted environmentalists by signing new clean-air legislation. Later, as the economy faltered, he was less willing to support environmental action that he claimed might slow economic growth. In 1992, he accommodated business by easing clean-air restrictions. That same year, at a United Nations–sponsored Earth Summit in Rio de Janeiro, Brazil, with 100 other heads of state, Bush stood alone in his refusal to sign a biological diversity treaty framed to conserve plant and animal species.

ECONOMIC AND DEMOGRAPHIC CHANGE

Republicans sought to reorganize the government against the backdrop of an economy that was volatile in the 1980s and early 1990s. As patterns of employment changed in an increasingly mechanized workplace, millions of workers struggled to survive the shocks. Under Republican supply-side economics, the business cycle moved from recession to boom and back to recession again. When Reagan took office in 1980, the economy was reeling under the impact of declining productivity, galloping inflation, oil shortages, and high unemployment. It revived in the early 1980s but faltered in the last years of the decade, giving way to a deep recession that lasted from 1990 to 1992 and underscoring the need for renewed productivity, full employment, and a more equitable distribution of wealth.

The Changing Nature of Work

Automation and other technological advances had a powerful impact on the American workplace and brought about a shift in the occupational structure of the working class. Because of such advances, the *New York Times* reported in 1990 in an article on the industrial Midwest that "Some factories look as if they have been hit by a kind of economic neutron bomb, which left assembly lines running at full speed but eliminated most of the people who worked on them." Formerly profitable jobs disappeared. One pulp-mill worker voiced gloom about the future: "I think the country has a problem. The managers want everything run by computers. But if no one has a job, no one will know how to do anything anymore. Who will pay the taxes? What kind of society will it be when people have lost their knowledge and depend on computers for everything?"

In human terms, the introduction of the computer (see Chapter 26) had other consequences as well. Now workers sat for hours before their screens. Some described the feeling of "floating in space" as they worked, or of being "lost behind the screen." Others worried about radiation from the monitor or muscular fatigue from sitting at a keyboard all day. Still others complained that they could no longer touch their work. As more Americans began to use computers, people who did not work with them complained about a growing "digital divide" that further increased the gap between rich and poor. Members of the middle and upper classes had easy access to computer technology, while less fortunate individuals, many of whom belonged to minority groups, found themselves left behind.

Yet even as the nature of work changed, people seemed to be working more. In past decades, leisure time had seemed to expand, and there was talk of a four-day workweek in the 1950s. In subsequent years, however, the amount of time Americans worked steadily rose so that in the mid-1990s, American employees worked many more hours each year than their counterparts in Germany or France.

In the process, they experienced more stress, as they attempted to juggle the pressures between employment and family life. Problems were particularly severe for women, still trying to cope with the pressures of a double load, as they maintained responsibility for the home even when working outside. Marriages came under significant strain. One 26-year-old legal secretary in California spoke for many as she summed up her frustration. Her husband, she noted, "does no cooking, no washing, no anything else. How do I feel? Furious. If our marriage ends, it will be on this issue."

The Internet and the World Wide Web

The Internet has become an integral part of our daily lives. More and more people use e-mail to communicate quickly with friends and colleagues around the world. Many Americans use the World Wide Web to make purchases ranging from books to automobiles. Others buy stocks online and rely on the Web to manage their portfolios. Historians and other scholars have come to depend on huge databases on the Web that are accessible from computers anywhere around the world.

The Internet has become an important tool for historical research. Historians can acquire census data on the Web. They can find essential statistical files, from both government offices and the private sector. They can examine huge collections of historical images. They can read the text of vital speeches. They can look at moving picture clips from the Spanish American War and listen to songs of the 1960s. But they need to be cautious in what they do. While the Internet provides access to a huge amount of material, the historian must evaluate it as if it was a more traditional source. But with that caution, it can be an extraordinarily useful tool.

While the Internet has only recently become an important source of historical information, it is not new. Its roots extend back 30 years, to the mid-1960s, when Americans were worried about the nuclear arms race with the Soviet Union at the height of the Cold War. After the Russians launched their *Sputnik* satellite in 1957 with a rocket that demonstrated the ability to send atomic weapons from one continent to another, American scientists dedicated themselves to catching up with and then surpassing the Soviets in space. To do so, they needed to develop their computer technology.

Scientists were also interested in figuring out how to maintain communication in the aftermath of a nuclear attack. As both the United States and the Soviet Union developed bigger and better atomic bombs and then in the 1950s began to create even more potent hydrogen weapons, it became clear that a full-scale nuclear war could wipe out a nation's ability to communicate with its distant military bases. The Department of Defense wanted to create a decentralized communication system that could continue to function even if part of it was wiped out.

In the early 1960s, scientists at the Massachusetts Institute of Technology developed the concept of timesharing, whereby different users at widely separated sites could use the same central computer at the same time. Another step forward came in the mid-1960s with the development of "packet-switching" technology, which broke down data into small, discrete packets that could be transmitted over telephone lines, using modems to connect the computers to the phone lines, and then reassembled when received by another computer at the other end.

Building on those steps, the Department of Defense established the Advanced Research Projects Agency Network, known as the ARPANET, in 1969. It linked together the computers of four institutions—the University of California campuses at Los Angeles and Santa Barbara, the Stanford Research Institute, and the University of Utah. Two years later, the system had expanded to include 23 universities and research centers around the country.

The system was hardly user-friendly in these early days. In an age before the advent of personal computers at home, or even office computers at work, only computer professionals, engineers, and other scientists mastered the intricacies of what were very complex systems. Once they did, however, they were able to communicate with one another through what became known as electronic mail, or e-mail.

The term *Internet* was first used to describe this decentralized network in 1982, and in 1986 the

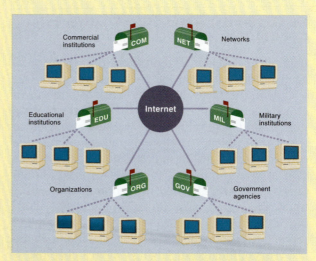

Internet and World Wide Web addresses are organized into domains, each indicated by a different three-letter suffix. Colleges and universities, for example, all use the "edu" designation.

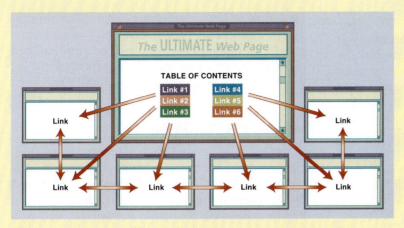

The World Wide Web links numerous Web pages together. By clicking the computer mouse on a highlighted item, a user can move easily from one linked page to another.

National Science Foundation created a network called the NSFNET with a better organized backbone for the entire system. In this new infrastructure, there were different domains, each marked by a different suffix at the end of an e-mail address, such as "edu" for educational establishments, "com" for commercial enterprises, and "gov" for government offices.

But even with improvements, the Internet remained hard to use. While computer experts could find all kinds of information, others found it difficult to access what they wanted. Then, in 1991, the University of Minnesota developed a system for finding information by accessing a huge number of databases, and they named it after the university mascot—the golden gopher.

At about the same time, another development made an even greater impact on Internet use. In 1989, Tim Berners-Lee and others at the European Laboratory for Particle Physics (known as CERN) in Geneva, Switzerland, developed a new system for information distribution. It was based on the concept of hypertext, which involved embedding links to other documents or pieces of information in the text of a document itself. While reading an article or essay on the computer, you could simply move to another document by selecting the appropriate link. This system became the basis for what came to be called the World Wide Web in 1991; over the next few years, it supplanted the gophers as the easiest way to maneuver the masses of information in cyberspace. In 1993, Mark Andreessen and others at the National Center for Superconducting Applications at the University of Illinois at Champaign-Urbana went a step further when they developed what they called Mosaic, which was a graphical Web browser. It was an easy-to-use piece of computer software that allowed you to click your mouse on graphics or icons as well as text in a document to move to another document or Web site. Andreessen and others then formed the Netscape Navigation Corporation, a private company, which marketed the Netscape Navigator to browse the Web. Microsoft's Internet Explorer provides another browser.

Reflecting on the Past Today, the World Wide Web is more accessible than ever before. But as more and more adults and children use the Web, legal issues remain to be resolved. What kinds of censorship are acceptable on the Web? How can writers, artists, and musicians maintain copyright protection for their work when the materials they produce are frequently instantly accessible on the Web? How can technology improve access to the Web, as telephone lines become choked with Internet traffic? How can we protect systems from "hackers" who use their ingenuity to break into commercial or government computer systems and disrupt the flow of information?

What kind of historical research might you do on the Web? How can you assess the veracity of the material you find on the Internet? What cautions are essential if you are to make the best use of Web sources?

Each chapter in this book contains a section at the end entitled "Discovering U.S. History Online." Take a look at the section in this chapter and try the various links. Which ones provide you with the most useful material? Look at the site on "The Gulf War." How could you use information here in pursuing a project on the struggle? What materials would be helpful that are not found here? What other sites can you find that provide additional material on this subject?

The Shift to a Service Economy

The scarcity of good jobs stemmed in part from the restructuring of the economy that occurred in the 1980s. In a trend that had been underway for more than half a century, the United States continued its shift from an industrial base, where most workers actually produced things, to a service base, where most provided expertise or service to others in the workforce. By the mid-1980s, three-fourths of the 113 million employees in the country worked in the service sector as fast-food workers, clerks, computer programmers, doctors, lawyers, bankers, teachers, and bureaucrats.

That shift, in turn, had its roots in the decline of the country's industrial sector. The United States had been the world's industrial leader since the late nineteenth century. By the 1970s, however, the nation began to lose that predominant position. After 1973, productivity slowed in virtually all American industries, and it remained lower than it had been in the past in the 1980s and early 1990s.

The causes of this decline in productivity were complex. The most important factor was a widespread and systematic failure on the part of the United States to invest sufficiently in its basic productive capacity. During the Reagan years, capital investment in real plants and equipment within the United States gave way to speculation, mergers, and spending abroad. Gross private domestic investment in national industries rose modestly during the boom years, though many companies became caught up in an acquisition mania that consumed even more resources. At the end of the 1980s, domestic investment was down—5.7 percent in 1990 and 9.5 percent in 1991. The energy crisis and rising oil prices (see Chapter 29) also contributed to the industrial decline. Finally, the war in Vietnam diverted federal funds from research and development with consequences that continued even after the conflict ended.

While American industry became less productive, other industrial nations moved forward. German and Japanese industries, rebuilt after World War II with U.S. aid and aggressively modernized thereafter, reached new heights of efficiency. As a result, the United States began to lose its share of the world market for industrial goods. In 1946, the country had provided 60 percent of the world's iron and steel. In 1978, it provided a mere 16 percent. So efficient and cost-effective were foreign steel producers that the United States found itself importing one-fifth of its iron and steel. By 1980, Japanese car manufacturers had also captured nearly one-quarter of the American automobile market, and they continued to hold a substantial share. The auto industry, which had been a mainstay of economic growth for much of the twentieth century, suffered plant shutdowns and massive layoffs. In 1991, its worst year ever, Ford lost a staggering $2.3 billion.

Workers in Transition

In the 1980s and early 1990s, American labor struggled to hold on to the gains realized by the post–World War II generation of blue-collar workers. The largest problems involved adjusting to the nation's changing economic needs. The shift to a service economy, while providing new jobs, was difficult for many American workers. Millions of men and women who lost positions as a result of mergers, plant closings, and permanent economic contractions now found themselves in low-paying jobs with few opportunities for advancement. Entry-level posts were seldom located in the central cities, where most of the poor lived. Even when new jobs were created in the cities, minority residents often lacked the skills to acquire or hold them.

Meanwhile, the trade union movement faltered as the economy moved from an industrial to a service base. Unions had been most successful in organizing the nation's industrial workers in the years since the 1930s, and the United States emerged from World War II with unions strong. In the years that followed, the percentage of workers belonging to unions dropped, from just over 25 percent in 1980 to barely over 16 percent a decade later. As the total number of wage and salary workers rose substantially between 1983 and 1993, the overall number of union members dropped from 17.7 to 16.6 million.

The pattern was visible in the example of U.S. Steel. It had once relied on a unionized workforce of 200,000 employees. In the early 1980s, it reconstituted itself as USX Corporation and shut many of its steel mills, while branching out into the more profitable oil business. The union—the United Steelworkers of America—lost half of its members in the process.

Union membership declined for a number of reasons. The shift from blue-collar to white-collar work contributed to the contraction. The increase in the workforce in the numbers of women and young people (groups that have historically been difficult to organize) was another factor, as was the more forceful opposition to unions by managers applying the provisions of the Taft-Hartley Act of 1947, which restricted the tactics labor leaders could use. At the same time, union organizing efforts fell off significantly.

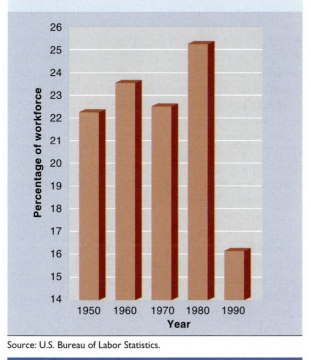

Union Membership, 1950–1990

The percentage of workers belonging to unions dropped dramatically after 1980 and continued to fall in the 1990s.

Source: U.S. Bureau of Labor Statistics.

Union vulnerability was visible early in Reagan's first term, when the Professional Air Traffic Controllers Organization (PATCO) went on strike. Charging that the strike violated the law, the president—who had once been a union leader himself—fired the strikers, decertified the union, and ordered the training of new controllers at a cost of $1.3 billion. The message was clear: government employees could not challenge the public interest.

Anti-union sentiments reverberated throughout the nongovernment sector as well, as a 1983 strike by Arizona miners demonstrated. Confronted by falling prices and company losses, the management of Phelps Dodge, one of the world's largest copper producers, decided to end the cost-of-living allowance that enabled workers, many of them Mexican Americans, to earn $12 an hour. When negotiations failed, workers struck, only to find that the company, working with anti-union experts at the University of Pennsylvania's Wharton School of Business, had hired permanent replacement workers. As the company president later acknowledged, "I had decided to break the union."

Strikers who kept their jobs found that their unions could not get favorable contracts. For exam-

ple, in 1984 the United Auto Workers (UAW) ended a strike at General Motors by trading a pledge that GM would guarantee up to 70 percent of the production workers' lifetime jobs for a smaller wage increase than the union sought and a modification of the cost-of-living allowance that had been a part of UAW contracts since 1948.

Farmers also had to adjust as the larger workforce was reconstituted. Continuing a trend that began in the early twentieth century, the number of farms and farmers declined steadily. When Franklin Roosevelt took office in 1933, some 6.7 million farms covered the American landscape. Fifty years later, there were only 2.4 million. In 1980, farm residents made up 2.7 percent of the total population; by 1989, that figure had fallen to 1.9 percent. As family farms disappeared, farming income became more concentrated in the hands of the largest operators. In 1983, the top 1 percent of the nation's farmers produced 30 percent of all farm products, while the top 12 percent generated 90 percent of all farm income. The top 1 percent of the growers in the United States had average annual incomes of $572,000, but the small and medium-sized farmers who were being forced off the land frequently had incomes below the official government poverty line.

The extraordinary productivity of the most successful American farmers derived in part from the use of chemical fertilizers, irrigation, pesticides, and scientific management. Government price-support programs helped, too. Yet that very productivity caused unexpected setbacks. In the 1970s, food shortages abroad made the United States the "breadbasket of the world." Farmers increased their output to meet multibillion-bushel grain export orders and profited handsomely from high prices in India, China, Russia, and other countries. To increase production, farmers often borrowed heavily at high interest rates. When a worldwide economic slump began in 1980, overseas demand for American farm products declined sharply and farm prices dropped.

Thousands of farmers, caught in the cycle of overproduction, heavy indebtedness, and falling prices, watched helplessly as banks and federal agencies foreclosed on their mortgages and drove

Work Stoppages, 1960–1990

Year	Number of Stoppages
1960	222
1970	381
1980	187
1990	44

Farm Indebtedness, 1950–1992

Farm indebtedness was a continuing problem in the postwar years. Even modest improvement in the mid-1980s and early 1990s did not change the overall picture.

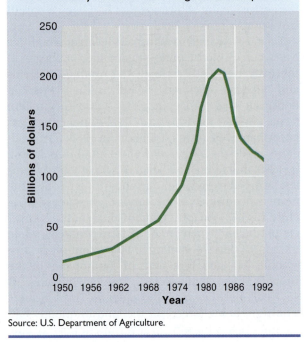

Source: U.S. Department of Agriculture.

them out of business. Dale Christensen, an Iowa corn grower, faced foreclosure in 1983 when the Farmers Home Administration called in his overdue payments on debts totaling $300,000. "I am 58 years old," he said. "My whole life has gone into this farm." He was one of many struggling farmers, who, in spite of government crop-support programs that cost more in 1982 than all welfare programs for the poor, could not make ends meet.

The Roller-Coaster Economy

The economy shifted back and forth during the 1980s and early 1990s. The Reagan years began with a recession that lasted for several years. An economic boom between 1983 and 1990 gave way to a punishing recession as the new decade began. It appeared that the United States had embarked on another boom-and-bust cycle as unsettling as that which had prevailed in the early years of the twentieth century.

The recession of 1980 to 1982 began during the Carter administration, when the Federal Reserve Board tried to deal with mounting deficits by increasing the money supply. Program cuts to counter inflation brought substantial unemployment in the workforce. During Reagan's first year, the job situation deteriorated further, and by the end of 1982,

the unemployment rate had climbed to 10.8 percent (and over 20 percent among African Americans). Nearly one-third of the nation's industrial capacity lay idle, and 12 million Americans were out of work.

Inflation, accompanied by heavy unemployment, continued to be a problem. The inflation rate, which reached 12.4 percent a year under Carter in 1980, fell after Reagan assumed office, to 8.9 percent in his first year and to about 5 percent during the remainder of his first term. But even the lower rate eroded the purchasing power of people already in difficulty.

The recession of 1980 to 1982 afflicted every region of the country. Business failures proliferated in every city and state, as large and small businesses closed their doors and fired employees. In 1982, business bankruptcies rose 50 percent from the previous year. In one week in June 1982, a total of 548 businesses failed, close to the 1932 weekly record of 612.

Detroit was one of the hardest-hit areas in the United States. An industrial city revolving around automobile manufacturing, it suffered both from Japanese competition and from the high interest rates that made car sales plummet. The Detroit unemployment rate rose to more than 19 percent and affected the entire city.

Even the Sun Belt—the vast southern region stretching from coast to coast—showed the effects of the recession. It had enjoyed economic growth fostered by the availability of cheap, nonunion labor, tax advantages that state governments offered corporations willing to locate plants there, and a favorable climate. Now it, too, began to suffer economic problems, and large areas began to stagnate. Overexpansion in the oil industry led to a collapse in prices that disrupted the economy in Texas, Oklahoma, Louisiana, and other oil-producing regions. Worldwide gluts of some minerals, copper for example, added to unemployment elsewhere in the Southwest.

Economic conditions improved in late 1983 and early 1984, particularly for Americans in the middle- and upper-income ranges. The federal tax cut Reagan pushed through encouraged consumer spending, and huge defense expenditures had a stimulating effect. The Republican effort to reduce restrictions and cut waste sparked business confidence. A voluntary Japanese quota on car exports assisted the ailing automobile industry. The stock market climbed as it reflected the optimistic buying spree. Inflation remained low, about 3 to 4 percent annually from 1982 to 1988. Interest rates likewise fell from 16.5 percent to 10.5 percent in the same period and remained thereafter under 11 percent. The unemployment rate at the end of the 1980s fell to below 6 percent nationally (though many of the new jobs that were created paid less than $13,000 per year). Between the start of the recovery and 1988, real GNP grew at an annual rate of 4.2 percent.

But the economic upswing masked a number of problems. Millions of Americans remained poor. Many families continued to earn a middle-class income, but only by having two full-time income earners. They also went deeply into debt. To buy homes, young people accepted vastly higher mortgage interest rates than their parents had. Stiff credit card debts, often at 20 percent interest, were common. Under such circumstances, some young families struggled to remain in the middle class. Blue-collar workers had to accept lower standards of living. Single mothers were hit hardest of all.

The huge and growing budget deficits reflected the fundamental economic instability. Those deficits provoked doubts that resulted in the stock market crash of 1987. Six weeks of falling prices culminated with a 22.6 percent drop on Monday, October 19, almost double the plunge of "Black Tuesday," October 29, 1929. The deficits, negative trade balances, and exposures of Wall Street fraud all combined to puncture the bubble. The stock market revived, but the crash foreshadowed further problems.

Those problems surfaced in the early 1990s, as the country experienced another recession. A combination of massive military spending, growth of entitlement programs, and tax cuts sent budget deficits skyward. As bond traders in the 1980s speculated recklessly and pocketed huge profits, the basic productive structure of the country continued to decline. The huge increase in the national debt eroded business confidence, and this time the effects were felt not simply in the stock market but in the economy as a whole.

American firms suffered a serious decline as corporate profits fell from $327 billion in 1989 to $315.5 billion in 1991. To cope with declining profits and decreased consumer demand, companies scaled back dramatically. In late 1991, General Motors announced that it would close 21 plants, lay off 9,000 white-collar employees the next year, and eliminate more than 70,000 jobs in the next several years. Hundreds of other companies did the same thing, trimming corporate fat but also cutting thousands of jobs.

The unemployment rate rose once again. In mid-1991, it reached 7 percent, the highest level in nearly five years. About 8.7 million Americans were without jobs, up 2 million since the recession began.

Around the nation, state governments found it impossible to balance their budgets without resorting to massive spending cuts. Reagan's efforts to move programs from the federal to the state level worked as long as funding lasted, but as national support dropped and state tax revenues declined, states found themselves in a budgetary gridlock. Most had constitutional prohibitions against running deficits, and so they had to slash spending for social services and education, even after yearly budgets had been approved.

After a number of false starts, the economy began to recover in mid-1992. The unemployment rate dropped, the productivity index rose, and a concerted effort began to bring the federal deficit down.

Population Shifts

As the American people dealt with the swings of the economy, demographic patterns changed significantly. The nation's population increased from 228 million to approximately 250 million between 1980 and 1990—a rise of 9.6 percent (as opposed to 11.5 percent in the 1970s) that was one of the lowest rates of growth in American history. At the same time, the complexion of the country changed. In 1992, the country's nonwhite population—African Americans, Latinos, Asians, and Native Americans—stood at an all-time high of 25 percent, the result of increased immigration and of minority birthrates significantly above the white birthrate.

The population shifted geographically as well. American cities increasingly filled with members of the nation's minorities. White families continued to leave for the steadily growing suburbs, which by 1990 contained almost half the population, more than ever before. In 15 of the nation's 28 largest cities—New York, Chicago, and Houston among them—minorities made up at least half the population. Minority representation varied by urban region. In Detroit, Washington, New Orleans, and Chicago, African Americans were the largest minority; in Phoenix, El Paso, San Antonio, and Los Angeles, Latinos held that position; in San Francisco, Asians outnumbered other groups.

The cities also grew steadily poorer. In Houston, for example, although increasing numbers of African Americans, Latinos, and Asians lived in the suburbs, most of the poorest minority families were concentrated in the city itself. As had been the case since World War II, commuters from the suburbs took the better-paying jobs, while people living in the cities held lower-paying positions. Mario Perez, a 27-year-old Latino immigrant, noted in 1991 that the increase in the number of Spanish-speaking immigrants in the nine years since he arrived in Houston made it easier to find a job but harder to secure well-paying work. Perez himself worked

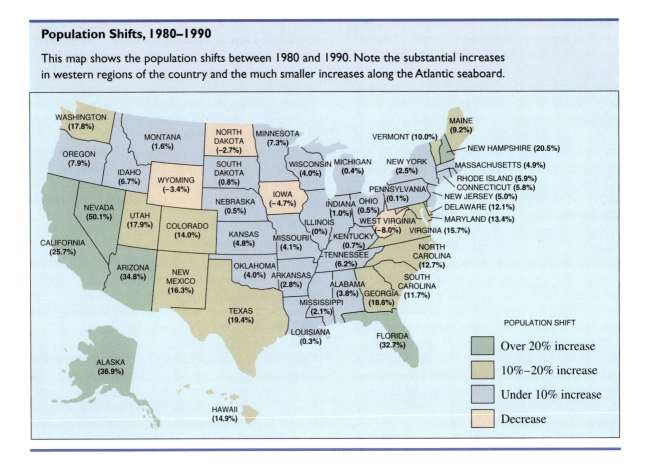

Population Shifts, 1980–1990

This map shows the population shifts between 1980 and 1990. Note the substantial increases in western regions of the country and the much smaller increases along the Atlantic seaboard.

seven days a week sweeping streets downtown and tending plants for $5.50 an hour.

At the same time, the population was moving west. In 1900, the Mountain and Pacific states contained about 5 percent of the nation's population. By 1990, that figure stood at 21 percent. The population of the nation as a whole rose by less than 10 percent in the 1980s, but the population of the West increased by 22 percent.

That population was becoming much more urbanized. In the 50 years following 1940, the six largest metropolitan areas in the West grew by 380 percent; the six largest in the East expanded by only 64 percent. By 1990, 80 percent of all westerners lived in metropolitan areas, compared to 76 percent of the people in the rest of the United States. As writer Wallace Stegner observed, the West "*is* urban; it's an oasis civilization."

With its urban development, the West became a pacesetter for the rest of the country. If the New England village was a symbol of the eighteenth century and the midwestern town was a similar symbol of the nineteenth century, then the western metropolis had special symbolic importance in the late twentieth century. Western cities were unbounded, open-ended, and sprawling in all directions. They seemed capable of expanding indefinitely. Horizontal, low-slung homes made western neighborhoods look very different from those in the Northeast. Tourism became a dynamic industry, with the West in the forefront. The motel, a western invention, made automobile travel easier. Western cities were among the most popular tourist destinations, drawing visitors from all over the world.

California was the nation's fastest-growing state, its population increasing in the 1980s by nearly 26 percent. Responding to a question about California's impact on the rest of the country, Wallace Stegner replied, "We *are* the national culture, at its most energetic end." Los Angeles became the most dynamic example of American vitality and creativity. The motion-picture industry exerted a worldwide impact. The city became a capital of consumption and served as a symbol of a dynamic national life.

FOREIGN POLICY AND THE END OF THE COLD WAR

In the early 1990s, the United States emerged triumphant in the Cold War that had dominated international politics since the end of World War II. In one of the most momentous turns in modern world

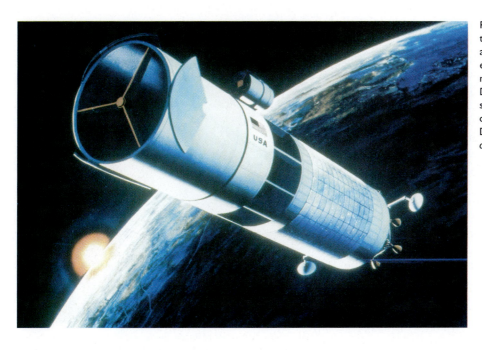

Reagan's Star Wars proposal drew tremendous criticism. Opponents argued that the program would be excessively expensive and would never work. This Department of Defense picture sought to demonstrate the potential of the program, officially known as the Strategic Defense Initiative. *(U.S. Department of Defense)*

history, communism collapsed in Eastern Europe and in the Soviet Union, and the various republics in the Soviet orbit moved toward capitalism and democracy. Other regions—the Middle East and Africa—experienced equally breathtaking change.

Reagan, Bush, and the Soviet Union

The Cold War was very much alive when Ronald Reagan assumed power in 1981. The new president asserted U.S. interests far more aggressively than had Jimmy Carter. Like most of his compatriots, Reagan believed in large defense budgets and a militant approach toward the Soviet Union. He wanted to cripple the USSR economically by forcing it to spend more than it could afford on defense.

Viewing the Soviet Union as an "evil empire" in his first term, Reagan promoted a larger atomic arsenal by arguing that a nuclear war could be fought and won. The administration dropped efforts to obtain Senate ratification of SALT II, the arms reduction plan negotiated under Carter, although it observed the pact's restrictions. Then Reagan proposed the enormously expensive and bitterly criticized Strategic Defense Initiative, popularly known as "Star Wars" after a 1977 movie, to intercept Soviet missiles in outer space.

In his second term, Reagan softened his belligerence. Mikhail Gorbachev, the new Soviet leader, watching his own economy collapse under the pressure of the superheated arms race, realized the need for greater accommodation with the West. He understood that the only way the Soviet Union could

survive was through arms negotiations with the United States that would help reduce his overextended budget. He therefore proposed a policy of *perestroika* (restructuring the economy) and

Mikhail Gorbachev was the Soviet leader who initiated the process that helped ease tensions with the United States and ultimately ended the Cold War. Gorbachev's policies provided for major readjustments in Soviet society, but those eventually tore the Soviet Union apart. *(AP/Wide World Photos)*

glasnost (political openness to encourage personal initiative). His overtures opened the way to better relations with the United States.

Concerned with his own place in history, Reagan met with Gorbachev, and the two developed a close working relationship. Summit meetings led to an Intermediate-Range Nuclear Forces Treaty in 1987 that provided for the withdrawal and destruction of 2,500 Soviet and American nuclear missiles in Europe.

George Bush maintained Reagan's comfortable relationship with Gorbachev. At several summit meetings in 1989 and 1990, the two leaders signed agreements reducing the number of long-range nuclear weapons, ending the manufacture of chemical weapons, and easing trade restrictions. The Strategic Arms Reduction Treaty (START) signed in 1991 dramatically cut stockpiles of long-range weapons.

The End of the Cold War

The Cold War ended with astonishing speed. Gorbachev's efforts to restructure Soviet society and to work with the United States brought him acclaim around the world but led to trouble at home. In mid-1991, he faced an old-guard Communist coup, led by those who opposed *glasnost* and *perestroika* and wanted to slow the process of change. He survived this right-wing challenge, but he could not resist those who wanted to go even further to establish democracy and capitalism. The forces he had unleashed finally destroyed the Soviet system and tore the USSR apart.

Boris Yeltsin, president of Russia, the strongest and largest of the Soviet republics, emerged as the dominant leader, but even he could not contain the forces of disintegration. Movements in the tiny Baltic republics of Latvia, Lithuania, and Estonia, culminating with independence in 1991, began the dismantling of the Soviet Union, and other Soviet republics likewise went their own way. The once-powerful superpower was now a collection of separate states. Although the republics coalesced loosely in a Commonwealth of Independent States, led by Russia, they retained their autonomy—and independent leadership—in domestic and foreign affairs.

Meanwhile, Communist regimes throughout Europe collapsed. In a series of remarkable developments that occurred at the same time and intertwined with the turbulence in the Soviet Union, many of the Communist satellites broke loose, rejected communism, and proclaimed a new commitment to democracy.

Boris Yeltsin, president of Russia, the largest of the republics in what had been the Soviet Union, became the most influential leader after Gorbachev's fall. But Yeltsin's efforts at economic reform met with serious opposition and led to his resignation as the century came to an end. *(Corbis-Bettmann)*

The most dramatic chapter in this story unfolded in Germany in November 1989. Responding to Gorbachev's softening stance toward the West, East Germany's Communist party boss announced unexpectedly that citizens of his country would be free to leave East Germany. Within hours, thousands of people gathered on both sides of the 28-mile Berlin Wall—the symbol of the Cold War that divided Berlin into East and West sectors. As the border guards stepped aside, East Germans flooded into West Berlin amidst dancing, shouting, and fireworks. All through the night, noisy celebrators reveled in what one observer called the "greatest street party in the history of the world."

Within days, sledgehammer-wielding Germans pulverized the Berlin Wall, and soon the Communist government itself came tumbling down. By October 1990, less than a year after the free movement of East Germans across their borders began, the two Germanys were reunited.

The fall of the Berlin Wall reverberated all over Eastern Europe. Everywhere it brought in its wake the pell-mell overthrow of Communist regimes. In Poland, the 10-year-old Solidarity movement led by Lech Walesa triumphed in its long struggle against Soviet domination and found itself in power in December 1990, with Walesa as president. Governing, however, sometimes proved more difficult than leading the revolt. The nation faced enor-

The Fall of Communism

In the late 1980s and early 1990s, the Soviet Union fragmented and lost control of its satellites in Eastern Europe. As many countries shown here declared their independence, Czechoslovakia broke into two nations, while Yugoslavia ruptured into a group of feuding states. **Reflecting on the Past** How widespread was the turbulence that led to the fall of communism? How quickly did the process take place? How did events in one country influence events in another country?

mous economic problems, and Americans had to decide just how much help they could afford to give.

In Czechoslovakia, two decades after Soviet tanks had rolled into the streets of Prague to suppress a policy of liberalization, the forces of freedom were

victorious. A month after the Berlin Wall dismantlement, playwright Vaclav Havel was elected president of Czechoslovakia. Like Walesa, he sought and received aid from the United States. But not even economic assistance could keep the nation intact,

The destruction of the Berlin Wall in November 1989 was a symbolic blow to the entire Cold War structure that had solidified in Europe in the postwar years. People grabbed hammers and joined together in tearing down the hated wall. Joyous celebrations marked the reunification of a city that had been divided for decades. *(Alexandria Avakian/Woodfin Camp & Associates)*

As communism fell, authorities in Eastern Europe removed statues of Lenin, one of the dominant figures in creating the Soviet state after the Russian Revolution. Here, a statue in Bucharest, Romania, is readied for removal with a metal cable that looks like a hangman's noose. *(Alfred/Sipa Press)*

as turbulence led to the creation of separate and independent Czech and Slovak republics. The same forces that culminated in the independence of Czechoslovakia brought new regimes in Bulgaria, Hungary, Romania, and Albania.

Yugoslavia, held together by a Communist dictatorship since 1945, proved to be the extreme case of ethnic hostility resurging amid collapsing central authority. In 1991, Yugoslavia splintered into its ethnic components. In Bosnia, the decision of the Muslim and Croatian majority to secede from Serbian-dominated Yugoslavia led Bosnian Serbs, backed by the Serbian republic, to embark upon a brutal siege of the city of Sarajevo and an even more ruthless "ethnic cleansing" campaign to liquidate opponents. The United States remained out of the conflict, unsure about what to do.

Early in 1992, Bush and Yeltsin proclaimed a new era of "friendship and partnership" and formally declared an end to the Cold War. After half a century of confrontation, the United States had won. Yeltsin abandoned the quest for nuclear parity—maintaining an arsenal equal to that of the United States—and agreed to cut back Russian conventional forces. The United States then extended aid to the former Soviet republics, which needed help in reorganizing their economies as free enterprise systems.

American Involvement Overseas

As the United States struggled to keep abreast of the momentous changes in Eastern Europe, it was equally involved with events in the rest of the world. Here again the nation sought to preserve stability as the Cold War drew to an end.

In Latin America, the United States intervened frequently as it had in the past, hoping to impose stability on the volatile region. Viewing Central America as a Cold War battlefield early in his presidency, Reagan openly opposed left-wing guerrillas in El Salvador who fought to overthrow a repressive right-wing regime. He was fearful that still another nation might follow the Marxist examples of Cuba and Nicaragua. The United States increased its assistance to the antirevolutionary Salvadoran government, heedless of a similar course followed years before in Vietnam. Efforts to destroy the radical forces failed, despite the expenditure of about $1 million a day. Then in 1989, a far-right faction won the Salvadoran elections and polarized the country. As fighting continued, U.S. officials despaired of finding a solution.

Nicaragua became an even bloodier battleground in the effort to promote stability. In 1979, revolutionaries calling themselves Sandinistas (after César Sandino, who fought in the 1920s against U.S. occupation troops) overthrew the repressive Somoza family, which had ruled for three decades. President Carter initially extended aid to the

Sandinistas and recognized the new regime, then cut off support to show his disapproval of their curbs on civil liberties and their alleged efforts to assist rebels in El Salvador. The Republicans adopted a far stronger position. Their 1980 platform pledged to replace the Sandinistas with a "free and independent" government. Once in office, Reagan circumvented congressional opposition to his efforts to defeat the revolutionary reformers and signed a National Security directive in November 1981 authorizing the CIA to arm and train counterrevolutionaries known as *contras*.

The *contras* began to attack from bases outside the country, and Nicaragua became enmeshed in a bitter civil war. When the war went badly for the *contras*, the CIA assumed the military initiative and mined Nicaraguan harbors, violating international law. Upon discovering these secret missions, Congress cut off military aid to the *contras*. Peaceful elections in early 1990 finally drove the Sandinistas out and brought the fighting to an end. Though the economy remained in desperate straits, the new regime seemed to offer the best hope of healing the wounds of the bloody conflict.

Reagan found it easier to maintain stability on the tiny Caribbean island of Grenada. The president

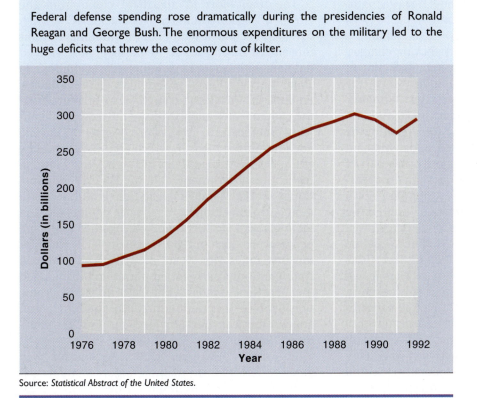

Federal Defense Spending, 1976–1992

Federal defense spending rose dramatically during the presidencies of Ronald Reagan and George Bush. The enormous expenditures on the military led to the huge deficits that threw the economy out of kilter.

Source: *Statistical Abstract of the United States.*

ordered marines there in October 1983, after a coup installed a government sympathetic to Fidel Castro's Cuba. Concerned about the construction of a large airfield, 2,000 marines invaded the island, rescued a number of American medical students, and claimed triumph. Though the United Nations condemned it, Americans cheered what the administration called its "rescue mission."

Middle Eastern and Central American concerns became entangled in the Iran-*contra* affair. In 1987, Congress learned that the National Security Council had launched an effort to free American hostages in the Middle East by selling arms to Iran and then using the funds to aid the *contras*, in direct violation of both the law and congressional will. The trial of Oliver North, the National Security Council official responsible for the policy, focused on his distortions and falsifications before congressional committees and on his destruction of official documents that could have substantiated charges of wrongdoing by top officials. Convicted in 1989, North received a light sentence requiring no time in prison from a judge who recognized that North was not acting entirely on his own.

Bush, too, was involved in a variety of episodes abroad. Despite memories of past imperialism, the United States invaded Panama in 1989; the reasons it gave were to protect the Canal, defend American citizens, and stop drug traffic. The campaign resulted in the capture of military leader Manuel Noriega, notorious for his involvement in the drug trade. Noriega was brought to the United States, tried, and after a lengthy trial, convicted of drug-trafficking charges.

The United States likewise found itself drawn into turbulent African affairs. In South Africa, the United States supported the long and ultimately successful struggle against apartheid. This policy, whereby the white minority (only 15 percent of the population) segregated, suppressed, and denied basic human rights to the black majority, was part of South African law. A resistance movement, spearheaded by the African National Congress (ANC) sought to end apartheid. Nelson Mandela and other ANC leaders refused to give up, despite fierce resistance to their efforts to achieve freedom. While the United States had long expressed its dislike of this ruthless system of segregation, in past years it had refused to go further in taking steps to weaken it. Large investments, naval ports, and a reluctance to oppose allies who still controlled African territory tempered U.S. resistance. Then the ferment within the United States, sparked by the civil rights movement and opposition to dictatorships in Central America, generated domestic pressure for a

Nelson Mandela served as a source of inspiration to black South Africans, as the long struggle against apartheid finally brought that system of rigid segregation to an end and led to the setting up of a biracial democracy with Mandela himself as president. *(AP/Wide World Photos)*

stronger stand. In 1986, over Reagan's objections, Congress imposed sanctions, including a rule prohibiting new American investments. The economic pressure damaged the South African economy and persuaded more than half of the 300 American firms doing business there to leave.

The final blow to apartheid came from the efforts of Nelson Mandela. The black ANC activist, who had become a symbol of the militant resistant movement during his 27 years in prison, steered his nation through a stunning transformation. In 1990, during Bush's presidency, Prime Minister Frederik W. De Klerk succumbed to pressure from the United States and the rest of the world which finally embraced the ANC cause. He freed Mandela and announced plans by which apartheid would be gradually overturned. Talks in South Africa between the white government and the African National Congress that Mandela led laid the groundwork for a smooth transition to a biracial democracy and Mandela and De Klerk worked together to ensure peaceful elections in 1994, in which blacks voted for the first time. After years of struggle, the African National Congress assumed power and dismantled the apartheid system. Mandela himself became president of this nation that was building itself anew. American aid provided support in transitional times.

Elsewhere in Africa, U.S. policymakers had greater difficulty in maintaining post–Cold War stability. Somalia, an impoverished East African

The Gulf War

When Iraqi leader Saddam Hussein invaded Kuwait in the summer of 1990, the United States formed a coalition to drive Iraq out. Operation Desert Storm began in early 1991 and routed Iraqi forces, while leaving Kuwait's extensive oil fields in flames. **Reflecting on the Past** How many Middle Eastern countries were involved in the Gulf War? What role did oil play in the events that unfolded during the war? Why was Israel vulnerable during the conflict?

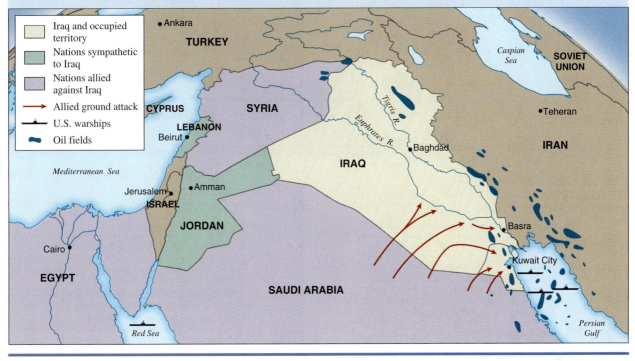

nation, suffered from a devastating famine, compounded by struggles between warlords that led to an almost total disintegration of order. In 1992, Bush sent U.S. troops to assist a United Nations effort to stop the starvation and stabilize the country, but those efforts proved unsuccessful in a struggle that continued into the twenty-first century.

A dramatic crisis occurred in the Middle East in 1990 when Saddam Hussein, the dictator of Iraq, invaded and annexed his oil-rich neighbor Kuwait. Hussein seemed intent on unifying Arab nations, threatening Israel, and dominating the Middle Eastern oil on which the West, including the United States, relied.

President Bush reacted vigorously. Working through the United Nations, as Harry Truman had done in Korea, the United States persuaded the Security Council to vote unanimously to condemn the attack and impose an embargo on Iraq. After Hussein refused to relinquish Kuwait, in mid-January 1991 a 28-nation coalition struck at Iraq

with an American-led multinational army of nearly half a million troops. In Operation Desert Storm, the coalition forces' sophisticated missiles, aircraft, and tanks swiftly overwhelmed the Iraqis. Americans were initially jubilant. Then the euphoria soured as Saddam used his remaining military power against minorities in Iraq. Bush's unwillingness to become bogged down in an Iraqi civil war and his eagerness to return U.S. troops home left the conflict unfinished. A year after his defeat, Hussein was as strongly entrenched as ever.

Meanwhile, the United States was involved in a larger, and ultimately more important, effort to bring peace to the Middle East. In the early 1990s, Secretary of State James Baker finally secured agreement from the major parties in the region to speak to one another face-to-face. A victory in the Israeli parliamentary elections in mid-1992 for Yitzhak Rabin, a soldier who recognized the need for peace and was ready to compromise, offered further hope for the talks.

A multinational coalition freed Kuwait after Iraqi leader Saddam Hussein—whose image appears on the signs at the anti-American demonstration in Baghdad—annexed the oil-rich land in 1990. The Persian Gulf War gave George Bush a quick victory, but the long-range results of U.S. involvement were questionable. *(Chris Morris/Black Star)*

Timeline

1980	Ronald Reagan elected president
1980–1982	Recession
1981	Reagan breaks air controllers' strike
	AIDS (acquired immune deficiency syndrome) discovered
1981–1983	Tax cuts; deficit spending increases
1983	Reagan proposes Strategic Defense Initiative ("Star Wars")
1984	Reagan reelected
1986	Tax reform measure passed
	Immigration Reform and Control Act
1987	Iran-*contra* affair becomes public
	Stock market crashes
	Intermediate Range Nuclear Forces Treaty signed

1988	George Bush elected president
1989	Federal bailout of savings and loan industry
	Fall of the Berlin Wall
1990	National debt reaches $3.1 trillion
	Sandinistas driven from power in Nicaragua
	Nelson Mandela freed in South Africa
	U.S. population reaches 250 million
1990–1992	Recession
1991	Persian Gulf War
	Failed coup in Soviet Union
	Disintegration of the Soviet Union
	Strategic Arms Reduction Treaty (START) signed
	Ethnic turbulence in fragmented former Yugoslavia

◆ *Conclusion*

CONSERVATISM IN CONTEXT

In the 1980s and early 1990s, the United States witnessed the resurgence of conservatism. The assault on the welfare state, dubbed the "Reagan Revolution," created a less regulated economy, whatever the implications for less fortunate Americans. The policies of Ronald Reagan and George Bush continued the trend begun by Richard Nixon in the 1970s. They reshaped the political agenda and reversed the liberal approach that had held sway since the New Deal of Franklin Roosevelt in the 1930s. In for-

eign affairs, Republican administrations likewise shifted course. Reagan first assumed a steel-ribbed posture toward the Soviet Union, then moved toward détente, and watched as his successor declared victory in the Cold War.

To be sure, there were limits to the transformation. Such fundamental programs as social security and Medicare remained securely in place, accepted by all but the most implacable splinter groups. Even the most conservative presidents of the past half century could not return to an imagined era of unbridled individualism and puny federal government. On the international front, despite the end of the Cold War, the nation's defense budget remained far higher than many Americans wished, and the nuclear arsenal continued to pose a threat to the human race.

Nor was the transformation beneficial to everyone. Periods of deep recession wrought havoc on the lives of blue-collar and white-collar workers alike. Working-class Americans were caught in the spiral of downward mobility that made them question the ability of the nation's economy to reward hard work. Liberals and conservatives both worried about the mounting national debt and the capacity of the economy to compete with Japan, South Korea, Germany, and other countries. Countless Americans fretted about the growing gaps between rich and poor. They fought with one another over what rules should govern a woman's right to an abortion. For the first time in American history, many children could not hope to do better than their parents had done. Reluctantly they tried to prepare themselves to accept a scaled-down version of the American dream.

✦ Recommended Reading

The Conservative Transformation

Samuel G. Freedman, *The Inheritance: How Three Families and America Moved From Roosevelt to Reagan and Beyond* (1996); U.S. Bureau of the Census, *U.S. Census of Population*, 1990; Vincent Virga, *The Eighties: Images of America* (1992).

David Chidester, *Patterns of Power: Religion and Politics in American Culture* (1988); Erling Jorstad, *Holding Fast/Pressing On: Religion in America in the 1980s* (1990); R. Laurence Moore, *Selling God: American Religion in the Marketplace of Culture* (1994); Garry Wills, *Under God: Religion and American Politics* (1990).

Paul Boyer, ed., *Reagan as President: Contemporary Views of the Man, His Politics, and His Policies* (1990); Lou Cannon, *President Reagan: The Role of a Lifetime* (1991); Ronnie Dugger, *On Reagan: The Man and His Presidency* (1983); Fred I. Greenstein, ed., *The Reagan Presidency: An Early Assessment* (1983); Godfrey Hodgson, *The World Turned Right Side Up: A History of the Conservative Ascendency in America* (1997); Haynes Johnson, *Sleepwalking Through History: America Through the Reagan Years* (1991); Lisa McGirr, *Suburban Warriors: The Origins of the New American Right* (2001); Edmund Morris, *Dutch: A Memoir of Ronald Reagan* (1999); William E. Pemberton, *Exit with Honor: The Life and Presidency of Ronald Reagan* (1998); Michael Schaller and George Rising, *The Republican Ascendancy: American Politics, 1968–2001* (2002); Garry Wills, *Reagan's America: Innocents at Home* (1985).

Colin Campbell, S.J. and Bert A. Rockman, eds., *The Bush Presidency: First Appraisals* (1991); Herbert S. Parmet, *George Bush: The Life of a Lone Star Yankee* (1997).

An End to Social Reform

Rodolfo Acuña, *Occupied America: A History of Chicanos*, 4th ed. (2000); Stephen Cornell, *The Return of the Native: American Indian Political Resurgence* (1988); Roger Daniels, *Coming to America: A History of Immigration and Ethnicity in American Life*, revised edition (2002); Susan Faludi, *Backlash: The Undeclared War Against American Women* (1991); John Hope Franklin and Alfred A. Moss, Jr., *From Slavery to Freedom: A History of African Americans*, 8th ed. (2000); David G. Gutiérrez, *Walls and Mirrors: Mexican Americans, Mexican Immigrants, and the Politics of Identity* (1995); Jacqueline Jones, *Labor of Love, Labor of Sorrow: Black Women, Work, and the Family from Slavery to the Present* (1985); Alejandro Portes and Rubén G. Rumbaut, *Immigrant America: A Portrait*, 2nd ed. (1996); David M. Reimers, *Still the Golden Door: The Third World Comes to America* (1985); Paul James Rutledge, *The Vietnamese Experience in America* (1992); Al Santoli, *New Americans: An Oral History: Immigrants and Refugees in the U.S. Today* (1988); Peter Skerry, *Mexican Americans: The Ambivalent Minority* (1993); Ronald Takaki, *A Different Mirror: A History of Multicultural America* (1993) and *A Larger Memory: A History of Our Diversity, With Voices* (1998); Studs Terkel, *Race: How Blacks and Whites Think and Feel About the American Obsession* (1992); Reed Ueda, *Postwar Immigrant America: A Social History* (1994); David Hurst Thomas, Jay Miller, Richard White, Peter Nabokov, and Philip J. Deloria, *The Native Americans: An Illustrated History* (1993); Roger Waldinger and Mehdi Bozorgmehr, eds., *Ethnic Los Angeles* (1996); Helen Zia, *Asian American Dreams: The Emergence of an American People* (2000).

Economic and Demographic Change

Robert M. Collins, *More: The Politics of Economic Growth in Postwar America* (2000); Kathryn Marie Dudley, *The End of the Line: Lost Jobs, New Lives in Postindustrial America* (1994); Arlie Russell Hochschild, *The Time Bind: When Work Becomes Home and Home Becomes Work* (1997); Jacqueline Jones, *American Work: Four Centuries of Black and White Labor* (1998) and *The Dispossessed: America's Underclasses from the Civil War to the Present* (1992); Michael B. Katz, *The Undeserving Poor: From the War on Poverty to the War on Welfare* (1990); Katherine S. Newman, *Falling from Grace: The Experience of Downward Mobility in the American Middle Class* (1988); James T. Patterson, *America's Struggle Against Poverty in the Twentieth Century* (2000); Kevin P. Phillips, *The Politics of Rich and Poor: Wealth and the American Electorate in the Reagan Aftermath* (1990); Juliet B. Schor, *The Overworked American: The Unexpected Decline of Leisure* (1991); John C. Teaford, *Cities of the Heartland: The Rise and Fall of the Industrial Midwest* (1993).

Richard B. Freeman and James L. Medoff, *What Do Unions Do?* (1984); Arthur B. Shostak, *Robust Unionism: Innovations in the Labor Movement* (1991).

Carl Abbott, *The Metropolitan Frontier: Cities in the Modern American West* (1993); Timothy Egan, *Lasso the Wind: Away to the New West* (1998); John M. Findlay, *Magic Lands: Western Cityscapes and American Culture After 1940* (1992); William G. Robbins, *Colony and Empire: The Capitalist Transformation of the American West* (1994); Richard White, *"It's Your Misfortune and None of My Own": A New History of the American West* (1991).

Foreign Policy and the End of the Cold War

George Bush and Brent Scowcroft, *A World Transformed* (1998); Paul Kennedy, *The Rise and Fall of the Great Powers: Economic Change and Military Conflict from 1500 to 2000* (1987); Walter LaFeber, *America, Russia, and the Cold War, 1945–1996*, 8th ed. (1993) and *Inevitable Revolutions: The United States in Central America* (1983); Robert Scheer, *With Enough Shovels: Reagan, Bush & Nuclear War* (1982); Laura Silber and Alan Little, *Yugoslavia: Death of a Nation* (1996); Strobe Talbott, *The Russians and Reagan* (1984); Allan M. Winkler, *The Cold War: A History in Documents* (2000).

Fiction and Film

Julia Alvarez's *How the Garcia Girls Lost Their Accents* (1992) is the fictional account of four young women from the Dominican Republic and their transition to American life. Tom Wolfe's *The Bonfire of the Vanities* (1987) is a novel about the arrogance of the upper class in New York—the masters of the universe—and the consequences when an accident occurs.

The film *Bedtime for Bonzo* (1951) shows Ronald Reagan the actor playing the part of a professor trying to teach morals to a chimpanzee. *Knute Rockne, All American* (1940) is another one of Reagan's films in which he plays the part of George Gipp (the Gipper), a Notre Dame football player. *The Life and Times of Harvey Milk* (1984) is an Academy Award-winning documentary about the gay San Francisco city supervisor who was murdered. *Wall Street* (1987) captures the sense of greed and corporate arrogance that created the tone for the 1980s. *When Harry Met Sally* (1989) is a film about the difficulties of relationships between men and women.

◆ Discovering U.S. History Online

Ronald Wilson Reagan
http://www.ipl.org/div/potus/rwreagan.html
This site contains basic factual data about Reagan's election and presidency, speeches, and online biographies.

Ronald Reagan Presidential Library
www.reagan.utexas.edu
This site offers selected pictures and written documents from the Reagan years.

Media, Advertising, and the 1984 Presidential Election
http://it.stlawu.edu/~quack/seminar/home.htm
A study of "the Reagan campaign's use of media, in the form of paid advertising and news coverage . . . [and contrasts it] with Mondale's approach, in order to demonstrate how different the campaigns truly were."

The Reagan Years
http://www.cnn.com/SPECIALS/2001/reagan.years
This site includes photos and speeches from Reagan's life, especially from key moments of his presidency such as Reaganomics, the Iran-Contra affair, and his views on the Communist empire in an attempt to contribute to the "debate [on] the legacy of [his] two-term presidency."

George Herbert Walker Bush
http://www.ipl.org/div/potus/ghwbush.html
This site contains basic factual data about George H.W. Bush's election and presidency, speeches, and online biographies.

Divining America: Religion and the National Culture in the Twentieth Century
http://www.nhc.rtp.nc.us:8080/tserve/twenty.htm
Using essays and primary sources, the site was "designed to help teachers of American history bring their students to a greater understanding of the role religion has played in the development of the United States."

U.S. Equal Employment Opportunity Commission
http://www.eeoc.gov/35th/
This government-sponsored site offers a history of the commission, from pre-1964 Civil Rights Act to the present day.

U.S. Forest Service History
http://www.lib.duke.edu/forest/usfscoll/index.html
Incorporating original documents and photographs as well as bibliographic references, this site presents "information about the history of the United States Forest Service, in the Department of Agriculture."

United States Environmental Protection Agency
http://www.epa.gov/history
A history of the agency, including a timeline from 1970–present, topical information, publications, collection search, and photographs.

The Forgotten Americans
http://www.pbs.org/klru/forgottenamericans/
Companion site to the film, this site offers a portrait of the "Third World conditions" experienced by the mostly Latino residents of U.S. neighborhoods outside the city limits in Texas, California, Arizona, and New Mexico, called *colonias*.

American Cultural History: 1980–1989
http://www.nhmccd.edu/contracts/lrc/kc/decade80.html
An informative breakdown of various cultural and economic trends during the 1980s, including Art and Architecture, Books and Literature, Fashion and Fads,

Education, Events and Technology, Music and Media, Theater, and Film and Television.

Global Economy

http://www.pbs.org/wgbh/commandingheights/lo

This Web site examines the "forces, values, events, and ideas that have shaped the present global economic system, including Reagan's introduction of 'supply-side' economics."

An Outline of U.S. Economy

http://usinfo.state.gov/products/pubs/oeon/
homepage.htm

This full-text volume presents the basics of the American economy as well as a brief history of major economic events.

Foreign Policy

http://globetrotter.berkeley.edu/clips/

This site has a three-part series "The End of the Cold War" that includes extensive news quotes on "The Search for a U.S. Strategy," "Europe's Search for a New Identity," and "The Collapse of Communism in Eastern Europe and the Shaping of a Western Response."

The Cold War

http://www.cnn.com/SPECIALS/cold.war

This is the companion site to the CNN series on the Cold War. It contains some material on the end of the struggle.

The Gulf War

http://www.pbs.org/pages/frontline/gulf

This site combines personal accounts with a chronology and general information about the war.

31 The Post–Cold War World, 1992–2002

American society became more and more aware of its multicultural past and present in the 1990s. Different groups competed with each other for positions in the marketplace and other public spaces as the gap between rich and poor continued to grow greater. *(Billy Morrow Jackson, Station, 1981–1982, Courtesy of the Artist)*

✦ *American Stories*

AN IMMIGRANT FAMILY STRUGGLES AS THE ECONOMY IMPROVES

In 1997, Marlene Garrett bundled up her three sleepy children—aged four, three, and one—and took them to the babysitter's home every morning at 5 A.M. "Mama has to go to work so she can buy you shoes," she told them as she left for a job behind the counter at a bagel café in Fort Lauderdale, Florida, that began at 6 A.M. This was a new position and she did not want to be late.

Marlene had come to the United States from Jamaica eight years earlier. She and her husband, Rod, had high hopes for a better life in the United States, and they were fortunate enough to be employed. But both of them held entry-level jobs and had to struggle to make ends meet. Rod worked in a factory making hospital curtains and brought home about $250 a week. Marlene had just left a $5.25 an hour job selling sneakers for her $6 an hour job at the bagel café. It was a small improvement, but the $200 she earned made it possible to pay the monthly rent of $400 and buy groceries. With luck, they could repair or replace the car, which had recently died, and perhaps begin to pay off their $5,000 debt from medical bills. They had no health insurance and could only hope that no one got sick.

Marlene was not happy about her babysitting arrangements. Her real preference was to stay at home. "Who's a better caretaker than mom?" she asked. But remaining at home was out of the question. Welfare might have been a possibility in the past, but the United States was in the process of cutting back drastically on its welfare rolls, and, in any event, Marlene was not comfortable with that alternative. "I don't want to plant that seed in my children," she said. "I want to work."

Marlene had few day-care options. She would have liked to have taken Scherrod, Angelique, and Hasia to the Holy Temple Christian Academy—her church's day-care center and preschool—but it cost $180 a week for three children and was beyond reach. Several months before, when she had been earning $8 an hour as a home health aide for the elderly, she had thought she could afford the church center and had even put money down for school uniforms for the kids. Then her car gave out and made it impossible to continue that job.

Instead of the Holy Temple Christian Academy, Marlene took the children to the home of Vivienne, a woman from the Bahamas who worked nights at the self-service laundry where Marlene did her wash. Vivienne's apartment was simple and clean but had no toys or books anywhere in sight. Most days, the children watched television during the 10 hours that Marlene was away.

The Garretts knew how important it was to stimulate their children. Reflecting longingly on the church center and what it offered, Marlene said, "The children play games. They go on field trips. They teach them, they train them. My children are bright. You would be amazed at what they would acquire in a year." But instead of a stimulating center, the Garretts had to settle for a place that was simply safe.

At a time when the administration of Bill Clinton was trying to reconfigure the welfare system, people like the Garretts found themselves left out. Florida, like many states, budgeted most of its child-care money for families moving off of welfare to jobs. People who had never been on welfare received nothing. As the executive director of a Florida child-care referral agency observed, "Many of these parents have no choice but to leave their children in substandard arrangements that are rotting their brains, and jeopardizing their futures."

Marlene refused to give up hope. Her children were on a waiting list for help from the state that might make the Holy Temple Christian Academy accessible. Meanwhile, she took a second job working nights at the local Marriott Hotel. She had to pay Vivienne more money for the extra hours, and she worried even more about the additional time away from the children, but felt she had no choice. "It is temporary," she said. "I am doing what I have to do."

Marlene and Rod Garrett were like millions of poor Americans who found themselves left out of the prosperity that returned to the United States in the mid-1990s. Despite rosy economic indicators, more than 35 million Americans still lived below the federally defined poverty line. Life was hardly easy for the Garretts or for other families who found themselves on the bottom side of the line. Then, soon after George W. Bush succeeded Bill Clinton as president in 2001, the economy faltered. Now even more Americans found themselves in the same straits as the Garretts.

The Garretts' struggle to care for their children—and for themselves—unfolded against the backdrop of the longest period of economic growth in American history. As a deep recession in the early 1990s lifted, the economy went on a tear. American corporations, increasingly operating in a multinational context, dominated the global economy. Though some countries, like Japan, experienced a slowdown in economic growth and became mired in a long-lasting recession, the United States prospered. Taking advantage of remarkable advances in communication technology, corporations found it easy to do business in a world smaller than ever before. With inflation low in the United States, the Federal Reserve Board kept interest rates down, and the easy availability of money encouraged middle- and upper-class Americans to invest in the stock market and mutual funds, often enabling them to realize large gains, at least on paper. The troubling budget deficit that had soared in the Reagan administration disappeared as the government, guided by Democratic president Bill Clinton, ran a surplus for the first time in years. The unemployment level dropped, yet for Americans at the bottom of the economic ladder, many of the jobs now available as a result of the relentless shift toward a service economy paid little more than the minimum wage, and people like the Garretts still found themselves struggling to survive. Conditions became even more difficult when the Democratic party cut back and reconfigured the welfare system to preempt the issue for their own political ends. The loss of that safety net became even more problematical after a tax cut promoted by Republican President George W. Bush cut government

income as a troubling recession refused to go away. Corporate fraud shattered investor confidence, and the stock market, which had risen for much of the decade, dropped dramatically.

Meanwhile, the foreign policy scene shifted abruptly. The cataclysmic events in Europe that ended nearly a half century of Cold War required the United States to redefine its international role. This led to substantial debate, as both Republicans, who controlled Congress for most of the 1990s, and Democrats, who controlled the White House for the same period, voiced reservations about playing an activist, and potentially expensive, role abroad. Then, as the new decade began, the United States confronted the menace of terrorism on a scale never known before. The attacks that destroyed the World Trade Center towers in New York City and left a gaping hole in the Pentagon in Washington, D.C., led to a war on terrorism and a fundamental reconfiguration of American foreign policy.

This chapter describes demographic shifts, reflected in the census of 2000, that changed the face of the American people. It highlights the revival of the economy that brought unprecedented prosperity for many but still failed to accommodate the needs of less fortunate Americans like the Garretts, and then records the even greater suffering as the economy fell apart. It examines the political struggle between Democrats and Republicans that brought the second presidential impeachment in American history. It notes the bitterly contested national election of 2000 and its conservative aftermath. Finally, it explores the continuing effort to define the American role in the turbulent and terrorist-dominated post–Cold War world.

THE CHANGING FACE OF THE AMERICAN PEOPLE

The United States changed dramatically in the 1990s, as the continuing influx of new immigrants reshaped demographic patterns. The overall population, as reported in the census of 2000, grew more rapidly than it had in the past several decades and reflected the steady increase in the number of non-white Americans.

The New Pilgrims

The second great wave of immigrants in the twentieth century changed the face of America. The number of immigrants to the United States in the 20-year period from 1981 to 2000 was approximately 17.5 million, making it the most voluminous period of immigration in American history. In the decade of the 1990s, close to 10 million immigrants were counted, just less than the 10.1 million immigrants recorded in the 10 years from 1905 to 1914, which stands as the all-time record for that span of time. Altogether, nearly one-third of the population growth in the 1990s stemmed from immigration.

Immigrants settled in the 1990s in a pattern resembling that of the previous several decades. Whereas most immigrants around the turn of the preceding century remained near the East Coast, or

Immigration, 1970–1998

This chart shows the significant rise in immigration after 1970, as the tightly restricted quotas in force from the 1920s to 1965 were liberalized. The steady rise in the 1970s and 1980s reflected the arrival of Asian and Latin Americans, while the spike in the early 1990s occurred because of the amnesty that legalized the status of many illegal immigrants who were now officially counted.

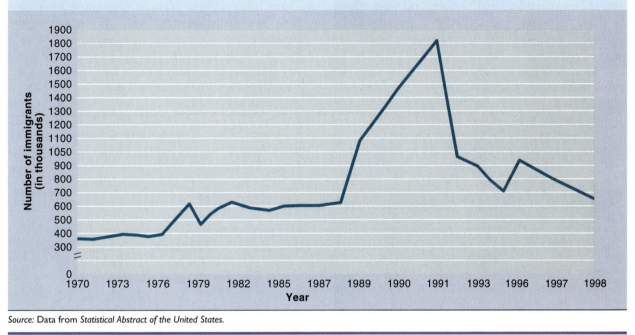

Source: Data from *Statistical Abstract of the United States.*

in contiguous states, in 2000, 39.9 percent of the foreign-born settled in western states, with only 22.6 percent of the foreign-born living in the Northeast. The shift was a result of larger demographic shifts in the United States. As the twentieth century began, the Northeast still dominated the economic and cultural life of the nation. New York City served as a magnet for immigrants, who often ventured no further after getting off the boat at Ellis Island. A hundred years later, the West was increasingly dominant. California had surpassed New York as the most populous state, and Los Angeles International Airport, known as LAX, had replaced Ellis Island as the port of entry for many immigrants.

The sources of recent immigration were similar to those of the 1970s and 1980s. In 2000, just over one-third of all immigrants—legal and illegal—came from Central America, while just over one-quarter came from Asia. The continuing influx was the result of factors that led immigrants to want to leave their home countries as well as factors that drew them to the United States. Faltering economies in many countries in Latin America led people living on the fringe to look toward the United States, where a

better life might be possible. Inhabitants of African nations, equally poor and faced with a crumbling infrastructure—as water and power sources deteriorated and roads sometimes became impassable—likewise saw hope for a brighter future in America, just as earlier immigrants had years before.

Immigration was not confined to the United States. Starting in the 1960s, Europe experienced its own wave of immigration, in a pattern that continued into the new century. Great Britain, France, and the Netherlands all had to deal with immigrants from former colonies. Germany experienced the arrival of people they called *gastarbeiter,* or guest workers, from southern Europe and Turkey, who were supposed to work in the factories and then go home, although many of them ended up staying.

The American influx was spurred by the Immigration Act of 1965 (see Chapter 28), which was aimed at curbing illegal immigration while offering amnesty to aliens who had lived in the United States prior to 1982. Part of Lyndon Johnson's Great Society program, this act authorized the impartial acceptance of immigrants from all parts of the world and was directly responsible for the greater numbers of Asians and Latin Americans. In later years, other legislative measures sought to rational-ize the immigration process. In 1986, Congress passed the Immigration Reform and Control Act, aimed at curbing illegal immigration while offering amnesty to aliens living in the United States. The Immigration Act of 1990 opened the doors wider, raising immigration quotas while cutting back on restrictions that had limited entry in the past. It also provided for swift deportation of aliens who com-mitted crimes. Two other measures in 1992 ex-panded eligibility slightly. In 2001, the United States and Mexico began to talk about how to ease the plight of Mexican immigrants and permit illegal ar-rivals to stay.

The rise in the number of immigrants fueled anti-immigrant feeling in some quarters. In the 1970s and 1980s, America's efforts to help immi-grants coincided with still-intact social-assistance programs of the liberal welfare state. Affirmative ac-tion programs aided both legal and illegal arrivals. Bilingual classrooms became more common, and multiculturalism, stressing the different values that made up a larger American identity, became a dom-inant theme in many schools.

Yet those efforts brought increasing resistance from Americans already here, particularly as the structure of the economy changed and good jobs became more scarce. At the same time, there was a cultural backlash, just as there had been in earlier eras. Opponents to immigration also worried about the challenge to America's character posed by new arrivals who clung to social patterns of their own. Americans were not alone in their fears. Europeans, too, were apprehensive at the threats to their way of

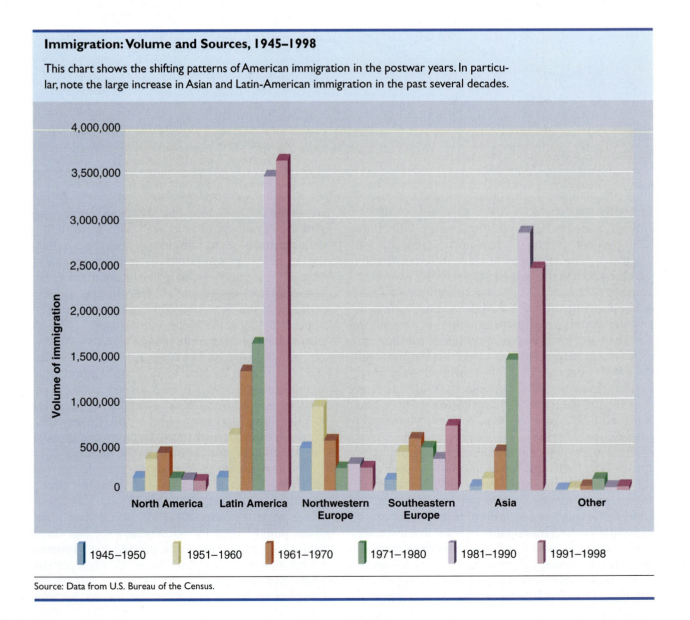

Immigration: Volume and Sources, 1945–1998

This chart shows the shifting patterns of American immigration in the postwar years. In particu-lar, note the large increase in Asian and Latin-American immigration in the past several decades.

Legend: 1945–1950 | 1951–1960 | 1961–1970 | 1971–1980 | 1981–1990 | 1991–1998

Source: Data from U.S. Bureau of the Census.

life. Opposition to the German *gastsarbeiter* became a political issue; in the Netherlands, Pim Fortuyn, a right-wing politician who had argued for extreme restrictions on immigration, was assassinated just before the 2002 general election in which his party had expected to do well and he had hopes of becoming prime minister.

That opposition, which echoed the anti-immigrant feeling of the past, included strenuous efforts to restrict illegal immigration. Resistance came to a head in California in 1994, where voters passed Proposition 187, denying illegal aliens access to public education and medical clinics. Just days after the election, a federal judge issued a preliminary injunction to prevent implementation of the ballot measure, which she made permanent several years later. Yet Proposition 187 provided a model for other states to follow and caught the attention of congressional members, especially Republicans, who gained control of Congress in 1994. Two years later, Congress passed legislation barring legal immigrants (who were not yet citizens) from receiving food stamps and disability assistance from the federal government. Meanwhile, toward the end of the decade, California ended its support for bilingual education, mandating English immersion instead and sparking a similar national drive.

Economic improvement, and the move toward full employment in the latter part of the 1990s, brought a political shift in the immigration debate. In 2000, pressure mounted to increase the number of visas for high-tech workers abroad, while a coalition of business groups and immigrant-rights organizations pressed for admitting more unskilled workers who could work in the service sector where there were unfilled jobs. Political considerations also played a part in the shift. Both Democrats and Republicans recognized the voting power of Latinos in particular and wanted to ensure their support.

Immigration issues became headline news at the end of the 1990s in the highly publicized case of six-year-old Elián Gonzales. In November 1999, he was miraculously pulled out of the water near Florida when a group of Cuban boat people trying to reach the United States drowned. His father, still back in Cuba, had not given permission for the boy to leave and wanted him back. Instead, the Immigration and Naturalization Service (INS) placed him in temporary custody with a Cuban cousin in Miami.

Elián became a pawn in a tremendous struggle. The Miami Cuban community, which hated Fidel Castro and his Communist regime, wanted the boy to receive asylum and stay in the United States. Others, including the INS, argued that the boy should be returned to his father in Cuba. In the end,

Attorney General Janet Reno authorized a raid that seized Elián and arranged for his repatriation.

The INS, already unpopular, attracted fierce criticism in the face of the terrorist attacks of September 11, 2001. It had allowed into the country immigrants from Saudi Arabia and elsewhere who had orchestrated the airplane hijackings that shocked the world. Now Americans began to look askance at Arabs or Muslims elsewhere in the country and to condemn the INS for its laxity in screening out potential terrorists.

The Census of 2000

The 2000 census reported a 13 percent increase in the nation's population, as the United States gained 32.7 million people in the 1990s to give a total of 281.4 million inhabitants. This expansion surpassed the previous 10-year record of 28 million people in the 1950s, in the midst of the baby boom after World War II. The rate of growth, which had slowed down over the past three decades, now accelerated in the 1990s as it reflected increased immigration and longer life expectancy.

While every state had a net increase in population, growth was greatest in the West, increasingly important in the economic, social, and cultural life of the nation. Altogether, the West as a whole gained 10.4 million people and expanded by 19 percent. Some areas showed extraordinary expansion. The Phoenix, Arizona, metropolitan area grew by 45 percent, while the Las Vegas, Nevada, metropolitan region expanded by 83 percent.

The United States remained about 69 percent white, with a 12 percent African-American and 11 percent Latino population. Latinos and blacks both predominated in urban centers and immigration entry areas. Latinos continued to flock to southern California, the Texas border region, and the south of Florida, and they also began to congregate in increasing numbers in places like Chicago and Denver, while at the same time settling in small towns all over the United States. Overall, their numbers increased by 38.8 percent. African Americans maintained their dominance in older northern cities such as Detroit and in Washington, D.C., while continuing to move into metropolitan suburbs, where they found changing employment and housing opportunities.

Nationally, the Asian and Pacific Islander population increased by 43 percent. In California, Asians showed the largest increase of any group. They now comprised nearly 13 percent of the state population and maintained their position as the third largest population group, after whites and Latinos. Much of the Asian population growth occurred in the sub-

Portrait of a Nation

The 2000 census documented changing population patterns and reported where different groups resided in the United States. Note the concentration of African Americans in the Southeast and the concentration of Hispanics in the Southwest. The Asian American population was greatest in the West, while American Indians, who had once roamed the continent, were now confined to a number of much smaller western areas.

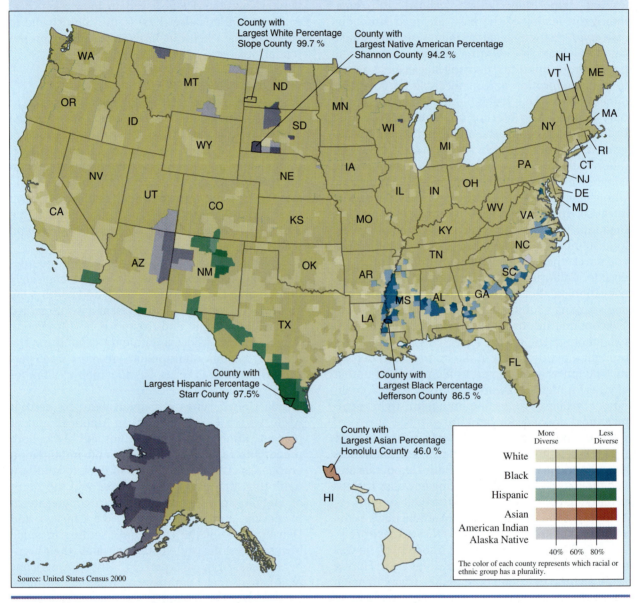

County with Largest White Percentage Slope County 99.7 %

County with Largest Native American Percentage Shannon County 94.2 %

County with Largest Hispanic Percentage Starr County 97.5%

County with Largest Black Percentage Jefferson County 86.5 %

County with Largest Asian Percentage Honolulu County 46.0 %

More Diverse — Less Diverse

White
Black
Hispanic
Asian
American Indian Alaska Native

40% 60% 80%

The color of each county represents which racial or ethnic group has a plurality.

Source: United States Census 2000

urbs, where the more affluent moved, though large pockets of poverty remained in places like Chinatown in Los Angeles and Little Phnom Penh in Long Beach.

The new census revealed that the combination of Latinos, African Americans, and Asians now outnumbered whites in California. This was the first time since 1860, when California began to provide accurate census data, that whites did not have a majority. State politics already began to reflect the shift. In 1998, Cruz Bustamante became the first Latino elected to statewide office in California since 1871, when he became lieutenant governor. This shift had enormous social and political implications. The United States, founded as a white man's country, had now developed into a nation where people of

Population Change for the Ten Largest Cities, 1990–2000

Most American cities grew in the 1990s, although some old industrial centers such as Philadelphia and Detroit lost population.

City and State	Population April 1, 1990	Population April 1, 2000	Change, 1990–2000 Number	Change, 1990–2000 Percent
New York, NY	7,322,564	8,008,278	685,714	9.4
Los Angeles, CA	3,485,398	3,694,820	209,422	6.0
Chicago, IL	2,783,726	2,896,016	112,290	4.0
Houston, TX	1,630,553	1,953,631	323,078	19.8
Philadelphia, PA	1,585,577	1,517,550	−68,027	−4.3
Phoenix, AZ	983,403	1,321,045	337,642	34.3
San Diego, CA	1,110,549	1,223,400	112,851	10.2
Dallas, TX	1,006,877	1,188,580	181,703	18.0
San Antonio, TX	935,933	1,144,646	208,713	22.3
Detroit, MI	1,027,974	951,270	−76,704	−7.5

Source: U.S. Census Bureau, Census 2000; 1990 Census, *Population and Housing Unit Counts, United States* (1990 CPH-2-1).

color were increasingly numerous and soon would be leaving their imprint on public policy in important ways.

One new feature of the 2000 census revealed the desire of large numbers of Americans to identify themselves as part of more than one racial or ethnic group. Nationwide, 2.4 percent of the American people identified themselves as multiracial. In Hawaii, 21 percent of all residents traced their heritage to two or more racial or ethnic groups. At long last, the United States was beginning to embrace its multicultural and multiracial heritage.

ECONOMIC AND SOCIAL CHANGE

In the 1990s, the American economy improved dramatically. Yet despite the revival, millions of Americans remained poor, and homelessness became an increasingly visible problem. Meanwhile, groups pushing for equality made significant gains, but they still faced resistance in their long, continuing struggle for fair treatment in the United States.

Boom and Bust

American economic recovery began in mid-1992, even as other parts of the world found themselves facing industrial problems. In Germany, where extraordinary economic growth had occurred in the post–World War II years, the economy—the largest in Europe—faltered. As the growth rate slowed, the unemployment rate, which reached 5.2 percent in 1990, rose steadily over the course of the decade, hitting 10 percent in 1997 (and going even higher in

the new millennium). Reunification of East Germany and West Germany came at a heavy cost. The Japanese economy, the second-largest in the world (after the United States), likewise encountered trouble. Japan had revived dramatically after World War II, and growth had continued into the 1970s and 1980s, when productivity was higher than in the United States. Then the American productivity rate caught up, as Japan found itself hemmed in with excessive bureaucratic regulation and a system of lifetime employment for workers that made it difficult for companies to retrench in hard times. Recession led to falling prices, and even while the unemployment rate was low (3.4 percent in 1997, 4.1 percent in 1998), the economy remained sluggish.

Against that backdrop, the American revival was even more remarkable. The promotion of big business in the Reagan era (see Chapter 30) spurred investment and led to significant economic expansion as large firms grew larger still and became even more involved in the global economy. The lowering of interest rates by the Federal Reserve Board revived confidence and promoted consumer spending. Productivity rose steadily throughout the decade, though not quite as quickly as it had in the 1950s and 1960s. Similarly, the national economic growth rate began to rise again, reaching 3.9 percent in 1997, while averaging 3 percent in the years since the recovery began. Growth, like productivity, was not as dramatic as it had sometimes been in the golden years of industrial development, but it was sustained in what became the longest expansion in American history. Inflation fell; in 1998, it stood at the lowest rate since 1965. The unemployment rate also declined, dropping from 7.8 percent in 1992 to

4.6 percent in 1997, with monthly rates occasionally even lower in the next several years. Taking credit for the recovery, President Bill Clinton declared that the drop in unemployment was "the latest evidence that our economy is growing, steady and strong, that the American dream is in fact alive and well."

One reflection of the return of prosperity was the soaring stock market. A willingness to invest in the market is often a good indicator of confidence in the nation's economic health. In the 1990s, millions of Americans became emboldened by the positive economic indicators and invested billions of dollars in mutual funds and stocks. This period was marked by a dramatic increase in the number of investors, reaching approximately 50 percent of the population in 2000. Some purchased stocks for themselves, often working on their own computers, without using a stock broker. Others purchased mutual funds, where experts took the money invested and used their expert advice to put together a diversified portfolio. Much of the investment was in the high-tech area, where people poured billions of dollars into start-up companies not yet making a profit, in the hope that they would take off. The market, which had inched upward in past years, now began a dramatic rise. The Dow Jones average topped the once-unimaginable 10,000 barrier in 1999 and quickly moved on past the 11,000 mark. Investors, most from the middle and upper classes, made considerable amounts of money in the market.

An even more important sign of economic health was the dramatic reduction in the budget deficit. A Democratic effort to preempt a Republican issue and hold down spending paid off, particularly as low interest rates encouraged economic expansion. In 1998, the United States finished with a budget surplus for the first time in 29 years. With $70 billion—the largest surplus ever—left over at the end of the fiscal year, Democrats and Republicans began arguing about how the money should be used. President Clinton and most Democrats favored using funds to bolster the social security system, which seemed likely to run out of money, while Republicans, who controlled Congress, preferred a politically attractive tax cut. Forgotten in the euphoria was the fact that the national debt—the total of all past deficits—remained over $5.4 trillion.

In these prosperous times, American companies embarked upon a wave of mergers like those around the turn of the century that created the great oil and steel corporations. In the defense industry, for example, Lockheed and Martin Marietta merged in 1994, while Boeing merged with McDonnell Douglas in 1996. In 1997, a record $1 trillion in mergers involving American companies took place

as huge conglomerates swallowed up smaller competitors in the interests of efficiency and ever-larger profits. One consequence of the mergers, however, was layoffs of workers who duplicated tasks and seemed superfluous. The jobs available to those looking for other work were often positions like those held by Marlene Garrett and her husband, introduced earlier in the chapter, which paid far less.

Then, all too quickly, the economy faltered. The soaring stock market of the 1990s finally reversed course. The bull market reminded some observers of the speculative bubble of the 1920s. Alan Greenspan, chairman of the Federal Reserve Board, warned in 1996 against "irrational exuberance" in the market, but most investors, especially those making millions of dollars, ignored his warning. Yet, as economist John Kenneth Galbraith warned as he studied the Great Crash of 1929, all bubbles must burst some day. In 2000, the stock market began to slide, as investors realized that many of the financial gains did not reflect commensurate gains in productivity. In 2000, the year ended with the major stock indexes—the Dow Jones Industrial Average and the Nasdaq Composite—showing their worst performance in decades, and in 2001 and 2002, the market continued to fall, wiping out the paper gains of millions of large and small investors.

The nation's overall growth rate began to slow as investment declined. Lack of confidence in the market, particularly in the high-tech area that had fueled the boom, led to a corresponding lack of confidence in the economy. As a recession began in 2000, a tax cut, described later in this chapter, further undermined the stability of the economy. Promoted by Republican George W. Bush after his victory in the presidential election of 2000, the tax cut was skewed in favor of wealthy Americans and not only failed to provide a necessary stimulus but contributed to the decline.

By early 2001, it was clear that the economy was slumping. In February, manufacturing fell to its lowest point in 10 years. Economists hoped that it would turn around quickly, but their hopes were shattered as it began to look as though improvement was still in the distant future. Unemployment rolls increased and applications for state unemployment benefits surged. *Newsweek* magazine ran a story asking the question everyone feared: "How Safe Is Your Job?"

Confidence in the economy was further eroded by growing reports of corporate greed and managerial fraud. Emboldened by deregulation in the 1980s, many corporations had taken advantage of lax oversight practices and made huge—and sometimes illegal—profits. Toward the end of 2001, the

Enron Corporation, a company that bought and sold energy, admitted that it had filed five years of misleading reports and declared bankruptcy. As the scandal grew, it became clear that the Arthur Andersen accounting firm had participated in providing cover for financial irregularities, reaping huge financial gains, but in the end losing clients when it faced an indictment for its role in the process. As the corporate empire began to tumble, the top executives cashed in their stock and made millions of dollars, while the company's workers, unaware of the looming catastrophe and prohibited from unloading stock, lost not just their jobs but their life savings as well.

Some people argued that the Enron case was an anomaly—a bad apple in the barrel—and contended that the rest of corporate America was in good shape. As 2002 unfolded, it became clear that many other companies had been falsifying their books and other accounting firms had likewise looked the other way. In the summer of that year, WorldCom, the telecommunications giant whose customers included the 20 million users of the MCI long-distance service, filed for bankruptcy in the largest case in American history. Acknowledging that it had improperly accounted for nearly $4 billion of expenses, it laid off workers and undertook a frantic effort to reorganize its finances. Just as Americans had discovered the abuses of big business during the Progressive period in the late nineteenth and early twentieth centuries (see Chapters

18 and 21), now they found themselves troubled by the corporate scandals in the daily news as the twenty-first century began.

For much of the decade, observers had pointed to the growing gap between rich and poor. Now, as the economy limped along at the start of the twenty-first century, more and more Americans found themselves in economic trouble. Millions who had prospered in the booming market of the 1990s found their gains wiped out, while those who had never had much remained marginalized.

Poverty and Homelessness

Poverty was a problem even in boom times. The Census Bureau reported in 1997 that 35.6 million people in the United States—the richest country in the world—still lived below what was defined as the poverty line of about $16,000 a year for a family of four. The percentage—13.3 percent—had fallen slightly in each of the past few years, but it was still sizable, especially considering that it included one out of every three *working* Americans. Worse still was the fact that in 1998, there were 900,000 more Americans living below the poverty line than in 1990.

Poverty in the United States was different than in other parts of the world, to be sure. People in American slums had more material benefits than many of the residents of Soweto, the huge slum just outside Johannesburg in South Africa. Homeless Americans were more fortunate than Cambodian

The homeless became far more visible in the 1990s. Here a man lies sleeping under a thin sheet of plastic, serving as his blanket, right in front of the White House in Washington, D.C. *(Bettmann/CORBIS)*

beggars who were often incapacitated by the explosions of land mines that still dotted their country years after the Vietnam War. Yet the American poor, like the poor in most other industrialized nations, still found themselves on the fringes of society, unable to cope on their own.

Urban Americans had the toughest time of all. Since the earliest days, the United States had glorified its rural heritage and its impact on national character. Even as population shifts led more and more people to live in cities, government programs often failed to provide fully for urban needs. As cities lost population to the suburbs in the last half of the twentieth century, they lost their tax base at the same time and could not easily meet the demand for services. Near the end of the twentieth century, the poverty rate in New York, Los Angeles, and Chicago hovered around 20 percent. In Cleveland, Detroit, Miami, and New Orleans, it was closer to 30 percent.

The gap between rich and poor increased significantly in the last two decades of the twentieth century. The efforts of the Reagan and Bush administrations in the 1980s and early 1990s to cut back on government spending and eliminate social programs that had provided services for the poor had a powerful effect in causing the growing gap. In 1999, it took 100 million people to equal the wealth of the top one percent. One study of household incomes during the last three economic cycles—in the late 1970s, the late 1980s, and the late 1990s—found that gains in the top 20 percent of families in those periods outstripped gains of the bottom 10 percent in 44 states. In five states—Arizona, California, New York, Ohio, and Wyoming—income of the bottom 20 percent fell, while it rose rapidly in the top 20 percent.

As always, minorities fared worse than whites. The net worth of a typical white household at the beginning of the 1990s was 12 times greater than the net worth of a typical black household and 8 times greater than the net worth of a typical Latino household. Minorities and women continued to lose ground faster than the rest of the population as the decade unfolded.

Just as the United States rediscovered its poor in the 1960s, so it rediscovered its homeless in the 1980s and 1990s. Even as unemployment dropped in the 1980s, the number of homeless quadrupled during that time. Numbers were hard to ascertain, for the homeless had no fixed addresses, but one estimate in 1990 calculated that 6 to 7 million people had been homeless at some point in the past five years. Another study noted that family homelessness in New York had risen between 1990 and 1995, with the largest increase coming among children nine years old and younger. A federal report released by the Secretary of Housing and Urban Development in 2000 noted that approximately 3.5 million people would become homeless at least once during the year, with 1.35 million of those children.

People became homeless for a variety of reasons. Some started life in disturbed families. Others fell prey to alcohol and drugs. Still others had health or learning problems that eroded the possibility of a stable life. For millions of working Americans, homelessness was just a serious and unaffordable illness away. While families in the past had felt a responsibility for taking care of their own, increased mobility in the twentieth century created a fragmentation that led more and more people to fall through the cracks. Though many Americans initially regarded the homeless as "bag ladies, winos, and junkies," they gradually came to realize that the underclass category included others as well.

Red, a homeless man in Las Vegas, Nevada, described his plight in 2000:

> I've been homeless for five years. It's getting worse. All they do at the shelter is give us food and a place to stay. I'm just maintaining. I can't get out of it at this rate. If I find a job and I put down the shelter address, they won't give you a job. At the blood blank, if they find out you're living at the shelter, they won't even let you donate blood. So I can't get money by donating blood.

As the federal government cut back on relief programs in an effort that had begun in the 1980s, private agencies had to pick up the slack. Goodwill Industries International reported a steady climb in the number of people it assisted with incomes well above the poverty line who still could not make ends meet.

Aging and Illness

The American population was older than ever before as the century came to an end. Between 1900 and 1994, when the population of the country tripled, the number of people over the age of 65 rose elevenfold and continued to rise in the next decade, reaching 33 million, or just about 12 percent of the population, in 2001. Underlying the rapid increase was the steady advance in medical care, which in the twentieth century had increased life expectancy in the United States from 47 to 74 years as the elderly were healthier than ever before. People once considered themselves old when they reached the age of 65; now, most 65-year-olds regarded themselves in a different light. Many Americans in their 80s continued to lead productive lives—participat-

American Population Aged 65 or Older, 1980–2040

The percentage of the American population aged 65 and older increased as the baby boom population began to age. This graph shows the steady increase up to 2000, and the projected increase for the next 40 years.

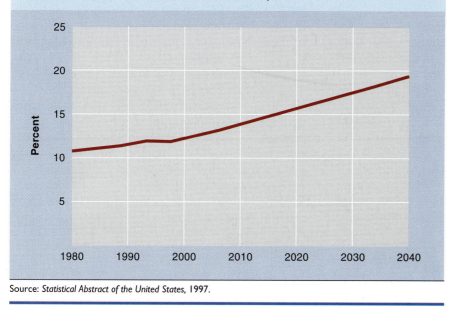

Source: *Statistical Abstract of the United States,* 1997.

ing in activities such as writing books, teaching classes, and consulting with corporate clients.

Changes in the United States were somewhat different than those elsewhere, particularly in the developing world. According to one estimate, the entire population of the globe 65 years and over was likely to more than double in the 1998–2025 period, while the youth population under the age of 15 would only grow by 6 percent. Even so, most dependents in the world were likely to be children in the coming quarter century. Only in the United States and other developed countries would elderly dependents outnumber those under the age of 15.

One component of the aging revolution in the United States was Viagra, a new drug designed to help men suffering from impotence that came on the market in the 1990s. Whether sexual dysfunction was a result of prostate illness, common among older males, or emotional distress, Viagra helped ailing men enjoy normal sex lives. Americans, including the elderly, now talked frankly about erectile dysfunction, just as they had talked openly about birth control when the birth control pill was introduced three and a half decades before. *Newsweek* magazine noted in 1998 that Viagra was the fastest-selling drug in history.

The elderly raised new issues in a nation suffering periodic recessions. Many wanted to continue working and opposed mandatory retirement rules

that drove them from their jobs. Legislation in 1978 that raised the mandatory retirement age from 65 to 70 helped older workers but decreased employment opportunities for younger workers seeking jobs. In 1986, federal legislation amending the Age Discrimination in Employment Act prohibited mandatory retirement on the basis of age for virtually all workers and created continuing problems for younger employees in the 1990s. The political power of the elderly became increasingly visible.

Generational resentment over jobs was compounded by the knotty problems faced by the social security system, which was established a half century earlier. Other parts of the world—Scandinavia, for example—provided social services out of general revenues and took such expenditures for granted. However, in the United States, contributions to the system were necessary to keep it solvent, and that became a problem as the population aged. As more and more Americans retired, the system could not generate sufficient revenue to make the payments due without assistance from the general governmental fund. In the early 1980s, it appeared that the entire system might collapse. A government solution involving higher taxes for those still employed and a later age for qualifying for benefits rescued the fund for a time, but many Americans in the 1990s wondered whether social security would survive. In 2001, the nation began to

RECOVERING THE PAST

Autobiography

As we reach our own time, the historical past perhaps most worth recovering is our own. Our own story is as valid a part of the story of American history as the tale of Revolutionary War soldiers, frontier women, reform politicians, and immigrant grandparents. In this computerized age, the person we need to recover is ourself, a self that has been formed, at least in part, by the entire American experience we have been studying.

Autobiography is the form of writing in which people tell their own life's history. Although written autobiographies are at least as old as the literature of the early Christians (for example, *The Confessions of St. Augustine*), the word *autobiography* dates from the late eighteenth century, around the time of the French and American revolutions. That is no accident. These momentous events represented the triumph of individual liberty and the sovereignty of the self. *The Autobiography of Benjamin Franklin*, written between 1771 and Franklin's death in 1790 (and excerpted here), is a classic celebration of the American success story. Franklin's work set the standard for one autobiographical form, the memoir of one's public achievements and success. The other brief autobiographical memoir, from the reminiscences of Elizabeth Cady Stanton, also reflects the tone and range of this tradition.

Not all autobiographies are written late in life to celebrate one's accomplishments. The confessional

---

Autobiographical Memoirs

Benjamin Franklin

DEAR SON,

I have ever had a pleasure in obtaining any little anecdotes of my ancestors. You may remember the enquiries I made among the remains of my relations when you were with me in England and the journey I undertook for that purpose. Imagining it may be equally agreeable to you to know the circumstances of my life—many of which you are yet unacquainted with—and expecting a week's uninterrupted leisure in my present country retirement, I sit down to write them for you. Besides, there are some other inducements that excite me to this undertaking. From the poverty and obscurity in which I was born and in which I passed my earliest years, I have raised myself to a state of affluence and some degree of celebrity in the world. As constant good fortune has accompanied me even to an advanced period of life, my posterity will perhaps be desirous of learning the means, which I employed, and which, thanks to Providence, so well succeeded with me. They may also deem them fit to be imitated, should any of them find themselves in similar circumstances.

Source: *The Autobiography of Benjamin Franklin* (1771).

Elizabeth Cady Stanton

Elizabeth Cady Stanton

It was 'mid such exhilarating scenes that Miss Anthony and I wrote addresses for temperance, anti-slavery, educational and woman's rights conventions. Here we forged resolutions, protests, appeals, petitions, agricultural reports, and constitutional arguments; for we made it a matter of conscience to accept every invitation to speak on every question, in order to maintain woman's right to do so. To this end we took turns on the domestic watchtowers, directing amusements, settling disputes, protecting the weak against the strong, and trying to secure equal rights to all in the home as well as the nation.

It is often said, by those who know Miss Anthony best, that she has been my good angel, always pushing and goading me to work, and that but for her pertinacity I should never have accomplished the little I have. On the other hand it has been said that I forged the thunderbolts and she fired them. Perhaps all this is, in a measure, true. With the cares of a large family I might, in time, like too many women, have become wholly absorbed in a narrow family selfishness, had not my friend been continually exploring new fields for missionary labors. Her description of a body of men on any platform, complacently deciding questions in which women had an equal interest, without an equal voice, readily aroused me to a determination to throw a firebrand into the midst of their assembly.

Source: Elizabeth Cady Stanton, *Eighty Years and More: Reminiscences, 1815–1897* (1898).

Confessional Autobiographies

Black Elk

And so it was all over.

I did not know then how much was ended. When I look back now from this high hill of my old age, I can still see the butchered women and children lying heaped and scattered all along the crooked gulch as plain as when I saw them with eyes still young. And I can see that something else died there in the bloody mud, and was buried in the blizzard. A people's dream died there. It was a beautiful dream.

And I, to whom so great a vision was given in my youth,—you see me now a pitiful old man who has done nothing, for the nation's hoop is broken and scattered. There is no center any longer, and the sacred tree is dead.

Source: *Black Elk Speaks,* as told through John G. Neihardt (1932).

Malcolm X

I want to say before I go on that I have never previously told anyone my sordid past in detail. I haven't done it now to sound as though I might be proud of how bad, how evil, I was.

But people are always speculating—why am I as I am? To understand that of any person, his whole life, from birth, must be reviewed. All of our experiences fuse into our personality. Everything that ever happened to us is an ingredient.

Today, when everything that I do has an urgency, I would not spend one hour in the preparation of a book which has the ambition to perhaps titillate some readers. But I am spending many hours because the full story is the best way that I know to have it seen, and understood, that I had sunk to the very bottom of the American white man's society when—soon now, in prison—I found Allah and the religion of Islam and it completely transformed my life.

Source: *The Autobiography of Malcolm X,* with the assistance of Alex Haley (1964).

---

autobiography, unlike most memoirs, explores the author's interior life, acknowledging flaws and failures as well as successes; it may be written at any age. The purpose of this type of autobiography is not just to reconstruct one's past to preserve it for posterity, but to find from one's past an identity in order to know better how to live one's future. The story of religious confessions and conversions is an obvious example. This form also includes secular self-examinations such as those by Maxine Hong Kingston in *The Woman Warrior* (1976), Piri Thomas in *Down These Mean Streets* (1967), or Maya Angelou in a series of five autobiographical sketches beginning with *I Know Why the Caged Bird Sings* (1969). The other two excerpts presented here are among the finest examples of confessional autobiography and suggest its variety.

These examples hardly convey the full range of the autobiographical form or how available to all people is the opportunity to tell the story of one's life. In 1909, William Dean Howells called autobiography the "most democratic province in the republic of letters." A recent critic agrees, pointing out:

> To this genre have been drawn public and private figures: poets, philosophers, prizefighters; actresses, artists, political activists; statesmen and penitentiary prisoners; financiers and football players; Quakers and Black Muslims; immigrants and Indians. The range of personality, experience, and profession reflected in the forms of American autobiography is as varied as American life itself.

Your story, too, is a legitimate part of American history. But writing an autobiography, while open to all, is deceptively difficult. Like historians, autobiographers face problems of sources, selection, interpretation, and style. As in the writing of any history, the account of one's past must be objective, not only in the verifiable accuracy of details but also in the honest selection of representative events to be described. Moreover, in fiction as well as history, the autobiographer must provide a structured form, an organizing principle, literary merit, and thematic coherence to the story. Many other challenges face the would-be autobiographer, such as finding a balance between one's public life and the private self and handling problems of memory, ego (should one, for example, use the first or third person?), and death.

Reflecting on the Past   To get an idea of the difficulties of writing an autobiography, try writing your own. Limit yourself to 1,000 words. Good luck.

consider establishing private retirement accounts as one part of the solution to the problem, but political agreement proved hard to attain, and the issue became much less compelling when the stock market faltered. Meanwhile, millions of elderly people wondered how they could afford the rapidly increasing cost of prescription drugs.

As Americans lived longer, they suffered increasingly from Alzheimer's disease, an affliction that gradually destroys a patient's memory and brings on infantile behavior. Diagnosis is difficult, and there is no treatment to reverse the ailment's course. The illness gained exposure in 1995 when the family of Ronald Reagan disclosed that the former president was suffering from the incurable disease.

Other illnesses affected old and young alike. The discovery of AIDS (acquired immune deficiency syndrome) in 1981 marked the start of one of the most serious diseases in the history of the United States—

As the AIDS epidemic caused more and more deaths, family members and friends began to create a huge quilt to celebrate the lives of those who had died. Each panel represented a different person. The quilt, shown here in Washington, D.C., was on display around the country and drew millions of viewers who came to remember those lost to the disease. *(Lisa Quinones/Black Star)*

and the world. Some nations found themselves decimated by AIDS. In China, for example, entire villages were infected with HIV (the human immunodeficiency virus that causes AIDS) as a result of unsterile practices in blood stations. In 2002, Russia faced a spiraling rate of infection and had 70,000 full-blown cases of AIDS, compared with 5,500 the previous year. Africa was hit even harder. One estimate from the United Nations, the World Bank, and the World Health Organization found that 34.3 million people in the world had AIDS, with 24.5 million of them in sub-Saharan Africa. Of the 13.2 million children in the world orphaned by the disease, 12.1 million came from the sub-Saharan region. In Kenya, some schools lost a teacher a month to AIDS. In Zimbabwe, estimates of life expectancy were expected to fall from age 61 in 2005 to age 33 in 2010.

While health conditions in the United States were better than those in many parts of the world, AIDS still had a corrosive effect. The sexual revolution of the 1960s had brought a major change in sexual patterns, particularly among the young, but now sexual experimentation was threatened by this deadly new disease. Although it seemed to strike intravenous drug users and homosexuals with numerous partners more than other groups at first, it soon spread to the heterosexual population as well. Babies with AIDS were born to mothers with the illness. AIDS became the leading cause of death in Americans between the ages of 25 and 44. The growing number of deaths—approximately 458,000 in 2001—suggested that the disease would reach epic proportions. That same year, some 800,000 to 900,000 Americans of all ages and ethnicities were living with HIV, which could burst into full-blown AIDS at any time. Advertisements in the national media advised the use of condoms, and the U.S. surgeon general mailed a brochure, *Understanding AIDS,* to every household in the United States. New drugs, taken in combination, extended the lifespan of those with the HIV virus and reduced the death rate in the 1990s, but AIDS remained a lethal, and ultimately fatal, disease. Despite medical advances, a cure remained elusive.

Minorities and Women Face the Twenty-First Century

Americans fighting for equality made gains in the 1990s. For African Americans, home ownership and employment figures rose. The numbers of murders and other violent crimes that involved blacks dropped. A record 40 percent of African Americans attended college in 1997, up from 32 percent in 1991. Yet African Americans faced constant reminders that Martin Luther King, Jr.'s dream of a color-blind America was not yet a reality. Incremental improvements often failed to erode racist ideas that were a legacy of American slavery. Incidents like the beating of black motorist Rodney King in Los Angeles in 1991 and the rioting that occurred the next year (see Chapter 30) made many people wonder just how much progress the civil rights movement had made. A survey in San Diego noted that the police there stopped African-American and Latino motorists more than whites and Asian Americans—a pattern that was common around the country. The 2000 census revealed that the nation was more racially and ethnically diverse than ever before, yet it pointed out that people still lived in neighborhoods inhabited by people like themselves. African-American historian John Hope Franklin, looking back in 1995 at the eight decades of his life, summed up common frustrations when he said: "Just about the time you sit down or sit back and say, 'Oh, yes, we're really moving,' you get slapped back down."

Affirmative action was one area where blacks faced a backlash. Resistance, grounded in continuing racism and reflecting opposition to new arrivals in other parts of the world, began at the state level and spread around the nation. Energized by their political victories in 1994, conservatives launched a powerful attack on the policy of giving preferential treatment to groups that had suffered discrimination in the past. Arguing that government leaders had never intended affirmative action to be a permanent policy, they pushed ballot initiatives and pressured public agencies to bring the practice to an end. The most visible of those was Proposition 209 in California, approved by voters in the election of 1996, which prohibited the use of gender or race in awarding state government contracts or admitting students to state colleges and universities. After victory in California, African-American businessman Ward Connerly, who had spearheaded the effort, established an organization called, ironically, the American Civil Rights Institute to help other states enact similar bans on preferences. When he declared that he wanted to create the kind of color-blind society Martin Luther King, Jr., had sought, black lawmakers and civil rights leaders blasted him for "spitting on the grave" of King's legacy.

The increasingly conservative Supreme Court also waded into the controversy. In 1995, the Court let stand a lower court ruling prohibiting colleges and universities from awarding special scholarships to African Americans or other minorities. In 1996, it declined to hear an appeal of a U.S. District Court

decision two years before in *Hopwood* v. *Texas* that prohibited the use of affirmative action in higher education. Meanwhile, other cases moved through the legal system. At the end of 2000, a federal judge ruled that the University of Michigan could use race in undergraduate admissions in the effort to promote diversity on campus. But early the next year, another federal judge ruled that the use of race in admissions at the University of Michigan Law School was unconstitutional. That decision was then overturned on appeal in mid-2002, setting the stage for another Supreme Court ruling, as both proponents and opponents waited anxiously to see what the court would decide.

The booming job market in the late 1990s was the most important factor in fostering better race relations. It provided new opportunities for people who had been unable to find jobs. A survey in 1999 reported that young black men in particular were moving back into the economic mainstream at a faster rate than their white counterparts, and crime levels were falling in areas where joblessness was declining. The jobless rate for young black men was still twice that for young white men, but the improvement was encouraging.

Even so, tensions that had existed throughout the twentieth century persisted. Issues stemming from continuing discrimination in finding jobs and persistent antagonism by the police erupted in the spring of 2001 in Cincinnati, Ohio. When a white policeman killed an unarmed black youth, confrontations around the city provided a bitter reminder of riots in the past. Five months after the riots, *The Cincinnati Enquirer* noted in a large front-page headline: "Races See Two Cincinnatis." The story observed: "In one, many white people feel safe and secure in their homes and neighborhoods, optimistic about their jobs and the futures of their children. In the other, many black people worry about daily survival—about becoming victims of violent crime and being stopped by the police, about being discriminated against in places where they work, eat and shop."

In early 2002, African-American television correspondent Ed Bradley pointed to changes he had seen in the course of his career. "When asked about progress," he said, "I'm often reminded of the old lady sitting in the church who says, 'It ain't what it ought to be, but thank God it ain't what it used to be.'" Bradley was right, but many African Americans wondered when further change would come.

Women likewise made steady progress in the 1990s. They were increasingly involved in academic programs and professions that had been closed to them several decades earlier. In 2001, for example, women made up 49.4 percent of all first-year law students, compared to 10 percent in 1970; that pattern was reflected in other segments of society as well. In the academic world that same year, women held 44 percent of all entry-level college teaching jobs, though they had only 14 percent of the most senior positions, revealing another common pattern. In addition, women worked as pilots on commercial planes and served on the front lines fighting the forest fires that broke out in the West in the summer of 2002. At the same time that there was substantial gender change in nearly every segment of the job market, there was still continuing resistance to inclusion at the top. Women started to become the heads of major firms (such as Carly Fiorina at computer giant Hewlett-Packard) as the glass ceiling, preventing women from rising to the top of the corporate ladder, began to crack in the 1990s, yet most leaders were still men.

Abortion remained a polarizing issue, particularly as anti-abortion activists sought to disrupt abortion clinics. They launched around-the-clock pickets, aimed at frightening away women seeking abortions. Physicians performing abortions found their lives at risk, and Barnet Slepian, a Buffalo doctor, became the latest casualty when he was killed in 1998 in his own home by a sniper shooting through a window. Abortion opponents also took aim at a seldom used, late-term procedure they called "partial birth abortion." Congress passed a measure banning the procedure, but President Clinton vetoed it. When some states passed their own restrictive measure, the courts stepped into the controversy, and in mid-2000, the Supreme Court, by a narrow 5–4 vote margin, declared that a Nebraska law banning the practice (and by implication, similar laws in 30 other states) were unconstitutional. That same year, when the Food and Drug Administration finally approved a drug known as RU-486, the so-called abortion pill, abortion opponents jumped into the controversy and sought—unsuccessfully—to attach conditions that would effectively eliminate its use. Abortion remained one of the issues dividing the American people.

The abortion debate was just one measure that created a backlash against the feminist label, even as men and women both accepted the changes brought by the women's movement. Women hesitated to be associated with what they still considered a radical fringe, and that affected how they identified themselves. In 1998, only 26 percent of working women said "To me, a career is as important as being a wife and mother," down from 36 percent in 1979. While young women took for granted the gains fought for and won by their mothers and grandmothers, fewer wanted to call themselves feminists.

Yet the feminist movement persisted and brought continued improvements in the lives of women. American feminists looked to their counterparts in Europe, where even more advances had taken place. Nations seeking to join the European Union had to accept its equal rights provisions. The government in France considered the issue of gender parity in political representation and in 2000 passed a measure mandating that in certain cases, there needed to be an equal number of male and female candidates. Backlash was much less common in Europe. Progress in the United States did not always come easily, particularly as demographic patterns changed. The 2000 census revealed that the number of families headed by single mothers had risen to 7.5 million, an increase of 25 percent since 1990. Still, despite problems, efforts to bring about equal rights continued.

Latinos likewise pushed for greater equality and had demographic change on their side. The 2000 census and subsequent studies based on the data provided noted that the Latino population spread farther and faster than any previous immigrant wave, even exceeding the influx of eastern Europeans in the early twentieth century. The Latino population increase of 38 percent since 1990 dwarfed the national rise. Metropolitan areas such as New York, Los Angeles, El Paso, and Miami still accounted for the largest numbers of Latinos, but many now gravitated to suburban areas, where they found homes and jobs. In 2000, 46 percent of all Latinos owned their own homes, compared to 42 percent a decade before, though that figure still lagged behind the national number of 66 percent.

The emergence of a sturdy middle class gave Latinos a greater voice in social and political affairs. In 1993, Henry Cisneros became secretary of housing and urban development, and Federico Peña became secretary of transportation in Bill Clinton's administration. At the end of the decade, with Latinos projected to become the nation's largest minority by 2005, Latino political figures became even more numerous and visible. In California, for example, both the lieutenant governor and the speaker of the assembly were Chicano, as was the mayor of San Jose. Democrat Loretta Sanchez, who defeated eight-term congressman Robert Dornan in Orange County, served in the U.S. House of Representatives. In the administration of George W. Bush, White House counsel Alberto Gonzales played a major role in making judicial appointments.

As the nation's overall unemployment rate dropped in the mid-1990s, the rate for the 12 million Latino workers likewise fell—from 9.8 percent in 1992 to 7.3 percent in 1997. Despite that drop, the rate remained higher than the rate for white workers. Meanwhile, median Hispanic household income fell, even as it rose for every other ethnic and racial group. Many Latinos found it difficult to make ends meet.

Latinos nevertheless had a growing impact on American culture. Though Hispanic students were three times as likely as whites, and twice as likely as blacks, to drop out of high school, they made their influence felt in other ways. Merengue music could often be heard in music stores or on the radio. Argentine steakhouses could be found in many cities. Use of the Spanish language became more and more common around the country. President George W. Bush himself used Spanish in appealing to this important electoral bloc.

Even so, Latinos faced many of the same difficulties as blacks. Proposition 209 in California, ending affirmative action at the state level, led to a drop in the percentage of Latino students in the first-year class at the University of California at Berkeley from 13 percent in 1997 to 7 percent in 1998. But aggressive efforts by university administrators to look more carefully at a variety of issues and to minimize the value attached to standardized tests led the percentage to increase in subsequent years.

Native Americans found they had less influence, in part because of their smaller numbers. In the 2000 census, only 4.1 million people, or 1.5 percent of the population, identified themselves as American Indian or Alaska Native. Yet Indians still managed to keep the causes that concerned them before the public.

Indians continued their legal efforts to regain lost land. In 1999, the federal government joined the Oneida Indians in a lawsuit arguing that state and local governments in central New York had illegally acquired 270,000 acres of land from them in the late eighteenth and early nineteenth centuries and wanted restitution. Now it was the turn of 20,000 landowners to be worried about the fate of their property. Meanwhile, Cayugas claimed a substantial section of the northern tip of Cayuga Lake, in upstate New York, while the Mohawks and Senecas fought to regain control over parcels of land they claimed had been wrongfully obtained in the past.

Some of these efforts met with success. In early 2000, the federal government returned 84,000 acres in northern Utah that it had taken from the Utes in 1916 when it sought to secure the rights to valuable reserves of oil shale. "We're trying to do the right thing, returning land to its rightful owners," Energy Secretary Bill Richardson declared.

Native Americans became more politically active in the 1990s. In the election of 1992, Ben Nighthorse Campbell was elected to the Senate from his home state of Colorado. (AP/Wide World Photos)

Indians also pressed successfully for the return of Indian skeletal remains, removed by white scientists and museum officials over the course of the last century. Ever since passage of the Native American Graves Protection and Repatriation Act of 1990, skeletons and sacred objects flowed back to the tribes where they belonged. In 1997, Harvard's Peabody Museum sent back the bones of nearly 2,000 Pueblo Indians in the largest single return of these remains.

Native-American women became increasingly active in the reform effort. Ada Deer, who had successfully fought the government's termination policy in the 1970s (see Chapter 29), served as Assistant Secretary of the Interior in the 1990s. Winona LaDuke, an environmental activist, directed the Honor the Earth Fund and the White Earth Land Recovery Project, fought needless hydroelectric development, and was singled out by *Time* magazine as one of the nation's 50 most promising leaders under 40 years of age. In 2000, she served as Ralph Nader's vice presidential running mate on the small Green Party ticket.

Many Indians still felt a sense of dislocation, captured by novelist Sherman Alexie in 1993. Asked what

Diminishing Tribal Lands

While Native Americans steadily lost their territory over a period of 200 years, in the 1990s, Indians filed lawsuits to regain tribal lands and were successful in some of their claims. *(Source: New York Times, June 25, 2000)*

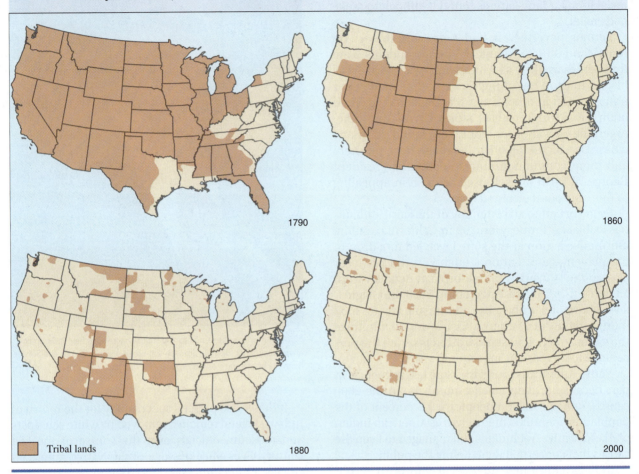

1790

1860

Tribal lands

1880

2000

---

it was like to return from the city to the reservation, he responded through the narrator in one of the stories in *The Lone Ranger and Tonto Fistfight in Heaven:*

> "It's like a bad dream you never wake up from," I said, and it's true. Sometimes I still feel like half of me is lost in the city, with its foot wedged into a steam grate or something. Stuck in one of those revolving doors, going round and round while all the white people are laughing. Standing completely still on an escalator that will not move, but I didn't have the courage to climb the stairs by myself.

An important symbolic gesture occurred in the last months of the Clinton administration. As the Bureau of Indian Affairs celebrated its 175th anniversary, Kevin Gover, head of the agency, reversed the pattern that had been so predominant in the past when he apologized for the nation's repressive treatment of Native Americans. "In truth, this is no occasion for celebration," he said. It was, rather, a time "for sorrowful truths to be spoken, a time for contrition." He spoke of "the decimation of the mighty bison herds, the use of the poison alcohol to destroy minds and body, and the cowardly killing of women and children." The suffering inflicted on the Indians "made for tragedy on a scale so ghastly that it cannot be dismissed as merely the inevitable consequence of the clash of competing cultures." Secretary of the Interior Bruce Babbitt called the bureau "a work in progress" and noted that now most of its 10,000 employees were Indians themselves.

Asian Americans enjoyed real success in the 1990s. With about 11 million people—approximately four percent of the national population—of Asian descent in the United States in 2000, there was a now critical mass. They came from a variety of cultures, to be sure, and Filipinos often had different experiences than Chinese or Koreans or Japanese, yet together they had an increasingly important impact on American society. Many of the children enjoyed remarkable educational achievements, making up a disproportionate share of the students at the most prestigious universities. In 2000, the student body at the Massachusetts Institute of Technology was 28 percent Asian American; at the University of California at Berkeley, the figure was 39 percent. In the middle of that year, President Clinton appointed Norman Y. Mineta as secretary of commerce, making him the first Asian American to hold a cabinet position.

Yet Asian Americans in the 1990s found themselves in an ambiguous position. While they had higher median incomes than whites, due in part to a dedicated work ethic, newcomers faced serious economic problems. Sometimes Asian Americans competed with African Americans and Latinos, as affirmative action programs limited the number of Asians who could be admitted in order to give other groups a chance.

A report in 2000 observed that many Americans still saw Asian Americans as secretive and inscrutable. That kind of reaction was frustrating. "Too many people in this country continue to see us in simple stereotypes," complained Paul M. Ong, a social policy professor at the University of California at Los Angeles.

Asian-American efforts to secure their own rights were complicated by the fact that two-thirds were immigrants, and most came to the United States after 1965. As the leader of one Chinese-American civil rights group noted, "Most don't know civil rights history. They may not understand the struggles of other minorities. But the fact is we are still seen as minorities in this country, no ifs, ands or buts about it."

The struggle for gay rights also continued, and slowly gays began to achieve their demands. In a major change in 2000, the Big 3 automakers—General Motors, Ford, and Chrysler—announced health-care benefits for partners of gay employees, in a move that covered 465,000 workers. That same year, Vermont recognized same-sex relationships through civil unions, though stopped short of permitting gay marriages. In 2002, the American Academy of Pediatricians announced its support of the right of gay men and women to adopt the children of their partners. The definition of a family was becoming broader as a result of gay activism. As the gay rights movement celebrated the 30-year anniversary of the gay rights parade commemorating the riot at the Stonewall Inn in Greenwich Village in 1969 that had sparked gay resistance, proponents noted that the event had changed from a protest to a party, and, as the *New York Times* observed, "that in itself is a sign of success."

Still, there was continuing resistance to gays playing a more visible role in American society. In

Asian Americans followed the example of civil rights activists to demand appropriate treatment. In an effort to counter decades of discrimination—and violence—some marched in 1993 to commemorate the thirtieth anniversary of the March on Washington in which Martin Luther King, Jr., and other activists demanded equality. (© *Corky Lee*)

1998, 21-year-old University of Wyoming student Matthew Shepherd died after being brutally beaten and tortured by two men troubled by his lifestyle. When actress Ellen DeGeneres came out as lesbian on television, both as a character in her sitcom and in real life, some viewers wondered if her public decision accounted for the eventual canceling of her show. While most American cities had thriving gay communities, there was still deep-seated resistance to gays living openly in some quarters.

The polarization about the acceptance of gays was most visible in a 5–4 Supreme Court ruling in mid-2000 that the Boy Scouts could bar gay troop leaders and even gay boys. The case had begun when the Boy Scouts had ousted James Dale, an assistant scoutmaster, after the organization discovered he was gay. Now, after a series of appeals, the Court declared that forcing the Scouts to accept gays violated the organization's rights of free expression and free association under the First Amendment of the Constitution.

Some Americans supported the ruling. But a growing number began to speak out in opposition. "I think discrimination within the Boy Scouts gets rid of the whole concept of what the Boy Scouts are all about," said Kevin Elliot, a 13-year-old eighth grader who was a scout himself. In the spring of 2001, filmmaker Steven Spielberg, a former Eagle Scout, resigned from an advisory group after 10 years of service, saying he could not serve a group practicing "intolerance and discrimination."

DEMOCRATIC REVIVAL

The 1990s saw a Democratic revival. After the success of conservative Republicans in the 1980s, challenging the assumptions of the liberal welfare state and advancing a more limited conception of the role of government, Democrats regrouped, reformulated their message, and followed the lead of the Republicans in relying on new forms of media to broadcast political appeals. The pattern in the United States reflected similar shifts in the rest of the world as more liberal politicians asserted that government needed to play a greater role in advancing the public welfare. Politicians in a variety of countries tried to recast their appeal in different ways, rather than trotting out tarnished notions from the past, to win office and then implement their plans. In Great Britain, the Labour party headed by Tony Blair took over from the Conservative party of Margaret Thatcher. In Germany, Gerhard Schroeder of the Social Democratic party unseated the more conservative Helmut Kohl of the Christian Democratic Union,

who had served as chancellor for 16 years. But in the United States, for much of the decade, even as the Democrats regained the White House, the Republicans maintained control of Congress and bitter partisan fighting was the result.

Democratic Victory

In 1992, the Democratic party mounted an aggressive challenge to Republican rule. After a fierce primary campaign, Governor Bill Clinton of Arkansas triumphed over a crowded field of candidates. Overcoming allegations of marital instability, marijuana use, and draft evasion, he argued that it was time for a new generation to take command. Forty-six years old, he had reached maturity in the 1960s and stood in stark contrast to President George H. W. Bush, now running for reelection, who had come of age during World War II. The third candidate in what became a three-way race was H. Ross Perot, a billionaire businessman from Texas who had made a fortune in the computer data-processing field. Stressing his independence from both political parties, he declared that he alone could provide the business experience and leadership the nation needed.

This campaign, more than any in the past, was fought on television. In addition to three televised presidential debates, the candidates appeared on

Bill Clinton was an exuberant campaigner who used his musical talent to attract support when he ran for president in 1992. Here he plays his saxophone on nationwide television on "The Arsenio Hall Show" in Los Angeles. (AP/Wide World Photos)

Presidential Elections, 1992–1996

Year	Candidate	Party	Popular Vote	Electoral Vote
1992	BILL CLINTON	Democratic	43,728,275 (43.2%)	357
	George Bush	Republican	38,167,416 (37.7%)	168
	H. Ross Perot	Independent	19,237,245 (19.0%)	0
1996	BILL CLINTON	Democratic	47,401,185 (49.2%)	379
	Robert Dole	Republican	39,197,469 (40.7%)	159
	H. Ross Perot	Reform	8,085,294 (8.4%)	0

Note: Winners' names appear in capital letters.

talk shows and interview programs. Perot energized his campaign with appearances on "Larry King Live." Bill Clinton used a post–Super Bowl appearance on "60 Minutes" to answer charges questioning his character and later played his saxophone on the "Arsenio Hall Show" and appeared on MTV. This reliance on the electronic marketplace reoriented American campaign politics. Although Bush's popularity rating was high after the success of the Persian Gulf War, many Americans were turned off when he reneged on his campaign promise of "no new taxes."

On election day, Clinton won 43 percent of the popular vote to 38 percent for Bush and 19 percent for Perot. The electoral vote margin was even larger: 357 for Clinton, 168 for Bush, 0 for Perot. The Democrats retained control of both houses of Congress, with more women and minority members than ever before.

The president-elect wanted to check the cynicism that was poisoning political life. In 1964, three-quarters of the American public trusted the government to do the right thing most of the time. Three decades later, after the deception of leaders in the Vietnam War and the Watergate affair, the number was closer to one-quarter. Clinton sought to shift the nation's course after 12 years of Republican rule with Cabinet nominations that included four women, four African Americans, and two Latinos. He held a televised "economic summit" to explore national options and demonstrated a keen grasp of the details of policy. In his inaugural address, Clinton declared that "a new season of American renewal has begun." He also spoke out on behalf of a "communitarian" initiative, in which Americans would be more concerned with their responsibilities to the larger national community than with their individual and collective rights, as he tried to revive a commitment to participate in public affairs that dated back to the early days of the republic.

Clinton soon found his hands full at home. Although the economy finally began to improve, the public gave the president little credit for the upturn.

He gained Senate ratification of the North American Free Trade Agreement (NAFTA)—aimed at promoting free trade between Canada, Mexico, and the United States—in November 1993 after a bitter battle in which opponents argued that American workers would lose their jobs to less well-paid Mexicans. He secured passage of a crime bill banning the manufacture, sale, or possession of 19 different assault weapons (though a much larger number of semiautomatic guns were not included in this bill). But he failed to win approval of his major legislative initiative: health-care reform. The United States lagged behind most other industrialized countries in the way it provided for public health. A national health-care system in Great Britain provided universal coverage. An even more extensive system in Scandinavia met all health needs. In the United States, people were largely expected to deal with their health needs on their own. Medicare took care of the elderly, and Medicaid provided some relief for the poor, but both were limited when compared to the coverage provided by other nations. "This health-care system of ours is badly broken," Clinton said in September 1993, "and it's time to fix it." Particularly troublesome were escalating costs and the lack of universal medical care, which left 35 million Americans with no medical insurance. Clinton's complicated proposal for a system of health alliances in each state provoked intense opposition from the health-care and insurance industries and from politicians with plans of their own. In the end, he was unable to persuade Congress either to accept his approach or adopt a workable alternative.

Republican Resurgence

Voters demonstrated their dissatisfaction in the midterm elections of 1994. Republicans argued that government regulations were hampering business and costing too much. They challenged the notion that the federal government was primarily responsible for health care and other such services. Capitalizing on the continuing appeal of the leadership of Ronald Reagan in the 1980s, they demanded a scaled-down role for the government. Republicans swept control of both the Senate and the House of Representatives for the first time in over 40 years. In the House, they made the largest gains since 1946, winning more than 50 races against Democratic incumbents. Some of the strongest and most senior Representatives, including Speaker Thomas Foley, lost their seats. At the state level, Republicans picked up 12 governorships and took control in seven of the eight largest states.

The election marked the end of the commitment to the welfare state. The 104th Congress moved aggressively to make good on its promises—outlined during the campaign in the Republicans' "Contract with America"—to scale back the role of the federal government, eliminate environmental regulations, cut funding for educational programs like Head Start, reduce taxes, and balance the budget. Newt Gingrich, as the new Speaker of the House of Representatives, pushed through changes in the House rules that provided him with far greater power in appointing committee members and moving legislation along. Under his leadership, Congress launched a frontal attack on the budget, proposing massive cuts in virtually all social services. It demanded the elimination of three Cabinet departments and insisted on gutting the National Endowment for the Humanities, the National Endowment for the Arts, and the Public Broadcasting System. When, at the end of 1995, the president and the speaker tangled with one another on the size of the cuts and refused to compromise on a budget, the government shut down and 800,000 federal employees found themselves temporarily "furloughed."

While the House of Representatives passed most of the measures proposed in the "Contract with America," only a few of them became law. The Senate balked at some; the president vetoed others. One of the most important ones passed was the unfunded mandates bill, stopping the government from demanding state or local action but failing to provide the funds for implementation. After all the attention it received, voters lost interest in the "Contract with America." As the election of 1996 approached, Newt Gingrich found himself out of favor, as millions of Americans began to realize that they would suffer from the cuts more aggressive Republicans sought.

A Second Term for Clinton

As Bill Clinton sought a second term in 1996, the Republicans nominated Senate Minority Leader Robert Dole as their presidential candidate. The 73-year-old Dole ran a lackluster campaign. His pledge to push through a sweeping 15 percent tax reduction failed to excite voter interest. Even supporters wondered how he would balance the budget at the same time. Stung by Democratic congressional defeats two years before, Clinton reshaped his own image and announced that the "era of big government is over." Like Tony Blair in Great Britain, who spoke repeatedly of a New Labour approach, Clinton co-opted Republican issues, pledging to balance the budget himself and enraging liberal supporters by signing a welfare reform bill that slashed benefits and removed millions of people from the rolls. At the same time, he posed as the protector of Medicare and other programs that were threatened by proposed Republican cuts.

Clinton's strategy worked. On election day, he won a resounding victory over Dole. He received 49 percent of the popular vote to 41 percent for Dole and 8 percent for H. Ross Perot, who ran again, though this time less successfully than four years before. In the electoral tally, Clinton received 379 votes to 159 for Dole. Yet the Republicans kept control of Congress. In the House of Representatives, they lost a number of seats but retained a majority. In the Senate, they added two seats to what they had won in 1994. Around the country, voters seemed willing to support Clinton, but not to give him the mandate he sought.

Partisan Politics and Impeachment

Democrats made small gains in the midterm elections of 1998. They worried about their prospects as election day approached, for Clinton had been accused by an independent prosecutor, appointed by the Justice Department, of having engaged in an improper sexual relationship with Monica Lewinsky, a White House intern. While Clinton denied the relationship at first, the lengthy report presented to Congress left little doubt that such a connection existed, and Clinton finally admitted to the relationship in a nationally televised address.

As Republicans in Congress began to consider impeachment, Americans outside of Washington felt differently. Disturbed at what Clinton had done in his personal life, they nonetheless approved overwhelmingly of the job he was doing as president; in fact, his approval ratings were higher than any of his presidential predecessors in the recent past.

Those sentiments were reflected in the 1998 midterm election. Republicans, who had hoped to score sizable gains in both house of Congress, maintained their 55–45 margin in the Senate, but lost five seats in the House of Representatives, ending up with a 223–211 margin that made it even more difficult to pursue their own agenda.

Despite that clear signal from the voters, House Republicans continued their efforts to remove the president. Just weeks after the election, a majority impeached him on counts of perjury and obstruction of justice. At the start of 1999, the case moved to the Senate for a trial, where Clinton fought to retain his office, just as Andrew Johnson had done 131 years before. In the Senate, presided over by the Chief Justice of the Supreme Court, a two-thirds vote was necessary to find the president guilty and remove him from office. After weeks of testimony, despite universal condemnation of Clinton's personal behavior, the Senate voted for acquittal. Democrats, joined by a number of Republicans, stood by the president, and with that coalition, neither charge managed to muster even a majority. The count of perjury was decided by a 45–55 vote, while the count of obstruction of justice failed on a 50–50 vote. At long last, the nightmare was over, and the country could deal with more pressing issues again.

Clinton was an enormously successful politician. Not only had he escaped conviction in the highly visible—and embarrassing—impeachment case, but he also managed to co-opt Republican issues and seize the political center. When he moved to reconfigure the national welfare system, to limit the number of years a person could receive benefits and to pare down the number of people on welfare rolls, conservatives were pleased while liberals were furious. Yet in other ways, he quietly advanced liberal goals, with incremental appropriations, even when he was unable to push major programs, such as his medical insurance scheme, through Congress. His administration's antitrust suit against the Microsoft Corporation aroused controversy. Although it was initially successful in court, it was partially overturned on appeal and eventually dropped after he left the White House. Suits against the nation's tobacco companies for deliberately misleading advertising in the face of known health risks were more popular with the public, and led in 1997 to a landmark $368 billion settlement to cover liability claims and provide reimbursement to the states for medical costs related to smoking. Throughout both terms, polls showed that Clinton remained popular (even when people disapproved of his personal conduct) to the end of his term in office.

Overall, in the words of the *New York Times,* Clinton demonstrated "striking strengths, glaring shortcomings." He came into office wanting to be a Roosevelt-like figure, with dreams of reconfiguring the role of government, but after the health-care debacle, he ended up instead quietly endorsing and implementing a variety of more modest causes. He faced more criticism—from the Right—than virtually any other politician, and it led to his impeachment. Yet he brought some of his troubles on himself. James Carville, his political consultant, once asked the president about his propensity for living dangerously, and Clinton replied, "Well, they haven't caught me yet." But that was before the Monica Lewinsky scandal. As he prepared to leave office, Clinton reflected, "I made one mistake. I apologized for it, I paid a high price for it and I've done my best to atone for it by being a good president." Most Americans, except for his virulent opponents, agreed.

Bill Clinton's relationship with Monica Lewinsky affected both the country and his own family. Here he heads off for vacation with wife, Hillary, and daughter, Chelsea, after the painful acknowledgment of the relationship to the nation. *(Brad Markel/Liaison Agency, Inc./Getty Images)*

THE SECOND BUSH PRESIDENCY

Republicans regained control of the White House in the election of 2000. Unable to oust Bill Clinton from the presidency by impeachment, they were determined to win back what they considered to be rightfully theirs in the conservative resurgence of the past 20 years. Texas Governor George W. Bush (son of former President George H. W. Bush—the first father–son combination since John Adams and John Quincy Adams), promised to return morality and respect to the White House, and appealed to those disturbed by Clinton's behavior.

The Election of 2000

The election of 2000 promised to be close. The strong economy gave Vice President Al Gore, the Democratic nominee, an initial advantage. Yet the Republicans, led by the younger Bush, insisted the country needed a change. Reflecting the profound difference in opinion about the overall role of government, the campaign revolved around what the government should do with the federal budget surplus. Republicans argued that much of the money should be returned to the public in the form of a tax cut. Democrats countered that such a tax cut would benefit only the wealthiest Americans, not ordinary workers, and said that the surplus should be used to bolster the ailing social security program and to pay down the national debt.

In the weeks before the election, polls showed that the race was virtually tied. They also showed that many Americans were not very enthusiastic about either nominee.

On election night, returns in several states were so close that the media found it impossible to say who won. As the returns trickled in, neither Bush nor Gore had captured the 270 electoral votes necessary to win the presidency. The electoral vote in Florida, one of the undecided states, was large enough to give the winner a victory. A recount, required by law, began, and Florida became a battleground as lawyers for both sides swarmed to the state to monitor the counting. Democrats and Republicans argued bitterly, in court and in the media, about how the recount should proceed. They also argued about which ballots should be counted. Some punch-card ballots, where a voter punched a hole next to the name of the candidate chosen, proved defective, and the particle of paper—called a chad—failed to drop off. Should such a ballot be counted if the intent of the voter was clear, even if the chad still hung by a thread to the card? And how could that intent be ascertained? Democrats also contended that in certain African-American precincts, voters had been turned away from the

In Florida—and other states—punch card ballots were sometimes defective, and if the little stubs of cardboard—called chads—were not pushed out entirely, the vote might be counted inaccurately. Here Judge Robert Rosenberg looks carefully at a disputed ballot during the manual recount in Florida. (AP/Wide World Photos)

polls. That charge was all the more significant since black voters around the country favored Gore by a 9–1 margin.

In December, more than five weeks after the election, after suits and counter-suits by both sides, the case reached the Supreme Court. In *Bush v. Gore*, the justices overturned a Florida Supreme Court decision allowing the recount to proceed, and ruled, by a 5–4 vote, with the most conservative justices voting in a bloc, that the recount should be curtailed, leaving Bush the winner. Although Gore won the popular vote by about 450,000 votes, Bush triumphed in the Electoral

Presidential Election, 2000				
Candidates	**Parties**	**Popular Vote**	**Electoral Vote**	**Voter Participation**
GEORGE W. BUSH	Republican	50,546,002 (47.87%)	271	51.0%
Albert Gore	Democratic	50,999,897 (48.38%)	266	
Ralph Nader	Independent	2,882,955 (2.74%)	0	

Note: The winner's name appears in capital letters.

College by a 271–266 majority. Ill feelings persisted as a result of the partisan ruling. Supreme Court justice John Paul Stevens wrote a scathing dissent, in which he argued: "Although we may never know with complete certainty the identity of the winner of this year's presidential election, the identity of the loser is perfectly clear. It is the nation's confidence in the judge as an impartial guardian of the law." This unusual election, like the disputed election of 1876 at the end of Reconstruction (see Chapter 16), had a profound effect on the course of the country.

The voting in congressional races was equally close. The new Senate was evenly split, with each party holding 50 seats. Republicans organized the chamber and gained all committee chairs, since Vice President Dick Cheney broke the tie. Yet five months after the new session began, Senator James Jeffords of Vermont, frustrated with the approach of the Bush administration, left the Republican party, giving control to the Democrats. Republicans also lost seats in the House of Representatives, leaving them with but a nine-vote majority.

The New Leader

George W. Bush had enjoyed an eclectic career before becoming president. Born into a political family, he had shown little interest in politics himself, gravitating into the Texas oil business and then gaining part ownership of a professional baseball team before running successfully for governor of Texas.

Bush was very different from Clinton. Whereas his predecessor was sometimes called a "policy wonk" who understood all the details of his assorted initiatives, Bush saw himself as a corporate chief executive officer (CEO) who established the broad outlines of policy but then left the details to others. Ronald Reagan had taken that approach, but Reagan used his actor's skill to communicate his vision to the American people. Bush, on the other hand, seemed inarticulate in his comments, stumbling over words and fracturing grammar unless a message was carefully scripted in advance.

Yet Bush had a tenacity that served him well. Author Gail Sheehy observed that "the blind drive to win is a hallmark of the Bush family clan." The new president, she said "has to win, he absolutely has to win and if he thinks he's going to lose, he will change the rules or extend the play. Or if it really is bad he'll take his bat and ball and go home." As president, Bush showed the same determination, driving himself hard then retreating in solitude to his ranch in Crawford, Texas, where he seemed happiest of all.

George W. Bush hoped to follow in the footsteps of his father, though he had much less political and practical experience in the world of public affairs. But Republicans flocked to him, and he triumphed in the disputed election of 2000. *(Suzanne DeChillo/The New York Times)*

Early in his presidency, Bush had to overcome the image of incompetence. On the eve of his first trip to Europe, a senior administration official observed, "The common European perception is of a shallow, arrogant, gun-loving, abortion-hating, Christian fundamentalist Texan buffoon." According to the *Japan Times*, Bush had to persuade Europe's leaders to take him seriously. That first trip went reasonably well, and over the next few years, Bush managed to establish relationships with such counterparts as Vladimir Putin in Russia, Tony Blair in England, and Vicente Fox in Mexico.

Promoting the Private Sector

As president, Bush knew what he wanted to do. He had the interests of corporate America at heart and intended to accommodate business demands. During the campaign, he talked about a tax cut, and this became his first priority. Supply-side economists, who argued successfully in the 1980s that lower tax rates were necessary to promote economic growth (see Chapter 30), became more influential in his administration. While Bush first promoted the tax cut to give the economy a short-term boost, when Democrats proposed an alternative that would have put money into consumers' hands more quickly, the administration countered that its measure was necessary to provide long-term incentives.

By mid-2001, the tax cut became law. It lowered tax rates for everyone, allowed more tax-free saving for education, and reduced estate taxes. The measure promised to save every taxpayer at least several hundred dollars a year, though top earners in the nation stood to save as much as $4 million a year. Though the administration tried to deny that more than 40 percent of the savings would go to the top 1 percent of American taxpayers, the measure was heavily skewed in favor of the wealthy. Meanwhile, the economy continued to falter as the growth rate slowed and a full-blown recession ensued.

Like his father and Reagan, Bush wanted to reduce the size of government and squelch its intrusions into private affairs, but at the same time, he sought to bolster the military. His first budget, for example, proposed deep cuts in health programs for people without access to health insurance. He argued in favor of private social security accounts, rather than providing federal money to keep the system solvent, even when the downturn in the stock market wiped out the savings of millions of investors. But his proposals for defense called for far greater spending, even before the terrorist attacks of September 11, 2001.

Bush infuriated environmentalists, who had been pleased with Clinton's efforts to protect America's national heritage. Quietly, the new administration moved to allow road-building in national forests, reversed the phasing in of bans on snowmobiles in national parks, and made it easier for mining companies to dig for gold, zinc, and copper on public lands. Under pressure from real estate interests, the administration sought to shrink legal protection of endangered species. And, catering to the interests of oil companies, it fought to promote drilling in the protected Arctic National Wildlife Refuge, even in the face of estimates that there was very little oil there to be found. When his own Environmental Protection Agency (EPA) issued a report in mid-2002 linking the use of fossil fuel (such as coal and oil) to global warming, Bush dismissed the study by declaring that he had "read the report put out by the bureaucracy," making it clear that he had no confidence in the judgments of the scientists working for the EPA.

FOREIGN POLICY IN THE POST–COLD WAR WORLD

As the Cold War ended, the United States had to examine its own assumptions about its international role. The world was now a different place. With extraordinary communications advances, it was more closely linked than ever before. Violence and upheaval in one part of the globe now had an almost immediate impact on other areas. In this setting, new questions arose: What kind of leadership would the United States exert as the one remaining superpower on the globe? How involved would it become in peacekeeping missions in violence-wracked lands? What kind of assistance would it extend to developing nations once the competition with the Soviet Union that had fueled foreign aid was over? How would it deal with the threat of terrorism? These questions, asked in different forms over the course of past centuries, helped shape foreign policy in transitional times.

The Balkan Crisis

In the Balkans, in Eastern Europe, ethnic and religious violence worsened in the mid-1990s. Yugoslavia—a collection of different ethnic constituencies held together by a Communist dictatorship—had collapsed in 1991. Muslims and Croats had fought bitterly with Serbs in the province of Bosnia as the world watched the Bosnian Serbs liquidate opponents in a process that came to be

George W. Bush loved the outdoors and spent as much time as he could at his ranch in Crawford, Texas. Here the physically active president is shown clearing cedar logs out of an oak grove. *(Eric Draper/ AP/Wide World Photos)*

called "ethnic cleansing" during the siege of the city of Sarajevo (see Chapter 30). Now, brutal killing escalated out of control, rape became commonplace, and civilians suffered most from the uncurbed violence. As the region became increasingly volatile, the United States remained out of the conflict, while the United Nations proved unable to bring about peace. In mid-1995, a North Atlantic Treaty Organization (NATO) bombing campaign forced the Bosnian Serbs into negotiations, and a peace conference held in Dayton, Ohio, led to the commitment of American troops, along with soldiers from other countries, to stabilize the region.

In 1999, a smoldering conflict in Kosovo, another of the provinces of the former Yugoslavia, led to war. In an effort to stop Slobodan Milosevic, the Serbian leader responsible for the devastation of Bosnia, from squelching a movement for autonomy in Kosovo, NATO, now 50 years old, launched an American-led bombing campaign. Milosevic responded with an even more violent "ethnic cleansing" campaign that drove hundreds of thousands of Kosovars from their homes. Even without the introduction of ground troops, this ultimately successful air assault was the largest allied operation in Europe since World War II.

Milosevic finally succumbed. When he refused to recognize the election victory of the opposition leader in 2000, hundreds of thousands of people demonstrated in the streets and declared a national strike. A week and a half after the election, protest-ers set fire to both the parliament and the state television station. Police officers joined the protesters and overthrew the leader who had wrought such havoc. Milosevic was arrested in 2001 and brought to The Netherlands to stand trial for crimes against humanity at the International Court of Justice in The Hague.

The Middle East in Flames

In the Middle East, Clinton tried to play the part of peacemaker, just as Jimmy Carter had done 15 years before. On September 13, 1993, in a dramatic ceremony on the White House lawn, Palestine Liberation Organization leader Yasir Arafat and Israeli prime minister Yitzhak Rabin took the first public step toward ending years of conflict as they shook hands and signed a peace agreement that led to Palestinian self-rule in the Gaza strip. In 1995, Israel and the PLO signed a further agreement, and the Israelis handed over control of the West Bank of the Jordan River to the Palestinians. A treaty between Jordan and Israel brought peace on still another border. While extremists tried to destroy the peace process by continued violence and assassinated Rabin in a move deplored worldwide, the effort to heal old animosities continued.

In 1998, Clinton once again played the role of mediator, this time facilitating an agreement leading to the return of land in the West Bank area to the Palestinians in return for peace between Arafat and Israeli leader Benjamin Netanyahu. As Clinton

President Bill Clinton helped orchestrate this famous handshake between Israeli Prime Minister Yitzhak Rabin and Palestine Liberation Organization Chairman Yasir Arafat in 1993. Though the two men had long been adversaries, they now began to work together to settle the bitter conflicts in the Middle East. *(AP/Wide World Photos)*

Siege in the West Bank

As Middle Eastern violence escalated out of control, Israeli forces in early 2002 responded to suicide bombings by mounting a massive siege of Yasir Arafat's headquarters in the West Bank—that area located on the West Bank of the Jordan River. Though the siege left Arafat unhurt, it undermined his authority and left the question of Palestinian leadership in doubt. **Reflecting on the Past** Why was the West Bank such a volatile area? Why did Israel mount a siege in the West Bank? Why did the siege undermine Arafat's authority?

LEBANON

Sea of Galilee

GOLAN HEIGHTS

SYRIA

• Haifa

• Nazareth

Mediterranean Sea

Netanya •

Nablus •

WEST BANK

Jordan R.

Tel Aviv •

Ramallah •

Jerusalem •

• Jericho

• Ashqelon

• Bethlehem

Dead Sea

Gaza •

• Hebron

GAZA STRIP

• Beersheba

• Dimona

ISRAEL

JORDAN

NEGEV

EGYPT

- Under Palestinian civil and security control
- Under Palestinian civil control, joint Israeli-Palestinian security control
- ■ Israeli settlement

prepared to leave office, he sought to seal a final agreement between the Israelis and the Palestinians, but this time he was not successful, as the Palestinians rejected a generous settlement offer, and the smoldering Middle Eastern tensions burst once more in flames that threatened to engulf the entire region.

The level of Mideast violence in the early twenty-first century was worse than it had ever been before. Arabs and Israelis had fought with each other repeatedly since the establishment of the state of Israel in 1948 (see Chapters 27, 28 and 29), and each conflict had left both victors and vanquished raw. Peace efforts culminating in relations with some of the Arab nations had promised to bring stability to the region. But the short-sighted Israeli policy of building settlements in occupied Arab land, and the Palestinian unwillingness to compromise at the negotiating table, culminated in a horrifying escalation of bloodshed following an intrusive Israeli visit to a holy Palestinian religious site in Jerusalem, a city claimed by both sides. Palestinian suicide bombers, some of them adolescents, wrought havoc on Israeli buses and in Jewish shops. A bomb exploded at Hebrew University in mid-2002, killing not just Israelis but Americans as well. Each time a deadly attack occurred, the Israelis counterattacked with equal violence in a never-ending spiral.

Bush was at first reluctant to intervene. Eventually, as the killing cycle continued, he moved from inattention to fumbling attention, becoming increasingly sympathetic to Israel as the suicide attacks continued. He lashed out at Yasir Arafat for not speaking out against the bombings, but was unable to bring the adversaries to the negotiating table. Meanwhile, many of the European nations, feeling that only the United States could help bring peace to the region, voiced dismay at American policy.

African Struggles

Africa also remained a source of concern to American policymakers who struggled to deal with a series of never-ending crises. Left behind as other parts of the world industrialized and moved ahead, the continent was also ravaged by the AIDS epidemic, which infected and killed far more people than in other parts of the world. Meanwhile, most other nations paid little attention to the region. During the Cold War, the United States and the Soviet Union had competed for the allegiance of African nations, but with the end of the conflict, that focus faded. Bill Clinton became the first

American president to travel to Africa, as he sought to dramatize international responsibility for assisting the continent, and he watched with satisfaction as Nelson Mandela handed over power in South Africa to his successor in a peaceful transition. But other areas proved more problematical. Six months after Clinton became president, a firefight with one faction in war-ravaged Somalia, in East Africa, resulted in several dozen American casualties. The United States was trying to promote stability in a region that lacked any central government at all (see Chapter 30) in what was a doomed effort from the start. The shooting prompted some Americans, still haunted by the memory of Vietnam, to demand withdrawal. Reluctant to back down as he groped to define his policy, Clinton first increased the number of U.S. troops, then in 1993, recalled the soldiers without having restored order.

The United States was similarly baffled by a crisis in Rwanda, in central Africa. There a fragile balance of power between two ethnic groups—the Tutsis and the Hutus—broke down. When the Hutu president died in a suspicious plane crash in 1994, hard-line Hutus blamed Tutsi rebels and embarked on a massive genocidal campaign that resulted in the slaughter of hundreds of thousands of innocent Tutsis and moderate Hutus. As the world followed the carnage on television, the United States, like many European nations, debated the possibility of intervention on humanitarian grounds but decided to do nothing. Eventually the killing stopped, although the friction between the rival groups remained.

George W. Bush was much less interested in Africa than his predecessor. He chose not to attend a conference on sustainable development held in South Africa in the summer of 2002, which gave a clear signal that the United States was more interested in its own business interests than in the economic problems of the less-developed world. When Robert Mugabe, the longtime ruler of Zimbabwe, appropriated the land of white farmers to give it to blacks and precipitated a major economic crisis that threatened starvation for many in the country, the United States did little at all.

Relations with Russia

In the area that formerly had been the Soviet Union, the United States continued to try to promote both democracy and free-market capitalism. It worked closely with Boris Yeltsin in Russia, and then with his successor, Vladimir Putin, who assumed power on the last day of the twentieth century and was then elected president in his own right in 2001. But Russia remained unstable, still caught up in the complications of a huge political, social, and economic transformation that was far from over.

George W. Bush recognized the need to work with Putin. In a series of meetings, both in Russia and in the United States, Bush developed a close working relationship with Putin, whose assistance he needed in maintaining European stability. The Soviet Union had ceased to exist, but the component parts still remained important in the larger international scene.

Terror on September 11

On September 11, 2001, three hijacked airplanes slammed into the World Trade Center towers in New York City and the Pentagon in Washington, D.C. The fires in New York from exploding jet fuel caused the towers to crumble, altering the skyline

The World Trade Center towers in New York City had dominated the skyline on the Hudson River. As two hijacked commercial airplanes crashed into the tall structures on September 11, 2001, both towers burst into flames and later collapsed, killing most of the people who were still inside. *(Steve Ludlum/The New York Times)*

forever. Altogether about 3,000 people died in the terrorist attacks. A fourth plane, probably headed for either the White House or the Capital, crashed in Pennsylvania when passengers fought back against the attackers.

The hijackers were Muslim extremists, most from Saudi Arabia, trained at flight schools in the United States, who belonged to the Al-Quaida network headed by a Saudi exile named Osama bin Laden. Osama bin Laden and his organization were headquartered in Afghanistan, led by the extremely conservative Muslim Taliban group that was seeking to impose the law of the Koran, the Muslim holy book, on civil society. Osama bin Laden and his associates were furious at the United States for its Middle Eastern policy of support for Israel, and they also hated its affluent and materialistic values that often conflicted with their religious values and values elsewhere in the world.

The terrorist attacks shattered America's sense of security, at least within its own borders. Irate at the unprovoked strikes, President Bush vowed to find and punish the terrorists. Like his father in the Gulf War a decade earlier, he put together a worldwide coalition to assist the United States, and he quickly launched a bombing campaign to smoke out Osama bin Laden and his network. Although the bombing, followed by attacks by ground troops in Afghanistan, defeated the Taliban and drove its members from power, the campaign failed to find Osama bin Laden. An international coalition attempted to assist in rebuilding Afghanistan, and Bush, who had spoken out vigorously against nation-building in his own electoral campaign, now found himself a reluctant participant in the process. Hamid Karzai became head of a new government, but the instability of his regime was reflected in threats—and attempts—on his life.

Terrorism, the United States discovered, was a complicated enemy. It was, of course, nothing new. For the last couple of decades, terrorism was a constant source of concern as the nation sought to avoid hijackings, kidnappings, and bombings before they occurred. Sometimes these efforts were successful; sometimes (as in a bombing at the World Trade Center in 1993) they were not. But nothing compared to this attack.

As Bush's approval ratings soared to over 90 percent, he vowed a lengthy campaign to root out terrorism wherever it surfaced in the world. He embarked on a massive governmental reorganization to create a new Department of Homeland Security to help prevent future attacks, and he also used terrorism to allow the government to encroach on individual liberties—in the interest of security—more extensively than in the past. Ironically, a president dedicated to smaller government now found himself in the forefront of an effort to give government an even larger role.

American Muslims were often the victims of the government effort. Some faced attacks by Americans angry at the terrorist strikes. Others were held, often without being charged with a crime, on the suspicion that they were somehow involved.

The anti-terrorism campaign escalated. In early 2002, Bush spoke out forcefully against what he called an "axis of evil," as he referred to Iraq, Iran, and North Korea. He was particularly intent on driving Iraqi leader Saddam Hussein from power. Hussein had launched the attack on Kuwait that had led to the Gulf War during the administration of Bush's father. While the United States and the coalition it had put together had won that war, the military had called off the campaign before toppling Hussein. Now Bush, arguing that Hussein was creating weapons of mass destruction, vowed to complete the task. Within his own administration, Secretary of State Colin Powell, inclined to a more restrained foreign policy, fought against Secretary of Defense Donald Rumsfeld and Vice President Dick Cheney, who were eager for an attack. Bush's argument that he could invade Iraq even without the support of Congress aroused a firestorm of protest both in the United States and around the world.

Timeline	
1991–1999	Ethnic turbulence in fragmented former Yugoslavia
1992	Bill Clinton elected president Czechoslovakia splits into separate Czech and Slovak Republics Riots erupt in Los Angeles
1993	North American Free Trade Agreement (NAFTA) ratified Palestine Liberation Organization and Israel sign peace treaty
1994	Nelson Mandela elected president of South Africa
1996	Bill Clinton reelected
1998	Budget surplus announced Bill Clinton impeached by the House of Representatives
1999	Bill Clinton acquitted by the Senate Stock market soars as Dow Jones average passes 10,000
2000	George W. Bush elected president
2001	Economy falters Stock market dips below 10,000 Tax cut passed Terrorists strike New York City and Washington, D.C.
2002	Recession continues and Dow Jones average drops below 8,000

✦ Conclusion

THE RECENT PAST IN PERSPECTIVE

In the 1990s, the United States prospered in a period of economic growth longer than any in its history. After weathering a recession at the start of the decade, the economy began to boom, and the boom continued for the next 10 years. Most middle- and upper-class Americans prospered. The budget deficit disappeared, and the government ran a sizable surplus. Yet not all Americans shared in the prosperity. Despite the drop in the unemployment level, many of the available jobs paid little more than the minimum wage, and people like the Garretts, met at the start of the chapter, had trouble making ends meet. Members of minority groups, whose numbers grew throughout the decade, had the toughest time of all.

Meanwhile, Americans worried about their role in the outside world. As they enjoyed their new-found prosperity, some were reluctant to spend money in an activist role abroad. They debated what to do about the defense establishment, which had begun to deteriorate, and were hesitant to become deeply involved in foreign conflicts where they had trouble ascertaining American interests. Then, in 2001, the brutal terrorist attacks on New York City and Washington, D.C., mobilized the nation. Recognizing at long last that terrorism threatened the entire globe, including the United States, they prepared themselves for an extended effort to try to bring it under control and to make the world a safer place. As they had in years past, in both World War I and World War II, the United States again sought to protect the democratic way of life for the American people and for people elsewhere as well.

✦ Recommended Reading

Historians have not yet had a chance to deal in detail with the developments of the immediate past, so full descriptions must be found in other sources, such as newspaper and magazine accounts. But a number of useful treatments about selected topics provide good starting points in various areas.

The Changing Face of the American People

Stephanie Coontz, *The Way We Really Are: Coming to Terms with America's Changing Families* (1997); Roger Daniels, *Coming to America: A History of Immigration and Ethnicity in American Life,* revised edition (2002); David M. Reimers, *Still the Golden Door: The Third World Comes to America* (1985); Paul James Rutledge, *The Vietnamese Experience in America* (1992); Al Santoli, *New Americans: An Oral History: Immigrants and Refugees in the U.S. Today* (1988); Jane I. Smith, *Islam in America* (1999); Ronald Takaki, *A Different Mirror: A History of Multicultural America* (1993) and *A Larger Memory: A History of Our Diversity, With Voices* (1998); Susan J. Tolchin, *The Angry American: How Voter Rage is Changing the Nation,* 2nd ed. (1999); Reed Ueda, *Postwar Immigrant America: A Social History* (1994); U.S. Bureau of the Census, *Statistical Abstract of the United States: 1994 & 1998,* U.S. Bureau of the Census, *U.S. Census of Population, 1990;* U.S. Bureau of the Census, *U.S. Census of Population, 2000* (as excerpted in the popular press); Alan Wolfe, *One Nation, After All: What Middle-Class Americans Really Think About: God, Country, Family, Racism, Welfare, Immigration, Homosexuality, Work, the Right, the Left, and Each Other* (1998).

Economic and Social Change

Rodolfo Acuña, *Occupied America: A History of Chicanos,* 4th ed. (2000); William Bamberger and Cathy N. Davidson, *Closing: The Life and Death of an American Factory* (1998); Dudley Clendinen and Adam Nagourney, *Out for Good: The Struggle to Build a Gay Rights Movement in America* (1999); Robert M. Collins, *More: The Politics of Economic Growth in Postwar America* (2000); Kathryn Marie Dudley, *The End of the Line: Lost Jobs, New Lives in Postindustrial America* (1994); Barbara Ehrenreich, *Nickel and Dimed: On (Not) Getting By in America* (2001); John Hope Franklin and Alfred A. Moss, Jr., *From Slavery to Freedom: A History of African Americans,* 8th ed. (2000); Juan Gonzalez, *Harvest of Empire: A History of Latinos in America* (2000); David G. Gutiérrez, *Walls and Mirrors: Mexican Americans, Mexican Immigrants, and the Politics of Identity* (1995); Arlie Russell Hochschild, *The Time Bind: When Work Becomes Home and Home Becomes Work* (1997); Frederick E. Hoxie, Peter C. Mancall, and James H. Merrell, eds., *American Nations: Encounters in Indian Country, 1850 to the Present* (2001); Christopher Jencks, *The Homeless* (1994); Jacqueline Jones, *American Work: Four Centuries of Black and White Labor* (1998) and *The Dispossessed: America's Underclasses from the Civil War to the Present* (1992); Michael B. Katz, *The*

Undeserving Poor: From the War on Poverty to the War on Welfare (1990); Linda K. Kerber and Jane Sherron De Hart, eds., *Women's America,* 4th ed. (1995); Kenneth L. Kusmer, *Down and Out, On the Road: The Homeless in American History* (2002); John Loughery, *The Other Side of Silence: Men's Lives and Gay Identities: A Twentieth Century History* (1998); Alice Mattison, Patricia Benedict, and Lezley TwoBears, eds., *As I Sat On The Green: Living Without a Home in New Haven* (2000); James T. Patterson, *America's Struggle Against Poverty in the Twentieth Century* (2000); Ruth Rosen, *The World Split Open: How the Modern Women's Movement Changed America* (2000); John C. Teaford, *Cities of the Heartland: The Rise and Fall of the Industrial Midwest* (1993); Joe William Trotter, Jr., *The African American Experience* (2001); William Julius Wilson, *When Work Disappears: The World of the New Urban Poor* (1996); Helen Zia, *Asian American Dreams: The Emergence of an American People* (2000).

Democratic Revival

Peter Baker, *The Breach: Inside the Impeachment and Trial of William Jefferson Clinton* (2000); Christopher Hitchens, *No One Left to Lie To: The Triangulations of William Jefferson Clinton* (1999); Haynes Johnson, *The Best of Times: America in the Clinton Years* (2001); Joe Klein, *The Natural: The Misunderstood Presidency of Bill Clinton* (2002); David Maraniss, *First in His Class: A Biography of Bill Clinton* (1995); Michael Schaller and George Rising, *The Republican Ascendency: American Politics, 1968–2001* (2002); George Stephanopoulos, *All Too Human: A Political Education* (1999).

The Second Bush Presidency

Vincent Bugliosi, *The Betrayal of America: How the Supreme Court Undermined the Constitution and Chose Our President* (2001); E. J. Dionne, Jr., ed., *The Election of 2000: Reports and Interpretations* (2001); Kathleen Hall Jamieson and Paul Waldman, eds., *Electing the President, 2000: The Insiders' View* (2001); David A. Kaplan, *The Accidental President* (2001); The New York Times, *36 Days: The Complete Chronicle of the 2000 Presidential Election* (2001); Larry Sabato, *Overtime! The Election 2000 Thriller* (2001); Jeffrey Toobin, *Too Close to Call: The 36-Day Battle to Decide the 2000 Election* (2001).

Frank Bruni, *Ambling into History: The Unlikely Odyssey of George W. Bush* (2001); George W. Bush: *A Charge to Keep: My Journey to the White House* (2001); Jacob Weisberg, ed., *George W. Bushisms: The Slate Book of the Accidental Wit and Wisdom of Our 43rd President* (2001); J.H. Hatfield and Mark Crispin Miller, *Fortunate Son: George W. Bush and the Making of an American President* (1999); Molly Ivins and Lou Dubose, *Shrub: The Short but Happy Political Life of George W. Bush* (2000); Elizabeth Mitchell, *W: Revenge of the Bush Dynasty* (2000); Stuart Stevens, *The Big Enchilada: Campaign Adventures with the Cockeyed Optimists from Texas Who Won the Biggest Prize in Politics* (2001).

Foreign Policy in the Post–Cold War Era

George Bush and Brent Scowcroft, *A World Transformed* (1998); Paul Kennedy, *The Rise and Fall of the Great Powers: Economic Change and Military Conflict from 1500 to 2000* (1987); Walter LaFeber, *America, Russia, and the Cold War, 1945–1996*, 8th ed. (1993) and *Inevitable Revolutions: The United States in Central America* (1983); Laura Silber and Alan Little, *Yugoslavia: Death of a Nation* (1996); Ronald Steel, *Temptations of a Superpower* (1995).

Fiction and Film

Sherman Alexie's *The Lone Ranger and Tonto Fistfight in Heaven* (1993) is a collection of stories about contemporary Indian life; Robert Olen Butler's *A Good Scent from a Strange Mountain* (1992) is a Pulitzer Prize–winning collection of short stories about Vietnamese immigrants in the United States. Joe Klein's *Primary Colors: A Novel of Politics* (1996), originally published anonymously, pro-

vides a vivid portrait of a politician very much like Bill Clinton. Alice Mattison's *Men Giving Money, Women Yelling* (1997) is a series of intersecting stories about the complexities of people's lives and relationships. Lorrie Moore's *Birds of America: Stories* (1998) is another collection of stories about modern culture and life, including one about a nuclear family involved in a meltdown.

Americanos: Latino Life in the United States (1999) is a documentary film about the impact of Hispanics around the country. *The Contender* (2000) is a movie about partisan political bickering; *Black Hawk Down* (2001) is a film about the bitter fighting in Somalia; *Philadelphia* (1993) is a movie about a lawyer who contracts the AIDS virus; *Lone Star* (1996) is a movie set in Rio County, Texas, that provides a vivid portrait of the frictions between Mexicans, Anglos, and African Americans; *Primary Colors* (1998) is the lively film made from the novel of the same name.

✦ Discovering U.S. History Online

United States Census 2000
http://www.census.gov/main/www/cen2000.html
Includes searchable data using the "American Factfinder" and "State and Country Quick Facts."

The Landscape of Asian America
www.asian-nation.org/history.html
http://www.asian-nation.org/immig.html
A broad look at the history of Asians in America up to the present time as well as details of immigration and present-day enclaves of Asians in the United States.

United States Economic Data
www.docs.lib.duke.edu/federal/guides/us_econdata.html
This site covers recent economic information under several categories: Labor, Employment and Earnings, Income and Poverty, Industry and Trade, National and Regional Accounts, and Price Levels.

Homelessness: Programs and the People They Serve
www.huduser.org/publications/homeless/homeless_tech.html
The full text of this detailed report on the state of homelessness at the end of the twentieth century is available online in pdf format.

WTO History Project
www.depts.washington.edu/wtohist/index.htm
This site seeks to document the protests that took place in 1999 against the World Trade Organization by examining the "range of people who turned out, the varieties of strategies and issues they brought to the streets and the meeting rooms, and the coalitions that emerged and failed."

William Jefferson Clinton
www.ipl.org/ref/POTUS/wjclinton.html
This site contains basic factual data about Clinton's election and presidency, speeches, and online biographies.

Clinton Presidential Materials Project
www.clinton.archives.gov
The official site for the ongoing collection of materials from Clinton's presidency.

Investigating the President: The Impeachment Trial
www.cnn.com/ALLPOLITICS/resources/1998/lewinsky
This site from CNN provides information and documents about the scandals surrounding President Clinton and his impeachment.

Election Collection 2000
web.archive.org/collections/e2k.html
This site contains links to 797 candidate Web sites and other sites covering the Election Day and its aftermath. The sites are presented in their archived state—that is, as they were at the time of the election.

George Walker Bush
www.ipl.org/ref/POTUS/gwbush.html
This site contains basic factual data about Bush's election and presidency, speeches, and online biographies.

A Nation Challenged
www.nytimes.com/pages/national/dayofterror
This site from the *New York Times* contains archives for six months of stories and accounts, including video images and pictures, of the September 11, 2001, terrorist attacks on the World Trade Center towers in New York City and the Pentagon in Washington, D.C.

Understanding Afghanistan: A Land in Crisis
www.nationalgeographic.com/landincrisis/
Current news from *National Geographic*, including maps, recent photographs, and lesson plans. The site also makes available online a few of the magazine's articles about Afghanistan, terrorist attacks, Islam, rescue work, and an archived Webcast of "National Geographic Explores a Changing World," a film screening and panel

discussion on the Middle East and Afghanistan after the events of September 11, 2001, accompanied by a discussion forum.

Picturing the Century: One Hundred Years of Photography from the National Archives
http://www.archives.gov/exhibit_hall/picturing_the_century
The photographs in this selection "depict both the mundane and high political drama, society's failings as well as its triumphs, war's ugliness as well as its bravery."

The Twentieth Century
www.cnn.com/SPECIALS/1999/century
A decade by decade look at the twentieth century via headlines, innovation, culture, and personalities.

THE DECLARATION OF INDEPENDENCE IN CONGRESS, JULY 4, 1776

The Unanimous Declaration of the Thirteen United States of America

When, in the course of human events, it becomes necessary for one people to dissolve the political bonds which have connected them with another, and to assume, among the powers of the earth, the separate and equal station to which the laws of nature and of nature's God entitle them, a decent respect to the opinions of mankind requires that they should declare the causes which impel them to the separation.

We hold these truths to be self-evident: That all men are created equal; that they are endowed by their Creator with certain unalienable rights; that among these are life, liberty, and the pursuit of happiness; that, to secure these rights, governments are instituted among men, deriving their just powers from the consent of the governed; that whenever any form of government becomes destructive of these ends, it is the right of the people to alter or to abolish it, and to institute new government, laying its foundation on such principles, and organizing its powers in such form, as to them shall seem most likely to effect their safety and happiness. Prudence, indeed, will dictate that governments long established should not be changed for light and transient causes; and accordingly all experience hath shown that mankind are more disposed to suffer, while evils are sufferable, than to right themselves by abolishing the forms to which they are accustomed. But when a long train of abuses and usurpations, pursuing invariably the same object, evinces a design to reduce them under absolute despotism, it is their right, it is their duty, to throw off such government, and to provide new guards for their future security. Such has been the patient sufferance of these colonies; and such is now the necessity which constrains them to alter their former systems of government. The history of the present King of Great Britain is a history of repeated injuries and usurpations, all having in direct object the establishment of an absolute tyranny over these states. To prove this, let facts be submitted to a candid world.

He has refused his assent to laws, the most wholesome and necessary for the public good.

He has forbidden his governors to pass laws of immediate and pressing importance, unless suspended in their operation till his assent should be obtained; and, when so suspended, he has utterly neglected to attend to them.

He has refused to pass other laws for the accommodation of large districts of people, unless those people would relinquish the right of representation in the legislature, a right inestimable to them, and formidable to tyrants only.

He has called together legislative bodies at places unusual, uncomfortable, and distant from the depository of their public records, for the sole purpose of fatiguing them into compliance with his measures.

He has dissolved representative houses repeatedly, for opposing, with manly firmness, his invasions on the rights of the people.

He has refused for a long time, after such dissolutions, to cause others to be elected; whereby the legislative powers, incapable of annihilation, have returned to the people at large for their exercise; the state remaining, in the mean time, exposed to all the dangers of invasions from without and convulsions within.

He has endeavored to prevent the population of these states; for that purpose obstructing the laws for naturalization of foreigners; refusing to pass others to encourage their migration hither, and raising the conditions of new appropriations of lands.

He has obstructed the administration of justice, by refusing his assent to laws for establishing judiciary powers.

He has made judges dependent on his will alone, for the tenure of their offices, and the amount and payment of their salaries.

He has erected a multitude of new offices, and sent hither swarms of officers to harass our people and eat out their substance.

He has kept among us, in times of peace, standing armies, without the consent of our legislatures.

He has affected to render the military independent of, and superior to, the civil power.

He has combined with others to subject us to a jurisdiction foreign to our constitution, and unacknowledged by our laws, giving his assent to their acts of pretended legislation:

For quartering large bodies of armed troops among us;

For protecting them, by a mock trial, from punishment for any murder which they should commit on the inhabitants of these states;

For cutting off our trade with all parts of the world;

For imposing taxes on us without our consent;

For depriving us, in many cases, of the benefits of trial by jury;

For transporting us beyond seas, to be tried for pretended offenses;

For abolishing the free system of English laws in a neighboring province, establishing therein an arbitrary government, and enlarging its boundaries, so as to render it at once an example and fit instrument for introducing the same absolute rule into these colonies;

For taking away our charters abolishing our most valuable laws, and altering fundamentally the forms of our governments;

For suspending our own legislatures, and declaring themselves invested with power to legislate for us in all cases whatsoever.

He has abdicated government here, by declaring us out of his protection and waging war against us.

He has plundered our seas, ravaged our coasts, burned our towns, and destroyed the lives of our people.

He is at this time transporting large armies of foreign mercenaries to complete the works of death, desolation, and tyranny already begun with circumstances of cruelty and perfidy scarcely paralleled in the most barbarous ages, and totally unworthy the head of a civilized nation.

He has constrained our fellow-citizens, taken captive on the high seas, to bear arms against their country, to become the executioners of their friends and brethren, or to fall themselves by their hands.

He has excited domestic insurrection among us, and has endeavored to bring on the inhabitants of our frontiers the merciless Indian savages, whose known rule of warfare is an undistinguished destruction of all ages, sexes, and conditions.

In every stage of these oppressions we have petitioned for redress in the most humble terms; our repeated petitions have been answered only by repeated injury. A prince, whose character is thus marked by every act which may define a tyrant, is unfit to be the ruler of a free people.

Nor have we been wanting in our attentions to our British brethren. We have warned them, from time to time, of attempts by their legislature to extend an unwarrantable jurisdiction over us. We have reminded them of the circumstances of our emigration and settlement here. We have appealed to their native justice and magnanimity; and we have conjured them, by the ties of our common kindred, to disavow these usurpations, which would inevitably interrupt our connections and correspondence. They, too, have been deaf to the voice of justice and of consanguinity. We must, therefore, acquiesce in the necessity which denounces our separation, and hold them, as we hold the rest of mankind, enemies in war, in peace friends.

We, therefore, the representatives of the United States of America, in General Congress assembled, appealing to the Supreme Judge of the world for the rectitude of our intentions, do, in the name and by the authority of the good people of these colonies, solemnly publish and declare, that these United Colonies are, and of right, ought to be, FREE AND INDEPENDENT STATES; that they are absolved from all allegiance to the British crown, and that all political connection between them and the state of Great Britain is, and ought to be, totally dissolved; and that, as free and independent states, they have full power to levy war, conclude peace, contract alliances, establish commerce, and do all other acts and things which independent states may of right do. And for the support of this declaration, with a firm reliance on the protection of Devine Providence, we mutually pledge to each other our lives, our fortunes, and our sacred honor.

JOHN HANCOCK

BUTTON GWENNETT
LYMAN HALL
GEO. WALTON
WM. HOOPER
JOSEPH HEWES
JOHN PENN
EDWARD RUTLEDGE
THOS. HEYWARD, JUNR.
THOMAS LYNCH, JUNR.
ARTHUR MIDDLETON
SAMUEL CHASE
WM. PACA
THOS. STONE
CHARLES CARROLL OF CARROLLTON
GEORGE WYTHE
RICHARD HENRY LEE
TH. JEFFERSON
BENJA. HARRISON
THS. NELSON, JR.

FRANCIS LIGHTFOOT LEE
CARTER BRAXTON
ROBT. MORRIS
BENJAMIN RUSH
BENJA. FRANKLIN
JOHN MORTON
GEO. CLYMER
JAS. SMITH
GEO. TAYLOR
JAMES WILSON
GEO. ROSS
CAESAR RODNEY
GEO. READ
THO. MÍKEAN
WM. FLOYD
PHIL. LIVINGSTON
FRANS. LEWIS
LEWIS MORRIS
RICHD. STOCKTON

JNO. WITHERSPOON
FRAS. HOPKINSON
JOHN HART
ABRA. CLARK
JOSIAH BARTLETT
WM. WHIPPLE
SAML. ADAMS
JOHN ADAMS
ROBT. TREAT PAINE
ELBRIDGE GERRY
STEP. HOPKINS
WILLIAM ELLERY
ROGER SHERMAN
SAMÍEL. HUNTINGTON
WM. WILLIAMS
OLIVER WOLCOTT
MATHEW THORNTON

THE CONSTITUTION OF THE UNITED STATES OF AMERICA*

PREAMBLE

We the People of the United States, in Order to form a more perfect Union, establish Justice, insure domestic Tranquility, provide for the common defence, promote the general Welfare, and secure the Blessings of Liberty to ourselves and our Posterity, do ordain and establish this Constitution for the United States of America.

ARTICLE I.

Section 1   All legislative Powers herein granted shall be vested in a Congress of the United States, which shall consist of a Senate and House of Representatives.

Section 2   The House of Representatives shall be composed of Members chosen every second Year by the People of the several States, and the Electors in each State shall have the Qualifications requisite for Electors of the most numerous Branch of the State Legislature.

No Person shall be a Representative who shall not have attained to the Age of twenty five Years, and been seven Years a Citizen of the United States, and who shall not, when elected, be an Inhabitant of that State in which he shall be chosen.

Representatives and direct Taxes shall be apportioned among the several States which may be included within this Union, according to their respective Numbers, *which shall be determined by adding to the whole Number of free Persons, including those bound to Service for a Term of Years, and excluding Indians not taxed, three fifths of all other Persons.* The actual Enumeration shall be made within three Years after the first Meeting of the Congress of the United States, and within every subsequent Term of ten Years, in such Manner as they shall by Law direct. The Number of Representatives shall not exceed one for every thirty Thousand, but each State shall have at Least one Representative; *and until such enumeration shall be made, the State of New Hampshire shall be entitled to chuse three, Massachusetts eight, Rhode-Island and Providence Plantations one, Connecticut five, New-York six, New Jersey four, Pennsylvania eight, Delaware one, Maryland six, Virginia ten, North Carolina five, South Carolina five, and Georgia three.*

When vacancies happen in the Representation from any State, the Executive Authority thereof shall issue Writs of Election to fill such Vacancies.

The House of Representatives shall chuse their Speaker and other Officers; and shall have the sole Power of Impeachment.

Section 3   The Senate of the United States shall be composed of two Senators from each State, chosen by the Legislature thereof, for six Years; and each Senator shall have one Vote.

Immediately after they shall be assembled in Consequence of the first Election, they shall be divided as equally as may be into three Classes. The Seats of the Senators of the first Class shall be vacated at the Expiration of the second Year, of the second Class at the Expiration of the fourth Year, and of the third Class at the Expiration of the sixth Year, so that one third may be chosen every second Year; and if Vacancies happen by Resignation, or otherwise, during the Recess of the Legislature of any State, the Executive thereof may make temporary Appointments until the next Meeting of the Legislature, which shall then fill such Vacancies.

No Person shall be a Senator who shall not have attained to the Age of thirty Years, and been nine Years a Citizen of the United States, and who shall not, when elected, be an Inhabitant of that State for which he shall be chosen.

The Vice President of the United States shall be President of the Senate, but shall have no Vote, unless they be equally divided.

The Senate shall choose their other Officers, and also a President *pro tempore*, in the Absence of the Vice President, or when he shall exercise the Office of President of the United States.

The Senate shall have the sole Power to try all Impeachments. When sitting for that Purpose, they shall be on Oath or Affirmation. When the President of the United States is tried the Chief Justice shall preside: And no Person shall be convicted without the Concurrence of two thirds of the Members present.

Judgment in Cases of Impeachment shall not extend further than to removal from Office, and disqualification to hold and enjoy any Office of honor, Trust or Profit under the United States: but the Party convicted shall nevertheless be liable and subject to Indictment, Trial, Judgment and Punishment, according to Law.

Section 4   The Times, Places and Manner of holding Elections for Senators and Representatives, shall be prescribed in each State by the Legislature thereof; but the Congress may at any time by Law make or alter such Regulations, except as to the Places of chusing Senators.

The Congress shall assemble at least once in every Year, and such Meeting *shall be on the first Monday in December, unless they shall by Law appoint a different Day.*

Section 5   Each House shall be the Judge of the Elections, Returns and Qualifications of its own Members, and a Majority of each shall constitute a Quorum to do Business; but a smaller Number may adjourn from day to day, and may be authorized to compel the Attendance of absent Members, in such

* The Constitution became effective March 4, 1789. Any portion of the text that has been amended is printed in italics.

Manner, and under such Penalties as each House may provide.

Each House may determine the Rules of its Proceedings, punish its Members for disorderly Behaviour, and, with the Concurrence of two thirds, expel a Member.

Each House shall keep a Journal of its Proceedings, and from time to time publish the same, excepting such Parts as may in their Judgment require Secrecy; and the Yeas and Nays of the Members of either House on any question shall, at the Desire of one fifth of those Present, be entered on the Journal.

Neither House, during the Session of Congress, shall, without the Consent of the other, adjourn for more than three days, nor to any other Place than that in which the two Houses shall be sitting.

Section 6 The Senators and Representatives shall receive a Compensation for their Services, to be ascertained by Law, and paid out of the Treasury of the United States. They shall in all Cases, except Treason, Felony and Breach of the Peace, be privileged from Arrest during their Attendance at the Session of their respective Houses, and in going to and returning from the same; and for any Speech or Debate in either House, they shall not be questioned in any other Place.

No Senator or Representative shall, during the Time for which he was elected, be appointed to any civil Office under the Authority of the United States, which shall have been created, or the Emoluments whereof shall have been encreased during such time; and no Person holding any Office under the United States, shall be a Member of either House during his Continuance in Office.

Section 7 All Bills for raising Revenue shall originate in the House of Representatives; but the Senate may propose or concur with Amendments as on other Bills.

Every Bill which shall have passed the House of Representatives and the Senate, shall, before it become a Law, be presented to the President of the United States; If he approve he shall sign it, but if not he shall return it, with his Objections to that House in which it shall have originated, who shall enter the Objections at large on their Journal, and proceed to reconsider it. If after such Reconsideration two thirds of that House shall agree to pass the Bill, it shall be sent, together with the Objections, to the other House, by which it shall likewise be reconsidered, and if approved by two thirds of that House, it shall become a Law. But in all such Cases the Votes of both Houses shall be determined by yeas and Nays, and the Names of the Persons voting for and against the Bill shall be entered on the Journal of each House respectively. If any Bill shall not be returned by the President within ten Days (Sundays excepted) after it shall have been presented to him, the Same shall be a Law, in like Manner as if he had signed it, unless the Congress by their Adjournment prevent its Return, in which Case it shall not be a Law.

Every Order, Resolution, or Vote to which the Concurrence of the Senate and House of Representatives may be necessary (except on a question of Adjournment) shall be presented to the President of the United States; and before the Same shall take Effect, shall be approved by him, or being disapproved by him, shall be repassed by two thirds of the Senate and House of Representatives, according to the Rules and Limitations prescribed in the Case of a Bill.

Section 8 The Congress shall have Power:

To lay and collect Taxes, Duties, Imposts and Excises, to pay the Debts and provide for the common Defence and general Welfare of the United States; but all Duties, Imposts and Excises shall be uniform throughout the United States;

To borrow Money on the credit of the United States;

To regulate Commerce with foreign Nations, and among the several States, and with the Indian Tribes;

To establish an uniform Rule of Naturalization, and uniform Laws on the subject of Bankruptcies throughout the United States;

To coin Money, regulate the Value thereof, and of foreign Coin, and fix the Standard of Weights and Measures;

To provide for the Punishment of counterfeiting the Securities and current Coin of the United States;

To establish Post Offices and post Roads;

To promote the Progress of Science and useful Arts, by securing for limited Times to Authors and Inventors the exclusive Right to their respective Writings and Discoveries;

To constitute Tribunals inferior to the supreme Court;

To define and punish Piracies and Felonies committed on the high Seas, and Offences against the Law of Nations;

To declare War, grant Letters of Marque and Reprisal, and make Rules concerning Captures on Land and Water;

To raise and support Armies, but no Appropriation of Money to that Use shall be for a longer Term than two Years;

To provide and maintain a Navy;

To make Rules for the Government and Regulation of the land and naval Forces;

To provide for calling forth the Militia to execute the Laws of the Union, suppress Insurrections and repel Invasions;

To provide for organizing, arming, and disciplining, the Militia, and for governing such Part of them as may be employed in the Service of the United

States, reserving to the States respectively, the Appointment of the Officers, and the Authority of training the Militia according to the discipline prescribed by Congress;

To exercise exclusive Legislation in all Cases whatsoever, over such District (not exceeding ten Miles square) as may, by Cession of particular States, and the Acceptance of Congress, become the Seat of the Government of the United States, and to exercise like Authority over all Places purchased by the Consent of the Legislature of the State in which the Same shall be, for the Erection of Forts, Magazines, Arsenals, dock-Yards, and other needful Buildings;

To make all Laws which shall be necessary and proper for carrying into Execution the foregoing Powers, and all other Powers vested by this Constitution in the Government of the United States, or in any Department or Officer thereof.

Section 9   *The Migration or Importation of such Persons as any of the States now existing shall think proper to admit, shall not be prohibited by the Congress prior to the Year one thousand eight hundred and eight, but a Tax or duty may be imposed on such Importation, not exceeding ten dollars for each Person.*

The Privilege of the Writ of Habeas Corpus shall not be suspended, unless when in Cases of Rebellion or Invasion the public Safety may require it.

No Bill of Attainder or ex post facto Law shall be passed.

No Capitation, or other direct, Tax shall be laid, unless in Proportion to the Census or Enumeration herein before directed to be taken.

No Tax or Duty shall be laid on Articles exported from any State.

No Preference shall be given by any Regulation of Commerce or Revenue to the Ports of one State over those of another: nor shall Vessels bound to, or from, one State, be obliged to enter, clear, or pay Duties in another.

No Money shall be drawn from the Treasury, but in Consequence of Appropriations made by Law; and a regular Statement and Account of the Receipts and Expenditures of all public Money shall be published from time to time.

No Title of Nobility shall be granted by the United States: And no Person holding any Office of Profit or Trust under them, shall, without the Consent of the Congress, accept of any present, Emolument, Office, or Title, of any kind whatever, from any King, Prince, or foreign State.

Section 10   No State shall enter into any Treaty, Alliance, or Confederation; grant Letters of Marque and Reprisal; coin Money; emit Bills of Credit; make any Thing but gold and silver Coin a Tender in Payment of Debts; pass any Bill of Attainder, ex post facto Law, or Law impairing the Obligation of Contracts, or grant any Title of Nobility.

No State shall, without the Consent of the Congress, lay any Imposts or Duties on Imports or Exports, except what may be absolutely necessary for executing it's inspection Laws: and the net Produce of all Duties and Imposts, laid by any State on Imports or Exports, shall be for the Use of the Treasury of the United States; and all such Laws shall be subject to the Revision and Controul of the Congress.

No State shall, without the Consent of Congress, lay any Duty of Tonnage, keep Troops, or Ships of War in time of Peace, enter into any Agreement or Compact with another State, or with a foreign Power, or engage in War, unless actually invaded, or in such imminent Danger as will not admit of delay.

ARTICLE II.

Section 1   The executive Power shall be vested in a President of the United States of America. He shall hold his Office during the Term of four Years, and, together with the Vice President, chosen for the same Term, be elected, as follows

Each State shall appoint, in such Manner as the Legislature thereof may direct, a Number of Electors, equal to the whole Number of Senators and Representatives to which the State may be entitled in the Congress: but no Senator or Representative, or Person holding an Office of Trust or Profit under the United States, shall be appointed an Elector.

The Electors shall meet in their respective States, and vote by Ballot for two Persons, of whom one at least shall not be an Inhabitant of the same State with themselves. And they shall make a List of all the Persons voted for, and of the Number of Votes for each; which List they shall sign and certify, and transmit sealed to the Seat of Government of the United States, directed to the President of the Senate. The President of the Senate shall, in the Presence of the Senate and House of Representatives, open all the Certificates, and the Votes shall then be counted. The Person having the greatest Number of Votes shall be the President, if such Number be a Majority of the whole Number of Electors appointed; and if there be more than one who have such Majority, and have an equal Number of Votes, then the House of Representatives shall immediately chuse by Ballot one of them for President; and if no Person have a Majority, then from the five highest on the List the said House shall in like Manner chuse the President. But in chusing the President, the Votes shall be taken by States, the Representation from each State having one Vote; A quorum for this Purpose shall consist of a Member or Members from two thirds of the States, and a Majority of all the States shall be necessary to a Choice. In every Case, after the Choice of the President, the Person having the greatest Number of

Votes of the Electors shall be the Vice President. But if there should remain two or more who have equal Votes, the Senate shall chuse from them by Ballot the Vice President. The Congress may determine the Time of chusing the Electors, and the Day on which they shall give their Votes; which Day shall be the same throughout the United States.

No Person except a natural born Citizen, *or a Citizen of the United States, at the time of the Adoption of this Constitution,* shall be eligible to the Office of President; neither shall any Person be eligible to that Office who shall not have attained to the Age of thirty five Years, and been fourteen Years a Resident within the United States.

In Case of the Removal of the President from Office, or of his Death, Resignation, or Inability to discharge the Powers and Duties of the said Office, the Same shall devolve on the Vice President, and the Congress may by Law provide for the Case of Removal, Death, Resignation or Inability, both of the President and Vice President declaring what Officer shall then act as President, and such Officer shall act accordingly, until the Disability be removed, or a President shall be elected.

The President shall, at stated Times, receive for his Services, a Compensation, which shall neither be increased nor diminished during the Period for which he shall have been elected, and he shall not receive within that Period any other Emolument from the United States, or any of them.

Before he enter on the Execution of his Office, he shall take the following Oath or Affirmation: "I do solemnly swear (or affirm) that I will faithfully execute the Office of President of the United States, and will to the best of my Ability, preserve, protect and defend the Constitution of the United States."

Section 2   The President shall be Commander in Chief of the Army and Navy of the United States, and of the Militia of the several States, when called into the actual Service of the United States; he may require the Opinion, in writing, of the principal Officer in each of the executive Departments, upon any Subject relating to the Duties of their respective Offices, and he shall have Power to grant Reprieves and Pardons for Offences against the United States, except in Cases of Impeachment.

He shall have Power, by and with the Advice and Consent of the Senate, to make Treaties, provided two thirds of the Senators present concur; and he shall nominate, and by and with the Advice and Consent of the Senate, shall appoint Ambassadors, other public Ministers and Consuls, Judges of the supreme Court, and all other Officers of the United States, whose Appointments are not herein otherwise provided for, and which shall be established by Law: but the Congress may by Law vest the Appointment of such inferior Officers, as they think proper, in the President alone, in the Courts of Law, or in the Heads of Departments.

The President shall have Power to fill up all Vacancies that may happen during the Recess of the Senate, by granting Commissions which shall expire at the End of their next Session.

Section 3   He shall from time to time give to the Congress Information of the State of the Union, and recommend to their Consideration such Measures as he shall judge necessary and expedient; he may, on extraordinary Occasions, convene both Houses, or either of them, and in Case of Disagreement between them, with Respect to the Time of Adjournment, he may adjourn them to such Time as he shall think proper; he shall receive Ambassadors and other public Ministers; he shall take Care that the Laws be faithfully executed, and shall Commission all the Officers of the United States.

Section 4   The President, Vice President and all civil Officers of the United States, shall be removed from Office on Impeachment for, and Conviction of, Treason, Bribery, or other high Crimes and Misdemeanors.

ARTICLE III.

Section 1   The judicial Power of the United States, shall be vested in one supreme Court, and in such inferior Courts as the Congress may from time to time ordain and establish. The Judges, both of the supreme and inferior Courts, shall hold their Offices during good Behaviour, and shall, at stated Times, receive for their Services, a Compensation which shall not be diminished during their Continuance in Office.

Section 2   The judicial Power shall extend to all Cases, in Law and Equity, arising under this Constitution, the Laws of the United States, and Treaties made, or which shall be made, under their Authority;—to all Cases affecting Ambassadors, other public Ministers and Consuls;—to all Cases of admiralty and maritime Jurisdiction;—to Controversies to which the United States shall be a Party;—to Controversies between two or more States;—*between a State and Citizens of another State;*—between Citizens of different States;—between Citizens of the same State claiming Lands under Grants of different States, and between a State, or the Citizens thereof, and foreign States, Citizens or Subjects.

In all Cases affecting Ambassadors, other public Ministers and Consuls, and those in which a State shall be Party, the supreme Court shall have original Jurisdiction. In all the other Cases before mentioned, the supreme Court shall have appellate Jurisdiction, both as to Law and Fact, with such Exceptions, and under such Regulations as the Congress shall make.

The Trial of all Crimes, except in Cases of Impeachment, shall be by Jury; and such Trial shall be held in the State where the said Crimes shall have been committed; but when not committed within any State, the Trial shall be at such Place or Places as the Congress may by Law have directed.

Section 3   Treason against the United States, shall consist only in levying War against them, or in adhering to their Enemies, giving them Aid and Comfort. No Person shall be convicted of Treason unless on the Testimony of two Witnesses to the same overt Act, or on Confession in open Court.

The Congress shall have Power to declare the Punishment of Treason, but no Attainder of Treason shall work Corruption of Blood, or Forfeiture except during the Life of the Person attainted.

ARTICLE IV.

Section 1   Full Faith and Credit shall be given in each State to the public Acts, Records, and judicial Proceedings of every other State. And the Congress may by general Laws prescribe the Manner in which such Acts, Records and Proceedings shall be proved, and the Effect thereof.

Section 2   The Citizens of each State shall be entitled to all Privileges and Immunities of Citizens in the several States.

A Person charged in any State with Treason, Felony, or other Crime, who shall flee from Justice, and be found in another State, shall on Demand of the executive Authority of the State from which he fled, be delivered up, to be removed to the State having Jurisdiction of the Crime.

No Person held to Service or Labour in one State, under the Laws thereof, escaping into another, shall, in Consequence of any Law or Regulation therein, be discharged from such Service or Labour, but shall be delivered up on Claim of the Party to whom such Service or Labour may be due.

Section 3   New States may be admitted by the Congress into this Union; but no new State shall be formed or erected within the Jurisdiction of any other State; nor any State be formed by the Junction of two or more States, or Parts of States, without the Consent of the Legislatures of the States concerned as well as of the Congress.

The Congress shall have Power to dispose of and make all needful Rules and Regulations respecting the Territory or other Property belonging to the United States; and nothing in this Constitution shall be so construed as to Prejudice any Claims of the United States, or of any particular State.

Section 4   The United States shall guarantee to every State in this Union a Republican Form of Government, and shall protect each of them against Invasion; and on Application of the Legislature, or of the Executive (when the Legislature cannot be convened) against domestic Violence.

ARTICLE V.

The Congress, whenever two thirds of both Houses shall deem it necessary, shall propose Amendments to this Constitution, or, on the Application of the Legislatures of two thirds of the several States, shall call a Convention for proposing Amendments, which, in either Case, shall be valid to all Intents and Purposes, as Part of this Constitution, when ratified by the Legislatures of three fourths of the several States, or by Conventions in three fourths thereof, as the one or the other Mode of Ratification may be proposed by the Congress; Provided that *no Amendment which may be made prior to the Year One thousand eight hundred and eight shall in any Manner affect the first and fourth Clauses in the Ninth Section of the first Article; and* that no State, without its Consent, shall be deprived of its equal Suffrage in the Senate.

ARTICLE VI.

All Debts contracted and Engagements entered into, before the Adoption of this Constitution, shall be as valid against the United States under this Constitution, as under the Confederation.

This Constitution, and the Laws of the United States which shall be made in Pursuance thereof; and all Treaties made or which shall be made, under the Authority of the United States, shall be the supreme Law of the Land; and the Judges in every State shall be bound thereby, any Thing in the Constitution or Laws of any State to the Contrary notwithstanding.

The Senators and Representatives before mentioned, and the Members of the several State Legislatures, and all executive and judicial Officers, both of the United States and of the several States, shall be bound by Oath or Affirmation, to support this Constitution; but no religious Test shall ever be required as a Qualification to any Office or public Trust under the United States.

ARTICLE VII.

The Ratification of the Conventions of nine States, shall be sufficient for the Establishment of this Constitution between the States so ratifying the Same.

Done in Convention by the Unanimous Consent of the States present the Seventeenth Day of September in the Year of our Lord one thousand seven hundred and Eighty seven and of the Independence of the United States of America the Twelfth IN WITNESS whereof We have hereunto subscribed our Names,

GEORGE WASHINGTON,
President and Deputy from Virginia

North Carolina	*South Carolina*	*Massachusetts*
WILLIAM BLOUNT	J. RUTLEDGE	NATHANIEL GORHAM
RICHARD DOBBS SPRAIGHT	CHARLES C. PINCKNEY	RUFUS KING
HU WILLIAMSON	PIERCE BUTLER	
		Connecticut
Pennsylvania	*Virginia*	WILLIAM S. JOHNSON
BENJAMIN FRANKLIN	JOHN BLAIR	ROGER SHERMAN
THOMAS MIFFLIN	JAMES MADISON, JR.	
ROBERT MORRIS		*New York*
GEORGE CLYMER	*New Jersey*	ALEXANDER HAMILTON
THOMAS FITZSIMONS	WILLIAM LIVINGSTON	
JARED INGERSOLL	DAVID BREARLEY	*New Hampshire*
JAMES WILSON	WILLIAM PATERSON	JOHN LANGDON
GOUVERNEUR MORRIS	JONATHAN DAYTON	NICHOLAS GILMAN
Delaware	*Maryland*	
GEORGE READ	JAMES MCHENRY	*Georgia*
GUNNING BEDFORD, JR.	DANIEL OF ST. THOMAS JENIFER	WILLIAM FEW
JOHN DICKINSON	DANIEL CARROLL	ABRAHAM BALDWIN
RICHARD BASSETT		
JACOB BROOM		

AMENDMENTS TO THE CONSTITUTION*

Amendment I

Congress shall make no law respecting an establishment of religion, or prohibiting the free exercise thereof; or abridging the freedom of speech, or of the press; or the right of the people peaceably to assemble, and to petition the Government for a redress of grievances.

Amendment II

A well regulated Militia, being necessary to the security of a free State, the right of the people to keep and bear Arms, shall not be infringed.

Amendment III

No Soldier shall, in time of peace be quartered in any house, without the consent of the Owner, nor in time of war, but in a manner to be prescribed by law.

Amendment IV

The right of the people to be secure in their persons, houses, papers, and effects, against unreasonable searches and seizures, shall not be violated, and no Warrants shall issue, but upon probable cause, supported by Oath or affirmation, and particularly describing the place to be searched, and the persons or things to be seized.

Amendment V

No person shall be held to answer for a capital, or otherwise infamous crime, unless on a presentment or indictment of a Grand Jury, except in cases arising in the land or naval forces, or in the Militia, when in actual service in time of War or public danger; nor shall any person be subject for the same offence to be twice put in jeopardy of life or limb; nor shall be compelled in any criminal case to be a witness against himself, nor be deprived of life, liberty, or property, without due process of law; nor shall private property be taken for public use, without just compensation.

Amendment VI

In all criminal prosecutions, the accused shall enjoy the right to a speedy and public trial, by an impartial jury of the State and district wherein the crime shall have been committed, which district shall have been previously ascertained by law, and to be informed of the nature and cause of the accusation; to be confronted with the witnesses against him; to have compulsory process for obtaining witnesses in his favor, and to have the Assistance of Counsel for his defence.

Amendment VII

In Suits at common law, where the value in controversy shall exceed twenty dollars, the right of trial by jury shall be preserved, and no fact tried by a jury, shall be otherwise re-examined in any Court of the United States, than according to the rules of the common law.

Amendment VIII

Excessive bail shall not be required, nor excessive fines imposed, nor cruel and unusual punishments inflicted.

Amendment IX

The enumeration in the Constitution, of certain rights, shall not be construed to deny or disparage others retained by the people.

* The first ten amendments (the Bill of Rights) were adopted in 1791.

Amendment X
The powers not delegated to the United States by the Constitution, nor prohibited by it to the States, are reserved to the States respectively, or to the people.

Amendment XI [Adopted 1798]
The Judicial power of the United States shall not be construed to extend to any suit in law or equity, commenced or prosecuted against one of the United States by Citizens of another State, or by Citizens or Subjects of any Foreign State.

Amendment XII [Adopted 1804]
The Electors shall meet in their respective states, and vote by ballot for President and Vice-President, one of whom, at least, shall not be an inhabitant of the same state with themselves; they shall name in their ballots the person voted for as President, and in distinct ballots the person voted for as Vice-President, and they shall make distinct lists of all persons voted for as President, and of all persons voted for as Vice-President, and of the number of votes for each, which list they shall sign and certify, and transmit sealed to the seat of the government of the United States, directed to the President of the Senate;—The President of the Senate shall, in the presence of the Senate and House of Representatives, open all the certificates and the votes shall then be counted;— The person having the greatest number of votes for President, shall be the President, if such number be a majority of the whole number of Electors appointed; and if no person have such majority, then from the persons having the highest numbers not exceeding three on the list of those voted for as President, the House of Representatives shall choose immediately, by ballot, the President. But in choosing the President, the votes shall be taken by states, the representation from each state having one vote; a quorum for this purpose shall consist of a member or members from two thirds of the states, and a majority of all the states shall be necessary to a choice. And if the House of Representatives shall not choose a President whenever the right of choice shall devolve upon them, before the *fourth day of March* next following, then the Vice-President shall act as President, as in the case of the death or other constitutional disability of the President.

The person having the greatest number of votes as Vice-President, shall be the Vice-President, if such number be a majority of the whole number of Electors appointed, and if no person have a majority, then from the two highest numbers on the list, the Senate shall choose the Vice-President; a quorum for the purpose shall consist of two thirds of the whole number of Senators, and a majority of the whole number shall be necessary to a choice. But no person constitutionally ineligible to the office of President shall be eligible to that of Vice-President of the United States.

Amendment XIII [Adopted 1865]
Section 1   Neither slavery nor involuntary servitude, except as a punishment for crime whereof the party shall have been duly convicted, shall exist within the United States, or any place subject to their jurisdiction.

Section 2   Congress shall have power to enforce this article by appropriate legislation.

Amendment XIV [Adopted 1868]
Section 1   All persons born or naturalized in the United States, and subject to the jurisdiction thereof, are citizens of the United States and of the State wherein they reside. No State shall make or enforce any law which shall abridge the privileges or immunities of citizens of the United States; nor shall any State deprive any person of life, liberty, or property, without due process of law; nor deny to any person within its jurisdiction the equal protection of the laws.

Section 2   Representatives shall be apportioned among the several States according to their respective numbers, counting the whole number of persons in each State, excluding Indians not taxed. But when the right to vote at any election for the choice of electors for President and Vice-President of the United States, Representatives in Congress, the Executive and Judicial officers of a State, or the members of the Legislature thereof, is denied to any of the male inhabitants of such State, being twenty-one years of age, and citizens of the United States, or in any way abridged, except for participation in rebellion, or other crime, the basis of representation therein shall be reduced in the proportion which the number of such male citizens shall bear to the whole number of male citizens twenty-one years of age in such State.

Section 3   No person shall be a Senator or Representative in Congress, or elector of President and Vice-President, or hold any office, civil or military, under the United States, or under any State, who, having previously taken an oath, as a member of Congress, or as an officer of the United States, or as a member of any State legislature, or as an executive or judicial officer of any State, to support the Constitution of the United States, shall have engaged in insurrection or rebellion against the same, or given aid or comfort to the enemies thereof. But Congress may by a vote of two thirds of each House, remove such disability.

Section 4   The validity of the public debt of the United States, authorized by law, including debts incurred for payment of pensions and bounties for services in suppressing insurrection or rebellion, shall not be questioned. But neither the United States nor any State shall assume or pay any debt or obligation incurred in aid of insurrection or rebellion against the United States, or any claim for the loss or emancipation of any slave; but all such debts, obligations and claims shall be held illegal and void.

Section 5   The Congress shall have power to enforce, by appropriate legislation, the provisions of this article.

Amendment XV [Adopted 1870]
Section 1   The right of citizens of the United States to vote shall not be denied or abridged by the United States or by any State on account of race, color, or previous condition of servitude.

Section 2   The Congress shall have power to enforce this article by appropriate legislation.

Amendment XVI [Adopted 1913]
The Congress shall have power to lay and collect taxes on incomes, from whatever source derived, without apportionment among the several States, and without regard to any census or enumeration.

Amendment XVII [Adopted 1913]
The Senate of the United States shall be composed of two Senators from each State, elected by the people thereof, for six years; and each Senator shall have one vote. The electors in each State shall have the qualifications requisite for electors of the most numerous branch of the State legislatures.

When vacancies happen in the representation of any State in the Senate, the executive authority of such State shall issue writs of election to fill such vacancies: *Provided,* That the legislature of any State may empower the executive thereof to make temporary appointments until the people fill the vacancies by election as the legislature may direct.

This amendment shall not be so construed as to affect the election or term of any Senator chosen before it becomes valid as part of the Constitution.

Amendment XVIII [Adopted 1919; Repealed 1933]
Section 1   After one year from the ratification of this article the manufacture, sale, or transportation of intoxicating liquors within, the importation thereof into, or the exportation thereof from the United States and all territory subject to the jurisdiction thereof for beverage purposes is hereby prohibited.

Section 2   The Congress and the several States shall have concurrent power to enforce this article by appropriate legislation.

Section 3   This article shall be inoperative unless it shall have been ratified as an amendment to the Constitution by the legislatures of the several States, as provided in the Constitution, within seven years from the date of the submission hereof to the States by the Congress.

Amendment XIX [Adopted 1920]
Section 1   The right of citizens of the United States to vote shall not be denied or abridged by the United States or by any State on account of sex.

Section 2   Congress shall have power to enforce this article by appropriate legislation.

Amendment XX [Adopted 1933]
Section 1   The terms of the President and Vice-President shall end at noon on the 20th day of January, and the terms of Senators and Representatives at noon on the third day of January, of the years in which such terms would have ended if this article had not been ratified; and the terms of their successors shall then begin.

Section 2   The Congress shall assemble at least once in every year, and such meeting shall begin at noon on the third day of January, unless they shall by law appoint a different day.

Section 3   If, at the time fixed for the beginning of the term of the President, the President elect shall have died, the Vice-President elect shall become President. If a President shall not have been chosen before the time fixed for the beginning of his term, or if the President elect shall have failed to qualify, then the Vice-President elect shall act as President until a President shall have qualified; and the Congress may by law provide for the case wherein neither a President elect nor a Vice-President elect shall have qualified, declaring who shall then act as President, or the manner in which one who is to act shall be selected, and such person shall act accordingly until a President or Vice-President shall have qualified.

Section 4   The Congress may by law provide for the case of the death of any of the persons from whom the House of Representatives may choose a President whenever the right of choice shall have devolved upon them, and for the case of the death of any of the persons from whom the Senate may choose a Vice-President whenever the right of choice shall have devolved upon them.

Section 5   Sections 1 and 2 shall take effect on the 15th day of October following the ratification of this article.

Section 6   This article shall be inoperative unless it shall have been ratified as an amendment to the Constitution by the legislatures of three fourths of the several States within seven years from the date of its submission.

Amendment XXI [Adopted 1933]
Section 1   The eighteenth article of amendment to the Constitution of the United States is hereby repealed.

Section 2   The transportation or importation into any State, Territory, or possession of the United States for delivery or use therein of intoxicating liquors, in violation of the laws thereof, is hereby prohibited.

Section 3   This article shall be inoperative unless it shall have been ratified as an amendment to the Constitution by conventions in the several States, as provided in the Constitution, within seven years from the date of the submission hereof to the States by the Congress.

Amendment XXII [Adopted 1951]

Section 1   No person shall be elected to the office of the President more than twice, and no person who has held the office of President, or acted as President, for more than two years of a term to which some other person was elected President shall be elected to the office of the President more than once. But this Article shall not apply to any person holding the office of President when this Article was proposed by the Congress, and shall not prevent any person who may be holding the office of President, or acting as President, during the term within which this Article becomes operative from holding the office of President or acting as President during the remainder of such term.

Section 2   This article shall be inoperative unless it shall have been ratified as an amendment to the Constitution by the legislatures of three fourths of the several States within seven years from the date of its submission to the States by the Congress.

Amendment XXIII [Adopted 1961]

Section 1   The District constituting the seat of Government of the United States shall appoint in such manner as the Congress may direct:

A number of electors of President and Vice-President equal to the whole number of Senators and Representatives in Congress to which the District would be entitled if it were a State, but in no event more than the least populous State; they shall be in addition to those appointed by the States, but they shall be considered, for the purposes of the election of President and Vice-President, to be electors appointed by a State; and they shall meet in the District and perform such duties as provided by the twelfth article of amendment.

Section 2   The Congress shall have power to enforce this article by appropriate legislation.

Amendment XXIV [Adopted 1964]

Section 1   The right of citizens of the United States to vote in any primary or other election for President or Vice-President, for electors for President or Vice-President, or for Senator or Representative in Congress, shall not be denied or abridged by the United States or any State by reason of failure to pay any poll tax or other tax.

Section 2   The Congress shall have power to enforce this article by appropriate legislation.

Amendment XXV [Adopted 1967]

Section 1   In case of the removal of the President from office or his death or resignation, the Vice-President shall become President.

Section 2   Whenever there is a vacancy in the office of the Vice-President, the President shall nominate a Vice-President who shall take the office upon confirmation by a majority vote of both houses of Congress.

Section 3   Whenever the President transmits to the President pro tempore of the Senate and the Speaker of the House of Representatives his written declaration that he is unable to discharge the powers and duties of his office, and until he transmits to them a written declaration to the contrary, such powers and duties shall be discharged by the Vice-President as Acting President.

Section 4   Whenever the Vice-President and a majority of either the principal officers of the executive departments, or of such other body as Congress may by law provide, transmit to the President pro tempore of the Senate and the Speaker of the House of Representatives their written declaration that the President is unable to discharge the powers and duties of his office, the Vice-President shall immediately assume the powers and duties of the office as Acting President.

Thereafter, when the President transmits to the President pro tempore of the Senate and the Speaker of the House of Representatives his written declaration that no inability exists, he shall resume the powers and duties of his office unless the Vice-President and a majority of either the principal officers of the executive department, or of such other body as Congress may by law provide, transmit within four days to the President pro tempore of the Senate and the Speaker of the House of Representatives their written declaration that the President is unable to discharge the powers and duties of his office. Thereupon Congress shall decide the issue, assembling within 48 hours for that purpose if not in session. If the Congress, within 21 days after receipt of the latter written declaration, or, if Congress is not in session, within 21 days after Congress is required to assemble, determines by two-thirds vote of both houses that the President is unable to discharge the powers and duties of his office, the Vice-President shall continue to discharge the same as Acting President; otherwise, the President shall resume the powers and duties of his office.

Amendment XXVI [Adopted 1971]

Section 1   The right of citizens of the United States, who are eighteen years of age or older, to vote shall not be denied or abridged by the United States or any state on account of age.

Section 2   The Congress shall have power to enforce this article by appropriate legislation.

Amendment XXVII [Adopted 1992]

No law, varying the compensation for the services of Senators and Representatives, shall take effect until an election of Representatives have intervened.

PRESIDENTIAL ELECTIONS

Year	Candidates	Parties	Popular Vote	Electoral Vote	Voter Participation
1789	GEORGE WASHINGTON		*	69	
	John Adams			34	
	Others			35	
1792	GEORGE WASHINGTON		*	132	
	John Adams			77	
	George Clinton			50	
	Others			5	
1796	JOHN ADAMS	Federalist	*	71	
	Thomas Jefferson	Democratic-Republican		68	
	Thomas Pinckney	Federalist		59	
	Aaron Burr	Dem.-Rep.		30	
	Others			48	
1800	THOMAS JEFFERSON	Dem.-Rep.	*	73	
	Aaron Burr	Dem.-Rep.		73	
	C. C. Pinckney	Federalist		64	
	John Jay	Federalist		1	
1804	THOMAS JEFFERSON	Dem.-Rep.	*	122	
	C. C. Pinckney	Federalist		14	
1808	JAMES MADISON	Dem.-Rep.	*	122	
	C. C. Pinckney	Federalist		47	
	George Clinton	Dem.-Rep.		6	
1812	JAMES MADISON	Dem.-Rep.	*	128	
	De Witt Clinton	Federalist		89	
1816	JAMES MONROE	Dem.-Rep.	*	183	
	Rufus King	Federalist		34	
1820	JAMES MONROE	Dem.-Rep.	*	231	
	John Quincy Adams	Dem.-Rep.		1	
1824	JOHN Q. ADAMS	Dem.-Rep.	108,740 (10.5%)	84	26.9%
	Andrew Jackson	Dem.-Rep.	153,544 (43.1%)	99	
	William H. Crawford	Dem.-Rep.	46,618 (13.1%)	41	
	Henry Clay	Dem.-Rep.	47,136 (13.2%)	37	
1828	ANDREW JACKSON	Democratic	647,286 (56.0%)	178	57.6%
	John Quincy Adams	National Republican	508,064 (44.0%)	83	
1832	ANDREW JACKSON	Democratic	687,502 (55.0%)	219	55.4%
	Henry Clay	National Republican	530,189 (42.4%)	49	
	John Floyd	Independent		11	
	William Wirt	Anti-Mason	33,108 (2.6%)	7	
1836	MARTIN VAN BUREN	Democratic	765,483 (50.9%)	170	57.8%
	W. H. Harrison	Whig		73	
	Hugh L. White	Whig	739,795 (49.1%)	26	
	Daniel Webster	Whig		14	
	W. P. Magnum	Independent		11	
1840	WILLIAM H. HARRISON	Whig	1,274,624 (53.1%)	234	80.2%
	Martin Van Buren	Democratic	1,127,781 (46.9%)	60	
	J. G. Birney	Liberty	7,069	—	
1844	JAMES K. POLK	Democratic	1,338,464 (49.6%)	170	78.9%
	Henry Clay	Whig	1,300,097 (48.1%)	105	
	J. G. Birney	Liberty	62,300 (2.3%)	—	
1848	ZACHARY TAYLOR	Whig	1,360,967 (47.4%)	163	72.7%
	Lewis Cass	Democratic	1,222,342 (42.5%)	127	
	Martin Van Buren	Free-Soil	291,263 (10.1%)	—	
1852	FRANKLIN PIERCE	Democratic	1,601,117 (50.9%)	254	69.6%
	Winfield Scott	Whig	1,385,453 (44.1%)	42	
	John P. Hale	Free-Soil	155,825 (5.0%)	—	

Year	Candidates	Parties	Popular Vote	Electoral Vote	Voter Participation
1856	JAMES BUCHANAN	Democratic	1,832,955 (45.3%)	174	78.9%
	John C. Fremont	Republican	1,339,932 (33.1%)	114	
	Millard Fillmore	American	871,731 (21.6%)	8	
1860	ABRAHAM LINCOLN	Republican	1,865,593 (39.8%)	180	81.2%
	Stephen A. Douglas	Democratic	1,382,713 (29.5%)	12	
	John C. Breckinridge	Democratic	848,356 (18.1%)	72	
	John Bell	Union	592,906 (12.6%)	39	
1864	ABRAHAM LINCOLN	Republican	2,213,655 (55.0%)	212	73.8%
	George B. McClellan	Democratic	1,805,237 (45.0%)	21	
1868	ULYSSES S. GRANT	Republican	3,012,833 (52.7%)	214	78.1%
	Horatio Seymour	Democratic	2,703,249 (47.3%)	80	
1872	ULYSSES S. GRANT	Republican	3,597,132 (55.6%)	286	71.3%
	Horace Greeley	Democratic; Liberal Republican	2,834,125 (43.9%)	66	
1876	RUTHERFORD B. HAYES	Republican	4,036,298 (48.0%)	185	81.8%
	Samuel J. Tilden	Democratic	4,300,590 (51.0%)	184	
1880	JAMES A. GARFIELD	Republican	4,454,416 (48.5%)	214	79.4%
	Winfield S. Hancock	Democratic	4,444,952 (48.1%)	155	
1884	GROVER CLEVELAND	Democratic	4,874,986 (48.5%)	219	77.5%
	James G. Blaine	Republican	4,851,981 (48.2%)	182	
1888	BENJAMIN HARRISON	Republican	5,439,853 (47.9%)	233	79.3%
	Grover Cleveland	Democratic	5,540,309 (48.6%)	168	
1892	GROVER CLEVELAND	Democratic	5,556,918 (46.1%)	277	74.7%
	Benjamin Harrison	Republican	5,176,108 (43.0%)	145	
	James B. Weaver	People's	1,041,028 (8.5%)	22	
1896	WILLIAM McKINLEY	Republican	7,104,779 (51.1%)	271	79.3%
	William J. Bryan	Democratic People's	6,502,925 (47.7%)	176	
1900	WILLIAM McKINLEY	Republican	7,207,923 (51.7%)	292	73.2%
	William J. Bryan	Dem.-Populist	6,358,133 (45.5%)	155	
1904	THEODORE ROOSEVELT	Republican	7,623,486 (57.9%)	336	65.2%
	Alton B. Parker	Democratic	5,077,911 (37.6%)	140	
	Eugene V. Debs	Socialist	402,283 (3.0%)	—	
1908	WILLIAM H. TAFT	Republican	7,678,908 (51.6%)	321	65.4%
	William J. Bryan	Democratic	6,409,104 (43.1%)	162	
	Eugene V. Debs	Socialist	420,793 (2.8%)	—	
1912	WOODROW WILSON	Democratic	6,293,454 (41.9%)	435	58.8%
	Theodore Roosevelt	Progressive	4,119,538 (27.4%)	88	
	William H. Taft	Republican	3,484,980 (23.2%)	8	
	Eugene V. Debs	Socialist	900,672 (6.0%)	—	
1916	WOODROW WILSON	Democratic	9,129,606 (49.4%)	277	61.6%
	Charles E. Hughes	Republican	8,538,221 (46.2%)	254	
	A. L. Benson	Socialist	585,113 (3.2%)	—	
1920	WARREN G. HARDING	Republican	16,152,200 (60.4%)	404	49.2%
	James M. Cox	Democratic	9,147,353 (34.2%)	127	
	Eugene V. Debs	Socialist	919,799 (3.4%)	—	
1924	CALVIN COOLIDGE	Republican	15,725,016 (54.0%)	382	48.9%
	John W. Davis	Democratic	8,386,503 (28.8%)	136	
	Robert M. La Follette	Progressive	4,822,856 (16.6%)	13	
1928	HERBERT HOOVER	Republican	21,391,381 (58.2%)	444	56.9%
	Alfred E. Smith	Democratic	15,016,443 (40.9%)	87	
	Norman Thomas	Socialist	267,835 (0.7%)	—	
1932	FRANKLIN D. ROOSEVELT	Democratic	22,821,857 (57.4%)	472	56.9%
	Herbert Hoover	Republican	15,761,841 (39.7%)	59	
	Norman Thomas	Socialist	881,951 (2.2%)	—	

Year	Candidates	Parties	Popular Vote	Electoral Vote	Voter Participation
1936	FRANKLIN D. ROOSEVELT	Democratic	27,751,597 (60.8%)	523	61.0%
	Alfred M. Landon	Republican	16,679,583 (36.5%)	8	
	William Lemke	Union	882,479 (1.9%)	—	
1940	FRANKLIN D. ROOSEVELT	Democratic	27,244,160 (54.8%)	449	62.5%
	Wendell L. Willkie	Republican	22,305,198 (44.8%)	82	
1944	FRANKLIN D. ROOSEVELT	Democrat	25,602,504 (53.5%)	432	55.9%
	Thomas E. Dewey	Republican	22,006,285 (46.0%)	99	
1948	HARRY S TRUMAN	Democratic	24,105,695 (49.5%)	304	53.0%
	Thomas E. Dewey	Republican	21,969,170 (45.1%)	189	
	J. Strom Thurmond	State-Rights Democratic	1,169,021 (2.4%)	38	
	Henry A. Wallace	Progressive	1,156,103 (2.4%)	—	
1952	DWIGHT D. EISENHOWER	Republican	33,936,252 (55.1%)	442	63.3%
	Adlai E. Stevenson	Democratic	27,314,992 (44.4%)	89	
1956	DWIGHT D. EISENHOWER	Republican	35,575,420 (57.6%)	457	60.5%
	Adlai E. Stevenson	Democratic	26,033,066 (42.1%)	73	
	Other	—	—	1	
1960	JOHN F. KENNEDY	Democratic	34,227,096 (49.9%)	303	62.8%
	Richard M. Nixon	Republican	34,108,546 (49.6%)	219	
	Other	—	—	15	
1964	LYNDON B. JOHNSON	Democratic	43,126,506 (61.1%)	486	61.7%
	Barry M. Goldwater	Republican	27,176,799 (38.5%)	52	
1968	RICHARD M. NIXON	Republican	31,770,237 (43.4.%)	301	60.6%
	Hubert H. Humphrey	Democratic	31,270,633 (42.7%)	191	
	George Wallace	American Indep.	9,906,141 (13.5%)	46	
1972	RICHARD M. NIXON	Republican	47,169,911 (60.7%)	520	55.2%
	George S. McGovern	Democratic	29,170,383 (37.5%)	17	
	Other	—	—	1	
1976	JIMMY CARTER	Democratic	40,828,587 (50.0%)	297	53.5%
	Gerald R. Ford	Republican	39,147,613 (47.9%)	241	
	Other	—	1,575,459 (2.1%)	—	
1980	RONALD REAGAN	Republican	43,901,812 (50.7%)	489	52.6%
	Jimmy Carter	Democratic	35,483,820 (41.0%)	49	
	John B. Anderson	Independent	5,719,722 (6.6%)	—	
	Ed Clark	Libertarian	921,188 (1.1%)	—	
1984	RONALD REAGAN	Republican	54,455,075 (59.0%)	525	53.3%
	Walter Mondale	Democratic	37,577,185 (41.0%)	13	
1988	GEORGE H.W. BUSH	Republican	48,886,000 (45.6%)	426	57.4%
	Michael S. Dukakis	Democratic	41,809,000 (45.6%)	111	
1992	WILLIAM J. CLINTON	Democratic	43,728,375 (43%)	370	55.0%
	George H.W. Bush	Republican	38,167,416 (38%)	168	
	Ross Perot	—	19,237,247 (19%)	—	
1996	WILLIAM J. CLINTON	Democratic	45,590,703 (50%)	379	48.8%
	Robert Dole	Republican	37,816,307 (41%)	159	
	Ross Perot	Independent	7,866,284 (9%)		
2000	GEORGE W. BUSH	Republican	50,456,062 (47%)	271	51.0%
	Albert Gore	Democratic	50,996,582 (49%)	267	
	Ralph Nader	Independent	2,858,843 (3%)	—	

STATES OF THE UNITED STATES

State	Date of Admission	State	Date of Admission
Delaware	December 7, 1787	Michigan	January 16, 1837
Pennsylvania	December 12, 1787	Florida	March 3, 1845
New Jersey	December 18, 1787	Texas	December 29, 1845
Georgia	January 2, 1788	Iowa	December 28, 1846
Connecticut	January 9, 1788	Wisconsin	May 29, 1848
Massachusetts	February 6, 1788	California	September 9, 1850
Maryland	April 28, 1788	Minnesota	May 11, 1858
South Carolina	May 23, 1788	Oregon	February 14, 1859
New Hampshire	June 21, 1788	Kansas	January 29, 1861
Virginia	June 25, 1788	West Virginia	June 19, 1863
New York	July 26, 1788	Nevada	October 31, 1864
North Carolina	November 21, 1789	Nebraska	March 1, 1867
Rhode Island	May 29, 1790	Colorado	August 1, 1876
Vermont	March 4, 1791	North Dakota	November 2, 1889
Kentucky	June 1, 1792	South Dakota	November 2, 1889
Tennessee	June 1, 1796	Montana	November 8, 1889
Ohio	March 1, 1803	Washington	November 11, 1889
Louisiana	April 30, 1812	Idaho	July 3, 1890
Indiana	December 11, 1816	Wyoming	July 10, 1890
Mississippi	December 10, 1817	Utah	January 4, 1896
Illinois	December 3, 1818	Oklahoma	November 16, 1907
Alabama	December 14, 1819	New Mexico	January 6, 1912
Maine	March 15, 1820	Arizona	February 14, 1912
Missouri	August 10, 1821	Alaska	January 3, 1959
Arkansas	June 15, 1836	Hawaii	August 21, 1959

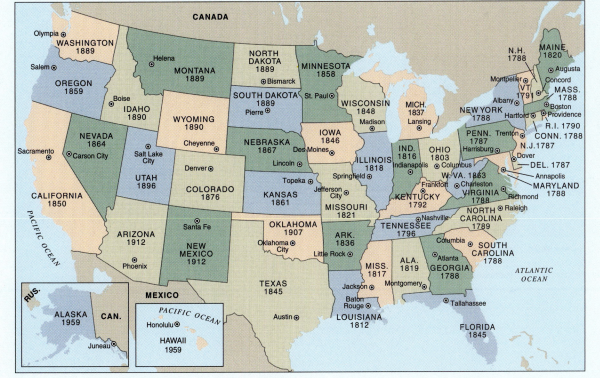

POPULATION OF THE UNITED STATES

Year	Number of States	Population	Percent Increase	Population per Square Mile
1790	13	3,929,214		4.5
1800	16	5,308,483	35.1	6.1
1810	17	7,239,881	36.4	4.3
1820	23	9,638,453	33.1	5.5
1830	24	12,866,020	33.5	7.4
1840	26	17,069,453	32.7	9.8
1850	31	23,191,876	35.9	7.9
1860	33	31,443,321	35.6	10.6
1870	37	39,818,449	26.6	13.4
1880	38	50,155,783	26.0	16.9
1890	44	62,947,714	25.5	21.2
1900	45	75,994,575	20.7	25.6
1910	46	91,972,266	21.0	31.0
1920	48	105,710,620	14.9	35.6
1930	48	122,775,046	16.1	41.2
1940	48	131,669,275	7.2	44.2
1950	48	150,697,361	14.5	50.7
1960	50	179,323,175	19.0	50.6
1970	50	203,235,298	13.3	57.5
1980	50	226,545,805	11.5	64.1
1990	50	248,709,873	9.8	70.3
2000	50	281,421,906	13.0	77.0

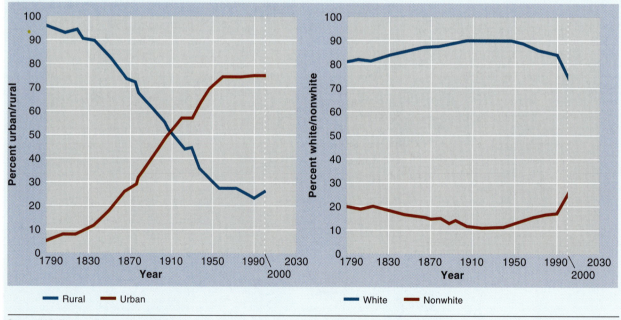

Source: U.S. Bureau of the Census estimates.

The World

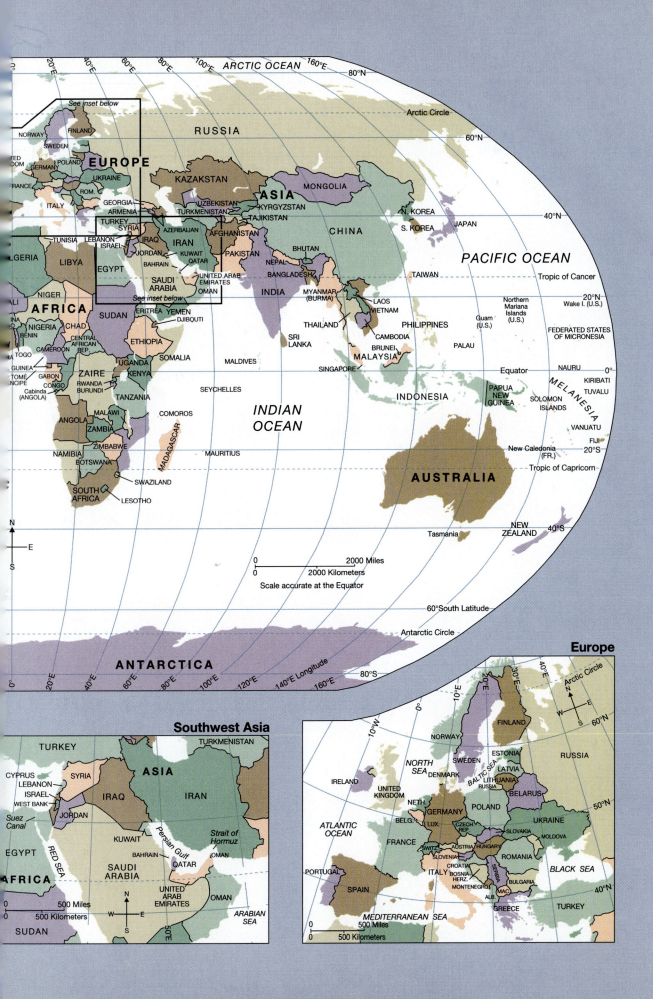